Crisis at Sea

New Perspectives on Maritime History and Nautical Archaeology

May 22, 2009

Congratulations on your impressive achievement!

Anchors Aweigh!

Love,

Uncle Rog & Aunt Debe

UNIVERSITY PRESS OF FLORIDA

Florida A&M University, Tallahassee
Florida Atlantic University, Boca Raton
Florida Gulf Coast University, Ft. Myers
Florida International University, Miami
Florida State University, Tallahassee
University of Central Florida, Orlando
University of Florida, Gainesville
University of North Florida, Jacksonville
University of South Florida, Tampa
University of West Florida, Pensacola

New Perspectives on Maritime History and Nautical Archaeology
James C. Bradford and Gene A. Smith, Series Editors

Maritime Heritage of the Cayman Islands, by Roger C. Smith (1999; first paperback edition, 2000)

The Three German Navies: Dissolution, Transition, and New Beginnings, 1945–1960, by Douglas C. Peifer (2002)

The Rescue of the Gale Runner: *Death, Heroism, and the U.S. Coast Guard*, by Dennis L. Noble (2002)

Brown Water Warfare: The U.S. Navy in Riverine Warfare and the Emergence of a Tactical Doctrine, 1775–1970, by R. Blake Dunnavent (2003)

Sea Power in the Medieval Mediterranean: The Catalan-Aragonese Fleet in the War of the Sicilian Vespers, by Lawrence V. Mott (2003)

An Admiral for America: Sir Peter Warren, Vice Admiral of the Red, 1703–1752, by Julian Gwyn (2004)

Maritime History as World History, edited by Daniel Finamore (2004)

Counterpoint to Trafalgar: The Anglo-Russian Invasion of Naples, 1805–1806, by William Henry Flayhart III (first paperback edition, 2004)

X Marks the Spot: The Archaeology of Piracy, edited by Russell K. Skowronek and Charles R. Ewen (2006)

Life and Death on the Greenland Patrol, 1942, by Thaddeus D. Novak, edited by P. J. Capelotti (2006)

Industrializing American Shipbuilding: The Transformation of Ship Design and Construction, 1820–1920, by William H. Thiesen (2006)

Admiral Lord Keith and the Naval War Against Napoleon, by Kevin D. McCranie (2006)

Commodore John Rodgers: Paragon of the Early American Navy, by John H. Schroeder (2006)

Borderland Smuggling; Patriots, Loyalists, and Illicit Trade in the Northeast, 1783–1820, by Joshua M. Smith (2006)

Crisis at Sea: The United States Navy in European Waters in World War I, by William N. Still Jr. (2006)

Chinese Junks on the Pacific: Views from a Different Deck, by Hans K. Van Tilburg (2007)

Rear Admiral William S. Sims, commander of U.S. naval forces in European waters, 1917–18. Courtesy of the Naval Historical Center.

Crisis at Sea

The United States Navy in European Waters in World War I

William N. Still Jr.

Foreword by James C. Bradford and Gene A. Smith, Series Editors

University Press of Florida
Gainesville/Tallahassee/Tampa/Boca Raton
Pensacola/Orlando/Miami/Jacksonville/Ft. Myers

Copyright 2006 by William N. Still Jr.
Printed in the United States of America on acid-free paper
All rights reserved

11 10 09 08 07 06   6 5 4 3 2 1

A record of cataloging-in-publicaton data is available from the Library of
Congress.
ISBN 0-8130-2987-2

The University Press of Florida is the scholarly publishing agency for the
State University System of Florida, comprising Florida A&M Univer-
sity, Florida Atlantic University, Florida Gulf Coast University, Florida
International University, Florida State University, University of Central
Florida, University of Florida, University of North Florida, University of
South Florida, and University of West Florida.

University Press of Florida
15 Northwest 15th Street
Gainesville, FL 32611-2079
http://www.upf.com

Dedicated to my grandchildren
Ashlyn Rose Still
Charity Jewell Still
Frank Harry Barton III
Jonathan Andrew Still
Kensley Blair Still

Contents

List of Illustrations

List of Maps

Foreword

Water is unquestionably the most important natural feature on earth. By volume, the world's oceans compose 99 percent of the planet's living space; in fact, the surface of the Pacific Ocean alone is larger than that of the total land bodies. Water is as vital to life as air. Indeed, to test whether the moon or other planets can sustain life, NASA looks for signs of water. The story of human development is inextricably linked to the oceans, seas, lakes, and rivers that dominate the earth's surface. The University Press of Florida's series "New Perspectives on Maritime History and Nautical Archaeology" is devoted to exploring the significance of the earth's water while providing lively and important books that cover the spectrum of maritime history and nautical archaeology broadly defined. The series includes works that focus on the role of canals, rivers, lakes, and oceans in history; on the economic, military, and political use of those waters; and upon the people, communities, and industries that support maritime endeavors. Limited by neither geography nor time, volumes in the series contribute to the overall understanding of maritime history and can be read with profit by both general readers and specialists.

Land warfare and sea warfare have been intimately linked throughout history, yet they are often studied apart from one another. This is particularly true with regard to World War I, where books on land warfare far outnumber those about the war at sea. Yet, World War I, while fought chiefly on land, was won at sea. Indeed, few other wars have so clearly shown the value of sea power. The armies of the Allies and the Central powers battled to a stalemate on virtually every front during the first year of the war. Germany did not break that stalemate on its Russian front until 1917, failed to break it in the West that same year, and, in the end, it was the Allies who broke through German lines in 1918. The basis for that breakthrough was laid at sea.

To grasp this point, one must understand the nature of the advantage that dominance of the sea confers upon the possessor. Control of the sea allowed Great Britain and France to transport their armies to the Western Front, often from their overseas empires; to support their allies, notably Italy and Russia; to seize German colonial holdings; and to launch attacks against the periphery of the Central powers, particularly the Ottoman Turks in Gallipoli, Palestine, and the Persian Gulf. Even more important, control of the sea provided the Allies with access to the resources of neutral nations around the world and allowed the Allies to deny access to those resources to the Central powers. Ultimately, World War I proved to be a war of attrition in which resources determined the outcome.

The war at sea also brought the most powerful neutral—the United States—into the war on the side of the Allies. Germany's attempt to break the stalemate on the battlefield by adopting unrestricted submarine warfare designed to starve Great Britain into submission, backfired. Combined with the Zimmerman Telegram, in which Germany sought an alliance with Mexico by promising that nation territorial gains at the expense of the United States, unrestricted submarine warfare precipitated an American declaration of war in April 1917, which marked the beginning of the end for the Central powers.

While much attention has been given the American contribution to victory on the Western Front, there has not before been a modern assessment of all the various operations of the U.S. Navy during the war. Within a month of the congressional declaration of war, Destroyer Division Eight crossed the Atlantic to join Royal Navy forces at Queenstown, Ireland, and together they first contained and then defeated the German U-boat offensive. At the end of May, the Cruiser and Transport Force was formed to carry troops of the American Expeditionary Force to Europe—a task it accomplished for nearly a million men without loss of a single life to enemy action. During the first week of June, the first naval aviation units reached France. They were harbingers of a force that eventually expanded to sixteen thousand personnel and five hundred aircraft that flew from naval air stations in France, Ireland, England, and Italy. In December, five American dreadnoughts, Battleship Division Nine, joined Britain's Grand Fleet at Scapa Flow in Scotland. A second American battleship division of three dreadnoughts followed and operated out of Bantry Bay, Ireland. By May 1918, the first of 121 American subchasers began operating in European waters, and two months later U.S. naval forces began laying the North Sea Mine Barrage, designed to bar German U-boats access to the Atlantic.

The operations of these forces have been chronicled in articles and books, as have the U.S. Marines and naval railway batteries that fought on the Western Front, the campaign against German U-boats in American waters, the Naval Overseas Transport Service, Anglo-American naval relations, and individual leaders, notably William S. Sims and William Benson. But until now there has been no synthetic overview of U.S. Navy operations in European waters during World War I. In addition to integrating these topics into a single study, Still also discusses topics such as logistics and the integration of new technology into operations that have received little coverage in other works.

James C. Bradford
Gene A. Smith
Series Editors

Preface and Acknowledgments

Crisis at Sea is a study of the United States Navy in European waters during World War I. It is the second of a proposed three-volume study of American naval presence in the Old World. The first volume, entitled *American Sea Power in the Old World: The United States Navy in European and Near Eastern Waters, 1865–1917*, was published in 1980. A planned third volume will cover the period between the world wars, 1919–41. *Crisis at Sea*, however, stands alone as a distinct work. The first volume focuses (as to a great degree will the proposed third volume) on naval operations and the Navy's presence as a diplomatic force in European waters. *Crisis at Sea* concentrates on naval activities during the war. It is not just an operational history, but I hope a balanced study of every aspect of the Navy in that geographical area during the conflict. Obviously, operations take up only a portion of the Navy's time. I have tried to balance operations and leaderships with sections on logistics, technology, and social history. A great many writers, both in the United States and abroad, have examined World War I naval operations, particularly convoying and antisubmarine warfare. From an analytical standpoint, I have added little new. Dr. Dean Allard, former director of naval history, taxed me with discovering a plan of Admiral William S. Benson, chief of naval operations during the war, for an offensive operation, possibly in the Baltic, but more than likely against German submarine bases. Although he evidently discussed this plan with British Admiralty officials, no documents relating to this plan came to light during my research. Nonetheless, there is circumstantial evidence that such a plan existed. I have placed considerable emphasis on logistics as the United States military, including the Navy, was preparing for the war that never occurred. German collapse was abrupt, and it took place before American and Allied military officials believed that it would. In the fall of 1918, the Navy was building bases and air stations, constructing more vessels, and shipping aircraft and material to the war zone in preparation for the war in 1919 and possibly beyond. The Navy Department was even ready to deploy the bulk of the fleet, including more battleships, to European waters if needed. Of course, the Armistice nullified the need for these plans and activities.

World War I witnessed the introduction into combat of a number of new ship types, weapons, and technologies. Wars act as proving grounds for untested weapons and new technologies, and World War I was no exception. Aircraft, submarines, subchasers, depth charges, radios, and listening devices are only a few that were tried out. Although few of them were American in origin, the Navy utilized and attempted to improve them.

The United States participated in coalition warfare for the first time in this conflict. I have attempted to discuss this cooperation on all levels from the president and cabinet down to the enlisted man. I have also discussed social and cultural issues in this cooperation. The millions of American servicemen who went to Europe in World War I encountered peoples, cultures, and customs that were totally alien to them. How did they respond? Rest, relaxation, and recreation (R&R&R) are important for morale. How did the Navy respond to these needs?

As I mentioned in *American Sea Power in the Old World*, it was my service with the Sixth Fleet in the Mediterranean that originally sparked my interest in American naval presence in European waters. Encouraged by Dr. Robert E. Johnson, my major professor while I was in graduate school at the University of Alabama, and the late Rear Admiral Ernest M. Eller, USN, former director of naval history, I began research on this topic. Thirty years ago the basic concept of *Crisis at Sea* was first considered. I envisioned a typical operational history, initially a single volume, covering the entire period from the early nineteenth century to the present. Even after the work evolved into a possible trilogy, the idea of a topical approach was not considered. It was only after I began writing that the basic outline was developed. The study has some over-lapping and a certain amount of redundancy. For this I apologize, but I considered it necessary at times.

Although research for this work began in the 1980s, it was really while I was the Secretary of the Navy's Scholar in Naval History at the Naval Historical Center in Washington, D.C., that I was able to focus on it. The eleven months that I spent in Washington away from my academic responsibilities at East Carolina University, Greenville, North Carolina, enabled me to virtually complete research and initiate writing. Unfortunately, my return to academia delayed work on the manuscript until I retired from teaching in 1994.

Inevitably a project of this length in scope as well as in time has indebted me to many individuals and institutions. Dr. William Dudley, former director of naval history, and his predecessor, Dr. Dean Allard, both did everything they could to further this work. Members of the staff at the Naval Historical Center, particularly those in the Ships History Branch, the Library, and the Operational Archives, were always extremely helpful. I cannot overemphasize the help of senior editor Sandra Doyle, who spent months carefully reading and correcting my manuscript. Dr. Allard, Dr. Harold Langley, and Dr. David Trask also read the manuscript, and their help is greatly appreciated. In the National Archives, Mr. Richard von Doenhoff, deceased, was most patient and understanding in my determination to wade through all the pertinent records. I am especially indebted to him for taking me back into that holy of holies, the stacks, to sift through dozens of boxes searching for documents. Other individuals who guided me to documents and manuscripts that I would never have been aware of include Mr. Donald R. Lennon, former director of the East Carolina Manuscript Collection, J. Y. Joyner Library, East Carolina University; Dr. Richard Sommers of the U.S. Army Military History Institute, Carlisle Barracks, Pennsylvania; Dr. Harold Langley, former curator of naval history at the Smithsonian; Dr. Fred Harrod of the U.S. Naval Academy, who steered me to some personnel records; Mr. Jan K. Herman, historian with the Navy's Bureau of Medicine and Surgery; and Professor Jon Sumida. At the Naval Institute in Annapolis, Paul Stillwell's knowledge of oral histories was invaluable. Dr. Geoffrey Rossano, Mr. Michael Simpson III, and Professor Pete J. Capelotti graciously allowed me to examine copies of manuscripts that were in private possession. I am still astonished at how Pat Guyette, librarian at the J. Y. Joyner Library, East

Carolina University, was able to find and obtain rare and obscure articles and books relating to the topic. I owe her a great deal for this. Ralph Scott of the J. Y. Joyner Library also provided me with some valuable assistance. Dr. Tom Adams, lately of Texas and presently of Paris, made it possible for me to use documents from the French Naval Archives, Vincennes, France, as well as a number of publications, by translating them from French to English. Ms. Alexandria Scarzo, a friend of my daughter, Captain Susan S. Jannuzzi, USN, translated a number of Italian documents for me. Dr. Sherwood Maynard, director of the Marine Option Program at the University of Hawai'i, Manoa, has been most helpful in having copied publications obtained on interlibrary loan. In the United Kingdom, Mr. N.A.M. Rodgers, formerly archivist/ historian at the Public Record Office, provided me with invaluable advice as to where to search for relevant documents in that repository. Mr. C. A. Goodfellow, librarian in Inverness, sent me articles from the *Inverness Courier* concerning the American Navy there. Ms. Norma Armstrong, head of Reference and Information Services for Edinburgh, provided me with copies of newspaper articles from the *Edinburgh Evening News*. Professor Forbes of the University of Glasgow not only took time to cull through the *Glasgow Herald* for me but also gave me a delightful anecdote from his father about American sailors in Scotland. I was most fortunate in my academic career to have outstanding students, especially those in the graduate program in Maritime History and Underwater Archaeology at East Carolina University. A number of them helped me with this study in various ways. They include David Cooper, Dr. Ray Ashley, Frank Cantelas, Dr. Robert Schneller, and Dr. Robert Browning. For a computer illiterate such as myself, the help of John Orr was indispensable. My gratitude to the University Press of Florida. The director, Meredith Morris-Babb and her staff cannot be praised too highly. Their patience and good counsel were extremely valuable. Finally, I thank my wife, Mildred, whose patience and understanding made this volume possible. Without that, I doubt if the book would have been completed.

As all who engage in historical research and writing well know, research is never completed. There are always potential sources that you would like to examine, but for one reason or another don't. That certainly is true of this writer. At some point, however, you must decide to get on with it and write! Nonetheless, I wish that I had spent more time examining records in the French Naval Archives and the British Public Records Office. I wanted to get to Rome to peruse Italian records but could never work it out. There are certain personal manuscripts in various repositories that I planned to examine, but I ran out of time. Particularly important are the Captain Tracy B. Kittredge Papers at the Hoover Institute on War, Revolution, and Peace, Stanford, California. There were a few books, primarily published in France and Italy, that I was unable to obtain copies of. Finally, I encountered two major problems in documenting this study. About halfway through the research, the National Archives reboxed the major collection of World War I naval records, rendering the citing of box numbers meaningless. Since it would not be realistic to go back through the hundreds of boxes to locate the new number for each box, I have followed the obvious procedure of using designated letters for the cited records. The introductory essay to the bibliography describes these records in more detail. Also, when we moved from North Carolina to

Hawai'i, one of the boxes of books and papers that were mailed never arrived. Unfortunately, it included a substantial portion of the bibliography used in this study. I have tried to resolve both problems as best I can, but there may well be errors, particularly in the citation of National Archives records. I, of course, assume all responsibility for the contents of this volume, including any errors.

Crisis at Sea is the published version of a somewhat longer manuscript. Copies of the manuscript are located in the Navy Department Library and the Manuscript Collection at East Carolina University, Greenville, North Carolina.

Introduction

The term *forgotten war* is often used in reference to the Korean War. World War I has also been characterized as a neglected war, at least the American involvement, especially the naval phase of it. The paucity of published scholarly works—books and articles—on World War I naval topics during the past quarter century or more suggests that indeed the "Great War," at least so far as naval history is concerned, has been generally ignored. In the 1975 supplement to *A Guide to the Sources of United States Military History* (Archon Books), William Braisted wrote, "the last full operational history of the Navy during World War I was completed more than a half-century ago." Today that is not altogether true as in 1994 the Naval Institute Press published Paul Halpern's excellent study, *A Naval History of World War I*, which does include the U.S. Navy's participation during the war. Nonetheless, there still is no up-to-date general history of the American Navy during World War I.

Why have historians "neglected" the Navy and its activities during the 1917–18 conflict? American involvement was relatively brief, lasting only eighteen months. Second, historians have been far more interested in the so-called neutrality period (1914–17), examining the issues of why the United States became an active participant, and the peacemaking period (1919–20) rather than the period of belligerency. In the third place, the Navy's role has been considered minor compared to that of the U.S. Army. Even Josephus Daniels, the secretary of the navy during the war, acknowledged this. After the June 1917 arrival in France of General John J. Pershing and the initial units of the American Expeditionary Force (AEF), American war correspondents concentrated on the land war and generally ignored the naval war. Throughout the postwar years, former sailors complained in magazines such as the ones published by the American Legion and Veterans of Foreign Wars about the neglect of their service.

The fact that there were no major engagements involving U.S. warships certainly contributed to this neglect. Few ships were lost, and few men in comparison to U.S. Army casualties. A large fleet of nearly four hundred ships and over seventy thousand men were gradually deployed in European waters. Naval units in Europe included bases, naval air stations, hospitals, supply depots, administrative offices in London and elsewhere, and even railway batteries. Units afloat included battleships, cruisers, destroyers, gunboats, converted yachts, subchasers, submarines, minelayers, minesweepers, auxiliary vessels, and seven Coast Guard cutters. Administratively, this force was under U.S. control; operationally, the American warships were assimilated with Allied naval units, a policy that contrasted to that favored by General Pershing. Whereas the naval policy of amalgamation was sound, it did contribute to the lack of awareness of the Navy's contributions both during and after the war.

Reveille in Washington

On March 20, 1917, President Woodrow Wilson held a cabinet meeting to discuss the crisis with Germany over unrestricted submarine warfare, attacks on neutral vessels without warning. The members of the cabinet unanimously favored war with Germany. Although Wilson did not divulge his intentions on that day, he decided upon war. Secretary of the Navy Josephus Daniels noted in his diary: "President was solemn. Very sad!"[1]

The administration began preliminary mobilization. On March 23, the Council of National Defense urged the attorney general to overhaul the nation's security laws. A plan for voluntary censorship of sensitive information was announced on the following day. During the last days of March, the president approved an increase of 157,000 men for the Navy and Marine Corps and accepted the secretary of war's decision to call units of the National Guard into federal service. American diplomats were withdrawn from Belgium. On March 25, the Atlantic Fleet was ordered to the Chesapeake Bay despite Daniels's belief that it was safer at the winter rendezvous, Guantanamo Bay.[2]

In his diary, Daniels mentioned a meeting of the General Board of the Navy to discuss "how we could protect American lives and ships."[3] The president had instructed the naval secretary to discuss the submarine menace with the General Board. When the secretary informed Wilson that the General Board was pessimistic about any effective defenses against submarines, he was told to establish a plan of cooperation with the British Admiralty. "As yet," the president wrote, "sufficient attention has not been given . . . by the authorities on the other side of the water to the routes to be followed to the British ports."[4] Franklin D. Roosevelt, assistant secretary of the navy, called in the British naval attaché. Among items discussed was the nature of naval contributions. Could the Navy base thirty American destroyers on the Irish coast? Quickly, the Admiralty sent back a "shopping list," which included deployment of a large force of destroyers to British waters operating from a base provided by the Admiralty and provision for U.S. naval forces in the North Atlantic, the Caribbean, the coasts of South America, and in Asian waters.[5] Daniels on March 26 ordered Rear Admiral William S. Sims to London to establish liaison with the British Admiralty, and President Wilson ordered a special session of Congress to meet on April 2.

At 8:20 p.m. on April 2, when the president entered the House of Representatives, he found waiting a subdued Congress and the members of the Supreme Court. Among them was the chief justice, Edward Douglas White, a veteran of the Civil War. Wilson's war message lasted but thirty-six minutes. At its end, he voiced the agony that had been forced upon him: "It is a distressing and oppressive duty . . . which I have performed in thus addressing you. . . . It is a fearful thing to lead this great peaceful people into war, into the most terrible and disastrous of all waters. . . . But the right is more precious than peace, and we shall fight for the things which we have always carried nearest our hearts—for democracy, for the right of those who submit to authority to have a voice in their own Governments. . . . [T]he day has come when America is privileged to spend her blood and her might for the principles that gave her birth and happiness and the peace which she has treasured. God helping her, she can do no other."[6] The Senate approved a declaration of war by 82 to 6, and the House followed by 373 to 50. The president signed the war resolution on Good Friday, April 6.

The news reached Europe almost immediately. "I first heard the news of the entry of America into the war in quite a dramatic fashion," a British naval officer recalled after the war. "We were out on a four day patrol in the North Sea . . . it was a raw misty morning . . . and we had just gone alongside an isolated lightship to give them some newspapers, when all at once out of the mist loomed a destroyer. Challenge and reply by searchlight Morse followed, and apparently being reasoned that we were not a Hun submarine, the destroyer sheered off to carry on her patrol. Just as she was disappearing again into the bank of fog her searchlight started morsing [code] to us once more. . . . 'America has declared war;' our searchlight replied, 'Good luck to her,' and we disappeared from each other to depart on our respective vigil."[7]

On the Western Front and on ships from the North Sea to the Adriatic, the news of the American intervention received mixed responses. Many felt relief, and others thought that it was about time, but everyone rejoiced. It is impossible to overestimate the improvement in the morale of the Allied forces.[8]

England was ecstatic. "London to-day is expressing its thanksgiving to America for taking her stand with the Allies," wrote one observer. "The great flagstaff of the Victoria Tower of the Palace at Westminster has hitherto been reserved for the Union Jack, to indicate that Parliament is sitting. For the first time in the history of Parliament the Stars and Stripes is flying alongside the Union Jack on the Victoria Tower. A historic incident indeed!"[9]

In Germany, the announcement of the U.S. entry into war surprised few, and certainly none of her leaders. Since the resumption of unrestricted submarine warfare early in February, American participation became increasingly probable. American entry did nothing to change Germany's belief in ultimate victory. Military officials were convinced that the United States could not train and transport to Europe an army in time to influence the outcome. Vice Admiral Eduard von Capelle, Admiral Tirpitz's successor as head of the German navy, declared in the Reichstag that the military significance of American intervention would be "zero, zero, zero!"[10] The German Naval Office reassured the press: "the American navy cannot possibly play a decisive role as far as we are concerned." On April 17, Captain Boy-Ed, formerly the Kaiser's naval attaché in Washington, argued that "in the foreseeable future there can be no talk whatever of American military aid to the Entente. This applies fully also to the American Navy."[11] One week later, the first six American destroyers departed from

Boston for European waters. At the Navy Department, preparations had already been made for what most considered inevitable. Daniels sent his aide, Lieutenant Commander Bryon McCandless, to the White House with a signalman. As soon as the president signed the war declaration, the news was wigwagged to the Navy Department. Lieutenant Commander Royal Ingersoll carried it to the communication office. Immediately an "Alnav" (all Navy) dispatch announcing the formal declaration of war was sent to all naval vessels, stations, and other installations.[12]

A diarist, Commander Joseph Taussig, wrote that night: "At 7:00 p.m. today the *Pennsylvania*, flagship of the Atlantic Fleet, sent the following signal to all vessels present at Base 2 [York River, Virginia], 'Mobilize for war in accordance with department confidential mobilization plan.'" On the destroyer *Fanning*, the boatswain's mate passed the word that Congress had declared war, but the crew had little time to contemplate the news. They spent the morning of April 7 "dragging for a [missing] . . . anchor and chain." On the *Cummings*, according to a junior officer, "There was no excitement. . . . A signal that the *Seattle*, flagship of the destroyer force, had mail for us, would have caused more bustle. War had been a possibility too long. Its novelty was lost."[13]

In August 1914, when the war began, few in the fleet and few Americans believed that thirty-two months later, the United States would become a belligerent, or that it would dispatch a large army to France and deploy hundreds of warships to European waters.

Although the United States initially declared neutrality, such a policy proved impossible to maintain. American business interests quickly took advantage of the conflict. Within a few months, millions of dollars in foodstuffs and war materials flowed across the Atlantic to the warring nations, primarily to the Entente powers. The British blockade of Germany and her allies proved to be effective almost from the beginning. American investors loaned large sums of money to the British and her allies. Influential British propaganda and German disregard of public opinion gradually increased pro-Allied sentiment. In time, the majority of the American people decided that a moral difference existed between the Allies and their enemies. Propaganda contributed to this belief, but the atrocities in Belgium, German espionage, and, of course, the sinking of the noncombatant *Lusitania* and other vessels carrying civilians were not propaganda. German submarine warfare eventually rendered neutrality impossible, although other motives also contributed to the outcome.

German submarine warfare had a dramatic effect on the public but little on the United States Navy. The number of built or authorized submarines grew during 1914–17, but little thought was given to the impact of undersea warfare on tactics or to the need for antisubmarine craft. The president and many of his cabinet members and advisors were ignorant of conditions in Europe. Wilson refused to send observers to the war zone. Only a few within the Navy Department such as Rear Admiral Bradley Fiske, the aide for operations, warned of being drawn into the war, but as the admiral later said: "if you brought up anything in connection with the efficiency of the Navy and its part in the war, why that was not good. We must avoid that subject."[14] Daniels and other naval officials were fully in accord with the president.

On the first day of August 1914, as the European nations mobilized for war, the General Board held a special meeting. Admiral Fiske requested the session to consider what action the Navy should take.[15] The Board discerned no immediate threat to American interests but agreed that difficulties might develop and recommended that the Navy begin preparations for possible involvement. The government did not act on this proposal and others that emanated from the Board, Admiral Fiske, and members of Congress. President Wilson, his cabinet, and the majority in Congress opposed improvements in the military establishment.[16]

Submarine depredations, particularly the sinking of the *Lusitania* in May 1915, finally forced the president to augment the nation's defenses. On May 7, 1915, a German submarine sank the Cunard liner *Lusitania* as she neared the end of a run from New York to Liverpool. More than 1,200 lives were lost, including 124 Americans. The sinking inspired cries for retaliation. There followed a "preparedness" debate in Congress that continued into 1916. The preparedness controversy is ironic because it had so little to do with possible intervention in the war.[17] This was especially true of naval expansion.

On July 21, 1915, when Wilson learned that the German government had ignored demands to halt submarine attacks against unarmed ships, he asked Secretary Daniels and the secretary of war to prepare programs that assured reasonable security.[18] The pacific president did not envision intervention, continuing to oppose military contingency planning. He sought to mediate the European conflict. Secretary of War Newton D. Baker said later, "From the time I came to Washington until we were nearly in the war . . . the President gave me the idea—although I could not quote anything he said—that to him the function of the United States was to be the peacemaker, and that the idea of intervening in the War was the last thought he had in the world."[19]

Nonetheless, Wilson's request for "reasonable security" led to naval preparations for possible war. Admiral William S. Benson, chief of naval operations, wrote in the late 1920s: "Immediately upon taking the oath of office [May 1915], I started in to prepare the navy for the struggle that I knew was ahead of us. I drew up an order . . . calling upon every bureau and office of the Navy Department to report not later than a certain date its preparedness for war, and to state in every particular where it was not prepared and what efforts were being made to make up the deficiency." In July, Secretary Daniels, suspicious of naval bureaucracy, created a consulting board of engineers and inventors headed by Thomas A. Edison, to advise the Navy on technological matters and industrial resources. The Bureau of Construction and Repair created a card index of yachts and yachtsmen. In 1916, Congress passed a naval appropriation act that, among other things, called for the creation of a naval reserve that included private yachts and yachtsmen. The Navy acquired 169 yachts from the New York Yacht Club alone. The Bureau of Medicine and Surgery instituted a survey of civilian hospitals on the Atlantic seaboard to identify potential naval personnel and worked out an agreement to cooperate with the Red Cross. The Bureau of Supplies and Accounts began an extensive study of logistical requirements. In 1916, it was authorized to procure "such quantities of provisions, clothing and general stores as may be necessary" and to "take immediate steps to fill to full capacity all stations along the Atlantic Seaboard with coal and oil, chartering such lighters or other bottoms . . . as may be necessary." The paymaster general made agreements with business firms throughout the country to acquire stores and supplies.

Other steps were taken to improve the Navy. The assistant secretary of the navy, Franklin D. Roosevelt, recalled later: "About four days after the declaration of war . . . I was sent for by Joe Tumulty to come over here to the White House. I came and there was the President, Barney Baruch, the Secretary of War, and the Chief of Staff. The President said, 'Roosevelt, I am very sorry but you, in your zeal, you have cornered the market in a great many essential supplies and you have to give up 50% of it to the Army." The chief of the Bureau of Navigation developed plans for new training camps. Admiral Joseph Strauss, chief of the Bureau of Ordnance, testified in 1921 that by the end of 1915, "conditions in regard to supply and production of ordnance were, on the whole, very satisfactory." He ignored the fact that the Navy had few depth charges in April 1917, and that those available were nearly worthless. Nonetheless, a great deal was accomplished in war preparations, particularly in logistics.[20]

Secretary Daniels also asked the General Board to draft a recommendation for new construction. The Board produced an ambitious program to make the United States Navy the equal of any in the world by 1925. The Board's proposed program, nearly identical to one prepared in 1913, emphasized the construction of capital ships, which did not reflect the exigencies of the European war.[21] At Daniels's urging, the Board later designed a more realistic program that envisioned construction of ten battleships, six battle cruisers, ten cruisers, fifty destroyers, a hundred submarines, and miscellaneous auxiliary craft. The ships were to join the fleet within five years. The administration did not take into account the possibility of coalition warfare. It emphasized defense of the nation and its territorial possessions, primarily in the Western Hemisphere. The president approved the Board's plan. From October 1915 to June 1916, Congress and the press debated massive naval expansion, a part of the preparedness controversy.[22]

The American public generally favored naval expansion. Some believed, including the former president Theodore Roosevelt, that Wilson's plan did not go far enough. Others thought it too ambitious. The advocates of a large building program, emphasizing capital ships, received a boost from widespread news coverage of the Battle of Jutland, the first large-scale fleet action of the war.[23] Wilson continued to push for his relatively moderate program, even after international tensions eased somewhat. On May 4, 1916, Germany agreed to the "Sussex Pledge," which the public and many in Congress interpreted as restricting submarine warfare, but various conditions limited its effectiveness.[24]

On May 18, the House approved a naval appropriation bill that rejected Wilson's program, but the Senate Naval Affairs Committee reported out a measure that accepted the president's entire construction program and reduced the completion time to three years. The bill passed the Senate overwhelmingly. Wilson supported the Senate version, and a joint conference committee finally agreed to it. The law, signed on August 29, 1916, authorized construction in three years of ten battleships, six battle cruisers, ten scout cruisers, fifty destroyers, and sixty-seven submarines. Sixty-six were to be laid down within the first year, including four battleships and four battle cruisers.[25]

The Navy was delighted with the program but later realized its glaring weaknesses. It provided a battle fleet, but it ignored the vital need for antisubmarine craft. "Oh for more destroyers! I wish we could trade the money in dreadnoughts for destroyers already built," Daniels recorded in his diary in April 1917, shortly after the declaration of war.[26] The naval secretary had finally begun to realize that destroyers and other antisubmarine craft were crucial for the type of conflict that the U.S. Navy would probably engage in. Unfortunately, only forty-seven destroyers were in commission and approximately fifty under construction or on order. Moreover, the United States lacked sufficient ship-building capacity to construct the large battleships and battle cruisers while also producing many additional destroyers. Despite opposition from the General Board and the CNO's reluctance, Daniels suspended the 1916 building program. Priority was given to destroyers and antisubmarine warfare (ASW) craft first and battleships last.[27]

Few of the new destroyers joined the fleet before the Armistice. The prewar navy fought most of the war.

Although the Navy had fallen from third to fourth place in the world, it was still impressive on paper. On November 1, 1916, it had 360 vessels. Of the thirty-seven battleships in commission, fourteen were considered first-class dreadnoughts, but only six (*Pennsylvania*, *Arizona*, *Oklahoma*, *Nevada*, *New York*, and *Texas*) mounted 14-inch guns. Ten others had become obsolete. The Navy had forty-four submarines (nearly all obsolete), seventeen small torpedo boats and gunboats, fourteen converted yachts, and forty-seven destroyers. The fleet was unbalanced, lacking high-speed, heavy, gunned battle cruisers and modern light and scout cruisers; it had few mine-layers and virtually no combat aircraft.[28] Overseas operations required transports, tankers, and supply ships, which were in short supply. The battle fleet, or the Atlantic Fleet, as it was designated, consisted of fourteen battleships, sixteen destroyers, and ten miscellaneous vessels.[29]

Although naval officers were concerned about readiness, the general public and members of Congress had little interest in the condition of the Navy. The fleet was in poor material condition at the outbreak of war. Ships are complex pieces of machinery and constantly in need of repair. During the congressional investigation of the Navy Department held in 1920, considerable testimony concerned the readiness of the ships, including those of the Atlantic Fleet. The final report of Congress concluded that "not more than one-third of the vessels of the fleet were in full materiel condition for war service on April 6, 1917, and that it then took from two to six months to put the balance of the fleet in such condition." The historian John Finnegan wrote: "Most of the . . . [Navy] ships were in need of repair, and 90 percent of them were not fully manned."[30] Rear Admiral Sims claimed that the fleet was unprepared when the United States declared war. "The outbreak of hostilities found many important naval units widely dispersed, and in need of repairs before they could be sent to the critical area."[31] "In the case of battleships . . . there was not a single vessel that was ready for war in April, 1917," testified an admiral who commanded a battleship division at that time. Although Admiral Henry Mayo, in command of the Atlantic Fleet, maintained that the fleet "was in the best state of preparedness it had ever been in," Captain Harris Lanning declared that the fleet did not undergo essential repairs and refit even after the breach in diplomatic relations. More than half of the destroyers needed refitting.[32]

About sixty thousand Regular officers and enlisted personnel manned the fleet of 1916. Although the first warships to sail for European waters had full complements, not more than 10 percent of the ships were fully manned at the war's outbreak. During the postwar naval hearings, the chief of the Bureau of Navigation testified that in the fall of 1916 he requested forty thousand additional men. Congress approved twenty-three thousand and the transfer of the state's naval militia to the Navy, enough to give the navy approximately the desired enlisted strength, but before these men could be transferred, enlisted, trained, and sent to the fleet, war broke out. Admiral Benson's decision to place armed guards on merchant ships exacerbated the personnel problem. In April 1917, all but two of the armored cruisers, several battleships, and other ships had partial crews or none.[33]

The Navy that joined the Allies in 1917, although under strength, was well trained, especially the Atlantic Fleet. This force was the country's first line of defense, created early in the twentieth century to guard the nation's coastline and possessions in the Caribbean. Its primary responsibility was to prepare for war by conducting maneuvers and tactical training as a unit. Admiral Mayo claimed that from 1915, "exercise of the Fleet in strategical and tactical problems was frequent and was increasingly directed to battle conditions. Special attention was directed to battle efficiency inspections and in these to the simulation of casualties in action and the Fleet steadily increased in efficiency for battle."[34]

During the fall of 1916, units of the fleet on maneuvers off Guantanamo Bay concentrated on gunnery practice. Gunnery had deteriorated throughout the Navy. Captain Charles P. Plunkett was appointed director of the Office of Target Practice and Engineering in order to improve gunnery. In 1920, he testified that the Atlantic Fleet's gunnery in March 1917 was at the "highest state of efficiency."[35]

Early in February 1917, when the United States broke diplomatic relations with Germany, Admiral Mayo placed the Atlantic Fleet on a war footing. "It was essential," he wrote, "that officers and men should become accustomed to war routine and war precautions." The destroyer force received extensive training with guns and torpedoes and "had a continuous success of tactical and strategical exercises." Commander Joseph Taussig, who took the first force of American destroyers to European waters, wrote in his diary: "[W]hile in Cuban waters during February and March, the Fleet was guarded by destroyer pickets and patrols, and by picket launches. All movements were made in screen formation, and the Fleet came north by an untravelled route with a destroyer screen, and ships darkened at night." Another destroyer officer recalled that the "personnel were in a remarkably well trained state of efficiency and readiness."[36]

In June 1917, a Royal Navy commander made a tour of American naval ships and stations to observe technological matters and personnel. He reported, "To those who wish to see, there is abundant evidence that for long past the entire American Navy has been thinking war; has prepared, trained and organized for it, and their absolute efficiency and readiness in all essential details leave a very pleasing impression."[37]

One striking failure gained attention during the 1920 hearings when a number of officers asserted that the Navy lacked contingency plans for war. Admiral Sims claimed, "although war with Germany had been imminent for many months prior to its declaration, there was nevertheless no mature plans developed or naval policy adopted in preparation for war." Rear Admiral Leigh Palmer stated, "we had no plans, only a mobilization sheet . . . stating the vessels which would be required for mobilization." Ernest King agreed with this assessment.[38] After meeting with American naval officers in Washington, the French naval commander in the Caribbean confided, "I have been constantly surprised that the American Navy . . . has prepared neither a plan of war nor acquired a clear conception of modifications caused in all naval branches by the actual war."[39]

Plans had been prepared but for a different kind of war. The plan for Germany was entitled War Plan Black. The Navy adopted it in 1913, and it remained in effect until the spring of 1917.[40] This plan was basically defensive in nature, envisioning a naval confrontation between the United States and Germany somewhere in the western Atlantic or the Caribbean. It was not abandoned or even significantly modified, although the German navy could not operate in distant waters. The Germans built submarines that crossed the Atlantic, but this capability made no impression on the prewar Navy Department. It continued to stress the concepts of "capital ships" and "big decisive battle" expounded by Alfred T. Mahan. In 1916, the General Board maintained that "commerce destroying is relatively unimportant." Control of the surface sea would decide future campaigns. Paradoxically, when the United States entered the war, the Allies dominated the surface, but as Russell Weigley has written, "submarines had made 'conventional command of the sea' appear a very bad joke."[41] The only plans initiated prior to the war declaration dealt with logistical matters, mobilization, and fleet organization.[42] The Navy Department did not establish a war plans division within the Office of Operations until the spring of 1917.

Until Captain William V. Pratt was appointed his assistant in July 1917, Admiral Benson had no staff and became so bogged down with detail that, according to the British naval attaché, "requests get put on one side after an answer has been promised for the following day" and were then forgotten. Pratt improved the work in the office of the CNO (chief of naval operations), but a satisfactory reorganization did not occur until March 1918.[43] Secretary Daniels resisted efforts to strengthen the Department. He was suspicious of career "blue coats." Early in his tenure as secretary, he strongly opposed the development of a general staff, considering it "Prussianism," and tried to block the creation of the Office of Chief of Naval Operations. The CNO's office was given the responsibility for making war plans in 1916, but bureaucratic power was concentrated in the General Board and the bureaus. These bodies reported directly to Daniels.[44]

Admiral Benson sought to prepare the Navy for war, but the novelty of his position and the pacifism of the naval secretary severely limited his activity. When Congress created the position of chief of naval operations, Daniels bypassed many senior officers and appointed Benson to the position. He was promoted to rear admiral and later to admiral. Benson successfully cultivated Daniels. In return, he maintained unswerving loyalty to the secretary.[45]

Benson's career was certainly unremarkable and did not seem to warrant advancement to CNO.[46] He was a southerner, born in Georgia six years before the Civil War. He endured the hardships of the war, including Sherman's march through Georgia, and Reconstruction. His inadequate formal education at least partly explains his poor academic performance at the Naval Academy, which he entered in 1872, one of the first southerners admitted after the Civil War. He finally graduated forty-third in a class of forty-six. Benson spent thirty-two years in service before attaining the rank of captain. Although proficient, he was never considered an outstanding officer. In 1909, he finally assumed command of a ship, the third-rate cruiser *Albany*, and later captained the new battleship *Utah*. After a tour as commander of the Philadelphia Navy Yard, Daniels made him the first CNO, probably because the secretary wanted an officer whom he trusted.

Benson always proclaimed his loyalty to the secretary, but he gained considerable power, responsibility, and independence. Benson seized every opportunity to strengthen his office and the fleet. Naval operations during the war remained largely in the CNO's hands, especially during the latter months of the conflict.[47]

Benson liked to characterize himself as a "plain sailor." Although generally respected in the Navy, he was considered a "stuffed shirt." Some suspected that his devout Roman Catholic belief and Anglophobia marred his performance. David Trask characterized Benson as an intense nationalist who examined nearly everything within the context of the future of the United States and the Navy.[48]

Benson endured extensive criticism. Wilson thought him "too prudent, too unimaginative, too early in training to do the necessary . . . thinking and planning."[49] Admiral R. A. Grasset, French naval commander in the Caribbean, wrote that Benson "is very little informed on the questions treated by the General Staff; his spirit is slow and he does not seem possessed of the moral authority that comports with his rank and functions." Admiral John Jellicoe, when first sea lord, described Benson as "very ignorant of sea warfare [as] he has never had his flag up afloat." Walter Long, who became first lord in 1919, decided that Benson was "not very quick at grasping any ideas other than his own."[50] Sims, who criticized Benson's policies during the war and afterward, nevertheless wrote in the fall of 1917: "It is very fortunate that we have such a man at the head of affairs," and later, "he is so darned honest and wants to do the best for everything and everybody." Rear Admiral Reginald Belknap wrote some twenty years after the war: "In hindsight, Benson measured up to his job fairly well, taking into consideration the long years of stagnation, the Secretary's singular character and the momentous problems to be met. Benson endured much that would have caused some others to resign. He was narrow in some views, but kept cool and in balance, would not allow himself to be stampeded, was neither hasty in decision nor arbitrary.

In administration he was the opposite of [William S.] Sims, inviting or submitting to too much detail. But to those who would accept responsibility he gave free rein and backed them. One could ask for no better support or confidence."[51]

Daniels respected Benson but protected his role as the coordinating authority in the Department. The CNO reported directly to the secretary, as did the bureau chiefs, the General Board, and other naval officials. The CNO tried to initiate coordination under his direction by organizing an advisory council of the bureau chiefs, but the secretary continued to receive the reports of the chiefs directly.[52] As the senior naval officer, Benson should have been permitted to advise the president, but Daniels's indecision and inflexibility stood in the way.

Little in Daniels's background suggested that he would become an influential secretary of the navy. A progressive newspaper editor from North Carolina, he long supported the perennial presidential candidate William Jennings Bryan. In 1912, he supported Wilson. Daniels's appointment as secretary of the navy was clearly a political payback from Wilson. The Tar Heel editor had no naval or maritime experience to qualify him for the position. Wilson allowed him unreserved control of the Navy and supported him to the end in spite of Daniels's unpopularity, his controversial programs and reforms, and even the disapproval of the president's second wife, who considered him a political liability.[53]

Josephus Daniels was a study in contradictions. A pacifist, he served as secretary of the navy longer than anyone except Gideon Welles. He became an ardent advocate of a powerful Navy second to none. A plump man with a round face, his rather bland and congenial demeanor disguised intelligence and shrewdness. An indifferent administrator, he had difficulty making decisions. When Daniels took office, he entertained an intense suspicion of naval officers, considering them aristocratic and un-American. Later he came to respect many of them, but his initial hostility and certain policies so alienated the officer corps that the majority remained critical of him. Daniels papered the walls of his office with antagonistic cartoons. Industrialists and politicians found him unyielding, but he dealt adroitly with Congress.[54]

The officer corps opposed many of Daniels's activities. He enforced a policy that no officer be promoted unless he performed sea duty required of his rank. He opposed a naval general staff. He refused to grant preferential treatment to the sons of officers who sought admission to the Naval Academy. He ruled that both staff and line officers use line titles. He attempted to abolish the terms *port* and *starboard*. He allowed enlisted men to enter the Naval Academy. He was accused of "coddling" enlisted personnel because he established academic departments to provide education. His most provocative order prohibited alcohol beverages on board naval vessels. One lieutenant purchased the largest hogshead of rum available and placed it on the deck of his vessel with a sign that read, "Josephus Daniels, God Damn Him."[55] A noted historian labeled Daniels a "modernizer" because he improved the caliber of enlisted men and improved the efficiency of the twentieth-century Navy.[56]

Not all officers, of course, disliked Daniels. Many of them found him friendly and courteous. William D. Leahy, the future admiral, considered him "an able man, a man of superior energy, of calm judgment, devoted to his work." Captain Pratt agreed: "I entered my war work, with all the dislike of him held by the average officer . . . [but he] was one of the best Secretaries the Navy ever had." Admiral James O. Richardson rendered a balanced verdict. "In my opinion, Josephus Daniels was a hard-working, conscientious, and honest man, who had a great yearning to make over the Navy into a greater and finer seagoing clan. He was devoted to what he believed were the interests of the government, and applied his energies vigorously to all aspects of the Navy, EXCEPT its war-making readiness and capabilities." Certainly he followed the president's wishes during the prewar period rather than those of the advance preparedness advocates.[57] Daniels deserves credit for improving the Naval War College. Ronald Spector commented, "it is somewhat ironic that the men who were later to accuse him of incompetence and lack of understanding of their profession derived much of their 'professional' outlook from the institution which he had helped to foster."[58]

Daniels eventually became a capable secretary of the navy because, as Pratt noted, he "learned to know the Navy" and after the intervention concentrated on wartime requirements. He made good use of the CNO and others during 1917–18, suppressing his penchant for social reform in favor of achieving victory at sea.

Daniels's assistant secretary, Franklin D. Roosevelt, also lacked important qualifications, although he manifested considerable affinity for the Navy throughout his life. An admirer of Alfred Thayer Mahan and an enthusiastic yachtsman, he wished to emulate his cousin Theodore, who had served as assistant secretary of the navy during the McKinley years. He was brought into the Wilson administration because of his name. Daniels selected him in great part to lessen the influence of the Republican Theodore Roosevelt.[59]

On paper, Daniels and Roosevelt seemed incompatible, products of different classes and cultures, but the two worked well together. Daniels was a religious fundamentalist who embraced rural mores. Roosevelt, educated at Harvard, belonged to an urbane New York family of wealth. Daniels's cautious, deliberate nature at times exasperated his impatient assistant. "J.D. is just too damned slow for words," Roosevelt told his wife.[60] Daniels was an Anglophobe, while Roosevelt greatly admired the British. Daniels was a pacifist, but the militant Roosevelt favored powerful armed forces, believing that war loomed on the horizon. He once said that he could run the Department better than Daniels. FDR was sometimes insubordinate, but Daniels tolerated Roosevelt's transgressions much as he did the hostility of the officers' corps. In later years, Roosevelt developed a grudging respect for the "chief."[61] Roosevelt aided Admiral Fiske and the "reformers" in their fight to establish a general staff, but, according to Dudley Knox, opposed the creation of the position of chief of naval operations. "He felt what was true, that the creation of this Office actually reduced the importance of his position."[62] Undoubtedly his relationship with the CNO was somewhat cool. Benson knew of the assistant secretary's insubordination and of his strong alignment with the "Sims camp."

How capable was Roosevelt? Daniels passively delegated some authority, which allowed some contributions from FDR.[63] Dudley Knox was critical, claiming that "His reputation . . . was that he was a dabbler and never saw anything through. He would take up a great variety of matters but on the whole was not very constructive."[64] Also his zeal led him to overstep this authority. He sometimes clashed with Daniels and various naval officers, especially on questions of preparedness.

Shortly after the United States severed diplomatic relations with Germany, a British naval officer wrote: "What difference is it going to make? They haven't got an army. We don't want their ships over this side, but they have got dollars."[65] Many American naval officers favored the deployment of warships mostly to the waters of the Western Hemisphere. On February 4, the General Board recommended a modification of the War Plan Black, the major change being "cooperation with the naval forces of the Allies for the joint protection of transatlantic commerce and for offensive naval operations against the common enemy." Admiral Benson approved but called for an independent naval force. He expected that the nation "may eventually have to act alone." Both the CNO and the Board stressed defensive measures, preparing to concentrate the fleet against German submarines in American waters.[66]

The Atlantic Fleet was anchored in the York River near Hampton Roads when orders were received on April 6 to mobilize for war. Its commander said, "I had no information as to any contemplated employment of any vessels in European waters in co-operation with the allies."[67] Nonetheless, the Department had begun to arrange naval collaboration. On March 24, Wilson wrote Daniels, "the main thing is no doubt to get into immediate communication with the [British] Admiralty . . . and work out the scheme of cooperation." Rear Admiral William S. Sims was soon sent to Great Britain with instructions to begin consultation with the Admiralty and other officials.

Who was to blame, if anyone, for inadequate preparations? Perhaps the traditional reliance on the citizen soldier and sailor slowed improvements in the armed forces. Or should one blame Wilson, Daniels, Benson, the General Board, Congress? Captain Pratt later insisted that no one person was to blame: "I think it correct to say that the greatest naval weakness lay not in the fleet, but in the Department itself. . . . The organization and administration of the Department was not fitted to cope adequately with the situation that faced it," not having enough time to reorganize before the war came.[68] Whatever the reason, when the die was cast, the Navy responded with vigor and determination.

When the United States declared war on Germany, President Wilson's administration included a sizable number of officials who were suspicious of Great Britain. These concerns deepened as some American leaders concluded that Britain was not doing everything it could to win the war, and that military and naval operations were basically defensive, especially the antisubmarine campaign. The CNO was quite pessimistic about British naval operations and felt strongly that the British had not been candid about the submarine peril. Daniels, according to a British officer who conferred with him, "appeared to be imbued with the idea that the apparent inactivity of the British Fleet represented a failure to prosecute the war with all the vigor demanded by the present situation." He added, "I met with this sentiment, not only from civilians, but also from Naval Officers."[69]

Did the nation develop its own naval strategy for the war, or did it adopt Allied designs primarily shaped by the most powerful sea power, Great Britain? The Navy's first and most important mission was to protect the nation's shores. This reality led initially to the retention of the bulk of the fleet in American waters, including antisubmarine craft, but as time passed the Navy deployed increasing numbers of warships and personnel to European waters in response to growing awareness of the naval crisis. Even the German U-boat campaign in the Western Hemisphere in 1918 failed to alter this trend.

In addition to coast defense, two other principles became central to Washington's naval policy. American leaders favored offensive inter-Allied operations on the part of the Allied navies. Also, seeking to protect American troop transports, the Navy gave priority to the use of its naval units in convoy and antisubmarine operations. The United States has traditionally preferred offensive naval operations and did so during 1917–18. President Wilson advocated attacks against fortified German ports, "destroying the hornets' nests" to end the submarine crisis. This exhortation, as much as anything else, was responsible for much of the criticism of the Royal Navy in Washington. Also, according to David Trask, President Wilson concluded that the Allied and Associated powers, if they desired a successful peace settlement, must inflict a decisive defeat on the Central powers. The Navy accepted Sims's argument that this assumption dictated reinforcement of the antisubmarine campaign.[70]

Admiral Sims largely defined U.S. naval policy, which came to reflect the views of the Allies, particularly Britain. Cooperation/collaboration became the keystone of Sims's actions while he was in command of U.S. naval forces in European waters. It required commitment to the point of "ignoring all questions of national pride."[71] He altered his original opinion (and policy) about a number of schemes such as undertaking the North Sea Mine Barrage, deploying battleships in European waters, and priorities for shipping troops and material to Europe. Sims adopted the Admiralty's view on nearly all issues, although he realized that he would endanger his credibility with Washington officials. He stressed the absolute necessity of concentrating American naval resources in order to neutralize the U-boat menace. All antisubmarine craft should be sent to European waters, and construction of ASW vessels should take place at the expense of capital ships and merchant vessels.[72]

Sims's support of deploying destroyers and other antisubmarine craft in the war zone materialized during his first week in London. He arrived on April 10 and immediately called on an old friend, Admiral Sir John Jellicoe, the first sea lord. At this meeting, described by Sims in *The Victory at Sea*, Jellicoe dramatically described the crisis at sea. Jellicoe "showed that the total sinkings, British and neutral, had reached 536,000 tons in February and 603,000 in March. . . . [S]inkings were taking place in April which indicated the destruction of nearly 900,000 tons." The astonished Sims then expressed his consternation. Jellicoe responded "as quietly as though he were discussing the weather and not the future of the British Empire. It is impossible for us to go on with the war if losses like this continue." Sims then asked what was being done to defeat the U-boats. Jellicoe replied: "Everything that we can. We are increasing our anti-submarine forces in every possible way. We are using every possible craft we can find with which to fight submarines. We are building destroyers, trawlers, and other like craft as fast as we can. But the situation is very serious and we shall need all of the assistance we can get." Sims observed that "It looks as though the Germans were winning," and the first sea lord agreed. "They will win, unless we can stop these losses—and stop them soon." Sims asked whether there was a solution. "Absolutely none that we can see now," Jellicoe announced.[73]

From the British viewpoint, Sims's presence in England proved exceedingly fortuitous. He arrived just after the United States declared war, he was a well-known Anglophile, and, equally important, he and the first lord were friends, a friendship that went back nearly two decades.[74] Jellicoe wrote later that "It was very necessary to bring home to the United States Navy Department the need for early action," and his friend Sims was the one to do it. Although Jellicoe later denied he had no solution for the submarine problem and that "we certainly were not in a state of panic,"[75] he was extremely pessimistic when he met with Sims because the antisubmarine campaign had failed abjectly to that point.

Lord Jellicoe identified three ways to end the submarine menace: "The first, naturally, was to prevent the vessels from putting to sea; the second was to sink them after they were at sea; and the third was to protect the merchant ships from their attack."[76] At first the Royal Navy adopted the second tactic. New weapons were introduced to sink U-boats, the most successful being the depth charge. Hydrophones were used with limited success to detect submarines below the surface.

Destroyers were the most effective ASW vessels, although they were originally designed to protect capital ships. Most of those available were assigned that mission. British ASW operations at first emphasized a system of surface patrols in U-boat–infested waters. These patrols absorbed most of the small craft in hand, but they were ineffective.[77]

Sims obtained information on the submarine war from documents and reports provided by Jellicoe and during conferences with Admiralty officials. He found it difficult to accept this material: "I delayed [four days] forwarding my first report . . . with a view of obtaining the maximum information. . . . I was also somewhat deterred by a natural reluctance to alter so radically my preconceived views and opinion as to the situation."[78] Jellicoe confided to David Beatty, C-in-C of the Grand Fleet, that he hoped "to get a good deal out of U.S.A. Sims . . . arrived here; he is quite sound and is acting whole-heartedly with me. I am telling him the situation frankly as it is necessary to let the USA realize that we want help at *once* in small craft and shipping. I hope to get a lot of destroyers over here very soon."[79] Sims realized that "Everything . . . reduced itself to the question of destroyers."[80]

Sims's initial report to the Department of April 14 stressed the calamity of the submarine crisis, which he deemed "very much more [dangerous] . . . than the people realize in America." He outlined the huge destruction of merchant shipping without a corresponding destruction of submarines. "The morale of the enemy submarines is not broken, only about fifty-four are known to have been captured or sunk," and new construction had replaced the losses. He urged an all-out deployment of destroyers and small craft, an appeal (often a demand) repeated in cable after cable during the following weeks and months.[81]

Five days later, Sims dispatched a much more extensive report. He detailed how he had gone about collecting information: "The evidence is conclusive that, regardless of any enemy diversions such as raids on our coast or elsewhere, the critical area will be made in the eastern Atlantic at the focus of all lines of communications." He discussed a variety of topics such as control of merchant shipping; utilization of antisubmarine measures and weapons such as zigzagging and depth charges; the fallacy of attempting to bottle up the submarines in their bases with nets, mines, etc.; and the use of submarines against submarines. He had raised the possibility of convoying (probably with an Admiralty official) but was told that "the area is too large; the necessary vessels are not available." Nevertheless, he considered it feasible. "I am now consulting with the Director of Shipping as to the practicability and advisability of attempting some approach to such a plan in case the U.S. is able to put in operation sufficient tonnage to warrant it."[82]

Sims later complained that more than two weeks elapsed before he received a reply to his first messages. On April 22, the CNO cabled that the president had approved the dispatch of six destroyers to British waters.[83] Nonetheless, Sims was convinced that Washington officials thought his "gloom and doom" reports unduly "alarmist." He urged a naval officer returning to Washington to impress upon the Department the "extreme gravity of the submarine situation abroad." He appealed to Herbert Hoover, returning to the United States after heading Belgium relief, to intercede with the president about the crisis. He also conferred with Ambassador Page and found him equally alarmed. "They think I am . . . pro-British and that I am being used," Sims confided to the ambassador. "But if you'll take it up directly with the President, they may be convinced."[84] Page fully supported Sims and exhorted Wilson and the secretary of state to send all-out naval support: "All the destroyers, and hundreds of armed sea-going tugs, yachts, . . . any kind of swift small ship."[85] Page continued to support Sims, but, like the admiral, he was viewed as a rabid Anglophile.

Sims was partially correct about the attitude of the Navy Department. Daniels found it difficult to believe that the situation was as desperate as Sims pictured it. As he observed in his memoirs, "Sims' grim news was in striking contrast with the buoyantly optimistic reports appearing in the British newspapers."[86] The reports from London, however, convinced Admiral Benson that the British might well lose and that sooner or later the U.S. Navy would have to face the German fleet. The CNO and his advisers also expected U-boats to shortly appear off the Atlantic coast. Some within the Department wanted to keep the powerful Atlantic Fleet intact, sending to European waters only a limited number of destroyers and small craft. They believed that the Navy Department was both psychologically and materially unprepared for large-scale deployment of men and ships overseas.[87]

Nonetheless, Sims was not entirely correct in attributing the silence from Washington to his "Anglophism [sic] or alarmism." Confusion and uncertainty reigned among the service's high command, both military and civilian, partly because the Navy lacked detailed operational plans. Plans to mobilize the fleet, purchase supplies, increase personnel by calling up reserves and recruiting volunteers, and establish training camps were approved before the outbreak of war and put into effect immediately with its declaration. The task of implementing these mobilization plans overwhelmed the woefully inadequate Navy Department. The Department of Opera-

tions under the CNO in theory had the responsibility for all operations and war planning, but Benson was still defining and developing a division of the Navy that had not
existed before 1915. For example, he had no authority over the bureaus and the General Board. He could monitor the fleet, but the Bureau of Navigation appointed ship
commanders. Other admirals were supposed to provide supplies, build new ships,
and maintain them in operating condition. The bureaus remained directly under the
secretary's control. If Operations recommended that a particular bureau take action
on something, the CNO had to get Daniels's approval. The secretary of the navy had
to sign all policy and major operational decisions, but he often procrastinated. Unduly frequent conferences of the staff, the bureau chiefs, the CNO, the secretary of
the navy, and other government officials compounded the confusion. These meetings dealt with a host of issues that required decisions on a myriad of items from new
construction to recruiting. Sims's communications were often lost in the bewildering
profusion of discussions. Sims never understood these circumstances. The delays of
1917 led to his accusation in 1920 that the Navy Department had not been prepared
for war and that it ignored his urgent requests for ships and personnel.[88]

Another cause of the "silence" out of Washington during the early weeks of the war
was the consultations with the Allies. These meetings eventually produced decisions
on cooperation with the Allies, including deployment of destroyers and other craft to
European waters. Sims was not informed of the first of these conferences, one with a
British mission, until it was over. "I learned of the [agreement] by accident," he testified after the war.[89]

From mid-April until July, Sims concentrated on persuading the Department to
accept his recommendations, especially the need to deploy destroyers in British waters. The CNO's decision to retain some antisubmarine craft to patrol the Atlantic seaboard greatly disappointed him. To Pratt, he wrote, "It would be very funny, if it were
not so tragic, the spectacle of many dozens of ships, destroyers, yachts, and so forth
parading up and down the American coast three thousand miles away from where the
vital battle of the war is going on."[90]

Admiral Benson admitted after the war that "My first thought . . . was to see that our
coasts and our own vessels and our own interests were safeguarded. Then when I was
satisfied that that was done as far as I could, with what we had, then to give everything
we possibly could for the common cause."[91] Daniels entrusted the allocation of destroyers to the CNO, who was determined to retain the number of destroyers thought required to protect the capital ships.[92] Although Benson tended to resist Sims's recommendations on the deployment of destroyers and other issues, his decisions, as David
Trask notes, were for the most part accepted, although grudgingly. Sims reacted to the
immediacy of the submarine crisis, whereas the CNO concerned himself with protecting the American coast and the possibility of British defeat. Nevertheless, Benson
agreed to the dispatch of antisubmarine craft as they became available.[93]

By June 1, twenty-four had appeared in British waters, and within a month twenty-
eight of the available fifty-two destroyers were able to conduct operations from Ireland. Admiral Albert Gleaves, who commanded the Atlantic Fleet's Destroyer Flotilla,
wrote in some anguish: "The first thing I noted in [the newspapers] this morning were

the glaring headlines of destroyers (my destroyers) in Europe and praise for Sims. . . . I feel as if I had died and been buried and that all my life and my career were finished and behind me." In his memoirs, he lamented, "Thus at the beginning of the war I lost my Force."[94]

Equally important, the Navy began to stress construction of antisubmarine vessels. The British mission arrived late in April to arrange naval cooperation and urged Wilson's government to build destroyers, sloops, and other smaller types. Benson and the General Board were opposed to this action because it kept the Navy from the capital-ship construction program intended to secure naval equality with Germany and Japan in such vessels by 1920. The Board, however, recognized that a substantial number of antisubmarine vessels had to go to European waters but decided that this requirement need not compromise the capital-ship program. On May 3, after surveying all potential ASW craft, including private yachts, it recommended the immediate dispatch of thirty-six destroyers and a tender to Europe and an additional one hundred ASW vessels as soon as possible.[95]

On July 6, a special board on antisubmarine warfare reported that 220 new destroyers were needed to combat the U-boats. Daniels and a reluctant CNO endorsed the report. The secretary sent it to the president, but it was not approved until September.[96] Few of the new destroyers arrived in European waters before the Armistice.

During the first week of July 1917, a series of cables crossed the Atlantic that settled the Department's policy. Captain Pratt informed Sims that the Department had little or no information about the operations of the British Navy. "In the spirit of cooperation what [are] the Admiralty's . . . conceptions. . . . Just what is their major plan? Is its fundamental conception offensive or defensive? What are the tactical details in general by which this plan is to be solved? Those are the things we want to know, and these are the things we have a right to know." He noted that the British and by implication Sims kept asking for help but did not provide supporting information. "The Admiral [Benson] is willing to recommend anything, any forces so long as he knows" the plans. Pratt mentioned the need to conduct offensive operations in two areas, the North Sea and the Adriatic. He specifically mentioned mining as "the strongest offensive agency" against submarines. Finally he insisted that these ideas were not his alone but reflective of a consensus in the Department.[97]

On July 3, Daniels sent a comprehensive declaration of American naval policy to Sims listing six fundamental objectives:

1. Full cooperation with the Allies against the submarine "compatible with an adequate defense of our own home waters."
2. Full cooperation to cope with problems and situations.
3. Concentration on ending the present conflict but in a way that would not "jeopardize" the main fleets.
4. Recognition that the Navy's primary responsibility was to protect lines of communication to the Allies.
5. Emphasis on offensive operations.
6. Willingness (a) to deploy antisubmarine craft not needed at home to Eu-

ropean waters; (*b*) to send the entire fleet if necessary; and (*c*) to discuss joint operations.[98]

The next day, President Wilson cabled Sims to criticize the British navy: "From the beginning of the war I have been surprised by nothing so much as the failure of the British Admiralty to use Great Britain's great naval superiority in any effective way." He asked what the Admiralty intended to do. He also endorsed a convoy system, unaware that the British had already approved this tactic.[99] The president sent a copy of his letter to Daniels implying that the United States should develop its own naval policy.

Finally, on July 5, Lord Northcliffe, an influential British publisher and confidant of the prime minister, reported from Washington the American dissatisfaction with British naval policy. He mentioned three themes advocated by the U.S. Navy—offensive operations, mining, and convoying. Arthur Pollen, an influential English journalist in the United States, reiterated Northcliffe's concerns. Sims referred to the American criticisms as "mob strategy."[100]

The timing of these four messages was no coincidence. They defined American naval policy and what was expected of the Allies. The Department also reacted to German policy. The undersea onslaught affected U.S. naval policy more than any other issue during the war. Finally, the Department recognized that the Royal Navy was far more powerful than its American counterpart and had accumulated more than three years of wartime experience.

Sims responded to Wilson on July 7 and to the naval secretary a week later, reemphasizing the necessity of maximum cooperation with the Royal Navy and the defeat of the submarine campaign. Although he favored deploying the Navy abroad, including battleships, he told Daniels that it could not be done because of logistical difficulties. He reiterated the need to send all light craft, including destroyers, to European waters. They were required to protect convoys. He advocated a switch from construction of capital ships and merchant ships to the building of antisubmarine craft. Finally, he criticized the Department's policy of retaining naval units in home waters that should be sent to the war zone. Trask maintains that "Nothing irritated Sims more than a persistent concern in Washington about coast defense in the Western Hemisphere."[101]

The recommendation to separate the destroyer screen from the battleships seemed contrary to the regnant Mahanian doctrine—concentration of all fleet elements—but Sims argued that the relevant concentration was in the English Channel and that the deployment of American naval vessels to augment the Allies was consistent with Mahan's doctrine.[102] This unique interpretation of Mahan's views reflected the onset of coalition warfare. It failed to resolve differences between Sims and the Navy Department. Wilson and Daniels were convinced that Sims was espousing British policy, and they were quite correct. Sims, however, had no other reasonable option. By August, the Department finally recognized the extent of the maritime crisis and gave priority to the use of American antisubmarine vessels in the war zone.

Nonetheless, fundamental differences over policy existed between Britain and the

United States. The Navy Department correctly viewed British naval strategy as basically defensive. The General Board concluded, "the defensive nature of this so-called policy is plainly indicated by the objects to be attained; . . . the leading words . . . [are] (1) protection (2) prevention."[103] Winston Churchill, when first lord of the Admiralty, advocated offensive operations both in the North Sea and the Mediterranean, but the British attempted only one, the attack at Gallipoli in 1915, a disaster that caused Churchill's downfall.

Traditionally the British navy used its sea power in wars against European powers to blockade enemy ports and control lines of communication. Close blockade was impracticable against Germany in World War I, but the Royal Navy established a distant blockade, keeping the battle fleet concentrated in the North Sea ports to keep the German High Seas Fleet in port and to control merchant shipping. In November 1917, the Admiralty declared the entire North Sea a war zone, prohibiting all traffic, including that of neutrals. A blockade was not officially proclaimed, but the British decree effectively closed German ports to trade. The prohibited area was changed from time to time, but it remained in effect even after the Armistice, imposing severe hardships on the German people. The United States, upon entering the war, in general prohibited the export of a variety of goods such as foodstuffs, coal, steel to neutrals, tacitly supporting the Allied blockade, but it did not engage in the search and seizure of neutral vessels.[104]

The blockade was designed to coerce the Central powers into ending the war by undermining the enemy's economy and to keep their fleets quiescent. The British Grand Fleet was based at Scapa Flow in the Orkney Islands and at Rosyth, Scotland, to control the North Seas, and the Channel Fleet maintained vigilance in the English Channel. Concentrated at Dover, it protected the vital cross-channel artery to France. The French and Italians operated in the Mediterranean, although Britain kept a naval force at Malta to protect the sea lane from the Suez Canal through the Strait of Gibraltar. The bulk of the fleet remained in the North Sea. As Paul M. Kennedy and Arthur J. Marder have emphasized, Great Britain could gain its principal objectives at sea by blocking the northern and southern entrances to the English Channel, standing on the defense, and sustaining the blockade to undermine Germany's economy.[105]

Britain's survival also depended upon control of the sea lanes to Commonwealth nations and neutrals. The Royal Navy deployed cruisers and small forces to carry out this responsibility. The introduction of submarine warfare, however, severely compromised these lines of communications. Nonetheless, the Admiralty refused to use significant elements of the Grand Fleet for this purpose. Although the C-in-C of the Grand Fleet in 1918 recognized the threat of the U-boats, his concern that the German High Seas Fleet might attempt a sortie into the North Sea prompted him to refuse transferring any of his destroyers to the Atlantic. The only major change in naval operations was to avoid fleet action, whereas in the past the Royal Navy sought out such an opportunity.[106] This cautious defensive tactic infuriated the Americans, particularly Wilson and his naval advisors.

German strategy was equally timorous; the fleet admirals would accept a full fleet action only in favorable conditions. Except for chance encounters, notably those at

Dogger Banks and Jutland, a stalemate persisted in the North Sea. This impasse clearly benefited the British, which suggests the essential soundness of this defensive posture. The joker was the submarine. Undersea warfare could not challenge Allied control of the North Sea, but it unquestionably threatened command of the Atlantic.

Admiral Sims exerted a powerful influence on naval policy, especially by interpreting directives from the Department to reflect his views. He did so without stimulating an official reaction until a controversy arose over the amount of compensation due to the British for repairs to American ships completed in British shipyards. Sims had approved payment. When Daniels learned of this decision, he sent what can only be called a severe reprimand to the force commander: "Department feels that in initiating policy [decidedly] contrary to the wishes and intentions of this government you have committed an error of judgment. In future do not initiate general policies of international character without first communicating with the Department, giving your views and obtaining views of this government through the Department, before taking up with foreign official matters affecting international policy."[107] In March 1918, Benson warned Sims not to change the department's policy without approval from Washington.[108] Nevertheless, Sims remained in his command throughout the war, conducting affairs through a staff in London that became known as "Simsadus," a rendition of "Sims, U.S. Admiral." This organization, unprecedented in American naval history, exerted profound influence during 1917–18.

Simsadus

On April 9, 1917, Admiral Sims and his aide, Commander J. V. Babcock, arrived at Liverpool, England. The voyage had been uneventful until their ship entered the harbor, but then it struck a mine. The passengers, including the two naval officers, were transferred by lifeboat to a small excursion steamer and landed at the quay. A representative of the Admiralty met Sims and escorted him by special train to London.[1]

Before leaving the United States, Sims claimed that Admiral Benson told him: "Don't let the British pull the wool over your eyes. It is none of our business pulling their chestnuts out of the fire. We would as soon fight the British as the Germans." Later the CNO half-heartedly challenged Sims's recollection of the remark. Daniels was equally explicit: "You have been selected for this mission not because of your Guildhall speech, but in spite of it."[2] In 1910, while commanding a battleship on a European cruise, Sims gave an informal speech at the Guildhall in London, in which he said, "if the time ever comes when the British Empire is seriously menaced by an external enemy, it is my opinion that you may count upon every man, every dollar, every drop of blood of your kindred across the sea." His remarks were widely publicized in England and the United States. This indiscretion evoked a reprimand from President Taft. Thereafter Sims was labeled an Anglophile, an accurate description. This reputation led to suspicion that in London he acted simply as a mouthpiece for the British Admiralty. The British, of course, were delighted with the selection of Sims and remained so throughout the war. At a farewell luncheon for Sims after the war as he prepared to return to the United States, one of those present remarked, "his presence in Washington will make a British Ambassador almost superfluous."[3]

Sims belongs to an elite fraternity whose members dominated a brief interlude of American naval history. David Farragut, David Dixon Porter, and Ernest King are also members of this select group. Admiral William V. Pratt later wrote, "probably no man in our recent naval history has left a more indelible stamp of his personality than Admiral Sims." Numerous naval officers and naval historians have expressed similar sentiments. Yet, as David Trask notes in an introduction to Sims's chronicle of the war years, *The Victory at Sea*, he is not as well remembered as other naval officers who held important commands during wartime. In contrast to Farragut, Halsey, Dewey, and John Paul Jones, only one full-length study of Sims has appeared, perhaps because he was an "armchair" admiral during World War I.[4]

William Sowden Sims was born to an American engineer and a Canadian mother on October 15, 1858, in the village of Port Hope on Lake Ontario, a fact more than once cited to explain his Anglophilism. Sims usually ignored remarks written about him, but he rankled at being referred to as Canadian rather than American. In 1872, his family moved to Pennsylvania, and he became a U.S. citizen. He entered the Naval Academy in 1876 despite a poor academic background, including inadequate foreign languages. This youthful deficiency later astonished the French because he became fluent in their language when he spent a year of study in Paris.[5] Sims graduated in the middle of his class in 1880 and received his commission two years later. His mediocre academic background possibly impelled him to read extensively later in life. The writings of Charles Darwin, Herbert Spencer, and above all Henry George stimulated him. He became an advocate of naval reform, joining a legion of political and social reformers during the Progressive Age from 1900 to 1921.

Sims's early career, according to one classmate, was less than brilliant, but "he was always full of life and fun. . . . He was always ready, willing and anxious to do his whole duty and do it well." Even then, however, he displayed impatience with what he considered stupidity and sham. He was "forthright to a fault, leaving no doubt about his views," as Trask put it, or as Admiral King wrote later, "all matters [to Sims] were clear white or dead black." He was unpopular with his seniors, whom he often called "Principal Dignitaries" or "P.D.s." Pratt considered him "impulsive." He was "indiscreet" to a fault, often exaggerating; as one naval officer wrote, "he lacked . . . the power of understatement." Others called him "loquacious," a nonconformist, a maverick, a muckraker, "a good deal of an iconoclast."[6]

With individuals outside his staff and supporters who disagreed with him, he was often intolerant, contentious, occasionally abrasive, and egocentric. Josephus Daniels noted that "Sims paid very little attention to the views of others." The confident Sims once wrote his wife: "There is no doubt whatever that my recommendations have been sound. . . . There is no possible mistake about this."[7]

Sims's impulsiveness, frankness, and at times tactlessness were refreshing to many writers and fellow naval officers. Hamilton Holt noted after an interview, "He is one of those men who apparently [do] not hesitate to say what he thinks." Another writer referred to him as the "*L'enfant Terrible* of the American Navy" because of his outspokenness, while a British journalist said that the admiral was no diplomat, "for his specialty is saying exactly what he means." Lord John Jellicoe, first sea lord, admired his "habit of speaking his mind with absolutely fearless disregard of the consequences." Fleet Admiral William F. Halsey later recalled that Sims "seemed to exult in affronting authority."[8]

Whatever the cause of his candid behavior, Sims admitted that he loved "to tilt at windmills," to uncover deficiencies and "smash idols." James Field argued that, like many reformers, Sims saw "hostility and conspiracy where there existed merely indifference, incompetence, or procrastination." Perhaps his conviction of rightness hardened his opinions. His superiors, however, were less tolerant. Many took offense at one time or another, including President Wilson, Secretary Daniels, Admiral Benson, the bureau chiefs, and many other senior officers. He shrugged off criticism and "wore official reprimands with as much credit as other men wear medals."[9]

Sims once remarked that luck often shaped one's career. His proficiency in French helped prepare him for service as naval attaché to France. An assignment as intelligence officer on the cruiser *Charleston* on the Asiatic Station during the Sino-Japanese War allowed him to compare foreign and American warships. Later, Sims's often lengthy reports impressed a youthful assistant secretary of the navy, Theodore Roosevelt. While serving on the battleship *Kentucky* during another Asian tour, he met a talented British officer, Sir Percy Scott, who exercised a profound effect on him

Important friends helped Sims, but he accomplished a great deal on his own. His analysis of foreign warships allowed him to identify the inadequacies of U.S. naval vessels, particularly battleships. The information about gunnery, especially "continuous-air firing," accumulated from Captain Scott and other British officers persuaded him to convey his concerns to the Navy Department. He bombarded the Department with critical reports and distributed copies to fellow officers. In 1901, he ignored the traditional chain of command and wrote directly to President Roosevelt about the "inefficiency of the Navy." Despite growing unpopularity with many senior officers, he became inspector of target practice in 1902. He brought about a considerable increase in the efficiency of gunners.[10] He was less successful in efforts to improve ship design and the administration of the Navy Department. However, he became an early advocate of the dreadnought, an all-big-gun battleship type, and helped persuade Roosevelt to arrange their construction. As one of the "young Turks" and other naval reformers, he supported Admiral Bradley Fiske's failed attempts to create a general staff.

Before Roosevelt left office, he awarded Sims the most coveted of all billets at that time, command of the new battleship *Minnesota*, but, after Sims made his Guildhall speech, he was exiled to the Naval War College in Newport, Rhode Island. His two years as a student were extremely beneficial; they allowed him to develop an understanding of higher tactical command. The Navy benefited because he applied War College methods to fleet problems, first on an experimental basis as commander of the Atlantic Fleet's Destroyer Flotilla and later on a practical basis as commander of U.S. naval forces in European waters during World War I.[11]

Sims's philosophy of command centered on two fundamental concepts: teamwork, or the "conference approach," and decentralized responsibility. He believed that the "organized team idea produced the maximum result of which the organization is capable."[12] Captain Twining, his chief of staff at Simsadus, observed that "Admiral Sims' theory of exercising his command . . . was to leave to his subordinate commanders all possible initiative and discretion; give them their mission, give them all the information he could, and leave it to them to carry out their duties according to their own ideas. . . . [He] never exercised any direct command from London of any of his forces." Captain Pratt considered that Sims "could detect the right qualities in another man and use them for the good of a cause. . . . [H]is personality ensures absolute loyalty."[13] He told his wife that he did not see documents until "they have been studied by the branch of the staff concerned, and usually an answer prepared for my consideration. . . . Even for a question of policy to be decided our 'planning section' . . . discuss it, study it, and reach a decision before [they] bring it to me. In any case, when a final decision is reached, I almost never write it. A tentative draft is composed, typewritten and brought to me for approval. . . . This will, I believe, make it clear how the organization works, and how small an amount of work it puts on me."[14]

Sims enjoyed a productive tenure as Destroyer Flotilla commander. He initiated a series of war games and maneuvers designed to develop teamwork between all types of ships. The term *band of brothers*, earlier used to describe Lord Nelson's devoted officers, was used to identify followers of Sims. Some officers of the flotilla withheld their homage. Ernest King admitted admiration for many of Sims's ideas but deplored his "exaggeration" and "temperament" and labeled him "a show off." Dudley Knox, who served in the Destroyer Flotilla and Simsadus, declared: "our personal relations [were] . . . never very cordial. In fact, temperamentally we are as opposite as the poles."[15] Nonetheless, the overwhelming majority of those who served with Sims in the flotilla were extremely loyal to him and valued their membership in the "band of brothers."

According to one authority, "no other American naval officer of this century has aroused such enthusiastic loyalty as he drew from the Destroyer officers based on Queenstown and Plymouth and those attached to the London Flagship." In this, the writer added, "he may be compared to Farragut and Porter—indeed, to the great Nelson."[16] Admiral Harold Stark, who served in Simsadus and later as CNO when Japan attacked Pearl Harbor, told his wife that "everyone looks at him and admires him— you and everyone at home can feel he is your admiral as well as ours because he belongs to all the United States and is worthy of it." Captain Reginald Belknap, who laid the North Sea Mine Barrage in 1918, wrote a few years after Sims's death that he was the most prominent of only a few naval officers who had "the strength of purpose" and the "unquenchable spirit" never "to accept discouragement, no matter how long . . . opportunity was deferred."[17] A veteran bluejacket testified that "Sims was the idol of the torpedo boat sailors because they believed that he was responsible for allowing them to wear dungarees when he commanded the Destroyer Flotilla. The soot and cinders from the stacks of the old coal burners kept them blackened all the time."[18]

On May 25, 1917, Commander Joseph Taussig, the commander of the first destroyers to arrive in British waters, wrote in his journal, "I can well imagine that Admiral Sims will be very popular over here, and there is no doubt in my mind but that he is the best man we could possibly have sent."[19] The Admiralty was delighted at his selection. British subjects from the king to schoolchildren came to admire him. The British press lionized him. His name was a "household word in England," according to an article in a London newspaper.[20] Vice Admiral Sir Rosslyn ("Rosy") Erskine Wemyss, Jellicoe's successor as first sea lord, observed, "I doubt very much whether any other United States Naval officer would have achieved the same result as he has." Lord George Riddell, an associate of Prime Minister David Lloyd George, wrote Sims, "You are one of the best bits of cement ever produced!" The admiral's personal secretary, an Englishwoman, told one of his staff after the war that, "Having Admiral Sims represent the Navy in England was one of the best things that ever happened to the Navy and the United States. . . . He is one of the biggest men I have ever known."[21]

"Admiral Sims is the Greek God of the navies," an Englishwoman remarked in admiration, and a biographer portrayed him as one of the handsomest naval officers ever to wear the uniform, a sentiment shared by many others.[22] His striking appearance stayed with him throughout his life. He was quite tall—6 feet 3 inches—and slender, "straight as a lance," and he maintained remarkable physical shape. He possessed short-cropped hair, gray by 1917, piercing blue eyes, and a pointed beard. Sims admitted that he grew his beard while studying in Paris. According to a reporter from *Le Figaro*, it gave him a "French look."[23] He was an immaculate dresser, whether in uniform or civilian attire.

Sims was dignified but friendly and nearly always in good spirits. He frequently voiced his well-known motto, "cheer up and get busy." An excellent speaker and accomplished raconteur, he enlivened both his conversations and formal talks with anecdotes and jokes. One French journalist called him a "gifted" and "elegant" speaker, perhaps in part because of his fluency in French. On occasion he would use the epithets and salty language traditionally associated with sailors.[24]

Sims reveled in cleanliness and physical conditioning. Throughout his life, he exercised vigorously. He cared nothing for blood sport, refusing invitations to attend "hunts," but enjoyed athletic games of all kinds. He played his favorite sport of tennis regularly. He encouraged those under his command to organize teams and leagues and play against teams from the armed services of other nations. He also enjoyed walking, even in damp London weather, indulging in brisk daily strolls to and from his office.[25]

Sims's obvious popularity in Great Britain annoyed some important officers and civilians at home. His critics were convinced that Sims was more British than American or at least so enamored of the British that he compromised his own country and its policies. Woodrow Wilson lost faith in Sims and might well have wished for his removal from the European command, saying at one time that "Admiral Sims should be wearing a British uniform."[26] Secretary Daniels and Admiral Benson deplored his Anglophilism. Rear Admiral Joseph Strauss recalled that even Captain Twining despaired of Sims's "subserviency" to the British.[27] Sims admitted to his liking for things British but denied that this sentiment influenced his decisions.

At first Sims served simply as an "observer" assigned to inform the Navy Department of British views on naval matters, but soon the decision to deploy thirty-six destroyers in the war zone and the imminent arrival of additional units required the establishment of a senior naval command. Although Daniels and Benson had reservations about Sims, he was the logical choice to lead the Navy in Europe. Already overseas, he enjoyed a useful rapport with the Admiralty and had exercised command at sea before the war. Sims was informed of his appointment on April 28, while the first six destroyers to come under his command were en route to Ireland. Neither the secretary of the navy nor the CNO anticipated the rapid deployment of U.S. naval forces to European waters in great numbers, nor did they realize that the new command would assume exceptional importance quickly. Benson tried to deemphasize the importance of Sims's assignment.[28] Rear Admiral Josiah McKean, one of the CNO's subordinates in Operations, testified during the hearings in 1920 that Sims appropriated "broader functions and reached for higher powers than it was intended he should have." The diarist Daniels recorded: "talked to Admiral F. F. Fletcher about Sims. He said he had warned me about Sims but agreed with me that Sims ought to go to London as observer, but not in command of forces."[29]

Some years after the war, Benson described Sims's command: "[Sims] . . . never commanded any naval forces. The destroyers sent over were immediately turned over to the Commander of the British Vice Admiral at Queenstown. Later on, when a battleship division was sent over, it was placed under command of the British Commander in charge of the Grand Fleet. They and all the rest of the naval forces in European waters were always subject to the direction of the Chief of Naval Operations." The former CNO also wrote, "I have refrained from coming out in the public press, in order to avoid anything like a Sampson-Schley controversy . . . among high ranking officers of the service which have followed other wars."[30] The feared controversy never achieved the notoriety of the Sampson-Schley imbroglio after the Spanish-American War in 1898, at least partly because of public aversion to mention of the war during the immediate postwar years.

Sims's actions during the war appear consistent with Benson's definition of his billet. Sims did not exercise "direct command from London of any of his forces," but he maintained administrative control, which meant to him that he was in control of all his forces, including the naval vessels. This was more a result of his philosophy of command and his belief in total amalgamation of Allied forces than a conception of his job as the CNO defined it. At times Allied commanders with American naval units under their control consulted Sims about operations. Also, Sims broke his flag on the tender *Melville* at Queenstown as commander of the U.S. naval force based there without objection from the Department. Sims maintained that he wore two hats, one as C-in-C of U.S. naval forces in European waters and a second as commander of the destroyer force. He ordered his chief of staff to create a staff in Queenstown parallel to Simsadus in London.[31]

Sims never received orders making him commander in chief of the U.S. naval forces in European waters, but he assumed the responsibilities and authority of a C-in-C. Sims and the Department agreed that as force commander he represented it in Europe at an advanced headquarters to coordinate naval affairs with the Allies.

The Department assumed that Sims was subordinate to Admiral Mayo, the commander of the Atlantic Fleet, in operational matters and to Benson in dealings with the Allies. Benson, Daniels, and Pratt did not agree that he held an independent command, but Sims thought so and acted accordingly.

Sims worked assiduously to create an autonomous command while professing loyalty to Benson's differing definition of it. Through frequent communications with the CNO, Pratt, and other Navy Department officials, and by passing his views through officers sent to Washington, he constantly sought to maintain his independence. "I can understand perfectly well the disposition there must always be at the Navy Department to make decisions, *even when they concern local affairs over here*," he wrote to Pratt. "Of course you know this is something which should be resisted as much as possible. The *responsibility* for local *disposition*, and for their success must necessarily be *on this side*."[32]

Although Sims did not write to Benson in this tone, his views reached the CNO, but he did not repudiate Sims's interpretation of his position, one that differed from his earlier instructions. Sims's powers may not have been as impressive as he describes them in *The Victory at Sea*, as Michael Simpson observes, but they were substantial. Although Admiral Benson informed Sims that he had the authority to distribute his forces as he saw fit, quite often the CNO decided such matters. Sims protested in vain to Pratt. He once informed his wife that he had not been "given any authority to change the duties of officers assigned to ships or stations by the department, but have assumed it. I am shifting [Admiral Henry B.] Wilson to Brest and have ordered [Admiral William B. Fletcher] home without consulting the department." When President Wilson arrived at Brest on the *George Washington* shortly after the Armistice, the battleships and destroyers assigned to escort him into port flew Sims's flag as commander of U.S. naval forces in Europe.[33] Probably Daniels and Benson considered that his administrative responsibilities warranted this.

Sims's subordinates sometimes were unsure of his command authority. One officer recalled that Sims had command of all U.S. naval vessels in European waters "except those at Scapa Flow." Rear Admiral Hugh Rodman, who commanded the American battleship division attached to the Grand Fleet, testified at the naval hearings that Sims's title as "Commanding United States Naval Forces in European Waters" was particularly misleading. He was a subordinate part of Naval Operations located in London. "He did not personally direct the movements of our fighting ships in the war zone."[34] Curiously Rodman later admitted that Sims was his superior officer. Admiral Harold Stark, a member of Simsadus during World War I, considered himself Sims's successor when he became commander of U.S. naval forces in Europe during World War II. Like Sims, he believed that his command was "the advanced headquarters of the U.S. Navy in Europe."[35] Rear Admiral Joseph Strauss, who commanded mine-laying operations in British waters, also questioned Sims's authority over him in his unpublished memoirs. Other senior officers, particularly Rear Admiral Henry B. Wilson, at times ignored the chain of command and consulted the Department directly. Sims insisted that his position was "precisely the same as that of General Pershing." A document prepared by his staff in late 1918 used exactly the same words and added, "The Department deals only with Admiral Sims' headquarters, and Admiral Sims in turn directs and coordinates the work of all the various groups under his general command."[36]

The Navy Department never resolved the ambiguity of Sims's position. He was quickly appointed to command the U.S. destroyers. On May 26, he was promoted to vice admiral, a decision that Sims considered premature. On June 14, he was designated the force commander of the United States Navy in European waters. According to "General Order No 218" adopted in 1916, a "force" was a major subdivision of a fleet and "is usually composed of all the vessels of that Fleet that are of the same type or class or that are assigned to the same duty." Benson informed Sims of this designation early in July 1917. Admiral Mayo insisted on this interpretation throughout the war and afterward. At the 1920 congressional hearings, he remarked firmly, "all officers on shore in Great Britain, including Admiral Sims, were under my charge."

Sims admitted that his force was under Mayo's command, although he believed that it was "to all intents and purposes a separate Force." Nevertheless, as early as June 1917, Mayo voiced his concern about the deployment of a considerable number of ships from the Atlantic Fleet to European waters without recognizing the "responsibility of the 'Commander of U.S. Forces Operating in European Waters,' to the Commander in Chief, Atlantic Fleet."

At the 1920 hearings, Sims stressed that his force was, "on paper at least," a part of the Atlantic Fleet, but he never received any orders from Mayo, and all his instructions came from the Navy Department. For example, in September the CNO cabled Sims that he would have the authority as force commander to distribute his forces as he desired, subject to Admiralty approval.[37] Admiral King later placed the blame for this confusing command structure on what he called "Daniels-Benson logic." "While the forces engaged in European waters and in convoy operations . . . were attached to the Atlantic Fleet," he wrote, "Admiral Mayo must be kept informed of their employment, these forces were to receive their orders directly from the Navy Department. With [this] . . . breech of military principles Admiral Mayo found it desirable from May 1917 onward to have some members of his staff in Washington [to] get firsthand information."[38]

Mayo and his staff were most unhappy with what they considered an unorthodox command structure, which placed American naval units directly under the control of British admirals. Sims understood their concerns but defended his conduct: "The situation is a particular one and it is so eminently satisfactory and so efficient that it would not be well to interfere with it."[39] When it became obvious that a large percentage of the fleet was to be deployed in European waters, Mayo lobbied to assume the European command. Commander Babcock, of Sims's staff, arrived in Washington on a fact-finding trip early in January 1918. During a conversation with one of Mayo's staff officers, he discovered that the Atlantic Fleet commander "will insist on going abroad on his flagship or in some other way *or* they must accept his resignation." Babcock informed Sims that "as long as the force over there was small and could be viewed as a single 'task group' he [Mayo] had no objection, *but*, now that other task groups had been created, viz—'mine barrier,' force, 'battleships,' submarine chasers, with probability of more tasks developing rapidly, the major activities of the Fleet were being transferred over there." When Mayo went to Great Britain in September 1917, he visited the Grand Fleet at anchor in the Firth of Forth near Edinburgh. To honor him, Admiral Beatty's flagship, *Queen Elizabeth*, flew Mayo's blue ensign with four white stars in place of the C-in-C's white ensign. Mayo was flattered, but, more important, he wanted to fly his ensign on his flagship in the war zone.[40]

On February 24, 1918, Mayo requested the European command. In a document entitled "Estimate of the Situation with Regard to the Efficient Development of the Operations of the Atlantic Fleet," he proposed to proceed in his flagship, *Pennsylvania*, to a British base in proximity to the Grand Fleet. Babcock, still in Washington, immediately informed Sims of the document. The aide credited Pratt with thwarting Mayo's effort to take over. Pratt, instead of going directly to the CNO, gave to Benson's aide an unsigned list of arguments clearly in favor of retaining Sims as European force commander. Why Pratt adopted this approach is unclear; Benson certainly knew or suspected that it came from Pratt. The CNO undoubtedly consulted with Daniels, but it was probably a foregone conclusion that neither would favor Mayo's desires. Relations between the CNO and the C-in-C, Atlantic Fleet, had deteriorated. While Mayo and his staff visited England during September 1917, members of his staff reportedly criticized the Navy Department before British officials. Mayo's decision to retain a permanent member of his staff in Washington was ostensibly to ensure effective liaison with the Department, but, according to King, the C-in-C. wanted to obtain firsthand information about the activities of the office of the Chief of Naval Operations and the various bureaus. Benson resented this arrangement. Sims informed his wife in August 1917 that "bad blood [existed] between the fleet and the Department," adding, "All sorts of things are done without consulting the C-in-C." In February, he mentioned to her a "war to the knife between the P.D.'s and the C-in-C." Relations between Mayo and Benson remained strained throughout the war and afterward. Daniels observed in March 1920 that [Mayo] had "not recovered his difference with Benson."[41]

In February 1918, Sims wrote Benson that rumors had reached him of Mayo's request to assume the European command. "I think you will realize that in case Admiral Mayo should be sent over here that my position would become impossible," he told the CNO. He wrote to his wife that he would "quit" if the Department gave in to Mayo's request. Commander Charles Belknap Jr., in Operations, informed Sims in March that it was unlikely that Mayo would go to Europe, but if it happened, the solution was to make "you Commander-in-Chief Europe. Then the forces would simply be transferred from one command to another."[42] This point was certainly unclear to the force commander and probably did little to ease his mind.

Mayo persisted: in April he proposed to steam to Europe with a powerful battleship force to cooperate with the Grand Fleet. According to King, the C-in-C feared that the Germans would use their fleet to attack the channel ports and help end the flow of reinforcements to France. The Germans had launched a massive offensive in March 1918, and by early in April the Allied armies fell back more than forty miles. Mayo made his proposal during this crisis to help alleviate German pressure, thinking that the timing would strengthen his case. He personally carried his scheme to Washington. Daniels and Benson, not surprisingly, did not favor the movement but agreed to present the proposal to the president. On April 15, Daniels recorded in his diary, "I saw the President and he agreed not to send."[43]

Sims remained uneasy about the unsettled command situation. On April 4, he wrote Pratt, "It would be of course a satisfaction if this question about the command over here could be settled one way or the other." He repeated his determination to request relief, if "a senior should be sent over." One obvious solution to Sims was to appoint him commander in chief of the European naval command, but the Department did not do so. Instead, as mentioned above, Daniels and Benson at different times sharply rebuked him for assuming too much power.[44]

As late as August, Mayo attempted to arrange a fleet movement to European waters. Daniels, probably to get him out of the way, agreed to send the C-in-C to Europe on a second fact-finding trip. Late in September, Sims wrote his wife that "I rather think it is definitely settled that there is no longer any question of his coming over here." Nonetheless, he remained apprehensive. In October, he told her of Mayo's visit and his cordiality but added: "I have regarded this friendliness with a certain amount of suspicion. I believe they [the C-in-C's staff] would like to get my approval of the scheme to send the Atlantic Fleet over here, to be based in a European port until after the war. It will not receive my support."[45]

Daniels certainly was at least partly to blame for the vagueness of Sims's authority. He was not impressed with Mayo, and also at that time Sims was not as offensive to Daniels as he later became. When Benson and Rear Admiral Leigh Palmer, chief of the Bureau of Navigation, recommended that an admiral be ordered to France, the secretary mentioned in his diary, "after cablegram from Sims it was clear that there ought to be only one command abroad." Daniels also came to accept the policy strongly advocated by Sims that the war would be won in Europe and that, if necessary, the fleet should be stripped of ASW vessels, which must be deployed to the war zone. This viewpoint was at odds with that held by Benson and Mayo, who feared that Britain might lose the war and the U.S. fleet would have to engage the Germans in American waters.[46]

The failure to clarify the naval chain of command satisfied neither Sims nor Mayo, but the latter's unhappiness with it was most understandable. Mayo had to watch helplessly as *his* junior commanded much of *his* fleet and received accolades. He retired six months after the war was over.

King thought Mayo a superior officer. He was "restrained and judicious," a "quiet man of remarkable ability" who was unequivocally "the best, the ablest and the most competent of all the flag officers" during World War I. Admiral Henry A. Wiley, who later served as C-in-C, U.S. Fleet, agreed with King. He stated, "If I were to criticize any quality or characteristic of his, I would say that he was too modest, and he didn't give a damn what any man thought of him." Even Sims admired Mayo, "a perfectly open-minded man and a man of the utmost integrity." He praised the C-in-C for his contributions after Mayo's trip to Europe in September 1917. However, the European force commander was surprised and obviously a little hurt when Mayo did not even mention his name in his report of that trip. In April 1918, he told his wife that his relations with all "on the other side [of the Atlantic] . . . except with the C-in-C are fine." In retaliation, he did not mention Mayo in *The Victory at Sea*.[47]

Sims's relations with the Navy Department, including its leaders—Daniels, the General Board, and the bureau chiefs—were often turbulent. In order to maintain unofficial communication with the Department, the European commander shuttled members of his staff to Washington on fact-finding missions. They were also to find ways of expediting shipment of the men and material. Finally, they were to advocate the views of Simsadus. Sims initially thought himself on good terms with members of the General Board and the bureau chiefs, but he soon learned differently. When Babcock visited Washington on one of his missions, he wrote that while conferring with the chiefs he was "forced into a number of very hot discussions. Captain McKean attacked me viciously . . . Captain [Roger] Welles [Director of Naval Intelligence] held me yesterday for a solid three hours in his office and such a tempest in a teapot you never saw." He added, "I think I deserve an iron cross for not . . . getting mad and making unfortunate statements."[48] During naval hearings in 1920, the president of the General Board and the bureau chiefs criticized the European commander.

Like theater commanders, past and present, Sims believed that his command was the most important in the Navy, and he pressed constantly for more staff, ships, support of all kinds, and authority over policy and his forces. In December 1917, he had a confidential meeting with Colonel Edward House, the leader of the mission sent to Europe in November 1917 "to improve communications" with the Allies. He confided to his wife that "[I] talk[ed] . . . about the position I had been placed [in], about the long delay in sending out a staff, about the opinions as to my being pro-British, etc., but I made it clear that I did not do so in criticism or complaint because as I stated, I had enough knowledge of the history of warfare to understand that in . . . all wars the relations between the seat of government and the 'front' were always [a problem]. . . . I also accentuated the advisability of relying upon the judgment of the man on the spot." Sims was convinced that House would carry the message back to Washington, but there is no indication that he did so.[49]

Criticism rarely affected Sims; his intense belief in the righteousness of his views served as armor. He constantly pressed the Navy Department to fulfill his requests. After one of Babcock's visits to Washington, he offered "one piece of advice. . . . Don't be deterred in making recommendations here for fear of stirring up rows or trouble here. . . . If we drive hard enough they don't dare turn us down. 'They' is not a person or persons. It is a big complicated system. . . . I don't believe it is possible to stir up any row over here which will do any harm." Sims followed this advice, and as Trask concluded, Sims ultimately managed to gain most of his ends, often because Benson in time accepted his advice. Ray Stannard Baker once said that Sims "was an efficient man, I should say, but think of a world ruled by men of that type!"[50]

Sims believed that Benson's trip to the war zone in November 1917 with the House Mission altered the CNO's views. He thought it a "pity that Benson did not come over months ago."[51] After extended meetings with Sims and Admiralty officials, he supported the British proposal to form an Allied Naval Council, to deploy a division of battleships with the Grand Fleet, to undertake a mine barrage in the North Sea, and to send over additional antisubmarine craft. Sims felt vindicated. "The visit of our people (Benson, etc.) will, I believe, prove of great benefit," he told his wife. "I believe that every single one of the recommendations I have been making for months past will be carried out. . . . What a pity they could have trusted to our judgment [earlier]."[52]

The House Mission placed Sims and Benson in close contact for the first time. The European commander concluded that Benson "really seems to have developed wonderfully in the two or three years he has been in the Navy Department, or else, I never appreciated what he was before, because he is such a quiet and non-assertive man." While in Europe, Benson investigated Sims, possibly at the instigation of Daniels, and concluded that his work was perfectly satisfactory.[53] Sims, a prolific correspondent, frequently wrote personal letters to Pratt and even semi-official letters to the CNO. Pratt sometimes shared with Benson his correspondence with Sims. Eventually the CNO refused to read them, candidly admitting to Sims, "I was afraid that the constant spirit of criticism and complaint that pervaded them at all times . . . would gradually produce a state of mind on my part that was undesirable."

Ultimately Benson's patience wore thin. In December 1917, he sharply criticized Sims. It was his duty to accept decisions of the Department.[54] Sims, however, continued to consider Benson "friendly" until the CNO took his place as the official American representative at the final meeting of the Allied Naval Council in November 1918 and sent the force commander back to London.

Captain Pratt worked strenuously to improve the Sims/Benson relationship. He greatly admired Sims. They became good friends. Pratt was also an Anglophile and willingly sought to support the force commander. As assistant to the chief of naval operations, however, Pratt was loyal to Benson and developed a great respect for him. He knew of Benson's conservatism and Anglophobia, but he also respected his dedication and above all his probity, telling Sims that "you will . . . learn to appreciate that rugged honesty which is the highest compliment I can pay him." Pratt shouldered a heavy load as Benson's assistant and carried it out ably. The British naval attaché in Washington, Captain Gaunt, informed the Admiralty that Pratt's appointment "made a very great difference to every thing. The difficulty before has always been that Admiral Benson dealt with the matters directly. Under the new regime," Gaunt added, "Captain Pratt is a very strong man. I can discuss things with him and he is very glad to do so, and he will go into details with me . . . and will get it done."

Pratt worked himself into a nervous breakdown toward the end of the war. Caught between two opinionated men, he managed this trying circumstance with "magnificent finesse," according to Gerald Wheeler, his biographer, but it contributed to his eventual exhaustion.[55] Pratt was not a striking or dynamic figure; he was short, quiet, "very cold, very impersonal," but he impressed superiors and subordinates with his intellect, knowledge, and hard work. President Franklin D. Roosevelt made him chief of naval operations in 1930.[56]

Roosevelt, like Sims and Pratt, was a strong Anglophile. He admired Sims, but the ambitious politician tried to avoid the bickering between Sims's headquarters and the Navy Department. Sims had had little personal contact with FDR until he finally persuaded his boss to let him visit the war zone in the summer of 1918. Sims was not impressed with him: he thought the young assistant secretary brash, naive, and a meddler in affairs of which he knew little or nothing. He also consumed the valuable time of various officials and naval officers. Nonetheless, Sims knew of Roosevelt's criticisms of Daniels and undoubtedly believed that he could use him against the secretary and his supporters. Little came of this notion during the war, but Roosevelt remained an admirer of Sims, even during the 1920 naval hearings, much to the disappointment of Daniels.[57]

Daniels supported Sims on many occasions. A retired rear admiral, Victor Blue, wrote to Daniels in 1927, "I will never understand Sims' attitude towards you after all you did for him—you made him what he became, contrary to the advice of many of the high ranking officers of the service."[58] The secretary of the navy did not like Sims, but he did not allow his feelings to affect his relations with the force commander. As Trask observes, Sims overpersonalized issues and decided that Daniels regularly opposed his recommendations. He told his wife shortly after the war: "It is practically certain that the Secretary and I must clash very seriously in the future, and it may well be the immediate future. . . . I have been and am still indignant of the treatment that has been accorded the Forces over this side."[59] His prediction came true during the naval hearings of 1920.

Sims insisted that the Navy Department was derelict in not responding sufficiently to his requests for competent staff officers. On May 31, 1917, he cabled the CNO: "the future security of the United States or at least the accomplishment of our purpose in entering this war will in a considerable degree be dependent upon the efficiency of the organization on this side. . . . It is therefore urgently requested that the Department approve a greatly enlarged organization with a view to insuring that the Department, Fleet, and the forces here are able to co-operate with the Allies to the maximum possible extent."[60] Pratt testified at the naval hearings in 1920 that "Admiral Sims had a just complaint. . . . He should have been allowed more assistants, and earlier," but he added that "It was impossible to meet all his demands." Competent staff officers were in great demand. The Office of Operations staff was itself very short of staff for many months. Sims had to compete with Benson for qualified officers. Many years later, Pratt stated: "In his entire naval career, Sims had never held an administrative job that I can recall, which required that he be the producing end. It may be quite wrong but one began to get the impression that it should only be necessary in order to receive bountifully. Yet, how were we to do it? Our own office in Operations was stripped to supply him with commissioned personnel. He had more officers attached to his staff than we had" at the end of the war. Josephus Daniels confided to his diary in 1920: "We had 3,000 officers and needed 8,000 & of course nobody had enough. Broke up Operations several times to help Sims."[61]

For several months, Sims's only staff officer, Babcock, used the "two-finger system" to type reports and correspondence. He carried the filing system in his pocket while traveling with the admiral. Sims reported to his wife in June: "Babby becomes more and more valuable. It would hardly be possible for me to get along without him. He does a heap of thinking and makes many valuable suggestions."[62] When Babcock nearly experienced a nervous breakdown, the Department finally ordered four additional officers to London along with ten enlisted men. One of these officers, Captain Nathan Twining, became Sims's chief of staff. Thereafter more personnel slowly trickled in. Nonetheless, late in October Sims informed the Department that he had only twelve people on his staff, which included those assigned to the naval attaché's office. Simsadus received a large increase of staff in November, when the armored cruiser *Huntington* arrived in England with the House Mission on board. Presumably with Benson's permission, some two hundred men of the ship's crew were transferred to Sims's force, the majority assigned to work in London.[63]

The strain on Babcock would have been much worse had he not received assistance from the U.S. naval attaché in London, Captain William D. MacDougall, and Ambassador Walter H. Page. The ambassador quickly formed a fast friendship with Sims. He provided an office along with stenographic and clerical help. MacDougall's small staff of four officers were placed at the admiral's disposal.[64] Out of necessity, the attaché and his staff became adjunct to Sims, but MacDougall was not under Sims's command, and his staff was assigned to duties not connected with Simsadus. At that time, the London attaché's office provided a clearinghouse for intelligence and other information from American naval attachés throughout Europe. It also passed on information obtained in the British Isles to the Navy Department.

Sims had to use the embassy's cable communications, which added to the burdens of MacDougall's staff. Only naval officers were allowed to encode correspondence, and his small staff could not absorb all of the cable traffic.[65] Soon MacDougall's paymaster and medical officer were transferred to Sims's staff. The attaché made temporary use of several reserve officers resident in London called to active duty, but in time they were also transferred to Simsadus.

An awkward command relationship developed between Sims and MacDougall. When he was simply an observer, Sims reported to the Department through the office of the naval attaché, but after he was raised to vice admiral and designated to command U.S. naval forces operating in European waters, he dealt directly with his superiors. The Department communicated directly with the naval attachés, who routinely replied directly to it. Sims was bypassed, which led to some confusion and irritation.[66]

In August, MacDougall was appointed intelligence officer on Sims's staff but continued as naval attaché. Whether MacDougall resented the additional responsibilities or was "temperamentally" unsuited for intelligence work, as Pratt was told, he quickly earned the ire of the British Admiralty. MacDougall became persona non grata to Admiral Sir Reginald Hall, the director of the Royal Navy's Intelligence Service. Sims wrote in confidence to Captain Roger Welles Jr., director of the Office of Naval Intelligence (ONI) that MacDougall had been "an actual detriment to me, rather than a help. . . . He can get practically no information about confidential matters." Welles also faulted the attaché's performance: "About all we have received from MacDougall has been stuff about materiel and little or nothing of military value." Sims and MacDougall clashed over British naval policy, but the admiral refused to refer the matter to either Benson or Daniels. The Admiralty, however, expressed its negative view of the attaché to Benson when he visited London.[67]

The CNO decided to replace MacDougall; after conferring with Sims, he made the force commander naval attaché. When the American consul in Liverpool inquired about his departure, MacDougall replied sarcastically, "He [Sims] will add Naval attaché to his other titles next week sometime."[68] Babcock assumed responsibilities for intelligence matters in Simsadus. In February 1918, the CNO placed all naval attachés in Europe directly under Sims.[69] When the United States entered World War I, the Navy had six attachés and two assistant attachés on station accredited to ten countries. By the time the Armistice was signed, the number had increased to fifteen. They provided Simsadus with considerable information, some of it valuable. Outside London, the most important attaché posts were in Paris and Rome.[70]

Sims also attempted to maintain some control in ports used by his force. Naval officers were ordered to ports in Great Britain, France, and to Genoa, Italy, to coordinate the operations of American naval vessels located at these places. The port officers' staffs included a communication section and personnel to deal with logistical matters. When possible, they cooperated with consuls and their staffs.[71]

The addition of the naval attachés and port officers created more work for Simsadus. Sims testified at the naval hearing in 1920 that the visit of Admiral Benson in November 1917 finally convinced the CNO "of the necessity of establishing a real advanced headquarters . . . with an adequate staff."[72] The European force commander bombarded Washington for additional personnel, frequently requesting specific individuals, most of whom had served with him in the Destroyer Flotilla, at the Naval War College, and elsewhere. On seven occasions he asked for Pratt, whom he wanted to become his chief of staff, but the assistant CNO had become nearly indispensable in the Department.

Nonetheless, Sims obtained many of the officers that he asked for, and more Reserve officers were assigned to his staff. By December 1, 1917, thirty-five people worked at Simsadus.[73] The Department did everything that it could to give him the personnel he needed. By Armistice Day 1918, Simsadus included 192 officers, 398 enlisted personnel, 62 Marines, and 310 civilians, a total of 962. Both American citizens and British subjects served in large numbers. For example, in August 1918, the workforce included civilian stenographers, typists, file clerks, photostat operators, housekeepers, and charwomen. When Admiral Mayo came to Simsadus headquarters in September 1918, a year after his first visit, he was astonished at the growth of Sims's staff. "He has a young Navy Department there," he wrote his wife. Earlier, Sims admitted to his wife, "this now really is a small Navy Department."[74]

The steady increase in Simsadus personnel led to a corresponding expansion in work space and quarters. Although Sims commanded an operating force of warships and maintained a flagship at Queenstown, he located his headquarters in London. Before World War I, all commanders in chief of American naval forces had commanded from the quarterdeck of a flagship. His policy of total integration with Allied navies, the probable expansion of his force, and the availability of modern communications, including ship-to-shore radio, extensive cables, and telephones, allowed Sims to remain ashore.

Initially the London "flagship" consisted of two rooms in the embassy. The admiral and probably also the Admiralty would have preferred to locate Simsadus in the Admiralty or nearby, but such an arrangement was both impracticable and politically unwise, considering Sims's well-known pro-British sentiments. Sims determined keep his staff either in or near the embassy.[75]

In August 1917, the Admiralty appropriated a private dwelling to house the growing American staff. "We rented the house furnished, just as it stood," Sims wrote. "We . . . [reduced] the twenty-five rooms to their original bareness, and filled every corner with office equipment. . . . At first we regarded the leasing of this building as something of an extravagance; it seemed hardly likely that we should ever use it all! But in a few weeks we had taken the house adjoining, cut holes through the walls and put in doors; and this, too, was filled up in an in creditably [sic] short time." In November, he told his wife that "The business is expanding all the time. We have outgrown the house we are in tho [sic] it had 23 rooms, and we are going into two more houses of the same size next door. There are 75 people in the building at present and more are coming all the time." In another letter, he reported that desks, chairs, file cabinets, and the like were taken off the *Huntington* and used in his headquarters. Staff members met U.S. naval vessels entering British ports to "borrow" office equipment.[76]

"The 'shop' is growing all the time," Sims noted in April 1918. "We are about to take over a 5th house." By summer, he had added a sixth house and finally in August a seventh. All were adjacent to each other with passages cut through walls that linked them together. The American embassy was located in Grosvenor's Square in the affluent district of Mayfair. Ever since the tenure of John Adams, the first U.S. diplomat accredited to the court of St. James, American officials have occupied buildings on Grosvenor's Square. Sims occupied quarters at the Carleton Hotel within walking distance of his headquarters.[77]

Sims's staff reflected his earlier command experiences at sea and certain aspects of the Admiralty's structure, particularly in the field of technical expertise. In July 1917, he outlined his conception of a minimum staff, which included (*a*) a chief of staff, (*b*) shipping and convoy officer, (*c*) antisubmarine warfare officer, (*d*) intelligence, (*e*) communications, (*f*) paymaster, and (*g*) two junior officers assigned as aides. The staff would divide into four sections: (*a*) Operations, (*b*) Material, (*c*) Secretarial, and (*d*) Communications. Early in 1918, the headquarters staff (Simsadus) had evolved into thirteen sections headed by a chief of staff and his assistant. In addition to the recommendations of July 1917, the staff included the following divisions: aviation, personnel, repairs, ordnance, medical, legal, scientific, and also a planning section. Several sections had subsections. For example, Intelligence, under Babcock, handled publicity, censorship, and counterespionage. The Navy Department created subsections that Sims did not request. In November 1917, one that included a Marine officer, four paymasters, and two enlisted men arrived in London to organize a "War Risk Insurance Office" under the Navy's Disbursing Office. Simsadus's paymaster absorbed this group. Assistant Secretary Roosevelt recommended the legal section, which was organized in August 1918. It dealt with legal problems such as claims against U.S. naval personnel for automobile accidents and property damage.[78]

Captain Nathan C. Twining, Sims's chief of staff, directed the headquarters. Pratt was Sims's first choice for this position, but Twining was on the admiral's list of the essential officers he sought for his staff. Twining had spent twenty-eight years in the Navy after graduating from the Naval Academy in 1889. A recognized ordnance specialist, he served as chief of the Bureau of Ordnance in 1913–14. He first served with Sims at the Naval War College, a tenure that led to his selection when Pratt was held in Washington.

Sims praised Twining highly in *The Victory at Sea*: "[He] would certainly have been a marked man in any navy; he had a genius for detail, a tireless energy, and a mastery of all the problems that constantly arose." Although Twining was a brilliant officer, Admiral John McCrea recalled that he was "like Admiral King—austere, cold, reserved, thorough, a plain, no-nonsense guy." Sims told his wife that Twining was "a very cold proposition. There is very little of the milk of human kindness about him." His personality led many in Simsadus to characterize him as a "Prussian." Sims also mentioned that the chief of staff "was very quiet . . . little small talk." Sims deemed Twining a valuable assistant, "a real tower of strength," but he admitted to his wife that his chief of staff did not like him. "I might almost say that he goes pretty near to disliking me; this is not due to any particular disagreeable qualities of mine but because he is so constituted that he cannot bear opposition." According to Admiral Strauss, Twining was quite outspoken and bitter about Sims's pro-British policies. Admiral King was close to the truth in noting that Twining served as a "useful balance wheel" for Sims. Despite their differences, Sims told his wife, "you may be sure I will give him full credit," and he did.[79]

The force commander marveled at the chief of staff's ability to function without much sleep. "He seemed to be working every hour of the day and night; yet, so far as was observable, he never wearied." The admiral did not realize that Twining might well have broken his health. Five years after the war, he was retired because of physical disability and soon passed away. Dudley Knox, who worked closely with Twining in London, called him "one of the most able of men. . . . [H]e was the best naval officer on the Navy List and his loss was really a tragedy."[80]

Twining arrived at the London headquarters in August 1917, and soon began to develop an efficient system of communications. When Congress declared war, government offices abroad, including military, used two methods to communicate with Washington. A dispatch agency acted as a clearinghouse for all official correspondence passing between Washington and its representatives in European countries. U.S. naval vessels deployed in European waters utilized this agency. Its employees routinely traveled back and forth across the Atlantic, carrying this "mail." The transatlantic cables offered an alternative. London served as the terminus for 90 percent of them. Other cables connected Europe with the other nations of the Western Hemisphere, but German submarines cut most of them early in the war. Messages that reached London were relayed to Europe and even to countries in the Near East. Two private companies controlled cable traffic, the Eastern Cable Company and Western Union and Commercial Cable Company. The former had a monopolized cable communication with the Mediterranean. The embassy in London managed official American cable traffic, including that of the naval attachés at the various embassies.[81]

The traffic connected with the American entry into the war and the rapid deployment of American warships in European waters quickly swamped both methods and threatened their security. Throughout the war, detachments of Marines guarded the agents who carried official pouches from London to U.S. ships bound for home. This mail service was slow and uncertain because of the U-boat menace, but U.S. naval forces in European waters used it extensively.[82]

The cable service had the theoretical advantage of being much faster, but dispatches were frequently delayed, depending upon their priority. Nevertheless, the cables provided the primary communication between the Navy in Europe and the Department. It was also the principal means of communicating with U.S. naval forces deployed in the war zone. During the summer of 1917, a cable was installed that linked Sims's headquarters with the transatlantic cable companies. The Admiralty's highly efficient cable service was placed at the disposal of the U.S. Navy. Communication specialists were attached to British naval cable and telegraphic offices, which enabled Sims to communicate directly with his forces.[83]

To augment existing communications, the U.S. Navy quickly developed a transatlantic radio system. By 1917, radio messages passed between the United Sates and Europe. The U.S. Navy established a Naval Communication Service in 1916. Even before the intervention, the Navy built several short-range stations. In April 1917, President Wilson assigned the Navy the responsibility of controlling radio operations, including two systems seized from the Germans. Others were added during the war, including a powerful station at Annapolis.

The United States gained access to certain radio stations of the Allies. Britain allowed early access. In July, the French government opened discussions with Washington officials to create direct radio contact. The Navy Department strongly favored a transatlantic station in France, and General Pershing endorsed the project in November 1917. In January 1918, agreement was reached to allow the United States to construct the station in southwest France. The Navy would build and control the station, which would revert to French ownership after the war. The station, however, was not completed until 1920. For several years the Lafayette Radio Station, as it was named, was the most powerful in the world.[84]

From London, Sims and his staff kept in close contact with facilities scattered from Murmansk in Russia to Corfu in the eastern Mediterranean and from Queenstown to the Azores. Extensive traffic flowed between Simsadus and Washington. Difficulties remained, although communications steadily improved during the war. No direct radio or cable link existed between Brest and London. Until late in the war, Simsadus depended upon a telephone link from Brest to Paris and radio or cable from Brest to London via Le Havre or Paris. To provide communications with numerous naval air stations and naval district offices in France, the U.S. Army Signal Corps constructed telephone lines that linked them to naval headquarters in Brest. They also laid a cable across the English Channel to connect directly with London. Communications with Gibraltar and the American naval officials in Italy remained undependable.[85]

All messages—cables, radiograms, and dispatches—were sent in code. Coding and decoding of messages required considerable time. Initially Sims delegated this task to the naval attaché's staff. MacDougall appealed to Washington for qualified officers in coding, "as the volume is beyond the capacity of officers attached." By August 1918, Sims's staff processed an average of five hundred dispatches a day and approximately the same number of other written communications. By the Armistice, more than two hundred thousand messages had passed between Sims's headquarters and the Navy Department alone. Gradually the Department increased the number of personnel involved in communications, including coding. In November 1918, 81 officers and 275 enlisted men were assigned to communications at Simsadus. Unlike the Army, which recruited women known as "Hello Girls" to serve as operators, the Navy depended upon its male personnel to run communications.[86]

The communication section worked closely with intelligence and censorship. The Navy had little practical experience with censorship. The British government, however, imposed strict censorship. It kept information about the Royal Navy out of the press. The Admiralty's chief censor, however, discovered that American journalists were determined to write about their navy. As H. C. Hoy explained in his study of British Intelligence, the American journalistic "technique is very different from that of their English brothers of the pen, and in their own country they are accustomed to a much easier accessibility to those who hold office." The problem was resolved, at least from the viewpoint of the Admiralty, when Sir Reginald Hall, the head of British Intelligence, entertained accredited American journalists at "tea" once a week and briefed them on what he could reveal. In addition, stories and news releases about the U.S. Navy had to pass through both American and British censors. The censors expurgated many stories, blacking out names of places, ships, and individuals.[87]

Admiral Sims was unhappy with the paucity of publicity about the Navy in European waters. "In this respect the army has us beaten to a frazzle," he wrote to Pratt. At a meeting of the English-Speaking Union in London, he admitted that the American people "had not been too accurately informed" about what the United States was contributing to the war effort, especially its Navy. Daniels agreed; during the spring of 1918, many more stories about the Navy began to appear in American magazines and press.[88]

For the first time, the Navy censored private correspondence. Every ship and naval facility assigned one or more men to this task. The sailors usually accepted censorship without complaint, although at times they tried to circumvent it. Rotated naval personnel and merchant seamen often mailed letters in a home port. If discovered, the writer and carrier were arrested. Sailors received a court-martial. The U.S. Postal Service maintained offices in Paris and London to conduct additional censorship. Also, the Navy Department in Washington inspected mail before distributing it.[89]

Shortly after war was declared, President Wilson created the Committee on Public Information (CPI) to manage censorship and publicity. The CPI established branch offices in London and Paris to channel correspondents approved by the committee and the War and Navy departments to the proper offices. Some problems arose between Simsadus and the committee. George Creel, who directed the CPI, tried to control information from the war zone by allowing only approved journalists to submit articles. However, a number of American reporters were based in Europe when war broke out, and a few others found ways to get over. The British and Sims's office accredited many of them without going through the committee. The committee also sent over a journalist named James Connolly, who wrote articles critical of the British navy and of Sims's policy of placing U.S. naval vessels under British control for operations. Both the British and the force commander considered him persona non grata.[90]

Daniels, a former newspaper editor, was unhappy with censorship, especially by the Allies. For this reason, he participated in the decisions of the CPI throughout the war. Nonetheless, after the publication of erroneous stories about American naval activities in European waters, he reluctantly accepted censorship.[91]

In April 1917, the Office of Naval Intelligence (ONI) was an insignificant unit under the command of Rear Admiral Roger Welles. During the war, Welles emphasized domestic rather than foreign intelligence. His office depended heavily upon naval attachés to provide foreign intelligence. Unfortunately, most of the attachés had no training in intelligence techniques. Neither Sims nor the British Admiralty was impressed with Welles's office. They also distrusted the Department's intelligence and its interpretation. Tracy Kittredge wrote in *Naval Lessons of the Great War* that the Navy Department: "resorted to many uncertain channels of information of varying degrees of reliability . . . such as Allied attachés in Washington. . . . Armed Guard officers were given orders to collect, in a week or ten days of their stay in port in England or France, a vast amount of information concerning war operations and experience . . . obviously beyond their capacity." The Department often acted on the recommendations of Allied attachés or Armed Guard officers even when these differed from those submitted by Sims. He never received information that the Department obtained from other sources, and the actions based on it.[92]

Sims understood the necessity of having an intelligence section in his organization. On May 31, 1917, he cabled the Department for an officer trained in intelligence work. Until one was assigned, he placed his personal aide, Babcock, in charge of intelligence and ordered a couple of activated reserve officers to assist him. Babcock remained in charge of the section, which increased to fourteen officers by the end of the war.[93] Sims developed intelligence doctrine and policy, and in doing so followed his usual pattern of challenging departmental officials, in this case Welles. Sims generally ignored him and gradually took control of intelligence activities in the European theater. In November 1917, he gained the CNO's permission to handle intelligence activities without referring to Welles. Later he persuaded Benson to require all naval attachés in Europe to channel pertinent information directly to his staff.[94]

Sims was content with his small intelligence staff because he believed that the Admiralty provided all the necessary information. Admiral William Hall, the director of British naval intelligence, got along very well with the American commander and briefed him daily, although the British carefully refrained from disclosing their sources. The Americans were evidently unaware of Room 40, the highly secret intelligence-gathering section of the British Admiralty. British cryptographers decoded much of the German wireless traffic, including messages to and from their submarines. This vital information enabled the Admiralty to monitor German U-boats. Simsadus received this data.[95]

Although the British willingly passed on vital information, they did not help the U.S. Navy develop its own cryptographic expertise. In time, officers at the different bases were assigned intelligence duties along with the attachés and their assistants. They coded and decoded messages and gathered information. One of these officers was an assistant surgeon aboard the tender *Leonidas* at Corfu. His fluency in German, according to his personal diary, allowed him to translate intercepted messages between U-boats and their bases.

Lieutenant Commander James H. Sayles, naval attaché in Paris and later intelligence officer at Brest, spent much of his time organizing a counterespionage system along the southwestern coast of France. The German navy possessed accurate information about maritime trade along that coast, particularly in the Bay of Biscay, which allowed U-boats to achieve considerable success in this area. Despite the efforts of

U.S. naval intelligence and French agents, they failed to curtail German espionage. French intelligence service also proved ineffective on the west coast of France. A small unit at Nantes worked with the French, but U.S. naval operations in French waters depended heavily upon British intelligence channeled through Simsadus.[96]

Admiralty officials believed that anti-British inhabitants of Ireland passed considerable information about convoy sailings and naval activities to the Germans. British officials were somewhat critical of American naval officers for being too "loose" when socializing in Irish bars.[97]

Sims did not consider naval aviation when he first organized his staff. Like most naval officers, Sims knew little about this relatively new branch. In 1910, the Navy Department officially recognized aviation in its organization, appointing an officer to conduct all correspondence concerning it. Seven years later, naval aviation remained in its infancy, consisting of one air station, fifty-four miscellaneous aircraft, and thirty active pilots. The French Commission, which reached the United States shortly after Congress declared war, asked for naval aviators. Admiral Benson, with Daniels's approval, agreed to send a detachment to France under the command of Lieutenant Commander Kenneth Whiting. Sims was not consulted: Whiting's verbal orders were simply to inform the naval attaché in Paris of his arrival and to contact the French minister of marine's office for directions.[98]

Sims did not place an American aviation detachment in France under his command until August 1917. It was officially designated the "United States Naval Aviation Forces, Foreign Service." Its commander, Whiting, reported directly to the Department through the naval attaché's office. Sims preferred to exercise direct control, but the attaché in Paris opposed a change. Early in August, the admiral took advantage of the opening of an office for U.S. naval aviation in France to ask the CNO to provide specialists to meet needs such as maintenance for dirigibles and aircraft maintenance. On August 21, he requested an officer of "administrative capacity" to take command of naval aviation. He wanted an officer of more rank than lieutenant commander and specified his choice, Captain Hutch I. Cone. Benson agreed, and during September Cone arrived in London.[99] He replaced Whiting as head of the naval aviation force in France and was designated aide for aviation on Sims's staff.

Cone, a native of New York who graduated from the Naval Academy in 1894, had no experience in aviation but was considered an outstanding administrator, having served as engineer in chief of the Navy and marine superintendent of the Panama Canal. He was also known for his fiery red hair. Admiral Yates Sterling Sr. believed that he was one of the navy's "most progressive and brilliant officers." He was one of Sims's best friends. On October 21, Sims wrote his wife: "It is a delight, and a great satisfaction to have Cone here. He is like a fresh breeze."[100]

Sims expected Cone to take charge of all U.S. naval aviation in the war zone. As Twining told the naval attaché in Paris, Cone was to "occupy . . . the same position with respect to our aerial stations, that Rear Admiral Fletcher [at that time in command of U.S. surface forces in French waters] occupies with respect to our floating forces in France, including the bases at Brest and Bordeaux." "His job is a very big one," Sims told his wife, "and he is just the man for it. . . . I have much confidence in his judgement [*sic*]."[101] Cone toured sites in Ireland and England to locate prospective naval air stations and reorganized the aviation staff in Paris. He established an organization similar to Simsadus.[102]

Cone ordered a final reorganization in August-September 1918. By that date, twenty stations scattered from Ireland to Italy were approaching completion and operational capability. Confusion over the command structure persuaded Cone to recommend changes. Admiral Wilson, who replaced Fletcher in the French naval command, assumed that when the naval air stations on the west coast became operational, they would join his command and serve under his district commanders. Cone responded that when the bases became operational, they were to be placed under French commanders of "Aerial Coastal Patrol." Sims confirmed this understanding. He reminded Wilson that "the same principle is followed, as has been followed in the case of our floating force, which in the view of the Force Commander, are not cooperating with the Allied Forces, but are operating with them as a part of them." As it happened, the French generally did not interfere with the American surface force under Wilson. For that reason, it was likely that "control [of our aircraft] will actually be exercised by U.S. naval officers." To Admiral Benson, however, he wrote that he anticipated some "difficulty . . . in the operations of our aircraft on the French coast. Owing to the relative location and number of the French Stations as compared to our own it will probably be impossible to attempt to operate our station[s] direct by our own operating commanders. The location of the stations and other conditions will render it necessary to work in conjunction with the French to a greater extent than is necessary with the surface craft."[103]

With Sims's approval, Cone wrote on July 19 to Captain Noble Irwin, chief of the Office of Naval Aviation in Washington, outlining his proposed reorganization. "Detach me from command of U.S. Naval Aviation, Foreign Service, and order me to report to the Force Commander as a member of his staff to look out for aviation matters for him. I will move with my headquarters' organization to London." He proposed to divide the naval air force in the war zone into five geographical "units," or districts. The Department approved Cone's recommendations, which took effect on September 1. Captain Thomas Craven, who had led the Operations Section in Paris under Cone, took charge of the French west coast stations. "Tireless Tom" or "Turn To" Craven, as he was known in the Navy, was appointed aide for aviation under Admiral Wilson. Whiting, who left the Paris headquarters in January, took command at Killingholme in England. Commander David C. Hanrahan, who had commanded the Q-ship *Santee*, assumed control of the Northern Bombing Group under the British vice admiral at Dover. Commander Frank R. McCrary, a lighter-than-air specialist, held a similar position under the British commander in chief for Ireland. Finally, Lieutenant Commander John L. "Lanny" Callan, the only aviator among the district commanders, took command of the American naval air stations in Italy. He was only one of two regular officers assigned to the Paris headquarters who had experienced combat. Like Whiting, Craven, and Cone, most were regular officers transferred to naval aviation, although they were not trained as aviators. Cone was wounded in October 1918, when the British mail steamer *Leinster*, on which he was a passenger, was sunk in the Irish

Sea. He once claimed that "eventually [it] . . . will be necessary to organize an air service separate from Army and Navy. . . . This aviation matter has very little of the Navy
connected with it."[104]

An effective staff needs three components: operations, intelligence, and planning.
Sims pressed the CNO to authorize a planning staff entirely separate from his administrative staff. He testified at the naval hearings in 1920 that he recommended the idea
some six months before its adoption.[105] The Naval War College endorsed a planning
staff when Sims was president. The staff established in London consisted entirely of
War College graduates. Sims claimed that Simsadus's planning section was the first "I
think . . . ever adopted by any navy,"[106] but the Admiralty had established a planning
division several months earlier. This division was founded when the Admiralty was
reorganized in 1917.

During 1917, the Admiralty came under attack from within and outside of the Royal Navy. The British worshipped the Royal Navy as their savior, but the submarine crisis shook their faith in this hallowed institution. The British press turned its editorial
guns on the Board of Admiralty. Many naval officers became disenchanted with the
Board. Even Lord Beatty thought that a clean sweep was the proper solution. Meeting with Prime Minister David Lloyd George on April 14–15, 1917, he complained
of the lack of a good staff organization, "no planning body . . . no executive body
. . . to make rapid decisions."[107] The prime minister made a number of important
changes during the next few months. A civilian comptroller was hired to separate operations from material concerns. One by one he replaced the members of the Board,
the culmination being the substitutions of the first lord of the Admiralty, Sir Edward
Carson, by Sir Eric G. Geddes, and the first sea lord, Admiral Jellicoe, by Admiral Sir
Rosslyn E. Wemyss.

These changes affected Sims's personal relationship with the Admiralty. Wemyss
proved friendly but not personable. Nevertheless, the change brought Sims into more
direct contact with Admiralty officials. When Wemyss initiated a daily conference
of the sea lords and other important staff members, Sims was invited to participate.
Sims observed early in 1918: "Things have greatly changed at the Admiralty. Admiral
Wemyss is as far as you can imagine from a detail man. . . . He will not allow any subject to be brought to him for discussion until after all those concerned have not only
thrashed it out and accumulated and collated a tentative decision for his approval or
disapproval . . . problems which are to be solved are put up to the Planning Section of
the Admiralty."[108]

Lloyd George identified planning as the weakest feature in the administration of
the Royal Navy. In July 1917, a planning section was formed in the Operations Division. Originally, its only duty was to plan; it did not initiate operations. Jellicoe was
not enamored of the new organization, but when Admiral Wemyss became first sea
lord, its duties were broadened to include the initiation of operational plans, which
greatly enhanced its influence.[109] Wemyss urged both Sims and Benson to create a
planning division in Simsadus.

On October 23, shortly after the Admiralty appointed a "director of plans," Sims
recommended a separate planning staff, one that would work in "close cooperation

with the recently established planning staff of the British Admiralty."[110] Undoubtedly it was no coincidence that a day earlier, the American author Winston Churchill, a former naval officer, sent a similar suggestion to President Wilson. The president deferred the matter to Daniels, who opposed it, hardly a surprise given his earlier opposition to the general staff concept. However, the secretary referred the matter to Benson, who placed it on his agenda for impending discussions in England.

After conferring with Sims and Admiralty officials during his November trip to London, the CNO asked Daniels to endorse a planning section. Such a group, "imbued with our national and naval policies and ideas," could influence Allied naval actions, particularly offensive operations favored in Washington. He argued that the new organization "will be in a position to urge upon the British any plan that promises satisfactory results."[111] Pratt sent a memo to Daniels stating that in his opinion the establishment of "a thinking staff should have been done some time ago." Daniels reluctantly agreed.

Captain Frank H. Schofield and Commander Dudley Knox were then ordered to London for this duty. Later two additional officers, both trained at the War College, were added to the section. Pratt handpicked these men, who were, according to Trask, a "group of unusually talented officers." Sims considered them "the ablest men of our navy in this particular line and I don't think there are many abler men of the kind in any navy." Benson was pleased when the American Planning Section was assigned office space with the British Plans Division in the Admiralty Building.[112] The first sea lord wanted to integrate the American planning staff with the Admiralty's planning division, but Benson refused, ever suspicious of British intent. Wemyss then recommended the assignment of the American planning officers to the staff of the Dover Patrol, the material section of the Admiralty, and the Operations section of the Admiralty. Sims, however, vetoed this proposal, perhaps because he doubted that the Navy Department would approve.

The section was formally organized on the day after Christmas 1917 and started to meet early in the new year. Its mission was "to make studies of particular problems, to prepare plans for future operations, and also to criticize fully the organization and methods which were already in existence."[113] Although the section could generate its own studies, the majority of their deliberations dealt with problems or questions presented by the force commander, the Department, and the Admiralty. At first, they agreed to consider proposals jointly, but when the staff doubled, they decided that each member would prepare his own critique. The planners discussed the individual findings and then adopted a common solution, which was submitted to Admiral Sims. These papers then were often presented to the Department and/or the Admiralty's Plans Division.[114]

The section prepared more than seventy memorandums, treating subjects that ranged broadly from an evaluation of the naval war early in 1918 to a prediction of German views on the naval terms of the Armistice. The section made recommendations concerning the deployment of subchasers, antisubmarine warfare, naval aviation, offensive operations in the Adriatic, and a mine barrage. Some were adopted, although the staff admitted that "rarely were our proposals frankly accepted." Sims, however, was enthusiastic about its success. In March 1918, he informed the CNO that the section was "having a very beneficial effect"; and in August that it had been most helpful to him. To his wife, he declared that its work "is beginning to be known pretty widely in governmental circles here."[115]

Despite Sims's opinion, it is questionable that the Planning Section influenced British policy and strategy very much. The American section met regularly with the Admiralty's Plans Division, and, according to Vice Admiral Kenneth G. Dewar, the assistant director of plans, "there [was] frank and cordial co-operation," but, with the exception of the Northern and Adriatic mine barrages, Admiral Wemyss and his key advisors gave no more than "lip service" to its work. One member of the Admiralty stated that the American Planning Section's "principal occupation is 'knocking the British Admiralty.'"[116] It probably was not a "nuisance," as one writer put it, but even the Planning Section admitted after the war that "there appeared constantly to be a strong and almost unanimous reluctance on the part of the British command to accept these doctrines." It probably influenced some decisions of the Allied Naval Council, but perhaps the section's greatest contribution, as Sims claimed, was the "tendency to establish mutual understanding as to methods of thought on military questions as between ourselves and the Admiralty." In other words, the planners helped to sustain cooperation between the two naval high commands.[117]

Admiral Benson was impressed with the section, and he decided to create a similar body in the Navy Department. In September 1918, Captain Harry Yarnell, one of the four members of the London section, was ordered to Washington to establish it. After the Armistice, the remaining three members of the section were sent to Paris as advisors to the CNO during the treaty deliberations.[118]

Sims fought hard to form an adequate staff, and Pratt did everything he could to send qualified officers. Although the headquarters continued to expand until the Armistice, as early as February 1918, he confided to his wife that he was quite pleased with his staff: "We now have an efficient and smooth running organization." In March 1919, he informed his successor: "It has always been my object to form an organization here which would run itself for all ordinary matters without the intervention of the man at the top. It was the only possible way that the business . . . could be conducted because there was a hundred times more to be attended to than any one man could give his attention to."[119]

3

Sims and His Commanders

Admiral Sims created a unique command structure whereby his commanders served both him and senior British officers. The American naval forces were effectively integrated into the Royal Navy. Fortunately his subordinates generally adhered to this policy of amalgamation.[1] Fourteen flag officers came under his command. Some served briefly, among them Rear Admirals Mark L. Bristol at Plymouth, Andrew T. Long in Paris, S. S. Robinson at Brest, N. A. McCully, district commander at Rochefort, Thomas S. Rodgers in command of a battleship division at Bantry Bay, and W.H.G. Bullard, in command at Malta and later Corfu. Others such as Henry B. Wilson and Albert Niblack remained with the European naval force for most of the war. Rear Admiral Hugh Rodman commanded a battleship division with the Grand Fleet from December 1917 until its return to New York early in 1919. Rear Admiral Philip Andrews commanded the base and coal-carrying fleet based at Cardiff. Charles P. Plunkett exercised the most unique naval command, a battery of 14-inch railroad guns on the Western Front. Rear Admiral Joseph Strauss directed the mine-laying force.[2]

Sims's method of command placed considerable responsibility on his subordinates, and he had to have complete trust in them. As with those assigned to his headquarters staff, he wanted to recommend individuals for important positions or at least be consulted about the selectees. He was granted neither of these options. During the congressional hearings of 1920 he testified that "at no time during the war was I permitted to select any subordinate flag commander."[3] This statement was not entirely correct; he recommended two of those appointed, Rear Admirals Herbert Dunn and W.H.G. Bullard. He complained to Pratt: "The responsibility of this billet is great enough for the Department to accord me the privilege of selecting the men to handle the situation for which I am responsible. . . . To say the least," he added, "the Department has had bad luck in people they have been sending me for certain billets," mentioning in this connection William B. Fletcher, Henry Wilson, and Joseph Strauss.[4] To Mark Bristol, he wrote, "I have rather protested to the principal dignitaries against sending officers over here for duty without consulting me, because that would run the risk of obliging me to work with people who were not personally in sympathy with my views and methods."[5] Pratt, who assigned many of the staff officers to Simsadus recommended by Sims, was not entirely successful with flag officers. Daniels made these appointments with the concurrence of the CNO. Only one, Rear Admiral Herbert O. Dunn, who commanded the U.S. naval base in the Azores, was senior to Sims. Several had been in his class at Annapolis. He encountered considerable difficulty with Fletcher and Wilson, the two who commanded U.S. naval forces in France.

Most regular officers, including those of flag rank, wanted a billet in the war zone. Among the senior officers who fruitlessly petitioned for assignments in Europe were Rear Admiral W. F. Fullam (in command of the Pacific Squadron at the time), Rear Admiral E. W. Eberle, and Rear Admiral Albert Gleaves. Gleaves, who was in command of the fleet's destroyer force, bitterly blamed Sims for the detachment of most of his force. Eventually he was given command of the cruiser force responsible for convoying. Eberle, the most persistent claimant; aspired to the command of the destroyer force at Queenstown. Sims strongly opposed it, believing that it would upset the effective command structure in place. In this case, Benson agreed with him.[6]

At the time of World War I, the senior naval officer corps constituted an elite fraternity. They were predominantly well born, a "naval aristocracy."[7] Cliques and informal alignments based on similar ideas, social relationships, and even loyalty to one's class at Annapolis existed in significant numbers. The "old-boy" network prevalent in the Navy of the pre–World War I years was as influential as its successors. Whether or not by design, some of those appointed to commands under Sims disliked him, notably Albert Niblack, Henry Wilson, Joseph Strauss, and Hugh Rodman. All four testified against him during the naval hearings. A certain amount of friction developed between Sims and nearly all of his flag officers, partly because he integrated their commands with local Allied commands and partly because they prized the traditional independence associated with flag rank.

Niblack ("Nibs"), who commanded American forces at Gibraltar, had been Sims's roommate at the Naval Academy and a good friend. He was one of only two officers in the service who called Sims "Billy." Their intimacy ended in 1902. Niblack was inspector of target practice at the time, and Sims criticized him for failing to improve gunnery. To add salt to the wound, Sims replaced Niblack as inspector of target practice. Thereafter, according to Yates Sterling, they were bitter enemies.[8] When Niblack took up his duties at Gibraltar, they carried out a cordial correspondence as "Nibs" and "Billy." But Sims later reprimanded Niblack for neglect of his responsibilities. After that they became "Sims" and "Niblack." Morison makes the case that Sims "never in his life displayed toward Niblack the rather savage intolerance which he reserved for those men of whom he was fond but who he believed had deserted his cause," a most questionable statement. When Niblack was appointed naval attaché to the Court of St. James after the war, Sims wrote poisonous letters about him to English acquaintances. To Lady Astor, for example, he wrote, "I assume that you will be interested in knowing what manner of man [Niblack] . . . is and what he stands for. . . . he is a Daniels man—one of the few men who supported the Secretary by his testimony before the Senate Committee. . . . While the appointment of this officer, as a reward for his services to Mr. Daniels, is quite understandable under the circumstances, it is unfortunate that a man should be sent to London who is also so anti-British. He has been twice Naval Attaché at Berlin, and is known not perhaps so much for his admiration for the Germans, as for his marked dislike of the British. . . . The above is, of course, for your own private ear. I do not want to injure Niblack in any way, much less interfere with his business; but, in view of his opposition to me while doing the best work I have ever done for our Navy, I think I am amply justified in assuming that his manifest prejudice may result, even unconsciously, in injuring me in the estimation of my friends."[9]

Sims's prejudicial remarks were unfair to Niblack, although he never mentioned Niblack's supposed Anglophobia to the department. Niblack got along extremely well with the British while at Gibraltar, which Sims admitted, writing in his memoir: "the Gibraltar force under Admiral Niblack performed service which reflected high credit upon that commander," although this tribute preceded the naval hearings. In his testimony, Niblack rated Sims's organization in London "as beautifully managed; very efficient." Whether Sims had anything to do with Niblack's short four-month tour as naval attaché in London is unknown, but during the immediate postwar years he appeared to decline. From April 1919 until September 1920, he served as director of naval intelligence, and, after his relief as naval attaché in London, he was appointed to command the U.S. naval forces in European waters. An officer at ONI observed that Niblack "could neither ask coherent questions nor pay attention to related answers." His predecessor in command of U.S. naval forces in European waters, Rear Admiral Philip Andrews, agreed with this assessment. "Nibs is up to his old stunts of gumming up the [works]," he wrote, to which Sims responded, "He can disorganize anything he gets his hands on."[10]

Rear Admiral Joseph Strauss commanded the American mine-laying forces in Scotland. Sims wrote Pratt: "I hope this will turn out to be satisfactory, but it seems to me that on general principles, the selection is not a good one. For a job of this kind we need a confirmed optimist, and you have sent me the leading pessimist of the Navy." The assistant CNO responded that the position required an admiral. Strauss was "picked . . . as being the most harmless and the one least apt to interfere with Belknap." Daniels wrote after the war that he selected Strauss because he had been chief of the Bureau of Ordnance: "I had come to have confidence in him as a great ordnance officer." The secretary added, "[Y]ou may not know . . . that Sims did not want Strauss."[11] The CNO placed Strauss under Sims's "entire control," and the force commander informed Strauss that for operations he was to serve under the local commander, in this case Admiral Beatty, who commanded the Grand Fleet. When Strauss and Beatty disagreed, Sims wrote an unusually tactful letter to his subordinate. He suspected that "the trouble has been caused largely by misunderstanding as to the actual division of authority." He reminded Strauss that his forces were under the "military control of the Allied Naval Commander in so far as concerns the actual operations." Beatty was also informed that Sims had given definite orders to Rear Admiral Strauss "to the effect that he is subject to your orders for operations."[12]

Despite this difficulty, the two American admirals got along quite well personally. They both liked sports, particularly baseball. In May, Sims wrote Pratt, "Old man Strauss is doing a good stunt and playing the game properly." Strauss made it clear in his memoirs that his relations with the force commander "were always quite satisfactory," but that he communicated with him only when necessary and generally ignored him.[13]

Sims did not complain about Rodman.[14] Benson was in Europe when the secretary appointed the Kentuckian to command the first American battleships sent to European waters during the war. While with the Grand Fleet, Rodman virtually ignored Sims. He sent weekly reports to Secretary Daniels, only communicating with the force commander in response to an enquiry or directive. Rodman made it clear in *Yarns of a Kentucky Admiral* and in his testimony at the naval hearings that he considered Sims a "liaison officer; a representative of the Office of Operations in Europe." "His title as 'Commanding United States Naval Forces in European Waters' is particularly misleading," he informed the congressional committee. "He did not personally direct the movements of our fighting ships in the war zone, as the public so generally believes."[15] Vice Admiral John McCrea, who served as Rodman's aide in 1920, noted that his superior supported Sims. Rodman considered him a friend until Daniels published a letter revealing that the former European force commander had presented a list of squadron commanders that placed Rodman eleventh out of twelve. He became extremely hostile toward Sims, writing to Daniels (whom he had held in contempt earlier), "I wish to combat [Sims's] . . . statements and help preserve the deservedly good name which the Navy earned during the war." According to the secretary, Rodman, responding to one of Sims's remarks, said: "I do not believe there is a particle of truth in that statement. . . . There are three kinds of lies—lies, damn lies and statistics." McCrea said that Rodman's original draft of his statement to the committee "blasted Sims," but it was toned down to dignified testimony. Early in 1918, at Admiral Beatty's recommendation, the Admiralty proposed to advance Rodman to vice admiral. Rodman was junior to the British flag officers commanding battle squadrons who were the equivalent of vice admirals. Also, the C-in-C's policy was to have individual flag officers in charge of battle squadrons to command all units on escort duty. Sims urged the promotion, but President Wilson opposed it as British interference. Rodman contradicted himself in his testimony of 1920 in order to defend the Navy against Sims. In his reports to Daniels during the war, he frequently mentioned the problems of American gunnery, but in 1920 he defended it.[16]

Rear Admiral Henry Baird Wilson, who briefly commanded the U.S. naval force based at Gibraltar before assignment in October 1917 to the command at Brest, probably annoyed Sims more than any other subordinate. They had not gotten along before the war, and Wilson tried with a great deal of success to treat his command as an independent force.

Sims blamed his trouble with Wilson on the distance between his headquarters and Brest and on poor communications, although it was just as far to northern Scotland and to Queenstown. President Wilson's decision to send an army, the American Expeditionary Force (AEF), to France enhanced the importance of the American naval presence in that country, but most of the difficulties with his force in France stemmed from the weakness of the French navy on the western coast, the inadequacy of surface combat ships and supporting facilities, the awkward command structure, and the personalities in play.

Lieutenant Commander W. R. Sayles was the U.S. naval attaché in Paris when Congress declared war. He had been acting naval attaché since August 1914 and spoke French fluently. His staff consisted of an assistant and a clerk. Until July 1917, he was "virtually in charge of the entire naval activities in France." His office had no mobilization plan. When the United States declared war, he on his own responsibility called to active duty several reserves residing in Paris.[17] Admiral Sims complained to the Department and again during the 1920 naval hearings that he was not told about the deployment of U.S. naval vessels in French waters and of plans to establish naval bases in France. So far as the French were concerned, the American admiral was not accredited: he was, in Sayles's words, "merely the Naval Representative so far as Great Britain was concerned." On June 6, Sims was informed of a flotilla of yachts to be deployed in French waters under his general command. He was officially appointed to the command of all United States naval forces in European waters on June 14, but it is not known when the French were notified of this action. Before his appointment, Sims met with French naval officials. On April 30, Sayles informed the American ambassador in Paris that in the future he would "report directly to Admiral Sims all matters of importance involving general policy of the United States Navy."[18]

Sims and Sayles did not know that Benson wanted to assign an admiral to command U.S. naval forces in French waters. On May 6, the French naval attaché in Washington cabled Paris: "A rear admiral will probably be designated to perform at Paris the same duties as Rear Admiral Sims at London." Secretary Daniels, however, was not in favor of it, assuming that the Navy needed only one command abroad. Sims may well have suspected that the CNO was considering a counterpart in France. On May 5, he journeyed to Paris and conferred with the minister of marine and other French naval officials along with Sayles. That afternoon, the American naval attaché recorded that Sims "through this office, telegraphed to the Secretary of the Navy that relations with the French Navy Department were very satisfactory."[19]

Nonetheless, the Department continued to communicate directly with Sayles, who acted as liaison with the French minister of marine. His office responsibilities included intelligence and information gathering, logistics, and communications. At Sims's instigation, Sayles was ordered to oversee maritime transportation from the United States. This task included negotiations with the French government for docks and other port facilities required to handle personnel and cargoes. Sayles's office informed Washington of the French decision to utilize St. Nazaire as the port of debarkation for the first contingents of the AEF. Through the naval attaché, French naval officials frequently ("incessantly," he wrote) requested information about ship sailings to France, the schedule for departure and arrival in French waters, their cargoes, and other matters. Sayles found it difficult to obtain such information. Admiral De Bon, the head of the French naval staff, called him in and told him that he "was in a fog as to what preparations to make in advance to receive the American Forces." Sayles promptly cabled Washington: "French Ministry of Marine constantly asks questions which I am unable to answer." Sims, testifying at the naval hearings, confirmed the naval attaché's statement, remarking that Sayles was informed of the deployment of yachts to French waters, but "no information had been given concerning their orders, or the prospective plans of the department for their operations. The result was that when they arrived, the French had made no plans for their reception."[20]

In June, the Department ordered Captain Richard H. Jackson to France to act as Sims's representative in Paris at the request of the French government. The arrival of Jackson and the American yachts under Rear Admiral William Fletcher in June set the stage for a confusing and inefficient command system. Sayles, Jackson, and Fletcher were ordered to report directly to Sims, but no effort was made to delineate their specific responsibilities.[21]

Captain Jackson, a native of Alabama, was a member of the Naval Academy class of 1888. He was aboard the *Trenton* when she was destroyed during the hurricane at Samoa in 1888. Shortly afterward, he was discharged from the Navy because he scored poorly on an examination for promotion to ensign. Nonetheless, because of his gallantry at Samoa, the Congress made him an ensign in 1890, the only naval officer ever commissioned in this manner.[22]

In 1917, Jackson was in command of the battleship *Virginia* when he received orders to France. Sims told him that his primary responsibility was to act as his staff representative in France and to conduct liaison with the French naval service. Nothing was said about establishing bases at St. Nazaire and elsewhere and locating sites for naval air stations. Yet Jackson reported to the CNO in August that the force commander "instructed me to take charge of the organization of the Bases and Aviation in France." When Sayles questioned his authority, Jackson wrote him that virtually all communications from the U.S. naval commands in France to Simsadus and those from Sims's headquarters to French commands were to go through his office. Quoting from Navy regulations, he informed Sayles that his major responsibility would be intelligence and that the attaché's office would come under his command. "I represent the Navy Department, particularly as regards Plans and Operations, as well as [being] Sims' representative." He soon informed Sims that he had sent an officer to St. Nazaire to witness the "arrival of each transport, to get them docked and to get them away." He also proposed to assign officers to command St. Nazaire, Bordeaux, and other ports that might receive American troops and supplies.[23] Sims had no such plan, which soon led to friction.

Early in September, Babcock, the force commander's aide, made a trip to inspect the American naval facilities along the French west coast. He warned Sims that relations between Jackson and Fletcher were strained because "there does not seem to be a good dividing line between the duties of Captain Jackson and Admiral Fletcher." Also, Fletcher complained of having to channel his communications to Simsadus through Jackson in Paris.[24] Shortly afterward, another member of Sims's staff visited the naval offices in Paris and Brest, and, like Babcock, noted jurisdictional conflicts. Whiting, in charge of U.S. naval aviation in France, was equally disgruntled. He mentioned that considerable information on French aviation was sent directly to Washington and not through Simsadus; "He [Jackson] won't send in any recommendations for the officers I ask for. He wants me to sit in a two-by-four room at the Ministry of Marine and decode messages, etc."[25] Sims and Twining made a quick tour of U.S. naval facilities in France, preparing to brief Admiral Mayo about them when he arrived in England. Apparently he did not mention the problems in France to Mayo, but soon Twining, at Sims's instruction, drafted a letter to Jackson emphasizing the force commander's dissatisfaction with his interpretation of his orders. Noting Jackson's official stationery, which labeled his post "Headquarters of United States Navy Department in France," Twining wrote: "nothing in the orders . . . gives you the command of any of our forces in France . . . your position being exclusively that of a Staff officer representing the Admiral in Paris. . . . The Admiral is of the opinion that you have on numerous occasions handled matters in such a way as to give the impression that you were acting with original authority instead of merely transmitting his wishes and those of the French Ministry to our Forces in France . . . [which] has caused such dissatisfaction and friction to the detriment of the efficiency of our operations." Twining then pointed out that Captain Cone was not under Jackson's authority as "you indicated" and that "you should be exceedingly careful to avoid the appearance of issuing orders to Rear Admiral Fletcher."[26]

Jackson responded that he understood Sims's orders; he found aviation and the bases in such a muddle that he had to do something about it. Jackson did not clarify matters. In October, Sims decided that Jackson's office would assume responsibility for all cables and correspondence originating in Paris and in Pershing's headquarters, while Fletcher would communicate with Simsadus directly by the Brest-Le Havre-London cable.[27]

Jackson continued to communicate directly with Benson. Pratt realized that this activity violated the chain of command and tried to have him recalled. So did Sims. Benson refused but ordered a reorganization of the American naval command in France. Sayles became intelligence officer under the American admiral in command at Brest, and Jackson became the naval attaché in Paris. He retained offices near the American embassy for himself and his staff, which had grown to six assistants, five civilian volunteers, and three clerks.[28] Difficulties with Jackson came to an end, and he served as naval attaché until the Armistice. Jackson enjoyed a distinguished career after the war, becoming commander in chief of the Battle Fleet, with the rank of vice admiral. He died in 1971 at the age of 105 years, at that time the oldest living military officer and the oldest graduate of a service academy.[29]

Sims did not succeed in removing Jackson, but he relieved Admiral Fletcher as commander of U.S. naval forces in French waters. William Bartlett Fletcher was a native of Vermont and a Naval Academy graduate in the class of 1882. His early career was not especially distinguished, although he was considered competent.[30] He received orders to command Squadron Three, Patrol Force of the Atlantic Fleet, and arrived at Brest with six yachts of this organization on July 4, 1917. After the arrival of another division of yachts a few days later, Fletcher had about fifteen naval vessels in hand prepared to begin operations in cooperation with the French.

Fletcher and his staff took up offices in a building near the French naval commander's headquarters. The Navy Department planned to establish a base at Brest and contemplated placing another one at Bordeaux. Fletcher, under instructions from Sims, was to command the shore facilities and the Patrol Force. The Bordeaux plan was discarded, but the base at Brest grew from a "small dilapidated building" that housed the entire staff, including Admiral Fletcher, to many facilities and several thousand people. Rear Admiral Henry B. Wilson, Fletcher's successor, also maintained his living quarters and those of his staff in the same building as his office.[31]

Sims's instructions to Fletcher were virtually the same as those of other subordinate commanders, to cooperate with the French and to function as part of the French naval force in the area. After conferring with French naval officials in Paris, Sims wrote to Admiral De Bon, chief of staff to the minister of marine, "It is my policy that the general nature of all operations to be performed by U.S. forces in French waters based on French ports should be indicated by the Ministry of Marine in the same manner as if these forces were actually French Forces." The force commander repeated this procedure to Fletcher shortly after the Paris conference, adding that "We must not in any way attempt to run a separate show. We must, as far as possible, keep the point of view that we are virtually a part of the French service—an addition to it but nevertheless a part of it."[32]

Within a few weeks, however, Sims began to modify his instructions to Fletcher. This departure was partly a response to communications from Washington, which stressed the priority attached to American troop transports and partly to the realization that French naval commanders allowed American transports to steam in French waters without adequate escort. One of Sims's staff warned Fletcher that he must ensure that the American ships were given sufficient escort. According to this officer, the patrol commander responded: "'You have changed your philosophy since your last visit.' . . . [He] explained then that some little time back he had received directions from the London office to the effect that our vessels must be considered in the light of French ships. The Ministry of Marine also received some communication, and had sent instructions to the [French naval commander] . . . at Brest to this effect. The [French commander] . . . told Admiral Fletcher that he hesitated to show these instructions as he felt that it was not quite fair that he [Admiral Fletcher] was being practically by-passed in the matter." When Sims received this information, he immediately informed Fletcher that priorities had changed: "The primary duty of the Forces placed under your command is the protection of troop transports and supply transports, whether inbound or outbound. . . . Your secondary mission is to cooperate to the fullest extent with the French forces assisting them in every way possible not in conflict with your primary mission. . . . While I desire to assist the French in every way, nothing must be done to interfere in any way with providing sufficient escort for our own vessels." Later he warned Fletcher, "[I]f we should lose a vessel owing to its not being properly escorted, no amount of explanation or shifting the blame to French shoulders would save either your head or mine."[33]

Testimony during Admiral Fletcher's court of inquiry in 1920 suggested that some confusion stemmed from his interpretation and execution of Sims's desires. When asked to describe his official relationship with the French command at Brest, Fletcher testified, "We operated in a measure independently and in a measure in cooperation with them, they being informed at all times of what we were doing." Captain Twining testified that Fletcher should have understood that he "had . . . to use diplomacy with the French. That he should regard himself as under the command of the French admiral who was senior to him, but at the same time to make sure that our forces were employed in the way in which . . . they should be employed," that is, as escort of transports. Whether Fletcher understood the necessity of tact in dealing with the French is unclear. He evidently followed what he considered to be Sims's instructions literally, that is, to follow the French lead regardless of consequences.[34]

Reports that American transports continued to pass through French waters without proper escort and other indications of difficulties at Brest prompted Sims on October 13 to notify Rear Admiral Wilson at Gibraltar that he (Sims) was considering swapping commanders, assigning Wilson to Brest and Fletcher to Gibraltar. Before this rearrangement occurred, the transport *Antilles* was torpedoed, an event that Sims had warned Fletcher to avoid. Sims concluded that the transport was not "sufficiently convoyed." Although it was widely believed that Fletcher was relieved because of the loss of the *Antilles*, Sims had decided at least to transfer him before this incident. The sinking made it impossible to transfer Fletcher. Both Sims and Twining testified at the Fletcher court of inquiry that the transfer of Fletcher was canceled because of British displeasure.[35] Instead, Fletcher was returned to the United States. Daniels approved Sims's decision, recording that Fletcher lacked "initiative and resource—is a paper Admiral and should not have been promoted."[36]

Sims stressed in communications to the Department that the escort situation was only one of the issues that persuaded him to act. Officers sent to Brest on inspection tours brought back stories of dissatisfaction among Fletcher's staff. They stated that Fletcher took on too much of the work himself. Also, when difficulties developed at St. Nazaire, the key port of debarkation for American troops, the force commander requested that Fletcher go there to investigate the circumstances. According to Twining's testimony, he did not make a trip to the port and did not send one of his staff. A member of Sims's staff who interviewed Fletcher said that "he had no time to visit the other ports in the zone of his activities." Virtually every officer who visited Brest reported disorganization at the port. Sims emphasized this deficiency when he reported the relief of Fletcher to the CNO. After Admiral Mayo spent a few hours at Brest, he concluded that the Brest force was "hampered in its operations by general unsuitability of the available vessels for high seas work, and by lack of organization and of general plans to serve as a guide in carrying out necessary work."[37]

When Fletcher learned of his relief, he demanded a court of inquiry. Sims refused, claiming that exigencies of war precluded the assemblage of the required officers. Fletcher was assigned to command a naval district in the United States. Fletcher was the only flag officer relieved of his command during the war.[38]

When Fletcher failed to persuade Sims to modify the reason for the relief from disobedience of orders to "temperamentally unfitted for the task," Daniels agreed to an official court of inquiry in 1920. The court's findings generally upheld Sims, but the court ruled that he should have granted more interviews to Fletcher, and that he relied too heavily on the reports of junior staff members. Sims felt some remorse, but, shortly after the court ended its deliberations, he wrote to Admiral Andrews that Fletcher was "the most complete case of inefficiency in command that I have ever run across."[39] Fletcher retired in 1921 and lived to the age of ninety-five before his death in 1957.

Under the circumstances, the European force commander had no choice except to remove Fletcher from the French command, but the disgruntled admiral was not completely at fault. The Navy Department did not help matters when it selected subordinate officers for Brest and Bordeaux before Fletcher was given the command. They were on site when Fletcher arrived and claimed that they were not under his command. Sims later placed Fletcher in command of all the bases and their officers. This decision did not foster increased efficiency.[40]

On November 1, Wilson arrived in Brest to replace Fletcher. Before breaking his flag on the *Prometheus*, his flagship, he made a quick trip to London, where Sims and members of his staff briefed him. He was a native of New Jersey who graduated from the Naval Academy in 1881. Commended for bravery during the Spanish-American War, he gained a reputation for his seamanship, smart ship handling, and ship keeping. Nonetheless, because of the extreme slowness of promotion, he remained a lieutenant for eighteen years. He did not receive his first command until 1908, after twenty-seven years in the Navy.[41] In 1916, he supervised the fitting out of the battleship *Pennsylvania* and later assumed her command. Designated the flagship of the Atlantic Fleet, the *Pennsylvania* was the most desired command in the Navy. After the advent of war, Wilson organized the Patrol Force of the Atlantic Fleet and became its commander. Several divisions of this force, all yachts, were sent to French waters under Fletcher; Wilson took additional units of the force to Gibraltar. While in command at Gibraltar and later in France, he retained command of the entire Patrol Force of the Atlantic Fleet.

Sims ordered Wilson, as he had with Fletcher, to escort all American convoys inbound and outbound in French waters and to cooperate with French naval authorities, although not at the expense of escort. Sims promised to provide an adequate number of vessels, particularly destroyers. The Department, however, was slow in reinforcing Wilson's force, and until late in 1918 those that arrived were second-rate, additional yachts and aged destroyers. Wilson did well despite his limited resources. Ships were torpedoed and sunk, but no transports with American troops aboard were lost en route to French ports. U.S. destroyers operating from Queenstown and British antisubmarine craft provided much of the escort until late in 1918, when modern destroyers replaced or reinforced Wilson's worn-out yachts operating from Brest. Wilson employed his smaller yachts in cooperation with French escorts for coastal convoys. By August 1918, the U.S. naval force in French waters under Wilson comprised thirty-three destroyers, sixteen yachts, nine minesweepers, and miscellaneous auxiliary vessels, operating from a large base at Brest and several smaller bases. Other facilities, including fifteen air stations and the Lafayette Radio Station, came under his command. In general, he directed these forces without interference from French naval officials. As he and others attested, including Sims, relations with the French remained quite satisfactory. Daniels praised Wilson highly, and Benson wrote to the secretary, "I am firmly of the opinion that the administration of vessels operating from Brest is more responsible for the failure of the much advertised German submarine campaign against our troop ships than any other one thing." Although the CNO may have exaggerated its accomplishments, Wilson's force made a significant contribution to the protection of troop transports.[42]

Nevertheless, Wilson caused Sims more aggravation than any other subordinate flag officer. The two came to dislike each other intensely before the war, probably when they served together on the battleship *Kentucky*, the flagship of Rear Admiral Robley Evans. The C-in-C of the Atlantic Fleet criticized Sims's crusade for gunnery improvements. The admiral's opinion carried over to many subordinates, including Wilson, who served first as navigator and then as executive officer on the *Kentucky*.[43]

Sims's correspondence with Benson and others contained frequent mention of his unhappiness with Wilson. Many of the admiral's comments dealt with Wilson's efforts to centralize his command of all American naval forces along the French west coast. At first, Wilson's attitude perplexed Sims. Evidently Sims learned that Wilson had criticized some of his actions and made "expressions of disloyalty, both before officers of the force and before other officers outside the force." Writing to Wilson, the force commander did not spell out the details of this "disloyalty," and Wilson did not reply.

Sims reported his concerns to Benson: "He [Wilson] has always been rather a puzzle." Sims mentioned that during two meetings with Wilson since he assumed the French command, "he was everything that could be desired." He wondered whether Wilson's criticism of him stemmed from their differences over improvements to target practice. Perhaps Wilson considered him "one of the most dangerous men in the service," or possibly he disliked his "impulsive temperament and rather boyish nature." He hoped to avoid "more trouble."[44]

The only issue of substance that arose between Sims and Wilson concerned a disagreement between the commander at Brest and Captain Cone, the head of American naval aviation in France. Cone's responsibility was to complete the establishment of naval air stations in France, after which they were to come under Wilson's control. The two differed over the timing of this transfer. Sims took Cone's side. Comments about Wilson to the CNO and to Pratt included disparagements such as "he has never grown up!" Curiously, he maintained that Wilson was "a loveable sort of a fellow and a very jovial companion due to the essential boyishness of his disposition and his high spirits and sense of duty." Benson never responded to Sims's complaints about Wilson. The naval commander in France replied only once to Sims, noting that he had been listening to rumors. Evidently, they were not all rumors. Sims wanted to recall Wilson and to replace him with either Rear Admiral William Rodgers or Rear Admiral William F. Fullam.[45] Wilson did not have to worry about his tenure, given his popularity in the Navy Department, particularly with Daniels and Benson.

By September 1918, the U.S. Navy in France had grown to an imposing force of more than twenty thousand men. To a great degree, this increase resulted from the expansion of the AEF. The disastrous defeat of the Italians at Caporetto, the withdrawal of Russia from the Allied coalition, and President Wilson's agreement to send a powerful army to France all contributed to this growth. Troops were needed to replace the depleted French and British armies, and only the United States had the necessary manpower. General Pershing made it clear to the secretary of war in December 1917 that the shipment of troops depended upon available escorts. General Tasker Bliss, the American military representative at the Inter-Allied Supreme War Council, wrote to

Benson on January 7, 1918, reporting Pershing's complaint that the lack of destroyers hindered the proper distribution of cargoes. The AEF commander wanted transports to go directly to a number of designated ports, but inadequate escort in French waters forced all merchant shipping to dock at Brest and St. Nazaire, where congestion at times seriously delayed off-loading. Bliss warned that "The matter of more efficient handling of our transports is every day a more and more burning question."[46]

Benson, whose trip to France in November 1917 had left him dissatisfied with the state of the naval force there, already had a plan in hand to reorganize the naval forces in France. His aide, Lieutenant Commander Andrew Carter, prepared this plan, which was based on the premise that "From the present outlook there can be little doubt regarding naval expansion in France. It is apparent that the Army is making preparations on a large scale the landing of supplies and troops." The War Department had determined to use additional ports. Carter recommended the division of naval activities in France into six categories: naval forces afloat, port organization and administration, aviation, intelligence, communications, and logistics. "Every naval officer, without exception, with whom I have discussed the question of naval policy in France seems to agree that the French administration of naval work is of a character which [indicates] we cannot place any reliance whatever in the naval cooperation which we had hoped to receive from them." Carter also proposed to divide the French west coast into districts with senior American officers in charge who would control shipping to ports in their jurisdictions. They would report to the American commander in France.[47]

Benson adopted the plan. He sent it to Sims on January 5, 1918, and also ordered Wilson, his staff, and Captain Jackson to discuss its implementation with the force commander. A second directive designated Sayles as intelligence officer under Wilson and made Jackson the naval attaché in Paris with the task of acting as liaison between Wilson and the French naval ministry. These changes gave Wilson more responsibility along with a new title. Sims recommended that Wilson's title should be "Commander United States Naval Forces in France," and Benson agreed to it.[48] Sims acquiesced in the reorganization plan without a quibble. It was a direct order from the CNO and obviously needed, and Sims was not as critical of Wilson as he became later. Wilson explained the new organization to Admiral De Bon. According to Jackson, De Bon was "pleased" with it, and the district organization was initiated on January 18, 1918.[49]

The reorganization took some time to function properly, especially the district commands. Admiral Mayo inspected U.S. naval activities in France shortly after the end of the war. He thought the organization basically sound but felt that the district commanders should have been given more authority. He recognized the obstacle to this augmentation: "the district commanders are working under French district commanders." Sims and Wilson agreed on the need to appoint officers of sufficient rank to "command respect and attention" from French officials and U.S. Army officers. At Sims's recommendation, probably following a suggestion from Wilson, Benson agreed that the naval districts should coincide with the French political and military administrative entities in the area, three *arrondissements*. The district commanders were based at Brest, Lorient, and Rochefort. They oversaw the major ports of St. Nazaire, Brest, and Bordeaux.[50] Later another district was added encompassing the port of Cherbourg. Port officers were detailed to ports within these districts opened to American shipping or naval activities. Communication offices, storehouses, a fuel depot, hospitals, and minor repair facilities were established in all the districts, and naval vessels were based in them. Nine minesweepers and one of the armed yachts were stationed at St. Nazaire, and a division of armed yachts was transferred from Brest to Lorient, but the majority of vessels under Wilson's command, including destroyers, continued to operate out of Brest. The number of shore-based naval personnel in the Lorient district increased dramatically to more than fifty officers and just over three hundred enlisted personnel. Barracks were under construction in all of them. Hotels, private residences, and buildings were requisitioned in Lorient and St. Nazaire to provide quarters and offices.[51]

The port officers managed all shipping under American control, including offloading of cargoes and the scheduling, organizing, and briefing for convoys. Before the war, the U.S. Navy had no experience in the administration of a port. Captain Twining drew up a set of instructions.[52] Port officers dealt with French officials in dealing with navigation laws and regulations, custom duties, pilotage and also with U.S. Army quartermaster officers to expedite transportation of troops and supplies to camps and storage facilities. They also cooperated with consular officials. Frequently, however, vessels under the control of the U.S. Shipping Board (USSB) ignored the port officers.[53]

Wilson wanted to centralize all U.S. shipping under his control and then delegate responsibility to the district commanders. This domain included transports of the naval command, the Army, the Shipping Board, and others managed by civilians. The CNO agreed with this objective but believed it impractical for political reasons. Admiral Mayo later noted the difficulties with shipping control, which he thought should have been under naval authority.[54]

The district commanders took charge of naval air stations when they became operational. Wilson contended that control should shift when they were commissioned and placed under American commanders. Captain Cone insisted that they should remain under his control until construction was complete and aircraft were ready to conduct flight operations. Sims supported Cone, although in his order to Wilson outlining the new organizations, he wrote: "In so far as the Aviation Stations in France are concerned, . . . Captain Cone will act under your orders." He should have "as free a hand as possible in the matter of developing, building up, and perfecting the details of the Aviation Service . . . without derogation to the military command residing in you as his immediate superior."[55] This ambiguous and contradictory communication precipitated much of the friction between the two admirals during the war.

In September 1918, Wilson was promoted to vice admiral. Sims was not at all happy about it, telling several subordinate commanders that neither he nor Benson had recommended it. It was "a personal selection of the Secretary." Sims informed Commander Percy Foote, the secretary's naval aide, that the promotion was unfortunate. He noted that the Admiralty wanted Admiral Rodman promoted to vice admiral because the British division commanders in the Grand Fleet held that rank, but the Department declined to act. Foote replied that the secretary was "fond" of Wilson; that he greatly admired him for his work in France, particularly in dealing with "social evils and moral conduct"; and that he "took great pleasure in making the appointment."[56] Sims might have considered the secretary's action a form of retribution against him because of his alleged disloyalty. Sims believed that Wilson "played the game" properly and that he did not.

The public announcement of Wilson's promotion included information that the newly promoted vice admiral would receive a fleet command, but Benson deemed Wilson "indispensable" at Brest and requested that he continue in the French command for the rest of the year. He assumed command of the Atlantic Fleet in February 1919. Sims protested: he sent Daniels a list of ten flag officers in order of preference who he said were qualified to command the fleet, but he did not include Wilson. He refused to recommend Wilson for a medal, although he decorated many of his London staff. This act angered the secretary and even Admiral Mayo, who recommended Wilson for the Distinguished Service Medal.[57]

Wilson retaliated during the naval hearings. Before his testimony, Rodman and Wilson discussed Sims: "Admiral Wilson was the more vocal," according to Rodman's aide. "He blasted Admiral Sims in every direction. He told of Admiral Sims' dissatisfaction with his, Wilson's, administration of the U.S. naval base at Brest, of Admiral Sims' visit to him and the threat that he had a mind to send him, Wilson, home. 'I shook my finger under his nose and said, 'don't forget, Admiral Sims, if I go home, you go home, too.'" Before the investigating committee, he downplayed Sims's contention that inadequate repair facilities and lack of fuel accounted for the delay in sending destroyers to Brest, suggesting that when he succeeded Fletcher, facilities at Brest "were adequate for quite a large force." Other testimony simply covered his activities in France.[58]

The naval forces based at Queenstown and Brest engaged in some rivalry. The destroyer skippers initially based in Ireland recounted that Wilson criticized them upon their transfer to Brest. Wilson believed that Sims favored the Queenstown command at the expense of the naval force at Brest in deciding the location of personnel and vessels. A retired officer wrote after the war that Wilson mistreated transferees from Queenstown "for no reason that I could see, except that we were working for Admiral Sims, whom he resented deeply."[59]

Sims's vindictiveness toward Wilson is difficult to understand despite hard feelings dating to prewar years. Benson, Daniels, FDR, and others rightfully gave him credit for his service at Brest. He cooperated effectively with French officials. Eventually the French gave him free rein with his forces.[60] He earned praise and promotion. If the war had continued, rear admirals would have commanded the naval districts under his authority.[61] The growth of the French command would have rendered his subordination to the European force commander increasingly awkward. Sims may have expected such a development.

Wilson was apparently popular or at least respected by his subordinates at Brest. Rear Admiral Newton McCully and Captain Thomas P. Magruder, two of the district commanders, were high in their praise of him. Magruder wrote in 1929, "I have served under many admirals, but from none have I received more courtesy, consideration and confidence than was accorded me by Admiral Wilson."[62] Wilson was equally attentive to war correspondents. One of them, James B. Connolly, lauded Wilson and his success but criticized Sims in wartime articles and later in books.[63]

Wilson cultivated popularity with considerable success. The French, particularly those in Brest whose respect for other nationalities was at times lukewarm, came to praise him. Eleanor Roosevelt wrote that Admiral Wilson "practically rules Brest and I am told has done much for the poor and is much beloved." The journal *Le Depêche* of Brest noted: "Admiral Wilson is now a well-known figure among us. He takes part in our daily life, shares in all our sorrows as well as in our hopes. Later, without doubt, the title of 'Citizen of Brest,' will be conferred upon him." The well-known Parisian magazine *L'Illustration* stated: "The indomitable will of our Allies is represented by Admiral Wilson. He has a countenance that you never forget. His quick manner of shaking your hand while looking you squarely in the face, the smile which, I dare say, follows up the orders he gives, his brief and concise speech, denotes a great firmness of character." A *Le Matin* reporter described Wilson as "large, 'svelte' [well groomed], alert and vigorous and young despite his graying hair. He has in his appearance a certain simplicity and charm that only years at sea could give him."[64] Like many naval officers, he often used profanity. The naval secretary might not have not known of this habit; he abhorred "strong or foul language."[65]

The French command under Wilson never had the esprit de corps that reigned in the Queenstown command. This difference probably stemmed from various dissimilarities, including prevailing types of ships, command structure, and personnel. Sims was quite proud of the Queenstown command with Admiral Sir Lewis Bayly, RN, in charge and Captain Joel R. P. Pringle, USN, as his chief of staff. Sims viewed the Queenstown organization as the model for all of his commands.

The Admiralty approved the Queenstown command in 1915. It assumed sole responsibility for offensive operations against German submarines lurking in the Western Approaches, that part of the Atlantic generally southeast of Ireland and England. All antisubmarine craft were supposed to concentrate at this base. At Beatty's recommendation, Admiral Sir Lewis Bayly was given the command. Arthur Marder wrote that "no happier choice could have been made than Bayly for the Queenstown Command, but few who knew him would have bet on this result."[66]

Bayly was sixty years old in 1917, having served nearly half a century in the Royal Navy. He was slight with a swarthy complexion, his face creased by years at sea. He had a beaked nose through which he blew or spoke through "with equal resonance." He never married and enjoyed few activities other than gardening. A teetotaler, he served distilled barley water at his dinners. He had little interest in social occasions. After taking the Irish command, he issued a request (really an order) that his officers should assume that they had completed all social calls.[67]

Bayly was an autocrat who acquired the reputation of a martinet. He was known as a hard, tough, unbending man and a stern disciplinarian. Admiral Robert Carney remembered him as "a very crusty old bird." A reporter described him as "curt, dry, exacting," lacking "imagination," and with "the manner of a rat-terrier towards people not of his own kind." He cared nothing for popularity with either the public or his superiors. "No man ever sought popularity less," a contemporary said. "[He had an] . . . almost cynical indifference to popular opinion." He was hostile to reporters and correspondents and on more than one occasion turned his back to photographers. One writer observed that Bayly was one of the few British admirals "whose photograph I never recollect having seen in any newspaper."[68]

Bayly was caustic and tart to the point of rudeness, perhaps a consequence of his reserved nature and absorption with his responsibilities. This trait, however, was something of a façade. Sims informed his wife that "You would find him shy, or rather diffident, for a day or so and after that one of the most entertaining companions. He is a very curious character."[69] He never wasted words on compliments. His method was to proceed directly by the shortest and quickest route, issuing "unequivocal [orders] with an economy in words and clarity of thought." One of the better-known anecdotes about him concerned a flotilla of British destroyers that arrived in Queenstown. When he ordered it to sea, the commanders delayed because of a gale. Bayly then ordered them back to their home base, and when the senior officer signaled, "sorry Destroyers were not much use to you," he replied, "Why say much!"[70] He had little use for the Irish people, especially after the Easter Rebellion of 1916, and they had little use for him.[71]

Bayly irritated many officers in the Royal Navy, having the reputation of being a "character." Called "Luragi" by those who respected him and "Black Bayly" by others, he was considered a nonconformist, and few held him in high esteem. Sir Henry Oliver claimed that Bayly "lacked vision," Lord Fisher considered him a "fool," and Sir Herbert Richmond contended that he was "obstinate as a fool, and . . . too stupid to convince."[72] Gordon Campbell, who won a Victoria Cross for commanding a Q-ship, referred to Bayly as the man "I admired more than any other." Sir Edward Evans, another British naval hero, wrote later, "I admired him as I have seldom admired any man." Winston Churchill and Jellicoe liked him, although the admiral considered Bayly "occasionally a little mad."[73]

Bayly did not suffer fools or weaklings gladly, even those among his superiors. As a young lieutenant in command of a small warship in the 1890s, he angered the admiral in charge of an opposing force during maneuvers when he claimed to have sunk the admiral's flagship by a torpedo in broad daylight. "You have done a very foolish thing," the admiral told him. Lord Chatfield, aboard the flagship at the time, wrote that "to me it was amazing that a lieutenant should have such audacity and when, quite calm and confident, he arrived on board we all felt rather sorry for him as he went down to the Admiral's cabin. But he soon emerged with a grim smile . . . and told how he had captured the [opponent fleet's] . . . torpedo boat the night before and saw no rule to forbid him to use her."[74] On one occasion, he took the prime minister ashore in his barge, and as the dignitary departed, he turned to Sir Dudley De Chair, later an admiral, and said, "what will you give me if I drown the Prime Minister?"[75]

Bayly's one soft spot was for Violet Voysey, a spinster niece whose loving care offered him the few amenities in his life. She acted as hostess at Admiralty House, the headquarters and residence of Bayly in Queenstown. According to Sims she was the only lady, except relatives, allowed to visit the house. Some quipped that Miss Voysey really ran the Queenstown command.[76]

Bayly was a keen student of naval operations. Unfortunately, he based many of his concepts upon British naval experience during the eighteenth and nineteenth centuries, often ignoring modern technology. Like Sims, Bayly considered himself an innovator in destroyer tactics. In 1907, he was selected to command the Destroyer Flotilla in the Home Fleet. In Bayly's words, "destroyers were then a comparatively new arm, and their capabilities when working in flotillas were not very well understood." Years later, he wrote the distinguished naval historian, Sir Julian Corbett: "I . . . [was ordered] to take up a billet as Commodore to organize the various destroyer flotillas and teach them war. . . . They had no idea what their duties would be in war (nor had anyone else.)"[77] Nonetheless, he impressed the Admiralty. He was promoted to flag rank and made president of the War College at Portsmouth. He commanded various squadrons before the outbreak of war in 1914. While in command of a division of pre-dreadnoughts in the Grand Fleet, he made various recommendations deemed impractical by Lord Jellicoe, the C-in-C, and his senior officers.[78]

Bayly never achieved appropriate rank and responsibility. In September 1914, he commanded the Channel Fleet, but the sinking of the battleship *Formidable* by a German submarine led to his removal. He demanded a court-martial unsuccessfully.[79] In some disgrace, he was banished to the Royal Naval College at Greenwich. In July 1915, the growing shipping losses to submarines in the Atlantic led to the creation of the Queenstown command, and Bayly took command of it. Although Beatty recommended him, Jellicoe was responsible for the appointment. Bayly never learned of this assistance or refused to recognize it.[80] He wrote Sir Roger Keyes in 1920 that "Jellicoe . . . never stirred a finger to help me when I was degraded and sent to Greenwich [which] made me feel that he either believed that the *Formidable* was my fault, or else felt glad that I was out of the way, so as to allow others to be advanced."[81] His anger was misplaced. Jellicoe thought that Bayly's removal was "unwise" and with Winston Churchill did what he could to help him.[82] The Queenstown command restored Bayly's enthusiasm for his work but did little to change his character.

The decision to deploy American destroyers to the Queenstown command caused Jellicoe to consider replacement of Bayly. His well-known attitudes and the assumption that he disliked Americans led to this possibility. In a letter to Pratt, Sims wrote: "Admiral Jellicoe expressed to me grave concern as to whether we would be able to get along with the Vice Admiral in command at Queenstown. He had, and still has, a reputation of being very difficult, and was supposed to have it in for all Americans because when he was Naval Attaché in Washington, he was practically fired out at the request of our people. . . . For a long time he had been at outs with the Admiralty." When Sims first met Bayly, "he was as rude to me as one man can well be to another . . . apparently deeply incensed at having been sent for. I do not know what they had been saying to him." Jellicoe apologized and offered to remove Bayly, but Sims demurred and soon visited Queenstown. "The Admiral received me very nicely but without enthusiasm. After about three days it became apparent that he quite approved of me." They soon became close friends.[83] Sims cemented his association with Bayly by arranging for the Admiralty to provide certain resources that Bayly needed to support operations out of Queenstown. He also helped mend Bayly's relations with his superiors, asking "both Jellicoe and Duff to let bygones be bygones, to forget all disagreements, and to disregard all misunderstandings, that may arise in view of our primary mission of *winning the war*."[84] It is not surprising that Bayly and his niece remained extremely close to Sims for the remainder of the war and afterward.

British naval officers who had some contact with Bayly after the Americans came under his command were astonished at his change in attitude. "This forbidding, almost inhuman disciplinarian had a heart!" one writer marveled. "In that strange personality," he wrote, "The British Navy had been aware only of a sort of Mr. Hyde. Was it due to the American naval officers that Dr. Jekyll suddenly became apparent?" Sims was "amused over somebody's remark that I discovered Admiral Bayly. There is enough of truth in it to make it amusing. I think it is true that our people have brought the British Navy to an appreciation of his intrinsic merit." He recounted to Benson a comment made by a British officer who "expressed the general astonishment of the British Navy in pretty nearly all ranks for the accounts they now have of what they consider the taming of Admiral Bayly. There was a common saying in the British Navy that what they ought to do with Bayly was to put him in an iron cage and feed him on raw meat, until war broke out, and then turn him loose on the enemy. They can't quite understand not only the respect in which he is held by our people, but the positive affection they all have for him and he has for them."[85]

The first meeting between the British admiral and American destroyer skippers set the tone for their extraordinary relationship. The first six destroyers arrived on May 3, under the overall command of Lieutenant Commander Joseph Taussig. He and his officers reported to Bayly at Admiralty House. After a brief exchange of amenities, the admiral asked, "Taussig, when will you be ready for sea?" The best evidence is that Taussig replied, "I shall be ready when fueled." Bayly then asked, "Do you require any repairs?" The reply was, "No sir." The Admiral finally asked, "Do you require any stores?" Taussig answered, "No sir." The Admiral terminated the call with welcome words: "You will take four days rest. Good morning."[86] In naval folklore, Taussig's legendary reply, known to every plebe at the Naval Academy, was simply "We are ready now, sir."[87]

Destroyer captains were expected to report to the admiral after a patrol. He addressed them by the name of their ship. According to Admiral William F. "Bull" Halsey, who commanded the *Benham* in 1917, "his greeting to me, reporting in after a cruise, would be, 'Good morning, *Benham*,' and almost before I had time to respond, he would invariably follow with, 'what is the condition of your ship?' Whatever its condition, you answered—if you were wise—'Quite all right, sir,' because Admiral Bayly held unpreparedness a crime more heinous than treason or mutiny." Roger Williams, who later became president of Newport News Shipbuilding, brought his destroyer in with a steering gear out of commission. Instead of requesting permission to miss his next patrol, Williams backed his vessel some five miles out of the narrow harbor, found room to turn her around, and proceeded to carry out his assignment, all "without any steering gear." Sims later wrote, "This officer never once mentioned to the Admiral the difficulties under which he worked, but his achievement completely won Sir Lewis's heart, and from that time this young man became one of his particular favorites."[88]

From the beginning, the admiral opened Admiralty House to the American skippers, and this hospitality cemented their affection for him. They were constantly entertained at lunch and dinner and were expected to tea when in port. A British officer who visited Queenstown during this period wrote that he "had heard . . . of the hospitality of Admiralty House, but one had to see it and feel it to appreciate what this 'home' atmosphere must have meant to these young American officers." "It is notorious," he added, "that Americans are vastly more homesick than British officers."[89] Relations became so close that they would sometimes go to Bayly or his niece with their personal troubles; Bayly "became not only their commander, but their confidant and adviser," wrote Sims.[90]

Sims attributed much of the success at Queenstown to Miss Voysey, Bayly's unmarried niece. The admiral and "the niece" joined forces, as John Dos Passos put it, to "rescue Uncle Lewis from the results of his own churlishness." In 1934, when Admiral Bayly and his niece were at a banquet in New York, Arthur Hepburn, later vice admiral, called on the attendees "to drink to the health of the *real* Commander-in-Chief at Queenstown, and the whole room rose to their feet and drank Miss Voysey's health with cheers."[91]

Admiralty House was pleasant, but it had a serious working side. Here Bayly was in his element. The American officers learned very quickly that the admiral commanded with an iron hand, believing strongly in discipline and efficiency. He did not interfere with the internal discipline of the destroyer force, concentrating instead on operational effectiveness. Nevertheless, he commanded with a human touch, recognizing that the American officers would make mistakes. When one of the American destroyers ran aground in a fog and had to be hauled off at high tide, Bayly, instead of ordering a court of inquiry, remarked to the luckless C.O.: "you know that is a strange coincidence. It was upon that identical rock that I ran my own first destroyer many years ago. Good morning, I shall expect you to put to sea again in twenty four hours."[92] Afterward, "a staggered and bewildered boy captain descended the hill to his ship again. A world of happiness welled up to and overflowed his eyes and blinded him. He still retained 'Uncle Luragi's' confidence, and, By God, he'd show 'Uncle Luragi' what sort of man it was he was trusting."

Nothing else in American naval history is quite like the relationship that developed between Bayly, a Briton, and the American officers under his command. Their rapport was based on enormous respect and love, a term rarely used in describing an official association between a commander and his men, particularly if the commander is a foreigner. A half century later, Admiral Charles Moore described his feelings about Bayly: "He was a very fine person, and I never knew an American admiral who wasn't criticized and abused and called names by his junior officers at one time or another. . . . But Admiral Bailey [sic] was admired and loved, I think by all the American naval officers over there." Even Halsey declared that "those who had the privilege of serving directly under him loved and respected him to a man."[93] Admiral Carney said in admiration: "I think they'd [the Admiralty] sent him to Siberia—put him down there at Queenstown. Well, actually, he wound up with the best-damned command in the outfit, except the Grand Fleet. And he made the most of it. He did a first class job."[94] One officer wrote to Sims in 1918: "I have a sweet taste in my mouth when I revert to Queenstown days. . . . Anytime [Bayly] . . . wanted to, he could walk over our prostrate bodies, so great did our affection for him become."[95] A note in the Bayly papers mentioned that when a rumor reached Queenstown that he was to be relieved of the command, the Americans prepared a "round-robin," asking the Admiralty not to remove their commander. Many American officers who served in the Queenstown command who transferred to other duty stations or ships during the war wrote letters of appreciation. Arthur "Japy" Hepburn gave perhaps the best tribute a commander can receive when he wrote, "I am proud to have served under your command, and I shall be prouder still, if, at any time hereafter, you shall give me the opportunity to show that my services are still entirely at your command."[96]

The attachment did not abate with the Armistice. In 1919, the British C-in-C of the Black Seas Squadron wrote Bayly: "I see a great many Americans out here, and hear a great deal of their opinions of their C-in-C at Queenstown. In fact when they once began on that subject it is difficult to get them to change it."[97] As late as 1933, a former Queenstown officer who had just been selected admiral gave Bayly most of the credit.[98] Letters from American officers who had served under him continued to arrive throughout his life. After leaving the European command, Sims wrote to Miss Voysey: "I doubt whether the Admiral realizes how far reaching his influence was, for it extended throughout all the American destroyer forces. Queenstown was the school which established the tactics and methods that all used, and the kindly headmaster of this school is very well-known throughout our service."[99]

The American naval officers privileged to serve in the Queenstown command thought themselves a "band of brothers," emulating the prewar destroyer flotilla.[100] After the war, they formed a Queenstown Association. Approximately 400 of the 750 officers who at one time or another served in the command joined it. In 1921, the association held its annual meeting in New York City, and Admiral Bayly (retired) attended it with his niece. Sims presented the keynote speech, and Bayly also gave a brief talk in which he said: "Over and over again—and I am not speaking in any way for effect it is perfectly true—that over and over again I have said to myself and in talking to my niece I have said to her, 'what does this mean?'"[101] In later years, the association contributed much of the funds needed to purchase a home for Bayly and his niece.

Bayly more and more enjoyed "his Americans," as he called them. "The new six destroyers are dining here tonight," he once wrote Sims. "Your boys are shaping splendidly. We had a game of dip and run on the lawn on Sunday after supper. . . . They had never played before and made 6 runs to our 2!"[102] In June 1918, King George V decorated Bayly. When congratulated, he "smilingly replied, 'Thanks, I guess it was intended as a compliment to the American Navy.'" To Jellicoe, he once quipped, "I shall be asking to be made an honorary admiral of the USN if I am not careful."[103]

The force commander wanted Bayly to meet American enlisted personnel as well as the officers. He and his niece went to the Men's Club and enjoyed the entertainment. Sims wrote: "his mere appearance at the Club is bound to have a good influence on the men. It is one thing to be serving under an Admiral that you never see and it is another thing to be serving under an Admiral whom you have seen smoking his pipe time and again."[104]

In his final report to the Admiralty, Bayly wrote of his admiration for the American officers under his command: "It is hard to express in words the singleness of purpose which animated them, the eagerness with which they set themselves to learn all the methods which had been tried, and to improve these methods. . . . In consequence they proved to be a most valuable asset to the Allies, and assisted magnificently to save a very dangerous situation." To one of the destroyer commanders, he wrote, "I can never express my gratitude sufficiently for the very able help you and your brother officers always gave us."[105] Admiral Bayly died in 1938. A British flag officer wrote an appreciation: "No man could have done more—possibly no one could have done so much—to bring the two Navies together and to inspire their officers and men."[106]

The American naval officer that Bayly most admired during and after the war was Joel Roberts Poinsett Pringle, who served him as chief of staff. Born in South Carolina during 1873, he was named after his famous ancestor, Joel Roberts Poinsett. Like many young men in the impoverished South after the Civil War, he quite early decided on a military career. A member of the Annapolis class of 1892, he later succeeded Sims in command of the Atlantic Fleet's Destroyer Flotilla in 1916, with his flag on the tender *Melville*. In June 1917, he took the second destroyer division to Queenstown, transferring his flag to the tender *Dixie*. At the time, he was forty-four years old, having served twenty-three years in the Navy.[107]

Sims, who considered himself in command of the American destroyer force at Queenstown, at first appointed Pringle (the senior officer present) as liaison with Admiral Bayly and his acting chief of staff. When Admiral Mayo visited England in September 1917, his staff noted that Pringle, a captain, directed the flotilla at Queenstown and that a rear admiral should take charge. Sims insisted that, although he was not the working commander of the destroyer force, he was so designated "*on paper*." He cabled Pratt, the assistant CNO, for support and evidently received it. The Queenstown command did not change. In July 1917, Pringle became Bayly's official chief of staff, the first non-British subject to appear on the Royal Navy's list as a member of an admiral's staff. This appointment entailed responsibility for both American and British vessels in the Queenstown command.[108]

Sims and Bayly continued to worry that the Department might appoint a rear admiral to replace Pringle at Queenstown. The force commander was well aware that Rear Admiral E. W. Eberle sought the command. In February 1918, Sims wrote Benson of the "delicate" situation at Queenstown. "The continuance of our good relations without friction of any kind, though it has often been threatened, are [sic] due exclusively to the very remarkable ability in this line of Captain Pringle. . . . He has ingratiated himself with Admiral Bayly to such an extent, and has been such a material help to him, that I sometimes doubt whether the Admiral could continue to hold down the position without such assistance. . . . I am telling you all this to try and make it clear that it would be a very grave mistake to make any change in conditions as they now exist at Queenstown." In March/April 1918, a series of articles appeared in various American publications that highlighted Sims's Anglophilism and claimed that he allowed American sailors to serve under a British admiral. The influential *Army and Navy Register* demanded the appointment of an American admiral to this command. On several occasions, Pratt reassured the force commander that the CNO contemplated no change, but as late as July 1918, Sims again voiced his concerns to the assistant CNO.[109]

Bayly was equally concerned. In December 1917, he wrote Sims: "Pringle is 100 percent. Whatever changes you make don't take him away." The British admiral had been impressed by Pringle even before they met. As the *Dixie* approached the entrance to Queenstown harbor, she entered a minefield laid by a German submarine the previous night. After he received a warning, he realized that it was high tide and continued into the harbor without changing course.[110]

The command arrangement at Queenstown seemed simple on paper. Bayly and his staff controlled operations. As Taussig wrote, "Admiral Bayly was the one we went to for orders as to when we would go to sea and what we were to do there. Our reports of operations were made to Admiral Sims (who considered himself in command of the American destroyers based in Queenstown) through Captain Pringle, his Chief of Staff. Copies of these reports were sent to Admiral Bayly." The American force administered itself. It was self-sufficient, retaining its own organization. "Captain Pringle was the officer we destroyer captains went to for everything pertaining to upkeep, maintenance, personnel, supply, discipline, in fact everything administrative," wrote Taussig, adding, "It all worked out beautifully, and was a most perfect example of efficient co-operation."[111] An officer from the Department who visited the command reported, "I have never imagined it possible to run operations of this magnitude and keep up the material with such an utter absence of formalities."[112]

Pringle was a brilliant naval officer. Rear Admiral Zogbaum observed that "by breeding and natural diplomacy [he was] just the man to deal with our British allies."[113] A genial, sophisticated man with a keen sense of humor who enjoyed stimulating conversation, he was quite the opposite of Bayly. Nonetheless, they got along extremely well.[114] In fact, Bayly grew to admire Pringle above all U.S. naval officers. In *Pull Together*, he wrote: "Pringle would have been an outstanding officer in any navy. [He was] a thorough disciplinarian, with a well-balanced mind and a lightening brain. . . . He was one of the greatest friends I have ever made, my *beau ideal* of what a naval officer should be." When Pringle died, Bayly wrote in the London *Times* that "he was a man of perfect tact and exceptional ability. . . . He was as universally liked as he was implicitly obeyed. He never once failed me during the war . . . his one idea being to do his duty; and no man ever did it better."[115] Two years after Pringle's death, Admiral Bayly presented a brass tablet commemorating Pringle, which was unveiled at a ceremony in Memorial Hall at the U.S. Naval Academy.[116]

Pringle, although a destroyer specialist, was not one of Sims's "band of brothers"; he did not serve with him before the war, but the European force commander quickly recognized Pringle's ability. Sims's fitness report for Pringle stated that he was "one of the most capable officers I have ever had the pleasure to serve with." Sims requested Pringle to serve as his chief of staff at the Naval War College when he assumed the presidency in 1919. Curiously, according to Sims, by then their relationship had changed. In 1918, the force commander wrote a letter to Pringle mentioning an oral report from one of his officers that U.S. naval personnel at Queenstown were drinking alcoholic beverages too heavily, and that it must stop. Pringle was offended; his relationship with Sims afterward remained good but formal.[117]

The connection between Bayly and Sims was never as close as that between the British admiral and Pringle, primarily because Sims rarely made the trip to Queenstown. Yet, they became friends. Bayly frequently invited Sims to Queenstown for the weekend or holiday; "Don't forget that this is your real home [away] from home, your stick is always in the hall," Bayly told Sims in July 1917.[118] Their friendship blossomed when Bayly wrote to the American admiral suggesting that he assume command at Queenstown while he took leave. Sims agreed: in June 1917, he became the first American naval officer to command a part of the Royal Navy.[119] He was delighted with the post because it jibed with his policy of total naval amalgamation. It received considerable attention in the press and helped to popularize the American naval effort.[120] Sims's interlude in Queenstown caused a passing alarm among the Irish, who evidently believed a rumor that Ireland had been handed over to the United States. Sims wrote his wife that the Admiralty's approval of his brief tour at Queenstown was "the most convincing evidence of [the] success in this business of cooperation." On the eve of the American admiral's departure for the United States in 1919, Bayly wrote, "We met as strangers; we worked as allies; we part as friends."[121]

"Pull Together"

The Queenstown command's success exemplified Anglo-American naval relations during the war. A majority of those writing about American naval relations with the Allies stress the extensive Anglo-American cooperation of 1917–18. Sims and his commanders went to the limit to work with the Allied navies, avoiding friction if at all possible. Sims wrote to Pratt: "I believe there is no case on record where Allies have cooperated together for any considerable length of time without more or less serious friction. I am out to make an exception."[1] From the arrival of the first U.S. warships at Queenstown until the Armistice, Sims advocated cooperation. On April 29, welcoming Taussig to Queenstown, he warned him to avoid friction "as long as it is practically possible." Similar warnings were given either orally or in writing to Wilson, Niblack, and other flag officers. Admiral Strauss, commander of the American mine-laying force in Scotland, received several communications from Sims, voicing his displeasure at apparent differences with Admiral Beatty. "I have been distressed from time to time by reports of bits of friction that have occurred . . . in connection with the laying of the mine barrage. . . . I think that in the interest of getting along within the war we should do everything we possibly can to avoid such incidents and to eliminate their causes. . . . I think in all probability that this trouble has been caused largely by misunderstanding as to the actual division of authority. This has been tried before in various ways among the Allies, and, so far as I know, it has never failed to cause friction except in those cases where the authority for operations is centralised and strictly defined. It is for this reason that I have placed our forces always under the senior Allied Commander in so far as concerns their purely military operations. . . . In a word . . . [your] relation to [Beatty] . . . should be exactly the same as though he were an American Admiral and our forces a part of his." To Niblack at Gibraltar, Sims cabled: "I do not consider it desirable to issue any orders that will limit the freedom of the British [admirals in the Mediterranean] . . . in using [U.S. ships] to defeat submarine campaign." The British vice admiral in command at Devonport complained to the Admiralty that the American officer in command of the American subchasers based at Plymouth issued orders without consulting him. "It is requested that I may be informed to what extent I am responsible for the employment of . . . U.S. Craft . . . in the Plymouth Command."[2] Surely the Admiralty consulted Sims, who must have responded that the American commander was under the operational orders of the British C-in-C at Devonport.

On at least one occasion, however, the force commander intervened in an order of a British C-in-C regarding the American naval operation. This involved the laying of the mine barrage in the North Sea. When informed that Admiral Beatty gave orders "contrary to those issued by the Force Commander or at least [he] . . . objected to the U.S. Mine Force laying mines in the locality ordered by you," Sims complained to the Admiralty, which countermanded Beatty's orders. Beatty opposed the mine barrage, but the U.S. Navy Department strongly favored it, and Sims was obligated to stress this view to the Admiralty.[3]

To Sims, cooperation/collaboration was really "consolidation" or "amalgamation." As he wrote in July 1917, "The paramount purpose of American naval activities was to "achieve maximum cooperation with the Allies." "Our attitudes and efforts," he wrote, "must be on the assumption that Allied and U.S. Services are one and the same service." Although not as inflexible as some writers claim, he tirelessly demanded "teamwork." Sims told a reporter that "The word cooperation ought to be struck out from the war dictionary and the word 'consolidation' written in its place. . . . This business of insisting on the preservation of its individual identity by one force or another is all wrong." To another he exclaimed, "Our destroyers! your destroyers!—I am tired of hearing of it. We have one fleet and it ought to be used as one." Admiral Mayo, after his second trip to the war zone, noted approvingly, "Co-operation has in many cases been carried to such an extent that the co-ordination necessary for efficiency has developed into practical consolidation."[4]

After the war, a document entitled "Summary of Activities of U.S. Naval Forces in European Waters" included the statement: "It is considered that the Principal accomplishment to be credited to the U.S. Navy in European waters is the degree and character of co-operation which it succeeded in carrying out in its joint operation with the French and British Naval Services." The French were most impressed with this. *Le Matin* reported, "Almost as soon as they entered the war the American navy without reserve placed themselves under the English admirals. They left aside their national independence to become simple units of the British fleet. The National sacrifice beneficial to the entire world was done to the great honor of the American nation and it forced those among us who in Europe have the habit of considering the Yankee as being aggressive, [and] vain to change our opinion."[5]

During the naval hearings, Sims had a sharp exchange with Senator Key Pittman. When the admiral mentioned teamwork with the French, Italians, and English, the senator remarked, "There is quite a difference between cooperating and being submerged." Sims snapped back: "They were not submerged. They were separate entities. . . . It is perfectly absurd to say that we subordinated ourselves to others."[6]

Yet, Pittman was not entirely wrong. Sims submitted a document that stated, "Admiral Sims believed from the beginning that the only effective way to throw the weight of the United States Navy into the war . . . was to use its available units to strengthen the weak spots in the other navies, and thus effect more vigorous conduct of the war." One of Sims's staff wrote years later, "All orders and plans for operations . . . came in fact from the Admiralty."[7] Captain Twining testified in a court of inquiry held shortly after the war that "Admiral Sims never exercised any direct command from London of any of his forces. He never, except when necessity arose, and it became apparent—he never issued anything more than a general instruction."[8]

General Pershing adopted an opposite policy. As Trask has written, he fought stubbornly for an independent army. In April 1918, when the American general reluctantly allowed units of the AEF to reinforce Allied armies decimated by a massive German offensive, Sims wrote his wife: "They [AEF] are now operating with the Allies, which is what the Navy did from the day our first vessels arrived. It has always seemed to me so natural and logical that we should do so." Secretary Daniels, who took every opportunity to censure Sims in his published memoirs, wrote that Sims, Herbert Hoover, and Ambassador Walter Hines Page all favored using American troops as replacements for British and French units, which "would have been fatal. Too often they sneezed when the British took Snuff."[9]

Sims's policy of cooperation/amalgamation complicated his relations with the Department. When he was invited to become an honorary member of the British Admiralty, President Wilson disapproved with an emphatic "no."[10] Benson had originally recommended approval, but later, when he learned that the king favored the proposal, he disapproved it.[11] The CNO approved (so he said) the attendance of Sims at daily meetings of the Admiralty. The American force commander made a good impression, not only because of his comments and "original views" but also because of "his humorous manner of expressing them."[12] Sims let his disappointment be known on more than one occasion.[13]

The British government was delighted with Sims's policy. Admiral De Chair wrote that "it is considered that the sea forces of the Allies should ultimately be mainly directed by the British Admiralty . . . and as the Navy . . . capable of greatest expansion of our Allies is that of the United States, it is of the greatest importance that the development of their sea forces should proceed along lines dictated by British war experience."[14] Undoubtedly in his initial meetings with Jellicoe and other Admiralty officials, the idea of unity surfaced immediately. The American admiral understood its necessity: "We were greatly outnumbered in ships, men, material and everything else in the game." He recognized the invaluable experience the British navy had gained in three years of war.

On April 18, a few days after Sims arrived in England, he cabled Secretary Daniels: "It would seem most advantageous that we should adopt existing British methods and base further developments only upon actual experience in co-operation with them." In May, he urged the deployment of as many antisubmarine vessels in British waters as possible: "The undesirability, from our own point of view, in breaking up the organization of our fleet is fully realised. It seems absolutely necessary, however, not to view our forces as an entity in themselves, but rather as an integral part of the combined Allied naval forces." In May 1918, a member of Simsadus explained: "if the U.S. squadrons were to be a source of real strength to the British squadrons with which they were to operate, they must become an integral part of those squadrons and adopt all the same essential methods of operating. . . . Consequently, the U.S. [forces] . . . in British waters had abandoned their own signals, . . . their own methods of fire control and concentration of fire, and had adopted the British methods."[15]

British naval officers were impressed with the single-mindedness of the U.S. Navy's support of integration. They had experienced so much difficulty with the French and Italians. Admiral Bayly said it was neither "Blood and Water" nor "cousins" but a "common cause" that persuaded the Americans to sacrifice their national identity and traditions so completely.

After the war, Jellicoe wrote, "I feel it is right to put on record the great admiration which we in the British Navy felt for the spirit of self-effacement displayed by senior American naval officers in placing themselves so unreservedly under the command of British naval officers, in order to ensure unity of control in British waters." His successor as first sea lord, Wemyss, was just as laudatory, writing to Sims about "the magnificent way in which the officers and men of your service have entered into a partnership with ours."[16] Not surprisingly, officials in Washington initially did not share the British enthusiasm for this "consolidation/cooperation." As Mary Klachko wrote, Sims's policy was "certain to create friction at home."[17] Nevertheless, American naval officers based in the United Kingdom were pleased with British reciprocity. Admiral Connolly later mentioned that the reason you never heard anything about it was "that everybody took it for granted."[18]

Naval cooperation with the Allies during the war and afterward was so emphasized that the "significant differences" have often been overlooked.[19] These conflicts concerned fundamental issues of policy, strategy, and assistance in the form of ships, men, material, and, of course, operations. Coalition warfare encounters pitfalls such as differences in national interests and aspirations, political and military personnel and organizations, and national strengths and weaknesses. Even disparities in social structure, culture, class, and etiquette created problems and misunderstandings.[20]

Although special telephone and cable lines linked Simsadus and the Admiralty, communications were far from efficient. In October 1917, Sims's aide assessed cooperation between the two naval headquarters. He emphasized that the "will" to cooperate was present, "but not the way. The fault lies with the machinery of carrying out the willingness. . . . [A]ll officers of the Admiralty are located in separate offices. They are, naturally, always busy. . . . [O]ur contact with the Admiralty resolves itself into visits to this or that office on specific details or only when there is some reason for seeing an individual of the Admiralty." He noted that the Admiralty was negligent in providing Simsadus with documents including confidential information. The British believed that the "U.S. Department is not entirely safe."[21] After Wemyss became first sea lord and the Planning Section began to function, communications improved significantly.

Undoubtedly, Sims's unswerving dedication to cooperation and harmony was in part a reaction to rampant disharmony among the Allies. Ambassador Page observed, "[N]othing could keep these nations together a week but dire necessity." Sims confided to Pratt, "The differences and jealousies between some of the Allies are almost unbelievable." He added, "We want to avoid everything of this kind."[22] He was much more successful than Pershing in this matter. The Allied Naval Council provided him a forum to demonstrate his country's willingness to cooperate. He had far more difficulty in persuading Washington to accept "unswerving cooperation" than with his own people.

Major problems during the summer and fall of 1917 rendered Sims's cooperation/

consolidation policy suspect in Washington. The president, Daniels, and probably Benson were convinced that the British "had pulled the wool" over his eyes.[23] They ignored Sims's denials. They also decided that British naval officials provided information to Sims that did not reach Washington. Early in July, Pratt wrote: "I feel that we do not get enough of the point of view over there. . . . [T]he facts, the cold facts are what we need. . . . [Benson] . . . wants to know not in any critical spirit, but in the spirit of utmost cooperation, what the Admiralty's strategical and tactical conceptions are. Just what is the major plan? . . . What are the tactical details in general by which this plan is to be solved. Those are the things we have a right to know. . . . We could work so much more intelligently toward the same united ends, if we knew a little more."[24] Sims replied to this concern with dispatches to the president, Daniels, and Pratt, but they did little good.

Concern over inadequate information and Sims's supposed subservience to the Admiralty influenced the decision to send a naval mission headed by Admiral Mayo to Europe. Sims approved the dispatch of naval officers to the war zone. He believed that Washington would acquire an improved picture of the situation and therefore accept his recommendations.[25] He also suggested that U.S. military officials participate in inter-Allied conferences, but the president vetoed this activity. Sims and Pershing were not supposed to attend a conclave in July, but Sims attended a naval conference as an unofficial observer.

But it was Vice Admiral Browning, C-in-C of the British North American and West Indian Station, who persuaded Wilson and his naval advisers to send a naval mission to Europe. He believed that the best way to clear up various misunderstandings and to establish close cooperation was for the Admiralty to invite senior officers to a conference in London.[26] Benson agreed: he selected Mayo and his staff to undertake the mission. Sims was delighted.

Before Mayo went to England, Daniels and Benson briefed him, and President Wilson also contributed to the Atlantic Fleet commander's instructions. Mayo was told to push for a more aggressive policy, especially offensive operations against the German submarine bases. He was also to negotiate with the British from the position of a "senior partner." Undoubtedly, he was also advised of the desire that the Admiralty communicate directly to Washington and not necessarily through Simsadus about naval requirements. Reaching England late in August, Mayo spent more than a week in discussions with Admiralty officials. He told the first lord that his trip was essentially to "ascertain in what possible way the Americans can more fully come into naval warfare," or so Lord Geddes understood its purpose.[27]

Although Jellicoe presented an agenda, much of the discussion centered on Mayo's concerns. In the conferences, two offensive measures were discussed, one introduced by the British and the other by the Americans. The first was a proposal to sink more than eighty vessels to block the exits that the German submarines used to depart from their bases. This was unacceptable to Washington officials; they did not think that it would work. The second was to lay a mine barrage across the North Sea. Although the British and Sims were skeptical, it was accepted when the United States agreed to provide the mines.[28] Other items were discussed, including convoying and new technologies in antisubmarine warfare. The British, supported by Sims, argued that convoying was the most effective method of dealing with the submarine. Geddes successfully recommended the expansion of the convoy system to the Mediterranean Sea. Mayo and his staff believed that the approval of the mine barrage was the most important decision reached in London. Mayo was disappointed with the conference, mainly because he felt that the participants talked in generalities rather than specifics. Both Jellicoe and Sims were pleased with Mayo's visit, the force commander because he believed that it would end the impression in Washington that he was simply a tool of the British, and the first lord because he expected that it would result in better cooperation and additional American naval assistance.

Mayo's trip did not end Washington's suspicions of both Sims and the British.[29] Few concrete agreements came out of the conference. One of the British representatives later wrote that the delegates should have discussed general naval strategy and the "fundamental question concerning the disposition of the Allied naval forces over the different theatres of war." Jellicoe's defense was that the agenda was based on Mayo's requests.[30] Nonetheless, Trask concludes that it was a considerable success, an important step toward improved naval coordination and a step toward the formation of the Allied Naval Council. Equally important, Washington obtained a firsthand account of the naval war, its prospects and future needs. Sims thought that Mayo's visit was most satisfactory. Mayo agreed that the defeat of the U-boats was "by far the most serious measure to ultimate victory" and strongly recommended the deployment of ASW vessels as soon as they became available.[31]

Mayo had not departed the war zone before the British became aware that his trip had not alleviated the Navy Department's suspicion that the Admiralty still did not consider it a "full partner." In an interview with Benson, the British naval attaché in Washington was told in some "bitterness" that Sims funneled selective information to the Department. The CNO mentioned two examples of information that the Admiralty had not communicated to him that came to him from other sources. One resulted from misinterpretation of a message from Sims, and the other was apparently a false rumor. President Wilson passed on to his naval advisors information received from two journalists. One, A.J.H. Pollen, was British, and the other was the American novelist Winston Churchill. After the war, Pollen denied that he had "engineered the naval misunderstanding," but he was certainly critical of his country's naval policies, and he was also aware of the information passed on to the newspapers concerning the "friction."[32] Churchill criticized the Admiralty for lacking an aggressive naval policy. He recommended what would later be designated the "Naval Planning Section" to achieve what he called "full partnership."[33]

Benson was not altogether pleased with the results of the Mayo's trip. He later regretted his intemperate comments made about it to Captain Gaunt, the British naval attaché, but the damage was done. After Gaunt expressed his concerns about the CNO's displeasure, he was ordered to London for consultations. The foreign secretary, the first lord, and the first sea lord held a long conference with Ambassador Page, who accepted their strong assertions that they had held nothing back from the American Navy. They recommended that Daniels and Benson journey to London and meet with

Admiralty officials. First Lord Sir Eric Geddes wrote Daniels, "We must endeavor to bridge over three thousand miles of ocean by close communication between yourself and myself, Admiral Jellicoe and Admiral Benson." Page endorsed a visit: "Our only job now—and everybody's job—is to win the war. Misunderstandings are crimes."[34]

To make matters worse, the problem leaked to the newspapers—"exaggerated" reports, according to Daniels. Officials in Washington assured the British government that the newspaper accounts had no foundation. Benson wrote a letter to Lord Jellicoe expressing full confidence in Great Britain and the Admiralty. Daniels emphasized in a communication to Secretary of State Robert Lansing that "No thought was entertained at any time that we were not receiving the fullest information from the Admiralty, or that they were failing in any way to cooperate." Daniels also held a press conference and reiterated this view.[35]

Two important developments stemmed from this episode. President Wilson agreed to send Benson to England, and messages from the Admiralty were forwarded simultaneously to Simsadus and the Navy Department. Communications to the Navy Department were channeled through the British naval attaché in Washington. Sims, who had recognized the difficulty, recommended this change to the Admiralty. The first lord also decided to assign personnel to ensure that reports and other documents were sent to Sims and Washington.[36] No further complaints about inadequate information emanated from Washington.

Admiral Benson's visit to Europe in November 1917 did a great deal toward improved cooperation. In September, amid the enthusiasm generated by Mayo's visit, the British suggested a general conference of the Allied and Associated powers to strengthen naval cooperation. Geddes repeated the invitation early in October.[37] The president was still reluctant to participate in "entangling conferences," but he finally agreed to send a fact-finding mission to Europe under his favored adviser, Colonel Edward M. House. The American delegation included Admiral Benson.

Arriving in London early in November, the House Mission remained in the war zone for nearly a month. Admiral Benson came away satisfied with the naval discussions. The CNO felt that he had got what he wanted, the creation of a naval planning section and agreement to conduct offensive naval operations with American participation. These decisions reflected close cooperation, but as Dean Allard has pointed out, Benson (and House) viewed them as an understanding that United States would become the "senior partner" in wartime naval affairs at some point.[38] British naval officials had advocated the placement of American naval officers in various administrative divisions within the Admiralty, but Benson insisted that his officers should become part of an American entity that would work closely with the British. The CNO undoubtedly expected that an American planning section would persuade the British to adopt more aggressive operations. Benson's optimism was misplaced. The United States did not replace Great Britain as the senior partner in the naval war, the Admiralty ignored most of the recommendations from the Planning Section, and with the exception of the North Sea Mine Barrage, the Americans did not succeed in stimulating major offensive operations.

Sims, British naval officials, and Benson were satisfied with the outcome of the discussions in Europe. The CNO went home with an agreement to deploy a division of battleships in European waters; to form an Allied Naval Council with Sims as the American representative; to dispatch additional ASW vessels; to create a planning section in London; to establish the North Sea Mine Barrage; and to base an American naval force in the Azores. The CNO also promised Sims additional personnel for Simsadus. Benson was determined to persuade the British to attack the German submarine bases, an operation that had President Wilson's strong support. According to the CNO's biographers, the British agreed to such a plan. The U.S. was to provide the necessary warships. It is possible that the British agreed to it to placate Benson. The CNO pressed the idea upon Admiral Beatty during a visit to the Grand Fleet, but the C-in-C claimed that such an attack could not occur until he acquired sufficient air power to guard his ships.[39]

The commission's departure for the United States left Sims convinced that Benson had finally accepted his recommendations, particularly the need for antisubmarine craft. More important, he believed that Benson would no longer consider him simply a British "tool." Sims was generally correct. Although differences between the force commander and the department surfaced on occasion, Sims's recommendations were taken at face value rather than as the desires of the Admiralty. Jellicoe wrote to Beatty that he considered the Allied Naval Conference "a waste of time," but he decided that Benson would do all he could "to help the general cause."[40]

Discord between the two services developed from time to time. The North Sea Mine Barrage generated controversy to the end of the operation. Disagreements surfaced over establishment of a naval base in Norway and the response to Italy, should it negotiate a separate peace with the Central powers.[41] As mentioned earlier, the Admiralty in good faith asked Washington to allow Sims to serve as an honorary member of the Board of the Admiralty. He attended daily conferences of the naval staff at the Admiralty, but Sir Eric Geddes preferred to give him a formal position on the Board, perhaps to prevent ruffled feelings. Benson was also to be appointed an "Honorary Lord of the Admiralty." Benson and apparently Daniels opposed it. The president disapproved with an emphatic "no," although Sims and the Admiralty did not learn of this decision for nearly two months.[42] The British media expressed indignation when Washington refused to allow officers and men to accept foreign declarations.[43]

Command controversies at times came to the attention of the Admiralty and Sims. Sims responded to some minor tensions. Welsh port officials treated naval colliers transporting coal from Cardiff to France as merchant ships. Liverpool officials, according to the American consul, prevented American military personnel leaving their ships without clearance from custom officials, a limitation that even applied to troops entraining to ports on the English Channel en route to France. An Admiralty investigation led to correction of this policy.[44]

Mutual distrust between the two countries appeared on occasion. British officials at first tolerated American exaggerations of their contributions to the war effort, but this restraint began to loosen during the summer of 1918. The Admiralty was dismayed in July, when the American government decided to continue the 1916 naval building program, which emphasized battleships. The first lord told FDR, then visiting in Europe, that the Allies already had an overwhelming superiority in capital ships. They needed antisubmarine craft. According to Geddes, the Royal Navy had shifted many destroyers to escort American troop transports, a decision that led to a decline in the destruction of U-boats. At his instruction, statistics were compiled that clarified the amount of British naval contributions in the war zone in comparison with the United States. Geddes traveled to Washington to press for enhanced naval contributions. A speech he gave angered Woodrow Wilson, who told Daniels, "I don't like it even a little bit." Colonel House had to intercede with Mrs. Wilson to get the president to see the first lord before he left the country.[45]

Other differences began to surface. The growing ascendancy of the American merchant marine and U.S. commercial activities overseas threatened leadership in this realm, especially in Latin America. Shortly before the war ended, the two countries disagreed over the disposition of German warships after the Armistice.[46] These differences set the stage for a breakdown of cooperation in the postwar world. Captain Edward McCauley, Roosevelt's naval aide during the European trip in 1918, wrote years later: "Everyone we met . . . seemed to appreciate the part the United States was taking in the war. . . . They whole-heartedly praised the work. . . . This attitude of friendliness and gratitude was so marked that, when I was again in London some years after the war, I was surprised to find the change in feeling. The British in general seemed to have forgotten how they had formerly felt about us."[47]

David Trask wrote that "coalitions rarely fight for exactly the same purposes," a circumstance that usually provokes disagreements, but the Anglo-American association was generally a refreshing departure.[48] As Arthur J. Marder wrote, "the general harmony of the Anglo-American naval effort . . . is a rare exception in the annals of wartime relations between Allies.[49] Although Sims's prediction that the "relations with this service [Royal Navy] . . . will have its influence for a hundred years to come" was overly optimistic, naval cooperation during World War I smoothed the way for excellent relations during World War II.[50]

U.S. naval forces in France also stressed cooperation but with varied success. Sims greatly admired the French naval chief of staff, Vice Admiral Ferdinand-Jean-Jacques-De Bon, but in contrast to his intimate relations with British Admiralty officials, Sims rarely dealt directly with him. The French needed American naval aid as much if not more than the British, but they did not give priority to naval affairs except those in the Mediterranean Sea, where French concerns were politicized to counteract Italian territorial ambitions. Georges Clemenceau once remarked that if the British destroyed the German navy it "would make a nice hole in the water" but would not win the war.[51] French naval forces along the Atlantic coast were extremely weak, consisting of a few small antisubmarine craft. The United States' entry into the war provided them with an opportunity to obtain additional antisubmarine vessels and the posting of American warships in their Atlantic ports. The U.S. government gave the French a few wooden subchasers, and a few warships were based in French ports.[52]

The Navy Department had little knowledge of the French navy when it began to deploy converted yachts and other armed craft to French waters. The French possessed only a few vessels that could cooperate with the Americans, and, more important, they were unable to provide adequate logistical support. When Admiral Benson returned from the war zone, he told Daniels that the "French on the Coast could do nothing. They lacked money and everything & Whatever is done there we must do." Rear Admiral Albert Gleaves, in command of the first convoy that transported American troops to France, noted that it was in "a rundown condition. . . . [T]hey have only one destroyer at Dunkirk, and in a recent destroyer action these boats, built for thirty-five knots, could only make eighteen."[53] Other difficulties stemmed from differing customs regulations, bureaucracy, language, and culture. Admiral Parker recalled that "we never integrated with the French Navy to the same extent that we had with the British." Taussig, who served both at Queenstown and Brest, concluded that "there is not the same co-operation here as . . . at Queenstown." He blamed the difference on what he called a dual command structure and "divided authority." Commander Whiting told the General Board that the system did not work because "The French are not a seagoing nation."[54] Captain Craven, in charge of naval aviation, blamed many of his difficulties while establishing naval air stations on "the necessity of co-operating with the French and of conforming to their views."[55] "The French and we have not the same idea of speed. They are perpetually in low gear," wrote Captain Byron Long. Shipping in the ports used by the Americans became a major headache, particularly in the Gironde. Problems with police and sanitation inspectors and the local pilots' association often delayed unloading of ships.[56] Sims persevered, informing Rear Admiral Marie-John-Lucien Lacaze, the French minister of marine, "that I wished him to consider the Forces under my command in France in all respects the same as tho they actually belonged to the French Navy."[57] However determined he was to carry out naval amalgamation in France, it proved unworkable.

Rear Admiral Fletcher's removal demonstrated the fragility of Sims's command policy. A few days after Fletcher was ordered back to the United States, his temporary successor was called into the office of Rear Admiral Zephinn-Alexandre-Antoine Schwerer, commandant of the French naval forces in the area of American naval operations. "Admiral Schwerer became quite excited," Captain T. P. Magruder reported, "and he spoke so rapidly that I could not gather all he said. The gist of it was, however, to the effect that *he*, not the American Commander, was responsible for operations on the West Coast of France. . . . [I]n case anything went wrong, he alone would be responsible."[58] Fortunately Rear Admiral Wilson arrived shortly after this interview and established excellent relations with both Admiral Schwerer and his superior, Vice Admiral Frederic-Paul Moreau, Maritime Prefecture of Brest.[59] The French Atlantic coast was divided into four political and military divisions. Admiral Moreau was not only prefect of the arrondissement that included Brest, but he was also in overall command of naval activities in other arrondissements in the area.[60] Schwerer commanded all forces afloat, including American forces.

Admiral Wilson stressed in interviews with newspaper correspondents and in his postwar book that he came under French command. "This is a French City; Admiral Moreau is the French admiral here; besides, his rank is higher than mine: I would not think of issuing an important order without first consulting him," he told an American correspondent. He reiterated this posture to a French writer: "The American

Navy operates in French waters and never have we had the idea to give an order which would not be approved by the French admiral." He also noted, according to a British account, that there had been no "question . . . raised as to the Chief Command of the two navies." In his book *The American Navy in France*, he wrote, "[L]ogically, all American forces on the west coast of France were under the command of the Senior French Naval Officer."[61] Nonetheless, he knew that in reality he controlled American naval forces, including their operations. Wilson informed the Naval Investigation Committee in 1920: "I always furnished the senior allied commander, Vice Admiral Moreau, a copy of the orders, as a matter of courtesy," adding, "any time at all he could have stepped in and stopped or changed my plans; but it was never done."[62] Captain Richard Jackson testified in the Fletcher court of inquiry that the French "were . . . quite willing for us to carry on our own work much in our own fashion, but we still had to preserve the appearance of working under their orders, and, therefore, a good deal of diplomacy and tact was required in the station at Brest."[63]

The French understood the reality of the command structure. Even when Daniels noted in his *Annual Report* for 1918 that "whereas practically all cooperation with the British is effected by operating as units under British control, cooperation with the French is arranged on a basis that leaves to the United States naval forces a very large measure of initiative," the French—usually sensitive to such pronouncements—did not take offense.[64] In September 1918, Admiral Schwerer pointed out to Moreau that the disparity between the French and American naval forces would rapidly force the French navy to lose control of all their operations. He emphasized that it was not a personality problem, that he got along very well with Admiral Wilson. The American admiral "has always shown proof of tact, often declaring that he considers himself under your [Moreau's] orders and under mine as well." Nevertheless, "the number of our vessels, but also all of our resources in material and personnel in our patrol service are much less than American resources. The slowness of repair work and slowness of administration is every evident compared to the activity and efficient methods of the Americans. . . . [B]y the force of these things they will end up supplanting us little by little in the direction of all these services. I might add that we would not have the right to take exception, since what is most important above all is to 'win the war.'" He concluded these dreary observations by noting "that the Department cannot by tomorrow greatly reinforce our squadrons; but we are placed in a situation that is a little humiliating, much less for our inferiority in vessels, than in material, personnel, and in methods of work. . . . [I]f Admiral Wilson is replaced his successor must one day or another demand control."[65]

The French minister did little or nothing; France's manpower shortage and other deficiencies rendered him powerless. He created a bureau to manage Franco-American naval relations, but the war ended before it could effect improvements. If anything, the American Navy increased its control over operations.[66]

The United States also entered into naval cooperation with Italy generally on an operational level. American naval air stations were established in Italy, and U.S. warships operated with units of the Italian fleet from Gibraltar and Corfu. Sims's attempts to coordinate with the Italians went primarily through the Allied Naval Council. His relations with Vice Admiral Thaon di Revel, the Italian representative on the council, were at times stormy. The council was organized because of problems in the Mediterranean and with Italy.

The British took the lead in advocating the creation of the Allied Naval Council. Lloyd George and his naval advisors wanted a naval body to parallel the Supreme War Council. They believed that such a group would allow them to dominate naval affairs.[67] The Allied Naval Council came into existence during Benson's visit to Europe in November 1917. The proposal for a council required the support of the United States. According to Sims, he attended a dinner at Sir Eric Geddes's house with Jellicoe and Benson at which the group decided unanimously to bring the proposal for a naval council before a conference of Allied naval leaders in Paris.[68] The conference convened a week later and agreed to the creation of the naval council "to ensure the closest touch and complete co-operation between the Allied Fleets." The ministers of marines and the naval chiefs of staffs of Britain, France, and Italy became members of the council. Sims was chosen to represent the United States, and Japan named a representative.[69] The Allied Naval Council was an advisory body, but Sims was convinced that the member nations would accept its decisions. He was convinced that naval decisions would "necessarily" be shifted to "this side," away from Washington. This change would enhance his influence in deciding the course of the naval war.[70]

The council held monthly sessions in London, Paris, and Rome. Sims always attended with members of his staff, including members of his Planning Section. The council discussed a whole range of issues, from ASW measures to intervention in Russia. Much of its debate concerned problems in the Mediterranean, including the intransigence of the Italians concerning offensive operations and their demands for naval vessels. Allocation of forces was always high on the agenda. The United States was the only nation that possessed uncommitted naval forces available for distribution. Great Britain and France could shift warships from one part of the war zone to another only if American vessels replaced them. "As Admiral Wemyss said to me the other day," Sims wrote to Pringle, "we [Great Britain and the United States] are the milk cows and the others are the calves. We are the only ones that have anything to give."[71] Sims generally followed the council's recommendations when assigning U.S. vessels.[72]

Although the council accomplished little, as Trask writes, it maintained a balance and a broad perspective on naval issues. Considering the divisions prevalent among the Allies and the lack of experience in coalition warfare, the council made a useful if limited contribution. Certainly Sims thought so, noting its efforts to end the submarine crisis. Even though convoying was adopted prior to the council's formation, it contributed to its implementation.[73]

The Navy's primary responsibility was to protect "the Army's lines of communication" and to support and cooperate with the AEF. Sims once told an Army chaplain that the naval force in European waters "are really a part of the American Army; that they are a part of the essential line of communication."[74] Support and cooperation took various forms. The Navy provided escorts for convoys and supported antisubmarine warfare. It also sent heavy guns, aviation units, and Marines to the Western

Front. The magnitude of American military commitment in the war zone taxed the services. These responsibilities collided and occasionally overlapped, a cause of friction, particularly in connection with shipping. Both the Navy and Army were involved in the transportation of troops and supplies, although the Navy manned the troop transports. Shortly after General Pershing arrived in France, he negotiated the permission of the French government to allow the use of certain designated ports. Initially St. Nazaire, Brest, and ports in the Gironde came under the AEF's jurisdiction. Pershing asked Premier Clemenceau to grant him total control of St. Nazaire, but the "Tiger" declined to do so. When the CNO ordered the reorganization of the U.S. naval command in France, he decreed the establishment of naval port officers. This development strained Army/Navy coordination in the French ports. The arrangement confused French officials, who did not know which American officers they were to work with. At times, conflicting instructions were sent to vessels entering particular ports. Admiral Wilson recommended that the Navy assume complete control of these ports, but when General Pershing objected the matter was dropped.[75] An agreement was worked out whereby the Army would control activities on land (unloading of cargoes and debarkation of personnel), and the Navy would control ships before and after docking, a system that generally worked well.[76] Considerable confusion arose in the ports when they did not receive adequate information about ship arrivals and their intended ports.

Transports loaded with troops and stores arrived unexpectedly in a particular port and could not be off-loaded because arrivals congested docks and other port facilities. Turnaround time increased drastically, some vessels requiring six weeks to unload. The Army blamed delays on four factors: shortage of stevedores, obsolescence of the ports, French control of port ship movements, and the refusal of the Navy to distribute ship arrivals to desired ports.[77] Simsadus explained that it did not have enough escort craft to protect ships steaming to some French ports. Escort improved after the transfer of destroyers from Brest to other ports during the summer of 1918. Congestion also eased when the Navy Department agreed to cable information about dates of arrival and the contents of cargoes to Simsadus, which then routed it to the appropriate Army port command.[78]

Disagreements arose over which ports to use because of increasing congestion as more and more ships brought troops and stores to France. Pershing wanted to designate additional ports for troop transports, but Sims balked because of escort limitations.[79] The problem was alleviated somewhat when the French agreed to allow large transports such as *Leviathan* to dock at Brest. In April, however, Pershing informed the force commander that the AEF was considering the use of Marseilles. Although Sims objected because of the serious submarine danger in the Mediterranean, the War Department persuaded naval officials in Washington to allow the use of the port for storeships. Sims did not approve of the French decision to allow the Army the use Le Havre for debarkation of troops. He insisted that the use of channel ports would enhance the danger of U-boat attacks.[80] Congestion decreased, but as the number of ships from the United States steadily increased, it remained troublesome until the end of the war.

Aviation caused the most significant discord between the Army and Navy. Both Pershing and General William "Billy" Mitchell, the first commander of Army aviation in France, opposed a separate naval air service.[81] Disputes developed over aircraft procurement and operations. Until the spring of 1918, however, there was very little disagreement. To coordinate aviation material and support, the Navy assigned an officer to provide liaison with the AEF air service and submitted requests for aircraft and parts to two agencies, one French and the other the American Army.[82]

Controversy stemmed from the organization of the Navy's Northern Bombing Group, whose mission was to bomb the German submarine bases at Ostend and Zeebrugge on the Belgian coast. The Army strongly objected, particularly Brigadier General Benjamin Foulois, Pershing's aviation chief at the time. The Army argued that the Navy's responsibility lay at sea, but the submarine pens were land targets. The Navy planned to use land bombers, available only through Army channels. When the issue was referred to Washington, the War Department learned that the Navy Department strongly favored the mission. It was offensive in nature, which the CNO strongly endorsed, and it targeted the bases of great interest to President Wilson. The War Department instructed Pershing to resolve the problem. He reluctantly agreed to the Navy's request and ordered the transfer of the necessary aircraft. Foulois strongly objected, an act that probably helped bring about his relief shortly afterward. The Army could not provide all the required aircraft, and many proved defective. The Navy ordered Caproni bombers from Italy, but difficulties with Army officials there, especially Captain Fiorello LaGuardia, delayed their delivery. The Navy never used the Caproni bombers. Late in August, the Northern Bombing Group began operations with other aircraft.[83]

Pershing protested mildly to Sims. The force commander denied responsibility. He mentioned an earlier offer to detail a liaison officer to the Army's aviation section "with a view of eliminating duplication of requests . . . and to which to date remains unacknowledged."[84] Sims, of course, strongly advocated cooperation at all levels, including the AEF. FDR reported after his visit to the war zone that were it not for the Navy, little interservice cooperation would exist, an exaggeration with a grain of truth. After the controversy over aviation, Sims detailed an officer to Pershing's staff. He informed President Wilson that he had "appointed a naval officer from my force as a member of General Pershing's Staff so as to keep us intimately in touch with each other. By this and other means we have been able to establish the best possible relations." He added, "While it might naturally be supposed that this [cooperation] was a foregone conclusion, I can assure you that the experience is pretty unique in combined warfare. It is really astonishing how much antagonism, not to say bitterness, has arisen from time to time between the naval and military forces of the same countries during this distressing war."[85]

Other Army-Navy relations did not cause friction. Pershing was particularly pleased with the railway naval guns sent to the Western Front. The five 14-inch naval guns were the most unique contribution that the American Navy made to the victory. Rear Admiral Ralph Earle, chief of the Bureau of Ordnance, was the architect of the idea.[86] These guns were to have been mounted on the battle cruisers approved by

Congress in 1916, but Daniels postponed construction of capital ships in favor of anti-submarine craft. In only six months, the Navy completed plans and specifications for a railway battery. The Baldwin Locomotive Works manufactured powerful locomotives and specially designed railroad cars, which were delivered to the Navy by May 1918. The guns, mounts, and trains were then shipped to St. Nazaire. In July, the first battery was ready, and Rear Admiral Charles P. Plunkett arrived to assume command of the batteries.

Plunkett was a Virginian whose father, an English immigrant, fought for the Union in the Civil War. He graduated from the Naval Academy in 1884. Ernest King admired Plunkett, "a man of dash and exuberance," as did the officers and men who served under him. He was called "Cy" or "Piedmont Cy." One of "Plunkett's Pirates," the sailors who manned the batteries, believed that the nickname came either from the Piedmont country in Virginia or because the admiral smoked Piedmont cigarettes, a popular brand during World War I. "I do know that he would smoke any cigarette you had including Bull Durham or Dukes Mixture and that he could roll a cigarette in a sixty mile gale and never lose a grain of tobacco." He added that Plunkett was "capable of mule-skinner's language . . . with eyes that could pierce through armor plate and a white mustache that reminded me of the old prospectors I knew in the rugged country of Colorado's mountains." The army officer who provided liaison between Plunkett and the Army later wrote that, when he first met the admiral: "He wore a pair of black—I said black—shoes beneath some badly rolled puttees. He didn't have on a blouse, but wore an enlisted man's rubber slicker open down the front, and badly rust-stained around the buckles. His battered campaign hat had no cord of any sort. He was strictly the least military object we'd seen in a couple of years—if ever."[87] Plunkett looked older than his fifty-four years in 1918. A tall man, he quite intimidated many French officers and officials, which is exactly what he wanted. He once offered FDR a commission and service with the Batteries if he could "swear well enough in French to steer a French train on the siding and let our big guns through."[88] A young army officer stationed with a nearby Army artillery unit was impressed with Plunkett's "common-folksy," attitude. He recalled the amazement registered on another officer who encountered the American admiral sitting eating a meal while in his undershirt.[89] Roosevelt was equally amazed when Plunkett greeted him dressed in a major general's uniform with a Sam Browne belt. The assistant secretary is supposed to have said with a grin, "You've forgotten your spurs."[90] His personnel wore army uniforms with naval insignias.

Pershing was anxious to get the guns to the front as quickly as possible, hoping to counteract the German "Big Bertha," but the huge German cannon was withdrawn before the battery could reach the front. Plunkett encountered considerable difficulty with French railway officials who protested that the thirteen-car trains loaded with guns and equipment were too heavy for the roadbeds and bridges and too large to clear depots, other buildings, and tunnels. After Plunkett checked the bridges and tunnels, he ordered the trains to the front despite French protests. On several occasions switches ahead of the trains were locked and were smashed open with chisels and sledge hammers.[91]

Thirty officers and five hundred enlisted men manned the batteries, mostly reservists who were selected because they were machinists, electricians, and former railroad workers. At the front, they were attached to an Army organization designated the Railway Artillery Reserve, composed of coast artillery units. The unit's commander was Brigadier General William Chamberlaine, a West Point graduate and like Plunkett, a Virginian, the only characteristic that they had in common. Chamberlaine was a martinet, so much so that, according to one of his officers, he regularly inspected the "cook shacks" to make sure that the "kitchen police" wore their blouses while "peeling the spuds and stirring the slum." Inevitably, the general and admiral clashed, one who did things solely by the book and the other who often flouted regulations. Plunkett's uniform outraged the general. The admiral, senior to the general, usually ignored him. AEF headquarters did not respond to Chamberlaine's complaints.[92]

Fortunately, the five batteries were scattered along both the American and French fronts, the trains moving them at six miles an hour to sites from which they fired on designated targets. They were used primarily to bombard German railway yards, bridges, and other logistical facilities. Their effective range was approximately 24 miles, although the maximum was 29 to 30 miles. They attempted to use aircraft for spotting, but poor visibility and difficulties with communications forced the battery commanders to use map coordinates. They used sextants and transits to aim their guns. Altogether they fired nearly eight hundred shells at their targets with considerable success. They severely damaged the railroad yards at Laon and the railroad that ran through Montmedy, Longuyon, and Conflans, the most important German line of communication, according to Sims.[93] Pershing was impressed and, if the war had continued, would have sought additional batteries.

In March 1918, a massive German offensive led Admiral Sims to order preliminary mobilization of available American sailors in France and prepared "to send them to the front in case the French . . . would like to have them for any work in which they could be of any use." He mentioned, for example, activities behind the lines such as driving vehicles and other means of transportation, digging trenches, and assisting communications. A member of Admiral Wilson's staff identified approximately seven thousand sailors for this purpose. General Ferdinand Foch, the newly appointed generalissimo of the Allied and American forces on the Western Front, said that they were not needed at the moment but that, if conditions changed, he would accept the admiral's offer.[94]

Combined inter-Allied operations that required American troops and sailors occurred when President Wilson decided to permit intervention in Russia, a decision that Pershing and the Army, who advocated concentration on the Western Front, did not favor. When the United States declared war in April 1917, Russia was in the initial stages of what is known as the "Russian Revolution," one of the most momentous events of the twentieth century. The majority of Americans, including U.S. Navy personnel, knew very little about Russia except that the country was one of the Allies. During the early months of the Revolution, the Allied leaders did not especially concern themselves with events in Russia, preoccupied as they were with the submarine crisis, mutinies in the French army, and failures on the Western Front. The new Russian government that assumed power after the czar's abdication continued to fight the Germans but with disastrous results. Nonetheless, the Western powers were satisfied as long as the Russian army tied up several hundred thousand German troops that, if freed for duty on the Western Front, could turn the tide against the Allies. This attitude changed abruptly in November when Communists, called Bolsheviks at the time, took control of the Russian government. Under Vladimir Ilyich Lenin, the new government decided to end its war with Germany. This event occurred in March 1918, when the Treaty of Brest-Litovsk confirmed the German victory on the Eastern Front and freed many divisions to fight in the West. These events caused the Allies, in some desperation, to intervene militarily in Russia. After an interminable delay, President Wilson reluctantly joined the intervention.[95]

The Russian Revolution did not materially affect American naval policy until the spring of 1918. Throughout most of 1917, the Russian government—with the support of the American ambassador, David R. Francis, and later Rear Admiral James Glennon, a member of an American commission sent to assist Russia led by Elihu Root—repeatedly requested naval vessels, armed trawlers, and destroyers to defend the Arctic coast, particularly the White Sea, against German submarines. The Navy Department rejected these requests. Sims argued that antisubmarine craft were needed everywhere and not enough were available to satisfy every demand. Sims also informed the Department that the deployment of U.S. destroyers in British waters allowed the Admiralty to send a destroyer division of the Royal Navy to the White Sea.[96]

Allied requests for American contributions to intervention in Russia began as early as December 1917 and gained intensity during the early months of 1918. The initial needs were warships, in this instance to reinforce the weak British naval force at Murmansk.[97] The Allied high command worried that German troops might attack from Finland toward the Murmansk area, including the port of Archangel. Murmansk would have made an ideal submarine base for U-boats. Archangel's harbor was free from ice during the summer months. During the summer of 1917, more than six hundred thousand tons of stores, including large amounts of munitions and coal, were landed at Archangel and placed in warehouses and on the docks. Until the signing of the Brest-Litovsk Treaty the British War Cabinet refused to consider intervention. The news of Russia's withdrawal from the war on March 3 prompted the Admiralty to request that the United States and France join in deploying cruisers to Murmansk. Lord Reading, the British ambassador to the United States, strongly advocated the dispatch of naval vessels to North Russia. The president, however, refused to sanction such a move until early in April. Evidently, the need to protect the supplies at Archangel persuaded him to provide at least token naval help.[98]

Wilson remained opposed to military intervention for several months.[99] Strongly supported by the War Department, he refused to divert troops from the Western Front. Strongly averse to interference in Russia's internal affairs, he favored the Russian people's effort to create what he considered a more representative government. Also he did not want to allow Japan to conduct a major military intervention into Siberia. Since the Russo-Japanese War, the United States had become increasingly hostile to Japanese territorial ambitions. The president, however, eventually distinguished

North Russia from Siberia, especially after the Supreme War Council, meeting on March 23, recommended the use of naval units to hold the Murmansk-Archangel area "as long as possible." Two days later, the Allied Naval Council meeting agreed to this initiative. A cable from Francis and the American military attaché to Russia endorsed deployment of an American warship to Murmansk "to join British and French who are cooperating with Soviet there" and added that Bolshevik officials approved the measure. Undersecretary of State Frank L. Polk forwarded the message to the secretary and mentioned that "high ranking military officers are [now] strongly in favor of this step."[100]

Nevertheless, Daniels and Benson were reluctant to send a naval vessel to North Russia, claiming that "the only vessels which are available to send to Murmansk are those operating in European waters," and all were involved with antisubmarine activities. On April 5, a cable went to Sims in effect stating that, if the Admiralty considered the presence of an American warship at Murmansk essential, the American vessel would have to come from his force. Sims, not surprisingly, replied that none of his vessels were available and added that "a pre–dreadnought battleship or armored cruiser from home waters" would do. When the president insisted that he was "anxious to [send a warship] . . . if it can be done without sacrificing more important objects," Daniels was left with no choice. Sims received notice that the *Olympia* was the only vessel available and would be ordered to Murmansk.[101]

The armored cruiser *Olympia* had been the flagship of Commodore George Dewey at the Battle of Manila Bay during the Spanish-American War. Commissioned in 1896, the 5,586-ton warship was the flagship of the Patrol Force, Atlantic Fleet, until she joined U.S. naval forces in European waters under orders for Murmansk. Late in 1917, the cruiser underwent refit to repair damage from a grounding. Ten 5-inch guns originally intended for the *Tennessee* replaced obsolete 12-inch guns.[102] Her commanding officer was Captain Bion B. Bierer, who had been recalled to active duty to perform escort duties. On May 20, the *Olympia* steamed out of Scapa Flow with two British destroyers. On board was British Major General Frederick C. Poole, recently appointed to head the Allied Mission in North Russia. Poole took along his staff, several French officers, and, according to an American bluejacket, "many cases of Scotch whiskey."[103] Four days later, the cruiser entered the Kola River and anchored at Murmansk.

Captain Bierer had no political instructions. He was to place his ship under the control of the Allied naval commander in North Russia, Rear Admiral Thomas Kemp, following the practice of cooperation. Although the Department approved this decision, the president made it clear that the American ship was not to participate in offensive operations against the Russians. Kemp later ignored this proviso when he employed a detachment from the ship in a military action against Russian forces. This operation, however, occurred after the Russian government ordered Allied forces to leave the area. Although Sims informed the Department that Kemp was instructed not to engage in land operations, his orders granted some latitude in this respect. The first sea lord informed him that he could use "the crews of the ships to stiffen local resistance against German or Finnish invasion." "It will be your duty," the British admi-

ral was told, "to hold the Kola Inlet with such naval forces as you have at your disposal
. . . and generally the coast of Russian Lapland lying between Kola Inlet and Norwegian frontier for the *Russians* against Finnish and German invasion." The American
sailors' confusion appears in the diary of a bandsman on the *Olympia*. On May 26, he
wrote: "We play a regular overture now for colors. 'Star Spangled Banner,' 'God Save
the King,' 'The Marseillaise.' Undecided about 'Lora, God Protect the Czar,' as we don't
know yet which side we are on."[104]

The Department was equally unsure of its responsibilities. Sims had reported that
the Allied Naval Council was opposed to deploying additional naval vessels to North
Russia, which would weaken antisubmarine operations, but the Supreme War Council favored military intervention. On June 22, the CNO advised Daniels that "in the
absence of definite information and views regarding the best line of action to pursue
in regard to Russia, the Department should depend upon Ambassador Francis to suggest the kind of action we must pursue." Francis, however, was at that time somewhat
isolated, having fled with other diplomatic delegations from Moscow to a remote
town. Nonetheless, his dispatches to the State Department constantly recommended
military intervention. Daniels wisely consulted with Secretary of State Lansing as to
identify "the attitude of the Allied Governments . . . and the policy of this Government in regard to maintaining naval forces in Russian ports." The secretary of state
noted that American policy had not changed; the American naval force was to assist the "Russian people against the Central Powers" but were not to undertake military actions without "instructions to do so."[105] Even as Lansing was stressing that the
administration's policy was the same, it was undergoing change. At the beginning of
June, the president, at the urging of the British, reluctantly agreed to limited military
intervention in North Russia. Wilson insisted upon a formal request from the Supreme War Council. He did not instruct the War Department to provide troops until
late in July.[106]

Even before American troops embarked for North Russia, the limited intervention
encountered difficulties. In mid-June, the Bolshevik government demanded the immediate withdrawal of Allied naval vessels in Russian waters.[107] The local authorities
in Murmansk continued to favor the Allies. On July 6, a number of Allied military
officials, including Captain Bierer, signed an agreement in Murmansk to provide military supplies, food, and protection to the local opponents of the Germans. Although
Olympia's captain clearly exceeded his authority, Sims and Washington officials ac-
ceded to his decision.[108] Authorities in Archangel, the location of the principal supply
dump, remained loyal to the Moscow government.

General Poole, in command of the Allied forces in North Russia, waited for the ice
to thaw and reinforcements to arrive before moving on Archangel. The city was on
the Northern Dvina River some thirty-five miles from its confluence with the White
Sea. Poole and his advisors believed that the Russians at Archangel would resist occupation. The British general wanted to wait for additional troops, but American
and British diplomats, including Francis, convinced him that an imminent anti-Bol-
shevik uprising at Archangel would fail without immediate Allied intervention. On
the night of July 30, an invasion force got underway. Although *Olympia* remained at

Murmansk because she drew too much water to navigate the Dvina, Captain Bierer, two officers, and fifty bluejackets sailed with the expedition, a violation of President Wilson's orders.[109]

Members of *Olympia's* crew performed a variety of tasks at Murmansk after the ship arrived there. On June 8, a landing party of a hundred officers and men went ashore to cooperate with a detachment of British marines. This force manned positions around the port to guard against an attack. They were billeted with the marines in log barracks and railway cars. When not on guard duty, they helped unload ships that brought supplies for the expeditionary force. The ship's crew also repaired and initially manned several Russian naval vessels in the harbor, including a torpedo boat and destroyers. Later, Russian crews took over the torpedo boat, but one destroyer remained in American hands; two officers and forty-seven enlisted men manned it. The destroyer escorted convoys in the White Sea.[110] On July 12, a terrorist bomb exploded in the home of a Russian officer. An investigation determined that sailors from the Russian battleship *Ashold* were responsible. A party of American and British sailors boarded the battleship and dismantled her guns. After the detachment of bluejackets left for Archangel, American sailors continued to occupy defensive positions in Murmansk.[111] During fourteen weeks of participation in the occupation, they never faced hostile action. The same did not apply to those sent to Archangel.

Murmansk, a town of rough wooden buildings and four thousand inhabitants, did not appeal to the Americans. Liberty usually consisted of walks in the hills and searches for food. Rations were short ashore and on the *Olympia*. A member of the ship's crew consumed only rice for breakfast one morning. "Eats are getting pretty low," he wrote, and later he continued: "Supper on the ship, white bread and delicious BEANS. The bread tasted like *Angel Food cake*." On another occasion, he observed: "Getting less to eat every day—Hash and beans today." Personnel on shore fared better. A gunner's mate mentioned the theft of cases of food when on working parties.[112] The twenty-two members of the ship's band went ashore nearly every day to play at various events. They later went to Archangel to help recruit Russians for a local military force. Although the band was evidently popular with the Russians, it did little to stimulate recruiting. A critical British diplomat refugee complained: "They have brought with them two orchestras, or 'bands' as they rightly call them, for one cannot qualify by any other name the bands of evil-doers made up by these ragtime players. The 'band' of sailors from the *Olympia*, which is rampaging around since our arrival in Archangel is going to constitute a danger to our ear-drums."[113]

General Poole's force landed at Archangel under protective fire from British and French naval vessels and occupied the town, forcing the Bolshevik militia to evacuate it. The American detachment did not take part in the initial assault; it came ashore the following day. In the subsequent weeks, the bluejackets joined in a number of actions.

A detachment of twenty-five men under the command of Ensign Donald M. Hicks went ashore to guard the American consulate and other designated sites, including the railway yards. They discovered a wood-burning locomotive with fuel on board and a full boiler of water. Hooking up two flat cars, the bluejackets climbed on them and mounted their machine gun. Evidently without orders, Hicks and his men steamed out of the yard and, shortly afterward, encountered the rear guard of the retreating Bolsheviks. They exchanged fire until the engine overheated, and they continued to give chase on foot until entrenched "Bolos" stopped them at a river crossing. They then returned some thirty miles to Archangel, carrying with them fifty-four Bolshevik prisoners.

Somewhat later this group advanced with Allied forces along the railway.[114] Resistance was slight at first but stiffened as the advance continued. On one occasion, a large contingent of Russian sailors launched a bayonet charge against Hicks's detachment and a force of French soldiers. Although the charge was repulsed with no American casualties, three bluejackets were wounded later. After a week of steady fighting, the Americans were withdrawn and returned to Archangel.[115]

On August 8, the Allies organized a naval brigade including one American officer and eight enlisted men. The brigade took over a motley collection of river craft, ranging from paddle wheel steamers to barges, and began to move up the Dvina River, acting in concert with forces ashore, which included Ensign Hicks's command. At the end of September, the flotilla had pushed about 250 miles up the river. According to one of the bluejackets, the Americans were housed on a coal barge pulled by a tugboat. Hicks's detachment moved parallel to the river. In their first encounter, they captured an armored car too damaged to use along with "thirty light wagons, horses, men and wives, to carry our equipment." He recalled that on August 19, "[W]e spent most of the day digging trenches to the front and rear of us. The following day we encountered about 500 'Bolos.' A small fight followed. . . . Our job at this time was to guard the transports and the local telegraph station, where we were shelled several times. . . . The following morning, we attacked a town." Afterward they returned to Archangel. Recent arrivals from the U.S. 339th Infantry Regiment replaced them. The flotilla had to return to Archangel because ice formed on the river.[116]

When American troops arrived, Bierer and his landing party returned to *Olympia*. As winter approached, both the French and Americans wanted to withdraw their ships from North Russia, but General Poole asked the Admiralty to arrange the retention of these vessels. Early in September, the first sea lord approached Sims about leaving *Olympia* in Murmansk. The French agreed to keep their warship in Archangel. Admiral Le Bon knew that the military forces depended upon naval support. The Department agreed to leave the cruiser at Murmansk and ordered Rear Admiral Newton McCully to assume command. It is not known why Daniels or Benson sent a flag officer. McCully took command at the end of October. His instructions from Sims placed him under Admiral Kemp, the senior naval officer, White Sea. Instructed to cooperate with the Allies, he was also expected to "make it clear that you are the sincere friend of the Russian people, and that American forces have no ulterior military or political motive inimical to Russian sovereignty."[117]

Olympia did not remain in Murmansk for the winter. Ambassador Francis became ill, and the cruiser transported him to London. Sims intended to return the cruiser to

Murmansk, but the CNO ordered her to the Adriatic Sea. Kemp was later informed that the gunboat *Yankton* would replace *Olympia*. McCully and his staff remained at Murmansk. Months passed before he regained a command.[118]

American naval and military forces lingered in North Russia for another year in what has been described as the "Forgotten War." The Navy Department deployed additional naval vessels there to support the ground forces, but they and their crews did not engage in combat.

Another aspect of Army-Navy cooperation requires mention. How well did Sims and Pershing get along? Despite certain entries in Daniels's diaries to the contrary, they appear to have coexisted well. Pershing in published remarks praised the Navy for its wartime service but said nothing about Sims, who in a confidential letter to the president stressed that the two "cooperated quite well," that they worked together in "the most complete harmony and sympathy." To his wife, he wrote, "I like him very much" and mentioned a meeting between the two after the Armistice.[119]

Pershing placed Brigadier General William Dawes in charge of transportation. The AEF commander was extremely concerned about obtaining adequate supplies of coal for the winter months. Dawes asked Sims for a collier, but the admiral told him that he did not have one in his force. Dawes informed Pershing, who in turn reported Sims's refusal to the War Department, which then pressured the Navy Department to assign a collier to the army.[120] Sims and Pershing disagreed on amalgamation, and differences arose over shipping and other logistical matters and aviation, but both recognized them as problems associated with interservice cooperation.

Despite inevitable difficulties in implementing the policy of cooperation/amalgamation, the U.S. Navy adapted successfully to coalition warfare. American naval forces in European waters steadily expanded and provided desperately needed help to the Allies. It also supported the AEF efficiently. Logistical support was developed to sustain these activities. The Navy established bases, and auxiliary ships were deployed either on station in European waters or assigned to logistical support on a regular basis. The ability of the U.S. naval forces in European waters to sustain themselves on a nearly self-sufficient basis earned the well-deserved praise of the Allies.

A Little Bit of America

U.S. Naval Facilities in Great Britain

The six destroyers under Commander Joseph Taussig departed from Boston for Ireland crammed with spare parts and ammunition.[1] As the heavily loaded warships plowed through the North Atlantic, Admiral Sims warned the Navy Department that logistical support for these vessels and others to follow them was a priority: "I cannot exaggerate the importance of our forces being followed immediately by adequate repair and supply facilities, particularly for all special repairs and needs peculiar to our ships. Facilities at Queenstown and neighboring bases greatly overstrained by volume of work and lack of labor."[2] The British Admiralty and later the Allied Naval Council made it absolutely clear to Sims and the Navy Department that American naval forces operating in European waters would have to be self-sufficient. Three years of war had badly overtaxed the Allies' ability to maintain their military forces. Throughout the war, a cardinal principle of U.S. naval policy was to rely on their own logistical resources.

American naval officers at that time had little knowledge of "pure" logistics or logistical theory, but the traditional policy called for U.S. warships to operate as independently as possible, particularly those deployed on distant stations. For practical reasons, the Navy purchased fresh provisions and bread locally and carried out minor repairs in private or governmental yards located within the cruising station. Chartered storeships periodically brought dry stores to the various stations and squadrons or at times stored them in leased warehouses. After the advent of steam, coal was either purchased locally or carried from the United States in colliers.[3]

Stephen R. Luce probably introduced the term *logistics* into American naval terminology, although Alfred T. Mahan also used it in his writings.[4] Logistics is the process of providing support for operating forces. The novelist Herman Wouk wrote, "the lifeblood of battle is logistics, a sort of colorless lifeblood noticeable only if it stops flowing, where upon the gangrene of non supply can be quickly fatal."[5] More than likely the noted military writer Antoine Jomini coined the term, mentioned in his *Precis de l'art de la guerre* first published in 1836.[6] The term has evolved from mere supply to a complex process. Even prior to World War I, an officer at the Naval War College, Commander C. T. Vogelgesang, stressed that "logistics comprehends all the operations outside the field of battle and which lead up to it—it regulates the execution of those movements which in combination become the function of strategy."[7]

The Board of Navy Commissioners, replaced by the bureau system in 1842, managed logistics during the first half of the nineteenth century. The bureaus created in the 1840s dealt with it until 1917. This bureaucracy had little difficulty supporting the few squadrons deployed abroad in peacetime and even during two major conflicts, the American Civil War and the Spanish-American War. The Great White Fleet's around-the-world cruise during 1907–1908 was considered an aberration.

Nonetheless, the Navy's bureaus in 1914 planned for possible involvement, particularly the Bureau of Supplies and Accounts (BuS&A). Before 1914, the Navy's supply system varied from management of the service's supply of clothing and provisions to control of fuel and repair parts. Ship allowances were established; a centralized general mess system and improved ration allotment were put into operation; a for-cash ship's store replaced the canteens that provided credit to the detriment of the bluejackets; an efficient procurement system was installed; specialized qualifications for paymasters (supply officers) were approved; and an extremely businesslike method of inventory and control of all stores became operational.[8]

In March 1916, the General Board recommended the compilation of data on the logistical requirements of the fleet in time of war. The new CNO, Admiral Benson, consulted with the bureau chiefs and created a "logistical committee" composed of representatives from the bureaus of Steam Engineering, Ordnance, Medicine and Surgery, Yards and Docks, Construction and Repairs, and Supplies and Accounts. The CNO selected Rear Admiral Samuel McGowan to head the committee.[9]

In the summer of 1916, McGowan wrote a long report to Daniels on the status of naval supply. He admitted the inadequacies of the logistical system. His staff compiled lists of food, clothing, and other stores for ships of various types. They computed fuel requirements. In order to place the information within the context of war, he sent a paymaster (supply officer) to the war zone. By June 1916, impressive strides had been made to improve the system and prepare it for war. The Navy created a stock catalog of standard supplies and materials; it ordered large quantities of clothing, dry stores, and fuel; and it constructed centralized warehouses, storage depots, and fuel dumps for both coal and oil.[10] As McGowan testified after the war, "The Navy's Supply System was so planned in advance . . . that when put to the test of war, it merely experienced an orderly expansion to handle adequately the increased volume of work without any radical change in method."[11]

The Department's war plans, including those of the various bureaus, presumed wartime concentration of the fleet in the Western Hemisphere. The logistical scheme devised by McGowan and the other bureau chiefs did not anticipate the deployment of naval forces to European waters. Although adequate supplies were available, the Navy possessed only a limited number of auxiliary ships to carry them to the war zone. Fortunately the buildup of ships and personnel abroad occurred deliberately and emphasized construction of antisubmarine craft. Some battleships and submarines were sent overseas, but the bulk of the fleet remained in home waters.

The tender *Melville* followed the initial unit of destroyers to Great Britain. She arrived at the base in Queenstown, Ireland, loaded with approximately three thousand

tons of cargo. With the exception of fresh provisions to be purchased locally, the supplies were considered adequate to serve twenty-four destroyers for six months.[12] The
Melville, which became the repair ship for the destroyers, carried everything needed
for minor repairs, including a year's supply of screws, bolts, and nuts. The allotment of
supplies, adequate in peacetime, was not enough in war. The policy of self-sufficiency
was neither possible nor practicable in the war zone. The Navy had to depend upon
the Allies. The British proved willing to help, but after four years of war they had limited capabilities. Nevertheless they provided vital support.[13] This included bases.

The Navy did not initially intend to establish bases in the war zone. Sims was told
that the Navy would not create facilities in Europe unless the "situation demands" it.
This policy reflected the assumption that most of the U.S. fleet, certainly the battle force,
would remain in the Western Hemisphere.[14] The Department soon became aware that
it must deploy many vessels to the war zone. It eventually established fourteen bases in
Europe, not including air stations.[15] A war correspondent wrote that "A naval base is a
place where naval operations begin and end—that is, the ships start out from the base,
return to the base and are directed from the base so far as their general orders are concerned. . . . The base is the source of supply, orders, repairs, and upkeep. . . . It combines
the function of manager, doctor, commissary, and purveys man and fuel power for
the ships. . . . It is a versatile and ubiquitous institution . . . where you can get anything
from a number of thousand young Americans crazy for a fight with the Huns to the
most delicate repair of an optical instrument; from a new boiler for a destroyer to
. . . an apple pie."[16]

The Irish port of Queenstown, now known as Cobh, became the first U.S. naval
base in the war zone. It was selected because of its proximity to convoy routes from
North American ports to the British Isles. The Royal Navy maintained a small dockyard and repair facility there to support antisubmarine craft, but Sims noted that it
had "practically been abandoned."[17] As more and more American destroyers arrived,
British ships were deployed elsewhere. Shore facilities, limited to a dock and fueling
depot on Haulbowline Island in the Cork River, were turned over to the American
Navy. Three private yards were located along the river between Queenstown and the
port of Cork.[18]

Four days after the first six destroyers arrived at Queenstown, Sims cabled the Department that "the British would help but they are strained nearly to the limit." He recommended that the *Melville* and *Dixie* should transport as many stores as possible. He
also urged the immediate dispatch of supply ships with meat and other provisions.[19]
Little space was available for storage. The first destroyers had no trouble unloading
extra stores and torpedoes, but the *Melville's* three thousand tons of supplies had to be
stored in a rented warehouse several miles from the base. Later the Navy leased additional warehouses and wharves at a site called Passage West located several miles upstream from the base. By the end of the war, Passage West had become the largest U.S.
naval supply center in the British Isles. BuS&A established purchasing and accounting
offices there, servicing U.S. naval forces as far distant as the battleships operating with
the Grand Fleet.[20] Cold storage facilities for frozen meat were leased in Cork. In 1918,

thirty prefabricated corrugated storage sheds were shipped from the United States to provide additional storage. Land adjacent to a dock belonging to a railway company was also purchased and a warehouse built on it.[21]

The supply officer at Queenstown (Base 6) took charge of naval aviation stores in Great Britain. It provided clothing, small stores, canteen supplies, and dry provisions to six air stations. The Bureau of Supplies and Accounts also obtained warehouses in Dublin, which distributed materials shipped from the States for use in the construction of air stations in Ireland. Because of the priority given to construction of air stations, the Navy was allowed to obtain materials on the open market. It purchased construction materials and equipment on open contract but also applied directly to Admiralty supply depots for their needs. An unfortunate result of the "open market" policy was to foster competition among the U.S. naval bases and stations in a severely restrictive market. It inflated prices. The problem was resolved to some extent when a central purchasing office was established at the Queenstown depot.[22]

During 1917–18, more than 17 million tons of food and millions of tons of other supplies were landed at Passage West and stored for later distribution. Inadequate transportation interfered with efficient storage. "Two-horse" carts had to be used to transfer supplies from docks to warehouses. A single narrow-gauge railway linked Cork and Queenstown. Few motor vehicles were available. Stores destined for American naval vessels and facilities elsewhere in the British Isles were unloaded at Queenstown and shipped by British coastal steamer. By October 1918, the supply depot had a four-month reserve of provisions.

In December 1917, a torpedo repair shop was set up at Haulbowline. Portable buildings were erected on the island to conduct repairs. This facility eventually succeeded in overhauling some four hundred torpedoes per month.[23]

The Department's decision to base thirty-six of the 110-foot wooden-hulled subchasers at Queenstown in July 1918 strained the seriously crowded port. No anchorage or mooring space was available either off Haulbowline or in Queenstown harbor because of the presence of repair ships, destroyers, and other vessels. The chasers were moved some two miles up the river. Most of them had to moor to buoys in the stream, a satisfactory procedure in calm weather but potentially harmful to fragile vessels in any kind of blow. The Navy's repair ships, some two miles away, were heavily committed to the destroyers. The tenders manufactured spare parts, but it was difficult to transfer them to the chaser anchorage because small boats and motor vehicles required for the move were rarely available. At times even food was scarce because of the lack of adequate transportation. When a chaser's hull required inspection, repairmen beached and careened the vessel. Space for personnel, stores, spare parts, and offices was available only in some barracks. The chaser detachment took over one of these buildings, forcing the occupants to move elsewhere. Space was at such a premium at Queenstown that a sort of "musical chairs" took place, and the game was played without disrupting operations, something of a miracle, according to one officer.[24]

In June 1918, Queenstown boasted a naval complement of more than seven thousand sailors. Eventually the Irish base became larger than any other American naval facility in Europe except Brest.[25] Quarters for naval personnel proved exceedingly difficult to locate. Housing for the personnel at the torpedo repair shop and others who could not find billets on the repair ships occupied an old farmhouse and a barrack once used by an Irish regiment. In November, a number of granaries were leased to provide housing and a training facility for replacements intended for the destroyer crews. Portable barracks were sent from the United States and assembled at the hospital and elsewhere.[26] Freshwater for the ships and many shore installations was never fully available, although American naval personnel laid pipes to the end. Many buildings were never heated, including the training barracks. American methods of solving the problems of housing, storage, and transportation impressed the local citizenry, but the physical changes stimulated concern.[27]

The senior U.S. naval officer at Queenstown was Captain Pringle, the chief of staff to Admiral Bayly and also the commander of all U.S. forces, including those afloat and ashore, in Queenstown and Cork except those at the naval air station. Bayly did not interfere in the administration of the American forces.[28] The system worked well. Repair ships proved so efficient that U.S. destroyers spent 66 percent of their time at sea. Spare parts, provisions and supplies were almost always available.[29]

The Navy established its first mobile floating advance base in Ireland, a logistical concept that proved invaluable in the Pacific during World War II. Rear Admiral George Dyer defined an advance base as a "temporary base located in or near forward areas . . . the primary mission of which is to support wartime operations of the Armed Forces."[30] Early in May, the British commission in Washington recommended Berehaven in Bantry Bay as a base for U.S. destroyers. The Department asked Sims to provide information about the facilities available for "housing and stores." He replied that the British used it as an advance base. It had a little hospital, and a small tanker and storeship provided logistical help. The site, he noted, "was near the main activity of submarines. . . . The British and French agree that our destroyer force should remain concentrated upon its own supply and repair ships . . . it [is] . . . essential to have the mobile force ready to follow shifting of main submarine activity."[31]

Eventually, a large number of American ships, including destroyers, battleships, submarines, and tenders, used Bantry Bay as an advance base. Some American officers were occasionally quartered in the small town of Berehaven, and sailors from the submarines occupied a few beach cottages. Admiral Mayo thought it "about as desolate, God forsaken appearing a place as any one could find."[32] No major shore facilities were established in Bantry Bay. Queenstown, about seventy-five miles to the north, provided general logistical support.

The U.S. Navy commissioned additional bases in England and Scotland. At some sites, the Navy took over established British bases. Elsewhere the Navy acquired property from private owners through requisition at the request of Admiral Sims. This procedure was used to obtain buildings for naval headquarters in London, hospitals, supply depots, and naval air stations. It also gained land on which to construct bases at Invergordon, Inverness, Cardiff, and Plymouth and a receiving station at Liverpool. Whenever possible, Admiral Sims insisted on the use "the existing machinery of the British Government," to avoid establishment of a "parallel system of purchase and supply."[33]

Liverpool became the site of two American naval facilities: a receiving ship and a medical stores depot. Also the overhaul and repair of destroyers based at Queenstown was accomplished at Liverpool. The receiving ship was at first ashore in the "Northwestern Hotel," and later personnel were billeted in some smaller hotels. The "receiving ship" provided lodging and travel vouchers for destroyer personnel whose ship was in a local yard. Officers and men arriving from the United States were funneled through Liverpool to various ships and shore duty in Europe, and those returning to the United States generally departed from that port.[34] The medical stores depot was established in a building leased from the Cunard Company. It became the central distribution point for medicines and stores sent to U.S. Navy hospitals, other medical facilities, and ships throughout the European theater. Until medical supplies arrived from the United States, the Red Cross provided them.[35]

In May 1918, the Navy decided to establish a base at Plymouth for a squadron of 110-foot submarine chasers. In 1588, Sir Francis Drake was engaged in a game of bowls there when the Spanish Armada was sighted, and the Pilgrims sailed from this port in 1620, beginning their voyage to the New World. Captain Richard H. "Reddy" Leigh, assigned to command the subchasers in European waters, selected Plymouth as his base. While an assistant to the chief of the Bureau of Steam Navigation, he supervised experiments with submarine listening devices. He was ordered to continue these investigations in England under combat conditions. Leigh believed that subchasers were ideal vessels to carry out his experiments.[36]

After sending inspectors to examine Plymouth, Sims approached the Admiralty for permission to requisition a privately owned complex known as the Victoria Wharf Company, which included a large deepwater basin, wharves, railroad tracks, warehouses, and vacant land. This property became U.S. Naval Base Number 27.[37] The warehouses were converted into barracks, mess hall, and store rooms, and certain private dwellings were turned over to senior officers and chief petty officers. Commander Theodore "Spud" Ellyson, who served at various times as the base's commanding officer, second in command, and operations officer, had to furnish his cottage: "install[ed] a bath, papered the walls throughout, select[ed] the carpet, and furnish[ed] the house throughout including curtains, linens, china, bed, chairs, kitchen utensils, and all arrangements."[38] Other officers rented rooms at the local yacht club and rooms in the city. Later two municipal wharves were requisitioned that overlooked the "Hoe," a renowned half-mile-long promenade in the community's center. The Americans built a repair shop to make minor repairs and assembled a small marine railway to haul chasers out of the water.[39]

The command structure at Plymouth resembled that at Queenstown. The local Royal Navy admiral, located at Devonsport, exercised operational command. Administrative control came under the senior American officer. Initially Commander Wilson Brown held the position, followed briefly by Ellyson. In June, Captain Lyman Cotton took over. After a certain amount of friction developed between the local British admiral and Cotton, Rear Admiral Mark Bristol, commanding the battleship *Oklahoma* at Bantry Bay at the time, was ordered to replace Cotton, who became his second in command. In October 1918, sixty-six subchasers, three destroyers, and one tender operated from the base. About three thousand naval personnel were stationed there. The Armistice aborted a plan to establish a training school for naval personnel who were in transit to bases elsewhere in the war zone.[40]

A small but vital base was built at the Welsh port of Cardiff. A few weeks after the AEF began to arrive in France, General Pershing's staff discovered a shortage of coal, which was needed to fuel locomotives that carried troops and supplies to inland locations and to heat quarters. The British had none to spare, and a severe coal shortage existed in France. Benson told a reluctant Sims that he must help meet the Army's requirements for coal. The force commander ordered the collier *Bath* at Brest to transport coal from Cardiff to Brest. A second collier, the *Nero*, was ordered to European waters to provide coal for the AEF. In October 1917, Sims informed the French government that the Navy would "insure that the United States troops in France are self-supporting in [coal]."[41]

Sims recommended the establishment of a base at Cardiff to handle shipments of coal to France and requested a flag officer to command the base and the coal carriers. He asked for Captain Charles F. Hughes, at that time in command of the battleship *New York* operating with the Sixth Battle Squadron of the Grand Fleet. Benson designated Cardiff as Base Number 29, but he promoted Captain Philip Andrews, commanding the battleship *Mississippi*, and assigned him to Cardiff.[42] Sims was pleased with the appointment as Andrews was a friend. Rear Admiral Andrews assumed his duties on September 25, 1918.

Sims asked the Admiralty to authorize acquisition of quarters for 250 men, a building for a 75-bed hospital, storehouses, and office spaces. Late in August a small hotel, the Angel Building, became base headquarters. It also provided quarters for officers and men. The Navy took over a vacant airplane factory, some small shipyards, and coaling facilities.[43] Efforts to obtain suitable buildings for barracks, mess hall, and hospital ran into local opposition. The mayor and other local officials urged that the Admiralty look elsewhere for suitable accommodations. Strong opposition also developed when British officials, at the Navy's request, attempted to acquire a women's teaching institute to provide space for a hospital. The belief that the war was nearing its end may explain local resistance, or perhaps it was a manifestation of the obstinacy often attributed to the Welsh.[44] The Navy also established submarine bases at the Barry Docks and in three nearby ports—Penarth, Newport, and Swansea.

Equipment and vehicles had to be shipped from the United States. Sims requested a supply ship loaded with desks, typewriters, clothing, lubricating oil, paint, and vehicles be shipped to the newly established base.

By October, some three hundred men had arrived and were billeted temporarily in private residences and small hotels in the city. Until renovations were completed, Andrews and his staff worked in the Merchant Exchange Building. Additional personnel arrived rapidly. By November 1918, 782 officers and 4,101 enlisted men, afloat and ashore, were assigned to the base. Andrews and his staff believed that the coal fleet would eventually consist of two hundred ships, but the Armistice immediately aborted growth.[45] The base remained active until late in the summer of 1919. By then a majority of the American troops had left France.

The two most unique bases established by the U.S. Navy in Great Britain during the war were located in northern Scotland near the picturesque towns of Inverness and Invergordon. In October 1917, after months of deliberation, the Admiralty agreed to create a combined U.S./British force that would lay an immense minefield across the North Sea, one of the two exits to the open seas available to the U-boats, the other being the Strait of Dover. On October 6, the Admiralty designated a board of naval officers known as the "Lockhart Leith Committee" to recommend suitable sites for U.S. mine depots in Great Britain. (Captain Leith was commanding officer of HMS *Princess Margaret* and senior officer of minelayers in the Royal Navy.) Five locations were considered—Dundee, Aberdeen, Leith, Invergordon, and Inverness, all on the northeastern coast of Scotland. Invergordon and Inverness were selected because of their access to rail and canal, the presence of repair facilities, the availability of buildings, their proximity to each other, and their closeness to the proposed minefield.[46]

Invergordon, a small fishing village of three thousand people located on Cromarty Firth, became a major naval base of the British Home Fleet. In 1914, the Royal Navy established a dockyard and a repair facility there. Invergordon also became something of a rest and recreation center for Grand Fleet personnel. Many officers, including Admiral Jellicoe, kept their families there.[47]

Inverness, the county seat located on Loch Ness, had a population of nearly twenty thousand people. An important railway center, it also served as the eastern terminus of the Caledonian Canal. Inverness exuded historical tradition: across the Firth was Culloden House, where Bonnie Prince Charles slept before he suffered crushing defeat at the hands of the British in 1746. Nearby was the ancient village of Fortrose and its ruined twelfth-century cathedral. As Admiral Sims later wrote: "the towns in which our officers and men found themselves . . . are among the most famous in Scottish history and legend. Almost every foot of land is associated with memories of Macbeth, Mary Queen of Scots, Cromwell and the Pretender."[48]

Among other things, Scotland is known for its whiskey. Invergordon and Inverness were home to renowned distilleries, Dalmore three miles from Invergordon and Glen Albyn at Muirtown on the outskirts of Inverness. Both were idle in 1917 because the British government severely curtailed the production of alcoholic beverages during the war. Citing the Defense of the Realm Act, it nationalized the liquor trade adjacent to munitions factories and military/naval bases, which included the distilleries at Invergordon and Inverness.[49] The distilleries consisted of one large warehouse each and several small buildings. Because these structures were clean, dry, and well ventilated, American naval officers believed that they would provide excellent living quarters for personnel. Secretary Daniels, a noted "dry," in an attempt at humor in his diary: "told naval officers [that the] war ended too soon. My purpose was to make G[reat] B[ritain] dry by taking over all distilleries for naval bases."[50]

"The only disadvantage attached to these two Distilleries," reported the Lockhart Leith Committee in a masterpiece of understatement, "is the large amount of Bonded whiskey in cask (Dalmore 6,100 casks and Glen Albyn 2,774 casks) which must be removed. . . . It is not thought advisable to leave this whiskey . . . with so many men on the premises."[51] When the American bluejackets arrived, some of them searched the distilleries in the hope that a barrel or so had been overlooked. One wrote that he considered the transformation of distilleries into naval bases "nothing short of an act of profanation."[52] An American correspondent who visited the bases with distilleries wrote: "Every time I tell [the] . . . story to my British friends tears come into their eyes. Fancy being in proximity . . . to six thousand barrels of pre-war whiskey."[53]

The Admiralty agreed to convert the distilleries into naval facilities. The large warehouses became barracks, the smaller ones offices and storehouses. "Sheds" were built to house the assembly of mines, to provide storage, and to conduct minor repairs. Admiralty representatives recommended heating for the facilities at the bases: "although it will be expensive, it must be remembered that Americans are accustomed to very hot rooms."[54] A dock was planned to serve lighters. In both communities, hotels were converted into either hospitals or officers' quarters. When space for quarters became virtually unavailable at Inverness, the American admiral in command of the mine barrage and his staff were offered Kingsmill House, owned by Sir Charles William D. Perrins of Lea & Perrins, the manufacturer of Worcestershire sauce. A large manor, it contained accommodations for sixteen officers, a library, lounging rooms, parlor, billiard room, kitchen, and dining saloon. The extensive grounds included gardens, tennis courts, a shooting preserve, and even a golf course.[55]

All manner of improvement took place. New telephone lines were run, fire mains laid, water systems upgraded, water closets (bathrooms, or "heads") and other sanitary devices installed, and commissary and messing facilities provided for the growing complement of American bluejackets and their officers. The British turned over gantry cranes, machine tools, and other equipment. Inverness was able to provide adequate electricity from the town's power plant, but a generator had to be installed to power the Invergordon base.[56] Both bases were barricaded and surrounded with barbed wire. "A place of great beauty," wrote a British naval officer, "was now turned into a grim series of buildings . . . which became . . . huge American camps. . . . All over . . . were American mottos and hieroglyphics."[57]

Because of the submarine threat, the disassembled mines could not be shipped directly from the United States to the bases. Instead the mines and mine stores were unloaded at Fort William (Corpach Village), the western terminus of the Caledonian Canal, and at the Kyle of Lochalsh, a railhead on Scotland's western coast. The eastern end of the railroad, like that of the canal, was located at Inverness. The mines were either received at Inverness or taken by rail to Invergordon. The Admiralty assembled about thirty-five self-propelled lighters to transport the mines on the canal. Admiral Sims assigned small detachments at both Fort William and the Kyle of Lochalsh to coordinate shipments of mines.[58] After the mines were assembled, they were loaded on barges and transported to minelayers anchored in the harbors.[59]

In November 1917, Admiral Benson assigned Commander Orin G. Murfin, an expert in the assembly and handling of mines, to take charge of the two bases.[60] Murfin, newly promoted to captain, arrived in England on November 23. After a briefing at Simsadus, he left for his new command. He was "agreeably surprised" at the distillery buildings but concerned over transportation facilities, lack of adequate docking, and the evident delay in bringing the bases to operational capability. "Labor is very scarce in Northern Scotland and the Admiralty is having difficulty in supplying men for the work," he wrote Sims. He urged the transfer of naval personnel to the bases as quickly as possible. The work, however, continued to drag, and Murfin continued to complain. The harsh Scottish winter contributed to the delays. "The weather has been unusually severe with heavy snows and considerable freezing," he reported to Sims. He even complained about the New Year holiday, "which is extensively celebrated in Scotland." The Admiralty considered the use of Royal Marine labor battalions to work on the bases, but apparently did not do so.[61]

The Admiralty committee estimated that approximately 1,800 men would be enough to run the bases. Murfin disagreed: he believed that a larger workforce was needed to prepare mines at the required rate.[62] The American base commander also bombarded the Admiralty with requests for housing and construction of needed facilities. He asked the Department to ship eight prefabricated buildings for use as barracks and mess halls and also vehicles and office equipment. These items did not arrive before the Armistice. At that time, approximately 20 officers and 2,000 enlisted personnel were stationed at the two bases, and an additional 120 men operated the western sub-bases.[63]

The American flag was raised at Base Number 18 (Inverness) on February 9, 1918, and at Base Number 17 (Invergordon) three days later. By February, each had received approximately five hundred bluejackets. Murfin remained in command of the bases until the fall of 1918, when he was ordered to the Mediterranean to construct a mining base.[64] After the war he rose in rank to vice admiral, became judge advocate general of the Navy, the commander in chief, Asiatic Fleet, and chairman of the board of inquiry that examined the December 7, 1941, attack on Pearl Harbor.

Mine warfare is an unusually dangerous naval activity. The base commanders feared an explosion like the infamous blast at Halifax. On one occasion, a fire broke out at Inverness in one of the buildings used to assemble mines. Fortunately, the building was empty; otherwise, as one official wrote later, "part of Scotland would have been missing." He also blamed the incident on the carelessness of American sailors who were having "a tea party with girls."[65] Murfin was concerned about adequate medical facilities for the bases and the mine-laying force. The British navy maintained a 100-bed hospital at Invergordon, and a public hospital at Inverness was open to American personnel. Both bases eventually created small dispensaries. The establishment of a large U.S. naval hospital at the nearby resort town of Strathpepper resolved the problem.[66] Strathpepper was one of a number of large U.S. naval hospitals established in Great Britain during the war, nearly all of them in former hotels.

When the United States entered the war in April 1917, the Navy's Bureau of Medicine and Surgery, responsible for the ill and infirm in the service, had no plan to establish hospitals in the war zone. Like the Navy as a whole, its prewar preparations presumed that the fleet would remain in the Western Hemisphere. As early as 1916, Rear Admiral William Braisted, the navy surgeon general in charge of the bureau, inaugurated planning for war. Secretary Daniels recorded that when the chairman of the House Appropriations Committee asked whether he agreed that the surgeon general's requested funding was not excessive, he replied that he did not think so, but

"Surgeon General Braisted is a very wise man," and his estimates should receive serious consideration.[67] The bureau concentrated on building up stocks of medicines and supplies, leaving it to the American Red Cross to prepare a mobilization plan for hospital units. Braisted later argued that because of the serious deficiencies of medical services in Europe, "no reliance can be placed on Allied accommodations. . . . [W]e should be prepared to take upon ourselves the care of our own sick and wounded."[68] He was most concerned about the Navy's lack of enough trained doctors, nurses, and corpsmen, particularly to operate shore-based medical facilities. Following the Army's lead, he worked out an agreement with the Red Cross to create five (later six) base hospital units that would be activated when war broke out. These self-contained units were staffed with doctors and nurses and stocked with needed medical supplies. They were formed in large metropolitan areas, frequently including personnel from the same hospital in the United States who were used to working with each other. In March 1917, the Navy officially accepted these units and enrolled them in the Naval Reserve. All of the units were sent overseas during the conflict, occupying large hospitals in Great Britain and France.[69] Four were established in the British Isles, including a 300-bed hospital in Queenstown, one of 50 beds in London for officers, one at Leith that could expand to 800 beds, and one at Strathpepper of 500 beds.[70]

The Navy's medical services ashore in Europe ranged from large hospitals at major bases to small sick bays and dispensaries at isolated facilities. The Bureau of Medicine and Surgery approved thirteen hospitals for the war zone. All became operational except one at Corfu. In many cases, existing structures were utilized, but approximately two hundred prefabricated buildings were shipped from the United States to supplement buildings available locally. At the end of the war, the Navy boasted four thousand beds in Europe, not including those available in sick bays on many ships at sea and in the numerous Allied hospitals available to American military and naval personnel on a no-cost basis. More than 300 medical officers, 42 dentists, over 200 female nurses, and approximately 1,000 hospital corpsmen and other medical personnel staffed the shore establishments.[71] In September 1918, the Navy assumed complete control of naval hospitals operated by the Red Cross.

Initially Admiral Sims informed the Navy Department that his force did not require additional hospitals,[72] but Dr. Braisted wanted his people in the war zone. He wrote to Dr. F. L. Pleadwell, the head of the medical section in Simsadus, urging him to intercede with Sims: "All we want is authority to send them over and the English and French to give up housing for them, a part or all of an existing hospital if there is such, or a house that could be used as a base hospital."[73] The surgeon general obtained permission to send a hospital unit to Brest, but none went to Great Britain until 1918. On January 14, 1918, Braisted ordered Dr. E. S. Bogert to London to persuade Simsadus and the Admiralty that they needed U.S. naval base hospitals in Great Britain. The Department's decision to deploy mine-laying squadrons and a battleship division to Scotland prompted the surgeon general to make this effort. Both operations might lead to substantial casualties, beyond the capacity of local medical facilities. The Navy set up dispensaries at both Inverness and Invergordon, but the medical officer sent to investigate deemed them inadequate. At Inverness, the dispensary occupied a very old lodging house/pub. "It was indescribably filthy and in poor repair. The place was full of odors resulting mostly from an imperfect sewage system. . . . It was the only place available within the limits of the base." The Bureau of Medicine and Surgery wanted to establish base hospitals at both mine bases but could not find suitable buildings. This difficulty stimulated a decision to locate one at Strathpepper.[74]

In London, Dr. Bogert found that Sims still opposed large hospital units in Great Britain. The force commander knew that the British did not favor their presence, and, more important, he was convinced that a major naval engagement would not take place in the North Sea. Nonetheless, he arranged a meeting between Bogert and Sir William Normar, director general, Medical Department of the Admiralty. Influenced by Sims's attitude, the American doctor was surprised when Normar informed him that he favored U.S. naval hospital units in Great Britain, particularly in Scotland. Bogert believed that the Admiralty's opposition disappeared when he explained that the hospitals would accept British as well as American patients. Also, he assured the medical director that the naval hospital units would support themselves, providing the personnel and equipment needed to function.[75] Sims then reversed himself. In February, Bogert recommended three sites—Strathpepper, Edinburgh, and Queenstown.

Strathpepper was considered an ideal hospital site. Lying approximately midway between the two mine-laying bases, it was located on the major rail line between Edinburgh and the South, enabling hospital trains to carry patients from the Grand Fleet's base at Rosyth to the hospital. Finally, excellent local support was available, the village having been the site of a health resort where for years visitors had come to take the "sulfur, Russian, Turkish, and other invigorating and health restoring baths." In addition to the "hydro-therapeutic" facility, which included a large pavilion used for concerts and entertainments, there were two large hotels and smaller bed and breakfast accommodations. An angry outcry came from local residents who claimed that the local economy depended upon income derived from the resorts. Bogert then agreed to permit civilian use of the baths during designated periods.[76]

Admiralty dockyard workers from Invergordon converted the resort into a hospital. Bedrooms became small wards and operating rooms. A large bathroom was transformed into a dental office. Heating and lighting fixtures and equipment were installed as were new washing machines in the former kitchen of a small hotel. Later, when the first bluejackets arrived, they converted other small hotels into surgical wards and several bed-and-breakfast places into clinics. Their efficiency impressed local citizens. A hotel manager, who thought that the work would take at least a month, was told that it would take only a few days. The sailors explained, "We did one of the largest hotels in London in three days!" Another resident wrote: "They are gems. On Monday they commandeered three large houses and to-day every stick of furniture has been removed and locked up in the hotel cellars. . . . Also the houses have been refurnished by these energetic sailors and everything is ready. . . . Never has the village been so hustled, but the American navy has so far won everyone's heart."[77]

Much to Bogert's dismay and Sims's irritation, the hospital personnel arrived before negotiations were completed to take over the resort. They arrived in February

and were assigned to temporary quarters; the doctors in London and the enlisted personnel in Inverness. The unit included sixty female nurses, the first to be sent overseas
during the war. Bogert did not know what to do with the nurses. The surgeon general
suggested that they be "loaned" to the Army or the British, but he admitted, "I doubt if
[the] unit would ever get them back." They were housed in Liverpool until their quarters were ready in Strathpepper. Equipment did not reach the hospital until April.[78]

Under Bogert's leadership, the Strathpepper hospital continued to expand. By the
Armistice, it had grown from the original 500-bed concept to 1,000 beds, primarily by
using the prefabricated buildings constructed for the Bureau of Medicine and Surgery
by the Bureau of Yards and Docks.[79] Four of these "hutment wards" were assembled
on the resort's lawn tennis courts, much to the chagrin of the tennis-playing members of the hospital staff. Inadequate transportation caused delay. A truck intended
to serve both as an ambulance and supply vehicle was ordered from the United States
but did not arrive until May. The hospital, located a half mile from the rail station,
received patients and supplies in horse-drawn conveyances until the arrival of the
vehicle.[80]

The second American naval hospital established in Scotland was placed in Leith,
a suburb of Edinburgh. The British naval medical director stressed the need to locate
the proposed hospital near the Firth of Forth, the anchorage of the Grand Fleet. The
British army controlled virtually all suitable sites in the area, which included an asy-
lum, a hospital for the deaf and dumb, and "the Lady Hostel," a school for females in
Edinburgh. A hospital in Leith, which the British army converted from a poorhouse
primarily for the use of the Royal Navy, was considered the most acceptable site.
British army officials balked until Sims, supported by Admiral Braisted, agreed that
the Leith hospital, as well as the one at Strathpepper, would admit wounded British
soldiers.[81] Bogert later told the surgeon general how "distressed" he was at the prolonged delay. The *Annual Report of the Surgeon General* for 1919 referred to "lengthy
pourparlers."[82]

Upon assuming control, the Americans immediately acquired a nearby hotel to
provide quarters for nurses and three residences in Leith for additional housing. Prefabricated huts were shipped from the United States but did not arrive before the
Armistice. If the war had continued, the 750-bed hospital would have added an additional 450 beds. Other improvements included laundry equipment, additional sanitation facilities, heating, and lighting fixtures. Although the British left beds and other
medical stores and equipment, a nurse wrote, "We found our equipment more convenient."[83] A traditional two-decker bus shuttled personnel between their quarters and
the hospital. The personnel from the base hospital unit, designated as No. 3, were all
from the California Hospital in Los Angeles.[84]

Queenstown was an obvious site for a base hospital. At first, Sims and Bayly considered local medical services adequate. But the rapid buildup of the U.S. naval force
there persuaded Admiral Braisted to recommend locating a hospital there.[85] Suitable
buildings for a base hospital were not available in town, and Irish opposition precluded placement elsewhere in Ireland. Captain Pringle and the *Melville*'s chief surgeon
agreed that the base required a "convalescent" hospital.[86]

Dr. Bogert made an inspection trip to Queenstown in February 1918 and determined that a 250-bed base hospital was needed rather than a convalescent facility. Sims withdrew his opposition to a hospital in Queenstown because the growth of U.S. naval activities in Ireland was expected to require seven thousand personnel by the end of 1918, and an old estate known as Whitepoint became available. It included a large house on some eleven acres of woodland directly across from the fleet anchorage. Fifty prefabricated buildings were ordered along with other necessary materials and equipment. Local labor was employed to prepare the foundations, lay water and sewage lines, and to construct drainage, plumbing, electrical power plant, and roads. Dissatisfaction with tardiness forced the Navy to use its own personnel. Another reason for delay, according to the officers who supervised construction, was the Irish custom of building "for all eternity." It was supposed to be a mobile hospital, but when ready for use, "nothing could . . . [have been] less mobile. . . . It is, therefore, a permanent institution."[87]

The prefabricated buildings arrived in May, but the hospital was not ready to receive patients until the middle of October. When the hospital staff, a medical unit organized by the Red Cross in Providence, Rhode Island, arrived in October, the buildings were still without electricity. A shipping strike in Cork delayed delivery of machinery for the power plant for more than a month. Oil lamps illuminated the first surgical operations. Until the X-ray equipment arrived, the technician took care of a cow donated to the hospital. His shipmates called him a "third-class cow's mate."[88] The buildings were scattered throughout the grounds among many trees and shrubs. A chapel, a YMCA recreation building, and a brig supplemented the medical buildings. The hospital functioned for less than a month before the start of the Armistice. Later it housed naval personnel from throughout Ireland while they awaited transportation to the United States.[89]

In London, Admiral Sims asked the Red Cross to locate a hospital at Aldford House, the prewar residence of Mrs. Frederick Guest, built on an entire city block on Park Lane. Early in the war, the Admiralty had converted it to a 50-bed hospital. After the American intervention, the Admiralty turned it over to the Red Cross to serve American personnel. Later the Red Cross transferred it to the Navy, primarily for the use of naval personnel stationed in the city, adding twenty-five beds.[90]

In October 1918, the Red Cross established a small hospital and dispensary at Cardiff, the site of the American Navy's coaling base. Three large houses were leased and converted into a forty-bed hospital, quarters for personnel, and an outpatient facility. When the Navy assumed control, a few weeks after its establishment, bed capacity was increased to two hundred. Although it became operational only a short time before the Armistice, the presence of the American naval coal-carrying fleet kept it open until the summer of 1919.[91]

Plymouth, the home of thirty-six subchasers, a tender, and destroyers, possessed a 30-bed hospital in a seven-room house. It included a small operating room, but serious cases were sent to the Royal Naval Hospital at Plymouth. Because of the influenza epidemic, the limited capacity of the British hospital, and anticipated expansion, the

U.S. naval medical officer strongly urged construction of a large hospital, but as in many other cases, the Armistice aborted the project.[92]

Naval air stations in Ireland and England had small dispensaries and sick bays. Eight small stations were established in Ireland at Bantry Bay, Berehaven, Castletowne, Lough Foyle, Lough Swilly, Queenstown, Wexford, and Whiddy Island, and two larger stations were set up in England at Eastleigh and Killingholme. Plans to place a station on the North Sea in Scotland were canceled because of the Armistice. The dispensaries at all of the Irish stations were prefabricated buildings, or "huts," two to four per station, averaging twenty beds each. Eastleigh had a dispensary of twenty beds, but temporary wards were added during the influenza epidemic in 1918. The naval air station at Killingholme, which had been a Royal Air Force station before the United States took it over in July 1918, had about 1,500 personnel at the end of October 1918 but no medical facility of any kind. A doctor and a few corpsmen were assigned there, but no building was available. The Red Cross provided medicines, but patients were sent to various British hospitals, the nearest one about eighteen miles distant. The Red Cross sent a portable hospital to the station, but it was never used because of the Armistice.[93]

In addition to Killingholme, the most limited medical facilities established were at the Kyle of Lochalsh and Fort William. Because civilian medical services were not available locally, the bureau ordered a doctor and two pharmacist mates to establish dispensaries.[94]

The doctor at Killingholme gave considerable credit to the Red Cross for providing medical aid, and Admiral Sims also commended its work with the Navy during the war. When the United States began to send military forces to Europe, the Red Cross was already well established there. The British headquarters were located in London and Dublin. Nine warehouses or depots stocked with medical supplies and equipment were located in England, six in Ireland, two in Scotland, and one in Wales. The London facility occupied a building that covered 50,000 square feet. Workers made thousands of splints, bandages and dressings.[95] Commanding officers and medical officers on ships and stations were permitted to draw medical supplies from the Red Cross. The Navy initially welcomed this assistance, but this access ended in the summer of 1918. According to an officer in the Bureau of Medicine and Surgery, "we had here on this side a dual arrangement which turned out badly."[96] The Bureau of Medicine and Surgery had established medical supply depots in Liverpool and Brest. The Navy Department issued a general order to take over Red Cross hospitals, "which could be used by the Navy and administer them as U.S. Naval Hospitals." In acknowledging this order, the medical officer attached to Sims's staff wrote, "It has been rather difficult to oppose the Red Cross and explain to them that we are entirely able to care for our own, on account of their driving force being based upon an intense, and I presume an unselfish enthusiasm."[97]

On October 8, 1917, American and British naval officials agreed to establish four seaplane stations and a kite balloon station in Ireland. This decision culminated a long series of conferences and negotiations concerning stationing American naval aviation units in Great Britain.[98] Although the British were interested in acquiring American aircraft and parts, they initially did not want to locate U.S. naval aviation units in the British Isles. However, in August, Sims, at the suggestion of the Admiralty, proposed that the United States assume the responsibility for air patrols in the waters off Ireland's southwest coast and cooperate with the British in the patrol of the English Channel. This initiative included the occupation of air stations.[99]

In September 1917, Captain Hutch I. Cone arrived in England to command naval aviation in European waters. He had authorization to establish fifteen air stations in the war zone. A number of locations had been selected already, primarily in France. Cone agreed to others, including five stations plus a second kite balloon station in Ireland. He also assented to an operational base at Killingholme. Later the Navy took over a British aircraft assembly and repair base at Eastleigh near Southampton.[100]

The Southeast of Ireland was selected because at that time American antisubmarine craft operated in adjacent waters and because the British did not place aviation units there. The seaplanes and the kite balloons were to cooperate in ASW operations. The seaplane stations had to be built. They were supposed to locate near the village of Aghada on the east side of Cork harbor in the vicinity of Queenstown; Wexford at Ferrybank on Wexford Harbor; Whiddy Island on the northeastern end of an island in Bantry Bay; and Lough Foyle, nine miles north of Londonderry.[101]

The engineer of the Bureau of Yards and Docks who inspected the sites contended that they would be difficult to build and maintain. Everything had to be constructed—the shipways, hangars, public works, and buildings. Essential building materials and local labor were unavailable, and the area lacked water and sanitation facilities. Admiralty officials agreed, but Sims refused to consider alternate sites. As usual, the solution was to ship the materials and equipment from the States.

To construct the stations, Yards and Docks proposed to send six to seven hundred skilled workers, but the idea was dropped because of labor sensitivity in Britain. A limited number of public works officers and essential personnel were eventually ordered to Ireland to supervise construction. They did not arrive until the preliminary groundwork (grading and construction of slipways, wharves, and foundations) was well underway. This work was done under Admiralty contract, using local civilian labor.[102] The grading began in December-January at the seaplane stations. Civilian workers continued until the summer of 1918, but several strikes delayed completion of concrete aprons, sea walls, and slipways. By summer, American naval personnel assumed much of the work.[103] They erected the buildings, hangars, and other facilities shipped from the United States.

The first such shipment arrived in March. A distribution center was set up in Dublin, using a warehouse "with no roof or floor." It was designated the United States Naval Aviation Supply Base, Ireland. When the air stations became operational, the supply depot was transferred to the Naval Air Station Queenstown (Aghada).[104] In addition to the usual labor problems, the delayed shipping of building materials and equipment forced the postponement of air operations. Prefabricated huts began arriving at the Dublin warehouse in April, but sections were often missing. Pre-assembled roofs often arrived before flooring and walls.[105] Even the tools and construction equipment rarely arrived on schedule. Other unanticipated problems occurred, for example, at the sites of Whiddy Island (Castletownbere) and Aghada. Barges and lighters were needed but nearly impossible to obtain. The builders at Whiddy Island leased two unsuitable local boats, a small speedboat and a motor sailer. A history of the U.S. naval air stations in Ireland revealed that "The greatest handicap suffered by the . . . Stations . . . in equipment was the lack of water transportation."[106] Excavation at Aghada was delayed until steam shovels, concrete mixers, dump cars, and other items became available. An immense steam shovel was found in an abandoned gravel pit. It was dissembled, loaded onto vehicles, and reassembled at Queenstown. Motor vehicles were scarce at all the sites. Several were leased from the Henry Ford plant at Cork; a few others were found elsewhere and used until suitable vehicles could be brought from the States. At Whiddy Island, transportation consisted primarily of carts pulled by horses.[107]

The Bureau of Yards and Docks had little experience in the design of naval air stations, having only one, the Pensacola Naval Air Station. It decided to build stations of similar design, concentrating them in a minimum amount of space and placing them as close as possible to each other in the working area. Each station contained barracks, mess halls, bakery and galleys, storerooms, an administration building, radio hut, carpenter shops, garages, machine shops, pigeon loft, gasoline tanks, piers, magazines, hangars, recreation facilities, power plants, water tank, and sick bay. With the exception of two cottages at Queenstown and two "ancient Irish mansions" at Wexford, all of the buildings for the different stations, ranging from hangars to latrines, were temporaries prefabricated in the United States, shipped to the building sites, and assembled by base personnel.[108] Whenever possible, building materials, furniture, and equipment were obtained in Great Britain, but most of it had to be shipped across the Atlantic.

NAS Queenstown was placed in commission on February 22, 1918, and the other three seaplane stations were opened soon after. At the end of March, small detachments manned all of the stations, but they did not become operational until September.[109] The lack of aircraft, maintenance equipment, and munitions caused this delay.

The U.S. Naval Air Station at Castletownbere (Berehaven) inaugurated operations in May 1918. Commissioning was delayed because a U-boat torpedoed the cargo ship that carried its equipment and stores.[110] Originally a kite balloon station built but evidently never manned by the Royal Navy, it was located near the mouth of Bantry Bay on a golf course. Because a majority of the ships operating out of the bay in 1918 were American, the U.S. Navy assumed control of the station. As Commander P. R. McCracy, in charge of the naval air stations in Ireland, wrote, Castletownbere was "the most logical port in Europe" from which to protect shipping in the Western Approaches.[111] Little new construction was required. Living quarters, administrative buildings, and workshops were available. The Americans erected messing and cooking facilities, a sick bay, and sanitation accommodations. When the U.S. personnel arrived, they built walks, resurrected lawns on the former golf course, and laid out small flowerbeds. The station planned additional changes and improvements, but they were not completed.[112] In July, most of the personnel and the balloons transferred to Brest. A small detachment remained until September, when the station was closed and the detachment was ordered to Queenstown.[113]

American naval air activities in Great Britain were generally confined to Ireland. With two exceptions, little thought was given to the establishment of U.S. naval air stations in England or Scotland. In August 1917, Lieutenant Commander Kenneth Whiting, then in charge of naval aviation forces in Europe, recommended an elaborate naval presence in the war zone, proposing to develop a dozen air stations on each side of the English Channel. Some of them were approved.[114] In his report, Whiting urged bombing of the German naval bases at Heligoland and elsewhere in the North Sea. The Admiralty was attracted to the idea and, after conferring with U.S. naval officials, agreed to transfer Killingholme Royal Air Force Station to the Americans. Killingholme was located in Lincolnshire on the banks of the Humber River approximately twelve miles from the sea. It lay on a landfill in extremely flat land. A twenty-foot rise in the tide pushed water onto the station. Mud flats ran for miles down to the sea.[115] From April 1 until July 20, the Americans and British occupied the station jointly under an RAF base commander. By August 1, six hundred American officers and bluejackets manned the station.

Initially the Americans at Killingholme lived in quarters vacated by British personnel. However, Sims, with Admiralty approval, decided to make it a major naval air station, with enlarged living quarters and other facilities. Supervised by naval engineers from the Bureau of Yards and Docks, the station's personnel erected the barracks and other buildings. Unlike the temporary wooden structures characteristic of U.S. air stations in Ireland and France, the buildings were made of brick. The station's medical officer wrote after the war: "In building the new huts the American civil engineer could not obtain brick layers, and it was considered by the British as quite impossible to build the huts properly. The Yankee genius, however, asserted itself. . . . His plan in brief was to put up the frame of the huts, and then put a portable partition up, against which the seamen brick-layers would lay the bricks, thus there was no chance for error and no necessity for plumb line. When the bricks were laid the portable partition . . . was removed."[116] Nonetheless, there was never enough housing for the American personnel, some of whom had to live in canvas tents. By November, fifty seaplanes flew out of Killingholme. Some two thousand men were stationed there.

Eastleigh, approximately five miles north of Plymouth, was the only other U.S. naval air station commissioned in England during the war. It was selected as an assembly and repair base for the Navy's bombing squadrons in France. Naval aviation officials originally planned to locate this facility in France, but the Admiralty made Eastleigh available. This offer and Eastleigh's proximity to Killingholme and the Dunkirk station led to the decision to situate it in England. Also it was an ideal repair and assembly base because the British had used it as a reception and storage park for aircraft before sending them to France. When the Americans assumed control, hangars, storehouses, and fuel tanks were ready, but they found few accommodations and facilities. For several weeks, the station's commanding officer, Lieutenant George de C. Chevalier, and his staff lived in a hotel and hired two taxis for transportation. The Navy planned to man the station with approximately five thousand personnel, a far cry from the British complement of a hundred. As with the other station projects in the war zone, the Bureau of Yards and Docks assigned a civil engineer to supervise expansion. Much of the construction material was imported from the United States. The builders obtained concrete and five carloads of roofing locally. Temporary tents provided by the Red Cross were set up as barracks, mess halls, and other structures until the completion of permanent buildings. Boilers that were intended for the power plant went down with a torpedoed ship. Fortunately, the Navy found replacements at the Portsmouth Navy Yard and in Scotland. The mess hall designed to accommodate four thousand men was a prefabricated structure of galvanized steel built in 130 hours. The workers buried piles of pipes and wiring. American personnel assembled most of the buildings completed before the Armistice. Furniture and other miscellaneous office equipment remained scarce. Few desks and chairs were at hand and only two typewriters. Benches and furniture were made from aircraft and motor crates. While the base was under construction, the first aircraft arrived for repairs. Tools were scarce with the exception of a lathe, a small screw machine, and a universal grinder. Essential machinery did not arrive until a few weeks before the Armistice.[117]

In the spring of 1918, the Admiralty requested that the U.S. Navy increase its air presence in the British Isles. In April 1918, Captain Cone wrote the CNO's aide for aviation, "I am constantly receiving requests, particularly from England, to take on new obligations; such as the manning and building of airship stations on the Channel, in the North of Scotland, manning more Irish stations, etc., etc., but I have consistently recommended that we have as many obligations now as I can see my way clear to meeting for the next year."[118] The British, of course, were hard pressed, lacking enough pilots and planes. The attrition rate on the Western Front was extremely heavy. In a September 1918 conference to develop plans for 1919, Admiral Sims agreed to establish or assume control over additional air stations along the eastern coast of England and Scotland. The end of the fighting occurred before this measure took effect.

The deployment of U.S. naval units to France and elsewhere in the war zone created a requirement for logistical support, especially to supply shore facilities. Brest became the most extensive American establishment. The Navy also located a large number of air stations along the French coast and sent aviation units to Italy and the Azores. Gibraltar and the island of Corfu provided sites for two U.S. surface bases.

The unexpected end of the war minimized the contributions of many naval installations, but their construction revealed the intense determination of the Navy to make its presence felt in every possible way in the theater of operations. Its experiences during 1917–18 provided considerable guidance during World War II.

U.S. Naval Facilities in France, the Mediterranean, and the Azores

President Wilson's decision to send troops to France committed naval support. The Navy had to provide escorts for convoys to and from France. It also had to establish bases and other facilities in France and in the Azores to maintain vessels and aircraft. Logistical facilities were also built at Gibraltar and Corfu.

France, like her British ally, experienced a deep crisis during the spring of 1917. A massive Allied offensive launched early in April failed and caused much loss of life. Demoralization spawned mutinies in the Army. The French navy, although not demoralized, could do nothing to thwart the German submarine campaign. Most of the French fleet remained in the Mediterranean. A mere handful of small patrol vessels were left to engage U-boats off the Atlantic coast and in the Bay of Biscay. American entry in the war was a godsend. The arrival of Yankee troops revitalized the poilu (French common soldier), and U.S. warships reinforced the hard-pressed French navy.

Representatives of the French navy soon appeared in Washington with a long shopping list. On April 13, a British observer reported various agreements, including the dispatch of six destroyers to European waters "to be based on a British or French port."[1] Admiral Benson preferred a French port, but Sims recommended concentration "as far to westward as practicable." When the destroyers were sent to Ireland, he received no information about a separate decision to base patrol vessels in French ports. "I learned of this by accident."[2]

This omission stemmed from various difficulties. The emergency overwhelmed the Department's small staff in Washington. The Department then viewed Sims simply as liaison with the Admiralty with no responsibility for France; the Department developed policy with no thought to the chain of command. Information passed through foreign naval attachés in Washington, American naval attachés, and diplomats abroad, and through Sims to the Admiralty. While naval officials in Washington negotiated with French representatives in Washington, Commander William R. Sayles, U.S. naval attaché in Paris, conferred with Admiral Lucien Lacaze, the French minister of marine, and Admiral Ferdinand De Bon, chief of the French naval staff (equivalent to CNO), about cooperation between the two navies. On April 24, Sayles urged Admiral Sims to meet with French naval officials. The admiral at first refused, emphasizing that he was not accredited to the French government, but, according to Sayles, changed his mind and met with Lacaze on May 5. Afterward he cabled the

Department that "relations with the French . . . very satisfactory. . . . [U]nanimous agreement that our destroyer force should remain concentrated" off the Irish coast.[3] The French minister of marine already knew that the United States had agreed to base patrol vessels at Brest and possibly at Bordeaux.

Late in April, a second French military mission arrived in Washington with more specific requests. Vice Admiral Paul-Louis-Albert Chocheprat, its senior naval advisor, proposed to send two divisions of six destroyers each and fifty patrol vessels to Brest and Bordeaux. Benson was receptive to the request. On April 20, he informed the paymaster general that the Department had agreed equip these bases. The French would provide land, and the Americans would build warehouses. Enough coal and oil was required at each base to supply a division of destroyers and twelve patrol vessels. On May 8, Admiral Lacaze ordered the district commanders to prepare for the arrival of the American naval vessels.[4]

On May 8, Daniels inquired of Sims, "what is your advice?" This message said nothing about deploying destroyers to the French ports. Sims replied that a presence in France was "desirable," but "it should not require transfer of necessary repair, supply and fuel vessels from mobile destroyer base. Urgent that destroyer force remain concentrated with mobile base." He obviously knew nothing about the decision to send vessels to France.[5]

Indecision in the Navy Department caused the confusion. Admiral Benson favored the French bases and initially agreed to station destroyers and other warships there. He began to hedge because of other commitments, the maintenance of a powerful fleet in the Western Hemisphere, and the dispatch of destroyers to British waters. On June 1, Captain William B. Fletcher was ordered to Brest with a force of eight armed yachts. No destroyers were assigned to his command.

Brest was the logical site for a U.S. naval presence as the largest French naval facility on the Atlantic coast was located there. The French government did not allow transatlantic vessels to use the port. It was in an excellent position to provide escort for convoys bound to and from French ports. The closest French port to the United States, Brest possessed one of the finest protected anchorages in the world. The harbor was deep and encompassed more than five miles of anchorage. During the war, only a limited number of wharves were available, forcing most large vessels to anchor. Brest became a major port of debarkation for the AEF.[6]

The city of Brest was located on the side of a hill flowing down to the harbor. Although Brest became notorious to doughboys camped in tent cities who often referred to it as "mud city," to the bluejackets it seemed attractive. "Never can I forget that ancient harbor with the old town cast into its green rim, the narrow high rock-walled entrance," an officer wrote later. The grandson of J. P. Morgan observed that "The place has a medieval look, very pleasant indeed." Another writer agreed: "All that was needed was to have the people in medieval dress."[7]

When the first U.S. naval vessels entered Brest early in July 1917, few preparations had been made to accommodate them.[8] Early in June, Admiral Lacaze sent an inspection team to Brest, including the American naval attaché Sayles, to determine necessary preparations for an American naval base. The minister of marine ordered placement of buoys and chains in the harbor, construction of a wharf, the building of a railroad to link the new wharf and the coaling depot, the provision of railway equipment, and the installation of electric lighting and water lines. Except for the buoys, no improvements had been completed when American vessels first arrived at the port.[9] The French did what they could to help, but they had little to give. Local officials sometimes procrastinated, worried about losing control in the face of American impatience. Admiral Bayly suggested a solution to Sims: "you ought to take 2/3 of the dockyard over; man it with your mechanics, and hoist the U.S. . . . flag over your 2/3 and the French Admiralty over the other 1/3."[10]

The commander of the first American vessels to arrive, Captain Frank Fletcher, was offered a small temporary facility, a "dilapidated building" on the waterfront. The French turned over several hastily evacuated rooms at the headquarters of the French naval patrol, but two weeks passed before the French provided facilities for stores. On July 19, Sims learned that "quantities of stores are now lying in the weather on the docks at the Navy Yard." A week later, Fletcher received a "comparatively new fireproof warehouse."[11] Shore personnel were housed in private residences. In September, the French government requisitioned the Credit Lyonnaise Building, a large structure that was converted into barracks and offices. After the war, Fletcher testified that "I always looked upon the base, so called at Brest, as more or less a fiction. We had nothing there except the stores that were brought with us or they sent to us."[12]

This description was probably accurate during Fletcher's tenure but not during that of his successor, Rear Admiral Henry B. Wilson. At Wilson's request, lumber, portable buildings, plumbing supplies, laundry equipment, portable latrines, water pipes, fuel oil pumps, motor trucks and other vehicles, wire, cable, hardware, tools, and building equipment were shipped from the United States. In May, the base's supply officer appealed to the French for additional storage, but many cargoes were diverted to other stations and bases.[13]

When Wilson arrived in October, his men lacked adequate quarters. By then a repair tender, the *Panther*, provided berthing for many of the shore personnel. Others were quartered on the yacht *Carola IV*. The yacht had arrived with the squadron in July, but in October she was declared unfit for active service. Her guns and depth-charge gear were removed, and she was converted into an auxiliary berthing ship. Reinforcements continued to arrive and had to be billeted in town. Wilson was also concerned about his personnel who had been confined for various offenses. He reported in November that twenty prisoners were restricted to the *Panther* and a number (exact number not given) incarcerated in a French prison while awaiting trial by general court-martial.[14]

To alleviate the housing (and brig) problems, the French turned over a large part of the "old chateau," one of the oldest fortifications in France, which previously had been a naval prison. When Wilson's staff inspected it, they found underground passages lined with dark, damp cells. Some accounts mentioned torture chambers, human bones, and even a guillotine.[15] Staff members decided to convert the chateau into a receiving and training facility, a prison, and a headquarters for the shore patrol. Considerable repair and replacement made the place habitable. On February 8, 1918, the facility was commissioned as the Carola Naval Barracks, named after the yacht moored at the Chateau's base.[16]

Carola Barracks continued to expand until the Armistice. By then the facility comprised sleeping quarters for more than 3,500 men, "with all the fittings of a proper Naval barracks," wrote Admiral Wilson. A galley, cafeteria, and mess halls were capable of feeding up to five thousand. Other facilities included classrooms, shore patrol offices, a ship's brig, band accommodations, supply offices, storerooms, a barbershop, a tailor shop, chapel, theater hall, and post office. A signal station was established on the chateau's rampart facing the harbor.[17]

American naval officials vainly requested additional buildings for barracks.[18] By November 1918, Wilson had some seventy officers and several hundred enlisted personnel on his staff. He requested a building adjacent to his headquarters, but the owner refused to vacate. French law, unlike British law, did not permit the government to seize property in wartime.[19] Eventually more than a hundred prefabricated "huts" were erected near the chateau and the hospital.[20] Gradually Wilson and his senior staff established offices and quarters in the original building. A French reporter wrote that the noises in the building suggested that "It could be the office of a large bank but in reality it is a room filled with machines that send American fighting men to the war."[21]

Drinking water was a serious problem in Brest as it was throughout France. Few residences or buildings had indoor water; the inhabitants had to rely on public hydrants or wells. Most of the American transports did not carry enough water for the return trip to the United States and had to obtain freshwater in France. Medical analysis dispelled rumors that the water was unfit for drinking. To provide adequate water, the base engineers laid pipes nearly five miles long to a small reservoir. Later the Army Corps of Engineers constructed a waterworks. At the Armistice, the Army was constructing a dam and reservoir on a nearby river, which would have provided some 23,000 gallons of water a day.[22]

Harbor facilities were inadequate, a difficulty that forced the use of lighters and barges to provide logistic support. Cranes had to be shipped from the United States. In August 1918, the *Favorite*, a Great Lakes salvage vessel, arrived at Brest. During the remainder of the war and for months afterward, this ship recovered damaged or sunken vessels in Brest and its vicinity.[23]

Fuel shortages, especially of oil, posed another major problem. At first, the port possessed only a small oil storage tank of seven thousand tons. Wilson's staff estimated that a squadron of destroyers would require at least twenty tons a month, and other oil-burning ships that used the base would aggravate the shortage. In December 1917, the French were asked to approve the construction of four additional tanks, three of 7,000 tons each for oil, and one of 150 tons for aviation gasoline. The French also approved Wilson's request that the tanks be connected to a fueling station established on the breakwater. This measure would allow oilers to pump fuel ashore and provide refueling for destroyers and other vessels. The U.S. Navy would provide the tanks (to be prefabricated and shipped to Brest), the pipe, and equipment for the fueling station if the French would lay the concrete foundations. The

Navy provided labor.[24] At the time of the Armistice, oil tank capacity rose to 28,568 tons.

To provide fuel for coal-burning vessels, the Navy brought in barges and lighters from Great Britain and some from as far as Russia to transport coal to ships in the harbor.[25] A nearby British air station provided airplane fuel.

The Navy Department planned a major expansion of the base at Brest and improvements at other French ports. In October, Wilson requested 9,500 additional personnel. This included 2,500 that would work on the two repair ships in shifts.[26] As in many other instances, the Armistice led to the cancellation of the project.

Wilson wrote after the war that "in selecting ports . . . the interests of the Army and Navy were somewhat different." The Navy's mission was to get troops and stores safely to France, whereas "the Army had to give full consideration to the great importance of distance and means of transportation from the point of discharge to the bases."[27] Nonetheless, the Army dictated the location of naval bases. In May 1917, a joint U.S./French army commission recommended the designation of Bordeaux, St. Nazaire, and La Pallice to serve as ports of debarkation for American troops in addition to Brest. Cherbourg petitioned for this task but was turned down.[28] The U.S. Army also assumed the responsibility of enlarging the designated ports. During the war, the Corps of Engineers built dozens of piers and warehouses, laid hundreds of miles of railroad tracks necessary to receive thousands of tons of freight as well as thousands of doughboys. As General James G. Harbord, who commanded Pershing's Services of Supply, wrote after the war,"The era of American . . . port construction in France was a time of miracles."[29]

In June 1917, the Navy Department ordered Commander John B. Patton, a retired naval officer with considerable experience in construction, to develop a base in the Bordeaux region. The ancient city of Bordeaux, renowned for the wines produced in the region, is located on the Garonne River about sixty miles from the sea.[30] Patton arrived early in July with virtually no instructions from the Department. The Navy Department had no operating directives for establishing bases abroad. The Army wanted a base at Bordeaux, which was a large port. Three of the five major rail systems in France went through the city.[31] Bassens, some six miles south of Bordeaux, became the Army's debarkation depot. Before the war, the French started to develop this site for deep-water vessels. Patton became the port officer at Bassens and initiated the renovation of warehouses and piers. U.S. Army engineers then constructed an elaborate system of piers and wharfs, warehouses, motor parks, a refrigeration plant, and other buildings. It also shipped in large cranes, locomotives, and cars and laid fifty miles of railroad tracks. By the end of the war, the engineers had completed a huge supply depot, including more than 1.5 million feet of covered storage with rail linkage to the hub at Bordeaux.[32]

The Navy was initially undecided about its plans for ports. Sims testified after the war that he recommended a plan to develop a naval base on the Garonne, but it was disapproved.[33] Patton, with Sims's approval, finally decided to develop a small base at Pauillac to support patrol and escort vessels. Pauillac was about halfway between Bordeaux and the ocean, and it had a rail connection to Bordeaux. Patton began to acquire land, lease buildings, contract for coal, and start building wharfs. By November 1917, vineyards, pastures, and local buildings were transformed into a small base with quarters and housing for personnel, a sick bay, mess hall, storerooms, and repair facilities. Pauillac served as a supply and fueling facility for U.S. escort vessels until the end of the war. At the completion of a patrol or escort mission, the naval vessels assigned to the area ran up the river and took on coal from colliers anchored in the stream or coal piles on shore. They also received water, provisions, clothing, lubricating oil, and the like.[34] Pauillac also became the site of a naval air station where personnel off-loaded aircraft components from cargo ships and assembled airplanes.

St. Nazaire was designated as Naval Base (9), but it never attained this status. Located twenty-five miles up the Loire River, it became one of the principal points of debarkation for American troops. The first contingent of the AEF to arrive in the war zone in June 1917 landed at St. Nazaire. Its artificial harbor contained basins created by a series of locks on the river. St. Nazaire had been only a small fishing village until Napoleon III decided to make it into a port capable of receiving oceangoing vessels. In 1917, it was a thriving town of more than twenty-five thousand people with shipyards, sawmills, and two docks in the basins. Nonetheless, it was too small to handle many ships or much freight.[35] Elsie Janis, the famous actress, wrote about the port, "Of all the holes, this is the prize." She and others critical of the port were appalled at the "smells" and the mud. U.S. servicemen, however, generally preferred St. Nazaire. It was not as old as the other ports; it had straight streets; and it had a beach. Sailors and soldiers lining the sides of ships entering the river in the summer months could see people (especially women) on the nearby beaches.[36]

Shortly after the arrival of the first American doughboys, Captain Jackson, U.S. naval representative in Paris, sent an officer to St. Nazaire to coordinate the arrival of transports and cargo ships from the United States, the only naval presence in the port. The AEF assumed control of all American military activities in the port, designating St. Nazaire as a military base and the surrounding region as a "military area."[37] Admiral Fletcher was urged to investigate the situation at St. Nazaire, but he did nothing. In September, Sims sent one of his staff to St. Nazaire and immediately proposed to establish a naval port office there. Commander Frank P. Baldwin was appointed to the position. In June 1918, thirty-three officers and enlisted personnel were assigned to St. Nazaire. The Army, however, still controlled the port. The naval detachment had control of escorts entering the harbor to refuel and ships that brought supplies for nearby naval air stations. During the final months of the war, a 75-bed naval dispensary and a small repair facility were approved but were still under construction at the Armistice. No escort or patrol vessel was based at St. Nazaire.[38]

Approximately halfway between Brest and St. Nazaire was Lorient, the site of an important German submarine base in World War II. With its two deep-water basins, Lorient was (and is) one of the finest fishing harbors in Europe. An obvious place for a naval facility, it was initially designated the site of a fuel depot for escorts, but Admiral Wilson decided to base a squadron of minesweepers there under the command of Captain Thomas P. Magruder. On December 14, 1917, ten of these vessels along with a converted yacht as flagship arrived at Lorient.[39]

Magruder discovered that the French admiral in command at Lorient opposed the presence of American ships, but the matter was referred to Paris, and the French admiral was overruled. In March 1918, Magruder moved his headquarters ashore. A limited amount of office space was available at the French arsenal, but there were no repair facilities and very little storage. Although Admiral Wilson requested prefabricated buildings, tools, equipment, and personnel from the United States in order to organize the base, only a small amount had arrived at the time of the Armistice.[40]

La Rochelle was never designated as a naval base, but a port officer was assigned to La Pallice, the commercial port of La Rochelle. This port consisted of a large but shallow basin entered via a narrow canal that could open only near high tide. The port officer at first was a reserve ensign with a staff of three enlisted men. Facilities included a small room in the corner of a warehouse, supplied by French authorities free of charge. La Rochelle had some importance, however. Two shipyards were located there with dry docks capable of handling the converted yachts. Also, the AEF began using the port to off-load cargo. It received most of the army's fuel.[41] Escorts accompanied cargo vessels in and out of La Pallice. By July 1918, the naval detachment had grown to seven officers and forty-six enlisted men. The bluejackets constructed a building near the docks for the port officer and his staff. No ships were based there, although it was planned to transfer some yachts there in 1919.[42]

The establishment of naval hospital facilities in France stemmed from the presence of a Marine detachment with the AEF and the deployment of naval and air units to protect convoys.[43] As early as June 1917, a small dispensary was situated in Brest. The French turned over a section of a French hospital that had been converted from a school. The Americans were allotted a floor and a half with some fifty beds. French medical officials resisted efforts to expand U.S. usage of the converted school, insisting that sufficient medical facilities were available in Brest.[44] But the small dispensary and French medical services in the city were not sufficient to service the growing American naval presence.[45]

Doctors and nurses from the Methodist Episcopal Hospital in Philadelphia, Pennsylvania, established Base Hospital Number 5 in Brest. Shortly after the United States entered the war, the surgeon general requested that the Philadelphia hospital organize a 250-bed medical unit to serve abroad. Like other base hospitals organized in urban areas, local suppliers provided equipment.[46] The hospital staff arrived in Brest early in October 1917 and immediately went to work in the small dispensary located at the French hospital.

Local authorities, finally recognizing the need for American medical help, searched for a suitable site.[47] Early in November, French authorities turned over a building on the outskirts of the city. Constructed more than fifty years before as a Carmelite convent, the French government acquired it as a convalescent facility. When the Americans assumed control, considerable renovations were necessary to make it usable as a hospital. Nevertheless, the hospital immediately began work while the process of scrubbing, painting, and renovating took place.[48] The general plan was to convert the chapels and large halls into large wards and the former nuns' rooms or cells into small wards. Later two prefabricated wooden buildings were assembled on the grounds, one for surgical use and the other for contagious cases. The religious aspects of the former convent were retained, including "mottos" in the nuns' rooms, for example, "*Sans Moi Vous Ne Pouvez*" (without me you can do nothing).[49] There was no sewage system, and one patient described the toilets as primitive. "Suffice it to say," he wrote, "that in common with many other animals, man is primarily a squatting animal. . . . [S]eats are apparently a luxury."[50]

The hospital was equipped with several surgical operating rooms, pathological laboratory, dental office, pharmacy, X-ray laboratory, mess halls, and galley. The doctors lived in hotels and apartment buildings. A large private residence was converted into a dormitory for the nurses. Enlisted personnel occupied several tents on the grounds. At the Armistice, the hospital was equipped to handle up to eight hundred patients at a time.[51]

As the U.S. naval presence expanded in France, so did the need for additional medical facilities. The Red Cross had large stockpiles of medical equipment and supplies in France as it had in Great Britain. The Red Cross initially supplied the base hospitals and dispensaries. Generally, dispensaries were established where naval detachments or port officers were located, including St. Nazaire, Rochefort, Bordeaux, Nantes, and Lorient. In the summer of 1918, the dispensary at Lorient was upgraded to a base hospital. Three hotels, formerly used to house Belgian refugees, were converted into a hospital. Later a resort/casino on the waterfront was added to the complex. A small pier fronted the resort, allowing patients to transfer from ships in the harbor directly to a medical facility. At the Armistice, the Lorient hospital was equipped to handle 150 patients. The Red Cross and the Bureau of Surgery and Medicine depot in New York City provided supplies.[52]

The dispensary at Bordeaux was on the verge of being converted into a hospital at the time of the Armistice. French contract labor constructed a small building near the docks. Thirty-five beds, an operating room, storerooms, a pharmacy, and a dentist office were housed in this building.[53] The dispensary at St. Nazaire was enlarged to a 70-bed facility by November 1918. A small three-room dispensary in Paris serviced the American naval staff there and personnel on liberty.

Dispensaries were placed at the sixteen different naval air stations in France. Many of the stations had had to use the nearest AEF hospital, but Navy medical officials were reluctant to allow this practice. The Army facilities were overcrowded; they kept incomplete patient records; and they discharged patients or even sent them to the United States without notifying the Navy.[54] The Bureau of Medicine formulated standard plans for prefabricated buildings used as dispensaries, but the structures varied in size depending upon how large the station was. They were subdivided into examination rooms, operating rooms, laboratories, and small wards.[55] Several stations borrowed large tents from the Red Cross to provide temporary shelter. The Moutchie Station used a brick building previously occupied by a French hospital staff. The kite balloon station at La Trinité leased a small hotel for its dispensary. Treguier Air Station took advantage of a French hospital located in the village of Treguier, which turned over five rooms to the Americans. Five days before the Armistice, naval fatigue parties completed a prefabricated building that served as a dispensary. In May 1918, the senior medical officer in France reported that all of the stations but Treguier, La Pallice, and the Northern Bombing Project had fully equipped dispensaries. The Red Cross stocked most of them.[56]

Dunkirk was the site of one of the air stations originally occupied by the Royal Navy. American personnel, including a doctor and a pharmacist mate, arrived in November 1917. Medical equipment was limited to that in "the doctor's personal bag" and items "borrowed" from the French. A room in a "very old and badly used" brick building served as a dispensary. Later a prefabricated building was erected but never used as a dispensary. The Red Cross also furnished tents for the Dunkirk dispensary. Because of constant bombing attacks, it was decided to evacuate sick and wounded personnel. The brick building continued to serve as the medical facility in Dunkirk until the Armistice.[57]

Pauillac, which became the largest U.S. naval air station in France, was staffed in December 1917 with two doctors and two pharmacist mates working in a one room, 5-bed dispensary in the station's former laundry. As with the other air stations' dispensaries, a wooden fabricated building was authorized; it was designed to hold forty-five beds. The new dispensary was inadequate even before it was completed because of the station's rapid expansion. Also the medical establishment there was to become the "central station" for special cases such as burns. In October 1918, the senior medical officer in France recommended acquiring a "lazaretto," a nearby French medical facility for contagious cases. Until this was authorized, the medical officer at the air station negotiated an agreement with the American Red Cross to utilize a small hospital of fifty beds at a chateau some three miles from the station. This hospital had originally been used to take care of French wounded. The Navy provided doctors and corpsmen and the Red Cross provided nurses. Later several tents were erected on the chateau grounds, bringing the total bed capacity to nearly a hundred.[58]

Neither the naval staff at Pauillac nor the Department was satisfied with this arrangement. The chateau owner refused to allow barracks on the grounds and banned patients with tuberculosis, meningitis, scarlet fever, and diphtheria. In August 1918, the Red Cross under an agreement with the senior medical officer organized a 300-bed hospital at a nearby cluster of buildings. The Bureau of Medicine and Surgery was not informed of this agreement. Admiral Braisted sharply reprimanded the senior medical officer: the Department "is not aware of any arrangement with the Red Cross regarding the building and equipping of a hospital at Pauillac." It was "contrary to . . . [Daniels's] attitude regarding duel arrangements of this character." He also informed Sims that additional medical facilities were not needed at Pauillac.[59] The Red Cross backed away, but the joint arrangement at the chateau continued while a new hospital was built on the station. At the time of the Armistice, four large buildings neared completion. Two large stone buildings, originally French military barracks, were turned over to the station medical officer and housed wards. The medical facility increased to 250 beds. By November, the staff included fourteen doctors, three dentists, and a large number of nurses and corpsmen.[60]

The Navy attempted to utilize the large French, British and U.S. Army hospitals scattered throughout France but encountered difficulties with transportation. Each station and base was allocated at least one ambulance, but not all had arrived before the Armistice. The senior medical officer in France also proposed the use of railways to transport patients, but the French government refused priority to hospital cases. On the whole, the Navy's medical facilities in France proved adequate, even during the flu epidemic.

Admiral Braisted wanted to supplement the shore medical facilities with hospital ships. As the admiral told the General Board, "Our idea of a hospital ship is a base hospital for the fleet."[61] In April 1917, the Navy had only one hospital ship, the *Solace*. According to one account, some two hundred Civil War cannons were embedded in concrete as ballast to prevent undue rolling, which led to the quip that she became "the most heavily gunned ship in the Navy."[62]

Shortly after the United States declared war, Braisted requested three additional hospital ships. Congress approved two, and suitable vessels were purchased from a steamship line and converted to hospital ships. *Mercy* was commissioned in January 1918, and *Comfort* in March. Both ships were capable of caring for approximately four hundred patients.[63] Shortly before the Armistice, Braisted recommended the addition of five more hospital ships.

In February 1918, the surgeon general recommended the deployment of the new hospital ships to European waters. He wanted to station one with the American battleship force attached to the Grand Fleet, and the other at Queenstown. Sims considered Queenstown harbor too crowded and that the Grand Fleet and the Scottish mine bases had sufficient medical support. The new hospital at Strathpepper, he wrote, was large enough to care for overflow.[64] However, the Admiralty's medical director, when informed of the idea, strongly favored it. They could serve as ambulance ships, relieving transports needed elsewhere. Sims reversed himself and recommended that they be sent over, but Braisted backed away. These vessels, he told the General Board, are "not to be used principally for transportation of the sick and wounded."[65] Admiral Benson then curtly informed Sims that *Comfort* and *Mercy* would be assigned to the Atlantic Fleet until needed elsewhere as hospital ships.[66]

Ironically, the hospital ships served as ambulances when they finally reached European waters. The flu epidemic of 1918 led Sims to urge their deployment to Brest as quickly as possible: "influenza and pneumonia in our own forces but particularly among troops arriving in transports is exceedingly grave and may develop into a great disaster and result in grave scandal involving both Army and Navy. Many deaths now occurring and many more expected. Immediate drastic measures should be adopted to avoid investigation by Congress with consequences which cannot be foreseen. The arrival of the two hospital ships as recommended would help materially to relieve conditions and would indicate that [the] Navy [was] endeavoring to care for the situation."[67] Three days later, *Comfort* received orders to steam to Brest, and the *Mercy* followed almost immediately. Both ships transported full loads of patients back to the United States.[68]

One of the Navy's most impressive construction projects was the Lafayette Radio Station. When completed in 1920, it was the most powerful in the world.[69] In November 1917, General Pershing urged this undertaking. Along with naval officials he feared that the enemy might cut the transatlantic cables and stop direct communication between Europe and the United States. The Navy was given the project. With French approval, the Bureau of Steam Engineering drew up plans and selected a site at a small isolated village, Croix d'Hins, sixteen miles southwest of Bordeaux. The first contingent of American naval personnel arrived late in April 1918.

The French agreed to prepare the site and build foundations for the towers and other structures. The Navy provided the structural steel, radio machinery, equipment, rolling stock, and material needed to complete the station, all of it shipped from the United States. The French were unable to provide the necessary skilled labor but refused to allow the Americans to bring in civilian workers. The Navy circumvented this decision by enrolling the workers as reservists, many of whom were exempt from normal military service because of age or disability. Supervisors and foremen were commissioned as reserve officers.[70]

French authorities also questioned technical matters and delayed construction. When Commander G. C. Sweet arrived in July to take command, he discovered "the French lack of cooperation." In September, he wrote: "I find that their ideas are rather hazy as to their share of the work to be done. . . . They had made no plans for the buildings and as yet have only an idea of the size of the plant."[71] By September, the Radio Station Detachment had grown to 623 men. Living and working conditions were fairly primitive. They bunked in storehouses and an unoccupied French army barrack. There was no galley. A local restaurant provided food. Water was a problem. Tracks were laid from a nearby mainline, and an abandoned engine was restored to working order by the American personnel, although it remained "temperamental."[72]

A station was finally completed with barracks, sick bay, laundry, recreation building, canteen, supply and administrative buildings, warehouses, carpentry and plumbing shops, all heated and electrically lighted. The four towers, 852 feet high, and the power plant were still under construction at the Armistice, but at the request of the French government, the United States agreed to complete the radio station.[73]

The French military commissions that visited Washington shortly after the United States declared war stressed the need for aviation personnel, especially pilots. A small detachment of 7 officers and 122 enlisted men were ordered to France. Its commander, Lieutenant Kenneth Whiting, agreed to send his men to French training schools. Without Sims's approval, he agreed to construct an American training station and three seaplane stations.[74]

While the Department considered this option, the French proposed a far more extensive program. It called for the Navy to develop twelve seaplane and three dirigible stations to become part of a French naval plan to establish fifty-two bases on the French coast, in the Mediterranean, and Africa.[75] On August 4, the Department agreed to the original proposal, and a month later to a total of fifteen stations "when practicable."[76] Sixteen stations were to be commissioned under U.S. naval control: Moutchie, Le Croisic, St. Trojan, Dunkirk, Pauillac, Brest, Ile Tudy, L'Aber Vrach, Treguier, Fromentine, Arcachon, Gujan, Guipavas, La Pallice, La Trinité, and Paimboeuf. The French agreed to prepare the first four stations, but Captain Jackson, the attaché in Paris, warned the Navy Department not to depend on this arrangement:

"In considering the whole situation in France in the matter of construction, material and personnel it must be constantly borne in mind that the country is practically exhausted in these respects." Jackson's pessimism was well founded; initial dependence upon the French delayed completion. The assignment of engineers from the Bureau of Yards and Docks to supervise construction did not resolve the difficulties.[77]

When it became evident that both the United States and France contemplated an extensive American naval air presence, Sims asked the Department to send all materials from the United States for barracks, shops, slips as well as tools, cranes, electrical equipment, "land and water transportation." He added, "Can this be done?" Sims's concern was justified. Whiting testified before the General Board in January 1918 that "at present there are 50,000 tons of material for seaplane stations waiting for ships to take it over. That is entirely building material, barracks, hangars, motor trucks, etc. No seaplane material has been received in France from the United States, and none will be for some time. The program is way behind what we said we could do some months ago. This has been caused in part by the contractors and in part by our lack of organization to see that this work was speeded up."[78]

The training school at Moutchie on Lake Lacanau was the first station to become operational. The French relinquished the station on July 17, 1917, when Lieutenant John L. Callum arrived with three enlisted men. The site was isolated; only one dirt road offered access, and the nearest railroad was nearly a mile away. In August, French workers began expanding the field and selecting building sites. The CO and his staff stayed at a nearby hotel, and the trainees and enlisted men lived in tents. One officer wrote, "I live three miles from the station in a summer hotel, with no fireplaces—only a candle for light, and not a sign of a bathroom."[79] One of the trainees wrote: "Our life here seems a lot like camp life I've done in the north woods. Our meals are cooked on a fire on the ground. We sleep in tents, bathe in the lake, and wash our own clothes."[80] In October, the first wooden hangar and a "mess hall made out of aeroplane boxes" became available.

At the new year, the station became functional, though it was still unfinished. Because of the labor problem, enlisted personnel took over much of the construction.[81] At the end of February, a recently arrived pilot wrote: "this is the nearest heaven I have been since I left home. Can you imagine real white bread, oatmeal with cream pie, a white tablecloth and napkins, and white clean china plates in France? I know it is hard but add to that real meat . . . and . . . a nice clean bed with spotless sheets."[82] By July 1918, the station consisted of administration, instructional, and engineering buildings, an armory, five hangars, barracks, a sick bay, and warehouses.[83]

On July 31, 1917, Captain Jackson wrote the CNO that "the most urgent need for American aviation in France today is the protection of American transports and commerce arriving at the mouths of the Gironde and the Loire [rivers]. . . . The French are undertaking the establishment . . . of stations [at these sites] and will provide quarters, sheds, shops, run-ways."[84] Le Croisic, eighteen miles from St. Nazaire, became the first of these facilities. It was given priority because of its location. Nearby St. Nazaire, the first port of debarkation for the AEF, quickly became a major shipping center.

Le Croisic was a small fishing village of some three thousand inhabitants located on the Bay of Biscay. Although the actress Janis referred to it as a "charming little fishing village," it was quite primitive by American standards. The station was located on two small islands directly in front of the main street. At high tide, the islands barely remained above water. The tide required the use of derricks to place aircraft in the water and retrieve them. The French provided some structures already on the site and acquired a complex known as the "Quilgare property," several buildings in the center of the town. They were converted into a sick bay, dental office, storehouse, brig, telephone office, and pigeon loft.[85]

A number of German prisoners, who Commander Whiting considered "the best workmen in France," were brought in along with American personnel to complete the station. Additional messing facilities were created from wood salvaged from aircraft and engine crates, a unique American enterprise employed in both France and Great Britain because wood was extremely scarce.

A skeleton crew of American personnel arrived at St. Trojan to begin operations in January 1918. The base was located on a long, narrow bank or island near the mouth of the Gironde River approximately twelve miles from Rochefort. The base was located on "pine covered sand dunes [and] gave the impression of a small sea-side resort, so quiet and beautiful was the spot." The site included a large vineyard.[86] Construction was started in November 1917. French labor cleared trees, and a group of Algerians graded it. After January, U.S. personnel assumed most of the work. Thirty-five bluejackets arrived at the end of January and were housed in a local hotel. They were given picks, shovels, and "a couple of hatchets" and put to work digging a well, constructing latrines, and grading. Concrete for the seawall, seaplane aprons, slipways, and foundations had to be shipped from the United States. Equipment, material, and personnel (later aircraft) had to be brought in by water. At the end of April, most of the barracks, hangars, and other buildings, twenty in all, were completed and personnel moved in from the village. The Algerians and civilian labor were sent away, leaving the bluejackets to erect radio towers, assemble prefabricated fuel tanks, and put in pipes and cables for water and electricity. Construction continued to be hampered by the slow arrival of needed materials. On Bastille Day, July 14, 1918, the station was formally commissioned and began operations.[87]

U.S. engineers often complained that European contractors wasted time by building permanent structures instead of temporary ones that could be assembled and disassembled quickly. At St. Trojan, the buildings were "admirably constructed of bricks made on the grounds: bricks are then covered with plaster."[88] French builders had far more experience with stone and brick structures because of the scarcity of wood. Both the French and the British thought well of the prefabricated huts or buildings that were assembled on virtually every American installation in the war zone. They also liked the wooden and canvas hangars that could be erected in a matter of days. A French naval officer wrote, "In all [U.S. naval] stations the new aircraft hangars were built after an American model entirely of wood; much higher than ours, and in an easily constructed manner since they had to be built nearly all at the same time by the same personnel of the different stations."[89]

Dunkirk was the last of the initial air stations developed in France. The site was selected because of its location across the English Channel from Dover a few miles from the Franco-Belgian border and the important German naval bases in the Ostend-Zee-brugge-Bruges area. The U.S. station was located in the port on a few acres of land. Its narrow waterfront allowed only small hangars and slipways. Working crews were continuously employed increasing the base through landfill. Nearby Allied airfields and the proposed U.S. naval air station lay within bombing range of German bases and large concentrations of enemy aircraft. The Germans bombed the Dunkirk area nightly when the weather permitted, including the U.S. installation at times.[90]

A French construction crew composed of soldiers, Moroccans, and local labor began work on the facility late in July 1917. The usual scarcity of materials and workers led to delays. The first draft of U.S. personnel arrived in October, and by the middle of month they had completed barracks and one canvas hangar.[91] They quickly made the station operational despite a recommendation that priority be given to building bomb shelters. In December, the French provided seaplanes, and on January 1, 1918, the station was commissioned.[92]

The formation of the Northern Bombing Group in the spring of 1918 expanded the presence of U.S. naval aviation.[93] Because seaplanes were not particularly successful in bombing the German bases, the Navy Department agreed to use land-based aircraft. It originally consisted of six day squadrons operated by the Navy and six night squadrons operated by the Marines. Six airfields in the area were requisitioned, and a headquarters was located near Calais. Naval personnel planned the stations and ordered the material from the United States. Because of the danger from bombing, canvas hangars were to be built and the familiar prefabricated buildings were placed on order. Much of this material did not arrive before the Armistice. Whenever possible, officers were temporarily quartered in chateaus and cottages, and enlisted personnel were housed in tents. The British turned over a number of unused hangars from an abandoned airfield. The officer in charge of construction wrote, "most of the work was done before the material arrived, thanks to the cooperation of the French and British authorities and the thieving tendencies of our own men."[94] The repair station was never built in France; it was relocated to Eastleigh in Great Britain.

The Navy established no other stations for land aircraft in France. The others, located on the Bay of Biscay from Brest to the Spanish border, were either for seaplanes, dirigibles, or kite balloons. A majority of them were new and had to be built "from scratch." A few of them, like Treguier and Paimboeuf were already built, and American naval personnel simply took them over from the French. In all of them, however, considerable renovation and modernization took place as U.S. naval aviation stations. Perhaps the most unique naval aviation facility was Pauillac.

Pauillac was the largest and probably the most important naval air station in France. It was located on the Gironde River about halfway between Bordeaux and the ocean. The commission of French and American officers who investigated possible sites for naval bases and station in the summer of 1917 recommended that a supply base be established at Trompeloup, a small village approximately a mile and a half from the town of Pauillac. Trompeloup developed around several docks built before the war to off-load passengers from liners when the tide was too low for the ships to reach Bordeaux. Railway tracks were laid between the village and Bordeaux. Neither the American Army nor Navy made much use of the facilities there until the naval aviation staff in Paris decided that it was an ideal location for a supply depot. In November 1917, Cone persuaded Admiral Sims to agree to establishing the Navy's aircraft assembling and repairing base for France near Trompeloup. He also agreed to its location for an aviation supply center.[95]

Pauillac Naval Air Station was commissioned on December 1, 1917, with the arrival of two officers and twenty-six enlisted men. Although the station took the name of the nearby town, it was actually built in and around Trompeloup. A vacant stone building, originally a steam laundry located near the piers, was taken over and converted into living quarters, mess hall, dispensary, and administrative offices. The officers were housed in a hotel in Pauillac. Additional personnel arrived rapidly, and by the beginning of the new year, some five hundred men were working at the station. The number nearly doubled the next month. To provide quarters and other facilities, the Navy began to purchase or lease buildings in the village. Many of them were demolished to make way for more "modern facilities." Living conditions, as usual, were primitive by American standards. Neither Pauillac nor Trompeloup had a central water supply or sewage system. The senior medical officer wrote that there was one bathtub in Pauillac, adding, "The toilet arrangements of Pauillac are probably as poor as any in France."[96]

As with other stations in the war zone, the Bureau of Yards and Docks drew up the plans for Pauillac. The plans called for some seventy buildings to provide living and working spaces for 1,000 to 1,500 officers and men. Land surrounding the village was purchased. The Navy attempted to secure the land directly from the owner, but the price was "so absurd" that at Captain Cone's request the French government requisitioned it. As one writer remarked, "In less than a year, a complete factory town with sawmills, sail lofts, machine shops, warehouses, hospitals, barracks, garages and a movie theatre sprang up where before were nothing but cow pastures, vineyards and an old Roman grave-yard." He marveled to see "7000 bluejackets bustling about their work, yard engines puffing and freight cars loaded with incoming and outgoing materials. . . . [It] made one think of a busy Navy Yard in the United States." In August 1918, there were five thousand personnel attached to the station, and the number continued to grow until the Armistice. The number fluctuated as Pauillac was a receiving station, and drafts were constantly coming and going.[97]

The increase in personnel necessitated revisions of the original station plans. Additional prefabricated buildings were ordered from the States. Also, portable steel was shipped in for shops and hangars. The French were able to provide some lumber (to be replaced by lumber from the United States) to construct mess halls, warehouses, and other buildings. Until a large mess hall was built, personnel used a former garage. It was so small that there was continuous serving from daylight to darkness. At one time, some fourteen sittings took place. In time, the mess hall was built out of seaplane crates. The French provided ten canvas hangars until wooden ones arrived. By the Armistice, NAS Pauillac had more buildings than any American aviation facility in the war zone but Eastleigh.[98]

Cone's office in Paris urged that a supply ship with refrigerator and deep cold storage capability be based at Pauillac, but Sims refused to recommend this, citing the shortage of supply ships. The Navy then approved establishing an ice and cold storage plant there, but the Armistice was signed before it could be built. Fortunately, the station was able to use the Army's refrigeration facilities in Bordeaux.[99]

Army engineers also laid some sixty tons of railroad track to create a marshalling yard, set up an electric plant and telephone system, put in a permanent sewage system and boardwalks. A 100,000-gallon water tank was shipped from the United States and installed.[100]

From December 1917 until shortly after the Armistice, Pauillac served as a supply depot for naval aviation. Stores and initially construction materials to build the different stations arrived regularly and were distributed. Aircrafts, engines, and spare parts started arriving in April and early May. At this aircraft assembly and repair base, some eighty-two seaplanes were assembled and 322 motors overhauled before the Armistice. Although Assistant Secretary of the Navy Roosevelt was impressed with its size and "feverish activity," he was critical of the length of time it took to get the station operational.[101] Ships continued to arrive with crated planes and stores even after the Armistice was signed. It would be one of the last naval air stations in France demobilized. In early 1919, it was turned over to the Army as a port for returning doughboys and equipment to the United States.[102] Pauillac had one major flaw; it was too far from many of the naval air stations and facilities, especially the Northern Bombing Group. This was a factor in the decision to develop the naval air station in Brest as an aircraft assembly center. Also, Brest was the key port in French waters for the arrival of cargo ships from the United States and their rerouting to other ports.[103]

The Naval Air Station, Brest, was located within the grounds of the French naval base adjacent to the port's inner harbor. At the request of the French navy, Captain Cone agreed to use the station for both seaplane and kite balloon operations. As with many of the air stations in France, private contractors were originally employed to build the facility. Because of labor problems and their inability to obtain material, the work was eventually taken over by the Americans, as at most of the stations. The first personnel assigned to the station reported in November 1917. Construction was underway, with most of the work being done by German prisoners of war and hired Moroccans. They were employed to build roads and lay the foundations for hangars and other buildings. Since concrete was not available, stone was broken up and used for the foundations. Temporary barracks from crates and canvas tents were used for personnel until lumber and prefabricated huts could be shipped from the United States. The French navy did what it could to get the station operational, providing, for example, hydrogen gas pumps and other equipment needed for the kite balloons.[104] Four concrete block and stone barracks were built by the French and American naval personnel. Nonetheless, construction was delayed not only because of the material problem but also because the bluejackets were frequently called away to help unload transports and cargo ships in the harbor, as well as to other construction projects.[105]

In August 1918, the French navy canceled the contract with private contractors. At that time, only ten buildings had been completed, although a number were under construction. U.S. personnel, despite being drafted for various projects, did complete two seaplane hangars, two radio towers, radio house and power plant, bomb storage building, machine shops, dispensary, galley, mess halls, and aprons. By November 1918, the station had living quarters for more than a thousand officers and men.[106] In July, while the station was still far from completed, flight operations for both seaplanes and kite balloons commenced. In September, station personnel began assembling aircraft, and by the Armistice more than sixty were operational and flown to other stations. One of these stations was NAS Ile Tudy a few miles south of Brest.

The naval air station at Ile Tudy began flight operations much sooner than Brest, partly because it was smaller and partly because it was an established French air station with two canvas hangars, radio tower and hut, and living quarters in a converted sardine cannery known as "usine Beziers." In a report on the station evidently prepared by naval aviation headquarters in Paris, it was stated that the French station was so small as to "be practically inoperative." American naval personnel began arriving in late November 1917 and immediately were put to work assisting the French contractor in completing the station.

By March, a number of wooden structures had been erected including a hangar, a storehouse, repair shops, and offices. Several stone buildings were built and used as garages and a storehouse for oil. The Americans considered the former sardine cannery "primitive" living quarters, so improvements such as indoor heads, water, and electric lights were installed. Finally, concrete aprons and launching ways connecting the hangar with the water were completed. The station became operational in April with aircraft supplied by the French.[107]

L'Aber Vrach was the most isolated of the U.S. seaplane stations in France. It was located on the small (sixteen acres) rocky island of Ehre at the southern entrance to the English Channel, some twenty miles from Brest. Although a railroad and highway ran along the coast, the island itself could be reached only by horse-drawn vehicle at low tide and by small, shallow draft boats at other times. The French government commandeered the island and turned it over to the American Navy but made no effort to plan or construct the station. It was built entirely by U.S. Navy personnel. The first detachment arrived early in February 1918 and immediately began grading, building roads and a boat landing. Until living quarters could be obtained, the bluejackets lived in the village of L'Aber Vrach and were ferried to and from the island in local fishing boats. Personnel moved to the island in March when twenty-three tents on loan from the Army and three portable French barracks were carried over on small boats and assembled. Later a few prefabricated barracks were erected.[108] A pier, walls, and several building foundations were built of stone, collected and hauled to the construction site by local women and children driving small two-wheeled carts. Lumber, concrete, and other materials needed for the station were unloaded from cargo ships at Brest and carried to L'Aber Vrach by a narrow-gauge railroad. The railroad had only one track with a small engine and cars running in one direction every other day.[109] There were no radios so signalmen on the mainland notified the station when material arrived. Transport on the island consisted of wheelbarrows and a few of the carts that came across at low tide. Much of it, however, including rocks, had to be hand-carried. Later a few motor trucks were brought across by lighter.

In July, various buildings including barracks were still under construction. Unfortunately, there were not enough tents or living quarters, and often newly arrived personnel had to sleep outside. "Our hammocks were spread on the rocks instead of being strung up," one former sailor recalled. Freshwater was not available on the island and had to be brought from the village in 55-gallon oil drums. Later, two 1,200-gallon steel tanks were placed on an old barge that periodically filled up at the village and then was towed to the island. Captain Taussig described a visit to the station in August: "They [American personnel] are doing all the work and have already much to show for their labor. Grading, building roads, and concrete sea wall for landing, barracks, etc. Two hangars, each capable of holding five large bombing machines are completed. The men are living in tents until the barracks . . . are completed. But they have a complete village where I noticed signs on various tents, 'shoe maker,' 'tailor,' 'post office,' etc. Their theater and recreation hall are run by the Y.M.C.A. in a long tent. . . . The men work hard and appear in the best of health and spirits. There are no eight hour work laws or labor unions to hamper them."[110] In October, signalmen completed running telephone and telegraph lines from the station to Brest. The station was still under construction when operations began in September. It was virtually completed shortly before the Armistice.[111]

NAS Treguier was located north of L'Aber Vrach, at the junction where two streams merged to form the Treguier River, approximately four miles from the ocean. The site was a difficult one for seaplanes. The river was narrow, winding, and shallow at low tide with rocks and mud banks scattered along the channel. The site was bounded by hills, and the frequent rain, fog, and low-lying clouds made flying almost impossible during the winter months. Yet the French established a station there in 1917, probably because of a narrow-gauge railroad that crossed the river there. Later the United States was asked to take the station over. The first Americans arrived in the middle of August 1918, one officer and three enlisted men. They found four small hangars, a few buildings, and an unfinished slipway and aprons.[112] Although additional drafts of men arrived, little construction work could be done until material was received. Six of the prefabricated "Dixie" barracks were completed in October as well as a mess hall and recreation center, but officer quarters were not ready for occupation until the day before the Armistice was signed. The hangars were enlarged, and aircraft arrived in September, but no operational flying actually took place during the war.[113]

Fromentine Naval Air Station was located on a bleak, desolate island in the Loire estuary, some thirty-five miles from the nearest town of any size. There were a few inhabitants on the island and a small village on the mainland directly across the half-mile stretch of water. The site was selected for a naval air station because of its proximity to the coastal convoy route between St. Nazaire and Brest and because the water between the island and the mainland was sheltered and suitable for seaplanes. The station was surrounded by water on three sides with a wire fence dividing it from the remainder of the island. The station was built entirely by U.S. naval personnel, starting in February 1918 and continuing until the Armistice. Initially the personnel lived in the mainland village, commuting to the island by a small steamer. In March, they were moved to temporary quarters—tents—on the island. The bulk of the building materials were brought from the United States. Transportation was a problem here as elsewhere along the French coast. Materials and personnel were carried by a narrow-gauge railroad to the village of Fromentine, and then usually hauled by wheelbarrows from the railroad station to a dock, loaded on small launches as well as the steamer, and carried out to the island. Some French labor, mostly elderly men and young boys, were employed to help in transferring materials to the dock. Hangars, storehouses, seven prefabricated barracks, mess hall and galley, and a hospital were built, along with roads, walkways, concrete aprons and slipways. The first seaplanes were delivered in June, but operations did not begin until August.[114]

Concern about U-boats using Spanish ports led to the decision to establish a seaplane base near the resort town of Arcachon. Located on the Gironde River, the town had a long association with the United States going back to American privateers using it as a supply base during the Revolutionary War.[115] The station was not actually located in the town but some eight miles farther downstream, on a sand strip that separated a large body of water known as the "Bassin d' Arcachon" from the Bay of Biscay. The station was built on the eastern side of the "Bassin" because the water there was sheltered and ideal for air operations. The French Ministry of Marine contracted on behalf of the U.S. Navy for the station's construction. In early November 1917, ground was broken. Construction material and fuel were off-loaded at the small port of La Teste, a few miles down the river, and transported by small, flat-bottomed sailing vessels to the seaplane station. The initial work of leveling, excavating, and filling was done by French laborers ("old men, women, and boys"); later a workforce of Singhalese arrived. In January, the Singhalese went on strike, delaying construction. U.S. naval personnel were then brought in to continue the work. The German spring 1918 offensive virtually stopped the shipment of building materials to the site, and very little work was done until July.[116] Personnel lived in resort hotels in the town and commuted to the station site until barracks were completed. Although the station was far from being completed, it was placed in commission in June. In August, the first hangar and slipway were ready and the first aircraft arrived, but initial flights were not made until October. On November 10, construction on the station was discontinued. At that time, a road linking the town across the island (covered with pine needles to provide traction), electrical lights, and water lines had been installed, and a galley, two mess halls, two barracks, an administrative building, storehouses, pump house, armory, two hangars and slipways, and a hospital had been completed. Still under construction were more barracks, two bathhouses, chief petty officer quarters, carpenter shop, laundry, post office, magazines, radio tower, commanding officer's house, officer quarters, sewer system, and a pier.[117]

Arcachon was also the location for a dirigible station. In November, Admiral Sims approved four dirigible stations to be located on the French coast at Arcachon, Paimboeuf, Rochefort, and Brest.[118] Later Guipavas was substituted for Brest as a station site. The Rochefort station was never built. Instead a kite balloon facility was established at La Pallice near La Rochelle, and a second kite balloon located at La Trinité. Each of the airship stations was to house a complement of four lighter-than-air craft that would be used to escort convoys. The French were to provide the airships.

The Arcachon dirigible station was actually located at Gujan, a few miles from the seaplane station. The station was never completed because of the lack of materials and personnel. There were never more than sixty men stationed at Gujan at any one time during the war, and usually half of that number. As at the seaplane station near Arcachon, all materials and supplies had to be brought in by small boats. A few roads were built, concrete foundations laid, and steel trusses anchored, but buildings, including prefabricated barracks, were never built. The men lived in tents. The equipment and tanks for the hydrogen were installed and some of the piping laid, but the Armistice ended the work. No dirigibles arrived, and in fact the station was actually never commissioned.[119]

The dirigible station at Paimboeuf near the mouth of the Loire did become operational. This was primarily because it was a functioning station under French command when turned over to the U.S. Navy. The first draft of Americans arrived in January 1918, but the station was not commissioned until March. The station consisted of a steel-skeleton canvas-covered hangar, a hydrogen gas plant, workshops and storerooms, a water storage tank, a radio shack with two eighty-foot towers, five barracks, officer quarters, galley, mess hall, brig, and shower building. A portable gasoline generator provided limited electricity. Although construction materials and prefabricated barracks were received on the site, no additional buildings except one to house the YMCA were built. Naval personnel with the help of a few French workers did construct a drainage system, roads, two piers, and a general upgrade of the facilities. The foundation for a second hangar was laid, but the hangar was never erected. Three dirigibles were turned over to the Americans, and the station commenced operations in June. By the Armistice, there were some five hundred officers and men stationed there.[120]

Guipavas, just north of Brest, was the site of a third dirigible station. The site selected was adjacent to a French dirigible station. By so doing, the French landing field, as well as equipment and some facilities, could be shared. Construction started in March 1918 but was still going on in November. Work was to be done entirely by American personnel. The first draft arrived without hammocks or sleeping bags and had to be housed with residents in the local village until tents could be obtained and erected. One of the prefabricated barracks arrived in late March and was assembled in a turnip field. In fact, the site was covered with dense underbrush, a few small gardens, and crisscrossed with hedges. The entire site was leveled, and then the building of roads and hangar sites commenced. The absence of proper equipment to erect the immense dirigible hangars (80 feet high, 60 feet wide, 600 feet long) delayed completion. On one occasion, two men were killed when temporary trusses collapsed. Naval working parties from the Brest Naval Air Station were frequently trucked in to work on the station. Nonetheless, as with the other U.S. naval air facilities in France, insufficient personnel and workers, as well as construction materials, so delayed construction that the station never became operational.[121]

Neither of the two kite balloon stations became operational. The La Pallice station was located near the port of La Rochelle in what was once a large wheat field. Construction was delayed until June 1918 to permit the wheat to be harvested. A small detachment of American personnel arrived in June and immediately erected a "Dixie" barrack. In the following weeks, additional barracks and buildings were erected, but as of November 11, the building to house the hydrogen gas equipment was still not completed. The station was never commissioned.[122]

The kite balloon station at La Trinite-sur-mer was located near a small fishing village on the Bay of Moroihan. The site was some six miles from the nearest railroad with only an unimproved dirt road linking it to the site. Construction began in March, and the station was ready for operations two months before the cessation of hostilities. As with the other stations, construction was delayed because of the lack of materials, equipment, and workers. Adequate construction tools and equipment were so scarce that large dishpans, taken from the galley stores, were used to carry sand from the beaches to roads and paths. Later wooden wheelbarrows, several shovels, picks, and two sledgehammers were obtained on loan from the village of Carnac. The French navy provided one motor truck to haul materials and supplies from the railroad. Fortunately, the French government was able to lease five summer beach cottages for use as barracks. A few civilians and Bulgarian prisoners of war did most of the actual construction. These prisoners along with a few American enlisted men erected a steel-framed balloon hangar and installed a plant for the production of the hydrogen gas. They also built an administrative building that housed a small medical dispensary. Additional structures, however, were never built. The first balloon was inflated in the middle of October. Several practice flights were made, but no actual operations were carried out.[123]

In August 1918, Captain Cone advised Admiral Wilson that no additional stations in France were to be established. The French minister of marine agreed. The American aviation commander would later complain that despite having to conform to French construction policies and procedures, inadequate labor and materials, as well as inexperienced officers to command the various stations, the Navy had actually built beyond its ability to equip. Not all of the stations were operational before the Armistice, yet those that were in many cases lacked aircraft or the necessary equipment, spare parts, and supplies to begin flight operations. Although the French, as Turnball and Lord wrote, were far too optimistic in their confidence about building the naval air stations, the construction delays were caused as much by the Americans' inability to deliver the needed materials as by the French.[124]

During the war, American naval forces were deployed also in Russian waters, the Azores, Gibraltar, and the Mediterranean. No bases or land facilities were established in Russia, where the British were depended on for logistical support. To some degree this was true at Gibraltar as well, where U.S. Naval Base Number 9 was established. As Admiral Niblack, in command of U.S. Naval forces at Gibraltar, wrote after the war, when the first American naval vessels arrived at the "Rock" in August 1917, there was virtually no available land to establish a separate base. Gibraltar is located on a narrow promontory near the southern tip of Spain. As the gateway to the Mediterranean, it has traditionally been strategically important. The British seized it in 1704 during the War of the Spanish Succession and obtained it by the treaty ending that war. It later became a Crown Colony and a naval base for the fleet. To provide shore facilities for the Americans, the British turned over to them an unused seaplane hangar in the Royal Dockyard, really a large warehouse. This became the American base, with everything from quarters for officers and men, galley, medical and dental dispensaries, to storerooms and repair facilities located there. The American commanding officer and his staff were allotted four rooms in the Tower Building, where other Allied officers were located. The British leased a house for Niblack's quarters. Unfortunately, it was unfurnished, and until furniture could be shipped in from the United States, he resided in a hotel. The British army later turned over to the Americans the Wind Mill Hill Barracks, which could house up to five hundred men. Finally, a small storeroom, a magazine for ammunition and one for depth charges were situated in the fort's casemate.[125]

U.S. medical facilities evolved from a sick bay in the seaplane hangar to a leased private residence known as "Glen Rocky." Until this dispensary was fitted out, the British naval hospital cared for American patients. The house had nine rooms, a kitchen, porch, patio, and outhouse on one-and-a-half acres of land. Extensive renovations were carried out, initially by Spanish workers and then, when they proved unsatisfactory, by Royal Engineers. The house was rewired for more electrical input, additional indoor plumbing for bathrooms and showers, temporary roofs over the porch and patio for conversion into a laboratory and a mess hall. When renovations were completed, the house would accommodate some forty patients. As the base expanded, the number of patients increased to more than forty. Six tents were erected on the ground. The chief medical officer recommended the creation of a hospital to double the patient capacity. This, however, was not done because of the end of hostilities.[126]

Base Number 25, the submarine chaser base established on the island of Corfu, was the most troublesome shore facility in European waters to support logistically. The distance from the United States, the presence of French, Italian, and British forces there, and the island's economy, primarily olive oil, all added to the difficulty in supporting thirty-six chasers, one tender, as well as shore personnel. The Allied Naval Council approved deploying the initial force of American subchasers to the Eastern Mediterranean in order to reinforce the Otranto Barrage.[127] In April 1918, Captain Richard H. Leigh, in command of the subchaser detachments in European waters, toured the area in search of a suitable site for a base. Leigh examined a number of ports including Brindisi, Bari, Taranto, and Gallipoli, before selecting Corfu. Although there was no suitable port available on the island, its proximity to the barrage made it acceptable for a base. The French and British turned over the use of Govino Bay for the subchasers. The British had used it as a temporary submarine base, and the French had an airfield there of which they agreed to allow the Americans to use part for shore installations. Leigh wanted more land adjacent to the airfield, land that was planted in olive trees and under Greek ownership. He was told that "in taking [the] land we would have to rent the olive trees and . . . olive trees had almost as many different owners as there were trees." Later he fortunately was able to negotiate with one of the owners who acted for all of them. She agreed to let the Americans use the land at no cost provided they did not damage the trees. In return, a pier that the Navy planned to have built in the bay would be donated to the owners when the base was demobilized.[128] The British turned over land on the northern side of the bay's entrance, which included a house used as a recreation facility by the sailors. The house continued to be used for recreation and as a mess by the American subchaser officers. A large warehouse was leased in a nearby village. Leigh wanted to use local labor to construct the pier and a road from the base to the main artery leading to the town of Corfu, but because he considered the quoted price too high, American bluejackets did the work. Repair facilities were nonexistent. Fortunately, the tender *Leonidas* arrived with the subchasers. Later two marine railways were shipped out but arrived too late to be of service. Leigh requested prefabricated buildings for barracks, dispensary, etc., but only three arrived in time to be erected before the Armistice. They were used as a hospital. The Bureau of Medicine and Surgery had approved the construction of a hospital on Corfu, but demobilization of the base after the Armistice made it no longer needed. Canvas tents were scattered among the olive trees for barracks, galley, mess hall, recreation, and stores. A British correspondent was most impressed with a galley stove and oven made from boiler iron by the seamen. Leigh's aide cabled Simsadus in May: "Cannot expect . . . help here, everybody has own building project. Advisable send everything from home." Yet, it was not until October 20 that the first ship loaded with construction materials and stores arrived from the United States. The cargo included lumber, cement, antiaircraft battery, three prefabricated buildings, lubricating oil for the chasers as well as spare parts.[129] As the base began to take shape, Leigh recalled in his memoirs, "The people around Corfu stopped talking of Govina [*sic*] Bay, and by now the topic of latest interest was 'doings at American Bay.'"

No bases were established in Italy, but a naval hospital was placed in Genoa and an air station at Porto Corsini. The naval air station's commanding officer, who had a sense of imagination, named the streets and buildings after places in New York City. The officers' quarters were on Riverside Drive; the enlisted personnel's barracks on the Bowery; the pay office on Wall Street, and the mess hall the Winter Gardens.[130] The U.S. Navy also had a training detachment stationed at Lake Bolsena and planned to commission a second air station at Pescara on the Adriatic. This station, however, was never completed and commissioned.

Bolsena was the site of an Italian naval air station. A small detachment of four officers and twenty-eight enlisted men were ordered there in February 1918. They lived and took their meals with the Italian personnel, and in general were supported by the Italians. In fact, in accordance with an agreement with the Italian government, the U.S. naval personnel were to be supplied with everything but food and clothing. No separate facilities were built or proposed for the Americans.[131] NAS Porto Corsini was commissioned in July 1918, when a contingent of 331 officers and men arrived there. The station was located some ten miles south of Venice. They were quartered in five brick barracks with no electricity and a primitive system of heating. The same was true of the sick bay, where minor operations were performed under kerosene lamps. The base also lacked proper sanitary facilities. Nicknamed "Goat Island City" by the

American personnel, few improvements were made either by Italian authorities or the U.S. Navy.[132]

At the request of the Navy, concerned about the prevalence of venereal disease among the armed guard of the numerous merchant ships that visited Genoa, the Red Cross leased a large private villa in the summer of 1918 and converted it into a 50-bed hospital. The villa had twenty rooms that were converted into wards and operating rooms. Other renovations included the installation of plumbing and sanitation facilities with a bathroom and toilet on each of the three floors, a laundry, and a new centralized heating plant. In September, the hospital with all of its equipment was turned over to the Navy. The staff was quartered in the hospital itself, but the chief medical officer admitted that if the number of patients increased, the personnel would have to be relocated outside the hospital. This did not occur, however, before it was returned to the Red Cross.[133]

In the spring and summer of 1918, the Allied Naval Council focused more and more of its attention on the Mediterranean. Among other decisions was one to establish new minefields similar to the North Sea Mine Barrage that was supposedly so successful.[134] Various locations for the mine barrages were proposed. Allied naval officials meeting in Malta in August agreed on two, one in the Strait of Otranto and the other in the Aegean. The Department approved the projects in September along with an agreement that the United States would supply the mines and the minelayers. A mine base would also have to be established. A number of possible locations were considered, including Corfu, Argostoli, Bizerta, Toronto, Petras, and Piraeus. Rear Admiral Joseph Strauss, in command of the North Sea Mine Barrage and the head of the American delegation to the Malta meeting, preferred Corfu, but Sims's Naval Planning Section recommended Bizerta in the French colony of Tunisia. Although the base would be 580 miles from the Otranto barrage and nearly 800 miles from the proposed field in the Aegean, the Planning Section considered this disadvantage was offset by the presence of repair (including dry docks) and fueling facilities and the area including the harbor was safe from air raids and torpedo attack. Sims accepted the Planning Section's recommendation.[135]

Unfortunately, the Planning Section got its information from reference works and data provided by the French. Captain Orin G. Murfin, who designed the U.S. mine bases in Scotland, was sent to Bizerta to examine local facilities and plan the new base. In October, he wrote Sims: "When I think that this place was selected for our work because of the '*Excellent Facilities*,' I have to laugh, serious though it is. There are absolutely no facilities of any kind, either ashore or afloat, and we must be prepared to go it alone, without any assistance from our French allies. Such a thing as a pier doesn't exist excepting at the dockyard, and that is so congested as to be out of the question for our purpose. . . . The place is impossible for us. Of all places that the local naval authorities had picked out for my inspection, the one I selected is the only one at all possible, and it lacks a great deal to make it suitable." It was apparently an abandoned airfield with a large hangar and a few small buildings. He also wrote that there was a shortage of water and fresh provisions; "No railroad rolling stock available—all handling of materials both from [mine] carriers and layers will have to be done by hand."

"The town needs cleaning and overhauling. . . . [I]*t doesn't possess a bath room*, and this game of bathing in a basin is growing irksome." He later admitted that the traditional substitute for a bath, "perfume," had been used.[136]

Nonetheless, the base was to be built there. The proposed base was to accommodate some one thousand men and the necessary facilities to assemble and house thirty thousand mines as well as a squadron of minelayers. Sims ordered Admiral Wilson in Brest to detail a construction force of some three hundred men as well as materials and tools from Pauillac NAS to Bizerta. Sims gave priority to the project. In order to save time he determined to secure the building materials, tools, and equipment in Europe, as much as possible from the bases in Scotland. The minelayers would also come from the force based at Inverness and Invergordon. The mines would have to be shipped from the United States. Material started arriving in late October, and by November 3, Murfin could inform Sims that the pier was nearly completed. Six days later, however, he was instructed to discontinue all work on the base. Two ships loaded with materials were turned around, and everything already at the site was turned over to the French.[137]

Quite early in the war, when it was apparent to naval officials that a coaling station was needed for the many coal burners in the fleet that were unable to carry enough fuel to cross the Atlantic, the strategic importance of the Azores became obvious. As Captain Pratt, assistant chief of operations, testified after the war: "We had from the very beginning made a study [of] . . . the Azores. . . . For the small craft we were endeavoring to send across . . . there was the necessity of providing a place in mid-ocean from which these craft could refuel. . . . If Portugal, as a cobelligerent, had not been in this war, it would have been for us a tremendously difficult problem to have gotten any of the yachts, any of the subchasers, any of the tugs, and a large percentage of the destroyers across, for the simple reason that they did not have the steaming radius to cover the 3,000 miles of ocean lying between us and the British shore."[138] However, what started as simply a coaling depot would evolve into a full-fledged naval base. The island was often referred to as the halfway stopping place between the United States and Europe. St. Michaels, on which Ponta Delgada was located, was some 1,200 miles from Newfoundland and 800–900 miles from Portugal.

There was the very real possibility that Germany would attempt to seize the islands or at least establish a submarine base there.[139] In May, Washington officials considered this a possibility, and even Admiral Sims recognized the threat. In July, he recommended that one of the older battleships and "perhaps one or two small auxiliary craft" be sent to the Azores "to prevent the use of those islands as a base."[140] The CNO was so concerned that he ordered destroyers, a submarine flotilla, miscellaneous small craft, and even a squadron of Marine aircraft to Ponta Delgada. On July 10, four days after the American consul in Ponta Delgada informed the State Department of the U-boat bombardment, Admiral Benson ordered a division of destroyers to the islands.[141] Even before the destroyers left the United States, Sims and the Admiralty were urging that the destroyers (750-ton coal burners) should be ordered to Brest, not Ponta Delgada. This was, of course, in line with the force commander's insistence that all destroyers should be concentrated in European waters. When Admiral Mayo arrived in London at the end of August, he was persuaded to recommend to the Department that submarines should be based in the Azores; that they would be equally if not more effective against enemy submarines than the destroyers. Finally, he came to agree that the destroyers were desperately needed for escort work. The CNO approved. Benson, however, remained concerned about the islands.[142]

The islands were on the southern flank of the important shipping routes followed by the transports carrying the American doughboys to Europe. Washington officials throughout the war feared that a German submarine would sink one or more of these transports with heavy loss of life. U-boat activities in the waters around the Azores increased these fears. As Admiral Sims mentioned in instructions to the U.S. naval commander there, a "primary reason" for the basing of a force there was to prevent the islands from being used by German submarines. Initially the question was, which harbor should be used or should American forces be dispersed among the islands? The Azores were comprised of nine islands. Ponta Delgada, on the island of St. Michaels, was selected because it had the most protected harbor. Later the CNO questioned Sims about the possibility of basing some naval forces in the Madeira Islands, but the force commander, supported by the British Admiralty, said they were not needed as the forces already in place were adequate.[143]

The Department informed Sims that the Azores and the waters to the Canary Islands came under his command. As the force commander later discovered, this was only partly correct. Benson's concerns resulted in much of the direction coming out of Washington. For example, the decision to base a force of Marines there originated in the Department. Sims was even told what naval units were to be assigned to the Azores. On September 5, 1917, the CNO informed him that "All forces [are] under your general instruction but we do not wish *Whipple*, *Truxtun*, and *Atlantic* moved from this general area." Sims argued that destroyers, including these three, should be concentrated in British waters and that a submarine flotilla would be adequate to combat U-boats in the islands. In time, the destroyers would be redeployed in European waters and their place taken by a gunboat and two armed yachts. The Department was willing to do this because of the presence of the submarines and a Marine air squadron.[144] The submarines were old, small, with fixed periscopes, and simply were not equipped to operate in those waters. The aircraft were not much better. In July 1918, the assistant naval secretary visited the island and wrote Daniels: "We have there a gun-boat with a cracked shaft, two old yachts which cannot go to sea and a sailing ship full of oil. On shore we have a Flying Detachment of the Marine Corps and four old type planes of which only two can occasionally get off the water."[145]

In February, the First Marine Aeronautic Company landed in Ponta Delgada with some one hundred men and ten aircraft and few spare parts. They were obsolete (one type was actually a trainer) with a two-hour cruising radius and no means of communicating with the shore. One by one they became inoperable. Later six somewhat larger flying boats were sent there. Their base was in an old quarry near the ocean where the Marines erected tents.[146]

Although Portugal was an associate of the United States in the war and contributed troops to the Western Front, the conflict was most unpopular with the Portuguese people. The government before and during the war years was in a state of turmoil with revolutions and civil war leading to the overthrow of several governments. Government officials in Lisbon, who feared that the United States had more interests than just establishing a temporary naval base there, looked upon American activities in the Azores with some concern. They were well aware that a large number of Azoreans wanted the islands to be annexed by the United States. Even some American officials favored this.[147] What compounded the situation was the apparent failure of the United States government, particularly the Navy, to inform the Portuguese government through the State Department of exactly what its plans were for the Azores. Often it was done after the fact, and in fact there was never a formal written permission for the Americans to establish a base at Ponta Delgada.[148]

There was considerable friction between the American commander and local officials shortly after the ships reached the port. In fact, local officials in Ponta Delgada had not even been notified that American warships were going to be based there. Difficulties first arose when the authorities refused to permit the destroyers to refuel. The American minister in Lisbon immediately got the government to allow the ships to be coaled. The senior naval officer wrote in October: "there seems to be a feeling, judging from the actions, or rather lack of information, that the local authorities give out that our position is dangerous to their welfare. . . . The question of stores and storage is serious. Local authorities do not seem to be inclined to grant us any concession whatsoever, as regard storage of necessary stores. . . . There was no end of red tape that had to be gone through before the gasoline . . . could be stored. Finally, after Lisbon granted permission to land the gasoline, I was given two arches in the breakwater in which to store it. In order to draw this gasoline out I have first to write an order which has to be [agreed to] by the Captain of the Port and then we can get it out." He was most critical of the port captain, calling him "lazy," and "a constant hindrance." When the port officer was approached about bricking in the arches, he quoted a price that was so high the Americans contracted for it themselves. Then he informed them they would have to pay rent on the arches. Some of the arches later became temporary quarters for submarine officers.[149] The American ships had to pay a mooring tax, other port taxes, and an export tax on provisions purchased locally. "When stores were transferred from one American ship to another, such as flour, canned milk, etc., the transfer could not take place until a permit from the customs office was obtained. It is submitted," the destroyers' commander wrote, "that a clear and concise understanding should be had through the Minister at Lisbon, if this place is to be used as a Base."[150]

The Navy paid considerable attention to the Portuguese Azores Islands, which were located on an important line of communications between the United States and Europe, but many problems dogged its efforts. A diplomat in Lisbon complained: "If the Portuguese Government would only understand just what we intended to do, . . . and that we are working with them and not against them in the campaign against the submarine . . . they would send such instructions as would be necessary to the local authorities at Ponta Delgada. It would wipe out the present friction."[151] On November 8, Portuguese officials in Lisbon informed the American minister that local officials in Ponta Delgada had been instructed to cooperate with the American Navy and to allow establishment of a temporary naval base.[152] Cooperation remained erratic even after Washington assigned a senior officer to command the base. Portuguese officials refused to permit the construction of a prefabricated building to store supplies but agreed to lease warehouses. On October 27, *Bushnell* and four *K*-class submarines arrived in Ponta Delgada. She unloaded five hundred tons of spare parts and stores before returning to the United States. Until the monitor *Tonapah* arrived to act as a tender, the submarine officers and crew took up quarters in the breakwater's arches, which they referred to as caves. As late as January 1918, the American consul informed the secretary of state that American naval vessels were not allowed to land ammunitions without a permit from Lisbon.[153]

A few business firms and families controlled economic interests in St. Michaels. The American senior officer there referred to one company as having "practically . . . a mortgage on every money making scheme in the island . . . and their prices are exorbitant." This company controlled water supply, lighterage, and repairs.[154]

The absence of adequate defenses for the harbor concerned the Navy. A few old coastal guns were considered practically worthless. The harbor was virtually an open roadstead. "It is quite possible," one officer reported, "for a submarine to steam along the coast at night and fire torpedoes directly into the harbor." He went on to say that the harbor was usually so congested with ships that a torpedo could hardly miss. Mines laid off the harbor's entrance also caused alarm because no minesweepers were stationed there.[155]

Admiral Sims, who had been told that the Azores lay within his command, requested a flag officer to command the base at Ponta Delgada. In November, Rear Admiral Herbert O. Dunn took command. Before Dunn's arrival, the senior naval officer present commanded American ships and facilities there. One of them, Commander Hugo Osterhaus Jr., later recalled that he commanded the "Azores area," from September 1917 to February 1918. During that period, "storehouses were rented and filled with material sent out at my request, oil and gasoline storage arranged for and large quantities kept on hand. An aviation field and 'beach' were located and prepared. . . . Guns for the defense of the harbor and town were requested. . . . The emplacements were well underway when I was detached. . . . With the British Vice Consul . . . I routed merchantmen, provided them with convoys, etc. Damaged merchantmen were sent for and towed in by our tugs. And repairs, surveys, etc. were all handled by me and my limited personnel on the many 'cripples' dropped off by the different groups passing through on their way to France." By the time Admiral Dunn relieved him, "the station was equipped and a running concern."[156] Although a great deal of work remained to be done, such as building a hospital, a radio shack, and the lease of additional buildings for administrative purposes and logistical support, the base was functioning when the admiral arrived.

Dunn did not assume command for nearly three months. In the middle of November, Washington requested permission for the admiral, his staff, and fifty Marines to take up residence at Ponta Delgada. The Lisbon government was informed that Dunn would not leave the United States until he secured clearance from Lisbon. In a second cable, the secretary of state requested that the admiral, his staff, the Marines, and vessels under his command be "exempt from all local taxes." A third telegram informed the Portuguese that the Navy wanted to station a squadron of Marine aircraft at St. Michaels.[157] The Portuguese government had not approved these matters when Admiral Benson, as a member of the House Mission in Paris, requested a conference with Affonso Costa, the Portuguese prime minister. The CNO mentioned the possibility of establishing bases not only in the Azores but in the Madeira and the Cape Verde islands. German submarines had recently shelled Funchal in the Madeiras. Finally, he expressed the desire to base three thousand Marines with a large number of heavy guns on St. Michaels. The prime minister told Benson only that he would consider these questions.

While the CNO was returning to the United States, Costa's government was overthrown. Portugal's new ruler, Sidonia Paes, was considered far more pro-German than his predecessor, having served as minister in Berlin before the war. Nonetheless, he made no effort to take Portugal out of the war. He also agreed to the American requests concerning the Azores except for the Marine presence. The Navy Department informed the Portuguese government that they were willing to defend the island with seventeen heavy pieces of artillery. Lisbon officials replied that they would provide the required three thousand men. Washington agreed to reduce the number by half, but the Portuguese balked once again. Even British intercession did not help.[158] Paes sent a military officer as governor of the Azores, whom Dunn later reported was most cooperative.[159] The admiral arrived at Ponta Delgada and assumed command on January 23, 1918.

Rear Admiral Dunn, a native of Rhode Island, graduated from the Naval Academy in 1877. Senior to Sims, he commanded a battleship division in the Atlantic Fleet when Congress declared war.[160] Upon assuming the Azores command, Dunn quickly recognized that he must assume both naval and diplomatic roles. To Sims, he wrote, "As we have not recognized the Lisbon government I have had to camouflage my diplomatic dealing and make them unofficial."[161] Until the end of May 1918, President Wilson refused to recognize the revolutionary government in Portugal. Dunn could not officially recognize the officials appointed by this government to run the Azores, but he had to deal with them. He also learned of a strong pro-German element among these officials. This information was passed on to the British government through Sims. Pressure applied to the Lisbon government led to the dismissal of the pro-German officials and the appointment of others loyal to the Allied cause, a change that helped the American admiral to obtain the necessary cooperation.[162]

Dunn brought two 7-inch guns to Delgada to protect the harbor. Fifty Marines served as gun crews. Local officials objected, claiming that Portuguese nationals should man the weapons. Dunn eventually persuaded them to let the Marines service the guns until Portuguese soldiers were taught to fire them.

Commander (later Vice Admiral) Ben Moreell, who later founded the Seabees, was the public works officer in Delgada. To haul one of the guns to its prepared emplacement, he secured twenty teams of bulls. They refused to move until he found a cow in "prime condition" and paraded her in front of the bulls. They followed the cow up the hill with "real fire in their eyes." Unfortunately, the cow did not stop at the prepared position and the gun was dragged into a fountain before it finally reached the emplacement.[163]

Dunn became extremely popular with the Azorean people. On one occasion, a crowd estimated at some eight thousand greeted him when he arrived at Ponta Delgada.[164] His popularity stemmed from efforts to help the local populace, A poor growing year for crops and the difficulty of importing food led to a famine. Wheat and corn were brought in, but bakers in St. Michaels charged exorbitant prices. Dunn then ordered the naval bakers to sell loaves at cost, which soon restored reasonable prices.[165]

Sims did not mention Dunn in his memoirs, although Dunn was loyal to him during and after the war. He clearly appreciated Dunn's handling of a sensitive political situation.[166] Dunn also earned the appreciation of the Navy Department.

Although few vessels were based at Ponta Delgada, a great many ships refueled and replenished there while crossing the Atlantic. To provide logistical support, the Navy made use of existing structures, including a large storehouse on one side of the harbor, several of the breakwater's large arches, bricked in and converted into storerooms, a fuel depot, and barracks. To provide storage for oil, a French sailing vessel was taken over and became a floating oil tank. At Dunn's request, the old monitor *Tonopah* was stationed there as a tender and repair ship for the submarines and other American vessels. Dunn flew his flag on two of the converted yachts, *Marietta* and *Margaret* (*Maggie*), at different times. Because neither was seaworthy, they became moored storeships.[167] The Department supplied prefabricated structures and construction materials for hangars, barracks, power and repair plants, and a radio station. A telephone system was put in to connect the various American installations. Trucks, automobiles, and motorcycles were also shipped to the island.[168]

In July 1918, the Bureau of Medicine and Surgery was instructed to establish a 26-bed hospital at Ponta Delgada. Three prefabricated buildings and several tents were set up in a park. These facilities proved adequate until the flu epidemic spread to the island. In October 1918, the hospital secured a large mansion in the town to provide additional beds and storage.[169] At the Armistice, the hospital staff of seventeen included two medical officers and one dentist.

During the period of American belligerency, Sims and his staff gave as much time, perhaps more, to logistics as they did to operations. The Navy was able to place forty-five bases and air stations in commission. and it constructed a plethora of hospitals and supply depots. Both the Allies and the Americans assumed that the war would continue into 1919 and even beyond. The large-scale expansion of bases, air stations, hospitals, and other facilities reflected that belief. During Sims's initial discussions with British Admiralty officials, he was told that the U.S. Navy, when operating in European waters, would have to become largely self-sufficient. The Americans succeeded in meeting this challenge.

The Train

The scarcity of skilled workers and labor unrest seriously affected U.S. logistical activities in the war zone. Years of war decimated the working force of the Allied countries, especially in Great Britain and France. Industry employed women, young people, children, older men, prisoners of war, and laborers imported from colonies.[1] Although the British armament industry experienced an increase in the labor force during 1917–18, a labor shortage persisted in Britain throughout the conflict. Ever-lengthening casualty lists forced the government to tap the civilian workforce for replacements.[2] Industries supported by the government attempted to offset the shortage by recruiting unskilled workers and later women.[3] Despite the constant need for "warm bodies" in the armed forces, workers in the armament industries remained at work. The number of civilians under the Admiralty's control expanded during the war. Between July 1917 and July 1918, the total grew from 750,000 to 887,000 workers, an increase of 18 percent.[4] Numerous strikes occurred in Great Britain during the war.[5]

The scarcity of skilled labor and worker unrest troubled construction, transportation, ship repair, and the loading and unloading of merchant ships. Officers in charge of U.S. naval activities stressed these conditions to explain delays. "No better command of the labor market than that of the Admiralty can be had, so we must bide our time," wrote Doctor Everett S. Bogert.[6] In Ireland the Irish struck so frequently that officers in charge of building American installations there were ordered to discharge Irish workers and replace them with American personnel.[7] Admiral Sims reported that the "English laboring man not only strikes at pleasure, but takes all of the usual holidays, and is not infrequently incapacitated for work on the day following the holiday." After the war, he said, workers "had tasted blood in the way of high wages and they were perfectly independent. They would work when they wanted to. They would take every holiday that came, and they would get drunk on many occasions."[8]

Sims and his staff were most concerned about difficulties at two repair centers: Liverpool and Newcastle-on-Tyne. American destroyers in European waters utilized the Cammell Laird Shipyard across the Mersey River from Liverpool to make repairs when others could not do so. On one occasion, the workers struck when the crew of an American destroyer started to paint their ship, a routine task in the American service. The unionized dockyard workers at Newcastle-on-Tyne threatened to walk out if the crew of the battleship *New York* cleaned and painted the ship's hull while she was in dry dock. The Americans ignored the threat, and the yard workers did not strike. British officials complimented the crews for this work, which permitted yard workers to concentrate on other tasks.[9] Captain Richard Leigh was in charge of installing listening devices on U.S. warships. He became involved in a controversy with British labor officials over whether this equipment came under new construction or repair work.[10]

Sims tried to persuade the British government to allow the importation of skilled labor from the United States. American workers enjoyed a much higher wage scale, and their presence in Britain might have created serious discontent among British labor. The Navy got around this obstacle. It enlisted skilled workers and sent them to various construction sites and repair facilities. Frequently naval facilities in European waters used enlisted personnel. Sims reported that at Queenstown "the entire available force including radio school were engaged in handling stores, working day and night when necessary as well as on Sunday."[11] The same practice also flourished in France.

Washington officials agreed to the establishment of naval facilities in France without extensive knowledge of conditions in that country, especially the condition of labor. By spring 1917, French casualties approached 1 million soldiers out of an army of 8 million. Sixteen percent of the French population was wiped out during the war, the highest percentage for any belligerent nation. To fill depleted ranks, the annual classes of conscripts stripped the farms and factories of able-bodied men. A half-million women worked in war industries during 1918, and an undetermined number worked outside the home.[12] France had to utilize women, the elderly, and children as unskilled workers. Hundreds of men from French colonies, particularly French North Africa, were brought in to expand the workforce, and thousands of prisoners of war were put to work.

Spreading discontent and even defeatism among the French military and the people in general compounded the labor problem. In the spring of 1917, entire French units mutinied. Workers and their families faced a declining food and fuel supply and escalating prices without increases in wages to offset scarcity and inflation.[13] Strikes occurred more and more frequently. In their anxiety to obtain American military and naval help, French officials made promises that they could not honor, among them an agreement to provide local skilled workers to repair ships and to build air stations and also unskilled workers to coal ships and unload cargoes.[14] Even when French workers were available, problems arose frequently. Mechanics at repair facilities and construction sites were unfamiliar with the American system of measurements. French stevedores under the control of contractors often refused to take orders from U.S. personnel. The personnel officer at the U.S. naval base in Brest reported that in general they had to discontinue the use of French workers to unload supplies from ships. "The local labor is poor as it consists of very young boys, old men, and the physically deficient."[15] French workers were hired in Brest to coal the American ship. One officer reported that the longshoremen were tough but cooperative. A sailor in *Reid* wrote: "Coaled ship today. About thirty Frenchmen helped in the morning but did not show up again after dinner." A quartermaster wrote after the war that French stevedores were so slow that they changed to the use of prisoners of war.[16] American facilities were not immune from strikes. In April 1918, more than eight thousand workers went out on strike at the naval arsenal in Brest, affecting repair work at the arsenal. Strikes delayed construction of many naval air stations.[17] Drafts of colonials, especially Algerian Kabyles (Berbers) and Moroccans, worked as unskilled laborers on the naval air stations. "They had no inclination to work, and at the slightest provocation would go on strike."[18]

When Americans first arrived in France, they were surprised to find prisoners of war working on the docks and air stations, and they marveled at their capacity for work, particularly the Germans.[19] A naval aviator observed that the German prisoners "are tickled at the wonderful treatment that they get here; that they work like slaves, twice as hard and twice as well as the French." Another officer was impressed with their "contentment."[20] A few Bulgarian prisoners were detailed to work on La Trinité Naval Air Station.

Sims became concerned because U.S. naval personnel performed an increasing amount of labor at American facilities and on board ships, but he had to utilize them as much as possible. The U.S. naval liaison officer in Paris warned that stevedores . . . of any description . . . [do not] exist."[21] He requested that the transport crews provide working parties to off-load their ships even at the expense of liberty, "owing [to a] great lack of labor and congestion [at] our terminal ports."[22] Even when workers were available, they were often extremely slow by American standards. The American officer in charge of the Lafayette Radio Station mentioned his frustrations at the "leisurely [way the French contractor was proceeding] with less than two dozen men."[23] On one occasion, repair work on the transport *Finland* proceeded so slowly that a detachment of U.S. Army engineers, camped near Brest, offered assistance.[24]

Similar problems with local labor developed at Mediterranean bases. In Gibraltar, Spanish workers did most of the work. Admiral Niblack considered their work "poorly done" and exorbitant in cost. Whenever possible, he asked the British Royal Engineers to help.[25] At Corfu, Greeks provided labor, but Americans found that few were available because of the intense competition for those available from the Allies forces on the island. To attract workers, the U.S. supply officer gave each one a pound of flour a day in addition to wages.[26]

The "dungaree legions" did most of the work. Bluejackets built air stations, working parties from the naval bases frequently off-loaded ships, and crews often had to coal their ships. "The major part of the efficient repair work on the ships had to be done by the men on the ships, who were at the same time doing the most active service afloat," wrote Admiral Wilson.[27] In Brest, fatigue parties from the naval air station almost daily helped build fuel tanks and unload cargo ships. "The cargoes of 32 ships were handled within a period of nine months," according to a history of the naval air station.[28] Naval personnel attached to the Northern Bombing Group based near Dunkirk, including air crews, built roads, dug ditches, and constructed camp facilities. "My first days' duties consisted of pulling up sugar beets," one sailor recalled, "although I had sixty hours in the air and had charge of . . . training planes at Pensacola." When Assistant Secretary Roosevelt returned from his trip to the war zone, he reported that the Pauillac Naval Air Station had "over 5,000 officers and men and practically the whole plant has been erected by our own bluejackets. This is true also of nearly all the other aircraft stations which dot . . . [the French] coast."[29] One sailor later wrote: "ours was the life of the pickaxe and the shovel, the paint brush and the wheel barrows. . . . We had to do all the painting, building roads."[30]

At Brest, St. Nazaire, and Bordeaux, working parties of Marine and Army personnel often helped unload ships. One of the *Seattle*'s officers wrote, "French stevedores, American sailors, and Marines, Negroes, and German prisoners worked side by side." Units of African-American soldiers assisted in this work.[31]

To alleviate the labor shortage, the Bureau of Yards and Docks proposed to send a working force of 1,500 men to France, but concern arose that American workers enjoying high wages might create difficulties for the French government. Later Admiral Sims requested two thousand men to help unload ships and distribute cargoes, but the war ended before it was considered in the Navy Department.[32]

By the Armistice, the Navy had fifty-four bases, stations, and other shore facilities in Europe. There were hundreds of buildings, barracks, hangars, piers, hospitals, and storehouses. This accomplishment impressed the Allies.[33]

Ship repair became a major issue in the war zone. Naval vessels in war operate under extraordinary strain and incur much more damage and require more upkeep during war than in peacetime, particularly modern steel-hulled warships with their intricate propulsion machinery. A captain at Queenstown remembered: "There was so much time at sea and so much damage at sea . . . [that it was] difficult to keep your ship in shape. . . . Our schedules of overhaul were continually being upset by emergencies of various sorts. You'd be placed alongside [a repair ship] . . . and scheduled for boiler overhaul, and before you ever got started, you'd be ordered to sea to fill in a vacancy or something would have popped up in the way of an unexpected convoy that had to be escorted, so, you could never really be sure what you were going to get done in the way of repairs."[34]

Sims requested shore repair stations, but the Navy lacked tenders and equipment. Also several hundred transports, cargo vessels, and tankers, which brought badly needed supplies as well as troops to the war zone, quite often needed repairs. The Allied governments promised to help, but little support was available except in Great Britain. An officer at Simsadus noted, "Throughout the war we have been practically entirely dependent upon England for all repairs, supplies, and assistance not obtainable from home."[35] The U.S. Navy had no dry docks or equipment required to remove and replace damaged hull sections and heavy machinery. Derricks or large gantry cranes were available only in Royal dockyards and in a few private shipyards in Great Britain, but new construction and repairs to British merchant vessels and warships absorbed much of their time.[36]

American naval forces in European waters utilized both the Royal dockyards and private shipbuilding establishments during the war. The seven Royal dockyards repaired or overhauled American vessels, but most of the work would be done at Haulbowline, Chatham, Devonport, and Rosyth.

Haulbowline was designated a Royal dockyard in the 1860s but did not become operational until 1894. The yard was small, although like all the other dockyards it had a large dry dock. In 1917, American destroyers at Queenstown shared the dock-yard with British escort craft until the departure of the British ships, when it became almost exclusively an American facility.[37]

Chatham, located in Kent on England's southeast coast, was one of the oldest dock-yards, having been established in the reign of Elizabeth I. After August 20, 1917, when the first American destroyer entered the dockyard to receive new depth-charge gear, an occasional U.S. warship was scheduled for work there.[38]

Devonport, a section of Plymouth, had one of the largest Royal yards, second only to Portsmouth. Ten thousand workers were employed at the yard when war broke out, a force that nearly doubled during the conflict. A few vessels were built during the 1914–18 period, but the yard devoted itself mostly to repair and refit. In September 1918, Devonport undertook to provide dry-docking and repair facilities for the American subchasers and destroyers based at Plymouth. Shortly before the Armistice, the Admiralty agreed to overhaul American submarines, although none were undertaken.[39]

Rosyth, on the Firth of Forth, was the site of the Royal dockyard in Scotland. In December 1917, the Ninth Battleship Division of the U.S. Atlantic Fleet—*New York* (flagship), *Wyoming*, *Delaware*, and *Florida*—joined the Grand Fleet at its anchorage in Scapa Flow. The American dreadnoughts stopped briefly at Rosyth to offload spare parts and extra ammunition. The Royal dockyard at Rosyth became the home base and repair facility for the American dreadnoughts.[40]

The American battleships, however, rarely visited the Rosyth dockyard; it was used primarily to take on coal and supplies. In general, British naval vessels, particularly battleships, required more scheduled upkeep and dry-dock time than their American counterparts. U.S. capital ships included trained personnel and facilities to handle routine repairs and even limited overhauling of machinery while on four-hour no-tice. The captain of *Texas* later wrote: "Each of our battleships was materially prac-tically self-supporting except for docking; each had a splendid machine shop fitted with modern machines and a foundry, capable of turning out fair-sized castings. The British were very deficient in this respect."[41]

In any event, the American ships required more work than the Rosyth yard could absorb. They were not ready for operations in the rough weather of the North Sea. Many of the hatches above the protective decks were not watertight. British engi-neers recommended smaller hatches and many other improvements such as slits in the conning tower, flash plates for the exposed batteries, salvage pumps, and broad-side fire direction for secondary batteries. None of the American battleships carried paravanes, a device that cut mine cables. German vessels, especially their submarines, often laid mines in harbor mouths, channels, and other navigable waters frequented by the Grand Fleet. A destroyer equipped with paravanes exploded three mines while leading the American battleships into Scapa Flow. The Navy Department agreed to provide paravanes to the American naval vessels with the Grand Fleet.[42]

The British navy employed the considerable private shipbuilding establishments on the River Tyne in northeastern England near Newcastle. A floating dry dock capa-ble of handling an American battleship was available there. The U.S. battleships were to use them for alterations and refits.[43] To complete all modifications, each battleship was scheduled to remain in the yard approximately ten days despite an objection from the naval superintendent in charge of repairs in the Tyne district. He complained that he would have to cancel work on a number of British ships. Admiral Sir David Beatty, in command of the Grand Fleet, insisted on it, and the Admiralty concurred. "It is not intended to dock and refit these ships again until 9–10 months after the date of . . . undocking at the Tyne so that as much work as possible should be done," Beatty wrote. He added that the ship's crew would assist in the work.[44] After the war, Admiral Hugh Rodman, commanding the American battleships, told the French attaché in Washington that none of his ships spent more than 10 to 12 days in dry dock. Actually *Delaware* remained in the dock for fifteen-and-a-half days.[45] Rodman's flagship, *New York*, was the first to enter the yard on February 19, 1918. *Delaware* followed on April 3, *Wyoming* on April 23, and *Florida* on April 23.[46] Later *Texas* and the U.S. minelayers attached to the North Sea Mine Barrage used the Newcastle establishments.[47]

In July 1918, Rodman recommended that the Sixth Battleship Squadron (so designated while in the Grand Fleet) be relieved by another division so that his squadron could return to the United States for overhaul. The Admiralty approved. In October, Sims recommended that Rodman's ships be replaced one at a time by the battleships in Bantry Bay. "This will provide so far as possible for making repairs in the United States," Sims cabled the Department. The Armistice was announced before this rotation could begin.[48]

What was true in Scotland was true throughout the British Isles. The Royal dockyards could not absorb all the work required by the American ships as well as necessary repairs on Royal Navy vessels. The problem was that the private yards had had to assume most of the repair and refitting of British naval ships. This was especially true of the concentration of yards in the northern English ports along the Tyne, the Clyde, and the Mersey. As Jon Sumida has pointed out, the wartime rate of naval refit and repair was some ten times that of peacetime.[49] In order to keep the fleet afloat and combat-ready, the government had had to sharply curtail merchant ship maintenance and new construction.

The American ships were an added burden. During the early months of American involvement in the war, there was little concern about the upkeep of American ships operating in British waters. The director of dockyards had overall responsibility for ship repairs under the Admiralty. His office worked with Simsadus to manage U.S. shipyard requirements. In August 1917, the Admiralty agreed to contract with Cammell Laird for work on the American destroyers based at Queenstown. This establishment with its seven dry docks was one of the largest and most famous shipbuilding firms in Great Britain.[50] Cammell Laird was located at Birkenhead on the Mersey River across from Liverpool. Other than its size, this establishment was selected to service the American ships because it was less than a day's steaming from Queenstown. Sims and the Admiralty agreed to rotate the destroyers three at a time for ten to fifteen days' refits. Later this policy was changed. After five hundred hours of steaming, the destroyers were to go in to the yard for five days; after four months, they were to receive a ten-day overhaul.[51] As with the battleships, the destroyers required extensive alterations. These changes included depth-charge racks, radiotelephones, closed bridges, and later blisters for listening devices. These modifications, except for the blisters, were based on British wartime experience. In addition, the hulls needed to be strengthened and other interior work carried out.[52] Although Pringle lauded Cammell Laird's work on the U.S. ships, at least one destroyer captain complained that his emergency cabin built by the company leaked "like a sieve."[53] The agreement gave to the U.S. Navy exclusive use of the yard for repair, although the shipyard was also building new construction at the time.

Cammell Laird would refit or repair ninety-five U.S. destroyers during the war. Nonetheless, because of labor problems, the Admiralty found it necessary to schedule the American vessels in other yards. On two occasions, strikes at the Mersey River facility resulted in destroyers being diverted to the Royal dockyard at Chatham and elsewhere.[54]

It was impractical for U.S. vessels operating out of Plymouth to go to Liverpool for upkeep. They were usually taken care of at the Royal Navy dockyard in Portsmouth or private yards in Southampton. American transports and auxiliary vessels also needed repairs. The shipyards along the Clyde River in Scotland repaired more than 1,500 vessels during the war, including six American ships.[55] The Queenstown-based destroyers and later subchasers and other American vessels deployed in Irish waters used the dry dock at Rushmore, a small village up the river from Queenstown. They also occasionally utilized the Dublin yards. The chasers that were temporarily based at Holyhead used a small private dockyard there for repairs. Yards at Cardiff and Bristol at times repaired American ships.[56]

British shipbuilding facilities generally handled upkeep for American vessels without a severe strain in 1917.[57] The year 1918, however, saw the development of a potential crisis that troubled British and American naval officials until the Armistice and even afterward. The problem was obvious—the deployment of large numbers of American ships in the war zone. By the beginning of 1918, U.S. naval forces in European waters consisted of 175 vessels, of which 131 were in British and French waters. Also, by that date convoys and individual ships from the United States carrying troops, equipment, fuel and supplies were arriving weekly, many needing repairs before making the return voyage.[58]

Early in the new year, members of Sims's staff met with Sir Thomas Bell, the Admiralty's comptroller, concerning the repair situation. In December, the Department had instructed Sims to negotiate an agreement for the repair of merchant vessels "of United States Registry" with the British. In introducing this issue to British officials, it was determined that the entire question of repair and upkeep for American vessels in British yards should be discussed. The British initially said that they could undertake no additional work on U.S. vessels beyond what had been previously agreed to.[59]

The major problem was manpower, not only in the trenches but in the industries as well. As Arthur Marwick wrote, "In a 'war of machines,' it was at least as necessary to look to the supply of machine users on the fields of battle."[60] So often in modern war the patriotic enthusiasm along with intensive recruiting, characteristics of the early stage of a conflict, seriously deplete a nation's workforce. This certainly happened

in Great Britain. Nor did matters improve. The charnel house known as the Western Front obliterated a large percentage of those who became involved in the deadly
struggle over no-man's-land. British military forces under Sir Douglas Haig had been
mauled in the summer and fall 1917 battles, particularly at Ypres. Haig understandably demanded that his thinned ranks be filled. He fully expected that in 1918 the
British army would bear the brunt of the German onslaught as the French were badly
demoralized, and the Russians left the war in January. Americans were arriving, but
it would be months, probably a year, before their numbers were vast enough to help
significantly.

Transporting these troops to France was a major problem. They were arriving too
slowly, partly because of inadequate shipping. To compound the problem, the German submarine campaign was at the beginning of 1918 still destroying more than
500,000 tons of shipping a month. As early as the summer of 1917, Sir Eric Geddes,
who in July was appointed first lord of the Admiralty, determined to build 3.1 million tons of merchant vessels during the following year. To achieve this as well as new
warship construction, he requested eighty thousand additional workers in the shipyards.[61] The question was, where would they come from? Shipbuilding as with other
war industries had already tapped women for employment in these industries. Only
a few thousand were employed in shipbuilding, but a surprisingly large number were
engaged in war work. By 1918, women in Britain comprised 60 percent of the workers in the manufacture of munitions.[62] Geddes hoped to get the bulk of the workers
he needed from the Army, and some 12,000 were actually released for shipyard work.
But the German spring offensive stopped this.

Even with an influx of workers, the Admiralty was reluctant to increase the amount
of work on American ships; this would certainly affect new construction. During the
first six months of 1918, British and American naval officials considered a number of
ideas to manage the shipbuilding problem. Among them was an Admiralty suggestion that the Americans establish a large repair base in one of the French ports. Sims
rejected this because no suitable site was available.[63] The Admiralty disapproved of
another proposal, to create and operate a repair base in Great Britain using American
labor. Sims also did not favor the idea. As he reported to the Department, importing American shipyard workers would (1) decrease the total output of new tonnage;
(2) absorb shipping, which was already short of the demand; (3) possibly create labor
unrest in Great Britain because of the difference in wage scales; and (4) impact the
already short food supply in Great Britain.[64]

Sims's arguments were persuasive, especially those on potential labor unrest. Wages
in American industries were already considerably higher than those in Great Britain,
and encouraging several thousand workers to give up jobs in the United States, travel
across the "submarine infested ocean," and put up with conditions that they were not
accustomed to would have required incentives such as bonuses and probably higher
wages. Also there was already considerable labor unrest in Great Britain. The powerful
trade unions—displeased over the "dilution" of their professions by the introduction
of women, semiskilled and unskilled workers, along with low wages, housing problems, and a decline in the quality and quantity of food—had struck on more than one

occasion since 1914.[65] One of the American destroyer officers recalled that while his ship was in the dry dock at Cammell Laird, "we had a frightful time with the civilian labor. We were there over Whitsuntide. On Whitsuntide Monday there was no work going on. Then the metal workers struck and then somebody else struck. We frequently didn't have any work going on the ship at all."[66]

Another American officer noted in his diary, "To add to our joy all the electricians employed in the Cammell Laird's yard had that morning gone out on strike, and the sole cause, I was told, was that in a neighboring munitions plant a foreman wouldn't join the Union; the munitions workers had Damn little sympathy for the boys in the trenches, I notice; or from the destroyer crews for the striking electricians."[67]

On March 15, 1918, Sims informed the Department that the Admiralty had agreed tentatively to dock and refit all U.S. vessels in British and French waters, assuming that dockyards and private establishments could be expanded; that materials, especially steel, could be obtained; and that labor was available. This was presumably the Admiralty's plan (Sims mentions a verbal agreement with the first sea lord on this). The force commander, in recommending its adoption, admitted that it would involve "withdrawal from the British Army of artisans . . . and United States making up the drain on the British Army." On March 21, the Germans launched offensive operation "Michael." Within days, the British front line divisions were badly decimated, and there was no likelihood of a significant number of men being permitted to leave the Army for industrial work, including shipbuilding. If anything, reinforcements had to be found. The British government appealed to Washington to approve supplying 120,000 troops per month for four months to strengthen the British army in France. The British would provide the shipping to bring them over. The War Department agreed, but General Pershing strongly opposed it, insisting that it was a calculated move to frustrate his efforts to create an independent American army.[68]

The negotiations over American troops affected the repair question. The British shipping problem was already acute, and the decision to provide transport for the doughboys would only aggravate it. On March 28, Sims cabled the Department that the Admiralty was willing to turn over to U.S. needs additional shipbuilding facilities. Marine railways and some equipment would have to be sent from the United States to adequately equip these yards. Sims then mentioned the manpower problem. According to him, the Admiralty would withdraw workers from new construction for the repair work. This situation could be met, he wrote, "by an agreement on the part of the U.S. to turn over to Great Britain an amount of new tonnage . . . which would be equivalent to the amount which would have been turned out . . . by the number of men employed on repair work for United States vessels."[69] Later, the Admiralty decided that five oilers would be acceptable as compensation for the repairs. Throughout the following months, the force commander would persist in urging the Department to agree to this plan.

President Wilson and his advisors, however, were opposed to this form of compensation. In obvious irritation, Geddes informed the War Cabinet that "apparently the United States Government is adopting the attitude that, whatever work of a Naval character we may do for them, whether it is in the building and maintaining British

Naval craft and doing more than our share of escorting . . . or whether it is in refitting their destroyers, . . . they should go on adding Merchant ships to the American flag [without any compensation in the way of ships to us]."[70] Geddes would travel to the United States, but he was unsuccessful in getting the Washington government to change its mind. Discord over this would linger into the postwar years. Nonetheless, the Navy got the repair facilities that it needed.

The Admiralty negotiated an agreement with Cammell Laird whereby it would undertake the upkeep of approximately 170 American destroyers per year. This would more than triple the number the yard overhauled before. The formula was based on eighty-five destroyers in European waters, and they would go through refitting twice a year rather than every four months. The Admiralty agreed to turn over the yard exclusively for the upkeep of the American vessels. Rather than three going through refit at a time, seven could be scheduled. Additional destroyers, including those operating out of French ports, would be divided up among the four Royal dockyards—Pembroke, Devonport, Portsmouth, and Chatham. This agreement would go into effect in January 1919.[71]

This agreement said nothing about other types of vessels, naval and merchant. However, the Admiralty in another accord agreed to repair hospital ships, troopships, supply vessels, and merchantmen sailing under the United States Shipping Board. Necessary upkeep for other combat vessels other than destroyers had been arranged earlier.[72]

Undoubtedly, Geddes felt that he had little choice. The destroyers were badly needed to provide escort for convoys, including those bringing supplies to Great Britain. If these ships could not be refitted in British yards, they would have to return to the United States, which would either weaken the convoys or force the Admiralty to withdraw destroyers from the Grand Fleet. As he wrote the War Cabinet, "It was obviously in the Allied interest that Great Britain should undertake this work as a destroyer refitted in United Kingdom yards can be of service in 14 days as against a probable period of 6 to 8 weeks if sent to America."[73]

In informing Washington of these agreements, Sims pressed the Department for an answer: "Does Department approve the principle of compensation to Britain in form of tonnage," he cabled on July 14. Much to his chagrin and anger, the answer some ten days later was no! "Department does not approve the . . . recommendation. . . . It is considered that just compensation (in the way of money) for labor and material can be fixed for the repair of American vessels."[74] The following day, Sims received a message with Daniels's signature—but, according to Benson's biographer, drafted by the CNO—that the "Department feels that in initiating policy contrary to the wishes and intentions of this government, you have committed an error in judgment. In future do not initiate general policies of international character without first communicating with the Department."[75]

Sims, clearly incensed at this reprimand, shot back: "I did not initiate a policy, but merely made a tentative suggestion of a possible method by which the difficulties in which we were involved in the matter of repair facilities . . . might be met. I have not at any time assured the British Admiralty that this plan would be approved by my Government, but have limited myself to saying that I thought it would receive sympathetic consideration. In this opinion I was apparently mistaken." Sims may not have been initiating policy, but he had made it clear that he favored the plan. The force commander also defended his interaction with the Admiralty: "If the instructions contained in the message referred to are to be literally construed, I would be unable at any time or in any circumstances to handle any new questions that might arise in which my approval was not to be final; but in every case in which the Department's approval might be involved I should be obliged to refer the matter to the Department before even entering into a discussion of it with foreign officials."[76]

Sims was right but wrong, and this apparent contradiction illustrates the problems of a theater commander interacting with policy-making officials on a national level, in this case the British Admiralty. Considering the circumstances, it was probably an inevitable dilemma and one not easily resolved. Washington officials were correct in reminding Sims of the boundary of his responsibilities, even though it was ill-defined. Benson attempted to clarify the situation by informing Sims that he had full authority to discuss "all matters dealing directly with naval policy" but that decisions concerning questions of "national policy" were to be referred to Washington.[77] Sims probably shook his head over this, but as Trask points out, for the remaining time that he commanded the American naval forces in European waters, he refrained from making commitments until he had received permission from the Department.[78]

The repair/compensation problem became increasingly political. By 1918, a serious shortage in food led to rationing. The public blamed this on the shortage in merchant shipping. In March, both Parliament and the press denounced the government for shortfalls in merchant ship construction.[79] The Admiralty's approach to Washington for merchant tonnage as compensation for repairs was one way of alleviating the shipping shortage. As Sims wrote, "Public opinion cannot . . . be ignored by responsible officials of the British Government and must influence very largely their attitude and action on any proposals affecting their shipbuilding program." He wrote his wife, "It seemed to me an astonishing piece of blindness that the principal dignitaries could not understand the psychological effect of the proposal that was made by the First Lord."[80]

Although Sims was certainly aware of the widespread Anglophobia in the Navy Department and in fact in the Wilson administration, he may not have been aware of the mounting suspicion concerning British shipping interests. In July, for example, reports reached Washington of British commercial advancements in Latin America at the apparent expense of the United States. Daniels, who confided in his diary, "Fear I will come out of the war hating English," was troubled that these activities might seriously damage the Anglo-American war effort.[81] Edward Hurley, chairman of the USSB, was convinced that the British were using the war to exploit their postwar aims in expanding their shipping interests. So was President Wilson.[82]

British suspicion over American intent was just as rampant. Washington's disapproval of the merchant tonnage and oilers for repair facilities convinced many officials in London that the United States was trying to build up both its Navy and merchant marine at their expense.[83] The United States' massive shipbuilding program in merchant ships met with increasing skepticism by Parliament, the War Cabinet, and the Admiralty.[84] "If the war continues for a few years we shall probably be left with a large fleet of warships and auxiliary vessels, and a large effort in merchant ship repair to our credit. On the other hand the Americans will have built up a mercantile fleet approaching that of Great Britain, whereas before the war they only owned one-fourth of our tonnage"; so warned Geddes in a report dated August 2, 1918.[85]

The repair/compensation controversy convinced Geddes that the United States was unable or unwilling to assume its share of the naval war. He so informed the prime minister.[86] However, the Wilson government refused to budge on the issue. Benson wrote Sims on September 30, "The Department is . . . still of the opinion that it would be unwise to enter into any agreement to pay for such repairs with new construction."[87]

This was sent while Geddes was in Washington. The first lord would make a quick trip to Washington in September to try to persuade American officials to accept the British positions concerning the issues of merchant and naval shipbuilding policies as well as the repair/compensation issue. Geddes arrival coincided with the initial peace feelers from Germany. Because of this as well as the growing Anglo-American tension, his mission accomplished little, except to deepen suspicion of Britain's postwar plans in commercial and naval affairs.[88] What started out as a problem concerning repairs had evolved into a serious political disagreement primarily concerning postwar economic rivalries in trade. Ironically, during the first eight months of 1918, British yards repaired only 151 American vessels, far fewer than the over 3,000 British vessels repaired during the same period.[89]

If the repair situation was serious in Great Britain, it was much worse in France. The American naval forces in French waters would grow from a squadron of converted yachts to a large force of destroyers, minesweepers, and other vessels. The arrival of hundreds of troop transports and cargo ships, many damaged, further strained the repair problem. The American naval forces in French waters were concentrated in the Bay of Biscay area. They were based at the same ports used by the AEF to off-load troops and supplies. All of these ports had limited repair facilities, but even those available could not be used because of the shortage of skilled labor. The most important repair facility was the arsenal in Brest, comparable to the Royal dockyards in Great Britain. It had a dry dock (a second one was uncompleted), a foundry where large castings such as propellers, engine cylinders, and rudders could be repaired and even manufactured, a number of docks, and the necessary facilities and equipment to conduct repairs on American vessels, but part of the yard had been converted to the manufacture of munitions. The major problem, however, was the lack of workers. This became most apparent when repair work on several of the converted yachts took far more time than necessary. As Admiral Wilson wrote after the war, "repair work [at the French navy yard] . . . was unsatisfactory, not so much as to quality, but as to the time it took to get the work done."[90] One sailor wrote that the navy yard had only one blowtorch. Nonetheless, for the first few months, the American ships operating out of Brest had no choice but to use the French yards. Admiral Richard L. Conolly recalled that his destroyer, *Smith*, had to go into the French navy yard after a big storm "to get patched up from the damage that we'd suffered, including the loss of our mast, and a hull pushed in from the impact of the waves. We had a lot of minor repair [also] which the French performed for us."[91]

The solution was originally to base repair ships at Brest. Two were ordered there by the Department. The tenders, however, could not handle all the work; much of it still had to be done by the French. In November, the Navy's repair officer at Brest recommended taking over and operating the French dockyards with American personnel. The Bureau of Yards and Docks considered the idea feasible, but Daniels opposed it initially for political reasons. He had misgivings for the same reason that he opposed sending American workers to Britain. French labor was paid so little that the presence of much higher-salaried skilled workers would create difficulties. The French minister of marine also opposed it.[92] Benson's visit to Brest, however, changed things. He was unhappy with the "very unsatisfactory condition" of vessels there. "A number of these vessels were tied up at Brest either undergoing or awaiting repairs," he wrote Sims. When informed of the CNO's criticism, Admiral Wilson blamed Benson's poor impression of the vessels under his command on a recently arrived squadron of fishing trawlers that had been converted into minesweepers. They were tied up while awaiting French mine-sweeping gear. Wilson repeated once again the opinion that the American naval vessels could not depend on timely repair because of the lack of skilled workers.[93] Sims forwarded Wilson's comments along with a report from Brest's repair officer recommending that a repair station be organized at Brest and that it be "developed from our own resources."[94]

The CNO instructed Wilson to investigate yards in French ports as potential sites for repair facilities. Benson wrote that as long as the tenders were used to the "maximum extent," he approved assuming control of French repair yards. In addition to Brest, St. Nazaire, Lorient, Rochefort, LaRochelle, Bordeaux, and Pauillac were examined. Wilson also asked the American naval liaison officer in Paris to discuss with the French Ministry of Marine the problem of adequate repair facilities. With French approval, Brest, Lorient, and Pauillac were recommended as sites for shore repair yards. However, the French were not willing to allow the naval repair yard at Brest to be taken over by the United States. Instead they recommended that a new facility be built there.[95]

The Department, with French approval, agreed to establish a repair facility on vacant land adjacent to the French naval dockyard. The dry dock, which had been under construction since before the war, was to be completed. Portable buildings, tools and equipment including cranes, were to be shipped from the United States for the proposed yard. A temporary building was erected on the site and equipped with lathes, drill press, and a small blacksmith shop, but it was September before the heavy equipment arrived. By the Armistice, the repair facility was 95 percent completed. The second dry dock was also made operational.[96]

The Department was slow in approving the Lorient and Pauillac sites. Commander Babcock, Sims's aide while on a fact-finding mission to Washington, wrote his boss that "Admiral Benson and McKean [Rear Admiral Josiah S. McKean was the assistant for material in the Operations Department] are very strong on this argument of keeping our bases mobile. I have explained to them that, due to the work of the Almighty in building the French coast, there happens to be but three ports that we can use, and hence there is not so much in the mobility argument."[97]

At Lorient, a small repair shop was established with French help to support ten minesweepers based there. Most of the tools, equipment, and portable buildings were shipped from the United States. Although the buildings and equipment did not arrive before the Armistice, the AEF and the French provided support in this regard, and in September the facility was in business.[98]

The same was generally true of the Pauillac facility. Buildings were never erected, and few of the tools and equipment arrived in time to be used. However, the presence of a large naval aviation repair facility at Pauillac as well as large commercial repair yards at Bordeaux enabled necessary repairs to be made.[99]

Although not a designated repair facility, an old dry dock (no pumps—water controlled by the tide) was used for minor repairs at Rochefort. Minor ship repairs were also carried out by Army vessels and at U.S. naval aviation bases.[100]

The Department was never enthusiastic about taking over French or for that matter any foreign repair facilities. It continued to emphasize mobile or floating bases and the need to be as self-sufficient as possible.

If repairs were a problem for U.S. naval forces in British and French waters, they were even more so for American vessels operating in northern Russian waters, the Mediterranean, the Adriatic, and the Azores. No effort was made to establish any kind of shore repair facility in North Russia or send a tender there. The British provided all logistical support for the few American vessels that were deployed at Archangel and Murmansk.

Gibraltar had a Royal dockyard. This yard was modernized toward the end of the nineteenth century with the addition of three dry docks, a coaling depot, cranes, and workshops. However, these facilities, located on very limited space, were heavily taxed, providing repairs and upkeep for British and other Allied warships. Adequate labor was theoretically available, primarily Spaniards and Moors from North Africa. There was considerable discontent and frequent strikes. Dockyard officials partially offset the problem by hiring local women to work in the various shops.[101]

In January 1918, Admiral Niblack, the CO of American naval forces at Gibraltar, requested a repair ship/tender. None were immediately available. Sims recommended the establishment of a shore repair facility. The superintendent of the dockyard agreed and turned over to Niblack two two-story wooden-frame buildings. One was designated to house machinery for repair work on the first floor, and electrical and radio repairs as well as an office on the second floor. The second building would be used as a barracks for the personnel. Niblack requested some seventy-five specialists to man the repair facility, as well as additional equipment, tools, and prefabricated buildings. The CNO, however, disapproved establishing the shore repair shop. Nonetheless, the American commander assembled a small repair shop in an abandoned seaplane hangar using personnel drafted from his squadron. In June 1918, Niblack wrote to Sims that U.S. naval activities in Gibraltar were steadily expanding, "but the real weakness is repair facilities. The Department has never yet told me that I am to get a major repair station." He complained about the old and decrepit ships under his command that were frequently breaking down. Because of the heavy workload at the dockyard, ships were being sent to Lisbon and Algiers for repairs.[102] In July, the department approved sending a repair ship to Gibraltar. Until then, Niblack had to depend upon his own ship crews and the British dockyard for repairs.

A base for subchasers was established on the island of Corfu at the entrance to the Adriatic Sea. There were no available repair facilities on the island, nor did the Americans organize a shore-based repair shop. The chasers depended totally upon the tender *Leonidas*, which had accompanied them from the United States to their new base.

Along with Corfu, the most difficult American base to logistically support, including repairs, was Ponta Delgada in the Azores. There were limited repair facilities there when the first U.S. naval ships arrived. Because of difficulties with the Portuguese government, only a small repair shop was established on shore—in one of the breakwater arches. Admiral Dunn, shortly after taking command in January 1918, requested that a repair ship be ordered there. He called Ponta Delgada "a trouble port" because so many ships in crossing the Atlantic needed repairs. The scarcity of repair ships led Sims to recommend approaching the Portuguese government about taking over the island's repair facilities, and whenever possible to send ships needing repairs to Lisbon. In August, Portuguese officials approved the U.S. assuming control of the repair facilities there, but because of their severe limitations in tools and equipment to work on modern ships, the situation remained unsatisfactory. The Department then agreed to station the monitor *Tonopah* as a tender in the port.[103]

Unlike other major navies of the world in the twentieth century, the United States Navy has been forced to develop and devise the means of providing the logistical support that would sustain their forces far from their home bases. One result of this was that American naval architects designed warships with considerable space for supplies and spare parts. The British navy had a large fleet of auxiliaries, but their warships and those of other European navies generally did not have the storage capacity of the American warships. Nor did they have shipboard repair facilities like U.S. naval vessels. They depended upon shore-based facilities and auxiliaries.[104] The need for operational mobility would also lead to the advance-base concept as well as the development of a series of highly specialized auxiliary vessels, individually designed to provide a singular logistical function. As Admiral Benson informed the Senate Committee on Commerce, "everything connected with the supplying of a naval force would be called an auxiliary."[105] The advance-base concept depended upon the "Train of the Fleet." The term *train* was adopted from the Army and referred to floating units or auxiliaries with the responsibility to support the fleet. This included fuel ships (tankers or oilers and colliers), storeships, refrigeration ships, ammunition ships, repair ships and tenders, transports for personnel, tugboats, mine planters, minesweepers, and hospital ships. As one naval officer wrote on the eve of the United States entering the war, "a principal purpose [of the train] . . . is to relieve the Commander-in-Chief [or commander of a warship] of the burden of logistics, so that he may devote his attention to tactics and strategy."[106] Although the term *auxil-*

iary squadron was occasionally used, by the beginning of World War I, "train" was in general use. "Mobile base" was also used interchangeably with "train" and "auxiliary squadron." In 1904, engineer A. C. Cunningham wrote an article published in the U.S. Naval Institute *Proceedings* entitled "The Movable Base." He suggested that a movable or advance base should consist of repair ships, fueling ships (at that time, coal colliers), ammunition ships ("equipment and magazine ships"), hospital, dry dock, refrigerator, and supply ships. Finally, in 1912, the Navy adopted the term *tender* in reference to vessels that acted as mother ships or mobile bases with specific types of warships such as destroyers and submarines.[107]

The train was basically a twentieth-century innovation. Until the 1880s, U.S. naval vessels, both sailers and steamers, depended upon their crew for minor repairs. When deployed abroad, they used foreign docking and repair facilities. Stores and other items, except perishable articles, were usually brought from the United States. Coal was obtained by contract with local merchants.[108] The creation of the so-called New Navy of modern steel warships and the Spanish-American War changed all this.[109]

The train concept probably originated with Rear Admiral George Melville, chief of the Bureau of Engineering from 1887 to 1903. It certainly was formulated during his watch as chief of the bureau. Melville should be considered the father of the Navy's engineering corps, probably the most influential chief in the bureau's history. He originally received the appointment because of being a highly publicized survivor of the ill-fated *Jeanette* expedition. During his more than sixteen years as chief, he was instrumental in the design of more than a hundred warship power plants, played a leading role in the emergence of the engineers corps on a par with the line, and during the Spanish-American War persuaded the Department to commission the first repair ship, an iron-hulled, schooner-rigged screw steamer named *Vulcan*.[110]

The General Board periodically examined the need for auxiliary vessels prior to 1917 and recommended the outfitting of a sizable number. A few were added to the fleet including additional repair ships. In 1911, three small repair vessels, *Dixie*, *Prairie*, and *Buffalo*, officially designated as "Destroyer Flotilla Repair Ships," joined the fleet. They were the first to be referred to as tenders as were the converted colliers *Vestal* and *Prometheus*, added to the fleet in 1913–14, and *Melville*, launched in 1915. In 1914–15, the first two submarine tenders, *Fulton* and *Bushnell*, were commissioned.[111] *Melville* was the first U.S. naval vessel designed and built from the keel up as a repair ship and appropriately would be the first to follow American warships into European waters during World War I.[112]

The Navy's auxiliary fleet in 1917 consisted of sixteen repair ships, twenty-four fuel ships (colliers and oilers), six supply ships, three refrigerator ships, two hospital ships, three minelayers, four tugboats converted into minesweepers, a few chartered cargo ships, and an assortment of tugboats, lighters, self-propelled barges, and other small craft.[113] In 1916, Admiral Benson had appeared before congressional committees in support of appropriations to add four hundred auxiliaries to the fleet. This number was based not on the probability of the United States becoming involved in the war, but as support for the powerful fleet of warships that the Navy would have under the proposed five-year naval construction program approved that year. Congress appropriated funds for fourteen auxiliaries in the Naval Act of 1916, but only converted merchant vessels would join the fleet before the war ended.[114] In March 1917, the General Board disapproved a recommendation that the Navy build a combination repair ship and floating battery. "While such a structure might be of military value in war, it is open to the objections of too low speed to accompany the fleet; poor maneuvering qualities, and its vulnerability . . . to submarines and raider attack."[115]

In January 1916, Congress created the United States Shipping Board with the responsibility of procuring ships to rebuild the nation's merchant marine, badly depleted from years of neglect. This agency would seize, purchase, and build thousands of ships, many of which would be taken over and operated by the Navy. In January 1918, the Shipping Board requested that the Navy man and operate all its vessels that entered the war zone. The Naval Overseas Transportation Service (NOTS) was created to carry out this responsibility. These vessels carried fuel and supplies for the Army and the Navy as well as troops. By the Armistice, NOTS had some 450 ships under its authority. NOTS, however, did not control many of the auxiliaries such as the hospital ships, minelayers and minesweepers, and repair ships or tenders that made up the train. Nor did it control any auxiliaries that were deployed and based in European waters during the war.

The repair ship *Melville* was the first auxiliary to reach the war zone after the United States entered the conflict.[116] The destroyer tender arrived in Queenstown on May 22, 1917. Displacing more than 7,000 tons and with a complement of four hundred officers and men, she was the largest repair ship in the Navy.[117] Shortly afterward the tender *Dixie* reached Queenstown.

The *Dixie* was built as a steam brig, launched in 1893. She was converted to an auxiliary cruiser and commissioned in the Navy during the Spanish-American War. After the war, she was again converted, this time to a transport, and she remained in that capacity until her third conversion, to a repair ship. She displaced 6,114 tons and carried a complement to European waters of approximately three hundred men.[118] Her CO was Captain Henry B. Price, who had fitted out *Melville* after her launching. *Dixie* was popular with the fleet at least partly because she had the first electric ovens in the Navy. They could bake more than 5,000 pounds of bread a day. After the end of World War I, Price referred to the *Dixie* as the "forces lubrication system and general adjuster of . . . bits of machinery."[119] Arriving in Queenstown on June 12, the tender was immediately sent to the advance base at Berehaven. She returned to Base Number 6 (Queenstown) on August 27, but late in 1918, with the arrival of submarines and battleships at Bantry Bay, she returned to Berehaven. In 1922, she was sold out of the Navy and scrapped.

Sims had had the foresight to strongly recommend to the Department that the tenders should be packed with everything required for an extended cruise. The repair ships were to replenish the destroyers so they carried more meat and dry provisions as well as spare parts and repair materials than were a normal allowance for a tender. Their inventories also included a year's supply of screws, bolts, and nuts, as U.S. standard screw threads were not used in Great Britain.[120]

The impact of these vessels was immediate and impressive. As soon as *Melville* arrived in Queenstown, all repair work was transferred from the British naval repair yard there to the tender, and according to Pringle, "except in cases of docking the yard has not been called upon for assistance."[121] He later reported that the tenders were handling repairs that prior to 1917 had been the responsibility of navy yards. "Before the war such a job order averaged about 100 a month. Since arrival in European waters they have increased to 350 for the first month, 470 the second month, and 600 the third month." In order to handle the enormous increase in work, the two tenders instituted round-the-clock operations. This necessitated a large increase in personnel. Both ships doubled their complements, with more than a third having to be quartered ashore. The tenders developed a policy whereby as soon as a destroyer returned from a patrol, engineering, supply, and representatives from the other departments went on board to determine what repairs were needed, supplies, etc. If repairs, replacement parts, or new equipment were required, the destroyer was then moved alongside *Dixie* or *Melville*. Usually, four destroyers were moored to a tender at a time. By November 1918, they were not only maintaining destroyers and other U.S. vessels but also doing work for shore facilities. *Dixie* even made a small flagstaff and engraved shield for an American diplomat.[122] The Queenstown-based tenders provided a precedent for the other repair ships deployed in European waters.

The deployment of naval units in French waters necessitated the need for local repair facilities. This force would number initially only a few converted yachts but within a year would include destroyers and various auxiliary vessels including tugboats, self-contained lighters, minesweepers, and repair ships. Although the French agreed to permit the Americans to utilize their repair yards, it was obvious from the beginning that they were totally inadequate. Sims's directive to be as self-sufficient as possible was even more urgent in France. On July 4, the first group of American warships entered Brest harbor, selected as the principal base and headquarters for U.S. naval forces in French waters. The American naval attaché in Paris toured Brest and later informed Sims that "repair facilities at Brest may be considered good, but there are few workmen there. There are none to be had."[123] Captain William B. Fletcher, first CO of the American naval force at Brest, totally agreed with Sims's mandate for self-sufficiency: "We should have facilities to handle ordinary repairs to vessels, because the dockyard is congested with work . . . work which has been necessary has taken time out of all proportion to what should have been necessary in order to complete it."[124] Throughout the period that an American naval force operated out of Brest, the length required to perform repairs in French yards was a frequent complaint by U.S. naval officers.[125]

The solution, as at Queenstown, was a repair ship. Fletcher as well as the American naval attaché in Paris urged that one be sent. Captain Richard H. Jackson, the naval attaché, suggested that the tender *Panther* would be suitable. Sims agreed and cabled the Department to send her or another one as soon as possible. He repeated this in a second message on July 18: "Repair facilities for patrol squadron in French waters very inadequate. Unless we can send repair ships, the patrol squadron's operations will be greatly restricted."[126] Sims preferred that another tender be stationed at Bordeaux, but when the Department suggested that one of the two at Queenstown be sent there, he backed down and only advocated a small repair facility on the waterfront at Pauillac, near Bordeaux.[127]

Despite these recommendations and others that reached Washington, it was not until the last day of August 1917 that the Department ordered a repair ship to Brest. The delay was caused because none were available. Sims requested that *Prometheus* be detached from the Atlantic Fleet and deployed to Brest, but Admiral Mayo, C-in-C of the fleet, objected. Benson finally decided to send *Panther*, which had tended a squadron of destroyers in the Azores.

He also informed the force commander that the *Bridgeport* would be ordered to Pauillac.[128] *Bridgeport* did not arrive in French waters for nearly a year, in August 1918. She was formerly the German merchant ship *Breslau*, seized when the United States entered the war. Because of damage to the ship by her German crew, she had to undergo extensive repairs and renovations before being commissioned. She never made it to Pauillac but remained at Brest as a base repair ship from August 1918 to October 1919.[129]

The deployment of two repair ships to Queenstown and the decision to send two to French ports determined the Department policy so far as repairs were concerned. In a memorandum to the Chief of the Bureau of Construction and Repair, the CNO informed him, "The present plans . . . contemplate carrying on, as far as possible, all repair work from repair ships. . . . The Department considers the repair [ships] . . . in the same general status as Navy yards located in this country."[130] At that time, the Department had not agreed to deploy battleships or minelayers, nor had it either envisioned the large number of naval vessels that would be based in European waters later in the war or considered the needs of the armada of cargo vessels and troop transports that would severely tax the repair facilities in Great Britain and France. In time, eight repair ships and one vintage monitor converted to a tender would be stationed at various American naval bases in the war zone. Among them, *Panther* was the third to deploy.

Panther arrived in Brest the last week in September 1917. She was originally an auxiliary cruiser built by William Cramp & Sons, Philadelphia, Pennsylvania, and launched in 1889. After the Spanish-American War, she was converted into a training ship and in 1907 into an auxiliary repair ship. *Panther* was small for a tender, displacing 4,260 tons with a complement of approximately 150 officers and men.[131]

Panther alleviated some of the repair problems in Brest, but her size and crew limited the work that could be done. The converted yachts that comprised the American naval force in French waters at that time were ill-prepared for the strenuous operations that were required of them. "Several of these vessels are not fit for service over here or anywhere else," reported the base's repair officer. "It is really humiliation to have them [French] see some of the bad material condition of some of these vessels."[132] To add to the problem, an increasing number of transports and cargo ships were discharging their troops and materials in French ports, many of them damaged by German submarines or heavy weather.

The French continued to do what they could. The French naval dockyard was virtually turned over to the Americans. The French workers, the base repair officer

wrote, "do it [the work] very well considering the handicaps of language, working different standards and lack of workmen. . . . They are not familiar with our system of
measurements. Our threads, pipe and bolt sizes are different."[133] The French services,
however, were never adequate, principally because of the lack of qualified labor. In
December, Sims cabled the Department: "additional facilities Brest urgently needed.
Panther [and French repair yards] unable to meet demands. . . . Propose assigning first
[repair] ship to arrive to Brest and none to Bordeaux." Rear Admiral Henry B. Wilson,
who relieved Fletcher in November, reiterated that the repair facilities in Brest were
totally insufficient. "Within the next six months," he warned, "there must be a great
expansion of the U.S. Naval Forces based on this coast in order to handle the shipping contemplated by the Army. By July 1 [1918] it is believed that there must be at
least seventy American destroyers in these waters." Another repair ship was urgently
needed, he added.[134] Although he would never have seventy destroyers operating under his command in French waters, his force did steadily increase. In January 1918,
Sims informed the Department that the "chief difficulty" of the naval forces operating in European waters was keeping the vessels in operating condition because of the
severely limited repair facilities.[135]

Admiral Benson while in Europe in the fall of 1917 toured the Brest naval facilities. Although he blamed Admiral Wilson's predecessor for not resolving the repair
situation, the CNO did agree that something would have to be done about it. The
question was, what? *Bridgeport*, which had been designated for the American naval
forces in French waters would not be ready for service for months. *Prometheus* was
ordered to Brest in her place.[136] *Prometheus*, displacing nearly 9,000 tons, was one of
the largest repair ships in the Navy. She had originally been built as a collier but was
converted into a repair ship in 1913. Shortly after the United States' entry into the war,
Prometheus was ordered to Bermuda to support the assorted warships and auxiliaries
that passed through the islands on their way to and from the war zone.[137] While in
Bermuda, she received orders to Brest, arriving there in mid-February 1918.

Prometheus's arrival in Brest was not as auspicious as the *Melville*'s in Queenstown.
Much to the surprise and irritation of some of the warship commanding officers, work
requests were at first turned down. "*Prometheus* began by refusing all our requests for
material and labor for alterations," an officer in *Reid* complained. He added, "I expect
we'll have trouble with her."[138] The problem was that she had been attached to the Atlantic Fleet as a repair ship for large vessels such as battleships and cruisers, not ASW
craft. "Apparently the ship did not have time to modify her equipment and supplies to
meet the demands of the duty with small craft," Sims informed the Department. For
several months after arriving in Brest, she worked primarily on large merchant ships
and transports, leaving to *Panther* and the dockyard repairs to the yachts, destroyers,
and smaller vessels.[139] It was August before the necessary equipment arrived so that
she could turn her attention to the yachts and destroyers.

A steady increase in the number and type of vessels along with expanded geographical responsibilities made it imperative for the Navy to establish additional repair facilities in European waters. Floating bases were preferred, but suitable vessels were scarce. In January, following the experience of the tenders at Queenstown,

Sims recommended that the Department approve a round-the-clock policy for the repair ships. He also requested additional "skilled mechanics" for these ships to be housed on shore. Secretary Daniels approved, ordering the different bureaus involved to give it priority.[140] There were two major problems to overcome in order to augment this policy—adequate trained personnel and housing. In order to implement the proposed three eight-hour shifts for each tender, their complements would have to be more than doubled. The Brest repair officer estimated that *Prometheus* "can work twelve hundred men," and *Bridgeport*, when it arrived, approximately a thousand. At Queenstown, where the two tenders there were already working twenty-four-hour days when required, seven to eight hundred men could be employed each. These ships, by dividing up their normal complement into sections, were already on a day-and-night schedule. Additional men could not be berthed on the ships; housing would be required on shore. Long before adequate housing could be secured, new drafts of skilled bluejackets arrived and had to be billeted on the ships. Hammocks were strung up in machine shops and other nonliving spaces. By September, all of the tenders in the war zone had gone on twenty-four-hour schedules, and as others arrived, they initiated it immediately. The Bureau of Yards and Docks was willing to send construction crews to erect new barracks, but Sims decided that they were not needed. Base personnel would handle the construction.[141] Housing for repair ship personnel was under construction at various bases when the war ended.

The twenty-four-hour workday in a seven-day work week was an important step in the development of mobile bases. Admiral William S. Halsey would later write in his memoirs that the maintenance of the destroyers operating out of Queenstown "was one of the best I had ever encountered. . . . [O]n return from a trip, no matter the hour of the day or night, the repair officer from the mother ship would come on board and request a list of necessary repairs." He went on to say that the repair ships assuming all responsibility for this work enabled the exhausted crews to get badly needed rest, and that the ships "were kept in such a state of repair that they were always able to respond to any call made on them."[142] Sims boasted to Niblack that the two Queenstown tenders handled more than 75 percent of the destroyer repairs. The Brest-based tenders became equally efficient.

In January 1918, the CNO informed Sims that other than *Bridgeport*, "no additional tenders would be available until August." This dispatch mentioned that four repair ships were already under orders to join the European forces in the period April-June. Benson later wrote that additional tenders "can only be secured by taking steamers from overseas service." The Department was reluctant to withdraw badly needed transports for conversion to repair ships but felt it had no choice. In examining the problem, the Department rejected the British policy of requisitioning commercial vessels. Instead, they favored utilizing naval vessels and going to the Shipping Board for replacements. This would be the policy followed, at least until August 1918, when Benson informed the European force commander that no additional vessels could be designated for conversion to tenders. Instead, emphasis would have to be placed on expanding shore repair facilities, something that the CNO had not wanted.[143] In May, the Planning Section in London took up the repair problem. It reported that one tender could maintain from eighteen to twenty-four destroyers or other ships. In projecting future needs, the Planning Section recommended that twelve would be needed by the end of 1919.[144] Both the Department in Washington and Sims's staff continued to wrestle with the repair problem. As one of the force commander's staff wrote, "more work on repair ship puzzle."[145] Among the merchant ships taken out of service and converted into repair ships were *Hannibal, Leonidas, Blackhawk, Buffalo, Savannah,* and *Bridgeport*. When the Armistice was signed, four more tenders, *Beaver, Camden, Prairie,* and *Rainbow* were in the yards undergoing conversion.[146]

Bridgeport had originally been designated as the tender/repair vessel for the minelayers and bases in Scotland. In February, the Admiralty agreed to carry out repair work for the American forces there. Sims then requested, and the Department approved, *Bridgeport* being sent to France. *Bridgeport*, originally a large twin-screw steel-hulled passenger and cargo steamship, displaced 8,600 tons. The German-built and -owned vessel was commandeered at New Orleans, where she had been interned since 1914. The Navy Department planned to transform her into a troop transport, but the need for repair vessels led to her conversion into a tender. Her equipment included an extensive machine shop, pattern shop, blacksmith shop, foundry for both brass and iron, and steam laundry. She had a cold storage plant, large and roomy sick bay, and even a facility to manufacture optical glasses. One of her junior officers recalled that she was undergoing repair work for various ships while being outfitted as a tender.[147] In March 1918, she joined the fleet as a destroyer tender. Although under orders to deploy to French waters, she was delayed for several months for escort duties between the U.S. mainland, Bermuda, and the Azores. Occasionally, she performed repair work while engaged in these activities. Captain E. P. Jessop, *Bridgeport*'s captain, wrote a formal complaint to Daniels: "Since leaving the United States on April 6, 1918, this vessel has been employed in convoying submarine chasers between Bermuda and the Azores. The original orders under which the Commanding Officer operated indicated that the vessel was to proceed to the coast of France . . . after completing the first trip to the Azores. Upon arrival at the Azores, quite a bit of repair work developed in the harbor. . . . If permitted to exercise the function for which she was originally designed, this ship would have been able in about three weeks time to have placed in operation 16,000 tons of shipping."[148] It was August before she was allowed to continue on to Brest. When *Bridgeport* arrived in Brest, *Panther* was ordered to the Azores.

Savannah, a submarine tender, reached the Azores with a submarine division shortly after the Armistice. She then returned to Charleston, South Carolina.

Hannibal, an English-built steamer, was purchased at the outbreak of the Spanish-American War and converted to a collier. In 1918, she was overhauled and outfitted as a repair vessel and was then deployed to Plymouth to support a squadron of thirty-six subchasers. *Hannibal* displaced 4,000 tons and carried a complement of 244 to the war zone. Admiral Bayly had wanted her stationed at Queenstown to act as tender for a squadron of subchasers there. "She can go to Weserford, Queenstown, or Berehaven, from all of which places chasers will work. She will save them having to hobble back here [Queenstown] to get their ailments put right." The tender, however, remained at Plymouth until after the Armistice.[149]

Leonidas had a similar background, being English-built and converted into a collier during the war with Spain. She also became a tender for submarine chasers, shepherding a pack of them to the island of Corfu in the eastern Mediterranean. At 4,264 tons displacement, she was slightly larger than *Hannibal* but had a smaller complement of officers and men. This was at least partly because every cranny and space was packed with supplies. The distance from support facilities in the United States made it crucial that she carry a maximum amount of spare parts, ammunition, gasoline, and other stores for the chasers. She even carried 120 tons of depth charges and complete engines for the small wooden warships.

Black Hawk was the only tender assigned to the Mine Force. A relatively new merchant vessel, launched in 1913, she was purchased by the Navy at the outbreak of war and converted into a repair ship. The 5,690-ton tender was ordered to Scotland as a replacement for *Bridgeport*. British repair facilities were unable to take care of the Mine Force's needs. *Black Hawk* was assigned to the North Sea Mine Barrage as a tender for the minelayers and, after the war, the minesweepers.[150]

Buffalo was also a veteran of the Spanish-American War. Purchased from the Brazilian government and commissioned as an auxiliary cruiser, from 1899 until 1917 she was both a supply and training ship before being converted into a destroyer tender. *Buffalo* was initially ordered to France to handle repair work on the Gironde River, based at Verdon, but after arriving in French waters in August, she was sent to Gibraltar. In September 1918, Rear Admiral Niblack, in command of U.S. naval vessels based at Gibraltar, wrote, "*Buffalo* has been the best thing that has happened to us yet, and she has taken the pressure off the dockyard here."[151]

With the arrival of submarines in the war zone—one flotilla based at Berehaven, Ireland, and the other in the Azores—tenders were needed for these boats. In contrast to surface vessels, submarine tenders not only acted as a repair facility and store depot but provided quarters as well. There were only two submarine tenders at the beginning of the war, *Fulton* and *Bushnell*. *Fulton* would remain at the submarine training base in New London, Connecticut, throughout the entire war. *Bushnell*, however, escorted four submarines to European waters and later became mother ship to seven *L*-class submarines operating out of Bantry Bay. A correspondent wrote that *Bushnell* "was a combination of flagship, supply station, repair-shop, and hotel. The officers of the submarines had rooms aboard her, which they occupied when off patrol, and the crews off duty slung their hammocks 'tween decks. The boat was pretty crowded, having more submarines to look after than she had been built to care for."[152] She was also the communication ship for the U.S. naval vessels in Bantry Bay. "'We live and learn' is a good motto, and war-time necessity has shown us new things. The *Bushnell* grew from an ordinary grammar school variety of tender at the beginning of the war to a regular college post graduate kind, with M.A. and Ph.D. and all the rest tacked on"; so one of the submarine officers recounted: "The way some big jobs were finished up would put any Navy Yard reputation to shame. 'Rewind a main motor armature—10 days.' 'Manufacture a new bow shutter—7 days.' Torpedoes were overhauled on the tender relieving the submarines of all that work. Spare parts . . . were made when none thought it could be done." He also mentioned that the tender took care of repairs for destroyers and other American and British warships operating out of the bay.[153]

It was perhaps only appropriate that the most unusual submarine mother ship was tender for a flotilla of obsolete submarines. In February 1918, the double-turreted monitor *Tonopah* escorted four *K*-class submarines and one *E*-class submarine to Ponta Delgada. She was launched in 1899 and commissioned *Connecticut* and renamed *Nevada* in 1901. To allow one of the new battleships to be named *Nevada*, the monitor was renamed *Tonopah* in 1908. Obsolete as a combat ship, she was converted into a submarine tender upon the outbreak of World War I. The monitor, like all of her class, was extremely slow and not very seaworthy. Nonetheless, she made it to Ponta Delgada safely. There the tender not only provided repair and supply facilities for the submarines but, with her two 12-inch guns, could provide fire support against U-boats. She had limited space, however, and unlike the other submarine tenders, no space for quarters. The submarine officers and crew had to be housed ashore.[154]

Halsey was not the only one impressed with the work of these ships. The surgeon in charge of the Navy hospital in Brest wrote his wife after visiting *Prometheus*: "This ship . . . is really a large machine shop afloat. . . . [H]ow they manage to get so many lathes, presses, forges, etc. in so small a space is a wonder to me."[155] One of the yacht officers wrote in admiration that the repair ships "could all but rebuild a vessel." They could retube boilers, a major repair job that usually required docking. The *Prometheus* repair officer bragged, "[T]he ship certainly has handled jobs from the 'biggest' to the 'littlest'—down to a smaller soldering job on Admiral Wilson's nose glasses." Another naval officer declared that "the repair gang on a tender can do anything from overhauling the main turbines of a destroyer to repairing the crew's Victrola." A *Bridgeport* crewmember claimed that they could "make anything" and added, "to prove it, we built a small automobile in our spare time. We made everything but the tires and a few small parts." Starters for liberty motors to be used on aircraft failed to arrive, so *Prometheus* manufactured seventy-seven of them. One tender with a furnace capacity of two thousand pounds as the extreme weight for a casting, cast an anchor for a submarine that exceeded its capacity by four hundred pounds. The commanding officer of *Bridgeport* told members of a professional engineering organization that his ship rebuilt the hull of a destroyer that had some 70 percent of the keel carried away. "The great advantage about the work over there was the fact that you were absolutely left alone. There was nobody to say 'you cannot do this' or 'you cannot do that.' We had to get the ships back. We were allowed to lay our own plans and go ahead and finish them, and the day *Bridgeport* left the port of Brest there was not a tug or lighter or ship that was not fully repaired, and everything that carried the United States flag was out of Brest three days after we left—we did a complete job." Admiral Wilson testified before a congressional committee after the war: "We repaired ships that had only 1 per cent flotation when they arrived in port. We repaired ships that had the whole bow knocked off of them, that had the whole bottom out of them, that were brought in by our salvage vessels."[156] The tenders in Brest also took on repair work for the Army transports, French escort vessels, and Army and Navy shore facilities. *Dixie* was even requested to make a small flagstaff with a brass eagle attached for a minister in Queenstown. The tender's captain responded, "though there are no brass eagles in store, I think some of the men on board can make one. . . . I don't know whether or not it will be an artistic success; for, despite the diversity of demands on the *Dixie*, this is the first request received for a brass eagle." On a more serious note, *Dixie* undertook to repair a destroyer that had been seriously damaged in a collision. Working twenty-four hours a day, she did the job "quicker and better than a dockyard," according to the tender's commanding officer.[157]

The repair ships attracted considerable attention among foreign naval officers, officials, and the press, probably more than any other type of American vessel. The British navy, among the Allies, was the only one with floating repair facilities, and their capabilities were far less than those developed by the U.S. Navy. Shortly after *Melville* arrived in Queenstown, Sims wrote to Roosevelt: "The *Melville* excites great interest. The British have nothing like her, as their distance [needs] render such vessels unnecessary."[158] Lord Jellicoe visited the ship and reiterated the force commander's remarks. Other prominent officials in Great Britain and France made a point of visiting these "marvels," and a reporter for the *Glasgow Herald* wrote of "the American gift for mechanical improvisation." The Liverpool *Journal of Commerce* predicted that *Melville* would become "a very historic ship."[159]

The French were equally intrigued by this type of ship. Raymond Poincaré, president of the French Republic, inspected *Prometheus* while on a brief trip to Brest. An article in a Paris newspaper referred to the tender as "an old mother ship hen surrounded by her chicks." The writer called her "extraordinary . . . certainly among all ships in [the] world unique." He described her "as a floating shipyard which can do everything. Cannot construct a new ship but it can make a new ship out of an old ship." In conclusion, the report stated that French naval experts were studying the repair ship, "and soon without a doubt the French Navy will have the same type of ship modified and perfected." What impressed a reporter from the publication *L'Illustration* was what he considered an efficient type of factory organization, "unencumbered by excessive hierarchical formality or rigid adherence to formalized bureaucratic procedures." To the author, this illustrated how Americans seemed to get things done. Rose, in *The Brittany Patrol*, concluded that the repair ship "won the admiration of our Allies, who depended entirely on shore stations for all such work."[160]

In evaluating the repair ships' impressive performance, officers on Sims's staff, as well as the commanding officers of the vessels themselves, attributed it to experience gained before the war, excellent plants, and above all the belief among the tender crews that they were an "integral part of the Flotilla," or force that they supported. "A spirit exists on board, in all ranks, which renders them just as keen and solicitous of the welfare of the [ships] . . . based upon them as . . . themselves. This is a condition which can never be obtained in Navy Yards of Repair Plants."[161] After the war, Sims asked Captain H. B. Price, who commanded *Dixie*, 1917–18, to assess the repair ships' success. In general, he reiterated other comments made about the vessels. "A large element of readiness, contentment and efficiency of the destroyers lie in the relationship and feeling existing between them and the parent ship, which is largely based on a mutual spirit of fraternity and cooperation, and mutual working for all-around efficiency of materiels. . . . The personnel of the parent ship should make the personnel of the [ships it supports] . . . always feel that they . . . are all one body working together." An officer on the submarine tender *Beaver* passed his observations concerning the responsibilities of a parent ship. His emphasis was basically the same as those who experienced tender duty during the war: teamwork, cooperation, and harmony. "We [meaning the submarine and tender] . . . must play the game like a team. . . . It is so very important . . . for all hands. . . . Our success as a *mobile fighting* Division . . . is going to hinge very much on just how well we all learn and practice this one idea." This concept that emerged in importance during World War I would characterize the relationship between tenders/repair ships and the force they were supporting in the future.[162]

The work of the repair ships was one of the most successful logistical operations during World War I. They alone, with the few shore-based repair facilities, contributed significantly to American naval self-sufficiency, which was the goal of Sims from the beginning. In addition to the tenders and repair ships, the ships' crews were trained to handle as much of their maintenance as possible. The Allies were surprised, for example, to discover that American crews performed work that was usually done in their navies in dry docks by civilian workers. Minor repairs as well as cleaning and painting were considered routine work for American sailors. The U.S. battleships that operated with the Grand Fleet impressed Admiral Beatty, and in fact the fleet, with their capability to handle most repairs. As one officer on one of the American dreadnoughts recalled: "We practically required no navy yard work at all. The British couldn't understand this." Captain R. R. Belknap, in charge of the mine-laying squadron for the North Sea Mine Barrage, wrote after the war, "Except for docking, we asked very little of the British in the way of repairs."[163] The final report of repair work in French waters concluded that work was handled in four ways: (1) by a ship of our own force; (2) by cooperation of the French; (3) by U.S. repair vessels stationed in French waters; (4) by U.S. repair units organized ashore. More than 75 percent of the repair work was done by American personnel.[164] All of the U.S. naval base commanders lauded their repair work.

With ship and shore facilities, the American Navy was able to handle most repair jobs. Fortunately, the Allies were able to manage heavy work and dry-docking. The battleships were sent to Newcastle and the destroyers to Liverpool/Birkenhead. Some yachts and submarines were worked on in Lisbon, Portugal. In some cases, however, where boilers needed replacing or retubing, the vessel had to return to the United States.[165]

On April 14, the day after the first American warships received orders to deploy to European waters, Admiral Sims in London cabled the Department recommending that seagoing tugs be sent to the war zone. Undoubtedly prompted to do so by the Admiralty, which had a severe shortage of these auxiliary craft, he wrote that they were needed to tow sailing vessels through "dangerous areas." He would repeatedly urge the need for these vessels throughout the war. In later messages, he stressed that the presence of these tugs would save valuable tonnage by rescuing torpedoed and stranded transports. Despite the admiral's characterization of the United States as "the country of tugs," few were available, either naval or commercial, and both the Navy and the Shipping Board insisted that they were needed, particularly towing fuel barges along the Atlantic coast.[166] The Department was not ignoring Sims in this regard. The Navy contracted for twenty-three seagoing tugs, and the Shipping Board even more. Like so many other vessels contracted for, however, they would not be finished until the war was nearly over. In the meantime, the Department did what it could. Twelve were purchased in August 1917 to be sent to Sims's command. By October, seven had arrived, towing submarines for duty in the Azores. They were assigned to French waters, Genoa, Gibraltar, and Queenstown. Gradually additional tugs arrived escorting subchasers. By the Armistice, nineteen seagoing tugs were scattered among the different U.S. naval bases.[167]

Supporting a naval force in distant waters required not only facilities and auxiliary vessels but supplies, equipment, and materials. Most of the equipment and much of the building materials needed to construct air stations and other facilities had to be shipped from the United States; everything from nails to prefabricated steel had to cross the Atlantic. Stores of all kind, including food, medicine, clothing, and spare parts for vessels, vehicles and aircraft, were supplied. Considering the magnitude of this kind of logistical support, the results were impressive.

"For Want of a Nail"

U.S. naval efforts to achieve self-sufficiency included materials, supplies, medical service, and fuel. Rear Admiral Niblack boasted, "In our Navy alone of all the navies of the world, we hold to the great fundamental principle that the Navy should man, own and operate its supply ships."[1] The Bureau of Supplies and Accounts prepared for war more effectively than any other entity within the Navy. Thanks to the foresight of its energetic chief, Rear Admiral Samuel McGowan, the bureau stockpiled supplies and created a system to get them to the fleet quickly.[2] By May 1918, the Navy's Queenstown Supply Depot had a reserve supply of provisions, clothing, and general stores for five months for the destroyers and four months for the aviation bases in Ireland and the battleship squadron operating with the Grand Fleet. McGowan ordered his staff to fill requisitions and requests from Sims and his staff on "the same day they were received." The British had an excellent transportation system, including rail that linked the various ports with Rosyth, the home base of the Grand Fleet.[3] The American supply depots used this system to keep stores and provisions flowing to the various ships and bases. The bureau decentralized in European waters. It supplied each base rather than creating a "central organization for material and supplies approaching in personnel and scope of activities that of the Bureau of Supplies and Accounts itself." The individual bases and floating forces handled their own supplies, including requisitions from the Department and local purchasing. The Allied governments promised to provide fuel and a variety of supplies. The bureau instructed its paymasters attached to European bases to use "the existing machinery of the [Allied] . . . governments for the purpose, and to make every effort to avoid "setting up a parallel system of purchase and supply."[4]

The first ships deployed to European waters, the six destroyers at Queenstown, filled every space with provisions and supplies. While they crossed the Atlantic, Sims arranged for the Royal Navy to provide them with British rations and other necessary supplies. The absence of a supply organization ashore to take charge of accumulated stores caused considerable confusion. This changed when *Melville* arrived and took charge of the supplies. The tender carried approximately three thousand tons of cargo to the new American base.[5]

The British supplied the destroyers well at Queenstown, but not always when the ships operated out of the advance base at Bantry Bay. One of *Conyngham's* officers confided in his diary, "We are in a bad way for stores, both fresh and dry." The situation improved significantly at the beginning of July, when the tender *Dixie* arrived in the bay with large quantities of provisions.[6] *Dixie* later returned to Queenstown, requiring ships that needed a tender to return to that port.

Although the tenders arrived with a large inventory, their stocks based on peacetime experience became scarce. Wartime operations created greatly increased demand. For example, *Melville*'s supply officer reported in August that the ship had nearly exhausted its supply of fittings, notes, screws, and bolts, despite having carried a year's reserve. Experience at Queenstown caused the bureau to increase the inventories carried on the tenders.[7]

In June 1917, the Department assigned the storeship *Celtic* to replenish the American naval force in European waters. *Celtic* discharged cargo first at Brest and then at the two Irish bases. She carried frozen meat, fresh provisions, and drystores. Adequate cold storage was available in Brest and Queenstown but not at Berehaven. After assessing this initial supply run, Sims recommended that his office coordinate the list of supplies and schedules of arrivals and departures from the bases. Sims wanted two storeships to make scheduled runs at least monthly to his forces, one to Queenstown and the other to Brest. The growth of Sims's force created a demand for more store/supply ships. The bureau assigned two older refrigerator supply ships, *Culoga* and *Glacier*, to the European run and in September sent *Bridge* to support the European forces. The four available ships could carry enough supplies for the American naval force in European waters if the Allies provided most of the vegetables and some of the meat and dry provisions.[8]

The expansion of U.S. naval activities in Great Britain required additional logistical support. At the request of the Bureau of Supplies and Accounts, two additional depots were established, one at Plymouth to service the vessels based there and the other at Southampton to service the American vessels engaged in cross-channel shipping and the naval aviation stations located in southern England.[9] In June 1918, Sims obtained two supply ships to support Queenstown rather than two for all of the European facilities. One carried frozen foods and the other general stores and dry provisions. A third vessel, *Glacier*, carried stores to the American naval forces in European waters but not specifically to Queenstown. In September, *Culoga*, the last of the four refrigerator/supply ships in commission, was assigned to transatlantic duty.

Distribution of supplies proved difficult. In general, all stores for the naval forces in Great Britain and France were channeled through two ports, Queenstown and Brest. The supply officer at Brest complained, "material comes all jumbled up at times for different Bases, that for the Base at first stop on bottom or mixed throughout shipment." He blamed BuS&A: "material comes first destination not marked and not accompanied by invoices or by information as to purpose intended." The supply officer at Queenstown claimed that during the early months of the conflict, "a great many discrepancies" occurred but eventually disappeared.[10] Rear Admiral Marbury Johnston, in command of the Naval Overseas Transportation Service in New York, placed much of the blame on Simsadus: "We load a ship with a cargo half of which is for Queenstown and half for Brest. If she is going to Brest first we put the Queenstown cargo on the bottom. When she gets over somebody says to send her to Queenstown first. Then when they get to Queenstown they have to take out the entire cargo to get the Queenstown cargo and then put the Brest cargo back."[11]

The shipment of aircraft parts caused the most trouble. In August 1918, Sims wrote the Department, "It is extremely unfortunate that, having completed practically all of our obligations as regards the construction of aviation stations in Europe, we are prevented from actual participation in the war offensively with American material due to the serious confusion in which Naval aviation shipments arrive in Europe." The historian Clifford Lord wrote, "We . . . built beyond our ability to equip."[12] Liberty motors were delivered damaged or without parts. Because of so many "mix-ups," the Department assigned an officer to each navy yard to monitor the shipment of radios and other aircraft parts. Assistant Secretary of the Navy Roosevelt was appalled at the situation when he was briefed on his trip to Europe. He told Sims that "Not a single American Navy airplane in France can operate offensively. Only 8 can fly. Propellers and gasoline pumps defective. Liberty motors short of parts improperly assembled. 8 starters received for 148 motors. . . . Trouble evidently lack of following up and proper factory and shipping inspection." At his recommendation, an investigating board examined the transportation system. The board blamed the problems on the "extreme speed under which the carrying out of the naval aviation program has been attempted."[13] Sims admitted that "mixed cargoes are troublesome" but noted, "the practice cannot be avoided and must continue if transatlantic tonnage is to be utilized to the maximum."[14]

Until January 1918, BuS&A transported stores and fuel to American naval forces. On January 8, however, a new organization, the Naval Overseas Transportation Service (NOTS), was to control all United States shipping other than troops to the war zone. The stores and fuel ships previously operated by the Bureau of Supplies and Accounts for the train were transferred to NOTS for the duration. Although the problem of distribution probably influenced the decision to create this new fleet of auxiliaries, the need to pool or concentrate all the vessels engaged in transporting cargoes to European waters—Army, Shipping Board, and Navy, led to its organization. NOTS tapped the Shipping Board for vessels and gained control of interned German liners. During World War I, the U.S. government seized nearly 700,000 tons of German shipping. Customs officials seized these ships, including sixteen liners, to prevent their sailing after war broke out in 1914. The U.S. Shipping Board converted fourteen of them, including *Vaterland* (renamed *Leviathan*) into troop transports. By the Armistice, NOTS operated 450 ships, displacing 3.2 million tons, manned by 95,000 American bluejackets. NOTS took control of all Army transport.[15] Although the Bureau of Supplies and Accounts and Sims's command followed a decentralized supply policy, NOTS attempted to centralize shipping.[16] It transported stores and provisions from New York City to bases and vessels in Great Britain, except Scotland, from Philadelphia to bases in the Mediterranean, Gibraltar, and the Azores, and from Norfolk to French bases.[17]

Warships, tenders, and other auxiliaries were pressed into service to transport supplies. The vessels that hauled the mines to Scotland for the North Sea Mine Barrage were loaded with provisions and supplies for the U.S. mine bases and minelayers and the battleships with the Grand Fleet. Oilers carried aircraft on open decks. Although Brest and Queenstown remained the major distribution points, stores were sent to other British, French, and Mediterranean ports when the Navy developed additional bases.

Norfolk was selected to service the battleships with the Grand Fleet and the mine bases because the mines for the barrage were loaded at that port. As early as November, shortly after the decision was made to deploy minelayers to Scottish waters, the Department was advised to ship all cargoes destined for the mine bases directly to those facilities because "rail shipment in England is extremely congested."[18] The first mine carriers to arrive brought with them approximately three thousand tons of provisions and stores. They were placed in leased warehouses in Aberdeen, from which they were distributed to the different ships and bases. Because of its rail connections, the British had a large supply depot at Aberdeen. A U.S. Naval Supply Center was established to service the mine bases, the battleships with the Grand Fleet, and the Naval Hospital at Strathpepper.[19]

The American battleships that arrived in Scapa Flow in December 1917 posed unique difficulties. The first four dreadnoughts to arrive in British waters carried a six-month supply of provisions. U.S. storeships could not easily replenish them. The most logical route from the United States to Scapa Flow and Rosyth passed through the waters between the Orkneys and northern Scotland, a hazardous area because of the frequent presence of German submarines. The Royal Navy maintained a regular supply system to its powerful fleet, and Admiralty officials agreed to treat the American battleships as they treated British ships. On Christmas Eve 1917, Admiral Rodman informed Sims: "We are now drawing fresh beef, mutton, and potatoes from the British but no other provisions, all other provisions, fresh or otherwise most come from the States. The British Fleet is practicing the most rigid economy in meats, and fats in particular, as well as in other articles of food. It is proposed to gradually introduce like procedure on our ships and practice the strictest economy." The squadron commander recommended that *Texas*, scheduled to join the fleet early in 1918, should transport supplies. "[E]very available space including flag officers quarters [should] . . . be filled with stores . . . [and] provisions, including preserved meats, canteen stores, and others in general use."[20] Despite the U-boat danger, he requested a supply ship by the first of April.

One U.S. supply ship did reach the Grand Fleet. *Bridge* arrived at Scapa Flow in March, carrying provisions, including too much frozen meat for the cold storage lockers, depth charges, spare motor launches, and other materials.[21] This storeship was the only vessel to replenish the battleships while they were with the Grand Fleet. The Department was unwilling to risk one of their few supply ships in those waters. The British recommended that the mine carriers transport the stores to the west coast of Scotland and ship them by rail to Aberdeen. From there, they could be sent to the Royal dockyard at Rosyth, loaded on British supply ships, and transported to Scapa Flow.[22]

The American battleships with the Grand Fleet depended upon the British for provisions more than any other U.S. naval activity or floating unit in European waters. An authority has stated that during World War I the supply of food was the least difficult of the Royal Navy's logistical tasks, but the Grand Fleet proved an exception. British enlisted naval personnel obtained their food from two sources—the Admiralty's store system and canteens. The British navy provided standard rations of staples such as meat, flour, potatoes, rice, and tea. These staples were considered nutritionally adequate but monotonous and even to some unpalatable. Occasionally the ships received sugar, butter, and, in season, peas, corn and other fresh vegetables.[23] The canteen was somewhat different from the ship's store, as it is known in the American Navy. Ship stores were found on U.S. capital ships and tenders; in the British navy, canteen ships were listed as auxiliaries of the fleet. They sold a variety of items at market prices, ranging from cigarettes and toilet necessities to fresh provisions such as eggs, cheese, bacon, butter, and vegetables. Enlisted personnel had a fixed allotment for canteen stores, but prices increased sharply during the war. Although the canteen system nearly collapsed because of its pricing, it proved helpful to both the British tar and the American bluejacket. A newspaper article published after the war said that the canteen ship sold out only once, "when the American Fleet arrived." The U.S. sailors "went aboard and cleared the store out of everything from dried kipper to strawberry jam, two articles of food which only an American sailor would dare to mix with impunity." The canteen ship established a schedule for the Americans tagged "Yankee days." According to the store manager: "It was nothing unusual for us to sell a thousand pots of honey and several tons of jam. Tripe and onions and marmalade was another of the Yankee's favorite dishes. . . . The most prodigal purchasers were certainly the Americans."[24] American sailors earned more than their British counterparts, and, although Admiral Rodman might recommend practicing "the most rigid economy," when the gobs had funds and the canteen was open, they supplemented their rations.

Throughout the stay with the Grand Fleet, British supply ships replenished American stores at Scapa Flow or from storehouses at Rosyth. An examination of the ships' deck logs suggests that special rations were distributed to American battleships as well as to the doughboys serving with British units on the Western Front. Coffee, for example, was sent to the American ships but not to the British. In March 1918, *Bridge* included in its cargo a load of oranges and lemons, a gift from California, but it is not known whether the fruit was shared with the British.[25]

American sailors did not like the British rations. One veteran recalled that they were "rotten." The American sailors had the unwanted privilege of eating a popular dish with British servicemen known as "maconochie stew," a concoction of meats and vegetables. It is likely also that they consumed horseflesh, the only meat available at times.[26]

American naval personnel elsewhere were not as dependent upon standard British staples as their countrymen in the Grand Fleet. Admiral Sims advocated reliance upon the British supply system for fresh provisions and certain dry staples to save space on supply ships, but in general shipments were left to BuS&A and their offices in the States and local commanders in the theater of war. Naval paymasters and supply officers on the different ships and bases could either obtain fresh provisions under Admiralty contract or use ship funds to purchase them on the local market. In Liverpool, however, local vendors refused to sell to American ships because of rationing.[27] U.S. warships under repair or overhaul at Royal dockyards were able to stock up with staples and canteen stores. Although Sims urged Washington to give priority to dry stores and other items not easily obtainable in Britain, the supply ships continued to bring fresh vegetables. *Bridge* brought 170,000 pounds of potatoes on one trip and had to take them back because they were plentiful and cheaper in Great Britain.[28]

Food shortages in Great Britain became so serious that at the beginning of 1918 the government imposed rationing primarily on meat and sugar. The American sailors did not recognize the privation faced by the British people. Rationing rarely affected them, particularly on their bases and stations. From the beginning, American naval supply ships regularly brought in provisions, and the British government did not restrict American purchases of food in local communities. Whether in Ireland, where, as one correspondent noted, "War rations did not prevail," or in Scotland, bluejackets voiced few complaints about food.[29] The one exception to the rule was in London. American personnel attached to Simsadus and the naval hospital had no general mess and had to take their meals in restaurants. For this reason, they had to use ration cards. Sims wrote his wife: "England [is] now on rations. It applies principally to meat and sugar. I have a card for each. The sugar allowance is less than one ounce. Each morning they give me a small envelope containing about one heaping dessert and that . . . is for all day. No sugar is seen at lunch or dinner. The same for butter." He could eat at the embassy lunchroom, where cards were not required. "I get plenty to eat at all times. There is always plenty of fish to be had.[30]

The availability and price of food varied from locality to locality. When the first destroyers in Queenstown arrived, they found food abundant and reasonable, but prices rose sharply, partly because of rationing and partly because local merchants became aware that the Americans paid well. Individual ships contracted with local vendors for fresh provisions. The *Maumee* paymaster wrote: "chickens [are] cheap, potatoes are plentiful and cheap and eggs high. There appears to be no fixed prices for meats purchased under British Admiralty contract." Sims, however, recommended to the Department that because of the high prices for provisions in Ireland, "it appears impossible to limit the ration cost to forty five cents per diem." He recommended an increase of at least ten cents.[31] In June 1918, an officer complained to his fiancée about the price of eggs. They "are so expensive . . . here that the mess cannot afford to serve them for breakfast so those that want eggs have to buy their own. . . . My private egg bill for one month was $24.50. If I don't eat eggs until Christmas I can get you a diamond ring with the egg money." A Cork newspaper blamed the exorbitant prices on the "wartime boom."[32]

The two mine-laying bases in Scotland obtained food locally without difficulty. The bases purchased from local vendors at prices frequently lower than those available under Admiralty contract. The U.S. supply officer attributed it to the fact that "our payments are prompt."[33] The supply officer at Base Number 29, Cardiff, found prices reasonable but food at times difficult to obtain. In the fall of 1917, an officer in

Reid wrote in his diary: "We [have] not been able to get any provisions at Cardiff. For supper . . . we had one third of a regular ration of Salmon and no one felt very cheerful."[34]

Sims's self-sufficiency policy was applied to U.S. naval forces based in France as well as in the British Isles. As the American naval attaché in Paris informed the Department upon the news that American warships were to be deployed in French waters, "stocks of coal, oil, and food steadily decreasing."[35] The availability of food for American naval personnel in France was about the same as in Great Britain except for some restrictions on local purchasing. "Chow is the best we have had yet," wrote a bluejacket housed in the receiving ship at Brest.[36] The sailors assigned to the naval air stations fared well, even those assigned to Dunkirk. Meals at the French air schools varied."[37] George Moseley thought his was quite good: "Can you imagine real white bread, oatmeal with cream, pie? . . . I know it hard [to believe] but add to that real meat—beef, pork and veal (no horse meat)."[38] Irving Sheely was not so pleased: "Our grub is getting poorer every day. Lots of meals all we get is black coffee and war bread. Sometimes the bread is sour and the coffee is strong enough to poison any ordinary man if he didn't get used to it."[39] Pilots at the Le Croisic Naval Air Station foraged to get food. An aircraft on convoy duty picked out a particular supply ship, invited the officers to dinner, and persuaded them to provide their station with supplies.[40] The Naval Railway Battery depended primarily upon French and AEF provisions.[41]

To a great degree, the American naval forces achieved self-sufficiency. The British generally provided coal, but petroleum products, repair facilities, and nearly all stores came from the United States. One officer recalled that provisions, "except for fresh vegetables, were almost entirely American, and so were all the other supplies."[42] The French navy in Brest allowed the use of their repair facilities, provided cold storage for refrigerated provisions, and encouraged the local bakeries to bake bread, using American flour.[43] Rear Admiral Conolly recalled that his shipmates arranged with a small bakery in the city "to bake white bread for us from navy flour." The baker was allowed to keep half of the flour for his use. "The baker was the happiest man in France. He said he had not been able to make good bread since the war started."[44]

The American Navy agreed not to purchase raw materials and provisions without the approval of the French government. The French claimed that approximately half of the Americans' supplies were obtained in country but offered little evidence to support this claim. American officials contended that most supplies originated in the United States.[45] In November 1917, the supply officer at Brest informed Simsadus that "the situation in regard to getting supplies gets worse every day. It has become so bad that the French were obliged to appoint a mission which now passes on all purchases for the U.S. exceeding a thousand dollars . . . stating whether the French government can spare the material requested for the use of the U.S. government. The Commission is not by any means a perfunctory one and has turned down many requests."[46] Provisions at times became so scarce that the Navy had to turn to the AEF.[47]

In the fall of 1917, the Department assigned two colliers, *Jupiter* and *Neptune*, to carry stores to Brest. On her first visit, *Jupiter* transported 5,000 tons of flour, 3,430 tons of oats, 250 gallons of benzene oil, 75 tons of coal, and 100 tons of munitions.

These ships made several trips before their transfer to NOTS. They continued to make trips to the war zone, carrying coal, general stores, and aircraft to several ports.[48]

The ships on escort duty out of Brest were at times short of provisions. A member of *Reid*'s crew complained that "Food was scarce and our rations were cut down so that we were really hungry most of the time." Later he wrote, "[T]he bread is gone."[49] Although the American ships at sea were occasionally short of rations, when in port and on liberty in Brest and other French ports the crews usually found food without difficulty. Personnel at the U.S. naval air stations in France generally fared better than those at the ports and ships. The Americans temporarily based at the French aviation training school at Moutchie were surprised at the quality of their food. One officer recalled that fresh meats, eggs, and vegetables were available in the vicinity of the stations but at high prices.[50]

The U.S. Navy encountered difficulty when it attempted to locate adequate water in France: the supply was insufficient and usually impure. Not enough water barges were available to service the American ships. In Brest, the total allowance was 350 tons for all U.S. vessels. Water rationing prevailed during the Navy's entire stay in Brest. Ships engaged in transporting or escorting troops and supplies to French ports were instructed to carry enough water for the round trip. Similar problems existed at the other U.S. naval bases and stations in France, but the situation at Rochefort was more acute than elsewhere. During the summer months of 1918, the civilian population could draw water only for a two-hour period each day.[51] A dam and reservoir were built on the Penfield River to hold 23 million gallons of water. It pumped water to the docks in Brest to smaller reservoirs. The new water supply increased dockside capacity to ten thousand tons per day, but the work was not completed until after the Armistice. The immediate recourse, however, was to boil all water and add chlorine to it. Chlorine was not available in France and had to be shipped in from the United States.[52]

Supply officers at the naval air stations in France obtained clothing, small stores, canteen supplies, and dry provisions from the naval bases at Brest, Lorient, and Rochefort. A naval air supply depot was established at Pauillac, near Brest, to serve as the distribution point for construction materials, equipment, aircraft, spare parts, and some general stores. Finally, whenever possible the various stations were to make use of local or open purchases, although French authorities required them to obtain permission. Officers at Pauillac and later at Bordeaux and Paris made local purchases to resupply the different stations. Although U.S. naval facilities in France did not compete with each other, they battled with the AEF, particularly over aircraft and spare parts. A step toward the curtailment of interservice rivalry occurred when the Navy's paymaster attached to naval aviation headquarters in Paris joined the General Purchasing Board of the AEF. This agency became the clearinghouse for the purchase of aviation materials in France. Later a Joint Army and Navy Aircraft Committee was formed to coordinate the purchase of aircraft and aircraft parts in Europe. The committee, with General Pershing's support, eased competition considerably.[53]

Although the entire naval force in European waters suffered from the chaos characteristic of transatlantic shipping during the early months of the war, the aviation section apparently was hit the hardest. For example, much of the construction material for the naval air stations in France went to Ireland by mistake. Stations were completed, but operations were delayed because of the "non arrival" of propellers, starting cranks, and radio equipment. The Irish stations had to borrow bombs from the British, although the Northern Bombing Group in France received enough to last for a year. A supply officer observed that cargoes often arrived in poor condition; "bills of lading and invoices were incorrect and incomplete. . . . [B]oxes did not contain what they were marked to contain. Practically no information [came] . . . from the states as to what material was ordered or as to what material was en route until same arrived." Seaplanes destined for Queenstown were delivered at Glasgow; those allotted to Eastleigh were unloaded at Brest. By the end of July 1918, only two storage batteries were received for use in naval aircraft. Only nine starters and twenty-five bomb gears arrived by September. Merchant ships were in such short supply that aircraft and motors were hastily loaded on oilers and transported to Europe.[54]

Naval aviation was so new that the Bureau of Construction and Repairs was unsure of its responsibilities for air stations in the war zone. It consulted other bureaus but received little information. The bureau finally determined that it would handle the aviation stations "in the same way as . . . ships acting separately." And it would respond to their requests as they would to any ship.[55] In contrast to the BuS&A, the Bureau of Construction and Repairs did not provide adequate logistical support to naval aviation in the war zone.

Transportation difficulties within France also caused delays in construction of the naval air stations. The railroad system was on the verge of collapse. The Americans had to depend upon the British transportation system to transfer materials from Pauillac to Dunkirk and the Northern Bombing Group. The stations scattered along the coast of the Bay of Biscay had to depend upon the inadequate railroad system and on motor sailers and two leased steamers for logistical support.[56]

The American forces at Gibraltar and in the Mediterranean were heavily dependent upon the Allies, especially at Corfu because of its distance from the United States. *Leonidas* carried only a three-month supply of dry provisions and small stores, extra clothing, and spare parts for the subchasers. Although fresh vegetables, olives, plums, and cherries could be purchased in season, very little was available locally. Sims claimed that adequate food was available on the island "on account of the excellent co-operation of the French. A French refrigerating ship is always available and the French Admiral has stated that our men will always have meat as long as his own men have it."[57] Captain Leigh, who established the base, remembered the difficulties of getting supplies to Corfu—"mostly food stuffs." He added: "All hands down there [at the French base] were eating black bread and not enjoying it. I had been ashore the day before when a small steamer from France was discharging cargo and noticed barrel after barrel of wine being landed, so I suggested to the Admiral less wine and more bread, flour, meat. He became quite agitated, not to say irritated, and a pained expression came over his face as he said, 'Why don't you know our men must have their wine—wine first then bread, yes.'" As the Americans discovered, provisions were scarce. A subchaser officer frequently mentioned limited supplies of food, writing on August 27, 1918, "We have no potatoes, bread, or meat"; on October 17, he wrote, "we were out of about all kinds of food; we had flap jacks for lunch."[58] Water was also scarce.

Water was "a precious article" at Gibraltar. With the exception of provisions and stores that the American naval vessels deployed to Gibraltar brought with them, the U.S. naval force depended on the British for all support, including fuel, frozen meats and other provisions, and water. There were reservoirs on the "Rock" collecting water from the surrounding hills, but in the dry months, barges brought it from Tangiers, Morocco. On more than one occasion, German U-boats sank the water barges en route to Gibraltar. Fresh vegetables from neutral Spain were purchased at local markets. Ships that escorted convoys to Italian ports obtained coal, water, and provisions at Italian navy bases. BuS&A never assigned a supply officer to Gibraltar; each vessel received an allotment of a thousand dollars for purchases on the open market. This money was expended in a few months, and despite requests from Admiral Niblack, the command did not receive additional funds.[59]

The detachment of American naval aviators stationed in Italy received provisions and stores by rail from the aviation supply depot at Pauillac. A paymaster/supply officer was never assigned to Italy, and few funds were available for local purchasing.[60]

Ponta Delgada, Azores, like Gibraltar, became a transition point for ships sailing between Europe and North America, and the Navy established a naval base there. Dry stores and provisions proved scarce at first. On October 25, 1917, the base commanding officer cabled the Department: "Urgently require dry provisions . . . practically dependent upon resources of the island. We will be entirely out in 5 or 6 days. Provisions are very high and of inferior quality. Stores such as engine oil . . . cordage, lumber, etc. prohibitive in price here."[61] Despite the high prices, the Navy continued to purchase what was needed, but the cupboard was nearly bare by the spring of 1918. "People in Ponta Delgada badly need supplies," Sims was informed. "Eggs and fruit are getting scarce. The Americans are eating the natives out of everything," an officer recorded in his diary.[62] Unlike Gibraltar and Corfu, the American personnel at Ponta Delgada were reprovisioned from supply depots in the United States.

The Navy found it difficult to provide logistical support for *Olympia* while she was deployed at Murmansk in northern Russian waters. The British shuttled a collier weekly, and some provisions and winter clothing were transported on these ships. Attempts to ship fresh vegetables failed because of "climatic conditions." The cruiser's personnel had to depend upon British support for provisions.[63]

With the exception of depth charges, bombs, and ammunition for aircraft machine guns, the American naval forces in the war zone received their munitions from the United States. British and French naval guns had different calibers than those carried on American ships. Unlike the ammunition ships (AE) of World War II, no auxiliary vessels were designated as ammunition transports during World War I. Naval cargo vessels carried them with other stores. Tenders provided spare torpedoes. Mines for the North Sea Mine Barrage were shipped on converted Great Lakes steamers. The British supplied depth charges, and others were shipped from the United States.[64]

Ammunition for the guns was never in short supply. Ordnance for the U.S. naval vessels were stored in the magazines of the Royal Navy and French navy.[65]

The Bureau of Surgery and Medicine established its own supply service for the American forces in European waters. Two supply depots were set up, one at Liverpool for the British Isles and a second at Brest for naval forces operating in France. The American Red Cross initially supplied medical items, and it maintained its help even after supplies arrived from the United States.[66]

Of all the materials in short supply, fuel oil was the most critical when the United States entered the war. The six destroyers sent to Ireland were the first American oil-fired warships to engage in combat. In 1917, the United States Navy was still in the process of converting its fleet to oil fuel, a revolution in technology second in importance only to the shift from sail to steam. The 1914–18 conflict was the first in which the belligerents became largely dependent upon motorized equipment on both land and sea. Lord Curzon's famous remark, "The Allies floated to victory on a sea of oil," perhaps an exaggeration, nevertheless illustrates the importance of this fuel.[67]

Although the French in 1909 became the first to announce the conversion of their entire fleet to oil, the British led the way. They did so reluctantly because the British Isles had no natural supplies of oil, although they possessed enormous reserves of coal in Wales. Admiralty officials recognized the many advantages of oil over coal. Although the Royal Navy began to convert its fleet to oil burners during the first decade of the twentieth century, it waited until 1912 to decide to build five oil-fueled battleships. By the outbreak of war in 1914, 45 percent of the British fleet burned oil, including nearly all the destroyers, but the bulk of the British battleship fleet still depended on coal mixed with oil. During the war, the number of oil-burning warships steadily increased; they did not build any more coal burners.[68] The Admiralty maintained a comfortable oil reserve until late in 1916, but the advent of unrestricted submarine warfare abruptly threatened the supply. By the spring of 1917, German sinkings of ships transporting petroleum and the continued increase in the number of oil burners in the fleet created a crisis that influenced Lord Jellicoe's candid talk with Admiral Sims shortly after the United States entered the war. During the early months of 1917, the Allies lost an average of a tanker a day.

The U.S. Navy entered the oil age slowly. The Navy remained cautious about switching to oil, primarily because of the fear that the supply would not be adequate to meet its needs. In 1910, the Navy still had few oil burners; only two battleships carried oil mixed with coal. The following year, the Navy took the significant step of approving the construction of *Nevada*, the first oil-burning battleship in the American fleet. By 1913, convinced that an adequate supply of petroleum was available, the Navy decided to build an oil-burning fleet. Never again, as Admiral Allston has written, did the United States Navy authorize or build new coal-fired ships.[69] By 1914, the Navy had in operation or under construction 4 battleships, 41 destroyers, 30 submarines, and a number of miscellaneous vessels—all oil burners. During World War I, the Navy's building program included 229 destroyers, 21 seagoing tugs, 49 minesweepers, and 60 Eagle boats, all using fuel oil; 20 submarines using diesel oil, and 442 subchasers using gasoline.[70] Nonetheless, most of the American fleet was still coal-fired when the United States entered the war. As late as 1918, approximately 250 naval vessels deployed on distant stations used coal as fuel.

The decision to deploy oil-burning destroyers in the war zone contributed to the growing petroleum crisis. Great Britain, who furnished most of the oil used by the Allied ships, seriously depleted its oil reserves. The British navy's monthly oil requirements jumped from 80,500 tons in January 1915 to 190,000 tons two years later. By 1918, the Grand Fleet contained 15 capital ships, 7 cruisers, and 125 destroyers dependent upon fuel oil. Tanker losses to U-boats further lowered the oil supply. "As demands went up tankers went down." Fuel oil stores were so low in February 1917 that Lord Curzon admitted, "the Fleet had to restrict its exercises." In June, the C-in-C of the Grand Fleet was told that the oil situation was "most critical," that all oil-burning vessels "except in great emergency were to be limited to three-fifths power." In July, British foreign secretary Lord Arthur Balfour cabled the British commissioner in the United States that unless three hundred thousand tons of fuel oil could reach Britain, immobilization of the Grand Fleet was threatened. This was the first of a series of urgent telegrams to the United States pleading for more oil and more tankers to carry it.[71]

Britain imported 80 percent of its fuel oil from the United States.[72] The United States had more than enough petroleum to care for its needs and those of the Allies. Difficulties arose over its transportation, not the supply. Before the American intervention, large numbers of tankers transported oil to the Allies. Afterward major differences with Great Britain materialized over this problem. The British inevitably turned to the United States for additional tankers. As one authority has written, "Since the Western Hemisphere . . . supplied the bulk of the world's oil, the Allies' main difficulty, therefore was one of transportation and not of basic supply." In every possible way, through Sims and Page in London and His Majesty's officials in the United States, the British government pressured Wilson's administration to provide more oil transports.[73]

The tanker problem illustrates the confusion and cross-purposes that troubled Washington during the early months of the war. In 1916, Congress approved a Council of National Defense composed of cabinet members and representatives of industry, business, transportation, and labor to advise the administration on economic mobilization. In March 1917, it created a Petroleum Advisory Committee chaired by Alfred C. Bedford, chairman of Standard Oil of New Jersey. It included representatives of the petroleum industry in the United States. The State Department reported the Allied fuel crisis to the committee. Although the committee acted only in an advisory capacity, it made decisions concerning petroleum matters. For example, in May 1917, it transferred seven American tankers from their former trade routes to the U.S.–U.K. route.[74] This change came at the request of the Admiralty. During April alone, five tankers were sunk and another four seriously damaged, a total of 72,000 tons. "It is therefore strongly urged that the United States should be asked to supply every oiler they can spare forthwith, and also to lay down as large a number of new oilers as is possible."[75] During May and June, the Navy sought to ensure that its force deployed in European waters had adequate fuel. It did not give priority to the Royal Navy.

On May 2, Secretary Daniels cabled Sims: "Can oil be obtained from any nearby fleet for the destroyers . . . or must the supply be from tankers sent from this side."[76] The Admiralty informed him that the destroyers could fuel from Admiralty stocks. "It is assumed that such supplies will be replaced by American oil ships bringing equivalent quantities to U.K."[77] At the end of the month, Sims, probably prodded by the Admiralty, inquired when tankers would arrive to replenish fuel. "It is most important, "he wrote, "that our forces were self sustaining and independent of material assistance," including fuel.[78] A few days later, the force commander informed the Department that during May the destroyers consumed 9,400 tons of fuel and that 8,000 tons were needed for June and 25,000 for July, when additional destroyers joined the Queenstown force. "Admiralty needs every gallon they can get, the situation being most critical, as reserve is but 2½ months and is rapidly diminishing."[79]

Sims's cables prompted several meetings in Washington between British officials, representatives of the Petroleum Advisory Committee, and the Navy Department. An agreement was reached to pool all petroleum products furnished to the Allies provided that the American naval forces in European waters were supplied from this stock. The primary objective of this arrangement was to permit the employment of "maximum transportation facilities both commercial and naval." Despite assurances from Washington, the Admiralty manifested concern about its transportation to the war zone. In the summer of 1914, the total tanker fleet numbered about 400 vessels, of which 260 were of Allied registry, nearly all British, and 140 American.[80] The overwhelming majority of those afloat in April 1917 were already involved directly or indirectly in the war effort.

In April 1917, the Navy believed that it had sufficient tanker tonnage. Four oilers, *Arethusa*, *Cuyama*, *Kanawha*, and *Maumee*, were in commission. *Arethusa*, 2,464 tons, was the first Navy oiler.[81] The Department's decision to concentrate on oil fuel for its new destroyers and the approval of the first oil-fired battleship in 1911 led to the construction of the other three. *Kanawha* and her two sister ships, *Maumee* and *Cuyama*, displaced 5,800 tons each.[82] *Maumee* was the first surface ship in the Navy to use diesel engines. She was also the first oiler to refuel U.S. warships at sea. The Navy had only four oilers in 1917 because a number of Navy colliers were equipped to carry fuel oil as well as coal, among them *Neptune*, *Proteus*, *Nereus*, *Orion*, *Jason*, and the ill-fated *Cyclops*. Together they could carry approximately two hundred thousand barrels of oil, but they were not used to transport fuel to Europe; they serviced the American and Allied ships in the Western Hemisphere and the Pacific Ocean. The colliers could carry only 2,930 tons of oil, not enough to warrant their use on the transatlantic route.[83]

The Navy obviously needed additional oilers. They were obtained during the war in four ways: regular naval construction, lease from private owners, purchase from private owners, and assignment by the U.S. Shipping Board. On May 12, a conference took place between Admiral McGowan and the administrative secretary to the chairman of the Petroleum Advisory Committee about the tanker shortage. The committee's representative complained that the Navy was forcing shipbuilding firms under contract to give priority to warship over auxiliary construction. This practice affected the construction of tankers.[84] A few weeks later the Navy decided to postpone its capital-ship program and give priority to antisubmarine craft and merchant ships. This action included a number of auxiliary vessels, including two oilers. The Navy originally planned to build twelve oilers but eventually asked for only four. The Naval Act of 1916 provided for fuel ships, including two oilers, but they were still under construction in 1917. The United States Shipping Board contracted for more than a hundred large tankers, but only three were completed before the Armistice.[85]

Admiral McGowan wanted to charter or requisition commercial tankers. In June, Congress passed the Navy Appropriations Act of that year, which gave the Navy the right to commandeer shipyards and ships during the emergency. On July 3, a conference convened at the Navy Department. Attending were representatives of the British government, the chairman of the Petroleum Advisory Committee, Admiral McGowan, and members of his staff. They agreed that the Navy needed additional tankers to meet its obligations in European waters. To determine the required tonnage, the British were requested to furnish information about their future needs, including monthly estimates if possible. Before the messenger arrived, however, the Navy decided to take over six commercial tankers and charter four others. Finally, the Navy requisitioned four small merchant vessels to transport miscellaneous cargoes of gasoline in drums, lubricants, and diesel oil in barrels. The tankers chartered or requisitioned were *Broad Arrow, John M. Connelly, Los Angeles, Sylvis Arrow, Frank H. Buck, Goldshell, Herbert L. Pratt, Chestnut Hill, Hisko,* and *Standard Arrow.* The four vessels commandeered were *Sioux, Manta, Carie,* and *Ozama.*[86]

The Navy's requisition of the six tankers annoyed the Petroleum Advisory Committee. At the same time, naval officials became irritated with the committee, convinced that it was exceeding its authority. On June 12, the British embassy informed the Foreign Office that the committee had advised it that two tankers (apparently commercial) were to be used to transport oil for U.S. and British ships through a pooling arrangement. Daniels, in a note to Secretary of State Robert Lansing, reported that the pooling arrangement was "formulated . . . without the knowledge of the Navy Department." "Will you," he added, "be good enough to invite the attention of the British Embassy to the obvious impropriety of attaching importance to the suggestions of private individuals [i.e., members of the Petroleum Advisory Committee] and basing thereon proposals to the Foreign Office concerning matters in which the responsible Departments . . . are vitally interested until such Departments have been consulted."[87] To make matters worse, when the Admiralty messenger carrying information about the fuel/tanker situation arrived in Washington, he conferred with the committee but not with Navy Department officials. Daniels wrote a sharp protest to the British embassy.[88] When the messenger finally conferred with naval officials, he surprised them with the statement that the Grand Fleet was no longer threatened by a shortage of fuel oil. He also informed them that the Petroleum Advisory Committee had agreed to provide 355,000 tons of fuel oil for the Allies during the next six months, approximately 20,000 tons a month in excess of the Admiralty's earlier estimate of need. A third of it was to be transported in the "double bottom" arrangement, a method that the Admiralty was extremely reluctant to accept because it would disrupt the delivery of badly needed supplies. The Admiralty strongly urged the use of additional tankers for this purpose.[89] This activity did nothing to reduce the Department's suspicions of British intent.

Distrust of the British was one of the elements that stimulated a growing belief that information was being withheld from them, a feeling that continued to grow until Admiral Mayo's trip in September. Wariness of their "Anglo cousins" permeated the Wilson government. Many believed that the British wartime shipping policy was developed with an eye to international trade in the postwar world, including Daniels and Edward N. Hurley, head of the U.S. Shipping Board. This opinion affected naval policy, including convoying, shipping, and ship construction.[90] It motivated Benson's warning to Sims to be extremely cautious "in lending your support to details of requisitioning proposals [of tankers] of any character." He stressed that the Department would place military necessities first and "settle the commercial complications later [and] will guarantee . . . so far as its own efforts are concerned . . . every measure it can to assist in safeguarding the military needs of the British fleet as regards the oil situation."[91] The CNO's and other naval officials' skepticism of British motive matched British mistrust of American intentions.

Hurley demanded that the British readjust the allocation of their tanker fleet before the United States would transfer more tankers to the U.K. route.[92] In October, Sir Frederick Black, head of the British Oil Mission in New York, wrote the chairman of the Petroleum Advisory Committee: "As you are aware, American trade in petroleum products is going on actively in practically every direction, involving much coastwise movement to refineries, etc. Also transport to markets which might admit temporary reduction such as Central and South America, West Indies, etc." He added, "a very moderate adjustment of that trade, falling infinitely short of the immense sacrifice made by Great Britain for her self and the Allies, would easily make good our deficiency."[93] In January 1918, he wrote to Hurley in anger: "Have read your cable to London re tankers with dismay. Failure to render immediate help in critical oil and food situation in Europe is most serious. . . . Much tonnage on American coast is now occupied in conveying manufactured products from south to north for purpose of luxurious consumption in automobiles."

Benson viewed the tanker problem, as he did everything else, from a nationalistic viewpoint.[94] Although some authorities believe that he was not as Anglophobic as some thought, he was extremely suspicious of the British. His suspicions abated somewhat after his mission in November-December 1917, but they never disappeared. In December 1917, American officials in Washington, concerned over the growing impasse with the British government over the tanker issue, sent Commander Foley and L. I. Thomas, a director of Standard Oil of New Jersey, to London to determine the extent of the fuel oil crisis and the Allies' future needs. Most important, they were to reconcile the differences between British and American authorities over tanker employment.[95] When Commander Foley arrived in England early in December, he found instructions to go to Paris and confer with the CNO. Benson warned him to proceed "with the utmost discretion" in dealing with the tanker issue. After he returned to Washington, Benson cabled Foley a message to pass on to Sir Joseph Maclay, minister of shipping: "Have been very busy on fuel oil since return. realize its critical effect. . . . Situation here is very critical and withdrawal of tankers will reduce output of fuel oil upon which you are depending. Production will be curtailed." Nonetheless, he informed Maclay that additional tankers would be assigned to the transatlantic route "voyage by voyage," depending upon priority based on "stock on hand" in the British Isles. He also urged the diversion of British tankers on low-priority routes to the U.S.–U.K. trade.[96] Bainbridge Colby, Wilson's fuel commissioner, took action to reduce the use of fuel oil in what he called "non-essential industries." "There is a very grave emergency in both England and France arising from the shortage of fuel oil," he wrote. "It threatens the scope and efficiency of our destroyer patrol in European waters; it threatens the efficiency of the British fleet. . . . [I]t involves also the safety and practicability of our entire transport and cargo service across the Atlantic."[97]

Foley and Thomas conferred with British officials over the oil/tanker issue and continued until the end of the war. They discovered that the British were apparently building up their Far East oil trade rather than transferring tankers to the Atlantic. This information convinced Hurley, chairman of the U.S. Shipping Board, that the British were not negotiating in good faith. Foley and Thomas also determined that the Royal Navy had adequate oil reserves for the near future. Following instructions from Benson, Hurley, and the Advisory Committee, they continued to recommend that the British transfer tankers from the East to the Atlantic but without success. When the British did not agree, they suggested the withdrawal of seven U.S. tankers from the U.K. trade and their reassignment to the French route or coastwise trade. Sims told Foley that the differences could not be resolved.[98]

The British position remained the same; more tankers were needed for the U.S.–U.K. route, which only the United States could provide. Admiral Wemyss, the first sea lord, reported to the War Cabinet, "The Navy is now dependent upon the good will of the United States for supplies of oil fuel and this dependence must continue unless and until alternative supplies can be developed." He added, "we [now] have no visible means of avoiding absolute dependence on the U.S.A."[99]

The changing of the guard at the Admiralty in January 1918 with Jellicoe and Carson out and with Geddes and Wemyss in along with Beatty as C-in-C of the Grand Fleet did nothing to change policy. For various reasons, including the shortage of oil fuel, British warships in the Grand Fleet and elsewhere were not very active. They increased their activity only in the face of a possible German threat.[100] In May, the comptroller of shipping recommended to the War Cabinet that the government should consider building ships that could carry either coal or oil. The oil situation, he wrote, was still most serious, and "owing to the lack of assistance from the United States and reduction in double bottom imports our reserve is falling."[101]

The ongoing tanker issue did not deter the Navy Department from giving priority to increasing tanker tonnage to meet the needs of its rapidly expanding force in European waters. Navy officials understood that this procedure would result from the pooling arrangement with the Admiralty and would increase the oil reserve. In October 1917, an unnamed officer in the Department wrote to the CNO that the number of oilers in naval service could be increased in one or two ways; to requisition and withdraw from commercial employment the required tankers ("this is the procedure adopted and persisted in by the British Admiralty") or to develop a tanker-mobilization plan that withdrew a limited number of tankers from the Shipping Board and commissioned them and to adopt an oiler-construction program. Benson favored the latter. Three weeks later, the Bureau of Supplies and Accounts recommended the acquisition from the Shipping Board of three tankers with a cargo-carrying capacity of 7,500 tons each. These vessels would be used to supply naval stations and bases on the Atlantic coast. In turn, this initiative would free other oilers to carry fuel to U.S. warships in European waters. In January, the Department even considered the British procedure of carrying oil in double bottoms, but Admiral Gleaves, in command of the transport service, strongly opposed this measure. He pointed out that the double bottoms were used to carry much-needed freshwater for both naval and AEF use in France.[102] The Navy rejected the double-bottom idea. In March, Daniels agreed to request authorization for twelve new oilers. By that date, a dozen tankers, both those of the Navy and the Shipping Board, transported approximately 84,000 tons of fuel oil to Great Britain per month. U.S. warships operating in the war zone consumed approximately 25,000 tons; the remainder was added to the reserve. The Department anticipated a 100 percent increase in oil-burning vessels in Europe, especially new destroyers, during the next six months, at least doubling the amount of required oil. In addition, the build-up of U.S. naval aviation in Great Britain entailed additional tanker space. The Department concluded that twelve new oilers would meet the anticipated American needs and the needs of the British navy. The U.S. Shipping Board agreed to build the tankers for the Navy.[103]

One matter bandied around within the Department was the fuel requirements that would result if the entire fleet had to be deployed in European waters. It was estimated that an additional 250 vessels would need 390,289 tons of coal and oil. Coal was available, but serious questions arose of the acquisition of tanker tonnage to supply the oil burners.[104] The Department's concern became reality in the summer of 1918, when three oil-burning battleships were deployed to Bantry Bay, Ireland.[105] The lack of oil fuel led the Admiralty strongly to oppose the dispatch of oil-fueled battleships to join the Grand Fleet. Instead the Navy deployed the Ninth Division of coal burners. The Admiralty reluctantly agreed to base American battleships at Bantry Bay and after considerable negotiation provided a small 4,000-ton tanker to support them.

For more than a year after the United States entered the war, the fuel problem did not concern naval units in France. Escorts out of Brest and other French ports were coal burners. The British provided coal for French naval needs, and the French in turn dispensed coal to the U.S. ships. When the naval air stations became operational, difficulties arose. The Navy and the AEF worked out an agreement whereby fuel and lubricants would come under a pooling arrangement. Cargo ships and tankers brought in petroleum products along with supplies from the British.[106]

The situation changed when the Department decided to base oil-burning destroyers in French waters to protect American troop transports. In August 1918, Sims informed the Department that anticipated oil consumption for these vessels would be approximately 30,000 tons a month.[107] Clemenceau appealed directly to Wilson for tankers. "These tank steamers exist," he wrote in his blunt fashion: "some are plying in the Pacific Ocean. . . . Others can be provided from the new fleet of tankers which [are] . . . now being built in the United States."[108] The American president could not agree; this appeal came in the midst of the growing demands from the British. He was well aware that the British supplied French requirements.

In September 1918, an American tanker carried fuel oil for U.S. naval forces operating in French waters directly to Brest.[109] Oil fuel was not shipped directly to France before September because of inadequate storage. As early as November 1917, the Navy Department informed the French that oil-fueled destroyers would be based at Brest. This deployment did not occur until the summer of 1918, when new petroleum tanks became available. Admiral Wilson disputed Sims's contention after the war that oil-burning destroyers were not based on the French coast because of inadequate oiling facilities. Wilson declared in the Naval Investigation Hearings of 1920 that, when he succeeded to the command, "facilities at Brest were adequate for quite a large force," but Sims was correct. Oiling facilities at Brest were inadequate in the fall of 1917.[110] The French navy at that time had five small oil tanks that held a maximum of five thousand tons of oil. The French navy refused to turn over these tanks to the Americans but agreed to permit them to build new ones. The Navy disassembled three 7,000-ton steel tanks at the Norfolk Navy Yard and shipped them to Brest. Additional tanks were to be installed at the other U.S. naval bases along the French coast, but they were still being assembled at the Armistice. The delay resulted from labor problems. By September, the tanks at Brest were almost ready, and Sims requested an oiler to carry 7,500 tons directly to Brest every eight days. Two oilers reached Brest in October, not one every eight days as the force commander requested, but sufficient to keep the oil reserve there at 27,000 tons.

The Navy's supply of fuel oil to its forces in French waters after September 1918 contrasted with the fuel policy that Sims established in May 1917. With the exception of the forces in the Azores replenished directly from the United States, the pooling arrangement with the Admiralty supplied American naval forces in European waters, including those in the Mediterranean. This arrangement also included the northern Russian waters, Gibraltar, and the Adriatic. French naval officials opposed the arrangement, insisting that all the fuel received from the British for naval operations in French waters should be allocated through them, including the American supply.[111]

Fueling the Adriatic force became its most vexing problem because of the extended supply line and because the subchasers deployed there used gasoline. In March 1918, the Navy Department agreed to base the first thirty chasers sent to the war zone at Corfu to reinforce the Otranto Barrage. Gasoline storage was not available at Corfu; the nearest tanks were at Augusta, Italy, three hundred miles from the American base. The British agreed to install storage tanks on Corfu, but the Admiralty requested a small tanker to transport the fuel to Augusta and a barge to carry it to the American base. The Department informed Sims that it did not have such a vessel. The tender

Leonidas, which accompanied the chasers to Corfu, carried enough gasoline for initial operations, and the British eventually provided the small tanker. She anchored at the American base, and the chasers came alongside to take on fuel. British colliers transported the gasoline to Gibraltar in deck loads. It was transferred to a tanker and carried to Malta and Augusta.[112]

U.S. subchasers were also based in Great Britain, seventy-two in Plymouth and thirty-six in Queenstown. Adequate gasoline storage facilities were available at both sites, but subsidiary fueling and repair stations were needed along the English and Irish coasts. An aide informed Sims that the chasers "eat up gasoline." The Admiralty provided storage tanks and two small coastwise tankers to transport the fuel.[113]

The Grand Fleet's oil fuel problem stemmed as much from difficulties of distribution and storage as from acquisition. The routes to the fleet's bases, either through the English Channel or around northern Scotland, were infested with U-boats. Many tankers had been sunk while refueling the fleet. The Admiralty stationed forty tankers, twenty each at Scapa Flow and Rosyth, to refuel the huge armada. This arrangement permitted a large percentage of the warships to fuel simultaneously should they have to sortie quickly. All the ships in the Grand Fleet were kept at four hours' steaming notice, but the oil burners, especially destroyers, needed "topping off" before getting underway. Shore tanks and storage barges were under construction at both bases. Early in 1918, the first eighty-ton bulk scows were used to carry fuel oil by canal from the Clyde to the Firth of Forth. However, eighty of these craft transported only six thousand tons a week.

Admiralty officials had studied the possibility of laying a pipeline to link oil terminals at Glasgow with the naval base at Rosyth. The project did not receive approval until American naval officials became interested in it. Although the oil situation in the Grand Fleet had no immediate affect on U.S. warships operating with the fleet because they were coal burners, Navy Department officials from Benson on down believed that sometime in the future additional American naval vessels, including oil burners, would deploy to the fleet. Commander Foley, probably on instructions from Washington, conferred with both the Admiralty and Admiral Beatty's staff. At Foley's request, a pipeline expert, Forrest Towl, the president of the Eureka Pipeline Company, was sent to Britain. After talking with British officials and inspecting the proposed location, he agreed to lay the line. Although the British considered him somewhat brash, his confidence impressed them.[114]

The British agreed to provide German prisoners to dig the trench and perform other construction work, to pay for the materials, and to build the storage tanks and pumping stations. The U.S. Navy agreed to have the materials manufactured and to provide a working party of skilled personnel and supervisor especially recruited for the project. In June 1918, six officers, including a doctor, a hundred enlisted men, the pipes and other materials, and provisions for six months arrived at Glasgow, and the work commenced in July. The thirty-six-mile line was completed in two months, but it could not operate until the pumping stations and storage facilities were ready. A shortage of riveters delayed the opening until November 1. The line had a capacity of 15,000 barrels a day.[115]

The tanker question was never resolved to the satisfaction of the Allies, particularly the British. Lloyd George's government pressured the United States for additional tanker tonnage up to the Armistice. American officials, receiving information constantly funneled to them from the Foley Mission, continued to believe that the British exaggerated the so-called oil crisis. They suspected that it was part of a design to strengthen British economic interests at the expense of the United States after the war. The tanker controversy, toward the end, contributed to the irritation that retarded wartime and postwar cooperation between Great Britain and the United States.[116]

During the conflict, Navy tankers transported 681,322 tons of fuel oil to the war zone, only a small part of the amount sent across the Atlantic. More than 2.5 million tons were shipped to the Allies during 1918 alone. Forty of the more than four hundred tankers used to carry this fuel oil were designated Navy oilers.[117] Despite dire British warnings, an oil crisis never developed; American ships in European waters experienced shortages, but this did not compromise their operational capabilities.

The supply of coal, the other fuel, never became a serious problem. The British who had nearly a monopoly of the coal trade for decades, provided almost all of the necessary coal for American naval forces in European waters. British coal resources, particularly the Welsh variety, considered the best marine coal in the world, proved sufficient to supply the American coal burners, their own ships, and those of the Allies. In 1915, the British had nearly four hundred colliers in service, but losses to German submarines reduced the number by two-thirds when the United States entered the war. Nonetheless, little difficulty arose in supplying vessels in home waters, including the American battleships operating with the Grand Fleet. The Admiralty assigned five small colliers to provide fuel for Rodman's division. The efficient British rail system carried coal from Wales directly to Rosyth, where it was loaded on colliers and carried to the fleet at Scapa Flow.[118]

It was more difficult to provide coal for the Allies and the Americans in France and elsewhere in the world. These needs included fuel to heat homes and buildings. As the winter of 1917 approached, the coal shortage in France became so acute that the government feared revolution. France received all of its coal from Great Britain. The majority of the ships in the French navy burned coal and had to be replenished from reserves located at the various naval bases along the Atlantic coast and the Mediterranean. The first American ships deployed in French waters were coal-burning yachts that the Navy converted into antisubmarine vessels. Initially the Department considered supplying the yachts by chartered collier. The Admiralty, preferring to use American colliers on other routes, agreed to provide coal for U.S. naval vessels operating in French waters. The Navy Department was willing to contract directly with the Admiralty for the coal, but it proved more practical to obtain coal from French depots. French and American naval vessels received their coal from the same coaling facilities, the French billing the Americans.[119] Because of the increase in American naval forces operating in French waters, coal consumption went from 7,000 tons a month in August 1917 to 25,000 tons a month a year later.

The fleet of transports and cargo ships carrying the AEF to France created another fuel problem. The hundreds of vessels that began to discharge their cargoes of troops and material in June 1917 continued until the end of the war. They required enough fuel, usually coal, to recross the Atlantic. In August, Sims, under strong pressure from the French, recommended that only ships with adequate bunkering space should be used in the "Bridge to France." This policy would help alleviate the coal shortage in France and also result in a rapid turnaround. Benson agreed, and every effort was made to enforce it. Extra bunkers were installed on some ships, and bags of coal were stored on open decks and in nooks and crannies.[120] Nonetheless, ships at times had to replenish their coal. Usually they coaled in the French port where they discharged their cargo, but on some occasions adequate supplies were not available and they went to Liverpool or Southampton before returning to the United States. In February, the Navy assigned two colliers, *Jason* and *Nereus*, to transport coal to France. The ships were too large to dock at Brest and lighters had to be used to unload the coal.[121] In May, the British began utilizing two small colliers to transport coal directly to Brest for the U.S. Navy. Admiral Wilson recommended the addition of three colliers on the transatlantic run to Brest because of "the large demand for coal . . . at Brest and the shortage of coal at the British sources," but this reinforcement did not take place before the Armistice.[122]

General Pershing was concerned about obtaining coal for the AEF. British officials told him that they could provide the coal but could not transport it. In October, the Army chartered three ships to carry coal from Cardiff to French ports. Throughout the winter months of 1917–18, the vessels engaged in the Army's coal trade increased in numbers. By the middle of August 1918, twenty-nine U.S. steamers, four Navy colliers, and 76,000 tons of Swedish time charters leased to the United States Shipping Board (USSB) engaged in this activity.[123] In July 1918, the USSB asked the Navy to assume total control of the Army coal service from Great Britain to France. Given the steady increase in colliers engaged in this activity, the Shipping Board became concerned about the lack of centralized control. Early in 1918, a Shipping Control Committee comprised of representatives of the three organizations was created to coordinate shipping. This group made the recommendation to concentrate the Army's coal activity under Navy control.[124] Although a majority of the colliers engaged in the transportation of coal from Wales to France belonged to NOTS, they came under Sims's command while operating in European waters.

In addition to nineteen vessels operated by the Army in the transportation of coal, the Navy assumed control of forty lake steamers. The USSB had taken over some sixty vessels that operated on the Great Lakes, brought them to the Atlantic seaboard, and utilized them in coastwise shipping. Many had transported ores on the Great Lakes and were easily adapted to carry coal. Ordered to British waters, they joined the other vessels engaged in the coal service. Altogether the Navy eventually operated seventy vessels that carried coal to France for the AEF. The potential crisis was avoided when the former Great Lakes steamers began to carry coal from Cardiff to French ports.[125] The War Department requested colliers from the Navy. In 1917, the Navy had fourteen colliers, eight in the Atlantic and six in the Pacific. Before the American entry into the war, naval officials considered this number adequate because of the belief that most of the fleet would remain in the Western Hemisphere. Even after the United States entered the conflict, few colliers were added to the fleet, and only one was deployed to the war zone. *Bath* was sent over to cooperate in the AEF's coal operations. Later three additional colliers taken over by the Navy joined *Bath*. Navy colliers under NOTS transported more than 1 million tons of coal during the war from Hampton Roads, all of it destined for U.S. military forces in France.[126]

The British fueled the minelayers based in Scotland, the auxiliary vessels that serviced the U.S. forces, and the transports that brought troops and supplies to U.K. ports. An article in the *Pall Mall Gazette* claimed that U.S. naval forces in the British Isles consumed 2 million tons of coal during the war. The minelayers used Scottish coal, although U.S. naval engineers considered it inferior to Welsh coal.[127]

Gibraltar became an important fuel depot for American naval vessels based there, and also for the ships, both naval and mercantile, that passed through on their way to French Atlantic ports and the Mediterranean. Because of the length of voyages from the United States to Mediterranean ports, the ships usually had to refuel at Gibraltar. The British kept their base there adequately provided with coal.[128]

The Azores, like Gibraltar, became an important transitional point for ships traveling between Europe and North America. The British possessed the only coal depot in the islands. The United States arranged for its vessels to use this facility. Coal occasionally arrived from the United States, but most of it was transported in British colliers and cargo ships, proceeding from the United Kingdom to ports in the Western Hemisphere. On one occasion, the supply fell so low that an emergency shipment of five thousand tons had to be sent from Great Britain.[129] The British possessed powerful economic interests in Portugal and the Portuguese colonies. They discouraged the United States from establishing a coal depot in the Azores, which might well have remained after the war.

The Bureau of Supplies and Accounts claimed after the war that ships under its direction carried 12,000 tons of gasoline, 130,000 tons of coal, 74,600 tons of fuel oil, and 1.2 million tons of miscellaneous supplies and provisions. After NOTS took over all cargo shipping, vessels under its control carried 1,090,724 tons of cargo, including 687,475 tons of fuel oil, for the Navy.[130] These statistics do not include spare parts and aircraft. Also, in assessing the supply system one must take into account the assistance of the Allies. Although statistics on this support have not been compiled, it was clearly substantial. As far as provisions were concerned, one correspondent insisted, "there never was a heartier, huskier, more healthy or better-nourished outfit in this universe" than personnel with the U.S. naval forces in European waters.[131] In the summer of 1918, prominent individuals in New York City organized a committee to "collect and deliver fresh fruits and vegetables, jams, preserves, etc. supplied free of cost." The stated reason for this committee's existence was information that the crews of British and American warships "got practically no fresh vegetables and no fresh fruit whatever, except what they pay [for] out of their own pockets." An indignant McGowan, when appraised of the committee and its objectives, said that the information was erroneous, and the committee was not needed.[132] On July 2, 1918, Sims cabled the Bureau of Supplies and Accounts: "All of the [bases and stations] . . . in France [are] full to capacity with provisions. Recommend that the next scheduled supply ship discharge its cargo at Plymouth."[133] Ships operating at sea often ran short of rations. A well-known publisher who served on one of the small subchasers wrote years later that during the eighteen months of his service in the Navy, nearly all on the chasers, he consumed at a conservative estimate about three thousand tons of beans.[134]

Construction and repair materials were in short supply in the war zone. Although lumber for constructing barracks and other structures was available in limited amounts, transports frequently brought stacks of lumber on their decks. Cement was hard to obtain. Steel for naval vessel repairs was a priority in shipping, but the British supplied most of it used on U.S. vessels.[135]

Although the U.S. Navy sought self-sufficiency in the war zone, it was neither possible nor practical. Even in France, which was far more exhausted than Great Britain, considerable help was forthcoming. During and after the war, the amount of assistance was exaggerated, and it proved expensive.[136] In May 1918, the director of the French Public Works in Brest wrote a detailed report of his department's aid provided to the Americans to help construct their bases and stations. He mentioned the construction of "numerous" projects, including the old chateau, a magazine for ammunition, renovation of various buildings, installation of telephones, water delivery by barges, "augmentation of water facilities in the Arsenal," coaling ships, construction of concrete foundation for fuel tanks, supply of pipes for fuel lines, and the construction of various air stations.[137] Although much of this was distorted and not entirely true, the French provided what they could.

Secretary of the Navy Daniels stated in his annual report for 1918 that "Every effort has been made to utilize existing facilities whenever possible rather than to duplicate the machinery of supply." In a memo prepared after the war ended, a member of Sims's staff wrote: "Throughout the war we have been practically entirely dependent upon England for all repairs, supplies and assistance not obtainable from home. . . . England['s] resources . . . [were] available to assist in administering our scattered forces. . . . Our forces in the Baltic, Adriatic, Salonika, Murmansk Coast, Gibraltar, etc. [were] . . . all fueled by arrangement with the Admiralty. Similar remarks apply to important [repairs], . . . docking, transportation of supplies, issues of naval supplies, lubricating oil, obtaining tugs, barges, floating equipment, etc."[138]

Allied logistical support was by no means free of cost. Charges were levied for everything from ship repairs to buoy fees at every level of government.[139] Although American officials accepted the assessments, they complained about some of the more unwarranted or exorbitant prices. Captain William Leahy, for example, was critical of the French for charging pilotage fees for American ships that had "come to save them from the Germans."[140] Soon after the American intervention, the government arranged a reciprocal agreement with the British whereby bills contracted by American naval forces within Great Britain or any of its possessions would be submitted monthly to the British financial representative in the United States. This procedure included private firms in the United Kingdom. For example, the Admiralty was to pay charges for repair work done in commercial shipyards on American vessels. The U.S. Navy would reimburse the Admiralty. The Admiralty submitted a monthly bill to the Navy with an itemized account of the help. Sims endorsed it and forwarded it to the

Department. Sims and the Department, particularly the chief of the Bureau of Supplies and Accounts, approved the plan because it eliminated the necessity of establishing a general accounting unit at Simsadus.[141] Problems surfaced from the beginning. Bills were not submitted monthly. Discrepancies occurred, at least partly because of different accounting practices and measurements. For example, gallons of gasoline were computed as 231 cubic inches in American gasoline and 277.42 in Imperial gasoline. What complicated the matter was that the Navy had agreed to replace a gallon for a gallon.[142]

But the most aggravating problem, at least from the British point of view, was the delay of compensation. This stemmed from the Navy's financial system. Congress made appropriations for specific bureaus and items. Sims, presumably prompted by the Admiralty, unsuccessfully recommended restitution from the Navy Emergency Fund.[143] The first sea lord attempted to get compensation for manpower used in the repair of American vessels, but President Wilson and his advisors rejected the proposal. At the Department's request, Sims's staff computed the man-hours required to work on American vessels.[144] The problem of compensation was not resolved until long after the war. FDR, after his 1918 trip to Europe, argued that the absence of an accounting officer in Europe was detrimental to the Department's business. He attempted without success to persuade Daniels to send him to Europe to organize and manage a business office.[145]

A less complicated procedure was used to reimburse the French. The ministry of marine charged a flat 20 percent fee for its help, including the work of private contractors. The French ministry of marine agreed to pay for contract work and seek reimbursement from the U.S. Navy. Labor cost became a major bone of contention, primarily because time and again U.S. naval personnel had to complete work started by French workers. Local taxes and fees posed another problem. For example, the chambers of commerce in the different ports had the responsibility of collecting funds to repay the national treasury for improvements to the ports. Foreign vessels, including warships, were not exempt from this duty. Bills were presented to the American government but apparently were never paid. Local port authorities also charged pilotage, docking, and other expenses related to harbor activities. As with British reimbursement, the matter was not settled until long after the war.[146]

The Navy's logistical support was far more efficient than the Army's. Captain William Pratt maintained that "Our total naval effort in this war consisted less in the operation of forces at the front than in [our] . . . logistical efforts.[147]

The "Gobs" Are Coming

Personnel

At the outbreak of war, the United States Navy included 79,182 officers and men, of which 67,6780 were regulars and the remaining 11,502 were reserves. Of this number, 44,447 manned the fighting ships, 7,610 operated the twelve old battleships used for training, and the remainder served on auxiliaries and shore stations.[1] As in most wars, patriotism was rampant early in the war; thousands of reservists and enlistees flocked to the colors. By the end of April, 111,175 men were in the Navy. Within a brief period, naval reservists on active duty surpassed the number of regulars. According to Daniels, at the Armistice the Navy contained 217,256 regulars and 271,571 reserve enlisted men, and 10,489 regular officers and 20,706 reserve officers for a total of 520,022.[2]

Many of the naval vessels, particularly those deployed to the war zone, carried more than their complement. Daniels opposed crowding too many men in a ship; his officers demanded "an absurdly large number of men." The *New York*, while operating with the Grand Fleet, had a crew of 1,444 enlisted men, although her complement was 902.[3] A committee of battleship officers investigated agreed that American naval vessels in European waters carried more men "type for type" than their British counterparts. U.S. warships conducted more shipboard activities than British ships, and a large number of enlisted personnel were "green" unseasoned "boys, and not experienced in this work."[4] Submarines based in Bantry Bay also carried an excess of officers and enlisted personnel. By the Armistice, approximately fifty thousand sailors manned the vessels and shore facilities in the war zone. Although the ships deployed abroad were fully manned, this was not always true for the shore facilities. Admiral Fletcher, when establishing his headquarters in Brest, handicapped for lack of personnel, temporarily employed Americans who had served as volunteer ambulance drivers before the United States entered the conflict.[5] The American naval facility at Gibraltar encountered the same difficulty.

During World War I, 5,328 blacks were enrolled in the Navy. A few were rated petty officers, including water tenders, electricians, and gunner mates, but the overwhelming majority were either messmen or coalheavers attached to engineering divisions. Fourteen black women served in the Navy.[6]

During the war, 11,880 women served in the Navy, all as enlisted nurses or yeomen. Of this number, 293 nurses served at hospitals and base units in England, Scotland, Ireland, and France. Several hundred female nurses were attached to Red Cross hospital units. An undetermined number of women served as yeomen overseas. Nearly all of them performed clerical and other nonmedical duties in the various hospitals.[7]

The Navy's expansion during the war resulted in the enlistment and commissioning of thousands of men, which accelerated promotions. Very few were advanced to admiral mainly because of an absence of first-rate captains, but also because the Navy did not need them. Rear Admiral William F. Fullam wrote sarcastically: "I have not noted any Admirals . . . leading fleets into battle these days. . . . It would appear that actual sea-fighting will be more or less confined to small craft and young officers." When war was declared, 2,394 experienced officers of the line were available, including 350 (two classes) recently graduated from the Naval Academy. Sims tried to assign regular officers to the destroyers, which he considered the first line of defense against the submarine. In August 1917, he informed the Department that each of the destroyers had five experienced line officers, but to keep this number he had to transfer officers from the tenders.[8]

For the regulars, the war created an opportunity for recognition and advancement, but as "Tip" Merrill noted, "The only way to get any glory out of this war is by being in Command. The skipper gets all the praise and glory and medals and the rest of the crew did their duty."[9] Sims frequently complained about his need of experienced middle and junior grade officers, but Benson refused to strip the Atlantic Fleet of most of its regular officers for duty with the European forces.[10] Generally, the reservists got along well with the regulars despite their inexperience. To calm fears that reservists, who did well in the war and who desired permanent commissions, would gain promotion over regulars, legislation specified a ceiling of lieutenant commander for reservists in the peacetime Navy.[11] Daniels consistently opposed expanding the regular force until 1916, despite a deficiency of 40 percent of officers and 20 percent enlisted personnel.[12]

In 1916, Congress approved a Naval Reserve. Under this act, thousands were enrolled before the United States entered the conflict. Forty thousand were mobilized immediately after the declaration of war and received orders to man the hundreds of vessels being commandeered for the coast patrol fleet. Many of them were transferred to ships destined for deployment overseas, although they expected to spend their time patrolling the coast near their homes.[13] Some states had naval reserves, but they were few in number and weak in training. Volunteer organizations existed, such as patrol squadrons organized by yacht clubs; many from these groups entered the Navy. The Army charged that the Navy pre-empted the best men, which forced Secretary Daniels to give up voluntary recruiting for conscription in August 1918.[14]

During the war, approximately eighty thousand men would be assigned to naval vessels and shore facilities in the war zone. (This does not include the two thousand Marines that served on the battleships, the cruiser *Olympia*, and as guards in London and the Lafayette Radio Station personnel.)[15]

Lack of experienced personnel, both officers and enlisted men, posed difficulties throughout the conflict. As new ships were commissioned, veteran officers and men were often transferred to them from naval vessels operating in the war zone. Draftees sent directly from the training stations and receiving ships replaced them. The short-age of officers necessitated assignment of reservists to responsible positions, at times including command of small craft such as subchasers. Gunnery, which excelled in the prewar Navy, deteriorated during the war. Admiral Beatty frequently criticized the poor gunnery of the Sixth Battle Squadron. When the American battleships were detached from the Grand Fleet to return home after the war, approximately half of their personnel were reservists. *Texas* deployed with a crew of which 75 percent were "green men."[16] During the first months that the ships served with the Grand Fleet, there were few changes in personnel; Rodman attributed the significant progress in efficiency to what he called "permanence in personnel."[17] The Bureau of Navigation sent Lieutenant Commander C. G. Davy to investigate personnel problems. He en-dorsed Rodman's plea to avoid rotation of officers serving on the battleships with the Grand Fleet. "It is my opinion that any change in officer personnel at this time would not only be inadvisable because of the consequent demoralizing effect it would have, but also because it would necessarily result in a loss of efficiency for the time being at least. . . . If the 6th Battle Squadron were assigned a six-month training period, for example, before taking its place in the battle line, the situation would be quite differ-ent. But the 6th Battle Squadron is actually *in* the battle line now."[18] Submarines were the one type that retained regular officers. To fill the billets of officers ordered home to take over new submarine construction, the Navy "fleeted up" (promoted) warrant officers.[19]

The majority of the naval aviators and the officers on board the armed yachts and wooden subchasers were reservists. Only 48 officers and 239 enlisted were assigned to naval and marine aviation before the war. Very few were sent to the war zone; naval aviation had to depend heavily upon reserves for its personnel. The much-publicized Yale units were all undergraduates at Yale University who volunteered for the Naval Reserve and paid for flight training and equipment either out of their own pockets or from donations. Other reservists, both officers and enlisted men, after receiving flight training in the United States, were posted to the various naval air stations under construction in Europe. About 2,500 officers and 22,000 men were attached to naval aviation units in the war zone.

The accomplishments of these organizations, according to Sims, were "largely the outcome of civilian enterprise and civilian public spirit."[20] Nonetheless, the lack of experienced regulars to take command of aviation stations and squadrons troubled Sims and his aviation advisors. In a report written after the war, the force commander wrote, "It was necessary to place inexperienced officers in positions of great responsi-bility." In a number of cases, reserve ensigns and lieutenants (jg) commanded squad-rons and stations. Sims tried without success to persuade the Department to promote these men to ranks representative of their responsibilities. He was equally concerned about advancements for the reserve officers commanding other vessels in his com-mand, particularly the yachts and the coal-burning destroyers.[21]

Although Sims admired reservists, he felt strongly that regulars should command the ships, and that a majority of ships' crews should be regulars. There were never enough experienced officers to satisfy Sims and his subordinates.[22] It was difficult for them to grasp the broader outlook of the Department, trying to cope with an ever-expanding Navy.[23]

Sims liked the "college boys" who crewed the subchasers. Not all had a higher education. A veteran recalled that among his shipmates was a Chicago cabbie, a tractor mechanic, a deserter who had reenlisted under an assumed name, a circus lemonade salesman, and a sailor who spoke five languages. Admiral Mayo recalled that a dentist commanded one of the Plymouth chasers.[24] Whatever their background, few had experience at sea. The CO of the subchaser detachment based in Ireland wrote, "Some of them had never seen nor heard of the Bluejackets Manual, and almost all of them were profoundly and cheerfully ignorant of much in the line of naval customs, procedure and regulations."[25] One of the Plymouth chaser captains, according to a veteran who served on his vessel, could not navigate. He recalled that after a patrol his commander, instead of heading directly to the base, always went north until he spotted land and then followed it back to port.[26]

"I do not think that the whole lot [of subchaser crews] contained 1 percent of graduates of Annapolis or 5 percent of experienced sailors," Sims wrote. The force commander preferred to place regulars in command of each division of subchasers (three vessels). He was convinced that in several instances ASW operations failed because of inexperienced reserve officers.[27] The Department admitted that it did not have enough experienced officers to command the 144 chasers sent to the war zone. One officer complained that the Bureau of Navigation refused to recognize that "a captain of one of these chasers on independent duty across the seas has a hundred times more responsibility than a 42nd officer on a battleship in home waters."[28] The Department tried to alleviate the problem in the subchaser units by promoting warrant officers and giving them command of a division of these vessels. Sims disapproved. "It is clearly a demonstrated fact that the average officer who has been commissioned from Boatswain, Gunner or machinist is not qualified for the command of a unit of Chasers operating against enemy submarines. While they may handle their own ships well . . . they do not possess that degree of skill, judgment, and quick decision which is essential to succeed in maneuvering a unit of chasers against any enemy submarine."[29]

Reservists manned the seven converted fishing trawlers deployed to French waters to sweep mines. The unit's commanding officer, a regular, wrote after the war that at his first conference with the vessels' captains, "to my amazement, I learned that several knew no navigation. Of the others, one had served only on sailing ships, one had been a pilot, one a refrigerating engineer experienced only with small boats in the Delaware River, and two had been fishing boat skippers." Shortly after taking command, Captain Magruder cabled Sims: "Most of the officers and men of the vessels . . . are reservists, many who have failed in the performance of their duty on account of lack of experience. . . . [M]any of the officers and men are holding ranks and ratings to which their qualifications and ability do not entitle them." Fletcher, while in command at Brest, complained to Sims that of the six reserve officers commanding trawlers, "one lost his ship, in my opinion unnecessarily, one was relieved on account of drunkenness, one has asked to be relieved and made second in command—reason experience." Two-thirds of his reserve commanding officers were "not at all fitted for their duties."[30]

Regulars commanded the armed yachts deployed in French waters, but the officers and men were nearly all reservists. Admiral Wilson wrote that the yacht crews included men "from more different walks of life than probably ever assembled on a man-of-war."[31] One of the *Margaret*'s crew later called his mates as "green a lot of landlubbers as ever stumbled down a gangplank for the first time. Only two were experienced, competent seamen. The rest varied from farm hand to designer of theatrical costumes, from city gangster to newspaper artist. . . . They looked good for nothing else than getting sick."[32] Rose wrote in his book about *Emerline* that his "crew was fairly intercollegiate with eleven colleges represented: Amherst, Brown, Cornell, Harvard, Lafayette, Lehigh, New York University, Trinity, University of Missouri, Union, and Yale. Most of these men were in the forecastle."[33] Harvard University undergraduates from the classes of 1918 and 1919 appropriately crewed the *Harvard*. Another yacht's officers included a fire insurance agent, a patent lawyer, a college physical education instructor, an advertising executive, a broker, an industrialist, and a "capitalist." A forty-year-old quartermaster was once New Jersey's tax commissioner. "It was quite something to hear the cultivated college speech issuing from a group of tarry sailors who were heaving up anchor."[34] Admiral Wilson, while in command of U.S. forces in France, was unhappy with his lack of regular officers. The reserve officers, he wrote, "are performing difficult and hazardous duty, for which they are not fitted by training or experience."[35]

The loss of the yacht *Alcedo* to a U-boat in October 1917 provided Sims with an opportunity to lament the necessity of assigning inexperienced reserve officers to naval vessels in the war zone. A court of inquiry concluded that the inexperience of the officer of the deck, a reservist, led to the loss. The force commander ordered an investigation of the officers with the yachts. The report noted the large number of reservists and inexperienced officers on the yachts and concluded: "The result is a condition of affairs that could not be much worse from any point of view; it is physically impossible for the Commanding Officer to be continually on the bridge . . . leaving the ship in the war zone [often] in the hands of totally incompetent officers." The report recommendation was that the commanding officer and at least two additional officers on each of the yachts should be regulars. Sims endorsed the report and forwarded it to the Department. The response was that regulars were not available, considering the Navy's overall personnel responsibilities. It proposed to remedy by transferring regulars from other ships in European waters. At that time, the only ships in Sims's force that had a majority of regulars were the destroyers, which already provided onboard training to prepare officers to return to the States and take new commands. The force commander considered this expedient unacceptable.[36]

Niblack's Gibraltar command also experienced steady depletion of regulars. Reservists gradually replaced regulars on his ships, including the Coast Guard cutters. Most of them did well, but they suffered from lack of training and experience. The gunboat *Nashville*, which spent its tour in the Mediterranean, had as navigator "a Boston Tech man who had studied surveying. He had a habit," the former commanding officer wrote, "when in sight of land, of cutting in the ship's position by taking bearings of the contour lines of the various . . . mountain ranges along the Spanish and African coasts and trying to plot them on naval charts. One evening, after working out a number of star sights, their intersection on the chart, representing our most probable position, was somewhere over the top of the Sierra Nevada mountains at about where the Alhambra is at Granada!" He added, "I went back to the bridge in a hurry."[37]

The Navy hoped to strengthen its regular force with the transfer of the Coast Guard for the duration. By law, this occurred immediately upon the declaration of war. The Coast Guard table of organization was not the same as the Navy's, but this and other anticipated problems were worked out by the two services before the transfer took place. One problem, however, that plagued the two services concerned enlistments. Coast Guardsmen could enlist for a year, and a significant number of enlistments ran out during the early months of the war. Until the law was adjusted to three years or the duration of the war, cutter personnel were constantly changing. For the cutters deployed in European waters, this proved unfortunate as it affected a ship's efficiency. Although the Coast Guard recruited thousands during the war, only approximately five hundred served at one time in European waters. They manned the cutters based at Gibraltar, and a number of officers were assigned to yachts. In order to provide the Coast Guard with naval methods and training, in September 1917 a "companion ship" was assigned to each of the cutters deployed in European waters.[38] There was a rivalry between the two sea services, likely more on the part of the Coast Guard than the Navy. Coasties liked to say that "when the Navy runs for port, the Coast Guard puts to sea." The bluejackets, on the other hand, considered the Coast Guard as a "sort of hybrid, half animal, half fish, a composite between a lighthouse keeper and a revenue shark."[39] There were, however, no problems between personnel of the two services in the war zone.

The outbreak of war seriously affected the Navy's normal training schedule. The regulation "boot" training for a recruit was four months. Although this period had often been violated in the past, it was ignored during the early months of the conflict. The need to fill wartime complements, which were considerably larger than in peacetime, along with the rapid commissioning of vessels, wrecked the training period. By June 1917, forty thousand men entered the Navy's four training camps, but their stay there was brief. Frederick Harrod, in his book *Manning the New Navy*, quotes an officer in the fleet as writing: "On Thursday evening we received a draft of about 100 boys from the Great Lakes Training Station. They had been under training only about one week, were only partially fitted out with clothing and that was in gunnysacks. They not only did not know anything about the Navy but they had never even been told about it."[40] Although the Navy did return to a longer training period, it was still less than that carried out before the war. A recruit wrote in his memoir: "Here was a real Navy 'snafu'—we were going overseas with less than a month training . . . to do what? We hardly knew how to wear our caps." This was in June 1918![41]

The Navy, in traditional fashion, determined that "boots" could finish their training while onboard ship. In August 1917, the CNO cabled Sims: "How many recruit seamen, firemen, machinists mates can be received on destroyers and tenders [and] put into training. . . . Necessary to train all extra men possible for new destroyers building." The force commander informed the Department that the Queenstown flotilla could absorb 1,500 men, 500 to be distributed among the ships and 1,000 to be housed in barracks.[42] Sims created a board of destroyer captains at Queenstown to formulate a plan for the training of officers and men and rotation for new construction. As Taussig notes in his journal, they were most concerned about maintaining the efficiency of the destroyers while at the same time addressing the needs of the expanding Navy. Their plan, which was adopted by the Department, called for the assignment of ten officers suitable to command destroyers, 75 junior officers, and 1,500 enlisted men to the flotilla. As soon as they arrived, personnel including commanding officers would be sent home to man the new destroyers. Later Sims requested that executive officers not be rotated, but whenever possible promoted to command within the flotilla. In November, Sims wrote to his wife: "They are sending us nearly 2,000 men to be trained for the new boats. This puts the training where the destroyers are and where the new men can acquire all the points about this very peculiar kind of warfare."[43]

This became a standard policy. Thousands of hastily trained recruits were sent over in drafts to replace "experienced" personnel, who were then returned to the United States to man new construction. Overcrowded ships were one unfortunate result of this policy. There were not enough officer and crew quarters. This was particularly true on the battleships.[44] Not all the units in the European force were used for training personnel. In general, there were few personnel changes in the battleships operating with the Grand Fleet. This was partly because no new battleships were to be constructed during the war, and partly because the Department planned to rotate vessels rather than men. The same was apparently true of other vessels. One of the destroyer *Whipple*'s crew wrote his mother, "nearly all of the men have been in the Navy a long time before the war."[45] The loss of regulars because their enlistments ran out was a problem that harassed many commanding officers. Regulations in effect during the first months of the conflict allowed these men to receive thirty days' leave so long as they reenlisted. Most of the regulars serving with the American naval forces in European waters, some 25 to 30 percent, requested that they be rotated back to the United States. There they could have their thirty days and then be available for re-assignment.[46]

Obviously, commanding officers from Sims down to ship captains were unhappy with the continuous turnover. This was especially true of regular officers. The force commander maintained a running argument with the Department over the need for additional officers in his force. He was particularly exasperated with the CNO's determination to retain experienced officers and petty officers in the Atlantic Fleet, especially the capital ships. He was also unhappy with the Department's decision to provide armed guards for merchant vessels. He did not believe that they would have any effect on German U-boat attacks, and at the same time they would deplete the pool of available personnel. Even before the outbreak of war, a large number of experienced petty officers in gunnery were transferred to the armed guard, and it continued after war was declared. Sims opposed it, pointing out that the submarine's great advantage was invisibility, that arming merchant ships simply resulted in submarines attacking while submerged. He also criticized transferring experienced personnel from battleships and other naval vessels to man the guns on merchantmen. Nevertheless, hundreds of merchant vessels carried armed guards during the war. "First to Fight—First to Give Their Lives—First Shot to Hit" was the motto of the armed guards. They sunk no U-boats during the war and hit very few. Their effectiveness was debatable, although one officer claimed in the 1920 congressional hearings on the Navy that armed guards drove off 113 submarine attacks. German accounts do not mention armed guards in describing attacks on U-boats.[47]

Experienced or not, the World War I sailor, officer, and white hat, regular and reserve, had a great deal of pride in the Navy and his place in it. This is evident in the many published and unpublished journals and memoirs of those who served in the service during the conflict. There is also the mystique of identifying with a ship, a naval tradition that has continued to the present. Although the Marines certainly have esprit de corps, the identification with *The* Corps, a sailor does not usually identify as much with *The* Navy as with a particular ship that he served in. He may well have served on a number of ships during his career or enlistment, but there is only one that he considers "his ship." That is one of the reasons why, as a World War I sailor wrote, there is a distinct difference "between the psychology of the soldier and that of the sailor."[48] Sailors often had (and have) nicknames for their ships. The destroyer *McDougal*, for example, was called "Madhouse"; the yacht *Margaret* was "Maggie." Other factors that he mentioned included the fact that, unlike the soldier, the sailor rarely faces what he called "the baser brutalities of war." Like aviators, his enemy is usually faceless, a ship (submarine) that he is trying to kill or be killed. Even in a combat zone, he spends much of his time swabbing decks, or standing watches, or tinkering with machinery, rather than enduring the constant strain of trench warfare or the terror of "over the top." Finally, there is the relationship with his officers. The World War I Navy was about as democratic as any naval force in American history. An amazing number of college students and graduates, as well as professionals, joined the ranks. A reporter visited a recreation hall at a training camp and was astonished at the apparent social rapport between officers and men playing billiards. When she quizzed one of the officers about this, he replied, "most of us come from the same colleges."[49] The traditional taboo of those on the quarterdeck becoming too familiar with the gob in the fo'c'sle was less apparent on the vessels that were crewed primarily by reservists, such as the subchasers. On destroyers and larger ships, however, it was generally present. A member of the destroyer *Reid*'s crew who was a college graduate and advanced in rank from a seaman to an ensign wrote in his diary: "On the beach the advantage was almost entirely on the side of my new berth. It was not possible to go ashore almost every afternoon when in port with a companion of similar tastes. The officers patronized different cafes from the men and had different ways of spending their time."[50] Brown, whose ship spent most of the war based at Brest, also admitted that sailors did not like to frequent the same establishments as the soldiers.

One thing that both the soldiers and sailors had in common, however, were nicknames. The World War I soldier is best known by the name *doughboy*, but he was also known as *Sammy*, a term that he disliked.[51] The American sailor had a number of names—*bluejacket, jack, jackie,* and *gob*.[52] The World War I sailor preferred *gob*. He did not mind *bluejacket*, could tolerate *jack*, but despised *jackie*. A number of newspapers carried an article that evidently originated at the Great Lakes Training Station claiming that sailors "hate" the term *jackie* because it was considered effeminate.[53] Samuel G. Blythe, a well-known reporter of the period, wrote an article in the *Saturday Evening Post* entitled "The Gobs." He wrote that *gob* is a generic term that applies to all sailors, even officers. For example, a commanding officer is often referred to as the "main gob." Blythe said that the term *gob* had been around five or six years before the war, and apparently it originated with the U.S. squadron in Asian waters.[54] In June 1919, a member of the Morale Division of the Bureau of Navigation wrote that *gob* was a term of derision and that a campaign should be undertaken to dissuade the sailors from using it.[55] It did gradually die out and was rarely used in the thirties.

Gobs, like doughboys, were anxious to get "over there" and do their part. Many of them felt as the writer John Dos Passos did, "Hell, I wanted to see the show."[56] What they discovered "over there" was not the war the doughboys found in the trenches in France, but in its own way it was a war just as exciting and as boring. This was particularly true of those who served on the warships that were deployed in the war zone or were on vessels engaged in convoy duty. As Frederick Harrod has pointed out, it is almost impossible to generalize about shipboard life. The type of ship, its age, its duties, and of course its geographical location were all factors that influenced a sailor's life. Service in *Olympia* at Murmansk was as different as night and day from crewing one of the 110-foot wooden subchasers operating out of Corfu in the Mediterranean. A bluejacket's life with one of the battleships with the Grand Fleet in the North Sea was quite unlike that of his counterpart on a destroyer operating out of Queenstown or one of the armed yachts cruising in French Atlantic waters. The larger and newer ships had more amenities such as barbershops, laundries, and canteens that improved living conditions for personnel. Discipline and dress codes were usually not as strict on smaller vessels. Sailors referred to destroyers as the "dungaree Navy," but in reality this could be applied to nearly all of the small craft in World War I.[57]

Shipboard routine and drills were standard on all U.S. Navy ships, regardless of type or location. Fueling was both a drill and replenishment. Whereas gasoline and fuel oil could be transferred at sea, coal was rarely replenished while underway in World War I. Rigs had been developed before the war to do so, but American coal burners, both naval and commercial, usually carried enough coal to cross the Atlantic. Although ship captains were strongly encouraged to carry sufficient coal to make the round trip, and many did, ships nevertheless had to replenish in European ports. In addition, the battleships, armed yachts, Coast Guard cutters, tenders, and other vessels attached to American naval forces in European waters were coal burners. Coaling ship, according to the bluejackets, was the dirtiest and the meanest job in the world. Coaling ship required nearly the entire crew, often including officers, and liberty would not be granted until the job was finished. It lasted from a few hours to as long as three days, working day and night, depending upon the size of the vessel and its bunkers. It was exhausting work, and in France, it was always done by the ship's crew. A *Reid* bluejacket mentioned in his diary that they heard rumors the entire time they were based in Brest that arrangements were being made to have French longshoremen do the work, but "they never materialized." Ponta Delgada in the Azores was the one base in the war zone where crews did not have to do their own coaling. In Brest, a few of the smaller vessels were lucky enough to tie up alongside a coal pier with bucket hoists, but most of them were coaled from barges while anchored in the harbor.[58] The French lighters, according to one veteran, were narrow and deep, unlike those used in the United States, which were relatively flat deck barges. On the French lighters, the coal was in holds and had to be dug by hand (shovel) from the top, loaded into canvas bags or wicker bushel baskets, and hoisted (often by hand) to the ship's deck. There the coal bags were emptied into the bunkers by way of canvas chutes.[59] Ideally, on the larger ships the work was done by sections. One section would work for eight hours on the coal pile and sixteen hours off. This was not always the case. Some commanding officers, determined to get their ship turned around as quickly as possible, would work all of his crew until the job was finished, holidays included. "Thanksgiving Day we coaled," an officer recorded in his journal. "Hardly a man could utter a prayer of thanks on that day, at least not while on the business end of a shovel in a coal lighter."[60]

The crews of the American battleships that joined the Grand Fleet had an equally strenuous time in replenishing coal. It started when they dropped their anchors. Because of the possibility of having to get underway quickly in case the German High Seas Fleet sortied, every ship in the fleet was required to be topped off with fuel as soon as she returned from patrol or exercises. On the occasion of the initial arrival of the American dreadnoughts, Beatty signaled the American flagship *New York* that colliers would come alongside the four battleships at 6:00 the following morning. When Rodman replied that they usually began coaling at 8:00, the C-in-C responded, "I will be on board your flagship at 0600 tomorrow." A British naval officer later boasted, "We in the British Fleet taught them the art of fast coaling."[61]

That is not all the British tars taught the Americans. At Queenstown, Admiral Bayly's officers were pleasantly surprised to discover that the American destroyer personnel were eager to learn from them. As one Annapolis-trained officer put it: "Green as we came to the job, . . . in comparison to their three years of hard experience . . . our taking over here was almost like a lot of boy scouts replacing a regiment of seasoned veterans in the trenches. . . . Let me tell you . . . that if we had had to find out all the wrinkles of the game ourselves—if they had not given us the benefit of all they had been paying in ships and men for three years to learn—it would have been a far slower business for us, and a far more costly one as well."[62] Other than information and suggestions concerning operations at sea passed from British to American officers in informal gatherings, there was little formal training except in signaling and radio operations. From the British point of view, the major problem was communications. Not only were British signalers and radio operators superior to Americans, but the signal flags, ciphers, and codes were all different. A British signalman was assigned to each of the destroyers for a month. It took that time to, as one of His Majesty's sailors put it, "to forget . . . what they had been laboriously taught for years. They had to master a different colored alphabet as it is glimpsed two miles away tangled up in halyards or half obscured by funnel . . . smoke." "The meaning of the [American] flags had nothing in common with the British."[63] Although Admiral Rodman and American writers declared that it took only a few days for the signal personnel on the American battleships to learn the British signal codes and use them efficiently, British observers from Admiral Beatty on down felt that they had "great difficulty in mastering" them. In order to master the British naval signal codes, the signalmen on *Texas* devised a Game of Flags, which they played regularly. "It was day and night work" for all the battleship signal forces, according to one officer. "Mistakes gradually diminished, until they faded completely away." The General Board was told that "Our signalmen are quite young and are poor in comparison with [the British]. . . . I believe ours are superior in intelligence and initiative. These [British] signalmen . . . have been doing nothing but signaling for eight or ten years. Some of them for 18 years."

The officer testifying before the Board also said that the same was true of radio operators. Radio signals were equally important, and in many ways more difficult to learn. But they did so, not only in the force at Queenstown, but elsewhere where the two navies cooperated. The French and Italians used the British system as well, so it had to be mastered throughout the American force operating in European waters. The Grand Fleet also allotted a month for the American signalmen to learn their system and codes. As the British liaison officer wrote, "the governing factor in the time required by a new ship before she is fully competent to operate in the North Sea is the training of the W/T operators."[64] Admiral Mayo was displeased with reports from Rodman suggesting that British methods of communication, staff work, gunnery, etc. were superior to that practiced by the American Navy. The British, however, did not consider all of their methods and procedures to be better. Admiral Sir Alexander Duff, the assistant chief of the naval staff at the Admiralty, considered American destroyer procedures such as those for lookouts to "give more protection to the convoy . . . than ours."[65] Admiral Carney would later say that many of the British naval officers at Queenstown were "somewhat irritated by our sea-keeping qualities and inclinations. They also rightfully felt that they knew a hell of a lot more about this game than we did—which they did, and we acknowledged this. On the other hand, as far as effectiveness was concerned, we felt that we were superior." The American sailor's proficiency in fire fighting was one exercise admired by the British.[66]

Inevitably, comparisons were made between the American and British naval personnel. In the Royal Navy, officers specialized, whereas American line officers were expected to become proficient in everything from driving a ship to running a division of men. Captain (later Fleet Admiral) Leahy testified before the General Board: "The British officers in general seem to have little information regarding anything but their own work." He added, "One turret officer came under my notice through failure of a solenoid in his sub-caliber firing mechanism. It was a casualty that could have been fixed in a minute by any turret officer in our fleet. He knew nothing about [it] . . . and sent for the electrical officer to fix it." Captain Plunkett agreed: "One of the most amazing things I have gotten from the English officers is, that outside of the Gunnery Officer, it does not seem that any other person in the ship knows very much about gunnery."[67] In general, the American bluejackets recognized that their British counterparts were vastly more experienced, but what surprised the British sailors was the Americans eagerness to learn, their proficiency at certain skills, and how quickly they accepted their methods and procedures. Some of the Royal Naval officers, however, considered them "amateurs."[68]

In the Grand Fleet, in addition to the intense training in British signals and codes, the Americans officers had to learn British operating procedures while at sea—tactical formations and exercises.[69] For the Americans and the British, gunnery was the most troubling problem.

The American battleship crews prided themselves on their gunnery. In the decade after the Spanish-American War, a revolution in naval gunnery in the Navy had resulted in American gunnery, according to one writer, becoming the best in the world or at least on a par with the British.[70] Service opinion continued to believe this until the United States entered the war. As various officers would later testify before Congress, experienced gunners were transferred to armed guard duty on merchant vessels and to ships brought into the Navy in the emergency. They were replaced with inexperienced men, volunteers, and reservists. This, they insisted, affected gunnery efficiency.[71] This argument was used to explain what the British considered poor gunnery on the part of the American battleships with the Grand Fleet. It must have been a shock to the ships' regular officers to learn after their initial gunnery practices that Admiral Beatty was disappointed and considered them inferior in gunnery to the British ships. Their gunnery was in the beginning "distinctly poor and disappointing," Beatty reported. Rodman was audibly unhappy and embarrassed when at target practice *Florida* fired a salvo over *King Orry*, the British target towing ship. A gunnery officer on HMS *Marborough* wrote in his memoir: "The American naval officer was to us an unknown quantity. To our surprise the first thing about them, which became apparent was their humble approach to the matter of making their ships battle-worthy. On arrival they had a long way to travel and knew it. In fact their shooting was appallingly inaccurate. However, under the forceful drive of Admiral Rodman and all such as was within our power to help and a general determination [by] the officers to learn quickly, in a few months they succeeded in moving from a state of poor efficiency to a reasonably high standard." It undoubtedly was equally disappointing to Sims, who had been one of the key figures in the development of efficient gunnery in the American Navy.[72] It was months before Beatty was satisfied with the battleships' performance. Rodman, when he later testified before the congressional committee investigating the Navy Department, insisted that the battleships' gunnery, other than the *Texas*, which had arrived several months after Rodman after an extended yard period from running aground, "were excellent," although "not perfect." *Texas* had joined the Grand Fleet carrying her "meat ball," a large "E" on each side of the after stack and elsewhere on the ship. The "E" informed the rest of the fleet that *Texas* held the coveted award for being the most efficient ship in the Navy for gunnery and engineering. Her initial gunnery exercises with the Grand Fleet, however, demonstrated that she was no better than the other U.S. battleships. Rodman characteristically verbally castigated the ship and its crew: "A mud scow should shoot better than the *Texas*. . . . Will you tell me what the British Commander in Chief must think of our trophy ship!" He then ordered the "E" painted over. As late as September 12, only two of the ships firing were considered satisfactory to the fleet commander. Rodman ignored (or forgot) the letter that he wrote to the Department three weeks before the Armistice extremely critical of the *Arkansas*'s gunnery practice.[73] *Arkansas* relieved *Delaware* in July 1918. Lieutenant (later Vice Admiral) John McCrea, a turret officer on *New York* in 1918, also lauded the battleship gunnery. "[W]e shot well; we really shot well, I thought," he remembered in his oral memoirs. The Atlantic Fleet's gunnery officer considered the initial poor gunnery to be simply "stage fright."[74]

Other factors affected American gunnery in comparison to the British, who, of course, had nearly four years of wartime experience behind them. Gunnery drill was a daily occurrence on the dreadnoughts.[75] As Admiral Rodman admitted after the war, the ships initially fired as they did in competition; that is, rapidity of fire was sacrificed for accuracy. They had to be indoctrinated with the view that the gun crews had to be trained to fire as quickly as possible. Admiral McCrea remarked that the U.S. battleships "shot much faster than did the British battleships, and that our marksmanship was better." His memory was at fault. An American officer from the Bureau of Ordnance assigned to the Grand Fleet for observations later wrote, "In some things they [the British] were ahead of us in gunnery; and in other important things, particularly in the line of fire control and powder, we were ahead of them."[76]

Second, the spread of their broadsides with their main batteries of 12- and 14-inch guns was far greater than that of the British battleships. According to Rear Admiral Sir Frederic Charles Dryer, the Admiralty's director of naval artillery and torpedo, they were "so excessive that the probability of getting hits at long range was small."[77] While at Scapa Flow, the American battleships were scheduled along with those of the British to undertake target practice at least once a month. They generally fired at a towed target at a range of six miles, although the towing ship often changed course and speed to challenge the gunners. They quickly ran out of practice ammunition, and since American gun calibers were different from the British, Rodman had to request a shipload as quickly as possible. They did improve, impressing even the British.[78] In addition, the British agreed with the Americans that their fire control was better. As HMS *Barham*'s gunnery officer admitted, "Spotting as practiced by the U.S. navy is a gift or the result of special training or both. . . . We cannot hope to introduce your system and must be content during the war to abide by ours."[79]

American gunnery was not particularly good throughout the force in European waters. Neither Sims nor his subordinate commanders prescribed training exercises and drills; it was left up to individual ship commanders. Admiral Wilson complained that the "demands upon his destroyers for escort duty makes it impossible to find time for regular target firing."[80] Some of the escort captains held target practice when practicable. The Coast Guard cutter *Seneca*, even while on convoy duty, would fire at a tin can attached to a boat hook to look like a periscope and let out from the ship by a long wire. The yacht *Sultana* periodically held target practice with both deck guns and machine guns. However, a destroyer officer later recalled that they became so endowed with depth charges that "we'd had no gunnery exercises and no torpedo exercises for a long, long time, if ever."[81]

The ships did have gunnery practice or at least gun drill as well as other drills whenever the commanding officer so ordered. A gob in *Wheeling* on convoy duty in the Mediterranean mentioned after the war, "Aboard ship routine life seldom varied and drills for torpedo defense, fire, collision, etc. were a part of our daily life."[82] Nonetheless, the strain from escorting convoys frequently in rough weather was not conducive for drills, even if a commanding officer wanted them.[83] During wartime, "Ropeyarn Sunday" was rarely observed. The gobs understood this but complained when drills and inspections were scheduled for Sundays while in port. "An Admiral is more important than God. 'Remembreth Sabbath day to keep it Holy' does not apply to the navy. A few months ago, President Wilson signed an order that: 'there shall be no more work on Sunday unless is absolutely necessary to the conduct of the war.' Painting on the Sabbath for admiral's inspection is absolutely necessary for war (must remember this when shipping over time comes)."[84]

Life on board the American naval vessels operating at sea in the "killing zone" was stressful and at times frightening. Some of the veterans recall that it was frequently tedious, "a long cold, wet, uneventful grind, with little to keep the tiring mind to the pitch of vigilance which must be maintained." "It is a very curious duty in that it would be positively monotonous, were it not for the possibility of being hurled into eternity the next minute," one destroyer officer wrote.[85]

Watches varied. Usual routine was to stand two four-hour watches in a twenty-four-hour period, but watch station, weather, and other factors often determined the length. For example, in extremely cold weather, lookouts were changed hourly. "My job was foretop lookout, one hour on watch, then two off," one destroyer sailor remembered. "Icy drizzle needled eyeballs, and the best eye wore out after sixty minutes of looking for submarines amidst the wreckage—cotton bales, butter-tubs, cabbage—that . . . strewed the ocean. Bridge and deck lookouts frequently carried automatic revolvers. What they were to be used for was puzzling until an order came down to fire on anyone caught smoking on deck after nightfall; there were strict instructions against smoking on open decks at night because the light could be seen by a lurking submarine." Since American ships carried more personnel than did their British counterparts, they usually assigned more lookouts (eight to ten in the yachts and cutters). "The number of lookouts available is truly remarkable," *Paducah*'s CO wrote, "but it is more remarkable how little they see."[86]

False alarms were frequent. Porpoises, floating spars, overturned lifeboats, birds, and other objects would lead to the alarm and General Quarters by nervous lookouts and officers of the deck. There are numerous accounts of guns being fired and depth charges dropped by mistake. On one foggy occasion, a hole caused by a toggle pin slipping out of its place created a whistling noise that sounded to the watch like a nearby vessel; on another pitch-black night, a destroyer collided with what was believed at first to be another vessel but proved to be a whale. The whale was draped over the ship's bow, and as the witness later recalled, "There were strict orders that under no circumstances was a ship to stop in the War Zone, so we proceeded with some tons of blubber impeding our progress."[87]

Destroyer service is not particularly pleasant for the recruit during his first few days at sea, and in fact for anyone until he gets his sea legs. Their long, slim lines and lightness (1,000 tons and under in World War I) made them particularly difficult vessels to ride. As a young ensign described it: "There is no motion on land or sea comparable to that of a destroyer. Rolling often in five-second jerks at an angle sometimes over 50 degrees. . . . There is combined with the roll a quick and violent pitching."[88] A former gob quipped years after the war that when a destroyer steamed eighty-five knots, it traveled thirty-five ahead and forty-five up and down. Another officer compared it to "rolling and bucking like a bronco," writing, "you can't exercise. You can hardly do any work, but only hold on tight and wipe the salt spray from your eyes."[89] "There are no cushioned corners, or padded smoke rooms or neat little sheltered nooks on a destroyer," a war correspondent wrote after his first experience on one off the Irish coast. "There is the deck. If you don't like the deck go below. If you don't like it jump overboard. . . . If you stay on deck . . . the only thing to do is to get hold of something and hang on. If you go below you have the walls of the ship to fall against—but heavens! How she shakes from the pound of the engines and how she smells from the fumes of the engine room."[90] Another reporter wrote: "By midnight the vessel was rearing like a frightened horse and rolling like a barrel churn. . . . A Western 'outlaw' had nothing on that boat. She would rear, shiver with rage just as though she were trying to shake the bridge off her back; plunge forward in a wild buck with her back humped and screws in the air. . . . I was lifted so often out of my bunk that I spent almost half the night in midair, and am now quite convinced of the possibility of levitation. By morning my sides were bruised from striking the sides of the bunk." He was shocked to discover, according to the officers, that "this was only half the blow."[91] One officer recalled that he was in his clothes six days at a time while escorting outbound transports for three days and inbound convoys for three days. "At sea I slept on the wardroom transom, behind a sort of line webbing to keep from rolling out."[92] Then there was the bluejacket who wrote: "[T]he life we destroyer men lead is awful. You woll [sic] so much you can't sleep an [sic] if you did go to sleep you would roll out."[93]

Seasickness was prevalent in all naval vessels operating in the war zone. Destroyers were notorious for inducing this condition among their crews. One officer said that in his opinion, "I don't think anyone escaped completely without getting seasick." New men "would invariably be seasick on their first voyage and they'd come to me when they got to port and say . . . 'I just can't stand this. I've got to go to a big ship. I can't live on these destroyers.' I'd say, 'well, just forget about it and wait until you make another trip and see how you feel.' And after a second trip usually they'd say, 'no, sir, I wouldn't leave here for anything.'"[94] One new seaman wrote, "I've got so tired of being sick that I've gone back to regular chow and resigned myself to living in the interior of a self-propelling machine shop with suicidal tendencies." Another one mentioned a crew member who "told his captain he would eat nothing but jam as that was the only thing on board that tasted the same in its wild flight going down and coming up." A *Fanning* bluejacket recorded in his diary that "sea sickness has almost reached the epidemic stage. The old salts are doubling up on watches because of the seasick on board."[95] This diary comment was in July, considered one of the more moderate months as far as the Western Approaches were concerned. According to a war correspondent who went out on patrol on a destroyer, their "crews do not loaf overmuch around deck. They can't. They live below decks, mostly strapped in when it is rough of canvas laced to four pieces of iron pipes, . . . called a bunk. Even strapped in so, they are sometimes . . . hove out into the passageway. It was a young doctor of the flotilla who said that, except for their broken arms and legs, his ship's crew were disgustingly healthy."[96] The winter months were much worse.

"Tip" Merrill, who came over on *Conyngham* and in the first destroyer division to be deployed in European waters, mentioned in his diary that even in May the waters off the Irish coast lived up to their reputation of "being the roughest stretch of water known to man." On May 25, he recorded, "Positively too awful to write about!" In June, he wrote that it was so much worse that "If the Huns were fools enough to go to sea in weather like [this] . . . they would have been licked long ago."[97] A British tin can officer concluded that "During the War my experience was that nine days out of ten the weather was vile" in the North Atlantic. From September until the following spring, storms were almost continuous, gales and half gales lashing up stupendous seas, creating misery for the destroyer crews. Virtually every account of destroyer service in those waters during the fall and winter months contains awesome details of these storms and the havoc they raised on the ships and their crews. A *McDougal* gob wrote years later that the crew lived "almost continuously in wet clothing, the vessel rolling thirty or forty degrees six times a minute for days on end, and bucking head seas that would raise the whole forepart of the vessel free of the water as far aft as the foremast. For over a week at a time our only food would be that which could be cooked in the coppers and eaten with spoons and forks directly from a tureen lashed to the table . . . the air below . . . was so foul that a man had to hold his breath as he went down the ladder. . . . The smell below was of stale air, unwashed bodies, vomit, and dampness. Bits of food and vomit swished from side to side on the deck against the after bulkhead. . . . We slept on our stomachs, our hands and feet stretched out to the edges of our bunks to hold us on. . . . One always felt weary and dull. You quickly lost all count of the days and begin to doubt if there really was a place without motion, vibration, reek of working metals, slosh of water and wind spray and cold."[98]

If this account seems too dramatic or an exaggeration, others said the same. J. P. Morgan's grandson Junius Morgan was a reserve officer on the *O'Brien*. A December storm, according to Morgan, made life "extremely uncomfortable. . . . Down below it seemed as if the entire ship would be pulled in two. She was bending and springing all the time and the green seas were coming over the forecastle in a way that threatened to smash in the decks. . . . By night our chart house was bent in, the forecastle gun was out of commission, most of the ammunition had gone out of the rack, the machine gun stands were bent and the bulkheads strained."[99] Another reserve officer wrote in later years: "On the bridge a constant deluge of water poured over us; a good thirty feet we stood above the water-line, and the wind, its violence augmented by our headlong speed, came like knife-blades through each crack or aperture in the bridge. Below decks . . . [was] the reek of fuel oil; topside all was water and the terrific wind. Just before sunset a huge cross-wave carried away the motor dory . . . just before we turned, another big sea had smashed in our motor sailer, the ship's only two boats. . . . When the weather is lively there is little [point] . . . going to bed on a destroyer, and on this particular trip, for instance, none of us removed his clothes from port to port. To wash is an absurd experiment. To try to shave is an indication of insanity."[100] Admiral Moore in his oral history (evidently based on a personal journal) mentioned a storm on November 25: "We immediately ran into terrific weather, heading into a head sea. We started out at 25 knots and slowed to 12 and eventually slowed down to eight. As we got clear of the south coast of Ireland, the sea shifted to the north and was on the beam, and we were hit by one terrific wave. . . . The after-davit of our motor dory storage was carried away at the deck. The dory was smashed. The sights on one of the torpedo tubes was completely carried away. The engine room ventilator was carried away. Our lathe, which was on deck just abaft the engine-room hatch, was smashed to smithereens and the electric motor was washed over the side. I was standing in water up to my waist on the bridge of the ship. We practically went under completely. . . . [T]hat's the kind of weather we had to put up with. Of course we got no sleep."[101] Merrill noted in his diary that in late December while escorting a convoy, "We got mixed up in a storm . . . the way the wind blew and the hail hailed and the rain rained was something worthy of appearing in any sailors diary. For three days we could make no headway against the NE wind. . . . Our main deck was awash practically the whole trip. . . . Both the *Trippe* and the *Jarvis* had their steering gear carried away." In the storm, he wrote, "about half of the convoy got lost, but presumably made it into port. The air was full of SOS's and reports of casualties during the four days but of course we couldn't answer them as we had our job all picked out for us" staying afloat. He mentioned a few days later that *Ammens* lost a stack and all her boats; *Trippe* "lost all boats and one man. Her stacks were collapsed into very remarkable shapes. *Parker* lost both masts."[102] Although this was in reality a hurricane (winds clocked at ninety miles per hour), other storms caused as much damage.

Often the small ships had no choice but to run before the storm. Convoys usually scattered, and it was impossible to stay with them at times. One ship, according to a bluejacket, had to "fly before it for three days, finally reaching Vigo, Spain. . . . I lived ten hours at a pace that counted for ten years, the most tense moment of my life being when, while the seas were breaking over us and we were crawling about the deck holding fast to everything that seemed fixt [sic] looking for a hatch cover that had become unfastened, we suddenly discovered that six . . . [depth charges] had become unloosed and were lurching about, butting the bulwarks with every roll of the ship."[103] The seas were often so rough that members of the crew not on watch were ordered to stay below deck. Wise captains, according to one writer, warned their crew that "if you have any writing, reading, sleeping, or anything except just existing to do, . . . better do it now," meaning before leaving port.[104] That included chow. Once the gale hit, it would be almost impossible to eat while sitting down, "not even in chairs lashed to stanchions and one arm free hooked around a stanchion." One was lucky to eat while propped in a corner or wedged against some immovable object. Even sitting was hazardous. "As we sat at supper in the wardroom" during a half gale, so wrote a correspondent, "the tablecloth slid with its load of food and dishes swiftly to the floor [deck]. The casual manner in which the steward accepted and swept up the ruin betrayed familiarity with the phenomenon. When he reset the table we held the tablecloth down and had gotten safely to the coffee when, with his cup poised at his lip, the skipper tobogganed on his chair back to the transom. Swallowing the coffee while she hung in balance he came back to us on the return roll." Warm food, however, was rarely available during a severe storm, certainly not for the crew.[105] "Gentle reader," one former gob wrote,

> imagine yourself perched on a camp stool with face to port and back to starboard—at the seamen's dining table—trying to steer a bowl of soup safely into your alimentary canal. The ship rolls 45 degrees and your stool and soup begin to slide at the same time. You hold the edge of the table with your left hand, clasp your spoon down hard into the bottom of the bowl to secure it, then cautiously push yourself to your feet, for the stool threatens to carry you across the compartment in a jiffy. . . . You quickly release your grip on the table edge and take the bowl in both hands to steady it. This leaves the soup suspended perfectly between zenith and nadir, fixed in relation to the bowl, and altogether incomparable if you weaken. Stated another way, the soup will not spill, although it may be getting cold. Yet, you must devise some way to eat. Your spoon and slice of light bread have been sliding all over the table, kept from hitting the wet deck only by a wooden flange. Before you can plan your campaign, your feet begin to slip and ere you can blink an eye you have slid four yards across to the starboard dining table, getting your feet hopelessly tangled up in the legs of a prostrate stool, bumping without demanding gangway into a shipmate who turns loose his soup so it fits perfectly down your neck. . . . but ere you have recovered from the confusion the ship rolls from 45 positive to the same negative and you rejoin your old friends the spoon and the bread where you left them. . . . You set the bowl down, cling to the table with your mighty right, hoping a lapse will come so you can swallow a spoonful and be happy. But the lapse does not come and the bowl goes caroming to the deck. . . . There was no use staying below to hear the mess cook rave; so I seized a cold potato between my teeth and followed it madly all the way to the chart house, where I feasted in peace. . . . Only a third arm could have made me happier. Every sailor needs one in this business.[106]

More than one doughboy, observing the struggling destroyers from the deck of a large transport, expressed admiration for the sailors. One regular who had fought in the Philippines Insurrection wrote: "Coming out of the jungle with clothes in rags and so little to eat, I was perhaps somewhat envious of the lot of the navy; but since seeing one of our ships, during the World War, met off the coast of Ireland by a fleet of American destroyers in a heavy sea to be escorted through the Irish Channel, I have felt differently. Those poor fellows were drenched in cold seawater, and buffeted about like dice in a box, their little boats standing first on one end and then on the other, with most of the crew sick, and I realized that they were cheerfully living a life which I could not have endured."[107]

The destroyer skippers, nearly all of them young regulars, "thrive[d] on it," as one captain wrote. "It's a damned sight easier than peace; everyone will work when he sees what he is working for."[108] Another tin can commander said: "This is like a game. . . . It spoils you for anything else."[109] As far as personalities were concerned, they were all types. Joe Taussig was a calm, rational person, who, according to his son, never raised his voice. "Tip" Merrill considered A. W. Johnson, his captain in *Conyngham*, to be "a gentleman and the most conscientious worker I have ever served with." Then there were the tense, nervous types. One veteran recalled his captain coming to General Quarters dressed in his uniform but without his pants. Mandy Lee, *Porter's* commanding officer was one who, according to one of his junior officers, "doesn't care a hang about anything. When the ship is in port he is ashore (getting drunk) and when we are at sea, he is asleep, so he doesn't worry us much." At sea, they expected the skipper to be sick, "but he is a sea dog all right." "The diarist considered Lee "a typical destroyer officer." "Whenever anyone ask me what job I want I always say the Skipper's." Admiral Carney considered Francis "Bones" Cogwell to be a great ship handler but also audacious.[110]

The crews of the small wooden subchasers suffered the most while operating at sea. These craft were deployed in the Irish Sea, the English Channel, and the eastern Mediterranean. In fact, there was probably more chronic seasickness on these boats than on any other type of American naval vessel in the war zone with perhaps the exception of submarines. According to Admiral Braisted, the Navy's surgeon general, 50 percent of the original crews had to be replaced "for the reason that they could not adapt themselves to the motion and were completely prostrated while at sea."[111] They suffered all the discomforts experienced by the destroyer sailors and more. Meals were just as much a problem, not only in the absence of hot food and often coffee while at sea but also in the necessity to eat while standing. There was no heating on these vessels initially, not a problem in the eastern Mediterranean, but clearly one in the channel and the Irish Sea (later hot water heating was installed, but it was never adequate). There was no forced ventilation, and air was provided through portholes and hatchways. Because they rolled excessively in any but the flattest sea, these openings were nearly always closed. In the "sweat-box or ice-box," depending on where the chaser was based, the decks nearly always leaked. As the surgeon general's report stated: "The thin wooden decks and hulls are penetrated by small amounts of water in any but the calmest weather; also moisture of condensation collects on the bulkheads and overhead . . . bedding is damp and even wet much of the time." In fact, it was not just the mattresses and covers that were wet but the men's clothing as well. No spaces escaped the water problem, and crew members including officers often remained damp the entire period at sea. Although many admired the small craft and bragged of their performances at sea, in one respect they were not good sea boats. As mentioned earlier, they rolled excessively, 140 degrees in seven seconds (70 degrees each way). Their powerful gasoline engines were loud and sent reeking fumes throughout the vessels. Yet these vessels were crewed mainly by reservists who were able to stand some of the toughest duty in the theater of war.[112]

The crews of the American battleships deployed with the Grand Fleet were not immune from bad weather and at times experienced considerable seasickness. They usually operated at sea fewer days than the vessels escorting convoys in the North Atlantic and farther south, but they went out weekly for exercises or escorting convoys to Norway. Seasickness was particularly prevalent among the "black gang" and in the compartments several decks down, where even in winter, because of inadequate ventilation, the temperature could hover at near 100 degrees.

If the North Atlantic had the roughest weather in the world in the winter, the Bay of Biscay was not far behind—certainly not to the sailors who manned the old yachts that spent the war escorting convoys in French waters. The *Nokomis* ran into a gale while escorting a convoy outbound from Brest. Despite 50-degree rolls, the ship survived and stayed with her convoy as the winds were blowing out of the east. "It's hell when you can't lye [*sic*] down, stand up, nor sit down," wrote one of the yacht *Sultana*'s sailors. "But still you have to put up with it."[113] Most of the yachts, however, escorted coastal convoys and were able to avoid the heavy weather that was so prevalent farther out at sea.

The other vessels based in European waters, although not as vulnerable to storms, had their own problems to contend with. The submarines at Bantry Bay and the minelayers in Scotland rarely operated in stormy weather. The small *E*-class submarines, however, with very little heat, had to struggle with the intense cold while out on eightday patrols. Fresh food would spoil after five days on patrol—even bread wrapped in wax paper would become moldy. Canned provisions and hardtack along with coffee were served the last three days. Odors from unwashed bodies, primitive heads, oil fumes, and the food—both cooked and uncooked—gradually got worse. They constantly had problems with moisture dropping from pipes and the overhang caused by condensation. Sleep was difficult, writing or reading nearly impossible. There was little light. They remained submerged during daylight and regardless of the weather had to surface at night to recharge storage batteries. According to a medical report, the sea conditions prevented all but a few of the boat's crew (those on bridge watch) from going on deck during the entire patrol. "In fact, daylight was not seen during this time." The result was a gradual deterioration of officers and men, both physically and emotionally. Seasickness was a universal problem in the boats. Fortunately, when they returned from patrol, the crew was berthed on the tender with hot food, showers, and clean dry bunks. However, whatever recreation they had, they found on the tender. Bantry Bay was isolated with virtually nothing available for recreation or amusement. Captain "Tommy" Hart, the flotilla commander, and other officers complained about this problem, but nothing was done. Hart even complained that no senior officer, Sims, Bayly, or Pringle, ever visited the flotilla while based at Bantry Bay.[114]

Minelayers could not operate in inclement weather, of course, because of the nature of their work, laying the North Sea Mine Barrage. The sailors of Battleship Division Six while at Scapa Flow were in a desolate part of the world, bleak, often cold and foggy. The Gibraltar-based vessels escorted convoys in both the Atlantic and the

Mediterranean. Weather was occasionally stormy in both oceans with the same effect on their crews as those in French and Irish waters. The western Mediterranean could get cold in the winter, cold enough to snow at times, and unlike the personnel of ships deployed in the North Atlantic, Mediterranean crews were not provided with winter clothing.

Although men were not standing watch all the time, there was little time for or interest in anything other than food while operating at sea. "During our four hours off watch," one Coast Guardsman recalled, "we had to do our eating and sleeping, as well as washing ourselves and our clothes, and it was always a scramble to get through with the two latter in order that we might turn in our hammocks."[115] Training, as mentioned earlier, was inconstant at best, and inspections of men and spaces were usually deferred to when they returned to base. Other than on the battleships, restrictions were relaxed concerning what to wear while at sea. Dungarees were most popular. Nonregulation sweaters were also popular. Often whatever was warm was the uniform of the day for officers and men. *Reid*'s gunnery officer on one occasion stood a watch wearing a suit of BVDs, a pair of shoes, and a pistol.[116]

Food served on board American naval vessels had improved significantly in the years before the war. Refrigeration and ice machines were a major improvement. Although not installed on all the ships operating in European waters, they were on the tenders that serviced the smaller vessels and submarines. Equally important were changes in meal preparations. Although the men continued eating in berthing areas, the Navy had adopted a system of centralized cooking.[117] Each mess—usually twenty men, but it varied considering the ship's size—had one member who was designated as mess cook. His responsibility was to pick up the food in the galley and carry it to the mess tables. The Bureau of Supplies and Accounts had a ration system of food types and quantity to be served for each meal, but it could not be strictly followed by the ships and shore facilities in the war zone. The bureau shipped dry provisions, canned goods, frozen meats, and occasionally potatoes and fruits, but supplies quickly ran out, and ships frequently went to sea on short rations. Fresh provisions and other items were obtained from the Allies or purchased locally. There were occasional surprises. Often, however, what was served depended upon what was available.[118]

Many gobs considered it at least acceptable. "The chow is bearable but not extra. We get butter twice a day and jam for supper. Plenty of meat, sausage and railroad hash. Plenty of spuds and onions. Hot cakes once a week." A former commercial fisherman wrote his wife, "the food is not fine but can make out on it."[119] But others agreed with the bluejacket who wrote in his memoirs: "To put it mildly, there was considerable grousing among the crew members on the subject of chow. To say it was poor would be to greatly understate matters. It was just plain lousy, if not putrid."[120]

The available food at times was inedible. One cook mentioned that on his ship, "the meat was rotting, caned [*sic*] goods swelling. Rats had been in the rolled oats." Another one mentioned spoiled meat and rancid butter. They lived on jam. Another diarist wrote: "We were given a lousy breakfast—rotten hash and that old standby—prunes. Many of the men are becoming sick."[121] A yeoman died on *Fanning*, and, according to a diarist, "The Chief Pharmacist Mate . . . diagnosed that his critical illness is caused from poor diet."[122] The medical officer for the subchaser detachment at Corfu reported that "the crews . . . suffered universally from constipation."[123] Obviously prunes were not a part of their diet.

Evidently the subchaser crews in the Mediterranean did not suffer as much from food shortages as did their fellow bluejackets on ships operating out of British and French waters. There were shortages, however. Milk was rarely available; "sugar ran low, canned preserves, and even flour for a time was unprocurable. Meat was always obtainable from the French fleet in the harbor."[124] The author of *Maverick Navy*, who acted as supply officer on one of the chasers, recalled that they had no refrigeration at all: "Slatted lockers installed on deck held our supply of potatoes, onion, and fresh vegetables while they lasted. . . . Meat on the long voyage was corned beef, ham, bacon, and frankfurters, also mincemeat, which came all prepared in ten-gallon kegs. This diet was varied with sardines, canned salmon . . . and canned tuna. We carried an assortment of canned vegetables as well as canned milk and butter. Staples were sugar, flour, salt, oatmeal, rice, macaroni, and dried beans. To alleviate the hardtack, served in lieu of bread, with every meal we had apple butter, a horrible Navy preparation."[125] The officers ate the same food as the enlisted personnel on the chasers as they did in the small submarines based at Bantry Bay. Fresh food would spoil on submarines after five days and since their patrols were usually eight days, canned provisions and hardtack along with coffee were served the last three days. Apparently officers on other vessels lived off the same food much of the time as the enlisted men, but not all of the time.[126]

Sailors were able to supplement their meals in various ways, legal and illegal. Canteens were found on larger ships and tenders where one could stock up on packaged crackers and cakes when available. Commanding officers often permitted certain foods, including meat and eggs (not liquor, however) to be purchased and brought aboard. It was not unusual to find members of the "black gang" cooking steaks using shovels, or boiling eggs.[127] It was not that uncommon for hungry sailors to purloin food from the wardroom or captain's pantry. On March 20, 1918, Wiggins wrote in his diary: "Some sailor stole the Captain's pie from the refrigerator. The Captain restricted all hands to the ship for one year or until the guilty sailor was apprehended." He added, "No liberty, no privileges, no confessions."[128]

Whenever possible, the crews were treated with traditional meals on holidays. Christmas and Thanksgiving were particularly emphasized. But convoys had to be escorted and patrols had to be carried out regardless of the weather or time of year. "Christmas Eve we picked up a convoy of eight ships," wrote an officer on *Chester*. "The weather was miserable, adding nothing to the enjoyment of the holiday season. If ever the moral [*sic*] of the crew was at a low level it was at this time. Christmas Eve and Christmas Day, several hundred miles from land. . . . The ship rolled, and pitched and tossed so badly that no mess tables could be set; our Christmas Dinner we ate while sitting on a greasy deck."[129] "We had a fine Thanksgiving diner [*sic*] in harbor and I had all the turkey I could eat," wrote one sailor. On rare occasions, usually holidays, ice cream was served but only the battleships and tenders had ice cream machines. None were available at shore facilities. As one newspaper account noted in an article with the headline "What Yanks Miss Most": "The answer is 'ice cream,' and maybe popcorn, sometimes peanuts. But always ice cream."[130]

British sailors generally admired and envied the American bluejackets for their much better pay and their living conditions on board ship. They were impressed with the barbershops, dentists, and ice cream machines on the larger ships. On all the ships, they were impressed with the quantity and quality of the food. Unlike in the British navy, where each mess had its own cook, the U.S. Navy had rated cooks for its enlisted personnel. Cooks then, as afterward, were selected not because of their experience or culinary skills but because they were available. One bluejacket wrote that their cook was a Maine Yankee whose profession was bricklaying. A cook was asked where he got his water for coffee. He replied that he "dipped it from over the side with a bucket."[131] A British sailor stationed at Gibraltar visited various American naval vessels there and later wrote, "They live very well . . . with the best of everything and we felt ashamed at being able to offer them only such a poor show in return." American ships, of course, were "dry ships," and this was the one exception to their admiration. One writer mentioned that *Melville* was a "happy ship, although as is the case with every vessel in the U.S. Navy, one can only drink water aboard her."[132]

Recreation was confined to the evening hours, if one was not on watch, and weekend days in port, for those not on liberty. In the days before television and radios, reading and writing letters home were the most common forms of relaxation. Music was popular. Gramophones, the early record players, were found on nearly all ships. Virtually every ship's crew included members with musical instruments from fiddles and mandolins to harmonicas. While operating at sea in submarine-infested waters, these instruments could not be played on deck.[133] Motion pictures, introduced on board naval vessels on a regular basis in 1903, were the most popular form of entertainment. Depending upon the availability and number of projectors, they were shown from one night a week to every night. USS *Harrisburg* operated three projectors every night, showing each movie twice "so that whether a man goes on or comes off watch at 8 o'clock he has his show."[134]

Some were more fortunate than others. The larger ships, particularly the transports, converted liners, and tenders, were roomy with space for organized entertainment. The tenders such as *Dixie* and *Prometheus* were usually in port, and as mother ships for a number of smaller vessels, acted as clearinghouses for motion pictures. They often hosted entertainment for the other vessels. They, along with other large ships, had jazz orchestras, bands, and even glee clubs. The musical ensembles performed during meals (lunch and dinner), before the movies, and during more formal organized entertainments such as smokers, happy hours, dances, and shows. Theatricals such as musicals, minstrels, and plays were always in demand on board ship and at shore stations as well.[135]

Shipboard entertainment was perhaps most important on the battleships with the Grand Fleet while at Scapa Flow. With the exception of a few hours on the beach in the Orkneys on July Fourth, liberty was unavailable for months, and the barren land surrounding the fleet anchorage provided little in the way of recreation. *Wyoming's* cruise book recognized this: "With the Grand Fleet amusement was a scarce article, and everybody knows that if fun and amusement are taken from the American 'gob' he will soon start some fun if he has to light a torch to a hay stack and run up and down the road yelling 'fire.' So we had to make amusements. First it was moving pictures, and they were shown both afternoon and night. Then they gave out and we were thrown upon our own resources." They would do everything from smokers to musicals and theatricals.

Gambling was widespread, "most anytime, anywhere," a sailor recalled. Craps, poker, and blackjack were zealously pursued especially on and immediately after payday. Even officers indulged in poker. Although against naval regulations, games were often "overlooked" or ignored by the naval authorities. A battleship gob described his berth deck on paydays as "a regular Monte Carlo." Another one admitted that he left the United States "flat broke . . . and got back flat broke." A chief pharmacist mate on *Mount Vernon* was for all practical purposes a professional gambler, running card games twenty-four hours a day while the ship was underway. Cockroach racing was both a popular and enterprising activity on some naval vessels. According to the commanding officer of a subchaser, "This was a serious money-making occupation!" A British sailor wrote in his memoirs that when the Americans on the battleships were bored, they would "cut three holes in the top of a cigar box, put a cockroach inside, and gamble on which hole it came out of."[136]

Sailors traditionally have kept pets on board ship, and the American bluejackets in World War I certainly followed this precedent. "Sailors have a great fondness for pets, and the men are always bringing them aboard," wrote a medical officer in his memoirs; "all kinds of pets, from marmosets to kinkajous. . . . One day a sailor from a submarine came back from liberty, carrying a baby skunk. The officer of the deck objected. . . . 'But you don't want to take it below decks where it's so crowded!' the officer persisted. 'Just think of the odor down there!' 'Let him get used to it!' said the sailor. 'The same as I did!'"[137] The writer does not say whether or not this occurred in the war zone, although he was there during the conflict. Monkeys, parrots, cats, rabbits, and even goats were mascots on various ships in European waters. There were at least two goats, a small Cuban goat on *Conyngham* and one that was brought to Glasgow from the States by bluejackets who were to commission the armed yacht *Nahma* there. Because of British regulations, the gobs secretly took the goat ashore, causing something of a ruckus with the local American consul and the naval attaché in London. The American consul, Horace Lee Washington, smoothed the matter over and wrote the attaché, "May good luck go with both the crew and the goat."[138] Dogs were the most popular pets, and there were a great many with the ships in European waters.[139]

Over 2 million doughboys were in Europe by the Armistice. As few American soldiers were stationed in the British Isles, their presence was usually temporary, primarily a result of debarking in Liverpool and Southampton. The overwhelming majority were based in France, where inevitably they came into contact with the sailors at St. Nazaire and the other debarkation ports and in Paris. A few sailors manning the railway guns were on the Western Front, and a few naval aviators were training and flying with U.S. Army units. On the whole, the doughboys and gobs got along fine. Some of the aviators disliked serving with the Army squadrons. The bluejackets' major complaint was that the soldiers did not appreciate what they were doing. They heard more than one remark by the AEF's "finest" on sailors fighting a war with good food and clean sheets while they survived in the muddy trenches. They also resented the *Stars and Stripes* as being nothing but a propaganda sheet for the Army.[140]

It is crucial to maintain good health within the military services in times of war. Secretary Daniels exaggerated somewhat when he claimed, "World War I was the first war in history where civilian and military leaders showed such practical concern for health and morals . . . as was evidenced by the American government."[141] Yet, the secretary was correct in his estimation of the importance that the Wilson administration placed on health. At the end of the conflict, the House Naval Affairs Committee declared that "the first battle of the war, that against disease, was won by the Medical Department of the Navy."[142] An article in the *American Legion Weekly* concluded that "men of the Navy were superbly healthy. In one 12 month period of the war the death rate among sailors was lower than for any previous years in peace."[143]

The Navy's Bureau of Surgery and Medicine under the capable leadership of the surgeon general, Rear Admiral William C. Braisted, started preparing the medical branch for war before the United States became officially involved. Congress granted at the Navy's request a large increase in funds for medical supplies and personnel. For the first time, medical personnel were assigned to destroyers. Initially, pharmacist mates were added to the ship's complements while medical officers were on the tenders. After war was declared and large numbers of doctors entered the service, medical officers were assigned to the destroyers. During the war, the Medical Corps personnel increased to 3,095 doctors, 485 dentists, 1,713 female nurses, and 16,564 pharmacist mates and other enlisted medical personnel. This included the organized hospital units that were deployed to the war zone as well as those who served with the Marine Brigade.[144] The Navy also initiated an education campaign emphasizing the importance of sanitation to health onboard ships. "A clean ship is a healthy ship" became the slogan of this drive. Foreign sailors visiting American warships often remarked on their cleanliness. In fact the U.S. Navy gained the deserved reputation of having the cleanest ships in the world.[145]

Nonetheless, "a clean ship" did not and could not prevent medical and health problems on board the ships. Even without the exigency of war, there would, of course, have been problems. The war simply exacerbated them. Ships became overcrowded as they were brought up to wartime strength. Overcrowding was the subject of complaints in the Senate that the Navy was neglecting the health of its sailors.[146] Transports were especially vulnerable with troops packed into spaces. The crews of the ships operating in the North Sea and patrolling the Western Approaches to British and French ports were subject at times to intense cold and frequent wet weather.[147] Cases of measles, mumps, diarrhea, tuberculosis, smallpox, chicken pox, meningitis, typhoid, diptheria, scarlet fever, malaria, and yellow fever affected many and killed some sailors with the American naval force in European waters. During the cold and wet months, the common cold was widespread. Skin rashes and constipation were prevalent on board the ships. A skin disease known as the "Irish itch" was a frequent source of complaint among the bluejackets on the ships based at Queenstown. Among the preventative measures, the most common was boiling clothing and "disinfecting the seats of the crew's head daily with live steam."[148] Measles and typhoid broke out on several ships that either were based in French waters or made port there. It was blamed on the drinking water. In fact, the bureau repeatedly warned medical officers to test local supplies of water before approving it for drinking. Transports were able to carry enough water for the round trip, but the vessels stationed in European waters had to depend upon local water. The surgeon general recommended that the ships and bases in the war zone use only distilled water.[149]

There are no statistics on malingering, but one retired pharmacist mate who served on a battleship with the Grand Fleet claimed that many of the crew were willing to do about anything to spend some time off the ship. When at Rosyth, "Men exposed themselves to mumps and other contagious diseases, hoping to become infected. . . . Others, cannier of method, suddenly developed wheezy wracking coughs. . . . The dampish climate made colds quite commonplace, and it was no easy matter for the doctors to distinguish between those actually sick and the malingerers."[150] There is no evidence that the morale of the overwhelming majority of sailors serving with the naval forces in European waters during the war was such as to create situations such as above.

There was considerable illness, including epidemics, among the naval forces. The battleship *New York*, when she first joined the Grand Fleet, had a siege of mumps. Twenty-seven cases were diagnosed in a period of three weeks. By the beginning of April, the ship had had some fifty-five cases. There were other epidemics on other ships. German measles hit *Melville* while underway for Queenstown.[151] But influenza was by far the most serious.

The influenza pandemic of 1918–19 is considered one of the deadliest viruses in history, comparable to the "Black Plague" that swept through Western Europe in the Middle Ages, killing millions. Influenza, or flu, or the grippe, or the "Spanish Lady," or "Flanders fever," or "Three-day fever," as the disease was commonly called, was even more devastating. It was a worldwide holocaust. More than 20 million people died—a conservative estimate as records are incomplete and statistics unreliable. It affected every continent, every nation, every stratum of society, every ethnic group, and every age group. The many remote islands in the Pacific were not immune from it. There is no discernable reason for its strange history, nor geographical pattern or obvious path of transmission. It followed no rhyme or reason in its appearance, attacking some, while mysteriously leaving others alone. It rampaged through the Grand Fleet in the spring of 1918 but did not seriously menace the American battleships attached to the fleet for months. German soldiers on the Western Front were seriously afflicted, but British Tommies were not. Doughboys crossing the Atlantic to France on transports had a much higher mortality rate than the naval crews. Ships returning to the United States from the war zone had far fewer cases than those going over.[152]

The influenza pandemic struck the military services earlier and more severely than the civilian population. The Army may well have had more than a quarter of its number down with the contagion at one time or another. Military camps in the United States became virtually huge hospitals with entire barracks taken over as wards. Bases were so crippled that the Army's chief of staff cabled General Pershing in November,

"Influenza not only stopped all draft calls in October but practically stopped all training."[153] The AEF was hit not quite so hard. The hospital admission rate in the war zone was approximately 64 percent of that of the soldiers in the States; 167 out of every 1,000 fell ill with the disease. Altogether 12,423 died.[154] A much larger number, however, died on the troop transports. As one authority has written, "The worst place to have an epidemic, like a fire, is in close quarters far from help, such as a ship on the high seas."[155] Troops were literally packed in the compartments of transports, making it likely that if one caught the disease, all in his immediately proximity would also come down with it. In the last six months of the war, while the pandemic was spreading rapidly throughout the world, 1.5 million doughboys crossed the Atlantic to British and French ports. Transports were often crowded with the sick and dead.

The cruiser *Minneapolis* moored at the Philadelphia Navy Yard in January 1918 saw the first noticeable outbreak of flu. Twenty-one members of her crew came down with the disease in a two-week period. Within a month, the Bureau of Medicine and Surgery was receiving reports of numerous cases in ships and bases scattered along the Atlantic seaboard. The Naval Radio School in Cambridge, Massachusetts, reported nearly 400 cases. In March, *Frederick* at the Portsmouth, New Hampshire, Navy Yard counted 147 cases and *St. Louis* in Norfolk, Virginia, 73.[156]

The epidemic spread to the naval forces deployed in the war zone. In April, more than 80 bluejackets (nearly 90 percent) at the Dunkirk (France) Naval Air Station came down with the "grippe," which was blamed on helping a nearby British squadron erect hangars. In March, a comparatively mild epidemic of influenza and pneumonia showed up among the naval personnel stationed at Brest and two U.S. naval air stations, Gujan and Fromentine. This was blamed on the French. It spread to the crews of escorts operating out of the French port. It tied up some ships. The yacht *Nokomis* was able to keep her scheduled patrols, despite having 38 men ill and 1 dead from the disease. One of the surgeons at the U.S. naval hospital in Brest wrote in early July that 30 members of a destroyer's crew became incapacitated with the illness. "We were thinking of taking them ashore so as to fumigate the ship when came the call of a torpedoed ship. Every man slid into place, fever, headache, bone ache and all, and away she beat it to sea and helped pick up the survivors."[157]

Influenza also spread among the American sailors based in Great Britain. The tender *Melville* at Queenstown had about 150 cases among her crew of more than 700, while the *Dixie* had 11 percent of her crew down with the disease throughout June. In June, it broke out in the submarine chaser squadron operating out of Plymouth. Only about 3 percent of the entire chaser force came down with the disease during June and July. The Sixth Battle Squadron with the Grand Fleet also experienced the epidemic. All of the ships had numerous cases but few deaths. *New York*'s sick bay, for example, treated 138 cases. Probably the submarines based at Bantry Bay, Ireland, were the hardest hit during the spring and summer months. On several of the boats from a third to a half of the small crews were infected. With no medical personnel assigned to the craft and with their crews facing the hardships they endured even under normal conditions while operating at sea, they nonetheless continued their assigned responsibilities. The *AL-2* was on the second day of a patrol when 13 out of her complement of 25 came down with the illness. She did complete her patrol. The *AL-9* had so many sick, according to her commanding officer, that diving stations could not be manned at all times. The submarine completed her patrol on the surface.[158]

In the Mediterranean, 92 members of the Gibraltar-based *Nashville* became ill while the gunboat was escorting a convoy to Bizerta. The converted yacht *Yankton* in April and May often operated with as many as half of her crew ill. One of *Chester*'s officers wrote in his diary that on May 13: "We picked up a convoy of 7 valuable ships. At that time the Spanish influenza was prevalent among the officers and men. More than 100 men were turned into the sick bay and hammocks that day, seriously crippling the working personnel." As with other American naval vessels in the war zone, *Chester* carried on with her escort duties despite a seriously depleted crew.[159]

Even the London headquarters staff of the American naval force in European waters (Simsadus) was hard hit by the epidemic. On June 30, Commander T. A. Thomson, Admiral Sims's chief medical officer, reported, "My entire office is out of commission with influenza including myself." Nonetheless, he predicted optimistically to Surgeon General Braisted at the end of July that there were only about 1,500 cases in the entire naval force and that the epidemic was about over.[160] Commander Thomson was tragically mistaken; a far deadlier strain had been sweeping through Asia, and even as he wrote the above, British civilians were dying by the hundreds. In June, 700 Londoners had died as well as more in other parts of the Isles.[161]

The new outbreak included the American subchaser detachment based at Plymouth. Beginning about the middle of August and continuing into November, some 15 percent of the personnel attached to the chasers and base were hospitalized with the flu. The base had only a small dispensary, and the usual procedure had been for the seriously ill to be transported to the nearby Royal naval hospital. During the outbreak of September-November, the hospital was so swamped with influenza patients from nearby British naval and military facilities that the Americans ill with the disease could not be admitted. Mild cases were confined to their quarters and ships. The base commanding officer informed Sims that "the efficiency of the Chaser Force . . . has been materially decreased . . . by a large number of cases of influenza among the personnel. In one case it was necessary to recall a boat from operations due to the small number of men available for duty." Only 4 American sailors at Plymouth died during the pandemic.[162]

Washington officials were not especially alarmed over the flu in August. Medical officers still reported evidence of the disease at home and abroad, but the number of cases was not cause for concern, nor were there an unusual number of deaths. This changed toward the end of the month. Cables arrived from Brest with the news of a massive and deadly outbreak among the French military personnel. At about the same time, the Department was notified of an eruption of the malady in Boston, initially targeting the bluejackets crowded on a receiving ship moored at the city's Commonwealth Pier. On the last day of August, as the city was focused on the local baseball stadium where Babe Ruth would pitch and hit the Red Socks to the American League Pennant, 106 sailors on the receiving ship came down with the flu. By the first week in September, more than 2,000 officers and men in the Boston area were stricken.

There were so many patients at Chelsea Naval Hospital that tents had to be erected on the lawn to handle the overflow. Before it was over, some 26 sailors in the Boston area had died from the disease. The local medical officials blamed it on congestion on the docks and moored ships; the Navy said it was probably brought in from European ports. Both ignored the presence of the disease among the port's civilian population and its presence in other parts of the country. Nonetheless, as one authority has emphasized, it was initially a naval affair. It would quickly spread among shore personnel up and down the Atlantic coast and to the large training center outside Chicago.[163]

The new epidemic reached the Atlantic Fleet and other shore installations in September. By the end of the month, the Great Lakes Training Station had nearly 10,000 down with the illness—so many that one sailor estimated that half of the barracks had been converted into temporary hospital wards. Flu swept through the naval facilities in Portsmouth, New Hampshire, including the prison and shipyard. Statistics are not available on how many at the prison came down with the illness, but according to a local newspaper, the number at the naval yard increased daily. On October 1, from 1,500 to 1,600 failed to come to work.[164] By the beginning of October, some 31,000 sailors, most of them on shore facilities in the States, had been stricken, and over 1,100 had died.[165]

In the war zone, the new and more deadly strain first appeared among the American naval force in French waters. One authority has described the fall flu epidemic among naval personnel in France as a kind of gradient starting and peaking at Brest and the other Atlantic ports in late September and decreasing inland.[166] This changed in October as the disease spread throughout France. Inevitably, Brest was battered by the disease. Even before influenza appeared in strength among Americans, the disease was ravaging French military and civilians in the district. To compound the situation, troopships from Norfolk, Boston, and other U.S. ports weekly debarked thousands of doughboys, many of whom suffered from the pestilence. Large numbers died and were buried at sea while others were carried ashore for internment. A sailor on the *President Grant* claimed years later that so many died on the transport that members of the crew when not on watch were required to prepare the deceased for burial. "I stood my watch in the radio room and when off watch I turned to and helped sew up some of the dead soldiers till my fingers bled. We used a palm and needle rig to cross-stitch thru the canvas."[167] Brigadier General Smedley Butler wrote his family after arriving in Brest on the naval transport *Henderson*: "We had a hell of a trip over, an epidemic of Spanish influenza breaking out among us. . . . We had at one time fully 500 cases of influenza. . . . I suppose it is one of the awful results of this devilish war . . . terribly hard to bear, this loss of your men when you can't help them." Shortly after, the huge liner *Leviathan* came in with 10,000 doughboys on board, 4,000 with the flu.[168]

The American naval vessels deployed in French waters were by no means immune from the pestilence. By September 15, the Navy hospital at Brest had admitted 200 patients with flu, while others with the disease remained in sick bays on their ships. A sailor on one of the patrol vessels wrote that "about 20% of the crew is in the hospital or on the sick list." An officer later recalled that "The destroyers in our group were pretty well stricken with it." On September 30, *Norma*'s medical officer reported 8 percent of her crew down with the malady. In *Brittany Patrol*, the author mentioned how the armed yacht *Emerline* "went to sea with half her crew sick." A boatswain mate, he added, "was moved to the Base Hospital, but after the first night he returned aboard. 'The men on either side of me died during the night,' he told us, 'and I decided that it was no place for anyone who wanted to live.'" The tender *Prometheus* had the thankless task of making wooden coffins for both sailors and soldiers. They "can't make enough," a *Reid* officer observed.[169]

Liberty was at first stopped and later restricted. Sailors could not enter stores, theaters, bars, and other public places. They were not permitted to leave the city without a pass. *Mount Vernon*'s skipper's solution was for his men to avoid the city while on liberty and instead spend their time at the Place Sainte Anne, a small beach several miles from the port. Liberty parties were marched there every morning. They were also sprayed with a disinfectant. Something must have worked, or perhaps *Mount Vernon* was one of the lucky ships as none of her crew came down with the flu.[170]

The epidemic, as usual, flowed and ebbed. On September 22, the chief surgeon of the U.S. naval hospital at Brest wrote, "The epidemic is thinning out." The following week, however, 250 more cases were admitted. On October 9 he wrote, "The epidemic has let up here." But it persisted well into December. On November 15, he reported that 629 patients from the forces afloat had been admitted to the hospital since the middle of September, of whom 65 had died. (This included both flu and pneumonia, which usually followed influenza, and most of the deaths were from that.) During the three-month period from September 15 to December 15, the hospital patient load averaged 800. The other naval hospital in France, designated primarily to take care of Marines and soldiers, also admitted sailors during the fall epidemic.[171] More than 2,000 American servicemen would die in Brest from influenza and complications.[172]

Naval personnel were not as affected by influenza at the other French Atlantic ports. At St. Nazaire, thousands of soldiers off the transports came down with the disease, but few sailors caught it. At Bordeaux, only 11 bluejackets were infected, 2 of whom died. The port officer at Lorient later reported two flu epidemics; one in September and a second one in December. Few men, however, came down with the affliction, and those who did had mild cases.[173]

The U.S. naval air stations in France generally reflected the "gradient" theory. La Trinité had a few cases in July and again in late November. La Pallice, with nearly 5,000 personnel, one of the largest of the stations, had what the medical officer called a "slight" epidemic. Approximately 300 were admitted to the hospital with flu, and another 400 confined in their barracks. One officer and 10 enlisted men died. Three of the stations experienced serious outbreaks. In October, nearly 90 percent of the personnel at the Dunkirk Seaplane Station were affected. The Northern Bombing Group reported 473 cases with less than 1 percent fatal. Moutchie Station in the Gironde counted 20 percent of its enlisted personnel catching the disease, with 2 deaths. The small air station at St. Trojan, near Rochefort, was devastated by the disease. The station's history mentioned that the epidemic lasted about three weeks, and that "there were days when the Station was unable to carry on operation because of it." During

September, half of the 360 men manning the station were ill and 7 died. Nonetheless, the mortality rate in the air stations was much lower than in the ports.[174] The small hospital at the isolated Lafayette Radio Station was not adequate for the number of patients. A large tent was erected for the overflow. Fortunately, only 3 deaths from the disease occurred at the station.[175]

As in France, the effect of the disease on American naval facilities and ships varied. The nearly 7,000 sailors with the mine-laying bases and ships at Inverness and Invergordon in Scotland got off lightly. They had about 200 cases in June and July, but in October and November averaged only 2 new cases a day. Only one ship, *Quinnebaug*, had a large number ill—so many, in fact, that tents and awnings were erected on the open decks to isolate those with the affliction until they could be transferred to a hospital. *Saranac* totaled 26 cases and *Lake Huron*, 25. The mine-laying personnel suffered only 2 deaths. None of the *Roanoke*'s crew came down with the malady. The squadron's commanding officer attributed the absence of the epidemic to the wearing of gauze masks and a quarantine imposed on the sailors. The Y was closed down, no liberty was allowed, and all athletic events outside the bases were canceled.[176]

Other American bases were not so fortunate. Queenstown, which had become the largest U.S. naval installation in the British Isles, saw a large number of cases. Throughout October, the number of new cases daily averaged from 25 to 35. When the new naval hospital at Whitepoint was open in late October, 150 patients were immediately admitted, all with the flu. They had been kept on board their ships or the two tenders in the harbor. According to the *Dixie*'s medical officer, the epidemic "threatened the entire crew." There were far too many for the sick bay, so the crew's messing compartments were taken over and used as wards. In October, there were 43 cases among *Melville*'s crew. The wooden subchasers on patrol in the Irish Sea had a difficult time as they had to depend on already overcrowded British medical facilities for help. Some of the ships, including destroyers operating out of Queenstown, were immobilized by the epidemic. Some 15 sailors at Queenstown died from the disease.[177]

The other American facilities in Ireland did not escape the disease. Nurses were sent to the Whiddy Island Naval Air Station to care for patients too ill to be transferred to Queenstown.[178] The station at Wexford escaped flu among its personnel despite the fact that a nearby town had from 3,000 to 3,500 cases with 5 to 10 fatalities a day. The Wexford commanding officer isolated his station from the town, allowing no one to enter or leave without a pass and allowing liberty only on Sunday where parties under an officer could hike in rural areas. The other stations generally followed Wexford's example. Other than at Whiddy, near Bantry Bay, there were no fatalities and few ill from flu.[179]

But it was the sailors stationed on the battleships and other U.S. naval vessels concentrated near Berehaven in Bantry Bay who suffered the most from the epidemic. By the middle of October, a third of *Utah*'s and *Oklahoma*'s crews were down with the flu. One of *Utah*'s officers recalled in his oral history that one Sunday in October he went hiking with several officers from *Oklahoma*, including the ship's gunnery officer, and a few days later the gunnery officer was dead from the flu.[180] *Nevada* experienced few cases until the second week in October, when the number began to escalate. As the ship's history said, "the end of a month found us riddled of the disease." A member of the ship's company wrote in his diary on October 21, "a large percentage of the ship's crew is sick with Spanish Influenza." Two days later, he remarked: "The general spirit is gloomy, everyone sees many of his shipmates groping around looking like hooded ghosts. . . . One can tell by the expression on each face that they are battling to their utmost to keep going, for this is the surest way to down the discease [sic]." He also mentioned in his diary that the sick bay line "is sometimes fifty or sixty feet long." During the week ending October 26, 7 sailors on *Nevada* died.[181] Altogether 11 of the *Nevada*'s sailors died. The battleship known far and wide in the Navy as the "Cheer Up Ship" had little to cheer about when the epidemic had run its course. Because of the lack of adequate medical facilities at Bantry Bay, the Red Cross agreed to send a 25-bed hospital with all the necessary equipment and supplies there. It was proposed at first to take over a large hotel in the nearby town of Glengariff and convert it into a temporary hospital. Instead, naval officials recommended that a tent hospital be set up on the shore near the fleet anchorage. The "hospital" was shipped from the Red Cross's warehouse outside London, by train to Holyhead, by steamer across the Irish Sea, and by truck to Cork and railway to Berehaven. There the hospital was installed in tents with naval medical personnel in charge.[182]

Personnel on the American dreadnoughts attached to the Grand Fleet were also seriously affected by the epidemic. The same was true of the British ships in the fleet. There were over 600 cases on the *Revenge.* The battle cruiser *Princess Royal* was so devastated by influenza that tugs were moored alongside to provide essential servic-es. Some of the ships, in order to go on patrol, had to borrow personnel from a sister ship.[183] In the American squadron, the *Arkansas* had 230 cases in one week; *New York* and *Texas* more than that. According to one former officer, *Arkansas* had "in excess of 1,200 cases"; this in a complement of approximately 1,500 men. "Everybody sick with the flu," a bluejacket on *Arkansas* dejectedly wrote in his diary. The flu, accord-ing to one veteran, "pretty well lay *Florida*'s crew out." Admiral Harry W. Hill in his oral history said: "On both *Texas* and *Wyoming*, we had more than half our crew in-capacitated at one time or another. They were so numerous they couldn't be handled in sick bay, and had to be taken care of in special areas set up in various places in the ship."[184] *Wyoming* got off the lightest with only 10 deaths with the disease. Admiral John McCrea, who was on the *New York* at the time, in his oral history said: "We had a hell of a time with it. We lost something around 14 or 15 people, including a couple of officers. There were ten officers . . . whose rooms were forward of the wardroom. I was one of the ten . . . and I was the only one in that part of the ship that didn't have the flu."

When the Grand Fleet had to sortie once during the epidemic, several British war-ships did not have enough healthy men to get underway. All of the American battle-ships, however, joined the fleet as it steamed out of the Firth of Forth. Fortunately, it was a false alarm; morale in the German High Seas Fleet had deteriorated to the point where it was unable to go to sea. Admiral McCrea said that if the German fleet had come out at that time, "the result could have been disastrous for the Grand Fleet. . . . [The epidemic] was bad, *bad*, I can tell you."[185]

For several weeks in October and November, the large American naval hospital at Leith was filled to capacity with men from the battleships. The surgeon general in his annual report stated that "It was the proud assertion of the United States Navy Base Hospital No. 3 [at Leith] at this time that never in one instance was a case . . . denied admittance, though it sometimes meant the temporary occupation of offices, etc."[186] Despite the large number of personnel in the squadron stricken with the disease, there were fewer than 30 fatalities on the American dreadnoughts.

Cardiff, Wales, operated more than twenty vessels carrying coal to France. By the fall, 1918 approximately two thousand naval personnel were based there. In early October, the flu swept through the shore installations and ships. The base, without medical facilities, had to turn to the Red Cross for help. The relief agency opened a small hospital to fill this gap, but it was quickly swamped with influenza patients. Whenever possible, the flu victims were sent to local hospitals, but they could not accommodate all the ill. A small hotel was taken over, and even the naval headquarters building was temporarily converted into a hospital. Before the fall epidemic had run its course, over 500 had contracted the disease, with nearly two dozen fatalities.[187]

Both U.S. naval air stations in England were affected by the epidemic. Flu first broke out at Eastleigh in September, and by the end of the month hundreds were down with it. "The only thing that worries me is the tremendous number of pneumonia cases in camp. One fellow died yesterday and another is sinking now."[188] By the second week in October, the number of cases had dropped to fewer than 100. Twenty sailors at Eastleigh lost their lives during the epidemic. At the Killingholme Naval Air Station, of the 1,500 sailors stationed there, 117 were infected with the flu, 16 caught pneumonia, and 6 died.[189]

The Mediterranean world suffered from the fall epidemic and so did the American naval vessels and facilities there. At Gibraltar, which had become the location of a sizeable U.S. base, Rear Admiral Albert Niblack, its commanding officer, reported to Sims: "The influenza ran through this place last spring and summer but has taken a fresh start. It is going through the Coast Guard cutter *Manning* now, and the Italian mail steamer *Giuseppe Verdi*, and neither of them are able to sail. Many other ships are crippled. We can not have any quarantine here, because of the thousands of laborers that come in and go out daily, from and into Spain." He added, "This grippe . . . is bound to go around the world and nothing can stop it. The best way is to let it take its course, keep clean and use sunshine."[190] There was plenty of sunshine in Gibraltar and elsewhere in the Mediterranean, but it, of course, did not stop the contagion.

It devastated Italy. The American naval air personnel stationed there were fortunate. Few caught the flu. At the Porto Corsini station, there were 37 cases out of a complement of 380 officers and men. In the nearby city of Ravenna, there were 220 fatalities among the Italian population. Approximately 60 Americans trained at the Royal Italian naval aviation school at Bolsena. The U.S. detachment there had only 12 that came down with the illness despite their quarters being only a couple of hundred yards from a village. Work was delayed at the Pescara base under construction as much of the workforce was ill from the flu, but there is no evidence that the few Americans there caught the disease. Only a few naval personnel were stationed in Rome, and none came down with the disease.[191]

The subchaser base at Corfu was the hardest hit of any American installation in the Mediterranean. Late in September, one of the chaser officers wrote in his diary: "Half of the crew are sick. As soon as one gets well another comes down." A month later, he wrote that two of his men had died of pneumonia, a high percentage considering the boats' small crews.[192] What was true of one chaser was generally true of all. On October 28, "Juggy" Nelson, the American commanding officer, cabled Sims, "Influenza Hurting." Four days later, he informed the force commander that he was concerned about "tax[ing] personnel [no] more than absolutely necessary."[193] The epidemic reached the naval base at Ponta Delgada, Azores, in September when a Japanese merchant vessel was towed into the port. She had been adrift with virtually her entire crew either dead or incapacitated from the disease. The flu quickly spread throughout the island. In late October, Rear Admiral Dunn, the commanding officer of the American base there, cabled that there were 15,000 cases among the island people and "practically without resources to meet situation." Thousands died, according to an American naval officer.[194] By October, every ship that entered the port landed stretcher cases. Afflicted base personnel averaged about 100 throughout the month. The small hospital was unable to handle the ill from transient vessels and the base. Tents were erected, but these proved inadequate. Finally a large private residence in the town was leased and converted into a 500-bed hospital.[195]

Far to the North in the Russian province of Archangel, American troops landed early in September. They brought the flu with them. By the middle of the month, it had spread among the Allied forces there, the Russian civilians, and the crew of USS *Olympia*. The American cruiser had been in northern Russian waters since May, but her personnel had been spared the earlier epidemic. By the middle of September, however, bluejackets were down with the illness. On September 23, a gob mentioned in his diary that about 50 were sick with the disease.[196] He does not mention the epidemic again. No record of the impact that it had on *Olympia*'s bluejackets has been found, including whether or not there were any deaths. The British cruiser *Glory* anchored nearby had several deaths and the U.S. Army units there suffered some 69 fatalities during the month.[197]

Admiral Sims, the European naval force commander, became increasingly concerned about the severity of the fall outbreak of influenza. In early October, he cabled the Department that "there is no doubt that this [epidemic] is now a greater danger to people on ship-board than the Submarine is." He appealed to Admiral Benson, the CNO, to immediately send two hospital ships to European waters. He also strongly urged Washington officials to reduce significantly the number of troops—up to 50 percent—per transport. "Many deaths," he wrote, "have occurred and many more expected. Immediate drastic measures should be adopted to avoid serious loss of life . . . [and] official public outcry and possible investigation by Congress."[198] The force commander also issued a general order stopping all leave in the war zone that involved travel.[199]

Largely, however, it was left up to individual commanding officers and medical officers to handle the crisis. Unfortunately there were few guidelines and even fewer effective medicines. Vaccines were virtually unknown in those pre-antibiotic days.

In general, they depended upon fresh air, bed rest, simplified diet, and quarantine. Physicians and nursing care were important, but often not adequate. Doctors were not available or ill themselves. Corpsmen were at times overwhelmed with responsibilities.[200] Quinine and aspirin (and whiskey) were the most common drugs used to treat flu victims. Preventatives from hot coffee to throat and nose sprays were tried on most ships and stations. However, one ship surgeon advised the Bureau of Medicine and Surgery that "the less medicine given by mouth," the better the chance of recovery. One naval air station in England required all windows in barracks left open at all times regardless of the temperature outside. The crew of USS *San Francisco*, while not on duty, were escorted by officers on long walks. On *Yankton*, the medical officer required all personnel to be issued two blankets. Many of the ships and stations ordered personnel to wear gauze masks, some even when they slept. Nearly every ship and station curtailed liberty. However, at Killingholme and the battleships with the Grand Fleet at Rosyth, it was encouraged. Afterward, the Bureau of Medicine and Surgery concluded that quarantine was the most effective preventative.[201]

The epidemic lingered on into 1919 before finally disappearing. The Navy, one authority claimed, kept more accurate records than did the United States Public Health Service concerning civilian cases. He concluded that at least 40 percent of the Navy's personnel had flu during the 1918–19 epidemics. This may well have been a conservative estimate since an undetermined number of sailors evidently did not report to sick bay. There were 5,027 deaths from influenza or complications, primarily pneumonia. This was more than twice as many as those who died from enemy action.[202]

The Navy was clearly affected by the pandemic. Crews were decimated, ships were delayed in sailing, medical facilities were badly taxed, but as the surgeon for the New York port of embarkation said, "We can't stop this War on account of Spanish or any other kind of influenza."[203] Navy veterans of the Great War never forgot the epidemic. In memoirs and oral histories, they recalled the suffering and dying. When one was asked, "What do you recall thinking and experiencing at the time?" he replied: "Mostly flu. Men were dying every day."[204]

No health problem, including flu, concerned Navy officers more than venereal disease. Although it could and at times did reach epidemic proportions, it was not epidemical.[205] The disease, nevertheless, had the potential to seriously affect a ship or station's crew and its operations. Yet, during the war the Navy's efforts to control VD were at best indifferent, this despite statistics in the surgeon general's annual report in 1918 stating that the percentage of cases had climbed during the conflict. Raymond Fosdick, the influential chairman of the Commission on Training Camp Activities, wrote after the war that the rate of venereal disease in the Navy was "considerably higher than that of the Army."[206] Ironically, it was the Navy that led the way before the war in the adoption of prophylaxis, the most successful preventative used during the war.

Dr. Braisted, the surgeon general, informed the Navy's General Board in 1917 that the prophylactic "packets" were originally obtained from the Germans.[207] Although he admitted that they were effective, under instructions from Secretary of the Navy Daniels in 1915, he ordered the discontinuance of their use. In addition, ships and stations were ordered to stop the selling of contraceptives either in ship stores or by individuals while on Navy property. Many of the Navy's medical officers opposed the orders, but the surgeon general refused to rescind them. Daniels policy was in part a reflection of the Progressive Era's reform crusade against vice, but it was far more his basic philosophy. Prophylactic treatment, he insisted, "would tend to subvert and destroy the very Foundations of our moral and Christian beliefs and teachings with regard to these sexual matters."[208] The naval secretary was a Progressive and determined moralist who preferred educational programs that stressed the dangers of VD. "I appealed to the youth to practice sexual continence," he wrote in his memoirs.[209] Captain Louis Poisson Davis, a retired naval officer and a fellow North Carolinian, called Daniels a "damn fool" for his obstinacy against prophylactics.[210]

The secretary's appeal for "continence" did not work, however, especially in the war zone. Despite the efforts of Daniels and his Progressive cohorts, Secretary of War Baker and Fosdick, Wilson's administration found it most difficult if not impossible to export its moral code to Europe. U.S. naval shore stations and vessels in European waters reported the number of venereal cases periodically, but no analysis of them or quantification was ever attempted. Some commanding officers, instead of reporting the exact number of cases, simply said that the number was small or high. Admiral Rodman, for example, mentioned that the battleships under his command experienced an unusually high percentage of venereal cases after their refits in Newcastle.[211]

Although the Navy's medical officers in the war zone were handicapped in their efforts to prevent VD, they still provided outstanding service. They handled a whole variety of health and medical problems from minor shipboard injuries to major ones caused by collisions and torpedo damage. Several thousand civilian doctors and dentists were taken in the service for the emergency, and many of them were assigned to European waters. In fact, by 1918 doctors were even being sent to destroyers. The small subchasers, however, did not rate medical officers; some of them had pharmacist mates; others did not. On at least one occasion, an injured seaman had to be operated on by the chaser's commanding officer.[212] Dentists were assigned to various tenders and stations. As one officer on a Gibraltar-based ship wrote, "The busiest men in the whole place are the two Naval Reserve dentists."[213] Probably many if not most of the American sailors had never had as much health care as in the Navy—that was certainly true of dental care.

Naval personnel in the war zone groused about food and conditions on board ship while operating at sea, and they were occasionally subject to illness. But morale was surprisingly good, at least partly because of recreational opportunities both on board ship and on shore, especially liberty and sports.

Map 1. French coast including the Bay of Biscay, where the U.S. naval forces were located. Courtesy of Paolo E. Coletta.

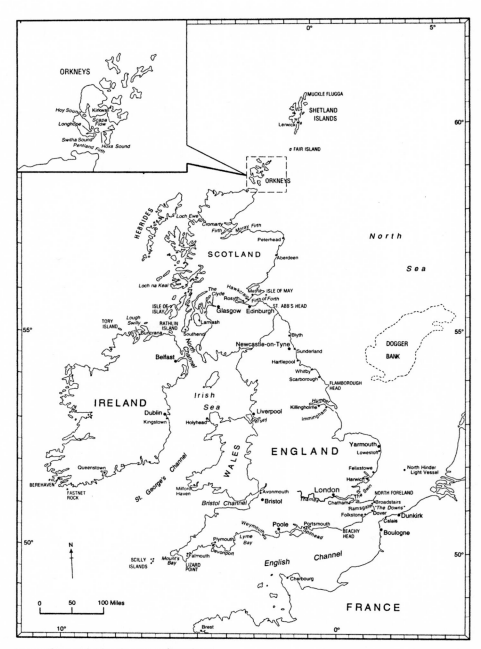

Map 2. The British Isles. Courtesy of P. Halpern.

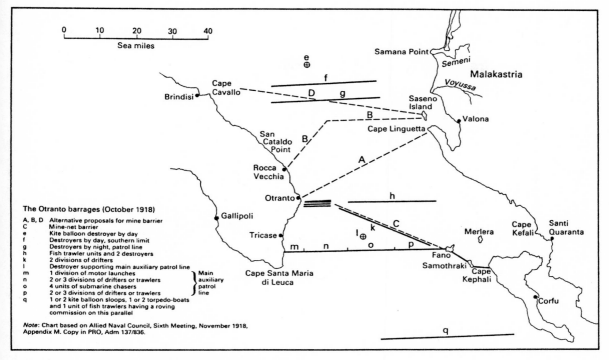

Map 3. The Otranto Barrages (October 1918). Courtesy of P. Halpern.

The Otranto barrages (October 1918)

A, B, D Alternative proposals for mine barrier
C Mine-net barrier
e Kite balloon destroyer by day
f Destroyers by day, southern limit
g Destroyers by night, patrol line
h Fish trawler units and 2 destroyers
k 2 divisions of drifters
l Destroyer supporting main auxiliary patrol line
m 1 division of motor launches
n 2 or 3 divisions of drifters or trawlers   Main
o 4 units of submarine chasers   auxiliary
p 2 or 3 divisions of drifters or trawlers   patrol
q 1 or 2 kite balloon sloops, 1 or 2 torpedo-boats   line
    and 1 unit of fish trawlers having a roving
    commission on this parallel

Note: Chart based on Allied Naval Council, Sixth Meeting, November 1918,
Appendix M. Copy in PRO, Adm 137/836.

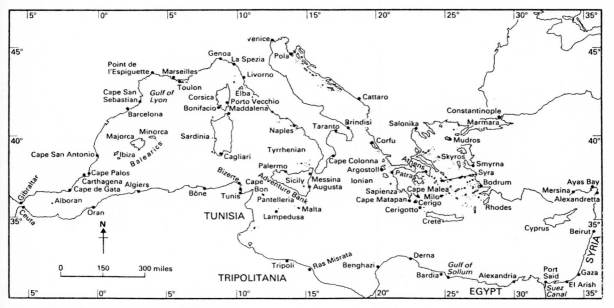

Map 4. The Mediterranean. Courtesy of P. Halpern.

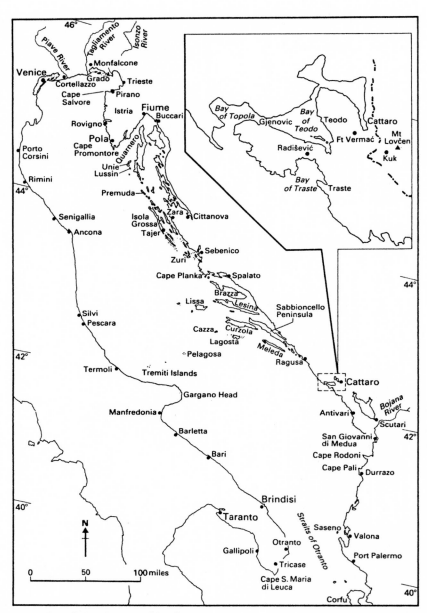

Map 5. The Adriatic. Courtesy of P. Halpern.

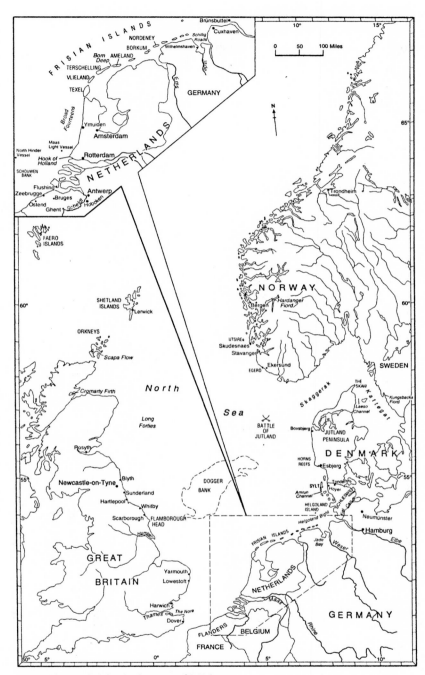

Map 6. The North Atlantic. Courtesy of P. Halpern.

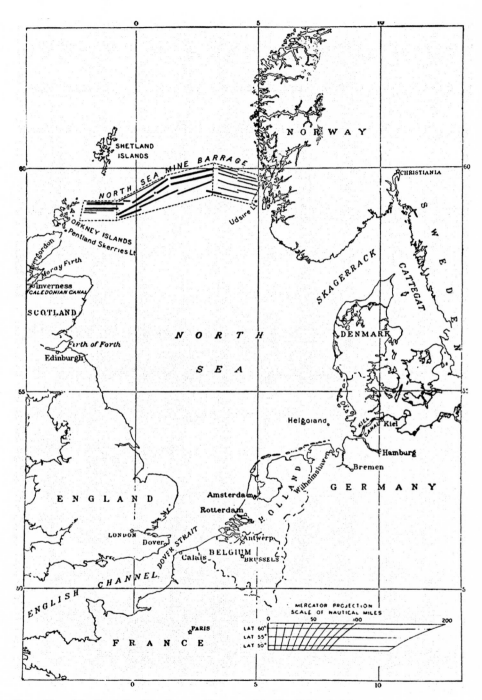

Map 7. Map of the North Sea Mine Barrage. Courtesy of the Naval Historical Center.

Figure 1. U.S. Coast Guard cutter *Seneca* in European waters, 1917–18. Courtesy of the United States Coast Guard Historian's Office.

Figure 2. U. S. Coast Guard cutter *Tampa*, sunk by U-boat while escorting convoy in European waters, September 1918. Courtesy of the United States Coast Guard Historian's Office.

Figure 3. At Queenstown, Ireland, in 1918; the third ship from the left is the USS *Terry*. The USS *Melville* is in the right background. Courtesy of Jack Howland and the Naval Historical Center.

Figure 4. USS *Porter* arriving at Queenstown, Ireland, May 4, 1917, as part of the first U.S. Navy force to take part in World War I. Courtesy of James C. Russell and the Naval Historical Center.

Figure 5. Rear Admiral Albert P. Niblack in command of the U.S. naval forces operating out of Gibraltar. Courtesy of the Naval Historical Center.

Figure 6. Rear Admiral Joseph Strauss, in command of U.S. mine-laying force. Courtesy of the Naval Historical Center.

Figure 7. Laying the North Sea Mine Barrage, September 1918. Courtesy of the Naval Historical Center.

Figure 8. USS *Aroostook*, a minelayer, in 1918. Courtesy of the Naval Historical Center.

Figure 9. Reginald Rowland Belknap, Captain USN CO Mine Squadron One, 1918. Courtesy of the Naval Historical Center.

Figure 10. U.S. Naval Base Number 17 in Dalmore, Scotland, and the mine-assembly sheds, 1918. Courtesy of the Naval Historical Center.

Figure 11. U.S. naval air station hangars in France, 1917–18. Courtesy of the Naval Historical Center.

Figure 12. *Curtiss H-16* going out for a test flight at Aghada. Queenstown, Ireland, 1918. Courtesy of the Naval Historical Center.

Figure 13. Admiral Henry B. Wilson, in command of the U.S. naval forces in France, with Captain Louis M. Nulton in 1920. Courtesy of the Naval Historical Center.

Figure 14. Semaphore signaling station at Park Au Dric, Brest, France, 1918. Courtesy of the Naval Historical Center.

Figure 15. USS *Covington*, torpedoed by *U-86* on July 1, 1918; *Covington* sank on July 2, 1918. Courtesy of the Naval Historical Center.

Figure 16. A convoy of twenty-five ships nearing Brest, November 1, 1918. Courtesy of the Naval Historical Center.

Figure 17. A 14–inch railway gun, Soissons, France, 1918. Courtesy of the Naval Historical Center.

Figure 18. The 110–foot wooden subchaser, the *SC 273*, 1918. Courtesy of the Naval Historical Center.

Figure 19. Destroyer USS *Caldwell* with dazzle camouflage. Courtesy of the Naval Historical Center.

Figure 20. USS *McCall* refueling at sea from the USS *Maumee* in an Atlantic gale, September 22, 1917. Courtesy of the Naval Historical Center.

Figure 21. *Quinnebaug* baseball team. Courtesy of J. W. Conroy.

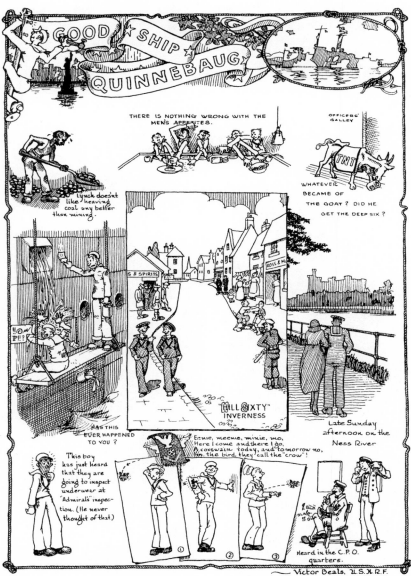

Figure 22. A cartoon by Victor Beals about life on board a ship. Courtesy of J. W. Conroy.

Figure 23. The USS *Black Hawk* Jazz Band. Courtesy of J. W. Conroy.

Figure 24. Liberty party at Inverness. Courtesy of J. W. Conroy.

Figure 25. USS *May* off Bermuda, an armed yacht on its way to the war zone in 1917. Courtesy of the Naval Historical Center.

Figure 26. USS *Pocahontas* with gun crews at drill, 1917. Courtesy of the Naval Historical Center.

Figure 27. *Left to right*: Admiral David Beatty, RN; Rear Admiral Hugh Rodman, USN; King George V; Vice Admiral William S. Sims, USN; Prince of Wales, on the USS *New York* in 1918, with the Grand Fleet, in the Firth of Forth. Courtesy of the Naval Historical Center.

Figure 28. The Sixth Battle Squadron off the French coast, awaiting the arrival of President Wilson, December 13, 1918.

Figure 29. USS *West Bridge*, torpedoed by *U-90* on August 15, 1918, is being surveyed for damage in a French dry dock. Courtesy of the Naval Historical Center.

For the Boys

Welfare

Before the twentieth century, the Navy paid little attention to the morale of its personnel. A sailor's free time on board ship or on liberty was his to do with as he pleased, except when an infraction of regulations occurred that seriously disrupted shipboard routine, work, or caused violence on shore or on the ship. This hands-off policy began to change in the twentieth century. In 1900, the Navy became more directly involved in welfare when it revised and published "Regulations for the Government of the Navy." Recreation and sports were addressed along with morale and other factors affecting the needs of naval personnel. This was partly a result of the temperance and other reforms popularized by the Progressive movement, and partly a result of the requirements for a better-educated and stable seaman in the new steel warships. By the time the United States entered World War I, the personnel were better educated and, in general, a reflection of American society at that time. At the same time, the Navy had become increasingly conscious about morale.

The primary responsibility for morale and the welfare of all personnel whether on shore or ship rested with the commanding officer. In the normal chain of command, he delegated this responsibility to the executive officer, who in turn leaned on the chaplain and/or another officer designated as "welfare" or "recreation officer." Few ships or stations, at least during World War I, had the luxury of an officer with welfare or morale as his sole responsibility, including the chaplain. For example, the chaplains with the U.S. battleships attached to the Grand Fleet helped decipher messages; others took charge of the laundry, barber, cobbler, and tailor shops, library, and photography laboratory.[1]

At the outbreak of war, Secretary Daniels reported that the authorized strength for the Navy's chaplain corps was the same as in 1841. At his recommendation, the ratio was changed, allotting one chaplain for every 1,250 personnel. According to *The History of the Chaplain Corps*, if the quota had been achieved, there would have been 480 chaplains, but only 203 chaplains served in the Navy during the war, 42 percent of the authorized number. Despite the secretary's claim that every ship had a chaplain, a majority of the ships did not, and as late as August 1918 a number of shore facilities were without one. Each of the battleships with the Grand Fleet had a chaplain, probably the most challenging service in European waters. The shortage in the naval force in European waters forced chaplains to support the spiritual needs of all men regardless of faith.[2] Sometimes political issues affected assignment. For example, Sims became apprehensive about a Roman Catholic chaplain assigned to Ireland: "at the present time the heads of the Catholic Church in Ireland are to all intents and purposes the enemies of the Allied cause. . . . I would not . . . hesitate for a moment to remove any Chaplain . . . that we found . . . opposing our wishes or meddling in our purely military affairs."[3]

The entry of the United Sates into the war caused thousands of volunteers to flood naval recruiting offices. New "boot" camps had to be established to train the recruits. The Department, particularly Secretary Daniels, gave immediate attention to the problem of welfare. The new camps were without any kind of entertainment—movies, libraries, or athletic fields. More troublesome were the temptations off base; prostitution and other vices quickly established themselves near new camps. Newton Baker, the secretary of the army, worked on a program to change "certain habits the public had ever associated with soldiering."[4] He was appalled at the drunkenness and debauchery among the soldiers mobilized in 1916 to deal with the Mexican crisis and the notoriety it brought to the Army. Daniels, a populist and zealous reformer of the Navy, concurred with his colleague.

American military and naval officials realized that recreation was "essential in the business of war."[5] On April 17, 1917, the naval secretary appointed a Commission on Training Activities, and the Army established a similar commission. With the president's approval, the two commissions were merged into a single agency with Raymond Fosdick as chairman. The commission would coordinate the activities of various organizations that dealt with servicemen such as the Young Men's Christian Association (YMCA), the Young Women's Christian Association (YWCA), Knights of Columbus (KC), and Salvation Army. The Red Cross did not come under the commission's direction.[6]

The two service secretaries became even more concerned about the problem of welfare when the administration decided to deploy a military force in the war zone. Fosdick's commission was given the responsibility for overseeing welfare activities overseas. In the United States, the organizations involved in the welfare program would create acceptable conditions in and around the various training camps and stations. Because of national and cultural differences overseas and the lack of control outside defined American military areas, conditions improved much more slowly and never became as satisfactory as they were in the States.

Admiral Sims created a section within Simsadus to deal with welfare. Initially, the Admiralty's censorship office acted as a clearinghouse for British efforts to entertain American sailors based in the United Kingdom. Later a group from the entertainment industry was formed to coordinate with Sims's staff.[7] When the first American ships arrived in Queenstown in May 1917, a move began to provide the sailors with organized recreation. The YMCA's interest in establishing one of their canteens may have provided a stimulus, and the British Sailor's Society approached Sims about building a "temporary Sailor's home for the special accommodation of his fleet." Sims was concerned about the enlisted personnel but opposed the Y's request to establish a canteen. "Religious feeling was so strong [among the Irish] . . . that under the advice of the British authorities, I felt impelled to decline" the offer.[8] In October, the Y tried again, but the force commander continued to insist that it was not advisable to establish huts in Ireland.[9] During the summer of 1918, a naval officer investigating personnel problems wrote, "there is no American Y.M.C.A. in Queenstown, and none is required." Yet the Y established a canteen and a large recreation hall at the naval hospital at Whitepoint, just outside Queenstown. The officers used the facilities of the Royal Cork Yacht and the Cork (golf) clubs. Junior officers dubbed the mooring station nearest the yacht club the "Gin and Bitters buoy."[10] The force commander wanted a club for the enlisted men, and one was made available. "The significant feature of this institution," he later wrote the Department, "is the fact that it is manned, operated, and managed by our own men and officers. This results in a much higher degree of popularity and usefulness than if it were manned and operated by outside organizations which always in the minds of the men carry a certain unavoidable stigma of charity."[11] Nonetheless, he later encouraged the Y to provide welfare centers elsewhere in Great Britain and France.

Initial funding for the proposed "Men's Club" came from American firms and citizens residing in London, presumably at the urging of Sims. A building and adjacent lots on the Queenstown waterfront were leased, and work started in June. It was formally opened on August 25, 1917. At that time, the club contained an auditorium used during daylight hours as a gym, a restaurant, canteen, billiard room, library, dormitory, shower/bath room, and restrooms. The announcement of the club's opening included the statement "no religion, no politics."[12] The tender *Melville*'s crew, who had been instrumental in constructing and outfitting the club, operated it. The "crew's entertainment allotment," accumulated from sales in the ships' stores and in the club's restaurant and canteen, funded the club's management and the entertainment. The Navy Department gave the tender permission to provide provisions at cost for the club's restaurant and canteen.[13]

The cancellation of all liberty to Cork (except commanding officers) placed more emphasis upon the club. In November 1917, Pringle reported to Sims that morale continued "very good . . . attributable to 'the influence of the Men's Club.'"[14] In the beginning, U.S. personnel provided the entertainment. *Melville* had a small string band. A much larger band was later organized from the various ships in the Destroyer Flotilla.[15] In time, an impressive amount of talent, both professional and amateur, was discovered in the flotilla. For no remuneration except the approbation of their shipmates, they performed as comedians, vocalists, and as actors in skits and plays. Sims wanted to send professional artists to perform, but Pringle preferred to feature his own personnel. He also requested movies. The censoring office in London provided both British and American films. American movies were extremely popular, particularly those featuring Mary Pickford and Douglas Fairbanks.[16]

In addition to the entertainment and movies, good food and a warm building attracted the sailors night after night. The restaurant specialized in steak and eggs, a traditional favorite with the American bluejackets. Pringle decided to allow all servicemen to enter the club. It quickly became popular with British sailors and soldiers stationed in Ireland, who traveled from as far away as Dublin to avail themselves of it. "Best of all," wrote a correspondent, "one could go to the Club and actually be warm and comfortable in the American style, a boon not to be lightly regarded in these islands, where people all winter long huddle in freezing rooms around lilliputian grates."[17]

Although VIPs visited many of the American military and naval installations in Europe, Queenstown probably hosted more than any other U.S. facility. They were taken to the club, and without exception they praised it. The British Admirals Jellicoe, Wemyss, and Bayly put in appearances.[18] Admirals Sims and Mayo were duly impressed as was Assistant Secretary of the Navy Roosevelt. Mayo wrote his wife that in the intermission between shows, "there was a lot of singing—the words being thrown on the screen, the orchestra playing the music and the whole audience joining in the singing. It was fine!" A British naval officer was enthusiastic about the singing: "It was exhilarating to hear the crowd of about 2,500 shouting 'Over There' to the accompaniment of the excellent band and with the words thrown on the screen so that we could also join in the chorus."[19]

In May 1917, the head of the YMCA in France wrote to the minister of marine, requesting permission to establish canteens, or "huts." When the first U.S. naval vessels arrived early in July, the Y awaited them. In June, USS *Walke* stopped off briefly in Brest. One of her officers wrote: "Met a couple of young Americans . . . who were just starting a Y.M.C.A. for American sailors. We promised to send our men to them next day."[20] Evidently Y authorities discovered, probably through Fosdick's office, that Brest was to be the site of an American naval installation. Three days after Sims was asked for "assurance," the Y headquarters in Paris informed the French navy that it would send two volunteers to the port to arrange for a canteen. They arrived early in June, leased the ground floor of a building, purchased a piano, billiard tables, and furniture, and prepared for the first liberty party.[21] Within months, Y "huts" sprung up in both France and Great Britain.

As American doughboys began to join the gobs in Brest and the surrounding area, French military authorities became concerned about the activities of the military personnel when on leave in the city. They feared that the absence of adequate recreation would have a negative effect on relations between the two countries. Admiral Moreau wrote: "Brest presents particular problems. . . . The French military . . . at local barracks not sports minded. Films and theatres are expensive." He mentioned that a French soldiers' organization in the port would invite Americans. The English had been admitted earlier. He admitted that a French officers' club was opened to Americans "but they don't go there often."[22]

The Red Cross, already established in Europe when the United States went to war, traditionally emphasized medical services and relief. For example, sailors who became ill while on leave or liberty in areas without naval medical service could turn to the Red Cross for help.[23] Although not affiliated with Fosdick's commission, the Red Cross provided "camp service," which included canteens for the AEF in Great Britain and to a lesser degree in France. The organization was willing to do the same for the Navy, but when it approached Admiral Sims, he put them off, saying that existing facilities met the Navy's needs. He later changed his mind and encouraged the Red Cross to step in where it was needed. For example, in Plymouth the Red Cross set up recreational facilities, a canteen and dining hall, and a dormitory. It sponsored dances, arranged with a local hospitality committee for teas and meals, established a free ticket program to use the local bath house, and even conducted hikes and tours. A canteen and club was opened in Dublin for American servicemen in transit. The Red Cross worked with the "American Welcome Club" in Edinburgh to provide everything from lodging to recreational activities in that city. It also became involved in providing quarters for sailors working or on leave in London. In December 1917, the Strand Imperial Hotel was leased and organized as a sailors' club. Rooms were available for a nominal charge. It was quickly occupied, primarily by personnel attached to London headquarters. Later two additional buildings were acquired and converted into living facilities.[24]

The Red Cross performed other services such as providing sweaters and warm clothes to sailors on duty in Great Britain and elsewhere; providing canteen services at the naval hospitals; and passing out doughnuts and coffee at train stations and even at the gates of bases. An effort was made to supply all the naval facilities, including hospitals, with libraries. Subchaser crews at Queenstown used a circulating library of five hundred books. Often when ships arrived from patrol, Red Cross representatives passed out "comfort bags" of items such as toothbrushes, toothpaste, soap, cigarettes, chocolates, and, at times, clothing. Boxes of assorted candies and other items were sent to the different facilities during the Christmas holiday period.[25]

The Red Cross sent staff members to open a center in Gibraltar, but they arrived after the Armistice. The chief Red Cross worker in Gibraltar later wrote, "I do not feel that we were given the opportunity . . . to show the Navy how much we could supplement their work and improve conditions."[26]

The Knights of Columbus, a service organization of the Catholic Church, was active in both France and Great Britain. Small in staff and number of facilities in comparison to the YMCA and the Red Cross, it opened clubs in Paris and London. The Knights also operated the only American service facility for doughboys and bluejackets in Aberdeen, Scotland, offering a dormitory, cafeteria, and music and reading rooms. KC representatives often met ships returning from patrol or escort duty at American bases in the British Isles and passed out free cigarettes and small religious and personal items. The Catholic organization wanted to locate in other parts of the war zone but generally could not because of the Fosdick commission's policy of avoiding duplication and the Navy's opposition. When the Knights approached Sims about establishing recreational centers at U.S. naval bases with two thousand or more men, he refused because of the need to concentrate oceanic transportation on essential materials. He ignored the fact that the YMCA needs, far greater than those of the Knights, used shipping space.[27]

The Christian Science Church emulated the Catholics in efforts to establish welfare centers at U.S. naval bases and stations in Great Britain. In several communities adjacent to American military facilities, they opened Christian Science reading rooms. During the flu epidemic of 1918, the Y hut at Inverness was quarantined, leaving open only the welfare center operated by Christian Scientists. In France, they established small reading rooms in Bordeaux, Paris, and Brest.[28]

In addition to the various service organizations under the Training Camp Commission's umbrella and the Red Cross, U.S. consular officials, especially in British and British colonial ports, provided considerable assistance to American naval personnel. In Newcastle, the American consul arranged for bluejackets to use the Admiralty's hostels while in port. In Liverpool, at the consul's request, the YMCA agreed to furnish the sailors rooms while their ship was repaired in the yard.[29] Consuls often handled funds cabled by relatives and even loaned money to stranded bluejackets. Railway tickets were frequently given to American servicemen who lacked funds to return to their base or ship. One sailor asked the American consul in Edinburgh to retrieve a cigarette lighter from a local pawnshop, sending money with the request.[30]

The YMCA was by far the most prominent organization in the war zone, the first and the largest, and the only one with the sanction of Congress and General Pershing. At the AEF's request, the Y agreed to operate post exchanges for the Army in France. Admiral Sims never permitted the Y to operate post exchanges at naval facilities under his command, but he allowed it to open centers in Brest and elsewhere in France. On June 15, 1917, the Y's director in Paris cabled New York: "four centres already running for sailors—five centres for soldiers and sailors . . . naval and military authorities cooperate magnificently." Two weeks later, a conference was held at Simsadus to discuss help from the Y for the Navy. Attending were the American naval attachés in London and Paris, Y representatives, and members of Sims's staff. They agreed to expand their facilities at Brest and open a center in London.[31]

From this modest beginning, the number of Y huts and centers operated for the benefit of naval personnel in the war zone grew to seventy-eight. They stretched from Gibraltar and Corfu to Archangel and Murmansk in northern Russia and the Orkney Islands. Approximately 90 percent of welfare services for all American servicemen came under the auspices of the Y. By the end of the war, the Y operated 135 centers for the Navy at 78 facilities and cities.[32] The majority of Sims's base and station commanders requested Y canteens. Rear Admiral Philip Andrews, in command of the naval base at Cardiff, pleaded for the establishment of a Y center, as did Admiral Niblack in Gibraltar.[33] For some reason, probably its isolation, none of the service organizations established welfare centers at Ponta Delgada in the Azores. Yet Ponta Delgada was exactly the kind of place that needed such a facility.[34]

In April 1918, the Y created a separate organization to work with the naval forces. The "secretaries" working with the Navy wore dark blue uniforms similar to those of warrant officers. The familiar red triangle of the Y was placed on the sleeve attached to an anchor. Also, the Y opened a chain of restaurants that served American food at the principal naval bases.[35] Admiral Sims had reservations about the restaurants, but since the Y had Secretary Daniels's support, he felt that he had no choice but to agree.[36]

The force commander also opposed the Y's efforts to place representatives on the battleships operating with the Grand Fleet. Admiral Gleaves, however, was not successful in keeping Y "secretaries" out of the cruiser and transport force. Much to his dismay, he was ordered to permit them to travel on naval vessels in his force, presumably as unofficial members of the crew. The duties of these men were unclear.[37]

Brest was the site of the largest Y complex in the war zone. From the beginning in June 1917 in a small building, the Y located fifty Y facilities of various kinds in the city and outlying areas. In December 1917, Sims wrote to the Y's European director, complaining that their establishments in Brest were "insufficient for the entertainment of the men on shore." The director responded that when the force commander visited Brest they had only five "rather small places, including two restaurants," in place, but they were expanding facilities there. As more and more Americans poured into the port, the Y continued to expand. In the spring, separate huts were established for the Navy, Army and the stevedores, mostly African-Americans.[38] In August 1918, the director of the naval hospital in Brest wrote, "The [Y] . . . is surely a busy one, they are running three restaurants, a hotel, a large Navy hut, I don't know how many Army centres, stevedore centres, moving pictures, canteens, spiritual work, a large money exchange place, and the Lord only knows what else."[39] The Hotel Moderne served officers. The Y also operated the only soda fountain in France, a doughnut factory, a cafeteria, an auditorium, athletic fields, a gym, and warehouses. Later the municipal theater was leased for plays and performances, entertaining up to three thousand soldiers and sailors at a time. The largest hut located in the city's center at the Place de Chateau served the Navy. Here bluejackets on liberty congregated daily to eat, shower, read, write, dance, enjoy entertainment, and get a haircut. "The Y.M.C.A. is more of an institution over here than it is in the average town at home. They furnish a mighty good recreation place and don't insist on coming around when you are trying to read or write and persuade you to lead a better life."[40]

The Y hut in Paris was located in a converted mansion. Few naval personnel were stationed there, and until late in the war few were allowed liberty or leave there. A soldier in Paris observed, "if an American is not at work, not at the theatre, not at a café, and not sightseeing, you may be sure to find him at the 'Y.'"[41]

St. Nazaire and Bordeaux had large Y centers. The canteen at Bordeaux looked like a "grocery store with its broad counter and wares stacked . . . in piles at the back."[42] Ethel Harriman and Helen Astor, both from prominent families, ran the Bordeaux hut. The entertainer Elsie Janis wrote afterward about her visit: "To the men, the names of Astor and Harriman meant nothing, but those two smiling blondes, frying eggs to order, meant a great deal. I heard one doughboy admit that the tall blonde 'egg slinger' at the 'Y' was some skirt!"[43] Most of the naval air stations in France had Y huts, although some of them were not ready for use until shortly before the Armistice. Because the La Croisic station was built on a small island, there was no space for a Y hut. The Y leased a theater building in the nearby village and installed electricity. The stage and seats were removed, and handball and basketball courts were laid out. In the evenings, the floor was rerigged with chairs for concerts and other entertainments.[44] The Navy's Lafayette Radio Station, located in a small village fourteen miles outside Bordeaux had a recreation building used by all of the welfare organizations.[45]

American naval air stations in Great Britain benefited from the presence of the Y, especially in Ireland, most of which were located in remote areas. Some of them were so secluded, according to the Y history, that "there was at first a ride to the end of a little branch railway. Next came a wait for a chance to take a tug or a drifter—a day's journey down some bay or lough. Finally a trip in a jaunting cart completed the last stage."[46] The first Y hut in Ireland opened at the Wexford Naval Air Station in June 1918, and the last at Bantry Bay, temporary home for submarines, battleships, and other U.S. warships. A large hut was erected on an island in the Bay.[47] In England, the largest Y center outside London was located at Killingholme Naval Air Station. A permanent recreation building, belonging to the Royal Air Corps, was turned over to the Y. The Y was also allowed to use several other buildings, including a large hangar, which was converted into a theater and concert hall. When a small temporary auxiliary field was established near Stonehenge, the Y followed with a tent that housed a piano and benches.[48] The naval air force's assembly and repair base at Eastleigh was fortunate in its Y facilities, although not at first. T. Francis Bludworth, in *The Battle of Eastleigh*, wrote: "Y Headquarters . . . originally consisted of a rather fair-sized tent with a hard cinder floor. The interior of the tent contained some pre-historic magazines, a few ancient checker-boards, and an antiquated victrola." Before the war ended, a brick structure was built to house the Y's activities.[49]

Plymouth, the site of both a British naval base and, early in 1918, an American base, was providential in that it was the home of the Astors, Nancy and Waldorf. Both were widely known. Nancy became the first female elected to Parliament. Shortly after Great Britain declared war, the Astors financed the construction of a Y canteen for Royal Navy sailors. When the prominent couple discovered that the United States planned to establish a base at Plymouth, they offered to lease and remodel a building suitable for the Y. The Y agreed, and early in April 1918 the center, known as "Forester's Hall," was opened with the usual amenities. "Motion pictures, boxing contests, and other forms of entertainment kept the men on the station at night." In addition to an auditorium, the building housed a handball court and reading rooms.[50]

American naval bases were not established at either Liverpool or Southampton, but they both had Y centers. They were important debarkation ports for American troops that landed in the United Kingdom. U.S. naval personnel manned many of the troop transports and crowded the cities on liberty. In addition, shipyards in both ports repaired American warships deployed in European waters.[51]

In the fall of 1917, the Department agreed to deploy a battleship division and later minelayers to Scottish waters. The Y was approached about providing welfare "at several points in the North confidential for the present."[52] When the American battleships joined the Grand Fleet, it was concentrated at Scapa Flow in the Orkneys. The Y was unable to establish a hut in the Orkneys because it was a restricted zone. Nothing could be done to help the American bluejackets until the Fleet returned to its home port at Rosyth on the Firth of Forth. Even then, liberty was not allowed for Edinburgh, fourteen miles from the base.[53] Nonetheless, a Y hut was opened in March 1918, on St. Andrews' Square in the heart of Edinburgh. The proprietors gave the Y permission to erect temporary buildings.[54] Shortly after the Armistice, thousands of American sailors from the battleships were given liberty and flocked to Edinburgh and the Y hut.

The North Sea Mine Barrage involved several thousand American bluejackets on a number of ships and four installations, two mine assembly bases, and two small depots on the west coast of Scotland. Prefabricated Y huts were set up at the Kyle of Lochalsh and Fort William, the two mine-shipping facilities. At Invergordon, the Y built a large building, and at Inverness, it leased a building known as the Northern Meeting House. It was converted into a typical hut with canteen, hostel, restaurant, and reading rooms. The Y also sponsored dances, athletic events, and other entertainments. Similar activities took place at Invergordon. Admiral Mayo was not impressed with the Y centers at the two bases, characterized as "a dreary and poor place." The facilities were "far below the average," he wrote the Department.[55] Mayo was equally displeased with the Y center established at the Strathpepper naval hospital. "This was in an old house, out of repair, dreary and cold, and generally makeshift."[56]

The British crown colony at Gibraltar, while not as isolated as Ponta Delgada, Corfu, or the Orkneys, still presented problems for Y officials. Land was unavailable in the crowded fortress, and vacant buildings were virtually nonexistent. But perhaps the greatest handicap was lack of interest on the part of the government officials there. Admiral Niblack wrote, "It is a curious fact that the British people [here] do not take much interest in what we call 'up-lift.'"[57] Because of its remoteness from acceptable leave areas and the absence of restaurants and recreation facilities for enlisted personnel, a Y facility was badly needed at Gibraltar. After the arrival of a new colonial governor who, Niblack wrote, was "very interested in Y.M.C.A. work," one was finally established. The Y located a building, leased it, and converted it into a hut with restaurant, lunch counter, and a clubhouse. "We are now pushing [Y activities] . . . rather hard here. The Y.M.C.A. is giving free exhibitions of movies four nights a week and our band plays in the Alameda Gardens one night, which means Gibraltar is amused five nights in the week by our Y.M.C.A." Niblack wrote after the war that "nothing could [have been] . . . finer than the contribution of the Y.M.C.A. here."[58]

Eagle Hut in downtown London was the most famous Y establishment in Europe during the war. It was a series of wooden buildings joined together and located on the Strand in the "Heart of [picturesque] Dickens Land." The Y and Americans resident in London provided the funds needed to construct the buildings and acquire land for a park. The first huts were finished in September 1917. At the opening ceremony, thirty-six veterans of the American Civil War marched up Fleet Street with a number of soldiers and sailors.[59] By November 1917, it added three dormitories that accommodated three hundred men, a restaurant that served a thousand men at a time, an auditorium, soda fountain, pool hall, laundry, tailor shop, telephone and money exchanges, lounges for reading and writing, and even a dentist. A reporter for the *Pall Mall Gazette* wrote, "I am not sure who was responsible for the original scheme, but the Eagle Hut is certainly the best and most tastefully equipped 'home' a lonely sailor or soldier could chance upon in a week's march." The London *Daily Chronicle* marveled that "the grounds of Eagle Hut of the American Y.M.C.A. are now a veritable oasis in the desert of Aldwych. . . . [A]s if by magic the rough ground which once formed the site of the old Olympic Theatre . . . has been converted into a garden fair with lawns, shrubs, and flowers."[60] At the peak of operation, 150 men and 400 women volunteers staffed the hut on a 24-hour-a-day schedule.

The Eagle Hut was the best known of the Y establishments and the most popular with servicemen. Unlike many other Y centers, the London hut did not encounter criticism. The American consulate in London received dozens of flattering communications from ship captains and other naval officials.[61] This outpouring contrasted with the widespread criticism of the Y during and after the war. A popular opinion was that the "damned Y" harbored draft dodgers and pacifists.[62]

The most damaging charge was the widespread opinion that the Y gouged servicemen. It charged for services at the canteens and restaurants, something that the Salvation Army, the Knights of Columbus, and other welfare organizations did not do. Stories circulated of claims that servicemen were overcharged or at least charged more for an item than at home, or that they were paying for donated items. The Y pointed out that General Pershing authorized it to operate post exchanges similar to those at camps in the States, and also that transportation costs were expensive. The Navy did not authorize the Y to operate the equivalent of post exchanges, although canteens were allowed to sell goods. A transport crew member on liberty in Brest wrote, "I went to the Y.M.C.A. and had a row with the lily-fingered 'canteen lizard' behind the counter over the prices he was charging me for some stuff, said prices being in excess of the ones in the advertisement." The *Stars and Stripes*, reporting on the opening of a new Y hotel in Paris, wrote that he was impressed except for the notices in rooms. "Rooms must be PAID FOR IN ADVANCE AND MEALS WHEN SERVED." "Very few World War veterans I have talked to had much use for the Y.M.C.A. in France," one ex-Navy gob wrote in his memoirs. A sailor from *Reid* mentioned having lunch with a Y worker who expressed disappointment at the "money-making tendency of the YMCA" and spoke of "much actual dishonesty" in the Y canteens.[63] The military tried to reassure its personnel that the welfare agencies were doing a good job. Pershing, who had some concerns about the Y, defended the organization. Naval headquarters in London issued a statement maintaining that complaints against the Y were investigated and found without foundation. "We have discovered no self-seeking, no shirking, and no taint of religiosity."[64]

Despite the criticisms, many of them justified, the Y contributed to the servicemen's welfare. During the war, the Y operated the largest system of hotels and restaurants in the world. According to Johnson Hagood, the prices charged "were just sufficient to cover actual expenses (less rent), and were from one half to one third current French prices." He also wrote that the Y distributed free $2 million worth of athletic goods and provided without cost $200,000 worth of musical instruments, 11,000 costumes, 30,000 copies of sheet music, and much of the entertainment, including some 70,000 movie shows.[65] During the flu outbreak in 1918, many American naval installations stopped all liberty and leave, confining personnel to their bases and stations. Often the Y centers provided the only outlet available to sailors during that period.[66]

The veterans who filled out questionnaires for the Army War College survey of World War I survivors were generally complimentary of the Y and its services, and so were many during the war. One young officer wrote, "I am very strong for the Y.M.C.A. A Secretary took me in tow and gave me ten victrola records and a box of books." He mentioned on another occasion that a Y worker presented him with a box of cigars, saying, "I know you boys don't see American tobacco." From a naval air station, a pilot wrote, "The Y.M.C.A. does splendid work here." A sailor at Killingholme mentioned the "wonderful work being done for us by the Y.M.C.A. It really deserves more praise than . . . it receives." The bluejackets on the station admired the Y secretary because he was willing to get in the ring and box with local pugilists. The athletic officer on *Charles*, disturbed at the criticism, stressed that the Navy "owe[s] the Y.M.C.A. not a little but a lot."[67]

Admiral Sims gradually came to recognize the Y's contributions: "Do not despise the Y.M.C.A. efforts at uplift. While I do not take so very much stock of the moral uplift part of it still the amusements that are afforded by the Y . . . are of great value." Admiral Niblack wrote after the war "that the Y.M.C.A. does not put over the door 'The wages of sin is death,' and expect people to frequent the place. They frankly beat the allurement of evil by counter attractions, and I speak frankly on the question, because there has been some mud-slinging."[68]

The Y also operated clubs for officers, including the Washington Inn located in London on St. James Square. It consisted of a series of eight small concrete-block buildings "radiating from a central court like the spokes of a wheel." The agreement between the Y and city officials was that the trees were not to be disturbed and the property would be restored to its former condition within a year after the war. The club included a library and reading room, recreation room where dances were held, a dining room, and a number of bedrooms.[69] Similar but smaller clubs were located at Edinburgh, Plymouth, Liverpool, Cardiff, and Southampton. The one in Plymouth was named the "Mayflower." Admiral Mayo considered it one of the most attractive and needed of all the Y establishments in the war zone.[70]

The Y leased two hotels for officers in Brest with both dining and sleeping facilities and an officers' club and hotel in Paris. One veteran of service organizations wrote, "The officers it must be said were a very difficult and exacting class to cater to, and it was from them that most of the unfavorable criticism came."[71] Although the gobs depended heavily upon the service organizations for much of their entertainment, this was not altogether true of the officers who sometimes organized clubs of their own. Traditionally, Naval officers were taught that they were an elite group, gentlemen, an "aristocracy." They were predominantly well born, generally from the upper and upper-middle social levels. The reserve officers—naval aviators from Yale, the yachtsmen from the New York Yacht Club, and other similar strongholds of wealth in the Northeast and Northwest largely belonged to this class. They understood that the distinction between officers and "other ranks" was enormous, indeed unfathomable, according to Karsten.[72]

Brest was the site of the first club organized by officers. In September 1917, a building was purchased and converted into a club. A surgeon at the local naval hospital wrote that the club "is going to be the centre of life here" but complained that it had only one bathroom.[73] By mid-1918, more than six hundred officers belonged to the club. Organized like clubs at bases in the States, the commanding officer served as president and officers had to be elected to membership. Because of this, the members considered the club to be "official." When Secretary Daniels got wind of it, he became incensed because the club served alcoholic beverages. The name was then changed to the Officers Mess. Any officer who paid a nominal fee could dine there.[74] When the war ended, the club was presented to the French navy as a permanent officers' establishment for the Allied naval services.[75]

Officers stationed at Queenstown did not found a club until late in the war, but the King's Hotel, which, as one writer noted, "is where every destroyer officer comes at least once between cruises," and the Royal Cork Yacht Club provided the Americans the amenities and service comparable to a regular officers' club. Many of the officers gathered for dinner or drinks at the Yacht Club before they returned to their ships. Admiral Halsey remembered many years later that "we dubbed it the 'Royal Uncork Yacht Club,' and devised a special decoration, the F.I.R. ['fell in river'], for officers who had difficulty retiring to their ships after an evening there."[76] When an officers' club was finally opened at Queenstown under the sponsorship of the Navy, many officers continue to use the Royal Cork Yacht Club as "recreational headquarters, where one could be assured of getting one or two glasses of excellent sherry."[77] King's Hotel was known for its coffee and its temperature. "Horribly cold room. A minuscule fire of coke burning in a tiny grate seems to be making no effort whatsoever to improve conditions." Pringle and Bayly wanted to open an officers' club in Queenstown, but it never occurred because of the Armistice.[78]

Because of the class system, ill-defined but still in place, American officers had opportunities, rarely afforded enlisted men, of visiting and being entertained in private homes and clubs throughout Great Britain. The same privilege existed in France despite a less structured social system than that in Britain.[79] A few officers had their wives with them. The Navy Department early in the war issued an announcement forbidding spouses to follow their husbands to the war zone, but a number evaded this restriction. Some of them went to Europe before the ban; others volunteered for the Red Cross and other welfare organizations. Despite Admiral Sims's disapproval, officers who had wives near their duty station usually leased apartments.[80]

A number of officers leased living quarters. If one had connections, as did a number of American officers, more sumptuous accommodations were often available. Vincent Astor, Junius S. Morgan,[81] and Hugo Koehler all were able to locate houses. Admiral Charles Moore recalled: "Koehler with all his Anheuser Busch money had established himself in Queenstown in supreme style. He had a beautiful estate, about ten acres of land around it, with lovely gardens. He appeared to greet us after we had all arrived in his house. He came down the stairs with sort of a purple dinner jacket coat and trousers, embroidered with little green wreaths, believe me, and black tie, and patent leather boots lined with red velvet. . . . Koehler was also entertained royally when he spent Christmas in London."[82]

Entertainment was available to officers and men not only in establishments provided by welfare organizations and clubs, but by the Navy and its personnel. Only one club was sponsored by the Navy, the one at Queenstown, but official recreational and entertainment activities appeared in all commands. Considerable entertainment was available on the bases and naval air stations and also on ships. The Department decreed that this entertainment was to be "wholesome," which meant that it had to be controlled either through welfare organizations or the unit itself. Not every ship or station had the desire or the talent to put on a theatrical or musical. Most of them held smokers or happy hours, a kind of variety show that included music—bands, orchestras, or individual sailors who played musical instruments. Bluejackets often performed an act such as comedy or impersonation.[83] Boxing was nearly always on the program.

"Thursday evening, August 1st was the best yet in the Happy Hour Club," claimed an article in the *Fixem*, the weekly paper of the Mine Forces at Inverness: "The program consisted of twenty events, including four boxing bouts. Mason, the painter gave a remarkable exhibition of bag punching. LaLonde was there to the minute on the juggling act. . . . Hamilton, Armasby, Rose, and Morrison had the quartette working in fine form but were a little bit stingy in answering the encore. Wigmore was a big hit in the kilty act, if only he had ordinary knees, we would take him for a native of the town. Merritt rendered a very nice number and we have to hand it to the boy, he certainly has the voice. . . . The bouts were all good exhibitions of the manly art."[84]

Minstrels, an American form of entertainment with comedians and musicians in black-face, were quite popular with the sailors. The Northern Bombing Group's "minstrels" performed at U.S. and Allied installations during the war and after the war put on shows in London and New York City.[85] The group's minstrel performers were not the only gobs to go "on the road." Musical ensembles, theatrical groups, and individual entertainers traveled to American and Allied bases, camps, and hospitals throughout Great Britain and France. Groups of bluejackets quite regularly performed in London before both servicemen and civilians. The *Daily Mail* was quite enthusiastic about a "Merry American Farce" at the Savoy Theatre.[86] *Oklahoma* produced a musical entitled the "O-Kay Follies—1918" while anchored in Bantry Bay. A portable stage, including a lighted runway extending into the audience, was built on the battleship's fantail. About thirty members of the crew danced, sang, and acted including, as the *New York Post* said, "the masculine members of the 'all girl' chorus." The show was later carried to New York.[87] *Delaware* put on a theatrical performance in a Boston theater when she returned from Europe. *Nevada*, also a unit of the battleship division in Bantry Bay, created theatrical productions. The "Cheer Up" ship put on minstrels, musicals, and concerts, featuring a jazz band and a barbershop quartet. The two latter groups performed throughout the United Kingdom and received considerable recognition in the London press.[88] The quartet was later discovered to have accepted money for its performances while receiving a travel allowance from the ship and free lodging. Admiral Sims, a former commander of *Nevada*, was quite irritated, considering it morally wrong and embarrassing to the Navy and the country.[89]

London was the high point for many of the Navy's performing groups in Great Britain. At one time, *Nevada*'s crew and a troupe from Base Number 18 (Inverness) were presenting shows at the same time in different London theaters.[90] The Inverness base's variety show included civilians recruited from the town, the only U.S. naval facility in Europe to allow females in its shows. The variety shows so popular with the sailors (and civilians) were modeled after vaudeville, which had emerged in the latter decades of the nineteenth century as the "principal commercial amusement of America's urban democracy."[91]

In the battleship division with the Grand Fleet, the traditional rivalries among the ships spilled over into theatricals and variety shows. The absence of liberty at Scapa Flow and the need to develop as many diversions as possible on board ship energized the efforts to put on these productions. Admiral Rodman strongly encouraged minstrels, vaudeville, and other types of entertainment, allowing officers to journey to Edinburgh and even as far as London to obtain sets and costumes.[92]

Shortly after the squadron joined the Grand Fleet, the American sailors were invited to shows held on several of the British warships. They were impressed with the professionalism of the performers, especially on HMS *Royal*, *Sovereign*, *Valiant*, and *Bellerophon*. *Wyoming*'s minstrel troupe, which had a reputation among the U.S. fleet, was so cowed by the British sailor/entertainers that, according to the ship's cruise book, the battleship's troupe "was thereafter used for impromptu after-dinner performances in the wardroom."[93]

While at Scapa Flow and later at Rosyth, a great deal of visiting and fraternizing occurred among the American and British ships. Movies were shown twice weekly, and their titles were usually flashed by signal flags throughout the fleet. When the American ships started putting on shows, a select number of British sailors and Americans from the various ships joined the ship's crew for the production. On one occasion, a crowd of nearly 1,500 attended a musical on *Texas*. Only three hundred seats were available, but viewers "climbed up on the superstructure, on the guns, or any old place they could freeze on." The writer added, "One little ensign was the hit of the bill as a 'Hula-Hula dancer.'" The Admiralty deployed a floating theater, *Gourko*, with the fleet. It had a stage and auditorium used to present plays, musicals and other forms of entertainment. Ships, including American vessels, reserved the vessel for a particular night or period, and she moored alongside the warship during that period.[94]

Wyoming engaged in entertainment other than in wardrooms. A competitive vaudeville show was organized among the American ships. Both *Wyoming* and *Florida* put on skits. *Florida*'s presented a song and dance revue called "The Scapa Flow Blues," while *Wyoming* offered a burlesque entitled "Somewhere on Sand Street." *New York* contributed its jazz band, which included thirty ukuleles, for the occasion. *Delaware*'s offering included two skits, "School Days," and "Feddah Johnson's Reunion," the latter a minstrel. More productions followed, each ship trying to outdo the other. The most talked-about show was a vaudeville presented on *Delaware* shortly before *Texas* relieved it, a take-off on *Chu Chin Chow*, a well-known London musical. *Delaware*'s presentation proved extremely popular with the American and British sailors, primarily because it was full of "gobs" acting as members of the opposite sex. The female impersonators were so effective that "many of the Limey sailors believed we had somehow contrived to corral a troupe of fair lasses to play the female roles."[95] After relieving *Delaware*, *Texas* joined in the competition and put on a show entitled "An Evening in Yankeeland." "I went to the *Texas* last night to their show," a young officer wrote his parents. "[It was] without a doubt the most beautiful and wonderful production I have seen done by amateurs."[96] *Wyoming*, however, topped the prize with her show entitled "HOP," a musical built around an imaginary liberty of two gobs in New York City. Admiral Harry Hill, an engineering officer on *Wyoming*, recalled that he participated in the show, playing a ukulele and singing "with a whiskey tenor" in "a little Hawaiian skirt." Although minstrels and variety shows were put on by U.S. naval personnel throughout the European force, none were as spectacular as those given in the Grand Fleet.[97]

Military bands were popular during World War I. In the nineteenth century, most military units had bands. Toward the end of the century, their function began to change from a purely military role to one of performing at concerts, dances, and other informal activities. Their programs and types of music changed to include light classical, popular dance, and music in vogue at the time. In World War I, jazz and ragtime had been added to their repertoire.[98] They also performed Hawaiian music. The martial music of John Philip Sousa remained popular, particularly his marches, many of which were dances.

Nearly every U.S. naval base and air station in Europe during the war organized a band or orchestra. Musical organizations ranged from three or four musicians to a full-size band of forty to fifty performers. The naval air station at Pauillac had a thirty-three-piece band, which the director hoped to increase to fifty. Most of the groups included vocalists and even quartets. The naval base at Brest had a large band named "USS *Carola* band" because it was housed at the receiving barracks of that name. L'Aber Vrach Naval Air Station did not have enough musicians to organize a band, but the small naval air station in Porto Corsini, Italy, had a ten-piece combo. All the battleships had bands, some more than one.[99] Not all ships, however, had organized music, particularly the destroyers and small craft. A band was formed at Queenstown with musicians drawn from all the ships based there. The organizational size and type often depended upon the number and variety of musical instruments available and personnel with musical talent. The Lough Foyle Naval Air Station had seventy-five musical instruments, far more than were put to use because of insufficient musical talent. Brest had a large band. Most of the musicians were amateurs, but professionals, either veteran members of Navy bands or musicians in civilian life, also took part. One ship, *San Francisco*, boasted that its entire aggregation was professional, the members having played at various theaters in and around New York. They enlisted when the ship was in dry dock in Brooklyn. Probably many of them resembled *Von Steuben's* Band, which had two alto horns, three cornets, a baritone horn, a trombone, two clarinets, and two basses. The leader, a chief yeoman, played the violin.[100]

The most popular musical organizations were the small jazz ensembles or orchestras. *Algonquin's* Jazz Band consisted of five pieces—violin, two banjo-mandolins, banjo, and piano, "when accessible." The total lack of sheet music was not of vital importance because all of the orchestra played by ear. "Many a time of an evening during a cold, uncomfortable trip, they would get together in the gang-way by the galley—the only place in those days with any suggestion of warmth. There was nothing that cheered us up and warded off the impeding glooms as did a little music and a song. . . . This little coterie compiled a fine record, playing many times at the YMCA rooms and hospitals both at Plymouth and Gibraltar, in the Coliseum at Lisbon . . . and at many affairs given—not only by the Americans, but by the British as well."[101]

Melville had a string band as did the battleship *New York* and the Pauillac Naval Air

Station. The two latter groups often played with nothing but ukuleles. The naval air station called its orchestra Hawaiian, while the battleship's was a jazz band that played music such as "The Dark Town Strutters' Ball" and "The Missouri Waltz." Its initial performance before British sailors was supposed to have been the first time that jazz had been played in the Grand Fleet.[102] The yacht *Emerline* had a seaman considered so talented by his fellow gobs that they purchased a piano and bolted it to the bulkhead in a large compartment below the main deck. Many of the naval vessels and shore installations had accomplished pianists. The most popular piano players in Brest, however, were not sailors but African-American stevedores. They performed frequently in the city and at nearby military facilities.[103]

At a number of the American bases, the different ships rotated performances in the entertainment centers and clubs. The entertainment depended upon the ship's talent. The battleships with the Grand Fleet and in Bantry Bay had no difficulty in providing a full night of music, vaudeville, and sports such as boxing and wrestling. Nearly every ship could put on a skit or theatrical. Individual acts such as comedians, vocalists, and mimics were interspersed in the performances. Nightly entertainment at the different naval bases and stations included more than music. Among the performers were magicians, contortionists, comedians, ventriloquists. The sailors wrote most of the skits and many of the plays, and burlesque and vaudeville acts. Lough Foyle Naval Air Station put on *Shove Off*, followed by *Aces Up*. Pauillac Naval Air Station presented *Cohen's Barber Shop*. Quite often ship or station personnel appeared with professional entertainers. The Coast Guard cutter *Seneca's* crew included an ex-cowboy who was a lariat artist.[104] Frequently the performances were inter-Allied as well as American. In Queenstown and Brest, soldiers and sailors from various nations participated in the entertainment. A seaman from *Reid* mentioned a performance at the end of which a Frenchman sang the "Marseilles," an Englishman sang "God Save the King," and an American sang the "Star Spangled Banner." When it was over, the audiences assembled outside the theater in ranks by nation. The Americans marched back to their ships "singing the hit of the evening."[105]

The ship bands and orchestras traveled around, performing at different military and naval installations, and also gave concerts in different towns and cities. When the battleship *Florida* went into the yard at Newcastle-on-Tyne for repairs, the ship's band led a detachment of sailors through the streets while the band played "Dixie" and other tunes.[106] The *Carola* band played three nights a week in Brest's main public square and in hospitals.[107] Captain Belknap wrote after the war, "The bands from our two [mine-laying] bases and from the *San Francisco* were in constant demand through all the neighboring country."[108] The naval band at Gibraltar played several nights a week at a park in the fortress before an appreciative audience of British sailors.[109]

Although the majority of the naval personnel performed during off-duty hours and did their normal ship work, some became full-time entertainers. One of them described the benefits of being in a jazz group: "What a War!! We worked, as a jazz band, at either the officers club in Brest or the Club in Tre-zir, and only on weekends or special occasions. The jazz group did not perform with the big band on parades or inspections, so the jazz band life was the greatest!"[110]

Bands from the AEF, British and French services, and even from the United States made concert tours that included American naval installations. The Boston Navy Yard "Star" Jazz Band gave a series of performances in the war zone. The band of the "Fighting Sixty-ninth" Infantry Regiment was one of the most popular. "I don't know when I've enjoyed anything as much for the band was very good indeed," wrote a gob based in Brest. "[T]here were two gray-haired French officers sitting just in front of us, and the Hawaiian stuff had them bouncing around on their seats like the chairs were hot. The band played what we asked for, mostly, so we heard Dixie and The Gang's All Here."[111]

Lectures were given once or twice a week, usually by a Y speaker or at times prominent individuals such as Admiral Mayo and Assistant Secretary of the Navy Roosevelt. They were pep talks. At Wexford, lectures included "The Ship That Cans the Submarine" and "American Relations to the World Crisis." The lectures at the naval air stations in France were similar: among them were "Modern Wars," "True Democracy," and "Do You Want to Kill the Kaiser?" Irving Cobb, humorist turned correspondent, was the most popular speaker.[112] In Great Britain, the minister of information furnished lecturers for various American facilities. John Masefield and Edmund Russell, among others, spoke on subjects from the history of the war to *Macbeth*.[113]

There was no USO in World War I, but efforts were made to mobilize professional entertainers and send them on tour in the war zone. The "Over There" Theater League under George M. Cohan and the "Redpath Lyceum Bureau" sent hundreds of actors and musicians to Europe.[114] Elsie Janis was the first and by far the most popular American entertainer. She made her first appearance before British and French troops months before the United States entered the war. Afterward, chaperoned by her mother and accompanied by a pianist, she spent as much time as she could in Europe. Constantly traveling to camps, bases, hospitals, and other military facilities, she resembled Bob Hope of a later era in her devotion to the entertainment of doughboys and bluejackets. An attractive, dark-haired, "breezy all-American girl," she sang, danced, did imitations, cartwheeled across a stage, and constantly joked with her enthusiastic audiences. Those who witnessed her performances never forgot her.[115] Janis also used her popularity to organize performing troupes among the military personnel. In Brest, she held auditions for a group called "The USS *Carola* Boys." Under her direction, they put on a minstrel show and were later invited to appear in Paris.[116]

Other entertainers followed Janis to Europe. The Liberty Quartet was one of the first. Their program ran from operatic arias to hymns, spirituals, and popular songs. They gave the first concert on *Prometheus* and other ships at Brest.[117] The Craig Company from Boston was one among other well-known performing groups that entertained the sailors. They presented several plays and readings from Shakespeare, and a musical comedy, *The Circus Girl*.[118]

Irene Franklin and her husband, Burt Green, with two other performers called themselves the "Broadway Bunch." Along with the "Electric Sparks," they performed in France and Great Britain, giving performances at the Eagle Hut in London on Armistice Day. The "Jesters," another theatrical troupe, spent several days on the

American battleships anchored in Bantry Bay, Ireland.[119] Often these small groups enlisted the help of the unit's musical talent to perform before the show and during intermissions.

Movies were just as popular with the World War I bluejackets as they were in World War II. Commanding officers and entertainment committees acquired as many movies as they could locate. All of the welfare organizations provided films, as did the U.S. and British governments. The movie business was lucrative for distributors who sold them to the organizations. The Committee on Public Information previewed and approved them. This committee also distributed documentaries and other "educational" films. They were designed to "inform" the military what the war was about, why they were "over there," and what the home folk were doing to back them up.[120] Films distributed to American naval facilities and ships in Great Britain also had to get the approval of the Admiralty's Censorship Office. The sailors enjoyed all the films, including the documentaries, but preferred movies with actors and actresses such as Mary Pickford, Charlie Chaplin, Mack Sennett, Pearl White, Mabel Norman, and Douglas Fairbanks. In Queenstown, "When a Fairbanks or a Pickford picture is shown—well the theatre, which seats at least 800, is packed with officers and men." Movies, like other forms of entertainment, provided ship personnel an outlet from the strain of operations at sea.[121]

Dancing became a popular form of entertainment. The waltz and quadrille had given way to the two-step, the foxtrot, ragtime, and "cheek to cheek." U.S. servicemen imported some of them. One was called the "Paul Jones," carried to Plymouth by the subchaser officers. The *Pauillac Pilot*, the newspaper of the U.S. naval air station, mentioned that station personnel introduced a dance called the "Doughnut Dance."[122] A frequent complaint in the writings of American sailors in France and Great Britain was that the local ladies could not dance. Ensign Corrigan in Invergordon wrote, "As far as looks and dancing went the girls were mostly good plumbers." In another letter, he said, "As far as dancing, they seem to think Fox Trot and One Steps are just one mad gallop and must be danced to the only American rag they know, 'Over There.'" An officer who attended a dance at Admiral Beatty's residence outside Rosyth commented afterward that "there wasn't a soul there who could dance—not the American way at least." Airman Kenneth MacLeish agreed: the "girls don't dance to music . . . they dance according to instructions, three steps, then a hop."[123]

Ships, stations and bases, welfare organizations, officers clubs, local communities, and Allied units and installations all sponsored dances. Ships usually leased a dance hall or other suitable building and appealed to the local Red Cross, Y, and other organizations for females. *Nashville*, while at Gibraltar, gave a dance. Each sailor had to pay $3.00 to attend. Most of the cruise books of the ships deployed in European waters mention dances.[124] Dances sponsored by the Y and other welfare organizations were usually open to all ranks and were often difficult to carry off successfully. Lady Nancy Astor described one that she went to near Bordeaux: "there were as many as a thousand sailors to about eight or ten girls. . . . There were so few of us that we had to have whistles, which we blew when the men might cut in. . . . When we went home we went with weary feet, feet positively black and blue." On at least one occasion when only a few females were present to accommodate the sailors, the "gob, not to be denied," paired off on the floor.[125]

World War I acted as a primer for the sporting boom that blanketed the United States in the decades after the war.[126] Yet in the beginning organized sports were a novelty to most of the new men entering the military services. Until the twentieth century, the Navy, as with the military as a whole, generally ignored sports. Boat races or regattas and occasionally boxing were the only organized sports approved and followed; even then, it was not a uniform policy throughout the service. Yet, the Navy in many ways mirrors and responds to national social forces. The late nineteenth century saw the emergence of organized sports in the United States to the point of becoming a national obsession. The phenomenal growth of sports finally persuaded the Navy to give heed to their potential benefits. By the time the United States entered the war, athletic competition was widespread in the Navy.

The Commission on Training Camp Activities created a division of physical training and athletics. Walter Camp, the well-known football coach, was appointed general commissioner of athletics for the Navy and provided liaison between the service and the commission. Initially, he concentrated his work on the training camps, but athletics followed the deployment of land and sea forces in the war zone.

The commission depended heavily upon the Y, the Knights of Columbus, and the other private organizations to shoulder the sports program overseas. The Y assumed most of the responsibility, especially in the AEF, but the Navy also benefited from assistance. Although most of the ships had athletic equipment, none was available at hospitals, bases, air stations, and other shore-based facilities. The Y also leased land for baseball diamonds, football and soccer fields, and even a few buildings for basketball and handball courts.[127] It sponsored professional athletics and sports directors who worked directly with the different installations. In Brest, for example, ten physical education directors from the Y supervised thirty-four athletic fields, nine tennis courts, and a basketball arena.[128] The Y frequently sponsored athletic events from baseball leagues to boxing matches to track meets.[129]

Athletic activity varied from place to place. Some ships and stations emphasized organized sports; others attempted to involve as many members of the crew as possible in physical activities. The *Harrisburg* history said, "We have recognized the ideal of true athletics, namely to get as many men playing as possible."[130] The forces afloat had fewer opportunities than those on shore. Ships stationed at the operating bases generally were unable to participate in organized league competition or send their athletes to sports events beyond their base. They often played "sandlot" baseball or "pickup" with other nearby vessels or within the ship's company. The medical officer at Plymouth reported after the war: "The Base and Submarine chaser divisions had representative baseball and basketball teams. These competed among themselves and the leaders challenged any U.S. Navy vessel that came into the port. The Base built up a football team but it lacked opponents when it was fully developed."[131] A destroyer officer at Queenstown wrote: "Today I couldn't help but think that it would be no particular hardship if we were deprived of shore liberty here altogether. We are permitted to go to the athletic field . . . with or without liberty."[132] Recreational activities became available to ship personnel when in a yard for repairs or refit. The Coast Guard cutter *Algonquin*, in a Lisbon repair facility, held a field and track meet with USS *Montauk's* crew. A boxing exhibition pitted the ships' pugilists against Portuguese and Spanish boxers.[133]

The battleships operating with the Grand Fleet had few opportunities to engage in sports. The cold and windswept barrier islands around the anchorage at Scapa Flow were not conducive to shore-based athletic activities.[134] After the fleet moved to Rosyth, boxing exhibitions on the ships, track meets, football matches, and baseball games were organized at fields on the shore. The different American battleships played baseball among themselves and with Canadian army teams stationed in Scotland.[135] The American battleship division presented a loving cup to the winner of the British sailing regatta, a competitive event held among the various ships of the Grand Fleet.[136]

The mine-laying squadron and bases at Inverness and Invergordon carried out an ambitious athletic program, encompassing nearly all of the popular sports. A squadron athletic officer was appointed to coordinate all sport activities. Boat races were held, but baseball was the most popular. Twelve teams were organized in the summer of 1918 and played 170 league games. They did not have baseball uniforms; dungarees became acceptable attire.[137]

The small ships—subchasers, converted yachts, gunboats, and even some of the old 700-ton destroyers—were often without proper athletic equipment and uniforms. They depended upon tenders and shore facilities. The ships involved in convoy work, especially those on the Atlantic routes, were well equipped with athletic gear but found little time to use it.[138] The turnaround in European ports was quick, rarely more than forty-eight hours, just time enough to refuel before heading back to the United States. As one NOTS history pointed out, "The Navy fosters athletics but the Sea does not."[139] Often sailors engaged in individual activities such as swimming, biking, fishing, boating, hunting, and especially walking.[140]

The tenders were probably best equipped of all of the ships to carry out organized athletic activities. They supported other vessels, including the distribution of athletic gear. They also frequently had the strongest athletic teams.[141] Although many of the ships had difficulty in taking part in organized sports, their crews were encouraged whenever possible to undertake some form of physical activity. Statistics of participation for the naval forces in the war zone are not available, but participation was extraordinarily widespread.[142]

Naval personnel based on shore had more opportunities to engage in physical activities. Naval installations were generally well equipped with athletic gear and facilities. Athletic directors created impressive sport complexes in the war zone. At Queenstown, for example, the Navy, using canteen funds, converted property at Ringaskiddy donated by the Admiralty into two baseball diamonds, two concrete tennis courts, and a track.[143] Teams traveled to distant camps and bases in Ireland and even England to compete with Navy, Army, and Allied athletes. Destroyer personnel were unable to compete; the players and athletes came from the tenders and the various units in the

Queenstown area.[144] Although the naval hospitals participated in organized sports, they had difficulty competing with the larger bases. The final report of the Strathpepper naval hospital admitted that tennis, lawn bowls, and croquet were more successful than the more popular team sports.[145] The isolated bases at Gibraltar, Corfu, and Ponta Delgada scheduled sporting events, but of course, they were confined to base and local ship personnel.[146]

Hiking (walking) and swimming were popular with all hands, but the water sport was limited to a few beaches in Brittany, Gibraltar, and Ponta Delgada. Officers and men stationed at the naval air facility at Porto Corsini swam in Lake Bolsena during the summer months. British waters were considered too cold. Tennis courts were usually available, and many naval personnel, including Admiral Sims, played regularly. Not many Americans played soccer at the time, but soccer fields abounded in the British Isles. American sailors were encouraged to learn the game, and some did so. Admiral Moore recalled how he occasionally took a group of men from his destroyer ashore at Queenstown and played soccer. "We didn't know anything about soccer. We didn't know the difference between rugby and soccer, but we had a big round ball, and we divided up sides, and we might have 15 people on a side, and we'd kick this ball around and run until we were exhausted. . . . But we did that to give the men something to do, and they just loved it."[147]

Golf was not one of the more popular sports in the United States until World War I. By 1917, however, an estimated 1 million Americans had taken up the game.[148] It quickly caught on with U.S. servicemen stationed in Great Britain. British naval officers were fond of the sport. From Scapa Flow to Queenstown, courses were available. "In the British Isles any old field becomes a golf course," one American officer observed.[149] With rare exceptions, however, these courses were not public, but private clubs. In typical British social practice, the clubs were opened to U.S. naval officers but not to enlisted personnel. The destroyer officers, when the first of them arrived in May 1917, were invited to the local club. Many went there at every opportunity. As the Americans arrived in other parts of Britain, they often took up the game. The minelaying squadron in Scotland held a golf tournament. The *Army and Navy Register* even noticed the growing popularity of the sport with American servicemen. "The American officers are becoming top notch golfers. Only a handful of them played the game 'back in the states,' but now every destroyer numbers three or four devotees of the sport."[150]

Track was popular with both officers and men; most stations had dirt or cinder tracks. Ship personnel were rarely involved in organized meets, although they participated in track, especially on holidays. Track was also a well-known sport in Europe, and Americans often competed with Allied personnel. The Killingholme Naval Air Station sponsored an "Anglo-American Sports Meet." Twenty events were scheduled with monetary prizes for each event.[151]

American sailors introduced the type of football played in the United States. Most of the stations and a few of the larger ships had veteran football players in their crews. Killingholme, for example, had a group that included college players from Cornell, Princeton, University of Missouri, Yale, and other institutions of higher learning. The team also included a few professional and semiprofessional players. In the fall of 1918, Killingholme played five games, nearly all with U.S. Army teams.[152] One hundred fifty-six ships and stations had teams. At the Felixstowe Royal Air Force Station, where American aviators and other personnel trained, a football game was held between the officers and men. According to one account, it was something of a grudge match and led to a number of minor injuries.[153] The game was popular with local inhabitants who joined the bluejackets in the stadium and around the field. At a game held in Brest between Army and Navy teams, Bretons in picturesque costumes and even some Chinese came to watch. "Of course the French didn't understand the game, but they enjoyed the tackling very much . . . and when a man would get his wind knocked out they would say, 'C'est bon. C'est bon. Il est Tres Malade.'"[154] American football was so popular with the people in Cardiff, Wales, that the players were entertained royally after each game. The Mine Force team in Scotland had the same experience.[155]

The U.S. battleships, while anchored at Rosyth, played each other regularly despite the unsuitable weather. "I went ashore this afternoon to see our football team play the *Wyoming*," an officer on *New York* wrote. "It was the usual muddy, cold rainy day and wasn't much of a game." *Arkansas's* paper, describing a game with another ship's team, mentioned the "sea of mud. . . . On account of the high wind and bad weather conditions no attempt was made to kick goals."[156]

In Scotland, American football attracted local citizens and curious British sailors. On one occasion, the weather and the field's poor condition limited scoring, which did not impress the "limeys." A few disparaging remarks that compared American football to soccer unfavorably led to several brawls and limited the number of spectators at the games.[157]

On the whole, however, the British tried to understand the game, although at times they found it difficult. The London *Daily Mail* attempted to describe it:

> In some respects (not many) American Rugby is like our own game, but is Ever so much more strenuous. . . . To those who saw it for the first time the American game was bewildering. . . . As illustrated in this game, it is the Very last word in tackling. Such tackling! In our English "Rugger" you can See two, perhaps three men in the grips at the same time, and "killing" the soil In an affectionate way; but these lusty boys from America do it by bunches. . . . It was part of the game for a man to prevent an opponent from getting at the Fellow with the ball, and if the side with the ball failed to advance more than Ten yards in 4 or fewer tries, called "downs,"—well the ball was surrendered To their opponents. . . . The players in the "scrum" [note a scrum is similar to A huddle in American football] adopt a more fan-shape formation than is the Case in our Rugby.

The author of this article noted with some amazement "sailors shrieked and danced with joy" after a particular play, and added, "Towards the end it is permissible for the players to go through all sorts of weird contortions" as the band played jazz music.[158]

In the U.S. Navy, boxing more than likely was second to boat racing as an organized sport. By World War I, it had become the most popular sport primarily because unlike baseball and other team sports it could be held on board ships. "Smokers," which had become an accepted term for an entertainment in a smoke-filled room, was adopted unofficially in the Navy for organized shipboard entertainment. Boxing bouts were usually the feature attractions.

In World War I, boxing became the most popular recreational activity with the bluejackets and the troops in the AEF. Ships and stations regularly held smokers, bouts, and matches among each other, with Army units and camps, and with Allied boxing teams.[159] Prize fighting was so popular with the sailors that many of the naval units contained experienced pugilists; some had bona fide professionals, in the service for the duration. Champions were usually recognized throughout the fleet.[160]

In the war zone, American naval boxing exhibitions open to the public attracted crowds of civilians, especially in Great Britain, France, and even Portugal. The crews of U.S. naval vessels being repaired in Lisbon held several matches, including one as a benefit for wounded Portuguese soldiers. A large coliseum where bullfights were usually held was filled to capacity with Portuguese soldiers and civilians as well as American sailors to witness the bouts.[161]

The British were most enthusiastic about boxing. "It is difficult for an American to understand the importance that the British attached to sport-boxing and prize fighting," Admiral Sims told his wife.[162] Boxing was just as popular with the British military services as with the Americans. Interservice matches were held whenever the two navies were present. Shortly after the American battleships joined the Grand Fleet, they issued a challenge to wrestle or box any British ship in the fleet. According to one British account, in the first match the British emerged victorious in every bout. At a smoker held by the British in Inverness and Invergordon, the American boxers won only one fight, the heavyweight bout. Some disagreement arose over the results, according to one American witness, which led to brawls that had to be put down by a Highland regiment.

In 1917, baseball was the leading spectator sport in the United States. During World War I, the national pastime became the military services' pastime. The Army and Navy made baseball their leading sport both at home and abroad. One authority wrote, "The Armed Forces Draft[ed] Baseball."[163] The Commission on Training Activities embraced the slogan "Every American soldier a Baseball player," which applied to the sailors as well.[164] Thousands of spectators viewed baseball games throughout the war zone.

Many of the ships deployed in European waters had bats, balls, and gloves, but some did not, and none of the newly established shore air stations and bases had athletic equipment of any kind. Newspapers in the United States publicized this need. Clark Griffith, the baseball commissioner, created a "Bat & Ball" fund. Youngsters turned in hundreds of old bats and balls, eager to help the cause. The major leagues also donated baseball equipment, including uniforms. The *Stars and Stripes*, the official newspaper of the U.S. military forces in Europe, reported early in 1918 that the YMCA had purchased $300,000 worth of athletic equipment for the services. The *New York Herald* said that more than 144,000 bats were shipped to France. The American Red Cross even secured uniforms and distributed them to various units and ships. A bluejacket on one of the converted yachts at Brest wrote: "Today we received a big wooden box containing—oh, joy!—not only balls, bats, and gloves, but uniforms bearing the name of our ship. Now whenever and wherever we can get ashore . . . the French are going to see baseball."[165] There was never enough to go around. A large shipment of athletic gear was lost when a U-boat torpedoed the transport that carried it. The Y and Knights of Columbus tried to arrange for the manufacture of equipment in France, but the finished products were far from satisfactory.[166]

Navy baseball made its initial appearance in European waters with the first American destroyers at Queenstown. The games played by American servicemen were the first that most Britons had ever seen. Commander Taussig wrote: "the baseball teams of *Melville* and *Trippe* were playing a game at the Mardyke Cricket Grounds for the Red Cross fund. So we took a jaunting cart to that place and arrived during the fifth inning. I think there must have been at least 3,000 people to see the game—which I believe was the first one played in Cork. It was a gay scene—so gay in fact that it was hard to realize that a war was going on anywhere. It seemed like a dream that only a few days ago I was out at sea with my ship shooting at a hostile submarine."[167] In June 1918, the Killingholme team played an Army aviation unit, which, according to a history of the air station, was the first American baseball game ever played in Hull. They also played the first game in Grimsby to help raise funds for a benefit for prisoners of war.[168] The battleships with the Grand Fleet may well have introduced the sport in Scotland. The American consul in Dunfermline believed so: "And to think it should all happen in the Kingdom of Fife where baseball has been an unknown quantity for 1000 years," he wrote.[169] Although the sport never replaced cricket in popularity with the British, at least one famous regiment, the Life Guards, caught "baseball fever." Three teams were formed with equipment borrowed from American units.[170]

Britons initially attended baseball games out of curiosity. Many, probably most, found the game an interesting but bewildering sport. British journalists often compared baseball to cricket or to "rounders," an old Scottish sport. One writer observed: "Baseball, in Englishmen's eyes, is noisy, nerve-wracking and upsetting. In the fact that cricket is *deliberate* and baseball *spontaneous*, we get, in my opinion, very close to the main difference in the English and American make-up." He admitted that "I never met a Yankee who could keep awake during a whole cricket game which isn't so surprising, seeing that a *real* cricket match can last three whole days." Finally, he stated: "cricket means much more to us than just two or three hours' sport in the open air. It is our way of building and training character."[171]

British writers also attempted to describe baseball and its equipment: "The batman's club . . . resembles somewhat an Indian club," or a policeman's truncheon. Another writer compared the baseball to a cricket ball but heavier. The *Daily Mail* carried a series of articles on the sport. One article entitled "Baseball Made Simple" included a typical ball field showing the diamond, bases, and the positions of the players. The article went into detail about innings, pitchers, strikes, outs, runs, etc. A second installment asked in boldface "when you see your first Baseball game, what should you watch. The ball, keep your eye on the ball. . . . When the game starts watch the pitcher.

He will not bowl the ball. He will throw it—throw it hard to [the plate]. . . . Watch the runners. When a run scores you will shout in loud applause. . . .[at least] some people do. Most Americans do." Another journalist pointed out that the pitcher was like a bowler, a catcher like a wicket keeper, and the striker like a batsman. He added in some admiration, "our cricket players must blush and tremble to watch." Britons who attended a baseball game for the first time were surprised at the noise of American servicemen shouting, screaming, whistling, singing, and cheering.[172]

Baseball was played by American sailors throughout the war zone. In Britain, cricket fields were occasionally used. Any level field could be adapted and a diamond laid out. At the naval station in Dunkirk, the beach was used for a field. The initial games were usually informal "sand lot" affairs. In time, however, teams were organized and leagues set up. By the Armistice, a majority of the ships and stations were involved in some kind of league.[173]

The American bluejackets with the Grand Fleet and the minelayers based in Scotland were rarely able to play a team with other than one of their own ships, although they occasionally played a team from a Canadian army unit stationed in the area. The minelayers had a twelve-team league, one for each of the ships. The original schedule called for 396 games during the season, but "Scottish mist" along with operations at sea reduced the season to fewer than two hundred games. Like elsewhere in the British Isles, the games attracted considerable attention from the local citizens.[174] The battleships were unable to play baseball until they left Scapa Flow for Rosyth. There, each ship recruited a team and began practicing every afternoon "whenever the weather was favorable." Trying out for the teams was popular with the ships' crews because, as one sailor recalled, it was one way they could get off the ship every day. *Texas* was the champion of the battleship squadron, and the crew considered their team invincible until the London naval headquarters team showed up loaded with big leaguers. The battleship's defeat was so humiliating that, as a bluejacket wrote later, "Baseball talk was strictly taboo thereafter." He added, "Our players looked a damned sight better on the long end of a swab than they did whiffing the air with a baseball bat."[175]

Leagues were organized throughout the war zone. In the London area, an Anglo-American League was established with four teams—Army, Navy, Army Air Corps, and a Canadian team. Industries such as DuPont financed it in part, supported by the Y and other welfare organizations. The league charged admission; a percentage of the gate went to war charities. Admiral Sims was not enthusiastic about the league at first, primarily because the Navy would not be able to field a competitive team. However, the force commander was a devoted baseball fan so the Navy joined the league. When Sims discovered that the Army teams had recruited players from various camps in England, he sent Admiral Rodman at Rosyth and Captain Pringle in Queenstown a list of bluejackets with baseball experience that included several major leaguers. At his request, a number of them were transferred to London. Pringle wrote, "I regard it as the sacred duty and in-alienable right of the Navy to defeat the Army whenever possible, and at any expense."[176]

The first big public game was played on May 21, 1918, on the field of the Chelsea Football Club before Sims assembled a competitive team. According to a note to Sims, much to his surprise, from nine to ten thousand spectators, mostly British subjects, viewed the game. The Navy lost their first game to the Army team, 7–6, but won the second one on Decoration Day. The city's newspapers carried announcements of the games, giving names of the teams and when and where they were scheduled to play. From then until after the Armistice, the teams played each other regularly, including exhibition games, throughout the British Isles.[177]

Admiral Sims was not the only one who searched for baseball players. Ship and station commanding officers also did so. As in the Army, professional and experienced players were scattered throughout the force. "Every battleship has a baseball team on which there are professional players and often as not there are big leaguers on the nine," wrote one journalist. USS *Carola* claimed that their team was the strongest in the Brest League because it was composed of "sea-going men, even if they were professional ball players before the war." Four former professionals anchored the Pauillac Naval Air Station's team. It did very well until it played an Army team whose pitcher was Grover Cleveland Alexander. "The reason we lost," a naval aviator wrote, "is that the team as a whole didn't stop one single ball that was knocked to them except one. The poor kids were so excited they didn't know they were anywhere near a baseball."[178]

Independence Day provided the occasion for the biggest game of the year. Nearly every station and ship in the American naval force in European waters played baseball on July 4, 1918. In Cardiff, Wales, five thousand spectators viewed a game between teams from two American ships. In Ponta Delgada, the game failed to attract local citizens because it was played at "siesta time." Games were played as far north as Murmansk and as far east as Corfu on that special day.[179] By far the most publicized baseball game played in European waters took place in London on July 4, 1918. The local press and newspapers throughout the British Isles and even in the United States carried announcements and stories of the event for days before it took place. Nearly three weeks before the game, Admiral Sims wrote his wife: "There's already much interest in the Army/Navy baseball game to be played on the 4th in the presence of the King. A great demand for seats. . . . The King is to invite 60 guests, and general [John] Biddle and I each invite 15 and everybody else will pay for their seats." Although President Wilson thought that it was a "mistake" to make the occasion an "official one," he agreed to send a note through Ambassador Page, thanking the king for "patroniz[ing] the American game."[180] On the given day, a crowd estimated at forty to sixty thousand filled every seat in the bleachers and stood around the field. The crowd included the king, queen, other members of the royal family, members of Parliament, British dignitaries including Sir Winston Churchill (who sported a large top hat and smoked "a six foot cigar"), a large number of American civilians resident in London, wounded Tommies, and a large number of American sailors and soldiers. Newspapers mentioned that the king planned to toss out the first ball and had asked an American to teach him how to do so. However, escorted by Sims, Biddle, and other officers, he handed the ball to the umpire.[181] When it was all over, the Navy won and the king missed tea. The *Stars and Stripes* reported that the Army team was consoled because it was not a league game and therefore did not count in the standings.[182]

Baseball was equally popular with the American servicemen and civilians in France. At Tarbes, a small town in the Toulouse area, the games played by AEF teams frequently attracted thousands of people. The French army decided to make baseball a part of their physical training and asked the Americans to help them obtain equipment.[183] Until diamonds were laid out, American sailors played pick-up baseball in the streets and public squares of Brest and were watched with a great deal of interest by the local inhabitants. The police finally decided that it was against the law and put a stop to the games.[184] At Dunkirk, the bluejackets played on the beach. According to one aviator, "The whole town turns out to watch it."[185]

Eventually, diamonds were laid out at every U.S. naval base and air station in France. Ships fielded teams but rarely participated in a league. Nonetheless, leagues were as popular as they were in Great Britain. Three interservice leagues were organized in France. In April 1918, the Paris League was formed with twenty-three teams, including Canadian teams and teams representing the American Ambulance Corps, the AEF, and the Navy. The Navy team was recruited from personnel assigned to naval aviation headquarters and other offices in the French capital. The games were played at Colombes, a Paris suburb where ten games could be played simultaneously.[186]

The Navy's shore bases and stations in France participated en masse in organized sports. Some of the aviation units were late in developing athletic facilities and organizing teams because their personnel were preparing their stations for operations. In contrast to the ships, the majority of which spent much of their time at sea, the shore installations were able to place more emphasis on fixed seasonable schedules. They were able to offer more athletic activities than the ships. These included handball, volleyball, wrestling, tennis, soccer, track, football, boxing, and baseball. Golf, hiking, biking, and swimming were usually available.[187]

Reading and writing were popular, especially correspondence with loved ones and friends back home. For the first time in American history, censorship was imposed, probably at the request of the British.[188] The Admiralty early in the war established a censorship program under Rear Admiral Sir Douglas Brownrigg, and it was probably at his direction that an agreement was worked out with Sims shortly after the first destroyer flotilla arrived at Queenstown. Both the Navy and the postal service set up censorship procedures in the United States. The postal censor, according to James Mock's *Censorship 1917*, found only two "indiscretions" in the Navy in European waters, both by officers from the Queenstown-based vessels.[189] Taussig wrote that his wife was "much disgusted (and so am I) the censor deleted parts of my letter. But I suppose this is one of the inconveniences of modern war . . . that we must put up with."[190] The Queenstown mail was channeled through the embassy in London; someone there may have censored Taussig's letter. He was not the only sailor in European waters to complain about censorship. Directives that originated at Simsadus went out to the various ships and stations, warning that violators of censorship rules would be in trouble. One rumor had it that a "Black List" existed of those who broke the rules and, if repeated, the perpetrator would be sent to a "concentration camp."[191] Enforcement proved spotty. The senior medical officer in Brest wrote his wife, "mercifully we have been spared the blanket order requiring every body's (including officers) letters read." A month later, he wrote that none of his outgoing personal correspondence had been opened "so far."[192] Some officers who assumed censorship responsibilities made no effort to censor their own letters.[193]

Assorted reading materials were available on naval vessels, shore installations, and in the reading rooms established by the welfare organizations. American newspapers were weeks old, British papers were heavily censored, and French papers were for the most part unreadable. The European edition of the *New York Herald*, and the *Stars and Stripes*, the "house organ" of the AEF, were the only up-to-date papers available. The gobs were understandably critical of the *Stars and Stripes* because it generally ignored the Navy.[194] Admiral Sims was well aware of this difficulty: "With the strict censorship in force in all Allied countries, the personnel get very little information of strictly service interest." No effort was made to provide them with a publication similar to the *Stars and Stripes*, although Simsadus issued bulletins periodically, which, according to the force commander, had "been found to be greatly appreciated by the personnel afloat."[195]

The Red Cross published a tabloid called the *Daily Bulletin* in Great Britain that was somewhat comparable to the *Stars and Stripes*. Although at first only one sheet (later two), it carried news from the United States, including coverage of the World Series and other sports. It was distributed to naval and army facilities throughout the British Isles. By October 1917, 75,000 copies were printed daily.[196]

Many of the ships and all of the shore facilities published papers or tabloids. NAS Pauillac, France, claimed that its *Pauillac Pilot* was the first naval unit paper published in European waters. A history of *Harrisburg* during the war concluded that their paper, *Sea Life*, had "unquestionably done more than other one thing to bind us together as a crew and to create that intangible but splendid *esprit de corps* which makes our ship so fearfully famous to our enemies and so famously friendly to ourselves."[197] Most of the ships and stations and the welfare centers carried small libraries of books and other publications.[198]

The YMCA established an extensive education program in Europe. Although not as elaborate as the Army's program, every naval shore installation offered Y-sponsored classes. The Queenstown base offered evening classes in typewriting and shorthand, and the Lough Foyle Naval Air Station offered classes in geography, arithmetic, trigonometry, algebra, French, English, history, geometry, physics, drawing, radio, and gas engines. French was part of the curriculum in every naval facility in France.[199]

Holidays were great occasions for the bluejackets. Whenever possible, the Navy, like the nation, gave its personnel a break for the day. The war at sea did not halt for holidays. Patrols went out and convoys received escorts. If weather permitted, a holiday meal was served to officers and men off-duty and to those on-duty when relieved.

During World War I, the Americans carried their holidays to Europe. The Allied nations had their fête days—Bastille Day in France and Guy Fawkes Day in Great Britain—but the Americans brought a new dimension of zealousness to their important holidays. At Queenstown in 1918, Memorial Day, sometimes called "Decoration Day," emphasized "patriotic features," including a pilgrimage to the graves of the *Lusitania* victims buried nearby. That afternoon, in typical holiday fashion, sport events dominated, and the evening entertainment centered on a concert and vaudeville show. Admiral Moore recalled that the crew of his ship just wanted to relax and to get ashore. The cruisers *Birmingham* and *Chester* were in Devonport, England, having just brought in a convoy. Their baseball and track teams competed against each other that day.[200] This was fairly typical throughout the war zone.

The U.S. forces in European waters observed Labor Day in 1917 and 1918. Even in Corfu, the American CO reported that the sport competition began early in the morning and lasted until the evening. Both French and British servicemen joined in. The naval air stations at Arcachon and Gujan in France joined to celebrate the day. A baseball game between the two stations was held at Gujan, and the Arcachon sailors entertained the Gujan personnel that evening with music and movies.[201]

Thanksgiving 1917 passed without much notice. Shore-based personnel and those whose ships were in port celebrated with sport events and evening entertainment. Many naval personnel in the war zone enjoyed turkey with all the trimmings. Storeships brought in tons of frozen birds. At Liverpool, where several American destroyers were undergoing repairs, the Red Cross provided the turkeys along with oranges, peas, potatoes, cauliflower, mince pie, white bread, butter, and candy. That night the mayor of Liverpool held a "dancing tea" for the American personnel.[202] Thanksgiving 1918 was not just another holiday. Coming two weeks after the Armistice was signed, all hands had reason to give thanks. The British by the thousands joined them in this uniquely American holiday.

Despite the war weariness of the Allies, Christmas 1917, at least on the surface, was a festive occasion. Before Christmas, trees with ornaments appeared in houses and buildings throughout the war zone. The American destroyers at Queenstown displayed garlands of holly and ivy from their mastheads. Naval vessels in France returning from patrol and escort duty spent Christmas Eve coaling ship "with victrola playing [carols] on the flying bridge and smutty youths struggling with shovels and baskets"[203] Commanding officers, welfare organizations, and Allied officials and citizens attempted to provide the servicemen with Christmas cheer. At the Eagle Hut in London, Father Christmas arrived with a gift for each of the approximately three thousand guests. In the Navy hospital at Brest, representatives of the Red Cross presented each patient with a comfort kit (pencils, writing paper, handkerchief, cigarettes, buttons, needles, soap, and candy). Similar kits were distributed to the crews of the naval vessels in the harbor. Every American shore installation held religious services on Christmas morning.[204] On the armed yacht *Emerline* at anchor in Brest harbor, several bottles smuggled on board were opened "to honor the occasion. Consequently [those that indulged] were most enthusiastic at the football game that afternoon."[205] Not all were filled with good cheer. Admiral Moore recalled a dismal Christmas. His ship was in Queenstown harbor. "I [was] waked up in the morning by music and sort of had a vague idea that we were being serenaded by something, and found it was a little joke of the Captain's. He brought the crews' phonograph up to the wardroom and played records, and he thought that was very amusing. It was an extremely dull and unpleasant day." He noted that even the Christmas dinner was "extremely poor." Undoubtedly, the holiday induced homesickness in a great many of the American sailors.

Benevolence and generosity toward the underprivileged, especially children, at Christmastime, is an American custom. The Navy continued this custom in the war zone. *New York*, the flagship of the U.S. battleships attached to Admiral Beatty's fleet, was awarded the name the "Christmas Ship" in 1915, when she entertained orphan children during the Christmas season, and its popularity persuaded Admiral Rodman to hold a similar event while at Rosyth. In December 1917, with the aid of the mayor of Edinburgh, 150 children were bused to the ship on Christmas Day, given dinner, entertained with Charlie Chaplin movies and the ship's band, and presented with gifts of clothes, shoes, toys and money.[206]

The personnel of the U.S. Mine Force at Inverness and Invergordon held a "Christmas Tree" for local children during the 1918 holiday season. The officers and men at the Cardiff naval base entertained some 1,500 children whose fathers had been killed during the war. The *Bridge* while in France played host to nearly five hundred children. Even at the naval air station in Porto Corsini, Italy, the American personnel entertained dozens of children from the local village.[207]

Not all charity went to children. The destroyer crews based at Brest collected funds to donate to the widows of French sailors lost at sea.[208] The U.S. mine bases in Scotland collected money to provide food packets for prisoners of war. The American personnel at NAS Killingholme held entertainments to raise money for prisoners of war held in Germany.[209] A French study of United States activities in Nantes and St. Nazaire during the war noted that the Americans were interested in a variety of causes—aid to orphans, refugees, and war victims.[210] A volunteer naval relief unit was formed to help rehabilitate the French city of Lille and the surrounding area. Hundreds of bluejackets with carpenter, brick-laying, and other building skills constructed dozens of houses.[211]

The Americans welcomed New Year's 1918 in typical American fashion with "as much noise and ceremony as the circumstance of war permitted." At midnight, the ships at anchor in Brest, Queenstown, other bases, and at sea rang the "ship's bell" and briefly blew their sirens.[212] For those ashore on liberty, it was an opportunity to celebrate. "I love Noo [sic] Year," wrote a naval aviator. "I was having a wonderful time with a little tissue paper hat on my head, and somebody had to go and spoil it by setting fire to the top. I didn't know it until my hair was on fire."[213]

The sailors in the war zone observed Independence Day in 1917 and so did Great Britain. The *Globe* of London commented, "nothing could be more symptomatic of the changes brought about by the war than the celebration of [American] Independence Day." The *Daily Telegraph* editorialized on July 5, 1917: "If one were called upon to name the most wonderful thing seen in this country since the opening of the war, one might well say that out of many marvels . . . none came near to the sight of the *Stars and Stripes* flying on the House of Parliament along with the Union Jack. Yesterday, by the King's order, the American flag flew not only from the Palace at Westminster, but from [all government buildings]. . . . But it was the flag at Westminster which gave the true symbolic touch." The *Times* (London) observed, "it was not so much Independence Day as Interdependence Day." "The Americans," the paper added, "were tactful in not reminding the British of their part in the holiday." The *Daily Mail* captioned its article on the Fourth, "The Day *WE* Celebrate."[214]

In July 1918, U.S. naval forces were scattered all the way from the Orkneys to the Azores and from Murmansk to Corfu. Wherever they were deployed, the bluejackets celebrated in one way or another. American aviators stationed at Lake Bolsena, Italy, were excused from flying and went to the nearby beach.[215] American and other national naval vessels "dressed ship" in honor of the occasion, flying flags from the halyards and mast tops.[216] The crews of ships at sea could do little but partake of a special meal and possibly view movies that night. A convoy that departed Genoa under American and Italian escort that morning encountered a German submarine, which ignored the holiday and torpedoed a merchantman. That night the convoy blundered into another U-boat, which left one ship sunk and others damaged.[217]

At Scapa Flow, most of the units of the Grand Fleet remained at anchor, but Admiral Rodman received permission to move the American battleships to the vicinity of Kirkwall, the Orkneys' county seat. "I told them to do what they liked. What they *can* do it is hard to say," Beatty said.[218] Liberty, which had been nonexistent for the bluejackets while with the Grand Fleet, was granted to half the ships' companies. They flooded the small town of a few thousand inhabitants. Although Kirkwall's amenities were limited, the Orcadians did what they could to help the Americans celebrate. The Stars and Stripes was flown from the town hall, and the cathedral bells rang every hour.[219]

Olympia was anchored in Murmansk harbor, Russia. At 8:00 a.m. on July 4, all of the men-of-war in the harbor dressed ship. "This was the big day," wrote a gob in his diary. "It started at morning Colors when we raised a big flag and two small ones at the mast heads and a Union Jack at the bow. All the other ships raised the Stars and Stripes. The French had a commission pennant about 50 feet long." The band went ashore, and a variety of activities, including a baseball game, took place in the town.[220] According to *Olympia*'s war diary, "while the band played, a large heterogeneous crowd endeavored to enter into the spirit of the game. However, it was very evident that most of them had never seen the game played before as they insisted on standing well within the foul lines."[221] At 6:00 p.m., according to a diarist, "we sat down to eat—100 American sailors and 30 Russians. First they brought out large plates of bread cut in thick slices and then some hamburger and sausages. Last came some chop suey, cake and tea with sugar. . . . [W]hooped it up on the boat coming back to the ship. It was a strange day."[222]

The French joined in the celebrations of Independence Day in 1918. In Brest, a parade took place, and the mayor gave a reception. He announced that the main square in the city would be renamed the "Place President Wilson." The chief medical officer at the naval hospital there wrote that he "never saw such crowds all day in the streets."[223] Paris "went mad," according to one observer. "There are but two subjects of conversation in Paris [today], the Fourth, and how many Berthas are going to fire on us before nightfall."[224] Houses and buildings by the thousands flew the Stars and

Stripes, and hundreds of American soldiers and sailors went through the crowds in the streets, pinning on miniature American flags.

Every U.S. base and air station in the British Isles celebrated the day with appropriate ceremonies. Admiral Moore mentions that they were surprised at Queenstown to see the British ships dress ship for July 4: "[T]here had always been the story which has persisted up until the present time that the British always arranged to go to sea on the 4th of July if there were any American ships in port so they wouldn't have a full dress ship and celebrate the 4th of July with us." If so, this departure did not take place at Scapa Flow and elsewhere where the two navies were together. In Gibraltar, an officer wrote that "The English tolerat[ed] . . . the good natured but noisy celebrating in view of the importance of the occasion." Even the Irish, far from enthusiastic about American participation in the war as a British ally, joined in the holiday. In Queenstown and Cork, shops closed and thousands flocked to see a baseball game between two destroyer teams.[225] In Cardiff, a special service was held at St. John's Parish Church with British and American officials and sailors in attendance. At the end, the organist played the "Star Spangled Banner." That afternoon, teams from two American ships played a baseball game, and the day ended with a reception and tea at city hall hosted by the lord mayor.[226]

The most elaborate celebration of "Liberty Day" occurred in London. All public buildings displayed the Stars and Stripes. Concerts, dances, teas, banquets, and speeches were held throughout the city, but the most publicized event was a baseball game played between American Army and Navy teams. Sir Winston Churchill addressed a joint meeting of American and British military and civilians officials at Westminster. This son of an English noble and an American mother said that "Deep in the hearts of the people of this island . . . lay the desire to be truly reconciled, before all men and before all history with their kindred across the Atlantic Ocean." He said that the war provided the opportunity for this reconciliation.[227]

Living conditions on shore depended on the facility and its location. Duty in London was better than in Queenstown or the Scottish bases, and Brest was more desirable than many of the naval air stations and also Gibraltar and Corfu. Quarters and barracks were at times primitive by American standards. Heating may have been inefficient or nonexistent, restaurants expensive, and regulations enforced more strenuously; but there was more recreation and entertainment, and best of all, they avoided the constant strain of sea duty in wartime.

Innocents Abroad

American sailors encountered a variety of problems in the war zone while ashore. Their transfer to Europe created difficulties from differences such as language and currency. Others were self-inflicted.

Although English was the common language of both the British and Americans, words, expressions, and meanings often differed considerably. For example, what Americans called a truck, the English called a lorry; a truck, to the English, referred to what Americans called a railway car. The cockney accent of London varied from those of the West Country, or Cornwall, or Yorkshire, or Lancashire. The Scots spoke Scottish, the people of Wales, Welsh or Cymric, and the Irish, Gaelic or Irish. One bluejacket recalled that "every other limey seem[ed] . . . to speak a different language, some said 'wot,' others 'what;' there were 'can't' and 'cawn't' and 'yer' and 'you.' . . . [O]ur language was probably as unintelligible to them as theirs was to us." American slang was as alien to the British as a foreign language. Although these differences caused some inconveniences, the common language mitigated them.[1]

In France, language posed serious difficulty, but the American bluejacket found ways to overcome it. The first Americans to arrive in Brest found signs in shop windows that read, "English spoken here." The sailors also made efforts to learn the language. "All the men are studying little dictionaries and they get wonderful results," wrote a junior officer on *Reid*. A few spoke "high school" or "college French," which was often not understood. By far, most of the sailors got by with a mixture of English and French complemented by sign language—"sailor French," as the local inhabitants called it.[2]

Currency posed more serious problems than language. The British monetary system frequently vexed the American sailor. When stationed in the British Isles, he was usually paid in pounds, shillings, and pence. American gobs referred to the large paper pound notes as "horse blankets," so thin that they disintegrated when wet. One sailor complained that the pound seemed to fluctuate from day to day: "I never did know how much I [had]." They called the copper pennies "clackers."[3]

American confusion over monetary differences was much stronger in France. Sailors on board ships going on liberty were required to exchange U.S. currency for francs, but they usually did not know the worth of the franc in American currency. As one sailor wrote, "a bushel basket of coppers as big as a cartwheel make you think you're getting something." They frequently gave the store owner or cashier a "fist full" of francs and took whatever change was offered. The director of the Navy hospital in Brest wrote about one of his men who insisted on being paid in U.S. currency and then exchanged it for francs, "'so I'll know how much I got.'" The *Stars and Stripes* recounted the tale of Brest-based personnel who crowded around a transport sailor just in from the States, "just to gaze at a one dollar or two dollar bill. . . . We just don't want to forget what real money looks like."[4]

In Gibraltar, the American dollar and the British pound both depreciated against the Spanish peseta. Most of the produce and other goods came from Spain, which led to inflated prices.[5]

The American sailors encountered many social and cultural differences in European waters. In 1917, few Americans had experienced contact with other nationalities. More than 2.5 million servicemen, including more than eighty thousand in the Navy and Coast Guard, traveled to Europe during the war. Most sailors were new to the service, and like the doughboys in the AEF, they were innocents abroad, with little understanding of the Allied people and their cultures. They observed Europeans from the standpoint of American culture. It was not simply a matter of respect for the different cultures; they had to adapt to them. They were tourists, although they were in Europe to make war—tourists making the "Grand Tour."

The Navy did not provide indoctrination in European culture for those ordered to European waters because of the need for speed, because the Navy had no experience of the circumstances, and because it was not considered necessary. For those going to Great Britain, it was assumed that the commonality of language, law, literature, and heritage would produce harmonious relations. Most Americans greatly admired their English counterparts. The American journalist Winston Churchill said, "there is no American so dear as not to feel a thrill when he first sets foot on British soil." Other Americans who visited the Isles during the conflict were imbued with this association. One wrote of the "best of feelings" between the personnel of the two navies; another said that "they were all friends and good fellows together"; and a third emphasized that they "are like old messmates." William Halsey declared, "we were not only comrades in arms but were very close friends." The British press lauded the "wonderful camaraderie that has sprung up between the American fleet and their British colleagues . . . and the . . . absence on both sides of any national or professional jealousy."[6]

A long tradition of rapport existed between British and U.S. naval officers. "It has been a rule," wrote Admiral George Dewey, "that wherever a British and an American ship meet, their officers and their crews fraternize."[7] They remembered the oft-quoted expression of the American commodore Josiah Tattnall, "Blood is thicker than water," when his small squadron cooperated with a British force in 1859 during an action in Chinese waters. Sims, then a commander, promised at a 1910 Guildhall banquet that, should Great Britain be threatened, "you may count upon every man, every dollar, every ship, and every drop of blood of your kindred across the seas." Naval officers of both countries truly believed that they were "brothers in arms."[8] Peter Karsten argued that they were Anglophiles because they "identified with [their] . . . British colleague[s] in every imaginable way, socially, professionally, ideologically, culturally, historically, and racially."[9]

During the war, U.S. naval officers often expressed their admiration for their British colleagues as they imbibed their professional expertise and experience and in-

dulged in their fellowship and hospitality. An officer on the destroyer *Walke* characterized the feelings of many American naval officers when he wrote: "We have met
some fine chaps in the British Navy. All here seem to be very anxious to make our stay
pleasant." Commander Walter Vernou informed the General Board that "absolutely
no friction of any kind" had arisen between the two services.[10]

The British were equally vocal in their regard for the Americans and their hospitality. "I must say I was very fond of working with the Americans and was a great admirer of them," a RN officer stationed at Queenstown wrote. Another recalled in his
memoirs: "I saw many U.S.A. naval officers serving on the staffs of Admirals Sims and
Rodman. They were first-class officers." Admiral William R. Hall, the head of British
naval intelligence, agreed. "I do not know what impressions these American military
officers make in France, but the American naval officers over here really mean business and there is a similar absence of the usual talk of the great deeds which the American Eagle is going to perform. The result is we get on extremely well." "Our American
friends [were] always a jolly lot of fellows," said one who served with the Grand Fleet.
The U.S. consul in Malta wrote that fourteen officers from U.S. subchasers on the way
to the Adriatic were invited to lunch with the local admiral and staff. "A nicer set he
never wishes to meet," the admiral is supposed to have said. An officer who worked
with Americans based at Gibraltar mentioned his acquaintance with them: "They
were all extremely keen on their job. . . . They were very generous to us, having us on
board to huge blow out dinners frequently and just before Christmas, they sent us a
large crate full of tobacco, pipes, cigarettes, and candy. . . . We felt ashamed at being
able to offer them only such a poor show in return. However, as the British Navy has
not yet gone dry we were able to make it up for them in other ways." [11]

A general feeling of respect and camaraderie for each other prevailed, but a certain
amount of awkwardness remained because of social and cultural differences, training and experience, and age. One American submariner noted, "While the Pukkah
naval officers, as the regulars of the British navy called themselves, were always polite
and sometimes very pleasant, still there seemed to be about them a restraint that was
more than a normal stand-offishness, as if they were glad we were there but resented
the necessity." He added, "Possibly [Hilaire] Belloc was right when he held that an
Englishman had far more in common with a Frenchman or even a German than with
an American."[12] Admiral Sir Herbert Richmond agreed: "to ignore national characteristics is most unwise. England is a very long way from America in social conditions,
however democratic the spirit of the present age may be. The mere fact that we employ
an interview committee is sufficient evidence of this; whatever may be the intentions,
there is no question that social attributes play their part in selection. They do not do
so in America."

American officers were generally older than their British counterparts, but the enlisted personnel were younger. Lady Beatty, the C-in-C's wife, after meeting a number of American naval officers at a reception, wrote her husband, "It seems a pity they
are so old." Beatty agreed, referring to Admiral Henry T. Mayo, in command of the
Atlantic Fleet, as a "dear old cup of tea who never did anything wrong in his life, an
impeccable old gentleman."[13] Other Britons tried to explain the differences: "To the

British Admiral his work is a religion, to the American it is business," wrote a newspaper correspondent. Another writer came to the same conclusion: "To the American naval officer of lesser rank the Admiral is not, as such, an object of veneration. He is an equal, entrusted by his fellows with larger powers; . . . [the American] pays deference to higher authority; to whom obedience is . . . a part of good manners. But the rigid etiquette of the British service bewilders the American. . . . The fact remains that the eminent virtue of the American consists in his disdain of the pompous and his ruthless contempt of the artificial. We shall never please America by talking eloquent nonsense."[14]

Allied as well as American naval commanders were determined to maintain good relationships. Well aware of the need for close cooperation and as little friction as possible, British admirals from Beatty to Bayly, as Roskill wrote, "worked [assiduously] . . . to foster it." Admiral Sims stressed it. On July 3, 1917, he informed all personnel under his command that they must achieve "maximum cooperation." He recognized that difficulties would occur but believed that once the United States got "into the game with these people all danger of friction would disappear." He downplayed to the press and even the Department any awareness of serious differences between Allied and American personnel, insisting that it was only "individual quarrels" over females, etc.

The admiral, however, glossed over the problem that strained relations had existed from the beginning. "There were those [naval officers] . . . who certainly weren't helping the 'entente cordiale,'" a war correspondent wrote. "They were just a bit condescending. And there were several of our fellows who could not forget the Revolution and the War of 1812." One officer recorded: "We hear of the fine receptions the British are receiving at the hands of the people at home while we are insolently ignored just as if we are invaders. The poor limejuicers did all in their power to drag us into this and after we did enter they begged for help."[15] Many Americans believed that they had come over to save the Allies, and the Allies, particularly the British, bitterly resented it. Robert H. Ferrell wrote, "a British soldier might ask if AEF stood for After Everything's Finished, and the American might reply no, it stood for After England Failed." Admiral Beatty's wife mentioned two drunken American bluejackets in Edinburgh shouting out a railway car window that "they had come over to finish the war."[16]

At the same time, many Americans were surprised that the British did not appreciate their presence. "What peeved Americans in London was to hear: 'Now that we've won the war the Yankees are coming!'" a journalist wrote. Admiral Robert B. Carney recalled, "They [the British] felt that we'd been a long time coming." When units of the AEF marched through London in mid-August 1917, people showed considerable enthusiasm, but when films of American intervention in the war were shown in the theaters, the audience evinced very little grateful response. A Navy veteran said that in Liverpool, "I heard for the first time YANKS GO HOME!" In Cardiff, various incidents occurred. A group of boys in a park shouted, "God damn Yanks." On November 9, 1918, a mob of civilians and sailors charged a gob, crying, "lynch him, kill the Yank." Shortly after the arrival of the first American warships, the U.S. consul in Cork reported to the State Department that "there is some slight English jealousy of the American Navy and of the popular inference here that its presence was necessary to come to the aid of the British war vessels." The poet Robert Graves, author of the moving war memoir *Goodbye to All That,* years later wrote, "American participation in the war, though officially welcomed, had never touched the British heart; and the Americans were accused of exaggerating their eleventh-hour services in France at the expense of those who had borne the heat and burden of the day."[17]

A number of the senior officers in the British navy were officially delighted at the presence of the U.S. Navy in the war but privately annoyed about it. Even Sims noted this "unfavorable attitude of British naval officers towards us." Admiral Jellicoe, whom Sims considered an old friend, had little time for Americans. Wemyss, his successor as first sea lord, had even less. He considered them "tiresome and sententious," and he once wrote Beatty, "I am suffering somewhat from 'Yankeeism'—disagreeable though not I believe, thank God, a fatal disease." Beatty himself was publicly friendly to American naval officials, particularly Admiral Rodman, but clearly patronizing. Shortly before the United States entered the war, Captain (later Rear Admiral) Roger Keyes wrote that he did "not at all like the idea of [the] U.S. as an ally. As such they will be a source of considerable embarrassment after the war."[18]

Much of this antipathy, certainly on the part of British naval officers, diffused as the war went on and mutual respect grew. Admiral Lionel Halsey, a member of the Board of Admiralty, wrote Sims in June 1918 that "any impression that may have existed in the minds of some Britishers that the Americans were vain talkers (and I think I may say it to you without offense that such an impression was current) has been entirely dissipated." Halsey's conclusion was not altogether true, especially as the war neared its end. Captain Lyman Cotton in Plymouth, writing a week before the Armistice, noticed "a change towards Americans in the last few weeks," adding, "when their backs were against the wall they welcomed us with open arms, but now rather resent our assistance." An American clergyman in London reiterated the naval officer's judgment shortly after the Armistice: "The feeling in England with regard to America is certainly, as the Scotch would say, 'on the north side of friendly,' and manifests itself in many petty, nagging ways." Several months later, he mentioned a sign in a store window that read, "Americans not wanted!" The Salvation Army's official history of its wartime activities determined that the most festering problem between the American military and the British was that "few Americans had any just knowledge or appreciation of the magnitude of England's efforts and sacrifice in the war, while many Englishmen only partly concealed the opinion that America had stayed out of the war a little longer than was compatible with self-respect."[19]

In contrast with the officers, little tradition of camaraderie existed between American and British enlisted men. As one former white hat wrote, "The educational and cultural gap was too large." The average gob in the U.S. Navy was considerably younger than his British counterpart. An article in a British military tabloid calculated that 99 percent of *Utah's* bluejackets were under the age of twenty-one years and eight months, leaving only 10 men in the ship's complement of 980 over the indicated age. The article went on to say that "there is not a big ship in the British Navy in which, apart from the artificers, ten per cent of the petty and chief petty officers are under 22."

Another writer noted that American sailors "are usually somewhat in the eager, irresponsible twenties, British tars are often men of sober middle age." British bluejackets signed up for a minimum of eight years, and usually they shipped over, whereas Americans enlisted for terms of four years and rarely reenlisted.

The Americans quickly became aware of the caste system prevalent in British society, including the military. The "British jack had, in his own social system, a place of his own. . . . Sons of 'gentlemen,' however, I use the word here in its British sense, did not join the Royal Navy as enlisted men," observed an American writer. Years after the war, a U.S. sailor concluded: "perhaps the weakness in the British Naval Service then was the caste system of that time. The ordinary British sailor was almost a nobody, as far as an officer is concerned." Another former bluejacket wrote, "we puzzled . . . [the British] with our disregard of their caste system, and they could not understand our gall in buying first-class tickets to everything unless they refused to sell them to us, which frequently happened."[20]

Several incidents occurred when British officers challenged American petty officers. They refused to accept the idea that American petty officers had far more authority than the British noncommissioned ratings. A number of American writers noted this difference. "We allowed our men far more freedom of initiative; certainly trusted them more; and there existed no hopeless social gulf nor brutal traditions of press-gang days in our service."[21]

Contact with British officers was professional, but with the enlisted personnel, it was primarily social. When given the opportunity, they fraternized with little friction. They were curious about each other. "All that I rec'lect o' the Yanks we used to run into on the China Station," one old salt exclaimed, "was that they was dressed diff'rent from us, talked diff'rent, and even swore diff'rent. The way they cussed struck me most of all. It was so earnest like." One of Sims's staff in London wrote after the war that "The Englishman is a very conservative person, who too often gives the impression that he is holding aloof; the American on the other hand, is very frank and talkative and apparently wishes to shake hands with the world."[22] American gobs considered the British tar quiet, reserved, argumentative, and slow to accept friendship but a "good fellow."[23] Several gobs mentioned the generosity of the British bluejackets, who paid for alcoholic drinks despite the fact that they were paid considerably less than their American counterparts.

A substantial number of American bluejackets did not care much for the British, and the British sailors did not care much for them. Secretary Daniels wrote that "there was friendship between A[merican] & B[ritish] officers but none between [the] sailors." "The American . . . cannot argue with the Frenchman but he can argue with the Englishman," concluded one of Sims's officers. The American consul in Queenstown noted the absence of friction between American and British seamen" but warned "it was to be, and I fear is still to be anticipated; as there is some slight English jealousy of the American Navy." A destroyer gob complained that British sailors came on board ship when they had a chance of bumming cigarettes, food, and the like. One crew requested to have their ship placed off-limits to British personnel during working hours.[24] A veteran remembered that "an anti-friendly feeling certainly did exist between the British sailor and us; nor could we seem to break that wall of suspicion, or whatever it was. We couldn't seem to strike up any friendly conversation, for they seemed curt in their answers, even sometimes a bit brusque." Nothing angered the British sailor more than the success of the American bluejackets with "their girls." "Turn yer' ead and orf they nips with yer missus," an English seaman complained. One white hat recalled: "While the men were not at home we made time. As soon as the men came home trouble started." American sailors in Queenstown would occasionally taunt their British compatriots: "Raz-berry! We got the girls, ain't we?"[25]

The difference in pay caused difficulties. An able seaman's pay in the U.S. Navy started at a dollar a day in 1917, whereas the British tar received approximately twenty-eight cents. A British author wrote: "Maybe the crux of the matter is to be found in the respective rates of pay in the two Services. . . . This fact, so often vulgarly advertised by their spurious generosity towards the British sailors, is the cause of much friction." British sailors bitterly referred to the American bluejackets as the "Millionaire Navy." Discontent on the lower deck had grown for a number of years, and association with the Americans exacerbated it. In January 1918, Admiral Beatty cabled the Admiralty: "In order to obviate disciplinary trouble and dissatisfaction immediate authority is requested to rate acting chief petty officers, the yeomen of signals, and petty officer telegraphers lent to ships of 6th Battle Squadron. Great dissatisfaction and discomfort is at present caused owing to the messing accommodations and general comparison with the petty officers 1st class, U.S.N. who are young men and mess with enlisted men by order of the Navy Department. . . . Matter urgent." The British press, noting the Americans' pay and living conditions, lobbied for better treatment of Royal Navy ratings. There was little improvement, however, and the unrest would continue into the postwar years.[26]

American and British sailors frequently got into brawls. One former bluejacket called it "a kind of love feast." The author of *Simsadus* wrote that the frequent arguments were "usually the training camp for a good old fashion fight." Fights occurred in every locality where the navies met. The British naval officer in command of the Otranto Barrage housed his personnel seven miles apart from the Americans as a "simple way" of preventing quarrels and fights.[27]

The British civilian had an opportunity to observe the American sailor in a different light as a tourist. His characterizations were generally flattering. They were both fascinated and curious about their "American cousins." "We are somewhat of a curiosity to the little English boys," an officer on liberty in Plymouth wrote. "Two of them followed a couple of us the other day until one of us said something, when one boy turned in wonder to the other and said 'they can speak English.'" Newspapers were full of articles about them, attempting to educate the Briton about the American. One of the courses of the National Home-reading Union for 1917–18 was entitled "American Principles and Ideals."[28]

Americans were frequently described as tall, "well-set up chaps." A letter writer to the *Daily Mail* judged that "they appear more slightly built than the British sailor, less ruddy, and a more wiry type. One receives an impression that they must be highly educated and have wrestled successfully with examiners." He added, "No doubt the tighter clothes and the little white caps they wear add to this slim youthfulness of appearance." A woman wrote, "They had good manners, dignified, unbending, and self conscious, quite different from our Tommy." Sims reported an interview with a reporter from the *Pall Mall Gazette* in which he was asked whether the U.S. Navy conducted specific training for its men on good conduct in public. "The reporter said that the editor himself had observed that our men not only conducted themselves very well on shore, but that it was noticeable that both officers and men were systematically polite in their intercourse with all classes of people."[29] A cockney proprietor of a pub told an American living in London: "Yerce, and I like what I've seen of 'em. No swank about 'em 'y' know—officers an' men, just pals together. Talks to yeh matey-like—know what I mean?—man to man sort o' thing. Nice, likeable chaps, I alwis finds 'em."

Certain habits of the Americans bothered the British. One diarist in London wrote: "A considerable number of American sailors are [in the streets.] They are almost invariably chewing something—gum or what?" Later he remarked that "The Americans have a curious habit of eating jam with everything—meat, puddings and cheese. . . . They are slow, untidy eaters."[30]

The British civilian tried hard to show hospitality to the American servicemen. Communities coordinated entertainment, recreation, and sporting events. Newspaper articles appealed for help in these activities. "But it is not only hospitality that is needed; we have to shed that misleading reserve of ours, which is so disconcerting to the men from overseas," the *Pall Mall Gazette* editorialized. "It is our national misfortune that we are shy with strangers, and consequently there is a danger that unintentionally we shall damp down the generous instincts of our visitors. For them we have the utmost friendliness, but if that friendliness is hidden beneath a cold and gauche reserve, what will it avail?"[31] The British achieved considerable success in these endeavors. American sailors were generally complimentary of them and their hospitality. The *Times* (London) with justifiable pride said after the war, "Thousands of Americans who came to this country with pre-conceived ideas about us, derived at second hand, who imagined that 'the Britisher was stand-offish, and frigidly reserved in his manner,' have gone away with an entirely different point of view." Some sailors disagreed; one wrote that "The English tried hard to please us, but there was always the feeling of dislike between us." One observer decried the Americans' arrogance: "We think we are tin gods on wheels and that other countries have no rights to their own customs."[32]

Cultural differences include food and drink, what we consume, how we consume it, when we do so, and the amount consumed. The American sailor confronted all of these in the war zone. He discovered, for example, that Europeans usually ate their meals at different hours from those to which they were accustomed. He often found the typical meal of a Frenchman or Briton to include less food than he was used to. Europeans frequently drank alcoholic beverages, usually ale or wine, with their meals. Finally, the exigencies of war affected the availability of food and drink.

In April 1917, most foods were still available in Great Britain, but certain items such as meat, sugar, and butter or margarine grew scarce. The shipping crisis created this shortage. For example, between February and June 1918, 85,000 tons of sugar were lost when ships carrying this product went down. Serious losses in ships that transported wheat and flour left Britain with only a two-month supply in the summer of 1917. Confectioners' shops and cafés no longer offered pastries and scones. Jams, which were popular with the English, gradually disappeared from the shelves. Periodically there occurred shortages of other staples such as potatoes and butter. The British government urged the consumption of less food with slogans such as "eat slowly, you will need less food" and "keep warm, you will need less food." Even beer and ale became scarce. It became common to see in the windows of pubs and taverns notices such as "no beer," "sold out," or "closed till Friday."

Early in 1918, the British government took its first step toward rationing. At first, butcher shops were to be closed two days a week. Then it decreed meatless days and issued regulations to control the consumption of dairy and bakery products and also fats. Finally, on February 25, the Ministry of Food announced the rationing of meat, butter, margarine, and sugar. Bread was not rationed and remained readily available. American servicemen were issued the ration cards and evidently used them without complaint. Rations for servicemen and the public remained adequate throughout the war.[33]

At first, officers dining in hotels or private homes were impressed with the quantity and quality of the food. Taussig, while in London during September 1917, was impressed with his dinners. "There may be some scarcity of food," he wrote, but "it has not reached the point where one cannot get anything they want as long as they have the price." Nine months later, American sailors arriving in Great Britain for the first time remarked on the food shortages and their effects on the people. They were "under nourished," one recalled. Another went so far as to say that they were "starving and needed help." A naval officer testifying before the General Board said: "In London there is often no meat on the bill of fare. I asked the waiter at the Ritz for some creamed potatoes and he said that there was no cream. I then asked him for some fried potatoes and he said he had no butter." The sailors depended upon the Y and other welfare centers for meals. Nonetheless, adequate food was available throughout the war, if one could pay the price. One authority concluded that in comparison to the other European belligerent nations, no serious food shortage occurred in Great Britain during the war.[34]

The American bluejacket was not very appreciative of British food. They generally disliked it, considering it "plain" and "tasteless." "The food was terrible for an American to try to stomach, so I went on a temporary liquid diet." wrote one "white hat." Another complained that "the food served in the average English restaurant was enough to drive strong men to drink and weaklings to baking soda. . . . It seemed that the highest aim of the English culinary art was to bedevil and bedamn all foods by devious processes during their preparation until there was no semblance of kinship between the original article and the finished product." The sailors voiced strong opposition to rabbit stew and mutton.[35] They were also disappointed with the beef. "Meat, ah! How I long for a piece of hamburg[er] steak with garlic." Fish and chips were available most of the time and became popular with Americans. According to an American naval officer, at least in one British community, the sailors consumed so much food locally that they "are causing a hardship now in town." The American bluejacket preferred to obtain his meals at the clubs and other entertainment centers that the Navy and private organizations established for them. He clearly preferred eggs and pancakes to Yorkshire pudding and beef and kidney pie.[36]

Food rationing did not apply to Ireland except in the "home counties." According to the American sailors, plenty of food existed in Ireland except for sugar. Taussig was impressed with the abundance of agricultural products. "It looked to me as if there was enough live stock and fields under cultivation to feed the whole of Great Britain." The people, he wrote, had ample food, but "the prices are very high." To remedy the sugar shortage, the U.S. Navy turned over to British authorities in Queenstown a million pounds of sugar.[37]

The Americans admired Irish cooking. A destroyer sailor exclaimed: "They make the most wonderful rye bread. They fixed the most wonderful eggs and ham they cooked on rocks." Another wrote: "There were two distinct steps to getting a meal. First, I went to a butcher shop and bought a pound of tenderloin at a price prohibitive to anyone but a Yankee. From there, I went to a grocery, and bought a can of peas, a jar of olives, and a can of pears. Next, after leaving the grocery, I walked up a short . . . street . . . and entered a little bakery, rather bare in its wartime necessities, and was greeted by a doll-like old lady. 'Evening Blackie.' 'Good evening.'" He then negotiated the preparation of his meal. "Miss O'Conners brought my sizzling steak, French fried potatoes, creamed peas, and olives."[38]

Of all the peoples in the United Kingdom, the American sailor found the Irish the most difficult because of the extreme poverty in Ireland in comparison to the rest of Great Britain and the apparent opulence of the Americans. This disparity led to jealousy and resentment among many of the Irish, especially those in the areas near the American bases.[39] The ancient hostility of most of Ireland toward the English and their desire for self-determination and independence also caused trouble. In 1916, with the support of the Germans, the Irish rebelled against British rule during Easter week. The revolt was put down, but three thousand people were killed or injured, and the British executed fifteen of its leaders. Afterward the militant organization known as Sinn Fein emerged as the most powerful extremist group in the country. Members endorsed a German victory because it was believed that such an outcome would result in Irish independence. A British naval officer stationed in Queenstown recalled that "the young men of Queenstown were in an ugly mood and would not make way for us on the pavement when we passed. . . . I, for one, slept with an automatic under my pillow at night."[40] Because of the unrest, the British had to keep a sizeable military force in the island, although it was badly needed elsewhere.

The local Irish greeted the Americans with considerable enthusiasm, mostly because the United States had a large Irish-American population. Initially, the American sailors got along well with the local populace. They found prices reasonable, food and drink plentiful, and females who were attracted to them or to their money. "Americans were treated like long-lost brothers by chance acquaintances and wined and dined in prodigal style," remembered a former gob. "The doors of Irish households stood ajar, and cheery words of welcome greeted visiting Americans wherever they went." Although he blamed the fine hand of John Bull for most of the words of warning that he and his mates had heard about the Irish, it became painfully clear that not all was "AOK" with the locals. "Almost came to blows with one of the rotters," he confided in his diary. Several officers at a movie theater got into a shouting match with what they called "Sinn Feiners." The American bluejackets also began to lose their respect for the Irish. A number of them commented on their laziness and slovenly work at the dockyard. In a conversation with Admiral Gleaves, Taussig condemned the Irish penchant for whiskey: "Liquor is the curse of the country; every other place is a public house." American naval personnel on liberty noticed the large number of young men of military age lounging around. British conscription excluded the Irish because of their suspect loyalty. Sailors began complaining of gouging by local businesses. Nonetheless, in the middle of June 1917, Admiral Sims reported to the Department that the Navy had no serious difficulties.[41]

A change in attitude toward the Americans began with the Sinn Fein. Admiral Sims believed that it was not just their hostility against the English but their openly "pro-German" posture. Shortly after the United States declared war, the American consul in Queenstown wrote, "[T]here is considerable feeling that the U.S. has deserted Ireland in joining England without exacting . . . any pledges on behalf of Ireland." The arrival of the first American destroyers and their enthusiastic reception led him to write, "it indicates that a great body of Irishmen have not been alienated from their esteem for the United States by the latter's alliance with the country which holds Ireland as a conquered province." Rumors circulated that the American ships had come to help the Irish against the British. "We were second in line entering Queenstown, with petticoats and green Sinn Fein flags waving from the windows of the gray stone houses. Up the River Lee, in Cork, we were hailed with 'Hurrah for America freeing Ireland.'" So wrote a naval officer early in May 1917. A British newspaper correspondent reported from Queenstown, "For two months after the American navy last May made this port one of their British bases, the Sinn Fein made it a 'Little Bit of Heaven' for the American bluejackets."[42]

By the latter part of July, this attitude began to change. American naval officials declared the movie houses in Cork off-limits to personnel because, when something about the United States was shown or the American flag was pictured on the screen, hissing and booing came from the crowd. They finally realized that the American Navy was not there to back them against the British or to ensure "Irish freedom." Although the Sinn Fein regularly held public meetings in Queenstown and Cork, it did not stimulate expressions of anti-American feelings. Early in August, however, American naval authorities became alarmed at the possibility of trouble between the sailors and the Sinn Fein. On August 11, liberty to Cork was canceled temporarily because of potential demonstrations and riots. Although the Sinn Fein became increasingly irritated with the American bluejackets' political views, probably they reacted most strongly to their popularity with the local women.[43] In the middle of August, incidents began to occur nightly. On September 1, Admiral Bayly informed the first sea lord of the disturbances. "I can quite understand it," he wrote; "the Sinn Feiners

and other rebels have for a long time been getting hold of the young American sailors in Cork and trying to persuade them that they are pulling chestnuts out of the
fire for England." Usually, however, young men harassed American bluejackets who
were escorting local females. The following day, an officer reported that several fights
broke out between "Sinn Feiners" and gobs. He also noticed that the Irish youth attempted to tear the clothing of the women with the sailors. "I happened personally to
notice while on liberty a gang of about 30 young men, armed with clubs, marching
on Merchants Street, Cork, whistling the 'Watch on the Rhine,'" recalled a sailor after
the war. Captain Pringle, concerned that serious trouble might occur, requested Bayly
to declare Cork off-limits to all American personnel. The admiral agreed, placing the
city out of bounds to all personnel below ship commanders, including the British servicemen as well as the Americans. Bayly and Pringle believed it would be a temporary
measure because Cork's business leaders would lose money, forcing the political leadership to halt the incidents.[44]

Sims reported to the Department on September 11 that "an efficient patrol" existed
in Cork and Queenstown.[45] Some Americans in Queenstown believed that putting
Cork out of bounds to the sailors was not entirely because of potential trouble. An
officer wrote that it was intended to "avoid any possibility of Americans fraternizing
with the Irish." In addition, a correspondent wrote that the restriction would prevent
the Americans from witnessing the "repressive means that an army of occupation
necessarily employs."[46]

The trouble spread to Queenstown, where groups of young men repeated the tactics followed in Cork. Roman Catholic clergy, critical of the relationships between
the sailors and the local females, encouraged the harassment. Local judges dismissed
assault and damage cases against the local males. Frequently the police turned their
backs on the difficulties. On September 11, a brawl occurred in Queenstown in which
a local man died from a head injury. A riot followed: when a large crowd of Irish men
began to tear up the cobblestones and hurl them at the sailors, the bluejackets retaliated. British troops were called in to restore order. The next day liberty was canceled
for Queenstown as well as Cork. A preliminary hearing determined that the injured
man died from falling against curbing and not from blows administered by Americans in the fighting. An American bluejacket was arrested and held over for trial but
was later released to American authorities. The gobs began to arm themselves.

Assistant Secretary of the Navy Franklin Roosevelt recalled years later that while
at Queenstown on an inspection trip he toured a machine shop on the tender *Melville*
and asked a chief petty officer what was under a large canvas covering. The chief "went
over and lifted up the canvas and there was the finest assortment of brass knuckles
and pieces of lead pipe that you ever saw. Captain Pringle said to the chief, 'What's
that for?' The chief with a grin said: 'Captain, sir, that's for the next liberty trip to Cork,
damn the Irish.'" As a writer mentioned after the war: "One naval battle that didn't
come off was the Battle of Cork."[47]

Although the *Examiner* (Cork) pooh-poohed the friction between the Irish and
the American bluejackets as "greatly exaggerated," others took it more seriously. Admiral Bayly wrote to Jellicoe of his fear of "big trouble later" and complained to the

first sea lord that the local civil authorities in Cork had made little or no effort to preserve peace. The first lord, Sir Eric Geddes, mentioned the ongoing troubles in Cork/Queenstown at a meeting of the War Cabinet, warning that the Irish difficulties might affect "our good relations with the United States." Although not discounting the Sinn Fein's influence, some British governmental officials considered the difficulties more social than political. The private secretary to the director of naval intelligence (DNI) described the incidents as rivalry between the U.S. sailors and Irish males over "colleens." "I think the Admiralty rather enjoyed the account of this inter-Allied engagement," he wrote. "It amused many of us to think that the American A.B. [able bodied seamen] had had to get quarter-deck advice to settle their differences with their rivals in love." The Foreign Office agreed that the relationships between the local women and the American sailors had instigated the trouble, and that the Sinn Fein seized upon it "to cause a scandal and make things disagreeable for the naval force." Whether they took it seriously or not, British officials seized an opportunity to damage American-Irish relations. British information offices released communiqués that "American transports were endangered" by Sinn Fein agents who trafficked with German submarines off the Irish coast. Although Admiral Sims agreed with British officials that the friction was more social than political, he and naval officials in Washington took it seriously. The American force commander refused to allow liberty to Cork until "some assurances are received from the civilian authorities as to their ability to suppress rowdyism and other difficulties which have arisen in the past." Sims publicly downplayed the problem, but in conferences and communications with Admiralty officials he took an entirely different stand.[48]

Local businesses and officials in Cork were concerned because the American sailors brought in badly needed revenue. On September 17, the city's mayor wrote to Admiral Bayly, urging him to drop the limitations on liberty. "I am sure that you will be quite safe in taking off the restrictions placed on Cork, and I am sure there will be no occasion in future for scenes such as caused the city to be put 'out of bounds.'" The admiral refused to act. On October 23, Bayly and Pringle met with Cork's mayor. Once again, the admiral refused to lift the restrictions when the mayor said that he could not guarantee protection for the sailors. Answering a list of questions put to him by the naval officials, it became evident that the mayor could not control his city.[49]

The enmity and the clashes that occurred during the fall of 1917 diminished in November and in the winter months. Occasional incidents took place, and the Irish retained their rancor toward the bluejackets. Not that all the Irish, even those in Queenstown and vicinity, were embittered, but enough were sufficiently up in arms to persuade the naval authorities to establish a sizeable shore patrol in the port. A report for the AEF estimated that 70 percent of the people in southern Ireland were "bitter at America for entering the war on the side of the Allies." Admiral Bayly, admittedly not an impartial witness, wrote, "It may truthfully be said that nine Irishmen out of ten [in southern Ireland] . . . cannot be trusted."[50]

As soon as the first incidents occurred between the Americans and Irish, Admiral Bayly assumed the responsibility of dealing with the problem. Sims accepted this decision without reservations and recommended it to the Department. Later, Assistant

Secretary of the Navy Roosevelt strongly endorsed the decision. Yet in February Sims informed the CNO that Pringle was to take "prompt and drastic political action in case the troubles of Ireland break out." He added, "It is this latter feature which is so worrying."[51]

The German offensive, which broke out in March 1918, caused the British government to introduce a new conscription act that included Irish males for the first time. This news led officials in Ireland to fear the worst. Southern Ireland offered strong opposition to conscription. Clashes occurred between the British and Irish in other parts of Great Britain. American commanding officers were instructed to warn their personnel to stay out of it.[52] British officials feared a full-scale rebellion in southern Ireland. They discovered that guns and other military hardware were being stolen and large groups of males were demonstrating and drilling. One gob on liberty in Queenstown on April 30 noticed "much Sinn Fein agitation." American and British naval officials were apprehensive about possible attacks against American military and naval establishments. Several naval air stations were under construction; a large supply depot was located in Dublin; naval units operated out of Bantry Bay; and Queenstown had become the hub of impressive naval activities.

Pringle and Bayly worked out a plan to protect American personnel and submitted it for approval. The admiral noted that in the past, "in order to prevent any chance of the U.S. Forces and Irish rebels from coming into armed conflict, I have protected [American personnel and property] . . . with British Forces, but this is no longer possible." The force that was available was not strong enough to do so, "and it is, in a manner derogatory to the U.S. Fighting Forces to see themselves protected by British soldiers." British and American authorities agreed that the British army had the responsibility of suppressing armed rebellion in Ireland, the Royal Navy the responsibility of protecting its property and personnel, and the United States the responsibility for all commissioned facilities, that is, those where the United States flag was flown. "In no case," the Admiralty agreed, "will United States' forces be available for the protection against Irish rebels of any property other than that covered by their own Flag." Yet the policy was unclear for the naval air stations and other facilities under construction or where the U.S. flag was not flown but American personnel were present. The United States would have the responsibility of protecting American property, but the British military would protect against "organized attacks." Without so stating, this arrangement required a joint effort. The Navy Department approved the plan but cautioned Sims that the "situation [was considered] . . . extremely delicate." The CNO cabled: "Utmost care must be exercised. Our forces should of course defend themselves against actual attack but the Naval Force of this Government should not take part in anything which could be construed as assisting in execution of Conscript Law in Ireland."

Consideration was given to dispatch U.S. troops to Ireland, presumably to help guard American property. Possibly troops would have been sent, if an armed force threatened the American facilities and personnel. Sims ordered line officers from the surface ships based at Queenstown to assume command of "outlying stations, . . . until the trouble is over."

The Admiralty was also concerned about logistical support if the Irish "rebels" caused an upheaval and blockaded services. The first lord surmised: "United States ships and men will be treated in [the] same way as we are, since the Southern Irish know well how friendly they are to us. But U.S. ships can feed themselves to a great extent from their repair ships and the U.S. stores on shore and since they burn oil fuel the coal labour will not interfere with them."[53] In the end, the British did not enforce conscription in Ireland, and the Irish did not instigate an armed rebellion that endangered American forces.

The U.S. naval air stations avoided incidents that might have stemmed from the "Irish Trouble." In April 1918, when most of Ireland went out on strike for a brief period, construction on the stations suffered, but it did not generally affect American personnel. The exception was at the station near Queenstown. Cork County remained a center of Irish unrest. American gobs on liberty, particularly if in the company of women, attracted hostile remarks and rude gestures. "The young ladies and the blue jackets are the source of trouble," wrote a destroyer officer. "Since the blue jackets can't go to Cork, the virtuous young ladies come to Queenstown." Captain Pringle canceled liberty to Queenstown whenever he received intelligence of a demonstration.

Cork remained out of bounds to servicemen despite periodic pleas from city fathers. Even so, occasional incidents occurred there. An American YMCA worker in uniform while walking down a street stimulated remarks such as "'There is a damned Yankee,' 'damned American,' and the like." "Suddenly," he later recalled, "a man emerged from a group, lifted a small cane, and struck me violently across the face, while his action was greeted by roars and shouts of laughter from his compatriots." A more serious incident occurred in late May, when four sailors, defying orders, went to Cork. Two of them became involved in a dispute, which injured one of them seriously. He later died. The local police arrested the sailors and turned them over to American naval authorities. They were tried by court-martial, convicted, and shipped back to the United States for imprisonment. Although the Irish were not directly involved in the incident, it promoted anti-American sentiment among the populace.[54]

Incidents occurred in the vicinity of Bantry Bay. Captain Roman C. "Rosie" O'Grady was in command of the U.S. submarine flotilla there. O'Grady, a loyal Irish-American, addressed a town-hall meeting of local inhabitants and criticized the Sinn Fein. He was assaulted, his jaw was broken, and he lost five teeth in the ensuing brawl. Lieutenant (later Admiral) Robert Carney recalled another donnybrook with local Irish males in a village near the bay. Another veteran remembered an incident when Irishmen pushed several American sailors into the bay as they waited at a dock for a liberty launch to take them to their ship.[55] An impressive number of the sailors stationed in Ireland went home with little or no sympathy for the Irish cause.[56]

American sailors got on best with the Scots of all the subject peoples in the British Isles. They also got on quite well with servicemen from the Commonwealth nations, especially Canada, New Zealand, and Australia.

In November 1918, Emile Boutroux, the philosopher and friend of William James, proclaimed in the highly respected journal *Revue des deux Mondes*, "If there were ever two peoples in this world who feel an instinctive attraction toward each other, they are the French and the American people."[57] A strong tradition of cooperation existed, going back to the American Revolutionary War, when the French helped the United States to gain its independence, lending military and diplomatic support that may have decided the outcome. When General Pershing, upon reaching France in June 1917, supposedly said, "Lafayette, we are here," he invoked this tradition. American entry into the war stimulated sagging French morale. Alexandre Ribot, the French minister, declared in the Chamber of Deputies: "The banner of the Stars and Stripes is about to float beside the Tricolor. Our hands are about to join and our hearts to beat in unison." American flags hung throughout Paris; in the cinemas, audiences applauded and cheered while the orchestras played the American national anthem, and a 101-gun salute was fired from the Eiffel Tower.[58]

This mutual attraction was to some degree superficial or exaggerated. The French derived a sense of relief that the Americans had come to help them win a disastrous war, and the Americans felt compassion. Yet the Americans and French were too different in language, habits, and temperament to expect to uniformly have desirable relations with each other. The language problem caused great difficulties on the Western Front, and it also created problems for the American naval forces.[59] As one gob wrote that "they can not understand Americans," and he could have added that the Americans had difficulty understanding the French: "It is both amusing and exasperating to see these Frenchmen—if you ask a Frenchie to do anything the first thought in his mind is of the obstacles and his eternal, 'c'est impossible.' Then he does it."[60]

When the Americans first arrived in the summer of 1917, the beautiful and picturesque countryside and the quaint towns impressed them. They found the people friendly. At some undetermined time, they began to refer to them as "frogs" because, as one sailor put it, they ate frog legs. It was not considered a term of derision, simply one of identification, as "limey" was for the British. The majority of the French sailors manning the ships along the Atlantic coast came from Brittany. The American sailor had little direct contact with his French counterpart socially. Language was the obvious barrier, although money was also a problem. "We don't fight much with the French gobs [because they] don't get paid enough for them to come where Americans hang out," wrote a diarist of the destroyer *Reid*. French naval officers were generally older than the Americans, and their enlisted personnel were either very young or much older. They were allowed to keep their beards, and more than one was described as being "gray bearded." Few drunken sailors were observed, but the *Reid* gob noticed that "when French sailors get drunk they generally link arms in a line which stretches from one side of the street to the other and march up and down, trying to sing." He added, "[T]hey don't seem to be as quarrelsome and destructive as our crowd."[61] It is impossible to generalize about the American bluejackets' attitude toward French sailors. The few references to them in the World War I questionnaires at the Army War College suggest that they had little respect for them.[62]

The bluejackets had far more comments about French civilians. A few sailors had the experience of being entertained in French homes and found them most hospitable. There are accounts of French generosity toward the Americans. Free drinks were occasionally offered by bar and café owners. One bakery merchant refused to accept pay from the gobs for bread. These were isolated cases. Americans in France during the war overwhelmingly felt that they were exploited. Secretary of War Baker, according to his colleague Daniels, said that the French were going to charge for the trenches American troops occupied. "'Then,' said Baker, 'we will evacuate at once.'" American sailors universally agreed that they were overcharged. One veteran sailor stated bluntly years later, "Our money was in demand."

In Brest, Admiral Wilson and members of his staff met periodically with the French district commandant, Vice Admiral Moreau, to discuss various problems including exploitation. The French officials admitted that they could do little to stop "elements of the population [from eliciting] gains." They agreed to order merchants and store owners to display their prices in a window or door of their establishment. Nevertheless, overcharging continued in Brest and throughout France as long as American servicemen were there. Everything from food to fuel was in short supply and in great demand, and no price controls existed as in Great Britain. One French writer claimed that the arrival of the Americans "coincided with rising complaints of local population because of rising prices." Then there was the popular illusion of American wealth among the French; "Toujours riches, les Americains." Everything began with speculation. "Americans have large salaries [which] . . . caused a furor to get dollars. Americans will buy anything. They spend money quickly. . . . Americans do not know how to resist these new types of pirates. . . . American [enlisted] sailors make as much as a French ensign. With their salaries they have come in and bought everything and have caused prices to rise in Brest," according to a French contemporary account. "Industrialists, unscrupulous shopkeepers, and girls by the thousands are attracted by the American dollar." There were incidents where American sailors victimized French merchants.[63]

The American sailors were also critical of the habits, customs, and living conditions that they observed among the French people of all classes. As the official history of the YMCA noted, "Whatever picture of life in France these men had conjured up, it is safe to say that imagination never approached the reality." "These people is so far behind times in some ways that you can't believe it till you're seen it," a sailor wrote home. "Everything is so strange over in this country, the people, the styles and customs, manners, and everything seems to be a few centuries behind time," a gob from Virginia wrote his mother. Another one exclaimed that "the most modern thing I have seen is electric lights." They often mentioned the quaint clothes, the wooden shoes that "clatter" on the streets as they walk, the substitution of perfume for bathing, and the absence of proper sanitation. They discovered that the majority of the French were indifferent bathers. In many French cities and most villages, indoor plumbing was a luxury that few could afford. Few houses had bathtubs. "They do their washing out of doors and every one washes in a pool built of stone and they all use the same water and never change it so it gets awfully dirty," one gob told his mother. He admitted, "I will not be sorry [to] get back where bath-tubs and plumbing are not looked on as luxuries for millionaires." The chief medical officer at the naval hospital in Brest mentioned to his wife that "one woman who owns an apartment . . . would not rent her place to English or Americans as they bathed too much."

Even Mrs. Daniels, wife of the secretary of the navy, who visited Brest shortly after the Armistice, was somewhat put out by the "tin pitcher of hot water delivered to a bedroom and served up in a tin basin as the substitute for the morning tub." The average American was scandalized at the personal uncleanliness of the average Frenchman, "appalled at his indifference to the dentist and his unfamiliarity with the toothbrush," as a member of the editorial staff of *Stars and Stripes* wrote after the war. A few were critical of the French proclivity for alcoholic beverages, particularly wine. One told his wife that in Brest, "every house is a gin mill or a wine House." He added, "The people hear [sic] don't drink any water."[64] The bluejackets were also critical of the use of roadsides for latrines and the slowness of the French in getting things done. "Tailors are slow, Bathhouses slow. One waits an hour sometimes for a meal which [an American restaurant] would turn out in thirty seconds," an exasperated American reported.[65]

The French were impressed with the American servicemen. According to an American author, one French staff officer, upon first meeting Americans, said in some surprise, "They are not the least American," an impression that quickly changed. According to a contemporary French writer, they admired the Americans for their ideals and values. American bluejackets were considered more disciplined than French sailors. A French writer described the Americans in St. Nazaire: "French men and women saw their streets being filled with large gay happy young men wearing [American uniforms]. . . . They all have the air of young cowboys from the American West. The American sailors were 'sveltes' and were nearly always larger than the French sailors. They walked along streets with chests out and their thin legs like ancient athletes with their hands in their pea jackets. The French called them 'Sammies.'"[66]

The French balanced admiration for Americans with some criticism. They particularly deplored American drinking and eating habits. They were unhappy at times with the American servicemen's relationships with local women. One writer decided that the French divided Americans into three classes: "The American who drinks nothing but water, the American who drinks everything but water, and the American who can't tell the difference between the French girl he can talk to and the French girl he can't." They considered Americans immature in many ways, particularly the young gob's penchant for mischief. The French naval guards frequently reported that American bluejackets "borrowed" launches and other small boats for cruises around the harbor or to return to their ship.[67]

The American sailors fascinated French children. Doctor Talley wrote from Brest: "It would amuse you to see gamin after gamin marching down the street whistling 'Hail, Hail, the gang's all here!' He feels a double pride, for he has been taught to whistle and taught a tune by a Sammie. The urchins are learning to whistle almost all the purely American tunes the band plays. . . . Wherever you see a sammie or sailor, you will see some French youngsters." Years later, one of those youngsters described his feelings when around the Americans: "The arrival of the Americans had been for us the realization of a childhood dream. We spent our free time hanging around [them] . . . with all of its adventure." The children quickly acquired a rudimentary understanding of English and American slang, using a combination of conversation with the Americans and a French-English dictionary. "Don't any of these people speak American?" was a common question with the gobs. Even on the command level, where interpreters were available, problems occurred because of miscommunication. The language difficulties aggravated the mutual distrust and animosity over prices. "If [a] madame or shopkeeper who felt she or he was being defrauded, the sailor responded, 'Oh! pas compri, madame or monsieur!' Again, if the sailor remonstrated, it was the madame or shopkeeper who pas compried." A sailor in Brest informed his mother, "You can't imagine how bad the boys want to learn French." In Nantes and St. Nazaire, about fifty individuals were hired to teach French to American servicemen. A French contemporary account said that "everyone is looking to learn English to help with [business] . . . transactions. English teaching establishments have sprung up everywhere."[68]

In general, the Americans, who were critical of British food, were most complimentary of French cooking. The availability, amount, and kind of foodstuffs depended on where and when one was stationed. Priorities in transportation, primarily rail, had a major impact on food distribution. Food was more plentiful in the summer of 1917. It was considerably more expensive in 1918 because of the growing shortages and inflation. France was far more self-sufficient than Britain in food production, but the government was forced to impose rationing and other regulations. White bread was prohibited; in its place French bakers sold what was called "war bread" made up of successive mixtures of different flours (wheat, barley, and rye) and, according to some, sawdust. Its color ranged from assorted shades of brown to gray, and it was doughy in texture, but even this bread became scarce and had to be rationed. In some parts of France, police had to control the queues because the bread was in such short supply. Meat could only be sold or served on certain days, and by 1918, horse meat was served in place of beef in many restaurants. Fish, the staple of French cuisine, was rationed and became expensive.[69]

Far more food was available in the country and on the coast, especially in Brittany. The naval doctor in charge of the U.S. base hospital at Brest concluded that "this section is [not] hard up for food." In another letter, he wrote, "They have fish, shell-fish, fruit, farm products, in fact, everything in greater profusion here than I thought possible." A bluejacket wrote that Brest had "many clean little restaurants about town run by families and we went to one run by an elderly couple. These small restaurants didn't put out large menus but what they offered was excellent. . . . We enjoyed it to the hilt. They saw how we cleaned up what they had to offer and Mother came out generously giving us seconds plus a generous glass of French red wine on the house." Conditions were less favorable in other places. One officer recalled: "[T]here was nothing to eat there. The French were starving. We'd take food over from the ship, and the sugar and the chocolate, things like that, and they'd cook for us." Another mentioned providing a baker with white flour from the ship, the bread being divided up between the baker and the ship's crew.[70]

The Americans evidently got on well with the Italians but had some problems with the Portuguese in Lisbon and Ponta Delgada, Azores, and considerable difficulty with French colonials. They brawled with the Algerians and the Tunisians in Bizerta. As in the past, ethnocentric American sailors showed little respect for the inhabitants of North Africa, considering them "semicivilized." Bluejackets on liberty in North African ports at times ignored warnings about local customs. They were informed of the inviolability of veils worn by Muslim women, but at least on one occasion an American gob was seriously injured when he ignored this warning. At the other end of the Mediterranean, Corfu was expensive, the food considered poor, and because of the prevalence of various diseases and the lack of sanitation, the American sailors based there were not encouraged to fraternize with the local population.[71]

The American sailors were popular with most Azoreans. Partly it was because so many Azoreans had immigrated to the United States. Dunn wrote to Sims: "We are solid with the people. The U.S. Ensign is seen flying over many private homes all over the island. It is a curious fact, more Azoreans . . . are in the U.S. than are now living here in the whole group of islands, U.S. 250,000, Azores, 230,000." At the same time, it was generally believed that the Americans had saved the islands from German occupation. When *Orion* fired on a German submarine on July 4, 1917, and supposedly drove it off, it sparked a spontaneous celebration in Ponta Delgada. As Secretary Daniels wrote, they named brands of cigars after the commander of the Orion, "and I know no more conclusive evidence of popular favor than that." The local population was still nervous when the American destroyers arrived a few weeks later. When *Lamson* fired a shot, calling for the return of the ship's crew on liberty, the audience in the local movie theater panicked, thinking that the German submarine had returned.[72]

The American sailor's relationship with the other sex while in the war zone is difficult to evaluate. The bluejacket who returned to home and family after the war seldom mentioned his experiences with women while "over there." In their diaries, memoirs, correspondence, and other writings, they were usually circumspect, often writing in generalities. Yet, it is clear from their writings and other information that large numbers engaged in sexual activities. Many Americans encountered a degree of social contact with women that they had never had before. Wherever the sailors went in the war zone, they found women eager to fraternize.

War affects social values. This is particularly true in geographical areas where the horror and hardship of armed conflict has a direct impact. In many ways, women are most affected, their lives disrupted. While their husbands, fathers, brothers, and boyfriends march off to war, they are left to cope with shortages of food, fuel, and other necessities, and the everyday drabness of life with few males around except the very old and young. Thousands took up war work. They did so for financial and patriotic reasons, but they also did so as a means of escape. Others joined the armed forces and welfare agencies such as the Red Cross and the YMCA. The Y employed approximately 3,500 American women as canteen workers in the war zone. These women were extremely popular with the American servicemen. As one sailor said after meeting a female Y worker, "Gee, it certainly is swell to see a girl that talks American." In his memoir of service in the Navy, a former officer in some bitterness wrote that it was these women, the "welfare workers, entertainers, YWCA's and others who had gone to France to 'dance with the soldiers and show them how to amuse themselves' . . . who tended to cause trouble."[73] Others looked for escape in social activities and relationships outside the home. An unusually large number sought male companionship. "Victorian morality was one of the war's first casualties. American 'innocence' followed soon after."[74]

American sailors in the war zone, particularly in the British Isles and France, were astonished at their popularity with members of the opposite sex. They encountered women socially in a variety of ways; at dances and other entertainments sponsored by local communities, groups, and organizations such as the Red Cross and the YMCA, in private homes and in shops, eating establishments and pubs, and on the streets. An American naval aviator in some amazement wrote his family, "There are literally thousands of girls who say they will show you around Paris, and it's a two-fisted fight to shake them off." In Brest and other ports, when American vessels came in, throngs of women crowded the dock where the liberty boats disgorged their loads of eager gobs and the streets leading from the landing. One bluejacket described his first liberty in Brest: "My feelings were those of a youngster enjoying one of his first Christmas mornings. . . . As we left the dock to walk up the steep hill we encountered an unexpected situation, the girls and there was a bevy of them, not a dog face among the lot. . . . They came forward to us as we left the landing wharf. One rather cute one put her arm in mine saying as calmly as though I had known her for years 'you jiggy jig with me. I jiggy jig with you.' . . . I had come from a different world. I was let down momentarily within [as I walked away]." In Queenstown and Cork in two and threes they stopped the American sailors, "blocking our way with a 'Hello Yank.'"[75] They also found them in brothels. One of the questions that the Army War College asked in its World War I survey concerned "consorting with women." The response was decidedly positive; "all we could," "as usual," "very much, mucho, mucho" were some of the answers.[76] The sailors were free with their money and also often brought "gifts" of candies, cigarettes, and scarce food items such as sugar and white flour.

American sailors were especially popular with the Scottish lassies, according to a sailor based in Inverness. In Edinburgh, dozens of them met the trains that brought liberty parties from Rosyth, and on more than one occasion, the bluejackets with their female companions blocked traffic, linking arms and marching down the narrow streets.[77]

The Americans generally found British women pleasant and attractive, with one exception. A surprisingly number of them remarked on their poor teeth, particularly the "Bonnie Scotch lassies." The minelayer USS *Saranac*'s cruise book included the comment: "This dame isn't what you'd call pretty but gee! The longer you stay, the better you like 'em; . . . Her teeth are fine—both of 'em. And they meet! O' course that's pure luck, but you gotta be thankful for something." This physical disfigurement was common among the English and Irish women. "Cripes! I thought the Scotch girls had bad teeth, but I believe the English girls go them one worse," wrote a sailor. Another destroyer gob based in Queenstown remembered that the Irish colleens seemed to be extremely interested in their teeth. "They would ask us to open our mouths so they could see better. Some even reached in with their fingers and pulled to make sure our teeth were real." He added, "Their own were yellow, snaggled, and chipped off almost to their gums."[78]

Long before the Americans arrived, British attitudes toward sexual morality were changing. One of the most popular songs of the first years of the war was "There's a Girl for Every Soldier," and as one authority wrote, "in most towns soldiers on leave found this to be only too satisfactorily true." The horror and austerity of war produced a "hedonism" unlike any found in British history. Arnold Bennett in his journal noted: "The sensual appeal is now really marked everywhere, in both speech and action, [and] on the stage. Adultery everywhere pictured as desirable, and copulation generally ditto." A gentleman in Liverpool, disturbed at the "antics" of American bluejackets, asked, "Am I to judge all Americans by the sailors I see in Liverpool?" The sailor to whom this was addressed, replied, "Am I to judge British women by the girls I've met here?"[79] This revolution in morality and behavior blanketed the entire nation during the war, but it was more pronounced in the cities, especially those close to military installations.

London posed the most challenges to the old morality. The author of an article published during the war in the YMCA magazine commented on the danger of prostitution. Titling his piece "The Greatest Battle of the War," he proclaimed that "more courage is needed on the streets of London than in the trenches of France. . . . [T]he opposing front trenches are manned by women." A shocked Marine captain who visited for the first time in November 1917 observed that the "streets are simply lined with women trying to pick up men." A bluejacket wrote in some bitterness after the war, "the lilies of Piccadilly Circus, Mayfair, and Rotten Row in many cases had turned out to be sharp-thorned thistles." Edward Bok, the well-known editor of the *Ladies' Home Journal*, was "surprised and depressed . . . at the uncontrolled solicitation of our boys by women on the London streets and in the hotel lobbies, lounges, and restaurants." His statement published in the *Times* and *Daily Mail* drew sharp response from the lord mayor, the chairman of the American Luncheon Club, and other officials.[80]

Other British cities notorious for the large number of women accosting American sailors during the war included Liverpool, Cardiff, Southampton, and Hull. "In Liverpool open solicitation is rife," reported the *Daily Mail*. Hull, the nearest city to the American naval air station at Killingholme, was described by British medical officers as the "dirtiest, most vulgar and immoral metropolis in England." However, prostitution was not considered a major problem in other cities with American bases nearby such as Plymouth and Edinburgh.[81]

Because of the British attitude toward prostitution, American authorities could do little. They strongly encouraged more acceptable options such as sports and supervised entertainment at Y centers and similar establishments. American naval headquarters in London attempted to keep the YMCA notified of the arrival of liberty parties. Y representatives then met the train and escorted the party to suitable lodging and to the Eagle Hut, where a talk was given on what the sailors should and should not do. This Y program was not carried out in other British cities.[82]

A women patrol and police made up of volunteers was probably the most effective measure in controlling vice. Two New Zealanders in London formed the Women's Patrol Service (WPS). In time, other nationals joined, including Americans after the United States entered the war. At the Armistice, nearly two thousand patrols operated

in Edinburgh, Birmingham, Glasgow, Bristol, Belfast, Portsmouth, Plymouth, Brigh-
ton, Nottingham, Southampton, Folkestone, Oxford, Cambridge, Grantham, Hull,
Newcastle (where it was known as the Women's Patrol Committee), and London.
London alone had more than four hundred patrols. Women police were recruited in
many of the cities as a result of a recommendation from American delegates attending
a conference convened by the British government to consider ways to remove "temptations" from servicemen from the United States and the Dominions. Although the
responsibility of the women police was much broader than that of the volunteers, they
spent much of their time in similar work.[83]

American efforts to export their country's moral code to France had little success. These activities generated considerable misunderstanding among a Latin people whose mores were considerably different. The French resented proselytism. This
"missionary" attitude did not filter down to the sailors. The French were tolerant of
the Americans who established relationships with women, even among the upper
classes. Officers and men were invited to homes, and French women quite often visited the living quarters of officers ashore. One authority wrote that the American sailors in Nantes and St. Nazaire were modest in behavior and in the "respect that they
showed to women. Scandal and debauchery were not the normal." Not all Frenchmen
agreed. According to an American minister visiting Brest during the war, a Frenchman told him: "The most dreadful thing of this war is not the loss of life of our men
and boys. To me, it seems to be the effect on our womanhood. How would you like
it if all the armies of the world were dumped on American soil? What effect would it
have on your young girls?" The minister added: "What could I say? Human nature is
much the same." The bluejackets were surprised at how easy it was to engage women
in conversation in cafés. They were also surprised that often they were invited home
to meet the family and invited back. The Americans characteristically brought gifts
in the form of food or other items from their ships. The sailors considered the French
women forward and aggressive. One French writer, in some amusement, wrote that
the Americans do not know how to resist these women, whom he referred to as a "new
type of pirate." A Marine aviator agreed, commenting that they were "not backward
about making advances."[84] A majority of the American sailors had never experienced
a situation where large numbers of females crowded the waterfronts awaiting the arrival of the liberty boats and congregated in the streets openly soliciting favors, even
in restaurants. The large number of brothels operating with the approval of the government was also a revelation to them.

When the first doughboys disembarked at St. Nazaire in June 1917, they and the
bluejackets that crewed the transports and escorts were granted liberty. For a period
of four months, no regulations were issued that governed their conduct with women.
The liberty regulations for the Navy were simple: keep out of any disturbances, keep
out of restricted areas, and obey the shore patrol. What was perhaps the typical attitude of the Navy in France is explained in the memoir of an officer who in mustering
a liberty party told them: "It is not my business to know how many of you will go with
a woman tonight. . . . It is my business to keep you out of trouble, such as being rolled
and robbed, or contracting a venereal disease. . . . If you go with a woman, there is an

old adage, which may make you popular, 'Treat a lady like a whore, and a whore like a lady.' Dismiss."[85]

St. Nazaire taught American military officials a painful lesson. "Twenty thousand Americans have disembarked at Saint Nazaire. A letter from my brother informs me that they are making a great uproar in the 'Red light' district of the town, and their military police have to use their truncheons." So wrote a Frenchman commenting on the arrival of the first Americans in France. The streetwalkers and six *maisons de prostitution* did a booming business. According to one French authority, the town with a population of approximately forty thousand had three hundred eating establishments that allowed prostitutes to solicit in them. The Army became concerned when statistics indicated that VD had reached epidemic levels at St. Nazaire. General Pershing's concern about VD led to a general order that declared brothels off-limits to American personnel. Contracting the disease was also declared a court-martial offense. Pershing's orders concerning VD were later amended to include all ports of debarkation.[86]

The St. Nazaire experience was duplicated wherever American sailors were based or went on liberty or leave. According to French authorities, the arrival of the Americans brought on a significant increase in the number of both licensed streetwalkers and "house prostitutes." At Brest, with its large concentration of American military personnel, the brothels and red-light district were placed out of bounds. Large numbers of streetwalkers and women then congregated near the docks. "I have mentioned the long line of steps leading up to the main street of Brest," a bluejacket wrote. "At the time of our first shore leave our launch deposited us at the landing stage and we proceeded to climb the stairs to the street. At that point, we came so abruptly upon a bevy of young ladies that we were quite taken aback. . . . We were so taken off guard as to stand speechless while, with giggles, and Gallic chatter, they took our arms and started up the street." They tried "a shore patrolman's soul," Stallings wrote in *The Doughboys*. Finally, both the Navy and Army issued orders forbidding American serviceman from being seen on the street with a French woman. French authorities reluctantly accepted the order on the ground that no decent girl would go out alone with a man.[87]

At La Rochelle, the military police and shore patrol took the name of any American serviceman seen with a French woman. If the woman was a prostitute, the sailor was ordered to captain's mast. Although the brothels in the city were out of bounds, it was possible for an officer to obtain a pass from the provost marshal to gain entrance. In Bordeaux, the local American military commander threatened court-marshal for any officer or enlisted man found entering a brothel or seen in public with a prostitute. Bishop Cannon said that Bordeaux was morally the worst place he visited in France. A doughboy agreed: "The city was even faster than Paris; for her women, indeed, this southern seaport may well blush. The number of most irresistibly attractive women on the streets who accosted us at almost every corner was amazing. We counted sixteen who spoke to us within half an hour."[88]

But there was no place like Paris! Thousands of American sailors went there on liberty during and immediately after the war. One authority estimated that seventy-five thousand prostitutes, professional and amateurs, practiced in the city during the war. A large percentage of them, especially the "amateurs," were from other parts of France, including women from the occupied regions, "husbandless women," and widows who found it impossible to make ends meet. Only a small percentage, about five thousand, carried on their profession in the regulated houses; the remainder walked the streets. More than 2,500 hotels were open in Paris during the war, most of them "houses of assignation." "America has as much to fear from the French women of Paris as from Germany," noted an American living in the city. A YMCA representative in Paris told of a group of Y workers who had gone to meet a train that brought American servicemen on leave: "300 of the boys came in, the Y.M.C.A. got forty and the balance went off with girls." An American naval aviator wrote from Paris: "I'm beginning to understand why so many American soldiers and sailors go wrong in Paris. . . . [T]he temptations now . . . are perfectly frightful. I have never been out walking in the evening that at least two girls didn't come up to me and grab my arm." A Frenchman recorded in his diary: "American sailors loll about on the terraces of the boulevard cafes. They make gestures to all the women. One feels they believe that they have only to lift their finger to secure any Frenchwoman they want."[89]

Premier Clemenceau offered to help establish official houses of prostitution for American military personnel, the common practice of the French and the other Allies. When Secretary of War Baker heard of the premier's proposal, he is supposed to have said, "For God's sake . . . don't show this to the President or he'll stop the war." Clemenceau and all French officials never accepted the American position and continued to complain of their determination to declare all French brothels out of bounds.[90]

Although nothing in writing has been found to indicate the Navy's policy toward prostitution, it followed the Army's directives. American jurisdiction over the ports of debarkation was unclear and occasionally led to friction between the local U.S. Army and Navy officials, but the military police and naval shore patrols covered red-light districts and designated houses of prostitution. The only order from Admiral Wilson's office about consorting with women canceled overnight liberty for married enlisted personnel. A standing order provided that no women with the exception of nurses, Red Cross, YMCA, and other female workers on official business associated with their organization could ride in U.S. naval vehicles.[91]

Elsewhere in the war zone where the United States had naval bases or stations, the regulations concerning prostitution were the same as in France. Known red-light districts and brothels were declared out of bounds, and shore patrols stationed in the vicinity were ordered to keep naval personnel out. The red-light district in Gibraltar was particularly notorious. One bluejacket on shore patrol referred to it as "the most sickening place I've ever seen." American authorities could do little about streetwalkers or those plying their trade in the restaurants and other public places, but they sent bluejackets caught with known prostitutes back to their ships or bases under arrest. At Ponta Delgada and Horta in the Azores, prostitutes frequently carried their business to anchored ships in bumboats.[92]

American women were present in the war zone. In addition to those holding U.S.

citizenship but living abroad, several thousand females were sent overseas specifically for war work. They included nurses, Red Cross workers, canteeners with the YMCA, Salvation Army volunteers, and telephone operators and messengers. Nearly all of them were located in the British Isles and France. A few officers' wives who despite official disapproval reached Europe frequently worked as volunteers with one of the welfare organizations or the Red Cross. Wives whose husbands served in the war zone were not permitted to use their passports. Naval officers were not given allowances for quarters if their wives were in the same location.[93]

Social contact between single American females and the sailors was common. Individual dates, although frowned upon, took place, particularly with officers. Nurses that became engaged or were married were automatically sent back to the States. Most of the fraternization took place in the canteens and other welfare and recreation centers and at dances and other entertainments. Dances were extremely popular. Frequently the only women present were American and at times so few in comparison to the number of males present that they rarely had time to rest. The Y, which created teams of chaperoned women to go from canteen to canteen dancing with the men, started to limit the number of dances each canteener was permitted to attend.[94]

According to one authority, the American serviceman abroad in World War I followed a "cultural double standard" in their association and attitudes toward women. The American girls were "nice" and "pure" and should be protected, whereas the foreign females were "loose" and "wicked."[95] Regulations protected the majority of American women in the war zone. Furthermore, by no means did all American servicemen, certainly not the sailors, look upon British, Irish, French, and other non-American women as immoral. Many of them married foreign women.

Many sailors were convinced that a large percentage of the women that accosted them wanted to marry them and go to the United States as an American citizen. "They get the screwey idea we're all rolling in dough, and they want to get married and go to the States," one bluejacket wrote. A destroyer gob recalled, "Most of the girls were out to get an American husband and did not scruple as to how they got him." In 1918, the American consul general in London wrote the State Department that a large number of American servicemen were marrying British females with unforeseen difficulties. A British subject, for example, lost her citizenship and was considered an alien upon marriage to a foreigner. At the same time, according to U.S. regulations, an American official could not register her unless her husband could provide proof of citizenship.

Estimates vary on the number of war brides. The *Pall Mall Gazette* said that six thousand French women married Americans in the twelve-month period from March 1918 to March 1919. A French bride wrote after the war that of the fifty thousand Americans considered permanent residents in France, 20 percent were veterans. However, another writer calculated that the Yanks married 3,059 French women. He also reported that they took to the altar 1,448 British wives, 88 from Luxembourg, 75 Belgians, and 40 Italians. The discrepancies can be partly explained by the fact that a great many American servicemen took their discharge in Europe and took up residence there. Also, considerable confusion occurred while arranging the transport of these brides to the United States. At the end of hostilities, the doughboys and sailors were returned to the States with little or no thought to the plight of their wives. In time, the Red Cross assumed this responsibility. The Navy agreed to provide transport under its supervision. Liverpool and Brest became the designated ports of embarkation for the brides. In France, a "squaw camp," as it was called, was established to house the war brides before they left for the United States.[96]

An article in the *New York Post* declared that "American Navy men were the 'champion marryers' of Uncle Sam's force in Europe during the Great War." Admiral Sims mentioned in an interview shortly before returning to the United States that a few hundred American sailors had married English brides. A correspondent who visited Queenstown early in 1918 wrote that "there have been some fifty marriages at this base." Several sources mentioned that the Americans based in Scotland had married "many" Scottish women but gave no figures. Perhaps the bluejackets married more Irish and British "colleens" rather than French women because, as one writer put it, "the fellows had much lingo trouble." A report prepared by the U.S. Naval Headquarters in Brest stated that by September 1919, 132 wives had been transported to the United States. A number of marriages occurred among the American force in Gibraltar and a few in the Azores. Perhaps the most unusual marriage took place in Bantry Bay, Ireland. One of the American submarines was used to carry the groom (an ensign) and wedding party, including a jazz band, to the village where the wedding was held. The submarine was decorated with evergreens and "various colored bunting."[97]

Not all associations had a happy conclusion. A study of Brest in World War I reported that a number of local wives married to Americans had been left behind when their sailor husbands returned to the United States. Most of the "husbands" were never heard from again. A British seaman's memoir of service in the war, including with the mine-laying force in Scotland, wrote that "many Scotch families around Inverness and Invergordon will ever regret the American sailors being quartered in these parts. . . . Many marriages took place, but inquiries after the war failed to find the 'husbands' who had gone home with promises to send for their wives."[98]

Despite some bitterness and criticism of American sailors, professional and personal relationships continued after the war. A unique example was the Queenstown Association formed by officers who served there during the war. They were deeply attached to Admiral Bayly, the Royal Navy officer in charge of the Queenstown naval command. His motto, "Pull Together," became the title of his published memoir and the symbol of the Queenstown Association. The unusual relationship between the British Admiral and the Americans formerly under his command was graphically illustrated when the Americans contributed enough money to purchase a retirement home for Bayly. British naval officers in the United States were invited to attend the association's annual banquets.[99] In 1929, U.S. naval veterans who served with the mine-laying forces in Scotland donated a large sum of money to help build a new hospital in Inverness. Periodically during the interwar years, both American and British veterans and writers emphasized the close bond that developed between personnel of their two navies and with the communities where they were based.[100]

Warships and Weapons

When the United States entered the war, it possessed a respectable navy. The force totaled 342 ships, including 37 battleships, 33 cruisers, and 66 destroyers. Many other vessels were under construction, which, when completed, were intended to make the United States a sea power "second to none." However, only a few were completed before the Armistice. Nonetheless, the Navy added 208 ships—87 private yachts, 39 tugboats, 8 tankers, 50 merchant ships, 12 passenger liners, and 12 fishing boats. The Navy also purchased or leased approximately 29,000 windjammers, motorboats, and barges. Several self-propelled barges purchased in England went to France and ferried troops from ship to shore. In addition, a crash shipbuilding program was initiated to provide destroyers and small antisubmarine craft such as the 110-foot subchasers. Finally, Coast Guard vessels were transferred to the Navy. By war's end, the Navy boasted 774 commissioned ships, more than doubling the total of April 1917. Of this number, 373 served in European waters.[1]

Initially, the Navy Department did not intend to send a powerful force of warships to the war zone. Its policy called for concentrating the fleet in American waters. Nonetheless, President Wilson's decision to order destroyers to British waters early in April 1917 inaugurated a steady build-up in European waters. The Department's policy of retaining most of the fighting force in the Western Hemisphere remained in place. More than half of the fleet either remained in home waters or escorted convoys. Throughout the war in all theaters American ships were in a minority, including antisubmarine craft that numbered more than two-thirds of the ships sent to European waters. In March 1918, 18 percent of the Navy's antisubmarine craft in commission were under Sims's command. By August, this had improved to 26.1 percent. In September, the Admiralty estimated that only 14 percent of the destroyers, 5 percent of the submarines, and 3 percent of patrol craft operating in British waters were American. The percentages for the Mediterranean were much lower. Two percent of destroyers and 3 percent of miscellaneous patrol craft in that sea were American, the remainder being British, French, Italian and Japanese.[2]

World War I, like other armed conflicts, was a proving ground for both ships and weapons. The employment of submarines was the most significant development in the naval war. The useful submarine was less than two decades old when the war broke out; although the major belligerents had submersibles, none were battle tested. Other ship types, especially destroyers, were first battle tested in World War I. Mine warfare was more extensive than in any previous conflict since the American Civil War. Technology and tactics evolved to combat the new weapons. Depth charges, Y guns, paravanes, and hydrophones, among others, were introduced in the naval war. The wartime use on board ship of telephones and radios (wireless) enhanced communication at sea. Many of these weapons and much of the equipment were in their initial stages of development. Little or no testing had been conducted under wartime conditions. It is also true, as Paul Kennedy has written, that operational policies based on these untried technologies often failed in combat.[3]

Even before the United States entered the war, the British had learned a great deal about the American navy's warships, weapons, tactics, and personnel, partly a result of the normal intelligence activities of naval attachés and observers and partly because of the conviction that the United States would eventually come to their assistance. In April 1917, British naval officials respected the American navy but recognized its inexperience and weaknesses.[4] Knowledge of U.S. warships increased significantly after several hundred American ships went to European waters. British and French officers and personnel freely visited the American ships. Although the older and converted vessels such as minelayers, gunboats, submarines, yachts, and even Coast Guard cutters attracted little but curiosity, the more modern destroyers and later the small wooden subchasers and battleships received serious attention. The tenders, repair ships, and the refrigerators, barber shops, and laundries found on some of the destroyers and larger ships impressed foreign officers. The cleanliness of the American ships surprised them. Considering wartime conditions, the Allied navies could be excused for neglecting the appearance of their ships. King George V noted after a visit to the Grand Fleet that the American flagship *New York* was "a most beautifully clean ship." When Admiral Sir Rosslyn Wemyss, the first sea lord, visited the U.S. destroyers at Queenstown in 1918, one of his staff wrote, "[The Americans] undoubtedly believe that cleanliness is next to godliness and that straight shooting and general efficiency go hand in hand with scrupulous cleanliness, which is, after all, only a form of discipline."[5]

American sailors were just as interested in the ships of the Allies, particularly the British. They were aware that living conditions, particularly for enlisted men, were much better on American ships. One officer told the General Board that "the impression that our ships have given to the officers who have seen both the British and U.S. ships is that we make the men more comfortable and they make the officers more comfortable." Generally, the Americans and British considered their modern ships as good as if not superior to those of the other.[6] At the same time, each navy discovered that the other had certain weapons, apparatus, machinery, communications, and structural features on their ships worthy of admiration or adoption. The British had the enormous experience of three-and-a-half years of combat, and the Americans took advantage of it.

The Americans soon adopted the British practice of camouflaging their ships. Although the concept of disguising ships by color schemes is centuries old, the British did not introduce it during World War I until 1917. At first, it was limited to merchant ships and antisubmarine craft, but in August 1918 a committee of the Admiralty recommended the application of camouflage to all vessels in the Royal Navy and merchant marine. British camouflage emphasized the "dazzle" design. Assuming that invisibility was impossible, the "dazzle" scheme aimed at deception. Various paint designs were supposed to distort a submariner's view. Initially, the U.S. Navy used the "dazzle" concept, but Secretary Daniels created a body to experiment with various designs, patterns, and paints. By the end of the war, the Navy had applied nearly five hundred different schemes. The majority were used on merchant ships and escorts, but specific designs were developed for submarines, subchasers, and even battleships.[7]

The six destroyers deployed in Irish waters in May 1917 were the first American warships to adopt the "dazzle" design. According to Commander Taussig, the colors used were white, black, two shades of blue, three shades of gray, green, and pink. One American officer, who observed the painting done in the British naval yard at Queenstown, wrote, "Our starboard side only is finished and looks like a dozen paint pots of different colors have . . . been capsized all over the ship." Marder is probably right in the assertion that "it is doubtful if any U-boat was ever deceived thereby, for you could not paint a false wake," but one U-boat commander admitted after the war that submarines might have been puzzled by this "mimicry."[8] The first U.S. warships to arrive in European waters and receive the "dazzle" scheme were the destroyers.

The World War I vintage destroyers trace their lineage directly to the *Smith* class begun in 1906 (716 tons, five 3-inch guns, four torpedo tubes, twenty-eight knots). They were the first destroyers labeled "flivvers" because of their light displacement. Between 1906 and 1911, the Navy built twenty-six of the "700-tonners" or "flivvers." They were enlarged to 742 tons and gained oil burners, greater fuel efficiency, more speed, greater range, and improved armaments.

In 1911, the General Board recommended the construction of a much larger class of destroyers, and Congress authorized eight vessels half again as large as the "flivvers," slightly over 1,000 tons. Beginning with *Cassin* (DD 43), twenty-five "1,000-tonners" were built. They displaced slightly over 1,100 tons and carried a main battery of four 4-inch guns and eight torpedo tubes. These turbine-powered, oil-fueled ships made nearly thirty knots, but, more important, they steamed 2,500 miles at twenty knots.

In 1915, Congress authorized another new class known as "flush deck destroyers" because of this architectural feature. They displaced approximately 1,200 tons and carried four 4-inch guns, a 3-inch anti-aircraft gun, and twelve torpedo tubes. Capable of reaching thirty-five knots under full steam, they were more seaworthy than their predecessors. Although 272 flush deckers, or "four pipers," were ordered, few of them reached European waters. The destroyers of the pre–World War I Navy were thought of as torpedo-boat destroyers. Originally designed for attack with torpedoes, destroyers eventually assumed the task of protecting the battle line, but in contrast to the destroyers of other navies, they continued to carry powerful torpedo armaments. Despite the experiences of the Allied and Entente destroyers during the first two years of the war, American counterparts continued to prepare for both defensive and offensive warfare. As a crew member of *McDougal* wrote, "In their own eyes, the [destroyer] crews were still torpedoboat sailors and called themselves that." Tactical exercises and maneuvers conducted before the war did not include antisubmarine warfare and convoying, their primary tasks during the war.[9]

The presence of U.S. destroyers with Allied naval forces led to comparisons of their vessels with those of the Allies, particularly with the British ships.[10] Admiralty officials and officers who examined or observed the American warships at sea were generally impressed with them. They commented favorably on their guns, machinery, and seaworthiness. Initially, however, British naval officials were concerned about the 1,000-tonners' and flivvers' sea-keeping qualities during the winter months. Admiral Bayly wrote to the first sea lord in October 1917: "I am afraid that the number of U.S. destroyers will not loom so large in the winter. They will not stand the weather like ours." Naval constructor Lewis McBride informed Sims that "The British boats being about 120 tons heavier . . . [than ours, will] undoubtedly result in a stiffer and stronger boat. . . . [T]here will arrive some stage of weather when the heavier British boat can be driven into a head sea at a higher speed than the lighter American boat."[11]

Much to their surprise, the U.S. destroyers, including the light flivvers, did extremely well in the winter months, weathering storms that kept British destroyers in port. "Tip" Merrill on *Conyngham* noted: "That night [November 14] we intercepted two W.T. messages from British destroyers to C-in-C saying the Irish Sea was too rough for Destroyers. None of our boats suffered." Two destroyers' commanding officers wrote to the Bureau of Construction and Repair that during the 1917–18 winter, "no American destroyers ever turned back or returned to port before the completion of assigned duty, except in cases of break down." The American destroyers could also remain longer at sea. British destroyers were designed to operate in the North Sea and waters close to home ports, whereas the American destroyers were built to serve on distant stations in the Pacific, Far East, and West Indies. However, the British destroyers were faster and more maneuverable. Their turning radius was far shorter than that of the Americans, a definite advantage in antisubmarine work. In testimony before the General Board, naval officers attributed the maneuverability of British destroyers to shorter hulls and flat sterns. One officer admitted: "It is quite probable that the reason our destroyers have only one definitely sunk German submarine to their credit in the war is . . . that they could not maneuver quickly enough. . . . This is not a case of quick acceleration of speed, which we now have, but of inability to turn."[12]

During 1917, the General Board held frequent hearings to consider improvements in destroyer design. Some of the recommendations were incorporated in the classes of flush deckers still on the drawing board, but surprisingly few changes stemmed from British designs. The most noticeable changes were the addition of a splinter shield for the bow guns; the placement of guns amidships carried on a raised platform, or "bandstand"; the addition of depth charges and Y guns; enclosure of the bridge; and strengthening of the bow. The latter improvement was a result of the amount of damage incurred by American destroyers in ramming or collisions. On the whole, however, the destroyers' wartime operations were, as one officer wrote, "highly specialized," Considerations that had determined the design of U.S. destroyers in the past should govern those in the future.[13]

The flush decker's design underwent certain modifications when they arrived in European waters. These included gun shields, ammunition boxes in proximity to the different deck guns, enclosed bridges with glass windows, captain's night cabin with bunk on the bridge or in the charthouse, additional girders forward of the bridge to strengthen the bow, depth-charge racks with hydraulic releases, shorter topmasts, crow's nests, cocoa matting on exposed decks to prevent slipping, and forced air ventilation in the forecastle.[14]

Four types of U.S. destroyers served in the war zone—the *Bainbridge* class, the flivvers, 1,000-tonners, and the flush deckers. In the fall of 1917, five of the 420-ton *Bainbridge* class, *Bainbridge*, *Barry*, *Chauncey*, *Dale*, and *Decatur* joined the patrol force at Gibraltar. Having served in the Philippines for several years, they were the oldest destroyers in the fleet, obsolete and barely seaworthy, but they valiantly escorted convoys in the Mediterranean.

The other three types received both acclaim and criticism. Both admirals Bayly and Sims considered the flivvers too small and to have insufficient fuel capacity to operate out of Queenstown and recommended their transfer elsewhere. Others claimed, however, that the 740-tonners generally were good vessels in the short, heavy seas during the winter off the Irish coast. The 1,000-tonners were rated high with both the British and Americans, especially their mechanical efficiency in the grueling convoy and patrol work in the Western Approaches. The American destroyers based at Queenstown, primarily the 1,000-tonners, spent 66 percent of their time at sea during the war. The British were impressed with the flush deckers, especially their speed, guns, and fire control system. Many of the naval officers who took command of them in the yards were disappointed, partly because of hasty and poor construction, and partly because of their performance. Admiral Carney later said, "I never did think much of them."[15] Nonetheless, American destroyers, regardless of the type, were the most desired U.S. warships in the war zone.

If the war had continued into 1919, Sims would have received new destroyers, but as it was he had to depend upon other types of vessels to escort convoys and conduct antisubmarine operations. Shortly after the United States entered the conflict, the Navy's deficiency in such vessels was recognized in the Department. Agents scoured the country in search of suitable craft, tugs, fishing boats, and oceangoing yachts. Large pleasure vessels were considered the most adaptable for combat purposes. Even before the United States entered the war, many of these vessels had been enrolled as a part of the reserve fleet. Later, when the yachts proved ill-fitted as warships, Daniels wrote: "[T]he truth is that I never signed a requisition for the purchase of any of these vessels except under protest because I knew they had not been constructed for the purpose for which we needed them but I appointed a board composed of three of the ablest civilians in the New York Yacht Club and three of our ablest officers to inspect them and buy those that were best. It was a case of either buying them or having no ships of that character to help us until our destroyer program could enable us to send much larger [ships]." Twenty-six yachts equivalent in size to destroyers were brought into the service during the war. Originally it was intended to employ them as patrol boats along the U.S. Atlantic coast, but the acute need for them in the war zone led to a change. Nearly all were deployed in the war zone, most of them in French waters.[16]

In April 1917, Secretary Daniels promised the French missions to the United States patrol craft as quickly as they were available. Yachts were the obvious solution.

Wealthy citizens owned these vessels, including J. P. Morgan, Vincent Astor, Mrs. E. H. Harriman, Frederick W. Vanderbilt, and J.W.C. Drexel. On May 8, five converted yachts, later increased to eight, were ordered to France. They were *Corsair*, *Aphrodite*, *Norma*, *Sultana*, *Vedette*, *Harvard*, *Christobel*, and *Kanawha II* (later *Piqua*). Two of them reached Brest on July 2. Seven more—*Alcedo*, *Remik*, *Wanderer*, *Guinevere*, *Corona*, *Carola IV*, and *Emeline*—arrived in the French port late in August. Others followed. Half of the first squadron of armed yachts to deploy to the war zone came from the New York Yacht Club. According to a war correspondent, a story "going around Brest" was about a junior officer gazing wishfully at one of the yachts. "'You look like you've seen that yacht before,' observed a brother officer. 'I have,' he replied. 'It was my Old Man's yacht before this war broke out.'"[17]

To fit out the yachts for war service, furnishings and decorations were shifted ashore, and carpenters removed the mahogany, teakwood, and oak panels, and added mountings for rifles on bulkheads. Plate glass windows were boarded up with storm shutters; berthing quarters for the crew were improvised by partitioning smoking rooms, libraries, and other compartments and building bunks, often in four tiers. The yachts that carried sails had their masts shortened or removed, and they received canvas-screened platforms or crow's nests. Bowsprits were also removed on *Corsair* and several others. The bows, quarterdecks, and fantails, with white pine decks, were covered with guns, depth-charge racks, and other paraphernalia of war. Galleys were enlarged to take care of crews more than three times the size of those in prewar days. The captains had the privilege of using the owner's quarters, while the ship's officers were assigned to other staterooms, more luxurious than those usually found on naval vessels. One of the yacht's captains gave a correspondent a tour of his command. "He led the way to the cabin—his cabin. 'lookit!' A four poster bed with brass legs! And lookit! A fireplace! . . . And lookit! My own private bathroom . . . and lookit!—a sunken marble tub! Who said it's a tough war?" The ships were painted navy gray and fitted out in various private and navy yards except for *Nahma*, which was transferred to the Navy at Glasgow and converted there. They received considerable attention from both the regular Navy and the public, acquiring names such as "suicide fleet" (flotilla), "tin fleet," "Easter egg flotilla," and "mosquito fleet abroad."[18] In the war zone, these vessels were used primarily as coastal escort, although two of them, *Kanawha II* and *Guinevere*, were converted to minesweepers. Eight yachts—*Arcturus*, *Cythera*, *Druid*, *Lydonia*, *Nahma*, *Surveyor*, *Venetia*, and *Wenona*—augmented the U.S. naval force operating out of Gibraltar. Because of their slowness, they were assigned to the Mediterranean as escorts.

The yachts were a mixed bag. Admiral Wilson said that they differed "materially from each other in size, seagoing qualities, and speed." They varied from *Corsair*, a large seagoing yacht capable of speeds up to eighteen knots, to *Christobel*, a small yacht of 248 tons that made at best nine knots. The majority of them, however, were too slow and light for antisubmarine work beyond coastal waters. Before leaving for Europe, they were strengthened to carry deck guns and small depth charges, but their fragility and slowness made them "unfit for the heavy duties assigned them." Some of them were so slow in anything but a moderate seaway that dropping a depth charge off the stern could seriously damage or even sink the vessel. More than one writer mentioned the story of a yacht skipper who decided to drop depth charges on a suspected U-boat. "'But sir,' protested the second in command, 'we are going so slow we might blow off our own stern.' 'All right, sonny,' answered the skipper; 'if we blow off our stern we'll bring in the bow. Drop 'em!'"[19] Regardless of their unfitness, by July 1918, seventeen converted yachts operated with the "Breton Patrol."

Writers wrote admiringly of these small improbable naval vessels, and sailors serving on other warships in the war zone often wrote or spoke sarcastically of the "joy" vessels, or "toy dreadnoughts." An officer on one of the destroyers out of Queenstown wrote of his brother on a yacht: "The yachtsman life on the French patrol based on Brest is pretty soft. They seem to think they have it hard to do three days out and three days in and anchor most of the day out and with a private bath for each officer. . . . Life is a dream. Of course they have to coal ship twice a week—rotten luck." Those who served on the yachts were at times just as critical. Frank Jack Fletcher, who became a well-known admiral in World War II, commanded the yacht *Margaret*, nicknamed *Maggie*. He considered his command a "nautical rubbish heap." John Mackenzie, who won the Medal of Honor while serving on a yacht, supposedly once remarked that the yacht was the most "damnable, wallowing, bucking, blistering craft I've ever laid eyes on . . . [a] misbegotten misguided hunk of cheese."[20]

Because of the desperate need for antisubmarine craft, twelve ancient New Jersey fishing vessels were converted into minesweepers. "When they outfitted these boats," one veteran recalled, "they [put] . . . all the stuff in a big gun and shot it at the hull. Then they loaded a machine gun with nails and bolts and shot that load after the first; and lo! out of chaos we have sweepers." Ten of the former fishing vessels were sent to French waters. Their equipment was so obsolete that the boats were useless until they were re-equipped.

At the beginning of the war, the Navy had only a rudimentary minesweeping organization of seven minesweeping tugs. These were retained on the east coast in case German submarines laid mines off various ports. As part of a contingency plan adopted before the war, fishing boats were purchased to strengthen the minesweeping fleet. Ten former "porgie boats," obtained in Norfolk and Philadelphia, were sent to Boston for refitting. These vessels were wooden with very little freeboard, approximately 160 feet in length, 25-foot beam, draft 14–15 feet with a displacement of about 450 tons. They departed the United States for France in August, but after an unsuccessful stint as escorts they were converted to minesweepers and organized as Squadron Four, Patrol Force.[21] Two sweepers, *Patapsco* and *Patuxent*, were also attached to the Mine Force based in northern Scotland.[22] The U.S. naval force in Scotland included ten minelayers.

The Admiralty was not impressed with the Navy Department's minesweeping policy. The few converted minesweepers deployed in European waters did not compare to the 646 in the Royal Navy. Under the Naval Construction Act of 1916, Congress appropriated funds for twelve new minesweepers, but they were still on the way in April 1917. They were designated as minesweeping tugs. Fifty-four additional sweepers were ordered in 1917, but they did not become available before the Armistice.[23]

Before 1911, the United States had no ship designated as a minelayer. Captain Cow-ie wrote, "In view of the fact that American ingenuity had been largely responsible for the pioneer development in mining technique, it is . . . somewhat remarkable that the year 1914 found the United States in much the same position as on the conclusion of the Civil War." Perhaps the American Navy's concept of mine warfare coincided with that of the British. Sir Eric Geddes once remarked, "Before the war, mine laying was considered unpleasant work for a naval man; an occupation like that of rat-catching, and not attractive."[24]

In 1908, the old cruiser *San Francisco* was ordered refitted as a "mine vessel." In 1912, she was designated a mine planter, the first of this type in the Navy. A year later, the Navy Department ordered a second vintage cruiser, *Baltimore*, converted to a minelayer. These two vessels could carry a combined capacity of 350 mines. They were the only mine planters in the Navy at the time the United States entered the war.

The decision by the American and British naval commands to lay a huge minefield in the North Sea during 1918 resulted in the deployment of the only two American minelayers to European waters, the converted cruisers *San Francisco* and *Baltimore*. Because of their limited mine-carrying capacity and the lack of British mine vessels, the U.S. Navy had to provide additional mine-laying ships. Eight former freighters were obtained from the U.S. Shipping Board. All of them had been involved in coast-al trade. They were redesigned to carry as many mines as possible on either two or three decks. Elevators were installed to lift the mines to the "launching" deck, where tracks transported them to large passageways cut in the stern. The mines were then dropped overboard to the rear. All of the converted minelayers were armed with a 5-inch gun on the afterdeck and two 3-inch guns on the forecastle. Four vessels were renamed *Roanoke*, *Housatonic*, *Canandaigua*, and *Cononicus*. They displaced over 4,600 tons and were 391 feet long with 48-foot beams and 20-foot drafts. Each carried from 800 to 850 mines. Two Old Dominion passenger vessels were renamed *Quin-neburg* and *Saranac*. They displaced only 3,700 tons and were in poor condition. The commanding officer of *Quinneburg* recalled years later that she had "canvas-covered decks like a ferryboat and all her internal fittings were of wood. . . . As her engines were completely shot, she had been retired from service." *Saranac* was in equally bad shape. Their hulls, much lighter in construction than the freighters, had to be signifi-cantly strengthened. Two Eastern Steamship Corporation ships, renamed *Shawmut* and *Aroostook*, displaced over 4,700 tons. Captain Belknap mentioned that a naval constructor who surveyed the two vessels recommended against them as "too light," but he disagreed, arguing that they had been built strongly enough to go around Cape Cod, and the Department finally agreed to their conversion. When recommissioned as mine planters, they carried three hundred mines each. The vessels finally reached Scotland early in July.[25]

In May 1917, the Admiralty inaugurated convoying from the British Isles to Gibral-tar. The British wanted to extend convoying to the Mediterranean but could not do so without the assistance of American warships. On June 7, Admiral Jellicoe appealed to the Navy Department for light cruisers and other escort types to be based at Gibraltar. A month later, the Navy Department agreed to deploy three light cruisers of the *Ches-*

ter class and six old gunboats. Shortly afterward, Daniels sent some of the converted yachts and six Coast Guard vessels.[26]

In 1915, Congress combined the Revenue-Cutter Service and the Life-Saving Service to form the United States Coast Guard. The act specified that the Coast Guard would operate as a part of the Navy in time of war or "when so directed by the President." In March 1917, when conflict with Germany appeared imminent, naval and Coast Guard officers drew up a mobilization plan. On April 6, 1917, all forty-seven Coast Guard vessels and their personnel were incorporated into the Navy.[27] This act made a large number of vessels available for refitting as antisubmarine craft. Late in July 1917, six of the larger cutters—*Ossipee, Seneca, Yamacraw, Algonquin, Manning,* and *Tampa*—were ordered to the war zone.

These vessels were comparable in size and tonnage to the 1,000-ton destroyers. However, they were considerably slower, with the fastest, *Algonquin,* making at best sixteen knots. To outfit them for wartime service, the Navy installed additional guns and depth-charge gear. The six cutters arrived at Gibraltar in August, September, and October at the rate of two per month and were designated as a squadron of the patrol force.[28]

Gibraltar became the operational base for a hodgepodge of American warships, including the oldest and weakest of those deployed to European waters during the war. In addition to the Coast Guard cutters, the motley collection included gunboats, cruisers, yachts, and some of the oldest destroyers in the fleet. Of the three light cruisers originally assigned to Gibraltar, only two, *Birmingham* (CL 2) and *Chester* (CL 1), were deployed in European waters. These two 3,700-ton cruisers were the fastest and most powerful American warships operating out of Gibraltar, serving as escort of ocean convoys, primarily to the British Isles.

Six old gunboats, slow and poorly armed—*Wheeling, Marietta, Machias, Nashville, Paducah,* and *Castine*—were assigned to the Gibraltar command. They joined the converted yachts and older destroyers as escorts for Mediterranean convoys. A seventh gunboat, *Sacramento,* was new, having been launched in 1914. Although *Sacramento* attained a speed of only twelve knots, she was used as an ocean escort out of Gibraltar.

The British were more critical of the Gibraltar-based American vessels, particularly those assigned to duties in the Mediterranean Sea, than any of the others operating with their naval forces. Admiral Niblack used his best ships, the cutters and cruisers, to escort Atlantic convoys, allocating the older, least seaworthy vessels, such as the 420-ton destroyers and gunboats, to the Mediterranean. Although the number of ships in the Gibraltar command was impressive, by December 1917 only about a third of them, twenty-five to thirty, were capable of challenging the German submarines. Even the two cruisers were rated third-class. In June 1918, the commanding officer of the gunboat *Marietta* sent a memo to Sims, detailing British criticism of the Gibraltar force. "One of the most common criticisms," he wrote, "was the slowness of American vessels . . . therefore their uselessness for escort duties." One British commander remarked, "I do not see of what earthly use such ships as yours are against submarines, you are out-gunned and you could never overtake a Hun." Admiral Sims admitted to these deficiencies but pointed out that the scarcity of antisubmarine craft in the U.S. Navy necessitated the deployment of these vessels to Gibraltar. In March, Niblack reported to the force commander that a third of his vessels were not operational because of breakdowns. On one occasion, the Gibraltar base commander held a conference of his ship captains and "tersely remarked that if there were not so many ships undergoing repairs he could not have had so many Commanding Officers present for a conference."[29] Neither Rear Admiral H. S. Grant, in command of British naval forces in Gibraltar, nor the Admiralty complained to American officials about the Gibraltar-based vessels; they were delighted to have them there.

During the last months of the war, the Navy began to shift some modern destroyers to the Mediterranean to replace older ones and to assign a division of the newly constructed wooden submarine chasers. The chasers were sent to the Mediterranean after much deliberation by the Navy Department, the Admiralty, the Allied Naval Council, and Sims and his staff.

After the early successes of the German U-boats, the British Admiralty began to commandeer fishing vessels, private yachts, and other small boats to support coastal convoying and antisubmarine operations. These craft were poorly fitted for this work. In 1915, the Admiralty contracted with the Electric Launch Company (ELCO) of Bayonne, New Jersey, for several hundred motor launches (MLs) especially designed for antisubmarine patrol. The ELCO-designed boats were wooden-hulled and initially 75 feet in length, but the more popular version was 80 feet long. ELCO MLs, popular with their crews, proved valuable in the waters around the British Isles and in French and Italian coastal waters.[30]

The success of these vessels prompted the United States Navy to follow suit. The Navy began to accumulate data on pleasure craft and other private vessels suitable for incorporation into the Navy and also began to develop a design for a wooden patrol craft. At that time, naval officials were concerned about protecting American waters. Assistant Secretary of the Navy Franklin D. Roosevelt strongly advocated construction of a fleet of small boats for coastal patrol. In February 1917, he held a conference with various bureau chiefs and other naval officials on shipbuilding, including the construction of small craft. The assistant secretary recommended 50-foot vessels as standard patrol craft for coastal waters, but the Bureau of Construction and Repair determined that both the 50-foot boat and the 80-foot ELCO launch were too small for the Navy's needs.

Instead, the Navy adopted a design by A. Loring Swesey, at that time vice president of the Herreshoff Manufacturing Company, the premier oceangoing power yacht firm in the United States. The design called for a flush-decked wooden-hulled vessel, 110 feet in length with a displacement of 75 tons to be powered by three gasoline engines of 220 horsepower. The Navy preferred a speed of seventeen knots, but, after they were loaded with fuel and ammunition, they made a maximum speed of only fifteen knots. Armament would later vary, but those that were deployed in European waters usually carried a 3-inch gun, two machine guns, and a Y gun for depth charges, as well as two depth-charge racks. In March 1917, before the United States entered the war, contracts were let for 355 of these subchasers, or SCs, as they were designated. The first was launched in May and commissioned early in August.[31]

No type of American naval vessel used in World War I received more publicity than the wooden subchasers. Their apparent fragility, difficult living and working conditions, nonregular Navy crews, and supposed successes captured the imagination of the American public. Stories about them appeared in newspapers, national magazines, and yachting and professional journals. They were called "sea terriers," "Cinderellas of the fleet," "the splinter fleet," and "sea fleas." At first, American naval officers expressed considerable skepticism as to their worth and usefulness. One officer who commanded a squadron of the subchasers wrote after the war, "when the 110 footers first came out—even before they were finished, in fact—a strong prejudice against them developed in the Navy and they were pretty freely condemned." Joe Taussig told the General Board that "they would not be of any use far from shore." The General Board agreed, giving its opinion that "the 110 [foot] subchaser is too small for an efficient offshore service against submarines," adding that the type was "adopted only as an emergency measure." Distrust of them among the officer corps continued long after they had proved their seaworthiness. Commander Babcock reported while on a trip to Washington: "As to the submarine chasers. . . . Boiled down, I might say that very few [in the Navy Department] have taken them seriously. No one apparently knew just what they were going to be used for, and many people responsible for their progress believed them to be practically useless." Sims had doubts, writing in July 1917: "I am sorry that so much emphasis has been put on building 110-foot boats. These are not able to keep on the sea if there is any weather and it would be much better to expend our energies on boats which would be really useful in these waters." He later recognized their utility but remained critical of their "submarine chasing."[32]

British officials were just as skeptical as their American counterparts. Sir Maurice Hankey, a member of the British War Cabinet, considered them "useless" and recommended that the cabinet use its influence to prevent the Americans from "wasting their resources on the construction of unsuitable classes of vessels for anti-submarine warfare." Admiral De Chair, a member of the Balfour Mission to the United States, visited the Brooklyn Navy Yard, where he observed "a dozen" chasers under construction. "They appear too small for their [designated] work," he reported to the Admiralty. Admiralty officials generally concurred. Captain Sir William Fisher, the director of the Anti-Submarine Division (DASD) opposed them, writing that he "was largely influenced by the unofficial remarks of U.S. Officers over here who think little of these craft. They were built, I understand, as an answer to any popular demand that might arise as a result of submarines operating on American coasts." Nonetheless, Admiral Mayo returned to the United States from his first mission to the war zone with a British request that the first seventy-two of these craft be sent to operate "more or less [in] . . . the waters of England and the North Sea." When Admiral Benson met with the first sea lord in November, he agreed to honor Mayo's recommendation. The French, desperate for coastal craft, also wanted these craft. The Wilson administration, unable to supply the French with all of the promised destroyers, agreed to sell them some of the subchasers. French naval personnel manned the first seventeen subchasers to cross the Atlantic. They arrived in December, and their performance led them to request additional chasers. Fifty were turned over to the French navy.[33]

By the middle of July, 41 subchasers operated out of Plymouth, including 6 originally assigned for "experimental work" and an additional 25 underway from the United States to Queenstown. In September, 102 American-manned subchasers had arrived in European waters, 35 operating with the Allied forces on the Otranto Barrage, 41 at Plymouth, and 36 at Queenstown and in the Irish Sea. The department promised 44 more, but the activities of German submarines in American waters delayed their deployment. Counting those turned over to the French navy, 170 of the 110-foot wooden subchasers were deployed in European waters during the war.[34]

The quality of these craft was debated during and after the war. Construction varied during the emergency of war. Many were built hastily of green timber with structural problems. Others were soundly built. They proved generally too slow for convoy work, especially in any but calm water. They rolled easily and without restraint even in moderate swells. They were wet sailers. As the surgeon general wrote, "[T]he thin wooden decks and hulls [were] penetrated by small amounts of water in any but the calmest weather." Their gasoline engines were also guzzlers, their cruising radius with one engine being approximately six hundred miles, half that with all three at work. They were notoriously hard on their small crews of two officers and twenty-four enlisted personnel. Ventilation below deck was poor, and gas fumes developed when underway. Some crew members suffered gas poisoning. A coal stove provided heat, which was most inadequate for those serving in the English Channel and Irish Sea. Fire on board ship was a serious threat on the wooden chasers. Fires broke out, but none of the vessels deployed in the war zone were seriously damaged or put out of operation. They carried only a small load of depth charges. Nonetheless, they were excellent "sea boats," much to the surprise of many senior officers. After the war, old salts raved about their seaworthiness, as did the small boat veterans and yachtsmen who "officered" most of them.[35]

The Allies were generally impressed with them. A French report stated that the ones they had received were "better than expected, and have proven themselves remarkable." The Italians, who had a well-deserved reputation in naval small craft, thought highly of them. The British reluctantly recognized their worth in the war zone, particularly in submarine hunting groups, but an Admiralty memo prepared shortly before the Armistice concluded, "these craft appear to require considerable structural improvement before they can be regarded as good sea boats." Although they did not destroy any U-boats, the Germans considered them a nuisance.[36]

Of the 440 subchasers launched during the war, several were lost at sea through fire, collision, running aground, enemy action, but none were lost because of stressful weather.

In March 1918, the Navy Department informed the Admiralty that a hundred of the "Ford Destroyers" were to be assigned to European waters. Called "eagle boats," these 200-foot antisubmarine craft were built at the manufacturing facilities of Henry Ford near Detroit, Michigan. They were a compromise between the larger, more sophisticated destroyers and the smaller, wooden-hulled subchasers. They were quickly built of steel. Sixty were completed, but only eight of them before the Armistice, and none reached the war zone before the end of the fighting.[37]

The U.S. Navy's neglect of undersea warfare before 1917 was not only in ASW craft and weapons but also in submarines. The submarine service was an orphan as far as the rest of the fleet was concerned. Submarines were considered "playthings" of little use to the surface Navy. Ironically, an American, John Holland, built the first workable submarine. The *SS 1*, commissioned in the Navy in 1900, was a *Holland* type. Gradually the number increased until by 1917 forty-four were in commission. Although the later boats were a significant improvement over the early *Holland* designs, they were small, underpowered, weakly armed, and intended as coastal defense vessels. They had serious deficiencies in torpedoes, deck guns, communication equipment, periscopes, living conditions, and engines. The *K* and *L* types, which made up all but one of the American submarines deployed in the war zone, had workable periscopes but poor magnification and focus and other problems. The engines were notoriously undependable. The diesel engines installed in the submarines built after 1910 were poor in design, workmanship, and quality, and generally remained so until after the war, when American naval constructors had an opportunity to examine German U-boat engines.

When the first five submarines reached the Azores, Admiral Herbert Dunn, in command of U.S. naval forces there, cabled London: "Condition of submarines here is such that successful operation against enemy vessels could not be carried out. Engines except USS *E-1* are unreliable, bow rudders practically useless." An Admiralty report concluded in August 1917, "good reason to believe that no class of U.S. submarines [are] . . . really satisfactory."[38] They clearly were far inferior to German and even British submarines. Although none of the American submarines operational in 1917 was capable of offensive operations, the British nonetheless requested that they be sent to European waters.

By the time the United States entered the war, the Royal Navy had achieved some success in the use of submarines against submarines. The Allies restricted their operations to designated areas to avoid surface vessels patrolling for U-boats. The inauguration of convoying with the reduction of patrolling persuaded Admiral Sims on June 2, 1917, to recommend the dispatch of American submarines to the war zone. He was convinced, as he testified after the war, that the "submarine was the most effective of all means of attacking and destroying a submarine." Although the European force commander complained that months passed before the Department agreed to send submarines to European waters, Admiral Benson responded promptly to Sims's recommendation.[39]

Three types of American submarines were based in the war zone, four of the *K* class and one *E* boat (*E 1*) at Ponta Delgada, Azores, and seven of the *L* class at Berehaven, Bantry Bay. The four *K* boats (*Ks 1, 2, 5,* and *6*) displaced 392 tons, 153 feet 7 inches in length, 16-foot 8-inch beam, and carried eight torpedoes and four launching tubes. *E 1* was even smaller. Launched in 1912, she was 135 feet 3 inches in length, a 14-foot 7-inch beam, and displaced 287 tons. She carried only four torpedoes for her four tubes. The seven *L* class (*Ls 1, 2, 3, 4, 9, 10*, and *11*) were all commissioned in 1916. They displaced 450 tons and were 167 feet in length with a 17-foot beam. They carried eight torpedoes and four launching tubes and a 3/23-inch deck gun. The *L* boats deployed in European waters were designated *AL* to avoid confusing them with British *L* class submarines. Regardless of class, they were unsuited for antisubmarine operations in the ocean. They were slow, ventilation was inadequate, periscopes were inferior, and they rolled heavily in any but extremely calm weather.[40] German submarines were larger, better armed, and overall much superior boats.

In December 1917, four battleships flying the Stars and Stripes—*Delaware, Wyoming, Florida*, and *New York*—joined the British Grand Fleet at Scapa Flow, the first of nine American battleships to serve in European waters during the war. *Texas* and *Arkansas* also joined the Grand Fleet, the latter replacing *Delaware*. In September 1918, three battleships—*Nevada, Oklahoma*, and *Utah*—were based at Bantry Bay until the Armistice was signed. *Delaware*, commissioned in 1909, displaced 20,000 tons. Considered by some the first dreadnought in the U.S. Navy, she carried a battery of ten 12-inch guns and a secondary battery of 5-inch guns. *Delaware*'s sister ship, *North Dakota*, was the first U.S. battleship powered by turbines. Six of the battleships sent to European waters during the war were turbine-powered; the sister ships *New York* and *Texas* had reciprocating engines. Twenty to twenty-one knots was the design speed for American dreadnought battleships, including those sent to European waters, but all of them could do better under flank speed. *Florida* claimed to be the fastest battlewagon in the fleet, but other ships disputed the claim. All but the two *Nevada*s were coal burners. *Nevada* and *Oklahoma* were the first oil-burning battleships in the American Navy. Each succeeding class of two battleships was considered an improvement on the previous class. They were larger, with displacements from 21,825 tons of the two *Utah*s to 27,500 tons for the *Nevada*s. Each succeeding class was armored and armed more heavily than its predecessors. Although *Nevada* at 575 feet in length (waterline) was 65 feet longer than the *Delaware* and *Utah* classes, their configuration or silhouette was generally the same. The number and location of gun turrets was the most noticeable difference.

Battlewagons were gun platforms, designed to engage an enemy at long range. *Utah* and *Florida*, launched in 1909–10, carried ten 12-inch guns in their main batteries, but *Arkansas* and *Wyoming*, launched in 1911, mounted the largest number of main battery turrets in a U.S. battleship, six turrets, each with two 12-inch guns. *New York* and *Texas,* launched in 1912, were the first American ships to carry 14-inch guns (ten each) in their main batteries. Two pairs of turrets were superimposed fore and aft, an arrangement that remained the standard battleship design for thirty-five years. *Nevada* and *Oklahoma*, launched in 1914, also carried ten 14-inch guns, three each in the extreme forward and after turrets and two each in the others. This class was the first in the U.S. Navy to have three-gun turrets, a design feature that became standard with the *Pennsylvania* and *Arizona*, launched in 1915. Although American dreadnoughts did not carry large batteries of various caliber guns, they had secondary batteries of 5-inch guns and anti-aircraft guns. The secondary battery was expected to protect capital ships from attacks by torpedo craft. The number of 5-inch guns varied from twelve in the *Utah* class to sixteen in the *Arkansas* and *New York* classes. The anti-air-craft gun was first installed on American warships in 1916, and each of the battleships received two 3-inch guns. American dreadnoughts also carried torpedo tubes.[41] Other differences existed such as the armor belt, location of the small boats, and interior arrangement, but these characteristics generally had no effect on the ship's performance during the war.

The cage or basket-latticed masts were the most distinctive features on American battlewagons during World War I. Although not totally unique to U.S. capital ships, they became a trademark. When the Sixth Battle Squadron steamed into Scapa Flow to join the Grand Fleet, many British sailors remarked on the unusual masts. These masts (usually two) were made of a network of intertwined metal tubing reinforced at intervals by steel rings that formed a cone-shaped tower. At various times the masts held searchlights, radio wires, range finders and fire control apparatus, signal yardarms, and even stationary lights both fore and aft to help ships keep in the line at night. These masts became standard starting with the *South Carolina* class, launched in 1908.[42]

The presence of the U.S. battleships with the Grand Fleet led to comparisons, official and unofficial, in both navies. Considerable debate occurred over the cage masts versus the British tripod masts. Everything was examined, from mast height and strength to the effect of gunfire and vibration while underway. Both the Admiralty and the Navy Department weighed changes. In time, both decided that each mast type had both strengths and weaknesses, and neither navy made a major change. In 1930, the U.S. Navy abandoned the cage masts.[43]

The Americans quickly discovered that some of their equipment, component parts, guns, and procedures did not work well in the North Sea under wartime conditions. The bridges on British battleships were completely enclosed, armored, and considerably larger than those on the American capital ships. Temporary canvas was used to enclose the bridges of the American warships. This measure did not protect bridge personnel from enemy fire, but it helped to deal with foul weather. Later the ships were rotated into yards, and permanent enclosed bridges were installed. After inspecting a British battleship, Admiral Rodman ordered the radio "shack," which also housed the telephone equipment, moved to a deck below the armor belt for better protection.[44]

Guns and gunnery attracted considerable observation and evaluation. Before the American battleships joined the Grand Fleet, American naval officers visited Admiral Beatty's command. According to Sims, two officers attached to the Bureau of Engineering told him that "in their opinion they should get back to America as soon as possible, and tell our people about the number of things they found in the Grand Fleet in which we are very distinctly inferior. This includes such fundamentally important things as fire control, concentration [of fire] and so forth." The Americans considered their powder, armor-piercing shells, and fuses superior to the British, but they were most impressed with the British star shells used to provide illumination at night. The secondary batteries on the American battleships were useless in the rough waters of the North Sea. They were mounted "tween" decks and below the main deck, a design flaw because they often could not be used in rough weather. Admiral Rodman wrote, "Our gun deck was flooded in our last run, to such an extent that not only were the guns useless, but the ports had to be kept closed to keep the water from flooding the gun deck." Unlike the British guns, the American 5-inch guns were not provided with spray shields. Admiral Rodman reported that *New York* could fire only two of her secondary guns while underway, and the commanding officer of *Texas* declared that while serving with the Grand Fleet he manned only two of his ship's 5-inch guns and two AA guns mounted on boat cranes. The range finders located on the top of turrets were also affected by the weather and had to be relocated.[45] The British agreed with American claims that the electrically operated centerline turrets on the U.S. battleships were more efficient than the British hydraulic turrets. An Admiralty report admitted that "The U.S. type of turret mountings enable the Americans to have the advantage of very considerable economics of weight and space as compared with British practice." Listing the absence of a shell room, hydraulic machinery, and other appendages, the reporters stated: "The above has a most important effect on the design of a ship as a whole, enabling either a larger armament to be obtained on a given weight or the weight saved to be utilized in some other direction. British designs of capital ships must appear at a disadvantage as compared with those of the U.S. on this account." Vice Admiral McCrea, who as a lieutenant was a turret officer on *New York*, insisted that the American turrets were better constructed: "if a shell hit the roof of the turret of a British ship, there was nothing to stop that shell going right straight through to the bottom . . . whereas our turrets were greatly subdivided . . . and I thought in that respect that we were much better, ship for ship."[46]

Considerable discussion arose over the quality of fire control systems.[47] Continuous aim firing was introduced in both the American and British navies during the first decade of the twentieth century, along with the necessary technology such as range finders, range keeper, plotting boards, range clock, and improved shipboard communications. The American fire control system, although based on the British model, was different in some respects. The two navies used different range keepers, although the American Ford range keeper was probably based on the British Pollen model. The British director controlled main battery fire from a tower, whereas the Americans used a plotting room in the ship's interior. The British placed a large range finder atop a mast, whereas the Americans installed several atop the turrets. The British system was far more automated than the American system, which placed heavy responsibility upon spotters and other gunnery personnel. Both claimed that their system was superior, but the American system was "not nearly as developed." Finally, the American battleship division gunnery officer deemed the American fire control system "awkward, slow, inaccurate under favorable conditions, and liable to be fatally so in the stress of battle."[48] American observers were impressed that the Royal Navy had developed salvo firing with its secondary batteries, utilizing directors located in towers. The U.S. battleships operating with the Grand Fleet could not use this method because of the location of their secondary batteries. The British also installed fire control systems in their smaller craft, including destroyers. In the summer of 1917, the

U.S. Navy began to place range keepers on cruisers and destroyers and later adopted directors.[49]

The British and American battleships made different interior arrangements. American officers admired the British ships' watertight integrity, particularly on the berthing decks. A British report on the *New York* concluded that it had "too many watertight doors especially at the ends of the ship." The doors were "closed at sea but in the event of damage they would inevitably leak if the bulkheads were strained and the water tightness of the ship would be seriously jeopardized."[50]

British observers frequently noted the presence of far more workshops, storerooms, and offices in American than in British battleships. They recognized that the U.S. ships were designed to function at sea in distant waters for long periods without access to repair yards and supply depots. British ships, however, were designed to operate close to their logistical facilities or to utilize the floating storeships that remained with the fleet. The British believed that the amount of space used for these purposes was excessive and limited effectiveness. Enlisted personnel messing arrangements were entirely different. The British messed by divisions in their living compartments, whereas the Americans designated spaces as "mess decks" for meals. Living conditions for American personnel impressed the British seamen who visited the American battlewagons. Showers, barbershops, laundries, bakeries, galleys with an assortment of appliances, and a dentist office all received acclaim. British officers, however, were not as laudatory, considering them "luxuries." They used too much water, too much electricity, and too much fuel. Their ventilation and heating systems, if damaged, could be detrimental to the ship's watertight integrity. "The seaman's head, on most of the British capital ships," one U.S. Naval officer pointed out, "is somewhat primitive, simply a trough with running water and a plank to sit on." Nevertheless, British officials defended their ships, at least the most modern ones, insisting that they were comparable to the Americans' in living conditions, ventilation, and sanitation. Their reports stressed the difficulties of providing such luxuries in a fighting ship. A committee of U.S. officers compared British and American ships shortly after the Armistice and claimed "that it was indisputable and cannot be gainsaid that the living conditions of the crews of the US ships are above comparison with those . . . in the British Service, and are second to none whatever. . . . The general impression of the Committee is that the British, at least theoretically, lay more emphasis upon the fighting qualities of their ships, while we lay an added stress upon the daily life of the ship."[51]

A number of other differences attracted attention. The American battleships with the Grand Fleet were coal burners, whereas Admiral Beatty had both coal- and oil-fueled capital ships. The radio and signal systems were quite different. The Americans used gyrocompasses, whereas the British preferred magnetic compasses. Admiral Beatty's staff was surprised to discover that American crews were not outfitted with metal helmets. A limited number of them were turned over to the Sixth Battle Squadron.[52] All U.S. naval vessels encountered these differences wherever they cooperated with the Allies. In addition, mines, torpedoes, depth charges, and the entire inventory of naval guns differed in size from those of the Allies. The British attempted to refit American ships with gear and equipment but found it difficult to "mate" American and British parts.[53]

American ships were not equipped with paravanes to cut moored mines. A British invention, the paravane was a metal device shaped like a "fish" or torpedo. Fitted with a rudder, fins, and steel teeth, they were attached to cables that towed them underwater on both sides of a ship. When the wire contacted a mine, the mine slid along the wire until the mooring teeth cut the mooring. Gunfire destroyed the mines when they floated to the surface. British battleships with the Grand Fleet were fitted with paravanes, and Beatty insisted on installing them on the American ships. In May 1917, the Admiralty provided working drawings of the paravane to the Navy Department. The Department developed different types, but those designed for the battleships were evidently not as efficient as the British ones. The *Texas* was the first American warship to stream a paravane manufactured in the United States. Both *Texas* and *Arkansas* were refitted with British paravanes after arriving in Scotland. Although warships operating with the Atlantic Fleet and those assigned to escort duty were equipped with paravanes, few American vessels deployed in European waters other than the battleships with the Grand Fleet received paravanes. Sims agreed with his flotilla commander at Queenstown that paravanes should not be attached to destroyers because they interfered with the use of depth charges.[54]

American battleships carried torpedoes, as did destroyers, submarines, and a few older vessels operating from Gibraltar. In April 1917, the Navy had an inventory of 2,096 torpedoes. Approximately half were carried on board the ships. The standard 18-inch Mark VII (MK 7) torpedoes were carried on the 750-ton destroyers and the E, L, O, and K submarine classes. The 1,000-tonners and flush deck destroyers carried the 21-inch Mark VIII (MK 8), as did the submarines built during the war. Although the British torpedoes were considered superior to the American version, no U.S. vessel in the war zone switched to them. As it happened, no American vessel fired a torpedo at an enemy during the war. Disuse led to rusting in the tubes. Heavy seas created difficulties, although a member of Sims's staff maintained that, when destroyers rolled and pitched, the tubes on destroyers did not dip in the water. The gunnery officers on the battleships with the Grand Fleet wanted to remove their torpedoes, but Admiral Beatty denied the request.[55]

The British originally developed the depth charge, or "ash can," as the weapon became known in the American Navy. They were steel cylinders filled with high explosives and fitted with a simple firing mechanism. After they were launched from a surface ship, the pressure of water set them off at designated depths. Depth charges were first used in combat in 1915. At that time, their effectiveness was severely curtailed because of their scarcity. Although production had increased by the time the United States entered the conflict, they were rationed throughout the rest of the war.[56] The United States Navy showed little interest in depth charges until a few months before the intervention of April 1917. In February, the Navy produced a small depth "bomb" of fifty pounds. A destroyer officer recalled that "There were no arrangements to launch them, and ships picked the strongest man in the crew to heave them over the stern when attacking a suspected periscope, oil slick, or unsuspecting whale." Admiral Carney called them "firecrackers, which wouldn't hurt you much if they went off." The American destroyers deployed to Ireland in May 1917 carried a few of the 50-pound charges, as did the yachts that reached French waters in the summer. They were quickly discarded as useless in favor of the British depth charges loaded with three hundred pounds of explosives. The American destroyers were fitted with racks located on the stern to house the charges, which were armed manually. A hydraulic system rolled them into the water. Commander Taussig stated that "most of us had not even heard that there were such things" as depth-charge racks. Like the British, the Americans initially were allotted only four per vessel, but by the middle of 1918, American destroyers carried up to twenty-four of the heavy explosives. The destroyers operating with hunting groups carried up to a hundred of the charges. American sailors had no experience with depth charges and at first were wary of dropping them out of fear of damaging their ship.[57]

None of the depth charges were totally effective. The American 50-pounders often failed to sink. The British charges were far more effective against submarines but were somewhat unstable and subject to premature explosion. In August 1918, a charge dropped from USS *Orizaba* exploded off the stern, killing a sailor and injuring nineteen. With specifications provided by the Admiralty, the Bureau of Ordnance began working on a more powerful depth charge. For reasons of "conformity," the bureau adopted the British-type container. Although they looked alike and weighed the same, there were differences. The American firing mechanism was a distinct improvement over the British one. The American charges were much safer. Nevertheless, at times they failed to explode. Both the Americans and British continued to improve their depth charges, each navy benefiting from the work of the other. In the fall of 1918, the U.S. Navy developed a 600-pound charge, which was manufactured but never used during the war.[58]

The potential of depth charges in antisubmarine warfare was readily understood, but until the fall of 1917, they were not very efficient. The weapons had to be improved to be effective, and the tactics of their use required development. The tactic generally used in the British and later the American navies was to drop one or two depth charges where a submarine was supposed to have submerged. This procedure rarely worked because the submarine easily moved. The charge had to strike the target and explode to damage or sink it. The British conducted experiments that proved that the more "cans" dropped over a geographical area as broad as possible, the more effective the weapons. Larger racks were introduced to carry up to thirteen depth charges on the stern of a vessel, and to provide a "spread," the British developed the Thornycroft Thrower, a kind of mortar. With two racks mounted on the stern and two throwers situated to fire the charges on each side of the vessel, an attacking vessel could fire a barrage of four. The Navy's Bureau of Ordnance also developed a kind of depth-charge thrower, the Y gun. The American version had two tubes or barrels at an angle of forty-five degrees from vertical. Mounted on the centerline near the stern, they threw two standard 300-pound depth charges in opposite directions at the same time. They were first installed in December 1917.[59]

Depending on the type of vessel and the availability of the different depth charges, an American antisubmarine vessel in the war zone could include any and all in its inventory. Some of the destroyers operating out of Queenstown carried racks, two Thornycroft Throwers, and a Y gun, enabling them to fire a barrage of six charges simultaneously. The wooden subchasers were fitted with two racks to carry ten charges and a Y gun. Torpedo tubes and guns located on the stern were removed to make room for the racks and throwers. In contrast to the Royal Navy, the U.S. Navy put more priority on the use of mines as a means of defeating the U-boats.

In 1916, the Department decided to establish a mine force by converting several old vessels to minelayers. At that time, the Navy did not have an acceptable standard mine. In 1917, the Navy's inventory of mines consisted of a few obsolete French-designed Mark IIs, and approximately 5,000 Mark III contact mines. The Mark IIIs were designed in Britain but built in the United States under contract with Vickers. They frequently malfunctioned; one out of every three mines exploded prematurely. The Bureau of Ordnance decided to develop its own mine that could be mass produced and that would explode whether or not the submarine made contact with it.

Although the Navy created a mine warfare program, very few in the service interested themselves in it, but the mine section of the Bureau of Ordnance was an exception. It concluded that a minefield laid across the North Sea from Scotland to Norway to block the entrance of German submarines to the ocean could play a major role in the defeat of the enemy. The difficulty was that existing contact mines were inadequate for use on such a minefield. A possible solution came in May, when Ralph Browne, an electrical engineer from the Massachusetts Institute of Technology, proposed the use of electricity to fire an underwater gun. The underwater gun proved impractical, but the section decided that the concept might be applied to a mine. Over the next few months, the mine section gradually put together a mine built around Browne's electrical device, which became the trigger or gun that exploded the mine. Although tests were conducted on individual parts of the mine such as the canister and firing mechanism, no comprehensive tests were carried out on a fully assembled mine before it went into production. In July, the mine, designated Mark VI (MK 6), proved so successful that in October the Department received permission to acquire a hundred thousand more.[60]

The Bureau of Ordnance was under pressure to develop a plan that would produce large numbers of mines quickly. It turned to the automobile industry for guidance. The bureau decided to apply the mass production techniques familiar to American industry but not to the Navy. The elements that made up the mine-firing mechanism—extender mechanism, mine case, anchor, antenna system, horn device, release gear, and buoy—were all engineered separately. Different concerns manufactured them and shipped them to a depot in Virginia for assemblage. The mines were then shipped overseas.[61]

The Mark VI mine was spherical in shape. It carried a canister of three hundred pounds of TNT and the firing mechanism. A copper antenna linked the firing gear with a buoy or float that was positioned just beneath the surface. The novel feature of the Mark VI was that, unlike contact mines, a submarine did not have to hit the mine to trigger it. The antenna was connected through a relay to a copper plate on the outside of the mine. The seawater, acting as an electrolyte of a battery formed when the steel hull of a submarine neared the antenna, generated a current sufficient to explode the mine. The mine was also attached to an anchor. Originally, it was proposed to use British anchors, but it was finally decided to manufacture them in the United States, generally based on the British design. The basic concept was that the mine would drop from a ship, sink to the bottom, and automatically detach itself from its anchor and float upward to a designated level beneath the surface.[62]

The first mines arrived in European waters in April 1918, and by the Armistice, 56,571 were planted in the North Sea. At that time, the United States and the Allies planned a second massive mine barrage, deploying the American MK 6 mines at the entrance to the Adriatic Sea.

The British, who had little enthusiasm for the North Sea Mine Barrage, rated the American mine a disappointment. Many were defective when activated in the barrage field. They were damaged either in shipment or in the assembling bases in Scotland. When the minefield was removed after the war, only 38 percent of the mines remained in their correct position. A large percentage broke away from their anchors. The most serious fault, however, were the numerous premature explosions.[63]

American naval officers were surprised at the British criticism, especially considering the difficulties that the Royal Navy had with its mines. On one occasion, British observers estimated that out of a field of five thousand mines, 40 percent blew up prematurely. The Americans insisted that it was only 4 percent. In November, when the barrage was completed, Sims accepted the estimate that "15 percent premature explosions may be considered as a fair percentage of the total number of mines laid," but not all accepted this figure then or later. A French history of the naval war claimed that 57 percent of the American mines exploded spontaneously. Although the German U-boat commander Michelsen was critical of the mines, some Americans adjudged them the most effective weapons used against the German submarines.[64]

Although ASW weapons absorbed much of the Navy Department's attention during the war, the submarine's unexpected success forced the Allied navies to examine the idea of locating submarines underwater. The Royal Navy created a small experimental station that concentrated on using hydrophones to detect sound waves transmitted though water. The hydrophone was a "passive" detection apparatus that relied entirely on reception of sound signals from the underwater environment rather than the reflection of sound signals emitted by itself. The device consisted of a sensitive underwater receptor linked to an operator with headphones. The early hydrophones were unsuccessful, primarily because they could not distinguish between submarine propellers and other noises such as surface ships. Despite the work of prominent British scientists and naval personnel, the hydrophone placed on ships never worked well.[65] The American Navy was equally unsuccessful. Several prototype "listening devices" were tested in the Gulf of Mexico, but the results were unsatisfactory. In February 1917, the Navy's Consulting Board headed by Thomas A. Edison became involved with the project. The board created a special group to study underwater detection. The Submarine Signal Company agreed to establish a research facility in Nahant,

Massachusetts. Academic scientists were also mobilized for underwater detection work through the National Research Council (NRC). The National Academy of Sciences created this council in 1916 to help governmental agencies obtain scientific expertise to support military-related research. In March 1917, the NRC established an antisubmarine committee to work with the Navy. Secretary Daniels created a Special Board on antisubmarine devices. Headed by Rear Admiral A. W. Grant, it included naval officers, representatives from the NRC, and each of the companies working at Nahant. Despite this semblance of unity, the civilian scientists with NRC worked in a hastily established research laboratory at New London, Connecticut, and the Nahant group cooperated with the Navy through Edison's Consulting Board. Despite Edison's criticism, Admiral Grant kept the rivalry in check. In June 1917, scientists from the two research groups met with naval officers and scientists from Great Britain and France to receive information and working models of underwater detection equipment. American underwater acoustic research after the three-day conference resulted in the mass production of the first underwater detection devices employed on American warships.[66] By fall 1917, these devices were ready for testing in the war zone.

The American underwater detection devices were hydrophones like those developed in France and Great Britain, but they differed significantly from those used by the Allies, particularly the Royal Navy. The U.S. Navy favored nonresonant hydrophones with a broad frequency response, whereas the British emphasized resonant or tuned hydrophones. The laboratory at Nahant developed the simplest version, the C tube, and an improved version called the SC tube. It was nothing more than piping in the form of an inverted T, the stem of which extended from inside the hull of a surface ship through its bottom and into the water. At each end of the crossbar was a sensitive diaphragm, a kind of rubber bulb that vibrated when it detected noise. A tube carried the sound to an operator. By rotating the cross bar, the operator determined the direction of the sound. A bearing ring or compass card was attached to the apparatus to ascertain the direction of the noisemaker. The M tube, which utilized multiple tubes and rubber bulbs rather than a single bulb on the end of the horizontal pipe, was also placed in production. Various series were developed for use in aircraft, submarines, and surface craft. Finally, the group at New London developed the K tube, modeled on a French detector. This type was supposed to have much longer range, but it lacked accuracy. It consisted of a triangle of metal pipe with a microphone at each apex towed behind a ship.[67]

The Americans were convinced that their detectors were much better than those used by the British and French but agreed that they had to be tested in combat conditions. In November 1917, Captain Richard H. "Reddy" Leigh, assistant chief of the Bureau of Steam Engineering and later commander in chief of the United States Fleet, was sent to Great Britain with a team of naval personnel and civilian scientists. During a two-week period in December 1917–January 1918, they conducted tests on both American and British ships off the English coast. In February, Admiral Sims ordered the destroyer *Aylwin* to work under Leigh. In April, a second destroyer, the Queenstown-based *Caldwell*, was fitted with listening devices. None of the tests were successful but they were not considered conclusive, primarily because the experimental equipment required that the vessel turn off its machinery and drift in silence in order to pick up the sound of an underwater submarine. This was not practicable; the submarine could disappear in the time needed for a destroyer to restart its engines and get underway. Towing the listening gear was considered a possible solution for the destroyers. The Americans were enthusiastic about the results. "Captain Leigh returned from two weeks with listening division in Channel," Sims cabled the Department. "His reports very favorable to American devices. All American equipment used throughout the test without damage. . . . Detection by American devices superior to that by English devices."

Two of Leigh's team of civilian scientists arrived back in Washington shortly after the tests and appeared before the General Board. They reinforced Sims's report that the American detection gear was more usable than the British. Their testimony was similar to Captain Leigh's report. They unanimously recommended that all antisubmarine craft should be equipped with the American devices; that the different devices should be used in conjunction with each other; and that hunting groups of several vessels, preferably the 110-foot wooden subchasers, should be organized to work together, using the devices. The American destroyers, initially equipped with British detection devices, were re-equipped with the American detection gear. Starting in August, those deployed to European waters received American detection gear before leaving the United States.[68]

Admiral Benson was impressed with the detection equipment. Its apparent success and potential fitted in with his oft-stated belief that every effort should be made to take the offensive against the submarines. He cabled Sims: "The numerous sinkings close in shore along the south and west coast [of the] United Kingdom impress upon us the tremendous possibilities of successful offensive operations by vigorous use of these tubes. It is desired you urge this point on the coming meeting of the Allied naval conference." At Sims's request, he allowed Leigh to remain in London as liaison with the Admiralty's Antisubmarine Division. Shortly afterward, Leigh was given the responsibility for all American anti-submarine tests in European waters. Sims was convinced that "the only effective solution . . . [to] the submarine problem lies in the field of listening devices." Although convoying had been effective in reducing merchant ship losses, "It is apparent," Sims wrote, "that we cannot hope to have sufficient escort vessels for adequate protection for some time, if ever." For that reason, Sims wanted to equip every antisubmarine vessel with some kind of underwater detection equipment. As his Queenstown commander wrote, "to install the most efficient type listening device that happens to be available at the time when there is opportunity to install."[69]

Despite initial optimism, further tests indicated that the American detection equipment had not been perfected, although an improvement on the British devices. Throughout the spring and summer months, experimentation continued, but results were disappointing. On August 10, Sims admitted in a report to the Department that "the practical development of sound detection devices is disappointing." The British developed ASDIC (later called SONAR in the U.S. Navy), but this equipment did not become operational during the war. The director of intelligence in the Admiralty

noted in March 1918, "The impressions left after the perusal of the hydrophone observations . . . are that the chances are so enormously in favour of the quarry as hardly to
justify the employment of the large number of craft and personnel at present engaged
on this duty."[70]

Despite the large amount of American acoustic equipment used on Allied vessels
during the war, they had little success in locating and destroying submarines. One
authority credited subchasers and Allied ships using the American devices with the
detection and destruction by depth charge of six submarines. The Americans claimed
that the acoustic gear affected German submarine operations, and one U-boat commander agreed: "Without doubt," he wrote, "these devices certainly made life difficult
for some of our submarines and at times materially assisted the enemy in their operations against them."[71]

Communications are extremely important in naval warfare, ship-to-ship, ship-to-
shore, and intra-ship. Traditionally, the U.S. Navy used visual signals to communicate between ships and ship to shore, employing designated flags and symbols. Lights
were added later to provide communication at night, but in fog and other inclement
weather it was often impossible to communicate.

The wireless telegraph (W/T), later called the radio, solved the communication
problem. Despite its advantages, wireless telegraphy developed slowly in the Navy.[72]
The outbreak of the war in 1914 and the demonstration of the radio's effectiveness
persuaded the Navy of its necessity. The American ships deployed in the war zone
quickly discovered that the British system was entirely different. "The Royal Navy
had highly selective but insensitive receivers, while the U.S. Navy receivers were the
exact opposite." Their signal flags, codes, and operating procedures mystified American signalmen. British radio sets installed on their warships were designed to give a
strong signal and to transmit and receive a multiplicity of messages at the same time
on different wavelengths. Their range was short, often less than fifty miles. The U.S.
Navy concentrated on long-distance communication.[73]

After the first destroyers arrived at Queenstown, the U.S. warships adopted the
entire British communication system. It was considered so much better that it was
gradually introduced into the Atlantic Fleet.[74] The mine-laying squadrons out of Inverness and Invergordon provided an exception. They established their own system,
continuing to use American flags and signals among the U.S. ships, and using British
flags and signals when communicating with Royal Navy ships.[75] An Inter-Allied Conference on communications in London in October 1917, agreed to adopt a common
signal code manual. The British, who agreed to prepare this manual, selected their
own manual and made it a multilingual publication.[76]

Although American naval radio technicians insisted that their sets were superior
to those of the British, an undetermined number of American warships operating
in the war zone were refitted with British radio equipment. The battleships attached
to the Grand Fleet, some of the Gibraltar-based U.S. vessels, and many of the subchasers received British sets. The vessels deployed to Corfu, however, had American
radiotelephones.

Most of the American destroyers and yachts were equipped with small 5-watt radiotelephone sets made by Western Electric Company. They had a range of approximately thirty miles under ideal conditions, but conditions were rarely ideal in the seas where they operated. On more than one occasion interference disrupted operations such as the rendezvous of escorts with a convoy.[77] American ships in French waters carried American equipment and used the American signal code, but shore-to-ship communication had to pass through French stations equipped with their equipment. Admiral Wilson worked out an arrangement to station American radio operators at the French naval radio facilities to share duty with French operators. American radiomen worked with American ships, and the French operators worked with French ships. Some American equipment was received, but the initial arrangement was applied to other naval stations that became operational, and it continued until the Armistice.[78]

Telephones for internal communication in American naval ships became standard, replacing voice tubes and messengers at the turn of the century. Radiotelephones, however, were not installed on American warships until 1916, initially on battleships, but also in 1917 on destroyers and smaller craft. Although telephone conversations had been held across distances of several thousand miles on shore stations, ship-to-ship and ship-to-shore transmissions were rarely successful beyond fifty miles. Under ideal conditions and in certain geographical areas such as the Mediterranean they generally worked well but not in the North Sea with its rough weather.

Radio communication with other ships in the war zone had its dangers. Submarines on the surface picked up the transmissions and located ships and convoys. When visual signals could not be seen or a message was too complicated for flags, escort commanders often passed instructions and information to other ships in a convoy by trailing a line with a buoy and a message, which the intended ship recovered. They also used a heaving line, which was hard to throw in rough weather.[79]

During World War I, American naval vessels were integrated into the fleets of other nations. As Admiral Rodman said of his command: "Always remember . . . that this squadron is not over here, as somebody put it, 'helping the British.' Nor are we 'cooperating' with the British fleet. Such ideas are erroneous. . . . Think of this great fleet . . . as a unit of force, controlled by one ideal, one spirit, and one mind, and of the American Squadron as an integral part of that fleet. Take, as an instance of what I mean, the change in our signaling system. We came over here using the American system of signals. Well, we could not have two sets of signals going, so in order to get right into things, we learned the British signals. . . . There are American ships here and British ships but only one fleet."[80]

During the war the Navy had problems with some of its weapons, particularly the Mark VI mines and listening devices, but on the whole weapons and equipment improved and worked well. The American warships operating in European waters ranged from modern to obsolete, but regardless of their age and their unsuitability for the work, they performed creditably.

Return of the *Mayflower*

The Introduction of Convoying

On the night of April 13, Commander Joseph Taussig was in Norfolk, Virginia, preparing to take his wife to a local dance. Although the United States had been at war for more than week, the only major change made during that week was to move the powerful Atlantic Fleet, including the destroyer division that Taussig commanded, up the York River, where nets and picket boats protected it. As the couple started out the door, the phone rang. The commander was informed that his division had received orders to sail at daylight for New York City "to fit out for distance service."[1] Taussig immediately left for his ship. Eleven days later the *Wadsworth*, Taussig's flagship, along with *Davis*, *McDougal*, *Wainwright*, *Conyngham*, and *Porter* stood out of Boston Harbor, under orders for Queenstown, Ireland. The six were selected because of material readiness and steaming radius. They were the newest destroyers in the fleet and in the best overall condition. Two of the ships, *Davis* and *McDougal*, were replacements for two of Taussig's original division that were unable to sail on time because of needed repairs.

Although Taussig's command resulted from the readiness of his destroyer division, it was a fortunate choice. In 1917, he was forty years old, the son of a rear admiral.[2] Taussig graduated from the Naval Academy in 1899, one year too late to participate in the Spanish-American War. However, he joined the USS *Newark*, one of the ships sent to China during the Boxer Rebellion. A member of the naval landing force that helped the international expedition to relieve besieged Peking, he was wounded in action and earned a commendation from Congress. While recuperating, he became friendly with a wounded British officer, Captain John Jellicoe, who was first sea lord of the Admiralty when Taussig arrived in Queenstown.[3]

Taussig was of medium height, but wiry and stocky. He had been an outstanding athlete at the Naval Academy, winning the Thompson Trophy his senior year.[4] He was described at various times as "blunt," "gutty," "caustic," and a "fighter," but his son characterized him as calm and rational. "My father was a very gentle person," Joseph Taussig, himself a naval officer, wrote; "he never raised his voice. He never used foul language." He was a "wonderfully immoderate moderate personality." He was intelligent but not an intellectual, according to his eldest daughter, Emily; practical and very sharp. Captain E.R.G.R. Evans (later Admiral Lord Mountevans), a famous British naval officer who was assigned as liaison with Taussig's destroyers, wrote in his book *Keeping the Sea* that "Taussig was full of brains and go, and I was very much impressed with him." Rear Admiral Frederick S. Withington believed that Taussig "had the best mind among the senior officers" in the pre–World War II Navy.[5] He would prove his worth in the months that he commanded destroyers in World War I.

After a stormy voyage of ten days, the destroyer flotilla approached the Irish coast. On May 3, a warship appeared, the British destroyer *Mary Rose*. After identifying the American vessels, she flew the international signal: "Welcome to the American colors." Taussig replied, "Thank you, we are glad of your company." The British ship then escorted the Americans into Queenstown.

The arrival of the American ships was no surprise. British and American officials were obviously aware that they had been ordered to Queenstown, and Admiral Sims, who was in France at the time, had sent his aide to represent him. The Admiralty, recognizing the enormous propaganda value of the arrival of the first American warships, had sent a motion picture photographer to record the event. In a few days, cinemas throughout the British Isles were showing the pictures. "British vessels are shown steaming out to welcome their new allies, and the American destroyers are first seen like specks on the horizon. Then the powerful *Wadsworth* comes into view. . . . No finer series of naval pictures have been shown since the war began," reported the *Pall Mall Gazette*. Another correspondent wrote "along the whole harbour front most of the houses and shops and all of the hotels hung out flags of welcome."[6]

The commanding officer of *Davis* wrote years later that his crew heard the bells of the cathedral chiming a carillonlike version of the "Star Spangled Banner." "We learned later that the priests had privately passed the word to the Irish people that 'here comes the Americans to free Ireland.'" Another officer mentioned the "swarm of small power boats in the harbor packed with cheering people." *McDougal's* crew observed a spectator in a window waving a pair of "fat women's drawers, which we took to be an advertisement."[7]

Queenstown harbor is the gateway to the port of Cork, part of a natural anchorage that is considered one of the best in the world. A narrow passage approximately two miles long leads to the harbor, and a "passage" up the Lee River opens to the upper harbor at Cork, several miles from the entrance. Forts located around the entrance and submerged nets protected the harbor. Prior to the war, the harbor was busy. Atlantic immigrant trade and later the liners used it. Occasionally, American warships stopped there en route to and from European waters.[8]

Queenstown (today Cobh) is located on the terraced side of Great Island overlooking the harbor. At the beginning of the war, it was a small, quiet Irish town of fewer than ten thousand people. The skyline was (and is) dominated by the St. Colmam Cathedral.[9] Close to it lies Admiralty House, the headquarters of Vice Admiral Lewis Bayly, RN, commander in chief, Western Approaches, and the senior British naval officer in Ireland. The town's streets were quite narrow, crisscrossing each other along the terraced hills. The exception was a wide thoroughfare running along the waterfront on which were located shops, pubs, small hotels, and the Royal Cork Yacht Club, the oldest such institution in the world, founded in 1720. Most of the houses and buildings in the town were gaily painted yellow, brown, and green.[10] Large ships could not unload at Queenstown, but they could at Cork. Shipyards, warehouses, and other maritime-related facilities dotted the riverside. The U.S. Navy later anchored its repair ships in the river and in time took over some of the buildings near Cork.[11]

On an island in the center of the harbor was the Royal Navy Dockyard, known as Haulbowline. The American destroyers moored to buoys between the yacht club and the dockyard, except for *Wadsworth* and *Conyngham*. They tied up at the navy yard's fuel dock, where dignitaries were waiting to greet Taussig. The destroyers began to refuel immediately. Supposedly the Haulbowline signal station asked Wadsworth if the crew needed supplies. The flagship, according to one gob, replied that it needed ten tons of ice. The signal then came back: "Sorry but there is not that much ice in all Ireland."[12]

After the ships were secured from sea detail and Taussig had briefly conferred with U.S. and British naval officials, the six commanding officers made the traditional courtesy calls on the American consul and local dignitaries.[13] They then proceeded to Admiralty House to report officially to Admiral Bayly. As mentioned earlier, this meeting impressed Admiral Bayly.[14]

Sims commanded the American naval units in Queenstown but made no effort to take charge, leaving matters entirely in the hands of Bayly and Captain Pringle. Nonetheless, the American destroyers operating out of Queenstown became popularly known as "Sims's Circus."[15] This command structure remained until the U.S. ships were withdrawn after the war. With a staff of two officers increased to four by 1918, Admiral Bayly controlled the operations of both British and American warships and later aircraft in the Western Approaches command. Admiralty House was his command center. He informed his commanding officers that they had three duties—to destroy submarines, to protect and escort merchant vessels, and to save the crews and passengers of torpedoed and mined ships. The first mission had priority.[16]

Bayly's efficient operational procedures were developed before the appearance of the Americans. From six to ninety warships, British and American, operated out of Queenstown from May 1917 to November 1918. Because of the congestion, the destroyer patrols returned to Queenstown after every second operational tour. Otherwise they usually used Bantry Bay as their base. Ships were constantly coming and going, patrolling, convoying, mine sweeping, etc. Bayly and his staff provided the ships with sailing orders as to when they would go to sea, where they were to go, and what their responsibilities were. When they returned and neared the harbor entrance, usually from four to six days after departing on their mission, each ship would be informed by signal where to go—to a buoy, fuel dock, or alongside the repair ship—if repairs were required. They would also be informed by signal any other relevant information as to their time in port. Routine port stays were three days, more if repairs so required. Admiral Bayly abhorred unnecessary paperwork, and, much to the amazement of commanding officers—who were used to requests and requisitions for fuel, supplies, repairs, etc., to be in triple—orders for the logistical support were given by signal without paperwork. An American naval officer sent by Washington to inspect the Queenstown command reported: "[M]y eyes have been opened by the direct, clear-cut efficient operating methods at this base. I have never imagined it possible to run operations of this magnitude and keep up the material with such an utter absence of formalities."[17]

British and American ships operated as an integrated force. The senior officer, whether British or American, was in command of a detachment sent out on patrol or as escorts. Within a week after the arrival of the first American ships, the Admiralty withdrew its few destroyers from Queenstown, leaving sloops, motor patrol boats, launches, and trawlers as the British units operating with the Queenstown command. Generally, after that American officers were senior. When courts of inquiry were held as a result of events such as a collision and an accident at sea, the panel was composed of both British and American naval officers, a policy followed at every joint command.[18]

On May 8, four days after they arrived in Queenstown, the first two American destroyers, *Wadsworth* and *McDougal*, followed four British warships out of the harbor on their first patrol. Four hectic days in port prepared them for combat. All unnecessary gear, spare parts, extra torpedoes and ammunition were removed. Topmasts were taken down to reduce visibility. At the British navy yard, racks and hydraulically operated gear for 300-pound depth charges were installed. British officers came on board bringing Admiralty confidential materials concerning communications, identification signals, shipping movements, etc. Royal Navy officers, signalmen, and radio operators were temporarily attached to the American ships to instruct in the British systems of signal flags and radio codes. Crash courses were held daily to familiarize the Americans with the British procedures and systems. An American sailor on *McDougal* claimed after the war that the signalmen on the U.S. destroyers had to learn in two weeks what British signalmen acquired over a period of seven years.[19]

Perhaps most important, Bayly and veteran RN officers instructed the inexperienced Americans in tactics to fight the U-boats. American naval personnel had virtually no experience in antisubmarine operations or even the weapons required to pursue such work. An enlisted man on *McDougal* recalled: "The officers had their classes too, and what they learned they pass down to the crew. It was not until then that we, and presumably the officers, had any idea of the new submarine warfare the Germans were waging. Our whole system of going to battle stations had to be speeded up, and the lookouts had to be instructed in how to look for submarines. We had it impressed on us that between sighting a submarine and firing on it before it submerged was a matter of seconds. Guns had to be loaded and ready, the gun crews at hand, and ammunition close by. There would be no time for unscrewing the weather caps on the telescopic sights and such."[20]

The Americans were told that ramming a submarine was an acceptable tactic, especially considering the instability of a destroyer operating at high speeds, and the submarine's low appearance in the water, which projected a small target. Admiral Bayly, however, cautioned against ramming periscopes as decoy periscopes were often mined. Commander E.R.G.R. Evans was among the British officers temporarily attached to the American flotilla. He had been widely publicized in the press for a night action in which his vessel, HMS *Broke*, sunk two German destroyers. Mutual admiration developed between Evans and the Americans. He went to sea with *Wadsworth* on the first patrol. "It took one very little time," he later wrote, "to appreciate that the American destroyer officers needed no one to 'hold their hands.' They were very quick of brains, keen, and enthusiastic."[21] Evans spent considerable time advising them about such things as zigzagging, color schemes, gun control, and depth-charge patterns. Destroyer officers were told that the destruction of a U-boat could be determined by oil floating to the surface, debris, papers, etc. Unfortunately, German submarine commanders understood this as well and often disguised their escape by discharging the supposed evidence.[22]

Admiral Bayly conferred with the American destroyer commanders the day before they went on their first patrol and later gave the same talk to commanding officers when their ships joined the flotilla. He stressed constant vigilance, the need to escort valuable ships, conditions under which survivors of sunken ships could be picked up, and areas of operation for each ship. The entire geographical area covered by the Queenstown patrol was divided into fifty-mile squares. Each ship was given one or more squares designated by latitude and longitude to patrol. There were not enough vessels to cover all the squares in the patrol area so squares were selected according to available intelligence on the location of U-boats and scheduled Allied shipping entering the area. Patrol squares were often changed on the basis of more recent intelligence.[23]

German submarines had been having what was described in another war and another place as a "turkey shoot." The night before the *Wadsworth* and *McDougal* left Queenstown, the sloop *Lavender* was torpedoed with the loss of the captain and twenty-one men; only one of dozens of Allied ships lost since the Germans resumed unrestricted submarine warfare in February 1917. The German U-boat attack was initially extremely successful. The Kaiser's naval command ordered more than thirty submarines into British waters to unleash a devastating offensive against Allied and neutral shipping.[24]

Few, however, recognized the war-fighting potential of the submarine in the pre–World War I years. Those who did viewed the submarine as an offensive weapon against surface warships. The knowledge that the submarine's greatest potential from a strategic point of view was in attacking merchant shipping was understood first by the Germans. The first sinking of a merchant ship by a German U-boat occurred on October 20, 1914. The first sinking without warning, the start of what became known as unrestricted submarine warfare, occurred six days later. The German naval staff began to see in the submarine a method of circumventing the British blockade and attacking Allied mercantile trade. Despite opposition from the Foreign Office, in February 1915, the Kaiser's government declared the waters around the British Isles to be a war zone and that Entente ships would be sunk without warning in those waters. Unrestricted submarine warfare was successful in terms of ships sunk and impact on the Allies economy, but of course, it brought the United States into the war and ultimately proved to be a major factor in Germany's defeat.[25]

In February 1915, Germany had only a small force of twenty-four operational U-boats, but undersea warfare on Allied trade quickly proved successful. Twenty-one merchant ships were sunk in March and double that number in August. In 1915, Allied losses in merchant shipping totaled 1.3 million tons, including nearly four hundred ships sunk by U-boats. In 1916, German success continued; some 964 ships totaling more than 2 million tons were lost to submarines. German U-Boat successes rose dramatically during the war from 52.3 percent of the tonnage sunk during the first year of the war (August 1914–July 1915) to 90.2 percent during the three-month period February–April 1917. During the first eighteen days of February, they sunk 121 British, 10 Allied, and 50 neutral ships, and this toll was only the beginning. The carnage mounted during the following weeks. In April, more than 900,000 tons of shipping was sent to the bottom. April, however, was the high-water mark for the rampaging U-boats. May sinking fell off more than a third (approximately 300,000 tons), and from June on, tonnage sunk averaged only about a third of the April record amount. As Arthur Marder notes, the situation was even more perilous because of the many ships damaged. In April 1917, more than 875,000 tons of Allied shipping was sunk by U-boats that conducted 133 raids and destroyed 458 ships.[26]

In January 1917, the Allied powers had at their disposal approximately 21.5 million tons of shipping, or 6 million tons more than the 15.5 million that was estimated was needed to carry on the war. One-third of this margin of safety was wiped out in the first quarter of 1917, and at the time the United States entered the war, the curve was sharply rising. By April, sinkings had become so frequent that one of every four merchant vessels that departed the British Isles failed to return. If the rate of sinkings continued at the April rate, Great Britain would be forced to surrender before the end of the year. Stephen Roskill suggests that it was not the introduction of unrestricted submarine warfare that brought Britain to the brink of defeat but rather "the steep rise in shipping losses [that] began some six months before unrestricted warfare was [re]introduced."[27] These impressive statistics explain why the Kaiser's naval advisors were convinced that the U-boat was the key to German victory, and why they persuaded him to agree to unrestricted submarine warfare early in 1917.

Antisubmarine warfare as a distinct form of naval warfare was born in the First World War. Until the introduction of convoying in 1917, it was generally ineffective. Prior to the opening of hostilities in 1914, the British Admiralty paid very little attention to underwater attack. A few experiments were made to develop equipment capable of locating submerged vessels, but all were failures.[28] A Royal Navy officer wrote after the war, "Had we in 1901 . . . concentrated on solving and developing submarine detection, the true bases of successful anti-submarine work . . . the desired result could certainly have been attained by 1914, and it is not too much to say that the whole course of the war would have been changed to our advantage and the length of the war shortened."[29]

The British and other Allied navies in 1914 had no detection equipment. In general, Allied ASW tactics agreed upon in 1914 were to blockade, attack German naval bases, and patrol the waters where U-boats operated. The Admiralty also followed a policy of dispersing merchant trade or routing ships in such a way that they could avoid (hopefully) submarines. New weapons were introduced, the most successful being the depth charge. Hydrophones were developed but with little success.

The lack of small craft was another problem. The British navy carried in its list only a few motorized launches before the war. At the beginning of the war, the British navy had fourteen auxiliary craft for antisubmarine and minesweeping work. The Auxiliary Patrol, as it came to be known, expanded until, at the end of 1914, 750 vessels were employed in the above duties. The number continued to grow until it passed more than 3,000 in 1917. During the conflict and the introduction of submarine warfare, the commandeering of hundreds of trawlers, drifters, whalers, yachts, and even steam paddle wheelers augmented these vessels. The Royal Navy primarily depended upon these craft for ASW operations. The Admiralty also placed under construction sloops and motor launches.[30] Other vessels such as submarines and Q-ships were employed for ASW work but were generally ineffective. Minefields could have been more effective if the British had produced enough mines and also if the mines were more dependable. Marder called them a "joke."[31] The Allied navies and later the United States placed armed guards on merchantmen to man deck guns, but few submarines were hit by their gunfire. Tactics used by these vessels changed very little until the adoption of the convoy system in 1917. In addition, mines, nets, arming merchant ships, and aircraft were all employed as antisubmarine measures.[32] The German navy lost twenty-two submarines in 1916 including four sunk by accidents and two through Russian action, an average of less than two destroyed a month.[33]

Admiral Sir John R. Jellicoe, who became first sea lord in December 1916, identified "only three ways of dealing with the submarine menace." The first was to prevent the vessels from putting to sea; the second was to sink them after they went to sea; and the third was to protect the merchant ships from attack. He favored the second approach, although it was the one that the Royal Navy had emphasized since the middle of 1915.[34] The British emphasis on a system of patrols as the proper way to defeat the U-boat is not surprising. "Attack" was a key word in the Royal Navy's vocabulary, the principle of constantly being aggressive, or carrying the war to the enemy. As one authority has written, "all its instincts were to go out and seek the enemy, and to destroy him; all anti-submarine warfare was conceived in terms of hunting the submarine to destruction."[35] A War Staff Paper dated February 1917 suggested, "too much stress cannot be laid on the necessity of enemy submarines being constantly harried and hunted and never allowed to rest."[36] The problem was that the system did not work and had never worked.

The Admiralty created two patrol forces (fleets) vaguely defined as coastal patrol and ocean patrol. These forces patrolled the channel and the shipping lanes to approximately 250 miles seaward of the British coast. Initially the patrols consisted of destroyers, sloops, and other light naval craft. As the submarine war expanded and most of the destroyers had to be withdrawn to protect the Grand Fleet and other duties, the auxiliary craft, armed yachts, trawlers, and drifters carried the brunt of this work. By 1918, the Auxiliary Patrol, as these forces were designated, operated out of a number of bases around the British Isles. Despite their large numbers, they had very limited success. In 1916, in approximately one hundred engagements with U-boats, Auxiliary Patrol vessels destroyed only seven.[37]

Unfortunately for the British, geography proved a liability, as shipping entering

ports in the United Kingdom had to follow certain defined routes. Although the patrols concentrated along these routes, the areas were too large to be patrolled by the
vessels available. Also the U-boats simply concentrated along these routes as well,
submerging when patrols were spotted and then surfacing to attack the merchant
ships. Patrolling for U-boats was like hunting needles in a haystack; it was, as Paul
Kennedy wrote, "uneconomic and hopeless."[38] During a ten-day period in September
1916, two or three U-boats cruised in the Western Approaches to the English Channel.
Despite a patrol force in the area that included 49 destroyers, 48 torpedo boats, and
468 auxiliaries, more than 30 merchant vessels were sunk with no loss to the German
undersea craft.[39]

In March 1917, the Admiralty initiated a redesigned patrol system concentrating on
the relatively narrow lanes used by ships approaching British ports. The idea was to
significantly reduce the area that had to be patrolled. It worked little better than the
old system; the area was still too large to patrol effectively with the craft available. (For
example, the southwest approach alone covered more than 100,000 square miles.)
The patrol vessels rarely saw, much less attacked, submarines. This policy, however,
was still being used when the United States entered the war.

The entry of the United States into the war in April 1917 provided a ray of hope in
what otherwise was a disastrous month for the Allies. This was certainly true of the
submarine war. Nine hundred thousand tons were sunk, a daily average of over thirteen ships. Admiral Sir Alexander Duff, director of the Admiralty's Anti-submarine
Division, wrote grimly on April 4, "The Southwest of Ireland has been a veritable
shambles for the last few days." Winston Churchill reiterated this, referring to that
important shipping lane as a "cemetery of British shipping."[40] Throughout April, only
two German U-boats were lost. Yet, on April 22, before the War Cabinet, Jellicoe recommended building more patrol vessels. The first sea lord's solution was simply to
continue the patrol and routing policy—just add more ships to patrol.

Although Sims would later acknowledge the failure of the patrol system, initially
he accepted it, emphasizing in his communications to Washington Jellicoe's plea for
light vessels to augment the patrols.[41] On May 11, he wrote the Department that "the
only apparent solution to the submarine issue lies in numbers of anti-submarine craft
with a view of sufficiently dispersing the enemy submarine effort so that shipping
losses will be reduced below the critical point."[42] Sims did not question British A/S
policy at that time, and neither did Washington. A patrol system was established in
the Caribbean and along the eastern seaboard of the United States.[43] The reason for
this was that the U.S. Navy had no antisubmarine doctrine when war was declared.
Commander P. Symington wrote, "Before the War it was assumed as an axiom that
the proper defense against submarines was speed and mobility and there seems to be
nothing to dispute this axiom." Although the writer was referring primarily to warships, a few months later a lecturer at the Naval War College noted, "only a few of the
younger officers in the Navy have any practical knowledge of . . . a submarine."[44] Sims,
the "father of the U.S. Navy's destroyer doctrine," paid little attention to ASW when
he commanded the Atlantic Destroyer Flotilla. Emphasis was on destroyers acting
in concert to attack enemy surface units.[45] In the summer of 1915, the Navy experi-

mented with using aircraft to search for submerged targets including submarines, but the results were inconclusive and there is no evidence that the Department paid any attention to them.[46]

In 1915, Rear Admiral Frank F. Fletcher, commander in chief, Atlantic Fleet, testified before the House Naval Affairs Committee that the torpedo was only a passing threat. A new weapon, he said, always "appeals to our imagination, and we are apt to say that it changes the history of warfare."[47] Although the admiral was minimizing the importance of submarines in order to stress that these vessels would have little effect on the importance of battleships, at the same time it suggests a prevalent belief on the part of senior officers in the Navy about submarine warfare.

The Navy's first ASW manual was published in April 1917, but it was almost immediately replaced by one used by the British navy.[48] This British guide, not surprisingly, emphasized patrol as the most effective means of eliminating the submarine threat. It also described the tactical weapons to be used, including depth charges. When the first six destroyers arrived in Ireland in early May, they carried only light depth bombs, considered worthless by the British.[49] "None of the Americans had ever seen a depth charge explode," another officer recalled years later.[50] Destroyer training in the U.S. Navy had not included depth-charge attacks.

Admiral Bayly also fully endorsed the patrol concept with the submarine's destruction as the main objective. It did not occur to Bayly or Jellicoe or evidently to a great many other naval officers that the objective was to get the merchant ships safely into port, not to kill U-boats. This conviction did not die easily. Those who refused to accept the idea that convoying was as much an offensive as a defensive tactic were the ones who became strong advocates of hunter/killer groups. It became apparent only gradually, and primarily after the war was over, that U-boats had little difficulty in avoiding both patrols and the hunter/killer groups, either by submerging or by taking advantage of their low silhouette to escape in the dark.[51] After the establishment of convoys, Bayly complained to the Admiralty that convoy work "hampered" patrolling. Later he endorsed convoying but reluctantly.[52] The admiral's force available for patrolling in April 1917 consisted of a few sloops, miscellaneous auxiliary craft, and the newly arrived American destroyers.

As *Wadsworth* and *McDougal* steamed out of Queenstown harbor on May 8, "Tip" Merrill mentioned in his diary, "at last the big hunt begins! . . . The six of us are standing out toward our patrol areas, and every man feels sure that he will be the hero instrumental in the sinking of the first Hun."[53] Perhaps inevitably, the inexperienced Americans started seeing submarines as soon as they had cleared the harbor. *McDougal* blazed away at a buoy with all guns, setting a record according to observers for "misses per gun per minute."[54] *Wadsworth* rammed what at first was believed to be a periscope but proved to be a boat hook. In the patrol area, the destroyers steamed through miles of wreckage, barrels, boxes, bales of cotton, crates, lumber, bits of gear, whole deckhouses, and dead bodies. Merrill spotted a body but did not report the sighting: "we could be of no help to him and he certainly would have been persona non grata on board by the time our tour is up," he wrote somewhat crassly.[55] Merrill also mentioned that one night "an old fisherman stood over toward us with a huge mine in tow. We were very much annoyed and yelled at him for god sake to change his course—we didn't want the damn thing. 'It's jolly well safe sir,' he said. 'I broke its horns off with one of me oars.'" Blackford, a petty officer on *McDougal*, wrote: "[W]hile we were on patrol, SOS signals filled the air. . . . The excitement or terror of the sender was easily noted in his sending."[56] Nervous lookouts caused the crews to go to General Quarters "at least half a dozen times" on sighting suspicious objects. On one occasion, the alarm was sounded because a crew member mistakenly let drop a depth charge. As Taussig observed in his diary: "If a submarine succeeds in torpedoing us it will not be so because we do not keep a good lookout. . . . The lookouts have been all eyes and there is nothing on the face of the sea that has not been reported—birds, fish, drift wood."[57] Admiral "Bull" Halsey mentioned steaming through a "regiment of empty champagne bottles," leading to the comment, "Guess the soldiers [on a transport his ship was escorting] . . . had a liquid breakfast."[58]

Wadsworth and *McDougal* remained at sea on patrol for four days before slipping into Berehaven, Bantry Bay, about twenty miles southwest of Queenstown. Bantry Bay was a relatively large sheltered anchorage used as an assembly point for patrol vessels. The British navy maintained fuel and storeships there. It would become an important anchorage not only for destroyers on patrol or escort duties but, in time, U.S. Navy tenders, submarines, and even battleships. Bayly planned to operate the American destroyers for six days at sea, then two days in port (either Queenstown or Berehaven), before sending them out again. This proved too hard on both ships and crews, so it was changed to five days at sea and three in port unless repairs were required. After two or three days there, the destroyers would resume patrolling an assigned area for five to six days before returning to Queenstown. This procedure continued as long as the patrol policy was in effect.[59] The change to escort of convoys modified the operating time. Destroyers assigned to escort convoys usually shepherded them or individual ships into either British or French ports before returning to their Irish base.

When Taussig on *Wadsworth* returned to Queenstown, he discovered that six additional American destroyers had arrived. Admiral Sims's and other officers' constant pleas for more destroyers had results, and over the weeks and months the number increased until thirty-five were assigned to Queenstown command. They became the backbone of Bayly's force as most of the British ships were ordered elsewhere.

Throughout May and into June, the U.S. destroyers patrolled their assigned areas with no confirmed success. According to Taussig, Admiral Bayly warned them that they might patrol for weeks and never see a submarine. This often proved to be the case. One destroyer veteran recalled, "You'd almost be glad to see a ship sunk, anything to cheer up the monotony of the patrolling."[60] But submarines or what were believed to be submarines were sighted, and whenever possible attacked. Despite a great many claims, the Admiralty credited the Queenstown flotilla with attacking, unsuccessfully, only two submarines in May.[61] Although most of the British were patient with the Americans as they learned "the game," occasionally they became exasperated with their "English-speaking cousins." "Both *Wadsworth* and *McDougall* [*sic*] yankee destroyers sighted submarines today without causing any reduction of the submarine menace," quipped a Royal Navy officer in his diary.[62]

Of course, the British were having no more luck than their "cousins" in eliminating U-boats, either by mining or patrolling. It was becoming increasingly clear that the patrol system was a failure. The Queenstown command alone was responsible for patrolling some 25,000 square miles of ocean. Even if the Americans and British had deployed most of their destroyers in the Western Approaches, it is extremely doubtful that the German submarine campaign could have been defeated or even severely curtailed. Prior to the adoption of convoying, merchantmen and transports were scattered all over the ocean as they plied, usually on their own, to their destinations. U-boats had little difficulty in locating targets. Naval vessels on patrol frequently were unaware of the presence of the submarine until a ship was torpedoed. By the time the patrol arrived, the submarine was gone. U-boats could spot patrol craft long before their own low silhouettes were discovered, and could, of course, submerge and slip away. As one authority has recently written, "patrol vessels were thus little more than casual irritations in U-boat routines."[63] Sims later said that patrolling was akin to searching for the "needle in the haystack." Although Jellicoe was pessimistic about the system of patrolling, he discerned no acceptable formula except the employment of more patrol craft. It took time to realize that convoys would force the submarine to come to them. No longer would single ships be scattered all over the ocean where submarines could easily locate them.

The frustrated Americans began to blame the patrol system. "The stupidity of the system was evident to every gob," an American sailor wrote years later, "but we supposed it was in the grand old tradition of the British Navy."[64] A destroyer officer wrote that ships "were always rushing to places where the submarines had been, but had just left." The cumulative effect, Marder wrote, was to make the U-Boat life "uncomfortable without finding the actual remedy."[65] In June 1918, Sims told the Allied Naval Council that probably it was a mistake to use a patrol system except when the convoy system was being organized.[66] Both Sims and Taussig defended the system after the war, but they questioned its effectiveness quite soon after American destroyers began to take part in it. On November 20, 1917, the force commander wrote, "[T]he results obtained by this method [patrolling] were wholly unsatisfactory." According to his biographer, the admiral concluded that the American ships were not being utilized efficaciously against the submarines and decided that convoying was the most acceptable solution.[67]

The Admiralty adoption of convoy did not end the system of patrols. Both Jellicoe and Sims believed that patrols were necessary but would require more destroyers and other antisubmarine craft. On June 24, Sims cabled the SECNAV: "impossible to carry on partial convoy and partial patrol system." Jellicoe used virtually the same words, adding that the patrol system "is very bad but unavoidable until complete convoy system introduced."[68] Antisubmarine patrols continued until the end of the war despite the fact that convoy escorts were more effective in ASW. Nonetheless, during the first six months of convoying, escorts sank four U-boats, the same number destroyed by antisubmarine vessels on patrol. Patrol forces in European waters and the Western Hemisphere absorbed more ships and men than convoy duty.[69]

Historians have debated the convoy system in World War I extensively because of the claims of the principal figures involved in its origin and their proponents. David Lloyd George, Sir Maurice Hankey, Vice Admiral Sir David Beatty, Admiral Sims, Secretary Daniels, and President Wilson have been credited with the decision to adopt convoying. Even King George V favored it and may have exercised some influence in its adoption. A French history claims that a member of the French naval general staff carried a demand to the Admiralty to begin convoying.[70] All advocated it at one time or another in 1917, but the honor does not belong to any one of them. A series of circumstances convinced the Admiralty of its necessity. Both Benson and Daniels initially had reservations about convoying and continued to favor patrolling. Early in July, Daniels queried Sims about the possibility of funneling all ships through a single lane and saturating it with antisubmarine vessels. Sims replied that not enough ships were available to provide adequate patrol.[71]

Convoying is the sailing of merchant ships in organized groups escorted by one or more warships. To sail in company was an eighteenth-century definition.[72] Convoying was a traditional system of protecting merchant shipping, employed by the British and others for centuries. After the conclusion of the Napoleonic Wars, convoying lost its appeal. During the century that followed, the few conflicts that occurred saw no serious threat to maritime trade, except the American Civil war, and despite threat from raiders, no convoying was implemented in that conflict. British concern with protecting vital trade with their colonies in case of war led to the adoption of a strategy of patrolling the sea routes or lines of communication that were usually followed by merchant ships. Alfred T. Mahan's writings certainly influenced the unpopularity or disinterest in convoying. British naval officials were particularly impressed with Mahan's argument that destroying an enemy's fleet was the most effective way to protect one's maritime commerce. Mahan, Admiral Philip H. Colomb, and other navalists writing toward the end of the nineteenth century emphasized convoying as a defensive strategy, clearly outdated. F. T. Jane described convoys as "a splendid prize already prepared for the enemy."[73]

The opposition to convoying that appeared in the writings of navalists such as Mahan and Colomb reflected their concern about surface raiders, but even after the submarine became a serious threat to maritime trade during the earlier stages of World War I, the British Admiralty continued to oppose it. Arguments against it emphasized its impracticability. Opponents noted that the speed of a convoy could not exceed the pace of its slowest ship; that long delays occurred while collecting ships for convoys; that congestion developed in ports from concentration of merchant vessels; that merchant vessels had difficulty keeping station in convoys; the increased danger of concentrating merchant ships rather than allowing them to steam independently increased the danger to them; and that the navies lacked a sufficient number of escorts.[74] Merchant ship owners and captains strongly opposed it. "Of all the novel routines that war has brought to seafaring, convoy work is, perhaps, the furthest apart from our normal practice," one merchant ship officer wrote after the war. "At first we were resentful of what, ill-judging, we deemed interference. Were we not master mariners, skilled seamen, able to trim and handle our ships in any state or case?" In time, however, they came to appreciate convoying.[75]

Convoying came to be accepted as an offensive strategy with the advent of the submarine. Admirals Beatty, Sims, and others recognized that concentrating ships in a convoy would attract submarines to the convoys. It would become easier to locate and destroy them. A great many naval officers, including Sims, grasped the fact that screens of destroyers had successfully defended undersea attacks against large naval units, particularly the Grand Fleet.[76]

Convoying was employed on a limited basis during the early years of the war. The French occasionally escorted small convoys in the Mediterranean. The British escorted troop transports from the Commonwealth nations and from ports in the United Kingdom to France. In 1916, convoys were introduced to protect food ships proceeding to Holland. In February 1917, the British began to escort ships carrying coal to France. Even an occasional convoy was organized on the east coast of Britain. In April, with Admiral Beatty's strong support, convoying was inaugurated along the Scandinavian routes. Despite notable success, the Admiralty steadily refused to endorse convoying until the last week in that month.[77]

On April 27, Admiral Jellicoe approved a memo that recommended the organization of a convoy system. The memo provided escorted convoys for all ships with speed under fifteen knots steaming from the Western Hemisphere to Great Britain. The Admiralty changed its policy because of the frightening shipping losses in April. Jellicoe now realized that Britain might well lose the war. Pressure from the prime minister, the first lord of the Admiralty, Sir Edward Carson, possibly Admiral Beatty, and even the French contributed to the decision. Finally, the United States' entry into the war potentially resolved the problem of locating adequate numbers of escorts.[78]

Sims's role in the adoption of the convoy system is unclear. Early in April, he began to attend frequent conferences with Jellicoe and other members of the Admiralty. Jellicoe later denied that Sims talked with him about convoying. Arthur J. Marder discovered nothing in the American admiral's April dispatches to suggest that he had done so.[79] Nonetheless, it is hard to believe that he did not at least mention convoying to the first sea lord. It certainly was bandied around within the Admiralty offices at that time. Knowledgeable writers contend that Sims played a role in its adoption, possibly a vital one. In 1925, Dudley Knox, then director of naval history in the U.S. Navy Department and a former member of Sims's staff, wrote to Thomas Frothingham, "Sims' influence was responsible for the adoption of it much earlier than would otherwise have been the case." According to a recent study on the submarine campaign, Sims understood the importance of convoying probably better than anyone else in authority.[80] Josephus Daniels claimed years after the war that Sims was instructed before departing for England to urge convoying strongly. In his first detailed report to Washington, dated April 19, he wrote that he had talked with the director of shipping about "the practicability and advisability of convoying." In *The Victory at Sea*, he noted that "a number of officers in the British Navy . . . kept insisting that it [convoying] be tried. In this discussion I took my stand emphatically with these officers."[81] Sims does not say that he discussed convoying with Jellicoe, but he clearly did so with at least one Admiralty official as well as an undetermined number of other British naval officers.

It is impossible to prove that Sims's advocacy of convoying influenced the Admiralty despite the statement of Lloyd George to that effect. During the early weeks of Sims's tenure in London, he met frequently with Lloyd George at social gatherings. The prime minister advocated convoying persistently and evidently gained support from the American admiral. An authority on the history of convoying wrote recently that "only two admirals in the 1914–18 war . . . understood the convoy system of warfare; one was Admiral Beatty, the other . . . Admiral Sims."[82] Sims wrote to his former aide, J. V. Babcock, after the war: "it would be a mistake for any American officer to publish, or authorize the publication of the claim that the influence of our officers was the determining factor in the adoption of the convoy by the Admiralty. . . . Our influence may have been the determining factor. It is at least probable that our influence accelerated the decision, but there is no single, authoritative statement to prove that this is true. . . . I think there can be no doubt that in the absence of our advocacy the convoy system would have been adopted before very long."[83] Sims was undoubtedly correct that, as one historian has written, "professional opinion was . . . moving swiftly in [that] . . . direction."[84]

Despite Josephus Daniels's praise of convoying, the Navy Department was initially opposed to its inauguration. The Department agreed early in May to use American destroyers on the way to European waters to escort merchant ships from Halifax, Nova Scotia. The Admiralty, however, decided against this expedient. On May 4, the British naval attaché in Washington reported that the Navy Department was "very strongly" opposed to convoying. Daniels's attitude toward convoying changed several times. He initially opposed it as "dangerous" but later became ambivalent, caught between the president, who strongly believed in it, and his naval advisors, who opposed it. The commander in chief, Atlantic Fleet, and the CNO and his assistants voiced their disapproval of convoying. Yet, according to Daniels, when he conferred with Sims before the admiral departed for London, he was told to press the Admiralty to adopt a universal convoy system and that the president, the secretary, and the General Board all supported it. Perhaps it was political opportunism.[85] After the war, one of Sims's staff in London wrote of a trip to Washington early in May 1917. He mentioned discussing convoying with Admiral Benson's assistants and discovered that "none of the officers in that office were in favor of a convoy system. . . . I could get no one to exhibit interest in [it]." Yet, in a cable to Sims dated July 2, Pratt, Admiral Benson's capable assistant, wrote: "Your assumption that merchant shipping should be escorted through the danger zone is absolutely correct. There has been no dissent there."[86] Whatever opposition to convoying had been present in the Department had apparently disappeared. Michael Simpson, in his introduction to *Anglo-American Naval Relations, 1917–1919*, asserts that the extension of the convoy system, once introduced, was extremely slow. "Much of the blame," he wrote, "for [its] . . . slow spread rests . . . with the Navy Department and with Benson in particular." He insists that President

Wilson finally intervened to force the Department to cooperate fully with the British. Daniels apparently said that the president was the first one that he heard mention the idea.[87]

On June 20, two months after Sims first mentioned convoying in a communication to the Department and weeks after the Admiralty had inaugurated the first trial convoys, Benson informed Sims of his opposition to convoying. "In regard to convoys, I consider that American vessels having armed guards . . . are safer when sailing independently."[88] William V. Pratt, Benson's wartime assistant, recalled that "Sims was quite wrought up about it, because Benson did not yield at first. . . . I was inclined to give Sims his own way, on the grounds that he being over there, must know better than we. However, a cold-blooded analysis of the matter does not make the convoy system that embodiment of all virtues, [as] Sims would have you believe. In fact in some cases, especially when shipping does not funnel into mouths like the English Channel and the Straights [sic] of Gibraltar, diversified and individual sailings, especially with ships of good speed, is far better." Both Benson and Pratt favored independent steaming to a midocean rendezvous. Then they could be grouped into convoys while passing through the dangerous war zone. As late as August 1918, the Department opposed escort of westbound convoys with the exception of very slow and poorly armed ships.[89] Although the Department reluctantly accepted convoying, it continued to insist that offensive operations such as mine barriers and the destruction or seizure of U-boat bases were more effective. Later it advocated the creation of hunter/killer groups of small craft rather than their use as escorts.

On May 3, the Admiralty inquired if the Navy Department would agree to use a destroyer squadron, then preparing to deploy to European waters, as escorts for a convoy of sixteen to twenty vessels. Admiral Gaunt cabled that the Department, particularly the CNO, opposed the plan. Benson, however, was willing to cooperate with experimental small convoys, groups of four vessels escorted by two destroyers.[90] Instead of convoying, the Department wanted to create a "heavily patrolled lane" through the war zone. The Admiralty responded that not enough patrol craft were available to sustain such a lane.[91] By that time (mid-July), the Admiralty was almost convinced that convoying was an acceptable antisubmarine tactic, having observed the success of convoys from Gibraltar to the United Kingdom and the U.S. east coast.

On May 24, the first Atlantic convoy departed from Hampton Roads, Virginia, and all of the twelve merchant vessels escorted by the Royal Navy reached British ports safely early in June. British warships escorted the initial Atlantic coast convoys. The first American convoy departed on June 14. It transported the first contingent of the American Expeditionary Force (AEF) to Europe. Destroyers from the Queenstown command rendezvoused with the convoy and escorted it into French ports. Eleven days later, American ships from Bayly's command escorted a merchant-ship convoy destined for British ports. These Atlantic convoys, which included seventy-one transports and merchant ships, reached their destinations without losses to U-boats. These successes persuaded the Admiralty with the agreement of the Navy Department to decide finally to implement a "limited system" of convoys.[92] Nonetheless, the initial Atlantic convoys were considered experimental; months passed before both the Admiralty and the Navy Department agreed to establish a "system" that encompassed all Atlantic shipping.

The convoy system as established by the Admiralty consisted of assembling, at selected ports, merchant ships and transports in groups of up to forty vessels. The British Admiralty recommended that an average convoy of from six to eight ships should be escorted in the war zone, or any area where enemy submarines were believed to be operating. There were, however, never enough escorts to completely carry out the recommendations. In practice, these initial convoys averaged about twenty to twenty-five ships.[93] North Atlantic convoys would be escorted from their point of origin to destinations in the war zone, usually British or French ports. As a convoy approached the submarine danger zone, usually several hundred miles in the Atlantic west of Ireland, additional escorts consisting of destroyers, sloops, and in French waters, armed yachts, would meet it. The strengthened screen would then escort the convoy to a predetermined point where the ships would scatter or disperse for their ports of destination. The ocean escort would then turn around and head back to their base. If the rendezvousing escorts had convoyed an outbound or westbound group of merchant ships, the ocean escort would shepherd them back to North America. The war zone escorts would whenever possible screen individual ships or groups to the ports. Additional escorts of the auxiliary forces consisting generally of small craft would joint the screen in British coastal waters. Ships from North America destined for ports on Britain's east coast were usually not escorted by the Queenstown command the entire way. As they neared British coastal waters, British escorts based in Devonport would meet them and escort them to various channel ports while the American destroyers would return to Queenstown. American destroyers from Queenstown primarily escorted ships destined for Irish and British west coast ports. Sims and the Admiralty believed that the Achilles heel of the system as devised was when the convoys split up for different ports. There were not enough vessels to adequately escort the separated merchant vessels to their destination. They were right. U-boats started concentrating in the approaches to the English Channel and coastal waters where the previously convoyed ships were then unescorted.[94]

In the Western Approaches, American destroyers usually made up the war zone escorts, for British and French ports. French destroyers were not available, and British destroyers' cruising radius was too limited. However, only British escorts convoyed in the North Sea, cross channel, and "for the whole of the escort work round the shores of Great Britain." British escorts were also used to screen British liners carrying American troops to ports in both the United Kingdom and France. British and French auxiliary vessels, however, joined the screen when the escorted ships reached coastal waters. American escorts were generally provided by the Queenstown command, although in 1918 a force of subchasers was stationed at Plymouth and provided escort for ships entering the channel. U.S. naval aircraft also participated in convoying.[95]

As a rule, a convoy would consist of from approximately sixteen to thirty-five ships sailing in a general order at agreed-upon intervals. The convoy's actual escorting formation as screen would depend upon speed of the ships (convoy speed would be that of the slowest ship), location (in the war zone, for example), weather conditions, and predetermined U-boat tactics. In general, the screen would include at least one escorting vessel zigzagging ahead of the convoy, one at the rear, the remainder concentrated along the flanks.[96]

In the weeks that followed the decision to adopt the convoy system, it was gradually put into operation. The Admiralty had approved the convoy committee's recommendations that every eight days, eight homeward (inward) bound and eight outward-bound convoys would leave designated assembly ports in the Western Hemisphere, Africa, Gibraltar, and the United Kingdom.[97] The important difference between convoying and the methods previously used was that antisubmarine vessels met and escorted the convoys to their destination, instead of simply patrolling the areas and lanes, searching for U-boats and escorting single ships through their patrol area.

The system approved in late June was for the North Atlantic trade only. It consisted of two from Hampton Roads per week. Sims was informed, however, that as soon as adequate escorts were available, six additional convoys would be inaugurated, two from New York City, two from Gibraltar, one from Canada, and one from no designated North American port for vessels with speeds of twelve to fifteen knots. The commander in chief, Grand Fleet, as well as other British naval C-in-Cs were notified that "the intention is that ultimately the whole trade with the exception of ships having a speed of over 15 knots shall be brought across the Atlantic under convoy."[98] Admiral Beatty was informed that in addition to the six North American convoys per week, two a week would originate from Gibraltar and one from Dakar, Morocco. He was also made aware that only inward convoys, those destined for British and French ports, would be escorted; outward convoys would be escorted only if there was a potential threat from a German surface raider. The Admiralty emphasized that the success of the convoy system depended upon the availability of escorts, particularly American, both for the deep-sea screen and the war zone. The British were willing to immediately organize a New York convoy if Sims would provide destroyers from Queenstown for the war zone escort. Sims agreed.[99]

On July 4, the first regular four-day convoy left Hampton Roads. Ten days later, the first convoy sailed from New York. By the middle of July, four homeward-bound convoys were departing every eight days, two from Hampton Roads, and one each from New York and Sydney, Australia. During the last week in July, regular convoys were introduced for ships bound for Great Britain from Gibraltar and Africa. July shipping statistics were convincing evidence of the success of convoying. During that month, 162 ships sailed in eight convoys from Hampton Roads; 45 ships in three convoys from Sydney; 37 ships in two convoys from New York. Of these 244 merchant vessels, two were sunk and another was lost after straying away from its assigned convoy. Marder and other writers have stressed that despite the initial success of these convoys, Jellicoe and others in the Admiralty remained skeptical and dragged their feet in expanding it.[100] Nonetheless, their success persuaded the Admiralty to initiate convoying in the South Atlantic, the Mediterranean, and outward-bound convoys from British ports, as soon as escorts were available.[101]

In August 1917, convoying for outward-bound groups was introduced. U-boats, with little success in attacking inward-bound convoys with their strong escorts, turned to the vulnerable ships returning to ports in the Western Hemisphere. The Admiralty hesitated in adding these ships to the system because of the lack of escorts. In order to do so, they came up with a rather simple solution. Escorts would screen an outward-bound convoy to a dispersal point outside the danger zone; then the escorts would break off and rendezvous at a pre-arranged point with a homeward-bound convoy. Ideally, the outward-bound merchant ships would assemble at Queenstown, but the anchorage was too restricted and crowded with warships for this to take place. As with the inbound convoys, the merchant ships sailed from various ports under coastal escort. The Queenstown-based destroyers would relieve the coastal escorts at a predetermined rendezvous and escort the convoy beyond the danger zone, where it would then separate to meet an incoming convoy. The outbound convoy would then come under protection of the ocean escorts. The system was effective, although it was most demanding for the escorts.[102] Considering the frequent fogs and rough seas in the Western Approaches, and the fact that for various reasons, convoys were delayed en route, it was an impressive accomplishment. There was some American opposition to escorting outward-bound convoys, but Sims favored it, and Washington then agreed to it.[103]

By October 1917, some four hundred to five hundred ships a month on the average were being escorted in and out of British and French ports. Modifications to the system continued into 1918. The Allied Naval Council discussed a recommendation by Admiral Wemyss that ocean convoying be extended throughout the world as needed. He mentioned that Germany had developed "cruiser submarines" with the range to extend their operations beyond the so-called danger zone.[104] In January, outbound convoying from French Bay of Biscay ports to the United States was introduced. Eastbound convoys, particularly those with troop ships, always had priority so far as escorts were concerned. Inbound cargo ships destined for French ports continued to sail with those headed for Great Britain in convoy, until April, when separate convoys from New York to French ports were inaugurated. The French government agreed to assign six cruisers from its relatively weak naval force in the Atlantic to these convoys.[105] American ships also joined in the escorting of convoys that ferried troops from Southampton to Le Havre. This was the safest convoy route throughout the war. No ships carrying troops were lost to U-boat attack on this route. A quartermaster on one of the American escorts wrote after the war that in twenty-one round trips they had sighted no submarines.[106]

Once the Allies and the United States initiated convoying, it spread like tentacles to various parts of the world—the Mediterranean, South Atlantic, Caribbean, and, to a limited degree, the Pacific. But the hub remained the waters around the British Isles and France. In order to determine the success or failure of convoying, the Admiralty kept detailed statistics, and even though from the beginning losses declined, it was not until September 1917 that there was enough evidence to conclusively prove that convoying was working.[107] As early as July, the Admiralty agreed to convoys leaving Hampton Roads and Gibraltar every four days, and New York City every eight days. By October 1917, convoys every eight days were departing from Sierra Leone, Dakar, Halifax (Nova Scotia), and Sydney.[108] Convoys from North America followed two general "lanes." A northern route that skirted the south coast of Ireland usually carried food and provisions, while a southern route carried troops and supplies into French ports in the Bay of Biscay. The escort screen for troop convoys was usually about three times as strong as that for cargo vessels.

The Gibraltar convoys to British and French ports were in one way the least successful of all the convoys in the system. Some twenty-seven ships in convoys to British ports were lost to submarine attacks in the months after convoying was introduced, the highest number of any route. The majority of the ships that comprised the Gibraltar convoys were slow "tramps," mostly British registry. They usually averaged seven to eight knots, but one was only five-and-a-half knots. Because of their slowness and the possibility of colliding with convoys on the North Atlantic route, they generally followed widely diverging routes. Routes were often changed during the voyage to avoid suspected submarines. A Coast Guard officer recalled after the war that at times a convoy would make "a huge arc, sometimes hundreds of miles from the coast and out of the ocean lanes." Another route "goes very near the land and often within sight of shore."[109] These convoys usually took twelve days to their destination. Ships exiting the Mediterranean bound for North America often sailed with the Great Britain convoys through the danger zone before leaving the convoy and heading west. These ships were not convoyed, nor were those from the United States destined for Mediterranean ports.[110] The Gibraltar/Great Britain convoys were for cargoes, although the ocean escorts frequently carried passengers, both military and civilian. The cruiser *Chester* once transported four prisoners to England, where they were to be tried as spies.[111]

A Gibraltar danger zone escort of British and American vessels and a similar group of "home water" escorts reinforced these convoys. The ocean escort took position some 600 to 800 yards in front of the convoy and constantly zigzagged across the oncoming ships. Straggling was characteristic of convoying in general, but the Gibraltar convoys seemed to have had more than its share. Coast Guard *Seneca*'s commanding officer recalled urging the skipper of a straying merchant ship by megaphone (radio silence was maintained) that he pick up speed and get back in position. The skipper, a "canney Scot," according to the American officer, replied, "I dinna ken, I dinna ken into position: This ship is no liner; she is an auld box."[112]

The danger zone escorts had more difficulty in rendezvousing with the Great Britain/Gibraltar convoys than others because of the different routes used, often making the convoy early or late. At times they failed to rendezvous, putting the lightly escorted convoy in more danger. On one occasion, according to an American escort officer, the convoy arrived at a rendezvous point thirty hours ahead of schedule, "so all the ships reversed course and steamed back for fifteen hours and then turned around . . . proceeding on the way according to schedule."[113] The Gibraltar/Great Britain convoys continued after the Armistice as protection against German submarines on their way home from the Adriatic.

According to Admiral Niblack, of the 225 convoys that sailed between Gibraltar and the United Kingdom during the war, two hundred of them, or almost 90 percent, were escorted both ways "solely by American . . . ships from Gibraltar." On December

6, 1918, he wrote to Sims that only 50 percent of all merchant ships were convoyed out of Gibraltar, including those escorted by U.S. vessels.[114]

Convoying was a relatively new experience for the U.S. Navy in World War I. It was also a new experience for the majority of the merchant officers and seamen manning the ships that would be involved in the system. Inevitably, there were problems. Inexperience, weather, faulty and poor equipment, the ships, and even the system itself created difficulties. Ships occasionally left convoy and headed for the wrong port. Merchant ship captains were notoriously independent and at times ignored orders. Admiral Sims repeatedly warned Washington of the lack of "discipline" on the part of convoys. As USS *Sacramento*'s commanding officer confided, "handling merchantmen in convoys is a difficult task requiring unlimited patience, tact, and considerable intelligence."[115]

Some of the troubles disappeared with time, but others lingered. Little could be done about the weather. The seas were often rough, and fog was frequently present as a convoy neared coastal waters. A former destroyer officer with the Queenstown command mentioned an incident to Sims where an American destroyer was in a dense fog off the Irish coast. An officer was sent ashore to get a "fix. The officer stepped ashore; found a donkey on the beach; road [*sic*] along the road, and inquired of a native what locality he was in. He returned aboard and with the 'fix,' the destroyer backed off, and set for Queenstown." The fog was so bad along the Bay of Biscay coast that ships occasionally ran aground. The leading ship in a convoy ran aground at Penmarch Point, south of Brest, in a dense fog. Fortunately, she blew her whistles warning of danger ahead, and the remainder of the convoy avoided the disaster.[116] Merchant ships, particularly, used their radios in the war zone despite repeated warnings. Although against convoy regulations they often kept their running lights lit at night to avoid collision.[117] For naval personnel on escorts, some preliminary training in tactics could be worked on at their bases or before joining a convoy, but much of it had to be acquired through actual experience. Inexperienced and nervous sailors that manned guns on the transports and cargo vessels often fired at anything afloat, from debris such as spars and rafts to fish, whales, birds, and at times fishing vessels whose silhouette looked like a U-boat. The log of *Edward Luckenbach* mentioned that her gun crews fired at a flock of gulls on the water. Not surprisingly, Allied and U.S. submarines and ships were occasionally fired at. On July 23, 1918, an unidentified transport opened fire on USS *L 3* and hit her, despite recognition signals by blinker light. No crew members were injured, but the sub had to limp back to port for repairs.[118]

By far collisions were the most serious problem. As the system expanded and there were more and more convoys crisscrossing the Atlantic, as well as in the Mediterranean, the possibility of a collision became increasingly a threat. Ships and convoys often blundered into each other, particularly at night or in bad weather. If a dense fog was hovering over the water when a convoy arrived at a port entrance, often it waited, sometimes underway, until the fog lifted enough so the ships could enter. On more than one occasion, collisions or near-collisions occurred during this period. One incident, according to a veteran of the transport *Von Steuben* ("Stew Bum") was so close that "when I combed my hair for quarters a little later there was [a] big lock of white hair."[119] In December 1917, the Coast Guard cutter *Seneca* was leading a convoy when she received a message from a British steamer, "That Italian astern has run into me and cut my stern bulwark down to the deck." This was immediately followed by another message, "We find one Italian on board. We don't know what's become of the rest."[120] A former bluejacket in destroyer *McDougal* recalled years after the war an incident where evidently "someone in London had routed an inbound and an outbound convoy into each other. . . . I watched the two meet head on. I could hear their sides scrape, the lifeboats rip off. Running lights were on, and ships were blowing passing or danger signals. But the visibility was less than a mile and other ships crashed. Ships bore down on us from both directions, sheering away just in time. The ship that struck us vanished," having sliced the ship in two. Some twenty-five feet of the stern "was cleanly cut as if a giant can opener had gone through." The destroyer was then towed into Liverpool.[121] An officer on *Porter* noted that when the convoy under his escort blundered into another convoy, "it looked as if a carnival was going on. Lights began to blink all over the sea. I saw a red light close aboard and told the quartermaster to call the captain. He said 'It's only a destroyer, sir.' I said 'you call the captain God damn quick.' Captains are paid for getting up when they are called. We were in the midst of a convoy heading in the opposite course to us and we went thru two lines of ships and saw ships arranged fantastically all over the ocean. A destroyer ahead would turn hard over and than a black hulk would loom up and we would do the same. When we were clear I heaved a sigh of relief and felt a few years younger."[122]

Other ships were not as fortunate. An English tanker rammed the transport *Pocahontas* at anchor in Gravesend Bay. Few collisions resulted in the loss of a ship, but Sims wanted a lawyer specializing in Admiralty law assigned to his staff "on account of the increasing number of cases of collision between United States vessels and foreign vessels in European waters . . . in which legal questions and possibly damages are involved."[123]

While in the danger zone, the convoy and escorts followed a predetermined zigzag scheme during daylight hours. Zigzagging was usually not carried out at night as it was usually considered not necessary and also it increased the possibility of collisions. As Leighton wrote in *Simsadus*: "Imagine thirty great ships all huddled together changing their courses every few minutes, and then imagine what havoc might be wrought if one ship made a mistake. Mistakes were made and havoc was wrought."[124] Whenever possible, convoys were scheduled to pass through the danger zone during night. The expectation was that the ships would enter harbor during daylight hours, but the exact time depended upon weather conditions, the speed of the ships, and other factors.[125] This policy had its disadvantages. Although it reduced the possibility of a submarine attack, it also created difficulties for the coastal escorts that rendezvoused with the convoys and individual ships.

Merchant ships had difficulty in keeping station in convoy, especially at night and while zigzagging. Commander Taussig wrote after the war: "Our chief difficulty with the convoys at first was the keeping of the ships together in a reasonably well defined formation. There was always a tendency to straggle."[126] One escort commander stated that station keeping was so bad that miles separated the van and rear.

Ships often picked up speed, creating a chain reaction as the other ships in the column had to do likewise.[127] Escort commanders such as Taussig usually stationed one of the escorts to patrol back and forth across the rear of the convoy formation to prevent straggling. The CO of the cruiser *Chester*, engaged in escort between Gibraltar and Great Britain, once dropped a "smoke box" astern of a straggler and signaled him that it was a submarine. According to *Chester*'s CO, the freighter nearly beat him back in convoy line.[128] The difficulties were compounded because convoys often included ships of various nationalities, many of which did not understand or abide by the need to either maintain station or zigzag. Escorts frequently had a most difficult time in trying to follow a zigzag pattern when convoying the fast liners.

During and after the war, naval officers debated the advantages of using zigzagging. At times, escort commanders and convoy commodores disagreed over zigzagging. One American naval officer who made frequent convoy trips across the Atlantic claimed that he never knew a British convoy commodore "to zigzag except as an exercise on the high seas, well outside the war zone."[129] While in the danger zone, the convoy and escorts would follow a predetermined zigzag scheme during daylight hours. The most common pattern followed was fifteen minutes thirty degrees to port, fifteen minutes thirty degrees to starboard, fifteen minutes straight ahead on the indicated course, but often the convoy commodore selected other courses.[130] Junius Morgan mentions in his diary the confusion caused by a convoy zigzagging one dark night: "We narrowly escaped being run down, and found out that *Rowan* and *Tucker* collided, and that one of the transports had fired on *Sterrett*. When the tangle was finally straightened out, all but *Jarvis* and *O'Brien* had been lost from the convoy."[131]

On more than one occasion, escort commanders reported narrowly avoiding a collision because of a merchantman following out an unknown zigzag pattern in the dark. Admiral Halsey recalled an incident in his memoirs where one of the escorting destroyers changed zigzag in the middle of the night without informing the rest of the convoy and escorts. "For four hours we vainly struggled to find out what she was doing and after much guess work we tumbled to the zigzag" she was following. They were lucky. Occasionally, zigzagging at night resulted in ships being separated. Escort commanders also tried to discourage zigzagging in dense fog and rain for the same reason.[132] In slow convoys, the escorts usually did the zigzagging. Neither speed nor zigzagging was totally effective. In warning escort commanders of this, Admiral Sims pointed out that a ship was torpedoed while not in convoy because she relied on her speed and zigzagging. Both the merchant ships *Antilles* and *Finland* were successfully attacked, although they were zigzagging and under escort at the time.[133]

Delays were a major concern, caused again by weather conditions but also by difficulties in assembling and routing ships for a designated convoy. Some ocean escorts had to be refueled at sea, usually causing a delay in arriving at a rendezvous. European waters escort commanders often complained of delayed arrivals of the convoys they were to meet. A twenty-four-hour delay was not uncommon, and several were nearly forty-eight hours late in reaching the rendezvous. AEF authorities in France admitted that the debarkation of troops was frequently held up for hours but blamed it on the absence of information about the number of troops on the arriving transports. This in turn delayed the convoy's sailing. Sims insisted that this information was cabled to his headquarters by the Department, which in turn was provided to Army officials as well as Admiral Wilson's staff.[134] When Admiral Sims was informed that a flotilla of six destroyers had been waiting forty-eight hours at Brest for the departure of a small convoy, he decided that in the future the Queenstown destroyers would not delay but keep to their scheduled return to base. They were required to refuel and replenish before meeting another incoming convoy.[135] The lack of escorts caused by delays often led to the postponement of convoy sailings, both east- and westbound. Admiral Benson voiced his and the European force commander's concern when he cabled Sims that despite the insistence by convoy commanders that they could rendezvous on time, "It has developed practically that the universal custom is to be late."[136] At times, the naval officers in charge of escorts were not informed in time to schedule the required vessels. On one occasion, the British C-in-C at Plymouth had to telephone the Admiralty for information and pass the details on to the escorts.[137] Escorts were also late in arriving at rendezvous. The French were notorious at this, but it was even true occasionally of American and British escorts as well.[138]

Speed was a major difficulty that was never entirely solved. Initially, convoys were organized consisting of ships of varying speeds, the policy adopted being that convoy speed would be determined by the slowest vessel. Fast vessels, initially fifteen and later eighteen knots or better, sailed independently. In August 1917, at the recommendation of the British minister of shipping, it was agreed to organize North Atlantic convoys on the basis of speed. After the loss of *Antilles*, all convoys were organized by speed, ranging from the slowest at six knots to the fastest, usually the large troop transports at eighteen to twenty knots. Ships of generally equal speed would be organized in convoys. There would be slow, medium, and fast convoys. The policy adopted at that time called for the slowest vessels, up to eight knots, to be in one convoy, and vessels whose speed was from eight to twelve knots in others. A third category included those whose speed ranged from twelve to eighteen knots. Ships with speeds of eighteen knots or better would continue to sail independently. However, there was a major exception to this rule. Ships carrying troops and their supplies were grouped in convoys without regard for their speed. This practice was modified early in 1918 and again in April. The War Department preferred to transport all troops in fast vessels for reasons of safety, but the German offensive in March 1918 and the need for troops quickly persuaded Pershing to urge the transport of troops to France in slower vessels achieving not fewer than eleven-and-a-half knots. The Navy agreed.[139]

Modifications continued throughout the war. The U-boats' effectiveness resulted in the division of eight-knot and twelve-knot vessels into separate convoys, and even the inauguration of convoys for vessels over eighteen knots. The availability of escorts determined these changes. High-speed vessels, such as the large liners, continued to sail independently until the Armistice.[140] The Atlantic convoy system attained an average of sixteen inward-bound convoys to Great Britain as well as an average of seven outward-bound convoys from British ports at sea at one time. By July 1918, 93 percent of oceanic traffic to and from the United Kingdom was convoyed.[141] Troop convoys and occasional convoys voyaged direct to French ports from New York. The Navy

Department scheduled troop convoys to follow a route not generally used by other convoys. Nonetheless, although the Atlantic Ocean is large, the area that comprised the war zone was restricted, and as the system evolved with dozens of ships traveling in all directions, centralized control became essential.

From its inception, the British assumed administrative control of the entire system. They had in place in London the nucleus of the best communication system in Europe and a highly developed intelligence service. On May 17, 1917, the Admiralty had created a convoy committee to study the question of operating regularly scheduled convoys. The committee later was given the responsibility of organizing and managing the system. The French and Russians accepted British management without question, as did the Italians in general and the Americans with one exception. The U.S. government insisted on maintaining control of convoys carrying American troops escorted primarily by American warships. The Navy Department administered these convoys.

At the beginning of the war, the U.S. Navy had only two small transports, and the merchant marine was not much better off. In 1914, Great Britain's merchant marine dominated oceanic shipping. It included 9,240 merchant ships amounting to 19,257,000 tons. The United States had only a third as many ships with about a quarter of the tonnage, the majority of which were small vessels in the coastal trade.[142] To rebuild the merchant marine, Congress, at President Wilson's recommendation, created the United States Shipping Board (USSB) to administer the nation's shipping industry. It was given the power to purchase and operate merchant ships. The board created the Emergency Fleet Corporation (EFC) to build the vessels required by the USSB. Thousands were purchased from private owners and laid down in shipyards throughout the country. It even requisitioned 163 vessels being built for the British, much to their irritation.[143] The British government throughout the war worried that the United States was attempting to supplant Great Britain in world shipping.[144] Most of the new construction was not completed in time to serve during the war.

In August 1918, the CNO demanded U.S. control of all convoys sailing directly to Bay of Biscay ports from the United States. Admiral Wilson strongly opposed it, informing Sims that "to take over control with present inadequate facilities may lessen obligation of French to furnish maximum escort."[145] The Admiralty and Sims disliked the American decision to run an independent convoy system, but Admiral Benson, with the support of Daniels, insisted on it. Sims believed the decision politically motivated, a correct assumption to some degree. Considering the Wilson administration's lack of confidence in the British navy at the time and the awareness of German U-boat successes, the determination to guard the American troops with their own ships is not surprising. Washington officials were most sensitive to the impact of the loss of one troop transport on American public morale. The Department was willing to place all but the troop convoys under British control and to continue to augment the number of escorts deployed in European waters. After the enormous increase in the number of troops sent to Europe, British escorts had to screen troop convoys.

Statistics on the number and nationality of escorts screening the troop convoys do not agree. Most American sources, but not all, conclude that U.S. naval vessels escorted 82.75 percent of American troops. Some American and British sources indicate that the percentage was much lower. The Admiralty, for example, claims that between March and September 1918, British naval vessels escorted approximately 140,000 American troops to Europe each month. Two-thirds of the U.S. troops brought over in the summer of 1918 came in British ships escorted in part by British vessels. Because of the complexity of the systems, it may well be impossible to determine an exact figure.[146]

Despite the awkwardness of two convoy systems, a convoy system within the broader convoy umbrella worked quite well. Some problems emerged at first. American naval authorities forgot to notify the Admiralty of the arrival of troop transports in British ports who steamed independently, causing some congestion in these ports.[147] Nonetheless, the system functioned remarkably well. The convoy system's centralized administration contributed to its success.[148]

All Allied convoy instructions went out through the British Admiralty except for American troop ship convoys, which were handled initially by the Navy Department and later with the cooperation of NOTS. Sims's headquarters in London established a section to coordinate convoy movements with the Admiralty, but this section confined itself to the American troop convoys. U.S. naval forces in France also had a section to coordinate convoying in French waters with the French and the Admiralty through Simsadus. American escorts operating out of Brest and other French Bay of Biscay ports generally followed British procedures.

Despite Washington's determination to give priority to troop convoys, the Navy continued to deploy destroyers to Queenstown. Sims persistently recommended the concentration of all destroyers in British waters. This practice led Secretary of War Baker to advocate the allocation of adequate destroyer escorts to the troop transports. Because the transports initially went to French ports, some of the officers in the Department wanted to shift the destroyers to French waters, but Sims, with British support, insisted that the French ports could not provide necessary logistical support to the American oil burners.[149] Nevertheless, as Daniels informed the president, "the absence of small craft for convoying is even more apparent on the French coast than on the English coast." In the meantime, a few decidedly inferior American antisubmarine craft shouldered the burden of convoy work in French waters.

Lafayette, We Are Here!

Convoys

Early in June 1917, the Department informed Sims that the first convoy carrying American troops to France would depart soon. Four groups or trains were formed with three to four transports under heavy guard in each one. The European force commander was instructed to provide additional destroyers to escort the convoys through the danger zone to St. Nazaire, the port of debarkation.[1] Sims ordered three divisions of six destroyers each to rendezvous with the convoy groups. There they would come under the control of the convoy group commanders. After shepherding the transports to St. Nazaire, they would return to Queenstown.[2]

The convoy left on June 14: in the foggy morning hours the armored cruiser *Seattle*, a commandeered German liner renamed *De Kalb*, the armed yacht *Corsair*, and three destroyers steamed out of New York harbor and quickly disappeared into the North Atlantic. Within a few hours, the other three groups passed through the submarine nets at the Narrows. Altogether ten small passenger liners carried fourteen thousand soldiers and Marines. The convoy also included four freighters loaded with supplies. Among the escorts were four cruisers, thirteen destroyers, and six other naval vessels to cover the most heavily guarded troop convoy to cross the Atlantic.[3]

Rear Admiral Gleaves, carrying his flag in *Seattle*, commanded the convoy. On May 29, he received orders to give up command of the Atlantic Fleet destroyer force and assume control of convoy operations. The admiral, who had been at odds with the Department because it had stripped his force of destroyers for European duty, was delighted with his new command. "If only they would make me vice [admiral]," he confided to his diary.[4] One of the destroyer captains complained that the convoy commander "was unfamiliar with war-zone technique [and] did things with his convoy that *we* knew was dangerous." Another destroyer skipper made this criticism known to the admiral and was promptly reprimanded.[5] Sims wrote his wife that he had to arrange the details for the escorts. "The Department made an *awful* mess of it—they tried to manage the details from Washington and even directed that the French Admiralty arrange some of the details while I was to manage others! It was such a dangerous proceeding that I was obliged to disobey all instructions and take charge of the whole business."[6] The American naval attaché in Paris informed the force commander and the Department that French naval officials were concerned at the inadequate information received concerning the convoy.[7]

On June 23, the destroyers on patrol from Queenstown received orders to join the convoy, and three days later the remaining destroyers left Queenstown. An officer on *Walke* commented in his diary: "we had a long trip ahead of us, the longest we had been called on to do and there was doubt that we could get away with it. Spent the day in nursing the ship along saving oil in every possible manner."[8] At 8:30 a.m. on June 23, a lookout on *Seattle* reported smoke on the horizon. Within an hour, six sleek destroyers from the Queenstown command took position with the first group's escorts. Gleaves is supposed to have signaled, "Gentlemen, you are ten minutes late." By the end of the day, some eighteen destroyers from the Irish base had joined the different groups.[9] As the destroyers maneuvered to take up their assigned positions, soldiers and Marines lined the sides of the transports and cheered. Years later, General of the Army George Marshall recalled: "a column of American destroyers broke out of the mist and bore down on us at top speed. The sea was rough and they made a very dramatic appearance cutting through the waves, pitching and tossing with every motion of the water. . . . They distributed themselves on the flanks of the transports, with much cheering back and forth between the sailors and soldiers." Another officer recalled sharing everyone's relief at seeing the American vessels, "plunging and rolling and looking, by reason of their queer camouflaging, like grotesque hobby horses, whose riders had just dismounted."[10]

The convoy observed radio silence to avoid detection. Only one message was sent out, confirming the place and time of the meeting between the destroyers and the convoy. Rendezvous was made without difficulty. Each division (six destroyers each) formed a scouting line when it arrived on the convoy's flank with individual ships at five-mile intervals. "Tip" Merrill was officer of the deck on *Conyngham* that day and later recorded the event: "more than one heart beat a little faster when the two areas of the service met some several thousand miles from home." This was the first use of U.S. destroyers to escort convoys through the war zone.[11]

Upon entering the war zone, tension mounted on board the ships. Nervous and inexperienced lookouts occasionally mistook debris and even wave action for submarines. An observer noted: "One of the merchant ships saw some fish close to us and opened fire at them. The splashes were right astern of us [*Walke*]. . . . The fragments howled over and around us."[12] A cruiser "gave a party" by firing several shots to starboard at an imaginary sub. Earlier *Seattle* fired at a supposed U-boat; two other ships fired at what they claimed were torpedoes. On June 26, the destroyer *Cummings* dropped a depth charge on what it thought was a submarine and claimed that it was damaged.[13] German records indicate that no U-boats were in the area at the time. George Creel, director of the Committee on Public Information, was anxious to publicize the crossing of the first troops. He released a story about the submarine attack, which was carried in U.S. newspapers. A few days later, a correspondent in London wrote an article that quoted unnamed destroyer officers who insisted that the submarine attacks were "floating spars or blackfish."[14]

On June 26, three days after the rendezvous with the destroyers, the first group dropped anchor in the Loire River off the town of St. Nazaire. Although the French promised an escort, only two small vessels joined the convoy as it neared the port. The

U.S. naval attaché in Paris later wrote, "The Admiral in command of the troop convoy had been told in Washington that he would be met by French destroyers, etc., and as a matter of fact they didn't exist."[15] German submarines apparently fired torpedoes and laid mines off the French coast, but none of the ships suffered damage. According to an Army officer, only one casualty occurred during the crossing, an animal, "and that was a mule."[16]

As the doughboys, stiff from the long voyage, began moving down the gangways, the escorting destroyers took on fuel. Sims ordered all the destroyers to Queenstown, including those that escorted the transports from New York. The Queenstown command had been left with only a few ships for patrol. *Seattle* remained at St. Nazaire for a few days to allow her crew liberty. "All the skippers went ashore and had dinner in a hotel. The food was very fine. The main piece de resistance was artichokes."[17] The destroyers were under orders to sail immediately after refueling, but Gleaves refused to detach those that came over with him. He ordered them to escort the returning convoy through the danger zone, noting the lack of French vessels to provide escort. Although the admiral was understandably concerned about the real submarine threat, Sims was unhappy with the order. "Vital shipping is being lost through delay in return of destroyers. . . . [T]hey must be dispatched immediately and not held for outgoing escort," he radioed the convoy commander. He added that French vessels should provide the escort, a puzzling statement considering the fact that he must have known that such vessels were unavailable. An indignant Gleaves sought to retain the destroyers that had sailed from United States, and he wanted at least one division of Queenstown-based destroyers to remain with the convoy through the danger zone. The convoy commander also informed Secretary Daniels that Sims was unwilling to provide adequate escort and requested that he "be directed to send Division of destroyers to furnish escort . . . through danger zone." Sims then agreed, much to the delight of the crews of the destroyers remaining at St. Nazaire.[18] Gleaves, who resented the depletion of his force to Sims when in command of the Atlantic Fleet destroyers, did not forgive Sims for this second affront.

Gleaves encountered difficulties with the civilian crews of the transports who refused to shift coal into bunkers for the return trip. Extra coal had been stored on all the vessels for the return trip. Because of the coal shortage in France, all vessels, including troop transports destined for French ports, were required if possible to carry enough coal for the return voyage, a procedure that continued even after the Armistice of 1918.[19] The first group of vessels finally departed St. Nazaire on Bastille Day, July 14, and the others left soon after. The Queenstown destroyers provided protection for each group through the danger zone.

The success of the initial troop convoy resulted in preparations to send the next one as quickly as possible. The Queenstown destroyers were to provide escort. Bayly was probably unhappy with this decision, but it was out of his hands. In accordance with the force commander's policy of total integration of U.S. forces with those of the Allies, the allocation of U.S. warships as escorts within the war zone was left to local C-in-Cs, but an exception was made in the case of escort for troop transports.[20] Bayly's command exercised primary responsibility, but Daniels informed Sims that the troop convoys had priority. The majority of the American destroyers in European waters were withdrawn from patrolling duties. On July 18, "Tip" Merrill noted: "The system has all been changed! Three divisions [of destroyers] have been formed for escorting purposes and the rest of the destroyers carry out the old routine. We are in one of the escorting divisions and we are bound for a rendezvous about 400 miles where we hope to meet 17 merchant ships." He later described their new responsibilities: "It is escort work entirely. We take a convoy of empties out to 15 or 17 west longitude where we meet a heavily laden convoy of 12 to 25 merchantmen from America or Africa or Australia. We escort them to 5 degrees west, and turn the Eastward bound ships over to British destroyers from Dover or Plymouth. Our escort splits up and we escort the individual ships bound for France or Irish Sea to their destinations. Another outbound convoy has formed by the time we get back to Queenstown. We take them out, if not we wait until one is formed."[21] As a rule, the destroyers operating out of Queenstown escorted outgoing convoys for three hundred miles before they shifted to incoming convoys. When destroyer escorts were sent out from Brest, they frequently met convoys five hundred miles out in the Atlantic.[22]

The priority given to troop convoys limited the number of vessels available for other duty in British waters. At a conference in the Navy Department, Gleaves, still irritated over Sims's refusal to allow the destroyers under his command to escort the homeward-bound transports, strongly opposed the dispatch of additional destroyers to the European command. Supported by Mayo, he argued that the destroyers should escort troop ships to and from Europe. The CNO compromised. Destroyers and other escort craft would deploy to European waters when they became available, but Sims was ordered to give priority to escorting. On July 28, the force commander received a cable from Daniels, stating that "the paramount duty of the destroyers in European waters is principally the proper protection of transports with American troops." As a result, troop convoys generally enjoyed a screen of European-based destroyers in the war zone that was somewhat more than three times as strong as the escort force assigned to cargo convoys.[23] This decision reflected Benson's conviction that the war would be won in the trenches. What affected the length of the war was the transport of American troops to the Western Front.[24] This position reflected the U.S. government's attitude, particularly that of the president and Secretary Daniels.[25] Secretary of War Baker also responded very sharply to Sims's "views": "I hope that it can be arranged so that no other duty assigned to the Navy destroyers in European waters need be allowed to interfere with what would seem to be the essential and primary duty to afford safe convoy to our troop transports through the submarine danger zone." Baker wanted the Navy to provide "heavy escort protection" to troop transport convoys both to and from France, but when it became evident that submarines posed no danger until convoys entered the war zone, he backed away from the latter demand.[26]

This debate reflected a fundamental difference in the use of American naval vessels. Sims wanted to fuse his force with the Royal Navy, accepting Admiralty control on the operational level. The British government believed that antisubmarine craft operating out of British bases should protect shipping to their ports. On July 13, the War Cabinet argued that the submarine was the one menace that might lead to defeat;

"it is most important to concentrate any possible effort on the protection of trade in the approaches to the United Kingdom."[27] Sims had to respect an order from the Navy Department, but he protested that the use of destroyers to escort troop ships would force suspension of patrols and escorts of food convoys destined for the British Isles. He also accepted the Admiralty's argument that the estimated eight to ten U-boats that Germany could deploy in the Atlantic could not attack the troop transports because of their limited cruising range and the absence of a support base.[28]

As Captain Pratt observed: "The point of view of Sims lay in England. Our point of view had its background in America. The impelling reason of the British was protection of food and war supplies in transit. Our basic reason was protection to our own military Force in crossing the seas."[29] It was only because of Sims's insistence that the Americans finally supplied a modest quota of destroyers to escort mercantile convoys. Even Sims ultimately accepted the need to place emphasis on the troop transports. "We of the Navy," he wrote Assistant Secretary of the Navy Roosevelt, "realize that there is no real naval war going on over here; that we are to all intents and purposes, a part of the lines of communication of the Army, or rather the defense force, keeping this line of communication open."[30]

The Admiralty and Sims were initially correct; Germany did not immediately attack troop transports. Early in May, Admiral Henning von Holtzendorff instructed U-boat commanders to avoid attacks on American ships because the Kaiser had refused to declare war on the United States. Even after American troops reached France, Germany did not make a formal declaration of war. As late as the fall, Germany hesitated to deploy U-boats in American waters to avoid antagonizing the United States further.[31] A British sailor on an escort voyage from Canada to Cherbourg wrote in October 1918: "The whole of France seemed to have been taken over by the Yanks. . . . It was a pity some of the German submarine commanders could not see the stuff that was slipping by them."[32]

More influential, however, was the German high command's conviction that it was more important to destroy merchant shipping than to torpedo troop transports. This view was based on the erroneous belief that the United States could transport only a negligible number of American troops to France before Germany won the war. The submarine, it was assumed, would force Great Britain out of the war by destroying the ships that provided sufficient supply to allow Britain to persevere.[33] Although the troop transports were left alone for quite some time, they were attacked later. Admiral Scheer, commander in chief of the German High Seas Fleet and later chief of the naval staff, admitted that "U-boats shadowed the [troop] convoys waiting for an opportunity to attack, but they were too well guarded." Five American transports were torpedoed, but only three went to the bottom. Those hit had unloaded their troops and embarked on the return voyage.[34]

The introduction of the convoy system had a profound effect; German U-boats discovered that heavily escorted ships were difficult to attack. "It is rare that escorted ships are being torpedoed," wrote a watch officer in the war diary of *Ericsson*,[35] although some German submarine commanders followed American destroyers out to the rendezvous.[36] U-boats gradually shifted their attention to more vulnerable targets, concentrating on unescorted outward-bound traffic. When these ships were placed under escort, submarine captains began to search for either vessels traveling independently or those that straggled from a convoy. During the last fifteen months of the war, ships sailing independently accounted for 85.5 percent of all losses in the war zone.[37] Sailing vessels were never convoyed and were supposed to keep out of the war zone. Nevertheless, some did so, and U-boats feasted on them. Submarines tried to intercept vessels in the vicinity of ports and also after convoys broke up and ships steamed independently to their destination. This tactic failed because the British and French concentrated their light antisubmarine craft in coastal waters.[38]

Admiral Karl Doenitz, a submarine officer in World War I who commanded Germany's submarine fleet in World War II, described the effect: "The oceans at once became bare and empty: for long periods at a time. . . . [T]hen suddenly up would loom a huge convoy of ships, thirty or fifty or more of them, surrounded by strong escort of warships of all types. The solitary U-boat, which most probably had sighted the convoy purely by chance, would attack, thrusting again and again and persisting, if the commander had strong nerves. . . . The lone U-boat might sink one or two of the ships or even several; but that was a poor percentage of the whole. The convoy would steam on."[39]

During the heyday of unrestricted submarine warfare, February through June 1917, thirty-one submarines cruised the seas, inflicting heavy losses on the Allies, but their number gradually dwindled. The number of U-boats responsible for the massive destruction in Allied shipping was relatively small. In March 1917, an average of forty submarines out of the total German and Austrian submarine fleet were at sea. In April, of 128 operational boats, an average of 47 went to sea. The number of operational U-boats climbed gradually, but the percentage at sea remained about the same.[40] U-boat losses were minimal. From the start of the war until 1917, forty-seven were lost, an average of less than two a month. From February through April 1917, ten more submarines were destroyed, but only seven of these by Allied antisubmarine vessels. In May, the average number at sea was forty-seven; in June, fifty-five; and forty-one in July.[41] Although during the three months of unrestricted warfare the percentage of U-boats lost to Allied action rose to 2.3 percent, the results and efforts were far below expectations. By 1917, the Germans built an average of seven boats a month. A few were lost to Allied warships, but most of them wore out and were sent to the yards for extensive refits and repairs. By the new year, approximately half of those at sea operated in the Western Approaches and in British waters at a given time. Even if the number had significantly increased, it would not have seriously affected the transportation of vital supplies and troops to the war zone. The convoy system proved remarkably effective. U-boat commanders preferred to attack by using gunfire because surface attacks held obvious advantages. The German submarine carried very few torpedoes, generally five; the use of deck guns extended its patrol. At the beginning of 1917, gunfire accounted for more than 60 percent of the Allied ships sunk. Convoying, however, forced U-boats into attacks while submerged; they attained few successes by surface attack after the summer of 1917. In the early months of restricted submarine warfare, the average

U-boat destruction declined by 700 tons a day. By the summer of 1918, the figure fell to about 275 tons and continued to drop. Unescorted vessels suffered most of the losses.[42]

Throughout the summer and fall of 1917, the protection of troop transports remained the major concern of the War and Navy Departments. On July 1, the Department informed Sims of the conversion of large and speedy liners such as *Leviathan* into troop transports and asked whether they should sail independently because of their relatively high speed. Sims replied that troop convoys and all ships, including troop transports, should be integrated into the convoy system. He mentioned his concern about congestion of convoys in the war zone, which might lead to "inadequate protection for some . . . convoy and hence the possibility of disaster." With the Admiralty's reluctant agreement, *Leviathan* and other converted transports sailed independently. Escorts met them when they entered the war zone. Their speed protected them from submarines.

Initially, the fastest ships, making over twelve knots, ferried the doughboys. Troopship convoys were generally somewhat smaller (four to five transports) than those transporting food, oil, and other supplies. According to Sims, they had three times as many escorts as the other convoys. The first troop convoys used St. Nazaire for debarkation, but when former liners joined the "Bridge to France," they landed at Brest, Bordeaux, and other French ports in the Bay of Biscay. Brest received its first troop convoy in November. The growing number of American troop and supply ships soon overwhelmed these ports. To alleviate this congestion, Sims recommended the use of British ports. The War Department agreed. Liverpool received the first contingents of American troops that arrived in the fall. They were shuttled by rail to channel ports and from there by boat to France. Later Southampton was added to the list. Those units that moved through British ports probably spent a few extra days in travel before reaching their camps in France, but it lessened the problems of the French ports. Also it reduced the strain on escorts based in British bases.[43] The Admiralty preferred that the troop ships remain together under escort, but the War Department thought it impracticable. By August 1918, British warships had escorted 62 percent of the American troops that debarked in English ports and all of the troops that crossed the channel to France.[44] Liverpool served as their port of debarkation until the German offensive of 1918, which led General Pershing to urge that the large transports steam directly to either Brest or Southampton. Disembarking these troops at either a channel port or on the Bay of Biscay saved considerable time, approximately two days if they were landed in France. Some large troop ships were diverted to Brest, although Liverpool remained the principal port then. In July, the Department determined to sail *Leviathan* in convoy with other large ships, believing that this expedient provided additional protection. U.S. naval officials feared a threat from surface raiders. Sims protested the decision because it depleted his destroyer force in order to furnish adequate escorts.[45]

Sims continued to stress the need to concentrate control of all shipping, including troop transportation, in the Admiralty, but the Department rejected his advice. It continued to organize the troop convoys, including those that landed their troops in British ports. The Admiralty was informed of all troop convoys in order to avoid conflict with other convoys. The Department also ordered the troop convoys to use "special lanes." Finally, whenever possible, the troop transports were instructed to pass through the danger zone at night.[46] Sims asked the U.S. naval liaison officer to the French navy in Paris to "handle the officials in the Ministry of Marine diplomatically, so that they will . . . allow us to run the show from one source, which must be in London."[47] The French agreed and promised to provide escort out to a hundred miles from their coast, but the force commander believed that they lacked the promised escorts. Later events confirmed this judgment.[48]

Unlike the French, who were enthusiastic about the constant arrival of American troops, British officials remained somewhat unimpressed, at least until 1918. They shared the general belief that the inexperienced AEF could not become effective until 1919, but the shipping problem was of more immediate concern. Understandably, they were most concerned with the necessity to protect the supply of the British Isles. The American desire to protect the troop convoys at the expense of the mercantile convoys deeply worried the Admiralty and the War Cabinet. They had little control over American troop convoys, an unsettling element.[49] Although the Admiralty's fears proved groundless, Sims continued to report them to the Department.

In August 1918, the Navy Department decided to take control of all supply convoys from U.S. to French ports. The Admiralty accepted the change with good grace; it was "a somewhat natural desire," wrote a British official, "especially in such Convoys as were chiefly American in character." The French were not as receptive. On August 24, Admiral Wilson informed Sims's liaison in Paris that the French admiral in command in Brest continued to insist that he had "authority to route" supply convoys "with the understanding that he . . . inform the [British Admiralty] and . . . act in cooperation with Admiral Wilson." By September, however, the French accepted the change, probably on orders from Paris.[50]

The buildup of the American army increased the difficulty of providing adequate escorts in French coastal waters. Initially, the army transports and cargo vessels used only St. Nazaire and Brest to land troops and supplies, but these ports became congested after the increase in the volume of troops, equipment, and supplies that arrived from the United States. The Army added to the number of ports it used, but this effort did not relieve congestion. This problem occurred in part because the Navy Department and Admiralty insisted that the convoys first enter Brest and St. Nazaire. Coastal escorts would then accompany them to other locations. The Army wanted the convoys to proceed directly to their ports of debarkation. Sims and the Admiralty opposed this practice because of the lack of sufficient escort vessels. In June 1918, after American destroyers arrived in French waters, the Army's wishes prevailed.[51]

Communications with the French suffered from serious deficiencies. Sims could not connect directly to Brest. Convoy administrators and Simsadus in London had to go through Paris to inform the naval headquarters in Brest of scheduled convoys.[52] Washington had to cable information to Brest through either London or Paris. Radio centers were not available in St. Nazaire, St. Lorient, and other ports. Because of the lack of radio communication in St. Nazaire, the Queenstown-based destroyers were often delayed there, awaiting outbound ships, a situation that infuriated Sims.[53] Information to these ports was usually channeled through Brest. Ships at sea beyond 250 miles lacked radio connections with the mainland. French radio codes and signals caused confusion. The commanding officer of the yacht *Wakiva II* reported that both he and the convoy commander of an incoming convoy could not communicate with the senior escort officer, who was on a French destroyer. The French complained that U.S. ships often failed to use correct call signs. American and French naval officials in Brest attempted to avoid mixing American and French escorts, but this option was rarely available.[54] French port officials complained with justification that they frequently did not receive notification of the arrival of merchant ships, an especially hazardous omission when channels had to be swept for mines.

The command structure suffered from significant difficulties. Sims's policy of subordinating his forces to local command placed Captain Fletcher and later Admiral Wilson under the local French admiral. Usually, the French did not interfere with American escort operations, allowing the commander of U.S. naval forces in France to exercise independent command. Fletcher received directions to escort all shipping and to make all patrol vessels available. Fletcher responded that he "had turned 12 of the yachts over to the French, and have only 3 for escort duty." He did not report that the yachts transferred to the French conducted escort operations along the coast because they were considered unfit for offshore service. Sims, however, believed that these vessels could have been used to escort transports up to fifty miles off the coast. He sharply informed Fletcher that his "head would roll" if one of the troop transports were sunk.[55] That is what happened.

The transport *Antilles* was torpedoed and lost on October 17, 1917. Fortunately, she was outward bound and carried no troops. Sims immediately relieved Fletcher and ordered him home, although he insisted that he had decided to do so before *Antilles* went to the bottom. A court of inquiry placed the blame on no single individual, pointing out that the transport had reduced speed to conform to the convoy speed of nine-and-a-half knots. She was not zigzagging, although she was scheduled to do so three minutes after being torpedoed. The court also found that the convoy did not have an adequate escort.[56] Fletcher's removal shocked French naval officials, especially Rear Admiral Zephinn-Alexandre-Antoine Schwerer, in command of patrol forces on the French west coast. The French admiral called in Fletcher's temporary replacement, Captain T. P. Magruder, and asked whether the American admiral was relieved not because of the Antilles but "anterior causes." At this point "Admiral Schwerer became quite excited, and he spoke so rapidly that I could not gather all he said. The gist of it was, however, to the effect that *he*, not the American Commander, was responsible for operations on the west coast of France. . . . [I]n case anything went wrong, he alone would be responsible." Schwerer sent the minister of marine a detailed report of the command situation. He mentioned the American demand for more escorts, "which *is absolutely impossible* . . . at the present state of our resources." He recommended that he should control the coastal convoys and the American commander the ocean convoys.[57] Two difficulties existed: insufficient numbers of American or French ships were available to provide ocean escort without the participation of both navies, and difficulties with the French escorts continued to trouble the ocean convoy system.

Admiral Fletcher was granted a court of inquiry after the war. Testimony clearly demonstrated that the principal reason for the loss of *Antilles* was the lack of sufficient escorts, but the hearing also identified serious deficiencies in Fletcher's command. It was these deficiencies that Sims said convinced him to replace the patrol commander.[58]

French/American policy for escort command was the same as that followed in the Queenstown command; that is, the senior officer, whether American or Allied, would take charge of the escort group. The American commanding officers assigned to the French coast were junior to the French naval officers, which placed French naval officers in command of the escorts, even if most of the vessels were American. On more than one occasion, this circumstance caused "a nice mess." French naval vessels assigned to a convoy in the danger zone sometimes failed to make the rendezvous, and the convoy had to proceed to its destination without adequate escorts. They also frequently left the convoy "before [its] arrival at point of dispersion." Sims and Washington officials were concerned about these problems but because of "the sensitive nature of it," made no official protests.[59]

The French had only four small destroyers on their west coast. On a number of occasions, Sims cabled the Department: "The inadequacy of the French Force is well known and numerous incidents have come to hand of this."[60] On several occasions, incorrect coordinates were given for incoming convoys, which caused the French-based escorts to miss a convoy entirely. The commanding officer of the transport *Henderson* reported: "Two French torpedo boats were sent out to meet the convoy on the first voyage, but they missed the convoy, and joined from far astern. On the second trip, no vessels met us until we were within one-half mile of the entrance of the port, and then two small motor boat patrol launches (about 40 footers) appeared, and one of them conducted the convoy into port." Both French and American ships escorted him on both voyages, but they could not keep up with the convoys.[61]

Corsair's commanding officer reported the difficulties in working under a French commander: "The senior officer of our escort was in a ship lacking efficient radio communication. . . . The Chief of the Escort did not require the ships to zigzag nor to assemble in line formation as per doctrine. . . . I do not believe it is advisable for the Chief of Escort to be a French officer acting with large convoys of American and English ships." Sims informed the American naval commander in France that the destroyers escorting convoys to French waters "indicate [a] lack of confidence on their part as to the co-operation . . . from the French in approaching the coast."[62]

The most serious problem, however, was the weakness of the naval force, both French and American. The Navy Department on more than one occasion requested the French to increase their escort force for the ocean convoys, but the French insisted that they were doing the best they could, considering their commitments. For example, in June 1918, they pointed out to Sims that they had to use most of their ships to escort troop transports from French North Africa. On more than one occasion, the number of French escorts assigned to an ocean convoy from the United States was reduced without notification to American naval authorities.[63] Convoy and individual ship commanders often complained of insufficient escort in French waters. Sims informed the CNO that "numerous incidents have come to hand where ordinary mercantile convoys well escorted in the English Channel were necessarily eventually turned over to an inadequate French escort."[64] Not enough ships, either French or American, were capable of joining the ocean screen. The French had only a few available, and until October, when five coal-burning destroyers arrived, the American Navy had only a few yachts in hand. By the middle of September, the American force numbered some fifteen yachts, but only three could operate outside coastal waters. Despite the addition of another seagoing yacht and a destroyer, the *Stewart*, at 450 tons the smallest in the fleet, Admiral Wilson admitted to Sims that "our work . . . has been, and continues to be, unsatisfactory and subject to criticism." Without reinforcements, especially destroyers, he doubted that conditions would improve significantly.[65] The Navy Department gave priority to the troop convoys but did not have enough vessels to accompany the ocean convoys even after the arrival of the destroyers. Early in November, Sims ordered Queenstown-based destroyers to screen convoys all the way to Brest, St. Nazaire, and other French ports. The Admiralty agreed to order British escorts to do the same, but the destroyers had to give priority to the troop convoys.[66] Often storeship convoys were delayed because escorts were unavailable.

The number of convoys steadily increased as the AEF built up its force in Europe. The number of ships carrying supplies to Pershing's troops grew from approximately twenty-five to thirty in March 1918 to more than double that number by the summer and continued to increase until the Armistice. Initially storeship convoys were started at regular intervals, usually every four or eight days, but later Admiral Wilson mentioned that on one day five separate convoys were routed westward from France.[67]

Starting in October 1917, two months after outward-bound convoys were organized in British ports, they began to form in French ports. Because of the escort problem, the French were reluctant to do so. Sims was dissatisfied with their reluctance and ordered escort of outward-bound convoys, insisting later that the American naval commander in French waters "has full authority to regulate all sailing . . . at his discretion in case he thinks necessary."[68] On December 29, Admiral Gleaves sent a detailed list of convoy delays from French ports to the CNO, stressing that "the lack of sufficient . . . escort is now a great source of delay, if not the greatest."[69] Available escorts usually screened outward-bound convoys for about forty-eight hours before detaching to rendezvous with an incoming convoy. At times, however, escorts, usually destroyers, would have to go much farther into the Atlantic. On one occasion, the destroyers *Reid* and *Flusser* steamed nearly a thousand miles to pick up a convoy. The escorts followed the British tactic of spreading out on a wide scouting line, the distance between escorts depending upon weather conditions. Troop convoys were small in number of vessels, but usually included large ships. In January 1918, three troop convoys containing seven transports reached St. Nazaire, and in July eight convoys of fifty-two troop ships arrived.[70] On June 20, 1918, Taussig formed an escort of sixteen destroyers to protect thirteen transports carrying fifty thousand troops.[71]

The coastal convoys often lacked sufficient escort. Admiral Wilson recommended the exchange of the small yachts for the Coast Guard cutters based at Gibraltar, but Sims did not approve. The force commander and the Navy Department had an inflated idea of the availability of French naval vessels for escort. At the Department's instruction, Sims asked the French to provide a list of their patrol forces on the west coast. Admiral Schwerer indicated that he had twenty-four vessels under his command capable of ocean convoying, but Wilson reported that only seven were "available to meet convoys." Altogether, he reported, only eighteen vessels were on hand to escort the ocean convoys. Schwerer estimated that he required twenty additional naval vessels capable of ocean escort work to provide adequate protection. Later the French admiral admitted that the "scarcity of . . . escorts is [fraught] with [disastrous] . . . consequences," but he could offer little help.[72] He transferred two destroyers from Bordeaux to Brest, but Wilson continued to warn that "Our force and that of French are over taxed and seriously behind in keeping tonnage moving westward." In January 1918, there were eight groups of escorts of four vessels each, three of them American to guard convoys along the dangerous Brest to Bordeaux route, all in daylight.[73]

A French commander controlled each coastal convoy. Because of the difficulty in navigation along the rugged coast of Brittany, local pilots accompanied the American escorts. Other than difficulties with communication, the arrangements satisfied American escort commanders. The initial group of four yachts, later increased to twelve, performed well.[74] Coastal convoys included ships that steamed to and from various French and British ports and storeships from the United States that came with convoys ordered to various French ports. Usually they arrived at Brest and then were escorted along the coast to their destinations. Ships bound for North America sailed independently until outward-bound convoying was introduced in October 1917. They were then concentrated at Brest for the return voyage under escort. In 1918, the system was changed again when shipping became too heavy for Brest alone. Convoys were organized at different locations such as Le Verdon near the Gironde River and north of Brest in Quiberon Bay. Some yachts were shifted to other French ports, including *Aphrodite*, *Corsair*, *May*, *Nokomis*, *Noma*, and *Wakiva II* at Le Verdon (Rochefort) early in 1918. These yachts with French vessels continued to escort coastal convoys when not screening outward-bound convoys. Coastal convoys sailed daily, varying from a few freighters or cargo ships to as many as thirty. One convoy from Brest to St. Nazaire stretched for more than fifteen miles with only four small escorts.[75] The coastal convoys also received considerable protection from aircraft, although at times they were more a nuisance than a help.[76] The convoying usually occurred at night until January 1918. Early in that month, a U-boat commander nicknamed "Penmarch Pete," operating off Penmarch Point, sank four ships in one convoy. His success persuaded American and French officials to abandon night convoys. Also, the British agreed to provide escorts for convoys sailing to and from British ports to Quiberon Bay, permitting the Americans and the French to concentrate on the coast south of the bay. One of the coal-burning U.S. destroyers was assigned to reinforce the American escort groups that protected the coastal convoys.[77]

Coastal convoys feared mines more than U-boat attacks; they endangered all ships that approached French ports. "On this job," an enlisted man wrote in his journal, "we have long since learned that our most dangerous enemy is not the submarine. First it is fog. Secondly, rocks, or perhaps mines."[78] German submarines operated in the channels along the French coast, including the heavily used passage that connected St. Nazaire to the bay. They even eased into the Brest channel at night, sowing mines and occasionally torpedoing an unsuspecting ship.[79] The shallow-draft yachts had little trouble with the minefields, but deep-laden merchant vessels fell victim to mines.[80] None of the American destroyers and troop transports hit a mine.

Nonetheless, both Washington officials and Sims were concerned about them. In July 1917, a squadron of minesweepers was organized in the United States and ordered to French waters.[81] After conversion, they deployed to Brest in September. Ten were eventually sent to France. Because of the desperate need for escorts, the squadron was disbanded and the sweepers assigned to convoy work, for which they were ill-suited. Fletcher cabled Sims that this decision was made after discovering that their minesweeping gear was inadequate. The French promised to switch some of their trawlers to mine work in place of the American vessels. In less than two weeks, however, the converted fishing vessels were returned to minesweeping because they were unfitted as escorts. One of them foundered in moderately rough seas near Brest only three days after the sweepers began convoy work. They were then outfitted with French minesweeping gear and based at Lorient near Quiberon Bay. The American minesweepers cleared the waters leading to St. Nazaire. They were fragile vessels. Two of the remaining nine went aground on rocks and were lost. A French minesweeping flotilla had similar duties at Brest.[82] Admirals Wilson and Sims considered both the American and French minesweeping forces inadequate and strongly urged an increase in their numbers.[83]

The inauguration of New York and Sydney convoys in July combined with the burden of the existing Norfolk convoys caused Admiral Bayly to warn Sims that patrol might have to be abandoned in favor of escort. "I am afraid that the Admiralty are beginning to think that our supply of destroyers is inexhaustible," he wrote with acerbity.[84] In August, Bayly notified the Admiralty that the convoy "scheme proposed by Admiralty will be incapable of being carried out with the force at present under my orders. To keep the men and machinery of the destroyers in working order with minimum of breakdowns of efficiency it is necessary for them to be in harbour three days out of eight. In addition they require five days boiler cleaning every 500 hours steaming."[85]

Admiral Gleaves boasted that the convoys under his command did not lose a single soldier on the eastward transatlantic run, although outward-bound ships with troops aboard were sunk. Thirty-nine American ships in American service, not including escorts, went down in European waters—one to mines, two to collision, two wrecked, and two to unknown explosions. German U-boats destroyed the remainder.[86] *Tuscania*, *Moldavia*, and the animal transport *Ticonderoga* were sunk. On September 30, 1918, *Ticonderoga*, without animals but with a load of liberty motors and a field artillery battery, developed engine difficulties and fell behind her convoy. A U-boat, waiting for such a stray, surfaced and opened fire with two deck guns. The ship was shelled for more than two hours before the crew abandoned ship. She sank shortly afterward with a loss of 215 men. The German admiral in charge of submarines during the war later wrote of this action, "The *Ticonderoga*'s "gun fire[ed] to the last, which is a praise-worthy example of the great courage of the American crew."[87] The British transport *Otranto* suffered the greatest loss on October 6, 1918, when she collided with another ship and went down with 356 American soldiers aboard.

More ships, including transports, were lost on the westward voyage. *Antilles*, a 6,878-ton ship under Army charter, had steamed four hundred miles west of Brest on October 15, 1917, after landing her troops and equipment at St. Nazaire. Second in a column of ships, she had just started a zigzag run when a torpedo struck home. Heavy seas made it impossible to launch lifeboats; the survivors jumped into the seas and clung to bits of wreckage. Sixty-seven of 237 seamen were lost.[88]

Two former liners belonging to the Naval Overseas Transportation service (NOTS)—the *President Lincoln* and the *Covington*—were sunk returning from Europe. The *President Lincoln*, 18,000 registered tons, was a former Hamburg-American liner seized when war was declared. Converted into a troop transport, she made five voyages to France, carrying five thousand soldiers on each trip. After her escort departed to rendezvous with an eastbound convoy, she was torpedoed on May 31, two days after leaving France. Shortly after 9:00 a.m. the German submarine *U-90* fired two torpedoes at the ex-liner; one tore through the vessel's side near the bridge and the other just aft the engine room. The captain, Commander Percy W. Foote, later Secretary Daniel's naval aide, realized that the ship was doomed and ordered abandon ship. The men did not panic. The engine crew blew the boilers and banked the fires before going topside; corpsmen removed the ill, including wounded soldiers from sick bay. Lifeboats and rafts were quickly lowered into the pitching seas. The two 6.50-inch guns on the after deck continued firing blindly until water began to cover the deck. The gun crews then stepped off into rafts. As they abandoned the ship, crew members waited in line to slide down a line and then swam to a nearby raft or boat. Officers yelled to them to get away from the ship to keep from being sucked under as the ship went down. As some of them paddled away, they yelled, "Liberty party shoving off, etc."[89] The vessel remained afloat for some twenty minutes until a third torpedo hit. With "a black cloud of soot and smoke shooting from her stack," she quickly plunged stern first to the bottom. Only 26 crew and passengers were lost out of 715 on board.[90]

After the ship went down, the hundreds of survivors were scattered over a large distance. As the officers began collecting the boats and rafts, *U-90* appeared among them. One sailor was taken on board, questioned, and then returned to his boat. The submarine captain sought the ship's captain or another officer, but all but one either assumed disguises or crew members concealed them. Lieutenant E. V. Isaacs, the ship's assistant gunnery officer, did not take off his cap and coat with the markings of an officer. He was made a prisoner. Isaacs, an Iowan, was but three years out of Annapolis. He remained on the submarine until it returned to Wilhelmshaven. He later escaped to Switzerland, returned to London, and reported in detail everything that he had learned firsthand about German U-boats. For this exploit, he was awarded the Medal of Honor.[91]

Both Admirals Sims and Benson believed that ships in convoy were most vulnerable to submarine attack when steaming in column; they instructed commodores to sail in line with escorts on all sides while in the danger zone. U-boat commanders gradually developed tactics to counteract convoying. They began to submerge under the protective screen to get inside the convoy and gain a position from which to attack. Admiral Sims estimated that 70 percent of submarine attacks were made inside the escort screen.[92] U-boats often trailed the convoy, awaiting an opportunity to attack.

When attacked, *Covington*, formerly the Hamburg-American liner *Cincinnati*, a 17,000-ton transport, was on her sixth trip, steaming at fourteen knots and zigzagging under escort. One of the former liner's crew mentioned that, when the torpedo struck, about half of the crew was watching the Douglas Fairbanks movie *The Lamb*. "There was a big explosion," he recalled, "followed . . . by a tremendous crash of shattered glass, and all the lights went out."[93] A single torpedo exploded in the boiler room, throwing a lifeboat against one of her stacks and flinging water over her masts. The U-boat immediately came under fire from escorts and transports, including *Covington*, but managed to escape. The crew abandoned ship so rapidly that codebooks and more than $43,000 in currency were left on board. The liner, although listing some twenty degrees to port and down by the stern, continued to float all night. The destroyer *Reid* came alongside at daybreak. One of the destroyer's officers wrote:

> She appeared deserted. One small oil lantern was burning on the forecastle. . . .
> The water was up halfway on her port topsides and a little red of her waterline
> was showing to starboard. Her decks were badly disordered. Her outboard lifeboats
> were all gone, but many others and a great number of rafts were still on
> deck. . . . There were no colors flying which made every one swear.

The following morning the decision was made to tow her to port. The captain and a volunteer crew of thirty men returned and discovered three survivors. The paymaster picked up the money and his records, but a lurch caused him to panic and leave a second time. A sailor then recovered the grip with the currency and records and put it in a boat. Three tugs were sent out from Brest to tow the disabled liner, but several hours later, she listed further. The crew members on board were removed, and shortly afterward *Covington* slipped under, leaving floating debris on the surface.

Another *Reid* officer wrote: "A terrible sight. Nasty feeling. Tried to get rid of it by shaking myself, but couldn't. Don't want to see it again."[94]

Two British chartered vessels transporting American troops, *Tuscania* and *Moldavia*, were also sunk. Both were prewar luxury liners that the Royal Navy commandeered and converted to troop transports. On February 5, 1918, *Tuscania* steamed with a convoy in the North Channel between Northern Ireland and Scotland. She had on board 2,179 soldiers of the Thirty-second Division. At 7:40 in the evening, *U-77* fired two torpedoes at the 14,000-ton former liner; one hit near the engine room, killing thirty-nine coal stokers. Several hours later she sank stern first, carrying some 310

American doughboys with her. *Tuscania* was the first troopship sunk while carrying Americans soldiers in European waters.[95] Fifty-six men from the Fourth Division died on May 26, 1918, when *Moldavia*, a British armed merchant cruiser, went down in the English Channel.

Very few torpedoed ships stayed afloat and reached port. According to U.S. naval records, not counting warships, only four American vessels or vessels "in service of the United States," *Rochester*, *Westward Ho*, *Westbridge*, and *Mount Vernon*, survived torpedo damage. However, this list is incomplete. *Finland*, although torpedoed in the Bay of Biscay, was able to return to port. Grant, in *U-Boat Intelligence*, wrote that on September 7, 1918, a U-boat torpedoed the transport *Persic* with 2,800 American troops on board, but it reached port.[96] On the morning of September 5, 1918, *Mount Vernon*, formerly the German liner *Kronprinzessin Cecile* of nearly 19,000 tons gross (32,130 displacement) steamed homeward bound at eighteen knots two hundred miles from Brest in a convoy of two ships screened by six escorts. At approximately 7:30 a.m., sailors on the mess deck heard a forward battery open fire. The order "General Quarters!" followed, but before all stations could be manned, a torpedo struck the ship amidships, destroying half the boilers and flooding machinery spaces. Thirty-five men died in the explosion, all in the boiler and engine rooms. The ship was saved because, as Admiral Wilson noted in his report, "every possible precaution had been taken prior to her torpedoing to anticipate just such an accident."

Captain Dismukes, the ship's commanding officer, later wrote: "Every member of the [ship's] complement realized fully well, because they had been taught, that being struck by a single torpedo will not sink the ship. . . . The officers and men . . . never had any other idea than that of saving the ship." The ship's executive officer wrote his father: "although the ship was mortally wounded with half of her boilers gone and 35 dead men lying under 20 feet of water . . . not a man flinched. I feel so honored to be associated with such a body of men that I can scarcely write of anything else."[97]

A seaman on the torpedoed ship gave a different account later:

We were just finishing breakfast and sitting at this table and there was a bump with a kind of subdued noise. It felt kind of like something hit the ship and pushed it over to one side. And then there was a sound like an explosion, and then the ship tipped to the port side—the side we were sitting on. And we just sat with nobody doing anything—just sort of stunned. . . . Everybody suddenly got up and we started running like hell and panic broke out . . . guys clogged the pretty wide stairway going up and it was jammed with the guys trying to get out. . . . I noticed a guy standing on the table right where I was, and he reached up and pulled . . . down . . . a rope that was going up through a ventilator. . . . I had never tried that before, but I climbed that God-damned rope with the knots and came out on the boat deck, where the life boats were. And Jesus, there was panic up there with shooting going on. They were shooting into the water but nobody knew what the hell they were shooting at. . . . We noticed that [the lifeboats] . . . were tied with these big hawsers, ropes; with all the salt water these ropes were just knotted in there. Christ you couldn't untie those if you were the strongest man in the world. . . . If you couldn't untie the ropes you would use [a] . . . hatchet to cut it loose. . . . [E]verybody in the life boat parties . . . [was] all chopping like hell, and there was nobody trying to untie the knots. And it was terrible because you would chop a boat and one end of it would come loose and swing loose before the other guy got his cut loose. And I think a few boats landed right side up in the water and they didn't even have the weather plugs in and they just got full of water and . . . sank. Other boats were hanging there by one end, and when the other end dropped the boat landed upside down.[98]

The boats were not needed; despite the gaping hole in her side, the ship did not sink. Under her own power but listing badly, she limped two hundred miles back to Brest. According to former Seaman Fix, she had to be "run into mud flats" to keep from capsizing. Concrete was used to fill the hole, and after three months *Mount Vernon* returned to her home port.

In contrast, the former liner *Finland*, manned by a civilian crew, panicked and nearly lost the ship when she was torpedoed on October 11, 1917, while westbound 150 miles out of Brest. Passengers and many of the crew immediately rushed to the boats and launched them, although no one ordered abandon ship. Even gun crews left their weapons and rushed for the boats, as did the ship's first and fourth officers, both civilians. Some jumped overboard. Eight lost their lives. The transport had a huge hole thirty feet across in its hull. However, she remained afloat on an even keel with undamaged engines and boilers. Under escort, Finland returned to Brest.[99] This incident influenced the decision to commission troop ships as Navy vessels manned by Navy crews.

Usually troop transports and cargo vessels with armed guards tried to fight back. About four hundred cargo ships carried armed guards of U.S. naval personnel. In October 1917, a U-boat shelled *J. L. Luckenbach*, a cargo ship armed with two 4-inch guns. *Luckenbach*'s guns replied as she tried to outrun her opponent. A running fight continued over four hours. American destroyers, escorting a convoy ninety miles away, picked up an SOS. The destroyer *Nicholson* immediately steamed to assist *Luckenbach*. Two hours into the battle, *Luckenbach* radioed that she was throwing her codebooks overboard and that most of the crew was abandoning the ship. One gun was out of action, but the other continued firing. When *Nicholson* radioed, "Do Not Surrender!" *Luckenbach* replied, "Never!" At 9,000 yards, the U-boat's gun started to register hits. One tore a hole in the ship's side and exploded in an empty compartment; another hit the hull near the waterline, rupturing the freshwater tank, the only supply of freshwater; a third entered the engine room and partially disabled the engines; and nine others damaged the ship. When *Nicholson* arrived and drove off the submarine, the freighter remained afloat but seriously damaged. Remarkably, no one was killed and only nine were wounded. The American destroyer sent a doctor and two other crew members on board to assist. *Luckenbach*, escorted by *Nicholson*, was able to continue her voyage, limping along at six knots, and reached Le Havre a day later.[100]

One troop transport, *HMS Olympic*, loaded with nine thousand American soldiers, rammed and sank *U-103* as she submerged.[101]

Historians generally agree that the German submarine offensive began to falter in September 1917. Tonnage sunk in that month totaled 351,748 worldwide, the lowest figure of the year to date. Of twenty convoys attacked before September, losses were extraordinarily light. Generally only one ship was sunk per convoy; and none lost more than two ships. By the end of September in the Western Approaches, of eighty-three inbound convoys consisting of 1,306 ships, 18 were lost to submarines; fifty-five outbound convoys of 739 ships lost only 2. Of thirty-eight convoys, consisting of 2,095 ships, only 20 ships went down, a rate of less than 1 percent.[102]

Ships, however, would continue to be sunk. Losses to submarines rose to more than 450,000 tons in October 1917 and remained at nearly that amount in December, but from then until the Armistice the rate declined significantly. Only 35 ships sank of the 16,102 that steamed in Atlantic convoys, mostly unescorted ships. The loss rate was a mere 0.2 percent.[103]

In September 1917, U-boat commanders shifted to new operational areas, concentrating in the Bay of Biscay and the waters around the British Isles, particularly the English Channel and the Irish Sea. These locations were far from those in which they had been successful before the introduction of convoying. Heavy U-boat losses occurred in September, ten (possibly eleven) compared to an average of just over four per month to that point in 1917.[104]

Allied efforts to counter U-boats in the English Channel were unsuccessful, excepting the escorts engaged in protecting convoys transporting troops and supplies between British and French ports, until the late fall of 1917. In November, the C-in-C, Devonport, recommended escort of all convoys passing through the channel. Before the Admiralty took action, the Milford Haven Command inaugurated convoying in the waters between Ireland and England. In that month, twelve escorted convoys passed through without losses. Despite this success, the Admiralty did not agree to convoying for all home waters until the middle of 1918.[105] American naval forces were not involved in channel escorts until late in 1918, when Plymouth-based subchasers joined channel escorts. Queenstown destroyers accompanied vessels destined for Liverpool and other ports in the Irish Sea. After the introduction of convoying, minimal losses occurred in both the channel and Irish Sea.

In April 1917, German submarines began attacking shipping in the vicinity of the Azores. The Allies and the United States did little about it at first. The U.S. Navy established a small coaling station in the Azores to refuel its "short-legged" vessels on the way to European waters but at first did not react to the U-boat presence. After the establishment of the convoy system, the islands became more important. Admiral Dunn wrote that because "our convoy routes passed north and south of the island [Ponta Delgada], if it had been in possession of the enemy, it would have seriously interfered with the successful transport across the ocean of troops and supplies."[106] When a U-boat bombarded Ponta Delgada in July 1917, the Navy Department decided to deploy warships to the Azores. On July 4, the Navy collier *Orion* drove off a German U-boat that attacked Ponta Delgada. The collier had stopped there to unload a cargo of coal to refuel American naval vessels plying to and from the war zone. In the fall of 1917, the Navy stationed a few small surface vessels and a flotilla of submarines in the Azores. The U.S. naval base at Ponta Delgada was expanded to support these units and vessels in transit. Periodically during the war the Navy considered the use of Ponta Delgada or another port in the islands as an assembly point for convoys going to the Mediterranean. Sims opposed the use of the islands for this purpose because it required the diversion of warships needed elsewhere. Although German submarines sunk fifteen ships between the Azores and Gibraltar during the period January-May 1918, the force commander told the Department in May 1918 that at that time only one U-boat was present in the waters around the Azores. Most of the losses were to passing submarines. In April, *U-262* was assigned to patrol the waters around the islands. She sank two ships, but the submarine skipper later wrote that traffic around the Azores "was slight."[107] In August 1918, the Department decided to base more destroyers at Ponta Delgada, but the Armistice was signed before their arrival. Whenever possible, Dunn held antisubmarine vessels for a few days before they proceeded to European waters. He sent them out on patrol. "Our duty," one destroyer sailor wrote, "consisted almost entirely of patrolling the waters adjacent to the islands . . . the procedure was for the destroyers to go out, either singly or in couples and run aimlessly around the ocean hoping that they might see a sight a sleeping submarine." The patrols never encountered one. Sims wrote that the "chief value of this base . . . was as an aid to Allied shipping rather than a means of fighting the submarine." Dunn certainly understood this point. "I keep the harbor gutted. No ship will stay a minute longer than necessary."[108] However, only a small percentage of convoys utilized Ponta Delgada.

Escorts would have been of little use if surface raiders had attacked a convoy. In the spring of 1918, British naval intelligence began to suggest that German surface ships might raid convoys. The Allied Naval Council discussed such a possibility during its first meeting in January 1918, but neither the British nor Admiral Sims took the threat seriously. In April, Admiral K.G.B. Dewar, the assistant director of the Admiralty's Plans Division, proposed to withdraw battleships from the Grand Fleet to escort convoys, but Beatty refused to consider this measure. Early in May, the possibility of a cruiser raid was brought to the attention of the American Planning Section with the suggestion that "American battleships should be employed to escort troop transports convoys." The British and American planning sections then drew up a plan that was forwarded to Washington. Admiral Benson agreed that battleships should be used to escort convoys and proposed to base a division of three battleships in European waters to serve as a fast task force. Pre-dreadnoughts could escort the convoys, and additional battleships based in North America could prepare to sortie. Convoys could be diverted to the Azores. The division of three battleships and escorting destroyers could rendezvous with them for protection. Because the American battleships were too slow to catch up with faster battle cruisers, the Navy Department hoped that either the British or Japanese would provide battle cruisers for the pursuit. The plan would become effective "upon receipt of broadcast radio and cable regarding enemy's escape from North Sea." In other words, the battleship escorts and task force would not deploy until British intelligence determined that German cruisers were on the loose.[109] Sims noted that no one could guarantee that warnings would be sent in time to prevent raiders from reaching the Atlantic convoy routes. Early in August, the Department agreed to deploy the battleship division to European waters immediately. At Sims's and presumably the Admiralty's recommendation, Berehaven in Bantry Bay became their operational base.[110]

Early in August, Rear Admiral Thomas S. Rodgers, in command of a battleship division with the Atlantic Fleet in Chesapeake Bay, was directed to get his division ready for deployment to European waters. One ship of the division, *North Dakota*, was in the yard undergoing an extensive overhaul. *Utah* was selected to join the other two units in the division, *Oklahoma* and *Nevada*. Sims requested that an oil-burning vessel replace the coal-burning *Utah*, but he was turned down.[111]

On August 12, *Oklahoma*, flying the flag of Rear Admiral Rodgers, and *Nevada* stood out of Hampton Roads. The voyage across the Atlantic was uneventful except that the *Nevada*'s gun crews fired at what they thought was a periscope but proved to be a floating spar. On August 23, the division entered Bantry Bay. "Well, here we are at last," wrote Rodgers to Sims, "and a great relief it is after seventeen months at Yorktown. My! But it got powerful full there."[112] Utah joined the squadron on September 12.

The command structure was somewhat awkward. Sims informed Rodgers that he was under his orders, but all other American naval forces in Ireland were under the British Admiral Bayly. The Admiralty preferred to channel orders concerning the battleships through Bayly, but at Benson's insistence they went through Sims. Bayly, in typical fashion, wrote the Admiralty requesting a clarification of command: "After very much experience I have always found that friction and misunderstanding are only avoided by a clear understanding beforehand, and that the policy of saying that things will be all right nearly always end in their becoming all wrong. Therefore, before they arrive, I suggest that you see Admiral Sims and send Admiral Rodgers a special letter stating that he is in command of his two ships only (or any other than may be added); that the *Bushnell* and submarines must remain directly under my orders."[113] Sims's instructions to Rodgers informed him that, when intelligence was received that raiders were out, twelve Queenstown-based destroyers would provide a screen for the battleship division. This measure would temporarily remove them from Bayly's command. Although obviously unhappy with the situation, Bayly, with the Admiralty's concurrence, agreed to this arrangement, but he told Rodgers that because of convoy commitments only six destroyers would be available to escort the division.[114] Bayly visited the battleships and came away impressed. "I like [Rodgers] . . . very much. He showed me the triple turrets the other day." According to *Oklahoma*'s captain, the British admiral equally affected the Americans.[115] Admiral Mayo came over on *Utah* for an inspection tour of U.S. naval forces in European waters. He had recommended deployment of all the dreadnought battleships to European waters under his command, but the CNO rejected the proposal.[116]

The Admiralty also objected to the diversion of convoys under their jurisdiction to the Azores in the event of a surface raid. Admiral Benson, however, insisted that troop convoys under American control were to go to the Azores when they received word that German raiders had departed their ports. Pratt wrote that convoys were under orders to scatter and later to rendezvous near the Azores when they received a single code word. Although the Department considered this procedure a drastic action, it was deemed necessary because the battleships were too slow to deal with German raiders and other vessels were unavailable to perform this duty.[117]

During the few weeks that the battleships were based at Berehaven, they were "under short sailing notice" similar to that of the Grand Fleet. On October 14, Rodgers received instructions to be ready for sea on an hour's notice. His division and escorting destroyers were ordered to rendezvous with an incoming convoy. A British submarine had spotted three raiders in the North Sea. *Nevada*'s commanding officer recalled in his memoirs: "at four o'clock in the morning we received a signal from Admiral Rodgers to be ready to get underway in two hours. This upset me very much as I knew it means information had been received that a raider was out." He was disturbed because he was being detached from the ship's command that day. "Sure enough, at eight in the morning the Admiral called all the Captains on board, told us he had received information that a raider was out and when the destroyers arrived from Queenstown at ten o'clock the Division would get underway and go out to meet the convoy."[118]

The division met the convoy and provided escort to its destination without incident. The battleships then provided a screen for a second convoy before returning to their base. Captain Charles McVay, who took command of *Oklahoma* the day it sailed ("I had only the clothes in my grip"), wrote that the operation was "what the British called a 'spasm.'" "Anyway, it was an experience."[119]

The alarm also forced the Grand Fleet to sortie. The Admiralty admitted later that no raiders had deployed from German ports. Admiral Fremantle wrote to Beatty, "There is no evidence whatever of any intention to send out raiders, nor do I think the political situation makes that likely." He referred to unrest in the German navy, which soon produced a widespread mutiny.[120]

The Navy Department arranged to rotate the battleships at Bantry Bay with the American battleships assigned to the Grand Fleet, but before the exchange began, the Armistice was signed. If the war had continued, Admiral Benson planned to rotate all the dreadnought-type battleships to European waters. The only one that did so was *Arizona*, which arrived in Berehaven on November 30. She then participated with the other units of the Sixth Battleship Squadron to escort President Wilson to Brest.

The battleships deployed to Ireland were called "fast battleships," but they were underpowered and could barely make twenty knots. If the German raiders came out, it was unlikely that the battleships could have caught them, but their primary objective was to protect the convoys, which they could do with their heavy battery of 14-inch guns.

Historians and participants from both sides agree that convoying was a great success. According to Sir Arthur Salter, statistics confirm that losses in convoy were less than 1 percent compared to an average of about 10 percent before its adoption. Of 16,693 ships that steamed in ocean convoy, 16,359 arrived safely at their ports of destination.[121] A former U-boat commander, Admiral Andreas Michelsen, admitted that "the greatest protection of the enemy commerce and the greatest difficulty of the submarines" was the convoy system.[122] Goerlitz, a diarist at the Kaiser's court, mentioned on July 13, 1918, that "His Majesty spoke exceedingly sharply on the failure of the U-boats to sink American transports." On August 8, he recorded, "urgent need to renew confidence in the U-boat war, which has been very much shaken by the report sent to his Majesty by the Naval Attaches abroad." On September 4, he mentioned a meeting with Albert Ballin, the director of the Hamburg-Amerika line, in which Ballin said that "The military plan had been to force a decision before the Americans entered the war and thus restore the balance which had been in our favour when Russia went out of the war. . . . The plan came to grief because of the failure of the U-boat war."[123] Admiral Sims stressed importance of the convoy system. "Without the assistance of the United States Navy, the vital lines of communication . . . could not have been kept open . . . [and] the Allies could not have won the war."[124] He did not mention that the contribution of the European-based escorts was vital to its success.

Escorts

Convoying has always required escorts. During World War I, escort work became the principal responsibility of the U.S. Navy. Warships to screen convoys were employed in the Western Hemisphere, on the transatlantic route to Europe, in the Mediterranean, and in British and French coastal waters. The Irish Sea became "as truly American as Long Island Sound," especially during the spring of 1918, when German U-boats shifted their operations to that area, making it "an infernal place." British ASW craft could not provide sufficient support. The American destroyers from the Queenstown command had to protect shipping in the area.[1] Destroyers were the favored ships for escort, but demand far exceeded the supply. The Department had to use every type of warship in its inventory and suitable civilian vessels to fill the gap until a crash building program provided the required escorts.

Robert Ferrell maintains that without the American destroyers "transatlantic convoys would have been impossible. . . . The U.S. Navy made the crucial difference without which the Allies would have lost the war in 1917–18."[2] Most of the American destroyers employed as escorts were based in European waters. Destroyers screened transatlantic or oceanic convoys at times, usually when ordered to deploy to European waters. They were detached from the convoys when they approached Queenstown or some other base.

Shortly after Congress declared war, the United States agreed to deploy destroyers in British waters and to send a number of armed yachts and miscellaneous vessels to conduct antisubmarine operations in French waters. Sims informed the Department that twenty destroyers were needed immediately. The first six destroyers set out for Europe on April 26.[3]

The General Board persuaded Secretary Daniels and Admiral Benson to send additional destroyers. Before the United States intervened, the Board recommended the dispatch of destroyers to the war zone as soon as the nation declared war. Within weeks, the Board received information that documented the devastating German submarine onslaught. On April 28, the Board informed Secretary Daniels that the success of the U-boats could lead to the defeat of the Allies. The United States must deploy as many patrol craft as possible in European waters. Five days later the Board advised the secretary to send "200 or more patrol craft . . . in the next two months. The fate of England would be decided during that period. This reinforcement was essential and must occur even if it became necessary to exclude other contributions." On May 15, the secretary forwarded a memo to the General Board for "information and guidance," which listed the construction of subchasers and destroyers as priorities numbers five and six. Top priority was to increase the strength and improve the material condition of the existing fleet, which included the battleships then under construction or on the drawing boards. The second priority was to arm merchant ships. Daniels and the chief of naval operations considered this measure a more effective means of defeating the submarine than convoys.[4]

The adoption of convoying confirmed the absolute necessity of deploying as many ASW craft in European waters as possible. The first sea lord and his advisors maintained that the Allies did not have enough escorts to establish an extensive convoy system without substantial American help. The French and Italians had few modern destroyers, which were concentrated in the Mediterranean. When the United States entered the war, the British had 279 destroyers in home waters. Admiralty officials insisted that the distribution of this sizeable force could not change, including nearly a hundred with the Grand Fleet.[5] Sims agreed that the Grand Fleet must retain its destroyer screen, but historians have generally disagreed. "There was no shortage of escorts in early 1917," declared John Winton. "The only blockages were mental ones. There were available and ready to start on convoy duties, 350 destroyers and sixty sloops, with sixty old cruisers and twenty-four old battleships. This was a truly staggering total of *very nearly 500 ships*. But large numbers of destroyers and cruisers were still used in patrolling empty ocean waters, or escorting single troopships." The British navy also had three hundred vessels in the Auxiliary Patrol that could be used as coastal escorts.[6] A number of American naval officers in European waters questioned the apparent refusal of the Admiralty to provide destroyers for convoy and antisubmarine operations.[7]

Sims along with many of his officers urged Washington officials to scrap the 1916 naval construction program, which emphasized capital ship construction, in order to build more destroyers and other small craft. The reluctant Navy Department eventually agreed to build more destroyers and delayed the construction of capital ships.[8]

Before President Wilson asked for a declaration of war, the British government organized a shopping list of American vessels, with destroyers at the top. On April 3, the Admiralty informed Captain Guy Gaunt, the British naval attaché in Washington, and Admiral Sir Montague E. Browning, in command of British naval forces in the West Indies, that it "attach[ed] [the] greatest importance to having as many U.S. destroyers as possible in our waters." Browning was ordered to travel to the United States. On April 10, he and Rear Admiral Maurice Ferdinand Albert de Grasset, in command of French naval forces in the West Indies, arrived at Hampton Roads. In meetings with Admiral Benson and Secretary Daniels, the two admirals stressed the need for destroyers and other small craft. The chief of naval operations was not encouraging. "The present naval policy [of the United States]," he told them, "was to maintain our Fleet intact until it would become apparent how it could be employed more effectively, but that we were ready to do our part in patrol of the Atlantic and Gulf Coasts." According to Benson's biographer, the CNO wanted to deploy only one or two destroyers to "show the flag" in European waters, claiming that this gesture would exercise a considerable moral effect. Two days later, however, an agreement was worked out to send six destroyers to British waters. Admiral Browning reported to the Admiralty that the assistance of Admiral Mayo and Assistant Secretary of the Navy Franklin Roosevelt led to the decision to send six rather than two. The French were promised ships as soon as they became available. De Grasset thanked Secretary Daniels, but he was disgruntled, complaining to Browning that "I [Browning] had got everything and that he [Grasset] had got nothing."[9]

A week after Browning and Grasset departed (April 14), large missions arrived from the two countries, bearing instructions to discuss joint war measures. The foreign secretary, Lord Arthur Balfour, headed the British mission, and René Viviani, a former vice premier, and Marshal Joseph Joffre led the French. Admirals Sir Dudley De Chair and P.L.A. Chocheprat served as naval representatives.[10] Admiral De Chair talked to Sims before leaving London, and the American admiral warned him that he would have difficulty persuading the Department to send "all of their destroyers to us." In Washington, De Chair conferred with Benson and the General Board. "I was received with great cordiality . . . but when I touched on the question of sending their destroyers to help us I found I was right up against it." De Chair later claimed that Assistant Secretary Roosevelt "finally succeeded in getting permission for thirty-six of their best destroyers to come to us as soon as possible." Roosevelt's role in the destroyer question is somewhat obscure. He pushed to send a great many destroyers to European waters. The General Board also recommended the dispatch of a large number of destroyers. More than likely, however, Balfour's meeting with President Wilson proved to be the decisive factor. Rear Admiral Albert Gleaves later wrote: "About this time Mr. Balfour arrived and went at once to the White House. After a conference with the president . . . it was decided to send all 36 destroyers. . . . Thus at the beginning of the war I lost my force!" He added, "I had a talk with Mr. Daniels and then went to Mr. Roosevelt's residence to talk with him, but with no results—except that I had the satisfaction, such as it was, of expressing my own views—which clearly did not make the impression I was seeking."[11]

The French were not as successful. Admiral Chocheprat presented a request for two divisions of six destroyers each and fifty patrol vessels. De Chair, however, opposed this measure. "I have rubbed it in how fatal it would be to disperse United States destroyers amongst different nations," principally the French, he informed the first sea lord. "But," he added, "there is a strong party who are anxious to conciliate [the] French." Conciliation produced a promise to send antisubmarine vessels, including armed yachts, when they became available, but not destroyers. When the French admiral called on Daniels before departing for France, he "bluntly through the Naval Attaché [Chocheprat did not speak English] expressed hope that our good sentiments would be followed accordingly to their claims for practical help." The French persisted in seeking destroyers but without success. The Wilson administration agreed to turn over a large number of the 110-foot subchasers as soon as they became operational and also to concentrate a sizable U.S. naval presence in French waters before the end of the war, including destroyers.[12]

The Admiralty's plans for the distribution of destroyers and other escort craft made the availability of U.S. warships a necessity to ensure the success of a convoy system.

Admiral Bayly wrote in his memoirs that it was impossible to escort convoys effectively without the American destroyers. "Before their arrival," he noted, "we had to protect the incoming trade . . . for the Channel and Irish Sea with 13 coal-burning sloops, a few trawlers, and an occasional destroyer for a short time."[13] Bayly, however, was strongly committed to patrolling, which was maintained in his command after convoying began.

Admiral Sims was convinced that the submarine crisis demanded the presence of American destroyers and other antisubmarine craft in the war zone, but he recognized that the proposal required a fundamental shift in U.S. naval doctrine. To send the U.S. destroyers independently would effectively dismember the battle fleet, contrary to the accepted Mahanist prescription, a comprehensive and concentrated battle fleet. He was well aware of the strong anti-British attitude that existed in the Navy Department at that time. Sims was delighted but also surprised when he learned that destroyers were to deploy in British waters. Sims later complained that for more than two weeks (April 10–22) the Navy Department did not respond to his appeal for destroyers and light craft. During this period, he apparently received only one cable from the Department, a communiqué from Daniels asking why it was not practicable to blockade the German coast and prevent the egress of submarines. Sims responded that the Allies had failed in efforts to do so.

On April 22, the CNO cabled the news that the United States would soon send six destroyers. Vice Admiral Mercier de Lostende, the French naval attaché in London, conferred with Sims and wrote a long report about his frustrations in dealing with the Navy Department: "After the naval conference held in Washington [April 10–14], the Americans decided to send a few torpedo boats to Europe and to reserve a large number in American combat squadrons. Admiral Sims declared this insufficient and asked, in order for their best military utilization, for all the torpedo boats of the American fleet capable of crossing the ocean to be sent to Europe." Sims testified after the war that he had been generally kept in the dark as to the Department's decisions. "I learned of this agreement [to send six destroyers] by accident. I was totally unaware that any conference had been held." Ambassador Page later commented on Sims's dissatisfaction. His "constant appeals for warships elicited the most inadequate response, his well-reasoned recommendations for meeting the crisis were frequently unanswered and at other times were met with counter-proposals so childish that they seemed almost to have originated in the brains of newspaper amateurs."[14] Although the Admiralty must have informed Sims of the deliberations going on in Washington in April, it is conceivable that much of it was passed on to him after the fact.

Throughout the summer months, Sims became increasingly convinced that convoying was necessary to counter the submarine. He equated the success of convoying with the availability of American naval vessels for escorts, particularly destroyers. On June 21, he wrote Daniels, "[T]he convoy system will defeat the submarine campaign if applied generally and in time." But, he added, "the immediate dispatch to this area of all possible destroyers and anti-submarine craft of any description is mandatory if the convoy system is to be effective."[15] On July 8, he reiterated his strong belief in the convoy system. "If . . . forces can be sent in time there is every reason to believe that convoy system can be sufficiently extended to defeat submarine campaign."[16]

Sims's communications to Washington began to underline the offensive nature of convoying. "This will be purely an offensive measure," he informed Daniels on June 29. "If we concentrate our shipping into convoys and protect it with our naval force, we will thereby force the enemy, in order to carry out his mission, to encounter naval forces which are not embarrassed with valuable cargoes."[17] He advocated the dispatch of all available light craft to European waters. On June 20, he wrote: "destroyers are, of course, the best and most successful anti-submarine craft, but their number, even if all . . . were sent, would not meet the demand. . . . It is therefore necessary to send any character of armed craft which can reach these waters—tugs, yachts, fishing vessels, small gunboats, towed if necessary by reserve battleships, [and] cruisers." On July 3, he pleaded, "cannot all destroyers Atlantic coast be sent and all revenue cutters." He sent similarly worded messages to Ambassador Page and asked him to appeal to the State Department and the president. "There are at least seventeen more destroyers employed on our coast, *where there is no war*," he complained to the ambassador. Page totally supported Sims and added his pleas to Washington. He also persuaded the British government to press Washington for more antisubmarine vessels.[18]

Several circumstances led to the Department's apparent indecisiveness about sending additional vessels. It was partly a result of the Navy's sluggish transition to the emergency of war, partly a consequence of Secretary Daniels's irresolution, and partly Benson's initial reservations about convoying. The CNO believed that armed guards on board merchant ships and transports would ensure their safety, and he hoped to retain most of the fleet in American waters. Another cause of delay was the belief prevalent in Washington that the British navy could provide many more vessels for escort.[19]

The Department's determination to retain destroyers and other light craft in American waters infuriated Sims. "How is it that they cannot see that this is as wrong as it possibly can be from a military point of view? . . . If there were any danger off our coast or if dangers should develop . . . you could send the forces back again . . . before any considerable number of the enemy could get over there."[20]

Nonetheless, Benson grudgingly ordered additional vessels to the war zone. On July 5, Sims received information that eight "patrol boats" were underway to France and that ten yachts would leave in ten days. Five *Preston*-class destroyers were headed for the Azores, and twelve trawlers and another yacht would leave home waters about August 10. "Department is strongly impressed with the necessity for adequate antisubmarine patrol in and off entrance of Gibraltar. Ten vessels, *Birmingham, Chester, Salem, Sacramento, Yankton, Macias, Casting, Paducah, Wheeling*, and *Marietta* are available to send across if considered that they can be of value."[21] Benson knew that most of these vessels were old and obsolete and was unsure of their suitability for escort. By August, the CNO had ordered the ten old vessels to Gibraltar along with yachts to French waters. Forty-five of sixty-eight destroyers in commission at the time were either operating in the war zone or en route to it.

Probably the CNO reacted to pressure from above. As Daniels informed Secretary of State Robert Lansing, they were willing to send "all anti-submarine craft not needed at home."[22] On June 9, Daniels cabled Sims: "Department considers it essential on account of the present sensitive public opinion that the escort . . . for the first [troop] convoy . . . be escorted by our own destroyers. . . . The soundness of your recommendations are [sic] recognized by the Department. . . . Please write giving outline plan for handling the European end of the escort duty for further convoys."[23] It is probable that the CNO's assistant, Captain Pratt, helped convince him to agree to send additional ASW vessels.[24] As early as May 12, Benson informed Admiral Mayo, "The Department fully appreciates the importance of maintaining a destroyer force with the battleship force," but he added that "it is necessary that as many destroyers as possible shall be employed on distance service." Only sixty-odd destroyers were then in service. On July 21, the secretary of the navy signed an order to build 266 new destroyers. Until they became available, however, the Department had to find other vessels considered adaptable for antisubmarine duty. The General Board provided an inventory of 201 vessels of all types. From this list, the Navy energetically selected yachts, gunboats, and other craft for service in Europe. Nevertheless, Sims and many of his officers in European waters then and after the war were convinced that ASW craft were needlessly held back.[25]

The Department ordered destroyers to the war zone despite strong recommendations from Admiral Mayo that they remain with the fleet. Admiral Albert Gleaves, in command of the destroyer force, Atlantic Fleet, noted: "On Friday (April 29) received orders to send Melville and six more destroyers to yards to prepare for distant service 'with all possible dispatch.' This robbed me of all my Force except Seattle."[26] Gleaves continued to press for retention of destroyers. In June 1918, he asked the CNO to keep all newly completed destroyers in the United States for escort duty "until a total of not less than twelve shall become available." Then the older ones could be sent abroad.[27] At the end of June, thirty-six of the available fifty-two destroyers were either in European waters or under orders to sail, not including five obsolete destroyers of the Preston class from Asiatic waters.

The destroyer question did not end with the decision to send thirty-six vessels to the British Isles. The initiation of convoying made it even more imperative to deploy antisubmarine craft. The Admiralty could or would not provide escort vessels for Atlantic convoying until adequate numbers of U.S. antisubmarine craft appeared in European waters. Jellicoe determined that at least seventy-two destroyers were needed for convoying. British destroyers were not available because of various concerns, among them fear of a sortie by the German High Seas Fleet, the possibility of enemy raids against locations on the English coast, and the need to protect hospital ships and troop transports in the channel. After the war, Daniels argued that "the British were married to the idea and never divorced it, that they must keep their destroyers attached to the fleet so as to defeat the German fleet when it came out." Although Daniels implied that the destroyers with the Grand Fleet could have been used for convoying because the High Seas Fleet never came out, he profited from hindsight.

Despite the battle of Jutland, it was reasonable in 1917 to assume that the Germans would sortie again.[28]

After Admirals Mayo and Benson visited Great Britain and France, additional destroyers were dispatched to the war zone. Eight arrived in August, three each in October and November, and seven in January 1918. By February, sixty-one were deployed in European waters along with a substantial number of yachts and other small craft based at French ports. This reinforcement stripped the battle fleet of most of its destroyers and small ASW vessels. The number of ASW craft in European waters slowly increased until by November 1918, 105 vessels were deemed suitable for escorting convoys, among them two cruisers, seventy-three destroyers, twenty-five armed yachts, five gunboats, five Coast Guard cutters, and two cruisers. Wooden subchasers, although used occasionally in the channel as escorts, were thought inappropriate for this work.[29] An Admiralty report of March 1918 recorded that only 16.2 percent of the auxiliary vessels deployed in home waters were engaged in escort, including American and British destroyers. The overwhelming majority, 819 vessels, carried out patrolling and minesweeping.[30]

In September 1918, the Admiralty concluded that "the convoy work of the United States destroyers in European waters is limited to the Atlantic. The whole of the convoy work in the North Seas, Irish Sea and Cross Channel is performed by British destroyers, which are also responsible for the whole of the escort work round the shores of Great Britain."[31] While this report is not entirely accurate because U.S. destroyers out of Queenstown escorted merchant ships in the Irish Sea and occasionally the English Channel, it suggests that the British shouldered most escort operations in British waters. German intelligence, which obtained accurate information about the number and location of U.S. naval vessels in European waters, concluded that American naval presence was "a negligible quantity."[32]

The Admiralty and the Navy Department faced the question of where to deploy escorts when they became available. The Western Approaches had priority at the Admiralty. The western coast of France was most important to the United States. Gibraltar, however, was also an important concern. The Admiralty wanted to station the five *Bainbridge*-class destroyers coming from Asia at Gibraltar. Although the Department recognized the need to reinforce Gibraltar, it initially hesitated to send destroyers. Twenty-two miscellaneous vessels were ordered there, including gunboats, converted yachts, and cruisers.[33] Because transports plying between Gibraltar and British ports entered waters frequented by U-boats, the entire screen usually escorted them to their destination. Units of the auxiliary patrol and later U.S. subchasers joined the convoys when they approached British waters. In the middle of August, Sims learned that six additional yachts were en route to France and five vessels to Gibraltar. Four others had orders for Gibraltar but were held up because of labor difficulties and congestion in the shipyards.[34] Although American naval vessels were deployed in Gibraltar as early as September, the cruiser *Sacramento* did not join the Britain-to-Gibraltar screen until November. Additional American warships based at Gibraltar reinforced this system, including the cruisers *Chester* and *Birmingham*, the armed yacht *Nahma*, and the Coast Guard cutters *Tampa, Algonquin, Seneca,* and *Ossipee.* Sims recommended convoying between Gibraltar and Hampton Roads, but it was not implemented until the spring of 1918. The usual reason, a lack of escorts, delayed its introduction.[35]

At Sims's request the destroyers from Asia went first to Queenstown, where they were fitted out with depth-charge gear and their officers and crew indoctrinated in ASW tactics. Later the force commander decided to order all antisubmarine craft to Queenstown for a brief period of training and the installation of equipment not provided in the United States. Indecision reigned over the choice of station for the old destroyers from Asia. The Department preferred the Azores, wishing to protect troop transports against long-range U-boats that had begun to operate in that area. Some consideration was given to deployment in French waters, but they eventually went to Gibraltar.[36]

The Admiralty continued to press the American government for escort craft. Admiral Mayo visited in London early in September and heard the familiar advice that all available antisubmarine vessels should move to European waters. He had misgivings about stripping the fleet of its light craft but loyally carried the British request with him. He also gained the impression that convoying worked well. He noted: "the first effect of convoying that an observer stationed 200 or 300 miles at sea would have noticed was that shipping seemed suddenly to disappear. In the days of individual sailings through the approach zones . . . No waters of the world were as crowded as these. Then, when the convoy system went into effect . . . The sea became deserted in appearance, simply because the ships which had once been scattered far and wide were now collected into compact groups. . . . A submarine far out at sea in search of prey might range there for days without seeing a single vessel."[37]

Benson and Mayo's trips to the war zone produced mixed results. They inspired commitments to continue sending destroyers to European waters as they became available, but at the same time the U.S. Navy significantly increased its responsibilities in the war zone, including deployment of battleships with the Grand Fleet, provision of minelayers for the North Sea Mine Barrage, and the establishment of additional naval presence in various areas such as the Azores and the Mediterranean. Later the Department agreed to create submarine hunting groups. All of these responsibilities required additional destroyers, but very few arrived after January. Between February 1 and November 1918, only twelve reached the war zone, increasing the number from sixty-one to seventy-three, a far cry from the number promised the Allies.

Despite contrary testimony delivered after the war, new construction of destroyers moved quite slowly. Also the Germans finally launched a submarine campaign in the western Atlantic off the coast of the United States during May 1918. The Navy Department immediately stopped sending destroyers to the war zone. As Lord Jellicoe wrote after the war, it was fortunate that Germany did not send U-boats to American waters in 1917: "[T]he moral effect of such action . . . would have been very great and might possibly have led to the retention in the United States of some of the destroyers and other small craft which were of such assistance in European waters in starting the convoy system."[38]

In December 1917, the Department approved a destroyer escort for the American ships assigned to lay the North Sea Mine Barrage. The Admiralty recommended sixteen destroyers. Washington then informed Sims that none were available for this duty except those in his command. Admiralty officials, after conferring with American naval officers in London, decided to provide the necessary destroyer support for the minelayers, "as it is preferable to use . . . [American destroyers] at Queenstown." To provide this protection, the Queenstown force was stripped of its remaining British antisubmarine craft (twelve sloops).[39]

Admiral Beatty also requested six American destroyers as escorts for the U.S. battleships that joined the Grand Fleet in December 1917. The Admiralty agreed to this, as did Admiral Rodman. An Admiralty official noted that "A screen of 6 destroyers is a small allowance for 5 ships." Although the Planning Section in London concurred, Sims disapproved:

> Will the proposed assignment of six destroyers to Battleship Division Nine be more effective in defeating the enemy's submarine campaign than the present assignment of the available destroyers? The answer to this question is obviously no. . . . Is the proposed assignment of destroyers necessary to retain command of the surface of the sea? The answer to this question is almost as obviously no as is the answer to the first. It is nearly two years since the enemy has made any bid for the command of the surface of the sea. His present position . . . would not require of him that he bring his High Seas Fleet into action. He is accomplishing his ends by attacking our communication with results which are certainly good and are apparently satisfactory to the enemy.

The Department sided with Sims's assessment and disapproved the deployment of American destroyers with the Grand Fleet.[40]

British destroyers had the responsibility of protecting the American dreadnoughts. Beatty and Rodman continued to request U.S. destroyers, and the Admiralty continued to concur. Beatty had to assign several of his destroyers to operate with the minelayers, which reduced the number available to screen the American battleships. The British commander in chief informed the Admiralty that if U.S. destroyers were not forthcoming, he must reduce the British destroyer force that protected the minelayers. Beatty opposed all efforts to decrease the number of destroyers operating with the Grand Fleet, and the Admiralty upheld him. On more than one occasion, the Navy Department complained about the refusal of the British to withdraw destroyers from the Grand Fleet for other purposes. No American destroyers were ever deployed with the Grand Fleet, although Sims agreed that in case of "extreme urgency," presumably if the High Seas Fleet came out, the "modern" destroyers based at Queenstown would be ordered to the North Sea. This deployment nearly occurred in October 1918, when the High Seas Fleet planned an attack. An American officer at Queenstown recalled that he received orders to prepare for a change of base. These orders were not executed because mutinies in the German fleet forced cancellation of the proposed sortie.[41]

Shortly after the United States entered the war, the French sought U.S. naval support along the Atlantic coast and Bay of Biscay, where submarines destroyed huge tonnage of Allied shipping. In 1914, the French navy ranked fourth in the world in tonnage, but a large percentage of the vessels were obsolete. The French government's decision to concentrate its most modern vessels in the Mediterranean left only a small force of destroyers and light craft to guard the western coast, not enough to contend with the U-boat onslaught. Little new construction reached the fleet. The government converted most of its shipyards to factories that manufactured shells and other arms for the Western Front. Ship repair facilities were lost. The need for antisubmarine craft became so desperate that the French government confiscated small fishing boats powered by sail armed with light guns and used them as patrol vessels. The decline in morale that affected all segments of the French civilian and military sectors also appeared in the French navy, but it did not experience mutinies. "Notwithstanding the paper strength of the French Navy as indicated by the records," Admiral Benson wrote after his return from Europe in December 1917, "I feel that should I fail to express the conviction that the French Navy is exhausted I should fail to state the whole truth. We cannot expect anything more from French naval operations on their western and northern coasts than what they are now doing as they have neither the trained men nor facilities to offer more."[42]

The French navy wanted American destroyers to deploy on their western coast. Although most of the U.S. destroyers were destined for Ireland, the French continued to press for some of them. On May 2, 1917, Rear Admiral Sir Dudley De Chair cabled Jellicoe that the French Commission was "much disgruntled" that the destroyers were going to Great Britain. The French minister of marine, Vice Admiral Dartige du Rournet, sent a personal letter to Assistant Secretary of the Navy Roosevelt on May 30, implying that some of the destroyers that were supposed to go to France had gone to Queenstown. "Admiral Sims is installing himself in a permanent manner in Queenstown and naturally he wants to keep the destroyers there." "Too bad," he wrote, "they would be very useful in France especially when troop ships start arriving."[43] In July, Sims sent an officer to confer with American and French officials in Paris. He reported that "We can send all sorts of ships here but some of them must be destroyers or the French will not be satisfied." The French, he wrote, "are too polite to say what they think, or feel, but I can see a decided feeling exists to the effect that the assistance being given the English is real and working, but the assistance give[n] to France is more in the nature of promise than anything else."[44]

Assistance was real, but not very impressive. The Department agreed to give the French the first fifty 110-foot subchasers. On June 1, Captain William B. Fletcher was ordered to assume command of eight yachts being fitted out for foreign service. They deployed to France as "U.S. Patrol Squadron Operating in European Waters." Later the designation was changed to the "Breton Patrol," or "Brittany Patrol," and finally to "U.S. Naval Forces Operating in French Waters." On June 20, Daniels informed Sims that twelve fishing vessels would also reinforce the patrol in France.[45] Two of the largest yachts, *Corsair* and *Aphrodite*, sailed for France as part of the screen for the transports that ferried the first contingent of troops to Europe. The remaining six— *Harvard*, *Sultana*, *Christabel*, *Kanawha II*, *Vedette*, and *Noma*—departed separately under Fletcher's command. They arrived at Brest early in July and began operating on Bastille Day. On August 30, a second division of seven yachts steamed to Brest. The name *Easter Egg Fleet* was attached to these yachts because of camouflage that covered them with every color in the rainbow.[46]

Although griping is normal for sailors, those serving on the yachts in French waters had some justification. They were generally fair weather sailors. The weather in the Western Approaches is notoriously bad in winter, but in the Bay of Biscay it is frequently nasty even in summer. One skipper later wrote, "The principal thing we had to fight was the weather."[47] Fog often appeared: ships lost sight of each other, and escorts lost their convoys. Escorts often searched more than a day for their convoys and returned to base without them. Westerly winds made it difficult for convoys to keep station and impossible for slower yachts to do so, which were often reduced to speed of a few knots. The fast troop convoys made at least eighteen knots. Seas built up as they rolled across the Atlantic and into the bay. Admiral Hoover mentioned that "the water outside of Brest was always rough. . . . We seldom went out there that it wasn't tough." A chief petty officer on the yacht *Westerly* recalled that on one occasion his ship attempted to leave Brest with a convoy but "was actually blown back." Unable to make headway, the ship dropped anchor and kept her engines turning over at two knots to keep from being dragged ashore. The commanding officer of the *Kanawha II* remembered a storm with gale-force winds and heavy seas that caused his ship to roll forty degrees.[48]

A December storm, possibly a hurricane, also seriously damaged the yacht *Corsair*. Heavy seas demolished hatches to the engine room and sleeping quarters, allowing tons of water to crash below deck. Two depth charges washed overboard and exploded under the stern. A survivor later wrote that nine depth charges rolled around on the deck without exploding. The ship finally limped into Vigo, Spain, remaining there only a short time because Spain, a neutral, would have interned the vessel after a stay of twenty-four hours. The yacht proceeded to Lisbon, Portugal, where repairs were made that allowed her to return to Brest.[49]

The destroyers were by no means immune from bad weather. On July 15, 1918, *Little* took on quantities of water. "It was necessary to slow down. Before the signal was sent we shipped a huge sea which walked along the forecastle carrying life lines, gun depression rail, ammunition box from anti-aircraft gun, cocoa matting, ammunition rank and fifteen rounds of 4" ammunition; buckled one frame in the deck, starboard side of chart house, bridge railing and smashed all the glass wind shields." Timothy Brown, who spent more than a year on the *Reid*, described weather conditions as his ship steamed on convoy duty out of Brest: "The *Smith* lost both her masts. . . . I never saw such waves. . . . I noticed that we were burning break-down lights, indicating that the ship was not under control. . . . The whaleboat . . . had been beat to pieces . . . the machinist's lathe was gone entirely, torn out of the deck to which it had been bolted. . . . The skipper had an SOS message ready to send, but the wireless was demasted and he didn't think it was of any use anyway." The ship eventually limped into a Portuguese village, made temporary repairs, and returned to Brest.[50]

Coastal convoys avoided much but not all of the heavy weather. The captain of *Cor-*

sair wrote of his first patrol: "This trip has been awful weather most of the time, rain, mist, wind, and fog. Nothing is dry on the whole ship." On one day it was so bad that *Emeline* sent a small boat ashore to ascertain her location. A merchant ship rammed *Wakiva*, which was escorting it.[51]

The first eight yachts cooperated with the French patrol of the coastal waters. They escorted merchant vessels through their assigned areas, rescued survivors of submarine attacks, and searched for U-boats. The CO of *Corsair* described his ship's work as "answering SOS calls, looking for submarines, and convoying merchant ships." They were no more successful than the Queenstown command in locating and destroying enemy submarines.[52] The yachts operated in pairs, which patrolled an area of the bay. Initially they operated at sea for four days (later changed to three) and rested in port for three. Four yachts patrolled at a time. Two of the smaller ones were assigned areas close to the coast; the larger ones were posted farther out. The yachts also joined French vessels to escort coastal convoys.

Patrolling continued after the convoy system began to operate in French waters. In September, Sims informed the Department that "the normal duty of our forces [in France] is a combination of escort duty, primarily of convoys, and of offensive operations off the coast." Five days after *Noma* began operations, it came under torpedo attack, the first action of the Breton Patrol. The yacht was not hit, and it did not locate the attacking U-boat. On the next day, the yachts observed the results of the submarine war as they steamed through upset lifeboats, debris, and other wreckage.[53]

The yachts operated in French waters for the remainder of the war, despite their serious limitations as escorts, especially for the transatlantic convoys. Only four yachts were considered seaworthy enough for these convoys. Destroyers were required to escort the transatlantic convoys, but none were assigned to French waters until September 1917.

Queenstown-based destroyers should have been transferred to Brest, but that port lacked adequate fueling and repair facilities.[54] Instead, Sims determined to use the Ireland-based destroyers to convoy troop transports to French ports, although this assignment taxed the vessels. The destroyers did not usually enter a French port with the transports but transferred the convoy to escorts based in France at a predetermined rendezvous. They then returned to Queenstown. Occasionally they had to refuel or wait for an outbound convoy. "If we told the folks at home that we had breakfast in France and supper in Ireland they would yell for a pulmotor," wrote a Queenstown destroyer officer.[55] The French craft then escorted the transports to their destination. This procedure displeased the Department in Washington, naval officials in France, and Sims's staff.

On September 20, at Benson's insistence, Sims agreed to shift the five coal-burning destroyers from the Azores to Brest. Logistics did not trouble these vessels because a destroyer tender accompanied them and coal was available in Brest. *Reid, Flusser, Preston, Lamson*, and *Smith* belonged to the 700-ton *Flusser* class, each carrying a battery of five 3.50-inch caliber guns. They were reasonably fast, steaming at a speed of twenty-eight knots. These vessels joined the "Brittany Patrol" late in October. Sims considered these vessels a part of the Queenstown command on detached service to Brest.[56]

In November 1917, two more destroyers arrived in Brest, *Monaghan* and *Roe*. These oil-burning members of the *Drayton* class, called "flivvers," were slightly larger and faster than the *Flussers*. Sims agreed to this assignment when the French decided to turn over a small oil tank to the American Navy in Brest. Large 7,000-gallon oil storage tanks shipped from the United States did not arrive until the summer of 1918.[57] The two *Draytons* participated in transatlantic escort until ordered to Brest. In December, *Warrington*, also of the *Drayton* class, arrived from Queenstown. In December, the first two *Truxtun*-class torpedo boat destroyers, *Truxtun* and *Whipple*, arrived from the Azores. They had been sent there to replace the five *Flussers*. In January, two more arrived, *Stewart* and *Worden*. These were some of the oldest combat vessels still in service, having been launched in 1899–1900.They were small, displacing approximately six hundred tons, and mounted a small battery of two 3-inch guns and six 6-pounders. At twenty-eight to thirty knots, they were fast, and they were seaworthy enough to undertake escort work in French waters.

At the beginning of 1918, the American combat surface force in French waters included fourteen armed yachts, eight destroyers, and ten trawlers, a weak force in the best of circumstances. Wilson informed Sims that "conditions on the Western coast of France are admittedly unsatisfactory,"[58] and they remained so, although a few destroyers reinforced the naval force in France.

In January 1918, Admiral Wilson reorganized his command, creating three districts at Bordeaux, St. Nazaire, and Brest.[59] This change responded to the War Department decision to send their supply ships directly to Bordeaux and St. Nazaire without first directing them to Brest. This decision prompted Sims, General Pershing, Admiral Wilson, and Captain Jackson, U.S. naval liaison in Paris, to request the assignment of additional destroyers to French waters to operate out of Bordeaux and St. Nazaire. The CNO cabled Sims, quoting Pershing's communication and suggesting that he allot more destroyers to French waters, presumably from Queenstown. Sims replied that "every additional destroyer sent [is] now being assigned to French Coast" and added that the "Need for destroyers in all areas [is] as critical as in past." He refused to reassign units of the Queenstown command to French waters, and Benson did not challenge his decision. When Wilson complained that the small destroyers were of "no value" for offshore work, Sims replied rather sharply: "this type of vessel has demonstrated its seagoing capacity by crossing the Atlantic in winter weather. . . . They are capable of offshore work to the extent of their radius."[60] The force commander mentioned that another destroyer was on the way, *MacDonough*, one of the oldest in the Navy and one of the smallest at 420 tons' displacement. She had to be towed part of the way across the Atlantic. Sims wrote optimistically to his subordinate in France, "in addition to the 5 seagoing yachts in your Forces, there are now 15 (16 counting *MacDonough*)." He added that the destroyer *Wadsworth*, the destroyer-yacht *Isabel*, and the yachts *Nokomis*, *Rambler*, and *Utowana* would shortly join his command.[61]

Sims failed to mention that *Nicholson*, the first "modern" destroyer based in France, arrived at Brest late in February. One of the 1,000-tonners deployed to the Queens-town command, she was a veteran of some nine months of patrol and escort work in European waters. *Jarvis* and *Wadsworth* followed soon. Sims once again specified that these destroyers were part of the Queenstown command under Bayly's orders. They were to escort troop transports to French ports and screen empty ships westward if their sailing coincided with the schedule of the Queenstown destroyers. Wilson considered this decision an infringement of his responsibilities, but he could do little about it.[62]

Late in May, Sims decided to transfer the destroyers already operating in French waters, still nominally under the Queenstown command, and other destroyers to Brest. The British agreed to repair French-based destroyers in their yards; the new oil tanks were nearly completed; and the need for destroyers operating out of France increased because the number of troop transports and supply ships that arrived from the United States rose weekly. The decline of French naval participation in the oceanic escort aroused concern when the number of French escorts for the New York convoys dwindled from four to six escorts to one "and in some instances [to] no escorts."[63] On May 24, Sims informed Admiral Bayly that twelve more of his destroyers would be deployed to Brest, including two new vessels coming from the United States and ten of the Queenstown command. The British admiral immediately informed the Admiralty of Sims's announcement, claiming that "It will be impossible to send 12 [destroyers] and at the same time carry out British Admiralty requirements with other convoys." The Admiralty, aware of the U.S. Navy's decision, did not protest. When the Queenstown commander requested six additional destroyers in August, the Admiralty again refused to send them. Bayly wrote bitterly, "I conclude that they [the American Navy] are also unaware of the straits to which we are driven."[64] A thirteenth destroyer from the Queenstown command was transferred to Brest late in July.[65]

On June 8, *Sigourney*, *Wainwright*, and *Fanning* arrived; on June 9, *Tucker*, *Winslow*, and *Porter*; on June 11, *O'Brien*, *Cummings*, *Benham*, and *Cushing*; on June 12, *Burrows*; on June 15, *Ericsson*, and on July 23, *McDougal*. Also in June two new flush deckers, *Little* and *Connor*, steamed directly from the States. Five more new flush deckers reached Brest before the Armistice. On August 19, Sims informed the Department that twenty-eight destroyers were based at Brest, of which five at a time rotated for repairs. He considered the remaining twenty-three adequate for the oceanic convoys. At the end of the war, thirty-three destroyers came under Wilson's command.[66] Despite the increase in destroyers operating out of Brest, the war-weary yachts continued to provide yeoman escort for the coastal convoys in French waters to the bitter end.

Sims still juggled his destroyer force as the war came to an end. He formed a few submarine hunting units with one destroyer each, but he had to reject requests for destroyers from the commanding officer of the three U.S. battleships at Berehaven and Admiral Niblack at Gibraltar. On October 9, he informed the Department that twenty-three of the next thirty-five destroyers that arrived in the war zone would go to Gibraltar and to French ports. The remaining twelve would be assigned to the Mine Force. Other arriving destroyers were to be organized into hunting groups. He wrote, "For offensive purposes, I deem it essential that at least four hunting groups of six destroyers each be organized." Only two more destroyers arrived in the war zone before the Armistice.[67] At the end of the war, seventy-three U.S. destroyers operated in European waters.

The American naval force based at Gibraltar also performed valiantly with a force that remained far weaker than the one employed along the French coast. The escorts were slow. Usually a British vessel or an American Coast Guard cutter, cruiser, or gunboat provided ocean escort from Gibraltar to an English port and screened another convoy back to Gibraltar.[68] Although the three American cruisers employed in this system were satisfactory, the Coast Guard cutters were too slow. The gunboat *Sacramento* was a laughing stock to the British. With a stick that "towered up to a prodigious height," she looked to a British officer like a Mississippi River "paddleboat." To another, she "looked very much like a submarine" at night. He added that on several occasions "we meditated firing at her."[69] Nonetheless she persevered and made a creditable showing. *Seneca* at 1,445 tons was the largest of the Coast Guard cutters deployed abroad during the war, but it was extremely slow. Sometimes described as "half a destroyer," she probably saw more action with U-boats than any of the other cutters. It was rumored on the cutter that she was on the blacklist of the German navy high command. Her exploits both before and during the war gained for her an inevitable reputation in the Coast Guard.[70]

Like merchant seamen, American sailors had no experience in convoy work or in combat with submarines. Admirals Bayly and Wilson blamed mistakes on young officers who were novices at sea warfare, including the regulars who manned the first destroyers to deploy in European waters and the volunteers and reserves who commanded most of the escorts. Bluejackets and officers had to learn by trial and error. Lights were left on at night; radios and blinkers were used far too often; convoys were missed because of poor navigation; depth charges were dropped at the wrong time; and guns fired at nonexistent submarines.[71]

Many escorts failed to meet their convoys, although one American destroyer captain recalled quite proudly, "it was our pride that we never missed meeting a convoy at the designated secret spot on time."[72] Occasionally a convoy arrived at a French port during the night, creating difficulties for the French pilots. Searchlights and beacons were turned on to help guide the ships into port. Despite protests from the French naval command, the Americans and British continued to schedule ocean convoys through the danger zone during the dark hours. In April, they made a slight modification. Convoys were allowed to pass through the danger zone in daylight for five days before and after the full moon. Beginning in February 1918, French coastal convoys and convoys from Great Britain to French ports were generally scheduled in daylight hours.[73]

Collisions were among the most dangerous experiences for vessels in the convoy system, involving escorts with convoyed ships and with other escorts at sea and in port. Admiral Bayly expressed concern over the number of collisions, which he blamed on "untrained youngsters," but he rarely demanded a court of inquiry, a standard practice in the U.S. Navy during peacetime. An officer who served in *Duncan* in the Queenstown command determined that one in three of the American destroyers in that command experienced "some sort of collision."[74] *Rowan* struck two other units in the command, the destroyers *Caldwell* and *Tucker*, but caused only minor damage.

In March 1918, the destroyer *Manley* collided with a British armed merchant cruiser. *Manley* was ordered to go alongside the British cruiser to pass sealed orders. According to her chief quartermaster, the destroyer made three attempts. On the final attempt, the cruiser turned left. The destroyer attempted the same maneuver, but it acted too slowly. She slid into a trough of a swell with the cruiser high on the crest. The cruiser slammed against the destroyer's stern, causing a depth charge loaded on a Y gun to explode. Other depth charges exploded as they rolled overboard. Seventeen feet of *Manley*'s stern was blown off, rupturing fuel tanks and launching sheets of flame and smoke. Witnesses on the destroyer *Terry*, two miles away, were convinced that the entire ship was on fire. *Manley*'s rudder was lost, and her propeller shaft was twisted outboard and down at a 35–40-degree angle, leaving the ship dead in the water. Casualties were heavy; thirty-seven were killed and all but eleven of the crew were wounded. They were evacuated to other escorts, leaving eleven men on board, including her commanding officer, Commander Robert Berry. Nineteen were killed on the cruiser, including a number of British soldiers who were standing at the rail and on the stern. *Manley* was towed into Queenstown for repairs. Berry was removed from the command because of "the way he handled the vessel," according to Sims.[75]

Collisions with merchant ships and transports were more numerous and far more deadly. In October 1918, the destroyer *Shaw*'s rudder jammed while escorting the giant British transport *Aquitania*. She headed directly toward the transport, and moments later *Aquitania* struck the destroyer, sheering off ninety feet of the American vessel's bow forward of the bridge and igniting a fire. The surviving members of the crew brought the destroyer under control and took her to port under her own power. Ensign M. F. (later Admiral) Schoeffel was on a nearby escort. He recalled rushing up on the deck when General Quarters was sounded: "all you could see was darkness and a great mass of flames over in the distance. . . . After awhile, as day broke, we saw a destroyer, which we had great difficulty in identifying, minus a bow and heavily on fire up forward. Then there was a bow floating keel up some distance away." Two of the escorts stood by the burning destroyer while the remainder continued with *Aquitania*. When picking up men in the water, a sailor on *Shaw* wigwagged: "Leave me. I am getting under way." The commanding officer, Commander William Glassford (later Vice Admiral), and a skeleton crew backed the vessel into a port forty miles away.[76]

On May 22, 1918, the freighter *Wabash* ran down the yacht *Wakiva II* and sank it. The fog was extremely thick at the time. "[W]e could just make out our mainmast from the bridge," wrote a sailor on another escort. Zigzagging had been discontinued because of the fog, and the various ships blew their whistles frequently. The freighter struck *Wakiva* near amidships, punching an eight-foot hole in her side. As the engine room filled with water, she began to settle by the stern and in fifteen minutes disappeared with two of her crew still on board. The *Wabash* rescued the rest of the crew.[77]

American escorts rammed other ships. In Liverpool, *Burrows* sank a tug. Several months later in heavy seas she ran down a French fishing vessel. Only two of the fishermen survived the accident. On October 19, 1918, another tug sank in Brest harbor when it collided with an American destroyer. *Benham* rammed the British warship *Zinna* and had to be towed to port. The court of inquiry found neither ship at fault. The two vessels were zigzagging on a dark and stormy night with no lights and little visibility.[78] In another storm, the yacht *Remlik*, according to a member of her crew, ran her bow "upon the deck of a Greek freighter." The writer does not say what happened to the yacht, but "No great harm was done."[79] Lieutenant (later Admiral) Merrill described a minor collision when a British freighter's stern rode over *Conyngham's* bow in heavy seas. The freighter lost a small boat, and the destroyer was not damaged, but it was so close that "for a few seconds Uncle Sam's million dollars worth of ship would not have sold for a 'tuppence.'"[80] On September 29, 1917, the yacht *Alcedo* radioed: "I have been rammed by convoy. Stand by." Although the yacht was not seriously damaged, less than two months later it was sunk. Admiral Halsey saw *McDougal* lose her stern to a convoyed ship. "We continued on our way. That is the heartless but absolutely necessary part of this game. The crippled must be slighted for the good of the uninjured."[81]

One American escort, the old *Bainbridge*-class destroyer *Chauncey* (420 tons displacement) sank after a collision. On November 19, 1917, 110 miles west of Gibraltar, the British merchantman *Rose* rammed her. Both vessels were steaming in regulated darkness at the time. Twenty-one men including the captain, Lieutenant Commander Walter Reno, went down with the ship; other escorts picked up seventy survivors. Sims later wrote to his wife: "I am sorry to say that the loss of the *Chauncey* was one of those things which in all probability could have been avoided. A man who was not qualified for the position, either by training or rank, was in charge of the vessel and all command officers were down below. I have declined to hold responsible the man who was in charge of the vessel, because he ought not to have been given that responsibility."[82]

Personal accounts of World War I sailors who served on escorts in European waters often mentioned receiving indirect fire from gunners on board merchant ships and transports when they attempted to target submarines. On January 9, a bluejacket on *Reid* noted that a lookout on a freighter claimed he spotted a periscope, which caused his ship to open fire along with the merchant vessels in the convoy. The next day "one of the freighters started shooting, her shells going in the water about fifty yards ahead of us, then skipping along the water and just missing another destroyer. That was the signal for merchantmen to open up with every gun they had and no place was safe."[83] *O'Brien's* CO wrote, "We were often in danger from the transports who would shoot at anything that turned up, including their own wake."[84] Another officer wrote that "at times the escort would have all it could do to avoid the shells, not to mention the trouble encountered in rounding up the convoy, which at the first alarm, would stampede to all points of the compass."[85] Some of the smaller escorting vessels, particularly the yachts, were mistaken for submarines and occasionally came under fire from nervous gunners. Many near misses were recorded, but few hit. An exception was the destroyer *Jenkins*, which received a direct hit from the former passenger steamer *New York*. One man was killed and four wounded.[86]

One writer concluded that U.S. naval vessels took part in fifty-seven mistaken attacks.[87] Errors of this kind were quite common among all the participants in the war. The author blamed these mischances on the advent of submarine warfare, but aircraft were equally to blame. He suggested that submarine defense was based on the fact that hostile undersea craft were exposed to their opponents for only a short time. Decisions had to be made quickly. Night attacks compounded the problem. According to one veteran, shortly after his destroyer reached Queenstown escorts received the order "to fire on all questionable objects and investigate after firing."[88] Other causes of unnecessary shooting included the absence of running lights, incorrect and delayed recognition signals, inexperienced crews and gunners, and the "heterogeneous" character of shipping.

Allied and American submarines were the most vulnerable. American submarines experienced twenty mistaken attacks during the war. None were sunk, and personnel avoided serious injuries.[89] Escort attacks on Allied submarines caused damage. On October 5, 1917, the armed yacht *Nahma*, searching for a reported German submarine near Gibraltar, spotted two submarines following a merchant ship. Assuming that the submarines were attacking the merchant ship, *Nahma* opened fire. A shot hit the conning tower of one of the submarines, mortally wounding two Italian sailors. The other submarine took a round through its conning tower that failed to explode. A court of inquiry found the yacht's CO negligent, but at the intercession of the Italian minister of marine he was not court-martialed, although he was removed from command.[90] In May 1918, Gibraltar-based American escorts fired on and depth-charged a French submarine, which surfaced in front of their convoy. The commanding officer and a seaman were killed and four wounded. An official inquiry found the deceased submarine commander at fault for ignoring instructions to avoid the area of the incident.[91]

Three American destroyers forced the British submarine *L-2* to crash dive until she struck the seabed at three hundred feet. She blew her tanks and rose rapidly. Crashing to the surface, she found the waiting destroyers, which opened fire and hit her. They stopped firing when they recognized the vessel's signal. The Admiralty official in charge of submarines complimented the destroyers' efforts. "In view of the small amount of conning tower exposed and the distance at which it was sighted . . . these vessels made a most remarkably efficient attack."[92]

McDougal escorted what was thought to be a small British coastal vessel for five hours one night only to discover at daylight that they had been protecting a U-boat. She submerged and disappeared before the destroyer could fire a shot.[93]

Surface vessels also suffered mistaken attacks. Fishing vessels came under fire when at a distance in poor light. At night, their silhouette looked like the conning tower of a submarine. British drifters and patrol boats, American subchasers, and even destroyers suffered similar experiences.

In June 1918, a unit of three subchasers on a hunting patrol in the Strait of Otranto picked up sounds on their hydrophones that they thought came from a submarine. They discovered two low-lying objects in the water. When neither responded to their recognition signal, they opened fire. They proved to be the British destroyers *Nymphe* and *Defender*. The American vessels immediately ceased fire, but *Nymphe* was hit, losing one of her engines. A court of inquiry justified the subchasers' response. The British naval commander at Otranto wrote that the American skippers "had no reason to suppose a British destroyer would be in that particular position."[94]

Similar incidents occurred elsewhere. A Brazilian squadron fired on three American subchasers in the Strait of Gibraltar but did not cause damage.[95] Commander Taussig reported early in June 1917 that *Wadsworth* targeted a British patrol vessel until she hoisted the British Ensign, identified herself by searchlight, and made smoke.[96] *Yankton*'s initial combat occurred while east of the Azores en route to Gibraltar. She fired more than fifty rounds of ammunition before lookouts recognized that the target was a fleet of small fishing vessels.[97] When an American escort captain whose ship received fire from an unnamed Allied warship ("the first shot missed my bows by a few feet, the second one carried away a stack") reported the incident to Simsadus, he commented, "I think greater cooperation is necessary."[98]

Submarines and surface vessels were not the only targets of eager American sailors. Any unidentified object afloat became fair game. As Taussig wrote, "When on escort duty, my fixed rule, if any one reported a periscope, was immediately to drop a depth charge." He added, "no chances could be taken."[99] The different objects that were fired on or depth-charged covered about everything likely to be found on or in the water, from the wake of ships and tide rips to fish, particularly porpoises, sharks, and whales. A retired officer recalled dropping sixteen depth charges on a tide rip before realizing what it was. Another recorded in his journal that he rammed an upright spar and dropped "ash cans" on it.[100] Another former junior officer wrote: "we noticed what looked like the periscope of a submarine just astern of [another escort]. . . . We fired at it, and he signaled: 'That was a piece of wood you fired at.' To which I replied: 'Yes, the same piece of wood you dropped a depth charge on.'"[101] A destroyer steamed at full speed with depth charges ready at what proved to be a white streak on the water caused by the sun shining through a small opening in the clouds on a smooth sea.[102] At least one large turtle became a target as did two white gulls flying close to the water. They looked "exactly like the feather of foam from the wake of a periscope."[103] Debris from sunken and wrecked ships and even ships themselves, usually wooden sailing vessels, were often attacked. On one occasion a destroyer depth-charged a wooden table with three legs shot off and one sticking up in the air.[104] Abandoned rafts and small boats with masts often caused the sounding of general quarters. Spars and buoys were also frequent targets. Admiral Halsey recalled that "Fish, particularly porpoises, sent my heart into my boots time after time. . . . At night, in phosphorescent water, a porpoise has a strong resemblance to a torpedo."[105] Assistant Secretary of the Navy Roosevelt, while on the destroyer *Dyer*, witnessed an attack on a mysterious "keg with a little flag on it."[106] German U-boats would at times try to trick eager Americans by disguising mines as periscopes, but it did not work. Admiral Halsey mentioned that destroyer crews had been warned of this "trick and we were on the lookout for them."[107] Mistaken attacks were so common that they at times were called "periscopitis."[108]

Despite the collisions, submarine scares, and the tension associated with service at sea in a combat zone, escort duty at times became monotonous. Patrols and escorts rarely sighted submarines, and they engaged an even smaller number. "This submarine-chasing business is much like the proverbial skinning of a skunk—useful, but not especially pleasant or glorious," a tin can officer wrote. He mentioned a month later that he welcomed mistaking a ventilator for a periscope and firing on it. "You have no conception of how gray life can get to be on this job."[109] A Coast Guard officer observed: "The average person, sitting at home during the war, and reading in the newspapers about the sinkings of vessels through submarine attacks, had the idea that U-boats were as thick as crows in a corn field, and that hardly a day passed without some thrilling battle with the enemy. This of course was not the case, and I knew of a British P-boat that had not sighted a submarine off the West coast for almost two years. Usually, it was a matter of luck, some vessels would always come in contact with them, while others cruised for months without even sighting a suspicious streak of foam."[110] "We never saw any German submarines ourselves," Admiral Wheeler remembered in an oral interview. "We did see several objects that we thought were German submarines' periscopes, but we were never able to actually identify them." Admiral Halsey wrote, "I cannot honestly say that I actually ever saw a German sub, although there were several occasions when I thought that I had seen one."[111] Personal accounts and reports time and again mention that U-boats submerged long before an escort could get into effective range. A bluejacket wrote that "quite frequently, in foggy weather, we would suddenly come on a German submarine on the surface charging batteries. . . . We would be in sight of each other a matter of seconds and wave to each other as we passed. They would be down and gone long before we could turn about and seek them out." A veteran recalled patrolling in the Bay of Biscay: "We might see a periscope briefly, but with our 12 knots or less, we couldn't go after them. . . . There was nothing we could do but hold our station." A shipmate agreed: "We have been in action only three times as our work was convoying and as we had to guard our ship, we could not leave to take the offensive except when actually attacked."[112] Another seaman told a war correspondent: "We sees Fritzie, or we don't. Mostly we don't, for he ducks under when he pipes our smoke." He added: "If he's stalkin' a convoy there's a chance of him givin' us time for a rangin' shot at him on the surface. Then we waltzes over to his grease and scatters a bunch of 'cans' round his restin' place."[113] They could only drop depth charges over the areas where submarines disappeared into the depths. Equally frustrating were frequent submarine sightings by merchant ships, often announced by blowing whistles and sending an SOS on the radio. American bluejackets began referring to the SOS calls as "(S)ame (O)ld (S)tuff."[114]

Nevertheless the submarines were present in considerable numbers. In convoys that *Seneca* escorted, twenty-one alarms of submarines occurred, of which seven were either mistaken or doubtful.[115] On November 5, 1917, the armed yacht *Alecto*, formerly owned by the Philadelphia millionaire George W. Drexel, was torpedoed and sunk in the Bay of Biscay. The explosion sent the shattered ship to the bottom in very few minutes, carrying with her twenty-one men. She was the first American escort to fall prey to a German U-boat.[116] The *Alecto* sinking was generally forgotten because of the loss of the destroyer *Jacob Jones* a month later.

Jacob Jones, a Tucker-class 1,000-tonner, was torpedoed on December 6, 1917, near the Isles of Scilly. *U-53* was responsible. Its commander, Hans Rose, was one of the most successful German submarine captains in World War I. Rose was one of the more humane submarine commanders. Often at considerable risk he radioed the location of ships that he torpedoed and towed boats loaded with survivors to within sight of land. Sims wrote after the war that Rose was "one of the few German U-boat commanders with whom Allied naval officers would be willing to shake hands."[117] Rose's torpedo struck the starboard side of the *Jacob Jones*. Within eight minutes, she plunged stern first to the bottom. Her tanks ruptured, but her fuel did not ignite. The explosion of the torpedo, exposure in cold water, and depth charges caused heavy casualties, sixty-four killed and missing. As *Jacob Jones* settled, her depth charges exploded, killing or wounding a number of men in the water. Rose sent an SOS that led to the rescue of the survivors, but not until most of them had been exposed to the frigid water and air for nearly seventeen hours. Lieutenant Stanton F. Kalk, one of *Jacob Jones*'s two officers who died, lost his life after swimming from raft to raft, helping men find places. Most accounts say that he drowned, but Merrill on *Conyngham*, one of the rescue ships, wrote that he succumbed on one of the rafts. "Just before he died he partially regained consciousness and asked if anyone could see the Statue of Liberty."[118]

No other American destroyer was lost during the war, although *Cassin* was torpedoed in October 1917, the first American destroyer to experience a U-boat attack. The explosion carried away most of the stern. She had only two depth charges on board. The explosion opened up the chief's quarters where fourteen men were located, but only one was killed. She was towed into Queenstown for repairs.[119]

The Coast Guard cutter *Tampa* was the last American escort sunk during the war and the greatest single loss. *Tampa*, originally named *Miami*, was a relatively new cutter, one of the larger Coast Guard vessels deployed to European waters, displacing more than 1,100 tons. Although not quite as large as a destroyer, she was heavier, having been built for the ice patrol. Operating out of Gibraltar, the cutter compiled an outstanding record. She successfully escorted eighteen convoys, altogether 350 vessels, on the Great Britain/Gibraltar run. She was never disabled and required only minor repairs despite spending more than 50 percent of her time at sea and steaming an average of 3,566 miles a month. On September 26, 1918, the day that a great Franco-American attack began in the Meuse-Argonne sector, *Tampa* was escorting merchant ships to Milford Haven, Wales. During the night, the convoy entered the Bristol Channel. *Tampa* left the convoy without informing the other escorts and steamed ahead. Possibly she spotted a submarine, although the night was extremely dark. Ships in the convoy heard a huge explosion. A search revealed nothing except a few pieces of wreckage and two bodies. A total of 131 men were lost, including 110 Coast Guard officers and seamen. Twenty-one passengers from Gibraltar were lost.[120]

Escorts frequently witnessed torpedo attacks. They could do little except drop ash cans, rescue survivors, and continue to screen the rest of the convoy.[121] They rarely found the U-boat that caused the sinking, and even more rarely did they destroy or damage the submarine. The Office of Naval Intelligence concluded that U.S. naval vessels claimed to have attacked enemy submarines on 256 occasions. In 183 of these, "there was definite chart evidence of a submarine in the vicinity."[122] American escort commanders, like World War II pilots, often took credit for sinking a submarine based on testimony from crew members or evidence such as oil and debris on the surface. A bluejacket wrote: "We sighted a U-Boat just off the port bow. She at once submerged. . . . The *Fanning* steered to the port and dropped one depth charge. . . . The depth charge sent a mountain of water a hundred feet in the air. Just as the geyser was receding, a second explosion erupted in the same area. . . . We chalked up another U-Boat." Merrill noted in June 1917 that "Some of the boats had thrills last week. *O'Brien* sank a submarine. *Winslow* almost ran alongside of one while running at high speed in a fog." In September, he mentioned that "The *O'Brien* got her second one a few days ago. The *Jacob Jones*, *Rowan*, and several other boats have in their claims also."[123] Conflicting claims were made because more than one escort frequently attacked a U-boat.

U.S. naval forces in French waters also engaged German U-boats on various occasions. The armed yacht *Noma*, shortly after arriving in Brest, had two actions with submarines. On August 8, 1917, she received an SOS from a ship, reporting that a U-boat had attacked her. Giving coordinates, she stated that the crew was abandoning ship. The vessel was the British decoy ship *Dunraven*, under the command of Captain Gordon Campbell. On approaching *Dunraven*, "on fire from stem to stern," *Noma* passed a submarine so closely that she could deliver only small arms fire. Two depth charges were dropped, both defective. The yacht then escorted the heavily damaged decoy ship, but she sank before reaching port. A week later *Noma* had a gun duel with a submarine. Before the U-boat submerged, the yacht approached within effective range. Neither vessel hit the other. In November, the yachts *Noma*, *Kanawha*, and *Wakiva II* reported that they fought two submarines, preventing them from attacking a convoy. They claimed to have sunk one of them. The Admiralty determined, however, that the vessel was seriously damaged but not sunk, a conclusion accepted by Robert M. Grant in *U-Boat Intelligence*.[124]

Christabel, one of the smallest armed yachts, put a submarine out of action by damaging it severely. The U-boat sought internment in Spain. In April 1918, *Christabel*, escorting a single vessel, sighted *U-56*'s periscope. The submarine was depth-charged and damaged so severely that she was fortunate to reach Santander, Spain.[125]

The old destroyer *Stewart*, all of 420 tons, while escorting a convoy in April 1918, attacked a submarine. Aircraft first sighted the U-boat and guided the destroyer to the site. Stewart dropped five depth charges, bringing large quantities of oil to the surface for several days. *Stewart*'s commanding officer claimed that the submarine was destroyed, an assertion supported by Admiral Wilson, but no U-boat was reported sunk or missing on that date. The destroyer was credited in Admiralty records as having seriously damaged a submarine.[126] Grant does not mention a German submarine lost that day in the area of the attack.

Mediterranean escorts were too weak to stop huge merchant-ship losses from U-boat attacks. After American warships joined the convoy work east of Gibraltar, losses continued to average over 100,000 tons per month, the exception being February, when less than 84,000 tons were destroyed. A steady decline in lost tonnage during the summer occurred until November, when U-boats succeeded in sending 10,233 tons to the bottom before the Armistice.[127] Escorts made frequent attacks on legitimate or supposed targets, firing their deck guns at what they described as periscopes and conning towers. Often they claimed success. Usually credit was given to all the escorting vessels who participated in the attack. On May 8, the small yacht *Lydonia* and a British sloop jointly attacked and destroyed a submarine. A week later the gunboat *Wheeling* and the armed yachts *Surveyor* and *Venetia* received credit for sinking a submarine after it torpedoed a ship in the convoy under their escort. In September, the gunboat *Paducah*, called by one of her commanding officers "without exception the most homely [ship] . . . afloat," attacked and possibly damaged a U-boat that threatened the convoy under escort. *Paducah*'s officer of the deck later recalled that shortly after the ship dropped a depth charge, "the whole gun's crew aft saw a long, black object break the water and lie quiet. They let out a yell, and everybody looked." They searched the area but found no evidence of a sinking. *Venetia* also was cited for damaging a U-boat and forcing her to enter Carthagena, where she was interned.[128]

The British Admiralty, which kept statistics of German U-boat activities, discredited claims most of the time. Reports of all attacks by U.S. escorts, British vessels, and ships of the other Allied nations were submitted to the Admiralty for evaluation. U.S. vessels were officially credited with twenty-four successful attacks on U-boats, including those damaged and those "known sunk." The Admiralty based its judgments primarily upon intelligence. Experience taught the Admiralty to be conservative in its evaluations. Often submarines claimed to have been sunk popped up again in radio reports or upon returning to port. Rose remarked in *Brittany Patrol*, "The disgusting part of this game is that you can smash a sub and send him to the bottom without knowing it, or you can be positive that you exploded a charge right up on his deck, and the next day he will be out torpedoing ships as usual."[129]

The destroyer "Ever-ready" *O'Brien* was the first American warship to put a U-boat out of commission. On June 16, 1917, while escorting a ship off the Irish coast, she sighted a submarine. The destroyer dropped a depth charge, but when it did not observe evidence of the submarine, she continued her escort duty. Later other ships detected large patches of oil at the site. The Admiralty credited *O'Brien* with slightly damaging a submarine but denied a second claim.[130]

Allen was involved in two depth-charge attacks that possibly resulted in the destruction of submarines. On February 1, 1918, she attacked a submarine in the Irish Sea. Commander Harold Cooke, the destroyer's commanding officer, claimed that three members of his crew saw a conning tower rise to the surface and then disappear. German records later revealed that *UB-63*, patrolling in the Irish Sea, disappeared and was probably sunk at around that time.[131] The Admiralty credited the U.S. destroyer with slightly damaging a submarine. *Allen* and *Patterson* may have sunk *UB-119* in May 1918. Oil, air bubbles, and debris were spotted on the surface where the submarine was last seen. The U-boat never returned from patrol. Nevertheless, the Admiralty ruled that the destroyers slightly damaged the submarine. On one occasion, the persistent *Allen* chased a German submarine for two days, dropping depth charges without success.[132] One of *Parker*'s officers claimed that in going after a submarine, the skipper, Commander Halsey Powell, inadvertently tripped a lever on the bridge, dropping two depth charges and seriously damaging a U-boat. The Admiralty confirmed the damage.[133]

Two American escorts received Admiralty blessings for definite kills. One was the armed yacht *Lydonia*, in the Mediterranean, and the other was the destroyer *Fanning*.[134]

Fanning, a "740-tonner," was one of a division of six destroyers that arrived in the war zone in June 1917. Commanded by Arthur S. Carpender, she joined the Queenstown command early in July. For nearly six months, *Fanning* participated in escort duty, occasionally dropping depth charges on suspected submarines but without visible results. Admiral Carney, an ensign on *Fanning*, remembers that November 17 was a "bleak and cheerless day as most winter days are on the south coast of Ireland." *Fanning* stood out of Queenstown as part of a convoy screen of eight escorts. Shortly thereafter, the convoy formed into four columns. Fanning discovered an oil slick. After a few minutes, she rejoined the screen. Almost immediately, a coxswain named David Loomis, called "eagle eyes" because of his keen sight, sang out that a periscope was off the port beam. He spotted what was known as a finger periscope because it was extremely small, usually showing only a few inches above the surface. The officer of the deck immediately ordered "left full rudder," and the destroyer circled toward the submarine, gaining speed as she did so. When the destroyer reached the spot where the periscope last appeared, the OD pulled the lever that rolled a depth charge over the stern track. *Conyngham* observed the explosion of the depth charge but at three thousand yards away was unable to lend assistance. *Nicholson*, next in line to *Fanning*, immediately cut away from the screen to join in the action. As she closed the spot, the submarine's conning tower appeared on the surface. Both destroyers opened fire, and *Nicholson* swerved alongside the U-boat. As the boat again disappeared below the surface, *Nicholson* dropped a second ash can. *U-58* settled to the bottom. Her captain, Amberger, decided that he must surface and surrender. Some accounts claim that the sub went down nearly three hundred feet, but George Fort, one of *Fanning*'s officers, said that the chart indicated a depth of only 165 feet.[135] Upon *U-58*'s reappearance, bow first, hatches popped open and crew members emerged, the first holding up a white shirt. Ensign H. W. Dwight Rudd, a junior officer, recalled the scene. "Out came the first Hun I, or anybody present, had ever seen in the War. I shall never forget the sight of that man as he ran frantically up and down the deck, his hands over his head. . . . Bees from out a hive had nothing on the crew of that submarine. They simply poured out of these hatches, until the deck was black with them."[136]

Fanning quickly maneuvered alongside while her guns and sailors armed with rifles trained on the submarine. Lines were secured, but her crew had already opened the sea cocks. She began to settle, breaking the lines as she gradually capsized. The German sailors jumped into the water and swam to *Fanning* where they were pulled on board. All but two of the forty-two crewmen survived the ordeal. As the Germans gained the tender *Melville*, they gave three cheers for *Fanning* and her crew.[137]

The American escorts spent as much time rescuing seamen as they did attacking U-boats. During the early months of the war, this activity violated standing orders. German submarines at times attempted to torpedo a vessel involved in rescue operations, but no American warships were torpedoed during such operations.[138] The Coast Guard cutters ignored the orders from the beginning. As one officer later wrote: "a strict interpretation of these orders would have meant leaving the surviving officers and crew to their fate. However, traditions of the sea and of the Coast Guard prevailed."[139] Sims later relaxed the order but warned his officers "to proceed with caution in rescuing survivors and never to slow down or to stop without reasonable assurance against possible presence of enemy." Later the orders were changed to permit two escorts to rescue survivors. One engaged in the rescue work while the other circled to protect the operation.[140] No instruction concerning rescue operations proved satisfactory to all forces, and many exploits were conducted with unusual intrepidity. According to one of her officers, the yacht *Corsair* probably rescued more torpedoed crews than any other yacht and possibly any other American escort. In June 1918, she towed the merchantman *Californian* stern first until she sank. In October, the yacht towed a severely damaged ship three hundred miles into port. *Corsair* was part of a screen when the transport *Antilles* was lost and for two hours rescued survivors. She was one of several escorts, including the small destroyer *Stewart*, that pushed through a mass of burning material, including ammunition cases, to escort lifeboats to safety.[141]

The cutter *Seneca*, like *Corsair*, became known for rescue operations. In June 1918, the convoy leader *Queen* was torpedoed and sank within five minutes. *Seneca*, the convoy's single escort, immediately steamed through the debris to rescue survivors in the water, saving all but six of the ship's crew. While involved in this work, the cutter's deck guns fired random shots toward the presumed location of the U-boat. None of the convoy's remaining ships was attacked.

Seneca is best remembered for the futile efforts of members of her crew to save the British collier *Wellington*. In September 1918, the collier was torpedoed while underway with a convoy headed for Gibraltar. Although the ship was not in immediate danger of sinking, the crew took to the lifeboats. Lieutenant Fletcher Brown and eighteen volunteers from *Seneca* and a few members of the collier's crew attempted to save the ship. The weather deteriorated. *Seneca* had to remain with the convoy. An SOS brought *Warrington* to the rescue, but the destroyer could not launch her small boats in the gale-force winds. The Coast Guards and the crew of *Wellington* lowered the remaining lifeboat with eight sailors on board, but as the remainder prepared rafts, the ship foundered. Survivors floated amidst the wreckage until retrieved.[142]

One of the most dramatic rescues occurred when the former Pacific and Orient liner *Orama* went to the bottom. *Orama* was one of the large ships converted by the British navy into an armed merchant cruiser. She was leading a convoy through an area where a submarine had attacked a ship a few hours earlier. The skipper of *Conyngham*, Commander Alfy Johnson, was senior officer in charge of the escort. He tried without success to persuade the convoy's commodore on *Orama* to change course and swing clear of the area. The British ship cruised several hundred yards in front of the convoy beyond the protection of the escorts. Johnson was still arguing with him when a U-boat torpedoed the liner. One of *Conyngham's* officers wrote in his journal: "[T]here was a sudden muffled explosion and a very distinct shock. A huge column of water flecked with wreckage rose under the portside of her bridge." As the destroyer steamed close to the torpedoed ship, she was "already beginning to list heavily to port and was settling by the head." It took *Orama* nearly four hours to sink. American escorts rescued 593 members of her crew. Johnson criticized the convoy commodore because he did not change course and remained ahead of the remainder of the convoy and its escorts. Admiral Sims, however, was also critical of the escort commander for allowing several escorts to move out of position to deliver messages to various ships and for dispersing the convoy.[143]

In discussing the reasons for the success of convoying, writers usually emphasize the percentage of merchant ships and transports ships sunk or damaged by German submarines. When the number of convoys and ships that the American escorts screened to and from ports in the war zone is calculated, their achievement appears most impressive. The destroyers operating out of Queenstown spent 50 percent of their time at sea. In June 1918, *Wilkes* was underway seventeen out of twenty-one consecutive days. Throughout the war, the destroyers averaged six thousand miles per month.[144] The escorts operating out of Gibraltar and French ports were not at sea as much, primarily because they did not have to operate as far from base as the Ireland-based destroyers.

Not all escort officers satisfied their commanders. Wilson, unhappy with the reserve officers on his yachts, requested regulars to replace them.[145] He also admonished escort captains for losing a convoy, failing to make a rendezvous on time, and attacking a submarine without sufficient determination.[146]

British naval officers admired the professionalism of American escort commanders. Captain D. J. Monro wrote after the war that "The escorts performed their duties in a seamanlike manner, and those of the U.S. Navy were past masters at this class of work."[147] British escort commanders accepted American criticism without offense. The British sloops were generally slower than the American destroyers and usually brought up the rear in a screen. Often they fell behind. When serving as senior American escort commander, Commander Frank Berrien frequently signaled the sloops to close up. On one occasion, he signaled HMS *Bluebell*: "you are of no use in your present position." Later, when the British and American officers gathered in the Royal yacht Club, *Bluebell's* commanding officer said, "I can always tell when Berrien is senior officer for the first thing I get is: 'ROTTEN BLUEBELL,' get in position."[148]

On one occasion a torpedoed ship sent out an SOS. A destroyer replied, "Coming to your assistance—give position, course, and speed." When nothing was heard, the destroyer repeated the message. Finally an unidentified radio operator came on the air: "POSITION OF TORPEDOED SHIP IS BETWEEN TWO DESTROYERS. HER SPEED IS EIGHT FEET AN HOUR, AND HER COURSE IS TOWARD THE BOTTOM OF THE NORTH ATLANTIC. SHE IS ALMOST THERE. GOOD NIGHT!"[149]

The prewar United States Navy did not develop operational doctrine for escort of convoys, and the British were of no help in this respect. The first American destroyer commanders to arrive in Queenstown recognized this deficiency. Taussig mentioned in 1921 that escort commanders issued differing orders to their escort groups. He said that the destroyer commanders not on escort duty met in July 1917 and put together a general doctrine "to cover the principal points" of escort work. Groups involved in escort operations experimented with various concepts.[150] In September, the proposed doctrine was turned over to Admiral Bayly, who, according to Pringle, was at work on a similar project. In October, the Queenstown commander held a series of meetings at Admiralty House to perfect the doctrine. The accepted text was published as an Admiralty document.[151] In the meantime, Sims cabled the Department a tentative outline of escort doctrine, parts of which Admiral Gleaves prescribed for use by his escorts.[152] The doctrine periodically underwent improvement. Admiral Wilson adopted a similar doctrine for the escorts under his command, based on the Admiralty document and the one promulgated by Gleaves, although Taussig, who arrived in the French command with a new destroyer, complained in June that the destroyer force under Wilson's command was without organization, "only a bunch of boats."[153]

The doctrine for the Queenstown destroyers included brief instructions concerning convoy station, communications, speed, zigzagging, operating procedures for both convoy and escorts under attack, rescue, and convoy command. To find a convoy without using the radio, destroyers were expected to form a scouting line approximately a mile apart from each other. All American escorts followed this procedure throughout the war. Later, the escort that first located a convoy was expected to send up a smoke column to establish a rendezvous.[154] When a submarine was sighted, the convoy dispersed with its screen except for two escorts who were expected to attack the submarine. Escorts were to avoid use of radios. The convoyed ships were not to use their guns against submarines while under escort. These instructions, especially those for the convoyed ships, were ignored at various times.

In general, the doctrine stressed that the first objective of escorts was to protect the convoy; the secondary mission was to rescue survivors and assist disabled vessels; and the third objective was to destroy the submarine. Some disagreement arose over the order of these objectives. Admiral Bayly issued an instruction on November 1, 1917, which stated that "the principal use of destroyers on this station are; (1) sinking of enemy submarines (2) protection of trade."[155] Although Admiralty instructions followed by American naval forces in European waters gave priority to protection of convoys, the destruction of enemy submarines remained important. Both British and American naval officers believed that convoying provided an ideal opportunity to destroy U-boats. Escorts went on the offensive against a submarine whenever possible. The British and American Planning sections stated in a memorandum on antisubmarine attack, "It is imperative that full advantage be taken of such contacts to destroy the enemy, to accomplish which the role of escorts of anti-submarine types must instantly be transported from defensive to offensive."[156] In May 1918, the Admiralty recommended that at least half of an escort force screening a convoy should attack a submarine when it was detected. The American naval command adopted this injunction.[157]

The use of depth charges altered with the increasing availability of this weapon. Initially, fewer than a dozen ash cans were allotted to American destroyers. British antisubmarine vessels carried only four as late as January 1917. ASW craft commanders were instructed to drop one only when they detected a U-boat. As output grew, the number of allotted charges multiplied. New ASW weapons such as Y guns were added to the antisubmarine arsenal. Tactics also changed. Ship commanders were permitted to drop on anything suspected of being a submarine. The expenditure of depth charges accelerated until in July 1918, American escorts dropped from two to three thousand a month. An escort often expended more than fifteen in a single barrage. *Fanning* dropped 111 in May 1918, "and only two were duds."[158] A destroyer officer recalled that "We dropped them upon the slightest provocation. The nearest suspicion of an oil slick upon the water was a good enough excuse to let go a dozen or more depth charges." The British and American planning sections agreed that depth charges quickly became the principal weapon for attacking submarines, although they accounted for "only a small number of successes." Too many ships were torpedoed with the loss of too few submarines.[159]

The Department agreed with the conclusion of Simsadus that depth charges were more effective than guns or torpedoes carried on antisubmarine vessels. As early as January 1918, the European force commander stressed the need for each ship to carry as many depth charges as it could and to use them "liberally." In May 1918, he approved laying a barrage of from twenty to thirty depth charges on each attack. This tactical practice depended on the availability of depth charges. The Navy contracted for ten thousand of the 300-pounders (Mark IIs) in July 1917, and twenty thousand more early in 1918, but supply to the European forces barely kept up with demand. In the Queenstown force alone, the destroyers expended approximately 250 a week by June 1918. Because British depth charges were similar to those of the Americans, they were used interchangeably. Sims, however, preferred the American charges because of the safety factor, keeping the British model in reserve. Nevertheless, Mark IIs never became available in sufficient numbers. American ships continued to carry British depth charges up to the Armistice. By then the Navy had contracted for a total of 72,000 of the 300-pounders. By August, the Queenstown force alone dropped an average of about a thousand a month. Depth charges sunk an estimated thirty-eight to forty-four submarines during the war. According to one writer, this volume resulted in an average expenditure of over a thousand for each submarine sunk.[160]

Escort commanders at times requested specific instructions concerning operations. Taussig wrote after the war of their preference for orders that "eliminated the necessity for the escort commander to issue a long detailed operation order each time we went out. Everything was covered, from the manner in which we leave port, to the manner of returning." Eventually escort commanders only had to state the time of departure "and the numbered position each destroyer would occupy in the screen. The rest became automatic according to the doctrine."[161] American naval forces in European waters were still at work on an acceptable doctrine at the end of the war. It included the concept of strengthening the escort's ability to attack submarines by increasing depth-charge weaponry. As Sims was informed, "we were finally able to develop a barrage a little over a mile long and 233 yards wide which, I think would have destroyed any submarine which happened to fall within it."[162]

American escorts in European waters contributed significantly to the antisubmarine campaign, although they made up only a small percentage of the total. Great Britain provided 70 percent of destroyers for all Atlantic convoy, and the United States approximately 27 percent. The British also employed more than three thousand auxiliary patrol vessels, mostly in coastal waters. The French contributed a few, but the U.S. Navy provided three-eighths of escorts for French coastal waters from August 1917 to November 1918.[163] American escorts destroyed only one U-boat and assisted in the destruction of three others out of a total of more than 170 destroyed during the war. The major objective of escorts was not to destroy submarines but to keep them from sinking ships. They succeeded in doing so. The submarines attacked only eighty-four convoys, 7.4 percent of 1,134. Although the percentage of American escorts in European waters was small, Admiral Bayly wrote that they made "All the difference."[164]

Comrades of the Mist

The North Sea

The Royal Navy adopted a defensive posture in 1914 and maintained it thereafter. It protected the nation's shores, vital maritime commerce, and the military force in France. The objective was to control the seas and thereby neutralize Germany's naval forces. The Grand Fleet was concentrated in the North Sea. Other naval forces remained in the English Channel to block German access to the sea. The Battle of Jutland in 1916 did not cause an alteration in this defensive approach, but the growing submarine campaign forced some changes. Admiral Jellicoe was at first convinced that victory would come from defeating or bottling up the German High Seas Fleet. By the summer of 1917, he recognized that Allied success required the defeat of the submarine menace. The Grand Fleet continued as a "fleet in being," preventing a sortie by German surface forces into the North Sea, but Jellicoe was no longer convinced that a successful fleet action would assure success. As first sea lord, he argued that the Grand Fleet should avoid adventures that threatened Britain's control of the North Sea. Admiral Beatty, who replaced Jellicoe in command of the Grand Fleet, endorsed this defensive strategy.

Many in Great Britain considered this posture indecisive. They believed that the Royal Navy should initiate offensive operations aimed at destroying the German naval bases. Among these advocates were Sir Winston Churchill, Admiral Fisher, and "young Turks" in the Admiralty and the Grand Fleet. Even Jellicoe favored a landing on the Flanders coast to seize or destroy the naval bases in that area. The prime minister, David Lloyd George, was most dissatisfied with Admiralty policies, one of the reasons for Jellicoe's eventual dismissal as first sea lord.[1]

When the United States entered the war, President Wilson and his advisors sought information about British naval plans. Admiral Sims was instructed to question the Admiralty officials, and officials in Washington queried the British naval attaché and visiting Allied naval officials. Secretary Daniels inquired why the British did not conduct a close blockade of the German coast. A French admiral said that the British considered it "extremely difficult." The idea of attacking German naval bases met with the same response.[2]

Early in July, President Wilson cabled Admiral Sims: "From the beginning of the war I have been greatly surprised at the failure of the British Admiralty to use Great Britain's great naval superiority in an effective way. In the presence of the present submarine emergency they are helpless to the point of panic. In my view this is not a time for prudence but for boldness even at the cost of great losses." Sims, who had decided that convoying was the solution to the submarine problem, replied that the American fleet should be concentrated in European waters to conduct antisubmarine and convoying operations. He also supported British naval strategy, a view that failed to change the president's impression that the Royal Navy was far too inactive.

Wilson became convinced that destruction of the German naval bases would resolve the submarine menace. Early in August, he offered this opinion to the officers and personnel on the battleship *Pennsylvania*, flagship of the Atlantic Fleet: "We are hunting hornets all over the farm and letting the nest alone. . . . I am willing to sacrifice half the navy[.] Great Britain and we together have to crush out that nest, because if we crush it the war is won. . . . We have got to throw tradition to the winds. . . . Every time we have suggested anything to the British Admiralty the reply has come back that virtually amounted to this, that it had never been done that way."[3]

Underlying the difference of opinion between the British and Americans over naval strategy was the desire of the president and his naval advisors to assume the leadership of joint American/British naval affairs. Sims and British officials for some time had urged the United States to send a naval mission to Europe and consult with Allied naval representatives. The president sent Admiral Mayo, commander in chief of the Atlantic Fleet. Meeting with Daniels and senior naval officers on August 16, he told Mayo that he desired plans in which the United States could "lead and be senior partner in a successful naval campaign." Wilson again urged the absolute necessity of offensive actions, using the analogy of "finding & ending the hornet's nest & destroying the poison or removing the cork." Mayo was also instructed to press for a mine barrage across the North Sea. Daniels was also willing to consider deploying battleships in European waters, but only if they would be used effectively.[4]

Jellicoe and other members of the Admiralty were well aware of American criticism. "There are a great many people in the United States who are entirely ignorant of war and who put forward proposals which are absolutely and absurdly impracticable . . . and . . . pouring them into the ears of the President," the first sea lord confided to Vice Admiral Browning. He responded that he had told Admiral Benson "as clearly as I could the practical unwisdom of acting against the enemy bases, or attempting to do so, without an army in conjunction, which is unfortunately impossible at the present." Jellicoe informed Beatty that he had instructed a committee to draw up a plan of "blocking the Germans." "The U.S. Navy Board keep[s] harping on an offensive," he wrote. "One cannot see the difficulties clearly except by having a regular plan of the operations systematically worked out. . . . We MAY find it a feasible proposition, though I don't think we shall."[5]

On August 18, the committee submitted a plan to the first sea lord. The objective was to block all the submarine exits by scuttling a large number of ships in them, mostly old merchant vessels filled with concrete. British troops would seize the heavily fortified islands of Wangeroog and Heligoland, which defended the approaches to many of these exits. Mines would be used in the Baltic Sea because of its depth. Jellicoe and most of his staff opposed this plan. It was considered impracticable because of difficulties in taking and holding the islands, the ineffectiveness of ships as obstructions, and the concern that these efforts, especially seizure of the islands, would draw the German fleet into a major battle in their waters. Beatty's staff developed a modified plan known as Operation ZZ, which substituted obsolete warships in place of merchant ships to block the Heligoland Bight. It made no mention of seizing the islands. When this plan was presented at the naval conference held in September attended by Mayo, it called for the use of forty warships, including at least fourteen American battleships.[6]

Mayo doubted that the United States could provide ships. It was also noted that mining the Baltic would violate Swedish and Danish neutrality. Only the Russian delegate strongly endorsed the plan. The delegates agreed to present the plan to their governments. Although President Wilson and the Navy Department had informed Mayo that they favored a more aggressive naval policy, including bombardment of the German ports, he apparently did not bring up this possibility during the conference. It is probable, however, that the admiral discussed the Americans' concerns with Admiralty officials before the conference. Mayo informed the Allied naval officials at the conference that he did not propose to recommend specific plans. The conferees agreed to "consider" the feasibility of offensive operations in German waters, using old warships, but Mayo doubted that it would come about. However, he succeeded in getting acceptance of the American plan to construct a mine barrage across the North Sea. Probably Jellicoe agreed to the mine barrage to pacify the Americans. A member of Mayo's staff later told the General Board, "it appeared to the American representatives that the plan was put up primarily as something to show that they had considered the subject, but it was not believed that they ever had any idea of attempting to carry it out."[7]

The American government rejected the blocking scheme as impracticable, a viewpoint shared by the Admiralty. It approved the construction of a North Sea Mine Barrage.[8]

Admiral Benson continued to favor attacks against German bases. He pressed this project when he joined the House Mission to Europe. The mission arrived in England on November 7. During one of his meetings at the Admiralty, the CNO raised the possibility of strikes on German submarine bases. "Before I left London," he wrote, "a very definite plan of operations was completed which will involve great risk and danger to our forces and the British forces; but I believe it is necessary and I assured the Admiralty officials that a certain number of our vessels would be fitted and assigned to participate in these efforts." Although no such plans have been found in the naval records, it is probable that the objectives were the principal German bases in the North Sea and possibly Zeebrugge and Ostend. They were attacked later: Sir Roger Keyes led a daring but unsuccessful raid. Admiral Richard Conolly recalled: "There was a plan at one time for some of our ships to participate in the attacks on Zeebrugge and Ostend, but the British . . . finally did the job. . . . I think it was unfortunate that we didn't [participate], because we had a lot of pre-dreadnoughts that were expendable." The Navy Department and the Planning Section at Sims's headquarters considered an attack on Heligoland, but both decided against it.[9]

After conferring with British naval officials, Benson met with representatives of the Allied Naval Council in Paris. Apparently the group did not discuss an attack on the German submarine, but the council approved the North Sea Mine Barrage, which the Americans considered an offensive operation. Benson also agreed to recommend the deployment of a battleship division to European waters.

On December 7, 1917, four battleships flying the United States flag—*Delaware*, *Wyoming*, *Florida*, and *New York*—joined the British Grand Fleet at Scapa Flow in the Orkney Islands, the first of nine American battleships to serve in European waters during the war. *Texas*, *Arkansas*, and *Nevada* also joined the Grand Fleet, the "*Arkie*" to replace *Delaware*, and *Nevada* to replace *Florida*. *Nevada* arrived after the Armistice, having been deployed in August with *Oklahoma* and *Utah* in Bantry Bay, Ireland. *Florida* went home with the rest of the squadron.[10]

The deployment of these ships demonstrated the flexibility of American naval policy during the war. The Navy's accepted doctrine was to concentrate the entire battle fleet into one powerful force. President Wilson's decision to send the battleships was in many ways the most important naval decision made during the war. It contradicted the Navy's doctrine and also the president's strong suspicions of British naval mistakes, which he voiced to Daniels in July 1917: "As you and I concluded yesterday, the British Admiralty has done practically nothing constructive in the use of their navy."[11]

Secretary Daniels was as critical of the British navy as Wilson, and so were a majority in the Navy Department, including Admiral Benson. Many were Anglophobes, but more important were their views on the use of the fleet. Aside from the doctrines of Admiral Mahan, two other elements influenced Benson's position. He was convinced that the United States must protect its future. To do so it must keep most of its naval power in the Western Hemisphere. If German raiders appeared in American waters, the Atlantic Fleet must deal with them. Benson and his subordinates were also suspicious of Japan. Relations between the two countries had deteriorated for years; many in the Navy Department believed that war was more than probable in the future.[12]

Admiral Sims challenged the Department's position shortly after the United States entered the war. On April 14, four days after he reached London, he mentioned the possibility of basing two divisions of dreadnoughts at Brest "for moral effect against anticipated raids by heavy enemy ships in the Channel out of reach of British main fleet." He denied that he violated doctrine when he urged the dispatch of various units to the war zone, although he was not a devoted follower of Mahan.[13] On July 6, Sims recommended preparation of all coal-burning dreadnoughts for duty with Admiral Beatty's Grand Fleet. Two weeks later, he passed on Jellicoe's request for four coal burners. They were to replace five pre-dreadnought battleships whose personnel could then man antisubmarine craft. The request was declined. Sims renewed it in August, but the Department remained firm in its opposition. "Sims again wanted four coal burning dreadnoughts to take the place of English ships," Daniels wrote, but the secretary wanted a plan for their employment other than replacement of British pre-dreadnoughts. When Mayo conferred with Allied naval officials in London, he discovered that the request for the battleships headed the British list of desired assistance. Admiral Benson's rejection of the British request reflected the United States' paramount need to prepare for "postwar possibilities," presumably the Japanese challenge.[14]

Within a month, the Department began to change its opinion. In testimony before the General Board, Commander William S. Pye, Mayo's chief of staff; Captain Frank H. Schofield from Sims's staff; and Captain Pratt all recommended deployment of battleships to European waters. The Board then gave its approval. Pratt cited improvements in Japanese-American relations as the major reason for favoring the British request, although he admitted that he offered his personal opinion and not that of either the CNO or Operations. Benson maintained his opposition until he met with Admiralty representatives in November.[15]

Early in November, the CNO journeyed to Europe. On November 10, Benson sanctioned the British request for four coal-burning battleships. He informed Colonel Edward M. House that he had tentatively agreed to send the "entire Atlantic Fleet to European waters in the spring provided conditions warranted such action." It is not known whether this decision reflected a new appreciation of "the awesome might of the Grand Fleet and the warmth of his reception" in England, as one authority suggests; the influence of Pratt, as another implies; the signing of the Lansing-Ishii Agreement with Japan on November 2, as a third writer argues; or the Admiralty's acceptance of the concept of a mine barrage in the North Sea, a pet project of the Department. Another circumstance might have influenced Benson—the British decision not to press for the decommissioning of pre-dreadnoughts. Instead, the Admiralty stressed the possible urgent need of the American battle fleet, and it accepted the American claim that the only a few U.S. battleships could serve in the Grand Fleet at a given time because of organizational and logistical considerations. Probably he believed that the ships would participate in "offensive operations" discussed with Jellicoe.

Perhaps more surprising than the CNO's change of heart was the turnabout of Secretary Daniels and presumably President Wilson. Daniels recorded a "Telegram from Benson suggesting 4 dreadnoughts to be sent to English fleet. We approved."[16] On November 25, the four battleships departed Hampton Roads for European waters.

Benson did not mention the possibility of sending the entire fleet in the spring, but he noted Admiral Jellicoe's agreement to rotate the American dreadnoughts until "all the fleet had had experience or conditions change." He referred to the ten coal-burning dreadnoughts in the Atlantic Fleet. The British desired only the coal burners. Because of the loss of tankers to German U-boats, they faced a severe shortage of oil. This difficulty necessitated the dispatch of older dreadnoughts because the more modern types burned oil. The Admiralty specified that the American ships should return to the United States for overhaul. Benson agreed, realizing that this measure would facilitate their rotation.[17]

Shortly after the four battleships joined the Grand Fleet, Sims cabled for a fifth, requesting *Texas*. British battle-line tactics called for two capital ships to operate together in a division of four. Without a fifth battleship, the American squadron could not do so. Daniels agreed: on January 30, 1918, *Texas* sailed for Scapa Flow.[18] In February, the Admiralty requested another change, the substitution of *Arkansas* for *Delaware*. The maximum range of *Delaware*'s 12-inch guns was less than that of the other American battleships. *Arkansas*, a sister ship of *Florida*, had the necessary range. Admiral Beatty declined when asked if he wished to retain *Delaware* along with *Arkansas*. The Department approved the request. *Arkansas* joined the American squadron in July 1918.[19]

Admiral Benson was prepared to rotate the entire fleet in entirety or by smaller units, but the British were reluctant either to increase or to modify the American units with the Grand Fleet. In January, the Admiralty informed Sims that it no longer favored rotation of a division in six months. The Department was informed that Admiral Beatty insisted upon "continuity" in the fleet. Beatty believed that it was taking an inordinate amount of time to bring the American battleships to the level of the British battleships. In June, the Admiralty considered a request for additional U.S. battleships but rejected the idea primarily because of Beatty's disapproval. The Admiralty's deputy chief of the naval staff wrote on June 12: "there is no denying the fact that the C-in-C has hitherto considered the U.S. battleships rather as an incubus to the Grand Fleet. . . . They have not even yet been assimilated to a sufficient degree to be considered equivalent to British dreadnoughts, yet for political reasons he does not care that the Grand Fleet should go to sea without them." Both Rodman and the Department were eager to deploy some of the modern oil-burning battleships to European waters, but the shortage of oil plus Beatty's attitude prevented it. In July 1918, the possibility the Germans might make a surface raid on convoys provided a reason to deploy additional American battleships. An agreement was reached to deploy a division of American battleships, including oil burners, in Bantry Bay, Ireland. On August 12, two battleships, *Nevada* and *Oklahoma*, departed Hampton Roads for Ireland, and *Utah* followed on August 30. After the Armistice, the fourth vessel in the division, *Arizona*, left to join the other three. On August 12, *Nevada* and *Oklahoma* passed *Delaware* as they left for Bantry Bay to return home from nine months' service with the Grand Fleet.[20]

In July, the Admiralty agreed to rotate a battleship to the United States for overhaul, a measure intended to relieve overtaxed dockyards and allow home leave for American personnel. Sims made the recommendation early in August. At first Benson disapproved, noting that the Navy's battleship strength in home waters had fallen rapidly. The matter rested until October, when Sims again requested action. This time the CNO agreed, but he recommended a plan whereby a battleship stationed at Bantry Bay would relieve one of the ships with the Grand Fleet. Another battleship would steam to Bantry Bay from the United States. In this way, Benson planned to attach some of his more modern battleships to the Grand Fleet. The Armistice came before the rotation could take place, but nevertheless, the oil burner *Nevada* sailed from Bantry Bay and joined the Sixth Battle Squadron on November 20.[21]

Rear Admiral Hugh ("Uncle Hughie") Rodman commanded the American battleships that joined the Grand Fleet. The General Board had recommended Rear Admiral Thomas S. Rodgers for the command, but Admiral Mayo and several other senior officers urged Rodman's selection. Daniels agreed, noting that he considered Rodgers "one of the most learned in the Navy, but I did not think his experience afloat and his lack of the spirit of comradeship, made him the ideal man for that service."[22] Rodman was promoted to rear admiral when selected for the command.

Rodman graduated from the Naval Academy in 1880, ranking second from the bottom in a class of sixty-two. His lack of academic prowess may explain why he had little time for "theory," although he once served as an aide to Mahan. Rodman referred to the famous naval officer as a poor seaman, "the swivel-chair artist with the fountain pen." Vice Admiral James O. Richardson, who served under Rodman, wrote, "I doubt that, after he reached the grade of lieutenant, he ever read a professional book." Yet Rodman became a superb seaman and ship handler, which enhanced his reputation. His career followed a fairly typical but inauspicious course. In 1905, he gained his first command, the gunboat *Elcano* on the Yangtze Station. In 1912, Rear Admiral Hugo Osterhaus selected him to command his flagship, the battleship *Connecticut*. He earned praise for his service as senior naval officer in charge of transportation at the Panama Canal. Rodman sat on the General Board when Daniels named him to the command of the battleship division about to join the Grand Fleet.[23]

Admiral Rodman was fifty-eight years old in 1917 but looked and acted much younger. He was a big man, over six feet in height. He was athletically built, loved hunting and fishing, but was disinterested in organized sports. His patrician face suggested a bulldog demeanor, an apparent contradiction, but one that reflected his character. He was known for his temper, his booming voice, and his salty language. A reserve officer wrote: "let the slightest mistake occur, then 'stand from under!' He is never sparing in reproach or criticism." Yet, away from his duties, Rodman was relaxed and even jovial. "I have seen him in 'tight positions,'" an officer remembered, "while everyone is more or less holding his breath, give orders sharply, briefly—then nonchalantly start to expound some absurdly irrelevant story to another officer on the bridge. . . . entirely confident in the outcome of the execution of his orders." A former aide recalled that Rodman "was always able and ready to ride with his decision." He demanded high performance in his command. He judged the captains under him severely, according to Pratt. Rear Admiral Harry W. Hill agreed, "He . . . demanded very high performance from everybody." He was particularly hard on his flagship captain, at times unfairly.[24]

Rodman was almost fanatical when it came to proper uniforms and cleanliness for both personnel and ships. No one escaped his vigilance. He personally inspected the different ships in his squadron. He dressed down a ship's commanding officer for dirt in his stateroom and ordered a reprimand for an officer on liberty observed with a dirty hat. Rodman was equally hard on enlisted personnel; according to one veteran, he "raise[d] . . . more rumpus about one spot we couldn't get out of our dress blues than the average man would kick up if he were being murdered."[25]

Rodman was a "subject of conversation," and tales were told about him. Secretary Daniels in his memoirs recounted the story of the admiral's visit to an English estate where he was introduced to a certain lady. "He said he understood her to be Lady Linlithgow or something like that. He did not catch the name and called her successively Lady Lithograph, Lady Linotype, Lady Linoleum. Finally seeing he did not get the name right the lady said, 'call me Mary,' and Marty she was all that evening." Admiral Hill recounts a story about the admiral sending his laundry ashore with a message as follows: "'Have admiral's washerwoman meet the one o'clock boat.' When the admiral got the copy of the message from the bridge, you could hear the roar all over the ship—because the message as sent read: 'Please arrange to have the Admiral's woman meet the 1 o'clock boat.'" He had his flag lieutenant send a corrected message, but "It read, 'Reference my message so and so, insert washer between Admiral and woman.'" When the U.S. battleships first entered the Firth of Forth, they received instructions to anchor just past the Forth Bridge, but they continued upstream. A signal from Admiral Beatty's flagship stopped the division. When Rodman was asked why he did not stop at the Forth Bridge, he supposedly replied that he was waiting for the fourth bridge. Not surprisingly, the British often had difficulty understanding his jokes. One, which made a number of British newspapers, described a visit by King George V to Rodman's flagship. While conversing with the dignitaries, he saw the British "beef boat," a refrigerator vessel, which carried meat to various ships in the fleet. The "beef boat" carried a flag with a large bull on it. Turning to the king, the admiral said, "This is the first time I have ever seen the royal standard of Great Britain flying officially— old . . . John Bull himself." Apparently British writers believed that Rodman had truly mistaken the flag. His wit even carried over to official signals. One of Lord Beatty's biographers wrote of a signal received from Rodman that read "have lost *Delaware.*" Beatty, "knowing full well what had happened," signaled, "Hope she is not sunk." Rodman then replied, "No, just mislaid."[26]

Rodman got along amazingly well with the British. Admiral of the Fleet Lord Chatfield wrote that Rodman was responsible for the successful Anglo-American cooperation in the Grand Fleet. His friendliness, wit, and obvious determination to get along attracted British officers who came in contact with him. One American naval officer speculated that the admiral's popularity with the British was a result of his "jovial, wholehearted smile" and added that to "Englishmen—the most reticent—his blunt, matter-of-fact, and to the point manner seemed a delightful revelation."[27]

Rodman enjoyed an extraordinary relationship with Lord Beatty, although in nearly every respect they were opposites. Beatty was a small man with intellectual interests. The American was ten years older than Beatty. They possessed different backgrounds and very different personalities. Rodman disliked naval officers that were products of wealth and privilege, and Beatty was such a person. After the war, Rodman praised Beatty highly in his testimony before a congressional investigating committee and in his autobiography. "He has my greatest admiration," Rodman wrote. "It was an honor and a pleasure to serve under him." Beatty called the American admiral by his first name (but not "Uncle Hughie") and "Old Rodman" in his correspondence with the first sea lord. Beatty frequently invited Rodman to dinner at Aberdour House, his mansion near Rosyth.[28]

The King of England became quite fond of Rodman. George V made two official visits and other "semi-private" visits to *New York* to meet with the American admiral whom "he greatly admired." Rodman delighted in "stirring things up," and the presence of royalty did not unsettle him. When the king lined up with Sims and Rodman to pose for photographs, Rodman joked about who would stand in the middle. The king knighted Rodman and did not take offense when the American refused to kneel. Rodman also got along "famously" with the Prince of Wales. In 1936, when George V died and the prince became Edward VIII, the new monarch invited the retired American admiral to serve as the official U.S. representative at the coronation. For the occasion, he once again flew his flag from *New York*.[29]

Rodman had few personal contacts with his commanders other than with the captains of his flagship, *New York*. Communication was carried out by written orders, signals, or by one of his staff. There were few conferences. Charles F. Hughes and Edward L. Beach commanded the *New York* while deployed in European waters. Both were excellent officers, although Rodman got along better with Hughes than Beach. Hughes was a "Downeasterner" from Maine, known as "Freddy" to his friends and "Walrus" to junior officers because of his drooping mustache. Rodman called Hughes an excellent seaman in his autobiography, although the admiral on at least one occasion took over command of the flagship in a difficult situation.[30]

Beach was just as capable a seaman but more cautious, a trait that at times irritated the admiral. Probably Beach's caution was a result of losing his previous command, the old armored cruiser *Memphis*. On one occasion, Rodman ordered the flagship to swing in extremely close to *Texas*. Beach refused. Rodman lost his temper. A shouting match followed, and, according to Beach's son, the admiral threatened with fists and had to be restrained.[31]

Rodman's division of four battleships left Hampton Roads late in November. The Admiralty specifically requested coal burners because of the oil shortage. Only eight coal-burning dreadnoughts were in commission. It was impossible to send four of the same class because the Navy had only two battleships in any one class. *New York*, *Wyoming*, *Florida*, and *Delaware* were selected because of their material readiness. The ships encountered a storm with winds approaching a hundred miles an hour, which followed them until they approached the British Isles. *Florida* and *Delaware* became separated, but they rejoined when they reached the English Channel. All of the ships suffered damage, but none of them required dockyard repairs.[32]

As the division entered Pentland Firth and neared Scapa Flow, a squadron of destroyers escorted them to the fleet anchorage. The American battleships came within sight of the powerful British fleet, and in column steamed slowly between the lines of the war-weary dreadnoughts. The day before, Admiral Beatty ordered the ship's crews to mass "in the most convenient part of the upper deck" and give three cheers as each of the American ships passed. Their bands were also to play the "Star Spangled Banner." One British sailor recalled: "We had just sat down to breakfast . . . when the order came: 'Clear lower-deck. Hands cheer ship.' With a lot of moaning all hands lined the rail all round the ship and as each American drew abreast of us, a very pompous old Commander announced through his megaphone: 'Three cheers for U.S.S. *Delaware*. Hip hip . . .' and as we waved our hats in the regulation manner the reply came: 'Hurray—' followed by a four letter word. . . . Lieutenants were frantically running from one side of the ship to the other but of course they never found out who it was—the four letter words always came from where they were not." The American crews were at quarters and returned the British salutations "cheer for cheer" but not the four-letter words. On *Wyoming*, a portable phonograph was placed near a radio transmitter and continued to play "The Yanks Are Coming," which evidently disrupted wireless communication within the British Fleet.[33]

Almost immediately after dropping anchor, the division coaled ship. When the American admiral was informed that his ships were required to steam on four hours' notice, he replied that U.S. ships were accustomed to twenty-four-hour notice before going to sea. The C-in-C then called a meeting of the U.S. squadron's chief engineers, who were "lectured to" by the fleet's chief engineer about procedures for keeping up steam. A Marine remarked: "'It was a new game, strange coal and stranger colliers, and we did not handle it well at first, but before long we had that darned Welsh coal trained so it would roll over and play dead.' Welcome to Scapa!"[34]

Seventy-odd islands make up the Orkneys. Only a few of the larger ones were inhabited, mostly by a few thousand hearty crofters and fishermen. Pentland Firth separated them from the mainland; a ferry connected the two locations at the closest point. The temperature was a few degrees warmer than on the Scottish coast, but ferocious winds seemed to produce very cold conditions. A few trees and very little of anything else grew except tundra grass and some wildflowers during the brief summer. Frequent gales occurred during the harsh winter. The islands in general surrounded a huge inland sea, Scapa Flow, a nearly landlocked amphitheater that covered more than 120 square miles. It was an ideal anchorage for the Grand Fleet, deep enough, without tidal current, and sheltered from the storms that lashed the North Sea. The navigable inlets or sounds were few in number. It was close to the North Sea and Atlantic Ocean, the maritime highways of German submarines and the High Seas Fleet. The British fortified the Orkneys early in the war and obstructed the inlets with barriers of sunken ships, drift nets, and minefields. They did not construct a base with shore facilities.[35]

Personnel attached to the Grand Fleet at Scapa Flow universally disliked it. Shortly after the Armistice, Admiral Beatty, speaking to the crew of HMS *Lion*, mentioned that units of the German High Seas Fleet were to be interned at Scapa Flow: "They are now going to be taken away and placed under the guardianship of the Grand Fleet at Scapa, where they will enjoy (laughter), as we have enjoyed the pleasures of Scapa (laughter)." One of the German naval officers wrote, "no place could be more godforsaken."[36] The *Wyoming*'s war cruise book referred sardonically to Scapa as a "famous Scotch watering resort . . . a wonderfully healthy place to live" but added that "a few months there would drive anyone at least half crazy." To Captain (later Admiral) Wiley, Scapa Flow "was the dreariest spot I have ever seen, and I have seen some dreary spots." He mentioned a popular saying among the enlisted men, "Yes Sherman said that war is hell, and yet he ain't seen Scapa Flow."[37]

In April 1918, the fleet moved to Rosyth, where conditions were much more favorable, but they continued to operate in the North Sea. Duty in the North Sea was miserable even on large battleships. Much of it, including the operational area of the Grand Fleet, was above the latitude of Sitka, Alaska, and St. Petersburg, Russia. It was nearly always stormy, rainy, and foggy. According to the *Wyoming*'s cruise book, the North

Sea was "the darnedest, most miserable body of water ever, especially in winter, a rotten place to sail, fish, or fight." An American jack reminisced, "I don't believe I saw the sun the whole year I was there." At times during the winter of 1918, the weather became so severe that turrets froze, and the bores of the guns became choked with ice and had to be cleared frequently. While at sea, the gun ports on the gun deck often could not be opened without flooding the deck. Shortly after the U.S. battleships arrived, two destroyers were lost with all hands except one while patrolling off Scapa Flow during a blizzard.[38] Rodman mentioned the "rigorous climate" to Sims and wrote that he considered it "very healthy indeed," but after the war he changed his mind: "The weather was terrific . . . arduous and dangerous." Ships operating in these waters were subjected to rough weather at any time, especially units of the Grand Fleet, which were usually required to maintain speeds of eighteen knots. In April, *Florida*'s wardroom pantry and galley were destroyed while screening a Scandinavian convoy.[39]

In January 1918, Admiral Beatty stated the mission of the Grand Fleet as "to defeat the enemy's fleet and to control communications in the North Sea," but certain qualifications came into play. The Grand Fleet did not intend to attack the German High Seas Fleet. The British posture was one of watchful waiting, a cautious approach adopted after Jutland and maintained during Beatty's tenure.[40] He assured the Admiralty that he wanted to take the offensive and possibly attack the German bases, but without additional light craft, particularly destroyers, such operations entailed great risk.[41]

For much of the war, the British ran small convoys of merchant ships from Scotland to Norway. They returned with dairy products, other foods, and badly needed timber. In October 1917, a German naval force attacked one of the convoys, destroying two British destroyers and scattering the convoy. On December 12, another convoy was attacked and annihilated, including the escorts.

The Admiralty decided to use battleships in the Grand Fleet to protect the Norwegian convoys. These operations began in mid-January and continued until the Armistice. The Grand Fleet also protected minelayers. Regardless of the type of operation, Beatty hoped that it would draw the High Seas Fleet out. To the C-in-C, the Scandinavian convoys were "bait," and the entire fleet was prepared to sortie if the Germans attacked a convoy. The American battleships participated in these operations. They were fully integrated into the Grand Fleet when they arrived at Scapa Flow. Rodman's command, designated as the Sixth Battle Squadron, joined the fleet's five battleship squadrons.[42]

Although Rodman's squadron was under the administrative control of Sims, it served under the operational command of Admiral Beatty. Even before the American ships arrived, Admiral Beatty developed mixed opinions about them. He believed that the ships and crews were inferior and their inexperience a great handicap. On February 25, he informed the deputy chief of the naval staff of the Admiralty that the efficiency of the American ships was far below that of their British counterparts. "Their gunnery was distinctly poor and disappointing; their tactical efficiency will be all right; they are learning rapidly, and are at present stationed in line of battle where their movements are not likely to interfere with the movements of the main battleships. They cannot, however, be the equivalent of the British Battle squadrons." As late as June, Beatty wrote his wife: "We had some shocks coming out as mines were reported. . . . *Florida* always, of course, causes some excitement. As at the critical moment her helm jammed and she sailed slap at the place where the mines had been reported, but they got her turned in time and she escaped. But these American ships are not very reliable and in a Fleet formation are something of a danger." For months after joining the fleet, the American ships were stationed approximately two-and-a-half miles from the rest of the fleet. Beatty feared a collision between one of the U.S. battleships and a British ship.

Rodman insisted in his communications with the Navy Department and naval officials that his squadron stood "very high indeed in the estimation of the . . . Commander-in-Chief Grand Fleet." He made this assertion in June when Beatty called the American ships "something of a danger" to the rest of the fleet. However, Beatty behaved tactfully in his relations with the Sixth Battle Squadron. For political reasons, if for no other, they were a part of his command, and he made the best of it.[43]

If nothing else, the Americans helped sustain the morale of their British comrades. Grand Fleet personnel had to endure extreme hardships in one of the most difficult parts of the world to fight a war. Sims passed on to Benson the remarks of a British officer: "One of the most fortunate things that ever happened to the Grand Fleet was the arrival of the American battleships. He expressed himself as quite unable to explain the very remarkable effect that this had had on the spirits and the morale of the British officers and men. He said they were 'fed up' to the last degree with confinement on board ship without any opportunity to go ashore sometimes for weeks at a time." Others, including Americans, commented on the excellent morale of the fleet. Spirits improved in January 1918, when the ships became more active, escorting convoys and protecting minelayers. Beatty recognized the impact of the American presence on both the fleet and the British public. Despite his professional misgivings, Beatty spared no effort in integrating the American force. He soon discovered that Rodman was just as eager to shape his squadron into a fully accepted part of the fleet.[44]

Fundamental problems had to be overcome before Rodman could achieve his goal. The British and American navies differed in organization, administration, tactics, and weapons. Nothing was done about the internal administration and organization of the ships except to recognize the differences. Rodman discovered that he was considerably older and more experienced than the other battleship squadron commanders who outranked him. Beatty recommended a temporary rank for Rodman comparable with those of his counterparts, but the Navy Department rejected the idea. Rodman later insisted that the difference in rank had no impact in his professional and personal relationship with the British admirals. At times he was the senior admiral afloat, and the British admirals served under him. He also reported to the Department that British squadron commanders were given more latitude than their equivalents in the U.S. Navy. "They are made acquainted with the policy of the Commander in Chief, and conduct their commands with more freedom of action, and are entrusted with more responsibility."[45]

Immediately after they joined the Grand Fleet, the American ships received British signals, codebooks, and other essential communication information. Rodman and others recognized that communications and gunnery were the most serious differences between the two navies. Although the American ships adopted the British communication system, months passed before Beatty was satisfied with their performance.

The same generalization applied to gunnery. The Grand Fleet's practice was to concentrate the fire of two or more ships on one of the enemy's. The U.S. battleships fired full-gun salvos, which created a broad barrage of shells with more spread than the fire of the British dreadnoughts, but they were slower. Although the Americans prided themselves on their accuracy, the British felt differently. During the massive German offensives of March-June 1918, the British War Cabinet considered requesting that the United States deploy additional battleships so that Beatty could release personnel to reinforce the British forces on the Western Front. Admiralty officials bluntly informed the War Cabinet that the U.S. battleships were not efficient enough to replace British dreadnoughts.[46]

Admiral Mayo, after visiting the Grand Fleet in September 1918 and going to sea on *New York*, reported that he observed no difference in British and American fleet operations except that the United States had no battle cruisers and "Rodman had no light cruisers, destroyers, or 'aero plane ships.'" Nevertheless, differences existed, particularly tactical formations. "The status of the 6th Battle Squadron," a visiting officer from the Navy Department observed, "is that, as it operates as a battle squadron, with a fixed task, the results of its effectiveness as a battle squadron will always be known, a condition of affairs different from that which would exist were our vessels scattered among the other battle squadrons. . . . Its status . . . is different from that of the ships . . . operating in home waters."[47] The battle squadrons steamed in six columns abreast, the Sixth Battle Squadron being designated a "wing squadron." When forming a battle line for a possible engagement, the American squadron might be in the rear or front, depending upon the direction of the Grand Fleet. As in all learning exercises, the Americans committed errors. One British naval officer later recalled "lighter occasions [while at sea], not excluding the at times somewhat startling manoeuvers of the American 6th Battle Squadron."[48] The Americans were expected to steam on four hours' notice at all times, and often on one-and-a-half hours' notice. Many of the ships hoisted an observation balloon to signal departure on two-and-a-half-hours' notice. These kite balloons remained up with gunnery observers in baskets hanging from them as the ships sortied in the North Sea.

The American battleships had one distinct advantage; they had facilities on board ship that allowed them to make all but major repairs. The Sixth Battle Squadron was always at full strength, whereas the British had to maintain replacement ships to relieve those in need of repairs. Repairs had to be done rapidly because of the requirement to get underway in four hours or less. One of Sims's staff wrote after inspecting the squadron: "When they first arrived on this side, they . . . expressed the opinion that it would be quite impossible to keep the machinery in readiness at all times unless they had the usual overhaul period which we are accustomed to in time of peace. They have learned since then, that not only is it perfectly possible to carry out all current overhauling while on four hours notice, but that the actual result is that the vessels are maintained in a better steaming readiness than they were in our peace days."[49]

Three days after the American ships arrived, they went to sea, a means of introducing them to the North Sea. It was the first of the so-called PZ operations, known as "Pee Zeds," a training exercise under combat conditions. "Of all the jobs that took us out to sea, we disliked most [the PZs] . . . that lasted to the very end." The Sixth Battle Squadron participated in one of these operations at least once a month. However, the crews were never informed whether the sortie was "for real." Beatty hoped to encounter German units. Because of the danger from German submarines, the fleet always got underway at night, usually steaming through either mist or fog into Pentland Firth and then into the North Sea. Mines posed a constant hazard in addition to the usual foul weather. Maintaining position in the squadron and the fleet while avoiding about a hundred ships steaming in the dark of night toward the same rendezvous required exceptional vigilance. The American ships did not suffer a collision during their tour with the Grand Fleet. They never encountered an adversary at sea, which one officer thought fortunate because "we were intensely occupied with the task of merging ourselves with the British navy." When daylight appeared, the fleet was scattered over a vast area. The captain of *Wyoming* wrote, "I never saw the whole fleet."[50]

The American squadron spent Christmas at Rosyth and returned to Scapa Flow early in January 1918. During most of that month, the squadron concentrated on training exercises. Poor weather prevented operations outside Scapa Flow and often forced cancellations of gunnery practices, much to Beatty's disgust.[51] On the last day of January, the fleet put to sea for a PZ exercise. The dense fog and generally bad weather prevented the maneuvers from taking place.

Texas finally arrived on February 11 after a rough crossing. The ship's motto and nickname was "come on *Texas*." The crew temporarily dropped the term after sailors from other ships began to say "come off, *Texas*," a reference to a grounding while leaving New York harbor. The ship received orders to prepare to go to sea after only forty-eight hours in Scapa Flow. As so often happened, rumors spread through the fleet that the "Germans were out." The ships were always to go to General Quarters or battle stations with guns manned and loaded when the Grand Fleet left Scapa Flow. *Texas* followed the rest of the Sixth Battle Squadron out of the anchorage with her guns manned, but lifelines, small boats, and other pieces of equipment, supposed to be unloaded or stored below, remained on the open decks. A British admiral is supposed to have observed her departure and said, "There's the good old *Texas*, not an inch out of station and steaming with the best of them," but Beatty told his wife that, although the exercise was a good experience for the newly arrived battleship in getting underway, it "took a long time about it."[52]

On February 6, Rodman received orders to escort a convoy to Norway. Earlier Beatty wrote his wife: "The American Squadron enjoyed themselves greatly while we were out, and did very well, and will do better next time. I am sending old Rodman out on an operation of his own, which pleases him and gives them an idea that they are really taking part in the war. . . . I trust they will come to no harm." On January 19, the Admiralty adopted a new policy, requiring that capital ships screen the Scandinavian convoys. These convoys sailed at intervals of three to five days; the screen was usually out from three to six days. Beatty decided to rotate the duty among his six battle squadrons. This procedure was popular with Grand Fleet personnel. It took them away from "watchful waiting" and into a more active roll. The C-in-C also believed that sooner or later one of these operations would lead to an encounter with units of the German fleet. The Sixth Battle Squadron screened a convoy without mishap, although some confusion occurred when several battleships claimed to have spotted submarines and torpedo tracks.[53]

One somewhat surprising result of this convoy duty occurred in the Navy Department. Admiral Benson, when first apprised of it, was sharply critical of Rodman's participation, which subjected his ships to possible submarine attack. Evidently Sims had not informed the CNO of the new operational policy and its effect on the American battleships. Benson's assistant, Pratt, mentioned the incident in his autobiography. "The CNO," he wrote, "directed me to prepare a wire containing what I considered an unnecessary reprimand, for a job well done." He added, "I said, 'Aye, Aye Sir,' but being entirely out of sympathy with Benson's point of view, I did not send the message, hoping Benson would forget it." but the CNO remembered and later reprimanded his assistant.[54] After Benson discussed the matter with Daniels, he asked Sims to clarify the practice of using the "dreadnought type" to escort the Scandinavian convoys. "This is contrary to our present conception of general strategy of Grand Fleet . . . and is likewise contrary to our own policy and conception of fleet-in-being whose principal role is watching until a[n] . . . enemy can actually be engaged." Sims's reply evidently satisfied Washington. Rodman was not censured, and his squadron continued to fulfill its escort responsibilities.[55]

A disagreement arose over a decision to use battleships to protect the ships that planted the mine barrage in the North Sea. Because the Department strongly supported construction of the mine barrage, it offered no adverse comments. Most of the opposition came from Beatty. He disliked the whole concept but was especially disgruntled because it interfered with Grand Fleet operations. He refused to accept the premise that, like the Scandinavian convoys, the mine-laying expeditions might draw out the German Fleet and give him the opportunity to attack it. Instead, he insisted that deploying a portion of the Grand Fleet to screen the minelayers, including battleships, would reduce its strength and might affect the outcome of an engagement. Nonetheless, the Admiralty ordered him to provide screens for the minelayers.[56]

Although mining operations began in the spring of 1918, the Sixth Battle Squadron was not called upon to provide protection until summer. It left Scapa Flow on June 30 with a supporting force of British light cruisers and destroyers. Rodman established a screen within sight of the minelayers. The light forces escorted both the mine carriers and the battleships.[57] After the barrage reached the Norwegian coast, the squadron provided one other screen for the minelayers early in August.[58]

Screening convoys, protecting mine-laying expeditions, and participating in training exercises occupied units of the Grand Fleet much of the time, including the Sixth Battle Squadron, but on occasion the entire fleet went to sea. Usually the fleet conducted PZ operations, but sometimes it responded to intelligence that the German fleet was out or about to come out. When Germany's spring offensive commenced, Beatty and some at the Admiralty suspected that the German General Staff might order the High Seas Fleet to sea, particularly if the military operations on the Western Front did not go well. They were partly correct. The German offensive was quite successful at first, but the High Seas Fleet ventured out to destroy a Scandinavian convoy. On April 23, Admiral Scheer's force left port and steamed into the North Sea. Before Beatty was informed of the sortie, he lost an opportunity to intercept Scheer. The American squadron escorted a convoy during the week before the German attack. Considering their lack of combat experience and other problems, it was, as Paul G. Halpern states, probably fortunate that the American battleships were not placed in harm's way on that occasion.[59]

On April 12, the Grand Fleet shifted its base of operations from Scapa Flow to Rosyth because the Admiralty concluded that the Grand Fleet was too far north to cut off raiding expeditions. Although Scapa Flow was used for gunnery and other training exercises, Rosyth possessed good anchorages in the Firth of Forth, a dockyard, and other facilities, and it served as the permanent base until the Armistice.[60]

On April 24, Beatty's powerful force steamed out in search of the High Seas Fleet. In a dense fog, 196 warships—including 31 battleships, 2 battle cruisers, 26 cruisers and 85 destroyers—cleared the Firth of Forth. The fleet was so large that it was anchored along the Firth in rows for a distance of more than four miles above and below the bridge that bears its name. It took the Grand Fleet several hours to leave the Firth. Rodman wrote later that in a constricted passage such as the Firth of Forth, the fleet in a single column would measure about sixty-five miles in length. The American sailors observed the ships steaming slowly down the Firth. The U.S. battleships were anchored above the bridge and behind them were the light forces. The Sixth Battle Squadron was the last battle squadron to get underway. After failing to locate the High Seas Fleet, the Grand Fleet reentered the Firth of Forth a few days later. Scheer was unable to locate a convoy. This circumstance and the breakdown of the battle cruiser *Moltke* prompted his return to base.[61]

In September, at a boxing smoker held near Rosyth, Admiral Beatty warned the hundreds of American and British soldiers present that, although the Germans were on the brink of losing the war, the Grand Fleet must remain ready to engage the enemy. He did not expect the German fleet to surrender without a fight. The German naval High Command knew that the end was near. It was determined to seek a final fleet engagement, even if it became what Admiral Von Hipper called "a death struggle."[62] Operations Plan No. 19, the German sortie, never materialized. During the night of October 29, German sailors rebelled and refused to get underway. Once again, Beatty and his fleet failed to engage the enemy. The squadrons went out in typically bad weather and returned to base two days later, after the German fleet failed to come out.

About the only excitement occurred when the American battleships blundered into a large flotilla of British destroyers during a pitch-black night and scattered them.

In what was described as a "wild night" and "worse day to follow," the destroyer flo-tillas finally regrouped despite extremely rough weather. After two days of this and finally realizing that the Germans were not going to appear, Beatty ordered the fleet home. The Sixth Battle Squadron went to sea only once again on November 7 to conduct gunnery practice.[63]

Memoirs of the American crews who served in the Grand Fleet and official papers, including the official deck logs of the Sixth Battle Squadron, give the impression that the ships frequently encountered submarines in the North Sea. A *Texas* Marine recalled that "one afternoon we ran across three of them [submarines] in a bunch and *Florida*, *Wyoming*, and *Texas* all took pot shots with their 5-inch guns." Years later, a former sailor graphically described an encounter with a U-boat:

> That funnel slowly emerging from the water was no ethereal phantom that would vanish with a shake of your head. God, no! This was the real McCoy! ... From aloft came cries of "Submarine! ... Submarine off the starboard bow!" ... [A] spurt of flame shot out from one of the five-inch guns. . . . Boy, what a hit! . . . Just aft the conning tower. . . . A shell from the *New York* shrieked through the air, hitting about ten feet for'd of the conning tower. . . . More shots ... raked the U-boat fore and aft. . . . Looking backward we saw her bow bound upward, her stern settle in the water. A spasmodic shudder shook her as the bow reached the peak of its ascent, then she slid down slowly and disappeared neath the waves.[64]

This account possesses the ring of authenticity, but no record exists of a German submarine lost in the North Sea on that day.

Rodman remembered that "attacks by hostile submarines on our battleships were not infrequent." After the war, a summary of the activities of the Sixth Battle Squadron stated that U.S. battleships had been attacked on six different occasions between their arrival at Scapa Flow and the Armistice. German U-boats lurked about, but the Americans exaggerated the number of encounters and torpedo attacks, the result of inexperience and extremely difficult conditions in the North Sea. German records rarely identify ships attacked as American, although they occasionally refer to the "Anglo-American" force. On February 8, three of the four American battleships at sea reported submarine attacks and torpedoes. The captain of *Wyoming* thought that these attacks might have taken place, but lookouts on his ship did not spot either submarines or torpedo wakes, and none of the ships in either the screen or the convoy took a torpedo. In June and July, the Sixth Battle Squadron reported submarine attacks on its ships. In every case, Beatty forwarded the reports but noted, "it is doubtful whether the reports [are] ... reliable." Admiral Wiley, who commanded *Florida* in the Grand Fleet, wrote, "For my part, I never saw evidence of a German submarine during my entire service on the other side" with one possible exception. He suspected that the submarines were probably porpoises.[65]

On October 14, 1918, *New York* struck a submerged object while entering Pentland Firth en route to Scapa Flow. The flagship was in the normal lane traversed by the Grand Fleet's battleships when it hit and probably sunk a submarine. Although no confirmation exists in the official British or German records, German submarines were operating in the vicinity of Scapa Flow at the time.[66] If *New York* was possibly the only American battleship with the Grand Fleet to inflict damage on a German U-boat, it unquestionably was the last. The war ended in a few weeks, and in December the Sixth Battle Squadron returned to the United States.

Throughout much of the twentieth century, battleships remained the most publicized warships in any navy. The battleships were fêted in New York when they returned from European waters but not the destroyers and other light craft that helped win the naval war in the Atlantic. Few visiting dignitaries in Great Britain were interested in trips to the American naval bases at Plymouth, Queenstown, and elsewhere but always wanted to visit Rosyth when the Grand Fleet was stationed there. A parade of naval officials from Admiral Sims to Assistant Secretary of the Navy Franklin D. Roosevelt, royalty, political figures, churchmen, and journalists descended upon Beatty's ships, including the U.S. battleships. Congressmen, the prime minister of Canada, the king and queen of Belgium, Prince Yorihito of Japan, and King George V of Great Britain all paid visits to *New York* and occasionally to other American ships. Even Samuel Gompers, the head of the American Federation of Labor, wangled an invitation. He also visited Admiral Beatty's flagship, *Queen Elizabeth*. Admiral McCrea recounted an anecdote of this event: "'You know, Rodman,' said Sir David Beatty, 'I think that you and I are about even. Our labor leader spat on your rug, and your labor leader, a guest at my table, was ill-mannered enough to criticize my cigar.'"[67]

Often these visits created hardships for the crews. Prior to the visit by the Belgian royal family, the Sixth Battle Squadron had been out for four days screening a convoy. Upon anchoring at Rosyth, the crews had to coal ship, and on *New York* the men had to stay up all night washing down the ship to get rid of the coal dust. An enlisted man wrote, "Kings are much trouble." An officer on *New York* witnessed a visit by a group of congressmen: "They surely were a wild looking bunch of apple knockers in their dirty and shabby clothes. Three or four were chewing gum, one smoked a cigarette during the inspection, while the prize bird chewed tobacco and spit on the beautiful clean deck. . . . One old Democrat got right in the middle of a division and shouted out so all the 'Boys' could hear him 'All this formality gives a pain in the gizzard!' The worst of it was they were going to a British ship this afternoon to inspect her as well. . . . The men were pretty disgusted, especially scrubbing up the tobacco juice stains."[68]

The king of England made by far the most publicized visits to the American ships. He made two trips to inspect the Grand Fleet. On July 20, he inspected *New York* and officers and enlisted men from the other U.S. battleships. It was the first visit by an English monarch to an American warship and the first time that the British Royal Standard flew beside the American flag on a U.S. warship. The king, who had been an officer in the Royal Navy, looked over the ship from stem to stern and from conning tower to the engine rooms. The laundry, bakery, and barbershop particularly impressed him. While in the engine rooms, at Rodman's request, he threw a few shovel loads of coal into the furnace. The coal supposedly had been well scrubbed in advance. George V later called *New York* "a most beautiful clean ship."[69] The king again visited the ship on November 20 to thank the crews for their service in the Grand Fleet and wish them a safe voyage to the United States.

What did the American battleships with the Grand Fleet contribute to the victory at sea? According to the *Pall Mall Gazette*, Admiral Beatty is supposed to have said that the Sixth Battle Squadron was "the last straw that broke the [German] camel's back."[70] Beatty knew better. The German government was quite aware of the American battleships with the Grand Fleet, but it made little impact on them. Historians agree that the British blockade contributed greatly to the defeat of Germany. Unquestionably the Grand Fleet's presence in the North Sea throughout the war dominated its enforcement. The American presence gave a boost to naval personnel with the Grand Fleet and to the long-suffering British public, but even the American sailors on the battleships later agreed that the destroyers on convoy and antisubmarine duty in the Atlantic came closer to "breaking the camel's back" than the Sixth Battle Squadron.

"The Pills of Perdition"

The North Sea Mine Barrage

On June 8, 1918, six United States naval vessels began to lay mines off the coast of Norway, the beginning of the North Sea Mine Barrage. The most extensive mining project in American history, the barrage was more than a year in the making. From the laying of the first mine until the last, it generated continual controversy between the British and the Americans. The two participants disputed its effectiveness for years afterward.

Before the United States entered the war, both navies studied the feasibility of such a project. The British rejected it because of the depth of the water in the North Sea, the number of mines required, and their unreliability. Evidently the American Navy's Bureau of Ordnance disagreed. A few days after Congress declared war, the Navy Department questioned the Admiralty about laying a minefield supplemented with nets across the North Sea. Its idea was to keep U-boats out of the open sea by utilizing mines to close their ports and destroy them if they ventured out. The British navy had created minefields in the Dover Strait and the Heligoland Bight but with disappointing results.

The Admiralty decidedly rejected the idea. Its opposition to the mine barrage concept continued throughout the summer months of 1917, and Admiral Sims agreed with the British. In mid-April, Daniels cabled Sims: "Is it not practicable to blockade German coast efficiently and completely, thus making practically impossible the egress and ingress of submarines?" Sims replied that the Admiralty considered it not feasible. In May, Navy Department officials, including Secretary Daniels, tried again: "Much opinion here is in favor of concerted efforts by the Allies to establish a complete barrier across the North Sea." On April 11, Admiral De Chair warned the Admiralty that the Americans were committed to the barrage. Both the Admiralty and Sims responded in strong terms against it. Admiral A. L. Duff, the deputy director in charge of antisubmarine operations, informed De Chair that the "method suggested [is] . . . quite impracticable. . . . The difficulty will be appreciated when total distance, depths, material and patrols required and distance from base of operations are considered." In any event, a barrage would not succeed. Admiral Fremantle, the deputy chief of the naval staff, was "hostile" to the barrage, according to the U.S. Naval Planning Section in London. He later referred to it as a "grandiose plan . . . received in this country with skepticism." The Planning Section also stated, "practically every influential British official afloat and ashore was opposed to the barrage except the British Plans Division."

Dudley Knox wrote years later that "British opposition to the plan at this stage was two fold in nature. First the question of the number of mines was stupendous, and secondary unless the [Strait] of Dover was closed, the North Sea Barrage would be of no use."[1]

In 1916, the British started to lay a barrage of mines and nets along the Belgian coast and across the channel just east of Dover and Calais. Work on the fields continued into 1917–18, but the minefields were never successful. German surface craft, operating out of bases in Flanders, frequently raided the fields, destroying parts of the barrage. British naval patrols were ineffective. The British mines were also often defective, at times encouraging German countermining. This result disillusioned the British. The proposed barrage across the North Sea required a workable barrage in the Strait of Dover.

Sims continued to voice opposition. According to Admiralty experience, he wrote: "all barrages whether of mines or nets or both are not an absolute solution for the following fundamental reasons. Nets do not stop submarines. Mine barriers cannot be wholly effective unless they could be maintained by patrol at all points. Few of the thirty thousand laid in Heligoland Bight may be watched but even if all would be patrolled it would not be wholly effective because the necessarily locally weak dispersed line of patrols can be broken by enemy concentrated attacks at any point and as often as may be necessary and mines dragged out thus releasing submarines."[2]

Nonetheless, the Department continued to develop the concept. American officials always insisted that the idea was born in the U.S. Navy Department, primarily in its Bureau of Ordnance. Even the president favored it, evidently as early as 1916. Assistant Secretary Roosevelt, with Daniels's approval, sent a memorandum to the president outlining a mining project across the North Sea. Wilson remained interested in the concept. Sims's opposition contributed to the president's unhappiness with him.

Benson had strong reservations about such a project, "perhaps not impossible but to my mind of doubtful practicability." As late as November, when Benson visited Great Britain, he still disapproved of the barrage. Although Roosevelt did not initiate the concept as some writers have suggested, he made it his special project and continued to push it before the secretary and Benson. Rear Admiral Frederick Harris, chief of the Bureau of Yards and Docks and a strong early proponent of the barrage said that if it has not been for Roosevelt, "there would have been no Scotch barrage"; and Commander Fullinwider, the co-inventor of the Mark VI (MK 6) mine, wrote in 1931, "I had been in the Bureau of Ordnance only a short time when I sensed the fact that if one wished to 'start something' the man to see about it was Roosevelt." Early in April, Fullinwider drew up a memorandum proposing a barrage. He carried it to the assistant secretary, who "showed me some sketches, prepared by the Bureau of Yards and Docks, outlining a scheme for closing the North Sea. At that time I had the impression that it was Roosevelt's own idea. . . . After submitting my memorandum to Roosevelt [and to his superiors in the Bureau of Ordnance] . . . I discussed the matter with the President. . . . I do not know who first laid the matter before Mr. Daniels. It may have been Roosevelt, or it may be that the President brought the subject up at a cabinet meeting. . . . [I]t was handled in a most informal manner in its early stages."

Frank Freidel, in his biography of Roosevelt, considered the North Sea Mine Barrage as the assistant secretary's "most notable achievement during the war."[3]

Roosevelt and others in the Navy Department tried in every way possible to persuade the Admiralty to consider the mine barrage. Sims received a communiqué every week or so concerning the issue, and various officers shuttling between Washington and London were requested to look into it, and American officials questioned British naval officers and others in the United States about the Admiralty's position. Lord Northcliffe, while on a mission in the United States, wrote the prime minister, "Our alleged inactivity in dealing with the submarines hampers our work as much as the question of Ireland." He mentioned that the U.S. Navy was most interested in "a continuous wall of mines at either end of the North Sea."[4] The Department discovered that not all in the British navy opposed the barrage, but its critics persisted in their negative evaluations. An American naval officer who returned from London reported: "Occasionally one hears statements that everything is subordinated to the antisubmarine campaign, but actually this doesn't appear to be so, for in any plan for attacking the submarines the needs of the Grand Fleet are first given consideration.... One officer of the Admiralty made what I thought a significant remark when he said, that two mine barrages [across the North Sea] had been proposed but disapproved because of the extent of the operations and the interference with the fleet." The Admiralty and Admiral Beatty continued to worry about the adverse effect of a barrage on the Grand Fleet even after the British finally approved its construction.[5]

The Admiralty began to undergo a change of heart toward the end of the summer. after the U.S. Bureau of Ordnance developed a new mine, the Mark VI.[6] Based on an estimate that the barrage required a hundred thousand mines, the bureau submitted a formal plan for a North Sea Mine Barrage on July 30. After Daniels gave his approval, it was formally proposed to the British. When the Admiralty rejected it, Admiral Mayo was ordered to bring it up at conference with the Allied naval leaders in London. The delegates began their discussions on September 4. Mayo argued that the mine barrage had more promise than convoying. Although no formal vote was taken, the conferees were not impressed with it. The Russian delegate opposed it outright; Admiral De Bon, the French delegate, said that it was not practical at present, and Admiral Sims did not support it wholeheartedly. Mayo years later stated that Sims "strongly opposed it." Admiral Jellicoe, the British delegate, however, did not voice disapproval. He merely said that such a project could not be undertaken without an adequate supply of mines and skilled personnel to assemble them. The British did not have these resources.[7]

Shortly before the conference convened, Jellicoe arranged for a committee of the General Staff to examine the barrage concept. Their report gave what Admiral Mayo considered a qualified approval; that is, if the United States provided the mines and skilled personnel, the British would cooperate. The first sea lord was well aware that influential Americans from President Wilson to Secretary Daniels and Admiral Benson were critical of British naval efforts, believing that the British were unduly conservative and opposed offensive operations. Jellicoe's qualified "acceptance" of the barrage was a political decision. One authority has written that it "did not represent a totally genuine conversion, for the British were anxious to conciliate the Americans with a view to extracting more naval assistance." Nonetheless, Mayo brought back with him an oral commitment and a draft proposal. Captain Reginald Belknap, the staff member in Operations in charge of mining, thought it quite informal—an unsigned, undated outline of the mining barrage from Jellicoe.[8]

The United States met the British conditions. The Admiralty sent a mine-laying specialist to the United States, who approved the new Mark VI mine. On September 19, the Admiralty ordered its director of plans to prepare a proposal. On October 17, Admiral Benson received a cable tantamount to formal acceptance of a North Sea barrage. Later the British ambassador handed Daniels a formal agreement in writing. The General Board approved the proposal on October 23, and during a cabinet meeting at the end of the month, the president authorized the project. Roosevelt then remarked to his boss, "I told you [the barrage would become a reality] . . . last May."[9] The Navy started its preparations before the final approval. As soon as Daniels heard of the British proposal, he authorized production of a hundred thousand Mark VI mines.

Everyone recognized the complexity of the project. The mines had to be manufactured, assembled, and shipped to designated bases in Great Britain. Ships to lay the mines would have to be obtained, converted, and equipped. Personnel must be trained and deployed to the designated bases. Originally, the Department considered sending civilian workers to Britain to assemble the mines, but the Admiralty strongly opposed this because of potential labor problems. The Department then agreed to provide naval personnel for this work. The Department asked the British to provide the sinkers for the mines, but the Admiralty insisted that it did not possess either the materials or the personnel required to produce them.[10] The major difficulty, however, was the choice of the location of the barrage, a question that led to considerable disagreement.

The general area for the field, the North Sea, was acknowledged without question. The initial British proposal, brought back to the Department by Mayo, recommended that it follow a line from Aberdeen, Scotland, to Ekersund, Norway. Proponents of this plan believed that the completion of the field and the Dover barrage would effectively bottle up the German submarines and raiders. Because the Germans frequently disrupted British mining fields off Heligoland and Dover, the barrage had to be placed far enough away from the Kaiser's naval bases to prevent minesweeping. On October 21, Admiral Benson asked Sims to confirm the Admiralty's approval of the Aberdeen-Ekersund line. Lord Jellicoe did so, and the American government gave formal approval.

In November, Benson went to Great Britain with the House Mission and brought up the mine barrier in discussions with Admiralty officials. Despite personal reservations about the project, he pushed vigorously for its implementation. During the conference and later at a meeting of the Allied Naval Council in Paris, Jellicoe did not mention a possible modification of the Aberdeen-Ekersund location, although he knew that Admiral Beatty and members of the Admiralty were already demanding major changes because of its impact on operations of the Grand Fleet.[11] On December

7, the Admiralty proposed to move the field northward to an area between the Orkney Islands and Bergen, Norway. The British offered several reasons for a relocation, including (1) the decision not to establish a mining base in Norway for diplomatic reasons; (2) the scarcity of vessels to patrol the entire barrage, especially the Norwegian portion; and (3) Beatty's strong objections to the original location. The new plan called for a 75-mile-wide channel on the western end to allow passage for convoys and especially vessels of the Grand Fleet. The barrage's eastern end would terminate at Norwegian territorial waters, which left a three-mile passage on that end. In the original plan, the barrage was divided into three sections. The Americans would have total responsibility for section A, the middle section, approximately 50 miles wide, extending 130 miles to the northeast. The Americans understood they would share responsibility for the others. The British were to lay the deep mines and the Americans the surface mines in section C, a 50-mile field extending from the east end of section A to Norwegian territorial waters, and section B, the area directly east of the American section extending to Scotland. The new plan eliminated American participation in sections B and C because surface mines were not to be planted in those areas. Beatty insisted on this plan, to allow surface vessels to pass over and because he lacked faith in the concept. The plan was later modified several times. Deep mining in both areas B and C proved unfeasible because the British-laid mines frequently failed to maintain their predetermined depth and often rose to the surface. This posed a threat to surface vessels. For that reason, Beatty ordered sweeping of the mines in B. He eventually agreed to let the American minelayers plant surface mines in B to a point ten miles from the Orkneys and extend the field in C to the north. He also agreed to provide patrols for area C, if a Norwegian base could be obtained, but he opposed the coercion of Norway to either provide a base or to allow British and American warships to enter its territorial waters. When it proved impossible to obtain a Norwegian base, he refused to patrol section C. Instead he later allowed the Americans to lay a surface field to complement the British deep field in that section. This field, however, would end at the edge of Norwegian territorial waters.[12]

Early in the war Norway declared neutrality, but this position was threatened by the Germans sending submarines and raiders through its territorial waters. The British government considered forcing Norway to declare war if it became necessary either to prevent German use of these waters or to seize a naval base. Admiral Beatty recommended dispatch of the Grand Fleet into Norwegian waters to stop German use of them, but the Admiralty opposed it. The decision to mine the North Sea made the idea of a naval base in Norway even more desirable because it would permit patrol of unmined areas, including Norwegian territorial waters. The British government, however, agreed in December 1917 to establish such a base if Norway gave consent. The U.S. Navy strongly favored a Norwegian base, but when President Wilson rejected the plan, it went by the wayside. The Norwegian situation became acute late in July 1918, when German U-boats began to traverse Norwegian territorial waters to avoid the North Sea barrage. On August 7, the British government demanded that Norway mine its own waters. According to one authority who examined German records, between July 11 and August 2 at least nine German submarines passed through Norwegian waters. In September, the Norwegians agreed to the mining, but because of the lack of mines and needed equipment, few were planted before the Armistice.[13]

The reluctant American acceptance of the modified plan did nothing to ease discord between the two participants. Major differences of opinion developed about (1) the nature of arrangements for the deployment of escorts for the minelayers and patrols of small craft to guard the fields; (2) the methods of surface mining; (3) British insistence on making gaps or channels in the barrage, principally one adjacent to the Orkneys to allow the passage of convoys and the Grand Fleet; and (4) the apparent ineffectiveness of the American mines, a consequence of the considerable distance between each mine, the depth of the mines and antennae, and premature explosions. These disagreements created the most serious breach between the American and British navies during the war.

Differences over methods of using light craft to patrol the minefields revealed a serious variance in attitude toward the North Sea Mine Barrage. The Americans were convinced that the mines would destroy or damage German U-boats. They believed that around-the-clock patrols of the entire barrage perimeter from Scotland to Norway by naval vessels were required for the success of the barrage. Patrolling would prevent German naval units from destroying the mines and reducing the field's effectiveness as they had done off Dover. The Admiralty insisted that insufficient craft were available for patrolling because of the demand for vessels to undertake convoying, guard the Grand Fleet, and support other antisubmarine activities.

The most important cause of disagreements over the doctrine for patrol of the minefields was British doubts about the effectiveness of the mines. They conceived of the barrage as a barrier to force the German U-boats into relatively narrow lanes where ASW craft would detect them. In February, an unsigned Admiralty memo declared, "until we have proved the efficiency of the American minefield we must look upon it as a bluff." Admiral Sims was informed that the Admiralty considered the "primary function of the Northern Mine Barrage . . . to restrict the available passage for submarines to such narrow limits as to permit of this area to be patrolled." A force of small craft designated the "Northern Patrol," was organized to traverse designated passages in the barrage and attack German submarines that they encountered. This plan called for considerably fewer vessels than under the American plan.[14]

Admiral Beatty's opinions decided matters. On December 28, the Admiralty agreed that the North Sea Mine Barrage would be under his "general direction." Two considerations governed his attitude toward it: strong reservations about its effectiveness and its consequences for the operations of the Grand Fleet. Admiral Sims wrote that the Admiralty always looked at the project in terms of its effect on "possible fleet actions," but "the [U.S.] Navy Department considered it almost entirely . . . an antisubmarine measure. So long as the Grand Fleet did not have its freedom of movement restricted . . . they had no objections to it and were rather inclined to favor it for the reason that it might help them meet the German High Seas Fleet."[15] Admiral Strauss recalled that shortly after arriving in Scotland to take command of the American mine force, he had a long interview with Lord Beatty. "He showed a minute knowledge of the whole scheme . . . but in saying goodbye, he remarked 'I am glad to find someone who believes in this barrage.' This remark staggered me a little; it meant to my mind that no British officer favored it."[16]

Beatty's opposition to the barrage, particularly the American role in it, divided the Admiralty. Lord Wemyss, the first sea lord, was placed in a difficult position. He constantly attempted to placate both Beatty and Sims. On August 15, he wrote to Beatty, "I sympathise with your feeling about the American mines, but I think it should be remembered that the decision was arrived at a time when the submarine campaign overshadowed everything and that drastic measures necessitating the whole-hearted co-operation of the Americans were required and this, I believe, was only possible to obtain by agreeing to the use of their mines." A few days later, he wrote the C-in-C to describe a difference of opinion about the effectiveness of the American mines: "Admiral Sims believes them to be more efficient than we do. I, on the other hand, believe them to be more morally effective than, probably you do. . . . It would indeed be a calamity if the Americans were now to chuck their hand in over the Northern barrage. You and I know very differently, but what I know better than you is how difficult it is to get these Americans into a sane, clear and sound state of thinking." The C-in-C then proposed to leave a 10-mile gap between the mine barrage and the Orkneys to permit the passage of his ships. Wemyss refused, pointing out that the "American Government desire[s] to complete the Northern Barrage from land to land, and nothing short of this will satisfy them; their views being that any gate in the barrage, however small, renders it ineffectual. If it is ineffectual, they consider that the whole of their great efforts and large expenditure is thrown away."

Beatty made notes on the margin of this letter. To the first sea lord's statement that Sims held strong views on the subject of the gap, the C-in-C noted, "So do I and I command the Sea—not Admiral Sims." When the first sea lord stressed that leaving the gap would have a "disastrous effect on our relations with the United States . . . [and] inevitably lead to the recall of Admiral Sims," Beatty scribbled, "Cannot believe this." Wemyss claimed an inconsistency between creating a gap and attempts to force the Norwegians into mining their territorial waters. Beatty then wrote, "The question can be re-considered when the territorial waters of Norway are mined." Wemyss favored the barrage, believing that it would have a definite impact on the "morale" of the German navy, particularly their U-boat personnel. "We should proceed on the hypothesis that the Northern barrage is effective," he suggested to Beatty. "The . . . barrage is the result of all the aspects of the Anti-submarine War. It is the keystone of our offensive anti-submarine policy." At his instructions, Sims was informed that the barrage "is functioning . . . in that no enemy submarines attempt to cross it. . . . It is certain that the enemy decided to avoid the dangerous area after they had tangible proof that this barrage was a reality and not a threat." Nevertheless, the first sea lord was most disappointed with the American mines and with what he considered Washington's refusal to grasp the problems of North Sea warfare. In September, he wrote Beatty, "Of course, our American friends, not having the responsibility that we have, do not look upon it from the same point of view as we do, and I am rather inclined to think that Sims is of opinion that all these matters are so simple that they can be settled by us here sitting round at a table."[17]

In August, Lord Balfour, the British foreign secretary, visited the Grand Fleet. He later wrote to Lord Robert Cecil, a member of the cabinet, "I found to my surprise a very sharp distinction between the views of the Admiralty and the views of the Commander-in-Chief towards the barrage." Although he provided wrong data, his letter created consternation when passed on to Wemyss. When Wemyss inquired about what he told Balfour, Beatty in some irritation replied: "I am at loss to understand what the fuss is all about. The Admiralty is fully aware of my views on the subject of the Northern barrage." The first sea lord insisted that both he and Beatty sign a paper stating that the C-in-C and the Admiralty shared the same view of the barrage. Beatty agreed. The matter died down, although in October Beatty issued orders to Strauss contrary to those desired by Sims and the Admiralty. These orders, which called for shortening mooring lines on mines already laid in the fields, would have seriously delayed the completion of the barrage. When Sims heard about it, he fired off a cable to Strauss asking whether the Grand Fleet commander "at any time issued any instructions to you concerning mine-laying operations contrary to instructions issued by me." Strauss's reply led to a meeting with Wemyss. The first sea lord assured Sims that Beatty would be instructed to cancel his order to Strauss. He noted that "Admiral Beatty was [the] source of much trouble to the Admiralty." In general, however, Wemyss got along better with Beatty than with his predecessor. Admiral Fremantle noted that, with a problem such as Beatty's difficulties with the mine barrage, the first sea lord "used to send me up to Rosyth to do my best with the C-in-C, and provided I sat quiet for the first hour of an interview, and gave him the full chance of declaiming against Admiralty iniquities, he was ready to hear and to give full weight to our case, and I was usually able to return having arrived at an understanding."[18] Beatty never accepted the mine barrage. In time, he wore down Wemyss on the ten-mile gap and received approval to keep it.

This outcome displeased the Americans. "It will be noted," the Planning Section at Sims headquarters in London stated, "that the original line extended from mainland to mainland, while the new line extends from island to island, and has in it passages completely navigable to submarines." Admiral Earle, chief of the Bureau of Ordnance, declared in a memo to the CNO that the plan is no longer American but British. It was "altered . . . so that its entire character has been changed, and because of this, the original faith placed in its effectiveness by the Department is no longer justified." Captain Belknap disagreed with the ordnance chief: "The change of location does not change the principle nor the plan as a whole." He also noted that the barrage was only one aspect of the naval war in the North Sea. Admiral Benson informed Sims that the proposed changes would "greatly diminish" the effectiveness of the barrage but admitted that his office was "not sufficiently informed on the intended disposition and employment of the Grand Fleet . . . to pass [judgment] upon the Northern Barrage, considered as only one part of the whole scheme of naval operations in the North

Sea." The CNO put far more credence in the Grand Fleet than in the mine barrage to disrupt German naval operations.

The British were most alarmed over the reputed failure of the American Mark VI mine. American authorities calculated that approximately 3 to 4 percent of the mines laid, about 150 of 3,385, detonated shortly after being dropped in the water. Because of the haste to develop and produce the mines, very little testing took place before they were shipped to Scotland. Explosions occurred when the first mines were laid and continued to the end. When one mine exploded, it often caused a domino effect; entire lines exploded in a spectacular fashion. Observers reported that many of them blew up as soon as they were deposited in the field. One British officer wrote that on one occasion about 150 went off in the course of an afternoon, "causing terrific concussions and shooting up great columns of water." He recalled that on another day about three hundred exploded: "the noise & concussion was tremendous and a huge mass of water was chucked up." Another officer noted: "This matter of the exploding American mines has set us all scratching our heads, and we consider that they probably all explode in the end. Perhaps they are badly made. . . . So what is the use of all this trouble." In March, Strauss expressed apprehension: "I am prevented from a feeling of assurance . . . by the fact that actual *experience* with the mine is very limited. . . . We can only hope for the best results." Despite optimistic reports from a British mining officer sent to the United States to observe tests of the mine, Admiralty experts were skeptical about it from the first. Belknap told the CNO that the British "can best be won over to the American mine by the successful outcome of the operation." The premature explosions did not surprise the American mine experts, and they were confident that they could resolve the problem. They never did.[19]

Mining operations were suspended until the minelayers discovered the cause of the premature explosions. Believing that they had solved the difficulty, the American minelayers sortied on August 8 to drop five thousand mines. However, after planting only 1,596 mines, the operation was canceled because the mines again exploded prematurely. A junior officer on *Shawmut* wrote: "Very great number of explosions [today], proportion larger than before. . . . This was most disconcerting. Instead of the explosions decreasing as experience was gained in the assembly and laying of the mines, the percentage had been gradually increasing and then had suddenly jumped to 19 percent on this excursion. Losses of 3 percent to 4 percent could possibly be tolerated, but this latter figure was absolutely prohibitive." Rear Admiral Daniel Mannix recalled that the explosions sounded "like the Day of Judgment! . . . These repeated explosions began to get on the men's nerves. . . . When the last mine had gone over we headed back to base. For a long time we could hear muffled explosions behind us."[20]

Admiral Beatty expressed considerable annoyance: "The situation as regards the American Mines and Northern Barrage is a very serious one. As I understand it the Admiralty allowed the Americans to jump us with their mine and accepted it on their own statements without taking sufficient steps to satisfy themselves as to whether it could or would do all that was claimed for it. That would have been justifiable if they were to be used in mining American Waters, but certainly not when they plant the infernal things in our waters." On more than one occasion, he criticized the American mines and minefield, writing that it was a waste of time, ships, and materials and recommended delay until the Americans perfected the mines.[21] The problem shook the first sea lord's normally calm demeanor. "The American mine-laying is unsatisfactory," he wrote Beatty. "Sims is always saying that the difficulty will be shortly got over, but apparently, they have not found a way to do so yet, and I tell him that it is out of the question deciding whether the Northern Barrage shall be taken further West until his material is on a more satisfactory basis." When one of the cabinet ministers suggested that the mining should be carried out only by the Americans, Wemyss retorted that "I should prefer to do it ourselves as then I should know it was carried out properly." Beatty agreed wholeheartedly with the first sea lord.[22]

The mine-laying force desperately sought to determine the cause of the explosions. At different times they blamed the problem on leaking mine cases, erratic washers designed to dissolve at a particular time, circuits, antennae not working properly, countermining, and an unduly sensitive exploding mechanism. Late in August, improved circuit breakers helped matters somewhat, but the premature explosions continued at an unacceptable level. The commanding officer of the cruiser *London* estimated that 50 percent of the mines exploded during the September 9 excursion. Even in October, after the problem was supposedly cleared up to some degree, the commanding officer of the Second Battle Cruiser Squadron, acting as escort, reported "constant detonations." The Bureau of Ordnance determined that the firing devices were at fault. New firing devices were installed and after various adjustments, premature explosions declined to 6 percent at the end of September.[23]

Other difficulties seriously delayed completion of the barrage. Converting and outfitting minelayers took weeks longer than expected, the last not arriving until the end of June. The minelayers and mine carriers were frequently delayed because of the slow arrival of stores and equipment. The British contributed to the delays by insisting on modifications to the mines and minefields. Admittedly, some of these changes were necessary. For example, after the American minelayers made four runs, they claimed that the mines were too deep and their antennae too long to be effective. They also concluded that surface mines were far more effective than those planted in deep water. Strauss told the General Board that changes would delay operations and "meant an immense amount of trouble" both in the United States and the mining bases. The first mines were not laid until June 6, nearly six months after the acceptance of the final plan.[24]

Mining operations were frequently held up or even postponed for a variety of reasons other than trouble with the mines. The British complained that Beatty could not approve a mission because Strauss's office did not provide required information on time or their preparations were not complete, although after the war Belknap insisted that "never was an excursion delayed on account of a ship's not being prepared." American ships were often delayed because either British escorts were not available or their minelayers were held up. When Strauss protested a delay, Sims reminded him that Beatty was in overall charge of the barrage. He also observed that "escort and protection of the mine forces engaged in laying the Northern Barrage constitute an additional demand on the already over-taxed light forces of the Grand Fleet." It became quite clear to the Admiralty that because of delays in the American destroyer-construction program, no destroyers were available unless they were drawn from the Queenstown force, an unacceptable option.[25] Neither could destroyers be withdrawn from the Mediterranean because of fears that Italy might leave the war, the need to protect the Otranto Barrage, and the need to maintain a watch on German ships in the Black Sea. The Admiralty in effect ruled that Beatty must provide protection for the minelayers.[26]

Even after the plan was adopted there were changes and delays causing more controversy. British insistence, led by Beatty, of nonmined passages on the east and west sides of the barrage continued to provoke most of the altercation with the Americans, what Marder would call a "first-class row." Captain Frank Schofield, a member of Sims's staff, stressed after the war that "American naval officers never lost sight of [the mission] to bar the exit of all German submarines from the North Sea. . . . We wanted an unbroken barrage from Norway to Scotland and from the surface of the sea to a depth of three hundred feet. . . . The British wanted that barrage to have two surface channels . . . for the use of the Grand Fleet. . . . Their persistent insistence upon it led to some very warm friendly differences with the British." Admiral Strauss, the commander of the American mining force, was a little more direct: "I will not prolong my account of the difficulties that were placed in my way by the British to prevent our making the barrage effective." First Sea Lord Wemyss, in his unpublished memoir, wrote that he agreed with the American position (which he erroneously called Sims's position): "The C-in-C eventually agreed to the eastern end of the barrage running to Norwegian waters, but that still left a gap of some three miles under Norway's control."[27]

The immense undertaking created a complex of deep mine fields from the northern Orkneys in the west to Norwegian waters just south of Bergen in the east. It consisted of three systems stretching throughout the length, each one to consist of a row of upper (surface), middle and lower level mines. Additional changes were made as the fields were laid. British mining experts had believed a submarine could be seriously damaged or destroyed if it struck an antennae of up to 70 feet, but later information convinced them that this was not correct; antennae were then shortened to as little as 35 feet for the surface mines. The barrage covered a distance of nearly 240 miles. It was fifteen to thirty-five miles wide. It spanned an area of approximately thirty thousand square miles.[28]

U.S. naval personnel began to land at the two mine bases in Scotland in January and continued to arrive in weekly drafts. The base at Invergordon was commissioned on February 9 and the one at Inverness three days later. Stores and equipment came in, but the first mines were not received until May 29. Work then started on assembling them and the thousands that followed. Approximately six thousand mines arrived weekly. Twenty-one merchant vessels transported them from the mining base in Yorktown, Virginia.[29]

In March, the converted cruiser *Baltimore*, the first American minelayer to arrive in European waters, was assigned to support a British mine-laying operation off the northern Irish coast. Using as its base a small British naval station at Lamlash, Scotland, *Baltimore* made five expeditions, laying 180 British mines on each sortie. The American minelayer was not equipped to handle British mines either on the ship or after they had been planted. The British provided little or no hydrographical information. The mines were laid close to the surface in a straight line approximately four hundred feet apart. Apparently the minefield neither damaged nor sank a German submarine. Late in May this project was suspended, and *Baltimore* steamed around the northern coast of Scotland to her new base at Inverness, joining five sister minelayers under the command of Captain Belknap.[30]

Belknap was clearly the best-qualified U.S. naval officer to head the American mining expedition. A member of the academy class of 1891, he first became acquainted with mining in 1907, when he served as naval attaché in Germany. During his three-year tour and again in 1914, when sent to Germany as an observer, he had a number of opportunities to examine that country's mine-laying program. He wrote many years later that his strongest impression at the time resulted from watching a demonstration of a warship loading some two hundred mines on steel tracks while the ship lay alongside a dock. Using similar tracks on board, the mines were quickly stowed in the ship.[31] Later, under Belknap's direction, U.S. minelayers were fitted out similarly.

In 1915, Belknap was ordered to command the converted minelayer *San Francisco*; later that year he received command of the Mining and Minesweeping Division, Atlantic Fleet, later designated the Mine Force. The division consisted of two minesweepers, including *San Francisco*, and two seagoing tugs. Belknap commanded the Mine Force until September 1917, when he became a staff member of the Department of Operations in charge of mining. When the North Sea Mine Barrage was approved, he was tapped to take charge of it. Daniels commented in his diary, "Will put Belknap in charge of the barrage in North Sea and of the mining division [with] . . . responsibility fully in [his] hands."[32]

Pratt thought highly of Belknap, recommending him to Daniels as "one of the most aggressive as well as one of the deepest thinkers" in the Navy. He remembered him as "a thoroughly efficient, intelligent, and able young officer." Vice Admiral Felix Johnson, who served under Belknap as a junior officer, considered him "the coolest shiphandler I ever saw," although he was blamed for running aground two of the minesweepers in his squadron. Rear Admiral Joseph Strauss, in command of the North Sea Mine Barrage and Belknap's superior, apparently wanted to court-martial him for this. Admiral Sims did not agree because he did not have an available replacement, but Strauss helped block Belknap's promotion to flag rank.[33]

Belknap organized the Mine Force, set up training schedules, and helped to select various vessels as minelayers and to oversee their alterations. Rear Admiral T. P. Magruder noted that Belknap "convinced the General Board of the feasibility of transporting and planting the great number of mines required for the barrage." The CNO had a high regard for Belknap and conferred almost daily with him while the barrage was planned. He credited Belknap for its accomplishments. The personnel of the Mine Force developed great respect for him, and he reciprocated, establishing relationships that continued through participation in the North Sea Mine Association until his death in the 1970s.

Admiral Strauss succeeded Belknap as Commander, Mine Force, Atlantic Fleet, in February 1918. Strauss graduated from the Naval Academy in 1889 and soon gained a reputation as an ordnance inventor. Josephus Daniels made him chief of the Bureau of Ordnance. He went on to command the battleship *Nevada*. Although recently designated rear admiral, he was still on the battleship when chosen to head the mine forces. Strauss gained his appointment in part because the Department wanted to appoint an officer of equal rank to the commander of the British mining force, but it came about because Rear Admiral Leigh Palmer, chief of the Bureau of Navigation, protested Belknap's appointment, which totally ignored the seniority system.[34]

At Belknap's insistence, he was made Commander Mine Squadron One, U.S. Atlantic Fleet, with additional duties as Strauss's chief of staff. Strauss generally allowed him to make the preparations for the barrage in the United States and later to conduct the mining operations in the North Sea. After the war, Belknap explained to Sims that "we worked always as a squadron, not merely as a lot of minelayers. Administratively, as well as tactically, the squadron was a unit, the squadron commander having, by regulations and exercise, the same degree and kind of responsibility as the commander of a battleship division—including the authority to convene court-martials—the same as a flag officer in all respects, except personal rank." Strauss spent much of his time administering the two mining bases and coordinating with the British and Admiral Sims's office in London.

Belknap claimed that the admiral was jealous of him: "officers who served with Strauss said that any suggestions put up to him had to be submitted in such a way as to make clear that it was His, Strauss's idea in the first place." Rear Admiral Philip Andrews, a classmate of Strauss, agreed with this assessment, calling him "sensitive and swayed by his feelings." Belknap recalled that when VIPs visited the American mine bases, Strauss often did not invite him to the receptions and dinners. Rear Admiral Bruce Canada, who commanded one of the minesweepers that took up the barrage, wrote after the war that "Strauss was indeed a vindictive man," although an officer who served as his aide while the admiral commanded the Asiatic Squadron in the 1920s wrote that he "had one of those meticulous minds which search out the why and the wherefore and will not accept generalities. . . . I found Admiral Strauss one of the most interesting men I have ever known."[35]

Strauss encountered difficulties with British naval officers, especially Beatty and Admiralty officials. Strauss later wrote, "The magnitude of the task assigned to the Mine Force was not my greatest concern; it was outweighed by the hidden determination on the part of our British allies not to permit its accomplishment, and at least to make it abortive by withdrawing from their share of the work which would have left a gap in the fence eastward from the Orkneys." Admiral Wemyss said that Strauss lied outright on one occasion and was relieved when the American admiral was ordered to the Mediterranean for a conference about a mine barrage in the Adriatic Sea. Although Sims informed the American Mine Force commander that Beatty had overall responsibility for the mine barrage, on a number of occasions Strauss appealed directly to Sims over Beatty's head. Twice the force commander sharply reminded Strauss that he was under Beatty's command. Sims gave "definite orders to Rear Admiral Strauss to the effect that he is subject to your orders for operations in a similar manner in all respects to Rear Admiral Rodman." On one occasion, however, when Beatty countermanded an order that had been approved both by Sims and the Admiralty, Sims demanded execution of the original order. Sims contradicted himself when he informed Strauss that, "It should, I think, be made clear to Admiral Beatty that except as his opinion may be asked by the Admiralty, his only connection with the laying of the American portion of the Northern barrage is to furnish escorting and supporting vessels and not the location in which it is proposed to lay mines." No record exists of Beatty's response. Sims's statement was sent to the American Mine Force Commander shortly before the North Sea Mine Barrage officially ended, so it is possible that Strauss never delivered it. Strauss claimed that "[Beatty] did not like me because I had forced them to carry out the plan to which they had agreed of providing a real barrier to the exit of the submarines." Strauss, however, insisted that he got along quite well with his British counterparts on the mine barrage.[36]

On March 29, 1918, Strauss arrived in Inverness and established his headquarters at the American mine base. Belknap remained in the United States to supervise the readiness of the Mine Force. On May 25, he arrived in Scotland with six minelayers. *Roanoke* was already there and *Baltimore* followed a few days later. Three mine planters and the repair ship *Black Hawk* arrived early in June. The first excursion of the American mine-laying squadron took place on June 8.

From June 8 to October 21, the minelayers carried out fifteen expeditions. Altogether the United States ships planted 56,611 mines. Some of them were conducted jointly with British minelayers; some laid only surface mines, and others laid mines at different depths. The lengths of the mine-laying runs varied from forty-six miles on the first one to more than sixty on later missions; the number of minelayers per expedition varied, depending upon availability and requirement. On the tenth expedition, September 27, the minelayers planted 5,520 mines in three hours and fifty minutes.

Weather caused delays, particularly fog. One American officer wrote, "fog was probably our major problem, but we handled that pretty well, keeping in formation by means of towing spars and very skillful handling of the ships." On the second expedition, in the middle of July, the fog was so thick "you could hardly see your hand in front of your face." As they returned to port, two ships, *San Francisco* and *Saranac*, went aground. *Saranac*, according to one sailor, ran "on the rocks at full speed." Both ships, however, were freed without serious damage. Both minelayers and escorts, and quite often the mine laying was halted or delayed until the fog lifted. During the fall months, the weather deteriorated, and by late October it became so difficult that an officer wrote, "when the winter comes . . . I for one want none of it." On the last expedition, the weather was so bad that squadron and escorts cruised around for more than twenty-four hours before laying a mine. A member of *Housatonic's* crew wrote: "the old tub was having all she could do to hold her own in the storm, but we were between two of our own mine fields and if we'd kept going into the storm (the best way to go) we'd have struck some of our own particular brand of punishment. We had to take it on our side and believe me, we did some rolling. . . . The next day it calmed down and we dropped our little black pills in the briny and beat it back to port." At times, the waves broke over the forecastle with such force that lookouts stood behind watertight doors and took position on their stations between waves. When the ships dropped mines, they steamed in line abreast, usually five hundred yards apart. Often the mine planter operated in relays; as soon as one layer finished unloading its mines, a second one immediately took over.[37]

Each expedition started when the ten minelayers, five from each of the two bases some thirty miles apart, rendezvoused at a given point, steamed northward, and joined escorts from the Grand Fleet. Then they proceeded to the designated starting point. Captain Belknap wrote later: "Ten ships laden with high explosive, navigating in mine-swept channels, in submarine thoroughfares, and near minefields beyond sight of fixed marks—compactness of the minefield demanding that the layers steam as near together as safe—necessity for keeping together in fog, darkness, or submarine attack—these were the conditions governing our tactics. . . . Precision and quickness of action while at sea were imperative, from start to finish." Belknap developed a system of flag hoists for tactical maneuvers such as speeds and turns. These signals differed from those normally in both navies. Upon the signal from the flagship, a red flag, the ships in line commenced to drop their mines. Navigational buoys were planted at the beginning and the end of a mining excursion. A mine was dropped every ten to twelve seconds. The mines were lined up on rails, the number depending upon the size of the ship, and they were pushed manually toward the opening at the stern. Belknap explained: "As the mines on the launching deck move slowly aft, those on lower decks move forward, to the elevators and up. Working spaces are cramped, passages narrow, bulkhead doors closed wherever possible. At the right time, a door will be opened, the portable section of mine track adjusted, the mines in that compartment hauled out, and the door closed again." It took from four to twelve seconds to drop a mine. As one sailor recalled, "that is one thing the crew are always willing to do faster than the officers want you to." When one planter had launched all her mines, another planter, steaming alongside, would quickly take her place. An excursion usually lasted approximately two days, although the drop of the mines took only from four to seven hours.[38]

Mine laying was exciting at first, but as one veteran recalled, "it . . . soon became real work; loading mines, steaming, watch, then coal ship each time putting on from 300 to 500 tons of coal." Another complained that it was no "fun to be on a mine layer, hitting port [after a mission] in the morning, coaling same afternoon, field day next morning, mines [loaded] that afternoon." To many of the sailors, the mines were "pills of perdition," or tin eggs, and to others they were "nails in the coffin of the Kaiser."[39]

Mine loading and laying was hazardous work, and the Navy did not award extra pay for it. Most members of the crews were volunteers. They trained for a brief period before leaving the United States, and whenever possible between expeditions, but even Belknap admitted that they were "green." They endured terrible ordeals, the constant threat from submarines, weather conditions, the possibility of breaking down and drifting into either one of their own mines or a German one, and the chance of an accident in the barrage area. At night they darkened ship, showing only running lights. Submarine alarms occurred on every expedition; escorts dropped depth charges and occasionally a nervous gun crew fired at supposed periscopes. During one excursion, as the ships headed up the coast of Scotland, torpedoes were fired at the ships. None hit, but one struck a large rock jutting out of the water and exploded. Accidents occurred. In a storm, *Quinnebaug*'s rudder became inoperable, and the ship had to anchor until it could be fixed, unable to avoid a drifting mine. "God help a ship whose engine broke down or rudder jammed during the mine laying!" wrote Belknap. "With a strong head wind, she would drift into the minefield, before even a destroyer could tow her clear." Only one minelayer, *Saranac*, broke down while on an expedition and had to return to base before planting her mines. On at least two occasions, the flagship hoisted the wrong signals and caused near-collisions. Despite trouble with the mines, the entire project was remarkably successful in operational terms. Only one sailor was lost overboard during an operation. Admiral Strauss recalled that, after the Armistice, Vice Admiral Sir William Pakenham, in command of one of the Grand Fleet's battle groups, told him, "I felt that Providence as well as great skill must have been on your side to enable you to go through a period of such dangerous service and yet take all home."[40]

If the barrage was operationally successful, its objective, the destruction and deterrence of German submarines, was far less impressive. The Americans argued that it was successful. According to them, the exact number of U-boats lost to the barrage could not be determined because of incomplete data, but an undefined number were lost. Even more important, they believed that the barrage damaged the morale of German submarine crews and contributed to the Armistice. In the *Summary of Activities of American Forces in European Waters*, the final report of Simsadus, the mine barrage received credit for having "a considerable morale effect on the German naval crews, for it is known that several submarines hesitated some time before crossing. Also, reports from German sources are that the barrage caused no small amount of panic in some of the submarine flotillas. It is also probable that the barrage played a part in preventing raids on Allied commerce by fast enemy cruisers." Daniels credits Sims with this statement, but it is doubtful that he believed it. During the final weeks before the Armistice, he notified the CNO that additional expeditions were needed to fill the many gaps in the barrage caused by premature explosions. On October 19, he informed Benson, "I am sorry to say that I am afraid the northern barrage is not going to prove effective." Considering his pessimistic attitude from the beginning, it is doubtful that he ever attributed success to it.

Strauss informed the chief of the Bureau of Ordnance in January 1919 that "it was the opinion of the Admiralty Staff in London that surrender of the German Fleet and final armistice was caused solely by the failure of the submarine warfare, which failure was admitted as soon as the mine barrage was found to be effective. In other words, our little stunt did the trick."[41]

Although the Admiralty believed that the antisubmarine campaign helped to persuade the Germans to accept an Armistice, neither the Admiralty nor the High Command of the British navy considered the North Sea Mine Barrage a significant influence. On November 1, the Admiralty's Plans Division, which had advocated the project in the first place, concluded, "As at present designed, the Northern Barrage does not appear to be a serious obstacle to submarines on the surface," nor can it, "by itself, be accepted as a complete solution of the submarine problem." Admiral Fremantle gave it credit for "hampering . . . the movements of the enemy submarines while on passage to their theatres of operation," but Admiral Beatty was never convinced that the barrage was either effective or worthwhile. Americans who participated in the barrage were miffed at the claims that it was a British accomplishment. Lord Jellicoe did not even mention the Americans in his comments about the barrage.[42]

What did the Germans say about the North Sea Mine Barrage, particularly its success? Neither Admiral Scheer nor Captain Michelsen, the German commander of submarines, considered the barrage a major problem for their U-boats. Michelsen believed that it was "considerably more dangerous to the enemy mine layers and mine sweepers than it was to our submarines." Scheer believed that mines were next to the blockade as the "chief cause of our collapse at sea" but credited British minefields in the Bight rather than the barrage in the North Sea. "So far as we could ascertain, we suffered no losses in U-boats from these mines," he wrote after the war.[43]

Historians and naval officers on both sides of the Atlantic have debated whether the mine barrage was a defensive or offensive measure.[44] Of course, it was both. They have also argued about the barrage's usefulness. Conclusions on the number destroyed ranged from two, the German estimate, to eight or more by various Americans. Robert Grant, the most careful authority on German submarines in World War I, determined that six definitely perished in the barrage and another one probably, but he did not believe that it was a success.[45] American historians also emphasized the morale and psychological effect of the barrage on German U-boat crews. David Trask perhaps best summed up this view, writing that "the barrage certainly injured the morale of the U-boat crews, causing a notable decline in efficiency."[46] Robert Ferrell, among others, suggested that, if the war had lasted longer, "the barrage might have proved its worth," but Admiral Hezlet argued that the absence of adequate patrols made it unlikely that the barrage would have prevented the U-boats from challenging it. A passage for U-boats through Norwegian territorial waters remained viable because the Norwegians never mined them.[47] More recent studies, especially those of Halpern, Marder, Roskill, and Simpson, state that the barrage was not worth the cost, estimated at more than $40 million, and the additional expenses of mines, ships, and personnel might have been better used elsewhere.[48] The North Sea Mine Barrage was one of a kind, however, and its lessons, like many others, were forgotten in the years before the outbreak of World War II.[49]

"Hunting the Huns"

When the United States entered the war, the U-boat absorbed much of the British Admiralty's attention. The British Grand Fleet had checkmated the German High Seas fleet, and the Royal Navy no longer expected much difficulty with surface forces elsewhere. In December 1916, Lord Jellicoe, the first sea lord, created the Anti-Submarine Division, which assumed the responsibility of coordinating the development of antisubmarine weapons and to some degree the use of those weapons. Operations, including those related to the antisubmarine campaign, were centralized in the operations and plans divisions. Nevertheless, the first lord and the chief of the War Staff controlled all operations, including ASW.[1] Jellicoe developed the final plans for convoying and the mine barrage.

Although convoying became the principal measure adopted to defeat the German submarines, many in the Admiralty and in the U.S. Navy Department preferred "offensive" tactics rather than methods they considered "defensive" such as escort. Among them were the CNO, First Lord Geddes, and First Sea Lord Wemyss. The first sea lord maintained after the war: "There was in the Admiralty an unfortunate defensive spirit. . . . To me it appeared absolutely necessary that the table must be turned and that we must hunt the enemy submarine instead of allowing him to hunt us." They were convinced that certain weapons, both under development and perfected, could locate the U-boats and destroy them. In October 1917, Admiral Bayly suggested the formation of a squadron of twelve destroyers to conduct a continuous antisubmarine patrol in waters preferred by German U-boat commanders. "If the twelve destroyers could be U.S.," he bluntly told the Admiralty, "I should greatly prefer it as I seem to get more work out of them."[2] The Admiralty experimented with patrols of destroyers and sloops without much success. In June 1917, the British created hydrophone-hunting flotillas. Known as the Auxiliary Patrol, these flotillas included motor launches, trawlers, converted yachts, sloops, and destroyers. More than a thousand of the smaller antisubmarine craft were scattered in the waters around the British Isles; the demands of the Grand Fleet and convoying left few of the larger vessels available for this work.[3]

When the United States intervened in April 1917, the Navy had not adopted doctrines for antisubmarine warfare or procedures to govern destroyer operations.[4] It lacked craft similar to the British motor launches or trawlers, which were suitable for antisubmarine operations. The first of a new type of light craft, the 110-foot subchaser was under construction, but these ships were intended for home waters. Few considered them sufficiently seaworthy for service elsewhere. Later in the war, the Navy decided that submarine "hunters" should include subchasers, submarines, aircraft, and even a mystery ship, but initially the Department judged the destroyer the best vessel to undertake antisubmarine work.

The Department gave extensive attention to the use of towed listening devices to supplement the destroyer's capabilities. Sims recommended the installation of listening devices on all destroyers deployed in European waters. On his authority, a destroyer was assigned to conduct experiments with the listening devices. On the last day of February 1918, the force commander informed the Department: "At present every effort is being made to make available destroyers for purely offensive work against Submarines. One United States destroyer with hydro-phone is now engaged exclusively in hunting operations and four others are so employed a large part of the time."[5]

The Admiralty, although interested in the hunting tactics, refused to divert its destroyers from escort and other duties to join in the experiments. Sims and Captain Leigh, the latter in charge of the experiments, were most anxious to establish hunting patrols in the Irish Sea because German submarines began to concentrate in that area. Strongly escorted convoys forced them to leave the Atlantic traffic arteries. They attacked ships after the convoys broke up and individual ships headed for different ports. The British deployed two patrols of three destroyers each in the Irish Sea in 1917, but an American destroyer patrol of three vessels engaged in submarine hunting did not begin operations until August 1918.

The first U.S. hunting group in European waters was made up of *Allen*, *Kimberly*, and *Caldwell*. The destroyer skippers created their own tactical doctrines and manuals. *Kimberly*'s commanding officer advised Captain Pringle at Queenstown, "Until the listeners in the destroyers have more experience in recognizing submarine sounds a just estimate cannot be made of the value of destroyers for hunting submarines." Another one of the destroyer captains suggested that, until the destroyers gained sufficient experience, the unit should remain intact without rotating. Sims endorsed this recommendation. Each time one of the Queenstown-based destroyers entered a yard for refit, it installed listening devices. The Navy had not settled on the best type. Some destroyers left the yards with equipment installed in blisters on the hull or keel; others carried towed types.[6]

Results were disappointing. After nine months of experimentation, the Navy still had not settled on acceptable tactical doctrine. The British and American hunting patrols in the Irish Sea were not coordinated and at times interfered with each other. In order to enhance the listening effort, destroyer commanders were ordered to stop their engines periodically and drift. In October 1918, Sims wrote, "it is the intention of the Force Commander to leave the actual stationing of the destroyer to the discretion of the Detachment Commander who is on the spot and can from his own experience . . . solve the problem in the best way." The day after this communication was sent, *Kimberly* found a submarine. The destroyer, while testing equipment, had stopped twenty-eight times to listen for approximately five minutes at a time. On the twenty-ninth stop, it made a contact. After determining the approximate direction of the U-boat, the destroyer got underway and launched depth charges. At this point, the destroyer lost contact with the submarine. Personnel assigned to the equipment were far too inexperienced to recognize a submarine sound. The major difficulty, however, was that the equipment did not work well. The American destroyers did not give up. Sims was told that despite poor results destroyers "*working together* in a comparatively small area" could locate and destroy a submarine.[7]

In October 1918, the Admiralty recommended that Sims send eight U.S. destroyers from the Queenstown force to the Bay of Biscay, where the Germans had concentrated half a dozen submarines. The Admiralty agreed to replace the American destroyers at Queenstown with British vessels. It preferred the American warships because they were fitted with antisubmarine equipment and were considered more effective than their British counterparts. Although the destroyer captains were "very keen . . . [for the] hunting," the force commander refused to divert the Queenstown-based destroyers. Instead he ordered the *Aylwin* and a detachment of subchasers from Plymouth to the bay. The British admiral in command at Plymouth protested what he considered an invasion of his authority as district commander. The chasers had a difficult time because of the rough seas and did not locate any submarines. On October 19, the force commander asked the Department to deploy twenty-four of the new destroyers organized in four hunting groups of six vessels each, but the Armistice occurred before this arrangement could take effect.[8]

Both Benson's staff and Simsadus searched for the most effective tactic for the hunting flotillas. The Planning Section called for a reduction in the number of destroyers used as escorts and their transfer to hunting units. Advocates of this plan argued that the success of the convoy system had forced German submarines to abandon the North Atlantic and to concentrate along the British coast. Both the Admiralty and Sims refused to endorse a decrease in escorts for convoys. The idea of attaching hunting units to convoys was considered, but it was never adopted, partially because the naval staffs in London concluded that destroyer hunting flotillas were not as effective as destroyers operating as part of a team with light craft, British trawlers, and American subchasers.[9]

When Admiral Mayo met with Admiralty officials in September 1917, he brought up the possibility of deploying 110-foot wooden subchasers to European waters. The first seventy of these small craft were about to become available.[10] Although the admiral proposed to deploy the first seventy-two of these vessels in British waters, British officials were doubtful of their usefulness. Sims and many U.S. naval officers shared this impression.

Sims was evidently not informed of Mayo's promise that the first subchasers would go to English waters. In March 1918, he complained, "I have never had complete information as to agreements reached by Admiral Mayo and by the Chief of Naval Operations in consultation with British Admiralty officials." He was informed in October 1917 that the subchasers would deploy in European waters, but he was not told of their assignments. On December 4, the Admiralty sent a recommendation that the initial group of chasers should go to ports on the English Channel. Between December and February, the Admiralty reversed itself, favoring the allocation of the first contingent of subchasers to the Mediterranean. Vice Admiral Rosslyn Wemyss, who replaced Jellicoe as first sea lord in January, probably made this decision.

On February 8–9, a special commission of the Allied Naval Council met in Rome to consider the Mediterranean situation. At this meeting, Sims agreed to send the first subchasers to the Mediterranean. Early in March, Sims—who was aware that some members of the Admiralty believed that the small vessels would be more useful in British waters than in the Mediterranean—requested a recommendation from the Allied Naval Council. "The Admiralty thinks," he informed the Department, "that the first 36 submarine chasers should be sent to the Mediterranean unless a radical change in the general situation should develop before their arrival."

On March 11–13, the Allied Naval Council recommended the dispatch of the first thirty-six chasers to the Mediterranean for use on the Otranto Material Barrage, a barrier of mines, nets, and vessels assembled to prevent submarines from leaving the Adriatic. The council also agreed that six to eight of these vessels would be assigned to British waters for "experimental purposes." It decided to take up the question of the "employment of the remaining 112 submarine chasers under construction . . . at a later date." Sims informed the CNO that the council should decide the distribution of the remaining chasers. "It seems extremely probable however that the greater part of these forces will operate in the waters contiguous to the British Isles where shore facilities can probably be depended on for repairs."[11]

When the CNO questioned the council's decision and whether it should determine the location of the American vessels, Sims replied that, although the body was purely advisory, allowing it to make these decisions would probably head off requests from other countries. The Department decided to accept the council's resolutions concerning deployment of the initial subchasers and also of others sent over during the war. Difficulties arose when members of the Allied Naval Council disagreed among themselves. The Italian representative wanted to send additional chasers to the Mediterranean as quickly as possible. The British wished to deploy the remainder of the chasers in the English Channel and the Irish Sea. Sims agreed with the British. Because of the apparent success of the new underwater listening devices, he wanted to concentrate vessels in British waters and organize submarine-hunting groups. He informed the Department: "The Force Commander is free to acknowledge that he did not lay particular stress upon the completion of the submarine chasers in the past. This was because he had not been informed of the progress of American listening devices. As soon as Captain Leigh came abroad with these devices, the value of the submarine chasers at once became apparent. . . . It is hoped that every effort will be made to expedite the arrival of submarine chasers equipped with listening devices." The Department agreed with him. Although the subchasers were too slow to run down the most recent classes of German submarines, destroyers were not available, and the new Eagle boats, more suitable, were not ready.

In March, the British government began to express interest in sending the small vessels to British waters. Sims changed his mind; he supported the Admiralty's request. Captain Leigh, who headed the tests of listening equipment, considered the 110-foot subchasers the most effective American vessel available for antisubmarine warfare. Destroyers were not available to join hunting groups.[12] At the March meeting of the Allied Naval Council, the British supported the council's earlier decision to send the first thirty-six chasers to the Mediterranean but proposed to assign the rest of the 144 subchasers designated for European waters to Gibraltar and British waters. The council, however, rebuffed the British proposal.[13]

In mid-January, Captain "Reddy" Leigh, was ordered to remain in Great Britain in charge of all subchasers in European waters. He noted that the United States was "doing absolutely nothing in escorting vessels along the Cornish coast"; that more vessels were lost in one month along this coast than were lost in six months along the French coast. "We should assist the C-in-C Devonport in some way which accords with his own view as to the best manner of protecting . . . ships passing through his area. . . . I do not believe that the sub-chasers can be satisfactorily used for this purpose, but it would meet the situation halfway at least if a part of the chasers were offered for escort work." Leigh, when informed of the Admiralty deliberations, told Sims that he could "see no reason why the present instructions in regard to the employment of sub-chasers should be changed." Sims was caught in a dilemma. From the initial deployment of U.S. naval forces in British waters, he had adamantly insisted on a policy of subordinating these forces to local British naval control, but he had been just as insistent that subchasers should not be used for escorting convoys. On October 30, he wrote a carefully worded letter to the Admiralty: "The Force Commander has no desire or intention to prescribe rules governing the employment of U.S. Sub chasers which will in any way hamper the Commander-in-Chief, Devonport, in their use," but "It is not believed that the Sub Chasers are suitable for escort duty." At Sims's recommendation, the Department put him in charge of all subchasers in European waters. By the end of the war, he had 170 of these small craft under his command scattered from Ireland to Corfu in the Adriatic Sea.

Captain Leigh was a Mississippian who graduated from the Naval Academy in 1891. He was assistant chief of the Bureau of Engineering when the United States entered the war. While in this position, he supervised the development of antisubmarine equipment and led a team to England to experiment with the listening devices developed in the United States. According to one account, Leigh "was an exceptionally fine [officer]. . . . He had the reputation of being an all-round Navy man, the type of officer that [Alfred T.] Mahan might have doted upon."[14]

Leigh and his boss, Sims, were convinced that subchasers would be most useful in the English Channel and the Irish Sea. By April 1918, the convoy system had reduced sinkings to less than one-half of 1 percent. Most sinkings occurred in coastal waters, especially in the channel and in the waters between Ireland and England, because as convoys reached the channel and the Irish Sea, the ships dispersed to different ports. "The convoys, as convoys, necessarily ceased to exist the moment that they entered these inland waters, and the ships, as individual ships, or small groups of ships, had to find their way to their destination unescorted by destroyers, or escorted most inadequately," Sims noted, adding that this procedure was the "one weak spot in the convoy system."[15]

In April, the Department agreed to base thirty-six chasers at Plymouth and the next thirty-two at Queenstown. Later it was decided to double the number at both Plymouth and Queenstown. The repair ship *Hannibal*, which had originally been sent to Plymouth, was ordered to Queenstown as tender for the subchasers there. American and British vessels overtaxed the repair facilities at Queenstown, whereas the American vessels at Plymouth could use the Royal Navy dockyard at Devonport. Admiral Wilson in Brest asked for a detachment of the 110-foot vessels, but Sims refused, explaining that the Plymouth detachment could cover the approach to Brest. In October, he was informed that eighteen chasers would be assigned to Brest after they underwent training in Plymouth. The Department was faced with urgent demands from Gibraltar and Portugal for submarine chasers, but only a few were sent from Plymouth to Gibraltar just preceding the Armistice. The subchasers to be based in Gibraltar were to intercept German submarines attempting to leave the Mediterranean, but none arrived before the Armistice.[16] The Admiralty wanted to merge those deployed in the British Isles with their small craft and use them to patrol the coast under British command, but Sims, backed by the Department, refused to agree. They remained in larger units under American command.[17] A British flag officer exercised overall operational command.

On May 9, six subchasers arrived at Portsmouth after a difficult crossing. An ensign on No. 143 recalled that his chaser "staggered up the face of each wave to be cuffed viciously and buried in a smother of white water that cast the hull broadside into the trough, there to fetch it up with a shattering jolt. I did not see how any structure built of wood could survive the wrenching onslaught of these great marching seas that lifted, battered, and dropped their victim to an endless succession of dizzying falls while the decks shouldered off tons of churning waters. . . . The crew, except for helmsman and engineers, were lashed along the lee side of the house, most of them in a torpor of misery, drenched and weary, too seasick to feel hunger or thirst, too numbed to know fear."[18]

While these vessels were struggling across the Atlantic, opinions were being exchanged and debated about their use. Captains Pringle and Newton McCully recommended the use of subchasers for convoy work. Pringle proposed that the subchasers accompany a convoy "not as escorts or for any defensive purpose, but solely for offensive action, the convoy . . . constituting the lure which would tempt the submarine to expose itself." Later Pringle recognized that they would be more effective working in small groups close to the coast. The Admiralty, Admiral Sims, and Captain Leigh agreed that they should operate independently or with a supporting vessel on offensive operations.[19] Time and again, Sims stressed the offensive nature of the subchasers. They were too slow to keep up with convoys in heavy weather; they had difficulty keeping station; and they could not carry enough fuel for extended voyages. Sims favored a plan recommended by Leigh to employ hunting groups of three to six subchasers (later upped to twelve) equipped with listeners, operating with an escorting destroyer. The idea was that the chasers would locate the submarine and the speedy destroyer would then depth-charge it. Leigh instructed the commanding officers of the various subchaser detachments to write their own tactical doctrine for "hunting." However, chaser COs disliked operating with other vessels because of the noise of accompanying vessels. They preferred to operate alone, using depth charges. Standard practice was to set depth charges to explode at fifty feet. On more than one occasion, exploding charges damaged equipment and the chasers and injured personnel. Later kite balloons and aircraft cooperated with the chasers. "They should operate in smooth deep water which submarines frequent, such as the south coast of England," Sims wrote. "The special usefulness of submarine chasers depends upon their listening equipment . . . and [this] . . . equipment is entirely useless in rough weather."[20]

The development of onboard tactics began during initial training in Rhode Island and continued during their deployment in European waters. Chaser personnel gradually learned how to use their listening equipment, especially how to identify various noises under water. Sims described their operations at sea:

> The fight against the submarine . . . was divided into three parts—the search, the pursuit, and the attack. . . . [T]he trained listeners . . . kept constantly at tension for any noise which might manifest itself under water. It was impossible to use these listening devices while the boats were under way, for the sound of their own propellers and machinery would drown out any other disturbances. The three little vessels therefore drifted abreast. . . . [S]uddenly, one of the listeners would hear something. . . . The commanding officer at once began talking [by radio] with the other two boats. . . . Unless all three vessels heard the disturbance, nothing was done. . . . When all three vessels obtained the direction as well as the sound it was a comparatively simple matter to define its location.[21]

The flagship had a plotting room. Here a crew member received reports from the other boats and charted them. Soon he issued a "fix," and the chasers rushed to that location and resumed listening. When the commander of the hunt believed that they were close to the submarine, he ordered a drop of depth charges. Sometimes a destroyer joined in the attack.[22]

The subchasers rarely made a hit. Too many difficulties worked against them: inexperienced personnel, weather, the maneuverability of the submarines, and, above all, imperfect listening equipment.

At Portsmouth, Lieutenant Commander David LeBreton of the destroyer *Aylwin* commanded the chasers. After several months of training, the chasers moved to Weymouth because Portsmouth was overcrowded with British warships. This small port was close to Portland, where the Royal Navy maintained a small repair yard. They were organized into two units of three vessels each. They followed an eight-day cycle, four days at sea and four days in port. *Aylwin* supported both units. They hunted between the Isle of Wight and the Eddystone light off Plymouth. When additional chasers arrived, the chasers covered a 63-mile section of the channel, running from Start Point near Plymouth to the Lizard. Later the area was extended to the Isles of Scilly. The vessels initially used British tactics. They steamed in line abreast, usually between five hundred and a thousand yards apart. During the few weeks that the chasers operated out of Weymouth, the weather in the channel was ideal. "Day after day the channel was as smooth as glass and we drifted nearly all day and took life easy, but always kept a careful watch and had the motors already ready for instant use. The chasers reported two submarines located and depth charged during this period. The first attack was broken off because of noise from a convoy; the only result being a load of fish killed by the depth charges exploding. The second, however, may well have damaged a U-boat."[23]

On June 12, twelve subchasers escorted by the American destroyer *Parker* arrived at Plymouth, a few miles south of Weymouth. A complex of gun batteries, nets, mines, and vessels guarded the port. Each time a ship entered or left the harbor, a small vessel led it through the mine and net fields. "Follow us—about three hundred yards astern—and we'll get you Yanks through the nets all right!" remembered a chaser commander.[24] Within two weeks, the six chasers and the *Aylwin* left Weymouth and joined the squadron at Plymouth.

Captain Lyman Cotten, who had been in charge of the small vessels during their trials, took command and conducted their shakedown cruises and training exercises. The command eventually included seventy-two subchasers, two destroyers, a tender, and shore facility, with more than three thousand personnel. Commander Theodore G. "Spuds" Ellyson, the first American to fly a plane off the deck of a warship, served as Cotten's executive officer.

Cotten was a North Carolinian who graduated from the Academy in 1898 and participated in the Spanish-American War, the Philippine Insurrection, and the expedition to China during the Boxer Rebellion. Noted for his musical abilities as both banjo player and composer, he once performed before President Theodore Roosevelt and Secretary of War William Howard Taft, singing several of his songs. While in Plymouth, the entire base and ship complement sung a composition of his called "The Sub-Chaser Song." Although popular with the regulars, he irritated the reservists that manned the subchasers. Leigh evidently got word of it and went to Plymouth to investigate. He informed Sims: "The impression is that he feels himself generally superior to those [reserve officers]; a sort of 'high and mighty individual' who should be approached with due reverence. . . . [I]t seems that all Officers are afraid to make suggestions for fear Captain Cotten will criticize them in an ugly way and accuse them of a general lack of ordinary intelligence. . . . Captain Cotten seems to resent suggestions even from headquarters." Sims called Cotten to London and remonstrated with him for "working the officers . . . too hard . . . and . . . [being] too hard on them." Ellyson wrote that this reprimand "cut me to the quick. . . . I have never worked . . . [anyone] half so hard as I have worked myself."[25]

Sims had a great deal of respect for Cotten, noting that Cotten "worked hard, intelligently, and with good results in establishing the base." Even before the conference, however, Sims had informed Cotten that a rear admiral would probably take charge of the base at Plymouth and that he would continue as chief and take charge of the subchasers. Cotten, according to Ellyson, tried to keep the command: "He isn't going to lay down without a fight." Cotten wrote his wife: "I am tired and blue and need cheering up badly. My work here has not been going badly, in fact quite the contrary, but I am being threatened with a relief. . . . Having done all the preliminary work of organization and getting things going properly, they now want me to turn over command to a rear admiral and stay on as a sort of chief of operations. . . . In other words

I am to continue to do the work and someone else will get the credit. . . . It does not seem fair." Cotten himself requested the appointment of a base commander, an officer junior or at least equal with him but not an admiral.

Cotten apparently got on well with Admiral Sir Alexander Bethell, the Devonport (Plymouth) commander in chief. On August 1, Vice Admiral Cecil F. Thursby relieved Bethell. The American commander did not get along with either Thursby or his chief of staff, Captain Adrian Keyes, brother of Sir Roger Keyes. Cotten insisted that he had an independent command. In the middle of July, he told his wife: "the matter of establishing the status of my force here was left entirely in my hands, and after avoiding one or two hazards I have done so to my complete satisfaction. My force is an independent one co-operating with the British rather than being incorporated into the British force with me as an aid [sic] on the Admiral's staff." Sims, if informed of this statement, would have issued a sharp reprimand. His policy was to integrate American forces with the British and place them under British commanders. Admiral Thursby assumed that this policy applied to Cotten's command. On August 30, Cotten wrote Leigh of a meeting that he had with Vice Admiral Thursby and his chief of staff: "He seemed to be provoked with the orders I had, and said he could not understand the philosophy of some one else operating a part of the force that was supposed to be operating under him. I told him that . . . I trusted that he understood my position, which called, not for divided loyalty, but for double loyalty, that is, loyalty to my own Force Commander and loyalty to Plymouth Commander-in-Chief. . . . He said that he understood my position thoroughly, and hoped to make his position clear to the Admiralty."

Thursby may have "understood" Cotten's position, but he did not appreciate it and so informed the Admiralty. When Sims learned of Thursby's displeasure, he wrote to the British admiral, reiterating his policy that American naval forces were to operate under the command of British commanders. Four days after writing to the British commander in chief at Devonport, Thursby heard that Rear Admiral Mark Bristol had been ordered to take command of American naval forces at Plymouth. Leigh wrote, "somehow things there did not go along as smoothly as we had hoped and it seemed best to put a high ranking officer of great diplomacy there to keep the ways oiled." Cotten later acknowledged the Plymouth command was really an admiral's command, but Sims preferred a captain to serve under a British admiral, an arrangement comparable to that of Pringle and Bayly at Queenstown. Cotten was the best-qualified captain for this position. Bristol later wrote: "I have found Cotten's work very good indeed. I think he had a hard time partly because he did not have enough rank and partly because he had some hard persons to deal with."[26]

Cotten remained with the chasers until end of the war. He became Bristol's chief of staff and retained command of the subchaser detachment at Plymouth. He and Bristol were friends. "I am glad to get a Rear Admiral that I know and like," he wrote his wife.[27]

Bristol was appointed acting rear admiral when he received the Plymouth command. Commissioned in 1889, he served on various ships and became an outstanding gunnery officer. In 1913, Captain Bristol became the director of naval aeronautics.

In March 1918, he received command of the battleship *Oklahoma* and was still with that ship at Bantry Bay when ordered to Plymouth. Bristol assumed the Plymouth command on October 24, but he had little time to grasp subchaser work before the Armistice. He shortly became high commissioner to Turkey and earned acclaim as a diplomat.[28]

Plymouth was an active station for operations and also a training and experimental facility. With the exception of the thirty-six chasers sent to the Mediterranean, all of them deployed in European waters were supposed to receive advanced training at Plymouth. Leigh's research team used the Plymouth-based subchasers to continue tests of the listening equipment. The chasers also experimented with hunting tactics. The results were reported to Simsadus and circulated to the other subchaser commands. For this, two American destroyers, *Aylwin* and *Parker*, were assigned to work with the chasers. Cotten requested additional destroyers and a submarine. An American submarine was ordered to Plymouth but never arrived because of the Armistice. A British submarine cooperated when weather conditions were acceptable. The tactical exercises led to an organizational change into operational units of six vessels each. This formation was copied from the British, who placed three trawlers and either a "P" boat or a destroyer in their hunting patrols.

The Weymouth chaser unit was the first scheduled for operations because it was considered "experienced" and understood British signals and codes. The other twelve ships were to go through training for twenty-one days and then become operational. Cotten introduced a rotating schedule of four days operating at sea, four days rest and repair, and four days of standby. The standby period was devoted to instruction and drills. "We were scheduled during our in-port periods to sit through long study periods and lectures at headquarters on stuff that we knew from trial would not work, owing to lack of visibility, sea conditions, or sound interference," wrote one of the *Weymouth* chaser officers later. For some reason, the crews were not allowed to drill with the 3-inch deck gun until Leigh discovered this deficiency and remedied it. Gunnery proved to be extremely poor, at least partly because of the unstable vessels. No record exists of a subchaser using her deck gun against a U-boat.[29] The three-part rotation continued until the Armistice, even after the number of chasers operating from Plymouth increased to seventy-two. The two American destroyers rotated four days out and four days in port.[30]

Weather influenced the rotation. The waters in the channel, the Isles of Scilly, and the Irish Sea are notorious for their roughness, especially after summer. Frequent gales raged, and the rise and fall of the tide sometimes reached twenty-three feet. Fog created serious difficulties. The small wooden vessels with their narrow beams were extremely uncomfortable in bad weather. Drifting on a flat sea was easy, but drifting in stormy weather with choppy cross-seas, tide rips, and large swells was very taxing. Moffat recalled a storm: "The motion was wild. I could see only intermittently the blue light on No. 177 from where I stood on the bridge, hanging on to a machine gun and spitting water. At times we were swept from astern by five feet of solid water. Two men at the wheel worked hard to keep the ship from broaching." The vessels leaked constantly. Everything below deck became damp, and the cooks rarely had an opportunity to prepare hot meals while at sea. Sea sickness was rampant; colds were common; and injuries frequent. Lieutenant Commander Hugo Kohler, who went out for a patrol of twenty-four hours, later said that between the roughness of the Irish Sea and the smell of gasoline, it was "murder." The acting head of the Queenstown detachment reported in October: "Everything possible is being done to expedite the work of making chaser decks watertight as this is considered the greatest step that can be taken to improve living conditions. . . . During recent patrols chasers have suffered considerable injury on account of heavy weather encountered . . . remaining at sea too long . . . [although it is] undoubtedly a fine exhibition of spirit, it has been made clear to commanding officers that it is unwise procedure to keep chasers at sea under conditions in which they cannot operate effectively and risk injury that may lay them up for repairs during periods when fair weather would allow them to operate effectively." Sims ordered chasers to seek sheltered waters whenever storms or heavy weather made it impossible for them to operate effectively. He also insisted on maintaining the rotation schedule of four days at sea, allowing the crews adequate time to recover after returning to port. A chaser engineering officer wrote after the war: "The life on the chasers was so strenuous in these turbulent waters that we were given an eight-day rest period. . . . After four days of being continually tossed and thrown about I have come in with every muscle in my body sore as a boil."[31]

Cotten and later Captain Arthur J. Hepburn complained about the inexperience of the chasers' commanding officers. Sims, who usually excused the reserve officers, was displeased with their performance. Describing a "hunt" near the Isles of Scilly, he wrote: "what was believed to be an excellent contact with a submarine [was unsuccessful] through inexperience of personnel. The officer-of-the-deck of the chaser that made the contact was formerly a tailor by trade and has had but six months' naval experience. Although the listener was sure he had a submarine, the contact was not followed up." A week later, he admonished Cotten about this failure and others: "Several instances have occurred lately where chasers have failed to make an attack after obtaining the fix of a submarine by sound or sight."[32]

The most serious problem was the ineffective listening equipment. While still operating out of Weymouth, a chaser patrol had drifted and listened for several hours without success when a submarine's conning tower unexpectedly surfaced astern of the patrol. Although the U-boat quickly submerged upon sighting the small vessels, the chasers were able to drop depth charges. The attackers observed oil and some debris, and the Admiralty later declared the submarine "missing." On August 26, Leigh tried to boost morale, notifying his detachment commanders: "Thirteen attacks have been made [by chasers] on what were thought to be submarines, and in six of the cases sound evidence has been verified by sight. . . . Several of the attacks justified the belief that the submarine was at least damaged." Nonetheless, as Ellyson wrote to his wife that day, "We have not gotten a Hun submarine as yet." One bit of encouragement, he noted, was that no ships had been sunk in his area of responsibility since the chasers arrived in Plymouth.[33]

On August 20, a detachment of thirty-six chasers arrived at Queenstown, Ireland. The Queenstown harbor and anchorage was so crowded with American and British naval vessels that only two small docks were available for the chasers. They moored six abreast while the remainder swung at anchor moored to buoys in the stream.

They were under the command of Captain Arthur J. Hepburn. A member of the Academy class of 1897, Hepburn was the battleship *South Carolina*'s executive officer when war broke out. Later he was attached to the Bureau of Steam Engineering and worked with Captains Leigh and Cotten at Newport in the chaser program. Hepburn, a brilliant officer, got along well with Admiral Bayly. On one occasion, Bayly wrote Sims that he was willing to take on an additional thirty-six chasers in his force only if Hepburn remained in charge, "and not be replaced by a more senior officer. Hepburn is quite 100%, pleasant to deal with, very able and keen, and knows how to deal with the youngsters. Therefore better Hepburn and thirty-six, than another man and seventy-two." In his published memoirs, Bayly mentioned Hepburn as the American officer "with the divine gift of humour."[34]

Only one element of the Queenstown detachment went on line August 22, a division of six chasers. The remainder were ready but lacked confidential publications needed to operate in the Irish Sea and the Western Approaches. The entire detachment was not considered ready to commence hunting operations until September 19. Three divisions of six vessels each were assigned to different areas. One operated out of Queenstown, a second out of Berehaven, and a third out of Holyhead. Plans were approved to base divisions at Weterford and Milford Haven, "depending upon the submarine activity," but this never took place. Two divisions remained in reserve to replace the active divisions periodically. Instead of the four-day operational period at sea followed by the chasers at Plymouth, those under Admiral Bayly operated at sea only three days before rotating to port; later the time at sea was extended from seven to eight days. They also used a most unusual identification system and code for their short-range radios that at times mystified British (and possibly German) listeners. A division or hunting patrol call sign was a phrase or jingle such as "High-low-jack," and "Corn-meal mush." Their codes came from Mother Goose, Aesop's Fables, the St. James version of the Bible, and from poems and stories. "Quack, Quack, Quack" sent with a call sign such as "High-low-jack" meant that patrols should "operate at once." Tactically, however, they followed the same routine of patrolling and drifting as the Plymouth vessels. Later Hepburn's vessels modified their tactics to change areas periodically both in patrolling and drifting. In the middle of October, the division at Berehaven was deployed to Holyhead because of increasing submarine activity in the Irish Sea. There they came under the command of Captain Gordon Campbell, who had won a Victoria Cross as commander of a Q-ship. This organization remained in effect until the Armistice.[35]

On September 2, a subchaser patrol, operating with the *Parker*, sighted a submarine on the surface, later identified as *U-53*, well known because of her commander, Hans Rose. The Plymouth-based vessels chased the submarine for nearly ten miles, using listening equipment to continue searching for the elusive submarine and dropping depth charges periodically. These attacks damaged *U-53*, but it returned to base and remained there for the rest of the war. Four days later, Plymouth-based chaser units located a submarine and sunk her. The listening equipment picked up hammer-

ing, and faint pops interpreted as pistol shots when the U-boat crew committed suicide, a more acceptable death than asphyxiation.

October brought in heavy weather and fewer submarines. Even false contacts were
extremely scarce. Only two contacts were made in November. After an hour's chase
one of them proved to be a British torpedo boat. During the night of November 8, a
submarine was depth-charged and probably damaged, the last one that the subchasers engaged during the war.[36]

Pickings were just as scarce in the Irish Sea. On one occasion, a group of three
chasers pursued a possible submarine for seven hours before finally depth-charging
the target with no visible result. According to a U-boat veteran interviewed shortly after the war, three vessels, probably subchasers, trailed his boat, dropping depth charges for more than an hour before it slipped away. One division was ordered to patrol
harbors along the Irish coast where German submarines were supposed to pick up
food and other supplies. According to an account written years later, the Queenstown
division destroyed two submarines. This claim is extremely doubtful. Nine German
submarines were lost in the Irish Sea in 1918 but none after the arrival of the subchasers. Hepburn in his final report listed only three contacts with German submarines.
Admiral Bayly understood the offensive nature of the submarine chasers and never
undertook to use them for other purposes.[37] The same was not true of the British admiral under which the Plymouth detachment came.

The British district commander at Devonport initially agreed to use the chasers primarily for hunting rather than patrolling. This policy changed when Admiral
Thursby became C-in-C of Devonport. Thursby believed strongly that the subchasers were not being used properly. He informed the Admiralty in October: "the submarines have been able to work off the coast in the vicinity of the hunting flotillas
in perfect safety. . . . [I]t is evident that the hydrophones are not yet sufficiently perfected to enable hunting craft to get into touch with the submarines unaided. . . . I
have, therefore, come to the conclusion that these forces could be better employed if
a system of convoys were introduced," using the chasers as a part of the escort. In the
past, the Admiralty strongly supported the American Navy's insistence on the use of
subchasers solely for offensive operations, but an Admiralty memo pointed out that
"it is easy to understand how a submarine can operate in the vicinity of chasers without being heard. . . . [T]he indiscriminate dropping of depth charges . . . appear to do
more harm than good."[38] Another communication noted that the Americans did not
protect the Cornish coast, where more vessels were lost in a month than in six months
on the French coast.

Sims had to face a dilemma. He had adamantly supported the subordination of
American ships to local British commanders, but he had been insistent in opposing
the use of subchasers as escorts. On October 30, he sent a carefully worded message to
the Admiralty. He indicated that he did not want to hamper the admiral commanding
at Devonport, but he once again argued that subchasers were unsuitable as escorts.
Then he restated his support for local British command of U.S. ships. "Senior Allied
Naval Officers should always have . . . authority . . . of all U.S. naval vessels operating
under his military command." In conclusion, he said, "If the Commander-in-Chief,

Devonport, considers the U.S. Sub-chasers allocated to Plymouth will prove of more value by employing them as escorts for convoys, he may do so."[39] Thursby used the subchasers as escorts during the few remaining days of the war.

The British admiral was correct in his view that hydrophones had generally been a failure. The Plans Division of the Admiralty concluded that the hydrophone had led to the destruction of only three submarines. This statistic related to all types of British and American vessels. Chasers equipped with hydrophones were directly responsible for the destruction of only one U-boat in British waters. Simsadus determined that the British-based subchasers made 37 sound and visual contacts and dropped 238 depth charges. Results were disappointing. Nevertheless, the subchasers were probably the most efficient type of vessel used to hunt submerged U-boats. This was the conclusion of Captain Andreas Michelsen, in command of German submarines with the High Seas Fleet. In an essay on Allied antisubmarine measures that was translated and published in the *Office of Naval Intelligence Bulletin*, Michelsen wrote: "The American subchasers were much more effective [than their French or English counterparts]. . . . They proved themselves dangerous opponents to the submarines after the listening devices were ready for service, on account of their speed and sea-keeping qualities." One authority has written that the submarine chasers were "no great factor in the anti-submarine fight" in World War I, but with sonar similar craft were quite effective in World War II.[40]

The Admiralty had more faith in submarines than in subchasers in antisubmarine warfare. Their submarines achieved impressive success.[41] This accomplishment persuaded Sims to recommend in June 1917 the dispatch of U.S. submarines to participate in ASW. On July 2, the CNO ordered "the twelve most suitable submarines on the Atlantic Coast fitted out for duty in European waters. Despite the admiral's order that they should deploy by August 15, it was more than two months later when the first four were towed out of New London, Connecticut, for the Azores. It January 1918, the final seven to serve in European waters during the war reached Ireland.

Because the newest submarines, the *O* class, were still not operational, the Department agreed to deploy *E*-, *K*-, and *L*-class submarines to European waters. In September, Admiral Mayo recommended that the Department send one division to the Azores and a second to Ireland. *K-1*, *K-2*, *K-5*, *K-6*, and *E-1* were designated Division Four, and the *L*-class submarines ordered to Ireland became Division Five. In October, three of the *K* boats left Philadelphia for New London. The crew believed that they were to undergo training: "The idea that they would be the first boats to go across hardly entered their minds, because requests for housing periscopes, bridges, and other equipment to be necessary for war work had been disapproved." Their own crews considered them unreliable. They had fixed periscopes; they had no bridges; and the machinery frequently broke down. Nevertheless, they were soon underway for the Azores with another *K* boat and with the tender *Bushnell* as escort. On October 27, they arrived at Ponta Delgada. Although Bushnell had been loaded with spare parts, fuel, food, and other necessary supplies, little planning had been done on operations. The tender was quickly unloaded and headed back to the States to escort the *L* class. The *K* boats were not designed for personnel to live onboard for a period of time. They quickly commandeered openings in a rock breakwater where an office and other "holes" for storerooms and quarters were located. The submariners, or "cave dwellers," as they called themselves, remained in these facilities until a storm blew in and drenched everything. Then they rented the third floor of a hotel in the town and acquired the use of a room in a nearby school. Four days after arriving in Ponta Delgada, the first submarine went on patrol. Later *E-1* joined the division. The submarines made many patrols for nearly a year, never fired a gun, and never saw a German U-boat. Although the Germans occasionally sent a submarine to the area, the obsolete American boats could do nothing to stop them. A bluejacket on the *E-1* later recalled, "My recollections of the war are of endless days of work, of bad weather, of the strain of search and of trying to escape destruction."[42] Both Admiral Dunn and Sims repeatedly requested improved modern submarines but without success. Dunn implied that his submarines were worthless for antisubmarine work and requested subchasers in their place.

On January 27, 1918, four *L*-class submarines, the tender *Bushnell*, and one tug arrived in Queenstown, Ireland, after an extremely difficult journey across the Atlantic.[43] The tender and three tugs left Newport on December 4, 1917, with seven *L*-class submarines under tow. Gales lashed the small force from the beginning. Before reaching Ponta Delgada, a tug and one of the submarines returned to the United States. On the leg from the Azores to Ireland, two more boats and a tug turned back because of the severe weather, but they eventually straggled into Queenstown. They later deployed to Bantry Bay because Queenstown was crowded with surface forces.[44]

In 1917, the Admiralty believed that the submarine was a most effective weapon against enemy submarines. British submarines were used principally as ASW vessels at least partly because the Allied blockade of German ports had driven that nation's commerce from the seas. The low profile of the submarine allowed them to approach another submarine without detection much more easily than a surface warship. The Admiralty agreed to the deployment of American submarines in the war zone because of this circumstance, although they were small coastal types. They could perform two vital duties: an offensive role as hunters against the U-boats and a defensive role as patrols off important seaports. The American Navy accepted the British viewpoint without question. "Admiralty experience," Sims informed Admiral Benson, "is that hostile submarines have almost invariably moved their hunting ground when they have discovered the presence of Allied submarines."[45]

Captain Thomas Hart initially commanded Submarine Division Five. He later gained fame early in World War II as commander in chief, Asiatic Fleet. In July 1918, he was ordered home to become director of submarines at the Navy Department, and Commander W. L. Friedell replaced him. The overall commander was Admiral Bayly, the Queenstown district commander, but the American submarines came under Captain E. Dumbar-Nasmith, RN, who reported to Bayly. Nasmith exercised operational control and, like Pringle, Hart, and Friedell, had administrative control. They reported directly to Sims on matters such as personnel, equipment, repairs, and supplies.[46]

Until early in March, the American submarines went through intense training under the direction of British submarine officers. Daily British and Yanks hunted each other in Bantry Bay's deep waters, firing torpedoes with dummy heads when one or the other was sighted through the periscope. American officers also went on patrol with the British submarines. One American lost his life when a submarine failed to return after a mission. He was the only casualty in the division while in the war zone. As much as possible, the submarines of Division Five applied British submarine doctrine, perfected in four years of war. American submarine experimented with hydrophones, but, according to Captain Hart, they were not very effective.[47]

On March 6, the first two American submarines left on combat patrol. The plan was to send out three submarines at a time as soon as all seven submarines completed their training and indoctrination. They were to operate for eight days and remain in port for eight days. One submarine at a time would have a double port period. Officers and enlisted men would live onboard the tender while in port. Hart's force patrolled the southwest coast of Ireland and the southern entrance to the Irish Sea. In August, declining German submarine activity in the Irish Sea led to the concentration of American submarines in waters west of Ireland. The areas to be patrolled were divided into squares designated as "billets" with patrol lines about thirty miles long running to about a hundred miles offshore. Bayly's staff selected the areas based on intelligence of U-boat operations. Whenever possible, a British officer went out with the American submarine on patrol to provide needed expertise.[48]

German submarines were larger and in general much superior to the American L class, but the Americans enjoyed a significant advantage that determined their basic tactics. The U-boats operating in the Western Approaches and the Irish Sea had to travel more than a thousand miles around the northern coast of Scotland, a most difficult voyage under the best of circumstances. Operating far from base and in hostile waters with limited oxygen, the German boats had to remain on the surface most of the time, submerging when they observed the smoke of an approaching ship. Often they made attacks on the surface. The American and British submarines were close to their base and could spend much of their time underwater. They usually came up at night to recharge their batteries, which supposedly gave them a great advantage, but for various reasons, they located few German submarines. According to the official report, American submarines sighted twenty-one U-boats and attacked four of them with torpedoes (L-class submarines did not carry deck guns) but failed to sink any. By a stroke of luck, a German submarine was destroyed when she fired a torpedo at an American boat. The torpedo evidently went out of control, circled, and struck the U-boat.[49]

The American torpedoes, like their counterparts in the early months of World War II, were notoriously ineffective. "Our torpedoes," Commander O'Grady wrote, "are so sensitive that a kiss on the nose is likely to set them off." Often they were erratic when fired, moving to one side or the other at the wrong depth. On one occasion, the *AL-11* encountered a U-boat on the surface dead in the water and for once got close enough to fire two torpedoes. One exploded prematurely and the other apparently dove under or astern of the submarine as she got underway. Because of their inexperience, submarine commanders sometimes failed to fire a full spread of torpedoes.[50]

The American submariners discovered that their major danger was not from the enemy but from friendly ships and aircraft. "My recollections of the war are . . . of trying to escape destruction, not so much by enemy ships as by those of the Allied nations," a submarine sailor recalled after the war. "The general practice of surface ships during the war was to fire at any periscope seen and then, as a second thought, make a slight effort to learn if it belonged to any enemy submarine. . . . The nerve wracking feature lay in the fact that under the rules of the game we could not fight back." The Executive Officer of Division Five wrote: "The destroyers and patrol vessels are the best things to avoid, and there is not a submarine in the division that has not been gunned by them at least twice. . . . Sometimes after a little gun play on the part of a destroyer there is an argument about signals." To prevent accidents of this kind from occurring, notices were sent out that Allied submarines would operate in particular areas, but radios were primitive and often failed to contact convoys approaching the Irish Sea from the United States. Submarines on patrol were issued recognition signals and rifle projectiles and grenades that, when fired, exploded into blue smoke. The warning indicated that the submarine was friendly, but approaching ships frequently ignored the signal. On one occasion, a ship opened fire with her bow and stern guns. The American submarine hoisted and waved a white blanket, but the ship continued firing until she passed astern and out of sight. Fortunately, the shells missed the submarine. On another occasion, two escorting destroyers, both American, fired on the *AL-2* when she surfaced to give her identification signal. The only casualty occurred when a shell exploded some thirty yards off the submarine, causing a cook standing on the bridge to break his front teeth. In another incident, *AL-10* came under fire from a destroyer and crash-dived, but then it surfaced while being depth-charged. After it made recognition signals, the surface ship came alongside, and the commanding officer discovered that the submarine captain had been his roommate at the Naval Academy. Two American submarines blundered into each other in the ever-present fog and fired their torpedoes at each other without success. On a dark night, *AL-9* was patrolling off Bantry Bay when a British destroyer steamed by. She was so close that the American CO heard the sight setters singing the ranges at the guns: "Two 'undred, one 'undred, no 'undred. Strike me pink! She's h'a bleedin' Yank."[51]

The seven *A* (*AL*) boats were the only American submarines to operate in European waters during the war. In October, Sims recommended that *O-* and *R*-class boats be deployed in the war zone, but the Armistice came before they arrived. Although the French government urged the Navy to send submarines to the Canary Islands or the northwest coast of Africa, the Americans opposed this measure. Sims said that additional submarines dispatched to the war zone should operate in British waters.[52] The only other American submarines in the war zone operated in the Azores.

A recent authority has written that the mission assigned to the American submarines that operated out of Ireland was "beyond their capability," but despite disappointing results in operations against U-boats, they achieved some success. Admiral Sims wrote that the presence of Allied or American submarines in a particular area frequently forced U-boats to abandon it. He also mentioned that they prevented the German submarines from operating in flotillas, or "wolf packs," as they did in World War II, although evidence is insufficient to substantiate this assertion. Nonetheless,

American submarines made an impact on German submariners. Michelson wrote: "American submarines . . . proved themselves dangerous opponents to our submarines. . . . [T]hese enemy submarines had only one mission, to attack our submarines, while our boats were charged primarily with the sinking of the maximum possible ship tonnage and could not be bothered attacking these enemy submarines." They also benefited because German submarines had to travel a long distance and had to cruise on the surface as much as possible during the day. He agreed that "On the whole, the [American] . . . submarine offensive exerted a measurable influence on our submarine activities, particularly owing to the resultant insecurity which was felt."[53]

During the latter months of the war, American-manned aircraft occasionally cooperated with submarines in antisubmarine activities. On June 5, 1917, the First Aeronautic Detachment arrived in St. Nazaire. This unit consisted of 7 officers and 122 bluejackets under the command of Lieutenant Kenneth Whiting. It was the first American military force to arrive in France. Lacking aircraft and under vague orders to cooperate with the French, they remained at St. Nazaire while Whiting went off to Paris to consult with the French naval authorities. The French were somewhat surprised, not having been notified that Whiting and his men were to arrive.[54] Their presence was also intended in some obscure way to "boost morale," although the means to accomplish this purpose were unclear.

The French government, along with the other Allies, knew that the United States was woefully weak in naval aviation. When the United States entered the war, the Navy had a total of fifty-four aircraft, none suited for combat, and a dirigible that could not fly. Personnel consisted of 48 officers and 230 enlisted men. Whiting's group was chosen from this group, most of whom were in training at Pensacola.

Whiting was determined to get into the war as soon as possible, and the French proved receptive. A 1905 graduate of the Naval Academy and a pioneer naval aviator (no. 16), Whiting was a handsome, hard-drinking, daredevil New Englander, who once had himself shot from the torpedo tube of a submerged submarine and who flew for the "pure, wholesome hell of it." Considered "impulsive," he often got into trouble with his superiors. He was selected for the command because he had been in command of the Pensacola Naval Aeronautic Station (later the Pensacola Naval Air Station). In a series of meetings with French naval officials, he worked out an agreement to allow the American aircrews and mechanics to train at French aviation schools. The American lieutenant also agreed, without authority, to man a number of French air stations. The French would supply the American stations with aircraft, spare motors and parts, instruments, and weapons—everything needed to equip combat aviation units and bases.[55]

Admiral Sims had no idea that a naval aviation unit had arrived in the war zone until the British Admiralty informed him of this event. This failure was probably an administrative oversight, a product of the vague relationship between Sims and Washington that existed during the early months of the war. Although Whiting had no orders to report to Sims, the admiral ordered the lieutenant to London. Although astonished at what Whiting told him, he approved the naval aviator's agreement with the French. Any other action would have probably resulted in discord with France, although Sims would have favored concentration of American naval aviation along the southern English and Irish coasts to cooperate in the protection of convoys. The Navy Department also approved the decisions, including the recommendation that the United States take over twelve seaplanes and three dirigible stations. Later Washington officials agreed to assume control of air stations in England and Ireland. In a report submitted toward the end of the war, Sims rebuked the Department for its "Lack of a definite, pre-arranged plan for the establishment of a Naval Aviation Force on Foreign Service."[56]

Despite Whiting's hope to "get to the front" as quickly as possible, months passed before a U.S. naval aviator flew a combat patrol. The Americans concentrated on training during this interlude. Until facilities for "advanced training" were established in Europe, the American aviators attended French schools. Later the British trained American naval aviators at Uxbridge, Rockhampton, Stonehenge, Cranwell, Eastchurch, and Leystown. Whiting's pilots went to Tours for flight training late in June. One of the Americans in this group later recalled that "none of us had had any ground school instruction and few of us had any idea about the theory of flight. Our instructors did not speak English and we did not speak French. . . . One leather flying coat, one pair of goggles and one crash helmet were issued to each group [of eight to ten student pilots] and these were passed from one student to another as his turn came to fly. . . . After each flight, the instructor would pull out a pasteboard card with a line drawn down the center. One side was written in English and the other in French. The instructor would explain all the mistakes you had made while in Flight. He gave you hell in French while pointing to the English translation. Perhaps it was just as well we did not understand his words."[57]

After Tours, the student pilots transferred to a station near Bordeaux where they received instruction in flying seaplanes. Finally, they went to a base on the Mediterranean to fly various types of French aircraft and to obtain instruction in skills such as gunnery and navigation. When they left the French schools as certified pilots, they had accumulated thirty to thirty-five hours of flying time. While the pilots went through their training, the observer/gunners and ground personnel attended other French schools.

Although American naval aviation personnel also trained with the British, the majority in the European theater went through the U.S. naval training facility established at Moutchie. Located on the Lake of Lacanau near Bordeaux, the facility was activated in late August, when fifty-four enlisted personnel who had undergone instruction at a French school arrived at the base. Early in September, the American pilots came in from Tours. This station, under the command of Lieutenant John L. Callan, one of the most experienced U.S. naval aviators, was nothing but a wilderness when he took over in July. It gradually took shape with the appearance of additional personnel and supplies. On September 27, Ensign Robert A. Lovett, later secretary of defense, made the first training flight from the station. The training of air crews, using French seaplanes, continued at Moutchie until the Armistice, although the station was never completed.[58]

Until the last few months of the war, the Allies provided all the aircraft used by American naval aviators in the war. The Americans flew an alphabet of airplanes with names such as Nieuports, Donnet-Donkauts (called DDs), Le Pens, Telliers, Spads, Sopwith Camels, Short 320s, Small Americas (H-4), Large Americas (H-12, H-16), DeHavillands (DH-1, DH-4), Capronis, Macchis (M.8, M.5), Bristol fighters, Avros, F2As, Henriot-Dupont HD-2s, and Breguat 14s. Some were bombers like the Capronis and DH-4s; some were fighters like the Bristols, Spads, and Camels; and some were seaplanes.

Most of the American pilots flew seaplanes. Curtiss developed the Americas in the United States, but they were improved in Great Britain. DeHavillands and DH-4s were also manufactured in the United States, some equipped with the famous Liberty engine. The first eight arrived in Ireland late in July 1918. Thirty-eight were being assembled at the time of the Armistice. The HS-1 was the only American aircraft to reach Europe during the war. The first was flown at Pauillac Naval Air Station on June 15, 1918.

World War I aviators often praised certain types of aircraft, but none of them was dependable. All were more dangerous to their crews than the enemy. The underpowered, low-performance flying boats gave the most trouble, but all types suffered from faulty engines and other malfunctions. They killed and injured more American aviators than the Germans and Austro-Hungarians. Personal accounts abound with mention of accidents. Wings broke apart, fabric peeled off, spars collapsed, machine guns jammed, bomb gear either failed to release at the proper time or released unexpectedly. Kenneth MacLeish, a Yale volunteer, mentioned an incident in which two seaplanes from the naval air station at Dunkirk were lost on patrol. One went out of control and crashed, killing one of the crew. The other landed to rescue the survivor but also started to sink. Another aircraft and motorboats finally rescued the downed airmen. After the war, veteran aviators criticized the aircraft they had flown. One referred sarcastically to the small Americas as having a ceiling of "maybe a hundred feet." Another claimed that the Donnet-Denhaut "was a treacherous machine to fly and would not fly at all when its Hispano-Sulsa motor quit." According to another pilot, "none of them were very good aeronautically." The vaunted Liberty engine was put in service before it was perfected, leading to frequent accidents. One aviator wrote, "We strewed those old Liberty-engined boats all over . . . the North Sea."[59]

The Navy's aviation force in Europe had to operate with flawed aircraft, and it encountered other problems. They lacked spare parts; indifferent maintenance and defective workmanship occurred before the aircraft were turned over to the air stations; and aircraft were received without necessary equipment. These deficiencies particularly plagued the airplanes that the French government gave to the Navy. Some were older models no longer used by the French air services. The major difficulty was that the French were unable to make good on their commitments because of shortages in materials and labor. Even those received from the United States were often deficient. The official war diary of the naval air station at Lough Foyle, Ireland, noted on August 1, 1918, that five flying boats from the United States were inoperable because of defective wings. Forty percent of the first shipment of American manufactured naval aircraft to France required overhaul, including stronger control wiring, before they could fly. Twenty-five percent of the "hulls" were damaged. Crated aircraft continued to arrive at the Pauillac station with warped wings and other defects. Crankshafts were manufactured on board the tender *Prometheus* and starters on *Bridgeport* at Brest. One veteran wrote: "We were held up for a long time in our flying due to the lack of spare parts. . . . [M]achines that crashed were carefully salvaged . . . [for] parts. . . . We heard a great deal of talk of the impracticability of the French motors because of the great amount of hand fitting done to them which made it almost impossible to interchange parts. However, you never know what you can do until you have to. We took crank-shafts, pistons, cylinders, and crank-cases from different motors and turned out rebuilt ones."[60]

To start the French pusher-type Tellier seaplanes, sailors known as "beach mules" pushed them into the water and hand-cranked the engines. A bomb broke loose from a defective bomb rack and exploded at the St. Trojan air station as the flying boat was pushed into the water. The crew and six "beach mules perished," and the aircraft was destroyed. Thirty-six officers, nearly all aviators, and eighty-six enlisted men died in naval aviation accidents that happened in the war zone. For the naval aircrews, the most dreaded accident was being forced to land at sea because of a "conked-out" engine or running out of fuel. Aerial navigation was still extremely primitive. The planes were equipped with a simple compass, and at high attitudes and in cold weather, the alcohol in the compasses sometimes froze. Late in the summer of 1918, the American aircraft were equipped with radios. They could only be used while the plane was airborne because the antenna was a wire reeled out by the pilot or observer while in flight. Aircraft on the water had to rely on a traditional communication system; at the Armistice, twelve pigeon stations operated in France with a supply of 1,508 birds either trained or in training as messengers. At the Pauillac Naval Air Station alone, seventy-eight pigeons carried 689 messages in one month, and of these, more than 200 were of an "urgent nature." Each aircraft carried three to four pigeons. Messages were tied to a leg. They were released while in the air by throwing them out away from the propellers or after the plane made a landing.

Downed aircrews frequently owed their lives to the pigeons. In November 1917, engine trouble forced down a Tellier seaplane from the LeCrosic Naval Air Station with three crewmen on board. Although three pigeons were released and reached their destinations, it took a search vessel three days to find the crew. The flying boat sank minutes after they were rescued. If possible, downed aircraft were towed in, but often they were abandoned if they were not repairable or the weather precluded towing.[61]

The naval air service in Europe included lighter-than-air (LTA) craft. Shortly before President Wilson's declaration of war, the Navy contracted for sixteen airships (blimps). These ships became operational during the war, but none were shipped to Europe. Instead, the Navy depended upon the Allies to supply airships.

The French minister of marine approached Admiral Wilson about establishing stations for dirigible-type aircraft. During fall 1917, the Navy Department agreed to build four LTA stations at Guipavas, Paimboeuf, Rochefort, and Arcachon (known as the Naval Air Station, Gujan).[62] The French agreed to provide the dirigibles, and twelve were turned over to the Navy. On March 1, 1918, the Navy commissioned the station at Paimboeuf. Two days later, an Astra-Torres airship made its first flight with an American crew. Two Zodiac types were soon added to the American squadron at Paimboeuf.

American naval officials had mixed opinions about LTA ships. They could remain aloft for nearly nine hours and could hover over a convoy because of their low speed. If one became inoperable while on patrol, it did not have to land but could drift back to land if the wind blew in the right direction. Airships were filled with hydrogen, an extremely hazardous gas. One American-manned dirigible was lost at sea because of a leaking valve, but the crew was saved. Although sailors on ships with airships as escorts were usually pleased to see one cruising above, others were not because of fear that their presence would lead U-boats to the convoy.[63]

Of more immediate concern to the Navy was the value of airships in the war zone. Because of their slowness and the influence of weather on them, dirigibles were of limited use in ASW operations. For these reasons, the Navy decided to restrict the number of airships and airship stations in the war zone. At the recommendation of Captain Hutch I. Cone, the head of U.S. naval aviation in France, the Department shelved plans for additional airship construction. Late in the war, however, naval officials in European waters became more receptive to expansion, adding new craft and assuming control of additional airship stations, especially in Great Britain. They were effective in escorting convoys and searching for minefields. On September 24, Captain Cone wrote, "Our small amount of experience over here would tend to show that dirigibles are invaluable and much less expensive . . . to accomplish the same amounts of escort as seaplanes."[64]

Kite balloons remained popular throughout the war. The Royal Navy first used kite balloons in August 1916. The British were so impressed with them that they were placed on ships as soon as they were manufactured. Kite balloons were the first standard aviation operational units on board U.S. naval vessels. These manned sausage-shaped craft were filled with hydrogen and attached to a ship by a winch-operated cable. They were towed at altitudes of several hundred feet while the ship was underway. In early July 1917, Admiral Sims sent an Admiralty want list for aviation to the Navy Department. It included a hundred large kite-balloon units "complete with trained men and officers." Only a few reached the war zone before the Armistice, but some patrol work was done with kite balloons supplied by the Allies. Small stations in Ireland and France prepared the balloons for use on warships engaged in convoying and ASW work. They were carried on destroyers, converted yachts, and even battleships. The 110-foot subchasers experimented with them unsuccessfully. British and American naval officials agreed that kite balloons were suitable for escort but not for patrol. By the end of the war, U.S. vessels used more than a hundred in European waters. Sailors, particularly on the smaller vessels, considered the "rubber cows" a nuisance because they were difficult to handle while underway in rough seas. They were also dangerous. Lightning struck the *New York*'s kite balloon during a heavy storm. Naval officials, however, found them useful for spotting torpedo wakes, observing the movement of ships behind fog banks and smokescreens, and even for fire control. The negative aspect was that they helped the enemy locate vessels flying kite balloons.[65]

Undoubtedly, LTA ships helped deter submarines from attacking escorted convoys. As early as December 1917, American-trained air crews for LTA craft underwent training on French airships. Patrols from designated American air stations in France began in February 1918, although the dirigibles and stations were still under French control. As more Americans arrived, the French gradually withdrew their personnel. Until the Armistice, the few dirigibles under American command escorted ships and convoys in and out of various French ports. Upon meeting convoys or escorts at sea, they used radio when possible or signaled with flashlight. They usually circled the ships under escort, flying at a height that allowed those on the ships to observe them. As one former crewman recalled, "We could see the khaki-clad doughboys looking like swarms of bees on the decks, wildly waving at the sight of the Stars and Stripes flapping from aft of our blimp." The French navy credited U.S.-operated airships with sighting five submarines, attacking three, and damaging two. American officials claimed that only one U-boat was spotted, and, although it was attacked, no damage was done. On October 1, 1918, a dirigible out of Paimboeuf came under attack from a surfaced submarine. Some thirteen shells from the German U-boat burst near the airship without seriously damaging it. The dirigible's one gun was inoperable, and efforts to bomb the sub proved futile because of headwinds that prevented the airship from getting into position.[66] The final flight of an American-manned airship escorted President Wilson to Brest early in December 1918.

Heavier-than-air craft were more successful than LTA ships in the submarine war. The French credited American naval planes flying out of U.S. naval air stations in France with twenty-seven submarines sighted, twenty-five attacked, twelve damaged, and four probably sunk. American figures are far more conservative: nine submarines sighted, eight attacked, three damaged, and two probably sunk. Accurate figures for the stations in Great Britain were difficult to compile. Patrol reports often included statements to the effect that they bombed "oil patches." They include mention of only three submarines sighted and attacked, one being damaged and the other sunk. British writers later contended that aircraft acting independently sunk but one submarine, but it was not by an American airplane. Possibly as many as thirty-nine attacks were made against German U-boats or what were considered submarines. The principal value of aircraft, however, was its effect on morale. Aircraft, upon locating a submarine, were expected to remain overhead, calling for a surface vessel and then guiding it to the target. German submariners were extremely fearful of aircraft, especially when on the surface recharging batteries.[67]

Kenneth Whiting initially outlined American naval policy for its aviation force in the war zone. He recommended the establishment of a chain of U.S.-controlled air stations along the French Atlantic coast and in Great Britain, and also an extensive program of advanced training for airmen. He advocated the use of American-manned aircraft to patrol the English Channel, and the Atlantic approaches to British and French ports, the creation of an air arm in the Mediterranean; and an offensive bombing campaign against the German submarine bases.[68] With modifications, U.S.

naval aviation followed this basic plan in Europe until the Armistice. The plan was refined in September 1917, when Captain Hutch Cone took command of American naval aviation in Europe. In a meeting with Admiralty officials, he agreed to develop seaplane and kite balloon stations along the south coast of Ireland in order to cooperate with American destroyers operating in the waters off that coast. He also agreed to build or take over one or more bases in England in order to join the British in air attacks on German naval bases. Cone also proposed offensive operations against the German submarines and their bases. Admiral Sims and the Navy Department usually accepted the advice of Whiting and Cone.[69]

Until the American air stations became operational, U.S. naval aviators flew with French and British squadrons. Flying seaplanes, they flew out of Felixstowe in England and Dunkirk in France and later from the American naval air station at Killingholme. The early flights conducted convoy patrol. In January 1918, American aircrews began to search for U-boats in the English Channel. Patrols from the U.S. naval air stations established in Ireland began in June.

American-manned aircraft conducted 4,689 patrols from fourteen bases, flying more than eight hundred thousand nautical miles. Most of the time, the patrols occurred without incident. Before the war, it was thought that a submarine could be spotted on the water by an observer in an aircraft from a distance up to ten miles. The British learned they could sight a submarine at best up to five miles away. Four-fifths of the submarines sighted were on the surface, and approximately one-fifth at periscope depth. Few attacks were made because submarine lookouts usually spotted an aircraft in time to allow the U-boat to submerge.[70] Usually the attacks were made in conjunction with surface escorts. Destroyers or other surface vessels sunk the majority of the U-boats damaged by aircraft. Admiral Sims's aide for aviation wrote after the war that "the destroyers almost always got the credit, whereas the aircraft, the indirect destructive agency, was really responsible for bringing the action in which the submarine was destroyed."[71] However, Lieutenant John J. Schieffelin was awarded the Distinguished Service Medal for attacking enemy submarines in the English Channel on July 9 and again ten days later. In both cases, he directed British destroyers to the scene, resulting in damage to the first U-boat and the sinking of *U-110* on July 19. In April, seaplanes from the Ile-Tudy Air Station attacked a German submarine and dropped a smoke bomb, which attracted a French warship and the American destroyer *Stewart*. The French claimed that these vessels sunk *U-108*, but, according to German records, she escaped. One aviator's memoirs mentioned "the absolute hit on a sub, in the Bay of Biscay on October 19, 1918. . . . just four days later, another plane was credited with disabling a sub." According to German records, none were lost in the Bay of Biscay during October. On one occasion the French complained that an American aircraft had bombed some fishing boats. At times the only result was that surface vessels, when reaching a position where a submarine was supposedly attacked, found dead fish floating on the surface. If time permitted, the fish were picked up and cooked later.[72]

The aviators engaged in routine patrol found it mind-numbing. An observer wrote after transferring from seaplanes to land planes: "Believe me I'm glad to because I hate those seaplanes. Also it's darned tiresome flying over water all the time. Also, I don't fancy a watery grave."[73] At least aircrews on patrol in French waters usually had convoys to occupy them, but those involved in the famous Spider Web rarely saw anything. The Spider Web was an area sixty miles in diameter that covered the eastern end of the English Channel. It centered on the North Hinder Light vessel, a well-known navigational marker in the middle of the channel. This patrol system blanketed a major U-boat transit route. Octagonal in shape with eight radiating arms, each thirty miles long, it extended from the corners of the octagon to the center, permitting a search of nearly four thousand square miles of sea. Normally U-boats took approximately ten hours to pass through the area. Seaplanes were the spiders. The British developed the system early in 1917, using aircraft from the Felixstowe and Great Yarmouth air stations. Aircraft from each station simultaneously patrolled overlapping sections of the Spider Web, searching for "flies," the U-boats.[74] These patrols were not without danger because part of the Spider Web was within range of German aircraft based at Zeebrugge.

American naval aircrews were introduced to the Spider Web when a small number of them were temporarily seconded to the British squadrons at Great Yarmouth and Felixstowe. In January, two of the Yale volunteers made their first combat flights on the Spider Web patrol. On April 25, 1918, German fighters shot down a Curtiss H-12 flying boat on which an American ensign flew as a member of the crew. Nearly a month later, a flying boat with another American on board developed engine trouble. After it landed in the water, a German aircraft destroyed it. The American was the only survivor. A German flier picked him up and he became a prisoner of war. The British tried to retaliate by sending five seaplanes to locate and attack patrolling German aircraft. Two American officers were members of the crews. The aircraft flew for nearly three hours, penetrating German-controlled air space. They finally ran into a large force of fifteen or sixteen fighters. There followed probably the greatest action fought between seaplanes during the war. Both the British and the Germans lost two aircraft in the dogfight. The Dutch interned the crews of the downed British aircraft, including one American.[75] Infrequently, one of the Felixstowe-based American pilots claimed to have sighted and bombed a submarine, but no aircraft with Americans on board were officially credited with damaging or sinking U-boats.

The Americans had no luck with the so-called beef patrol. Two or three times a month small convoys of merchant vessels made trips from a British port to neutral Holland and back. Rumors had it that the ships carried good British beer to the Dutch and Dutch beef back to Great Britain. Felixstowe-based aircraft, including those with American aircrews, participated in the beef patrols, escorting the ships to and from Holland. They did not encounter enemy aircraft during these patrols.

In July, American aircraft from their recently commissioned station at Killingholme, joined the Spider Web patrols. Killingholme, at the mouth of the Humber River, was the site of a large British seaplane base before it was turned over to the U.S. Navy. Originally, the station was to be used to train American naval aircrews to bomb German naval bases. At a conference between Admirals Beatty and Benson early in November 1917, the Grand Fleet commander emphasized the need for aggressive action against the German submarine bases with aircraft. The CNO, who was enthusiastic about any action that would go after the "hornets in their nests," agreed to provide naval air support. Because the bases were beyond the range of aircraft flying from fields in Great Britain or France, an ambitious scheme was approved that called for the use of lighters (barges) to carry the aircraft to within range of their targets. The lighters were to be towed by destroyers to a designated spot where the planes were off-loaded from the lighter. An American pilot recalled that "The lighters were built so that they could let water in the back end of them, and this would make the tail end of the lighter sink." The planes rested on carriages that would roll into the water and disengage. In order to take off, an aviator wrote, "We had the destroyer go full speed in front of us to make the water rougher, because to break the suction of a sea plane taking off you must have enough bloom on the water to break that vacuum." After completing their mission, they would return to Killingholme. The British began to experiment with the use of lighters in September 1917. These flights were designed to permit British flying boats to extend their patrols into the Heligoland Bight and other territorial waters under German control. American naval aviators while attached to British squadrons at Felixstowe participated in what were called "lighter stunts." According to one of the American pilots, the lighter flights were popular with the aircrews.[76]

The Americans, however, were determined to use the lighters to launch "concentrated" squadron attacks against the German naval bases at Kiel, Wilhelmshaven, Hamburg, and Heligoland. The first operation was planned for April 1918, with Hamburg the target. The operation was delayed and later canceled because lighters and aircraft failed to arrive from the United States. The Department agreed to provide fifty flying boats and fifty lighters. They began arriving at the station in the summer. On July 30, the U.S. Navy formally assumed command of the Killingholme station. Some experiments were carried out with the American aircraft and lighters, but no combat operations were undertaken before the Armistice. In August, the British Admiralty abandoned the concept; intelligence determined that the Germans were aware of the lighter project and planned to use fast surface craft to disrupt the operations. An Admiralty official recommended, however, that "the Americans should be permitted to continue their efforts to develop their force for overseas bombing operations on which they set great store." He added that while they probably would not succeed "within measureable time . . . they will have had good training for operations of a more practicable nature."[77]

The Department and Sims's headquarters, primarily the aviation section, expended great time and energy in an attempt to get a bombing offensive underway, especially the so-called Northern Bombing Project. The scheme centered on the American naval air station at Dunkirk. Its importance lay in its location on the English Channel, the closest point in Allied territory to the submarine bases at Zeebrugge, Ostend, and Bruges. German submarines, upon leaving their Belgian bases, had to exit through the channel, which was shallow in that area, requiring the U-boats to remain on the surface vulnerable to attack. The Germans recognized that to defend their bases and submarines they had to maintain control of the air. Several squadrons of aircraft, both fighters and bombers, were concentrated in range of Dunkirk. They bombed the Dunkirk air stations frequently, nearly nightly when the weather permitted, and fighters patrolled the channel, attacking Allied aircraft, usually flying boats. Dunkirk was also within range of long-range guns, which shelled the town day and night.[78]

Dunkirk was extremely dangerous duty. The U.S. naval air station located in the city and on the harbor began flying operations at the beginning of January 1918, employing seventeen French flying boats. Even before then, U.S. naval aviators flew with French and British squadrons in the area to gain combat experience. Shortly after the station became operational, Captain Cone complained to a friend in the Office of Operations, that "we have the station at Dunkirk . . . but we have no pilots completely trained as fighters . . . and it would be little short of murder to send our pilots out against the Germans at this station." Because of this problem, he agreed to concentrate on operations against submarines rather than attacks on the bases. Patrols were limited to the channel off the French coast because the adjacent Belgian coast was too dangerous.

The flying boats flown by the American pilots were no match for the German fighters. After an inspection trip to Dunkirk, Captain Alfred Cunningham, USMC, recommended the dispatch of at least four Marine Corps fighter squadrons to Dunkirk to protect the flying boats. Commander John Towers, the assistant director of naval aviation in the Department, testified before the General Board that "no matter how many bombing machines we put out" to bomb the U-boat bases in Belgium, "if there are no [fighters] . . . there to protect them it is a useless sacrifice."[79]

American pilots at Dunkirk disliked the slow, obsolete French aircraft. Rest and relaxation were difficult to find because of the German shelling and bombing. "We get bombed every night," one naval officer wrote home, "but that isn't bad. The worst thing is that big gun up the line which shoots a shell five feet high, 17 inches in diameter, and weighing 1,900 pounds. Last night they shelled us from five-thirty until five this morning every three or four minutes. . . . That really is a bit hard on one's nerves." The bombardment affected the aircrews that had to get up before daylight for the dawn patrol. A pilot at Dunkirk wrote: "I've lived about thirty years in the past three weeks. . . . I've been on every kind of patrol—high and low—day and night. I've taken part in every kind of a stunt—good weather and bad. But I'm getting use to it, or else I'm dead tired, because I don't lie awake anymore, even when old 'Loegenboom' is busy dropping shells at the doorstep. This long-range shelling is a joke in the daytime, but it is perfectly awful at night, because old 'mournful Mary,' the town siren, is so fearfully regular and businesslike."[80]

American naval aviators were second to French and British squadrons in the Dunkirk area to fly land aircraft, often fighters called "small scouts." This assignment provided experience in going over the lines into German-occupied territory. Kenneth McLeish, one of the Yale volunteers, wrote his family in April 1918: "Cheer Ho! The whole gang of you. I am so happy I can't see straight. I'm actually on fighting patrols and I actually fly over Hun land. . . . We went way behind Hun lines. You could see the line stretching away in the distance, marked on either side by flecks of smoke from artillery and back aways, the captive balloons, mere specks so far down."

The first raids on the German naval air and naval bases were carried out while flying with the Allies. Sopwith Camels were rigged with small bombs and used in daylight assaults. On April 10, McLeish participated in a strike against Zeebrugge. It was supposed to be coordinated with a naval attack to block the mole and prevent U-boats from using the port. Although the naval assault was delayed, the air raid did take place. McLeish noted that anti-aircraft fire was so intense that he was unable to get close to the naval base and eventually dropped his bombs on another target. Two days later, seven RAF aircraft, carrying several American crew members, attempted a daylight raid. It was inconclusive because of anti-aircraft fire and a large number of German Albatross fighters,[81] but the American aviators gained combat experience that would help when the Northern Bombing Project finally became a reality.

The Northern Bombing Project was the most ambitious air operation conceived by the U.S. Navy during the war. If it had been carried out as planned, the operation would have involved a large number of aircraft and personnel. Some disagreements and vagueness clouded the origin of the project. The Department, especially Admiral Benson, was interested in any proposal for offensive operations against the German bases. This commitment led to the abortive effort to utilize lighters and the decision to develop Dunkirk into a major naval air station. Despite disappointing results from these efforts, the Navy remained committed to bomb the submarine bases. By the spring of 1918, it became a priority in the Department and the General Board. The force was to include thirty flying boats and two hundred land-based fighters. Initially the CNO, believing that the British would target the submarine bases with their aircraft, wanted to concentrate the group's aircraft over Dover and the English Channel. Marine land-based aircraft would protect American seaplanes on patrol. After conferences with the British, Sims and his staff urged Benson to approve round-the-clock bombing of the submarine bases by the Marines' aircraft because flying boats were too slow and vulnerable. The Department, while approving the concept of continuous bombing day and night, initially refused to abandon the use of floatplanes but later relented. The British hoped that the build-up of American naval air strength along the Dunkirk-Calais front would enable their squadrons to transfer elsewhere.[82]

Originally, the Northern Bombing Group (NBG) planned to operate with a day wing and a night wing, each consisting of six squadrons. In May, the Navy's failure to obtain sufficient aircraft resulted in a reduction to a total of eight squadrons, four night and four day. The Navy stopped the employment of flying boats and also fighter escorts at sea because none were available. Marine and Navy pilots were shifted to bombers. The RAF convinced Sims and his advisors that well-armed bombers flying in tight formations could effectively defend themselves against attacking enemy planes. The squadrons were to be located in the Dunkirk area with an assembly/supply base at Eastleigh, England. The initial force was taken from units already operating in European waters, but in June additional personnel began to arrive from the United States. Captain David Hanrahan, although not an aviator, was placed in charge. U.S. naval aviation in the Dunkirk area was at first under French command, but in June the Northern Bombing Group, including the station at Dunkirk, was transferred to the British vice admiral commanding at Dover. Pershing wanted to control all American "air activities" in the Dunkirk-Calais area, but Sims decided to maintain British naval command. The group was ready to begin flight operations in July, but they were yet to acquire aircraft. The group planned to use DeHavilland DH-4s for day bombing and the huge Italian three-engine Capronis for night operations.[83]

The Navy's decision to use land aircraft and attack land targets led to controversy with the Army. Although the War Department accepted Secretary Daniels's argument that submarine bases were legitimate targets for naval aircraft, the AEF's aviation staff opposed it. Pershing eventually acquiesced, but disagreements arose over the allocation of aircraft. The War Department finally agreed to turn over two hundred DH-4s being manufactured in the United States. When the first fifty-two were assembled in June at Pauillac, they were discovered to be seriously defective, so much so that they had to be returned to the United States. The others were never delivered. The British provided DH-9s in their place. The Navy had even more trouble with the Capronis intended for night operations. In order to obtain them, the Navy agreed to provide the Italians with raw materials shipped directly from the United States. The Italians promised at least two hundred of the night bombers. Nineteen were eventually delivered, but only eight were flown to naval stations in France. The rest were either unable to fly or lost en route. Those that reached their destination were unreliable because of faulty engines and other structural weaknesses, according to American inspectors.[84]

By the middle of August, the Northern Bombing Group still lacked day bombers and had only a few defective Capronis to conduct night operations. Sims's aviation staff seriously considered cancellation of the project but finally agreed to proceed, using any type of appropriate aircraft.[85] On the night of August 15, a single Caproni, the only one flyable, bombed the submarine pens at Ostend. This raid was merely a token gesture; combat missions utilizing both day and night squadrons did not begin for nearly two months. Until then the Navy and Marine aviators assigned to the Northern Bombing Group flew with British squadrons. A few of them flew American-built DH-4s and British-built DH-9s, which began arriving at the group's fields in September. Within a few weeks, however, they stopped bombing the submarine bases in Belgium. The great Allied offensive late in September and early October forced the German armies to abandon their last positions in France and Belgium. This withdrawal sacrificed their naval and air bases in Belgium. Railroads, canal locks, supply and ammunition dumps, and airfields took their place as targets. With this change in mission, control of the group passed from the Royal Navy to the British army and later to Marshal Ferdinand Foch, in command of the Allied armies. On November 4, Sims ordered Captain Hanrahan to report to the marshal "for duty when his command is ready in all respects to begin offensive operations." He apparently did not comply with this order before the Armistice. At that time, the group still had only thirty-five aircraft, six Capronis, twelve DH-4s, and seventeen DH-9s, of which approximately half were operable. Its complement of personnel was nearly full strength, including a force of 250 officers and 2,400 enlisted men in northern France and approximately the same number at the Eastleigh repair station.[86]

The Navy's other mission, antisubmarine patrol and escort operations, was not neglected during the last six months of the war despite the priority of attacks on the submarine bases. During this period, naval officers in Washington and London debated the advantage of land planes versus seaplanes and whether to abandon the latter in favor of the former. It was generally agreed that on a one-to-one basis land planes were superior to seaplanes. Allied flying boats could not stand up to German land aircraft. In a personal letter to the director of naval aviation in August 1918, Captain Cone wrote, "I am of the opinion that it will not be very long before we will restrict very greatly the use of seaplanes and use land machines for many things for which we use seaplanes at this time."[87] Yet the Department continued to insist on the use of seaplanes. However, Cone's recommendation was carried out in areas where German land aircraft challenged American naval aircraft. In the middle of September, the Navy abandoned the air station at Dunkirk and transferred the float planes stationed there to Pauillac.

Despite the argument that land planes could replace flying boats engaged in patrol and escort, seaplanes carried out these operations until the Armistice. The British adopted the use of frequent patrols to force U-boats below the surface and keep them there, making it extremely difficult for submarines to surface in daytime. The Americans used the same tactic in the English Channel, the Irish coast, and the Bay of Biscay. This approach became increasingly effective in 1918, when the Germans shifted their underwater operations mostly to coastal waters.

During the last two weeks in September, members of Sims's staff, including Cone, held a series of meetings with officials of the Admiralty and the French air ministry to decide air policy for 1919. They endorsed the policy followed up to that time. The Americans decided not to build new air stations; to maintain their naval air strength in England and Ireland at the existing level; and to continue concentration on the bombing offensive. However, Cone noted in a letter to Captain Noble Irwin, director of naval aviation: "The trend of affairs here is undoubtedly toward the practical abandonment of the patrol method of anti-submarine campaign with aircraft, and the adoption of the escort of convoys. In other words, following exactly the experience of the surface craft . . . the great amount of effort of miles flown on patrol is not sufficiently productive in submarines sighted and bombed." Cone's information came almost entirely from data provided by the Admiralty based on intelligence relating to German submarine operations in the North Sea and the channel. Late in September, U-boat activity in those areas diminished to a mere trickle of its operation a year earlier. Robert Grant points out that German submarines remained a serious threat as they passed through the North Sea Mine Barrage into the Atlantic. American naval aircraft continued patrols and convoy escorts off the Irish coast and the Bay of Biscay to the Armistice.

In July, the Navy began to experiment with joint air-surface operations against U-boats. Although the primitive nature of air-to-surface communications created serious problems of coordination, the Department approved the tactical employment of subchasers and flying boats in antisubmarine operations. This tactic did not produce an attack against a German submarine.[88]

Patrol and escort work at sea was tedious, but with the exception of the English Channel off the French/Belgian coasts, it was not extremely dangerous, although often uncomfortable. World War I aircraft had open cockpits and lacked heating apparatus. They encountered rain, fog, mist, and bone-chilling cold. Kenneth MacLeish wrote his family in April 1918 of the "torture" he endured when flying at thousands of feet above the surface. "I had on a pair of silk gloves next to my hands, a pair of rubber gloves over that, and then a pair of fur-lined, fur-covered flying gloves. To my mind that combination is the warmest possible, yet I froze two fingers absolutely solid, and my thumb and one other finger were frost-bitten. The altitude gave me the worst headache I've ever had. . . . [It] affected me strangely. At first it was nauseating, then I felt weak and dizzy. . . . The veins around my ears expanded enormously at every heartbeat, and cut off my hearing entirely, so that when my heart throbbed I couldn't even hear the terrific roar of my motor." He later talked about a nose, lips, and cheeks so frozen that they "all turned brown and peeled off." At times the oil in the machine guns, gauges on the instrument panel, and alcohol mixture in the compass froze, but he added, "by George, I wouldn't give it up for all the love, money, and marbles on earth."[89]

Patrols over the channel and missions over hostile territory were far more hazardous for the American naval aviators than other activities. Combat occurred frequently over Flanders and the coastal waters near Dunkirk because the Germans fiercely contested control of the air in those areas. Aircraft and crews were lost, primarily because of human error and their unreliable airplanes. MacLeish was killed in October in a dogfight with a number of Fokkers. Surprisingly, only eight officers and eleven enlisted became casualties, and only two naval aviators were made prisoners of war. Most of the casualties were not killed in action. One naval aviator, David Ingalls, became an ace, downing five German aircraft and a kite balloon. A few others, including MacLeish, shot down one or two, but American naval aviators destroyed fewer than two dozen enemy aircraft. Seaplanes on patrol or convoy escort had no opportunity to down hostile aircraft, but their accomplishments were more impressive than those of the naval pilots who destroyed German planes and balloons. After the establishment of coastal air stations, German U-boats off the west coast of France failed to attack air-escorted convoys successfully. During the last ten months of the war, only three ships were torpedoed or destroyed in the area between Penmarch and Ile d'Neu patrolled by American naval aircraft. Previously the toll averaged one Allied ship per day.[90]

The American naval air effort was small in comparison to its allies, but as Paul G. Halpern wrote, it expanded rapidly during the latter months of the war. The Navy used twenty bases in the war zone manned by twenty thousand officers and men. The Allies in great part furnished their aircraft and balloons, but American-built planes arrived in increasing numbers during the fall months. Following the British example, a temporary deck was built on the turrets of the battleship *Texas* to experiment with aircraft. Like other aspects of U.S. naval activities in European waters, aviation grew rapidly at the time of the Armistice.[91]

Less than three months before the Armistice was signed, Assistant Secretary of the Navy Roosevelt, making a fact-finding mission to Europe, reported to Daniels that naval aviation was by far the most troublesome activity of the U.S. Navy in European waters. Much difficulty stemmed from logistical failure. Aircraft, spare parts, and equipment arrived slowly, and when they appeared, they were often damaged or defective. Roosevelt blamed a large part of the difficulties on the fact that naval aviation was sort of an orphan with an "indistinct and indefinite relationship . . . between [it] . . . and the different bureaus." He reported to Admiral Sims essentially the same observations. The force commander appointed a board, called the "Westervelt Board" after its head, Commander George Westervelt, to investigate the aviation problem. The board's report stressed the absence of prewar planning, dependency upon the Allies and the U.S. Army, and chaotic transportation. The crux of the problem lay in Washington; too little was done to correct deficiencies.[92]

Nonaviators such as Captains Hutch Cone and David C. Hanrahan took command of U.S. naval aviation in the war zone. Even air stations were commanded by youthful and inexperienced reservists. An ensign commanded NAS Queenstown in part because senior officers with aviation experience were not available but also because most flag officers, including Sims, possessed little or no understanding of aircraft and their role in naval warfare. Sims placed Hanrahan in command of the Northern Bombing Group after the *Santee* fiasco.

The Q-ship *Santee* was the most misguided U.S. naval effort in European waters during the war. Although the German navy introduced the Q-ship concept, the British navy adopted it and gained some success with it in antisubmarine warfare. The Q-ships were usually tramp steamers, intentionally designed to appear inoffensive and as easy prey. Although British-manned Q-ships (called "queer ships" by sailors) destroyed an impressive number of German submarines during the early years of the war, they had become ineffective when the United States entered the conflict. By then German submarine commanders were far more proficient at recognizing them. Sixteen Q-ships were lost to submarine attacks in 1917.[93] Nevertheless, the naval conference in London during September 1917 recommended the continued use of decoy ships. Several weeks earlier, Sims urged the dispatch of a "mystery" ship and two submarines to the Azores, but, according to Sims, a request from personnel in the Destroyer Flotilla at Queenstown precipitated the decision to outfit a Q-ship. The idea was to take volunteers from the flotilla to man the ship. Sims recommended it and arranged the possible loan of a Q-ship from the Royal Navy. The Department gave its approval, and on October 23, Sims informed Captain Pringle that HMS *Pargust* was to be turned over to the American Navy for this purpose. "It is desired," Sims wrote, "that every ship of the Force be represented in the complement [of 75] as finally selected."[94]

Nevertheless, Captain Hanrahan, the ship's commanding officer, selected his officers "from among his friends" in the Destroyer Flotilla. Admiral Moore later recalled, "He wanted people who would be good-natured, extroverts, able to get to sea and to stay for months at a time, and all to act their part properly as a Q-boat officer." Some of the flotilla captains were quite irritated at Hanrahan. Taussig, in some relief, wrote in his journal, "No officers on the *Wadsworth* [his ship] volunteered to go." "Tip" Merrill noted: "My application went in to-day. Not that I want to go to her—I certainly don't—but a call for volunteers is a dare and I am too weak not to take a dare."[95] Hanrahan, however, had no trouble in quickly filling his complement of officers and men. Too many volunteered, including forty enlisted men from *Wadsworth* alone.

A native of Chicago, Hanrahan entered the Naval Academy in 1894 and later followed the normal ship-to-shore rotation of duty stations. In 1910, he was promoted to lieutenant commander and ordered to command the destroyer *Balch*. A full commander in 1917, he took command of USS *Cushing* and Division 7, Destroyer Force, Atlantic Fleet. His division followed the initial American destroyer division to Queenstown, arriving on May 24. For six months, *Cushing* performed patrol and convoy escort work. According to Taussig, Hanrahan requested the Q-boat assignment.[96] Despite Hanrahan's flair, reminiscent of Halsey, he was one of the few destroyer captains under Sims who did not become rear admirals.

Nicknamed the "Iron Duke," Hanrahan exhibited a paradoxical nature. Taussig was not too fond of him and his "overbearing personality." Yet Sims commended Hanrahan as a "tower of strength," and Bayly honored him by flying his admiral's flag in *Cushing* for the first time on an American ship. Admiral Moore later remembered that Hanrahan "hasn't changed a bit. Just as unpopular. Just as popular. Just as wild, jolly, bad-tempered, violent and mild as ever. That was just the kind of a person he was." Moore considered him a good organizer and disciplinarian. "We were really all quite fond of Dave Hanrahan in spite of his peculiarities." MacLeish, who later came under the Iron Duke's command, agreed with Moore: "He's the most fascinating character in the Navy. I've never seen a man with so much personal magnetism. He has marvelous Irish humor, and he's always on the go. He hasn't any idea what he's doing, but he's always doing something, and he always gets balled up."[97] *Santee* was one of those "ball ups."

Hanrahan named the Q-ship *Santee* after an old sailing frigate laid down in 1820 that became a school ship and later barracks ship at the Naval Academy before she sank at her moorings in 1912. When the Americans took over *Pargust* on the eve of Thanksgiving 1917, the British had already fitted her out as a Q-ship. Hanrahan made a few modifications including the installation of a periscope disguised as a stovepipe, which enabled a member of the crew below decks to make observations. Commander Gordon Campbell, the most successful Q-ship captain in the Royal Navy, inspected the *Santee* and later wrote: "She was the very last word in fitting out. I had the honour of being invited to go over her and make comments, but it was impossible to suggest any possible improvements."[98]

The "improvements" were of little or no use, for *Santee*'s shakedown cruise out of Queenstown on December 27 was her only venture to sea. Sims wrote his wife, "this is the shortest cruise of this kind on record." While underway for Bantry Bay to begin training, a German submarine torpedoed her. In a typical Q-boat tactic, Hanrahan immediately launched his lifeboats with the "panic party." The German U-boat commander, wise to these tactics, did not surface. When it became obvious that the ruse has failed, the lifeboat party was recalled, and the damaged vessel was towed stern-first back into Queenstown. A damage report later concluded that the *Santee* had remained afloat because her hold was full of lumber.

The Q-ship never again made a cruise under American command. In March 1918, at Hanrahan's recommendation, the ship was returned to the Royal Navy. The officers and men of the destroyer flotilla regretted the failure. Moore said: "Well Hanrahan was the joke of the town. He had sworn that he would shave his mustache if anything of this sort happened to him. So, he appeared without a moustache."[99] Shortly after *Santee* was decommissioned, Hanrahan was appointed to command the Northern Bombing Group.

In postwar inquiries, the British and American navies recognized the significant role of convoying in the defeat of the submarines but also concluded that offensive operations against the U-boats would have been far more effective if some of the weapons had been perfected such as mines, hydrophones, and suitable "hunting craft," including aircraft. They were convinced that in time the hunter-killer concept would have become increasingly successful. Although this conclusion was debatable, no one questioned Sims's statement in a circular letter sent throughout the force in September 1918 that "the prewar belief that submarines were very vulnerable has been disapproved in the most unmistakable manner."[100]

The Mediterranean

On August 16, 1917, the gunboat *Sacramento* entered Gibraltar. She was the first of a large contingent of American warships assigned to operate out of the British fortress. Its responsibility was to patrol the waters leading to Gibraltar from both the Atlantic and the Mediterranean. When convoying was extended to cover the routes to Gibraltar and into the Mediterranean, the *Sacramento* and other American vessels at Gibraltar became escorts. American presence in the Mediterranean expanded with the arrival of subchasers in the Adriatic and aviation units in northern Italy.[1]

The Mediterranean Sea was quite familiar to the United States Navy. As early as 1801, an American naval squadron cruised that sea. Warships flying the Stars and Stripes would periodically venture into those waters. Shortly before Congress declared war in April 1917, the cruiser *Des Moines* left the Mediterranean. Four months later, *Sacramento* dropped anchor in Gibraltar.

On the day after *Sacramento* arrived, the cruiser *Birmingham* with Rear Admiral Henry B. Wilson on board entered the harbor. The Navy Department appointed Wilson to the command of "The U.S. Patrol Forces Based on Gibraltar." The Navy Department, however, officially designated the force there as "Squadron Two, Patrol Force, U.S. Atlantic Fleet." The Navy Department also placed Wilson in command of U.S. naval forces operating in French waters, but Sims separated the two upon the arrival of the yachts at Brest under Fletcher. At a meeting with the senior officer at Gibraltar, it was agreed that the American naval vessels would escort convoys "both east and west of here"—that is, in both the Mediterranean and the Atlantic.[2]

Other units arrived regularly: the gunboats *Nashville* on August 18, *Machias* and *Castine* on August 22, along with *Wheeling* and *Paducah* and six Coast Guard cutters, *Ossipee*, *Seneca*, *Manning*, *Yamacraw*, *Algonquin*, and *Tampa*. The gunboats were in the Gulf of Mexico because of the Mexican situation when the United States entered the war. They were recalled to their base in New Orleans, fitted out for distance service, and, after refueling in Norfolk, sailed independently for Gibraltar. By September 1, the Patrol Force numbered thirteen vessels. Additional units deployed to Gibraltar, including a squadron of five obsolete destroyers nicknamed "the dirty five."[3] In December, the yachts began to arrive—*Druid*, *Wenonah*, *Arcturus*, *Lydonia*, *Cythera*, and *Venetia*. The latter vessel came from San Francisco by way of the Panama Canal and New York. It escorted subchasers across the Atlantic and, upon arrival at Gibraltar, reported for escort duty within twenty-four hours.[4] In 1918, the force reached forty-one vessels with 314 officers and 4,660 enlisted personnel. Wilson's tour at Gibraltar soon came to an end. On November 25, 1917, he was ordered to the command of U.S. naval forces at Brest, France.

His relief was Rear Admiral Albert P. Niblack. A native of Indiana, he graduated in 1880 from the Naval Academy, where he roomed with Sims.[5] "Nibs," as he was known in the service, had a most diverse career. His first ship command was the steam tug *Iroquois* in 1903–4. From 1907 to 1910, he commanded training vessels at the Naval Academy and then the cruiser *Tacoma*. In 1913, the recently promoted captain took command of the battleship *Michigan*. While in this command, he participated in the attack on Vera Cruz in April 1914. In the years preceding the U.S. intervention in World War I, he returned to the Naval War College, served on the General Board, and commanded a division of battleships. He was promoted to rear admiral in August 1917.

His peers characterized Niblack as witty, affable, and cheerful. He also had a reputation as an author, having published frequently in the U.S. Naval Institute *Proceedings*. Niblack was a favorite of Secretary of the Navy Daniels, partly because "Nibs" was interested in improving the lot of enlisted men, particularly career petty officers. He often talked about giving them more privileges such as overnight liberty if they accepted the responsibilities associated with these privileges. For example, commanding officers usually refused to permit liberty on the day before a ship coaled, but Niblack did so while in command of *Michigan* with impressive results.[6] He was popular with enlisted personnel but had difficulty with certain officers. Sims wrote him a confidential "personal" letter while Niblack was in Gibraltar, informing him that his staff had received an unusually large number of communications from officers complaining about him. The Gibraltar force commander defended himself, but it is true that there were more requests for transfers from Gibraltar than in other commands in the European theater.[7]

Niblack enjoyed a successful tour as commander of U.S. naval forces in Gibraltar. Sims told him in no uncertain terms that cooperation with the Allies meant that he must subordinate his command to British naval authorities. He accepted this injunction without a murmur. On several occasions, he boasted to Admiral Sims that he had no responsibility for command decisions: "Hardly a day passes that Admiral [Heathcote] Grant, [British senior naval officer at Gibraltar] does not telegraph, or make some suggestion to Malta, with regard to orders that are issued in the Mediterranean. I keep my fingers out of the pie almost entirely. As far as I am concerned, the situation is personally not at all difficult, it is very pleasant." Niblack later testified before the Naval Investigation Committee that "The allied forces [in the Mediterranean] . . . were under the command of Admiral Gauchet, of the French Navy at Corfu. To that extent I was under him. Vice Admiral [Sir Somerset Arthur Gough] Calthorpe, at Malta, was in charge of the Mediterranean convoy system, and to that extent I was on . . . [his] staff." Niblack reported to Calthorpe through Grant. This chain of command worked well, at least from Niblack's perspective. Sims later accused Niblack of anti-British sentiments, but he showed no such prejudice while he was in command at Gibraltar. In his testimony before the Naval Investigation Committee, he mentioned his harmonious relations with the British. "Nothing . . . could have exceeded the friendly spirit of co-operation and helpfulness of the British naval and military authorities, and all our relations with the allied forces were free from friction or 'holding back' from cordial co-operation," he wrote later. The British were apparently quite happy with him. Niblack told Sims that Grant was "an extremely able man and our relations could not be more satisfactory." Later he confided to Sims: "We all have our little jokes and mine is always with Admiral Grant. He takes me aside about every ten days and gives me a heart-to-heart talk about what he is going to do with the Brazilian Squadron, the submarine chasers, the listening devices, the radiotelephones, the Ford Boats, and the new destroyers. I always laugh and say that I never cook a rabbit until I catch it."[8]

Niblack was responsible for the American warships operating out of Gibraltar, escorting convoys in the Atlantic and the Mediterranean. After January 1918, a commission of officers at Malta under Admiral Calthorpe formulated policies for the Mediterranean, including Gibraltar. Until the fall, the U.S. Navy did not have an official member of the commission, although Captain Richard Leigh briefly worked with it. Niblack told Sims that he acted as an unofficial member of the commission because Calthorpe at times asked for his advice. "To my mind," the Gibraltar commander wrote Sims, "he is satisfied that we do not have any liaison officer at Malta and feels that the present arrangement is best."[9] More than likely Niblack had heard that Sims wished to send a senior naval officer to Malta. He had already informed the force commander that he was "willing to go there or stay here.[10]

Sims had other intentions. On July 28, he suggested to the CNO that because of the rapidly increasing American naval presence in the Mediterranean, "it is very desirable that we have an officer of flag rank stationed with the other similar officers at Malta with the Commander-in-Chief." He went on to state that he did not favor appointing this officer to the command of all U.S. naval forces in the Mediterranean; the appointee should be junior to Niblack, who was "doing well at Gibraltar." The Admiralty approved this arrangement, and on August 17, the Department transferred Captain W.H.G. Bullard from command of the battleship *Arkansas* to Malta with the rank of temporary rear admiral. The Department went a step further than Sims's recommendation and designated Malta as Base Number 28 with Bullard in command while serving as liaison officer with Admiral Calthorpe.

Bullard arrived in Malta on August 23.[11] No American warships were stationed there, and no facilities were established before the Armistice. Bullard was ordered to the Adriatic shortly before the Armistice. Niblack remained the senior U.S. naval officer in the Mediterranean until the end of the war.

The command situation at Gibraltar seemed to work well, but as with other commands under Sims, occasional problems came to the surface. Admiral Benson in a meeting agreed to divert the five destroyers assigned to the Mediterranean (coming from the Philippines) to Italian waters. The British and French, however, preferred to use them to reinforce the Americans at Gibraltar and serve as escorts. Admiral Wilson, shortly after taking the Gibraltar command, told the Italian liaison officer there that he was willing to use his gunboats to escort convoys from Gibraltar to Genoa and even to send vessels under his command to the Adriatic. Sims insisted that all recommendations for the deployment of American vessels in the European command were to pass through him and to be decided upon by the Allied Naval Council.[12] Niblack apparently made no effort to assign his ships to particular responsibilities, leaving the decision to Sims and Grant, working through the Admiralty.

The command structure in the Mediterranean was confused and extremely controversial. . . . Although Niblack was apparently in accordance with the Gibraltar command, some evidence suggests that Admiral Grant's command was not satisfactory to the officers commanding British warships that used the base and at times to the British Mediterranean commander in chief. Niblack several times insisted to Sims that he and Grant got along well, but he admitted that relations were strained between Gibraltar and Malta. He informed Sims of "a very lamentable lack of similarity in views between here and Malta, much in my opinion, to the disadvantage of Malta, where this station is regarded as an adjunct to be stripped to furnish the means to carry on operations in that region." Nevertheless, relations between Grant and Admiral Calthorpe were fairly satisfactory.[13]

Throughout the war, naval command in the Mediterranean remained a hodgepodge. Until Italy entered the war in the fall of 1915, the British and French controlled Allied activity. The French concentrated their naval force in the Mediterranean, leaving the Atlantic coast unprotected, and the Royal Navy maintained a sizeable fleet in the region. French Vice Admiral Dominique Gauchet was technically in command of Allied naval forces operating in the Mediterranean, but neither nation was willing to subordinate its fleet under a unified command. As Marder wrote, "the villain was the parochial mind . . . a symptom of the disease called national prestige."[14]

The entry of Italy as an ally exacerbated the situation. The Treaty of London signed in 1915 promised Italy, among other things, substantial land along the Adriatic Sea, if it entered the war on the Allied side. Italy did so, with the proviso that for the remainder of the war she would ensure naval command of the Adriatic Sea. The Italian government stubbornly resisted every effort by the Allies to create a unified naval command in the Mediterranean, including the Adriatic. The Italian navy willingly sacrificed naval collaboration in the Mediterranean to maintain control in the Adriatic, seeking to make significant gains in the area at the expense of Austria-Hungary. The British divided the Mediterranean into naval districts with flag officers in charge who often preferred independence, which at times affected cooperation. This attitude of independence was very much to the advantage of German and Austro-Hungarian submarines. Marder held that "Each Admiral did the best for his own area and cared little about his neighbor's problem."[15] In July 1918, a partial solution to the command problem came about when the Allied naval authorities agreed to the appointment of a British vice admiral to command all of the British naval forces in the Mediterranean and head a central authority at Malta with the responsibility of managing the convoy system in that sea. Because of Admiral Gauchet's decision to remain in Corfu with his battle fleet, the British vice admiral at Malta assumed control of the antisubmarine war in the Mediterranean.[16]

The American Naval Planning Section in London rather naively suggested the appointment of an American admiral as C-in-C of all naval forces in the Adriatic. Sims passed this proposition to the Department. Benson approved it, and it was brought before the Allied Naval Council, where the Italian representative strongly opposed it. Although never pressed to the point where it might cause a confrontation with the Italians, the Americans were definitely interested in making the Adriatic an American command. The United States was prepared to deploy a powerful force there if the Allied Naval Council approved its recommendations, but Italy would never have agreed to give up control of the Adriatic.

The Allied Naval Council was established in November 1917 to a great degree because of the Mediterranean problem. Both British and French naval officials persuaded Admiral Benson that such a body might "induce the Italians to use their vessels to the best possible advantage for the common cause." The council would hold a number of sessions during the war. It was "a very useful institution through which the Allied and Associated Powers arranged those over-all naval plans on which they were able to agree." Nonetheless, the council was without executive powers and generally failed to solve the problems in the Mediterranean Sea. Almost from its inception, Sims considered the Mediterranean situation, especially the issues involving Italy, the "most troublesome question" that the council would have to handle. In April, after attending a meeting of the council, Sims confided to Benson that "the trouble is that the Italians distrust both the French and British very seriously." He could have added the Americans, but Italo-American relations were not as strained then as they were later. After subsequent meetings, he wrote that the disagreements with the Italian representative at the meetings of the naval council had gotten so heated "that it makes any naval conferences more or less a farce in so far as concerns such essential questions as unity of command and unity of effort in the Mediterranean."[17]

The Italian government was determined to acquire the vast areas promised in the Treaty of London. To accomplish this end, the Italian navy in the Adriatic was to remain on the defensive throughout the war, avoiding the possibility of being defeated by the Austro-Hungarian fleet. Despite many efforts by the Allies to persuade them to assume the offensive, the Italians refused to comply. Commander C. R. Train, U.S. naval attaché in Rome, was convinced that the government believed it would fall should Italy suffer a naval defeat in the Adriatic. After a "prolonged and heated" discussion in June 1918, the British General Douglas Haig remarked: "Their [the Italian representatives] objective seemed to be to stay in port and keep their fleet safe. I was disgusted with their attitude."[18] During the meeting, the American General Tasker H. Bliss was asked what all the shouting was about. He replied, "[T]hey are all at sea except the Italian admiral who won't go there." Lord M.P.A. Hankey, secretary to the British Committee of Imperial Defense, said: "Revel [the Italian representative on the council] was an altogether contemptible person. Yesterday he distinguished himself by saying that he could not join the Italian fleet at Taranto with the French fleet at Corfu, because the voyage between the two ports was too dangerous for ships going to and fro to dock."[19] The Italians would not accept a foreigner as supreme commander of naval activities in the Mediterranean if the arrangement included the Adriatic. They refused to reduce their fleet in the Adriatic to augment operations elsewhere, including convoying. Vice Admiral Thaon di Revel was the major architect and proponent of this policy. As both chief of staff and C-in-C of the fleet, he was by far the most powerful figure in the Italian navy. He became a thorn in the side of the Allies and the United States because of his championship of Italy's naval policy. Sims considered him an obstructionist, confiding to Benson that he did not believe the Italian navy would accomplish anything of significance until Revel was removed from his positions.

The United States had limited interests in the Mediterranean until December 1917, when it declared war on Austria-Hungary. Nonetheless, the command issue affected the American navy and its operations in the Mediterranean. Niblack observed to Sims: "Unfortunately unity of command is not yet fully attained in the Mediterranean where five navies are working, without counting the Greeks and Brazilians which also are coming. . . . In some of my recent official letters I have tried to indicate how many compromises have to be made in the Mediterranean on account of the different interests. . . . [T]here is not the slightest friction here in any way with the British, but the Italian and British relations are rather difficult."[20] Nibs stayed out of it, but other American officials in Washington and London did not.

The Navy Department strongly favored a unified command in the Mediterranean, believing that it would lead to more aggressive action on the part of the Allied navies, particularly the Italian. Daniels instructed Sims to push for it in the Allied Naval Council and requested the secretary of state to pressure the Italian government. According to Daniels, President Wilson told the secretary of state to talk with the Italian ambassador and "tell him how embarrassing it was." Nelson Page, the American ambassador to Italy, took up the matter with Sidney Sonnino, the Italian foreign minister. He vacillated, informing Page that he "had nothing against the idea of a single commander . . . provided that a regard . . . and liberty of action . . . be left to [the] commander of all Italian Navy touching operations in the Adriatic."[21]

Assistant Secretary of the Navy Franklin D. Roosevelt tried to persuade the Italian government to accept a British admiral as supreme commander in the Mediterranean. Roosevelt asked Daniels to allow him to go to Europe and observe the activities of the Navy. He was finally permitted to make the trip in July 1918. After meetings with Lord Balfour and Geddes, he wrote to Daniels, "As you know the Italians have refused to play ball in the Mediterranean situation, and after I look over the lay of the land a little more, I think I can determine whether it would be a good thing to go to Rome."[22] He decided to go, partly because Geddes asked him to do so but also because of his overweening confidence that he could get the Italians to cooperate. After all, he wrote his boss, "the Italians may not love us, but at least they know that we have no ulterior designs in the Mediterranean."[23] He arrived in Rome on August 8, and for three days he met with senior officials from the foreign minister to Admiral Revels. His efforts were unsuccessful and might have been somewhat detrimental. He evidently irritated some Italian officials, including the naval chief of staff, despite his view that the Adriatic should remain under Italian control.

Roosevelt puzzled the Italians and the French, who wondered who he was and whether his ideas reflected American policy. Both governments suspected that the British were using Roosevelt. The French went so far as to query their minister in Washington about Roosevelt and his mission. The French government was particularly annoyed at Roosevelt's support of Lord Jellicoe to become supreme commander in the Mediterranean. Daniels had to assure the secretary of state that his assistant was not authorized to "say who command[ed]." He was allowed only to indicate that the United States supported the concept of a supreme commander. Neither the naval secretary nor President Wilson was pleased with Roosevelt's foray into diplomacy. It may have been an "education" for FDR, as one writer put it, but it was also an embarrassment.[24]

The Italian attitude toward the United States involved a contradiction. President Wilson's well-publicized fourteen points of peace and other pronouncements alarmed the government, but they desperately wanted American products and war supplies. They would have preferred American materials without their presence in the Adriatic, but when they realized that the United States was going to join the fight, they reluctantly requested American aircraft, warships, and even troops. This activity grew after the disaster at Caporetto in the fall of 1917, when the Italian northern front collapsed under German/Austro-Hungarian pressure. Caporetto influenced President Wilson's decision to ask for a declaration of war against the Austro-Hungarian Empire. Congress agreed and declared war on December 10, 1917. As winter approached, the Italians found themselves desperately short of fuel, especially coal. The General Board was informed that the Italians had threatened to withdraw from the war if they did not receive sufficient deliveries of coal. An American naval aviator at Porto Corsini wrote his parents: "We'll have no fires this winter. Coal costs $112.00 per ton; there is no wood."[25] The Italian crisis also persuaded the Navy Department to send additional help such as ships and aircraft. The CNO, however, was concerned: if the United States sent assistance, "it commits us to a policy of active participation in operations in and around the Mediterranean Sea." Benson understood that contributing substantial aid to Italy was clearly as much a political as a military action because it might result in clashes with Austro-Hungarian military/naval units, although the United States was not at war with Austria-Hungary at that time. The Italian government continued to the end of the war to request the presence of additional American warships in the Mediterranean to provide escorts for convoys. A few tugboats were sent to Genoa and later Naples, but the Italian request for subchasers and yachts was turned down. Most of the promised aid never reached Italy because of construction delays and differing priorities.[26]

The Mediterranean situation remained awkward for the rest of the conflict and into the immediate postwar months. Nonetheless, cooperation on an operational level was successful, particularly in connection with the Otranto Barrage, convoy work out of Gibraltar, and aviation.

The Italian catastrophe at Caporetto occurred when Admiral Benson, a member of the House Mission, was en route to Europe. Undoubtedly, the possibility of an Italian collapse weighed heavily upon many of the Allied officials that he met in Europe. Benson instructed Sims to investigate the possibility of providing military aide, including aviation. Evidently the government in Rome asked for naval personnel to man certain Italian stations. The Italians were prepared to train U.S. pilots for duty on the Western Front. To determine exactly what the Italians were proposing, Lieutenant

John Lansing Callan was ordered to Rome in December.[27] Callan discovered that the Italian head of naval aviation, Captain L. de Filippi, was willing to accept Americans to train as aviators, but he expected them to serve in Italy. He also strongly urged that the United States Navy assume operational control of two or three seaplane bases. The Italian navy would furnish the aircraft, spare parts, and equipment.

Callan inspected the three proposed stations, all on the Adriatic. He opposed the occupation of a base designed to handle eighty large Caproni bombers, considering commitments in France. However, he liked the other two located at Porto Corsini and Pescara and advised Captain Cone to take them over.[28] Three months passed before the Department approved Callan's recommendation. Benson and Sims were reluctant to act because of the emphasis placed on establishing the Northern Bombing Group. They also wanted to make sure that the Italians would provide the needed aircraft and support.[29] In April, Sims recommended acquisition of the two stations, and Benson consented on May 8.

Callan was appointed to command U.S. naval aviation forces in Italy, but in October Commander Charles R. Train, the naval attaché in Rome, relieved him. Train retained both positions until the end of the war. Operational control, however, fell to the Italian vice admiral commanding at Venice.[30] Both Callan and Train unsuccessfully urged the acquisition of additional stations.

The Italian navy had a pilot training school on Lake Bolsena, sixty miles north of Rome. Although the Department delayed occupation of the two operational stations, it agreed to assume control of the training facility. In February, the Italians transferred the station to the United States. The first group of seventy-three trainees arrived soon. Although most of those trained at Lake Bolsena served in France, about seventy remained in Italy and flew with the American contingents there.[31]

The station at Pescara never became operational, but the one at Porto Corsini became a thriving American city known to the sailors who were stationed there as "Goat Island City."[32] The first detachment of 331 men arrived in Porto Corsini in July 1918. It was located at the mouth of a canal about ten miles from Ravenna and seventy from Venice. Flight operations from this base were difficult. Flying boats had to take off and land on a narrow canal that was approximately a hundred feet wide.[33]

The Navy's mission at Porto Corsini was to bomb Pola and Trieste at night and also to drop leaflets during the day. The pilots also made weekly photographic flights over the two Austro-Hungarian ports and flew routine patrols along the coast to guard against surprise attacks by Austro-Hungarian warships. The station never had more than twenty-one aircraft to carry out its missions, approximately half of them operational at a given time. Austro-Hungarian aircraft frequently raided Porto Corsini, but, although the attacks disrupted sleep, they did not inflict any casualties.

Occasionally the opposing aircraft engaged in dogfights over the Adriatic. Late in July, seven Austro-Hungarian pursuit planes attacked five American planes, two bombers and three fighters. One Austro-Hungarian fighter was shot down, and an American seaplane was forced to ditch in the water. Fortunately, another plane in his flight landed and rescued the pilot. In retaliation, the Austro-Hungarians bombed the station that night. During the next four days, both sides tried to bomb each other out of existence, the most intense operation undertaken by a U.S. naval aviation unit during the war.[34] The unit spent September and October raiding and scouting Pola and other Austro-Hungarian ports. In October, the Italian naval air force and the Americans launched a combined raid of forty-three aircraft on Pola, avoiding losses despite heavy anti-aircraft fire. By the last week in October, however, Austria-Hungary sought an Armistice, which was signed on November 4.

Gibraltar was the hub of the Atlantic-Mediterranean convoy system. More than a "convenient coaling station, hospital, and minor fitting base for the Royal Navy," it provided a gateway through which passed one-fourth of Allied shipping during the war.[35] Admiral Grant, the British naval commander at Gibraltar, wrote afterward that "in general, Gibraltar presented a somewhat unique position during the war, being the 'clapham [sic] junction' of all convoys to and from the Mediterranean and being neighbored by the coast of a neutral country, Spain, to the northward, and to the southward by the coast of Morocco, neutral. There was a narrow stretch of water between neutral ground through which all mercantile traffic was obliged to pass."[36]

Beginning as early as June 1917, the United States received requests from the Allies and from its diplomatic officials to deploy warships to the Mediterranean. The Allies, especially the Italians and British, were reluctant to do so, but they suffered extensive losses to U-boats in the Mediterranean as well as elsewhere.[37] Sinkings in May reached 150,000 tons and in June 130,000. As in the Atlantic, the Allies did not have nearly enough light vessels to counter the submarines. The United States, not having vested interests in the Mediterranean and not yet at war with Austria-Hungary, paid little attention to this area during the early weeks of American belligerency. Eventually the serious situation there persuaded Washington officials to offer some assistance. After meeting more pressing requirements, the Navy was left with a hodgepodge of miscellaneous vessels, including antique gunboats of Spanish-American War vintage, Coast Guard cutters transferred to the Navy, private yachts commandeered for the duration, and a few light cruisers. Wilson and his successor, Niblack, were given no detailed orders from either Washington or Sims. Like other American units, they were instructed to cooperate with the Allies, in this case the British. Because of their vague orders, Wilson and later Niblack assumed that the British C-in-C at Gibraltar was to control American ships, including escort and patrol work in the Mediterranean and the western approaches to Gibraltar. On September 20, the Admiralty informed Admiral Grant that American ships were not to operate in the Mediterranean beyond the danger zone that ended approximately thirty miles east of Gibraltar. This decision reflected the fact that the United States was not at war with the Austro-Hungarian Empire.[38]

Until December, when the United States declared war on Austro-Hungary, the American warships based at Gibraltar operated principally in the Atlantic, the cruisers and Coast Guard cutters escorting convoys to and from Great Britain and the gunboats patrolling the danger zone.[39] However, the introduction of convoying in the Mediterranean depended on the availability of escorts, including American vessels. More than likely the convoy system would not have been started in the Mediterranean without the presence of United States naval vessels and the promise of others.[40] Convoying had been employed in the Mediterranean from the beginning of the war. The Italians escorted merchant ships between Gibraltar and Genoa, using twelve warships, months before the British introduced the system in the Mediterranean. The Italian escorts later were incorporated into the British system. The British organized some convoys in the Mediterranean before they established a comprehensive system. These convoys usually consisted of two or three ships, often troop transports, with a single escort. Vice Admiral G. A. Ballard, the British commander at Malta, organized convoys of four or five ships that steamed from Malta eastward to Alexandria and westward to Gibraltar. These were usually convoys of four or five ships escorted by four armed trawlers.[41] None of the other Allies followed suit, and because of the British zonal arrangements under different commanders, Ballard's approach did not proliferate throughout the Mediterranean. Generally the British preferred to disperse ships without patrols. The French adopted fixed patrolled routes. As in the Atlantic, neither method succeeded.

In April 1917, at a naval conference held in Corfu, the Allies decided to modify the system. Whenever possible, ships were to follow patrolled routes in coastal waters during night hours only, anchoring in protected waters during the day. Fast ships that followed open water routes were to sail independently or in convoy on randomly dispersed routes. Although this policy required far more escorts than were available, it remained in effect until September. The British shouldered most of the load. Nonetheless, escorts for convoys were more multinational in the Mediterranean than elsewhere. For example, a Genoa convoy screen included a U.S. yacht, an Italian armed merchantman, and two trawlers, one French and the other Portuguese.[42] French vessels cooperated as much as they could, but the French navy was woefully short of ASW craft in the Mediterranean. The Japanese contributed fourteen destroyers to the Mediterranean, the first arriving in April 1917. Other than a few British reinforcements, these were the only vessels available to strengthen the Allied naval force in the Mediterranean until the arrival of the Americans.

The American ships assigned to escort duty in the Mediterranean worked well with their allies, despite criticism of the organizational procedures. One commanding officer wrote, "The haphazard or random assignment of escort vessels as now in effect at this base produces the minimum of efficiency." His vessel, *Cythera*, engaged in escort duty, had "not once, with possibly one or two exceptions . . . left Gibraltar with an escort vessel that she had been in company with before. No two senior officers of the escort have ever had the same plan of attack or plan of guarding the convoy." Admiral Grant placed the names of available vessels in a hat for a "drawing" to select those to be assigned to a particular convoy. When queried about the procedure, Niblack said that it worked "Beautifully." Apparently, unlike the escort officers at Queenstown and Brest, those operating out of Gibraltar made no effort to develop antisubmarine and escort doctrines, probably because of the heterogeneous collection of ships that made up the escort force. *Cythera*'s CO, like Taussig at Brest, recommended the creation of permanent escort squadrons that would operate as units under a permanent senior officer, but Grant did not adopt this procedure.[43]

In August 1917, Vice Admiral Sir Somerset Gough-Calthorpe was appointed com-

mander in chief of British naval forces in the Mediterranean. He arrived at Malta
with instructions to establish a comprehensive Mediterranean convoy system. The
Admiralty had already run a successful test convoy between Great Britain and Gibraltar. On October 3, the first "through" convoy left the United Kingdom for Port Said,
Egypt. One or more warships provided escort. Additional escorts provided protection in defined areas such as British waters and the approaches to Gibraltar. Calthorpe
was never enthusiastic about convoying, preferring more offensive operations and
the Otranto Barrage, but he faithfully carried out Admiralty orders and expanded the
system.[44]

American warships were sent to Gibraltar to escort convoys. The cruisers and cutters, the best seagoing vessels, were assigned to the ocean convoys proceeding to Great
Britain. The gunboats, unsuitable for convoy work, patrolled the danger zone in the
approaches to Gibraltar. These vessels and other naval vessels operating out of Gibraltar had very little offensive capabilities. The Navy Department agreed to send fifteen yachts to Gibraltar, but most of them went to France. Two yachts, *Yankton* and
Nahma, joined the Patrol Force at Gibraltar in September; and three others followed
in the fall. Their bunkers carried enough coal to escort convoys, but they were poorly
armed except for *Nahma*, which carried five 3-inch deck guns and one anti-aircraft
gun.[45] Sims had the tender *Melville* at Queenstown stripped of her 5-inch guns and
placed them on the cruisers at Gibraltar. Other vessels received additional armament
including the Coast Guard cutters and the five destroyers that arrived from the Philippines in December. Until the spring of 1918, their depth charges consisted of a small
supply of the ineffective 50-pounders. In August, the armed yacht *Venetia* attacked
a U-boat and expended her entire load of twelve 50-pound charges without noticeable effect; the submarine got away. Shortly afterward, *Venetia* was fitted with racks
to carry thirty 300-pound charges. Niblack cabled the force commander, "The depth
charge business has saved the day down here, and I am slapping bomb throwers on
everything as fast as the Dockyard can do the work."[46] The difficulty was that the
American vessels were two slow and frequently broke down. According to the commanding officer of the gunboat *Marietta*, one American escort was so slow that, when
she dropped astern of her convoy to "kick up a straggler," she required nineteen hours
to regain her position. "[Her] top speed was not near the speed of the convoy—eight
knots."[47] Admiral Niblack wrote Sims, "These ships are worked to their full capacity
until they break down, and then we repair them and break them down again." The admiral referred to his vessels as "a lot of junk," but he was most critical of the gunboats.
One of them had been built for use on Chinese rivers; another had fired the first shot
in the Spanish-American War. "It is positively wasteful to put money for repairs into
[these ships] . . . they . . . are terribly unreliable. I am going to recommend that one
or two of them be sent home while they can get there."[48] The five *Bainbridge*-class destroyers were nearly as unreliable. They had all served in Asiatic waters for years. One
had sunk to the bottom and remained there for several months before being raised
and refitted. A war correspondent wrote that a machinist's mate was court-martialed
for inadvertently dropping a monkey wrench through one of the destroyer's bottoms.
Perhaps this account was a sea story, but the ships were overdue for scrapping. A

Coast Guard officer considered the Patrol Force a counterpart of the "Suicide Fleet" of yachts that operated out of Brest. "Such a conglomeration of good and bad vessels had never before been seen in Gibraltar."[49]

Admiral Grant was also disappointed with the performance of the American warships. "The U.S. Ships are mostly not of recent date and cannot be relied on to perform the continuous work which the shortage of ships throws on them," he informed the Admiralty. Because of "frequent breakdown of the U.S. Patrol vessels" and the assignment of nine American ships to ocean escort duty, he had to reduce the number of ships available to patrol the danger zone. The American warships assigned to Gibraltar were in poor condition, but they were not much worse off than the other naval vessels operating out of Gibraltar. Niblack informed the Naval Investigation Committee after the war that "We had at Gibraltar what was called a hat pool, and every morning at a conference the Italian, British and French [and American] officers present drew out of the hat the ships that were available and distributed them for escort work, and if we would enter a ship to sail and something would happen, we would have to substitute another." "Angels could do no more," he told Sims, "Possibly devils could, but it is hard to be a devil with the . . . type of ships we have here, most of which are on their last legs."[50]

As early as October, American warships capable of escort duty were occasionally assigned to the Mediterranean despite the possibility of encountering an Austro-Hungarian U-boat. This was improbable because in July 1917 Austro-Hungarian submarines were ordered not to attack American warships or merchant vessels. Austro-Hungarian U-boats generally remained clear of areas where American naval vessels patrolled.[51] On October 3, Admiral Wilson reported that *Sacramento* and *Castine* were on escort duty between Gibraltar and Oran, Algeria.[52] American gunboats and yachts were assigned to the Gibraltar-to-Genoa route when they began operations in January 1918. Convoys on this route were weakly escorted despite the frequent complaints of merchant ship captains. The Gibraltar-to-Marseilles route also generated concern. Italian warships including destroyers usually escorted convoys from Marseilles to Genoa.[53] Until the Genoa convoy was begun, merchant vessels destined for Genoa sailed independently, staying as far away from land as possible. Fast vessels were safe, but slower vessels were vulnerable to submarine attacks. When convoying was initiated, no vessels, regardless of speed, were permitted to sail independently.

Eastward-bound convoys usually hugged the Spanish coast within the three-mile limit. Escorts remained outside the neutral boundary but within sight of the convoy. Those bound for Oran, Bizerta, and elsewhere in North Africa went to a point on the Spanish coast, waited for nightfall, and then dashed across the sea to North Africa. In September 1917, a regular convoy system was started between Gibraltar and Oran, usually with American escorts. Between September and the beginning of 1918, sixty convoys under the protection of American vessels sailed from Gibraltar to Oran and Algiers. On January 1, 1918, Oran convoys were abolished in favor of convoys to Bizerta.[54] Those bound for French and Italian Mediterranean ports continued along the Spanish coast. The escorts occasionally "strayed" into Spanish waters, close enough to see buildings and fields under cultivation. One sailor on an American warship even recognized the statue of Christopher Columbus on the quay in Barcelona as they steamed past the city. Another bluejacket recalled the snow-capped mountains of the Sierra Nevada and the "dinky, dirty, little huts squatting along the coastline." A diarist described his view as they passed along the coast: "Passed the city of Almeria, Spain this A.M.; also an immense plateau—extended far inland. Lot of vineyards to be seen through binoculars. Just can't describe the beauty of it all—so won't try." The CO of USS *Surveyor* apparently believed that he had been ordered to stay within Spanish waters while guarding a convoy. According to the ship's yeoman, the vessel passed through "the Barcelona lobster fishing grounds, tearing up several nets and swamping a smack or two. If there's one thing in arm waving cussing and hollering in Spanish we got it and plenty of it. We didn't stop to see if any were hurt or drowned. The skipper said he was carrying out his orders to stay within the 3-mile limit and that he was going to do it regardless [of] a few Spanish cuss words and lobster nets." Niblack, however, was adamant about respecting Spanish neutral waters. He once countermanded one of Grant's orders to the CO of *Bainbridge* that would have taken the ship within the neutral zone.[55] In February 1918, when U-boats began to seek out targets in Spanish waters, Admiral Calthorpe ordered the Gibraltar-to-Genoa route shifted to the open sea. A month later, however, the Spanish waters route was reinstituted when intelligence had indicated that the submarines had moved their operations elsewhere.[56]

Niblack constantly grappled with the problem of escorts. Because of the limitations of his vessels and the necessity of frequent repairs, he had to juggle his available ships for ocean escorts and convoy work. Frequent requests for additional convoys could not be met because the system was already stretched to the limit. The Italians wanted to initiate convoys from the United States to Italian ports similar to those that went to France and Britain, but the requisite vessels did not exist. In July 1918, Grant told the Admiralty that he needed at least sixteen additional vessels for escort work, not counting those needed for add-on convoys. Niblack bluntly informed Sims, "We have not enough escort ships here for the work so it is only a question of certain convoys being neglected." Four to six vessels escorted nearly all Mediterranean convoys, regardless of their size and speed. A few vessels capable of thirteen knots or better steamed independently, but none under that speed. In July, Niblack recommended the transfer of several faster vessels engaged in ocean escort to the Mediterranean because the Admiralty had gradually increased its complement of vessels assigned to the United Kingdom–Gibraltar convoys.[57] Sims approved, but Niblack had to wait until September to begin shifting his Coast Guard cutters to the Mediterranean.

The American ships at Gibraltar carried more than their share of the load. On October 17, 1918, Sims was informed that Niblack's force in July and August operated at sea more than half of the time in July and August. They supplied 25 percent of the escorts for Mediterranean convoys and 70 percent of those for the Atlantic.[58] Old gunboats and yachts did most of the Mediterranean escorts. A volunteer reserve officer quipped: "Yachting in the Mediterranean. . . . This is what your millionaire pays his good money for."[59] Shipping losses in the Mediterranean were heavy. In the last five months of 1917, submarines destroyed 160 ships, including many under escort. American warships usually provided at least one of the escorts. Fewer than fifty German and Austro-Hungarian submarines inflicted these losses. Eventually the increased use of convoys greatly reduced shipping losses. During the final twelve months of the war, 11,509 ships were convoyed in the Mediterranean, but fewer than 150 went to the bottom.[60]

Sims was well aware of shortages in the Mediterranean. He wrote Niblack: "It has not been possible to replace any of [your] . . . vessels or provide warships more suitable for convoy work, owing to the greater needs of other areas." Although several hundred destroyers and other ASW craft were under construction in the United States, the shipyards fell behind schedule. Two developments forced Sims to allocate a limited number of destroyers to the Mediterranean. One was the Army's decision to send supply ships to Marseilles; the other one was the necessity of providing destroyers to units of ASW teams assigned to the Mediterranean.[61]

The rapid buildup of the AEF resulted in serious congestion in the French Atlantic ports. To ease the problem, the Army began to divert supply ships to Marseilles. Sims expressed strong reservations, pointing out the success of U-boats in the Mediterranean, the weakness of the escort there, and the fact that the voyage to Marseilles was 1,400 miles longer than to the Atlantic ports, "all in submarine waters." Nevertheless, the Army dispatched its first vessels to Marseilles in June. Despite inadequate escort, they reached their destination and returned to the United States. To provide a stronger escort for the Army convoys, in July Sims ordered the new destroyers *Gregory* and *Dyer* to Gibraltar. They were fast and well armed. Admiral Calthorpe was most impressed: "beautiful craft. I wish we had them for the Dardanelles or Otranto, they are too good for the escort work they are engaged on."[62] Sims informed Niblack that the two vessels were the first of ten planned for his command. He was allowed to use the destroyers for other purposes such as patrolling as long as it did not interfere with their primary responsibility of protecting the Army's supply ships. They were ordered to operate directly under the American admiral at Gibraltar rather than Calthorpe at Malta. The force commander took this step after receiving word from Niblack that Calthorpe intended to use the new destroyers to escort convoys between Gibraltar and Genoa. These convoys would include the Army transports, which were to be detached at Marseilles. Sims refused to put the destroyers under the British Mediterranean commander because the Army vessels were much faster than the Genoa convoys. Later the destroyers were placed under Calthorpe's command but only in a technical sense. The frequent arrival of supply ships deterred Niblack from using them for patrolling or as replacements.

By July, seventeen Army transports had been routed to Marseilles via Gibraltar. Each convoy consisted of two to three merchant vessels escorted by one of the two destroyers. In September, two additional destroyers, *Luce* and *Stribling*, arrived at Gibraltar.[63] Niblack never received the last six of the promised destroyers, but veterans *Parker* and *Israel* arrived from British waters.

In May 1918, Admiral Sims recommended the deployment of *Parker* and *Israel* along with *Downes* to the Mediterranean. They were to cooperate with subchasers in antisubmarine missions—"hunting," not convoy work. The Department, however, instructed the force commander to hold off the deployment of the destroyers to the Mediterranean because they were needed to ensure "the safety of the troop . . . [transports to France]." "This is what I call a paper alibi," Sims wrote Niblack.[64] *Parker* and *Israel* finally reached Gibraltar early in November and conducted antisubmarine exercises with subchasers in the waters around Gibraltar.

On October 29, the Admiralty informed Admiral Sims that the Austro-Hungarian government planned to capitulate and that German submarines based in Austro-Hungarian ports had received orders to return home. They would pass through the Strait of Gibraltar on their way north. Admiral Grant decided to establish a barrage of all available vessels across the strait. *Parker*, *Israel*, and a flotilla of eighteen subchasers that had just arrived from the United States joined the barrage. Because of the scarcity of gasoline, only eight chasers operated at one time. They patrolled the strait for a period of four days, using their listening gear and occasionally getting what was considered a "contact." On several occasions, chasers and destroyers dropped depth charges after deciding that the contact was a U-boat. One subchaser officer later reported that the American naval vessels detected four U-boats, two of which came under attack.

Despite the concentration of Allied and American ships, they failed to either sink or damage a U-boat; fifteen of them slipped through and returned to their bases in Germany. A Brazilian squadron of cruisers and destroyers en route to Gibraltar from South America blundered into the barrage during a rain squall and opened fire on several subchasers. At a distance, the subchasers' silhouettes looked like submarines' conning towers. None was hit. The U-boats got in one last blow as they egressed the Mediterranean. The British battleship *Britannia* was torpedoed with heavy loss of life, the last ship sunk by a submarine during the war.[65]

German and Austro-Hungarian submarines operating from bases in the Adriatic gained enormous success despite extensive efforts to stop them. When Italy entered the war in May 1915, she withdrew her naval forces from the Adriatic, leaving Austria-Hungary in control of that sea. The Italians, with French and British assistance, established a blockade across the Strait of Otranto at the entrance to the Adriatic Sea but made no effort to challenge the Austro-Hungarian navy. At the time, Austria-Hungary had only twenty-two small coastal submarines, none capable of operating in the Mediterranean. In November 1915, the German government agreed to deploy U-boats in the Adriatic. They could venture into the Mediterranean; operating as far west as Gibraltar. At one time, thirty-two German U-boats operated from Austro-Hungarian bases. Later, improved Austro-Hungarian submarines cruised out of the Adriatic. By 1918, 30 percent of Allied shipping losses occurred in the Mediterranean.[66]

The Allied High Command strengthened the barrier across the Strait of Otranto. Rear Admiral Mark Kerr wrote later: "If the Straits of Otranto had been closed to them [submarines], their next nearest base would have been Constantinople, and after that Germany itself." Kerr commanded British naval forces in the eastern Mediterranean. His superior, Admiral Calthrope, C-in-C, Mediterranean, agreed with him. He preferred a more offensive antisubmarine policy that placed emphasis upon the Otranto Barrage, even if it meant reducing the number of convoy escorts.[67] However, the material barrage across the strait never grew strong enough to stop the enemy submarines, even after the addition of forty miles of fixed nets and minefields. When the first American naval vessels arrived in the summer of 1918, more than a hundred drifters, thirty armed trawlers, motor launches, destroyers, and even submarines with supporting balloons and aircraft were deployed at the barrage. Seven U-boats were lost during the war either in the Adriatic or the Mediterranean, but it is impossible to determine the exact number destroyed on the barrage. Only two kills were confirmed.[68]

Initially American interest was not tied to the barrage; the Navy had a broader purpose—to conduct offensive operations in the Adriatic designed to limit or stop U-boat operations. In January 1918, the Naval Planning Section presented to Sims a plan that envisioned combined operations against Austria-Hungary in the Adriatic. The force commander presented it to the Allied Naval Council's second meeting in Rome on February 8–9, 1918. It called for the use of troops supported by naval vessels to seize the Sabbioncello Peninsula temporarily. It was located on the Dalmatian coast a few miles north of the Austro-Hungarian naval base at Cattaro. Raiding parties were to interrupt all land and sea traffic that linked Cattaro to repair facilities at Pola and other Austro-Hungarian entrepôts. Also a number of nearby islands were to be taken and fortified for use as bases. The plan recommended a mine barrage from the island of Curzola near the Sabbioncello Peninsula to Gargano Head on the Italian coast. Finally, they advocated bombardment of Cattaro, using Allied naval vessels and American battleships. The planners, however, assumed that the forces employed in the operations, both land and sea, would include troops from the Allies with an American admiral in command. Sims stressed that the United States would supply most of the naval vessels, mines, and at least ten thousand troops, presumably Marines.

The Italians strongly opposed the operation. They considered the utilization of American troops "fanciful" and impracticable. They were adamantly opposed to an American commander. They also feared that the United States would not withdraw its forces when their presence was no longer needed.[69]

When Sims took the plan to the Allied Naval Council, he did so without permission from the Navy Department. More than likely he expected that Washington would approve it, assuming that it gained approval. He also recognized that it fitted with both President Wilson's and Admiral Benson's advocacy of offensive operations. It is probable that the British Admiralty had at least been told of the concept and the force commander had obtained some sort of tentative approval.[70] He might have expected Italian consent because of America's disinterested presence in the area.[71] He undoubtedly did not expect its adoption at the February meeting. The council agreed to consider the plan at its next meeting, but Sims returned to London pessimistic about Italian support.[72]

The plan with certain modifications was again put before the Allied Naval Council at its third meeting on March 12–14. Earlier, Sims received qualified approval from Admiral Benson despite the strong reservations of Captain Pratt.[73] The British generally favored it, although the Admiralty proved unwilling to commit more than limited naval participation. Admiral Calthorpe noted that it would complement his barrage plan for the Strait of Otranto.[74] The Italians remained critical of the proposed operation. They insisted that any supreme commander in the Adriatic should be Italian. Sims responded that he did not care which nation the commander came from as long as he was a "fighter." The Italians also questioned American estimates of the forces, especially troops, needed to carry it out, the availability of adequate logistical support, and even the need for such an operation. Finally, they voiced concern that the failure of the operation might shatter the Italian public's declining morale. Nonetheless, the plan was approved, but because it required land forces, it was referred to the Supreme War Council.

The military representatives of the Supreme War Council met with members of the Allied Naval Council on March 14, and after less than an hour of discussion decided to "defer it for further consideration."[75] This result was the end of the plan, although Sims persisted for another month or so. The German offensive on the Western Front, which began on March 21, eliminated any chance that it would be adopted in the near future. Italian opposition to the planned operation continued in the following months. On June 10, Sims wrote Benson: "It has been made evident by the attitude of Italian authorities . . . that Italy will not agree to the proposed Adriatic project. . . . It is also probable that the French, while not adopting the same extreme attitude of opposition, will not give support to the proposed plan if its execution were to be at the expense of the Otranto Barrage. In view of [the above] . . . I deem it inadvisable to push our plan further at present."[76] The plan was never resurrected. In mid-September, the Naval Planning Section in London put together another detailed plan to attack Cattaro, but the Armistice was signed before it was approved for consideration by the Department.[77]

The only activity that might have made the United States a major player in the Mediterranean was the mining of certain narrow seas. In January, the Naval Planning Section emphasized the need to create mining barrages in the Adriatic similar to the one being developed in the North Sea. "The Department's attitude," Admiral Benson wrote Sims, "is that the mine barrage when properly placed and adequately guarded by patrol craft, supports, and sufficient friendly submarines, promises to be one of the cheapest and most efficacious methods of combating the hostile submarine."[78] Influenced by the optimism of the Navy Department, Sims was persuaded to include a proposed mine barrage in the plan to conduct offensive operations in the Adriatic. When the Allied Naval Council met in March, other Mediterranean barrages were placed on the table. The American Planning Section expanded its proposals for minefields to include the Aegean and other areas. The British were divided between placing a minefield across the northern Adriatic (Ancona, Italy, to Grossa Island) and the idea of using American mines to strengthen the Otranto Barrage. The French favored the Aegean barrage, but the Italians opposed anything that might possibly interfere with completion of the Otranto Barrage. Finally, the Navy Department called for a barrage from Sicily to Cape Bon on the African coast. Naval officers, probably from the Bureau of Ordnance, predicted that such a barrage could greatly decrease submarine activities in the Western Mediterranean. On May 24, Admiral Benson notified Sims that military priorities elsewhere, especially on the Western Front and the North Sea Mine Barrage, precluded the proposed Adriatic mine barrage in the Adriatic. For this reason, the Department favored the Sicily–Cape Bon project: "If the Western Mediterranean were made safe by a barrage from Sicily to Cape Bon and the Straits of Messina controlled, the Eastern Mediterranean situation would be no worse than it is at present, while the ability of the US to transport both men and supplies particularly to French and Italian western Mediterranean ports would be greatly facilitated." The Allies opposed the Sicily–Cape Bon proposal at the July meeting of the Allied Naval Council. Its obvious weakness was that the enemy could continue to prey on Allied shipping plying the eastern Mediterranean or exiting from the Suez Canal. The divergent positions were partly clarified at the July meeting of the Allied Naval Council and a meeting in August called by Admiral Calthorpe held on Malta. Priority was given to the completion of the Otranto Barrage. Next in line was the Aegean project, and last was the Sicily–Cape Bon concept. Admiral Benson reluctantly accepted this decision.[79]

Sims ordered Admiral Strauss to attend the Malta meeting. Strauss later wrote that he deemed the meeting highly successful: "At first the Italian representative refused to permit a mine barrier to be placed further north in the Adriatic than Cape Santa Maria de Leuca, which is at the very toe of the 'boot.' I informed the conference that it was doubtful whether our mines would be operable in such deep water." The conference then agreed to move the barrier farther north "to a line between Brindisi and the island of Sasseno" in shallower waters. From the American point of view, the conference was not a success. Sims was critical of the Otranto Barrage net/mine barrier, and neither he nor the Department considered giving priority to a barrage in the Aegean. None of the delegates except the Americans favored the Sicily–Cape Bon site. Ironically, this site was also quite deep. When the conference ended and the Department was informed of the results, the Bureau of Ordnance admitted that it had not developed a mine effective at depths below 1,200 feet. The Department also informed Sims that it did not have sufficient amounts of mooring cable to plant mines below 250 feet of the surface. In September, Admiral Benson instructed Sims to abandon insistence on the Sicily–Cape Bon plan in order "to produce the unity of effort so essential to success." The CNO agreed, reluctantly, to accept the decisions of the Allied Naval Council, including the American assumption of responsibility for laying mines below the Otranto Material Barrage. He accepted the Aegean project with the reservation that because the United States was not at war with Turkey, the British must lay the portion of the barrage in that country's waters.[80]

Strauss expected to get the Mediterranean mining command. The Navy Department insisted on an American admiral, but the Admiralty assigned a rear admiral senior to Strauss to command their mining squadron in the Mediterranean. Sims then decided to allow Strauss to serve under the British admiral. Strauss lost out on another matter. After the Malta conference, he visited potential sites for a mining base on Corfu. Sims, supported by the Bureau of Ordnance, selected Bizerta, Algeria.[81] The entire business became moot when the Allies signed an Armistice with Turkey on October 30, and with Austria-Hungary on November 3.

Corfu became the site of an American naval base, established to support a flotilla of 110-foot subchasers. The Department's decision to deploy a large number of the small vessels to the war zone prompted considerable discussion among the Americans and the Allies. The British, French, and Italians all wanted as many as they could get. A conference of naval officials held in Rome on February 8–9 decided to send a detachment of the subchasers to reinforce the Otranto Barrage. Admiral Calthorpe initially opposed this decision, principally because of the difficulty in providing gasoline. He wanted to employ them on the Palestinian coast.[82] After the first detachment of subchasers spent a few days at Malta, Calthorpe changed his mind: "These vessels promise well, and I should be very glad of any reinforcements of this type of craft which it is found possible to send."[83] Sims wisely turned the matter over to the Allied Naval Council. Meeting in mid-March, the council "reached the unanimous conclusion that in view of the present political and submarine situation, about thirty of the chasers should be used in connection with the Otranto Barrage." The Department approved this decision, agreeing to assign thirty-six to the barrage.[84]

Sims ordered Captain Leigh to confer with the Italian authorities. After discussions with Commodore Sir William Archibald Howard Kelly, in command of the British Adriatic force, and Vice Admiral Gauchet, the French admiral in command of Allied forces in the Mediterranean, Leigh recommended the location of a base on Govino Bay in Corfu. Leigh wrote a naval officer in Washington, "The matter of selecting a base was a very serious one, there being practically nothing left which could be used. . . . [Y]ou will see from my report that [the site selected] . . . is not a very satisfactory one, but still I think we can get along quite nicely with it."[85]

The Americans encountered major logistical problems before the base became operational. Labor and materials were not available on the island and had to be brought in from the United States. The tender *Leonidas* was ordered as mother ship for the chasers. The lack of gasoline on the island posed the most serious problem; Allied vessels operating from there used either coal or diesel. The Italians had fuel storage tanks at Augusta, Sicily. When the United States informed the British that they did not have a suitable oiler, the Royal Navy supplied one to transport the gasoline from Augusta to Corfu. When the American sailors arrived, they built a pier and other facilities.[86]

The first nine subchasers arrived at Corfu on June 4 after a thirty-two-day voyage from the United States. On June 28, the remaining twenty-one shepherded by *Leonidas* entered the bay after brief stops at Gibraltar and Malta. While the larger group was in Gibraltar, a patrol aircraft spotted and bombed a U-boat on the surface twelve miles west of the British colony. Admiral Grant, with the concurrence of Niblack, immediately ordered the subchasers to locate and destroy the submarine. For more than a day, the American vessels searched for it. Depth charges were dropped in the vicinity of a U-boat moving to the east. The U-boat, evidently damaged by the air attack, was later observed in Sardinia Bay.

At Niblack's request, the subchasers were delayed to mount an operation against what was described as a submarine base in Sardinia. On May 19, the American vessels reached the target. After several hours of "listening" and dropping depth charges, they returned to Gibraltar. British authorities later admitted that smuggling and other illegal activities had occurred in the area, probably including the sale of supplies to the submarines. Niblack defended the operation as good experience, "very valuable for their future operations."[87]

The stop in Malta was to obtain recognition flags and lights and confidential publications for the Mediterranean theater. Also, it allowed Admiral Calthorpe to inspect the chasers. Some of the vessels received minor repairs and painting; others escorted ships into Malta. The chaser crews on escort duty got their first taste of submarine activity in the Mediterranean. Two chasers followed up a radioed SOS from a sinking ship. "There was wreckage of all sorts, bulkheads, the wing of a bridge, beds, mattresses and numerous other pieces and articles. . . . [W]e came to an area covered with cases of lemons. Here we lay to, and putting over the wherry proceeded to load our decks. . . . The lemons were so thick in the water that the crew just leaned over the side and hauled the cases aboard. [Subchaser] Number 128 picked up seventy-two cases of lemons, six cases of soap, three fenders, and many other articles. Although we had not seen a submarine, we felt we had made the trip worth while."[88] The British C-in-C asked for some of the subchasers to do escort work, but Sims refused the request. Leigh was instructed to inform the Allied naval commanders that the subchasers were to be used for "hunting enemy submarines and for no other purpose, except in an emergency." *Leonidas* and the last of the thirty-six chasers destined for Corfu finally left Malta during the second week of June.[89]

Corfu lies in the Ionian Sea. To the east, about three or four miles, is the mountainous Albanian coastline, often a subject of painters because of its picturesque beauty at sunrise and sunset. The island is forty miles long and twenty wide. Although the island is renowned for its loveliness, attracting thousands of tourists over the years, it had been involved in war and conquest from the ancient Phoenicians and Romans to the Italians, French, British, and Greeks in the years before World War I. When the American sailors were stationed there, the island abounded with ruins of the classical age and modern villas. The palace of Kaiser William I overlooked the bay where the American ships were moored. Admiral Sims waxed poetic when he described the presence of the American bluejackets in Corfu: "There was a certain appropriateness in the fact that the American college boys who commanded these ships—not much larger than the vessel in which Ulysses had sailed these same waters three thousand years before—should have made their base on the same island which had served as a naval station for Athens in the Peloponnesian War, and which, several centuries afterwards, had been used for the same purpose by Augustus in the struggle with Anthony."[90]

Although "a very jewel of a place," as a newspaper correspondent put it, Corfu was far from a Mecca of civilization. The people were poor; the climate was hot and dry; food was expensive; and liberty was rare. The only town of any size was Corfu, six miles from the American base. Because of disease and unsanitary conditions, it was out of bounds most of the time. Flies, fleas, and mosquitoes inundated the base. The men swung hammocks between the olive trees. Later tents were erected and bunks were built out of gasoline crates.[91] The island was crowded with military personnel—Greeks, Italians, French, British, and even the remnant of the Serbian army evacuated to the island in 1916. Somewhat isolated from their allies, the Americans had little to do with them, except when they joined French, Italian, and British naval units in the Otranto Barrage.

Captain Leigh, who remained on Corfu to initiate the subchaser force in ASW operations, later wrote that the commanders of the subchasers were "full of enthusiasm and ready for immediate service; except that they had [not] the haziest idea of how to hunt submarines. . . . They were equipped with sound devices, but did not know how the darned things worked."[92] Leigh and his assistant, Lieutenant Commander Edward E. Spafford, instituted a training program. Later the Italians provided a submarine to assist in training exercises. This cooperation ended when one of the chasers collided with the submarine. Training continued even after operations commenced on the barrage. In September, the exercises were moved to Gallipoli, not far distant from the scene of the Allied disaster earlier in the war.[93]

A conference of American and British naval officers approved operational procedures for the chasers. The small vessels were divided into three squadrons of twelve each. Each squadron was deployed on the barrage for four days, later extended to six, and then spent four in port. The chasers formed a line across the forty-mile strait from Albania to the Italian coast. To the north of the line were patrolling destroyers; to the south were the fixed nets and drifters, trawlers, motor launches, and kite balloons. The chasers ran for ten minutes toward one shore and listened for five, and then they reversed the procedure. At night they drifted, turning on their listening equipment. If they made a contact, a unit of three subchasers converged on the presumed submarine position and attacked with depth charges.[94]

In July, Leigh departed for London, leaving in command Captain Charles "Juggy" Nelson, who led the subchasers and tender on the voyage from the United States. The United States Navy has had its share of unusual characters who left their mark on the service—legendary figures such as John "Mad Jack" Percival, Louis M. "Old Guts" Goldsborough, and William "Wild Bill" Kirkland. "Juggy" Nelson was certainly in this category. Born in Baltimore Maryland, he was a member of the Academy class of 1898. He made a name for himself at the Academy, not as a result of his academic endeavors, graduating 138 out of 139, but because of his athletic prowess and his antics. The class of 1898 graduated months early because of the Spanish-American War. Nelson was assigned to the cruiser *New Orleans*, where he gained his initial recognition for gallantry. He evidently was in a launch on picket duty and with a fireman swam to the beach when he was discovered and fired upon by Spanish soldiers. As legend would have it, they plunged into the surf, "followed by rifle bullets, brickbats, and curses in choice Castilian." His commanding officer put him under suspension for deserting his ship, but as one writer put it, "Juggy's reputation was made."[95] In the post–Spanish-American War days, he served in the Far East, where among other exploits he delivered a baby. He then entered submarine duty, commanding *Plunger* and later *Porpoise*, earning Admiral Charles Lockwood's praise as one of the "makee-learn university of hard knocks" with the new vessels. In December 1917, he was appointed to command the *Leonidas* and the submarine chasers ordered to the Mediterranean.[96]

Sims was pleased with Nelson. He wrote in *The Victory at Sea*: "Indeed, the American Navy possessed few officers more energetic, more efficient, more lovable, or more personally engaging than Captain Nelson. . . . [His] rotund figure, jocund countenance, and always buoyant spirits were priceless assets to our naval forces at Corfu. . . . He had the supreme gift of firing his subordinates with the same spirit that possessed himself." One of his chaser officers mentioned a conference during which "Juggy" said, "Well, boys, I wouldn't swap my job with anybody, either in heaven or on earth, for we have the greatest little assignment for hunting 'Huns' that one could wish for."[97]

After Leigh left Corfu, Nelson spent as much time as he could with the chasers on the barrage. Leigh pleaded with Sims to send regular officers because the "personnel of chasers [were] entirely untrained [and] need constant supervision of [an] experienced officer." Lieutenant Commander Paul H. Bastedo and Lieutenant F. Loftin were promptly ordered to Corfu. The two took command of two of the three squadrons, permitting Nelson to spend time completing the base. At the beginning, the crews were excited about the prospect of hunting U-boats, but as the days went by and no submarines were spotted despite numerous supposed contacts, the euphoria began to wane, particularly when the majority of their "pursuits" proved to be friendly destroyers, "or, as it was expressed in a private letter, the chasers were chasing 'circulating pumps.'"[98] The crews were frustrated because noise from Allied vessels constantly interfered with their listening devices. Months later, Sims wrote that inexperience kept them from separating noise generated by submarines from those of surface vessels. Nelson's reply said nothing about experience but stressed the efforts of the barrage commander to reduce the interference: "It is believed that no greater effort could have been made by any man than has been made . . . to have all vessels passing through the area observe listening periods." He admitted that it was difficult to persuade ship commanders to stop their vessels for "set periods while in waters traversed by enemy submarines." At times more than two hundred vessels joined the barrage, adding to the confusion. Chaser officers were told that Allied vessels would neither penetrate the barrage nor leave their assigned area; therefore any contact should be considered hostile. This claim proved untrue. After the war was over officials recognized that the primitive listening equipment could not differentiate between submarine and surface vessel noise. It often identified large fish as possible targets. One night a chaser followed an unusual sound, "a sort of squeaking," for hours before identifying it as a damaged screw on a trawler. Admiral J. H. Godfrey blamed the barrage's failure on the listening equipment: "We did not know that it was of no use."[99]

Unfortunate incidents occurred. A British destroyer failed to give recognition signal, and a chaser put a 3-inch shell in her boiler room. A few days later, a British destroyer opened fire on one of the subchasers but did not hit it. In the hearing that followed, the destroyer's commanding officer said that he was "dreadfully sorry," but that "anyone seeing one of those chasers at night for the first time would take it for a submarine." Allied surface vessels frequently identified the small American vessels as U-boats, but none were damaged.[100]

Although only one submarine was discovered on the surface, the subchasers made numerous contacts. Captain Usborne, the barrage commander, wrote after the war that British and American vessels made over 150 contacts, and a submarine was sighted in sixty-three instances. A U-boat captain commented on a submerged cruise through the barrage. Listening equipment picked up his boat. When he looked through his periscope, he observed chasers within a thousand yards and closing. "We submerged to deep soundings, but when we put up the periscope again at 7:30 P.M. our pursuers are still there and within three cables' length of us." Eventually the submarine escaped.[101] Although the barrage affected morale, U-boats continued to pass through it. Although the American vessels were given credit for one destroyed submarine, it is doubtful that they sunk any.[102]

Living conditions were Spartan, both on board the small vessels and in the base. Days and nights in the Adriatic were hot, often over a hundred degrees. The crews usually remained on the open deck, even sleeping there. When in general quarters, night-time stays on deck were not allowed because they might interfere with the guns and depth-charge racks. Often they remained at General Quarters throughout the night, "tearing around in the darkness at full speed, hoping that a stray floating mine don't get you." Another sailor added: "We were always out of depth charges and rolled so hard that it was impossible to bring our guns to bear." The chasers in the best of conditions were rough sea boats. During gales, which became more frequent as summer came to a close, they were nearly uninhabitable. "Many a day cooking was an impossibility," one officer remembered. "Eating became a fine art, of the impressionistic school, to be sure, plastered all over one's person, as it were." Regardless of the sea conditions, little recreation was available while operating at sea. Reading and poker were the most popular activities. Occasionally, a few men were allowed to go swimming, but this pleasure was rare because of sharks. "We do not see or hear anything on this barrage," an officer wrote. "The men are so sick of this small ship with no chance for liberty or exercise that they do a great deal of grumbling." A chaser veteran of the barrage wrote after the war that "We averaged twenty-two cruising days a month, leave was unknown but once in a great while we got midnight liberty."[103] Conditions in port were not much better. The crews slept on the open deck or in tents. Liberty to Corfu was not allowed, and until the YMCA appeared, the sailors had few opportunities for recreation. Much of the time was spent repairing the wooden vessels and power plants that broke down frequently. "The boats are all slowly going to pieces," one officer complained in August.[104] The *Leonidas* was well equipped with tools and spare parts, but the crews were responsible for repairs and upkeep. Yet they kept going to the end, buoyed by the conviction that they were destroying or at least harassing the U-boats.

On the night of September 29, twelve chasers under the command of Captain Nelson were ordered to sea, destination unknown. The next morning they entered Brindisi, where they learned that they were to become part of a task force organized to attack the Albanian port of Durazzo. The Italian navy planned the mission, but the French persuaded them to agree to it. Durazzo, a naval base, was also a logistical center for the forces of the Central powers that fought the French in the Balkans. The

French told the Italian government bluntly that they intended to attack Durazzo unless the Italians did so.

The American ships joined naval units from all the Allied nations fighting in the Mediterranean except the Japanese. A powerful fleet of Italian battleships, cruisers, destroyers, and torpedo boats joined British light cruisers, British and Australian destroyers, and the American chasers. Some submarines, including several French boats, joined the expedition. Not all the ships were to join in the attack on Durazzo. Some, including the submarines and Italian battleships, were to patrol north of the port to make sure that the Austro-Hungarian navy did not send powerful reinforcements from Cattaro.

The chasers waited in Brindisi for two days before getting underway on the sixty-mile crossing to Durazzo. Nelson was ordered to make sure that the chasers carried at least four days' stores. "Juggy" always carried a wicker chair to sit in. He selected the fastest vessel in the squadron as his flagship. After reaching Brindisi, Nelson boarded the British flagship and received his orders. When he returned, he exclaimed, "We are going to have a real party!" While in Brindisi they were not allowed liberty and were ordered to avoid conversation with anyone off their vessel. Guards were posted to ensure strict observance of this order. The crews passed the time examining their vessels and weapons, sleeping, and on the last night getting together for a jazz concert. At the end they sang "The Star Spangled Banner."[105]

The subchasers got underway shortly before daybreak on October 2. One of the chasers fouled its propeller on an underwater obstruction and had to be left behind. The chasers were placed in the vanguard followed at some distance by the rest of the fleet; altogether thirty-five vessels made the attack supported by aircraft, and the rest provided a screen to the north of Durazzo. The weather was rainy; the sea too rough for cooked meals.

The chasers' role in the attack was somewhat unclear. Nelson and his second in command, Lieutenant Commander Bastedo, attended a meeting in Commodore Kelley's flagship, but the commodore generally ignored the American officers and their responsibilities. They later conferred with the commanding officer of the British destroyer squadron, an acquaintance of Nelson's from Corfu, and developed a tentative plan. Six of the chasers were to screen the bombarding force as it entered the bay, while the remaining six patrolled off the bay's northern and southern capes. Their primary duty was to guard against submarine attacks.

Because of their early start, Nelson's small force arrived off Durazzo approximately an hour before the rest of the attacking group. They cruised around six miles off the port outside of artillery range but clearly within sight. One officer recalled that Nelson wanted two enemy destroyers in the harbor to come out and fight: "It was a real Indian war dance about four or five miles outside the harbor . . . because the boats just kept going around in a big circle."[106] The Austro-Hungarian destroyers got up steam with the intention of "coming out" and eventually steamed within range of the chasers, but by that time the attacking force arrived and began to make its initial bombardment run. The force did not achieve surprise; the smoke of the approaching Allied ships could be seen within minutes of the chasers' arrival.

The Italian armored cruisers—supported by destroyers and motor torpedo boats and screened by the chasers—were to enter the port from the south, run parallel to it, and depart at its north end. The British cruisers meanwhile were to steam to the north end. When the first attacking force cleared the port, the British cruisers entered and steamed south, again screened by the American vessels. While the ships in the bombarding line were firing on the two destroyers and vessels in the harbor, aircraft were also attacking. The Allied ships came under fire from batteries of heavy guns located on the bluffs around the port, but none suffered serious damage. The three chasers on the inboard screen came under fire, the only American vessels to experience it, but they were not damaged. Allied intelligence had mentioned the presence of nets and minefields, but evidently the bombarding force remained outside of them. The screening force of chasers spotted two mines on the surface. It destroyed the first one by gunfire. The second floated in the path of the British ships as they commended their bombardment. One of the chasers went alongside the mine, forcing the cruisers to steer around it.[107] One account mentions that the chasers were sent ahead of the bombarding units to clear the minefields and mark a passage through the field with flags attached to small flats, but no evidence supports this claim.[108]

The northernmost section of three chasers experienced the most action. They encountered two Austro-Hungarian submarines, *U-29* and *U-31*. *U-29* was in the harbor as the bombardment commenced and immediately got underway to attack the Allied ships. *U-31* was returning from a patrol and was still outside the port when the attack began. The chasers spotted them and attacked. They fired their 3-inch guns at the periscopes and dropped depth charges, but neither U-boat was sunk nor seriously damaged. The Americans claimed that they destroyed both boats, a claim initially supported by the Allies. Later the number was reduced to one, and an official inquiry of the Austro-Hungarian navy decided that none were sunk.[109]

The Allies described this engagement as a great victory, but it was nothing of the sort. A massive force bombarded what a recent authority referred to as a "miserable third-rate Albanian harbour," with a few Austro-Hungarian warships and merchant vessels under the protection of six batteries of coastal guns. The expedition sunk a merchant vessel, damaged a second, and destroyed a few buildings in the town. An Austro-Hungarian naval officer later wrote: it "was quite a ridiculous action, on one side 3 armoured & 3 light cruisers with large flotillas, on the other side two 400 ton destroyers and one small torpedo boat and one Austro-Hungarian submarine and 2 old 6[-inch] guns on the coast. The destroyers lost 3 men."[110]

A great deal was written about this engagement in the American newspapers.[111] They described it as a victorious surface engagement that involved American naval vessels, the only fleet action that U.S. naval forces engaged in during the war. It demonstrated the growing presence of the United States in the Adriatic. Although an Austro-Hungarian naval officer later claimed that "We hardly knew the presence of Americans in the Adriatic Straits," if the war had continued, additional warships, possibly including battleships, would have joined the subchasers.[112]

In May, the Admiralty queried Sims about the possibility of deploying U.S. battleships to the Mediterranean. It feared that the Germans would gain control of the Russian Black Sea Fleet as a result of a secret agreement when Russia agreed to peace in January. Sims and Benson were unable to agree to this deployment because the United States was not at war with Turkey.[113] The crisis over the Russian fleet eased, but the Allies continued their interest in sending some of the American battleships to the Mediterranean and the Adriatic. None had ever been deployed to these areas during the war.

Destroyers were promised for the Otranto Barrage to cooperate with the chasers as part of "killer-hunter" groups, but the two vessels allocated for this purpose remained in the vicinity of Gibraltar, and others were not sent until after the Armistice. Destroyers, including the few new ones arriving from the United States, went elsewhere. At the request of the British commanding officer of the Otranto Barrage and the endorsement of Captain Leigh, Sims agreed in September to recommend that an additional thirty-six chasers should join the Otranto Barrage. Commodore Kelley proposed to base them at Gallipoli, where the chasers initially assigned to the barrage received some of their training.[114] No additional units reached the Mediterranean before the Armistice ended the conflict.

Early in October, both the Germans and Austro-Hungarians sent simultaneous notes to the Allies requesting an armistice. The Armistice was delayed until November because both sides argued over the terms. While the belligerents bickered, the Allied leaders and the Americans began to think of demobilization. On October 19, Commodore Kelley held a conference at Corfu to discuss the dismantling of the barrage. Nelson immediately reported the gist of the discussion, mentioning that he was informed that his force would retire to Gibraltar, and asking whether he should continue construction at the base. Sims replied that the barrage would not be broken up until an Armistice was signed with Austria-Hungary. The chasers were to remain at Corfu until he received different instructions.[115] On November 3, American forces in the Mediterranean and Adriatic received orders from Sims to abstain from attacking Austro-Hungarian vessels.[116] That day, Austria-Hungary agreed to an armistice. The Otranto Barrage was discontinued four days later.

Historians agree that the Otranto Barrage was a failure. Although Trask doubts that any submarines were destroyed in the barrage, other historians conclude that two U-boats were definitely destroyed along with two "possibles."[117] The enormous expense of ships, men, and material, which could have been used elsewhere, was wasted in the ill-defined barrage. The Allies could have concentrated on improving the convoy system in the Mediterranean. Convoying was less successful in the Mediterranean than elsewhere. The loss rate of merchant vessels was generally higher; of 11,509 ships convoyed, 136 were sunk, for a loss rate of 1.2 percent. Admiral Niblack attributed the convoy system's difficulties in the Mediterranean to three elements: geography, the slowness of cargo ships, and the inferior escort ships. By "geography" he meant the fact that the Mediterranean was relatively narrow, limiting the number of possible routes. Nevertheless the system, weak as it was, was a success.[118] Merchant ship losses dropped dramatically when they steamed in convoys rather than independently. Vessels allocated to the barrage, even the subchasers, could have been used as escorts. More than likely the mine barrage that the U.S. attempted to construct was ill-conceived.[119]

At the time of the Armistice, the United States Navy had seventy-five ships and 5,542 officers and men in the Mediterranean and Adriatic. According to an analysis of the Navy's accomplishments in the Mediterranean, probably prepared at Niblack's headquarters, it furnished 25 percent of the escorts for local Mediterranean convoys and over 70 percent of the escorts for the ocean and deep-sea convoys. If the war had continued, American naval presence in the Mediterranean would have expanded significantly. In September, the General Board wrote Daniels, "in the future our operations [in the Mediterranean] . . . will grow perhaps more than those of any other power."[120]

The Eleventh Hour of the Eleventh Day of the Eleventh Month

The Armistice

The final collapse of the Central powers began in the Mediterranean and adjacent seas, when Bulgaria requested an armistice on September 26. Turkey followed four days later. The disintegration of the Austro-Hungarian Empire and its military and naval forces took place in October and early November. On the Western Front, from August into the fall months, Allied and American armies systematically drove the German forces toward their border. Early in October, Germany made its first overture for an armistice in an appeal to President Wilson, proposing to settle on the basis of his fourteen points. Political upheaval in Germany, which led to the abdication of the Kaiser, and intense negotiations among the Allies over terms of an armistice delayed the signing for more than a month.

The naval war continued during this period much as before, but events in October finally persuaded naval officials that the end was near. On October 5, the first sea lord, Admiral Wemyss, wrote Beatty: "Events are moving rapidly. . . . [W]e have arrived at a moment when either the war collapses or when the most likely psychological moment, if ever, has arrived for the High Seas Fleet to make some demonstration."[1] Wemyss was right, although events did not work out as he expected. On October 20, the German chancellor gave in to Wilson's demands and, despite vigorous opposition from Admiral Scheer, ordered the end of the submarine campaign and the return of the U-boats to home ports. The German naval commander still believed that some sort of victory was possible if he could defeat the Grand Fleet. Perhaps a naval sortie might persuade the German High Command to resume submarine warfare. Scheer ordered the High Seas Fleet commander, Rear Admiral Franz Hipper, to attack shipping off the Flanders coast and the Thames estuary to bring out the British fleet. The operation was scheduled to begin on October 30, but during the night German sailors on various ships mutinied and refused to weigh anchor. The operation was then canceled, ingloriously paralyzing the High Seas Fleet. The Armistice signed on November 11 included a naval clause that required Germany to turn over the submarine fleet to the Allies and the United States and the internment of the surface ships. To some British and American naval officers, the Armistice came as a great surprise.[2]

Nevertheless, by the second week in November, many naval officers knew that negotiations for an armistice were taking place. Then occurred what became known as the "false Armistice," the "greatest fake news story in all history."[3] This episode stemmed from a chain of misinformation. On November 7, at about 11 a.m., Admiral

Wilson received a dispatch from Captain Richard H. Jackson, the U.S. Navy's representative in Paris, announcing that the Armistice had been signed. The newspaper correspondent Roy Howard by chance was in Wilson's office at the time and without permission cabled the news to the United States. There, without confirmation, the United Press spread it throughout the country. Wilson provided the local newspaper and the base bandmaster with the news. At the time, the Navy band was presenting a concert in Brest's large city square near the admiral's office. The bandmaster immediately passed the news on to the crowd, which led to a celebration that continued well into the night. The news spread like wildfire throughout the war zone. The minelayer *Saranac* received a signal, "hostilities over," as did other American naval vessels. It led to premature celebrations throughout the world. Later that afternoon, word arrived that no armistice had been signed.[4]

The details of this incident are still unclear, but evidently it originated with someone in the Paris office of the French army's Intelligence Bureau. A German delegation was on the way to France on that day to discuss armistice terms. A great deal of radio and other traffic passed between various military offices. This cacophony may have led to the erroneous information that eventually reached Admiral Wilson's office.[5]

Admiral Wilson wrote years after the war that "no harm had been done . . . and the people had had a good time. . . . And goodness knows they needed one and deserved one. The only effect was that the premature jollification rather took the edges off the celebration of the true Armistice four days later."[6] Nevertheless, millions of people throughout the world were upset when they learned of the mistake. Captain Jackson was recalled, and even Admiral Wilson came extremely close to censure and a reprimand. That afternoon, Admiral Moreau, the prefect commanding the district around Brest, angrily denounced the American admiral for not requesting "my authorization nor for any confirmation before publicizing this news. . . . [H]e only communicated to me later verbally through my aide." Wilson later wrote that the next day he visited Vice Admiral Moreau: "I had heard he was a bit upset by the turn of events, and when I saw him he appeared to be very serious. I asked him if he had been disturbed by last night's premature jollification, etc. He replied 'yes.' Crowds kept marching up and down the rue de Siam . . . the street on which is situated the Prefecture, his residence and office—and kept him awake most of the night." The French admiral might have added that the American naval vessels moored in the harbor turned on their sirens and searchlights and fired rockets during the night. Wilson remembered that in their meeting Moreau "gradually thawed out and laughed heartily with me. . . . We parted the best of friends as usual."[7] Sims wrote his wife later that he received the same telegram as Wilson, but "Anybody should have known that the Armistice could not have been signed so quickly." Wilson wrote Daniels a report on the incident. Although the incident did not hurt his career, Wilson collected everything published on it. He condemned Daniels's version of the incident in *The Wilson Era: Years of War and After, 1917–1923*, which did not appear until 1946.[8]

When the official announcement finally came on November 11, Brest celebrated again. At noon, the French ships in the harbor fired a salute, and sirens and whistles added to the din as did the cannon mounted on the fortifications. By 3:00 in the afternoon, the city's entire population packed the streets. An American officer on liberty recorded: "When Brest celebrates, all of Brest joins in." Groups of French sailors, civilians, and American servicemen snaked through the streets singing and dancing. To get some of the Americans off the streets, the Y and other welfare centers held dances. Even the Red Cross nurses at the nearby naval hospitals gave a dance.

What most Americans remember about the following day and night was the drinking of alcoholic beverages. The French called it a "Sacred Drunk." A bluejacket recalled that a tavern owner broke out a bottle of wine, vintage 1870, which had been hidden for fifty-two years under the building. Unfortunately, it had turned to vinegar. A destroyer officer wrote a couple of days later that "Everybody in Brest was drunk from the celebration. I went ashore the night that the Armistice was signed and at 5 everybody had 'ballast,' at 6 they were 'three sheets in the wind,' and at 8 they were making those little cognac zigzags and at 9 PM they were all 'up to a million.' I never saw so many people snowed under before." *Porter's* officer of the deck who had duty that evening was disgusted when "about fourteen officers [from several destroyers] . . . including a couple skippers . . . snake danced" up his gangway. "I told [the Captain] . . . that after our crew had behaved so well [on liberty that it was unfortunate] to have a load of soused officers from other ships visit us." One of *Reid's* officers mentioned in his journal that the celebrants were still going strong three days later. The other French ports with American servicemen experienced the same phenomenon. Two days after the Armistice, they were still celebrating in Bordeaux. One sailor recalled that the "main streets were four to five inches deep with confetti."[9]

Paris was the scene of a frenzied celebration for three days. As one American naval officer said many years later, it "was like nothing that I've ever seen or heard of. . . . It was really the most fantastic thing that I think ever happened." There were thousands of American servicemen, including sailors, in Paris on November 11 so that, as one writer wrote, "the celebration appeared in places to acquire an American flavor." Aviators at the New York Bar concocted a drink called *L'Armisticee*, which contained champagne for France, gin for Great Britain, whiskey for the United States, port for Portugal, Chianti for Italy, sake for Japan, arrack for Greece, and rum for Liberia.[10]

Not all American bluejackets stationed in France were able to join in the Armistice celebrations. The crew of the yacht *Nokomis* spent most of November 11 fighting a fire that had broken out on an ammunition ship anchored nearby. A transport loaded with gas shells "stacked 4 deep on the deck" reached a French port on November 11 and was immediately ordered to sea to dump the cargo. At Gibraltar, *Ophia*, a transport carrying ammunition, came into port during the night of November 11, flying a distress flag because she was on fire. The signal was either ignored or not observed. Very lights and rockets from the ship were assumed to be part of the Armistice celebration. When nearby vessels recognized the fire, they could not muster adequate fire parties because nearly everyone had gone on liberty. One of *Ophia's* crew later said that "the harbor was lit up by the flames . . . but still we received no help. This was about six o'clock. About seven . . . ran the good ship aground." She then exploded and finally woke up the base and town. Ships scrambled out of the harbor as sailors from the tender *Buffalo* arrived with fire equipment. Only two men died, one stuck in a porthole as he attempted to escape.[11]

U.S. naval personnel that made up the subchaser force and tender *Leonidas* based at Corfu had the distinction of celebrating two armistices, one with Austria signed on November 3, and the other with Germany just over a week later. The news of the armistice with Austria was received by radio on *Leonidas*. The chasers, a number of which were out on patrol, were immediately signaled to cease attacks on submarines. A chaser officer later wrote: "This signal sounded as though it had been our custom when in a bad mood to run out in the straits before breakfast, sink a couple of subs, then come back and eat. It . . . gave a most fitting finish to our Adriatic endeavors. The American ships welcomed the news with blasts of their whistles. The following day, the chasers cruised in column through the anchored Allied ships and as they passed the French flagship, firing their Y guns loaded with grease to make smoke rings." The French replied by playing the "Star Spangled Banner." The news of the armistice with Germany was received with less fanfare. The whistles blew again, and liberty was approved for Corfu. Although "thousands of French sailors were singing and dancing in the streets, the Americans were more subdued, thinking of going home."[12]

A great many American naval vessels were at sea that day, patrolling and escorting convoys. Most of them had no time to celebrate. Although the vessels had been informed that the U-boats had been ordered to their bases, they feared that some submarines had not received the message or might refuse to abide by it. The torpedoing of the British battleship *Britannia* in the Strait of Gibraltar on November 9 did nothing to lessen their concerns. *Nokomis* was escorting a convoy in the Bay of Biscay on November 11 when it spotted an apparent periscope. The captain knew that German U-boats from the Adriatic were passing through the bay on their way to Germany and told his officers to "shoot hell out of them" if one was discovered. *Nokomis* dropped depth charges but observed nothing further. The destroyer *Cummings*, also escorting an eastbound convoy, dropped a few depth charges when a transport gave the submarine signal "but to no avail."[13]

The Armistice was celebrated joyously in the British Isles. In Southampton, local students beating tin buckets and trays and blowing bugles led parades of British, French, Belgian, American, and Italian soldiers and sailors, munitions workers, land girls, WRENS, and others up and down the main street. American bluejackets from the naval vessels in the yards at Liverpool and across the river at Birkenhead as well as from the transports in the harbor flocked into the port. As elsewhere, the celebration brought the city to a standstill. One officer later wrote, "I never saw so many drunk women in my life." The Plymouth city fathers tried to curb drunkenness by closing the bars and pubs, but, as one officer remembered, adequate alcoholic "resources" were obtained to throw quite a party.[14]

November 11 in London defied description. Admiral Sims, however, tried to describe the scene in a letter to his wife: "when [the] armistice was signed London really cut loose. Practically all work stopped. Employees in all kinds of business left their work and went out into the streets. The block of buildings which we and the [American] Embassy are now occupying had every window filled, and a great part of the people went outdoors. . . . Our sailormen, stenographers, messengers, marines, etc. all joined in [the celebration]. They commandeered one of our biggest 3-ton trucks which made tours around the neighborhood cheering all hands. Three or four dozen of the sailors formed in line ahead with their hands on each others shoulders and marched through the neighborhood bearing an American flag and were followed by a couple of dozen of our messenger boys carrying a flag stretched out between them. . . . I heard later that they marched around in front of Buckingham Palace and were invited by the Guards to march in on the parade. They attracted the attention of the King who came out and made a few remarks to them." Thousands stood in front of the palace, some even climbing onto the Victoria statue, waiting for the king to appear on the balcony. While the crowds continued to concentrate in Trafalgar Square, Piccadilly, and Haymarket, Sims and his key officers went to dinner and then to the theater to see the revue *Hullo Janis*, staring Elsie Janis. The audience recognized the admiral and gave him three cheers when he was both entering and leaving.[15]

Queenstown received the news of the Armistice with a great deal of equanimity. The overwhelming majority of the Irish people were at best ambivalent at the announcement, and many were downright disappointed. Even the sailors based there showed little of the exuberance found elsewhere. One American destroyer officer remembered that his ship's crew was assembled on the forecastle, where the captain read the news. "Then we fell out and I heard the chief boatswain's mate say under his breath, 'What are we supposed to do? Cheer?'" *Stevens*'s captain was in his stateroom when he received a dispatch with the news of the Armistice. He ordered the boatswain's mate to pass the word that the war was over. "I listened for the shouting and the tumult, but heard nothing much above the usual hum of the ship's noises." Another officer wrote: "There was no commotion aboard the ship, and no blowing of whistles, or noise of any sort. Queenstown seemed to think nothing of the event." *Melville*'s deck log for November 11 did not mention the Armistice. *Dixie*'s log acknowledged it but did not comment.[16]

The American ships in Bantry Bay welcomed the news in several different ways. The submarines maintained their in-port disposition alongside the tender as did the battleships *Utah* and *Oklahoma*. As one bluejacket recalled, "it was just another day." One of *Oklahoma*'s officers remembered no "overt celebration. . . . I think we took it thankfully but quietly." *Nevada*, the "Cheer Up" ship, certainly lived up its name that day: "Then came our little celebration on shipboard. Major Braumbaugh [the Marine CO] donned a bathrobe and with a Turkish towel entwined about his head in true turban style, acted as the drum major, leading the band in our parade about the ship. Following the band came the crew, headed by the majority of the officers, dressed in any costume that was available in short order, all marching in the prison lock step and forming a seemingly endless line wiggling about the upper decks." "It was a glorious day," said the ship's cruise book.[17]

American bluejackets with the mine-laying bases in Invergordon and Inverness joined the local Scottish people, parading through the towns. At Invergordon, the base's brass band and drill company started the parade, and local Scottish military units joined in.[18] A number of minelayers were at sea when the news was received. They immediately returned to base.

Nowhere among the American and British sailors was jubilation more exuberant and more visible than in the Grand Fleet, although the 11:00 a.m. announcement did not lead to a spontaneous celebration. Admiral Beatty made a general signal to the fleet that the traditional method of commemorating an occasion, "splicing the main brace," would be carried out at 1900 (7:00 p.m.), meaning that each British sailor would receive an additional tot of rum. The signal also included "Negative 6th B[attle] S[quadron.]" There would be no rum ration for the American bluejackets because their ships were dry. Although it was Monday, the C-in-C also announced "make and mend," the equivalent of the British "rope yarn Sunday," a holiday from work except for duty sections. South Carolina congressman James F. "Jimmy" Byrnes, on a "fact-finding" mission with two other congressmen, was talking with *New York*'s commanding officer when he received a message: "When he read it, he took several steps before he paused and then said quietly, 'I am sure you will be interested to learn that the terms of the armistice came into force at eleven o'clock.' He offered no other comment or explanation."

Little happened on the ships during the afternoon. A *Texas* gob wrote, "We loafed in unaccustomed idleness." Those going on liberty caught the 1500 boat. On the British ships, one by one, brooms were secured to the truck of the masts as a symbol of victory, the sea having been swept clear of enemy ships. Not all were able to join the fun. One of *Wyoming*'s officers mentioned in his oral history that because of the prevalence of flu on board, "we just had to sit there and listen to other people celebrating. . . . We had the old yellow flag up at the mast head and that was all there was to it."[19] *New York*'s deck log mentioned the presence of three congressmen but was strangely silent otherwise. A *Texas* sailor wrote after the war: "Evening colors were made; the ships winked on their riding and standing lights, the lights on their gangways. Christ, whadda ya know. We don't hafta darken!"

Everything changed shortly after 7:00 p.m. Marine Major (later General) del Valle was officer of the deck on *Texas*: "Now, that was something. That was the night that the whole Fleet was lit up, and I'm not kidding. The lights were on, and everybody was drunk—the whole bloody Fleet." A British sailor claimed that the Americans "started the fireworks." Eugene Wilson insisted that "an old tanker alongside the dock at the Rosyth Yard began tooting her siren, spelling the word 'peace' in Morse over and over again. . . . In a moment a thousand whistles took up the refrain." All the ships anchored for miles up and down the Firth of Forth joined the chorus. Sirens screamed, foghorns boomed, ships bells rang, every ship's band began to play. Thousands of sailors massed on the decks, banging pots, pans, and any other object that made a racket, each ship trying to outdo the others. A *Texas* bluejacket wrote: "It was a volume of sound, never of its kind, perhaps, equaled in intensity before." Then signal guns started to fire red, green, and white stars, lighting up the sky and water as they floated lazily down. Very pistols joined in. Probably not a very shell remained in the fleet after that night. Searchlights came on and played on the flags of the Allies that had been raised on the truck and elsewhere.

On ships throughout the fleet, pandemonium reigned with little or no check from the officers. They often joined in. Snake dances of shouting officers and men, some beating galley tinware and ringing dinner bells, others carrying brooms and swabs, weaved around the decks. "Some of the coalheavers from below came up with ash rakes and shovels." "Some were dressed as comedians, some half dressed." One British sailor wrote in his memoir: "I was amazed when I saw an American sailor climb aloft up the ship's trellis mast with a can of paraffin slung around his shoulders. Reaching the crow's next, he proceeded to pour the paraffin all over his clothes, then with an air of nonchalance he set fire to himself. Giving a wave to the watchers below the human torch dived fifty feet into the water, everyone giving him a tremendous cheer."[20] Thousands, including the bands, manned small boats and began visiting and serenading other ships. One officer later wrote that "it is probably unnecessary to record that the Americans did most of the visiting" to British ships, where they were offered rum, champagne and other alcoholic beverages. Toasts were drunk to the president, to the king, to Admiral Beatty, and to the United States and the Allies. Boats full of British bluejackets also went from ship to ship. A boat from *Repulse* sent a case of whiskey to *New York*. It was placed in the junior officer's wardroom, but during the night senior officers frequently appeared to indulge. According to a British admiral: "every officer except the Admiral [Rodman] celebrated the Armistice at times in the junior officer's wardroom." The officer of the deck on another American dreadnought recalled that "about 9:30 we saw a row boat coming in our direction with an officer standing up in the stern giving them the stroke, but nobody paying any attention to him. They turned out to be officers from one of the British ships and they were in every costume going. You never saw such rigs. I was the only officer on deck . . . that could receive them and as they were all pretty well lit, I had my hands full from being hugged and shaken hands with. They said they felt sorry for us when they saw the 'negative Squadron [sixth] B.S.' in the signal and had come over to cheer us up. Upon closer view I saw that every one of them had a bottle of gin or champagne." The bottles were taken down to the wardroom where "in about five minutes . . . [those present] . . . were 'splicing the main brace.'"[21]

All in all, it was a fitting occasion. "A party like that comes only once in a lifetime," an American officer wrote. "But it is a bad ending," confided a British officer in his diary. A correspondent observed: "The officers and men of the American Fleet received the news with mixed feelings. They rejoiced at the prospect of getting home, but they never fired a shot in anger, and they would have dearly liked to have been in something big before the end came." A *Texas* bluejacket agreed: "Despite the spontaneous spirit of revelry, the majority of the crew harbored a feeling of disappointment. . . . [T]he hope that had burned deep within all of us during the long, dreary North Sea days was that we would take part in the greatest naval battle of all time." "I cannot speak for the fleet," one of *New York*'s officers said, "but speaking for myself I am disappointed." The same was true of many of the British despite four years of war. Admiral Beatty felt "cheated." He and many of his officers and men wanted a Trafalgar-like engagement to break "the Sea Power of the Hun forever." Even after the celebration, he kept submarine measures in effect: "The armistice has been signed but it is doubtful whether there is sufficient authority in Germany to enforce it." Personnel on open decks were ordered to carry gas masks.[22]

The surrender of the German fleet ten days later ended once and for all the hopes of a massive surface engagement. Before the signing of the Armistice, Allied and American diplomats and military officials discussed the fate of the German navy. Some wanted them surrendered, and others recommended internment. The eventual agreement resulted in either the surrender or destruction of the German submarines, and the internment of the surface fleet, or at least most of it. When no neutral nation proved willing to assume the responsibility of hosting the interned ships, the British proposed Scapa Flow, and it was chosen.[23]

Operation ZZ, the internment of the surface vessels, took place on November 21. The Grand Fleet met the German High Seas Fleet off the Scottish coast and escorted it to the internment site in Scapa Flow. Admiral Beatty sent a cruiser to guide the Germans through the minefields. The crews on the Allied and American ships realized that the enemy ships were coming when lookouts spotted the cruiser's kite balloon. Approximately 370 Allied ships from submarines to battleships were formed in a double line twenty miles long and six miles across. Beatty, suspicious that the Germans might not surrender without a fight, sent out a general signal to the fleet, cautioning them that a state of war still was in effect. Guns were trained on the approaching ships and readied for immediate loading and firing. The fire control centers were fully manned, and directors and range finders continuously plotted the range of the German ships. These precautions were taken despite instructions to the Germans that they were to disarm their weapons, including the removal of their breach blocks.[24]

The American Sixth Battle Squadron lined up along with the units of the Grand Fleet and other Allied ships to receive the German ships. If there had been tension on the American ships the night before, it was not apparent on *Texas*. A reporter found a party going in the wardroom. A jazz band serenaded a crowd of American and British naval officers and a number of women, mostly British officers' wives and daughters. Admiral Sims and members of his staff arrived from London that day and dined with Admiral Rodman on board *New York*. Reveille sounded extremely early at approximately 2:00 p.m. The fleet got underway out of the Firth. The battleships sortied by squadrons in order. At dawn, they went to General Quarters. When the German ships slowly made their way through the huge armada, the Allied ships reversed themselves and steamed parallel to the units of the High Seas Fleet. The Sixth led the battleships because it was the last to come out. Sims later described the occasion to his wife: "I doubt if you could be made to realize what an imposing spectacle. . . . We were of course all wishing for the fairest possible weather in order that the photographic records of the ceremony might be taken and exhibited in all of the cinematograph theatres in the world. So for a wonder the sun came out and shone continuously throughout the day."[25] An American Marine who witnessed the day's events wrote, "It was a wonderful, almost terrible, sight; and it gave one a feeling of embarrassment in looking on at another's shame."[26]

A few days after the surrender, the American battleships left the Grand Fleet. On the eve of their departure, Admiral Beatty said, "you won't forget your 'comrades of the mist,'" nor did they.[27]

The battlewagons were not the first American warships to depart for home waters; destroyers, yachts, and other craft began to leave their European bases late in November. At the same time, Simsadus began the process of dismantling the various air stations and bases in European waters. Land, buildings, equipment, and military armament were returned to their original owners. Some small vessels were transferred to the Allies. Demobilization of the U.S. naval forces in European waters continued into 1919 and even beyond.

During this process, publications began to appear that analyzed the U.S. Navy's contribution to the war effort. Various naval offices, including those of Daniels, Sims, and even Admiral Wilson, compiled statistics to illustrate American naval involvement in the war. Personnel casualties for the Navy during the war totaled 6,929 enlisted men and 438 officers. Of the enlisted fatalities, 5,352 were attributed to disease, including the influenza epidemic. Another 1,193 died as a result of accidents. Only 384 were killed in action. Thirty-eight officers died in combat, 284 of disease, and 116 through accidents. Less than 1 percent of the 53,402 American servicemen who died in battle during World War I were in the Navy.[28] Ship casualties were relatively light. The Navy lost forty-eight naval vessels, about half to submarines. Collision, mines, and miscellaneous causes account for the others. Auxiliaries and transports made up a majority of the losses. The destroyers *Chauncey*, *Jacob Jones*, and the Coast Guard cutter *Tampa* were the only American warships lost to enemy action in European waters during the war.[29] The British Admiral W. C. Pakenham wrote an American naval officer shortly after the war: "I thought Providence as well as skill must have been on your side to enable you to pass through a period of such dangerous service, and yet to take all home."[30] He referred to the American battleships with the Grand Fleet, but his observation applied to the entire U.S. naval force in European waters.

After the war, it was not uncommon for boisterous American veterans' organizations, ethnocentric politicians, and crass tourists to claim that the United States saved the Allies. The Allied peoples bitterly resented these pronouncements, particularly in Great Britain and France. Considering that enormous casualties wiped out an entire generation of young men and brought on economic deprivation, many among the Allies harbored anger toward the Americans who came in only after nearly three years of exhausting conflict. One writer lamented that the United States intervened only after the Allies "had already done most of the dirty work."[31] Others denigrated the participation of the American Navy in the war, giving the Royal Navy total credit for the victory. Even Sir Winston Churchill, an admirer of the United States, belittled the U.S. Navy's role.[32] French writers have been divided on the U.S. Navy's part, and the Germans generally believed, as Michelson wrote, that its contribution "was never of decisive importance."[33]

Secretary of the Navy Daniels and Admiral Sims agreed that the Army made a greater contribution than the Navy. "This was an army war," Sims wrote his wife, "and the army should receive more recognition than the navy." He added, "The trouble seems to be that the navy did not win any battles—which bears out my statement—that you must shed blood to deserve recognition."[34] The general consensus, however, is that both services contributed to the victory.

Certainly the United States accepted the basic strategy of the Allies for both land and sea warfare.[35] Also, and of equal importance in evaluating this first instance of coalition warfare in the martial experience of the nation, is that its naval force in the war zone was placed under the command of the Allies. This practice held true for all of the Allies, but it especially applied to the Royal Navy. The subordination of U.S. naval vessels to another nation's command on the strategic and operational level, although unique during World War I, was repeated in World War II and later in the North Atlantic Treaty Organization. Admiral Sims's policy was amalgamation, not simply cooperation. He "believed from the beginning . . . that the only effective way to throw the weight of the U.S. Navy into the war without delay was to use its available units to strengthen the weak spots in the other Navies." So wrote one of his officers as the war wound down.[36] This approach was the opposite of General Pershing's method. He fought long and hard for a separate American Expeditionary Force rather than integrating his units with those of the Allies. Considering various elements such as logistical requirements, types of vessels needed for the submarine war, and the Department's policies, it is extremely doubtful that Sims could have commanded a separate naval force operationally, even if he had desired to do so.[37]

Historians and others who wrote about the war, including his critics, agree that Sims was the right man to command American naval forces in European waters. His rapport with the Allied leaders was nearly universal. Admittedly, he accepted, generally without question, their naval policies and supported them fiercely in his relations with Washington officials. He possessed a sound grasp of the naval war and its requirements. He looked at the war from the perspective of a theater commander, which at times led to conflict with the secretary of the navy and the CNO. Despite differences, in time the Navy Department usually accepted his recommendations. Daniels often appointed his subordinate commanders without soliciting his advice. He had minor difficulties with several of them, but on the whole they were effective. Sims relieved only one of them. Before the war, Sims had been one of the proponents of a general staff. He created one for the Navy in European waters in London. He also established a planning section that became a model for those established in the Admiralty and the Navy Department.[38]

In coalition warfare, cooperation and good relations are highly desirable not only at the top but exceedingly helpful throughout the ranks. Disagreement and friction appeared at times, but on balance the American Navy maintained a commendable association with the Allies on all levels in the war zone.

Allied naval strategy generally followed the precepts of Alfred Thayer Mahan, seeking to gain control of the seas by means of blockade and by seeking to destroy the German fleet in a decisive battle such as Trafalgar. These objectives never changed despite the inconclusiveness of the fleet engagement at Jutland and the introduction of convoying.[39] In 1917, the teachings of Mahan also dominated American naval policy, but under the influence of Sims they were sacrificed because of the nature of the war.

Responding to his demands for the deployment of antisubmarine craft to the war zone, the Navy Department, however reluctantly, gradually abandoned its desire to concentrate the battle fleet.[40]

This change in doctrine was a direct result of the submarine crisis and the introduction of the convoy system. Although the Admiralty could have introduced convoying without American antisubmarine craft, it did not do so and never seriously considered it. According to Marder, a small number of British warships engaged in convoy work. As late as October 1918, it contributed only 257 escorts, a mere 5.1 percent of the slightly over 5,000 ships in commission. "The total is still a mere 15 percent, if we add some 500 ships which served as escorts or in support from time to time." He added that "the bulk of the escort forces were over-age destroyers, sloops, and other craft."[41] The U.S. Navy eventually deployed nearly four hundred ships to the war zone, a large percentage of which engaged in antisubmarine activities. In addition, the cruiser and transport force of the Atlantic Fleet, under Rear Admiral Albert Gleaves, consisted of destroyers, cruisers, and overage battleships. Although not part of the U.S. naval force in European waters, they escorted transports and merchant ships to and from the war zone. The U.S. Navy in 1917 was a second-rate force compared to the Royal Navy, certainly in number of ships, but it contributed more to the convoy system than did the British navy.[42]

Robert H. Ferrell states bluntly that "without American destroyers transatlantic convoys would have been impossible." Perhaps an exaggeration, but American escort craft were crucial to the convoy system, and convoying was a major element in the defeat of the submarine. The Navy Department deployed antisubmarine vessels to European waters a few at a time, and Admiral Benson held back ships out of concern for the Western Hemisphere, but Admiral Beatty refused to release any of his destroyers for convoy duty. Nonetheless, enough American antisubmarine craft were operating out of British and French ports, including Gibraltar, by the fall of 1917 to make a highly significant difference. The Queenstown command exercised the vital responsibility of escorting transports through the Western Approaches. As Admiral Jellicoe wrote Bayly after the war, "You have the satisfaction of knowing how greatly the Queenstown command contributed to the final victory." He added, "I suppose that no one realizes that more than the United States Navy."[43] As far as the Navy was concerned, the American contribution was more than "moral" or "psychological," as some writers have stated.[44] The containment of the submarine was not decisive by itself. It was only one of the military operations that contributed to the economic, political, and moral collapse of the Triple Alliance. Nevertheless, as Schmitt and Vedeler wrote about the submarine, "This revolutionary instrument of war was not a decisive weapon, but it was the nearest thing to that weapon that came out of the war."[45]

An impressive number of writers have stressed the impact of the blockade, which was maintained until the signing of the Treaty of Versailles, as the most important factor in German defeat. Certainly the Grand Fleet held the German High Seas Fleet in check throughout the war, and, as Jerry W. Jones states, was the real power behind the antisubmarine campaign. In a broad sense, the Allies and the United States won because of a combined sea, land, and air blockade that gradually exhausted Germany's economic and military power.[46] Allied and American control of the seas allowed them to transport men and material to the war zone safely. Command of the seas was not complete until the submarine threat was brought under control. The American Navy contributed to the blockade's success not only by emphasizing antisubmarine warfare and convoying but indirectly by deploying battleships with the Grand Fleet. The North Sea Mine Barrage and the Otranto Barrage contributed to the blockade, both of which included American naval participation.

Probably the mine barrages were not worth the large amount of fiscal resources, manpower, and vessels allocated to them. Few U-boats were destroyed, and German submariners claimed after the war that they had little difficulty avoiding them. The same judgment applies to the hunter groups. The available technology could not locate submerged U-boats. Nothing proved effective until the invention of SONAR. American naval vessels sunk or damaged very few U-boats.[47] American naval aviation was on the verge of contributing substantially to the war effort by November 1918, but, lacking adequate resources, it made little impact. In the application of operational logistics, the U.S. Navy proved effective from the beginning.

The bureaus made contingency plans, and a number of them moved beyond planning to implementation before the American intervention. Yet they did not envision the support of a large military and naval force deployed thousands of miles from the home base. Operational logistics during modern warfare, including World War I, is an incredibly complex business. The task of moving men and materials to the points where and when required in the proper quantity and sequence is essentially a naval mission. Despite the immensity of the task, the Navy carried out this responsibility in World War I with surprisingly few "foul-ups."[48] Self-sufficiency became a major objective of the American naval forces in European waters during the war. The strain of four years of war on the Allies made this practice essential. To a great degree it was attained, particularly in repairs, but considerable logistical support came from the Allies.[49]

These observations do not mean that the United States Navy was prepared to fight the war. After the war, Sims claimed that it was largely unprepared, and a drawn-out partisan investigation by the Senate Naval Affairs Committee did not produce significant conclusions. Both Sims and those who said that the Navy was prepared—Daniels, Benson, and the bureau chiefs, among others—were correct. The Navy prepared for the wrong kind of war in the wrong place. Preparation rested on the presumption of a war in the western Atlantic, where fleet actions would predominate, not a struggle in European waters, where antisubmarine craft and U-boats would fight it out. Admiral Mayo insisted that the fleet was as ready for war as it could be in April 1917 but agreed that "the material unpreparedness of the vessels in reserve and out of commission, and the shortage of personnel, was due primarily to the national policy of strict neutrality with its resultant effect of a failure to prepare against war." He stressed that a navy ready to fight a war "can not be built and trained in a year or two." It was the responsibility of the political leaders to foresee the possibility of conflict and to order the necessary preparations.[50]

When war was declared, the U.S. Navy was on the brink of becoming a first-level naval power. The United States had twenty-three pre-dreadnoughts and fifteen dreadnoughts in April 1917, and *New Mexico* and *Idaho* were launched shortly after. The naval bill of 1916 provided for a sustained construction program of 156 ships of all types, including 10 battleships and 6 battle cruisers, to be laid down before July 1, 1919. This construction program was severely modified because of the need for antisubmarine craft during the war and the Naval Disarmament Treaty of 1922. None of the capital ships approved in this bill was completed during the war. The Navy did not deploy its newest and most powerful battleships in commission in 1917 in the war zone during the conflict. The desperate need for destroyers and other antisubmarine craft led to laying down 267 destroyers, but few reached European waters. Several hundred wooden subchasers and Eagle boats were built to conduct ASW operations, but few of the Eagle boats were commissioned before the Armistice. In general, the U.S. Navy in European waters fought the war with older vessels and converted yachts, many of which were obsolete. Fortunately, this motley collection of naval vessels did not have to engage in combat with enemy surface ships. They fought submarines. Although rarely successful in sinking or even seriously damaging any, they succeeded in keeping them away from vital convoys. The Allies could not have won without American help, including naval support.[51]

The Navy derived very few lessons from its deployment of vessels to the combat zone. It forgot the devastation caused by submarine warfare; and it ignored the potential of air power; it disregarded the effectiveness of convoying; it lost sight of the necessity to prepare for war, at bottom a responsibility of the civil authority, which was, as usual, abandoned in the face of public lack of interest. The generation that governed the United States at the approach of World War II, including the president, had firsthand knowledge of what had happened twenty years before. The Navy grasped the importance of logistical support. Efforts were made to develop the train, to strengthen operational support, and to improve naval technology during the interwar years. Although the fleet included aircraft carriers, as far as most of the Navy was concerned, the battleship remained the decisive weapon. Mahan remained in vogue. The Navy returned to its historic peacetime role of showing the flag.

Notes

Chapter 1. Reveille in Washington

1. Entry for April 22, 1917, in Cronon, *The Cabinet Diaries of Josephus Daniels, 1913–1921*, 118, hereafter cited as Josephus Daniels, *Cabinet Diaries*.

2. Entry for March 25, 1917, ibid., 121.

3. The General Board, created in 1901, was an advisory body of naval officers.

4. Link, *Wilson: Campaigns for Progressivism and Peace*, 409.

5. Admiralty to Beatty, April 6, 1917, ADM137/1946; Barclay to Foreign Office, March 20, 1917, ADM137/1436 in the Public Records Office, London. Hereafter Admiralty records are cited as ADM, and the Public Records Office is cited as PRO.

6. Walworth, *Woodrow Wilson*, 2: 100.

7. Maxwell, *The Naval Front*, 176.

8. Hurd and Bashford, *Sons of Admiralty*, 247; Schoultz, *With the British Battle Fleet*, 275.

9. Entry for April 20, 1917, in MacDonough, *In London during the Great War*, 189.

10. Quoted in Reiners, *The Lights Went Out in Europe*, 218.

11. Herwig, *Politics of Frustration*, 128–29.

12. Josephus Daniels, *The Wilson Era: Years of War*, 339; Josephus Daniels, *Our Navy at War*, 1.

13. Entry for April 6, 1917, in Taussig, *Queenstown Patrol*, 3; Wiggins, *My Romance with the Navy*, 75; entry for April 6, 1917, M. W. Larimer Diary, University of Virginia Library, Charlottesville, hereafter cited as UVA.

14. Quoted in Trask, "William Shepherd Benson," 4. See also Coletta, *Sea Power in the Atlantic and Mediterranean in World War I*, 60; and Woodward, "The Military Role of the U.S. in World War I," 122–23. "Aide to operations" was senior naval officer until the position of "chief of naval operations" (CNO) was created.

15. Fiske, *From Midshipman to Rear Admiral*, 544–45.

16. Finnegan, *Against the Specter of a Dragon*, 24–25. See also Schilling, "Admirals and Foreign Policy," Ph.D. diss., 49–50.

17. Finnegan, *Against the Specter of a Dragon*, 37–40.

18. Link, *Wilson, Confusion and Crisis*, 33. See also Cuff, *The War Industries Board*, 34. The third *Lusitania* note warned Germany that the American government would regard another submarine attack on a passenger ship as "deliberately unfriendly."

19. Quoted in Trask, *The AEF and Coalition Warmaking*, 4.

20. For Strauss's testimony, see U.S. Congress, Subcommittee on the Committee on Naval Affairs, *Hearings: Naval Investigation*, 66th Cong., 2nd sess., Washington, D.C.: GPO, 1921, 2803; hereafter cited as *Naval Investigation*. For Bureau of Supplies and Accounts, see Confidential Memo, Dec. 1, 1918, Box 1802, Records of the Bureau of Supplies and Accounts, Record Group Number 143, National Archives and Records Service, Washington, D.C., hereafter cited as RG143; History of the Bureau of Supplies and Accounts during the War, Subject File ZU, Record Group Number 45, Naval Records Collection of the Office of Naval Records and Library, National Archives and Records Service, Washington, D.C., is hereafter cited as RG45. National Archives and Records Service is hereafter cited as NA. Bureau of Supplies and Accounts is hereafter cited as BuS&A. For Bureau of Medicine and Surgery, see various files, in the 13000 series, in Records of the Bureau of Medicine and Surgery, Record Group Number 52, NA, hereafter

cited as RG52. See also file 14258-A-3 in Box 795, Correspondence Concerning Ships, 1915–1925, Entry 105, Records of the Bureau of Ships, Record Group Number 19, NA, hereafter cited as RG19. For the Naval Consulting Board, see Finnegan, *Against the Specter of a Dragon*, 114–17, and Cuff, *The War Industries Board*, 15–17. See also Press Conference, April 6, 1937, in *Complete Presidential Press Conferences of Franklin D. Roosevelt*, 9: 249–50; and von Doenhoff and von Doenhoff, *Patriots and Guardians*, 9. The Benson memoir is in the William S. Benson Papers, Library of Congress, Washington, D.C. Manuscript collections in the Library of Congress are hereafter cited as LC.

21. Brooke, "The National Defense Policy of the Wilson Administration," Ph.D. diss., 160–61.

22. Ibid.; Testimony of Admirals William S. Benson and Charles J. Badger, *Naval Investigation*, 1142–75, 1819–23, 1840.

23. Finnegan, *Against the Specter of a Dragon*, 162.

24. The *Sussex* was a British passenger ship torpedoed March 26, 1916. The United States demanded the cessation of unrestricted submarine warfare or "the Government can have no choice but to sever diplomatic relations." German-American relations improved after the pledge. It helped Wilson win reelection by demonstrating that his firm policy toward Germany was effective.

25. *U.S. Statutes at Large*, 39, part I, 556–619; Link, *Wilson, Confusion and Crisis*, 336–38.

26. Entry for April 11, 1917, in Josephus Daniels, *Cabinet Diaries*, 132–33. See also W. J. Williams, "Josephus Daniels and U.S. Navy's Shipbuilding Program during World War I," 17–18.

27. W. J. Williams, "Josephus Daniels and U.S. Navy's Shipbuilding Program during World War I," 17–25.

28. *Ships' Data U.S. Naval Vessels, November 1, 1916*, passim. Jellicoe, *The Crisis of the Naval War*, 153; Kittredge, *Naval Lessons of the Great War*, 191; Hurd and Bashford, *Sons of Admiralty*, 248–49; Rodman, *Yarns of a Kentucky Admiral*, 261–62.

29. Mayo, "The Atlantic Fleet in the Great War," 349.

30. Finnegan, *Against the Specter of a Dragon*, 189–90; copy of report in Bowling, "The Negative Influence of Mahan on the Protection of Shipping in Wartime," Ph.D. diss., 284.

31. Quoted in Kittredge, *Naval Lessons of the Great War*, 81. Kittredge's book offers a good condensation of the hearings.

32. Ibid., 165–66, 190, 192.

33. Gleaves, *The Admiral*, 135–36; Charles C. Gill Memoirs, Operational Archives, Naval Historical Center; hereafter cited as OA; the Naval Historical Center is hereafter cited as NHC; Hanrahan to Sims, 1920, Box 62, William Sowden Sims Papers, Manuscript Division, LC. Braynard, *The Story of the Leviathan*, 1: 108; Alden and Allan, *The United States Navy: A History*, 339; *U.S.S. Seattle during the War*, 17–18. See also testimony of Admiral Rodgers, *Naval Investigation*, 1168–69; and Dudley W. Knox to Frothington, 1925, Box 9, Dudley W. Knox Papers, LC.

34. Kittredge, *Naval Lessons of the Great War*, 163–65, 171–73, 191; *Naval Investigation*, 520, 2794–95; Bowling, "The Negative Influence of Mahan on the Protection of Shipping in Wartime," 294. Mayo's manuscript on the Atlantic Fleet in Reel 5, Josephus Daniels Papers, LC.

35. Plunkett is quoted in Kittredge, *Naval Lessons of the Great War*, 184. For gunnery problems, see Klachko (with Trask), *Benson*, 42–43; see also *Annual Report of the Secretary of the Navy*, 1916, 22–24.

36. For Mayo quote, see Mayo, "The Atlantic Fleet in the Great War," 349. See also Gill Memoirs, OA; entry for April 6, 1917, in Taussig, *Queenstown Patrol*, 5.

37. Richard Downs, June 27, 1917, ADM137/1621. See also his report dated July 22, 1917 in ADM137/1621.

38. Kittredge, *Naval Lessons of the Great War*, 80, 166–67, 174; *Naval Investigation*, 420, 521;

King and Whitehill, *Fleet Admiral King*, 109. Abrahamson, *American Arms for a New Century*, 174; Knox to Frothington, Oct. 28, 1925, Box 9, Knox Papers, LC.

39. Quoted in Herwig, *Politics of Frustration*, 161.

40. War Plan Black was one of a number of contingency plans prepared by the Naval War College for possible conflict. Each plan was given color designation, for example, "Orange" for Japan and "Blue" for Great Britain.

41. Weigley, *The American Way of War*, 193; Costello, "Planning for War: A History of the General Board of the Navy," Ph.D. diss., 146; Schilling, "Admirals and Foreign Policy," 16.

42. Yerxa, "The United States Navy in Caribbean Waters during World War I," 182–83; V. Davis, *The Admiral's Lobby*, 128–30; Trask, "Benson," 7; Klachko, *Benson*, 41.

43. G. E. Wheeler, "William Veazie Pratt, U.S. Navy," 41; Gault to Admiralty, July 5, 1917, ADM137/1437; Klachko, *Benson*, 106–7. Benson's papers in the manuscript collection, LC, clearly indicates his penchant for detail.

44. "U.S. Naval Administration in World War II, Guide No. 18, CNO Aspects of Logistic Planning," 12–18, copy in Naval Department Library. Abrahamson, *American Arms for a New Century*, 170–71; Furer, *Administration of the Navy Department in World War II*, 110–11; Coontz to Senator Hale, June 5, 1920, copy in the Samuel McGowan Papers, LC.

45. Klachko, *Benson*, 24–26; Trask, "Benson," 3–5.

46. For Benson's prewar career, see Klachko's biography. A brief biographical sketch is in Bradford, *Admirals of the New Steel Navy*, 300–329. See also a summary of his career in Cogar, *Dictionary of Admirals of the U.S. Navy*, 2: 222–23; and C. G. Reynolds, *Famous American Admirals*, 29–31.

47. Benson to Pratt, Nov. 23, 1918, Box 102, Area File, 1911–1927, RG45. See also Klachko, *Benson*, 104–5, and Furer, *Administration of the Navy Department in World War II*, 111.

48. Trask, "Benson," 20. See also Charles W. Moore Oral History, Columbia University; and Zogbaum, *From Sail to Saratoga*, 257; Thomas Craven's comments in "Aviation U.S.N., from Its Beginning until Spring of 1920," ZGU subject file, RG45.

49. To Daniels, July 29, 1917, Box 13, Daniels Papers, LC.

50. Quoted in Herwig, *Politics of Frustration*, 161. See also Jellicoe to Beatty, Nov. 9, 1917, in Patterson, *The Jellicoe Papers*, 2: 225–26. Long quote in Harries and Harries, *The Last Days of Innocence*, 83.

51. Sims to Pringle, Nov. 13, 1917, Box 79, Sims Papers; Sims to Fullam, Feb. 20, 1918, Box 59, Sims Papers, LC; Belknap to McGrann [1919] date and year unreadable, Reginald Belknap Papers, LC. Weigley, "The Principle of Civilian Control, from McClellan to Powell" 27–58; Ferrell, *Woodrow Wilson and World War I*, 37–38; Woodward, "The Military Role of the United States in World War I," 122–23. According to a Wilson biographer, the president was more interested in naval affairs than in the Army and had once thought of enrolling at Annapolis. Walworth, *Woodrow Wilson*, 108. See also Daniels, *The Wilson Era: Years of War*, 41.

52. Klachko, *Benson*, 38; Coletta, "Josephus Daniels," in Coletta, *American Secretaries of the Navy*, 2: 540.

53. Still, *American Sea Power in the Old World*, 185.

54. There is no adequate biography of Daniels. See Morrison, *Josephus Daniels*. See also Cronon's introduction to the Daniels *Cabinet Diaries*; Jonathan Daniels, *The End of Innocence*; Coletta, "Daniels," in Coletta, *American Secretaries of the Navy*, 2: 525–81; Bartlett, "Secretary of the Navy Josephus Daniels and the Marine Corps," 190–207; Karsten, *The Naval Aristocracy*, 13. For Daniels's unpopularity in Washington, see Pepper, *Philadelphia Lawyer*, 117–18; Longworth, *Crowded Hours*, 260; Powers Symington, "The Navy Way," Navy Department Library, hereafter cited as NDL; W. J. Williams, "Josephus Daniels and the U.S. Navy's Shipbuilding during World War I"; "Daniels" entry in Herwig and Heyman, *Biographical Dictionary of World War I*, 125.

55. Quoted in Bartlett, "Secretary of the Navy Josephus Daniels and the Marine Corps," 191.

See also Cronon's introduction to Josephus Daniels, *Cabinet Diaries*, vii; Hassler, *With Shield and Sword*, 268; Coletta, "Daniels," 526–27. For Daniels's efforts to impose his moralistic views on the Navy and others, see Mrs. Josephus Daniels, *Recollections of a Cabinet Minister's Wife*, 147; *New York Herald*, Sept. 14, 1917; Daniels, *The Wilson Era: Years of War*, 52–53; Morrison, *Daniels*, 64–66, 74–76; Coletta, "Daniels," passim. For social issues, particularly his efforts to improve the lot of enlisted men, see Harrod, *Manning the New Navy*, 29–31; Ferrell, *Woodrow Wilson and World War I*, 32. Richard McKenna, the author of *Sand Pebbles* and a career enlisted man, wrote an essay titled "The Wreck of Uncle Josephus," in which he stated that Daniels ("Uncle Josephus") was known to the enlisted personnel of the prewar Navy as a kind of "do-gooder" and as a "defier of admirals," who "trampled upon traditions" (in *The Left-Handed Monkey Wrench*, 159).

56. Harrod, *Manning the New Navy*, 28. See also Coffman, *The War to End All Wars*, 88.

57. W. J. Williams, "Josephus Daniels and the U.S. Navy's Shipbuilding during World War I," 8; Harries and Harries, *The Last Days of Innocence*, 58. Leahy quote in William D. Leahy Diary, LC; Pratt quote in William Pratt, "Autobiography," William V. Pratt Papers, OA. Spector, "Josephus Daniels, Franklin Roosevelt, and the Reinvention of the Naval Enlisted Man." Richardson, *On the Treadmill to Pearl Harbor*, 462.

58. Spector, *Professors of War*, 126.

59. Trask, "FDR at War," 14. FDR wanted to go to Annapolis, but his mother persuaded him to go to Harvard. Roosevelt sublimated his naval interests in the collection of manuscripts and other naval memorabilia.

60. K. S. Davis, "No Talent for Subordination," 5.

61. Kilpatrick, *Roosevelt and Daniels*, passim; Ferrell, *Woodrow Wilson and World War I*, 32; Hassler, *With Shield and Sword*, 268; Jonathon Daniels, *The End of Innocence*, 215–18; N. Miller, *FDR: An Intimate History*, 138–40; Freidel, *Franklin D. Roosevelt: The Apprenticeship*, 304.

62. Knox to Frothington, Oct. 28, 1925, Box 9, Knox Papers, LC. See also Klachko, *Benson*, 28.

63. K. S. Davis, "No Talent for Subordination," 7.

64. Knox to Frothington, Oct. 28, 1925, Box 9, Knox Papers, LC.

65. Entry for Feb. 4, 1917, Packer Journal, Packer MS, Churchill College, Cambridge.

66. Plan in *Naval Investigation*, 1102–3.

67. Quoted in Kittredge, *Naval Lessons of the Great War*, 195. The decision to concentrate the fleet in the Chesapeake Bay area in case of war was made the year before the United States entered the war. See memo from SecNav, April 27, 1916, Reel 1, ME-11, "World War One," microfilm, NDL, hereafter cited as ME-11.

68. Pratt, "Autobiography," OA. Admiral King agreed with this assessment. See King and Whitehill, *Fleet Admiral King*, 110.

69. Stackhouse, "The Anglo-American Convoy System in World War I," Ph.D. diss., 52–61. "Pinky" to Sims, Sept. 13, 1917, Box 23, Sims Papers, LC; Wilson to Daniels, July 2, 1917, copy in M. Simpson, *Anglo-American Naval Relations*, 78. See also Lord Northcliffe to War Cabinet, July 5, 1917, ibid., 84. He was head of a British mission to the United States in 1917. See also Love, *History of the U.S. Navy*, 504; speech of Wilson, Aug. 11, 1917, copy in Box 5, Special Correspondence, Joe Tumulty Papers, LC.; Maurer, "American Naval Concentration and the German Battle Fleet," 168. For Anglophobe sentiments in Washington, see Bowling, "The Negative Influence of Mahan on the Protection of Shipping in Wartime," Ph.D. diss., 220–21. M. Simpson, *Anglo-American Naval Relations*, 62.

70. Trask, *The AEF and Coalition Warmaking*, 168. These strategic policies are discussed in more detail in later chapters. See also Nenninger, "American Military Effectiveness in the First World War," 126.

71. Sims, *The Victory at Sea*, 45.

72. Trask, *Captains and Cabinets*, 64, passim.

73. Sims, *The Victory at Sea*, 8–9.

74. Ibid., 7–8.

75. Jellicoe, *The Submarine Peril*, 70–71; Marder, *From the Dreadnought to Scapa Flow*, 4: 147–48.

76. Quoted in Marder, *From the Dreadnought to Scapa Flow*, 4: 70.

77. For the U.S. Navy and the patrol system, see pp. 472–73 in this volume.

78. Sims to SecNav, April 19, 1917, CP subj file, RG45.

79. April 12, 1917, Patterson, *The Jellicoe Papers*, 2: 156.

80. Sims, *The Victory at Sea*, 36.

81. Sims to SecNav, April 14, 1917, CP subj file, RG45; Sims, *The Victory at Sea*, 374–76.

82. To SecNav, April 19, 1917, in Sims, *The Victory at Sea*, 377–84; Page to SecState, April 16, 1917, Reel 1, ME-11. The introduction of the convoy system and Sims's role in it is discussed in more detail in chapter 13.

83. Entry for April 19, 1917, in Josephus Daniels, *Cabinet Diaries*, 136.

84. Hendrick, *The Life and Letters of Walter Hines Page*, 2: 278; A. H. Miles to Sims, March 16, 1920, Box 72, Sims Papers, LC; Hoover, *An American Epic*, 16.

85. Hendrick, *The Life and Letters of Walter Hines Page*, 2: 198–99; W. F. Bell, "American Embassies in Belligerent Europe," Ph.D. diss., 154–55; Cooper, *Walter Hines Page*, 378–81; *Naval Investigation*, 4, 71.

86. Josephus Daniels, *The Wilson Era: Years of War*, 70.

87. Sprout and Sprout, *The Rise of American Naval Power*, 363.

88. His accusations led to the highly publicized hearings held before the Senate Naval Affairs Committee, which opened on March 9, 1920.

89. *Naval Investigation*, 121.

90. July 3, 1917, Pratt Papers, OA. See also Sims to CNO, June 20, 1917, Box 3, Area file, RG45.

91. *Naval Investigation*, 1849–51.

92. Schilling, "Admirals and Foreign Policy," Ph.D. diss., 87.

93. Trask, "Benson," 11–12. See also Allard, "Anglo-American Differences during World War I," 75–76.

94. Albert Gleaves, *The Admiral*, 139; entry for May 19, 1917, diary, Albert Gleaves Papers, LC. See also Gleaves to Padgett, Aug. 9, 1917, Gleaves Papers. According to Admiral Mayo's son, who was an officer in the Navy in World War I, his father strongly opposed stripping the Atlantic Fleet of the destroyers. To Dunn, Feb. 13, 1931, Mayo Papers, LC.

95. To Daniels, General Board File 425, General Board Records, OA. See also Braisted, *The United States Navy in the Pacific*, 294–95, 300–301; Trask, *Captains and Cabinets*, 74.

96. Testimony of Capt. McKean, Sept. 4, 1917, General Board Hearings; See also Braisted, *The United States Navy in the Pacific*, 295–96, 300; Schilling, "Admirals and Foreign Policy," Ph.D. diss., 101–3.

97. Pratt to Sims, July 2, 1918, copy in Box 368, Daniels Papers, LC.

98. Trask, *Captains and Cabinets*, 94; Maurer, "American Naval Concentration and the German Battle Fleet, 1900–1918," 168–69; *Papers of the Foreign Relations of the United States, 1917*, Supplement 2, 116–17, hereafter cited as *Foreign Relations*, followed by year.

99. July 4, 1917, *Foreign Relations, 1917*, Supplement 2, 117–18.

100. For Northcliffe's message, see July 5, 1917, TP subj file, RG45. For Pollen's, see Sept. 7, 1917, to Geddes, and Sept. 17 to Sir Philip Kerr, copies in hands of author provided by Dr. Jon Sumida. See Sims to wife, Aug. 30, 1917, Box 9, Sims Papers. Sims had no qualms about using

journalists to further his policies as well. He mentioned a number of discussions with Winston Churchill; "am supplying him with the dope about the situation," to wife, Sept. 24, 1917, Box 9, Sims Papers. See also to wife, Sept. 15, 1917, ibid.

101. Trask, *Captains and Cabinets*, 89. See also Sims to Daniels, July 16, 1917, TP subj file, RG45; to Wilson, July 7, 1917, ibid.

102. See G. T. Davis, *A Navy Second to None*, 290.

103. October 16, 1917, Hearings. For an outline of British naval policy, see report of Admiralty's Plans Division, Nov. 17, 1917, ADM137/2706.

104. Owen, "The United States Navy and the Allied Blockade in the Last War," 206–12; Daniels to SecState, Feb. 20, 1919, *Foreign Relations, 1918*, Supplement 1, 933–36.

105. P. M. Kennedy, *The Rise and Fall of British Naval Mastery*, 243; Marder, *From the Dreadnought to Scapa Flow*, 2: 41.

106. Marder, *From the Dreadnought to Scapa Flow*, 4: 40–42. Knox to Frothingham, Dec. 12, 1925, Box 9, Knox Papers, LC.

107. Entry for March 23, 1918, in Josephus Daniels, *Cabinet Diaries*, 293. Daniels to Sims, July 25, 1918, TT subj file, RG45. Benson's biographers claim that the CNO drafted this cable to Sims. Klachko, *Benson*, 117. See also Trask, *Captains and Cabinets*, 197.

108. For a succinct discussion of this problem, see Allard, "Admiral William S. Sims and United States Naval Policy in World War I."

Chapter 2. Simsadus

1. Morison, *Admiral Sims and the Modern American Navy*, 341, hereafter cited as *Sims*.

2. Josephus Daniels, *The Wilson Era: Years of War*, 67.

3. *Pall Mall Gazette*, March 15, 1919.

4. Pratt, "Autobiography," in William V. Pratt papers, OA. Wygant, "Admiral Sims as I knew him," 1088–92; Mitchell, *History of the Modern American Navy*, 146. See also Hough, *The Great War at Sea*, 313; Wheeler, *Admiral Veazie Pratt*, 424; McGrann to Belknap, Dec. 3, 1936, Jan. 16, 16, 1937, Belknap Papers, LC. Belknap wrote an article on Sims published in the *Bulletin of the Military Order of the World War*. Copy in Belknap Papers. See also Handley and Sarty, *Tin Pots and Pirate Ships*, 196–97. Morison's biography of Sims is considered the standard work on the admiral. Its highly laudatory nature is not surprising considering the fact that he was married to Sims's youngest daughter at the time it was written. Rear Admiral Reginald Belknap questioned Morison's ability to write a biography of Sims, stressing, perhaps not surprisingly, that Morison had never served in the Navy. Belknap's wife (who knew Mrs. Sims) told him, "Mrs. Sims knows he [Morison] has to make a living." Belknap to Mike, March 4, 1940, Belknap Papers, LC. The most balanced biography is a brief study by David Trask in "William Sowden Sims: The Victory Ashore," 275–90. See also Hagan, "The Critic Within"; Herwig and Heyman, "Sims" entry in *Biographical Dictionary of World War I*, 318; Bowling, "Convoy in World War I," master's thesis, passim. There are also biographical summaries in C. G. Reynolds, *Famous American Admirals*, and Cogar, *Dictionary of Admirals in the U.S. Navy*.

5. *Le Figaro*, Aug. 15, 1917; *New York Telegram*, Dec. 13, 1918; Thompson, *Take Her Down*, 236.

6. Quoted in Morison, *Sims*, 24. For several anecdotes of his early career that illustrate his "impatience," see Meriwether, "Four American Admirals." Meriwether was a shipmate of Sims on the *Swatara*, 1883–86. Trask, "Sims," 282; King and Whitehill, *Fleet Admiral King*, 91, 127; Coffman, *The War to End All Wars*, 93; Pratt, "Autobiography," OA; Belknap to Mike, March 4, 1940, Belknap Papers, LC.

7. To wife, Aug. 7, 1917, Box 9, Sims Papers, LC; Josephus Daniels, *The Wilson Era: Years of War*, 270; Karsten, *The Naval Aristocracy*, 114.

8. Holt, "A Talk with Admiral Sims," 409; *Literary Digest*, July 7, 1917; *Daily Mail* (London),

Jan. 8, 1918; Jellicoe, *The Crisis of the Naval War*, 116; Halsey quoted in Coffman, *The War to End All Wars*, 93.

9. Paine, *Roads to Adventure*, 433. See also Baldridge, "Sims the Iconoclast," 183; Field, "Sims," 614; Wygant, "Admiral Sims as I Knew Him," 1091; H. H. Smith, "Sims—the Bold," *Navy and Merchant Marine* 1 (July 1917); B. Hayes, *Hull Down*, 269–70.

10. For Sims and Scott, see Padfield, *Aim Straight*, 120–23, 141–42, 152–53, 282–83; Admiral Sir Frederic Dreyer, in *The Sea Heritage*, wrote: "Scott and Sims will go down in history as having taught how to shoot with accuracy and to load with speed. This had a tremendous effect in two world wars" (34). One of Sims's peers at the Naval Academy wrote that Sims was extremely interested in gunnery while serving on the *Swatara* in the early 1880s. Ellicott, "Recollections of Admiral Sims," 319. Among those who received Sims's reports and was critical of him was Alfred Mahan. See Mahan to Luce, Nov. 16, 1901, to Theodore Roosevelt, Oct. 8, 1901, in Seagar and Maguire, *Letters and Papers of Alfred Thayer Mahan*, 3: 178–80, 234. Rear Admiral French E. Chadwick, however, was one of the senior officers who supported him. See Chadwick to Sims, Jan. 16, 1909, in D. D. Maguire, *French Ensor Chadwick, Selected Letters and Papers*, 455–56. Captain W. H. McCrann, who was gunnery officer on the *Brooklyn* when it was the first American warship to experiment with Scott's techniques, wrote that Sims began his push for reform while on the staff of Rear Admiral George C. Remey and with the strong encouragement of the admiral. See McGrann to Bristol, April 6, 1927, copy in the Belknap Papers, LC. Morison in his biography of Sims says that he began his "reform" work while on the *Kentucky* (78–99). See also Symington, "The Navy Way," NDL.

11. Hattendorf, *Sailors and Scholars*, 88–89.

12. Morison, *Sims*, 294–96; *Literary Digest*, June 21, 1919; manuscript, n.d., Box 42, William S. Benson Papers, LC.

13. Twining testimony, Case 10662, Fletcher Court of Inquiry, RG125, NA. See also Land, *Winning the War with Ships*, 96; Pratt, "Autobiography," OA; Morison, *Sims*, 302–3; Shafter, *Destroyers in Action*, 46–47; G. E. Wheeler, *Pratt*, 74–75; Pratt to Daniels, Nov. 12, 1917, Reel 65, Daniels Papers, LC.

14. To wife, June 4, Aug. 7, Sept. 26, 1917, July 20, 1918, all in Box 9, Sims Papers, LC.

15. Harris Laning, "An Admiral's Log," II, NDL; Pratt, "Autobiography," OA; Shafter, *Destroyers in Action*, 46–48; Morison, *Sims*, 293–94; King and Whitehill, *Fleet Admiral King*, 91; Knox to Frothington, Nov. 9, 1925, Box 9, Knox Papers, LC.

16. Hattendorf, *Sailors and Scholars*, 143; Morison, *Sims*, 302–3; Pratt, "Autobiography," OA; L. W. Johnson, "A Junior Officer with Admiral Sims," 1141; Alden and Earle, *Makers of Naval Tradition*, 324.

17. To Keupie (?), Jan. 19, 1919, Stark Family Papers, private possession of family. Copy provided author by Michael Simpson III. See also Dunn, *World Alive*, 270; Cotten to wife, July 21, 1918, Lyman Cotten Papers, University of North Carolina Library; Belknap to McCrann, May 24, 1939, Belknap Papers, LC.

18. Blackford, *Torpedoboat Sailor*, 92. Adams, *Witness to Power*, 87; Buell, *Master of Sea Power*, 49; Connolly, *Sea-Borne: Thirty Years Avoyaging*, 205–8; General Holland M. "Howlin Mad" Smith, USMC, called Sims narrow-minded. "Sims' viewpoint was a relic of the peculiar form of snobbery regarding the Marines common in the Navy at that period." H. M. Smith, *Coral and Brass*, 48–50.

19. Entry for May 25, 1917, in Taussig, *Queenstown Patrol*, 43.

20. *Daily Mail* (London), March 26, 1918. Among the prominent British subjects who lauded Sims in their memoirs and correspondence were Admiral Sir Percy Scott, *Fifty Years in the Royal Navy*, 154; Fisher to Sims, Dec. 29, 1918, in Marder, *Fear God and Dread Nought*, 3: 561; Repington, *The First World War I*, 2: 507; Hoy, *40 or How the War Was Won*, 271; Griff, *Surrendered*, 180; Brittain, *Pilgrims and Pioneers*, 141–42; Murray, *The Making of a Civil Servant*,

97–98; Hankey, *The Supreme Command*, 2: 584–85; Riddell, *Lord Riddell's War Diary*, 250–51; Addison, *Four and a Half Years*, 2: 357; Patterson, *Jellicoe: A Biography*, 39–40. See also Marder, *From the Dreadnought to Scapa Flow*, 5: 123–24; *Chicago News*, March 5, 1919; Land, *Winning the War with Ships*, 112.

21. Riddell to Sims, April 13, 1919, Box 81, Sims Papers, LC; Wemyss quote in Hough, *The Great War at Sea*, 313. See also Hurd and Bashford, *Sons of Admiralty*, 251.

22. Field, "Sims," 616; *New York Telegram*, Dec. 23, 1918; Ellicott, "Recollections of Admiral Sims," 319; Harries and Harries, *The Last Days of Innocence*, 76–77.

23. *Le Figaro*, Aug. 15, 1917. See also Holt, "A Talk with Admiral Sims," 394; Paine, *Roads to Adventure*, 432–33; Reuterdahl, "Admiral Sims," 9; *Le Temps*, Aug. 8, 1917; Sims to Bernard, Aug. 13, 1917, Box 47, Sims Papers, LC.

24. *New York Post*, April 8, 1919, March 13, 1920; *Le Figaro*, Aug. 15, 1917; Zogbaum, *From Sail to Saratoga*, 125; Beston, *Full Speed Ahead*, 132–33; Anonymous, "The Very Human Admiral," 93; Holt, "A Talk with Admiral Sims," 394.

25. Robertson, *From Private to Field Marshal*, 352. Robertson and Sims occasionally traveled to Paris together during the war. O'Hara, *World War at Its Climax*, 253–54; *New York Telegram*, Dec. 23, 1918; *Our Navy* 15 (Sept. 1921): 45; *St. Louis Post Dispatch*, April 27, 1919; *Times* (London), Oct. 1, 1936.

26. Quoted in Braisted, *The United States Navy in the Pacific*, 430. For other examples of Wilson's criticism, see entry July 21, 1917, in Josephus Daniels, *Cabinet Diaries*, 178; entry for May 7, 1919, Dr. Cary T. Grayson Diary in Link, *The Papers of Woodrow Wilson*, 58: 500; entry for May 7, 1919, Edith Benham Diary, ibid., 530–31; Wiseman memo, July 13, 1917, ibid., 43: 173. See also Oliver Pilat, *Pegler: Angry Man of the Press*, 116–17; and Wheeler, *Pratt*, 128.

27. Strauss Papers, OA.

28. G. E. Wheeler, *Pratt*, 104; Coletta, *The American Naval Heritage in Brief*, 203. In May, he wanted to send another admiral to represent the Navy in France, but Daniels refused. Trask, *Captains and Cabinets*, 86.

29. Entry for March 30, 1920, in Josephus Daniels, *Cabinet Diaries*, 511; *Naval Investigation*, 1769.

30. Benson Papers, LC. The Schley-Sampson controversy was over which one of the two won the Battle of Santiago during the Spanish-American War. It would divide the Navy and simmer for years.

31. Twining testimony in Case 10662, Fletcher Court of Inquiry, RG125; Sims to Pringle, Oct. 10, 1917, Box 79, Sims Papers, LC; Knox to Frothington, July 16, 1925, Box 9, Knox Papers, LC.

32. Quoted in Trask, *Captains and Cabinets*, 13; see also ibid., 163–64. In *Naval Investigation*, 1202–3, Pratt outlines Sims's duties.

33. M. Simpson, *Anglo-American Naval Relations*, 55. Morison, *Sims*, 365; SecNav to Sims, June 6, 1917, Reel 8, ME-11. See also Niblack testimony, *Naval Investigation*, 1027–30; "Recollections" in Harold Cooke Papers, LC.

34. For Rodman's testimony, see *Naval Investigation*, 843–44.

35. M. Simpson, *Admiral Harold R. Stark*, 232.

36. "A Brief Summary of U.S. Naval Activities in European Waters," Aug. 5, 1918, subj file TL, RG45; Sims to wife, Oct. 21, 1917, Box 9, Sims Papers; Sims to Pratt, Aug. 11, 1917, Box 78, Sims Papers, LC. See also William F. Halsey Memoirs in William F. Halsey Papers, LC. June 5, 1916, ZO subj file, RG45; Sims to wife, June 15, 1917, Box 9, Sims Papers, LC.

37. Sims testimony, *Naval Investigation*, 15; Trask, *Captains and Cabinets*, 163; Sims to wife, June 8, 1918, Box 10, Sims Papers, LC; Sims to Niblack, no date but before Mayo's visit to Europe, Box 24, ibid. For Mayo's insistence that Sims's forces were under his command, see Mayo to CNO, April 9, 1917, Reel 1, ME-11; Mayo to CNO, June 13, 1917, file 28754-20: 46 in Box 54, Confidential Files, 1917–1919, General Records of the Navy Department, RG80, NA, hereafter

cited as Confidential Files, RG80; *Army and Navy Journal* 57 (Jan. 24, 1920): 642; Plunkett to Sims, n.d., Box 78, Sims Papers; Mayo, "Atlantic Fleet in the War," Reel 57, Daniels Papers, LC.

38. King and Whitehill, *Fleet Admiral King*, 114–15.

39. To Pratt, Aug. 30, 1917, Box 23, Sims Papers, LC; Bradford, "Henry T. Mayo," 267–70; Sims to Pringle, Sept. 3, 1917, Box 77, Sims Papers, LC. See also "Mayo" entry in Herwig and Heyman, *Biographical Dictionary of World War I*, 247–48.

40. Hunter, "American Admirals at War," 35; Babcock to Sims, June 24, 1918, Box 144, Sims Papers. Mayo's flag was also flown on the destroyer HMS *Broke* when he and Jellicoe went on board to watch a bombardment of German positions on the Belgian coast. Taffrail, *Endless Story*, 329.

41. Belknap to McGrann, May 29, 1939, Belknap Papers, LC. Belknap served in Operations for six months before going to the war zone to develop the North Sea Mine Barrage. See also entry for March 29, 1920, in Josephus Daniels, *Cabinet Diaries*, 511; Sims to wife, Aug. 9, 1917, Feb. 25, 1918, Box 9, Sims Papers, LC.

42. Belknap to Sims, March 14, 1918, Box 48, Sims Papers, LC; Sims to wife, Feb. 15, 25, 1918, Box 9, ibid., Sims to Benson, Feb. 15, 1918, Benson Papers, LC.

43. Entry for April 14, 1918, in Josephus Daniels, *Cabinet Diaries*, 299; Zimmerman, "George W. Goethals and the Reorganization of the United States Army Supply System," Ph.D. diss., 28; King and Whitehill, *Fleet Admiral King*, 124–25; Finnegan, *Against the Specter of a Dragon*, 190.

44. Sims to Pratt, April 4, Aug. 30, 1918, Box 78, Sims Papers, LC; Sims to Dept., June 4, 1918, TL subj file, RG45; Trask, *Captains and Cabinets*, 198; Belknap to Sims, March 11, 1918, Box 48, Sims Papers, LC; Pratt to Sims, May 5, 1918, Box 78, ibid.; Sims to Pratt, May 18, 1918, Pratt Papers, OA; Babcock to Sims, July 24, 1918, TL subj file, RG45.

45. Mayo to CNO, Aug. 10, 1918, Reel 5, ME-11; Sims to wife, Sept. 25, Oct. 12, 1918, Box 9, Sims Papers, LC.

46. G. E. Wheeler, *Pratt*, 94–97; Morrison, *Daniels*, 100; entry for May 7, 1917, in Josephus Daniels, *Cabinet Diaries*, 148. Daniels wrote in his account of the war, probably to "salve" Mayo's feelings, that he expected "that the time would come when the entire Fleet would be sent abroad [under] . . . Admiral Mayo . . . but the character of the war [at that time] . . . made it impractical." Josephus Daniels, *Our Navy at War*, 361.

47. Wiley, *An Admiral from Texas*, 174–75; King and Whitehill, *Fleet Admiral King*, 145. Sims to Pratt, Sept. 1, 1917, Box 78, Sims Papers, LC; Sims to wife, March 3, 1918, Box 9, and April 10, Sept. 23, 1918, Box 10, ibid.; Bradford, "Mayo," 273; Trask, *Captains and Cabinets*, 153.

48. Jan. 24, 1918, Box 144, Sims Papers, LC. See James Fife Oral History, Columbia University. For Admiral Thomas Hart's comment, see Leutze, *A Different Kind of Victory*, 41. See also G. E. Wheeler, *Pratt*, 118–19.

49. Sims to wife, Dec. 9, 1917, Box 9, Sims Papers, LC. Coletta, "The American Naval Leaders' Preparations for War," and comment by Joseph Dawson, 161–89.

50. Baker, *American Chronicle*, 325. See also Trask, *Captains and Cabinets*, 100, passim; Babcock to Sims, Jan. 24, 1918, Box 144, Sims Papers, LC. See also Emmett to Sims, June 22, 1917, TD subj file, RG45. Later Babcock modified his recommendations concerning the "row" with the Department. "Avoid any that could be used as ammunition against you," he wrote in February 1918. Letter, Feb. 28, 1918, Box 144, Sims Papers, LC. For a view that differs from Trask's, see Klachko, *Benson*, 114.

51. Oct. 30, 1917, Box 9, Sims Papers, LC.

52. Sims to wife, Dec. 1, 1917, Box 9, Sims Papers, LC. See also Sims to wife, Dec. 6, Nov. 10, 1917, ibid.; Trask, *Captains and Cabinets*, 181–82; Klachko, *Benson*, 88–96.

53. Sims to wife, Nov. 9, 15, 1917, Box 9; Oct. 12, Nov. 5, 1918, Box 10, Sims Papers, LC. See also Coletta, *Sea Power in the Atlantic and Mediterranean in World War I*, 64.

54. Dec. 23, 1917, Box 49, Sims Papers, LC; Benson to Sims, Sept. 24, 1917, quoted in Wheeler, "William Veazie Pratt," 41–42.

55. G. E. Wheeler, "William Veazie Pratt," 41. See also Pratt to Sims, Oct. 28, 1917, Box 9, Sims Papers, LC; Gaunt to Admiralty, July 5, 1917, ADM137/1437. Wheeler's biography of Pratt, a relatively unknown but gifted naval officer, is excellent.

56. Moore Oral History, Columbia University; Land, *Winning the War with Ships*, 135–36; Zogbaum, *From Sail to Saratoga*, 428.

57. G. C. Ward, 465–68. All the biographies of Roosevelt describe his European trip. See also Elliott Roosevelt, *F.D.R.: His Personal Letters*, 374, passim.

58. May 7, 1927, Reel 42, Daniels Papers, LC. Morison describes essentially the same story concerning Fletcher's fitness reports, but Blue is not mentioned, nor is Daniels. See *Sims*, 306–11. Blue, a North Carolinian and good friend of Daniels, was chief of the Bureau of Navigation at the time Fletcher was in command of the Atlantic Fleet. See also entries for March 8, 1920, in Josephus Daniels, *Cabinet Diaries*, 205, and Trask, *Captains and Cabinets*, 138.

59. Jan. 25, 1919, Box 10, Sims Papers, LC; Trask, "Sims," 290; entry for April 17, 1920, in Josephus Daniels, *Cabinet Diaries*, 519.

60. May 31, 1917, TL subj file, RG45.

61. *Naval Investigation*, 226–27; Allard, "Sims," 103; Pratt, "Autobiography," OA; entry for March 8, 1920, in Josephus Daniels, *Cabinet Diaries*, 505. Charles A. Pownall Oral History, U.S. Naval Institute, hereafter USNI.

62. Sims, *The Victory at Sea*, 240–43; Sims to wife, June 13, 1917, Box 9, Sims Papers, LC; Babcock to Gilmore, July 17, 1917, TL subj file, RG45; Sims to Pratt, July 6, 1917, file 830, U.S. Embassy London Records, Records of the Foreign Service Posts of the Department of State, RG84, NA; *Naval Investigation*, 5–6, 207; Naval Attaché London to SecNav, June 1, 1917, TL subj file, RG45.

63. Sims to Pratt, July 6, 1917, file 830, U.S. Embassy London Records, RG84; SecNav to Sims, July 30, 1917, ibid.; SecNav to MacDougall, Aug. 6, 1917, TL subj file, RG45; Sims to Dept., Oct. 23, 1917, ibid.; *Naval Investigation*, 223; Sims to wife, Nov. 15, 1917, Box 9, Sims Papers, LC.

64. MacDougall to First Secretary, American Embassy, London, Aug. 6, 1917, copy in TL subj file, RG45; Sims, *The Victory at Sea*, 240–43; *Naval Investigation*, 204–5; Cooper, *Walter Hines Page*, 379–80.

65. MacDougall to SecNav, July 6, 1917, TL subj file, RG45.

66. Sims to MacDougall, June 13, 1917, ibid.

67. Benson to SecNav, Nov. 16, 1917, Box 42, Benson Papers, LC; Klachko, *Benson*, 95; Dorwart, *The Office of Naval Intelligence*, 123–24, hereafter cited as *ONI*; Pye to Benson, Aug. 7, 1917, Box 4, Benson Papers, LC; Benson to SecNav, n.d. (not sent), Box 5, ibid.; Babcock memo, Oct. 25, 1917, copy in Harold R. Stark Papers, OA; Daniels to Naval Attaché, Paris, Aug. 30; Benson to Sims, Aug. 28; Daniels to MacDougall, Aug. 30.; Benson to SecNav, Nov. 16, 1917, all in Reel 2, ME-11; Sims to Welles, Oct. 19, 1917; Roys to Welles, Sept. 29, Oct. 2, 1917, all in File 21500-610, Box 91, Confidential Correspondence, 1913–1924, Records of the Office of the Chief of Naval Operations, RG38, NA, hereafter cited as Confidential Correspondence, RG38; Sims to wife, Oct. 14, Nov. 15, 1917, Box 9, Sims Papers, LC; Trask, *Captains and Cabinets*, 164. LCDR J. H. Roys was one of Welles's staff in ONI.

68. Washington to MacDougall, Dec. 7, 1917, and MacDougall to Washington, Dec. 5, 1917, in File 830, Liverpool Consulate Records, RG84.

69. Daniels to Naval Attaché, Paris, Aug. 30, 1917; CNO to Naval Attaché, London, Aug. 30, 1917; to Sims, Aug. 28, 1917, Reel 2, ME-11; Sims to Welles, Oct. 10, 1917, file 21500-610, Box 91, Confidential Correspondence, RG38; CNO to naval attachés, Oct. 4, 1918, Reel 12, ME-11; Benson to Sims, Feb. 10, 1918, TL subj file, RG45; Gade to Sims, May 3, 1918, ibid.

70. Packard, *A Century of U.S. Naval Intelligence*, 62–65

71. Long to Belknap, July 1, 1918, OF subj file, RG45.

72. *Naval Investigation*, 226.

73. Memo in Benson Papers, Box 42, LC.

74. Mayo to wife, Sept. 29, 1918, Henry T. Mayo Papers, LC; Leighton, *Simsadus*, 152; G. E. Wheeler, *Pratt*, 104–5; memo for Captain Knox, July 24, 1935, in TL subj file, RG45; Sims to wife, Aug. 9, 1917, Box 9, Sims Papers, LC; Pownall Oral History, USNI. Daniels claimed that the total number of personnel at the London headquarters was 1,200. Josephus Daniels, *Our Navy at War*, 357.

75. "A Brief Summary of U.S. Naval Activities in European Waters," Aug. 5, 1918, TL subj file; *Naval Investigation*, 3280.

76. Sims to wife, Nov. 6, 15, 1917, Box 9, Sims Papers, LC; Sims, *The Victory at Sea*, 244–45. See also to MacDougall, n.d., TL subj file; RG45; Leighton, *Simsadus*, 151; Chapple, *We'll Stick to the Finish*, 190.

77. Sims to wife, April 21, 1918, Box 10, Sims Papers, LC. See also Strauss, "Recollections," OA. Because so many officers sought rooms in Mayfair, a British writer observed that Mayfair had become the "club land of the Dominions and the United States." Playne, *Britain Holds On*, 334. According to another British writer, one new American officer tried to take up residence at the Athenaeum Club in Waterloo Place. When Sims was informed of this, he is supposed to have replied, "My boy . . . I guess I'd as soon ask for the Houses of Parliament or Buckingham Palace as your Club Athenaeum." Taffrail, *Endless Story*, 343. Interestingly, the American embassy and headquarters of the C-in-C, U.S. Naval Forces, Europe (CINCUSNAVEUR) are still located on Grosvenor's Square. In a brief "Biography of U.S. Navy London, Headquarters, Simsadus, London," World War I is not mentioned. See also Morison, *Sims*, 366.

78. SecNav to Simsadus, Nov. 23, 1917, copy in Box 5, Benson Papers, LC. For a detailed description of the staff, see "A Brief Summary of U.S. Naval Activities in European Waters," Aug. 5, 1918, TL subj file, RG45. This document also includes a chart showing the breakdown in organization of U.S. naval forces in European waters. See also *Naval Investigation*, 256–58; Kittredge to Stark, March 24, 1942, item 158, COMNAVEU File, OA. For development of a gunnery subsection, see F. McNair sketch in Furlong, *Class of 1905*, 325–27. For the Legal Section, see Freidel, *FDR: The Apprenticeship*, 355; memo, Oct. 17, 1918, TL subj files, RG45. See also land claims in Box 26, General Correspondence, 1917–19, US Naval Operating Forces Europe, in Records of the Navy Operation Forces, RG313, NA, hereafter cited as Records of the Navy Operation Forces, RG313; Legal Section, U.S. Naval Forces Operating in European Waters, in Records of Boards and other Special Units, 1896–1938, RG125; See also Stuart Farrar Smith Diary in the LC. Smith was a naval constructor who Sims sent to various bases and stations.

79. Sims, *The Victory at Sea*, 250–51; Sims to wife, Aug. 24, Dec. 15, 1917, Feb. 25, 1918, Box 9, and Feb. 13, 1919, Box 10, Sims Papers, LC; Strauss, "Recollections," OA; Pratt, "Autobiography," OA; J. L. McRae Oral History, USNI; "Raymond Perry Rodgers Neilson," in Furlong, *Class of 1905*, 346–47. Strauss confirmed the personal dislike between Sims and Twining. See also King and Whitehill, *Fleet Admiral King*, 129.

80. To Frothington, June 12, 1925, Nov. 9, Knox Papers, LC.

81. Gurney, "The U.S. Dispatch Agency in London," 189.

82. Ibid., 190–91. See also Benson to Simsadus, July 12, 1917, Reel 4; Sims to CNO, June 8, 1918, Reel 3; Niblack to Sims, July 7, 1918, Reel 20, ME-11. For communication problems, see also various documents in DP subj file, RG45.

83. Howeth, *History of Communication Electronics*, 238; Sims to Admiralty, Aug. 30, 1917, Reel 2, ME-11; Memo, 1919, TL subj file, RG45; entry for July 2, 1917, Foley Diary, QC subj file, ibid.

84. For French-American radio communication, see *Foreign Relations, 1918*, Supplement 2,

836–44; Howeth, *History of Communication Electronics*, 234–44; *Annual Report of the Secretary of the Navy*, 1918, 22–23; Hooper, "The Lafayette Radio Station," 410–14; Bastedo to Hooper, Feb. 21, 1918, Stanford C. Hooper Papers, LC; Hooper address, Sept. 6, 1918, copy in ibid.; "Brief Summary of U.S. Navy in France, November 11, 1918 to October 1, 1919," Z file, OA; *Naval Investigation*, 2576–77; Sims to Dept., July 18, 1918, Reel 4, ME-11; Copeland, "Steel Tower Construction at the World's Greatest Radio Station," 1903–20.

85. William S. Sims file, item 158, COMNAVEU Files, OA; Leighton, *Simsadus*, 12; *Naval Investigation*, 887; Jackson to Sims, Jan. 16, 1918, Reel 19, ME-11; Sims to Wilson, Jan. 20, 1918, ibid.; H. B. Wilson, *An Account of the Operations of the American Navy in France during the War with Germany*, 77–82.

86. MacDougall to SecNav, July 6, 1918, Reel 38, Daniels Papers, LC; "Summary of U.S. Naval Activities in European Waters," Z file, OA; *Annual Report of the Secretary of the Navy*, 1918, 22; "The Navy Ruled the Waves," *American Legion Monthly*, Aug. 1936, 32–33; "This Is Station GOB Broadcasting," ibid., Jan. 1934, 36–37. For the "Hello Girls," see Schneider and Schneider, *Into the Breach*, 177–83. Dr. James E. Talley, in his journal (actually letters to his wife in the form of a journal), wrote that there were a large number of "Hello Girls" working in Brest. Entry for Aug. 25, 1918, James E. Talley Papers, OA.

87. Seldes, *Tell the Truth and Run*, 26; Nutting, "Squelched by the Censor"; Hoy, *40 or How the War Was Won*, 84–85. See also W. James, *The Eyes of the Navy*, 165–66. Blythe, "Removing the Mufflers"; *Literary Digest*, Nov. 1918, 17.

88. Rogers to Irwin, March 20, 1918, Box 105, CPI 17-A1, Records of the Committee on Public Information, RG63, NA; memo from Daniels to Rogers, March 29, 1918, ibid.; Sims to Pratt, April 29, 1918, Pratt Papers, OA. O'Hara, *World War at Its Climax*, 49–56.

89. Mock, *Censorship 1917*, 107–8. See Reel 10, M1092 for abstracts concerning this problem.

90. Sims to Daniels, Nov. 20, 1917, Box 23, Sims Papers, LC; Connolly, *Sea-Borne*, 194–95; Creel to Daniels, Aug. 13, Nov. 24, 1917, Reel 47, Daniels Papers; Navy Dept. Clerk to Creel, Nov. 28, 1917, ibid.; memo from Blythe to McConnaugh, n.d., ibid.; Paine, *Roads to Adventure*, 415–19; entry for Jan. 26, 1920, in Josephus Daniels, *Cabinet Diaries*, 488; *Chicago Herald Examiner*, Jan. 25, 1920, copy in Box 50, Sims Papers; Warren I. Titus, "Winston Churchill, American, A Critical Biography," Ph.D. dissertation, New York University, 1957, 458–64. This was later published in book form as *Winston Churchill*. See also Ferrell, *Woodrow Wilson and World War I*, 202–3.

91. Entry for July 5, Sept. 20, 1917, in Josephus Daniels, *Cabinet Diaries*, 172–73, 208; Josephus Daniels, *The Wilson Era: Years of War*, 221; Gramling, *AP: The Story of News*, 264–66; *Daily Telegraph*, Sept. 17, 1917.

92. Dorwart, *ONI*, 123; Dorwart, *Conflict of Duty*; Deacon, *The Silent War*, 116–17.

93. Sims to Dept., May 31, 1917, TL subj file, RG45; Sims, *The Victory at Sea*, 250. MacDougall was briefly assigned to head the intelligence section.

94. Dorwart, *Conflict of Duty*, 7–8.

95. Beesly, *Room 40*, 245, 246; Hoy, *40*, 271; James, *The Code Breakers of Room 40*, 200–201; Roosevelt to Daniels, Oct. 16, 1918, Box 46, Assistant Secretary of the Navy Files, Franklin D. Roosevelt Library, National Archives and Records Service, Hyde Park, N.Y., hereafter cited as FDR Library. Marder, *From the Dreadnought to Scapa Flow*, 4: 266–68; *Naval Investigation*, 255; Deacon, *The Silent War*, 117–34; Love, *History of the U.S. Navy*, 507.

96. Sims to Wilson, July 8, 1918; Wilson to Sims, May 21, July 8, 1918, Reel 20, ME-11; "History of the U.S. Naval Attaché, American Embassy Paris," File E-7, Box 12302, RG38; W. F. Bell, "American Embassies in Belligerent Europe," Ph.D. diss., 237–38. Memoir note by LTJG Leon Clemens, from papers in possession of his son. The Germans were quite successful in espionage activities in Ireland. The United States was evidently not involved in counterespionage operations there.

Bayly, *Pull Together*, 182–83. The Navy Department in Washington attempted to organize a cryptographic bureau but gave it up in July 1918. They failed to decipher a single cipher or code message. Yardley, *The American Black Chamber*, 199–200. Wilson to Moreau, Aug. 24, 1918, and reply, Aug. 27, 1918, French Naval Archives, Vincennes. Deacon, *The Silent War*, 123.

97. Moore Oral History, Columbia University; G. Campbell, *Number Thirteen*, 112; Bayly, *Pull Together*; entry for May 25, 1917, in Josephus Daniels, *Cabinet Diaries*, 157.

98. Whiting to the Navy Dept., July 20, 1917, Reel 1, ME-11; Cone to Wilson, April 3, 1918, Reel 4, ibid.; Roscoe, *On the Seas and in the Skies*, 63–64.

99. Sims to CNO, Aug. 16, 1917, Reel 3, to CNO, Aug. 21, 1917, Reel 2, ME-11; Lord, "History of Naval Aviation," NDL.

100. Sims to wife, Box 9, Sims Papers, LC; Stirling, *Sea Duty*, 124; biographical sketch of Cone in ZB files, OA; Turnbull and Lord, *History of United States Naval Aviation*, 122.

101. Sims to wife, Sept. 26, 1917, Box 9, Sims Papers, LC; Twining to Jackson, Aug. 28, 1917, GP subj file, RG45.

102. Progress Report, U.S. Naval Aviation Forces, Foreign Service, March 15, 1918, microfilm, NDL.

103. Sims to Benson, May 14, 1918, Reel 4, ME-11; Sims to Wilson, May 24, 1918, G subj file, RG45; Wilson to Sims, May 9, 1918, ibid.; Cone to Wilson, April 3, 1918, Reel 4, ME-11; Wilson to District Commanders, Feb. 15, 1918, Box 490, subj file, RG45.

104. Cone to Irwin, Jan. 22, 1918, GA subj file, RG45. See also Cone to Irwin, July 19, 1918, GL subj file, RG45; Cone to Sims, June 22, 1918, GP subj file, RG45; Lord, "History of Naval Aviation," NDL; Sims to Wilson, May 24, 1918, GA subj file, RG45; Sims to Dept., Aug. 16, 1918, Reel 5, ME-11; Sims to Dept., Aug. 29, 1918, GA subj file, RG45; Sims to all commands, Aug. 25, 1918, Reel 10, ME-11; Sims to Admiralty, June 12, 1918, Reel 4, ME-11; Cone to Simsadus, June 6, 1918, Reel 8, ME-11; Cone to Wilson, May 22, 1918, GP subj file, RG45; Admiralty to Sims, June 26, 1918, ADM137/2241; Sims to Admiralty; "History of the U.S. Naval Air Stations, Ireland," ZPA subj file, RG45; MacLeish to family, June 2, 1918, in Rossano, *The Price of Honor*, 169.

105. *Naval Hearings*, 227.

106. Hattendorf, *Sailors and Scholars*, 90.

107. Marder, *From the Dreadnought to Scapa Flow*, 4: 167–72; P. M. Kennedy, "Britain in the First World War," 57. For the reorganization of the Admiralty, see L. Gardiner, *The British Admiralty*, 334–47. *The Naval Staff of the Admiralty: Its Work and Development*, 76–81; "The Admiralty and the War," in *Naval Annual, 1919*, 200–213; Owen, *No More Heroes*, 84–87.

108. Jan. 19, 1918, Box 29, Sims Papers, LC. See also the "Wemyss" entry in Herwig and Heyman, *Biographical Dictionary of World War I*, 351.

109. Navy Dept., *The American Naval Planning Section in London*, 451; Marder, *From the Dreadnought to Scapa Flow*, 4: 195.

110. TL subj file, RG45.

111. Klachko, *Benson*, 95; Trask, *Captains and Cabinets*, 165; *Naval Investigation*, 227; Benson to Pratt, Nov. 1917, Box 15, Benson Papers, LC; memo, Jan. 2, 1918, Reel 10, NA microfilm pub. M1092.

112. Sims to wife, March 16, 1918, Box 9; Babcock to Sims, Feb. 11. 1918, Box 144, Sims Papers, LC; Trask, *Captains and Cabinets*, 166; memo, Dec. 30, 1918, in M. Simpson, *Anglo-American Naval Relations*, 183–84. Pratt's list of recommended officers with brief comments about why each was suitable for the Planning Section is in Reel 65, Daniels Papers, LC. Sims wrote his wife that Benson selected Schofield and Knox, but Pratt submitted their names to the naval secretary. Nov. 19, 1917, Box 9, Sims Papers, LC. Pratt to SecNav, Nov. 12, 1917, Reel 65, Daniels Papers, LC.

113. Sims, *The Victory at Sea*, 126.

114. Navy Dept., *The American Naval Planning Section in London*, 312; Benson to Simsadus,

April 17, 1918, Reel 14, ME-11; Memo, Jan. 2, 1918, in M. Simpson, *Anglo-American Naval Relations*, 145–48.

115. Sims to wife, March 16, 1918, Box 9, Sims Papers, LC; to Benson, March 7, 1918, in M. Simpson, *Anglo-American Naval Relations*, 280; Aug. 16, 1918, Reel 5, ME-11.

116. Sims memo for Schofield, Oct. 25, 1918, Box 82, Sims Papers, LC.

117. Sims to Benson, Aug. 16, 1918, Reel 5, ME-11; Trask, *Captains and Cabinets*, 166; Navy Dept., *The American Naval Planning Section in London*, 491–92; Marder, *From the Dreadnought to Scapa Flow*, 5: 124; Stackhouse, "The Anglo-American Atlantic Convoy System in World War I," Ph.D. diss., 59–60.

118. Parsons, *Wilsonian Diplomacy*, 158; Albion, *Makers of Naval Policy*, 90; Babcock to Sims, Feb. 11, 1918, Box 144, Sims Papers, LC; Benson to Sims, July 7, 1917, TL subj file, RG45. Not all U.S. naval officers were impressed with the need for a planning section. Admiral Strauss, who wrote in his recollections about the evils of having too much staff, questioned the need for such a section. "The reason for [the section] . . . I have not yet quite understood." "Recollections," OA.

119. Sims to Knapp, March 28, 1919, Box 69, Sims Papers, LC; to wife, Feb. 15, 1919.

Chapter 3. Sims and His Commanders

1. Sims to Admiralty, Sept. 9, 1918, ADM137/1984.

2. For Rodman and Plunkett, see pp. 83, 84, and 413–16 in this volume.

3. *Naval Investigation*, 7.

4. April 16, 1918, Box 78, Sims Papers, LC.

5. Aug. 26, 1918, Box 24, Sims Papers, LC. See also to Bristol, Sept. 2, 1918, Mark Bristol Papers, LC.

6. Sims to Pringle, Jan. 24, 1918, Box 79, Sims Papers, LC; Sims to Benson, April 16, 1918, Box 49, Sims Papers, LC; Sims to Pratt, May 18, 1918, Pratt Papers, OA; Sims to wife, May 6, 1918, Box 10, Sims Papers, LC; G. E. Wheeler, *Pratt*, 118–20; Still, "Albert Gleaves"; entry for May 25, 1917, Latimer Diary, UVA. See also Sims to Cone, Aug. 21, Box 145, Sims Papers, LC.

7. Karsten, *The Naval Aristocracy*. See especially chapter 2.

8. Stirling, *Sea Duty*, 95–96. See also Morison, *Sims*, 17, 128–29. For Niblack's biography, see brief sketch in ZB file, NDL.

9. Aug. 18, 1920, Box 143, Sims Papers, LC. Mrs. Astor replied on November 20, referring to Niblack as "that pitiful creature." For similar remarks, see also Sims to MacAfee, Aug. 18, 1920, Box 143, Sims Papers, LC; and Morison, *Sims*, 128.

10. For Niblack at ONI, see Dorwart, *Conflict of Duty*, 9–16, quote on 10. For Andrews's remark, see to Sims, March 12, 1920, Box 46, Sims Papers, LC. See also Andrews to Sims, Jan. 1, 1920, and Sims to Andrews, Dec. 7, 1920, Box 46, Sims Papers, LC; Niblack testimony, *Naval Investigation*, 1028–38. Niblack would retire in 1923 and would die five years later. "Albert Parker Niblack," in *DAB*, 480–81; C. G. Reynolds, "Albert Parker Niblack," in *Famous American Admirals*, 236–37. For his command at Gibraltar, see pp. 479–80 in this volume.

11. Daniels to Rodman, May 23, 1929, Reel 59, Daniels Papers, LC; Sims to Pratt, April 16, and Pratt to Sims, April 30, 1918, Box 78, Sims Papers, LC. Captain Reginald Belknap had been sent over to establish the mine-laying bases and command the squadron of minelayers. He was the mine expert in the Navy at the time, and both Sims and Pratt would have preferred that he remain in command. See chapter 17 for Strauss's biography and for his command of the mine barrages.

12. Sims to Strauss, Sept. 7, 1918, Strauss Papers, LC; ADM to C-in-C Grand Fleet, Oct. 9, 1918, ADM137/1964.

13. "Recollections," OA; Sims to Pratt, May 18, 1918, Pratt Papers, OA. See also Belknap to Sims, March 11, 1918, Box 48, Sims Papers, LC; and Corrigan, *Tin Ensign*, 190.

14. For Rodman's service in the war zone, see chapter 14.

15. *Naval Investigation*, 854–57; Rodman, *Yarns of a Kentucky Admiral*, 269; Pratt, "Autobiography," OA; G. E. Wheeler, *Pratt*, 104. See also notes from Rodman in Box 81, Sims Papers, LC.

16. J. W. Jones, "U.S. Battleship Operations in World War I," Ph.D. diss., 106–9, 163–64. This dissertation has been published as a book entitled *U.S. Battleship Operations in World War I*. John L. McCrea Oral History, USNI; Josephus Daniels, *The Wilson Era: Years of War*, 500–501.

17. History of the U.S. Naval Attaché, American Embassy, Paris, 1914–1918. File E-9, Box 12302, RG38; J. R. Green, "The First Sixty Years of the Office of Naval Intelligence," master's thesis, 61, W. F. Bell, "American Embassies in Belligerent Europe," Ph.D. diss., 229–36.

18. History of the U.S. Naval Attaché, American Embassy, Paris, File E-9, Box 12302, RG38; *Naval Investigation*, 124–25; Benson to Sims, June 6, 1917, copy in case 10662, Fletcher Court of Inquiry, RG125.

19. History of the U.S. Naval Attaché, American Embassy Paris, File E-9, Box 12302, RG38; entry for May 7, 1917, in Josephus Daniels, *Cabinet Diaries*, 148; French Naval Attaché, Washington, to Paris, May 6, 1917, copy in TP subj file, RG45. See also Trask, *Captains and Cabinets*, 86.

20. *Naval Investigation*, 124–25; History of the U.S. Naval Attaché, American Embassy, Paris, File E-9, Box 12302, RG38. Sayles was informed that the yachts would leave the United States on approximately June 1. No additional information was provided. The cable did request information about coal and stores. Daniels to Sayles, May 21, 1917, Reel 1, ME-11.

21. Sayles to Babcock, August 8, 1917, Box 23, Sims Papers, LC. For the French request for a senior officer, see Sims to Department, May 30, 1917, Reel 1, ME-11.

22. R. C. Smith, "A Grand Old Man," 19.

23. Jackson to Sims, Aug. 31, 1917, TV subj file, RG45; Aug. 13, 1917, P subj file, RG45; Sims to Jackson, Aug. 3, 1917, copy in case 10622, Fletcher Court of Inquiry, RG125; Sims to SecNav, Aug. 9, 1917, Correspondence with ADM William S. Sims, Entry 113, Box 5, Correspondence, Reports and Related Records, 1887–1940, RG19, hereafter cited as Sims Correspondence, RG19; Jackson to Benson, Aug. 10, 1917, Box 4, Benson Papers, LC.

24. Sept. 9, 1917, Logistics file, RG45.

25. Lord, "History of Naval Aviation," NDL, 372.

26. Sept. 28, 1917, copy in Case 10622, Fletcher Court of Inquiry, RG145. See also Twining testimony in ibid.

27. Jackson to Twining, Oct. 5, 1917, copy in Case 10622, Fletcher Court of Inquiry, RG125; Sims to Jackson, October 16, 1917, Reel 2, ME-11.

28. W. F. Bell, "American Embassies in Belligerent Europe," Ph.D. diss., 236; Report of trip, November 1917, Box 42, Benson Papers, LC; Jackson to Benson, January 5, 1918, Box 6, Benson Papers, LC; Pratt to Benson, n.d., Box 6, Benson Papers, LC; *Naval Investigation*, 255; Jackson to Benson, Jan. 24, 1918, Box 6, Benson Papers, LC; Babcock to Sims, Feb. 10, 1918, Box 14, Sims Papers, LC.

29. R. C. Smith, "A Grand Old Man," 19–20; Vice Admiral Bernhard H. Bieri Oral History, USNI. When FDR made his tour of France in 1918, Jackson irritated him by being overprotective. Characteristically, Roosevelt did not forget what he considered Jackson's "lack of tact and good manners." Ward, *A First-Class Temperament*, 399, 401. Jackson's personal papers are in the Hoover Institution of War Revolution and Peace Archives, Stanford University, but contain nothing on his World War I experiences.

30. Richardson, *On the Treadmill to Pearl Harbor*, 71; Cooke, "Recollections," LC. Fletcher biography in ZB file, OA.

31. For the development of this base, see chapter 6. See also R. W. Kauffman, *Our Navy at*

Work, 59–65; entry for June 11, 1918, Taussig Diary, Naval War College; Memo to French Marine Ministry, June 29, 1918, French Naval Archives, Vincennes; *Broadside*, Dec. 6, 1918; Dinger to Foley, Sept. 22, 1917, P-Brest, subj file, RG45; War Diary, Commander, U.S. Patrol Squadron, entry for July 13–14, 1917, OE, subj file, RG45; Sims to Chief of Staff, French Minister of Marine, Paris, July 30, 1917, subj file P-Brest, RG45.

32. Sims to Admiral De Bon, July 30, 1917, case 10662, Fletcher Court of Inquiry, RG125; Sims to Fletcher, August 3, 1917, ibid.; Sims to SecNav, August 9, 1917, Reel 2, ME-11.

33. To Fletcher, Sept. 24, 1917, ibid.; Sims to Fletcher, Sept. 12, 1917, Box 104, Confidential Files 1911-27, RG80; Daniels to Sims, Sept. 26, 1917, case 10662, Fletcher Court of Inquiry, RG125.

34. Testimony of Fletcher, Sims, Twining, and Captain Long, Case 10662, Twining Court of Inquiry, RG125.

35. For the sinking of the *Antilles*, see chapter 14. See also Sims to Wilson, Oct. 13, 1917, Box 371, Confidential Files, 1917–19, RG80; Sims to Fletcher, Sept. 27, 1918, Box 104, ibid.; OpNav to Simsadus, Sept. 29, 1917, ibid.; Sims to Benson, Oct. 15, 1917, Box 104, ibid. There is considerable documentation on this in Box 104, ibid. See also Sims to Pratt, Oct. 15, 1917, Box 78, Sims Papers, LC; Sims to Pringle, Oct. 19, 1917, Box 79, Sims Papers, LC.

36. Case 10662, Fletcher Court of Inquiry, RG125. For *Antilles'* loss, see p. 370. Entry for Dec. 5, 1917, in Josephus Daniels, *Cabinet Diaries*, 243. See also entry for Nov. 6, 1917, 233, ibid.

37. Mayo report to SecNav, Oct. 11, 1917, Box 104, Confidential Correspondence, 1917–1919, RG80; Daniels to Sims, Sept. 26, 1917, and testimony of various officers in Case 10662, Fletcher Court of Inquiry, RG125; Dinger to Foley, Sept. 22, 1917, P-Brest subj file, RG45.

38. For examples of what the newspapers wrote, see the *New York Herald*, Jan. 5, 1918; *New York Sun*, January 5, 1918; *New York Times*, Jan. 5, 1918; *Chicago Daily Tribune*, Jan. 4, 1918. See also *New York Times*, April 1, 1920.

39. April 26, 1920, Box 46, Sims Papers, LC; Sims to wife, Oct. 21, 1917, Box 9, ibid.; Mason to Sims, Jan. 8, 1920, Box 57, ibid.; Sims to Benson, Oct. 22, 1917, Box 23, ibid.; see also findings of the Fletcher Court of Inquiry, Case 10662, RG125. The *Army and Navy Journal* carried the court proceedings in its April 1920 issues.

40. Patton to Twining, Aug. 10, 1917, and Patton to Sims, Sept. 19, 1917; Sims to Fletcher, Sept. 24, 1917, all in TT subj file, RG45; *Naval Investigation*, 124-27.

41. Biographical sketch, OA; Belknap to McGrann, May 24, 1939, Belknap Papers, LC; John H. Hoover Oral History, Columbia University.

42. Dec. 19, 1918, Box 36, Daniels Papers, LC, for statistics on Wilson's force in August 1918. See also entry for August 1918, McCauley Diary, Box 191, Assistant Secretary of the Navy Files, FDR Library. For Wilson's testimony, see *Naval Investigation*, 904.

43. Belknap to McGrann, May 24, 1939, Belknap Papers, LC. Although at the Naval Academy at the same time, they served in only one other ship together, the *Tennessee* early in their careers. In a letter to Benson, Sims hints that some of his trouble with Wilson possibly can be traced back to "his efforts to improve target practice." Jan. 14, 1918, Box 23, Sims Papers, LC. See also Morison, *Sims*, 250–54.

44. To Benson, Jan. 14, 1918, Box 23, Sims Papers, LC; to Wilson, Jan. 14, 1918, Box 91, ibid. Admiral Hoover in his oral history suggests that Wilson's dissatisfaction with Sims stemmed from the fact that Wilson was senior to him, "at least on the Navy List." Although Wilson was promoted to captain before Sims, Sims was promoted to rear admiral before Wilson.

45. Rodgers to Sims, Sept. 27, and Sims's reply, Oct. 10, 1918, in Box 81, Sims Papers, LC; *Army and Navy Journal*, June 12, 1920; Josephus Daniels, *The Wilson Era: Years of War*, 496; Stuart Smith's diary for May 17, 1918, Stuart Smith Papers, LC. See also Sims to Benson, March 7, 18, April 1, June 14, Sept. 17, 1918, Box 49, Sims Papers, LC; to Pratt, May 18, 1918, Pratt Papers, OA; Cone to Twining, May 23, 1918, GA subj file, RG45.

46. Jan. 7, 1918, Box 78, Confidential Files, 1917–1919, RG80.

47. Carter Memorandum, Dec. 5, 1917, Box 25, Confidential Correspondence, 1911–1927, RG80. See also Benson to Simsadus, Dec. 14, 1917, CP subj file, RG45; Wilson to Sims, Dec. 28, 1917, P subj file, RG45; Benson's report of 1917 trip, Box 42, Benson Papers, LC; Benson unpublished memoir, ibid.; Klachko, *Benson*, 101–2; Beers, "U.S. Naval Port Offices in the Bordeaux Region," 22.

48. Sims to Benson, Jan. 11, 1918, P-Brest subj file, RG45. Wilson's title had already gone through several changes. At Twining's recommendation, it was changed from "Commander Patrol Force," to "Commander Patrol Squadrons," to "Senior Naval Officer, France," to the one recommended by Sims. Twining to Halligan, Dec. 5, 1917, OF subj file, RG45. For Benson's orders concerning the plan, see January 5, 1918, P-Brest subj file, RG45; Sims to Wilson, Jan. 6, 1918, P-Brest subj file, RG45; Wilson to District Commanders, Jan. 18, 1918, PM subj file, RG45.

49. De Bon to Jackson, May 9, 1918, French Naval Archives, Vincennes; Jackson to Benson, Jan. 24, 1918, Box 6, Benson Papers, LC.

50. Brief History of U.S. Navy in France, Nov. 11, 1918–Oct. 1, 1918, ZO file, OA. For the Rochefort command, see McCully to Wilson, Dec. 31. 1918, ZP subj file, REG45. See also McCully Diary, particularly entries for Jan 16, Feb. 4, Oct. 5, and Dec. 31, 1918, Newton A. McCully Papers, LC.

51. Mayo to Dept., Dec. 11, 1918, Box 25, Confidential Correspondence, 1917–1919, RG80; "U.S. Naval Activities and Developments in St. Nazaire," Dec. 15, 1918, Logistics file, RG45; Magruder, "The Navy in the War," 21; Sims to Wilson, Jan. 11, 1918, copy in Andrew T. Long Papers, UNC–CH; Sims to Dept., Jan. 11, 1918, Reel 19, ME-11; *Naval Investigation*, 886; Sims to Wilson, Jan. 11, 1918, Box 104, Confidential Files, 1917–1919, RG80. See also Husband, *On the Coast of France*, 26–30. For the Rochefort District, see Weeks, *An American Naval Diplomat in Revolutionary Russia*, 129–30. Captain (later Rear Admiral) N. A. McCully was the district commander at Rochefort.

52. Twining testimony, case 10622, Fletcher Court of Inquiry, RG125; Beers, "U.S. Naval Port Offices in the Bordeaux Region," 5–10; "A Brief History of the U.S. Naval Forces in France, 11 Nov. 1918 to 1 Oct. 1919," ZO file, OA. Problems concerning shipping persuaded Sims to appoint port officers for St. Nazaire and Bordeaux in September 1917 (Beers, *Naval Port Offices*, 5–12).

53. Beers discusses these problems in detail in *Naval Port Offices*, passim. See also Husband, *On the Coast of France*, 29–30.

54. Wilson to Sims, May 9, 1918; Benson to Sims, June 11, 1918; Sims to Wilson, June 17, 1918, Reel 4, ME-11.

55. Sims to Wilson, Jan 12, 1918, Box 104, Confidential Files, 1917–1919, RG80; Cone to Irwin, Jan. 12, 1918, ibid.

56. Foote to Sims, Sept. 27, Nov. 7, 1918, Box 58, Sims Papers, LC; Sims to Foote, Oct. 10, 1918, Box 58, Sims Papers, LC. See also Sims to Niblack, Nov. 4, 1918, Box 76; and Sims to Rodgers, Sept. 24, 1918, Box 24, Sims Papers, LC; Benson to Simsadus, Sept. 23, 1918, Reel 6, ME-11; *New York Times*, Aug. 29, 1918.

57. Sims to wife, Jan. 10, 1919, Box 10; to Cone, Jan. 17, 1919, Box 52; to Daniels, January 13, 1919, Box 53, Sims Papers, LC; entry for February 3, 1920 and note, in Josephus Daniels, *Cabinet Diaries*, 410; *New York Post*, Feb. 3, 1920; *Fleet Review* 11 (April 1920): 21; *Chicago Tribune*, Dec. 27, 1919.

58. *Naval Investigation*, 905–10; *New York Times*, April 6, 1920. See also Halligan to Sims, Jan. 3, 1920, Box 63, Sims Papers, LC.

59. Hunter to Taussig, May 1, 1940, Joseph K. Taussig Papers, NWC. See also Zogbaum, *From Sail to Saratoga*, 275, 286–89; Leighton, *Simsadus*, 42; Ralph C. Parker Oral History, Columbia University; Hoover Oral History, Columbia University; Wilson to Sims, May 22, 1918, Box 91, Sims Papers, LC. Taussig, who served on both stations, does not mention rivalry or re-

sentiment but does point out that there were differences in organization. Wilson asked him to take an administrative position at Brest, which he turned down. Taussig, "Destroyer Experiences during the Great War," 404; Taussig to Sims, June 23, 1918, Box 87, Taussig Papers, NWC.

60. Unpublished memoirs, Box 42, Benson Papers, LC; Daniels, *The Wilson Years: Years of War*, 496–97; Harbord, *The American Army in France*, 375; Benson to Daniels, Nov. 10, Dec. 19, 1918, Reel 42, Daniels Papers, LC; Daniels to Benson, Jan. 4, 1919, ibid.; Roosevelt report, Oct. 15, 1918, Box 46, Assistant Secretary Navy Files, FDR Library.

61. Wilson to Twining, Oct. 4, 1918, PM subj file, RG45.

62. Magruder, "The Navy in the War," 20; entry for Oct. 6, 1918, McCully Diary, McCully Papers, LC. He made a point of visiting and meeting the doctors at the two naval hospitals located in the port. The medical director of one of them called Wilson a "corker, keen, alert, democratic, knowing his job." Entry for Aug. 3, 1918, Talley Letters, OA. See also the entry for August 25, 1918, and Dr. Quion to Dr. Braisted, Oct. 28, 1918, file 131000, RG52, and W. A. Maguire, *Rig for Church*, 68–69.

63. Connolly, *Navy Men*, 242–43. See also Connolly, *Sea-Borne*, 209; and Crozier, *American Reporters on the Western Front*, 192. He was equally successful in his dealing with AEF officials. Harbord, *The American Army in France*, 375. Wilson's tour in command of the Atlantic Fleet was generally successful, although his health was a problem. When he was relieved as C-in-C, the fleet's enlisted personnel presented him with a loving cup. *Our Navy* 15 (Dec. 1921): 12. In July 1921, he reported for duty as superintendent of the Naval Academy at Annapolis and remained in this position until he retired on his sixty-fourth birthday in 1925. Wilson died in New York City on January 30, 1954; he was ninety-three years old.

64. *Le Matin*, May 17, 1918; *L'Illustration*, June 29, 1918, 623; Paine, *The Corsair in the War Zone*, 135–36; entry for Jan. 11, 1919, in Elliott Roosevelt, *F.D.R.: His Personal Letters*, 448. The *New York Times* said that he was the most popular man in Brest (see Dec. 17, 1918). Vice Admiral Moreau, the prefect in Brest, after the war offered Wilson honorary presidency of the Naval Officers Club in that port. Wilson accepted. See Moreau to Minister of Marine, April 27, 1919, Wilson to Moreau, April 8, 1919, French Naval Archives, Vincennes. During the four years that Admiral Wilson presided over the Naval Academy, he gained an enviable reputation and was a superintendent greatly admired by the midshipmen, which, as Rear Admiral Kemp Tolley wrote, was rare as most of the superintendents "remain a shadowy figure to the mids." Jack Sweetman, who has written an excellent history of the Naval Academy, noted, "One thing that struck me, from the recollections of everyone who set eyes on him, is that he was a physically imposing man." Sweetman quoted Admiral Holloway: "Wilson must have been: 'absolutely the beau ideal of a white-haired, ex C-in-C supe' 'one of the handsomest, most distinguished and immaculately groomed men I have ever known' . . . and on in that vein" (letter to author, Feb. 11, 1985). "We thought he was the greatest individual we'd ever seen. . . . [H]e was just about the sharpest guy that ever came down the pike," said Charles D. Griffin in his Oral History, USNI.

65. Charles D. Griffin Oral History, USNI; Sweetman to author, Feb. 11, 1985; Tolley to author, Feb. 18, 1985, letters in author's possession. For other comments about Wilson by individuals who were midshipmen at the Naval Academy when he was superintendent, see Frederick Stanton Withington Oral History; Rear Admiral Schuyler Neilson Pyne Oral History; Walter C. W. Ansel Oral History, all in USNI. Rear Admiral Hoover, who served with him in the pre-war Navy, said almost the same things about Wilson then (see his oral history). See also Sweetman, *The U.S. Naval Academy*, 174. Quoted in Sweetman letter to author, Feb. 11, 1985.

66. *From the Dreadnought to Scapa Flow*, 4: 121. See also Roskill, *Admiral of the Fleet Earl Beatty*, 129; and Bayly, *Pull Together*, 201.

67. Chatterton, *Danger Zone*, 68–69.

68. Taffrail, *Endless Story*, 328. See also Admiral Robert Carney Oral History, Columbia University; Paine, *Roads to Adventure*, 418–19; Pilat, *Pegler*, 73; Connolly, *The U-Boat Hunters*, 82; Connolly, *Navy Men*, 164–67; Bartimeus, "Admiral Sir Lewis Bayly and the American Navy," 637. Captain J. P. Pringle, who became his chief of staff while the Americans were under his command, wrote that "Admiral Bayly [has] an intensive dislike of publicity in any form. . . . [His] general mode of life does not lend itself to anecdotes." Pringle to Babcock, July 11, 1918, Box 24, Sims Papers, LC.

69. Feb. 10, 1919, Box 10, Sims Papers, LC. FDR came to the same conclusion as Sims. See Freidel, *Franklin D. Roosevelt: The Apprenticeship*, 351.

70. *Broadside*, Oct. 25, 1918; Marder, *From the Dreadnought to Scapa Flow*, 2: 363. See also Chapple, *We'll Stick to the Finish*, 222.

71. McBride testimony, Dec. 31, 1917, General Board Hearings; Ireland, *Ireland and the Irish in Maritime History*, 328.

72. Marder, *Portrait of an Admiral*, 134; Fisher to Asquith, Jan. 28, 1915, in Marder, *Fear God and Dread Nought*, 3: 147–48; W. James, *A Great Seaman*, 115.

73. Jellicoe to Jackson, August 7, 1915, Patterson, in *The Jellicoe Papers*, 2:177; G. Campbell, *Number Thirteen*, 108; Evans, *Keeping the Seas*, 147. See also Gilbert, *Churchill: The Challenge of War*, 3: 39; Churchill, *The World Crisis*, 160; Bartimeus, "Admiral Sir Lewis Bayly and the American Navy," 636, copy in the Admiral Sir Lewis Bayly Papers, Imperial War Museum, London, hereafter cited as IWM.

74. Chatfield, *The Navy and Defense*, 17–18.

75. De Chair, *The Sea Is Strong*, 157.

76. Sims, *The Victory at Sea*, 68.

77. June 1920, Bayly Papers, IWM. See also "Bayly, Sir Lewis," in *Dictionary of National Biography, 1931–1940*, 54–55; F. Green, *Our Naval Heritage*, 338–39; Chatterton, *Danger Zone*, 65–66. Marder wrote that at the outbreak of war British destroyers "lack[ed] . . . tactical training. Bayly's principal interest . . . was to keep them as continuously at sea as possible with no special task to perform."

78. Goldrick, *The King's Ships Were at Sea*, 24. For Bayly's early career, see Chatfield, *The Navy and Defense*, 17–18; Gretton, *Winston Churchill and the Royal Navy*, 157–59; Bennett, *Charlie B.*, 334–37.

79. Bywater and Ferreby, *Strange Intelligence*, 149; Paine, *Roads to Adventure*, 418–19. For the planned attack on Borkum, see Marder, *From the Dreadnought to Scapa Flow*, 2: 177–89; Dewar, *The Navy from Within*, 166–67; Patterson, *The Jellicoe Papers*, 1: 36, 67–69, 83–87; Gilbert, *Churchill*, 3: 19–21; Gretton, *Winston Churchill and the Royal Navy*, 201–7. For the loss of the *Formidable*, see W. James, *A Great Seaman*, 145; Dewar, *The Navy from Within*, 168–70; Marder, *From the Dreadnought to Scapa Flow*, 2: 98–100.

80. M. Simpson, "Admiral William S. Sims, U.S. Navy and Admiral Sir Lewis Bayly, Royal Navy: An Unlikely Friendship and Anglo-American Cooperation, 1917–1919," 68, hereafter cited as "Admiral Sims and Admiral Bayly."

81. Feb. 19, 1920, in Halpern, *The Keyes Papers*, 47.

82. See Jellicoe to Vice Admiral Sir Alexander Bethell, Jan. 22, 1915, in Patterson, *The Jellicoe Papers*, 1: 128; Jellicoe to Jackson, June 24, 1915, ibid., 169–70; Marder, *From the Dreadnought to Scapa Flow*, 2: 361–62.

83. Sims to Pratt, Aug. 30, 1917, Box 23, Sims Papers, LC. Jellicoe recounted this meeting later to Daniels, entry Jan. 4, 1920, in Josephus Daniels, *Cabinet Diaries*, 480.

84. May 30, 1917, copy in Bayly Papers, IWM. An excellent study of the unusual relationship between Sims and Bayly is M. Simpson, "Admiral Sims and Admiral Bayly."

85. To Benson, April 2, 1918, in M. Simpson, *Anglo-American Naval Relations*, 159; to his wife, Sept. 23, 1918, Box 10, Sims Papers, LC. See also Bartimeus, "Admiral Sir Lewis Bayly and

the American Navy"; M. Simpson, "Admiral Sims and Admiral Bayly," passim; and Mounte-vans, *Adventurous Life*, 121.

86. Quoted in Taussig, "Destroyer Experiences during the Great War," 2036; Glassford, "A Leader of Men."

87. Taussig, *Queenstown Patrol*, 188 n. 84. Taussig does not mention the incident in either his published or unpublished accounts, but he agreed in a letter written years later that he said something of that sort. Taussig to Bryant, Nov. 7, 1946, Naval Historical Collection, Naval War College. For different versions, see "note" in Taussig, "Destroyer Experiences during the Great War," 2036; Gady to CNO, June 8, 1917, DE subj file, RG45; Sims to CNO, May 11, 1917, OE subj file, ibid.

88. Sims, *The Victory at Sea*, 70. For Halsey's comments, see Halsey and Bryan, *Admiral Halsey's Own Story*, 30. See also Halsey's MS dated March 30, 1918, copy in OA.

89. Brownrigg, *Indiscretions of the Naval Censor*, 254–55. See also Paine, *Roads to Adventure*, 425–26, 432; entry for June 11, 1917, Charles Russell Journal, USS *Walke* file, ZC files, OA; for cricket, see Bayly to Sims, July 19, 1917, Box 47, Sims Papers, LC; entry for June 6, 1917; entry for June 6, 1917, in Taussig, *Queenstown Patrol*, 49–50.

90. Sims, *The Victory at Sea*, 66–66. See also FDR to Daniels, July 27, 1918, copy in Box 53, Sims Papers, LC; entry for July, 1918, McCauley Diary, Box 191, Roosevelt Papers, FDR Library.

91. Note in Bayly Papers, IWM. See also John Dos Passos, *Mr. Wilson's War*, 262; Sims, *The Victory at Sea*, 71; Simpson, "Admiral Sims and Admiral Bayly," 70.

92. Glassford, "A Leader of Men," 11.

93. Halsey, *Admiral Halsey's Own Story*, 30.

94. Carney Oral History, Columbia University.

95. Courtney to Sims, April 4, 1918, Box 52, Sims Papers, LC.

96. Hepburn to Bayly, Jan 25, 1919, Bayly Papers, IWM. A large number of these letters can be found in the Bayly Papers, IWM. For other accounts of the American naval officers' attitude toward Bayly, see Sims, *The Victory at Sea*; Bywater, "Notes on the American Navy," 80; a note attached to a letter that Sims wrote April 29, 1917, Reel 1, Taussig Papers, NDL; Pownall Oral History, USNI.

97. Seymour to Bayly, Aug. 1, 1919, Bayly Papers, IWM.

98. Charles Bryant to Bayly, Jan. 14, 1922, Bayly Papers, IWM.

99. July 11, 1919, Box 10, Sims Papers, LC. Bayly had a sign mounted near the gangway of the American destroyer tender *Melville* with the slogan "Pull Together." This later became the title of his memoirs and was the adopted logo of the Queenstown Association. U.S. Naval Institute *Proceedings* (Aug. 1934): 1156. For an example of Bayly's influence on tactics, see Halsey, *Admiral Halsey's Own Story*, 36, 106.

100. Charles Maddox to Bayly, Dec. 30, 1930, Bayly Papers, IWM. The term had been used by those who served in the destroyer flotilla of the Atlantic Fleet under Sims before the war; in Queenstown it was more widely used to include those Americans who were in the command.

101. Copy of Bayly's talk in Bayly Papers, IWM. DeLany, *Bayly's Navy*, 36; Delaney, "Pull Together," 19; *Times* (London), March 9, 11, 1921. A copy of Sims's speech is in the records of the association's records in Naval Historical Foundation, Washington Navy Yard, Washington, D.C.

102. July 6, 1917, Box 47, Sims Papers, LC.

103. Dec. 19, 1917, Add 49009, Jellicoe MS, British Museum. For remark about decorations, see Baldridge to Sims, June 16, 1918, Box 47, Sims Papers, LC.

104. To Pringle, Jan 24, 1918, Box 79, Sims Papers, LC. See also letter to Pringle, Jan 17, 1918, ibid.

105. Bayly to Davis, Nov. 1, 1919, in Louis P. Davis Papers, East Carolina University Manuscript Collection. For Bayly's report, see Dec. 31, 1918, in M. Simpson, *Anglo-American Naval Relations*, 318–20. A copy of the report is in *Navy* 24 (Aug. 1919): 103.

106. *Times* (London), May 26, 1938.

107. Biographical sketch, ZM file, OA; "Vice Admiral Joel Roberts Poinsett Pringle" 1–2; *Baltimore Sun*, March 31, 1943. For background, see also Zogbaum, *From Sail to Saratoga*, 263–64. See also Courtney to Sims, April 4, 1918, Box 52, Sims Papers, LC.

108. Sims to Pringle, Sept. 3, 6, 1917, Box 79, Sims Papers, LC; Bayly to Sims, July 20, 1917, in M. Simpson, *Anglo-American Naval Relations*, 244; G. E. Wheeler, *Pratt*, 121; Bayly, *Pull Together*, 222.

109. Sims to Benson, Feb. 28, 1918, Box 49, Sims Papers, LC; to Pringle, April 19, 1918, Box 47, ibid.; Pringle to Sims, April 24, 1918, ibid., Sims to Pringle, May 6, 1918, Box 79, ibid.; Sims to Benson, July 28, 1918, Box 47, ibid.; Sims to Pratt, April 29, 1918, Pratt Papers, OA; G. E. Wheeler, *Pratt*, 119–21; *Army and Navy Register* 56 (March 16, April 6, 1918); *New York Tribune*, March 21, 1918; *Washington Post*, April 14, 1918.

110. Bayly, *Pull Together*, 253.

111. Taussig, "Destroyer Experiences during the Great War," 224, 233. See also FDR to Daniels, July 27, 1918, Assistant SecNav files, Box 45, FDR Library; Sims to Wilson, Sept. 5, 1917, Box 23, Sims Papers, LC; and Bayly, *Pull Together*, 222.

112. Davy to Baldridge, May 17, 1918, copy in Box 47, Sims Papers, LC.

113. Zogbaum, *From Sail to Saratoga*, 264.

114. For Pringle's social interests, see G. Campbell, *Number Thirteen*, 111; and Arpee, *From Frigates to Flat-Tops*, 171.

115. September 29, 1932.

116. *Times* (London), July 30, 1934; Delaney, *Bayly's Navy*, 32.

117. Sims to Babcock, Dec. 1, 1924, Box 144, Sims Papers, LC. See also Pringle Fitness Report, 1919, copy in Box 79, ibid. On background to Pringle's death, see H. Kent Hewitt Papers, OA; unpublished memoir of Admiral William Stanley, William Stanley Papers, LC; "Vice Admiral Joel Roberts Poinsett Pringle, U.S. Navy," 2.

118. July 6, 1917, Box 47, Sims Papers, LC.

119. Bayly to Sims, May 30, 1917, Box 47, Sims Papers, LC.

120. *Army and Navy Register* 55 (Sept. 8, 1917): 57; Morison, *Sims*, 381–82.

121. Bayly to Sims, March 8, 1919, in M. Simpson, *Anglo-American Naval Relations*, 135, 186; Sims to wife, June 13, 1917, Box 9, Sims Papers, LC; *Literary Digest*, Nov. 23, 1918, 18.

Chapter 4. "Pull Together"

1. June 7, 1917, Area file, 3, RG45; See also Trask, *Captains and Cabinets*, 83. Sims later predicted that the cooperation with the Royal Navy "will have its influence for a hundred years to come." Although perhaps too optimistic in general, it has proven true. See to wife, June 8, 1918, Box 9, Sims Papers, LC, and Captain Tracy B. Kittredge, "United States-British Cooperation."

2. Thursby to Admiralty, Sept. 2, 1918, ADM137/0221; Sims to Niblack, July 14, 1918, Reel 4, ME-11; Sims to Strauss, Sept. 7, 1918, Box 24, Sims Papers, LC. See also Sims to Strauss, June 28, 1918, AU subj file, RG45; and C-in-C Grand Fleet to Admiralty, Aug. 29, 1918, SFM137/1984. See also Sims to Taussig, April 29, 1917, copy in M. Simpson, *Anglo-American Naval Relations*, 212–13, and Sims to Rodman, May 2, 1918, Box 23, Sims Papers, LC.

3. Thomson to Strauss, Oct. 22, 1918, AU subj file, RG45. For Beatty and the North Sea Mine Barrage, see chapter 17.

4. Mayo to SecNav, Nov. 5, 1918, copy in Box 2, Ernest King papers, LC; *San Francisco Chronicle*, May 16, 1918; *Baltimore Sun*, May 26, 1918; *Observer* (London), May 26, 1918; P. Scott, *Fifty*

Years in the Royal Navy, 154; Hough, *The Great War at Sea*, 313; *Naval and Military Record* 33 (June 11, 1919): 377; *Independent* 98 (April 17, 1919): 93; Trask, *Captains and Cabinets*, 83, 134; Sims memo, July 3, 1917, TT subj file, RG45. See also Beston, *Full Speed Ahead*, 131; "Admiral Sims in the Team-Work for Victory," 374.

5. *Le Matin*, Aug. 15, 1918; copy of the "Summary" in Z file, OA.

6. *Naval Investigation*, 366.

7. Kittredge to Stark, March 24, 1942, Stark Papers, OA. Sims actually said the same, *The Victory at Sea*, 248. Sims quoted in *Naval Investigation*, 300.

8. Case 10662, Fletcher Court of Inquiry, RG125. For an example of his General Order to operating forces, see Order No. 10, Aug. 11, 1917, TL subj file, RG45. See also campaign order No. 2, Nov. 10, 1917 in ADM137/1437.

9. Josephus Daniels, *The Wilson Era: Years of War*, 319. He does not explain why amalgamation would have been fatal. See also Sims to wife, April 8, 1918, Box 10, Sims Papers, LC; Trask, *Captains and Cabinets*, 206–7.

10. Entry Nov. 26, 1917, in Josephus Daniels, *Cabinet Diaries*, 242.

11. Entry for Jan. 31, 1918, ibid., 274.

12. Fremantle, *My Naval Career, 1880–1928*, 238. See also remarks of Admiral Sir Frederick Dreyer, in tribute to Sims upon announcement of his death. *Times* (London), Oct. 2, 1936.

13. Sims to Pratt, April 29, 1918, Pratt Papers, OA.

14. To First Sea Lord, June 25, 1917, ADM137/1436.

15. Dated May 6, 1918, TT subj file, RG45; see also Sims to Daniels, April 18, May 11, 1917, in M. Simpson, *Anglo-American Naval Relations*, 210, 223; *Christian Science Monitor*, April 9, 1919; Morison, *Sims*, 388–89; *Scientific American* 120 (April 12, 1918): 374; Kittredge, "United States-British Co-Operation."

16. Undated paper in the Bayly Papers, IWM; Wemyss to Sims, March 28, 1918, Box 90, Sims Papers, LC; Jellicoe, *The Submarine Peril*, 82. See also statement of Admiral De Chair, June 7, 1917, ADM137/1436; and review of Sims, *The Victory at Sea*, copy in WS subj file, RG45; Marder, *From the Dreadnought to Scapa Flow*, 5: 25. British newspapers and tabloids were effusive in their admiration for this cooperation. See for example, *Evening News* (Edinburgh), July 27, 1918; *Naval and Military Record* 38 (Jan. 28, 1920): 56. See also the article by Arthur Pollen, "America and the Naval Revolution"; and *Army and Navy Journal* 56 (Feb. 1, 1919): 774–75.

17. Klachko, *Benson*, 67.

18. Conolly Oral History, Columbia University; *Sunday Times* (London), April 21, 1918; copy of newspaper article in Reel 1, Taussig Papers, NDL; Niblack to Sims, Dec. 11, 1918, CG subj file, RG45; Historical Sketch of Administration of Destroyer Flotillas Queenstown during the War, March 12, 1919, ZP subj file, RG45; H. Holt, "A Talk with Admiral Sims," 409.

19. Allard, "Anglo-American Naval Differences during World War I," 75.

20. For differences in American and British naval organizations, see Churchill, "Naval Organization, American and British"; Sims Report, June 21, 1918, Reel 4, ME-11. For an example of how change in individuals affects policy, see Sims to Pringle, Jan. 17, 1918, Box 79, and to wife, Jan. 16, 1918, Box 9, Sims Papers, LC. This concerns replacement of Jellicoe with Wemyss. See also Stackhouse, "The Anglo-American Atlantic Convoy System in World War I," Ph.D. diss., 55–57.

21. Babcock memo, Oct. 28, 1917, copy in Stark Papers, OA.

22. Smythe, *Pershing: General of the Armies*, 31; Sims to Pratt, May 18, 1918, Pratt Papers, OA.

23. Emmet to Sims, June 22, 1917, copy in M. Simpson, *Anglo-American Naval Relations*, 68–69; See also Stackpole, "The Anglo-American Convoy System in World War I," Ph.D. diss., 52; and Daniels, *The Wilson Era: Years of War*, 86; Klachko, *Benson*, 78.

24. July 2, 1917, copy in M. Simpson, *Anglo-American Naval Relations*, 76–77. Admiral Gaunt, the British naval attaché in Washington, said basically the same thing in a cable to the Admiralty. July 5, 1917, ibid., 82–84. See also Tumulty to Wilson, June 29, 1917, copy in ibid., 71.

25. Sims to Wittlesey, Aug. 29, 1917, Box 23, Sims Papers, LC.

26. Browning to Jellicoe, July 20, Aug. 10, and Browning to Benson, July 26, 1917, in M. Simpson, *Anglo-American Naval Relations*, 90–91, 93–94; Page to SecState, July 13, 1917, file 830/251a, London Consulate, RG84; Page to SecState, July 24, 1917, file 763.5959, "Records of the Department of State Relating to World War I and Its Termination, 1914–29," NA microfilm M367, hereafter cited as M367; Daniels request to U.S. Embassy, London, July 28, 1917, file 763.6059, M367; entry for July 24, 1917, in Josephus Daniels, *Cabinet Diaries*, 182; Page to SecState, July 31, 1917, *Foreign Relations, 1917*, Supplement 2, 151; Lansing to Page, Aug. 15, 1917, ibid., 161.

27. To David Lloyd George, with enclosure, Aug. 29, 1917, in M. Simpson, *Anglo-American Naval Relations*, 94–95. See also Admiral Mayo's notes on the purpose of his visit, Aug. 29, 1917, in Link, *Wilson Papers*, 44: 86–88. Also there is a copy of these notes as well as correspondence and other documents relating to the trip and Admiral Mayo's interest in personally assuming the European command in Box 2, Ernest King Papers, LC. For Jellicoe's account of conference, see *The Crisis of the Naval War*, 168–81; and *The Submarine Peril*, 71–81.

28. Allard, "Anglo-American Naval Differences," 78; Mayo to Benson, Sept. 5, 1917, Box 5, Benson Papers, LC; *Naval Investigation*, 597. For a detailed plan of the blocking scheme dated August 7, 1917, see item 49008, Jellicoe MS.

29. For Mayo's reports, see September 1917, in M. Simpson, *Anglo-American Naval Relations*, 97–104, 203–8. See also Sims to Pratt, Aug. 30, Sept. 5, 7, 1917, ibid., 95–96, Sims Papers, Box 78, LC; Allard, "Anglo American Naval Differences"; Trask, *Captains and Cabinets*, 149–52; Bowling, "The Negative Influence of Mahan on the Protection of Shipping in Wartime," Ph.D. diss., 162–69.

30. Schoultz, *With the British Battle Fleet*, 284–95. See also Mayo's detailed report of the conference, Sept. 8, 1917, Box 5, Benson Papers, LC.

31. *Naval Investigation*, 597; Mayo to Daniels, Oct. 11, 1917, UP subj file, RG45.

32. Pollen to Roosevelt, Sept. 26, 1917, in M. Simpson, *Anglo-American Naval Relations*, 107–8; Pollen to Editor, *Manchester Guardian*, Oct. 29, 1925, in the Pollen Papers. Copy provided by Dr. Jon Sumida. See also M. Simpson, *Anglo-American Naval Relations*, 61; entry for Sept. 24, 1917, in Josephus Daniels, *Cabinet Diaries*, 210.

33. To the President, Oct. 22, 1917, in Link, *Wilson Papers*, 45: 19–24.

34. Page to Daniels, Sept. 21, 1917, in M. Simpson, *Anglo-American Naval Relations*, 113. See also Geddes to Daniels, Oct. 13, 1917, ibid., 115; Notes, Sept. 13, 1917, ADM137/1437; Page to SecState, Sept. 21, 1917, file 287551-20:158, Confidential Files, RG80; Gaunt to Jellicoe, Sept. 10, 1917, in M. Simpson, *Anglo- American Naval Relations*, 104; Spring Rice to Foreign Office, Sept. 12, 1917, ibid., 105; Gaunt to Hall, Sept. 12, 1917, ibid., First Sea Lord to Gaunt, Sept. 13, 1917, ibid., 106.

35. Daniels to Polk, Oct. 10, 1917, in M. Simpson, *Anglo-American Naval Relations*, 114. See also entries for Sept. 28, Oct. 10, 1917, in Josephus Daniels, *Cabinet Diaries*, 210–11, 218; Lansing to Page, Oct. 6, 1917, file 763.72/7185a, General Records of the Department of State, RG59; Daniels to Page, Sept. 28, 1917, ibid. For concern about newspapers, see Butler to Buchan, Oct. 23, 1917, ibid., 125; Gaunt to Admiralty, Oct, 6, 1917, ibid., 113; Navy Dept. Memo, Oct. 7, 1917, ibid., 112; Memo, Oct. 6, 1917, ADM137/1437; Spring Rice to Balfour, Oct. 8, 1917, ibid., Benson to Jellicoe, Oct. 22, 1917, in M. Simpson, *Anglo-American Naval Relations*, 116–17; Butler to Buchanan, Nov. 10, 1917, FO 395/85. This file includes clippings from American newspapers.

36. Butler to Bayly, Nov. 7, 1917, FO 395 Memo, Oct. 6, 1917, ibid.; Memo, Oct. 8, 1917, ibid.; Memo, Oct. 17, 1917, ibid.; Memo, Dec 4, 1917, ibid.; Oct. 11, 1917, ADM137/1437.

37. To Daniels, Oct. 13, 1917, file 830, London Embassy Records, RG84.

38. Allard, "Anglo-American Naval Differences during World War I," 78. See also Trask, *Captains and Cabinets*, 175–82.

39. Klachko, *Benson*, 93–94. See minutes of Naval Conference, Paris, Nov. 29, 1917, Box 40, Benson Papers; undated report of trip, Nov. 1917, ibid.; Nov. 30, 1917, in Patterson, *Jellicoe Papers*, 2: 229.

40. Trask, *Captains and Cabinets*, 179–82.

41. For Norway, see chapter 17; for Italy, see documents in ADM137/2180.

42. Trask, *Captains and Cabinets*, 193–94; Page to SecState, Jan. 29, 1918, file 763.72/8698. RG59; Daniels to SecState, Feb. 3, 1918, file 763.72/8736, ibid.; Memo, Aug. 3, 1918, in M. Simpson, *Anglo-American Naval Relations*, 169.

43. *Daily Chronicle* (London), Aug. 7, 1918. See also Daniels to Wilson, July 28, 1918, Reel 65, Daniels Papers, LC.

44. Considerable correspondence in 832 files, Liverpool Consulate, RG84 on this problem. For Cardiff, see memos Jan. 1, 1918, ADM137/1621, and Oct. 4, 1918, ADM137/2260. For other problems at Liverpool, see Zogbaum, *From Sail to Saratoga*, 278–80.

45. Wilson to Daniels, Oct. 2, 1918, in Link, *Wilson Papers*, vol. 51; entries for Oct. 9, 1918, ibid., 275–80, 315–16; Daniels to W. W., Sept. 26, 1918, ibid., 124; Geddes to FDR, Aug. 31, 1918, 49: 410–13; Geddes Memo, Sept. 19, 1918, ADM 137/1622; "Naval Effort—Great Britain & United States of America," Aug. 2, 1918, ADM116/1810. See also Sims to Benson, Sept. 6, 1918, Roll 40, M1140; FDR report to Secretary of Navy, Oct. 16, 1918, Assistant Sec. of the Navy Files, Box 46, FDR Library; *Scotsman*, Oct. 25, 1918; Trask, *Captains and Cabinets*, 299–312; Parsons, *Wilsonian Diplomacy*, 142–48.

46. Geddes to War Cabinet, Nov. 7, 1918, ADM1167/1771; M. Simpson, *Anglo-American Naval Relations*, 482–85; Kaufman, *Efficiency and Expansion*, 192–93.

47. Note to his diary, Box 191, FDR Assistant Sec. of the Navy Files, FDR Library.

48. Trask quoted in Wallach, *Uneasy Coalition*, 21.

49. Marder, *From the Dreadnought to Scapa Flow*, 5: 128.

50. Kittredge, "United States–British Cooperation, 1939–1942." For Sims's quote, see to wife, June 8, 1918, Box 9, Sims Papers, LC.

51. Porch, "The French Army in the First World War," 205. For the Mediterranean situation, see chapter 19.

52. French naval attaché, Washington to Ministry of Marine, May 3, 5, 1917, French naval archives, Vincennes; French Minister of Marine to FDR, May 30, 1917, Assistant Sec. of the Navy Files, Box 25, FDR Library; Daniels to Sims, July 10, 1917, Box 53, Sims Papers, LC.

53. Quoted in Hoehling, *The Great War at Sea*, 190; entry for Dec. 20, 1917, in Josephus Daniels, *Cabinet Diaries*, 253. See also entries for Jan. 24, 27, 1918, Stuart Smith Diaries, LC. The American naval force would have to be as self-sufficient as possible. Mayo to SecNav, Sept. 17, 1917, Mayo Papers, LC; Sims to French Minister of Marine, Oct. 23, 1917, French naval archives, Vincennes. For problems with French logistical support, see chapter 6 on logistics; for operations in French waters, see chapter 14. See also L. C. White, *Pioneer and Patriot*, 88–89.

54. Jan. 18, 1918, General Board Hearings; entry for June 11, 1918, Taussig Diary, Taussig Papers, NWC

55. "Progress Report Naval Aviation Stations, France, Nov. 11, 1918," GA subj file, RG45.

56. Beers, *Navy Port Offices in the Bordeaux Region*, 26–29, 38–39, 44; Long to "Charlie" July 1, 1918, OF subj file, RG45. See also entry for June 12, 1918, Taussig Diary, NWC; and Parker Oral History, Columbia University; Zogbaum, *From Sail to Saratoga*, 245; *Fleet Review* 10 (Nov. 1919): 31; Marcosson, *S.O.S. America's Miracle in France*, 26–27. For a brief examination of similar problems with the AEF, see Wallach, *Uneasy Coalition*, 139–40; Pamard to Minister of

Marine, Aug. 22, 2928, French Naval Archives, Vincennes. The British navy also had problems with the French navy. See W. James, *A Great Seaman*, 155–56.

57. See Leigh to Sims, July 30, 1918, Box 70, Sims Papers, LC; Sims to De Bon, Aug. 5, 1918, French Naval Archives, Vincennes. To wife, Aug. 9, 1917, Box 9, Sims Papers, LC. See also testimony of Captain Richard Jackson, Fletcher Court of Inquiry, Case 10662, RG125. The American force based at Corfu came under French control. Cooperation apparently there was much better. See Leigh to Sims, July 30, 1918, Box 70, Sims Papers, LC; Sims to De Bon, Aug. 5, 1918, French Naval Archives, Vincennes.

58. Magruder to Sims, Oct. 27, 1917, CP subj file, RB45.

59. For biographies of Schwerer and Moreau, see Taillemite, *Dictionnaire des marins Francais*, 241–42, 309. See also Neeser, "Les patrouilleurs Americains sur les cotes de France."

60. "Powers of the Prefets Maritimes," Oct. 29, 1917, copy in OF subj file, RG45. See also Magruder, "The Navy in the War," *Saturday Evening Post*, 21.

61. *American Navy in France*, 17. See also R. W. Kauffman, *Our Navy at Work*, 244; *Le Matin*, May 17, 1918; *Pall Mall Gazette*, May 17, 1918. Daniels never accepted the fact that American forces in France were under French command.

62. *Naval Investigation*, 904.

63. Case 10662, Fletcher Court of Inquiry, RG125. The same was true of the naval air stations. See Paine, *The First Yale Unit* 1: 34–35. For a different viewpoint see Le Roy, *La guerre sous marin en Bretagne*, 92–93.

64. *Annual Report of the Secretary of the Navy, 1918*, 396. See also Josephus Daniels, *Our Navy at War*, 100

65. Schwerer to Moreau, Sept. 13, and Moreau's reply, Sept. 19, 1918, in French Naval Archives, Vincennes. Moreau also in a memo reviewed the correspondence that he had from Schwerer concerning relations with the Americans and said that as early as November 1917 he had requested a report of the relations, which he never received. Jan. 12, 1918, ibid.

66. De Bon Report, February 2, 1918, French Naval Archives, Vincennes. See also Pamard to Division Chief, Aug. 22, 1918, French Naval Archives, Vincennes; Cone to Sims, May 22, 1918, Reel 4, ME-11. See chapter 14 for operations in French waters.

67. Trask, *Captains and Cabinets*, 175–77.

68. Sims to Pratt, Nov. 21, 1917, Box 78, Sims Papers, LC.

69. Geddes to War Cabinet, Dec. 11, 1917, in M. Simpson, *Anglo-American Naval Relations*, 142–43; C. Seymour, *The Intimate Papers of Colonel House*, 3: 298; Klachko, *Benson*, 97–99.

70. To wife, Feb. 15, 1918, Box 9, Sims Papers, LC.

71. June 17, 1918, Box 79, Sims Papers, LC.

72. See, for example, Sims to naval attaché, Rome, subj file, Box 564, RG45; Sims testimony, Case 10662, Fletcher Court of Inquiry, RG125; to Pratt, April 4, 1918, Pratt Papers, OA.

73. Trask, *Captains and Cabinets*, 180; Sims to Pratt, April 4, 1918, Pratt Papers, OA; Villary to Sims, Dec. 30, 1917, QC subj file, RG45; memo by Italian Representative, Allied Naval Council, January 1918, ibid. For the Mediterranean problems, see chapter 19 on the Mediterranean.

74. *Stars and Stripes*, July 19, 1918.

75. Beers, *U.S. Naval Port Offices in the Bordeaux Region, 1917–19*, 44–49. See also report on ports, Nov. 28, 1917, French Naval Archives, Vincennes.

76. Long to "Charlie," July 1, 1918, OF subj file, RG45; Hagood, *The Services of Supply*, 283; Roger Williams to Sims, Oct. 15, 1918, Box 91, Sims Papers, LC; General William W. Atterbury to Sims, Box 47, ibid. There was friction between Army and Navy officials over responsibility for controlling personnel in the port cities. See chapter 9 on personnel.

77. Ramsey, "Delivering the Goods," Ph.D. diss., 74–75.

78. Benson to Sims, Aug. 5, 1918, Reel 5, ME-11; Ferrell, *Woodrow Wilson and World War I*, 59; Palmer, *Newton D. Baker: America at War*, 2: 11.

79. Sims to CNO, Jan.1, 1918, TV subj file, RG45. There is considerable correspondence concerning this problem in this file.

80. Sims to Dept., June 3, 1918, Reel 4; Sims to Comfran, Brest, Aug. 27, 1918, Reel 10, ME-11; Pershing, April 10, 1918, Box 79, Sims Papers, LC; Pershing to Biddle, May 5, 1918, Reel 4, ME-11; Pershing to Biddle, May 10, 1918, Reel 20, ibid.; Pershing to Simsadus, London, June 4, 1918, Reel 4, ibid.; Benson to Simsadus, June 4, 1918, ibid.; Huston, *The Sinews of War*, 357.

81. W. Mitchell, *Memoirs of World War I*, 136; Pershing to Sims, May 10, 1918, Reel 4, ME-11. The Army aviation service in France had serious command problems. During its first year, six officers commanded it.

82. Cone to Irwin, Nov. 16, 1917, TV subj file, RG45; Cone to Sims, May 17, 1918, ibid.; Cone to Sims, May 22, 1918, Reel 4, ME-11.

83. Cone to Sims, May 17, 1918, Reel 12, ME-11; Sims to Pershing, June 7, 1918, Reel 4, ibid.; Sims to Pratt, June 14, 1918, Pratt Papers; Cone to Sims, June 26, 1918, Reel 4, ME-11; Lord "History of Naval Aviation," NDL; Turnbull and Lord, *History of United States Naval Aviation*, 136–89; Coffman, *The War to End All Wars*, 197. For operations, see section on naval aviation in chapter 18.

84. Sims to Pershing, May 16, 1918, Sims to Major General G. T. Bartlett, January 24, 1918, Pershing to Sims, May 10, 1918, all in Reel 4, ME-11. See also Lord's "History of Naval Aviation," NDL. There is considerable correspondence concerning problems in coordination between the Army and naval air service in France in TV subj file, RG45.

85. Sims to Wilson, July 13, 1918, in Link, *Wilson Papers*, 48, 604–5. See also Sims to Dept., May 29, 1918, Reel 4, ME-11; Sims to Pratt, April 29, 1918, Pratt Papers, OA; Pershing to Sims, August 11, 1917 and Sims's reply the same day in Box 23, Sims Papers; FDR report, Oct. 16, 1918, Assistant Sec. of the Navy Files, Box 46, FDR Library.

86. *The United States Naval Railway Batteries in France*, 1–2. This booklet originally published in 1919 and reprinted in 1988 is the most detailed account of these guns.

87. Bill Cunningham, "K.O. by Sailor Guns," *American Legion Magazine*, Aug. 1939, 44; Tighe, "Plunkett's Pirates," NDL. See also King and Whitehill, *Fleet Admiral King*, 128–29; Coontz, *From the Mississippi to the Sea*, 117–18. Another account said that his nickname was "Si." Connolly, *Navy Men*, 240.

88. Josephus Daniels, *The Wilson Era: Years of War*, 265.

89. Cunningham, "K.O. by Sailor Guns," 42.

90. Quoted in Magruder, "The Navy in the War," 121.

91. Jenkins, "Why Hard-Boiled Crew Liked Plunkett," 178, 185; Magruder, "The Navy in the War," 121; Tighe, "Plunkett's Pirates," NDL.

92. Williams to Sims, Oct. 15, 1918, Box 91, Sims Papers, LC; Cunningham, "K.O. by Sailor Guns," 43–44.

93. Sims, *The Victory at Sea*, 340.

94. Sims to wife, March, 29, 1918, Box 9, Sims Papers, LC; Sims to Wilson, March 30, 1918, Reel 19, ME-11; Ministry of Marine to Jackson, April 3, 1918, Reel 4, ibid.; Sims to Wilson, April 6, 1918, ibid. See also Sims to Jackson, July 29, 1918, Reel 9, ibid. Interestingly, the Navy Department wanted the naval personnel to be a separate unit such as a division under Navy officers.

95. The literature on the Russian Revolution is, of course, enormous. For a perusal of some of the historiography on American intervention, see Eugene P. Traini, "Woodrow Wilson and the Decision to Intervene in Russia: A Reconsideration," *Journal of Modern History* 48 (Sept. 1976): 440–61.

96. Russian Chargé to SecState, April 21, May 1, 1917, *Foreign Relations, 1917*, Supplement 2, 32–33, 48–49; SecState to Francis, May 3, July 10, 1917, ibid., 52, 123; SecState to Russian Chargé, June 2, 1917, ibid., 83; Francis to SecState, June 14, 1917, 101, ibid.; Daniels to Sims, April 22, 1917, Reel 8, ME-11; Benson to Sims, July 19, 1917, ibid.; Sims to Dept., Sept. 21, 1917, Reel 1, ibid.;

Sims to Bayly, Oct. 29, 1917, Box 23, Sims Papers, LC; entry for May 3, 1917, in Josephus Daniels, *Cabinet Diaries*, 145–46; Sims to Dept., May 24, 1917, U subj file, RG45; Francis to SecState, SecState to Daniels, May 28, Daniels's reply, May 31, 1917, file C-20-24, Box 54, Confidential Files, 1917–19, RG80; Francis to SecState, July 12, 1917, file 28754-20:46, Confidential Files, RG80; see also considerable correspondence in file 20:34, ibid. Memo, July 12, 1917, 763.72/5854, Roll 45, M367. As early as September, the Department began assembling charts of the Russian Arctic coast. Memo, Commandant, Washington Navy Yard, Sept. 1, 1917, Reel 10, M1092.

97. French Embassy, London, to Foreign Office, Dec. 7, 1917, ADM137/1704; Monograph Number 7, Feb. 9, 1920, "A History of the White Sea Station, 1914–1919," 11–14, ADM137/1731.

98. W. W. to Lansing, April 4, 1918, in Link, *Wilson Papers*, 47: 246; F. O. to Reading, March 12, 1918, ADM137/1704; Memo, March 2, 1918, ADM 137/1704; "A History of the White Sea Station," ADM137/1761; Sims to Dept., March 3, 1918, Reel 8, ME-11; Dept to Sims, March 5, 1918, ibid.; Kennan, *The Decision to Intervene*, 55–57.

99. See, for example, F. O. to Reading, March 20, 1918, F.O. 371/3305.

100. Polk to Lansing with enclosure, April 2, 1918, in Link, *Wilson Papers*, 47: 226–27; Sims to Benson, April 25, 1918, Box 49, Sims Papers, LC; Memo, March 23, 1918, Box 174, Tasker H. Bliss Papers, LC.

101. Benson to Sims, April 5, 9, 1918, Reel 4, ME-11; Daniels to W. W., April 5, 1918, in Link, *Wilson Papers*, 47: 263; W. W. to Daniels, April 8, 1918, ibid., 47: 290; various documents and correspondence in "Polk Drawer 85," Edward M. House Papers, Yale University Library; Adm memos, April 4, 12, 1918, ADM137/1704; W. W. to Daniels, April 6, 1918, Box 14, Daniels Papers, LC; Sims to Benson, April 8, 1918, in M. Simpson, *Anglo-American Naval Relations*, 160; Sims to Dept., April 12, 1918, OS subj file, RG45. See also Bacon, "Russian American Relations," Ph.D. diss., 167–69; Olszewski, "Allied Intervention in North Russia," Ph.D. diss., 28–30; Trask, *Captains and Cabinets*, 210–14; Long, "Civil War and Intervention in North Russia," Ph.D. diss., 23–24. Beers, in *U.S. Naval Forces in Northern Russia*, offers the most detailed account of the Navy's role in North Russia. See also Kennan, *The Decision to Intervene*, 245.

102. Memoir of C. V. Jackson, copy in possession of author; news release, Feb 4, 1918, OS subj file, RG45. See also *DANFS*, 5: 152–53.

103. Entry for May 20, 1918, Diary of Thomas S. Hatton, copy in author's possession; see also Jackson, "Mission to Murmansk," 83.

104. Hatton Diary, copy in author's possession. See also Sims to Dept., April 14, 1918, Reel 4, ME-11; Wemyss to War Cabinet, April 16, 1918, ADM116/1810; Sims to Dept., May 1, 1918, Reel 20, ME-11; Sims to Dept., May 14, 1918, W-6 file, subj file, RG45; Admiralty to Kemp, May 16, 1918, ADM116/1807; Geddes to War Cabinet, May 30, 1918, ADM116/1808; Kennan, *The Decision to Intervene*, 275–76, 447. The German high command did plan a major offensive toward the Murmansk area, but it was never carried out. Halpern, *Naval History of World War I*, 136.

105. Lansing to Daniels, July 1, 1918, Box 95, General Records of the Navy Dept., RG80; Benson Memo to Daniels, June 22, 1918, Box 35, Daniels papers, LC; Francis to SecState, April 30, May 20, June 14, 1918, *Foreign Relations, 1918, Russia*, 1: 541; 2: 474, 485; Sims to Dept., June 15, 1918, Reel 4, ME-11; Trask, *Captains and Cabinets*, 213–16.

106. Long, "American Intervention in Russia," 53–56.

107. Morris to SecState, June 20, 1918, Records of the Department of State Relating to the Internal Affairs of Russia and the Soviet Union, 1910–29, Roll 14, M316; Cole to SecState, June 21, 1918, ibid.; Francis to SecState, June 20, 1918, in *Foreign Relations, Russia*, 1: 564–65.

108. Lansing to President, Sept. 13, 1918, in Link, *Wilson Papers*, 51: 79–80; Lansing to Daniels, Oct. 14, 1918, in *Foreign Relations, Russia*, 2: 556–57; Lansing to Francis, Oct. 16, 1918, ibid., 2: 558.

109. Entry for July 30, 1918, Olympia War Diary, copy in OS subj file, RG45; Long, "American Intervention in Russia," 57; Long, "Civil War and Intervention in North Russia," Ph.D. diss.,

196–97; Rhodes, *The Anglo-American Winter War with Russia*, 21–24; Goldhurst, *The Midnight War*, 85–86; Dobson and Miller, *The Day They Almost Bombed Moscow*, 61–63; Weeks, "An American Naval Diplomat in Revolutionary Russia," Ph.D. diss., 131–32. As early as the middle of April, the first lord said that the military occupation of Archangel "is extremely necessary." Wemyss to War Cabinet, April 17, 1918, ADM116/1810. See also War Council to Poole, June 5, 1918, ADM137/1704; Francis to SecState, July 7, 22, 1918, in *Foreign Relations, Russia*, 2: 496, 503–4; Francis to SecState, Aug. 1, 4, 1918, ibid., 1:, 624–29.

110. Bierer to Francis, Oct. 21, 1918, OS subj file, RG45; McCully to Sims, Oct. 26, 1918, W-6 file, ibid.; Hunt, *One American*, 112.

111. Jackson, "Mission to Murmansk," 84–87; Diary of Thomas Hatton, various entries from June 8 to Nov. 12, 1918, copy in author's possession; Bierer weekly reports to Sims, July 6, Aug. 10, 17, 1918, Reel 37, M1140; entries for July 17, Aug. 3, 1918, *Olympia* War Diary, copy in OS subj file, RG45.

112. See Jackson, "Mission to Murmansk," 85–86; quotes from various entries in Thomas Hatton Diary, copy in author's possession.

113. Entry for Sept. 4, 1918, in Robien, *The Diary of a Diplomat in Russia*, 287. See also various entries in diary of musician Thomas Hatton, copy in author's possession.

114. Goldhurst, *The Midnight War*, 94–95; Rhodes, *The Anglo-American Winter War with Russia*, 26–27.

115. Hicks report, Sept. 7, 1918, Reel 8, ME-11. See also Long, "Civil War and Intervention in North Russia," Ph.D. diss., 230–32. Long's study includes Soviet accounts of the actions; entries for Aug. 2–25, 1918, *Olympia* War Diary, copy in Intervention in Russia file, ZO file, OA. See also Gordon, *Quartered in Hell*, 7–8. *Bolos* was a name given to Bolsheviks by either the British or the Americans.

116. Gordon, *Quartered in Hell*, 8. Gordon quotes from accounts by two American seamen with both Hicks expedition along the railroad and the one on the river (see 53–56); see also Burton to Kemp, Dec. 18, 1918, ADM137/1711; Bierer report, Aug.21, 1918, Roll 37, M1140.

117. These instructions originated with the Navy Department. FDR to SecState, Nov. 1, 1918, Roll 17, M316; Sims to McCully, Oct. 10, 1918, Reel 8, ME-11. See also Weeks, "A Samaritan in Russia," 13; Kemp to Admiralty, Sept. 7, 1918, ADM137/1717; ADM to Sims, Sept. 5, 1918, ADM 137/1704; Bierer to Francis, Sept. 4, 1918, OS subj file, RG45; Le Bon to Admiralty, Sept. 20, 1918, ADM137/1704; Lansing to Francis, Sept. 11, 1918, Box 182, Breckinridge Long Papers, LC; Sims to CNO, Sept. 17, 1918, WA subj file, RG45; Sims to Bierer, Sept. 28, 1918, Reel 8, ME-11; Francis to SecState, Oct. 9, 1918, *Foreign Relations, Russia*, 2:, 555.

118. Jackson, "Mission to Murmansk," 89; Sims to Dept., Nov. 10, 1918, Reel 8, ME-11; Sims to Admiralty, Dec. 16, 1918, ADM137/1713; Francis to Sims, Nov. 19, 1918, Box 24, Sims Papers, LC.

119. Sims to wife, April 14, 21, Dec. 13, 1918, Box 10, Sims Papers, LC; Sims to the President, Aug. 2, 1918, in Baker, *Woodrow Wilson: Life and Letters*, 8: 313–14, hereafter cited as *Wilson*. See also Trask, *Captains and Cabinets*, 202–3; and Smythe, *Pershing*, 16.

120. Dawes, *A Journal of the Great War*, 1: 28–35. This collier and others assigned to transport coal were then assigned to Sims's command.

Chapter 5. A Little Bit of America: U.S. Naval Facilities in Great Britain

1. Entry for May 6, 1917, in Taussig, *Queenstown Patrol*, 23.

2. April 28, 1917, in *Foreign Relations, 1917*, Supplement 2, 47. See also Still, "Anglo-American Naval Logistic Cooperation in World War I," 213; and Still, "Logistical Support for U.S. Naval Forces Operation in European Waters in World War I," 283.

3. "Supplies in War," n.d., paper in Samuel McGowan Papers, LC. See also Still, *American Sea Power in the Old World*, 39–55.

4. Stanley L. Falk, introduction to Thorpe, *Pure Logistics*, xx; Albion, "Logistics in World War II," 97; J. D. Hayes, "Logistics—the Word," 200.

5. Wouk, *The Glory*, 467.

6. Macksey, *For Want of a Nail*, 5.

7. Quoted in Hattendorf, *Sailors and Scholars*, 133. See also Hattendorf, "Technology and Strategy," 127–28, 137; and Dyer, *Naval Logistics*, 5.

8. For these developments see Allston, *Ready for Sea*, 124–60.

9. Memo with references to the Committee, August 3, 1916, file 127046, Records of the Bureau of Medicine and Surgery, NA RG52, hereafter cited as RG52.

10. McGowan to SecNav, June 19, 1916, Reel 546, Daniels Papers, LC; L. B. Bell, "McGowan," master's thesis, 60–61.

11. Quoted in "The Bureau in World War I," 100. See also "U.S. Bureau of Supplies and Accounts," in World War II Administrative Histories, copy in Navy Department Library; Dyer, "The Supply Department in War Time"; Josephus Daniels, *Our Navy at War*, 350–51.

12. Historical sketch of administration of Destroyer Flotilla at Queenstown during the war, March 12, 1919, ZD subj file, RG45, hereafter cited as "Destroyer Flotilla at Queenstown"; History of Bureau of Supplies and Accounts in the War, file 427-5, Box 430, Records of the Bureau of Supplies and Accounts, NA RG143, hereafter cited as RG143.

13. "Summary of U.S. Naval Activities in European Waters," Z file, OA. See also Historical Sketch, Headquarters, Dec. 5, 1918, ZT subj file, RG45, and *Annual Report of the Secretary of the Navy*, 1918, 174, and *ONI Monthly Information Bulletin*, May 15, 1919, 33, hereafter cited as *ONI Monthly Bulletin*; and memo, 1919 in TL subj file, RG45; *Fleet Review* 10 (July 1919): 35–36; *Daily Telegraph*, June 13, 1917.

14. Aug. 17, 1917, Reel 2, ME-11.

15. The Department designated numbers for thirty bases including those in the Western Hemisphere. Tangier Sound was number 1, Queenstown, number 6, and Bizerta (actually never completed), number 30. Paragraph 5354 of Naval Instructions as adopted in 1918 defined a base as "a point from which naval operations may be conducted and which is selected for that purpose. Its essential feature is an adequate anchorage for a fleet with its auxiliaries." Copy in folder 1, ZO file, WWI, OA.

16. Bythe, "At a Naval Base," 109.

17. Sims to Dept., May 11, 1917, in M. Simpson, *Anglo-American Naval Relations*, 221.

18. *Naval and Military Record* 37 (January 1, 1919): 13; Malcolm F. Schoeffel Oral History, USNI; Destroyer Flotilla at Queenstown, March 12, 1919, ZD subj file, RG45; "The Great War: The Great Boom," 39; Sims to SecNav, June 1, 1917, P-Queenstown subj file, RG45.

19. To SecNav, May 8, 1917, in M. Simpson, *Anglo-American Naval Relations*, 219. The *Dixie* was also a tender ordered to Ireland.

20. Destroyer Flotilla at Queenstown, March 12, 1919, ZD subj file, RG45; memo, August 5, 1918, Box 65, Logistics file; RG45.

21. Sims Rept., April 17, 1918, Reel 4, ME-11.

22. Aide for Supplies and Transportation to CO U.S. Naval Air Stations, Ireland, Dec. 28, 1918, ZPA subj file, RG45; Pringle to Sims, March 24, 1918, Box 27, General Correspondence, 1917–1919, USNAVOPFOR, London, Headquarters, Records of the Navy's Operating Forces, NA RG313, hereafter cited as RG313; "Progress Report," U.S. Naval Aviation Forces, Foreign Service, headquarters, Paris, March 15, 1918, microfilm, NDL; Cone to Sims, Nov. 5, 1917, Reel 2, ME-11.; Destroyer Flotilla at Queenstown, March 12, 1919, ZD subj file, RG45.

23. Sims to Bureau of Ordnance, June 23, 1918, Box 7, Logistics file, RG45; Mayo to wife, Sept. 14, 1918, Mayo Papers; entry for Nov. 1, 1917, in Josephus Daniels, *Cabinet Diaries*, 230; Sims to Navy Dept., Nov. 14, 1917, Reel 10, M1092; Sims to OpNav, June 1, 1918, Box 10, RG19. A hospi-

tal, naval air station, and a training establishment were added to the U.S. Navy's Queenstown command in 1918.

24. Hepburn to Sims, Aug. 21, Nov. 30, 1918, SD subj file, RG45. See also Sims to Dept., April 30, 1918, Reel 20, ME-11; "The Great War: The Great Boom," 37–39.

25. Chatterton, *Danger Zone*, 362; *Cork Examiner*, Dec. 6, 1918.

26. *Evening Echo* (Cobh), May 5, 1977; Chatterton, *Danger Zone*, 362–63.

27. *Naval and Military Record* 36 (June 5, 12, 1918): 365. 389.

28. Roosevelt to Daniels, April 5, 1918, in Kilpatrick, *Roosevelt and Daniels*, 43–44; Cooke, "Recollections," LC.

29. Mayo Report, Oct. 8, 1918, copy in King Papers, LC; "Queenstown Ireland U.S. Naval Base, 1917–1919," in Coletta and Bauer, *United States Naval and Marine Corps Bases: Overseas*, 386–87, hereafter cited as *Bases, Overseas*; Memo, Dec. 24, 1918, in M. Simpson, *Anglo-American Naval Relations*, 317–18; Leighton, *Simsadus*, 23.

30. Dyer, *Naval Logistics*, 120; Eccles, *Operational Naval Logistics*, 87–89.

31. M. Simpson, *Anglo-American Naval Relations*, 219; entry for May 12, 1917, Joseph Fagan Diary, Mariners' Museum.

32. Mayo speech, n.d., Mayo Papers, LC. See also *Naval Investigation*, 43; Chapin, *The Lost Legion*, 25; "Bound for Bantry Bay," 296; Thompson, *Take Her Down*, 223.

33. Memo, Dec. 1918, ZT subj file, RG45; memo, n.d., Box 7, entry 136, RG125; Still, "Anglo-American Naval Logistic Cooperation in World War I," 230 n. 23.

34. Memo, date unreadable, ZPO file, subj file, RG45; Pilat, *Pegler*, 81–82; Washington to Stark, Feb. 18, 1918, file 832, Liverpool Consulate Records, RG84.

35. Bogert to Braisted, Feb. 9, 22, March 19, April 4, 1918, file 127046, RG52; Murphy to Pringle, June 10, 1918, file 12535, ibid.; Sims circular letter, May 3, 1918, file 127046, ibid.

36. Pratt to Daniels, Nov. 12, 1917, in M. Simpson, *Anglo-American Naval Relations*, 123–24; Sims to Admiralty, May 10, 1918, Confidential Correspondence, 1917–1919, RG80; entries for May 1918, Richard Leigh revised Journal, Richard H. Leigh Papers, Florida State University; Moffat, *Maverick Navy*, 101.

37. Memo No. 32, May 30, 1918, in Navy Dept., *The American Naval Planning Section in London*, 235–37; Historical Sketch of U.S. Naval Base No. 27, Dec. 23, 2928, ZP subj file, RG45.

38. June 19, 1918, Theodore Gordon Ellyson Papers (microfilm), NDL Ellyson to Sims, Dec. 23, 1918, ZP subj file, RG45; Sims to SecNav, June 21, 1918, Reel 4, ME-11; Medical Officer, Base 27, to Bureau of Med and Surgery, Oct. 7, 1918, file 130212, RG52; Med Officer to Bureau of Med and Surgery, Feb. 1919, file 132564, ibid.; *Naval and Military Record* 36 (Dec. 4, 1918): 773; Section Engineer, Plymouth Report, June 26, 1918, ADM137/2507. See also the file on Plymouth in ADM131/66. For Ellyson's comments to his wife about his quarters, see June 17, Aug. 29, 1918, Ellyson Papers, ND.

39. Cotten to Sims, Aug. 7, 1918, OD Subj file, RG45; Ellyson to wife, June 18, 1918, Ellyson Papers, NDL.

40. Sims to Bristol, Sept. 10, 1918, Bristol Papers, LC; Cotten to Hepburn, July 9, 1918, P-Plymouth subj file, RG45; Base CO to Sims, Dec. 23, 1918, ZP subj file, RG45; entries for Oct. 1918, revised Leigh diary, Leigh Papers, FSU; Memo for Admiral Sims, Aug. 14, 1918, Box 52, Sims Papers, LC; Cotten to wife, Aug. 4, 12, Sept. 7, 1918, Lyman Cotten Papers, UNC-CH. See also Bristol to Sims, Nov. 6, 1918, Box 50, Sims Papers, LC; Ellyson to wife, Aug. 4, 7, 17, 1918, Ellyson Papers, NDL; Sims to Benson, July 28, 1918, in M. Simpson, *Anglo-American Naval Relations*, 167. Entries for Oct. 1918, revised diary of Leigh, FSU; *Naval and Military Record* 37 (Feb. 19, 1919): 119. Cotten to Leigh, August 30, 1918, P-Plymouth subj file, RG45; Sims Report, July 11, 1918, Reel 4, ME-11; Sims to Benson, July 28, 1918, Box 49, Sims Papers, LC; Base CO to Sims, Dec. 23, 1918, ZP subj file, RG45; Davy to Force CO, June 27, 1918, Report of Personnel, NA subj file, RG45; memo, August 4, 1918, subj file, ibid.

41. To Minister of Marine, Oct. 3, 1917, Reel 2, ME-11. See also Benson to Sims, Sept. 20, 1917, ibid.; Sims to Dept., Sept. 26, 1917, Reel 3, ibid.; "Summary of U.S. Naval Activities in European Waters," Z file, OA; Dawes, *Journal of the Great War*, 28–35. Sims claimed that Army authorities failed to inform him of coal difficulties until a "few days" before the War Department intervened in Washington. Sims to Dept., Sept. 22, 1917, Reel 3, ME-11.

42. Sims to CNO, August 9, 1918, P-Cardiff subj file, RG45; to CNO, August 9, 1918, Reel 9, ME-11; Leighton, *Simsadus*, 88–89. No explanation has been found as to why Andrews was selected over Hughes. Andrews was not a favorite of Daniels so the promotion to flag rank and command at Cardiff was an important career step for him. Hughes was not hurt professionally by being passed over this time. He would later become CNO. See also Morison, *Sims*, 292; Morison, *Josephus Daniels*, 52; entry for Jan. 30, 1921, in Josephus Daniels, *Cabinet Diaries*, 594; C. G. Reynolds, *Famous American Admirals*, 156–57.

43. Fife, *The Passing Legions*, 297; Andrews to Sims, Oct. 5, 1918, P-Cardiff subj file, RG45; to Sims, Oct. 21, 1918, Box 46, Sims Papers, LC; memo, for Secretary of the Admiralty, Oct. 22, 1918, ADM137/2260.

44. Andrews to Sims, Jan. 9, 1919, P-Cardiff subj file, RG45; memo for Secretary of the Admiralty, Oct. 22, 1918, and memo for Senior Naval Officer, Law Courts, Cardiff; and Admiralty to Andrews, Nov. 30, 1918, all in ADM137/2260.

45. Army coal trade, Summary of U.S. Naval Activities in European Waters, Z files, OA.

46. Report, October 31, 1917, ADM137/1962; memo and enclosures on conference held October 30, 1917, Roll 37, M1140. See also CO U.S. Mine Bases to CO Mine Force, Sept. 2, 1918, AN subj file, RG45; Force Commander to Bureau of Ordnance, Nov. 2, 1917, Roll 37, M1140. For the deliberations as well as the mine barrage itself, see chapter 17.

47. Griff, *Surrendered*, 146.

48. Sims, *The Victory at Sea*, 298.

49. Donnachie, *A History of the Brewing Industry in Scotland*, 232–33.

50. Entry for April 27, 1919, in Josephus Daniels, *Cabinet Diaries*, 401. See also Jonathon Daniels, *The End of Innocence*, 287.

51. Report of Committee, Oct. 30, 1917, Roll 37, M1140.

52. *Literary Digest*, Feb. 15, 1919, 96.

53. Bythe, "The Pills of Perdition," 34.

54. Baker to Admiralty, Nov. 18, 1917, ADM137/1962. See also *Inverness Courier*, Dec. 6, 1918.

55. Mayo to wife, Sept. 26, 29, 1918, Mayo Papers, LC; Report of Committee, Oct. 30, 1917, Roll 37, M1140.

56. CO, Mine Bases to CO, Mine Force, Sept. 21, 1918, AN subj file, RG45; Murfin to Sims, Jan. 16, 1918, ibid.

57. Griff, *Surrendered*, 180.

58. Memo for Chief of Bureau of Ordnance, March 1, 1919, Simon P. Fullinwider Papers, National Museum of History and Technology, Smithsonian Institution, Washington, D.C., hereafter cited as Smithsonian; testimony of Admiral Strauss, General Board Hearings, NDL.

59. Mayo to CNO, Nov. 20, 1917, AN subj file, RG45; Rpt. Oct. 31, 1917, ADM137/1962; R. Richmond to *Torch*, Sept. 7, 1976, copy in World War I Survey Research Collection, U.S. Army Military History Institute, Carlisle Barracks, Pa., hereafter cited as "WWI Survey Research Collection, AMHI." See also Navy Department, *The Northern Barrage and Other Mining Activities*, 62; Report of Keith Committee, Oct. 31, 1917, Roll 37, M1140.

60. Bureau of Ordnance, Navy Department, *Navy Ordnance Activities, World War, 1917–1918*, 122.

61. Admiralty report, October 31, 1917, Roll 37, M1140; January 16, 1918, AN subj file, RG45;

Murfin to Fullinwider, Dec. 4, 1917, Fullinwider Papers, Smithsonian; to Sims, Dec. 3, 1917, copy in ibid.

62. Schuyler to Admiral Earle, Nov. 26, 1917, copy in Fullinwider Papers, Smithsonian. Lieutenant Commander George Schuyler was supply officer for the bases. A member of the assembly crews at Invergordon estimated that they could assemble fifty mines an hour "if things went right." Richmond to *Torch*, Sept. 7, 1976, WWI Research Collection, AMHI.

63. Conaga to Gilpin, April 5, 1918, Box 3, Assistant SecNav Files, FDR Library; Murfin to Sims, Dec. 3, 1917, AN subj file, RG45; Sims to Department, Dec. 7, 1917, Roll 10, M1072; Sims to Bureau of Ordnance, Dec. 8, 1917, copy in Fullinwider Papers, Smithsonian.

64. CO Mine Bases to Sims, Sept. 21, 1918, AN subject file, RG45.

65. Griff, *Surrendered*, 180–81.

66. Murfin to Sims, Jan. 16, 1918, Box 16, Logistic file, RG45; to Sims, Dec. 3, 1917, AN subj file, RG45; Belknap, *The Yankee Mining Squadron*, 23.

67. Josephus Daniels, *The Wilson Era, Years of War*, 190.

68. Testimony of Braisted, *Naval Investigation*, 2598–99; Surgeon T. W. Richards to Surgeon General, USN, March 17, 1917, and reply dated March 20, file 127046, RG52; Richards to Braisted, Aug. 22, 1917, ibid.

69. Davison, *The American Red Cross in the Great War*, 57; G. W. Gray, "The Red Cross and the Navy," 424–27; Dock et al., *History of American Red Cross Nursing*, 691; Fenney, "History of Navy Nurse Corps," vol. 7, Navy Nurse Corps Records, OA. Captain E. R. Stitt, a naval surgeon during the war, would later state that the Navy Base Hospital Unit was first used successfully during the war. It is unclear if the concept originated with the Navy or the Red Cross. "Activities of the Bureau of Medicine and Surgery in Time of War," Aug. 21, 1925, RG15, NWC.

70. Sims report, Aug. 24, 1918, file 127046, RG52; *Annual Report of Secretary of the Navy, U.S. Navy, 1918*, 176–77; *Annual Report of Surgeon General, 1918*, 23, 82, 103; *Activities of the Bureau of Yards and Docks, Navy Department, World War, 1917–1918*, 125–26, hereafter cited as *War Activities of the Bureau of Yards and Docks*.

71. *Naval Investigation*, 2599; memos to operations, June 15, July 10, 1917, file 127046, RG52.

72. To Thompson, Jan. 31, 1918, file 127046-0.012, RG52.

73. July 14, 1917, file 127046, RG52; see also S. Franklin Martin to Daniels, August 11, 1917, ibid.

74. W. Graham Greene to MacDougall, June 17, 1917, PH subject file, RG45; F. L. Pleadwell, surgeon and Assistant Naval Attaché to Braisted, June 24, 1917, file 127046, RG52.

75. Bureau of Medicine and Surgery to Naval Medical Supply Depot, May 1, 1917, file 125135, RG52; entry for July 8, 1917, in Josephus Daniels, *Cabinet Diaries*, 174.

76. Memo for Assistant SecNav, July 2, 1918, File 131000-D14, RG52; *Annual Report of Surgeon General, U.S. Navy, 1919*, 246. See also Thompson to Braisted, Nov. 30, 1917, file 127046, RG52; see H. D. VanSant, American Consul, Edinburgh to Robert Peet, American Red Cross, May 13, 1918, file 814.2, Edinburgh Consul Papers, RG84; Bogert to Braisted, Jan. 9, 1919, file 132570, RG52; see also his reports dated Feb. 9, 27, 1918, file 127046, RG52; *Annual Report of Surgeon General, U.S. Navy, 1919*, 196–97; Mayo to wife, Sept. 29, 1918, Mayo Papers, LC.

77. Entry for March 19, 1918 in Andrew Clark, *Echoes of the Great War*, 229–30. See also Bogert to Braisted, April 8, 1919, file 132564, RG52.

78. Braisted to Bogert, February 27, 1918, file 127046, RG52; Bogert to Braisted, April 4, 1918, ibid.; Hickey, "The First Ladies in the Navy," master's thesis, 68–69.

79. *War Activities of the Bureau of Yards and Docks*, 125–26; Braisted to Thompson, June 8, 1918, file 127046, RG52. A large number of the buildings were built and shipped abroad for various hospitals and dispensaries.

80. Bogert to Braisted, March 19, 1918, file 27046, RG52.

81. Bogert to Bureau of Medicine and Surgery, August 19, 1918, file 131000, RG52; Bogert to Braisted, Feb. 22, 27, March 19, April 4, 1918, file 127046, RG52.

82. Quoted in Dock et al., *The History of American Red Cross Nursing*, 723. See also *War Activities of the Bureau of Yards and Docks*, 126; *Annual Report of Surgeon General, U.S. Navy, 1919*, 194.

83. "A Sick Bay in Scotland," 36–37.

84. Bogert to Braisted, Feb. 18, 1918, file 120476, RG52.

85. *Annual Report of Surgeon General, U.S. Navy, 1918*, 57; *1919*, 265; Destroyer Flotilla at Queenstown, March 12, 1919, ZP subj file, RG45.

86. Thompson to Braisted, Dec. 19, 1917, file 127046, RG52.

87. Johnson and Miller, "A Navy Base Hospital Overseas," 11. See also Thompson to Braisted, March 4, 1918, file 127046; Bogert to Bureau of Medicine and Surgery, Aug. 19, 1918, file 131000, RG52; Sims to Department, Feb. 20, 1918, file 127046, RG52; Sims Report to CNO, February 28, 1918, Reel 3, ME-11; *War Activities of Bureau of Yards and Docks*, 112–126; *Pall Mall Gazette*, May 13, 1918; Miller to Bureau of Medicine and Surgery, Oct. 31, 1918, file 131000, RG52; Roosevelt to Daniels, July 29, 1918, in M. Simpson, *Anglo-American Naval Relations*, 164; "Historical Sketch of Base Hospital No. 4," Dec. 10, 1918, PH subj, RG45.

88. Philbrick, "Navy Undress Blues," 20–21.

89. *Navy and Military Record* 36 (Nov. 28, 1918): 765; Hickey, "The First Ladies in the Navy," master's thesis, 68–69; *Annual Report of Surgeon General, U.S. Navy, 1919*, 111. According to the surgeon general's *Annual Report*, the brig was never used (ibid., 198).

90. Commission to Great Britain: Military and Naval Relief, WWI, file 941.11/08, Records of the National Red Cross in National Archives Gift Collection, NA RG200, hereafter cited as RG200.

91. Dock et al., *History of American Red Cross Nursing*, 724–25; Base CO Cardiff, to Sims, Oct. 5, 1918, P-Cardiff subj file, RG45.

92. Medical Officer, Plymouth to Bureau of Medicine and Surgery, file 130212, RG52; *Annual Report of Surgeon General, U.S. Navy, 1919*, 260.

93. Sanitary Report, Killingholme, Dec. 31, 1918, file 130212, RG52; med. officer, Killingholme to Braisted, Nov. 3, 1918, file 131000, RG52; *Annual Report Surgeon General, U.S. Navy, 1919*, 242–43, 246–48, 268; Freeman to Braisted, Nov. 3, 1918, file 131000, RG52; Bludworth, *The Battle of Eastleigh*, 41–43; Braisted to Lane, June 26, 1918, file 127046, RG52; Progress Report, U.S. Naval Aviation, Foreign Service, March 15, 1918, microfilm, NDL.

94. Grow to Bureau of Medicine and Surgery, June 28, 1918, file 131000, RG52.

95. Fife, *The Passing Legions*, 71; Report of the American Red Cross of Commission for Great Britain (to December 31, 1918), Part II, Camp Service, file 941.11/08, RG200.

96. J. A. Murphy to Thompson, May 27, 1918, file 127046, RG52. See also Thompson to Braisted, April 16, May 4, 1918, ibid. General Order, Navy Department, February 15, 1918, file 941.52, Box 843, RG200; *Annual Report of Surgeon General, U.S. Navy, 1919*, 21.

97. Thompson to Braisted, Aug. 21, 1918, file 127046, RG52; see also Braisted to CO USS *Baltimore*, Aug. 5, 1918, file 125/35, RG52; Sims to Dept., Aug. 16, 1918, Reel 5, ME-11.

98. Pound to Wemyss, Sept. 29, 1917, in M. Simpson, *Anglo-American Naval Relations*, 111.

99. Sims to Daniels, August 3, 1917, GP subj file, RG45. See also Lord, "History of Naval Aviation," 351–52, NDL; Turnbull and Lord, *History of Naval Aviation*, 122–41; "U.S. Naval Aviation in World War II: DNCO (Air) Aviation Shore Establishments, 1911–1945," NDL, 91–189, hereafter cited as "Aviation Shore Establishments," Summary of U.S. Naval Activities in European Waters, Z file, OA; *ONI Monthly Bulletin*, May 15, 1919, 36–41. For a brief description of the various stations, see Coletta and Bauer, *Bases, Overseas*, 2: 361–75.

100. Lord, "History of Naval Aviation," NDL, 388; "Aviation Shore Establishments," NDL, 102–3; OpNav to Sims, Nov. 12, 1917, Reel 2, ME-11.

101. Cone to Sims, Oct. 6, 1917, GP subj file, RG45.

102. Progress Report, March 15, 1918, U.S. Naval Aviation Force, Foreign Service, microfilm, NDL.

103. K. Hayes, *A History of the Royal Air Force and United States Naval Air Service in Ireland 1913–1923*, 29–34, hereafter cited as *A History of the USN Air Service in Ireland*. See also *American Legion Magazine*, June 1921, 33.

104. Davy's Report, June 27, 1918, NA subj file, RG45.

105. "Aviation Shore Establishments," 116, NDL; Lord, "Naval Aviation History," 428, NDL.

106. "History of the U.S. Naval Air Stations, Ireland," ZPA subj file, RG45.

107. K. Hayes, *A History of the USN Air Service in Ireland*, 30–33; History of the U.S. Naval Air Stations, Ireland, ZPA subj file, RG45; U.S. Naval Air Station Wexford souvenir, copy in Mayo Papers, LC; Cooke, "Recollections," LC; "Whiddy Island," ZPA subj file, RG45.

108. K. Hayes, *A History of the USN Air Service in Ireland*, 29–31; "An American Naval Air Base"; Coletta and Bauer, *Bases, Overseas*, 362; *War Activities of the Bureau of Yards and Docks*, 418.

109. *United States Naval Aviation, 1910–1980*, 26–28; Force Commander to Sec of State, Air Ministry, Admiralty, Aug. 2, 1918, Reel 5, ME-11, 26–28. As of 1994, some of the structures and concrete aprons at Whiddy Island were still there but "much overgrown," according to one who saw them. M. Rathbone to the author, Aug. 7, 1994, letter in author's possession.

110. Sims to Dept., April 13, 1918, Reel 4, ME-11.

111. Quoted in "Aviation Shore Establishments," 157, NDL; CO U.S. Naval Air Stations, Ireland to Assistant Secretary of the Navy, Jan. 27, 1918, ZPA subj file, RG45.

112. Medical Officer, Castletownbere to Bureau of Medicine and Surgery, July 3, 1918, file 130212, RB52.

113. Memo, Secretary Air Ministry, Sept. 20, 1918, ADM137/2927; Bayly to Sec Admiralty, June 28, 1918, ibid.; M. Rathbone, "Berehaven & West Cork Naval Operations, 1900–1922." MS provided by author.

114. "Aviation Shore Establishments," 159–60, NDL.

115. *Annual Report of Surgeon General, U.S. Navy, 1919*, 247; J. Carl Harrison letter to author, Dec. 7, 1989; Admiralty to Admiral commanding East Coast of England, Dec. 14, 1917, ADM 137/2241.

116. Freeman to Force Commander, Dec. 31, 1918, file 130212, RG52. See also CO RAF Group to RAF Headquarters, July 11, 1918, ADM137/2241; and *Annual Report of Surgeon General, U.S. Navy, 1919*, 248.

117. *The Battle of Eastleigh*, 20–22, 26, 88–90, 118; *War Activities of Bureau of Yards and Docks*, 422; "Aviation Shore Establishments," 180–82, NDL.

118. April 27, 1918, GP subj file, RG45. See also "Aviation Shore Establishments," 149–50, NDL; Lord, "History of Naval Aviation," 477–80, NDL. The British request included other geographical areas such as Gibraltar, Alexandria, and the Adriatic.

Chapter 6. U.S. Naval Facilities in France, the Mediterranean, and the Azores

1. Browning to Admiralty, April 13, 1917, in M. Simpson, *Anglo-American Naval Relations*, 33.

2. *Naval Investigation*, 121–22, 129; Sims to Dept., April 16, 1917, O subj file, RG45; entry for April 16, 1917, in Josephus Daniels, *Cabinet Diaries*, 135.

3. Copy in *Naval Investigation*, 122. See also Sayles report to Dept., ZPA subj file, RG45; Blumenthal, *Illusion and Reality in Franco-American Diplomacy*, 39.

4. Memo in French Naval Archives, Vincennes. See also memo from Admiral De Bon, May 5, 1917; Admiral Chocheprat to Lacaze, May 3, 1917, ibid.; entry for April 26, 1917, in Josephus Daniels, *Cabinet Diaries*, 142; Benson memo to Paymaster General, April 20, 1917, file 187-11,

RG143; "Memorandum of Measures to Assure an Effective Cooperation in Europe between the American Navy and the French Navy," April 27, 1917, Reel 58, Daniels Papers, LC. See also Klachko, *Benson*, 68–69. A Paris newspaper carried an article dated April 4 reporting that governmental officials from the Brest region had signed a resolution urging the French government to make the port an American naval base. "To do so would be the best means of launching the project which has been long under consideration for making Brest a Transatlantic terminus." Quoted in the *Cork Examiner*, April 4, 1917.

5. Daniels to Sims, and Sims reply, both dated May 8, 1917, O subj file, RG45. Even the French were a little mystified as to American intent. As late as May 22, Admiral De Bon told Sayles that he "was all in a fog as to what preparations to make in advance to receive the American Forces." *Naval Investigation*, 123.

6. Charles G. Helmick Oral History, ECU; Rose, *Brittany Patrol*, 51–53; entries for April 15, June 22, Oct. 1, 1918, George P. Slayback Jr. Memoirs, NDL; entries for Oct.-Nov. 1917, Timothy Brown Papers, State Historical Society of Wisconsin, Madison, hereafter cited as WisHistSoc; *The Log of the U.S.S.* Northern Pacific; H. A. Gibbons, *The Ports of France*, 148–55; R. B. Holt, *The History of the U.S.S.* Harrisburg, 80; Murdock, *They Also Served*, 19–21; Moffat, *Maverick Navy*, 70; H. B. Wilson, *The American Navy in France*, 11, 14–15; "Notes on Brest," *ONI Monthly Bulletin*, Dec. 1, 1917. See also file P-Brest, subj file, RG45; Coletta and Bauer, *Bases, Overseas*, 374–84.

7. Quoted in *The Log of the U.S.S.* Northern Pacific, 39. See also Sullivan, *With the Yanks in France*, 24–25; Husband, *A Year in the Navy*, 140; Vaughan, *An American Pilot in the Skies of France*, 43–44, hereafter cited as *The Gates Diaries and Letters*; entry for Nov. 23–24, 1917, Junius S. Morgan Diary, NHF; Cottman, *Jefferson County in the World War*, 103; entry for Nov. 26, 1917, in Schueler, "A Gob's Letters Home during the First World War," AMHI; entry for Oct. 1, 1918, Slayback Memoir, NDL; *New Brunswick, New Jersey, in the Great War*, 128. Reginald Wright Kauffman, *Our Navy at Work*, 63. See also Oct. 20, 1917, Dr. James E. Talley Papers, OA; *Log of U.S.S.* Northern Pacific, 39. Entry for Oct. 20, 1917, Talley Letters. See also Reginald Wright Kauffman, *Our Navy at Work*, 63. Harbord, *The American Army in France*, 375, 479; H. A. Gibbons, *Ports of France*, 149–54; "Brest and Le Havre," 275. The port's transatlantic trade did not significantly increase after the war, primarily because Le Havre was much closer to Paris.

8. *Naval Investigation*, 124.

9. "Installation . . . of a Base for American Patrol Ships," June 4, 1917, French Naval Archives, Vincennes.

10. Dec. 12, 1917, Box 23, Sims Papers, LC. See also McBride testimony, Dec. 31, 1917, General Board Hearings; Distr. CO to Bureau of Supplies and Accounts, April 21, 1918, Box 63, Logistics file, RG45.

11. Fletcher to Sims, Aug. 9, 1917, Reel 3, ME-11; Jackson to Sims, July 19, 1917, TV subj file, RG45; Dinger to Foley, Sept. 22, 1917, P Brest, subj file, RG45; Murdock, *They Also Served*, 20; Rose, *Brittany Patrol*, 60; Fletcher to Sims, July 13, 1917, OS subj file, RG45.

12. Fletcher Court of Inquiry, Case 10662, RG125. See also "Notes on Brest," Dec. 1, 1917, P file, Brest, Bases, subj file, RG45.

13. Guger to Bourgain, May 10, 1918, French Naval Archives, Vincennes. See also various files in General Correspondence, 1910–1926, Records of Bureau of Yards and Docks, NA RG71.

14. War Diary, Base 7, Brest, 1917, Box 8, Logistics file, RG45.

15. *The Log of the U.S.S.* Northern Pacific, 39; Murdock, *They Also Served*, 29.

16. CO Carola IV to Wilson, Dec. 11, 1918, OF subj file, RG45; *American Legion Magazine*, April 1937, 35; H. B. Wilson, *The Navy in France*, 102–3; *New York Herald*, January 26, 1919; *L'Illustration*, July 27, 1918.

17. Brief History of U.S. Naval Forces in France from 11 November 1918 to 1 October 1919, ZO file, OA; Wilson to Sims, Aug. 30, 1918, Logistics file, RG45; *New York Herald*, Jan. 26, 1919.

18. Prefect to Minister of Marine, June 29, 1918, French Naval Archives, Vincennes. See also Minister of Public Works, Brest, to Minister of Marine, July 25, 1918; and Admiral De Bon to Vice Admiral Commanding Brest, July 28, 1918, ibid.

19. Minister of Marine to Vice Admiral, Préfet Marine in Brest, March 22, 1918, French Naval Archives, Vincennes.

20. *American Legion Magazine*, April 1918, 36.

21. *Le Matin*, May 14, 1918.

22. *Naval Investigation*, 887; H. B. Wilson, *The American Navy in France*, 103, 110–13; *The Log of the USS* Northern Pacific, 40; medical officer, USS *Leviathan* to Bureau of Medicine and Surgery, Aug. 14, 1918, file 131000-D14, RG52.

23. H. B. Wilson, *The American Navy in France*, 95–97; Air War, 1912–25, file N258-A14, Box 796, RG19.

24. Wilson to Vice Admiral Moreau, Préfet, Maritime, Brest, Dec. 13, 1917; Moreau to the Minister of Marine, Dec. 16, 1917, French Naval Archives, Vincennes.

25. Cutcheon to French Minister of Marine, February 21, 1918, French Naval Archives, Vincennes; Memo, October 27, 1918, ADM137/1622; *Naval Investigation*, 887; H. B. Wilson, *The American Navy in France*, 111–12; entry for April 16, 1918, Slayback Memoirs; Robert Loder to wife, n.d., Loder Papers, Mariners' Museum.

26. Wilson to Dept., Oct. 11, 1918, Box 10, General Correspondence, 1911–22, RG19.

27. H. B. Wilson, *The American Navy in France*, 13–14.

28. Marcosson, *S.O.S.*, 68–69; *New York Herald*, June 24, 1917, "History of the U.S. Naval Attache," American Embassy File E-7. Bot 12302, RG38.

29. Harbord, *The American Army in France*, 162.

30. For Bordeaux, see Beers, *U.S. Naval Port Offices in the Bordeaux Region, 1917–1919*, passim; Coletta and Bauer, *Bases, Overseas* 2: 374–75; Lajugie, *Bordeaux au XX siecle*, 15–17; H. A. Gibbons, *The Ports of France*, 238–49.

31. H. A. Gibbons, *The Ports of France*, 245.

32. Marcosson, *S.O.S.*, 75–77; Coletta and Bauer, *Bases, Overseas* 2: 375; R. A. Hayes, *Secretary Baker at the Front*, 138–39; Harbord, *The American Army in France*, 163–64, 372; Courteault, *La vie economique a Bordeaux pendant la guerre*, 27–35. This is a detailed study of American construction at Bassens and Bordeaux.

33. *Naval Investigation*, 122–29.

34. Beers, *U.S. Naval Port Offices in the Bordeaux Region*, 36; testimony of Comdr. Dinger, July 29, 1918, General Board Hearings.

35. Harbord, *The American Army in France*, 162, 374–75; H. A. Gibbons, *Ports of France*, 201–2; F. Gibbons, *And They Thought We Wouldn't Fight*, 64–66; Coletta and Bauer, *Bases, Overseas*, 2: 383–84; Marcosson, *S.O.S.*, 72.

36. Some agreed with Janis. See S. Young, *Pen Pictures of the Great War*, 85; Sullivan, *With the Yanks in France*, 48; entry for June 27, 28, 1918, Latimer Diary, UVA; Janis, *So Far So Good*, 33, 193; Tighe, "Plunkett's Pirates," 27, NDL.

37. Capt. Long testimony, Fletcher Court of Inquiry, Case 10662, RG125; See also testimony of Capt. Twining, ibid.

38. Fletcher Flag Secretary testimony, Fletcher Court of Inquiry, Case 10662, RG125; H. B. Wilson, *The American Navy in France*, 114.

39. George Van Deurs Oral History, USNI; Fletcher testimony, Fletcher Court of Inquiry, Case 10662, RG125; Coletta and Bauer, *Bases, Overseas* 2: 381–82; *Army and Navy Journal* 57 (April 24, 1920): 1030.

40. H. B. Wilson, *The American Navy in France*, 127–29; Coletta and Bauer, *Bases, Overseas* 2: 381–82; Magruder, "The Navy in the War," 31.

41. Harbord, *The American Army in France*, 373.

42. H. B. Wilson, *The American Navy in France*, 115–16; Rose, *Brittany Patrol*, 179–80; Murdock, *They Also Served*, 66.

43. Curl, "Installation and Development of Hospital Facilities in France," Report to Wilson, Dec. 10, 1918, file 131000-D14, RG52.

44. Talley to wife, Nov. 4, 10, 1917, Talley Letters, OA.

45. Curl to Wilson, Dec. 10, 1918, file DH, subj file, RG45; Harrison to Braisted, June 20, 1917, file 127046, RG52; cablegram, French Minister of Marine to French naval attaché, Washington, July 19, 1917, ibid.

46. For the history of this hospital, see Major R. W. Morgan, "Dr. James E. Talley, Lieutenant Commander (MC) USNR, A Navy Department in France, 1917–1918," copy in Office of the Historian, Bureau of Medicine and Surgery, Washington, D.C. This paper is based on the letters of Dr. Talley, who was second in command of the hospital. Copies of his letters are in OA. See also "Brief History of Base Hospital No. 5, Brest, France," in Historical Files, Bureau of Medicine and Surgery; Herman, "Naval Base Hospital No. 5"; and "Base Hospital #5," ZPA subj file, RG45; A Brief Summary of U.S. Naval Forces in France, Nov. 11, 1918–October 1, 1919, OA.

47. Jackson to Force CO, Oct. 10, 1917, file 127046, RG52; Curl to Braisted, Oct. 22, 1917, ibid.

48. Talley to wife, Nov. 10, 1917, Talley Letters, OA.

49. A Brief Summary of U.S. Naval Forces in France, Nov. 11, 1918–Oct. 1, 1919, OA; Murdock, *They Also Served*, 82.

50. Murdock, *They Also Served*, 83. See also Reginald Wright Kauffman, *Our Navy at Work*, 204–5; Curl to Wilson, Dec. 10, 1918, DH subj file, RG45; *Annual Report of Surgeon General U.S. Navy, 1919*, 191–92; "Base Hospital No. 5," ZPA subj file, RG45; A Brief Summary of U.S. Naval Forces in France, Nov. 11, 1918–Oct. 1, 1919, OA.

51. Curl to Braisted, Dec. 10, 1918, file 131000, RG52; Wilson to Sims, Aug. 30, 1918, Logistics file, RG45; Herman, "Naval Base Hospital No. 5," 326; "A Brief Summary of U.S. Naval Forces in France, Nov. 11, 1918–Oct. 1, 1919," OA.

52. H. B. Wilson, *The American Navy in France*, 99–100; A Brief Summary of U.S. Naval Forces in France, Nov. 11, 1918–Oct. 1, 1919, OA; Curl, to Braisted, Aug. 1, 1918, file 131000, RG52; *Annual Report of Surgeon General U.S. Navy, 1919*, 254.

53. Curl to Braisted, Sept. 6. 1918, file 130212, RG52.

54. Curl to Wilson, Dec. 10, 1918, file 131000-D14, RG52.

55. H. B. Wilson, *The American Navy in France*, 100.

56. Lane to Braisted, May 31, 1918, file 127046, RG52. See also "Summary of Annual Sanitation Report," ZPA subj file, RG45.

57. Meals, "The Air Station at Dunkirk", 9–22; *Annual Report of Surgeon General*, 241.

58. Lane to Murphy, Aug. 1, 1918, file 127046, RG52; Curl to Braisted, file 131000-D14, ibid.

59. Braisted to Curl, Aug. 13, 1918, file 12706, RG52.

60. Curl to Braisted, Oct. 18, Dec. 10, 1918, file 131000, RG52; McArthur to Braisted, Oct. 22, 1918, file 13107, RG52; Senior medical officer, Pauillac to Braisted, Sept. 6, Dec. 8, 1918, file 130212, RG52; Garrison to Braisted, Sept. 18, 1918, file 131000, RG52.

61. Testimony, Feb. 8, 1918, General Board Hearings.

62. Riske, *United States Hospital Ships*, 5. See also entry for May 17, 1917, in Josephus Daniels, *Cabinet Diaries*, 147.

63. *Annual Report of Surgeon General U.S. Navy, 1918*, 63–64; Dunbar, "The Hospital Ship *Comfort*." In World War I, medical officers commanded hospital ships, but auxiliary merchant marine officers actually operated the ship. See Oman, *Doctors Aweigh*, 103. This was changed in 1921, when the Department approved allowing line officers to command hospital ships.

64. Testimony of Braisted, Feb. 8, 1918, General Board Hearings; Dept. to Sims, Feb. 25, 1918,

file 127046, RG52; Bogert to Braisted, Feb. 27, 1918, ibid., Sims to Dept., March 1, 15, 1918, ibid.; Sims to Dept., March 2, 1918, OH subj file, RG45.

65. Testimony, Nov. 1, 1917, Feb. 8, 1918, General Board Hearings; Thompson to Braisted, March 4, 10, 1918, file 127046, RG52; "Extracts from Admiralty Memo," March 16, 1918, OH subj file, RG45.

66. March 8, 1918, Reel 3, ME-11; Murphy to Thompson, May 27, 1918, file 127046, RG52.

67. Sims to Dept., Oct. 5, 1918, file 130212, RG52.

68. Dunbar to Braisted, Nov. 7, 1918, file 125135, RG52; *DANFS* for both ships; Department to Commandant, 3rd Naval District, New York, Oct. 8, 1918, OH subj file, RG45.

69. Originally named the Liberty Radio Station, its name was changed to Lafayette by President Wilson's order. For histories of the station, see Copeland, "Steel Tower Construction at the World's Greatest Radio Station"; Hooper, "The Lafayette Radio Station"; *War Activities of Bureau of Yards and Docks*, 367–79; "Brief Summary of U.S. Navy Forces in France, Nov. 11, 1918 to Oct. 1, 1919," ZO file, OA.

70. This was the same procedure that was used to provide workers for laying the fuel pipeline in Scotland. *War Activities of Bureau of Yards and Docks*, 367–68; Hooper, "The Lafayette Radio Station," 405; "Brief Summary of U.S. Navy in France, Nov. 11, 1918 to Oct. 1, 1919," ZO file, OA.

71. To Hooper, Sept. 6, 1918, Hooper Papers, LC. See also L. C. White, *Pioneer and Patriot*, 88–89.

72. *War Activities of the Bureau of Yards and Docks*, 369–70.

73. "Brief Summary of U.S. Navy Forces in France, November 11, 1918–October 1, 1919," ZO file, OA.

74. Lord, "History of U.S. Naval Aviation," 121, NDL; LeRoy, *La guerre sous-marine en Bretagne 1914–1918*, 51–53; Coletta and Bauer, *Bases, Overseas* 2: 365–72; "Aviation Shore Establishments," 99–100, NDL; Edwards, "U.S. Naval Air Force in Action." See also Whiting testimony, Jan. 16, 1918, General Board Hearings.

75. Whiting testimony, Jan. 16, 1918, General Board Hearings.

76. Lord, "History of U.S. Naval Aviation," 350; Benson to Sims, August 24, 1917, Reel 2, ME-11; Whiting testimony, January 16, 1918, General Board Hearings. See also LeRoy, *La guerre sous-marine en Bretagne 1914–1918*, 50.

77. Quoted in Lord, "History of U.S. Naval Aviation," 351, NDL. See also Sims to Dept., Aug. 4, 1917, Reel 2, ME-11.

78. Jan. 16, 1918, General Board Hearings; see also quote in Lord, "History of U.S. Naval Aviation," 351–52, NDL; Sims to Dept., Aug. 30, 1917, Reel 2, ME-11.

79. Paine, *The First Yale Unit*, 15. See also entries for July 31, Aug. 1 & 2, 1917, in John L. Callan's Diary, LC: "The men in the tents, however, fared much worse during the cold winter of 1917–18."

80. Sheely to Lewis, in Sheely, *Sailor of the Air*, 67.

81. George C. Moseley, letter from Feb. 28, 1918, in *Extracts from the Letters of George Clark Moseley during the Period of the Great War*, 147, hereafter cited as Moseley, *Extracts from Letters*.

82. Elliott Roosevelt, *F.D.R.: Personal Letters*, 435.

83. Coletta and Bauer, *Bases, Overseas* 2: 370

84. Reel 2, ME-11.

85. "U.S. Naval Air Station Le Croisic, France," MS in ZPA subj file, RG45; "History of U.S. Naval Aviation, French Units," MS in NDL. Van Wyen, *Naval Aviation in World War I*, 46; Coletta and Bauer, *Bases, Overseas* 2: 369; Lord, "History of Naval Aviation," 137, NDL; Janis, *The Big Show*, 35.

86. "United States Naval Air Station, St. Trojan," ZPA subj file, RG45.

87. CO NAS St. Trojan to Cone, Nov. 30, 1918, ZPA subj file, RG45; "St. Trojan," ZPA subj file, RG45; "History of United States Naval Aviation: French Unit," NDL; Coletta and Bauer, *Bases, Overseas* 2: 371–72.

88. District Medical Officer to CO, St. Trojan, Sept. 24, 1918, file 130212, RG52. See also *War Activities of Bureau of Yards and Docks*, 425; Lord, "History of U.S. Naval Aviation," 138–39, NDL.

89. Pamard to Division Chief, August 22, 1918, French Naval Archives, Vincennes.

90. Meals, "The Air Station at Dunkirk," 9–10; Coletta and Bauer, *Bases, Overseas* 2: 390; Alfred Cunningham, "Report of an Aviator's Observation Trip to France and England," January 1, 1918, microfilm, Navy Department Library.

91. Johnson to Van der Veer, Oct. 12, 1917, G subj file, RG45. See also "Progress Report, U.S. Naval Aviation Forces, Foreign Service, Headquarters, Paris," microfilm, NDL.

92. Entry for Nov. 15, 1917, in Sheely, *Sailor of the Air*, 74; "Progress Report, U.S. Naval Aviation Forces, Foreign Service, Headquarters, Paris"; *Flying Officers of the U.S.N.*, 24.

93. For the Group, see chapter 18.

94. "Hubert Burnham," in Furlong, *Class of 1905*, 40; Sims to Dept., April 27, 1918, Reel 19, ME-11; Coletta and Bauer, *Bases, Overseas*, 2: 390–91.

95. Sims to Dept., August 21, 1918, Reel 2, ME-11; Conger to Irwin, Nov. 16, 1917, file 127046, RG52; "Naval Air Forces in European Waters, Pauillac," ZPA subj file, RG45; Cone to Sims, Nov. 22, 1917, ibid. For the CNO's visit to Pauillac, see his report in Box 46, Benson Papers, LC.

96. To Bureau of Medicine and Surgery, Jan. 1, 1918, file 130212, RG52; Garrison, "The United States Naval Air Station, Pauillac, Gironde, France"; "Pauillac," ZPA subj file, RG45; Hawks, "The Battle of Trompeloup," 1–2.

97. Pamard to Division Chief, August 22, 1918, French Naval Archives, Vincennes; Sitz, "A History of U.S. Naval Aviation," NDL; See also *War Activities of Bureau of Yards and Docks*, 421; Sims to Jackson, Dec. 7, 1917, Reel 3, ME-11; Cone to Sims, Dec. 22, 1917, Box 10, General Correspondence, 1917–1919, USNAVOPFOR, RG313.

98. *War Activities of Bureau of Yards and Docks*, 420; Garrison, "Pauillac," 612; "Pauillac," ZPA subj file, RG45; Mayo to wife, Oct. 31, 1918, Mayo Papers, LC; Elliott Roosevelt, *F.D.R.: Letters*, 436; Public Works Officer, Pauillac to Cone, date unreadable, Box 26, General Correspondence, USNAVOPFOR, RG313.

99. Sims to Dept., August 21, 1917, Reel 2, ME-11; Benson to Sims, Dec. 12, 1917, Reel 18, ibid.; Garrison, "Pauillac," 612.

100. Garrison, "Pauillac," 612; Jackson to Sims, Dec. 12, 1917, Reel 18, ME-11; "Pauillac," ZPA subj file, RG45.

101. Elliott Roosevelt, *F.D.R.: Personal Letters*, 436–37.

102. Hawks, "The Battle of Trompeloup," 2.

103. "Naval Air Station, Brest," ZPA subj file, RG45; *War Activities of Bureau of Yards and Docks*, 430.

104. Memo, ONI, Jan. 19, 1923, PA subj file, RG45; Memo for Director General of Naval Construction, October, 1917, Series 59, eb39, French Naval Archives, Vincennes.

105. Historical Account of Naval Air Stations, France, ZPA subj file, RG45.

106. *War Activities of Bureau of Yards and Docks*, 432–33; *American Legion Magazine*, October 1928, 65.

107. "History of the United States Naval Air Station Ile Tudy, Finisterre, France, March 16, 1918" copy in ZP subj file, RG45; "Progress Report, 1917, U.S. Naval Aviation Forces," Foreign Service, Headquarters, Paris, microfilm, NDL; "History of United States Naval Aviation French Unit," copy in NDL; Le Roy, *La guerre sous-marine en Bretagne, 1914–1918*, 98–104, 201–5. This is the most extensive study of American naval aviation in Brittany.

108. McKelvey, "Construction of the U.S. Naval Air Station L'Aber Vrach, France, World War

I," copy in OA. McKelvey was the officer in charge of building the station. See also "History of United States Naval Aviation French Unit," microfilm, NDL.

109. CO Richards Memoirs, copy in author's possession.

110. August 8, 1918, Taussig Journal, NWC.

111. "History of United States Naval Aviation French Unit," microfilm, NDL.

112. Ibid.

113. "U.S. Naval Air Station, Troquier," ZPA subj file, RG45; *War Activities of Bureau of Yards and Docks*, 436.

114. "History of United States Naval Aviation French Unit," microfilm, NDL; *War Activities of Bureau of Yards and Docks*, 419; *Annual Report Surgeon General*, 1919, 244.

115. For a brief history of the station, see "U.S. Naval Air Station, Arcachon," ZPA subj file, RG45.

116. During that period, a majority of the naval personnel were transferred to work on the Pauillac Naval Air Station.

117. "U.S. Naval Air Station, Arcachon," ZPA subj file, RG45; "History of United States Naval Aviation French Unit," microfilm, NDL.

118. Cone to Wilson, Feb. 20, 1918, Reel 19, ME-11.

119. "History of United States Naval Aviation French Unit," microfilm, NDL; Sitz, "A History of U.S. Naval Aviation," NDL.

120. "History of United States Naval Aviation French Unit," microfilm, NDL.

121. Ibid.; *War Activities of Bureau of Yards and Docks*, 435.

122. Kite Balloon Stations, PA subj file, RG45.

123. Memo, CO U.S. Kite Stations, January 19, 1923, PA subj file, RG45; "History of United States Naval Aviation French Unit," microfilm, NDL; *Annual Report of Surgeon General, 1919*, 252.

124. Wilson to Cone, Aug. 6, 1918, GP subj file, RG45; memo on conference, Aug. 20, 1918, ibid.; "Progress Report, Naval Aviation Forces, Foreign Service, Headquarters, Paris," microfilm, NDL; GA subj file, RG45; Turnbull and Lord, *History of Naval Aviation*, 121.

125. Niblack, "Putting Cargos Across," copy in ZCP subj file, RG45; Niblack to Roosevelt, Dec. 6, 1917, Box 47, Assistant SecNav Files, FDR Library; Report on Gibraltar, n.d., P-Gibraltar subj file, RG45 Hamilton Cochran Papers, Coast Guard Library.

126. Niblack to Bureau of Medicine and Surgery, July 26, 1918, file 13100-D14, RG52; *Annual Report Surgeon General, 1919*, 245; Niblack, "Putting Cargos Across," ZCP subj file, RG45.

127. For this barrage and American participation in it, see chapter 19.

128. Leigh memoirs, Florida State University; Leigh to Sims, April 17, 1918, OD subj file, RG45; Leigh to Tompkins, April 16, 1918, Logistics file, RG45; Sims to naval attaché, Rome, May 6, 1918, Reel 12, ME-11.

129. Nelson to Sims, Oct. 28, 1918, Box 11, Logistics file, RG45; *Times* (London), Oct. 25, 1918. See also Leigh's memoirs, Florida State University; Sims to Leigh, May 31, 1918, Reel 12, ME-11; Nelson to Sims, July 1, 1918, Box 1802, Records of the Bureau of Supplies and Accounts, RG143, hereafter cited as BuS&A, RG143; Sims to Nelson, August 3, 1918, Box 11, Logistics file, RG45; Sims Report, July 24, 1918, Reel 4, ME-11; Sims Report to Dept., Aug. 24, 1918, Reel 5, ME-11; Spafford to Simsadus, May 18, 1918, Reel 12, ME-11; Chambers, *United States Submarine Chasers in the Mediterranean*, 47, hereafter cited as *Submarine Chasers in the Mediterranean*; *War Activities of Bureau of Yards and Docks*, 127.

130. Wayne to mother et al., Nov. 25, 1918, Wayne Duffett Papers, Emil Buehler Naval Aviation Library, National Museum of Naval Aviation.

131. *Annual Report Surgeon General, 1919*, 239–40.

132. Lord, "History of U.S. Naval Aviation," NDL; *Annual Report Surgeon General, 1919*, 260–61.

133. Commanding Officer, USS *Nashville* to Niblack, April 24, 1918; Lannon to CNO, July 24, 1918; Medical Officer, U.S. Naval Hospital, Genoa to Bureau of Medicine and Surgery, Sept. 20, 1918, all in file 131000-14, RG52; *Annual Report Surgeon General, 1919*, 192–93.

134. For the background to this, see Trask, *Captains and Cabinets*, 278–79. See also chapter 19.

135. Memorandum No. 53, "Mine Base in the Mediterranean," Sept. 23, 1928; Navy Dept., *The American Naval Planning Section*, 384–86, 517; Duncan, *America's Use of Sea Mines*, 69–71; Sims to Admiral De Bon, Sept. 27, 1918, AM subj file, RG45.

136. Oct. 11, 16, 24, 1918, AM subj file, RG45.

137. Murfin to Sims, Nov. 1, 3, 1918; Sims to Murfin, Nov. 9, 1918, AM subj file, RG45; Sims to Wilson, Oct. 7, 11, 1918, Reel 10, ME-11; Sims to Dept., Oct. 14, 1918, AM subj file, RG45; Strauss to Grangemouth, Oct. 10, 1918, AU subj file, RG45; BuOrd to CNO, Oct. 8, 1918, Box 71, Confidential Files, 1917–19, RG80.

138. *Naval Investigation*, 1452–53; Benson to Proctor, July 10, 1917, OS subj file, RG45, American Consul to State Dept., July 6, 1917, copy in ibid.

139. Gorlitz, *The Kaiser and His Court*, 323.

140. To Benson, July 30, 1917, in M. Simpson, *Anglo-American Naval Relations*, 248–49. See also Gleaves to CNO, July 20, 1917, Reel 1, ME-11; Josephus Daniels, *Our Navy at War*, 276–77; Daniels testimony, 2717, and Pratt testimony, *Naval Investigation*, 1452.

141. Benson to Sims, Sept. 5, 1917, P-Ponta Delgada subj file, RG45; October 25, 1917, Reel 2, ME-11; to Dept., Oct. 15, 1917, ibid.

142. SecState to Legation, Lisbon, March 21, 1918, 811.345/48; Daniels to SecState, Feb. 13, 1918, file 811.345.68; Page to SecState, March 7, 1918, 811.345.77; Lansing to American Embassy, London, Feb. 13, 1918, Reel 19, ME-11; State Dept. to American consul, Ponta Delgada, March 15, 1918, Reel 10, M1092; Foreign Office to Page, Feb. 21, 1918, Box 375, P-Ponta Delgada subj file, RG45; Reading to SecState, Feb. 23, 1918, file 811.345/74, RG59; Livermore, "The Azores in American Strategy-Diplomacy," 197–211, 206–7. May 19, 1918, Reel 4, ibid.; *Naval Investigation*, 139–40, 1453.

143. Benson to Sims, Sept. 5, 1917, in M. Simpson, *Anglo-American Naval Relations*, 255; August 31, 1917, Reel 3, ME-11; Sims to Proctor, Aug. 30, 1917, Box 375, P-Ponta Delgada, 1 Reel 3, ME-11; Benson to Simsadus, Oct. 2, 1917, ibid., Benson to Simsadus, April 2, 1918, Reel 19, ME-11.

144. *Naval Investigation*, 1452–53. Portugal had entered the war as an ally of Great Britain and France in March 1916. The Azores were colonial possessions of Portugal. For correspondence concerning establishing a coaling station in the Azores, see file 811.3456/26, RG59. See also Coletta and Bauer, *Bases, Overseas*, 2: 389–92.

145. Entry for July 18, 1918, in Kilpatrick, *Roosevelt and Daniels*, 45–46.

146. E. C. Johnson, *Marine Corps Aviation*, 13; Lord, "History of Naval Aviation," NDL; entry for Dec. 14, 1918, Brown Papers, WisHistSoc; entry for May 28, 1918, Taussig Journal, NWC.

147. Dunn to Sims, Dec. 29, 1918, Box 55, Sims Papers, LC; Sims to Dunn, May 7, 1918, ibid.; Birch to SecState, Nov. 23, 1917, 8112.345.54, RG59; *New York Times*, April 13, 1918.

148. For a discussion of the complex diplomacy concerning the Azores in American-Portuguese relations during World War I, see Livermore, "The Azores in American Strategy-Diplomacy," 197–211.

149. Thompson, *Take Her Down*, 142–43; S. O. to Sims, Oct. 10, Dec. 1, 1917, P-Ponta Delgada subj file, RG45; to SecNav, Oct. 25, 1917, file 28754-27-5/6, Confidential Files, 1917–1919, RG80.

150. Proctor to Dept., Aug. 17, 1917, file 28754-18:99, Confidential Files, 1917–1919, RG80; Osterhaus to SecNav, Oct. 25, 1917, file 28754-27, 5/6; Sec State to American Minister, Lisbon, Aug. 16, 1917, 811.345/28a, and American Minister, Lisbon, to SecState, Aug. 20, 1917, 811.345/29, RG59; Proctor to Sims, Aug. 15, 1917, Reel 3, ME-11.

151. To the counselor of the Department of State, Oct. 12, 1917, 811.345/40, RG59. See also SecState to Lisbon, Oct. 17, 1917, 811.345.41, RG59.

152. Birch to State Dept., Nov. 5, 1917, copy in Reel 10, M1092; Birch to SecState, Nov. 8, 1917, 811.345/45, RG59.

153. January 14, 1918, Reel 10, M1092; CO USS *Wheeling* to Dept., Oct. 25, 1917, ibid.; Hart to Dept., Oct. 28, 1917, file 18–194, Confidential Files, 1917-1919, RG80. For series of cables on warehouses, see file 811.345/2a, RG59; unknown Azorean writer to Dunn, Dec. 19, 1918, file 853B.00/2, Paris Peace Conference Records, RG59.

154. CO Azores Detachment to Sims, Jan. 3, 1918, Box 5, Entry 113, RG19.

155. CO USS *Panther* to Dept., Aug. 17, 1917, file 28754-18:99, Confidential Files, 1917–1919, RG80; Sims to Dept., Oct. 15, 1917, Reel 2, ME-11; Osterhaus to Sims, Dec. 20, 1917, Ponta Delgada subj file, RG45.

156. To Sims, May 27, 1930, Box 76, Sims Papers, LC.

157. To Legation, Lisbon, Nov. 13, 20, 27, 1917, file 811.345/51a, 52, 56, RG59.

158. Benson to Sims, Sept. 5, 1917, in M. Simpson, *Anglo-American Naval Cooperation*, 255–56; Sims to Benson, July 30, 1917, ibid., 247–49.

159. Liston to SecState, Jan. 3, 31, 1918, file 811.345/63, 66, RG59; Daniels to SecState, December 17, 1917, file 28754-27:5, Confidential Files, 1917–1919, RG80; *Naval Investigation*, 2719; Livermore, "The Azores in American Strategy-Diplomacy," 205–6.

160. Biographical sketch, OA; Cogar, *Dictionary of Admirals*, 76–77.

161. Feb. 3, 1918, Box 55, Sims Papers, LC.

162. Foreign Office to Portuguese President, April 20, 1918, copy in P-Ponta Delgada subj file, RG45; Sims to Dept., Feb. 13, 25, April 19, 1918, ibid.

163. *Shipmate* 43 (Nov. 1980): 9; Dunn to Sims, Feb. 3, 1918, Box 55, Sims Papers; Wood to SecState, March 30, 1918, 811.345/83, RG59; Fleming, RN to Admiralty, April 25, 1918, copy in P-Ponta Delgada subj file, RG45; Sims to Dept., April 19, 1918, ibid.; Sims to Dept., August 23, 1918, Reel 10, ME-11.

164. Entry for July 1918, Roosevelt Diary, Box 191, Assistant SecNav Files, FDR Library; Wilson to American Embassy Paris (for Benson), Jan. 18, 1919, file 853B.00/3, RG59; Daniels testimony, *Naval Investigation*, 2718.

165. Sims to Dept., Feb. 15, Sept. 10, 1918, Reels 19, 10, ME-11; Benson to Simsadus, Sept. 4, 1918, Reel 10, ibid., ONI to CNO, May 14, 1918, P-Ponta Delgada subj file, RG45.

166. To Dunn, May 7, 1918, Box 55, Sims Papers, LC.

167. Entry for June 6, 1918, Taussig Journal, NWC; Sims to Benson, Nov. 24, 1917, Box 5, Sims Papers, LC; Dunn to Sims, Feb. 3, 1918, Box 55, ibid.; Embassy, London, to Embassy, Portugal, May 4, 1918, 834 file, London Embassy Records, RG84; Sims to Dept., Oct. 15, 1917, Reel 2, ME-11; Birch to SecState, Oct. 10, 1917, file 27.5, Confidential Files, 1917–1919, RG80; Josephus Daniels, *Our Navy at War*, 277; Hart to Commander Submarine Force, Nov. 6, 1917, Box 1, Allied Submarines Operations, WWI, OA.; Sims to Dept., April 15, 1918, Reel 10, M1092; Proctor to Sims, Aug. 28, 1917, P-Ponta Delgada subj file, RG45; *Naval Investigation*, 137, 2718–19; Fleming to Admiralty, April 25, 1918, ibid.

168. Various documents, General Correspondence, 1916–1925, Records of the Bureau of Yards and Docks, NA RG71; CO Azores Detachment to Dept., Dec. 22, 1917, Reel 10, M1092.

169. *Annual Report Surgeon General, 1919*, 188–89; Bureau of Medicine and Surgery to CO Azores, Sept. 21, Oct. 9, 1918, file 131000-D14, RG52; CO Hospital, Azores to Sims, Sept. 5, 1918, file 130212, RG52.

Chapter 7. The Train

1. Schmitt and Vedeler, *The World in the Crucible*, 319.

2. Sumida, "Forging the Trident," 221–22; Hardach, *The First World War*, 79–80, 86–87; Reid, "The Impact of the War on British Workers," 226–27.

3. Hardach, *The First World War*, 79; Thomas, "Women and Work in Wartime Britain," 318.

4. Sumida, "Forging the Trident," 9; Hardach, *The First World War*, 86.

5. Reid, "The Impact of the War on British Workers," 227.

6. To Braisted, April 11, 1918, file 127046, RG52. For other remarks concerning labor problems and the American hospitals, see Medical Officer, Plymouth, to Bureau of Medicine and Surgery, Feb. 1919, file 132564, RG52; and Carpenter to Chief of Staff, Destroyer Flotilla, Dec. 10, 1918, P subj file, RG45.

7. Cooke, "Recollections," LC: Pringle to Sims, April 19, June 12, 1918, Box 79, Sims Papers, LC; "Whiddy Island," ZPA subj file, RG45; Naval Air Station Wexford, Souvenir, copy in Mayo Papers, LC; Brownell testimony, April 25, 1918, General Board Hearings.

8. Sims testimony, Fletcher Court of Inquiry, Case 10662, RG125. See also Sims to Dept., June 1, 1918, subj file P-Queenstown, RG45.

9. Rodman to Sims, May 23, 1918, in *ONI Semi-Monthly Compilation*, ser. 63 (Nov. 1918): 2353–54; A. E. Smith, "The Sixth Battle Squadron," 56–57; Blackford, *Torpedoboat Sailor*, 102; Simon, "Both by Land and by Sea," 27, NDL. See also Senior Naval Officer, Liverpool, to Commander-in-Chief, November 30, 1917, Reel 18, ME-11.

10. Leigh Journal, FSU; Wiley, *An Admiral from Texas*, 214.

11. To Dept., May 27, 1918, P subj file, RG45; See also entry for July 11, 1918, Foley mission, QC subj file, ibid.; Pringle to Simsadus, March 20, 1918, Box 27, General Correspondence, 1917–1919, USNAVOPFOR, RG313.

12. Robbins, *The First World War*, 167; J. Williams, *The Home Fronts*, 217; Talley to wife, Feb. 13, 1918, Talley Letters. See also Becker, *The Great War and the French People*, 251–301.

13. Fridenson, "The Impact of the War on the French Worker."

14. *New York Times*, Feb. 27, 1919.

15. To Simsadus, June 27, 1918, NA subj file, RG45. See also Dinger to Foley, Sept. 22, 1917, P file-Brest subj file, RG45; superintendent, Transportation to CO Pauillac, Feb. 15, 1919, ZPA subj file, ibid.

16. Lynch Memoir, WWI Research Collection, AMHI; entry for April 15, 1918, Slayback Memoirs, NDL; entry for Nov. 26, 1917, Brown Journal, WisHistSoc.

17. H. B. Miller, *Navy Wings*, 229; Lord, "History of Naval Aviation," NDL; *Flying Officers of the U.S. Navy*, 32–33; Sayles to Simsadus, April 29, 1918, Reel 20, ME-11.

18. "History of the United States Naval Aviation French Unit," microfilm, NDL. See also "United States Naval Air Station, St. Trojan," ZPA subj file, RG45; and Bell to CO Naval Forces, France, March 11, 1918, Box 8, Logistics file, RG45.

19. Testimony, Jan. 16, 1918, General Board Hearings.

20. MacLeish to Beloved, Nov. 17, 1917, Kenneth MacLeish letters, private possession, copy provided author by Geoffrey L. Rossano. Lynch Memoir, WWI Research Collection, AMHI; entry for July 12, 1917, Joseph Fagan Diary, Mariners' Museum; "History of United States Naval Aviation, French Unit," NDL. Admiral Benson, when he visited France, was not impressed with them. See his report, Nov. 1917, Box 42, Benson Papers, LC.

21. To Sims, July 10, 1917, TV subj file, RG45.

22. Sims to Dept., Dec. 13, 1917, Reel 2, ME-11.

23. L. C. White, *Pioneer and Patriot*, 88; H. B. Wilson, *The American Navy in France*, 28.

24. Josephus Daniels, *Our Navy at War*, 105.

25. Niblack to Bureau of Medicine and Surgery, July 26, 1918, file 131000-D14, RG52; Cochran MSS, Cochran Papers, Coast Guard Library.

26. Joy to CO Submarine Chaser Forces, Distant Service, July 7, 1918, Box 1802, RG143.

27. H. B. Wilson, *The American Navy in France*, 127; Holt, *U.S.S.* Harrisburg, 80, 84; CO USS *Henderson* to CO Cruiser Force, April 4, 1918, OS subj file, RG45; Report on Personnel, June 27, 1918, NA subj file, RG45; entries April 16, June 19, 1918, George Slayback Memoirs, NDL; Sims to Wilson, Dec. 13, 1917, Reel 2, ME-11.

28. ZPA subj file, RG45.

29. Report, Oct. 15, 1918, Box 46, Assistant SecNav Files, FDR Library; *American Legion Magazine*, March-May 1930, 71. See also Hawks, "The Battle of Trompeloup," 1.

30. Philbrick, "Pharmacist's Mate, 3d Class," 55.

31. *U.S.S.* Seattle *during the War*, 44; Haygood, *The Services of Supply*, 106.

32. Sims to Dept., Oct. 18, 1918, Reel 10, ME-11; Lord, "History of U.S. Naval Aviation," NDL.

33. *New York Evening Mail*, Feb. 24, 1919.

34. Moore Oral History, Columbia University.

35. Memo, 1919, TL subj file, RG45.

36. Sumida, "Forging the Trident," 11.

37. MacDougall, *Royal Dockyards*, 159. See also Thompson, *Take Her Down*, 222–24. For American use of the yard, see entry May 14, 1917, Aaron Stanton Merrill Diary, Manuscript Collection, UNC-CH; and Charles J. Wheeler Oral History, USNI.

38. Entry for Aug. 20, 1917, Fagan Diary, Mariners' Museum; entry for February 20–21, 1918, Latimer Diary, UVA.

39. Gill, *Plymouth: A New History*, 172–73; Admiralty Superintendent, Devonport to Admiralty, Oct. 31, 1918, ADM137/1527; *Marine Engineer and Naval Architect* (Oct. 1919): 56; excerpt from Daily Reports, Feb. 7, 1919, Reel 10, M1092; entries for Aug. 25–27, 1918, Charles Russell Journal, USS *Walke* file, CZ file, OA.

40. C-in-C Grand Fleet to Admiralty, Dec. 9, 1917, and reply, Dec. 15, 1917 in ADM137/1973; CO Div 9 to Force CO., Dec. 13, 1917, Reel 8, ME-11. P. Kennedy, "Britain in the First World War," 44; Sumida, "British Naval Operational Logistics," 456; 24; entry for April 28, 1919, in Josephus Daniels, *Cabinet Diaries*, 402. MacDougall, *Royal Dockyards*, 173, 178; Report on Rosyth Naval Base, July 31, 1914, PF subj file, RG45. Benson report of trip, Nov. 1917, Box 42, Benson Papers, LC; MacDougall, *Royal Dockyards*, 178. Christie, *Harbours of the Forth*, 9, 119. Wiley, *An Admiral from Texas*, 208–9. See also Sims to Pratt, June 14, 1918, Pratt Papers, OA; H. Whittlesey, Office of Naval Intelligence memo, June 2, 1918, Box 10, Sims Papers, LC; Report of H. O. VanSant, American Consul, Dunfermline, Scotland, Nov. 19, 1918, file 850.4, Dunfermline records, RG84; Sims to Rodman, Dec. 20, 1917, Box 23, Sims Papers; Sims to Benson, Dec. 20, 1917, Box 49, ibid.

41. Rodman to Benson, Dec. 19, 1917, file C-18-323, Confidential Files, RG80

42. For the recommended alterations, see correspondence files in entry 113, Box 10, Sims Correspondence, RG19; Sims to Dept., Dec. 19, 1917, Reel 2, ME-11; Dept. to Sims, Jan. 24, 1918, Reel 10, M1092.

43. For historical background to these yards, see Dougan, *A History of North East Shipbuilding*, 132–37; Bird, *The Major Seaports of the United Kingdom,* 43–44.

44. Feb. 13, 1918, ADM 137/1973.

45. ADM137/1973; Seine to Minister of Marine, Jan. 21, 1919, French Naval Archives, Vincennes.

46. Rodman to Dept., Feb. 17, 1918, BB subject file, RG45. For the refitting, see "Summary of U.S. Naval Activities in European Waters," Z file, OA; Twining to Dept., May 17, 1918, Box 117, Sims Papers.

47. Beatty to Admiralty, Sept. 28, 1918, ADM137/1984; *A Brief History of the U.S.S.* Texas, 80–81; Rodman to Sims, Oct. 19, 1918, Reel 8, ME-11.

48. Sims to Admiralty, Oct. 15, 1918, ADM137/1622; Rodman to Sims, July 27, 1918, ADM 137/1898; *Naval Investigation*, 231.

49. Sumida, "British Naval Operational Logistics," 453; *Marine Engineer and Naval Architect*, 7.

50. *ONI Semi-Monthly Compilation*, ser. 61 (Oct. 3, 1918): 3403–4; Historical sketch, Headquarters, Dec. 5, 1918, ZT subj file, RG45; Sims to Dept., Aug. 15, 1918, Reel 5, ME-11. The American Civil War raider CSS *Alabama* was built in the yard. One sailor recorded in his diary that the "destroyers *Fanning* and *Wadsworth* . . . are docked in the same drydock the battleship *Alabama* of Civil War fame was built." Entry for Feb. 14, 1918, in Wiggins, *My Romance with the Navy*, 117.

51. To Palmer, Sept. 25, 1917, Box 23, Sims Papers, LC.

52. Murdock, *They Also Served*, 89–90; Sims to Melville, May 14, 1918, Reel 4, ME-11; Moore Oral History, Columbia University; Sims Report, August 9, 1917, PF subj file, RG45; Sims to Dyer, Aug. 9, 1917, Reel 2, ME-11; Sims to DD Flotilla, Aug. 23, 1918, Reel 5, ibid., entry for Oct. 16, 1917, Morgan Diary, NHF.

53. Moore Oral History, Columbia University; Pringle to Sims, Sept., 5, 1917, Box 79, Sims Papers, LC.

54. Taussig testimony, Dec. 4, 1917, General Board Hearings; entry for Aug. 16, 1917, Merrill Diary, in Merrill's Papers, UNC-CH; *Syren and Shipping* 90 (Jan. 1, 1919): 49; *Cork Examiner*, Dec. 30, 1918; *New York Sun*, Aug. 4, 1918. The Cammell Laird Archives has forty-eight photographs of U.S. destroyers receiving alterations and repairs.

55. Scott and Cunnison, *The Industries of the Clyde Valley during the War*, 78–79, 204. Peebles, *Warshipbuilding on the Clyde*, does not mention repair to U.S. ships.

56. Moore Oral History, Columbia University; Wheeler Oral History, USNI; Sims to Dept., July 30, Aug. 9, 1918, Reel 9, ME-11.

57. Memo, British and American naval efforts compared, 1918, ADM137/2710.

58. Memo on repair situation, March 28, 1918, Box 60, Sims Papers, LC.

59. Sims to Daniels, Jan. 23, 1918, TT subj file, RG45.

60. Marwick, *The Deluge*, 56.

61. Sumida, "Forging the Trident," 227–28.

62. Schmitt and Vedeler, *The World in the Crucible*, 319. Also by the fall of 1917, some seventy thousand POWs were working in Britain, mostly in agriculture. R. Jackson, *The Prisoners*, 140–41.

63. Entry for Feb. 22, 1918, Stuart F. Smith Diary, LC; Sims to Dept., Feb. 28, 1918, Box 10, Entry 113, RG19.

64. Memo, March 28, 1918, Geddes folder, Box 60, Sims Papers, LC.

65. Reid, "The Impact of the War on British Workers," 236–37; Thomas, "Women and Work in Wartime Britain," 318–22.

66. Moore Oral History, Columbia University.

67. Entry for Sept. 4, 1918, Forbes Diary, in Box 58, Sims Papers, LC. See also Sims to SecNav, June 1, 1918, P-Queenstown, subj file, RG45; memo, June 13, 1918, Box 10, Entry 113, RG19; American Consul, Liverpool, to Tobey, Liverpool Consulate Records, Aug. 18, 1917, 830 file, RG84; entry for Aug. 15, 1917, Latimer Diary, UVA; Blackford, *Torpedoboat Sailor*, 102–3. For problems with the Merseyside workers including shipbuilders, see Waller, *Democracy and Sectarianism*, 270–71.

68. Coffman, *The War to End All Wars*, 171–72.

69. Memo, March 28, 1918, Geddes folder, Box 60, Sims Papers, LC.

70. Memo dated Aug. 26, 1918, ADM116/1810. See also Geddes memo, Aug. 2, 1918, ibid.

71. Report of subcommittee called for by Maintenance Committee, April 5, 1918,

ADM116/1798; Sims to Pringle, May 7, 1918, Box 79, Sims Papers, LC; Sims Report to Dept., June 5, 1918, Box 10, Entry 113, RG19.

72. Sims to U.S. Naval Officer, Liverpool, June 12, 1918, File 830, Liverpool Consulate Records, RG84; to Admiralty, May 8, 10, 1918, copies in ibid.

73. Aug. 26, 1918, ADM116/1810.

74. Benson to Sims, July 24, 1918, Reel 9, ME-11.

75. TT subj file, RG45; Klachko, *Benson*, 117. See also Parsons, *Wilsonian Diplomacy*, 138.

76. July 26, 1918, Reel 4, ME-11. See also Trask, *Captains and Cabinets*, 198.

77. Klachko, *Benson*, 117.

78. Trask, *Captains and Cabinets*, 295. See also Sims to Dept., August 15, 1918, Reel 5, ME-11.

79. Sumida, "British Naval Administration and Policy in the Age of Fisher," 25.

80. Quoted in Klachko, *Benson*, 117; see also Sims to Dept., August 15, 1917, Reel 5, ME-11.

81. Entry for April 5, 1918, in Josephus Daniels, *Cabinet Diaries*, 299. See also Safford, *Wilsonian Maritime Diplomacy*, 150–51.

82. Safford, *Wilsonian Maritime Diplomacy*, 153–54; Wilson to Hurley, August 29, 1918, in Link, *Wilson Papers*, 49: 374–75.

83. Safford, *Wilsonian Maritime Diplomacy*, 155.

84. Ibid.; Trask, *Captains and Cabinets*, 293–94; Reading to Wiseman, August 28, 1918, copy in Link, *Wilson Papers,* 49: 454.

85. "Naval efforts, Great Britain and U.S.," ADM116/1810.

86. To David Lloyd George, Aug. 28, 1918, in M. Simpson, *Anglo-American Naval Relations*, 507–9.

87. Reel 6, ME-11.

88. For this trip, see Safford, *Wilsonian Maritime Diplomacy*, 160–61; Trask, *Captains and Cabinets*, 295–311; Klachko, *Benson*, 118–20. See Geddes report, Oct. 8, 1918, in M. Simpson, *Anglo-American Naval Relations*, 529–32; Geddes to Daniels, Oct. 10, 1918, ibid., 534; Admiralty memo on results of the trip, Oct. 1918, ibid., 535–39.

89. Memo, Director of Statistics, Admiralty, Sept. 22, 1918, ADM137/2710.

90. H. B. Wilson, *The American Navy in France*, 69. See also Daniels to Sims, July 10, 1917, Box 53, Sims Papers, LC; Sims to SecNav, Aug. 9, 1917, Box 5, entry 113, RG19.

91. Conolly Oral History, Columbia University. See also Schueler to Mom, Nov. 14, 1917, "A Gob's Letters Home during the World War, 1917–1919," WWI Research Collection, AMHI.

92. De Bon to Inspector General of Material, Jan. 18, 1918, French Naval Archives, Vincennes.

93. Wilson to Sims, Dec. 28, 1916, Jan. 14, 1917, P subj file, RG45; Benson to Simsadus, Dec. 18, 1917, ibid. See also Magruder to Wilson, Jan. 2, 1918, OF subj file, RG45; Wilson to Sims, Jan. 3, 1918, ibid.

94. Dinger to Sims, Dec. 24, 1917, Reel 10, M1092.

95. Jackson to De Bon, Feb. 16, 1918, French Naval Archives, Vincennes; Smith to Sims, Feb. 12, 1918, Logistics file, RG45; Daniels to Bureaus, Feb. 4, 1918, file 27-14, Confidential Files, RG80; Palmer, Chief of Bureau of Navigation, to Benson, Dec. 24, 1917, Box 10, copy in entry 113, RG19; Sims to Dept., Feb. 28, 1918, ibid.; Benson to Simsadus, Jan. 31, 1918, Reel 3, ME-11; Benson to Sims, March 1, 1918, Reel 10, M1092.

96. "Brief History of U.S. Naval Forces in France," ZO file, OA; H. B. Wilson, *The American Navy in France*, 71–74; Rose, *Brittany Patrol*, 112, 122, 298; Chief, Bureau of Steam Engineering, to CNO, March 4, 1918, Box 9, entry 113, RG19; Fry to G. E. Burd, March 4, 1918, Box 79, Confidential Files, RG80. The Army considered establishing a repair yard in Brest for its transports but opted to use the Navy's facilities.

97. Babcock to Sims, n.d., Spring 1918, Box 144, Sims Papers, LC.

98. H. B. Wilson, *The American Navy in France*, 72–73.

99. Ibid.; Smith to Sims, February 12, 1918, Logistics file, RG45.

100. Mayo to wife, Oct. 3, 1918, Mayo Papers, LC; Cone to Sims, date not legible but 1918, Box 52, Sims Papers, LC; H. B. Wilson, *The American Navy in France*, 117; entry for June, 1918, Michael Bathrop Diary, Smithsonian.

101. "Report of Events at Gibraltar, 1st to 15th Jan, 1918," Senior Naval Officer, Gibraltar, to British C-in-C, Mediterranean, ADM137/760.

102. Sims to Dept., Jan. 19, Feb. 26, 1918, Reel 19, ME-11; Niblack to Sims, June 21, 1918, Box 76, Sims Papers, LC; Sims to Benson, May 20, 1918, Reel 4, ME-11; Niblack to Sims, June 21, 1918, Reel 20, ME-11; Sims to Dept., June 22, 1918, ibid., Niblack to Sims, July 29, 1918, P-Gibraltar, subj file, RG45; MacDougall, *Royal Dockyards*, 159; holograph from Oliver, dated Nov. 24, 1917, in Halpern, *The Royal Navy in the Mediterranean*, 295; Niblack to "Billy," May 28, June 21, Sept. 10, 1918, Box 76, Sims Papers, LC; Admiralty dispatch for Niblack, January 19, 1918, Reel 10, M1092; Calthorpe to Geddes, Sept. 4, 1918, ADM116/1809; Cochran MS, Cochran Papers, Coast Guard Library. Other vessels operating in European waters were occasionally sent to Lisbon for repairs and overhaul. Simsadus to Dept., Feb. 2, March 6, 12, 18, 1918, Reel 10, M1092; Paine, *The Corsair in the War Zone*, 194–95.

103. Dunn to Sims, Jan. 30, 1918, Reel 19, ME-11. For Ponta Delgada, see pp. 137–39.

104. "Comparison of Provisioning and Supply Systems of United States and British Navies," January 1919, *ONI Semi-Monthly Information Bulletin* (Feb. 1919): 110–11; T. Wilson, *The Myriad Faces of War*, 78–79

105. Congress, U.S., June 22, 1916, *Hearings before the Subcommittee of the Committee on Commerce, U. S. Senate*, 64th Cong., 1st sess., 1916.

106. Belknap, "The Auxiliary Squadron," 639.

107. Cunningham, "The Moveable Base"; Jackson and Evans, *The New Book of American Ships*, 182, 187; Coletta, "The Destroyer Tender," U.S. Naval Institute *Proceedings* 84 (May 1958): 91; Stanley, "War Time Repairs in the Navy," 731–32; Memo, General Board Subject file, 420-15, Box 408, RG80; "The Fleet Train," in R. Gardiner, *The Eclipse of the Big Gun*, 165–71.

108. Still, *American Sea Power in the Old World*, 37–40.

109. Ibid., 12, 138–39.

110. For Melville, see J. D. Long, *The New American Navy*, 1: 154; R. W. King, *Naval Engineering and American Sea Power*, 35; *Dictionary of American Biography*, 6: 521–22; *History of the Bureau of Engineering Navy Department during the War*, 76.

111. Costello, "Planning for War," Ph.D. diss., 267–69; Still, *American Sea Power in the Old World*, 139; G. T. Davis, *A Navy Second to None*, 179, 2236-227; Sprout and Sprout, *The Rise of American Naval Power*, 310–11, 319, 326–27, 335. Ferraby, *The Grand Fleet*, 115; For *Melville*, see *Norfolk Virginia Pilot*, Aug. 9, 1946; "Mobile Logistic Support Force: Auxiliary Ship Navy," 3–4.

112. The tenders would assume additional responsibilities during the war, responsibilities that would become standard in the years afterward. For example, they began to handle the disbursing duties for the smaller ships. Burns, "The Flotilla Disbursing Office," 1–2.

113. Navy Dept., *Ships' Data: U.S. Naval Vessels* Ships, Nov. 1, 1916, 132–38.

114. Finnegan, *Against the Specter of a Dragon*, 162–63; *Hearings before the Committee on the Merchant Marine and Fisheries*, House of Representatives, 64th Cong., 1st sess., 239–56; *Hearings before the Subcommittee of the Committee on Commerce, U. S. Senate*, 64th Cong., 1st sess., 181–209. The bill approved only one additional repair ship. In May 1918, the American Naval Planning Section in London recommended eight new tenders for the destroyers being built, one tender for each of the twenty-four destroyers. Memorandum No. 24, May 2, 1918, in Navy Dept., *The American Navy Planning Section in London*, 205–6.

115. File 420-5, Box 67, General Board Records, RG80.

116. The collier *Caesar* provided logistical support for U.S. warships engaged in protecting American interests in the Mediterranean prior to the war declaration.

117. The various volumes of the *Dictionary of American Naval Fighting Ships* (*DANFS*) give brief biographies of all the tenders including *Melville*. See also *Melville*'s deck log in RG45.

118. Shafter, *Destroyers in Action*, 219–20. For comments on serving on the tender, see entry for May 22, 1917, Latimer Diary, UVA.

119. To Bayly, Dec. 31, 1918, Bayly Papers, IWM. For *Dixie*, see Neeser, *Our Many Sided Navy*, 144–45; Neuhaus, "Fifty Years of Naval Engineering in Retrospect," 24–25; Foley, "The Cruiser *Dixie*." For a biographical sketch of Price, see file in ZB file, NDL.

120. Sims to Daniels, May 8, 1917, in M. Simpson, *Anglo-American Naval Relations*, 219–20.

121. Pringle to Sims, July 15, 1917, Reel 3, ME-11.

122. Price to Sims, Nov. 3, 1918, Box 79, Sims Papers, LC. See also the two ships deck logs, various entries, RG24; Taussig, "Destroyer Experiences during the Great War," 383; DeLany, *Bayly's Navy*, 12; Sims to Dept., June 15, 1917, Reel 1, ME-11; address by Taussig, copy in Taussig Papers, LC; Pringle to Sims, Sept. 7, 1917, Box 1, Entry, 113, RG19; Chapple, *We'll Stick to the Finish*, 218; *Sphere*, Oct. 26, 1918, 66.

123. Daniels to Sims, July 10, 1917, Box 53, Sims Papers, LC. See also memo of agreement between French and American representatives in Washington, n.d., copy in Reel 58, Daniels Papers, LC; memo, French Minister of Marine, May 8, 1917, French Naval Archives, Vincennes; translation of memo of French engineering office, June 4, 1918, TT subj file, RG45.

124. July 20, 1917, P subj file, RG45.

125. See, for example, Hinton to mother, Dec. 1, 1918, Richmond folders, WWI Archives, Virginia State Library; Conolly Oral History, Columbia University.

126. To Dept., July 18, 1917, Reel 1, ME-11.

127. July 18, 1917, file C-27-39, Confidential Files, 1917–1919, RG80; Sims to Dept., Aug. 7, 1917, Reel 3, ME-11.

128. Dinger to Koester, July 28, 1917, file 11-27, Box 8, Logistics file, RG45; Jackson to Benson, Aug. 10, 1917, Box 4, Benson Papers, LC; Fletcher to Sims, Aug. 16, 1917, Box 8, Logistics file, RG45; Jackson to Sims, August 14, 1917, TV file, subj file, RG45; Dinger to Foley, Sept. 22, 1917, P-Bases, subj file, RG45; Sims to CNO, Aug. 29, 1917, OS file, *Prometheus* subj file, RG45; Benson to Sims, Aug. 30, 1917, Reel 1, ME-11; Sims to Dinger, Sept. 6, 1917, Box 54, Sims Papers, LC.

129. *DANFS*, 1: 156.

130. Memo, Aug. 30, 1917, Entry 13, Box 10, RG19.

131. *DANFS*, 5: 210.

132. Dinger to Foley, Sept. 22, 1927, PF-bases, Brest subj file, RG45.

133. Ibid.

134. To Sims, Dec. 15, 1917, PF subj file, RG45; Sims to CNO, Dec. 13, 1917, ibid.

135. To Dept., Jan. 14, 1918, file 28754-1-18: 345, Confidential Files, RG80.

136. Benson to Sims, Dec. 8, 1917, Reel 2, ME-11; Benson Report, Nov. 1917, Box 42, Benson Papers, LC.

137. *DANFS*, 5: 392–93; Reginald Wright Kauffman, *Our Navy at War*, 175–76.

138. Entry for Aug. 11, 1918, Brown Journal, WisHistSoc.

139. June 27, 1918, N subj file, RG45. See also Sims to Bayly, June 8, 1918, Box 47, Sims Papers.

140. Sims to Dept., Jan. 8, 1918, Reel 3, ME-11; Daniels to Bureaus, Feb. 4, 1918, file 27-14, Confidential Files, RG80.

141. Babcock to Sims, July 9, 1918, file 611-120, Box 201, RG71; Babcock to Sims, n.d., Box 144, Sims Papers, LC; Sims to Dept., Jan. 14, 1918, Reel 3, ME-11; Repair Officer, Brest to Wilson, Sept. 25, 1918, file C-27-76, Confidential Files, RG80; Sims Report, May 4, 1918, Reel 4, ME-11; Sims to Niblack, Sept. 22, 1918, Box 24, Sims Papers, LC.

142. Memoirs, William F. Halsey Papers, LC.

143. Memo for CNO, Oct. 20, 1917, OH file, subj file, RG45; Benson to Sims, Aug. 1, 1918, Reel 8, ME-11; to Sims, Jan. 31, 1918, Reel 3, ibid.; to Sims, March 6, 1918, OH subj file, RG45.

144. May 8, 1918, memo No. 24, pp. 205–6. See also Dept. to Sims, Feb. 27, 1918, Reel 3, ME-11; Sims to Dept. March 8, 1918, ibid.

145. Entry for May 30, 1918, Stuart Smith Diary, LC.

146. *History of the Bureau of Engineering Navy Department during the War*, 78; Benson to Simsadus, January 31, 1918, Reel 3, ME-11.

147. Sims to Dept., Feb. 27, 1918, OS, *Bridgeport* subj file, RG45; Reed, "The *Bridgeport*," 17; See also MSS in the Fullinwider Papers, Smithsonian.

148. May 28, 1918, OF, *Bridgeport* subj file, RG45; *Bridgeport* file, Ships History Branch, NHC; Dept. to Sims, May 22, 1918, Reel 10, M1092.

149. To Sims, Sept. 13, 1918, Box 47, Sims Papers, LC.

150. MSS in Fullinwider Papers, Smithsonian; Strauss testimony, 1919, General Board Hearings; *DANFS*, 1: 128–29.

151. Sept. 3, 1918, Box 24, Sims Papers, LC. See also Sims to Wilson, Aug. 7, 1918, Reel 9, ME-11; Sims to Niblack, Aug. 8, 1918, ibid.; Wilson to Sims, June 10, 1918, Reel 20, ME-11; Sims to Dept., Aug. 8, 1918, OS file, *Buffalo* subj file, RG45.

152. Beston, "With the American Submarines," 690–91.

153. Grady, "War History of Submarine Division Five," n.d., n.p., copy in *Nautilus* Memorial and Submarine Force Library and Museum.

154. *DANFS*, 5: 51; Buranelli, Maggie *of the Suicide Fleet*, 253–54; Thompson, *Take Her Down*, 124–26, 153.

155. Entry for Feb. 13, 1918, Talley Letters, OA.

156. *Naval Investigation*, 910. See also address of Capt. Earl Jessop, *Transactions of the Society of Naval Architects and Marine Engineers* 27 (1919): 341, and Blythe, "At a Naval Base," 21, 106–7; Wilson to Sims, Feb. 26, 1918, P-Brest subj file, RG45; Reed, "The *Bridgeport*," 17–18; "American Destroyers in the War," 90–91; Parker Oral History, Columbia University; Rose, *Brittany Patrol*, 177. Duncan S. Ballantine, in his book *U.S. Naval Logistics in the Second World War*, was mistaken when he claimed that the World War I repair ships could not do this job and the vessels had to return to the United States for retubing; see page 24.

157. Price to Sims, Nov. 3, 1918, Box 79, Sims Papers, LC.

158. May 31, 1917, Box 82, Sims Papers, LC; Sumida, "British Naval Operational Logistics," 456.

159. *Glasgow Herald*, Oct. 25, 1918; *Journal of Commerce* (Liverpool), Nov. 1, 1918. See also Geddes to Calthorpe, Sept. 12, 1918, in M. Simpson, *Anglo-American Naval Relations*, 544; testimony of Capt. Todd, April 20, 1918, General Board Hearings; Sims to Dept., Oct. 10, 1918, Reel 6, ME-11; Pringle to Sims, July 15, 1917, Reel 3, ibid.; Churchill, *A Traveller in War Time*, 39; "American Destroyers in the War," 91; *New York Herald*, European edition, Dec. 28, 1918.

160. Rose, *The Brittany Patrol*, 177; see also *L'Illustration*, June 29, 1918; *Le Matin*, May 28, 1918; *Le Figaro*, Aug. 18, 1918; H. B. Wilson, *The American Navy in France*, 75.

161. Price to Sims, April 23, 1919, Box 79, Sims Papers, LC.

162. Sims to Dept., May 4, 1918, Reel 4, ME-11; Price to Sims, April 23, 1919, Box 79, Sims Papers, LC; "Co-operation," Jan. 19, 1921, "Data on U.S.S. S/M, Series 4, 1915–1928, Box 2, OA. See also Bieg, "War and Naval Engineering," 545–47.

163. Belknap, *Yankee Mining Squadron*, 14; Louis Poisson Davis Sr. Oral History, ECU; see also entry for May 29, 1918, Brown Journal, WisHistSoc; Strauss to the Admiral, Invergordon, Box 10, Logistics file, RG45.

164. "A Brief Summary of U.S. Navy in France, Nov. 11, 1918 to Oct. 1, 1919," ZO file, OA; Naval Forces Operating in European waters, Final Report, Dec. 1918, ZT subj file, RG45.

165. Ballantine, *U.S. Naval Logistics in the Second World War*, 23–24; Brassey and Leyland, *The Naval Annual*, 78.

166. Sims testimony, *Naval Investigation*, 78–83; McKean testimony, ibid., 1712–13. See also Secretary, the Admiralty, to Sims, Jan. 14, 1918, copy in OH subj file, RG45; Minutes of the 49th Meeting of the Tug Distribution Committee, Sept. 23, 1918, ADM139/1622.

167. *The Bureau of Engineering Navy Department during the War*, 41; Sims to Dept., Jan. 28, 1918, copy in *Naval Investigation*, 79; Number of Seagoing Tugs in European Waters, OH file, subj file, RG45; Dept. to Simsadus, Dec. 1, 1917, ibid.; Sims to *Melville*, Sept. 4, 1917, ibid., Sims to Secretary, Admiralty, Jan. 18, 1918, ibid.; Long to Twining, Feb. 11, 1918, ibid.; Sims to Dept., Feb. 19, 1918, ibid.; Sims to *Melville*, Aug. 14, 1918, Reel 9, ME-11; Sims to Wilson, Aug. 20, 1918, Reel 10, ibid.; Sims to Dept., Oct. 18, 1918, ibid.; Sims to Admiralty, June 27, 1918, ADM137/1622; Admiralty to Sims, July 11, 1918, ibid.; Strauss to Sims, July 23, 1918, ibid. Four tugs under Army control were also sent to French waters, but these were harbor tugs. Sims requested an undetermined number of yard tugs for his command, but evidently none were received. He did receive one salvage vessel assigned to Brest. Sims to Wilson, May 6, 1918, Reel 10, ME-11. See also Clephane, *History of the Naval Overseas Transportation Service in World War I*, 44.

Chapter 8. "For Want of a Nail"

1. Niblack, "Putting Cargos Across," CZ subj file, RG45.

2. Memo to McGowan, Dec. 1, 1916, Box 1802, RG143; "History of Bureau of Supplies and Accounts during War," ZU subj file, RG45.

3. Ellis, *British Railway History*, 305.

4. History of Bureau of Supplies and Accounts during the War, ZU subj file, RG45; Sims to Dept., April 30, 1918, Reel 20, ME-20; Mayo Report, Box 376, P-bases subj file, RG45. For McGowan's and the bureau's work in Washington, see Allston, *Ready for Sea*, 174–91.

5. History of Bureau of Supplies and Accounts in the War, file 427-5. Box 430, RG143; Destroyer Flotilla at Queenstown, March 12, 1919, ZD file, subj file, RG45; Sims to Navy Dept., April 27, 1917, TT file subj file, RG45; Op order No 1., U.S. Destroyer Force, European Waters, April 29, 1917, copy in Taussig Papers, NWC; Wheeler Oral History, USNI; Page to SecState for SecNav, May 10, 1917, file 834, London Embassy records, RG84.

6. Entries for May 4, 5, 16, and June 20, 1917, Fagan Diary, Mariners' Museum; Destroyer Flotilla at Queenstown, March 12, 1919, ZD file, subj file, RG45. *Dixie* would return to Queenstown early in September because of the inauguration of the convoy system and the need for repair facilities at Queenstown.

7. Supply officer, *Melville*, to Pringle, Aug. 16, 1917, P-Queenstown, subj file, RG45; History of Bureau of Supplies and Accounts in War, file 427-5, Box 430, RG143.

8. Pringle to Sims, July 10, 1917, Box 54, Logistics file, RG45; Sims to Dept., Aug. 9, 1917, Reel 2, ME-11; Sims to Dept., 29, 1917, OH subj file, RG45; Sims memo and McGowan response, Aug. 29, 1917, Box 71, Sims Papers, LC; Dept. to CO Train, Atlantic Fleet, OS subj file, RG45; Allston, *Ready for Sea*, 185.

9. Chief of Staff, Destroyer Flotilla, to U.S. Destroyer Flotilla, Jan. 21, 1918, Box 10, Logistics file, RG45; Sims Report, Aug. 16, 1918, Reel 5, ME-11.

10. Destroyer Flotilla at Queenstown, March 12, 1919, ZP subj file, RG45; Lyon to Snead, Aug. 28, 1918, Logistics file, Box 54, RG45; Sims to SecNav, Aug. 9, 1917, Box 9, Entry 113, RG19.

11. Testimony, General Board Hearings, Feb. 6, 1918.

12. "History of Naval Aviation," NDL. See also Turnbull and Lord, *History of United States Naval Aviation*, 143–44; Sims to SecNav, Aug. 21, 24, 1918, Reel 16, ME-11.

13. Hooper to Blakes, Nov. 5, 1918, Hooper MS, LC; Pamard to Div. Chief, Aug. 22, 1918, French Naval Archives, Vincennes. "History of Naval Aviation," NDL; Roosevelt to Simsadus, Aug. 18, 1918, Reel 10, ME-11

14. Sims Report to Dept., Aug. 16, 1918, Reel 5, ME-11; Pringle to Sims, March 6, 1918, OS subj file, RG45. For its effect on the AEF, see Zimmerman, *The Neck of the Bottle*, 116–17; Hagood, *The Services of Supply*, 52–53; Harbord, *Leaves from a War Diary*, 149.

15. For the History of NOTS, see Clephane, *History of the Naval Overseas Transportation Service in World War I.*

16. Ibid., 27–28, 34–35; Gaunt to Jellicoe, Nov. 15, 1917, in M. Simpson, *Anglo-American Naval Relations*, 338; *ONI Semi-Monthly Compilation*, ser. 63. Oct. 1918: 209.

17. History of the Bureau of Supplies and Accounts during the War, file 421-5, Box 430, REG143.

18. Thompson to Braisted, Nov. 23, 1917, file 127046, RG52.

19. Schafter to COs bases 17 and 18, Feb. 7, 1918, Logistics file, Box 54, RG45.

20. File C18-300, Confidential Files, RG80.

21. Sims to Dept., Feb. 28, 1918, OS file, subj file, RG45; Riddle, CO of Bridge to Rodman, March 24, 1918, ibid.

22. Rodman to Dept., Jan. 26, 1918, Box 10, Logistics file, RG45; memo on supply arrangement for Sixth Battle Squadron, March 30, 1918, G-1-C 1918, Provisions shipment, RG45; CO Mine Forces to Sims, April 6, 1918, Reel 8, ME-11; Sims to CO Mine Force, Aug. 7, 1918, Box 63, Logistics file, RG45.

23. Sumida, "British Naval Operational Logistics," 450, 451–52.

24. Ibid.; For the Grand Fleet's canteen ship, see *Daily Mail* (London), June 7, 1918; *Pall Mall Gazette*, Feb. 12, 14, 1918; *Daily News* (London), Feb. 14, 1919.

25. Allen, *Sails to Atoms*, 31.

26. Hayward, *HMS Tiger at Bay*, 156; Shrader, "Maconochie's Stew," 118–19; interview (subject's name not readable) in WWI Research Collection, AMHI.

27. The Directory of Victualling, Admiralty, Oct. 15, 1918, ADM137/2260; Washington, U.S. Consul Liverpool to Schafter, Feb. 21, 1918, file 814.2, Liverpool Consulate Records, RG84.

28. Bureau of Supplies and Accounts to SecNav, Dec. 17, 1917, Box 5, Entry 113, RG19. See also Sims to Dept., July 31, 1918, OS subj file, RG45; Mayo to CO Train, Sept. 12, 1918, file C-21-76, Confidential Correspondence, RG80.

29. Chapple, *We'll Stick to the Finish*, 215. See, for example, Smith to Bureau of Medicine and Surgery, July 3, 1918, file 130212, RG52; Freeman to Force Commander, December 31, 1918, ibid.; Blythe, "At a Naval Base," 21; Kleinatland, "A Saga of World War I," in author's private collection; *Annual Report of Surgeon General U.S. Navy, 1919*, 247; Chase, *Benjamin Lee, 2d*, 228; Sheely to mother, December 9, 1917, in Sheely, *Sailor of the Air*, 101, 112; *U.S.S.* Wyoming: *At War in the North Sea*. For the doughboy's attitude toward English rations, see Goddard, "Relations between American Expeditionary Forces and British Expeditionary Forces," AMHI.

30. Feb. 26, 1918, Box 9, Sims Papers, LC; Rowcliff testimony, March 6, 1918, General Board Hearings.

31. Sims to Dept., July 17, 1917, copy in 1-2.5/889, RG59; entry for Oct. 10, 1917, William Tomb Diary, UNC-CH. See also Beston, *Full Speed Ahead*, 86; Chief of Staff, Destroyer Flotilla, to U.S. destroyers operating in European waters, Jan. 21, 1918, Box 10, Logistics file, RG45.

32. *Evening Echo*, May 5, 1977; to fiancée, June 6, 1918, Witherspoon Family Papers, AMHI.

33. Memo for CO Mine Forces, Oct. 31, 1918, Box 10, Logistics file, RG45; "Logistics," unpublished notes in Fullinwider Papers, Smithsonian.

34. Entry for Oct. 1917, Brown Journal, WisHistSoc. For the mine bases, see War Diary, USS *Sacramento*, Jan. 9, 1918, Reel 19, ME-11.

35. Sayles to Dept., May 13, 1917, P subj. file, RG45.

36. Post to Mom, August 9, 1918, Post MS, LSU. See also Moffat, *Maverick Navy*, 78.

37. The surgeon at the base hospital in Brest frequently raved about the food. On Oct. 20, 1918, he wrote, "Just think of it, I have had a piece of each of apple, cherry, and pumpkin pie

this week." For comments about food see Talley to wife, Oct. 19, Nov. 4, Dec. 2, 1917 and Feb. 1, July 8, and Oct. 20, 1918, Talley Papers, OA.

38. Moseley, *Extracts from Letters*, 147.

39. Sheely to mother, June 20, Oct. 20, 1917, March 17, 1918, in Sheely, *Sailor of the Air*, 33, 67, 107. See also Moseley, *Extracts from Letters*, 181; Memoirs of Joe Cline in *Naval Aviation in World War I*, 13; MacLeish to Beloved, April 27, 1918, in Rossano, *The Price of Honor*, 150.

40. Paine, *The First Yale Unit*, 2: 54–55.

41. Stephenson, "With a Naval Railway Battery in France," 840.

42. Conolly Oral History, Columbia University.

43. Fletcher to Sims, Aug. 9, 1917, TT file, subj file, RG45.

44. Moffat, *Maverick Navy*, 78. Conolly commanded the destroyer *Smith*.

45. Adams, "André Tardieu and French Foreign Policy," Ph.D. diss., 349–50.

46. Conger to Tobey, Dec. 22, 1917, Box 64, Logistics file, RG45.

47. Entry for Sept. 25, 1917, Stuart Smith Diary, LC.

48. *Literary Digest*, Nov. 17, 1917, 217.

49. Entries for Nov. 1917, Feb. 23, 1918, Brown Journal, WisHistSoc.

50. *Flying Officers of the U.S.N.*, 33; entry for Feb. 28, 1918, Moseley, *Extracts from Letters*, 147; Sims to SecNav, June 1, 1918, Reel 4, ME-11; King and Whitehill, *Fleet Admiral King*, 137–38.

51. Brief History of U.S. Naval Forces in France, ZO file, OA; H. B. Wilson, *The American Navy in France*, 110–11; Robert E. Tod MS, n.d., Box 88, Sims Papers, LC; Wilson to Sims, Jan. 23, 1918, Box 8, Logistics file, RG45.

52. H. B. Wilson, *The American Navy in France*, 110–11; Tod MS, Box 88, Sims Papers, LC. Tod was in charge of the project. He also had the help of U.S. Army engineers. Sims to Dept., Jan. 21, March 18, 1918, Reel 19, ME-11; Hatch to Sims, Feb. 16, 1918, ibid.; Braisted to Chief, Bureau of Yards and Docks, July 18, 1918, file 130212, RG52; Sims to Wilson, Aug. 26, 1918, Reel 10, ME-11.

53. The best discussion of the competition is Lord, "History of Naval Aviation," NDL. See also Conger to McGowan, Nov. 26, 1917, Box 19, USNAVOPFOR, Europe, General Correspondence, 1917–1919, RG313; "Progress Report, U.S. Naval Aviation Forces, Foreign Service, Headquarters, Paris," microfilm, NDL.

54. Grenshaw to Perkins, May 22, 1918, OS subj file, RG45; Sims to Admiralty, Aug. 2, 1918, TT file, ibid., Sims to Dept., Aug. 14, 1918, Reel 5, ME-11; Benson to Simsadus, Aug. 23, ibid.; Aide for Supplies and Transportation to CO U.S. Naval Air Stations, Ireland, Dec. 28, 1918, ZPA subj file, RG45; Sims to Wilson, Aug. 14, 1918, Reel 9, ME-11; "History of the U.S. Naval Air Stations, Ireland," n.d., ZPA subj file, RG45; Conger to Tobey, March 15, 1918, box 63, Logistics file, RG45; Lord, "History of Naval Aviation," NDL.

55. Wilson to Chief of the Bureau of Construction and Repairs, Aug. 30, 1917, Box 10, Entry 113, RG19.

56. Aviation Progress Report, Sept. 30, 1918, GA subj file, RG45; Lord, "History of Naval Aviation," NDL; "Progress Report, U.S. Naval Aviation Forces, Foreign Service, Headquarters, Paris," microfilm, NDL; Sims to Admiralty, June 1, 1918, Reel 4, ME-11.

57. July 24, 1918, Reel 4, ME-11.

58. Kipp Diary, author's private collection. See also "Standing Order Related to Stores to U.S. Naval Base No. 25," June 12, 1918, Box 1802, RG143.

59. CO, USS *Lydonia* to CO, Patrol Squadron, Gibraltar, Feb. 27, 1918, OS subj file, RG45; Entry for May 15, 1918, Kipp Diary, author's private collection; Sims to Dept., Aug. 29, 1917, OH subj file, RG45; memo, CO Patrol Squadron, Gibraltar, September 3, 1918, file 631, RG26; undated journal, Hamilton Cochran Papers, Coast Guard Library.

60. *Annual Report, Surgeon General 1919, U.S. Navy*, 239–40.

61. Osterhaus to SecNav, file C-48, Box 105, Confidential Files, RG80.

62. Entry May 1, 1918, Kipp Diary, author's private collection. See also Sims to CO Azores, May 1, 1918, P-Ponta Delgada subj file, RG45; extracts from August, 1917, Deck Log of USS *Panther*, RG45.

63. Sims to Dept., Oct. 10, 1918, Reel 8, ME-11.

64. Wilson to Simsadus, Aug. 14, 1918, Reel 9, ME-11. Bureau of Ordnance cable, Feb. 21, 1918, Reel 10, M1092; Strauss to Bureau of Ordnance, Aug. 28, 1918, Box 10, Logistics file, RG45; Rodman to Sims, May 14, 1918, ZOB subj file, RG45; Admiralty to C-in-C July 30, 1918, ADM137/1973.

65. Bureau of Ordnance cable, Feb. 21, 1918, Reel 10, M1092; Strauss to Bureau of Ordnance, Aug. 28, 1918, Box 10, Logistics file, RG45; Rodman to Sims, May 14, 1918, ZOB subj file, RG45; Admiralty to C-in-C, July 30, 1918, ADM137/1973.

66. Thompson to Braisted, March 12, April 17, 1918, file 127046, RG52; Braisted to Curl, Dec. 2, 1917, ibid., Curl to Braisted, Oct. 29, 1918, file 131000, ibid.; Memo for Assistant Secretary, July 2, 1918, ibid.; H. B. Wilson, *The American Navy in France*, 104; Report of officer in charge, American Red Cross, Great Britain, n.d., file 941.11, Box 842, RG200; Benson to Simsadus, Nov. 24, 1917, Reel 10, ME-11.

67. Venn, *Oil Diplomacy in the Twentieth Century*, 35. See also Davenport and Cooke, *The Oil Trusts and Anglo-American Relations*, 29–30.

68. Sumida, "British Naval Operational Logistics," 460–65; G. Jones, "Admirals and Oil Men," 107–10; Macksey, *For Want of a Nail*, 5–6.

69. Josephus Daniels, *Our Navy at War*, 283; DeNovo, "Petroleum and the United States Navy," 548, 641–44; Maurer, "Fuel and the Battle Fleet," 60–77; Allston, *Ready for Sea*, 154; John J. Fee, "The Rise of American Naval Power," in R. W. King, *Naval Engineering and American Seapower*, 79–80.

70. Hamilton, "A Short History of the Naval Use of Fuel Oil," 43.

71. Geoffrey Jones, "The British Government and the Oil Companies," 657–58. See also *Home Waters*, pt. 9, May 1, 1917–July 31, 1917, Naval Staff Monograph 19, no. 35, Aug. 1936, 1253, copy in National Defense Library; Still, "Anglo-American Naval Logistic Cooperation in World War I," 218; Burke, *Britain, America, and the Sinews of War*, 155; Davenport and Cooke, *The Oil Trust and Anglo-American Relations*, 30; Denny, *America Conquers Britain*, 231.

72. G. Jones, "The British Government and the Oil Companies," 119; Venn, *Oil Diplomacy in the Twentieth Century*, 38.

73. Entry for July 2, 1917, in Josephus Daniels, *Cabinet Diaries*, 171; Page to Lansing, June 26, 1917, in M. Simpson, *Anglo-American Naval Relations*, 70; Admiralty to De Chair, May 25, 1917, ibid., 6; W. Long, *Memories*, 259.

74. Wilkerson et. al., *The American Petroleum Industry*, 274.

75. Director of Shipping to War Cabinet, May 5, 1917, MT 23/743; British Embassy to Department of State, n.d., *Foreign Relations, 1917*, Supplement 2, 595–96. Lord Jellicoe wrote that the shortage of "oil fuel reserves became serious towards the end of April, 1917." See Jellicoe, *The Submarine Peril*, 171.

76. Reel 8, ME-11.

77. Benson quotes cable to the Paymaster General, May 8, 1917, Box 4580, RG143.

78. Sims to SecNav, May 30, 1917, Box 65, Logistics file, RG45.

79. To Benson, June 5, 1917, Box 4, Benson Papers, LC. The British used metric tons to measure petroleum supply and usage; Americans used both gallons and barrels.

80. Benson to Sims, June 8, 1917, Box 4, Benson Papers, LC; paraphrase of talk from F. O. to Washington Embassy, June 18, 1917, Box 4580, RG143. Although the Navy Department agreed to the pooling arrangement, it reserved the right to rescind it if so desired. FDR to McGowan, June 25, 1917, Box 4580, RG143.

81. For a detailed discussion of the first four oilers, see Wildenberg, *Gray Steel and Black Oil*,

5–15. These early tankers were designated as fuel ships. The term *oiler* (AO) became an official designation in the post–World War I years, although it was used during the war.

82. *DANFS*; Oilers, QC subj file, RG45; Jackson and Evans, *The New Book of American Ships*, 184–85.

83. Havès, "Coal Wagons of the Sea," 18–21; Henritz, "U.S. Navy Colliers," 163–64; Van Deurs, "What Happened to *Cyclops, Nereus,* and *Proteus*—The *Langley's* Missing Sisters?" 60–64; History of the Bureau of Supplies and Accounts during the War, ZU subj file, RG45.

84. Conference memo, McGowan to FDR, May 12, 1917, Box 9, Assistant SecNav Files, FDR Library.

85. Hamilton, "A Short History of the Naval Use of Fuel Oil," 53; SecNav to USSB, April 4, 1918, C-31-72, Box 78, Confidential Files, 1917–1919, RG80; Ratcliffe, *Liquid Gold Ships*, 71; History of Bureau of Supplies and Accounts during the War, ZU subj file, RG45. The USSB acquired twenty-six tankers during the war including the three that were built. See appendix 1, "List of Vessels That Served in the Naval Overseas Transportation Service as of 1 November 1919," in Clephane, *History of the Naval Overseas Transportation Service in World War I*, 213–46. See also Hamilton, "A Short History of the Naval Use of Fuel Oil," 52–53. Ratcliffe states that U.S. yards built 316 tankers between 1917 and 1921 but does not say how many were completed during the war. Ratcliffe, *Liquid Gold Ships*, 71.

86. McGowan to SecNav, July 3, 1917, McGowan Papers, LC. FDR to SecState, Aug. 11, 1917, file 102.5/946, RG59; Daniels to Sims, July 26, 1917, Reel 1, ME-11. Sims had earlier informed the SecNav that to date none of the oil provided the Queenstown-based destroyers had been replaced. July 17, 1917, Reel 1, ME-11. See also memo for chairman, Shipping Board, Oct. 18, 1917, in "U.S. Petroleum Mission to Europe," ZQ subj file, RG45.

87. Quoted in Petroleum Mission to Europe, ZQ subj file, RG45. See also entry for July 26, 1917, in Josephus Daniels, *Cabinet Diaries*, 183; McGowan to SecNav, July 12, 1917, copy in Box 3, Assistant SecNav Files, FDR Library.

88. FDR to SecState, Aug. 11, 1917, file 102.5/946, RG59.

89. Memo for CNO, Aug. 20, 1917, Reel 2, ME-11.

90. Trask, *Captains and Cabinets*, 170–72.

91. September 1, 1917, Reel 2, ME-11.

92. Black to Hurley, January 9, 1918, ibid.; Hurley to Page, Nov. 17, 1917, *Foreign Relations, 1917*, Supplement 2, 637–38.

93. Black to Bedford, Oct. 11, 1917, file 3930, Box 90, RG32.

94. Allard, "Anglo-American Naval Differences During World War I," 75–81.

95. Wilkerson et al. *The American Petroleum Industry*, 276.

96. January 7, 1918, Reel 3, ME-11.

97. Colby to W. S. Gifford, Director, Council of National Defense, January 12, 1918, file 3930, Box 90, RG32.

98. Entry for January 16, 1918, Foley Diary, QC file, subj file, RG45. See also Thomas and Foley to Hurley, March 29, 1918, Reel 3, ME-11; records in the Foley Mission files, QC file, subj file, RG45. For Daniels, see entry for Feb. 12, 1918, in Josephus Daniels, *Cabinet Diaries*, 278.

99. January 3, 1918, ADM 116/1810, Geddes Papers, University of California at Irvine; see also Sims to Dept., March 9, 1918, Reel 3, ME-11; to Benson, Feb. 28, 1918, Box 49, Sims Papers, LC; to Hurley, March 8, 1918, Reel 3, ME-11; Royden, British War Mission to Hurley, Dec. 7, 1917, RG32.

100. T. Wilson, *The Myriad Faces of War*, 628; Knox to Frothington, June 9, 1922, Box 7, Knox Papers, LC.

101. Note for the War Cabinet, May 3, 1918, MT 25/201.

102. Memo dated October 20, 1917, OH file, subj file, RG45; McGowan to Benson, Nov. 7, 1917, C-31-1, Box 78, Confidential Files, RG80; Gleaves to CNO, Jan. 7, 1918, C-31-71, ibid.

103. Daniels to chiefs, various bureaus, March 8, 1918, C-31-1, Box 78, Confidential Files, RG80. See also Foley to Dept., March 8, 1918, Reel 3, ME-11; Moore Oral History, Columbia University.

104. Memo from Bureau of Supplies and Accounts to CNO, March 22, 1918, C-31-1, Box 78, Confidential Files, RG80.

105. For this deployment, see Chapter 16.

106. Hatch to L. S. Lorient, May 7, 1918, Box 65, Logistics file, RG45; "Progress Report, U.S. Naval Aviation Forces, Foreign Service, Headquarters, Paris," microfilm, NDL; Dudley to Supply Officer, U.S. Naval Forces, Paris, May 18, 1918, GA subj file, RG45.

107. To Dept., Aug. 25, 1918, Box 65, Logistics file, RG45; Benson to Hurley, Aug. 28, 1918, C-31-C, Box 78, Confidential Files, RG80.

108. Sharp to Wilson, Dec. 15, 1917, in Link, *Wilson Papers*, 45: 302–3.

109. Gudger to Bureau of Supplies and Accounts, Feb. 21, 1920, Box 4580, RG143; Hach to Admiral Wilson, April 29, 1918, Box 65, Logistics file, RG45; entry for Jan. 3, 1918, Foley diary, Foley Mission, OC subj file, RG45.

110. Quoted in the *New York Times*, April 6, 1918. Taussig agreed with Sims in his article on Brest published in the U.S. Naval Institute *Proceedings* 49 (March 1923): 403. Foley Diary, Foley Mission, QC subj file, RG45.

111. Allston, *Ready for Sea*, 187–88.

112. Memo, 1919, TL subj file, RG45; Admiralty to Sims, March 16, 1918, OD file, ibid.; Sims to Dept., April 16, 1918, ibid.; Sims to Dept., April 14, May 23, June 4, 9, 1918, Reel 12, ME-11; entries for April 12, 27, 1918, Foley Diary, Foley Mission, QC subj file RG45; Sims to Wilson, June 8, 1918, Reel 4, ME-11; Wilson to Jackson, June 9, 1918, Reel 12, ibid.; Leigh to Sims, June 10, Reel 12, ibid.; Leigh to Sims, April 17, June 11, 1918, Box 65, Logistics file, RG45; entry for Nov. 3, 1918, Kipp Journal, author's private collection; Leigh Memoirs, Florida State University; Sims to Niblack, Nov. 13, 1918, Reel 12, ME-11; Tobey to Wilson, Sept. 20, 1918, Box 65, Logistics file, RG45; memo, March 18, 1918, ADM137/1621.

113. Memo, Director of Stores, July 15, 17, 1918, ADM137/2709; Walker to Malloy, April 20, 1918, OS file, subj file, RG45. For Sims's aide's quote, see Box 144, Sims Papers, LC; no date but probably spring 1918.

114. Callahan to Admiral Peoples, Dec. 18, 1920, Reel 47, Daniels Papers, LC; Foley, "Petroleum Problems of World War," 1806; entry for Dec. 7, 1917, Foley Diary, Foley Mission, QC subj file, RG45; Black to Bedford, Oct. 15, 1917, and Bedford's reply, Oct. 18, 1917, Reel 47, Daniels Papers, LC; "Building a Pipe Line across Scotland," 16.

115. Sims to Benson, March 7, 1918, Box 49, Sims Papers, LC; Sims to Dept., March 13, 1918, Reel 3, ME-11; Hurley to Black, July 30, 1918, ibid.; memo by Daniels, April 5, 1918, Reel 47, Daniels Papers, LC; Bureau of Supplies and Accounts Memo, April 5, 1918, Box 765, subj file, RG45; memo for McGowan, Sept. 10, 1918, Reel 5, ME-11; Sims to Dept., Sept. 8, 1918, ibid.; entry for Sept. 17, 1918, Foley Diary, Foley Mission, QC subj file, RG45; memo, Bureau of Supplies and Accounts, Oct. 16, 1918, file C-31-71, Confidential Files, RG80; *Scotsman*, Nov. 20, 1918; Barstow report of inspection trip to pipeline, Nov. 18–20, 1918, Reel 47, Daniels Papers; "Oil Pipe Line across Scotland," H. D. Vansant, American Consul, Dunfermline, Scotland, Nov. 22, 1918, in Dunfermline Consulate files, file 834, RG84.

116. Geddes to Lord George, Aug. 26, 1918, in M. Simpson, *Anglo-American Naval Relations*, 508; Trask, *Captains and Cabinets*, 294–95; Klachko, *Benson*, 117; Rowcliff to General Board, May 6, 1918, General Board Hearings, Wilkerson et al., *The American Petroleum Industry*, 278–79. See also entries in Foley Diary, April-October, 1918, Foley Mission, QC subj file, RG45.

117. Ships' Data U.S. Naval Vessels, Nov. 1, 1918, 446, 550; Stackhouse, "The Anglo-American Atlantic Convoy System in World War I," Ph.D. diss., 253; Clephane, *History of the Naval Overseas Transportation Service in World War I*, 211.

118. Memo, Plans Division, June 5, 1918, ADM137/2709; Sumida, "British Naval Operational Logistics," 467–69. See also E. Wilson, *Wings of the Dawn*, 5.

119. State Department to French Prefect, Brest, Aug. 4, 1917, French Naval Archives, Vincennes; Sims to First Sea Lord, July 16, 1917, Box 65, Logistics file, RG45; memo from First Sea Lord to Sims, July 21; Dept. to Sims, July 15, 1917, all in ibid.; Hilton to CNO, July 22, 28, 1917, Reel 1, ME-11; Sims to Dept., August 26, 1917, ibid.; Fletcher to Sims, Sept. 9, 16, 1917, OF subj file, RG45.

120. Sims to Dept., Aug. 30, 1917, Reel 2, ME-11; Murray L. Royar Oral History, USNI; Sims to SecNav, Jan. 21, 1918, CP subj file, RG45.

121. Sims to Dept., Feb. 24, 1918, Reel 19, ME-11; Sims to Dept., Feb. 28, 1918, Box 4395, RG143; R. B. Holt, *History of the U.S.S.* Harrisburg, 95; Wilson to Sims, Sept. 20, 1918, Box 65, Logistics file, RG45.

122. Sept. 25, 1918, Box 65, Logistics file, RG45. See also Sims to Pringle, May 28, 1918, Reel 20, ME-11.

123. *ONI Monthly Bulletin* (May 15, 1919): 26–27. See also Sims to CO, Patrol Squadron on French coast, Oct. 4, 1917, and to CO, *Bath*, Oct. 4, 1917, Reel 2, ME-11.

124. Sims to Dept., July 7, 1918, Reel 4, ME-11; Hurley, *The Bridge to France*, 101.

125. Sims to Wilson, Aug. 2, 1918, Reel 5, ME-11; "Summary of U.S. Naval Activities in European Waters," Z file, OA. Dudley Knox wrote to Frothingham after the war that "these ships really encountered greater danger than any other class of American ships for the reason that they never went to sea except in the war zone. They did not sail in convoy but individually and rarely if ever with any escort." March 18, 1926, Box 8, Knox Papers, LC; Dawes, *Journal of the Great War*, 28–35.

126. History of Bureau of Supplies and Accounts during War, ZU subj file, RG45; memo on auxiliary vessels, OC file, ibid.; Clephane, *History of the Naval Overseas Transportation Service in World War I*, 211.

127. Correspondence in file 502, Box 4395, RG143 on this topic; *Pall Mall Gazette*, March 6, 1919. See also Freeman, "Coaling the Fleet," 17.

128. Niblack to Sims, Feb. 3, 1918, Reel 9, ME-11; Sims to CO Patrol Squadron to be based at Gibraltar, Aug. 20, 1917, Box 64, Logistics file, RG45; see also undated journal of Hamilton Cochran, a Coast Guard officer on a cutter based at Gibraltar, in Coast Guard Library.

129. Sims Report, June 21, 1918, Reel 4, ME-11; Benson to Sims, June 1, 1918, ibid.; History of Bureau of Supplies and Accounts during War, ZU subj file, RG45; Bureau of Supplies and Accounts to CNO, July 25, 1917, Box 4395, RG143; Benson to Sims, Sept. 6, 1917, Box 4850, ibid., British Ambassador, Washington, to Daniels, July 9, 1917, Box 4395, ibid.

130. McGowan to Daniels, March 31, 1920, Reel 57, Daniels Papers, LC; Clephane, *History of Naval Overseas Transportation Service in World War I*, 211.

131. Blythe, "At a Naval Base," 21.

132. McGowan memo to Daniels, Aug. 8, 1918, Reel 57, Daniels Papers, LC. See also Allston, *Ready for Sea*, 190–91.

133. OS subj file, RG45. For examples of overstocking, see Sims Report, Aug. 16, 1918, Reel 5, ME-11.

134. Peter Smith to Sims, Aug. 29, 1931, Box 89, Sims Papers, LC.

135. CNO to Bureau of Supplies and Accounts, Jan. 2, 1918, file 421-5, Box 428, RG143; Dawes, *Journal of the Great War*, 2: 78–79. The AEF provided the Navy with some lumber, much of which was purchased in Switzerland.

136. The French charged the United States 20 percent to cover their expenses. *War Activities of the Bureau of Yards and Docks*, 429.

137. To Minister of Marine, May 9, 1918, French Naval Archives, Vincennes.

138. "Summary of U.S. Naval Activities in European Waters," Z file, OA; "Historical Sketch," Headquarters, Dec. 5, 1918, ZT subj file, RG45.

139. Furlong testimony, Oct. 3, 1918, General Board Hearings; Tobey memo, Nov. 8, 1918, Box 42, Logistics file, RG45.

140. Quoted in Adams, *Witness to Power*, 36. See also CO, *President Lincoln*, to Naval Port Officer, St. Nazaire, Feb. 19, 1918, File C-1-155, Confidential Files, RG80.

141. "Historical Sketch," Headquarters, Dec. 5, 1918, ZT subj file, RG45; Memo, n.d., Entry 136, Box 7, RG125; Sims to Wilson, Aug. 2, 1918, Reel 5, ME-11; Tobey to Operations, Box 42, Logistics file, RG45; Daniels to Sims, June 2, 1917, Box 42, ibid.; Sims to SecNav, May 30, 1917, TT subj file, RG45.

142. Pringle to all COs, July 23, 1917, Box 64, Logistics file, RG45; Property Accounting Office memo: May 12, 1922, Box 4580, RG143.

143. Sims to McGowan, July 16, 1918, Reel 4, ME-11; McGowan to Sims, July 18, 1918, ibid.

144. Geddes to Daniels, Oct. 10, 1918, Reel 36, Daniels Papers, LC; Sims to Dept., Oct. 12, 1918, Reel 6, ME-11; Twining Report, Oct. 28, 1918, ibid.

145. FDR Report, Oct. 16, 1918, Box 46, Assistant SecNav Files, FDR Library; Freidel, *FDR: The Apprenticeship*, 353.

146. Mcguire to Beale, Jan. 15, 1934, WA subj file, RG45; War Diary, U.S. Naval Forces in France, April 17, 1918, Box 10, Logistics file, RG45; memo, April 16, 1920, Box 42, ibid.

147. Quoted in Allston, *Ready for Sea*, 191.

Chapter 9. The "Gobs" Are Coming: Personnel

1. Thomas Washington, Chief of the Bureau of Navigation to Daniels, May 21, 1920, Reel 64, Daniels Papers, LC. A large number of the Navy's auxiliaries were manned by civilian seamen.

2. Ibid.; Josephus Daniels, *The Wilson Era: Years of War*, 126.

3. Josephus Daniels, *The Wilson Era: Years of War*, 131.

4. Notes on British and United States Naval Personnel, Jan. 1919, in *ONI Monthly Bulletin* (Feb. 1919): 111.

5. Entry for Sept. 1, 1917, War Diary, Commander U.S. Patrol Squadron, file OE subj file, RG45.

6. Nalty, *Blacks in the U.S. Military*, 91.

7. Godson, *Serving Proudly*, 65, 72–73; Ebbert and Hall, *The First, the Few, the Forgotten*, 11. Ebbert and Hall's book emphasizes women in the Marine Corps. Josephus Daniels, in *The Wilson Era: Years of War and After*, ignores women as naval nurses (see 211).

8. Fullam to Gleaves, May 3, 1918, William F. Fullam Papers, LC. See also Trench to Fullam, Oct. 6, 1918, ibid; Wheeler, *Pratt*, 101–2. Sims to SecNav, Aug. 9, 1917, Box 9, Entry 113, RG19.

9. Entry for October, n.d., 1917, Merrill Diary, Merrill Papers, UNC-CH.

10. See, for example, Lansing to Sims, Aug. 26, 1918, and Sims's reply, Sept. 16, 1918, in TD file, subj file, RG45.

11. Karsten, *The Naval Aristocracy*, 361; "memorandum," n.d., Morgan Diary, NHF, NHC. Reservists, particularly aviators, did complain at what they considered too many regulations at times. See MacLeish to "Pal," April 30, 1918, in Rossano, *The Price of Honor*, 152–53.

12. Donald Mitchell, *History of the Modern American Navy*, 191; Sprout and Sprout, *Rise of American Naval Power*, 319; Josephus Daniels, *The Wilson Era: Years of Peace*, 249; Taussig testimony, *Naval Investigation*, 1837–38.

13. Cooke, "Recollections," LC; Perry, *Our Navy in the War*, 242.

14. Finnegan, *Against the Specter of a Dragon*, 102; Harrod, *Manning the New Navy*, 36.

15. Millett, *Semper Fidelis*, 307

16. Plunkett testimony, *Naval Investigation*, 521.

17. To Mayo, May 6, 1918, Mayo Papers, LC. See also J. W. Jones, "U.S. Battleship Operations in World War I," Ph.D. diss., 159–62. For the gunnery problem, see chapter 16.

18. Report on Personnel, June 27, 1918, NA subj file, RG45. See also Sims to Bureau of Navigation, June 27, 1918, ibid.

19. Report on Personnel, June 27, 1918, NA subj file, RG45.

20. Sims, *The Victory at Sea*, 327–28; History of U.S. Naval Air Stations, Ireland, n.d., ZPA file, subj file, RG45; Roscoe, *On the Seas and in the Skies*, 86.

21. Sims to Dept., June 27, 1918, NA subj file, RG45; Sims to Dept., May 26, 1918, Reel 4, ME-11; History of U.S. Naval Air Stations, Ireland, ZPA subj file, RG45. For Sims's report, see Lord's MS on the "History of Naval Aviation," NDL.

22. Sims to Dept., Sept. 11, 1918, Reel 5, ME-1; Wiley, *An Admiral from Texas*, 179–80; Harry W. Hill Oral History, Columbia University; Sims to Dept., Sept. 11, 1918, Reel 5, ME-11; Lansing to Sims, Aug 26, and Sims's reply, Sept. 16, 1918, TD file, subj file, RG45.

23. Lansing to Sims, Aug. 26, and Sims's reply, Sept. 16, 1918, TD subj file, RG45. Sims to Dept., June 27, 1918, NA subj file, RG45; Sims to Dept., May 26, 1918, Reel 4, ME-11; History of U.S. Naval Air Stations, Ireland, ZPA subj file, RG45. For Sims's report, see Lord's MS on the "History of Naval Aviation," NDL.

24. "Atlantic Fleet in the War," copy in Reel 57, Daniels Papers, LC; Coffman, *The War to End All Wars*, 115–16. See also Reginald Wright Kauffman, *Our Navy at Work*, 17–18.

25. Hepburn Report, Nov. 30, 1919, OD subj file, RG45.

26. Payne questionnaire, World War I Research Collection, AMHI.

27. Sims, *The Victory at Sea*, 207. See also Brassey and Leyland, *The Naval Annual 1919*, 73; Sims to Dept., Aug. 13, 1918, Reel 5, ME-11.

28. Thompson to Leigh, May 10, 1918, copy in Cotten Papers, UNC-CH.

29. Sims to Bureau of Navigation, Oct. 21, 1918, OD subj file, RG45; Palmer to Sims, July 25, 1918, ibid. See also Sims Report, Aug. 1, 1918, Reel 5, ME-11.

30. Wilson to Sims, May 3, 1918, OF subj file, RG45; Magruder to Wilson, Jan. 2, 1918; Magruder, "The Navy in the War," 21; Magruder to Sims, Oct. 29, 1917, NA subj file, RG45; Fletcher to Sims, Oct. 27, 1917, OE subj file, ibid. See also Wilson to Force Commander, Jan. 2, 1918, OF file, subj file, RG45.

31. H. B. Wilson, *The American Navy in France*, 25.

32. Buranelli, *Maggie of the Suicide Fleet*, 12. See also Paine, "Our Navy on the French Coast," 14.

33. Rose, *Brittany Patrol*, 36; Davy, Report on Personnel, France, June 27, 1918, NA subj file, RG45.

34. Whitaker, *Hunting the German Shark*, 96–97. See also Whitaker, "Toy Dreadnoughts," 10–11; Battey, *70,000 Miles on a Submarine Destroyer*, 266.

35. To Sims, Nov. 11, 1917, NA subj file, RG45.

36. Conn to Sims, Nov. 11, 1917, Wilson to Sims, Nov. 17, 1917, Opinion of Court of Inquiry of the Loss of the USS *Alcedo*; Palmer to CNO, Nov. 17, 1917, Palmer to Sims, Nov. 17, 1917, all in OF subj file, RG45.

37. Commander P. E. Speicher, "Some Experiences with Mediterranean Convoys during the World War," lecture delivered at the Army War College, June 9, 1922, copy in AMHI.

38. Bertholf to Chief, Bureau of Navigation, May 11, 1917, July 22, 1918, file 631; RG26; Halligan to Commander Patrol Force, OF subj file, RG45; Sims to CNO, Aug. 15, 1917, OK file, ibid.; Cochran MS, Coast Guard Library; R. E. Johnson, *Guardian of the Sea*, 44–45; Halligan to vessels concerned, Sept. 1, 1917, OF subj file, RG45. For a detailed account of the Coast Guard in World War I, see Larzelere, *The Coast Guard in World War I*.

39. Whitaker, "The Mediterranean," 51; Harry L. Whitney et al., "A Brief Retrospective Summary of Our Work and Experience in the World War Aboard the U.S.S. *Algonquin, C.G.,* 1917–1919," copy in Cochran Papers, Coast Guard Library.

40. Harrod, *Manning the New Navy,* 85. For enlisted training in World War I, see Besch, *A Navy Second to None,* passim.

41. CO Richards Memoir, copy in author's possession. The author, who was in the Navy in the early 1950s, had only two weeks of "boot camp," plus one reserve cruise when he was assigned to a ship.

42. To Palmer, Sept. 25, 1917, Box 23, Sims Papers, LC; Benson to Sims, Aug. 30, 1917, Reel 2, ME-11.

43. Nov. 6, 1917, Box 9, Sims Papers, LC. Sims to CNO, Jan. 8, 1918, Reel 3, ME-11; entry for Oct. 5, 1917, entry for Oct. 5, 1917, in Taussig, *The Queenstown Patrol,* 149–50. For Sims's later efforts to address the problem, see Sims to Dept., May 9, 1918, Reel 4, ME-11; and Davy, Report on Personnel, June 27, 1918, NA subj file, RG45. This was the Navy's counterpart to the War Department's policy of training men in France.

44. Entry for Oct. 26, 1918, Division Nine War Diary, OB subj file, RG45; Moore Oral History, Columbia University; Levell, *"War on the Ocean,"* 23.

45. Post to mother, Aug. 22, 1918, Post Papers, LSU; Summary of Activities of U.S. Naval Forces in European Waters, Z file, OA; Sims to Dept., Aug. 6, 1918, Reel 5, ME-11; to Dept., Oct. 3, 1918, Reel 6, ibid.; Benson to Sims, April 15, 1918, Reel 19, ibid.; Sims to Wilson, Aug. 14, 1918, Reel 9, ibid.; Ross letter to author; *Illustrated London News,* Aug. 24, 1918.

46. Davy, Report on Personnel, June 27, 1918, NA subj file, RG45; Trask, *Captains and Cabinets,* 189–90; G. E. Wheeler, *Pratt,* 103–5; Niblack to Sims, March 18, 1918, Box 76, Sims, Papers, LC. Trask, *Captains and Cabinets,* 198–99; Wheeler, *Pratt,* 103–5; Niblack to Sims, March 18, 1918, Box 76, Sims Papers, LC; Farley to Sims, July 16, 1918, Box 24, Sims Papers, LC.

47. *Naval Investigation,* 1002, 1066–68; Gleichauf, *Unsung Sailors,* 10–11; G. E. Wheeler, *Pratt,* 106; Clephane, *History of the Naval Overseas Transportation Service in World War I,* 15–18. *Naval Investigation,* 1006. See also *American Legion Magazine,* March 1935, 42.

48. Beston, *Full Speed Ahead,* 253. See also Hicken, *The American Fighting Man,* 390.

49. Richardson, "My Visit to Our Sailor Boys," 26. See also Battey, *70,000 Miles on a Submarine Destroyer,* 266–67; Beston, *Full Speed Ahead,* 50–52.

50. Entry for June 22, 1918, Brown Journal, WisHistSoc.

51. Fraser and Gibbons, *Soldier and Sailor Words,* 250; *Pall Mall Gazette,* May 8, 1918.

52. "Jack Tar," used in the mid-nineteenth century, was no longer in popular usage. There is no evidence that the term *swabby* was used in World War I.

53. *New York Herald,* Oct. 17, 1918; *New York Evening News,* Aug. 24, 1918; *Broadside,* Sept. 25, 1918, 9.

54. Oct. 5, 1918, 6, 737–39. See also "What Is a Gob?" *Naval Reserve* 1 (Feb. 1918): 7; "Gobs, Not 'Jackies,'" 11; Beston, "My Friends, 'The Gobs,'" 62–63; Battey, *70,000 Miles on a Submarine Destroyer,* 302; *American Legion Monthly Magazine,* Dec. 1919, 46.

55. Gallent to Hall, June 16, 1919, Box 15, Morale Division files, RG24.

56. Quoted in D. M. Kennedy, *Over Here,* 185.

57. Harrod, *Manning the New Navy,* 146–50.

58. Husband, *A Year in the Navy,* 108–9; Battey, *70,000 Miles in a Submarine Destroyer,* 290. For the Brown quote, see his journal, n.d., WisHistSoc.

59. Malcolm Schoeffel Oral History, USNI. See also Ralph Helm Comford, "The Log of a United Sates Marine," Ralph Helm Comford Papers, P.C. 872, Personal Papers Collection, USMC Museum.

60. Entry for Nov. 28, 1917, Bellitteri journal, Marino Bellitteri Papers, ECU.

61. R. F. Nichols Memoir, Peter Liddle Archives. See also A. E. Smith, "The Sixth Battle Squadron," 54; McClellan, "American Marines in the British Grand Fleet," 143; Hayward, *HMS Tiger at Bay*, 159. See also Brown and Meehan, *Scapa Flow*, 69–71.

62. Quoted in Freeman, *Stories of the Ships*, 248–49.

63. Bartimeus, "Admiral Sims and His Fleet," 578; DeLany, *Bayly's Navy*, 11.

64. Aylmer to the Captain of the Fleet, March 2, 1918, ADM137/1898. See also F. Hunter, "Backing Beatty," 330; W. H. Miller, *The Boys of 1917*, 127; Broome, *Make A Signal!* 177; Signals—British and United States in *ONI Semi-Monthly Compilation*, ser. 60 (Nov. 1918): 2445–48; Rodman, *Yarns of a Kentucky Admiral*, 269; Mayo to Dept., Nov. 1, 1918, Box 10, Entry 113, RG19; Rowcliff testimony, May 6, 1918, General Board Hearings; Hutchinson, "The Sixth Battle Squadron," 266; entry for May 7, 1917, in Taussig, *The Queenstown Patrol*, 27–28; Davy Report on Personnel, June 27, 1918, NA subj file, RG45. For the game, see the Victor Blue Papers, UNC-CH.

65. Duff to Barthell, Sept. 10, 1917, Duff MS, National Maritime Museum, Greenwich, UK (hereafter cited as NMM); Mayo to Rodman, July 12, 1918, Mayo Papers. See also Freeman, *Stories of the Ships*, 263; M. Simpson, *Anglo-American Naval Relations,* 327; Report of Committee of U.S. Officers on Comparison between British and American Warships," Dec. 10, 1918, ibid., 358–60.

66. Entry for June 7, 1918, unknown seaman's diary, JOD/198, NMM; Carney Oral History, Columbia University.

67. Plunkett testimony, Oct. 2, 1917, Leahy testimony, Oct. 2, 1918, General Board Hearings.

68. See, for example, entry for Dec. 20, 1917, G. C. Harper Diary, Churchill College.

69. Hutchinson, "The Sixth Battle Squadron," 266. See also Lewis Ross to author, n.d., in author's possession.

70. Morison, *Sims*, 241; Sprout and Sprout, *The Rise of American Naval Power*, 275.

71. Mayo to SecNav, Nov. 1, 1918, Box 10, Entry 113, RG19; Plunkett testimony quoted in Kittredge, *Naval Lessons of the Great War*, 184–85.

72. Beatty to Wemyss, Jan. 31, 1918, Wemyss MSS; Rodman to Dept., March 2, 1918, OB subj file, RG45; Wemyss to Beatty, March 30, 1918, Beatty MS, NMM; Friedman, *U.S. Battleships*, 171–73; *Le Matin*, Aug. 15, 1918. See also chapter 16 on the battleships. Not all the British Grand Fleet personnel thought that the American ships had shot poorly in the initial practice. See entry for Jan. 24, 1918, Attrill Diary, Imperial War Museum, UK (hereafter IWM).

73. Rodman testimony, *Naval Investigation*, 859; See Oct. 20, 1918, OS subj file, RG45.

74. John McCrea Oral History, USNI; Bingham to Rodman, April 2, 1918, Bingham Papers, LC

75. Murmane, *Ground Swells,* 177.

76. McCrea Oral History, USNI; Rowcliff to Hoffman, May 11, 1918, USS *Arkansas* File, Ships History Branch, NHC.

77. Dreyer, *The Sea Heritage*, 455; Roskill, *Admiral of the Fleet Earl Beatty*, 243–44.

78. Rodman to Bingham, March 15, 1918, copy in Daniels Papers, LC; Egerton to Bingham, July 21, 1918, Bingham Papers, LC.

79. Egerton to Bingham, July 21, 1918, Bingham Papers, LC; See also Furlong, *Class of 1905*, 164.

80. Testimony of Leahy, Oct. 2, 1918, General Board Hearings.

81. Schoeffel Oral History, USNI; W. J. Wheeler, "Reminiscences of World War Convoy Work," 387. See also various entries, April-June 1918, Bathrop Diary, Smithsonian.

82. Stewart W. Gretzinger in S. Young, *Pen Pictures*, 79–81.

83. Lawrence to Kate, July 12, 1918, Lawrence Papers, WisHistSoc. This young reserve officer gives a most detailed account of a day at sea in 1918, describing what the officers and men did during the day.

84. Entry for Oct. 20, 1918, Joubert S. McCrea Journal, WWI Research Collection, AMHI.

85. "A Destroyer on Active Service," 545; Maxwell, *The Naval Front*, 185. See also Taussig, "Destroyer Experiences in the Great War," 69; Coffman, *The War to End All Wars*, 108.

86. USS *Paducah* manuscript, Wheeler Papers, Coast Guard Library; Cochran MS, Coast Guard Library; Journal of William R. Dawson, typed copy, n.d., in author's possession. See also Dunn, *World Alive*, 268

87. *American Legion Magazine*, March 1937, 38; ibid., April 1931, 31; Durlacher, "The Phantom Whistle," 721; entry for July 21, 1917, Russell Journal, USS *Walke* file, Z file, OA; "A Destroyer in Active Service," 545; Freidel, *Over There*, 54–55.

88. Quoted in Coffman, *The War to End All Wars*, 107. See also Mason, "Out with the Fog-Hounds," 413; Hunt, *One American*, 107.

89. "A Destroyer in Active Service," 546; *American Legion Magazine*, Aug. 1929, 43.

90. Blythe, "Contact!" 89.

91. Whitaker, "Smashing Hun Submarines with Sims."

92. Holloway, "Recollections, 1915–20," 19.

93. "A Sailor's Letters," Oct. 21, 1918, Box 56, Sims Papers, LC.

94. Moore Oral History, Columbia University.

95. Entry for July 11, 1917, in Wiggins, *My Romance with the Navy*, 93. See also Wallace, *A Sailor's Log*, 7–8; and Carney, "The Gob's Log," 27.

96. Connolly, "Our Dauntless Destroyer Boys," 9.

97. Entries for May 25, June 16, 1917, Merrill Diary, UNC-CH.

98. Blackford, *Torpedoboat Sailor*, 111–12.

99. Entry for Jan. 19–24, 1917, Morgan Journal, NHF.

100. Husband, *A Year in the Navy*, 247–49.

101. Moore Oral History, Columbia University.

102. Entries for Dec. 20, 24, 1917, Merrill Diary, UNC-CH.

103. Quoted in Freidel, *Over There*, 37–38.

104. Freeman, *Sea-Hounds*, 121; Levell, *"War on the Ocean,"* 27.

105. Whitaker, "Smashing Hun Submarines with Sims"; Connolly, *The U-Boat Hunters*, 195; Beston, *Full Speed Ahead*, 99; Coffman, *The War to End All Wars*, 107.

106. Battey, *70,000 Miles on a Submarine Destroyer*, 333–34.

107. H. L. Scott, *Some Memories of a Soldier*, 363.

108. Entry for June 10, 1918, Alexander Forbes Diary, copy in Box 58, Sims Papers, LC.

109. Quoted in Mason, "Out with the Fog Hounds," 418.

110. *Shipmate* 49 (Aug. 1986): 8; entries for March 23, 24, 1918, Kurfess Diary, OA; unidentified sailor, WWI questionnaire, World War I Research Collection, AMHI; entry for Nov. 1917, Merrill Diary, UNC-CH.

111. *Annual Report, Surgeon General, U.S. Navy, 1919*, 263. See also F. Green, *Our Naval Heritage*, 346–47.

112. Nutting, *Cinderellas of the Fleet*, 84–85; *Annual Report Surgeon General U.S. Navy, 1919*, 263; Edgar L. Bancroft in S. Young, *Pen Pictures*, 10–11; Blythe, "The Sea Terriers," 16, 83; Coffman, *The War to End All Wars*, 116–17.

113. Entry for June 18, 1918, Bathrop Diary, Smithsonian; Lawrence to Kate, Sept. 15, 1918, Lawrence Papers, WisHistSoc.

114. E. Brown, "Submarine Division Five," 849–53; Grady, "War History of Submarine Division Five," *Nautilus* Memorial and Submarine Force Library and Museum; Hart to Admiral, June 20, 1918, *Bushnell* File, Ships History Branch, NHC; Leigh memo, Nov. 15, 1918, TT subj file, RG45; Davy Report on Personnel, June 27, 1918, NA subj file, RG45; Leutze, *A Different Kind of Victory*, 60

115. Cochran MS, Coast Guard Library. See also Battey, *70,000 Miles on a Submarine Destroyer*, 272.

116. Entry for July 1, 1918, Brown Journal, WisHistSoc; Moore Oral History, Columbia University; Mason, "Out with the Fog-Hounds," 412.

117. Post to Edith, Oct. 22, 1918, Post Papers, LSU.

118. Harrod, *Manning the New Navy*, 148–49.

119. Loder to wife, Oct. 27, 1917, Loder Papers, Mariners' Museum; Post to Mother, Oct. 1, 1918, Post Papers, LSU.

120. George P. Slayback Memoir, NDL. See also entry for Dec. 1917, Brown Journal, WisHistSoc.

121. Entry for Friday, July 19, 1918, Slayback Memoir, NDL; unidentified sailor questionnaire, WWI Research Collection, AHMI; Inman letter to author, Nov. 17, 1989, in author's possession.

122. Entry for Jan. 28, 1918, Wiggins, *My Romance with the Navy*, 116.

123. *Annual Report Surgeon General U.S. Navy, 1919*, 267.

124. Chambers, *Submarine Chasers in the Mediterranean*, 46.

125. Moffat, *Maverick Navy*, 60–61.

126. See Lawrence to Kate, Oct. 17, 1918, Lawrence Papers, WisHistSoc; entries for March 2, 5, 1918, Kurfess Diary, OA; C. S. Alden, "American Submarine Operations in the War," 1023–24.

127. Royar Oral History, USNI; entry for Dec. 22, 1917, Brown Journal, WisHistSoc; Blythe, "Deep Sea Scouting," 28; entry for July 19, 1918, Slayback Memoir, NDL; *Broadside*, July 19, 1918, 30.

128. Wiggins, *My Romance with the Navy*, 121. See also *American Legion Magazine*, Aug. 1940, 32.

129. Balladeer, "The Cruise of the U.S.S. *Chester* in European Waters, 1917–18–19," Balladeer Papers, ECU.

130. *Naval and Military Record* 36 (Dec. 4, 1918): 773. See also Loder to Sweet hart, Dec. 1, 1917, Loder Papers, Mariners' Museum. For other accounts of holiday meals, see Stirling, "American Armed Yachts in the War Zone," 278; and *Torch* 30 (Jan. 1983): 5.

131. Boland, "The U.S.S. *Pocahontas* during the War," 461.

132. *Sphere*, Oct. 26, 1918, 66; C. M. Eady Memoir, IWM. See also *Daily Mail*, Dec. 27, 1918.

133. Hicken, *The American Fighting Man*, 213; Levell, "*War on the Ocean*," 17; "A Brief Retrospective Summary of Our Work and Experience Aboard the USS *Algonquin*," in the Cochran Papers, Coast Guard Library; Young questionnaire, World War I Research Collection, AMHI; Chapple, *We'll Stick to the Finish*, 210.

134. R. B. Holt, *History of the U.S.S.* Harrisburg, 129. See also *Arklight* 1, no. 12, copy in the papers of Eugene E. Wilson, microfilm, NDL; Karsten, *The Naval Aristocracy*, 92.

135. E. Kennedy to mother, Jan. 20, 1919, Richmond folder, Virginia War History Commission Records, Virginia State Library; Cooling, "Making Morale on a Man O' War," 31; Corrigan, *Tin Ensign*, 150.

136. Moffat, *Maverick Navy*, 120; W. G. Gerrard Memoir, Peter Liddle Archives; Paul Peter Fix, "World War I Bluejacket," Oral History, NHF; Murmane, *Ground Swells*, 178 (see also 255); Richmond and Hahn Questionnaires, World War I Research Collection, AMHI; Tighe, "Plunkett's Pirates," NDL; entry for March 8, 1918, Kurfess Diary, OA; entry for Nov. 11, 1917, Latimer Diary, UVA; Kleinstland, "A Saga of World War I"; Zogbaum, *From Sail to Saratoga*, 262; Wiggins, *My Romance with the Navy*, 92.

137. Oman, *Doctors Aweigh*, 120.

138. Washington to MacDougall, July 16, 1917, and MacDougall to Washington, July 14, 1917 in 834 file, Liverpool Consulate Records, RG84. For *Conyngham*'s goat, see Forbes diary, n.d., in

Box 58, Sims Papers. For rabbit, see entry for Oct. 1917, Brown Journal, WisHistSoc; and Battey, *70,000 Miles on a Submarine Destroyer*, 271.

139. See for example, Moffat, *Maverick Navy*, 103; Freeman, *Sea-Hounds*, 88; Moore Oral History, Columbia University; *Torch* 27 (June 1981): 3; Lawrence to Kate, Dec. 2, 1918, Lawrence Papers, WisHistSoc.

140. The tabloid rarely ran articles about the Navy, but when it did they were laudatory. See, for example, issues for March 1, Dec. 6, 1918. See also *Chicago Sunday Tribune*, Sept. 13, 1918. MacLeish to "Beloved," May 30, 31, June 2, 22, Aug. 8, 1918, in Rossano, *The Price of Honor*, 166–68, 170, 178, 198.

141. Josephus Daniels, *The Wilson Era: Years of War*, 187.

142. Ibid., 190.

143. Miles, "Ain't It the Truth," 12.

144. Josephus Daniels, *The Wilson Era: Years of War*, 190–91; I. W. Williams, "With Destroyers in the War Zone," 403–4. "Front Line Sailors of the A.E.F.," 20–27, 47. Most of the female nurses were provided by the American Red Cross. Kernodle, *The Red Cross Nurse in Action*, 159. The Navy did have a Nurse Corps approved by Congress in 1908. See Dock et al., *The History of American Red Cross Nursing*, 686–87, and Schneider and Schneider, *Into the Breach*, 108–9, 112–13.

A pharmacist mate on *Leviathan* was fourteen years old when he enlisted (said he was eighteen). Letter to author from his widow dated Dec. 5, 1989, enclosing article entitled "America's Youngest Legionnaire." For general medical history during the war, see Garrison, *Notes on the History of Military Medicine*, 195–98 (little information on naval medicine).

145. Pugh, "Education and Sanitation Aboard Ship," 254–66; See, for example, McCrea Oral History, USNI; and Davy, "Report on Personnel," June 27, 1918, NA subj file, RG45.

146. Josephus Daniels, *The Wilson Era: Years of War*, 192–93.

147. I. W. Williams, "With Destroyers in the War Zone," 403–6; Surgeon General to CNO, March 13, 1918, file 125125, RG52; to Chief, Bureau of Navigation, April 19, 1918, ibid.

148. CO *Wilkes* to Bureau of Medicine and Surgery, Jan. 14, 1919, file 130212, RG52.

149. Braisted to CNO, Oct. 19, 1918, file 130212; RG52; *Annual Report Surgeon General U.S. Navy*, 1918, 168. For other reports concerning drinking water, see file 130212, RG52. For statistics of health conditions in the fleet, see the *United States Medical Bulletin* for Aug. 21, 1917, March 1918, April 4, 1918, and June 16, 1919 in ibid.

150. Murmane, *Ground Swells*, 321.

151. Destroyer Flotilla at Queenstown, March 12, 1919, ZP subj file, RG45; Medical officer, *New York*, to Bureau of Medicine and Surgery, Feb. 10, 1918, April 25, 1918, file 125135, RG52; *Annual Report of the Secretary of the Navy*, 1919, 2318.

152. William N. Still, "Everybody Sick with the Flu," *Naval History* 16 (April, 2002): 36–40.

153. Quoted in Coffman, *The War to End All Wars*, 82. See also Crosby, *Epidemic and Peace*, 31–32; and Gabriel and Metz, *A History of Military Medicine,* 2: 251.

154. Coffman, *The War to End All Wars*, 83; Crosby, *Epidemic and Peace*, 205.

155. Quoted in Crosby, *Epidemic and Peace*, 121.

156. *Annual Report of Surgeon General U.S. Navy, 1919*, 367–68. For the epidemic at the Portsmouth (New Hampshire) Naval Shipyard, see Winslow, *"Do Your Job!"* 119.

157. Talley to wife, July 8, 1918, Talley Letters, OA. See also Talley to wife, June 30, 1918, ibid.; Lawrence to Kate, Nov. 18, 1918, Lawrence Papers, WisHistSoc; Meals, "The Air Station at Dunkirk," 12–13; "History of United States Naval Aviation French Units," NDL.

158. Thompson, *Take Her Down*, 250–51; Alden, "American Submarine Operations in the War," 1031; *Report of Secretary of the Navy, 1919*, 2201–2; Grady, "War History of Submarine Division Five"; E. W. Brown, "Submarine Division Five," 847. For the Sixth Battle Squadron, see *Annual Report Surgeon General U.S. Navy, 1919*, 150–51; McCrea Oral History, USNI; VanSant

to Secretary, American Red Cross, April 30, 1918, file 814.2, London Embassy Records, RG84; Medical officer, *New York*, to Bureau of Medicine and Surgery, June 26, 1918, file 125135, RG52; Marwick, *The Deluge*, 257; *Report of Secretary of the Navy*, 1918, 2414. For the subchasers at Plymouth, see *Annual Report Surgeon General U.S. Navy, 1919*, 261–62; Medical Officer Plymouth to Bureau of Medicine and Surgery, February 1919, file 132564, RG52. For Queenstown, see Destroyer Flotilla at Queenstown, March 12, 1919, ZP subj file, RG45.

159. Balladeer, "The Cruise of the U.S.S. *Chester* in European Waters, 1918–1919," in the Bellitteri Papers, ECU; Willoughby, *Yankton—Yacht and Man-of-War*, 211; Medical officer, Nashville, to Bureau of Medicine and Surgery, June 8, 1918, file 125135, RG52; Crosby, *Epidemic and Peace*, 26.

160. Thomson to Braisted, July 26, 1918, file 2127046, RG52; to the Bureau of Medicine and Surgery, ibid.

161. T. Wilson, *The Myriad Faces of War*, 650; J. Williams, *The Home Fronts*, 258.

162. Cotten to Force CO, Aug. 9, 1918, OD subj file, RG45; Medical Officer, Plymouth to Bureau of Medicine and Surgery, Feb. 1919, file 132564, RG52; Medical Officer, Plymouth to Bureau of Medicine and Surgery, Oct. 7, 1918, file 130212, ibid.; *Annual Report Surgeon General U.S. Navy, 1919*, 261–62; Moffat, *Maverick Navy*, 122–23.

163. *Annual Report of the Secretary of the Navy*, 1919, 2246; Sanderson, "The Worst Disaster in Recorded History," 114; Crosby, *Epidemic and Peace*, 45–46, 56–57; Hoehling, *The Great Epidemic*, 24–25; Coffman, *The War to End All Wars*, 82; *Portsmouth Herald*, Sept. 17, Oct. 1, 1918; Wilson to COs, all ships and stations in France, Sept. 2, 1918, file 130212, RG52.

164. Burch, "I Don't Know Only What We Hear!" 23. The author mistakenly considered the station Army rather than Navy. See also Report of Medical Officer, USS *Mercy*, Oct. 31, 1918, file 130212, RG52; Morrisey, "The Influenza Epidemic of 1918," 11–19.

165. Crosby, *Epidemic and Peace*, 48.

166. Ibid., 153.

167. Alex Breth statement, WWI Research Collection, AMHI. See also Connolly, *Sea-Borne*, 210–11.

168. Oct. 5, 1918, in Venzon, *General Smedley Darlington Butler*, 205–6; Thomas, *Old Gimlet Eye*, 247.

169. Rose, *Brittany Patrol*, 299; entry for Oct. 19, 1918, Brown Journal, WisHistSoc; Medical Officer, *Norma*, to Bureau of Medicine and Surgery, file 130212, RG52; John H. Hoover Oral History, Columbia University; Post to Nelvis, Sept. 28, 1918, Post MS; Wilson to Sims, Sept. 15, 1918, NA subj file, RG45; Murdock, *They Also Served*, 81; Talley to Braisted, Sept. 15, Nov. 15, 1918, file 130212, RG52.

170. *The U.S.S.* Mount Vernon, 134–35. See also Medical officer *Tenadores*, to Bureau of Medicine and Surgery, "at sea," file 132212; RG52; Holt *U.S.S.* Harrisburg, 80; War Diary, Brest, Dec. 20, 1918, OF file, subj file, RG45; John C. Taylor to folks, Oct. 2, 1918, John Clayton Taylor Papers, ECU.

171. Base Hospital No. 5, Historical File, Bureau of Medicine and Surgery, Washington, D.C. See also Connolly, *Navy Men*, 240–42; Autobiography of W. D. MacCourt, Hospital Corpsman, copy in the author's possession; Talley to Braisted, Nov. 15, 1918, file 130212, RG52; Talley to wife, Sept. 23, 29, Oct. 9, Talley Letters; *Annual Report of Surgeon General U.S. Navy, 1919*, 191–92.

172. *Army and Navy Journal* 56 (1918), 979.

173. *Annual Report of Surgeon General U.S. Navy*, 1919, 241, 254–55; Hoehling, *The Great Epidemic*, 104.

174. Curl to Surgeon General, Oct. 18, 1918, file 131000, RG52; H. B. Wilson, *The American Navy in France*, 101. For the individual air stations, see Medical officer, La Trinité, to CO, Nov. 30, 1918, file 120212, RG52; Garrison, "The United States Naval Air Station, Pauillac, Gironde

France," 613; Garrison to Surgeon General, Nov. 7, 1918, file 131000, RG52; Medical Officer to Force Commander, Nov. 30, 1918, file 130212, ibid.; "History of U.S. Naval Aviation French Units," NDL; District Medical officer to District Commanding Officer, Sept. 24, 1918, file 130212; Robert Gilbert memoir, typed from his journal, in possession of author; *Annual Report Surgeon General U.S. Navy*, 1919, 241, 150, 256.

175. Hooper, "The Lafayette Radio Station," 28–29.

176. Belknap, *The Yankee Mining Squadron*, 89. See also *Christian Science War Time Activities*, 820–21; and Albert Harris letter, Nov. 1977 in World War I Research Collection, AMHI; Corrigan, *Tin Ensign*, 101; *New York Herald*, Jan. 20, 1919; Memo for Bureau of Medicine and Surgery, Oct. 20–26, 1918, file 130212; *Annual Report Surgeon General, U.S. Navy*, 1919, 246.

177. Destroyer Flotilla at Queenstown, March 12, 1919, ZP subj file, RG45; Force medical officer to Sims, Nov. 1, 1918, file 125135, RG52; Flotilla Surgeon's reports, Oct. 12, 19, 1918, file 131000, ibid.; Force medical officer to Bureau of Medicine and Surgery, Oct. 26, 1918, file 130212, ibid., Carney Oral History, Columbia University; Dock et al., *The History of American Red Cross Nursing*, 727–28; Capelotti, *Our Man in the Crimea*, 30; *Naval and Military Record* 36 (Nov. 6, 1918): 717; Levell, *"War on the Ocean,"* 44.

178. Dock and Pickett, *History of American Red Cross Nursing*, 728.

179. CO Naval Air Stations, Ireland to Force Commanding Officer (Aviation), Dec. 30, 1918, file 130212, RG52; Medical officer, Wexford to Bureau of Medicine and Surgery, Dec. 21, 1918, ibid., "History of U.S. Naval Station, Wexford, Ireland," ZPA subj file, RG45.

180. *Oklahoma General Recall* 4, no. 3 (Sept. 1977); Todd, *USS Oklahoma*, 20; Olaf M. Hustvedt Oral History, USNI.

181. Rodgers to Sims, Oct. 26, 1918, OB subj file, RG45; Guy Ricketts Diary and Memoirs, Smithsonian.

182. Hustvedt Oral History, USNI; Thompson, *Take Her Down*, 261; Memo for Bureau of Medicine and Surgery, Oct. 26, 1918, file 130212, RG52. See also Wilkinson, "The U.S.S. *Nevada* and Her Experiences in the War," 1; *USS Nevada: The Cheer Up Ship*, 8. CO subchaser detachment to CNO, Oct. 12, 1918, file 131000-14, RG52; J. W. Jones, "U.S. Battleship Operations in World War I," 203–4; Fife, *The Passing Legions*, 246–47; Bassett to Sims, Nov. 23, 1918, MR subj file, RG45.

183. McCrea Oral History, USNI; Bush, *Bless Our Ship*, 82.

184. Harry Hill Oral History, Columbia University; Straubat to Anderson, Dec. 1, 1977, in WWI Research Collection, AMHI; entry for Oct. 24, 1918, Pressprick Diary, copy in author's possession; *ONI Monthly Compilation*, ser. 64 (Dec. 15, 1918): 2524; Memo for Surgeon General, Oct. 6, 1918, file 130212, RG52. Murmane, *Ground Swells*, 258–59. See also entry for Oct. 23, 1918, Pressprick Diary; Rodman to Sims, Oct. 26, Nov. 2, 9, 1918, OB subj file, RG45; Rodman to Dept., Nov. 9, 1918, ibid. See also Daniel Schenk Memoir, Smithsonian. On using masks, see *Annual Report Surgeon General, U.S. Navy*, [1919?], 67. More than one doctor recommended whiskey as a "cure." One correspondent wrote, "The service cure in Brest was to get next to a quart of rye whiskey, and stay by it, and when that was gone, get a replacement." Connolly, *Sea-Borne*, 211.

185. A. E. Smith, "The Sixth Battle Squadron," 57; Bush, *Bless Our Ships*, 82; Marder, *From the Dreadnought to Scapa Flow* 5: 170–73.

186. *Annual Report Surgeon General, U.S. Navy 1919*, 151. See also "A Sick Bay in Scotland," 36–41.

187. Base CO to Sims, Oct. 5, 1918, P-Cardiff subj file, RG45; Memo for Surgeon General, Oct. 12, 1918, file 131000, RG52; Fife, *The Passing Legions*, 294, 299.

188. MacLeish to Beloved, Sept. 23, 1918, Rossano, *The Price of Honor*, 216.

189. Medical officer to Bureau of Medicine and Surgery, Nov. 30, 1918, file 130212, RG52;

"Sanitary Report, Dec. 31, 1918, ibid.; Freeman to Braisted, Nov. 3., 1918, file 131000, RG52; Memo from medical officer to Surgeon General, Oct. 5, 1918, ibid.; Bludworth, *The Battle of Eastleigh*, 43, 45.

190. October 18, 1918, Box 24, Sims Papers, LC.

191. Medical officer, Bolsena to Bureau of Medicine and Surgery, Nov. 19, Dec. 23, 1918, file 130212, RG52; Medical officer, Porto Corsini, to Bureau of Medicine and Surgery, Dec. 1, 1918, ibid.; Medical officer, Naval Headquarters, Rome to Force CO (Aviation), Nov. 30, 1918, ibid., Lord, "History of Naval Aviation," NDL; Wayne Duffett to family, Oct. 18, 30, 1918, Wayne Duffett letters, Emil Buehler Naval Aviation Library.

192. Entries for Sept. 24, 26, Oct. 22, 1918, Kipp Diary, copy in author's possession.

193. Extract from General Report sent to Bureau of Medicine and Surgery, Sept. 27, 1918, file 130212, RG52; Nelson to Sims, Nov. 2, 1918, reel 12, ME-11; to Sims, Oct. 28, 1918, Box 11, Logistics file, RG45; Medical Officer patient report, Nov. 3–12, 1918, ibid.

194. Nutting, *The Cinderellas of the Fleet*, 188; *Report of the Secretary of the Navy*, 1918, 2245; Dunn to Sims, Oct. 27, 1918, Reel 10, ME-11.

195. *Annual Report Surgeon General, U.S. Navy, 1919*, 188–89; Dunn to Sims, Oct. 9, Dec. 5, 1918, file 130212, RG52. No information has been located of the number of American deaths (if any) at Ponta Delgada.

196. Entry for Sept. 23, 1918, Thomas Hatton Diary, copy in author's possession.

197. Crosby, *Epidemic and Peace*, 148–49. The daughter of a seaman who served on the *Olympia* in Russian waters mentioned a letter written in 1919 by her father from the Adriatic Sea in which he said that flu was on board the ship again, but it "is not so bad as the one we had in Russia." Ann Cantrell to author, April 21, 1987, copy in author's possession.

198. To Dept., Oct. 5, 18, 1918, file 130212, RG52. Different message, same date, in ON subj file, RG45. See also Sims to wife, Oct. 12, 1918, Box 10, Sims Papers.

199. To Benson, Oct. 11, 1918, Box 49, Sims Papers, LC. See also USS *Birmingham* war diary, Oct. 10, 1918, OS subj file, RG45.

200. MacCourt Autobiography, copy in author's possession.

201. The files in RG52, particularly file 130212, contain reports from virtually every ship and station medical officer concerning measures they took as preventatives. See also *Stars and Stripes*, December 13, 1918; Pugh, "Education and Sanitation Aboard Ship," 255–66; Willoughby, *Yankton—Yacht and Man-of-War*, 227–28; Moffat, *Maverick Navy*, 122–23; Kleinatland, "A Saga of World War I," author's private collection.

202. *Annual Report of Surgeon General, U.S. Navy, 1919*, 354; Coffman, *The War to End All Wars*, 84; Crosby, *Epidemic and Peace*, 206.

203. Quoted in Sanderson, "The Worst Disaster in Recorded History," 113.

204. Unidentified sailor's questionnaire, WWI Research Collection, AMHI. See also Oman, *Doctors Aweigh*, 226.

205. The Navy's efforts against vices, including prostitution, will be treated elsewhere. This section concentrates on VD and the health problems it created.

206. Fosdick, *Chronicle of a Generation*, 162.

207. General Board Hearings, Nov. 1, 1917.

208. Quoted in Schaffer, *America in the Great War*, 103. See also Harrod, *Manning the New Navy*, 135; and Brandt, *No Magic Bullet*, 114.

209. Josephus Daniels, *The Wilson Era: Years of War*, 195–97. See also Brandt, *No Magic Bullet*, 58–59.

210. Louis P. Davis Oral History, ECU. See also Gulick, *Morals and Morale*, 33; Smythe, "Venereal Disease," 701; Ferrell, *Woodrow Wilson and World War I*, 62.

211. J. W. Jones, "U.S. Battleship Operations in World War I," Ph.D. diss., 123.

212. Moffat, *Maverick Navy*, 115–18.

213. Cochran Memoir, Cochran Papers, Coast Guard Library.

Chapter 10. For the Boys: Welfare

1. Drury, *The History of the Chaplain Corps*, 1: 181.

2. W. A. Maguire, *Rig for Church*, 73–76; *Christian Science War Time Activities*, 318; Beston, *Full Speed Ahead*, 172–75; Drury, *History of the Chaplain Corps*, 1:172, 188; Davis to Force Commander, Aug. 2, 1918, Box 11, Logistics file, RG45; Josephus Daniels, *The Wilson Era: Years of War*, 201–2.

3. To Bayly, June 8, 1918, Box 47, Sims Papers, LC.

4. Quoted in P. Borden, *Civilian Indoctrination of the Military*, 102.

5. *Literary Digest*, Feb. 15, 1919, 97.

6. Entry for April 17, 1917, in Josephus Daniels, *Cabinet Diaries*, 189. See also Harrod, *Manning the New Navy*, 131; Brandt, *No Magic Bullet*, 59; and Fosdick, *Chronicle of a Generation*, 142–43.

7. Welfare Section to Chief of Staff, Simsadus, November 25, 1918, TT subj file, RG45; *Daily Mail* (London), June 12, 1918. The British Sailors Society approached American officials about a canteen for sailors. Capper, *Aft-From the Hawsehole*, 228.

8. Sims to Director, YMCA France, Dec. 22, 1917, MR subj file, RG45.

9. Memo of meeting with Sims, Oct. 22, 1917, 814 file, London Consulate Records, RG84.

10. *Cork Examiner*, Nov. 29, 1918; Davy, Report on Personnel, June 27, 1918, NA subj file, RG45. Entry for May 7, 1917, Taussig, *The Queenstown Patrol*, 28, Note 98, 189; Taussig, "Destroyer Experiences during the Great War," 234; Moore Oral History, Columbia University.

11. June 21, 1918, Reel 4, ME-11.

12. Copy in Box 95, Logistics file, RG45.

13. Pringle to Sims, Oct. 19, 1917, Box 79, Sims Papers, LC; Destroyer Flotilla at Queenstown, March 12, 1919, ZP subj file, RG45. See also "The United States Naval Men's Club," brochure, copy in Logistics file, Box 95, RG45; Pringle to Brownrigg, Oct. 19, 1917, ibid.; entries for July 3, 9, 26, 1917, Fagan Diary, Mariners' Museum; *Glasgow Herald*, Oct. 25, 1918; entry for September 8, 1917, Latimer Diary, UVA. Before the war ended, the club had paid off its debt and had accumulated a cash reserve. Mayo to wife, Sept. 14, 1918, Mayo Papers, LC; Sims to Dept., Box 95, Logistics file, RG45; Sims Report, June 21, 1918, Reel 4, ME-11; *Army and Navy Journal* 56 (March 16, 1918): 1067; entry for June 30, 1917, in Taussig, *The Queenstown Patrol*, 72.

14. Box 379, subj file, RG45.

15. Entry for July 26, 1917, Fagan Diary, Mariners' Museum; Whitaker, "Sims' Circus When it Gets Shore Leave"; Leighton, *Simsadus*, 32–33. See also Whitaker, *The German Shark*, 96–97.

16. Entry for Feb. 26, 1918, Kurfess Diary, OA.

17. Beston, *Full Speed Ahead*, 96; Chapple, *We'll Stick to the Finish*, 222; The United States Naval Men's Club Brochure, copy in Box 95, Logistics file, RG45. Cooking was done on huge gas ranges and a grill in full view of the diners. See Press Release, copy in WS subj file, RG45.

18. Taussig later wrote that "it was rumored" that Bayly would not visit the club until an American destroyer "brought in a German submarine." He did so after *U-58* surrendered to the *Fanning*. Taussig, "Destroyer Experiences during the Great War," 235.

19. Brownrigg, *Indiscretions of the Naval Censor*, 255; Mayo to wife, Sept. 14, 1918, Mayo Papers, LC; FDR to Daniels, July 27, 1918, Box 45, Assistant SecNav Files, FDR Library. See also *Naval and Military Record* 36 (Aug. 14, 1918): 524; entry for Sept. 26, 1917, Latimer Diary, UVA; Blackford, *Torpedoboat Sailor*, 122–23; Churchill, *A Traveler in War Time*, 42.

20. Entry for June 7, 1917, Russell Journal, USS *Walke* file, CZ file, OA; Memo to Sims, May 23, 1917, TT subj file RG45.

21. Darius A. Davis to Commandant De Salners, French Ministry of Marine, May 17, 26, 1917, French Naval Archives, Vincennes; Sayles to Sims, May 18, 1917, TRP subj file, RG45; Mayo,

"*That Damn Y,*" 21–22. Later two prominent American ladies, Mrs. Vincent Astor and Mrs. Theodore Roosevelt Jr., took charge of this first Navy canteen in France. Schneider and Schneider, *Into the Breach*, 126. For the YMCA in the war years, see Odell, "Spiritual Realities and High Explosives," 697–703; Hopkins, *History of the Y.M.C.A. Movement in North America*, 485–503; *Summary of World War Work of the American YMCA*, 12–23; Taft, *Service with Fighting Men*, 2: 94, 464–65.

22. To General in command of Eleventh Regiment, Jan. 17, 1918, French Naval Archives, Vincennes; Moreau to the French Minister of Marine, Jan. 24, 1918, ibid.

23. VanSant, American Consul, Dunfermline, to American Red Cross, April 10, 30, May 30, 1918; to chaplain, USS *New York*, April 30, 1918; and to E. W. Austin of the American Red Cross, all in file 814.2, Dunfermline Consulate Records, RG84.

24. Armstrong, Report of Bureau of Naval Services, American Red Cross Commission to Great Britain, file 941.11/08, Box 842, RG200; Fife, *The Passing Legions*, 91, 300–301; "Plymouth Red Cross," in file 941.08, Box 840, RG200; Page to Davidson, July 31, 1917, TT subj file, RG45; Memo for Admiral Sims, May 26, 1918, Box 91, Sims Papers; entries for Aug. 27, 29, 1917, in Josephus Daniels, *Cabinet Diaries*, 197–98. John F. Hutchinson's book, *Champions of Charity: War and the Rise of the Red Cross*, does not address either World War I or the Navy.

25. Report of the American Red Cross Commission for Great Britain, Part 2, Camp Service, file 941.08, RG200; Fife, *The Passing Legions*, 284–85; Schneider and Schneider, *Into the Breach*, 95; Kleinatland, "A Saga of World War I," author's private collection. The Red Cross, however, did not provide athletic uniforms. Austin to VanSant, American Consul, Dunfermline, May 18, 1918, 814.2 file, Dunfermline Consulate Records, RG84.

26. Acker to Armstrong, Feb. 10, 1919, 959.61 file, Gibraltar, RG200.

27. Memo to Dept., Feb. 28, 1918, Reel 3, ME-11; P. Borden, *Civilian Indoctrination of the Military*, 12; Egan and Kennedy, *Knights of Columbus in Peace and War*, 1: 264–79, 323–26. Fosdick was also concerned about the "multiplication of social agencies" but was unable to do much about it. Fosdick, *Chronicle of a Generation*, 170. The Irish Catholics were hostile to the Y probably because it had been traditionally a British institution.

28. *Christian Science War Time Activities*, 178–79, 318–21, 326–29.

29. Chief Housing Officer to U.S. Consul, Newcastle, Aug. 2, 1918, file 886, Newcastle Consulate records, RG84; Consul Washington to CO USS *Conyngham*, March 20, 1918, file 832, Liverpool Consulate Records, ibid.

30. O'Neill to American Consul, n.d., Edinburgh, 832 file, Edinburgh Consulate Records, RG84; Washington, American Consul, Liverpool to Tobey, Aug. 8, 9, 1917, file 832, Liverpool Consulate Records, RG84; Consul, Dunfermline, to Secretary of State, May 23, 1918, file 814.2; Dunfermline Consulate Records, ibid.; to Grant Forbes, London, October 22, 1919; to Skinnon, Dec. 18, 1917, file 833, ibid.; to Logan Ramsay, Nov. 4, 1918, file 851, ibid.

31. Report of meeting, July 10, 1917, file 814, London Consulate Records, RG84; Quoted in Mayo, "*That Damn Y,*" 20. Only the Brest site was identified.

32. *Summary of World War Work of the American YMCA*, 13; Hopkins, *History of the American Y.M.C.A. Movement in North America*, 409.

33. Mayo, "*That Damn Y,*" 48; Niblack, "Putting Cargos Across," ZCP subj file, RG45.

34. *Our Navy* 12 (Feb. 1919): 28.

35. *New York Herald*, Apr. 3, 1918; entry for May 14, 1918, Brown Journal, WisHistSoc.

36. See the memo of May 26, 1918, NA, subj file, RG45; Schneider and Schneider, *Into the Breach*, 123.

37. Gleaves to Transport Force, April 5, 1918, NA subj file, RG45; Force Transport Officer to Gleaves, June 29, 1918, ibid.; Memo for Admiral Sims, May 26, 1918, Box 91, Sims Papers; Schneider and Schneider, *Into the Breach*, 123; Taft, *Service with Fighting Men*, 2: 381.

38. Sims to Carter, Dec. 22, 1917, NA subj file, RG45; Carter to Sims, Jan 14, 1918, Box 91, Sims

Papers; entry for May 15, 1918, Talley Letters, OA. F.D.R. would later write that soldiers continued to use the Navy Y facilities "as there is no place provided for them in town." To mother, Jan. 11, 1919, in Elliott Roosevelt, *F.D.R.: Personal Letters*, 449.

39. Talley to wife, entry for Aug. 25, 1918, Talley Letters, OA.

40. Entry for Oct. 1917, Brown Journal, WisHistSoc. See also Taft, *Service with Fighting Men*, 1: 99–102; Rose, *Brittany Patrol*, 57, 250–52; Vaughan, *The Gates Diary and Letters*, 44–45.

41. Sullivan, *With the Yanks in France*, 35. See also M. Baldwin, *Canteening Overseas*, 18–19.

42. M. Baldwin, *Canteening Overseas*, 49–53.

43. Janis, *So Far, So Good*, 198.

44. "History of U.S. Naval Aviation, French Unit" copy in NDL; U.S. Naval Air Station, Le Croisic, France, ZPA subj file, RG45.

45. Copeland, "Steel Tower Construction at the World's Greatest Radio Station," 1918. See also CO Richards Memoirs, author's private collection; Naval Air Station, Tranquier, France, n.d., ZPA subj file, RG45.

46. Taft, *Service with Fighting Men* 1: 75–76.

47. MacNaughton to Sims, Sept. 12, 1918, Box 91, Sims Papers, LC; "U.S. Naval Aviation Forces Foreign Service," Recreation Bulletin No. 6 (June, 1918); in GA subj file, RG45. See also "Y.M.C.A. Girls in Emerald Isle," *New York Post*, Feb. 20, 1919, and U.S. Naval Air Station at Lough Foyle, ZPA subj file, RG45.

48. Sanitary Report, December 31, 1918, Killingholme, file 13212, RG52; *Fleet Review* 9 (Dec. 1918): 20–21; entry for May 2, 1918, Charles Fahey Diary, LC; Taft, *Service with Fighting Men*, 1: 75.

49. Bludworth, *The Battle of Eastleigh*, 114.

50. Medical officer, Plymouth, to Bureau of Medicine and Surgery, February 17, 1919, file 132564, RG52; *Naval and Military Record*, April 17, 1918, 253; Report of Committee, American YMCA London, December 3, 1917, file 814, London Consulate Records, RG84; D. Sinclair, *Dynasty*, 295; Walling, *The Story of Plymouth*, 248–49; Langhorne, *Nancy Astor*, 78.

51. Report of Committee, American YMCA, file 814, RG84, London Consulate Records. This file contains numerous references to the Y activities in these two ports. See also Washington to Noll, Feb. 19, 1918, file 814.2, Liverpool Consulate Records, RG84; Washington to Leighton, Aug. 22, 1917, 820 file, ibid.

52. Report of Committee, American YMCA, London, Jan. 8, 1918, file 814, London Consulate Records, RG84.

53. They did establish a canteen in the Orkneys after the Armistice to service the American sailors on the minesweepers removing the North Sea Mine Barrage. *Army and Navy Journal* 51 (June 28, 1919): 1912–13. The structure that housed the Y was named the "Birds' Nest" because American minesweepers were named after birds (ibid.); Taft, *Service with Fighting Men*, 1: 78.

54. *Evening News* (Edinburgh), Aug. 31, 1918. See also American Consul, Edinburgh to Consul-General, London, Dec. 17, 1917, file 822, Edinburgh Consulate Records, RG84; *Scotsman*, March 4, April 28, 1918.

55. To SecNav, Nov. 20, 1918, Box 10, Logistics file, RG45. See also Report of Committee, YMCA, London, March 4, 1918, file 814, London Consulate Records, RG84; Tomb to Belknap, Nov. 3, 1918, Belknap Papers, NHF; Historical data, mine bases, Sept. 21, 1918, ZA subj file, RG45. See also Simon P. Fullinwider memoir, Fullinwider Papers, Smithsonian.

56. To wife, Sept. 27, 1918, Mayo Papers, LC.

57. To Sims, Sept. 18, 1918, Box 24, Sims Papers, LC.

58. "Putting Cargos Across," ZPC subj file, RG45; Niblack to Sims, Sept. 18, 1918, Box 76, Sims Papers, LC; entry for Aug. 6, 1918, Eady Memoir; IWM: Cochran memoir, Cochran Papers, Coast Guard Library.

59. *Daily Chronicle* (London), Sept. 4, 1917.

60. July 18, 1918; *Pall Mall Gazette*, Aug. 25, 1917. See also conference notes, YMCA meetings, July 10, Aug. 8, 1917, 814 file, London Consulate Records, RG84; *Kansas City Star*, Nov. 21, 1918; Taft, *Service with Fighting Men*, 2: 80–81; *Summary of World War Work of the American YMCA*, 20–22; *Cork Examiner*, Sept. 4, 1917; *Daily Telegram* (London), Sept. 7, 1917; Mayo to wife, Oct. 8, 1918, Mayo Papers, LC; Wiggins, *My Romance with the Navy*, 100; *New York Herald*, April 28, 1918; Stuart, "All for 'Our Boys' in London," 686–87; *Army and Navy Journal* 55 (Sept. 8, 1917): 46.

61. See vol. 71, London Consulate Records, RG84. See also Wiggins, *My Romance with the Navy*, 100.

62. Apparently there was some substance in the pacifist argument. Ambassador Page wrote to the secretary of state informing him of letters from YMCA workers obtained through British postal censorship that indicated "extreme" pacifism (Jan. 16, 1918, 814 file, London Embassy Records, RG84). See, for example, letter from Lylse to father, Dec. 3, 1917, vol. 71, London Consulate Records, ibid. See also entry for Sept. 12, 1918, Brown Journal, WisHistSoc; and Coffman, *The War to End All Wars*, 78–79. See P. Borden, *Civilian Indoctrination of the Military*, 108–9.

63. Entry for Nov. 20, 1918, Brown Journal. See also Tighe, "Plunkett's Pirates," NDL; *Stars and Stripes*, April 5, 1918; Jimmy Lynch to family, March 26, 1918, Lynch Letters, Virginia War History Commission Records, Virginia State Library. See also Todd, *USS* Oklahoma, 17; Schneider and Schneider, *Into the Breach*, 122–23; Cornebise, *War As Advertised*, 104–5; Gulick, *Morals and Morale*, 22; Sullivan, *With the Yanks in France*, 35–36, 46–47; Ferrell, *Woodrow Wilson and World War I*, 63–64; Harrison, *With the American Red Cross in France*, 259–67. For the Y's explanation, see Odell, "Spiritual Realities and High Explosives," 701–2; Hopkins, *The American YMCA Movement in North America,* 497–502.

64. Quoted in Mayo, *"That Damn Y,"* 357–58. For the Army, see Cornebise, *War As Advertised*, 106–7.

65. Cornebise, *War As Advertised*, 88–89. See also Schneider and Schneider, *Into the Breach*, 123; Cornebise, *War As Advertised*, 106–7.

66. See, for example, Duffett to family, Sept. 4, 1918, Duffett Papers, National Museum of Naval Aviation.

67. *Our Navy* 13 (May 1919): 41; entry for Oct. 26, 1918, in Chase, *Benjamin Lee, 2d*, 273; letters for April 5, Sept. 15, 1918, Talley Letters; *American Legion Magazine*, May 9, 1940, 35; W. A. Maguire, *Rig for Church*, 77–78; *Fleet Review* 9 (Dec. 1918): 24; 10 (July 1919): 27; *United States Naval Air Station Killingholme*, 21.

68. Niblack, "Putting Cargos Across, ZCP subj file, RG45; Sims to Niblack, Sept. 1918, Box 24, Sims Papers, LC.

69. *Summary of World War Work of the American YMCA*, 22; Taft, *With the Fighting Men*, 1: 79; YMCA Committee, London, June 6, 1918, file 814, London Consulate Records, RG84; Sykes, *The Life of Lady Nancy Astor*, 206; Sinclair, *Dynasty*, 296; Chase, *Benjamin Lee, 2d*, 152.

70. To wife, Oct. 10, 1918, Mayo papers, LC. See also Ellyson to wife, Oct. 8, 1918, Reel 1, Ellyson microfilm, NDL. In Liverpool, the Midland Railroad donated the use of the Adelphi Hotel, which it owned, as an officers' club. Midland Railroad to Washington, American Consul, Liverpool, Sept. 1, 1917, file 832, Liverpool Consulate Records, RG84; Pringle to Washington, Sept. 24, 1917, 820 file, ibid.; Niblack, "Putting Cargos Across," ZCP subj file, RG45; *Glasgow Herald*, April 30, 1919.

71. Walker, *Venereal Disease in the American Expeditionary Forces*, 193.

72. Karsten, *The Naval Aristocracy*, xiii, 51–52; P. Borden, *Civilian Indoctrination of the Military*, 125–26.

73. Letter, Oct. 19, 1917, Talley Letters, OA. See also Paine, *The* Corsair *in the War Zone*,

200–201. No information has been located to explain who started it and where the money came from.

74. Sims to Pringle, June 9, 1918; Pringle to Sims, June 12, 1918, Box 79, Sims Papers, LC; Hayes, *Hull Down*, 227; Braynard, *The Story of the* Leviathan, 1: 177; letters for July 14, 27, 1918, Talley Letters, OA.

75. Paine, *The* Corsair *in the War Zone*, 201.

76. Taussig, "Destroyer Operations in the Great War," 383; Connolly, *The U-Boat Hunters*, 108; Thompson, *Take Her Down*, 221, 225; Halsey, *Admiral Halsey's Story*, 27.

77. Morgan Diary, n.d., NHF; Zogbaum, *From Sail to Saratoga*, 243

78. Beston, *Full Speed Ahead*, 85; entries for March 13, 20, 1918, Kurfess Diary, OA. Kurfess said that the Royal Cork Yacht Club was most popular with the commanding officers; junior officers preferred the hotel.

79. The Ellyson Papers in the NDL have numerous references to being entertained in Plymouth. See also Moffat, *Maverick Navy*, 118–20; Taussig, "Destroyer Experiences during the Great War," 404; and American Consul to SecState, Jan. 6, 1918, file 832, Liverpool Consulate Records, RG84.

80. See, for example, Zogbaum, *From Sail to Saratoga*, 267–73; Fletcher testimony, Case 10622, RG125.

81. Of the J. P. Morgan and family and later commodore of the New York Yacht Club.

82. Moore Oral History, Columbia University. See also Peter J. Capelotti, *Our Man in the Crimea*, 25–26.

83. For a French impression of entertainments on *Prometheus*, see *Le Matin*, May 28, 1918.

84. Vol. 1, no. 1 (Aug. 5, 1918): 2.

85. *New York Herald*, April 6, 1919. See also Ruggles, *The Part the U.S.S.* Von Steuben *Played in the Great War*, 36; CO Richards Memoirs, copy in author's possession; *Fleet Review* 9 (Sept. 1918): 26–27; L. J. Collins, *Theater at War*, 97.

86. *Daily Mail* (London), Feb. 6, 1918; *Summary of World War Work of the American YMCA in North America*, 13; Hopkins, *The American YMCA Movement*, 409; *New York Herald*, European edition, Jan. 3, 1919; CO Richards Memoirs, copy in author's possession. This memoir is a detailed account of how one sailor became involved in a group of entertainers from L'Aber Vrach Naval Air Station that performed in Brittany and later Paris.

87. *New York Post*, Jan 6, 1919. See also the *Oklahoma General Recall* 11 (Jan. 1975): 6; and ibid. 4 (Dec. 1977): 355.

88. *Sporting News* (London), November 6, 1918; *Pall Mall Gazette*, Dec. 9, 1918; *Daily Graphic* (London), Dec. 14, 1918. See also *Fleet Review* 9 (Sept. 1918): 26–28; and Sims to Anne, Sept. 23, 1918, Box 10, Sims Papers, LC. See also F. J. Egger to author, April 18, 1988, in author's possession.

89. Sims to Chaplain Duff, Feb. 19, 1919; memo for Admiral Sims, Feb. 16, 1919; Duff to Sims, March 5, 1919, all in Box 54, Sims Papers, LC.

90. Pringle to Sims, Dec. 8; Sims to Pringle, December 9, 1918, Box 79, Sims Papers, LC.

91. Dulles, *History of Recreation*, 218–19.

92. Rodman to Sims, May 14, 1918, ZOB subj file, RG45; Murmane, *Ground Swells*, 256.

93. In addition to the *Wyoming* Cruise Book (*U.S.S.* Wyoming: *At War in the North Sea, 1917–1918*), see Nicholson to author, July 20, 1987, copy in author's possession. Nicholson served on *Texas*.

94. Brown and Meehan, *Scapa Flow*, 67; "In the North Sea," 18. See also Schubert, *Come on Texas*, 168; Egger letter to the author. For the movies, see Wilson Oral History, Columbia University; and Beston, *Full Speed Ahead*, 158.

95. *Fleet Review* 9 (June 1918): 24–25; (Aug. 1918): 34–35; Murmane, *Ground Swells*, 255–57; *Torch* 3 (May 1983); Boswell Notes, Peter Liddle Archives; Egger letter to author.

96. Entry for July 28, 1918, Witherspoon Diary, Witherspoon Family Papers, WWI Research Collection, AMHI. This diary entry gives a good description of the show.

97. Hill Oral History, Columbia University; *U.S.S.* Wyoming: *At War in the North Sea, 1917–1918*; *A Brief History of the U.S.S.* Texas, 41; The Story of the U.S.S. Texas 4–10. See also Burrows, *Scapa Flow and a Camera*, 35. For other Navy minstrel groups, see "U.S. Naval Air Station Le Croisic, France." ZPA subj file, RG45; *Fleet Review* 9 (Dec. 1918), 30; CO Richards Memoirs, copy in author's possession; Talley to wife, Feb. 24, 1918, Talley Letters, OA.

98. Dulles, *A History of Recreation*, 368–69.

99. Wilson to Sims, Aug. 30, 1918, Box 10, Logistics file, RG45; CO Richards Memoirs, copy in author's possession; U.S. Naval Aviation Forces, Foreign Service Recreation Bulletin, Aug. 5, Sept. 14, 1918, GA subj file, RG45; Land W. Latimer to author, Nov. 19, 1989, letter in author's possession; *Arklight* 1, no. 21, 1918, copy in Eugene E. Wilson Papers, Reel 1, NDL. This paper was published by USS *Arkansas*.

100. John A. Beatty Memoir, WWI Research Collection, AMHI. See also *Fleet Review* 10 (Jan. 1919): 29; *Fixem*, Aug. 5, 1918; History of USS Naval Air Station Lough Foyle, ZPA subj file, RG45; see also *American Legion Magazine*, Dec. 1939, 36.

101. Niblack to Sims, Sept. 19, 1918, Box 24, Sims Papers, OA; "A Brief Retrospective Summary of Our Work and Experience in the World War aboard the USS *Algonquin*," unpublished MS, Hamilton Cochran Papers, Coast Guard Library.

102. Entry for June 22, 1918, F. Foxen Diary, Peter Liddle Archives; U.S. Naval Aviation Forces, Foreign Service Recreation Bulletin No. 17, Sept. 14, 1918, GA subj file, RG45; entry for July 3, 1917, Fagan Diary, Mariners' Museum. See also R. B. Holt, *U.S.S.* Harrisburg, 129.

103. Rose, *Brittany Patrol*, 94; Murdock, *They Also Served*, 32.

104. Wheeler, "Reminiscences of World War Convoy Work," 386–87; Chase, *Benjamin Lee, 2d*, 272; U.S. Naval Aviation Forces, Foreign Service Recreation Bulletin No. 13, Aug. 5, 1918, GA subj file, RG45; Bulletin No. 5, May 25, 1918, ibid.; Willoughby, Yankton—*Yacht and Man-of-War*, 214.

105. Entry for Oct. 1917, Brown Journal, WisHistSoc.

106. Entry for Feb. 26, 1918, Witherspoon Diary, Witherspoon Family Papers, WWI Research Collection, AMHI.

107. Entry for Oct. 16, 1918, Brown Journal, WisHistSoc; entry for Aug. 8, 1918, Taussig Diary, NWC.

108. Belknap, *The Yankee Mining Squadron*, 87.

109. Entries for Aug. 4, Oct. 21 and 28, 1918, unknown seaman's diary, JOD/198, NMM.

110. CO Richards Memoirs, copy in author's possession.

111. Entry for Nov. 1917, Brown Journal, WisHistSoc. See also U.S. Naval Aviation Forces, Foreign Service Recreation Bulletin, No. 13, Aug. 5, 1918, GA subj file, RG45.

112. Murdock, *They Also Served*, 70–71.

113. *United States Naval Air Station Killingholme*, 51.

114. Cornebise, *War As Advertised*, 107.

115. Schneider and Schneider, *Into the Breach*, 156. *The Big Show* is an autobiographical account of her experiences in the war.

116. Autobiography of W. P. McCourt, copy in author's possession.

117. H. B. Wilson, *The American Navy in France* includes a list of important visitors and entertainers who gave performances in Brest, 170–76. See also Evans and Harding, *Entertaining the American Army*, 24, passim.

118. Ibid., 71.

119. Entry for Sept. 22, 1918, USS *Oklahoma* Deck Log, RG24.

120. D. M. Kennedy, *Over Here*, 353.

121. *New York Sun*, April 28, 1918; Murdock, *They Also Served*, 50; Chase, *Benjamin Lee, 2d*, 201.

122. Neither of these was described. See Ellyson to Nina, Oct. 20, 1918, Reel 1, Ellyson Papers, NDL; *Pauillac Pilot*, Sept. 7, 1918.

123. Corrigan, *Tin Ensign*, 106, 152; Rossano, *The Price of Honor*, 87; Weiss Questionnaire, WWI Research Collection, AMHI; Ellyson to wife, Aug. 28, 31, 1918, Reel 1, Ellyson Papers; Chase, *Benjamin Lee, 2d*, 217–19; *Cork Examiner*, Jan. 20, 1919.

124. E. V. Whited Memoir, Smithsonian. See also R. B. Holt, *U.S.S.* Harrisburg, 12; *Inverness Courier*, Dec. 3, 1918.

125. Murmane, *Ground Swells*, 345. For Astor quotation, see *Literary Digest*, Feb. 1, 1919.

126. Sammons, *Beyond the Ring*, 48–49; Betts, *America's Sporting Heritage*, 36; Filene, *Him/Her/Self*, 93–94; Cozens and Stumpf, *Sports in American Life*, 195.

127. Stumpf, *Sports in American Life*, 198–200; P. Borden, *Civilian Indoctrination of the Military*, 126–28; History of Lough Foyle Naval Air Station, n.d., ZPA file subj file, RG45; *Our Navy* 13 (May 1919), 41; Mayo, *"That Damn Y,"* 26.

128. Taft, *Service with Fighting Men*, 1: 102.

129. See, for example, memo, Dec. 22, 1917, P subject file, RG45

130. R. B. Holt, *History of the U.S.S.* Harrisburg, 136.

131. To Bureau of Medicine and Surgery, Feb, 1919, file 132564, RG52.

132. Entry for April 24, 1918, Kurfess Diary, OA; Moore Oral History, Columbia University.

133. Cochran MS, Coast Guard Library.

134. *Fleet Review* 9 (July 1918): 28.

135. Ibid.

136. F. T. Hunter, *Beatty, Jellicoe, Sims, and Rodman*, 132; *Westminster Gazette*, November 20, 1918; Rodman to Beatty, Oct. 10, 1918, copy in Reel 59, Daniels Papers, LC. See also *Fleet Review* 9 (Oct. 1918): 56.

137. *The Northern Barrage: Mine Force*, 88–89; *Fixen* 1 (Aug. 5, 1918): 3, copy in the Belknap Papers, LC; *Fleet Review* 9 (Sept. 1918): 31–32.

138. R. B. Holt, *History of the U.S.S.* Harrisburg, 134. See also Rose, *Brittany Patrol*, 57.

139. Holt, *History of the U.S.S.* Harrisburg, 134

140. For examples of these activities, see entry for Sept. 9, 1917, Russell Journal, USS *Walke* file, CZ Files, OA; Corrigan, *Tin Ensign*, 102–3, 189–91; Duncan, "Before and After," *Marksman* 1 (April 20, 1919): 1–2; Richmond questionnaire, WWI Research Collection, AMHI; Ellyson to wife, Aug. 14, 1918, Reel 1, Ellyson Papers, NDL; Koehler to mother, Jan. 28, 1919, private collection; provided author by P. J. Capelotti. See also Capelotti, *Our Man in the Crimea*, 34–35.

141. See, for example, the *Bridgeport* in *Our Navy* 13 (Sept. 1919): 51; *Dixie* in *Fleet Review* 9 (Oct., Dec. 1918): 27, 31.

142. Thompson, *Take Her Down*, 192.

143. Destroyer Flotilla at Queenstown, March 12, 1919, ZP subj file, RG45; *New York Herald*, July 5, 1918.

144. A valuable and detailed source for athletic events in the war zone are the recreation bulletins published weekly by the U.S. Naval Aviation Forces, Foreign Service. Copies can be found in the GA subj file, RG45.

145. Medical officer to Sims, Jan. 7, 1919, file 132570, Box 604, RG52.

146. For Gibraltar, see Nelson to Niblack, Oct. 18, Nov. 5, 1918; Niblack to Patrol Squadron, Gibraltar, Nov. 15, 1918, all in Box 94, Logistics file, RG45.

147. Duffett to family, July 30, 1918, Duffett Papers, National Museum of Naval Aviation; Moore Oral History, Columbia University; *Kansas City Star*, Aug. 10, 1918.

148. Dulles, *A History of Recreation*, 242, 357. Considering the climate in Europe, basketball would have been an ideal sport. However, it was purely an American game at that time, one of

the few major sports that was not derived from an English sport. Only a few basketball courts were built in the war zone during the war.

149. Thompson, *Take Her Down*, 192.

150. *Navy and Military Register* 35 (Dec. 18, 1917): 754. See also Chapple, *We'll Stick to the Finish*, 130; entries for July 27, Aug. 13, 18, 20, 21, Sept. 3, 1917, Russell Journal, USS *Walke* file, CZ Files, OA; entry for May 9, 1918, Kurfess Diary; OA; Beston, *Full Speed Ahead*, 94; entry for June 12, 1917, in Taussig, *The Queenstown Patrol*, 57; *The Northern Barrage: Mine Force*, 89,

151. *United States Naval Air Station Killingholme*, 17.

152. Ibid., 19; *Fleet Review* 9 (Dec. 1918): 22; entry for Oct. 26, 1918, Chase, *Benjamin Lee, 2d*, 272; Sanitary Report, Killingholme, Dec. 31, 1918, file 130212, RG52; Bludworth, *The Battle of Eastleigh*, 102.

153. Paine, *The First Yale Unit*, 81.

154. Entry for Nov. 28, 1918, Brown Journal, WisHistSoc.

155. Entries in Bases logs, RG24; Clarence Anderson questionnaire, WWI Research Collection, AMHI.

156. *Arklight* 1, no. 23, copy in Reel 1, Wilson Papers, NDL; entry for Oct. 22, 1918, Witherspoon Diary, Witherspoon Family Papers, AMHI.

157. Murmane, *Ground Swells*, 328–33.

158. Nov. 29, 1918. See also the *Army and Navy Record* 36 (Dec. 1918) 813, for a description of a game played at Weymouth.

159. Dulles, *A History of Recreation*, 226

160. Sammons, *Beyond the Ring*, 50; Cooling, "Making Morale on a Man-of-War," 31; Harrod, *Manning the New Navy*, 134; F. T. Hunter, *Beatty, Jellicoe, Sims, and Rodman*, 137; *The Story of the USS* Texas, 56; *Fleet Review* 9 (Oct. 1918): 28; U.S. Naval Aviation Service Foreign Service, Recreation Bulletin No. 3: 10, May 25, August 10, 1918, GA subj file, RG45; Tighe, "Plunkett's Pirates," NDL; *Chicago Tribune*, March 1, 1919.

161. "Edinburgh's Poor Bairns," *Fleet Review* 9 (Sept. 1918), 39–40; *New York Herald*, Aug. 3, 1918.

162. May 11, 1918, Box 10, Sims Papers, LC.

163. H. Seymour, *Baseball*, 1: 330 (see also 337–40).

164. Ibid., 333.

165. Quoted in Murdock, *They Also Served*, 56. See also the *New York Herald*, March 16, July 2, 1918; Betts, *America's Sporting Heritage*, 136–37; H. Seymour, *Baseball*, 1: 332; Wycoff, *Ripley County's Part in the World War*, 164–65.

166. H. Seymour, *Baseball*, 1: 332.

167. Entry for July 29, 1917, in Taussig, *The Queenstown Patrol*, 83. For baseball at Queenstown, see *Fleet Review* 9 (Oct. 1918): 28; entry for June 18, 1917, Merrill Diary, UNC-CH; entry for July 25, 1917, Fagan Diary, Mariners' Museum; *Cork Examiner*, July 26, 1917; Sterne, *Over the Seas for Uncle Sam*, 64–65. For baseball throughout the Navy in World War I, see GA-1 subj file, RG45.

168. *Killingholme Naval Air Station*, 15, ZE file, OA; *Fleet Review* 9 (Dec. 1918): 21–22.

169. VanSant to the *New York* athletic officer, May 29, 1918, file 840.6, Dunfermline Consulate Records, RG84. See also F. T. Hunter, *Beatty, Jellicoe, Sims, and Rodman*, 135–37; Burrows, *Scapa Flow and a Camera*, 18; *Scotsman*, July 25, 1918.

170. *Daily Mail*, September 7, 1918.

171. Wile, *Explaining the Britishers*, 19–21. See also the *Cork Examiner*, July 17, 21, 1917.

172. *Daily Mail*, June 28, July 4, 1918; *Pall Mall Gazette*, Aug. 5, 1918; *Cork Examiner*, July 17, 26, 1917.

173. MacLeish to beloved, April 15, 1918, in Rossano, *The Price of Honor*, 142; Paine, *The First*

Yale Unit, 2: 297; Mims, "Take Me Out to the Ball Game," 110; Corrigan, *Tin Ensign*, 81–83, 188–90; Hewitt to Canage, Aug. 6, 1918, copy in Belknap Papers, LC.

174. *The Northern Barrage: Mine Force*, 88; Corrigan, *Tin Ensign*, 85; *Fleet Review* 9 (Oct. 1918): 25; (Sept. 1918): 31–32; 10 (July 1919): 35; *Fixen* 1 (Aug. 1918): 3; Belknap, *The Yankee Mining Squadron*, 49–50, 87.

175. Murmane, *Ground Swells*, 272, 301–2. See also the *Arklight* 1, no. 38, in Reel 1, papers of E. Wilson, NDL; *The Story of the U.S.S. Texas*, 65–68; Rodman to Sims, May 23, 1918, OB subj file, RG45; U.S. Naval Aviation Foreign Service Recreation Bulletin No. 1, May 11 1918, GA subj file, RG45.

176. Pringle in Queenstown would not permit teams to travel to Dublin or even Cork to play other teams. Pringle to Sims, May 30, 1918, Logistics file, RG45. See also *American Legion Magazine*, May 1930, 33; U.S. Naval Aviation Foreign Service, Recreation Bulletin No. 5, June 5, 1918, GA subj file, RG45; Corrigan, *Tin Ensign*, 29–30. To Sims, May 30, 1918, Logistics file, RG45; May 24, 1918, ibid.; Sims to Pringle, June 3, 1918, Box 53, Sims Papers, LC; Sims to wife, May 18, 1918, Box 10, ibid.; Rodman to Sims, May 28, 1918, Box 81, ibid.; Cross to Sims, April 22, 1918, Box 53, ibid.; H. Seymour, *Baseball*, 3: 344; *Pall Mall Gazette*, Aug. 1, 1918.

177. Mims, "Take Me Out to the Ball Game," 109; *Daily Telegraph*, May 31, 1918; *Daily Mail*, May 20, 1918; *Pall Mall Gazette*, May 20, 1918; Wilson Cross to Sims, May 21, 1918, Box 53, Sims Papers, LC.

178. MacLeish to "pal," Aug. 6, 1918, MacLeish letters, private collection provided author by Geoffrey Rossano. See also excerpt from the letter in Rossano, *The Price of Honor*, 197. See also U.S. Naval Aviation Foreign Service Recreation Bulletin No. 3, May 25, 1918; Bulletin No. 17, Sept. 14, 1918; Bulletin No. 10, Aug. 10, 1918, all in GA subj file, RG45; *Our Navy* 12 (Sept. 1919): 51; H. Seymour, *Baseball*, 3: 337–38; Cooling, "Making Morale on a Man O' War," 31; History of Pauillac Naval Air Station, Feb 15, 1919, ZPA subj file, RG45.

179. Translation of Ponta Delgada newspaper article dated July 6, 1918. in Box 55, Sims Papers, LC; copy of article from the *South Wales Daily News*, July 5, 1918, in part 7, Cardiff Consulate records, RG84; Corrigan, *Tin Ensign*, 144.

180. To Daniels, July 1, 1918, Reel 65, Daniels Papers, LC. See also Sims to wife, June 13, 1918, Box 10, Sims Papers, LC. For newspaper accounts of the scheduled event, see *Daily Mail*, June 26, 27, 29, 1918; *Daily Sketch*, June 29, 1918; *Daily News*, July 3, 1918; *Boston Herald*, June 13, 1918; Beston, *Full Speed Ahead*, 201.

181. *Daily Mirror*, July 7, 1918; *Daily News*, July 6, 1918; Sims to wife, July 6, 1918, Box 10, Sims Papers, LC; Blythe, "At a Naval Base," 109; *Literary Digest*, Aug. 10, 1918. Later he signed a new ball, which was mounted in a case and presented to President Wilson. For photographs of the event, see *Illustrated London News* 151 (July 13, 1918).

182. *Stars and Stripes*, July 7, 1918; *Daily Chronicle*, July 5, 1918; *Literary Digest*, Aug. 10, 1918; J. F. Newton, *Preaching in London*, 99; Beston, *Full Speed Ahead*, 202–3.

183. *Kansas City Star*, Aug. 21, 1918; and *Chicago Tribune*, Paris edition, May 3, 1919.

184. Halleran to CO Brest, Feb. 2, 1918, NA subj file, RG45.

185. MacLeish to "Beloved," April 27, 1918, in Rossano, *The Price of Honor*, 149–50.

186. *New York Herald*, April 11, 1918; U.S. Naval Aviation Foreign Service, Recreation Bulletin No. 5, June 10, 1918, GA subj file, RG45; H. Seymour, *Baseball*, 3: 342.

187. Willoughby, *Yankton—Yacht and Man-of-War*, 214–15; Niblack, "Putting Cargos Across," ZCP subj file, RG45.

188. Entry for March 28, 1918, Moseley, *Extracts from Letters*, 154–55. See also U.S. Naval Aviation Foreign Service, Recreation Bulletin No. 3, May 25, 1918, GA subj file, RG45.

189. Hoy, *40 or How the War Was Won*, 84; Mock, *Censorship 1917*, 109.

190. Entry for June 12, 1918, in Taussig, *The Queenstown Patrol*, 56.

191. MacLeish to "Beloved," March 3, 1918, in Rossano, *The Price of Honor*, 109.

192. Talley Letters, May 29, June 26, 1918, Talley Papers, LC.

193. See, for example, the Ellyson correspondence to his wife in the Ellyson MSS, reel 1, NDL.

194. Cornebise, *The Stars and Stripes*, 108. See also the April 12, 1918 issue for a tongue-in-cheek criticism of this by a bluejacket. For one of the rare articles about the Navy, see the June 9, 1919, issue.

195. To CNO, June 27, 1918, NA subj file, RG45.

196. Fife, *The Passing Legions*, 342–45.

197. R. B. Holt, *History of the U.S.S.* Harrisburg, 134. See also FDR diary letter in Elliott Roosevelt, *F.D.R.: Personal Letters*, 436.

198. Cooling, "Making Morale on a Man O' War," 31; Taft, *Service with Fighting Men*, 2: 104.

199. U.S. Naval Air Station Lough Foyle, ZPA subj file, RG45; U.S. Naval Aviation Forces, Foreign Service Recreation Bulletin No. 7, June 10, 1918, GA file, ibid.; Bulletin No. 17, Sept. 14, 1918, ibid. For the Army's program, see P. Borden, *Civilian Indoctrination of the Military*, 134–37.

200. U.S. Naval Aviation Forces, Foreign Service Recreation Bulletin No. 6, May 1918, GA subj file, RG45; entry for May 30, 1918, Balladeer Diary, Balladeer Papers, ECU; Charles Moore Oral History, Columbia University.

201. U.S. Naval Aviation Forces, Foreign Service Recreation Bulletin No. 10, Sept. 14, 1918, GA file, RG45; Nelson to Simsadus, Sept. 14, 1918, Box 10, Logistics file, RG45; *Our Navy* 12 (Dec. 1918): 65.

202. Fife, *The Passing Legions*, 132; Rose, *Brittany Patrol*, 131.

203. Rose, *Brittany Patrol*, 15.

204. *Cork Examiner*, Dec. 26, 28, 1917; letters for Dec. 23, 25, 26, 1917, Talley Letters, OA; entry for Dec. 26, 1917, Brown Journal, WisHistSoc; Whitaker, "Sims' Circus When It Gets Shore Leave."

205. Rose, *Brittany Patrol*, 15.

206. *Edinburgh Evening News*, Dec. 25, 1917; Rodman to Navy Dept., Dec. 30, 1917, C-31-1, Confidential Correspondence, 1917–1919, RG80; F. T. Hunter, *Beatty, Jellicoe, Sims, and Rodman*, 132; entry for Dec. 27, 1917, Packer Diary, Packer MS, Churchill College; Rodman, "The Christmas Ship," 888; Rodman, *Yarns of a Kentucky Admiral*, 274–75; "*New York*'s Christmas Party," 18; "Edinburgh's Poor Bairns," 36–37; A. E. Smith, "The Sixth Battle Squadron," 54–55; *Scotsman*, Dec. 2, 1918.

207. *Inverness Courier*, Dec. 26, 1918; Jan. 3, 1919; Andrews to Sims, Dec. 28, 1918, P-Cardiff subj file, RG45.

208. Talley to wife, May 22, 1918, Talley Letters, OA; *American Legion Magazine*, Dec. 1931, 47–48.

209. Duffett to family, Dec. 26, 1918, Duffett Papers, National Museum of Naval Aviation;

210. Nouailhat, *Les Americains a Nantes et St. Nazaire*"; Roger, *Les Americains a Brest pendant la premiere guerre mondial*; *United States Naval Air Station Killingholme*, 17; speech of Reginald Belknap, June 1, 1940, Belknap Papers, NHF.

211. "A Brief Summary of U.S. Naval Forces in France, November 11, 1918–October 1, 1919," OA; Josephus Daniels, *Our Navy at War*, 361; *Stars and Stripes*, May 9, 1919.

212. *New York Herald*, January 1, 1918.

213. MacLeish to "Beloved," in Rossano, *The Price of Honor*, 74–75. See also Thompson, *Take Her Down*, 305.

214. July 4, 1917. See also *Globe*, July 4, 1918; *Times* (London), July 4, 5, 1918; *Daily Telegraph*,

July 5, 1917; C. H. Hunter, "Anglo-American Relations during the Period of American Belligerency," Ph.D. diss., 706–7.

215. Duffett to family, July 4, 1918, Duffett Papers, National Museum of Naval Aviation.

216. Willoughby, Yankton—*Yacht and Man-of-War,* 229–33.

217. For celebration on ships, see *American Legion Magazine,* Dec. 1939, 39.

218. Jameson, *The Fleet That Jack Built,* 238.

219. Hewison, *The Great Harbour-Scapa Flow,* 167; *Orcadian,* July 11, 1918. For those not on liberty, the *Florida* held a smoker. *Fleet Review* 9 (Sept. 1918): 24–25.

220. Entry for July 4, 1918, Thomas Hatton Diary, copy in author's possession.

221. Entry for July 4, 1918, OS subj file, RG45.

222. Entry for July 4, 1918, Thomas Hatton Diary, copy in author's possession.

223. Talley to wife, July 5, 1918, Talley Letters, OA; see also Admiral Wilson to Kerney, July 5, 1918, Box 343, file CPI-18A1, Records of the Committee on Public Information, RG63.

224. Adams, *Paris Sees It Through,* 286–87. "Big Bertha" was the name given to huge German artillery pieces (420mm mortars) firing on the city from the German lines.

225. *Sun* (London), July 5, 1918; Sims to Dept., July 11, 1918, Reel 4, ME-11; Moore Oral History, Columbia University; *Naval and Military Record* 35 (July 10, 1918); Pringle to Sims, July 6, 1918, Box 79, Sims Papers, LC; *Fleet Review* 9 (Dec. 1918): 21; entry for July 4, 1918, Balladeer Diary, Balladeer Papers, ECU.

226. *South Wales Daily News,* July 5, 1918, copy in part 7, Cardiff Consulate records, RG84. For other celebrations in Great Britain, see the *Daily Chronicle* (London), July 5, 1918.

227. *Edinburgh Evening News,* July 4, 1918; Taft, *Service with Fighting Men,* 2: 85–86; *Scotsman,* July 5, 1918; *Daily Mail,* June 26, July 5, 1918; Mims, "Take Me Out to the Ball Game," 109–10. See also Cottman, *Jefferson County in the World War,* 104–10.

Chapter 11. Innocents Abroad

1. *USS Nevada: The Cheer Up Ship*; Murmane, *Ground Swells,* 235–63; Freeman, "Getting Together: How the Officers and Men of the British and American Ships in European Waters are Making Acquaintance," 564–65; *New York Evening News,* Aug. 4, 1918.

2. Entry for Oct. 1917, Brown Journal, WisHistSoc; S. Young, *Pen Pictures,* 12; entry for Sept. 1917, Merrill Diary, UNC-CH; *The U.S.S. Mount Vernon,* 135; *Stars and Stripes,* Nov. 15, 1918; Blackford, *Torpedoboat Sailor,* 113.

3. Townsend, *One Man's Navy,* 165. See also Braynard, *The Story of the* Leviathan, 1: 137. *New York Herald,* Aug. 11, 1918.

4. Nov. 15, 1918. See also entry for Jan. 3, 1918, Talley Letters, OA; Townsend, *One Man's Navy,* 166; entry for Oct. 1917, Brown Journal, WisHistSoc; Frank S. Schueler to "folks," Nov. 26, Dec. 9, 1917, in "A Gob's Letters Home during the World War, 1917–1919," AMHI; Lovell, *"War on the Ocean,"* 20; Reginald Wright Kauffman, *Our Navy at War,* 248; entry for Dec. 20, 1918, Everett Hart Diary, in Wycoff, *Ripley County's Part in the World War,* 202.

5. Niblack to Simsadus, April 17, 1918, Reel 19, ME-11.

6. *Pall Mall Gazette,* June 5, 1917. See also Churchill, *A Traveller in War Time,* 46; Halsey Memoir, LC; Strauss, "Recollections," LC; Dreyer, *The Sea Heritage,* 236; Chapple, *We'll Stick to the Finish,* 189; Paine, *The First Yale Unit,* 88; M. Simpson, *Anglo-American Naval Relations,* 213–14; *Daily Mail,* May 17, 1918; *Glasgow Herald,* July 27, 1918; *Naval and Military Record* 37 (Dec. 24, 1919); Leighton, *Simsadus,* 33, 35; Connolly, *Navy Men,* 226; Freeman, "Getting Together," 451–52.

7. Quoted in Hurd and Bashford, *Sons of Admiralty,* 249.

8. Karsten, *The Naval Aristocracy,* 107–16; Still, *American Sea Power in the Old World,* 15. See also *Naval and Military Record* 37 (Dec. 24, 1919); *Times* (London), Oct. 25, 1918.

9. Karsten, *The Naval Aristocracy*, 116. See also C. H. Hunter, "Anglo-American Relations during the Period of American Belligerency," Ph.D. diss., 684–745.

10. Dec. 4, 17, 1917, General Board Hearings; Halsey Memoir, LC; entry for Aug. 18, 1919, in Josephus Daniels, *Cabinet Diaries*, 431; M. Simpson, *Anglo-American Naval Relations*, 66; entry for Sept. 1, 1917, Russell Journal, USS *Walke* file, CZ file, OA; *New York Herald,* Jan. 21, 1919; C. King, *Atlantic Charter*, 193; Ellyson to "Nim," June 5, July 5, 24, 1918, Ellyson Papers, NDL.

11. E. M. Eady Memoirs, IWM. See also entries for Dec. 4, 9, 13, 1917, Jan., Spring, July, 1918. ibid.; entry for Oct. 6, 1917, Midshipman Lycelt Gardner Diary, IWM: Consul Sanderson to Page, June 24, 1918, file 830/40, London Embassy Records, RG84; Cowan to Sims, May 9, 1918, Box 89, Sims Papers; Griff, *Surrendered*, 184; Sherston to Bayly, Sept. 23, 1919, Bayly Papers, IWM; entry for Dec. 1, 1917, R. Goodrich Diary, IWM; Hall to Lord Bertie, Aug. 31, 1917, FO800/181; H. H. Smith, *A Yellow Admiral Remembers*, 324; Moffat, *Maverick Navy*, 98–99; Paine, *The First Yale Unit*, 83; Brownrigg, *Indiscretions of the Naval Censor*, 257; Goodenough, *A Rough Record*, 97; Freeman, "Getting Together," 451–53; Paine, "Hide and Seek Afloat," 16; H. Holt, "Behind the British Fleet," 26; Freeman, *Stories of the Ships*, 264–67.

12. Thompson, *Take Her Down*, 172–73. Belloc was an English essayist and poet born in France. See also entries for June 10, Aug. 20, 1917, Merrill Diary, UNC-CH. One authority has suggested that southern Americans were more Anglophobic than were officers from other parts of the United States. Watt, *Succeeding John Bull*, 18. The author has found no evidence to substantiate this, at least for the World War I period.

13. Quoted in Roskill, *Admiral of the Fleet Earl Beatty*, 230. See also Lady Beatty to Beatty, Dec. 10, 1917, Beatty MS, NMM; Richmond Folio Dairy, n.d., entry RIG/1/5, Richmond Papers, NMM; Freeman, *Sea-Hounds*, 84. Admiral Rodman considered American junior officers more competent than their British counterparts—reason, methods of education. Capt. Saint-Seine to Minister of Marine, Jan. 21, 1919, French Naval Archives, Vincennes. Entry for Oct. 10, 1918, in Munson, *Echoes of the Great War*, 252. See also Bayly speech, Feb. 19, 1921, Bayly Papers, IWM; Cornford, "The United States Navy," 264–69; *Daily News* (London), Oct. 25, 1918; *Journal of Commerce* (Liverpool), Nov. 1, 1918; *Pall Mall Gazette*, June 1, 1918; entry for July 8, 1917, in Taussig, *The Queenstown Patrol*, 74–75; *Army and Navy Journal*, June 28, 1917; *Naval and Military Record* 36 (Jan. 23, 1918): 54; Symington, "The Navy Way," NDL, 332; Paine, *The First Yale Unit*, 83. A study of American Army officers in World War I mentions problems of U.S. officers introducing themselves; also British social customs, etc. Goddard, "Relations between American Expeditionary Forces and British Expeditionary Forces," AMHI.

14. Quoted in Trask, *Captains and Cabinets*, 83. See also Sims to SecNav, May 7, 1918, Box 94, Log file, RG45; Sims interview, Sept., 1918, Box 50, Sims Papers, LC; Sims to wife, June 8, 1918, Box 10, ibid.; *New York Herald*, Jan 21, 1919; Roskill, *Admiral of the Fleet Earl Beatty*, 264; Bayly speech, Feb 19, 1921, Bayly papers, IWM; Land to Trotter, July 21, 1921, Box 1, Land papers, LC.

15. Entry for July 22, 1917, Fagan Diary, Mariners' Museum. See also Connolly, *Navy Men*, 226; CO Barracks, Queenstown, to Sims, Feb. 18, 1918, NA subj file, RG45. A Ph.D. dissertation on Anglo-American relations suggests that there was no "personal conflict" between the personnel of the two navies. Even at the time it was written, there was considerable evidence that such conflict existed. See C. H. Hunter, "Anglo-American Relations during the Period of American Belligerency," Ph.D. diss., 727.

16. To Beatty, Jan. 22, 1918, Beatty Papers, NMM; Ferrell, *Woodrow Wilson and World War I*, 119.

17. Graves and Hodge, *The Long Weekend*, 32–33. See also Connolly, *Sea-Borne*, 197; Carney Oral History, Columbia University; Munson, *Echoes of the Great War*, 207; MacDonough, *In London during the Great War*, 210–11; Frost to SecState, May 8, 1917, *Foreign Relations, 1917,*

Supplement 2, 79; Clarence Anderson Questionnaire, WWI Research Collection, AMHI; Sims to wife, June 29, 1918, Box 10, Sims Papers, LC.

18. Keyes to wife, Feb. 14, 1917, Halpern, ed., *The Keyes Papers*, 1: 373. Sims and his officers had a high opinion of Keyes. Sims to SecNav, May 30, 1918, UB subj file, RG45; Navy Dept., *The American Naval Planning Section London*, 202. See also Sims to wife, June 29, 1918, Box 10, Sims Papers, LC; Wemyss to Beatty, undated, Beatty Papers, NMM; Jellicoe to De Chair, Nov. 7, 1925, De Chair Papers, IWM; Watt, *Personalities and Policies*, 30 n. 3. Jellicoe expressed his negative opinion of Americans after the war. He gave no evidence of this during the period that he was first sea lord.

19. Taft, *Service with Fighting Men*, 1: 74; Halsey to Sims, June 16, 1918, Box 62, Sims Papers, LC; Cotten to wife, Nov. 4, 1918, Cotten Papers, UNC-CH; Braynard, *The Story of the* Leviathan, 1: 149; Newton, *Preaching in London*, 108; Harvey Miller, "Uncle Sam—He Also Ran," 1.

20. *Naval and Military Record* 36, new ser. (Feb. 20, 1918): 121; Blackford, *Torpedoboat Sailor*, 136; Kleinatland, "A Saga of World War I"; Beston, *Full Speed Ahead*, 141–44. See also Murmane, *Ground Swells*, 239; Freeman, *Sea-Hounds*, 85.

21. Blackford, *Torpedoboat Sailor*, 134–36; Kleinatland, "A Saga of World War I;" entry for May 8, 1918, William F. Kurfess Diary, OA; Thompson, *Take Her Down*, 234.

22. Leighton, *Simsadus*, 34; Freeman, *Stories of the Ships*, 269; Beston, *Full Speed Ahead*, 145–46. See also L.G.W. White, *Ships, Coolies, and Rice*, 216; *Daily Mail*, May 28, 1918; entries for June 22, 28, July 4, 1918, F. Foxton Diary, Peter Liddle Archives.

23. Freeman, *Stories of the Ships*, 278–87; Murmane, *Ground Swells*, 241–42; Beston, *Full Speed Ahead*, 145; *New York Post*, Dec. 21, 1918. A study on relations between British and American soldiers in World War I done at the Army War College reached the same conclusions. See Goddard, "Relations between American Expeditionary Forces and British Expeditionary Forces," AMHI.

24. Freeman, *Stories of the Ships*, 275–76; entry for Aug. 17, 1919, in Josephus Daniels, *Cabinet Diaries*, 431; Leighton, *Simsadus*, 34; Murmane, *Ground Swells*, 241–42; Blackford, *Torpedoboat Sailor*, 103. For other comments, see Daniel Schenk Memoir, Smithsonian; unidentified seaman letter, Dec. 10, 1918, JOD/198, NMM.

25. Kleinatland, "A Saga of World War I"; undated newspaper article by W.J.B. Newman in newspaper file, Virginia War History Commission Records, Virginia State Library; Murmane, *Ground Swells*, 237–38; M. S. Brown, "Life Overseas on the Yankee Sub-Chasers," 19; Wiggins, *My Romance with the Navy*, 35; J. S. Kleinatland to author, March 3, 1987, in author's possession; entry for March, 1918, in Brown Journal, WisHistSoc; Thompson, *Take Her Down*, 19; Sims to SecNav, July 2, 1917, Confidential Files, 1917–1919, Box 54, RG80; Griff, *Surrendered*, 182. The questionnaires are found in the WWI Research Collection, AMHI. See especially the Gravis and Hahn questionnaires. American sailors had considerably less trouble with British soldiers, but still there was some friction. Blythe, "Removing the Mufflers," 77.

26. W. G. Gerrard Memoir, Peter Liddle Archives; Evans, *Keeping the Seas*, 159; G. Campbell, *Number Thirteen*, 111; Pilat, *Pegler*, 73; *Register of the Commissioned and Warrant Officers of the United States Navy & Marine Corps*, Jan. 1, 1918, 361–65; C-in-C to Admiralty, Jan. 6, 1918, ADM137/1964; Hoy, *40, or How the War Was Won*, 264, 272; *Daily Mail*, May 25, 1917; *Naval and Military Record* 36 (Feb. 13, 1918): 94; *Observer*, Jan. 5, 26, 1919; *Our Navy* 15 (Dec. 1921): 13. For the British sailor during the war, see Liddle, *The Sailor's War*, 125–36; Carew, *The Lower Deck of the Royal Navy*, xii–xiii, 72–91, 110–13, 192–93. The latter book discusses the problem of pay and living conditions in detail. See also Knock, *"Clear Lower Deck,"* 35; and Griff, *Surrendered*, 182.

27. Baker, *The Terror of Tobermory*, 69; Richard H. Leigh memoirs, Florida State University; Leighton, *Simsadus*, 34; Buranelli, *Maggie of the Suicide Fleet*, 74–75; Cochran, "Life at Sea,"

Cochran MS, Coast Guard Library; Griff, *Surrendered*, 182; Adams, *Paris Sees It Through*, 92. See also below for additional details on brawling.

28. *Manchester Guardian*, Oct. 12, 1917. See also entry for Aug. 30, 1917, Russell Journal; USS *Walke* file, CZ files, OA.

29. Feb. 15, 1918, Box 49, Sims Papers, LC. See also *Daily Mail*, May 23, 1917, May 15, 1918; *New York Herald*, Aug. 14, 1918; Munson, *Echoes of the Great War*, 229; *Literary Digest*, Aug. 31, 1918; *New York Evening News*, Aug. 4, 1918; Goddard, "Relations between American Expeditionary Forces and British Expeditionary Forces," AMHI.

30. Newton, *Preaching in London*, 98; Munson, *Echoes of the Great War*, 249, 255.

31. *Pall Mall Gazette*, May 10, 1918; *Times* (London), July 4, 1919.

32. Frank Schueler Questionnaire, WWI Research Collection, AMHI; entry for Oct. 27, 1919, Bellitteri Journal, Bellitteri Papers, ECU; D. Reynolds, *Rich Relations*, 2; *Times* (London), July 4, 1919. For good opinion of the British, see questionnaires in WWI Research Collection, AMHI. See also entries for Aug. 1, 21, 1917, Fagan Diary, Mariners' Museum; Bellitteri, "The Cruise of the USS *Chester*, 1917-18-19," Bellitteri Papers, ECU; Sterne, *Over the Seas for Uncle Sam*, 98–99; *New York Herald*, July 7, 1918; *Living Age* 300 (Jan.-March, 1918): 62; S. Young, *Pen Pictures*, 15; Newton, *Preaching in London*, 61; Braynard, *The Story of the* Leviathan, 1: 137; Picard to Sims, Aug. 14, 1917, 830 file, London Embassy Records, RG84; *Daily Mail*, May 17, June 20, 1918.

33. Sims to wife, Feb. 26, 1918, Box 9, Sims Papers, LC; Lyle to Mason, n.d., Box 71, London Consulate Records; RG84; J. Williams, *The Home Fronts*, 193, 247–49; Peel, *How We Lived Then*, 79; Dewey, "Nutrition and Living Standards in Wartime Britain"; T. Wilson, *The Myriad Faces of War*, 648–49; Patterson, *Portsmouth: A History*, 136–37; Brown and Meehan, *The Imperial War Museum Book of the First World War*, 226–27; Schmitt and Vedeler, *The World in the Crucible*, 318; Pitt, *1918*, 35–37; Marwick, *The Deluge*, 191–99; Von Schoultz, *With the British Battle Fleet*, 313; Blythe, "At a Naval Base," 21; T. Wilson, *The Myriad Faces of War*, 537; Hardach, *The First World War*, 230–31.

34. T. Wilson, *The Myriad Faces of War*, 465; Cdr. Rowcliff testimony, May 6, 1918, General Board Hearings; entry for Sept. 16, 1917, in Taussig, *The Queenstown Patrol*, 122; Moore Oral History, Columbia University; Dewey, "Nutrition and Living Standards in Wartime Britain," 210; Blythe, "At a Naval Base," 21; entry for Aug. 29, 1917, Russell Journal, USS *Walke* file, CZ files, OA; Paine, *The First Yale Unit*, vol. II, 287. See also questionnaires in the WWI Research Collection, AMHI, particularly Walter Arnold and Leslie Merrill.

35. Murmane, *Ground Swells*, 265, 371; autobiography of W. D. MacCourt, copy in author's possession; entry for Oct. 18, 1917, Woodworth Diary, Hoover Institute Archives; entry for June 11, 1917, Latimer Diary, UVA; Taft, *Service with Fighting Men*, 2: 68, 74; unsigned letter to newspaper editor, Columbus, Indiana, unnamed newspaper, Dec. 8, 1918, copy in War History Records, Indiana State Library. See also questionnaires in WWI Research Collection, AMHI.

36. Entry for May 19, 1917, Fagan Diary, Mariners' Museum; Braynard, *The Story of the* Leviathan, 1: 150; Freidel, *Over There*, 35.

37. Entries for May 20, June 12, 1917, in Taussig, *The Queenstown Patrol*, 39, 55–56; Schaffer to Washington, Feb. 18, 1918, file 814.2, Liverpool Consulate Records, RG84.

38. Blackford, *Torpedoboat Sailor*, 120–21. See also Todd, *USS* Oklahoma, 20; Beston, *Full Speed Ahead*, 85–86.

39. Leighton, *Simsadus*, 32–33.

40. Fitch, *My Mis-spent Youth*, 237. See also entry for May 20, 1917, Fagan Diary, Mariners' Museum; *Chicago Tribune*, Nov. 6, 1919.

41. Sims to Dept., June 15, 1917, Reel 1, WE-11; Taussig "notes," June 27, 1918, WS subj file, RG45; entry for May 30, 1917, Merrill Diary, UNC-CH; entry for May 7, 1917, Kurfess Diary, OA; n.d., Morgan journal, NHF; *Naval and Military Record* 36 (Aug. 7, 1918): 18–19. For opinions on the Irish, see the questionnaires, WWI Research Collection, AMHI; Murmane, *Ground Swells*,

304–5; *Cork Examiner*, May 18, 1917; Wiggins, *My Romance with the Navy*, 92; entries for June 8, 15, 1917, Fagan Diary, Mariners' Museum; *Fleet Review* 2 (Jan. 1920), 15. The Irish Convention (a congress with delegates) was in session during the first year that the U.S. Navy was in Ireland. There is no evidence that difficulties between the Irish and American sailors were discussed. See Lyons, *Ireland since the Famine*, 386–89; McDowell, *The Irish Convention*.

42. Frost to American Consul General, London, April 21, 1917, file 811, Cork, U.S. Consulate Records, London, RG84; Frost to SecState, May 8, 1917, file 27914-334, RG59, M580; Dunn, *World Alive*, 268; Sims, *The Victory at Sea*, 83; entry for July 5, 1917, Latimer Diary, UVA; C. H. Hunter, "Anglo-American Relations during the Period of American Belligerency," Ph.D. diss., 649; copy of newspaper article, Nov. 4, 1917, in FO395/85; *Philadelphia Public Ledger*, Nov. 8, 1919.

43. Reagan to Sims, Nov. 19, 1919, Box 82, Sims Papers, LC; Farrell to Sims, Nov. 4, 1919, Box 83, ibid.; *Chicago Tribune*, Nov. 19, 1919; Taft, *Service with Fighting Men*, 1: 60–67. American sailors were prohibited from going to Sinn Fein meetings, but at least one American naval officer, disguised in civilian clothes, did so. It is not clear if he did this on his own or under orders of naval officials to obtain intelligence. See P. J. Capelotti, *Our Man in the Crimea*, 25–29; and information provided the author by Professor Capelotti. By no means were all inhabitants in the Cork/Queenstown area unhappy with the Americans. For example, see letter to editor, *Cork Examiner*, Sept. 25, 1917; copy of a letter from a local doctor passed on to Sims, Oct. 2, 1917, Box 23, Sims Papers, LC.

44. Entry for Aug. 11, 1917, Russell Journal, USS *Walke* file, CZ files, OA; *Washington Post*, Sept. 5, 1917; *New York Herald*, Sept. 5, 1917, Blackford, *Torpedoboat Sailor*, 24; entry for Sept. 4, 1917, in Taussig, *The Queenstown Patrol*, 113; *Daily Chronicle*, Sept. 4, 1917; *Cork Examiner*, Sept. 4, 1917; Pringle to Sims, Sept. 7, 1917, Box 79, Sims Papers, LC; entry for Sept. 7, 1917, Louis P. Davis Papers, ECU; undated newspaper article in FO395/85; entries for Sept. 2, 5, 1917 PRO; entry for Sept. 2, 1917, Clarence Moore Diary, NHF; Lauer Journal, USS *Burrows* file, CZ files, OA; Bayly to Jellicoe, Sept. 1, 1917, in Patterson, *The Jellicoe Papers*, 2: 202; Sims, *The Victory at Sea*, 84–87; Cooke, "Recollections," LC; Thomas Robbins to P. Capelotti, copy in author's possession.

45. P-Queenstown subj file, RG45. See also *Fleet Review* 2 (Jan. 1920): 15; Sendel to Sims, Nov. 4, 1919, Box 84, Sims Papers, LC.

46. Thompson, *Take Her Down*, 228; *Washington Post*, Sept. 6, 1917.

47. For the death and riot, see Blackford, *Torpedoboat Sailor*, 110–11; n.d., David Jenkins Diary, NWC; *Irish Independent*, Sept. 12, 1917. See communication to Daniels, Feb. 28, 1920, and Rear Admiral Harry Knapp to Wright with enclosures, March 15, 1920 in 841d .00/173 file, RG59, M580. For Sims's account of the incident, see Sims, *The Victory at Sea*, 85. There is no evidence that any compensation was granted. For the clergy's role in the friction, see undated newspaper article in FO395/85 PRO; Hartley, *The Irish Question as a Problem in British Foreign Policy*, 151; entry for Nov. 19, 1918, Forbes Diary, copy in Box 58, Sims Papers, LC. See also *New York Herald*, Nov. 6, 1919; *Irish Independent*, Sept. 20, 25, 1917; Report on Crime, Cork, Oct. 2, 1917, CO904/104; entry for Sept. 5–6, 1917, Clarence Moore Diary, NHF; Sims Report to Dept., Sept. 15, 1917, OB subj file, RG45; Ryan to Senior Officer *Conyngham*, Sept. 9, 1917, Logistics file, RG45; Bayly to the County Inspector, Cork, Sept. 8, 1917, copy in ibid.; entry for Sept. 9, 1917, Fagan Diary, Mariners' Museum. Sims confirmed the machine shop story of FDR. See Sims, *The Victory at Sea*, 87. See also Blythe, "Removing the Mufflers," 77; Freidel, *F.D.R.: The Apprenticeship*, 352; and Freidel, *Over There*, 39–40; entry for Sept. 10, 1917, Latimer Diary, UVA.

48. See, for example, Sims's secretary to Mrs. Harrington, Oct. 6, 1917, Box 23, Sims Papers, LC; Sims Report to Dept., Oct. 23, 1917, file C-47-62, Box 104, Confidential Files, 1917–1919, RG80; FDR to Daniels, July 27, 1918, Box 24, Sims Papers, LC; Hoy, *40 O.B.*, 273–74; Bayly to Jellicoe, Oct. 9, 1918, ADD49009, Jellicoe Papers, British Museum; Geddes memo to War

Cabinet, Sept. 19, 1917, Geddes Papers, ADM116/1806; Butterfield to Bayly, Sept. 17, 1917, copy in P-Queenstown subj file, RG45; *Cork Examiner*, Sept. 8, 1917; Director of Information, Nov. 13, 1917, FO395/85; Wiggins, *My Romance with the Navy*, 121–22; Hartley, *The Irish Question*, 158–61, 182.

49. Copies of documents and answers in Confidential Correspondence, 1917–1919, file C-42-62, Box 104, RG80. See also *Cork Examiner*, Sept. 14, 1917; and Evans, *Keeping the Seas*, 157–59.

50. Thompson to "Doctor," March 1918, file 127046, RG52; entry for Jan. 21, 1918, Lauer Journal, USS *Burrows* file, CZ files, OA; Goddard, "Relations between American Expeditionary Forces and British Expeditionary Forces," AMHI; Bayly to the Secretary of the Admiralty, April 28, 1918, ADM137/1512.

51. Sims to Benson, Feb. 28, 1918, in M. Simpson, *Anglo-American Naval Relations*, 276; Sims to Dept., Nov. 26, 1917, Reel 10, M1092; FDR to Daniels, July 27, 1918, Box 45, Assistant SecNav Files, FDR Library.

52. Cotten biographical sketch in Governor J. Melville Broughton Papers, Department of Archives & History, Raleigh, N.C. Cotten was in command of the U.S. Naval Base at Plymouth.

53. ADM memo, April 4, 1918; Bayly to Secretary of the Admiralty, April 4, 24, 1918; Pringle to Force Commander, April 4, 1918; Bayly to Military Officer, Ireland, April 16, 1918; Bayly to Sims, April 24, 1918; Bayly to Pringle, May 5, 1918; Sims Force Instruction No. 15, May 11, 1918; all in ADM137/1512. See also Sims to Pringle, May 18, 1918, Box 79, Sims Papers, LC; Pringle to Sims, April 27, 1918, ibid.; Goddard, "Relations between American Expeditionary Forces and British Expeditionary Forces," AMHI; Geddes to War Cabinet, April 28, 1918, ADM116/1810; Benson to Sims, May 17, 1918, Reel 20, ME-11; Sims to Dept., May 19, 1918, Reel 4, ibid.; Sims Reports, April 17, 23, 1918, ibid.; Wiggins, *My Romance with the Navy*, 124.

54. Wiggins, *My Romance with the Navy*, 125, 128; entry for April 25, 1918, Kurfess Diary, OA; Sims reports, May 22, 27, 1918, O subj file, RG45; Sims to Dept., May 29, 1918, Reel 4, WE-11; White to C.O. Naval Air Station, Queenstown, Aug. 12, 1918, Box 7, Logistics file, RG45; Sims Circular, Aug. 30, 1918, Box 94; ibid.; Pringle to Sims, Aug. 22, 1918, Box 79, Sims Papers, LC; entry for Oct. 3, 1918, Brown Journal, WisHistSoc; Price to Sims, Nov. 3, 1918, Box 79, Sims Papers, LC; CO Naval Air Station, Queenstown, to CO, July 23, 1918, Box 7, Logistics file, RG45; E. T. Clark, *Social Studies of the War*, 50.

55. Land, *Winning the War with Ships*, 102; Todd, *USS* Oklahoma, 18; Carney, "The Capture of the *U-58*," 8.

56. Memo on Irish conditions, Sept. 12, 1918 in Link, *Wilson Papers*, 49: 545–46; Freeman, *Sea-Hounds*, 91–92; *Chicago Tribune*, Nov. 6, 1919; entry for Sept. 1, 1918, Lauer Journal, USS *Burrows* file; Leighton, *Simsadus*, 32–33; Blackford, *Torpedoboat Sailor* 78; *Times* (London), Nov. 20, 1920; n.d., Brown Journal, WisHistSoc; Freeman, *Stories of the Ships*, 281; *New York Times*, Nov. 5, 1919; *New York Sun*, May 24, 1918; American Consul, Queenstown to SecState, Feb. 3, 1921, 841d/311, RG59, M580. The *Cork Examiner* continued to insist that the majority of the American sailors stationed in Ireland left with good feelings toward the Irish. The author in his research found only two (one officer and one enlisted man) who did. Admittedly, it is difficult to generalize about the attitude of the sailors toward the Irish based on the small percentage who wrote memoirs. Nevertheless, they often indicated a general attitude of dislike or hostility toward the Irish. See also comments by writer Ralph Paine in the *New York Sun*, May 24, 1918. An article about the presence of the U.S. Navy in Ireland during World War I in the *Cork Evening Echo* dated May 4, 1977, does not mention any difficulties between the local populace and the American sailors. It emphasized the prosperity of thousands of local citizens who were employed at the dockyards. "Money flowed freely, and business firms, shopkeepers and publicans benefited substantially from the boom." *Marine Magazine*, Feb. 1919, 17; questionnaires, WWI Research Collection, AMHI.

After the war, Sims in his published works and speeches blamed the Sinn Fein for the "Irish troubles," accusing them of pro-German sympathies that prolonged the war. Irish Americans reacted strongly against the admiral. There is considerable literature on this. See, for example, Entry 114, RG80; file 117, roll 186, Warren G. Harding Papers, Ohio Historical Society, the Daniel T. O'Connell Collection, Irish-American Historical Society, and the Sims Papers in LC. See also Carroll, *American Opinion and the Irish Question*, 170–74, Ward, *Ireland and Anglo-American Relations*, 246–47, and Morison, *Sims*, 482–86.

57. Quoted in Strauss, *Menace in the West*, 53.

58. J. Williams, *The Home Fronts*, 205, 271.

59. D. E. Nolan, "A Study of Anglo-American and Franco-American Relations during World War I, Part II, Franco-American Relations," AMHI.

60. Quoted in "What the American Soldier Thinks of the French," *Literary Digest*, June 29, 1919, 47–48. See also George to Kate, Sept. 15, 1918, Lawrence Papers, WisHistSoc; Bullard, *Personalities and Reminiscences of the War*, 329–31; Esher to Robertson, July 18, 1917, Viscount Oliver Esher, *Journals and Letters*, 4: 130; entry for Jan. 4, 1918, Stuart F. Smith Diary, LC.

61. Entries for Nov. 1, 26, 1917, Feb. 4, 1918, Brown Journal, Brown Papers, WisHistSoc; Post to mother, Aug. 11, 1918, Post MS, LSU; entry for June 8, 1917; Russell Journal, USS *Walke* file, CZ files, OA; Louis P. Davis Oral History, ECU; Paine, *The Corsair in the War Zone*, 223; Loder to family, Dec. 17, 1917, Loder Papers, Mariners' Museum; Battey, *70,000 Miles on a Submarine Destroyer*, 68.

62. Pownall Oral History, USNI.

63. Nouailhat, *Les Americains a Nantes et St. Nazaire*, 103, 168; Moreau to Naval Minister, Jan. 24, 1918, French Naval Archives, Vincennes; Roger, *Les Americains a Brest pendant la premiere guerre mondiale*, n.p.; copy in ibid.; Lepotier, *Brest, porte oceane*, 290–91; entry for June 24, 1918, in Josephus Daniels, *Cabinet Diaries*, 314; Mannix, *The Old Navy*, 253; Ferrell, *Woodrow Wilson and World War I*, 119; "What the American Soldiers Thinks of the French," *Literary Digest*, June 28, 1919, 48; *American Legion Magazine*, Jan. 1929, 45; entries for Sept. 4, Nov. 1, 191?; entries for June 20, 1918, Slayback Memoir, NDL.

64. Mrs. Josephus Daniels, *Recollections of a Cabinet Minister's Wife*, 169; Taft, *Service with Fighting Men*, 1: 126, newspaper article, n.d., Virginia War History Commission Records, Virginia State Library; Loder to Mildred, Jan. 27, 1918, Loder Papers, Mariners' Museum; Watson, "A Profile of the Tennessee Servicemen of World War I," Ph.D. diss., 51–52; Rose, *The Brittany Patrol*, 55; Duncan, "Before and After," 1–2; letter dated Oct. 21, 1918, "A Sailor's Letters Somewhere in France," in Box 56, Sims Papers, LC; Schueler, "A Gob's Letters Home during the World War, 1917–1919," AMHI; Talley to wife, March 13, April 28, 1918, Talley Letters, OA; Ferrell, *Woodrow Wilson and World War I*, 119; Loder to sweetheart, Nov. 16, 1917, Loder Papers, Mariners' Museum; F. D. Baldwin, "The American Enlisted Man in World War I," Ph.D. diss., 220.

65. S. Young, *Pen Pictures*, 54; Wycoff, *Ripley County's Part in the World War*, 166; entry for March, 1918, Brown Journal, WisHistSoc; Julius to Folks, Jan. 20, 1919, Letters of Sol Cohen and Julius Cohen, Illinois State Historical Library; Lawrence to Kate, Sept. 15, 1918, Lawrence Papers, WisHistSoc; Tighe, "Plunkett's Pirates," NDL.

66. Nouailhat, *Les Americains a Nantes et St. Nazaire*, 120. See 177–78, 195, ibid.; Freeman, *Stories of the Ships*, 247.

67. Graves and Hodge, *The Long Weekend*, 93; Chevrillon, *Les Americains a Brest*, 125; Pamard to Division Chief, lst Section, Aug. 22, 1918, Sorette to Comma. Talley to wife, June 7, 1918, Talley Letters, OA; Jestin, "*Histoire vecue du camp Americains de Pontanezer pendant la guerre de 1914–1918*, 218–36; Nouailhat, *Les Americains a Nantes et St. Nazaire*, 133.

68. Post to mother, Aug. 9, 1918, Post MS, LSU; entries for Oct. 1917, Nov. 22, 1917, Feb. 2, 1918, Brown Journal, WisHistSoc; S. Young, *Pen Pictures*, 12; entry for Sept. 1917, Merrill Di-

ary, UNC-CH; *The U.S.S.* Mount Vernon, 135; *Stars and Stripes*, Nov. 15, 1918; Blackford, *Torpedoboat Sailor*, 113; Coffman, *The War to End All Wars*, 134; *Literary Digest*, June 2, 1919, Loder to sweetheart, Oct. 10, 1918, Loder Papers, Mariners' Museum; diary entry for June 20, 1917, in Sheely, *Sailor of the Air*, 33–36; Murdock, *They Also Served*, 74–75; Autobiography of W. D. MacCourt, copy in possession of author; Thoumin, *The First World War*, 358; Jestin, *Histoire vecue du camp Americains de Pontanezen pendant la guerre de 1914–1918*, 218–36; Nouailhat, *Les Americains a Nantes et St. Nazaire*, 134–35; Roger, *Les Americains a Brest pendant las premiere guerre mondiale*, n.p..; Talley to wife, June 7, 1918, Talley Letters, OA.

69. J. Williams, *The Home Fronts*, 201–3, 263–65, 271; Sheely to Lewis, July 20, 1917, in Sheely, *Sailor of the Air*, 38; Lawrence to Kate, Aug. 9, 1918, Lawrence Papers, WisHistSoc; Summerbell, *A Preacher Goes to War*, 33; Moseley, *Extracts from Letters*, 38; Falls, *The Great War*, 170; "Nelson Goss," in Furlong, *Class of 1905*, 177; Wiggins, *My Romance with the Navy*, 91; Talley to wife, July 27, Oct. 9, 1917, Talley Letters, OA; entry for July 24, 1918, Taussig Diary, NWC; Schueler, "A Gob's Letters during the World War," AMHI.

70. Entry for Sept. 29, 1918, Slayback Memoir, NDL; entries for Dec. 1917, Jan. 18, 19, Feb. 24, March, 1918, Brown Journal, WisHistSoc; Forbes to Mrs. Maxwell, Dec. 13, 1917, Alexander H. Cathcart and Family Papers, Minnesota Historical Society; Talley to wife, Oct. 27, Nov. 21, Dec. 4, 1917; King and Whitehill, *Fleet Admiral King*, 138; Hoover Oral History, Columbia University; A. C. Murray, *Master and Brother*, 166–67; entry for July 21, 1918, Taussig Diary, NWC; Paine, *The Corsair in the War Zone*, 63; MacLeish to Beloved, April 9, 1918, in Rossano, *The Price of Honor*, 136.

71. Schueler, "A Gob's Letters Home during the World War," AMHI; *New York Evening Post*, July 2, 1918; Rose, *Brittany Patrol*, 55; Autobiography of W. D. MacCourt, copy in author's possession; Hoover Oral History, Columbia University; Watson, "A Profile of the Tennessee Servicemen of World War I," Ph.D. diss., 52; entry for June 13, 1918, Brown Journal, WisHistSoc, 80; Speicher, "Some Experiences with Mediterranean Convoys during the World War," AMHI; various questionnaires, WWI Research Collection; entry for Oct. 1917, Brown Journal, WisHistSoc; Slayton to CO Division One, Destroyer Force, Aug. 1, 1917, OS subj file, RG45; U.S. Naval Aviation Foreign Service, Recreation Bulletin No. 7, June 22, 1918, GA subj file, RG45; MacLeish to Beloved, Feb. 13, 1918, in Rossano, *The Price of Honor*, 98–99; Surgeon Shaw to Office of Naval Intelligence, July 15, 1918, file 126881, RG52; entry for May 31, 1918, Taussig Diary, NWC; Kennedy to Mary Kennedy, Dec. 21, 1918, Richmond folder, Virginia War History Commission, Virginia State Library.

72. Dunn to Sims, May 7, July 14, 1918, Box 55, Sims Papers, LC; Dunn report in *Naval Investigation*, 2719; Commander Hayward, Jan. 26, 1918, General Board Hearings; Josephus Daniels, *Our Navy at War*, 275–76; Battey, *70,000 Miles on a Submarine Destroyer*, 40.

73. Mannix, *The Old Navy*, 250; Schneider and Schneider, *Into the Breach*, 122–23; M. Baldwin, *Canteening Overseas*, 45; *Literary Digest*, Feb. 1, 1919.

74. MacLeish to Beloved, Dec. 16, 1917, in Rossano, *The Price of Honor*, 67; Blackford, *Torpedoboat Sailor*, 76; entry for June 20, 1918, Slayback Memoir, NDL; MacLeish to family, Nov. 10, 1917, in Rossano, *The Price of Honor*, 40; Loder to sweetheart, Oct. 20, 1918, Loder Papers, Mariners' Museum.

75. In addition to the questionnaires, see Rossano, *The Price of Honor*, 67.

76. *Manchester Guardian*, Dec. 7, 1918; Murdock, *They Also Served*, 92–93; Murmane, *Ground Swells*, 265; *The Story of the Texas*, 45.

77. *The Saranac: U.S. Mine Squadron One*, n.p.; Blackford, *Torpedoboat Sailor*, 76; Moffat, *Maverick Navy*, 108; Braynard, *The Story of the Leviathan*, 1: 137; Leslie Merrill questionnaire, WWI Research Collection, AMHI; Griff, *Surrendered*, 180–81; *Fixem*, copy in Belknap Papers; Corrigan, *Tin Ensign*, 133; *Newport Recruit* (Oct. 1918): 28; Murdock, *They Also Served*, 405.

78. Entry for Sept. 29, 1918, Slayback Memoir, NDL; entries for Dec. 1917, Jan. 18, 19, Feb. 24,

March, 1918, Brown Journal, WisHistSoc; Forbes to Mrs. Maxwell, Dec. 13, 1917. Alexander H. Cathcart and Family Papers, Minnesota Historical Society; Talley to wife, Oct. 27, Nov. 21, Dec. 4, 1917; King and Whitehill, *Fleet Admiral King*, 138; Hoover Oral History, Columbia University; A. C. Murray, *Master and Brother*, 166–67; entry for July 21, 1918, in Taussig Diary, NWC; Paine, *The Corsair in the War Zone*, 63; MacLeish to Beloved, April 9, 1918, in Rossano, *The Price of Honor*, 136.

79. Hibbert, *The English: A Social History*, 701; Marwick, *The Deluge*, 109–10; J. Williams, *The Home Fronts*, 186–87; entry for Oct. 24, 1918, in Flower, *The Journal of Arnold Bennett*, 238.

80. *Times* (London), Sept. 24, 1918; *Daily Mail*, Sept. 25, 1918; Vandercook, "The Greatest Battle of the War," 590; entries for Oct. 9, 14, 1918, McCully Diary, LC; Murmane, *Ground Swells*, 310–11, 365–67, 376–77; "Information on Entertaining Liberty Parties in London," Aug. 1, 1919, Box 11, Morale Division General Correspondence, RG24; entry for Nov. 13, 1917, Cunningham, *Marine Flyer in France*, 7.

81. Sanitary Report, Killingholme, Dec. 31, 1918, file 130212, RG52; *Annual Report Surgeon General, USN, 1919*, 243, 247–50; *Daily Mail*, Sept. 27, 1918; Quatemilt Memoir, WWI Research Collection, AMHI; Memo, Assistant Provost, Oct. 1, 1918, Base Section 3, Box 69, RG120.

82. Vandercook, "The Greatest Battle of the War," 591.

83. David Mitchell, *Women on the Warpath*, 213, 218–21; Beardsley, "Allied Against Sin," 221; Ms. Merz to American Consul, Newcastle, April 24, 1918, file 886, Newcastle Consulate Records, RG84; Keys to Fosdick, Sept. 6, 1918, Box 1, Fosdick Papers, Princeton University; Schneider and Schneider, *Into the Breach*, 134–35; *Summary of World War Work of the YMCA*, 23; Taft, *Service with Fighting Men*, 1: 84.

84. Cunningham, *A Marine Flyer in France*, 31; Roger, "*Les Americains a Brest le pendant la premiere guerre mondiale*"; Summerbell, *A Preacher Goes to War*, 19; Murdock, *They Also Served*, 66–67; Tighe, "Plunkett's Pirates," NDL; entry for Oct. 27, 1918, Kurfess Diary, OA; entries for June 20, 21, 29, 30, 1918, Taussig Diary; entries for Aug. 7, 8, Sept. 4, Nov. 16, 1917; and Sept. 30, 1918, NWC, Brown Journal, Brown Papers, WisHistSoc. Brown said that a large percentage of the American officers on board the ships based in Brest leased apartments ashore. See also Nouailhat, *Les Americains a Nantes et St. Nazaire*, 178; Paine, *The First Yale Unit*, 13–14. Two officers smuggled their French girlfriends on board their ship dressed as sailors. Unfortunately, the ship was torpedoed and the ruse discovered when the two females were rescued. Entry for Aug. 16, 1918, Lauer Journal, USS *Burrows* file, CZ files, OA; entry for Aug. 14, 1918, Brown Journal, WisHistSoc.

85. Moffat, *Maverick Navy*, 75.

86. Brandt, *No Magic Bullet*, 103–5; Schaffer, *America in the Great War*, 103–4; F. D. Baldwin, "The American Enlisted Man in World War I," Ph.D. diss., 205–6; MO, Seattle to Bureau of Medicine and Surgery, July 18, 1917, file 125561, RG52; Cecil to CO, Base Hospital, Oct. 4, 1917, ibid.; Corday, *The Paris Front*, 263; Stallings, *The Doughboys*, 212–13; H. Young, *A Surgeon's Autobiography*, 308–12; Walker, *Venereal Disease in the A.E.F.*, 66, 84–88; Lake, "Giving the Boys His Best," 593; Taft, *Service with Fighting Men*, 2: 116; Garrison, *History of Military Medicine*, 204; Nouilhat, *Les Americains a Nantes et St. Nazaire*, 127.

87. Walker, *Venereal Disease in the A.E.F.*, 68; Stallings, *The Doughboys*, 208–9; entry for June 20, 1918, Slayback memoirs, NDL; Murdock, *They Also Served*, 21–22.

88. Cannon, *Bishop Cannon's Own Story*, 204, 297; Sullivan, *With the Yanks in France*, 119–20; entry for March 21, 1918, Kurfess Diary, OA; F. D. Baldwin, "The American Enlisted Man in World War I," Ph.D. diss., 210; Report on VD, 1918, Box 1, Fosdick Papers, Princeton University.

89. Entry for May 26, June 1, 1918, Brown Journal, Brown Papers, WisHistSoc; MacLeish to Beloved, Dec. 4, 1917, in Rossano, *The Price of Honor*, 54–55; Huddleston, *In My Time*, 46–47; J. E. Moore, "Venereal Campaign in Paris District of the American Expeditionary Force," 1158–59.

The quote from an American citizen in Paris is in Brandt, *No Magic Bullet*, 108; See also Corday, *The Paris Front*, 259–61, 263; Summerbell, *A Preacher Goes to War*, 46–47; Tighe, "Plunkett's Pirates," NDL; Andrew T. Long Memoir, Andrew T. Long Papers, UNC-CH.

90. Ferrell, *Woodrow Wilson & World War I*, 62–63; entry for April 27, 1918, Brown Journal, Brown Papers; Nouailhat, *Les Americains a Nantes et St. Nazaire*, 169–70; D. M. Kennedy, *Over Here*, 186–87; P. Borden, *Civilian Indoctrination of the Military*, 114–17; Brandt, *No Magic Bullet*, 104–5; Freidel, *Over There*, 79–82; Schaffer, *America in the Great War*, 104–5; Cecil to CO Base Hospital No. 1, Oct. 4, 1917, file 125561, RG521.

91. Hough to COs of all ships and bases in France, July 23, 1918, Box 94, Logistics file, RG45; Medical officer to CO Naval Air Station, Gujan, Nov. 1, 1918, file 130212, RG52. There is a memo dated Jan. 24, 1918 in the French Naval Archives, Vincennes, from Admiral Moreau to the French Naval Minister, of a meeting with Admiral Wilson and local political officials. The items discussed included "surveillance of prostitutes," but no details of the meeting are included. See also Navy Port Officer, Bordeaux, to Provost Marshal, Oct. 11, 1918, Base Section 2, Box 134, A.E.F., Service of Supply, RG120; Talley to wife, July 14, 1918, Talley Letters, OA. For disagreements between American Army and Navy officers over jurisdiction in the different ports, see chapter 5.

92. Entry for Oct. 19, 1918, George Marek Diary, Virginia War History Commission Records, Virginia State Library; Buranalli, *Maggie of the Suicide Fleet*, 120–21; CO *Lydonia* to Niblack, Feb. 27, 1918, OS subj file, RG45; Shaw to Office of Naval Intelligence, July 15, 1918, file 126811, RG52.

93. McGowan to SecNav, Nov. 27, 1918, Reel 57, Daniels Papers, LC; Zogbaum, *From Sail to Saratoga*, 268–69; Schneider and Schneider, *Into the Breach*, 123.

94. Entry for Oct. 15, 1918, Forbes Diary, Box 58, Sims Papers, LC; Corrigan, *Tin Ensign*, 160–61; entry for Oct. 16, 1918, Brown Journal, WisHistSoc; *Pauillac Pilot*, Sept. 7, 1918; Schneider and Schneider, *Into the Breach*, 132; newspaper article in Columbus, Indiana, paper, n.d., copy in War History Records, Indiana State Library; *New York Post*, Feb. 20, 1919; Talley to wife, July 24, 1918, Talley letters, OA; Sims to Pringle, May 6, 1918, Box 79, Sims Papers, LC. Canadian nurses also attended the dances and were often considered as "American." See entries for July 14, 22, 27, 1917, in Sheely, *Sailor of the Air*, 38–42.

95. Schneider and Schneider, *Into the Breach*, 134–35, 266–67.

96. American Consul General to SecState, Sept. 11, 1918, File 133, London Consulate Records, RG84; Hicken, *The American Fighting Man*, 302–3; *Pall Mall Gazette*, March 8, 1919; "My A.E.F. Husband," *American Legion Weekly*, July 10, 1925, 6, 20–21; Fife, *The Passing Legions*, 167–71; *New York Herald*, European edition, May 28, 1919; Brown to American Consul, Dunfermline, Jan. 13, 1919, file 834.2; Dunfermline Consulate Records, RG84; Van Sant to Crass, Jan. 1, 1919, ibid.; Blackford, *Torpedoboat Sailor*, 139; Murmane, *Ground Swells*, 312; entry for Oct. 27, 1918, Kurfess Diary, OA; Harrison to author, Dec. 8, 1989; Davis to SecState, Jan. 6, 1920, and enclosure; Lansing to Jusserand, Nov. 27, 1918, and enclosure; De Chambrun to SecState, June 22, 1919; Lansing to Jusserand, Aug. 1, 1919; Jusserand to Lansing, Sept. 26, 1919; Lansing to Jusserand, Oct. 21, 1919; all in *Foreign Relations, 1918*, Supplement 2; 771–78. There are no statistics on the number of children born to the wives who were transported to the United States.

97. Thompson, *Take Her Down*, 284–85; *Cork Examiner*, Feb. 20, 1918; entry for March 8, 1918, Brown Journal, WisHistSoc; Sims to Pringle, May 6, 19198, Box 79, Sims Papers, LC; *Naval and Military Record* 36 (July 3, 1918): 428; questionnaires, WWI Research Collection, AMHI; *Our Navy* 12 (Feb. 1919): 40; *Fleet Review* 9 (Dec. 1918): 25; Beston, *Full Speed Ahead*, 60; *New York Herald*, April 17, 1919; *New York Post*, April 1, 1919; "A Brief Summary of U.S. Naval Forces in France, November 11, 1918–October 1919," OA. There is a large number of letters in the Aberdeen Consular Records, 1918–1919, concerning marriages to Americans. RG84.

98. Skinner, American Consul General to SecState, Sept. 11, 1918, file 133, London Consul-

ate Records, RG84; Sims Circular Letter, Sept. 9, 1918, copy in file 832, Cork Consular Records, RG84; Hicken, *The American Fighting Man*, 303; Griff, *Surrendered*, 182; Roger, *Les Americains a Brest le pendant la premiere guerre mondiale*. An American sailor based in Brest in a conversation with a French naval officer and wife was told that it was a good thing for "our men [to] leave a good many children behind them when they went home . . . as all our men were so big and strong they ought to have fine healthy kids." Entry Nov. 14, 1918, Brown Journal, WisHist-Soc. Some British women, not clear whether married to Americans or not, subscribed to the *Fleet Review*, the Navy's enlisted magazine of the period. See vol. 2 (Feb. 1920), 20. See also questionnaires, WWI Research Collection, AMHI.

99. DeLany, "Pull Together," *Shipmate* 40 (Oct. 1977): 19–20; DeLany, *Bayly's Navy*.

100. *Times* (London), July 4, 1919; Niblack, "Putting Cargos Across," ZCP subj file, RG45; Walling, *The Story of Plymouth*, 258; Golert to Belknap, April 11, 1919; *Inverness Courier*, April 9, 1919; in Belknap Papers, NHF.

Chapter 12. Warships and Weapons

1. "U.S. Navy Ship Force Levels, 1917–1989," Dec. 8, 1989, Ships History Branch, NHC; M. Simpson, *Anglo-American Naval Relations*, 55; Josephus Daniels, *Our Navy at War*, 355; French Naval Attaché to Minister, Sept. 17, 1917, French Naval Archives, Vincennes; Admiralty, *Supplement to the Monthly Navy List, Showing the United States Naval Forces Operating in European Waters, Corrected to November 1, 1918*, 362–402. I have used the SecNav's figures. See also *New Country Life*, Aug. 1918, 33; *American Legion Magazine*, June 1929, 41; memo, Sept. 10, 1918, ADM137/1622; Simsadus to Dept., Sept. 8, 1918, Reel 5, ME-11.

2. Parsons, *Wilsonian Diplomacy*, 121–22; Beharrell to Geddes, Sept. 22, 1918, ADM116/1209; *Army and Navy Journal*, August 17, 1918, 1949; "U.S. Navy Ship Force Levels, 1917–1989"; memo by Geddes for War Cabinet, Aug. 2, 1918, in M. Simpson, *Anglo-American Naval Relations*, 504–6; Geddes to Lloyd George, Aug. 26, 1918, ibid., 507; British Naval Mission to the United States, memo, Sept. 22, 1918, ibid., 520–24.

3. P. Kennedy, "Britain in the First World War," 54.

4. Hurd and Bashford, *Sons of Admiralty*, 248–49.

5. Brownrigg, *Indiscretions of the Naval Censor*, 256–57; Sims to Benson, June 14, 1918, copy in Pratt Papers, OA. See also *Navy and Military Record* 37 (March 19, 1919): 177; memo no. 30, May 24, 1918, in Navy Dept., *The American Planning Section in London*, 231; H. Borden, *Robert Laird Borden*, 838; Davy, "Report on Personnel," June 21, 1918, NA subj file, RG45; Chapple, *We'll Stick to the Finish*, 210–11; Sims to wife, June 8, 1918, Box 10, Sims Papers, LC; McCrea Oral History, USNI; entry for July 22, 1918, King George V Diary, Windsor Castle. Royal Navy officers kept up their tradition of "mess jackets and dress uniforms" during wartime whereas the U.S. Navy abandoned the tradition for the duration.

6. Sims to Benson, June 14, 1918, copy in Pratt Papers, OA; Report of Committee of US Officers on Comparison between British and American Warships, Dec. 10, 1918, in M. Simpson, *Anglo-American Naval Relations*, 358–60; testimony of Comdr. Rowcliff, May 6, 1918, General Board Hearings.

7. The ships in the Grand Fleet had been camouflaged, but it was soon dropped as "too confusing to other ships in formation." Wiley, *An Admiral from Texas*, 186; entry for Dec. 7, 1917, Marder, *Portrait of an Admiral*, 282.

8. Hashagen, *U-Boats Westward!* 163–65; Marder, *From the Dreadnought to Scapa Flow*, 4: 89; *New York Sun*, Nov. 24, 1918. For the Queenstown command, see Beston, *Full Speed Ahead*, 63; entry for Sept. 1, 1917, Latimer Diary, UVA; entry Aug. 21, 1917, in Taussig, *The Queenstown Patrol*, 104–5. For British developments in camouflage, see Report of "Dazzle Painting Committee," Aug. 1918, Crease Papers, Ministry of Defense Whitehall Library, Scotland Yard, London; R. Gardiner, *The Eclipse of the Big Gun*, 204–5; Gibson and Prendergast, *The German*

Submarine War, 177. For U.S. Navy developments, see Slosson, *The Great Crusade and After*, 51; Crowell and Wilson, *The Road to France*, 2: 509–11; Whitaker, "Smashing Hun Submarines with Sims." The best discussion of camouflage is Stackhouse, "The Anglo-American Atlantic Convoy System in World War I," Ph.D. diss., 359–69. See also Murphy, "Marine Camouflage," 28–32, 72; Alan Bemend, "Principles Underlying Ship Camouflage," *International Marine Engineering* (Feb. 1919): 90–93; R. F. Sumrall, "Ship Camouflage, Deceptive Art," U.S. Naval Institute *Proceedings* 74 (July 1971): 68–71.

9. Friedman's *U.S. Destroyers* is the standard study. See also J. D. Alden, *Flush Decks and Four Pipers*, 1–5; Shafter, *Destroyers in Action*, 50–51; *Jane's Fighting Ships of World War I*, 141–44; Silverstone, *U.S. Warships of World War I*, 107–14; Blackford, *Torpedoboat Sailor*, 34; R. Gardiner, *The Eclipse of the Big Gun*, 110; R. W. King, *Naval Engineering and American Seapower*, 94; Friedman, *U.S. Destroyers*, 33–34, 40–47; Ray Ashley, "The Return of the *Mayflower*," May 3, 1991, copy in author's possession. Thirty-nine flush deck destroyers were commissioned before the Armistice.

10. A search in the French Naval Archives produced no comments on American warships. No observations on U.S. warships by Entente nations other than Great Britain have been found. There is one Italian intelligence report on the wooden 110-foot subchasers. See "Report of an Italian Officer on Subchasers," Sept. 19, 1918, OD subj file, RG45. There are comments on American auxiliary vessels, particularly the repair ships, by the French. See chapter 8.

11. McBride to Sims, Box 1, Entry 113, RG19; Bayly to Jellicoe, Oct. 7, 1917, add 49009, Jellicoe Papers. See also Sims to CNO, Nov. 3, 1917, copy in *Naval Investigation*, 168; Kearny testimony, Sept. 5, 1917, General Board Hearings.

12. Entry for Nov. 23, 1917, Merrill Diary, UNC-CH; H. Holt, "A Talk with Admiral Sims," 394; Furlong testimony, Oct. 3, 1918, General Board Hearings; Vernou testimony, Dec. 17, 1917, ibid.; Taussig testimony, Dec. 4, 1917, ibid.; Du Bose testimony, Oct. 17, 1917, ibid.; Johnson testimony, Dec. 4, 1917, ibid.; Fairfield to Bayly, June 15, 1917, ADM137/651; Jellicoe, *The Submarine Peril*, 102; *New York Evening Post*, Jan. 19, 1918; Louis P. Davis Oral History, ECU; Davis to Bureau of Construction and Repairs, May 20, 1918, Davis Papers, ECU; Sims to Bureau of Construction and Repairs, Oct. 13, 1917, Box 1, Entry 113, RG19; "We Are Ready Now," *Review of Reviews*, 531–32; Sims, *The Victory at Sea*, 59; Friedman, *U.S. Destroyers*, 46; Lt. Cdr. Francis Craven, "Destroyer Design for the U.S. Navy," *ONI Monthly Information Bulletin* (March 15, 1919): 37.

13. Chandler, "American and British Destroyers," 579–80; "The American Destroyer," *Scientific American*, Dec. 28, 1918, 515; Friedman, *U.S. Destroyers*, 46; Murdock, *They Also Served*, 76–77; *Glasgow Herald*, Oct. 25, 1918.

14. Henry Kieffer Memoir, USS *Parker* file, CZ files, OA; Moore Oral History, Columbia University; entry for July 25–26, 1917, Forbes Diary, Box 58, Sims Papers, LC; Pringle to Sims, July 15, 1917, Reel 3, ME-11; CO *Manley* to CNO, Dec. 19, 1917, OS subj file, RG45; Davis & Davis to Bureau of Construction and Repairs, May 20, 1918, Louis P. Davis Papers, ECU; testimony of Taussig and Johnson, Dec. 4, 1917, General Board Hearings. There is considerable material in Box 1, Entry 113, RG19, concerning these modifications. See particularly Mayo to SecNav, Oct. 7, 1917. See also Blackford, *Torpedoboat Sailor*, 109.

15. Robert B. Carney Oral History, Columbia University; Sims to Bayly, Nov. 20, 1917, Box 47, Sims Papers, LC; Friedman, *U.S. Destroyers*, 45, 46; Taussig, "Destroyer Experiences during the Great War," 396–402; Coletta and Bauer, *Bases, Overseas* 2: 386; Craven, "Destroyer Design for U.S. Navy," 36–37; Roosevelt journal letter, July 26, 1918, Elliott Roosevelt, *F.D.R.: Personal Letters*, 386; Pringle to Sims, March 11, 1918, Box 79, Sims Papers, LC; *New York Herald Magazine*, Jan. 5, 1919; Pringle to Sims, July 16, 1917, Reel 3, ME-11.

16. Forbes, *J. P. Morgan, Jr.*, 98; Parkinson, *The History of the New York Yacht Club*, 258–60; CNO to Mayo, May 8, 1917, Reel 1, ME-11; Daniels to Sims, Dec. 15, 1917, Box 23, Sims Papers, LC.

17. Franklin Roosevelt was a member of the club and possibly the one instrumental in persuading it to take the lead in leasing the yachts to the Navy for a "dollar a month" (see Parkinson, *The History of the New York Yacht Club*, 257–58); Some were leased at this price; some were purchased by the Navy. Perry, "They're in the Navy Now," 33–38; Connolly, *Navy Men*, 243.

18. There is considerable literature on the armed yachts. See Stirling, "American Armed Yachts in the War Zone"; Breckel, "The Suicide Flotilla," 661–70; *Literary Digest*, March 22, 1919; Whitaker, "Our Tin Fleet in the First Battle Line"; Husband, *On the Coast of France*, 6–21; Husband, *A Year in the Navy*, 122–23; Reginald Wright Kauffman, *Our Navy at Work*, 2–3; Rose, *Brittany Patrol*, passim; Connolly, *Navy Men*, 243; Paine, "Our Navy on the French Coast." See also entry for July 3, 1917, in Josephus Daniels, *Cabinet Diaries*, 184. For individual yachts, see Husband, *A Year in the Navy*, 156–62 (*Christabel*); "The oldest and smallest of the yachts deployed in war zone," in Cooke, "Recollections," NDL; *Havenhill (Pa.) Sunday Record*, Jan. 22, 1928; Twining to Wilson, Sept. 8, 1917, OF subj file, RG45; Collins to Macunn, June 19, 1917, file 530, Glasgow Consulate Records, RG84. There is considerable information in file 834, 1917, in the Liverpool Consulate Records, RG84. Tibbott, "'Broadway' Sailors," 59–65; R. R. Moore, "*Corsair*, Most Famous of Steam Yachts"; Paine, *The Corsair in the War Zone*. For conversion, see ibid., 8–11; Perry, *Our Navy in the War*, 242–44. For *Isabel*, see J. D. Alden, "The Yacht That Was a Destroyer." *Isabel* was the only one of the yachts to be designated a destroyer. For details on many of the yachts, see Hofman, *The Steam Yachts*. Nations on both sides converted yachts into armed naval vessels. See *Jane's Fighting Ships of World War I*, passim; Arnold, Medea: *the Classic Steam Yacht*, 129–48.

19. Quoted in Blythe, "The Breton Patrol," 7; see also Ruth Wright Kauffman, "Small but Valiant"; "With the Yankee 'Suicide Fleet' in French Waters," *Literary Digest*, March 22, 1919. 19. Leighton, *Simsadus*, 39. See also Benson to Sims, Sept. 7, 1917, Reel 2, ME-11; and H. B. Wilson, *The American Navy in France*, 23

20. Pownall Oral History, USNI; Howell, *Medals of Honor*, 255–79, on John Mackenzie. See also Buranelli, Maggie *of the Suicide Fleet*, 4, 17–18; Whitaker, "Toy Dreadnoughts," *Land and Water* 71 (Sept. 19, 1918): 10–11; Whitaker, "Our Toy Dreadnoughts," *Century Magazine* 96 (June, 1918), 801. These two articles by Whitaker are the same with different introductions. See also entry for Oct. 31, 1917, Latimer Diary, UVA.

21. Hinkamp, "Bringing in the Sheaves"; Hinkamp, "Pipe Sweepers"; Hinkamp, testimony, July 28, 1918, General Board Hearings; "Work of the American Mine-Sweeping Squadron," *Rudder* (April 1919): 180–81; "History of Squadron Four Patrol Force," OF subj file, RG45; Moser Melia, "*Damn the Torpedoes*," 28–29; H. B. Wilson, *The American Navy in France*, 123–26; Magruder to CO Patrol Squadron, Jan. 2, 1918, file C18-324, Confidential Files, 1917–1919, RG80; Loder to wife, Oct. 18, 1917, Loder Papers, Mariners' Museum; Hurd and Bashford, *Sons of Admiralty*, 256–57; *Philadelphia Public Ledger*, Sept. 20, 1919; scattered correspondence in Box 5, entry 113, RG19 concerning decision to deploy minesweepers to French waters. See also Magruder to Sims, July 18, 1917, OF subj file, RG45; Magruder, "The Navy in the War," 21.

22. Moser Melia, "*Damn the Torpedoes*," 28.

23. Memo: A Comparison of British and American Naval Effort, ADM137/2710; Moser Melia, "*Damn the Torpedoes*," 34.

24. Quoted in Belknap, *The Yankee Mining Squadron*, 99 n. 34. See also Cowie, *Mines, Minelayers, and Minelaying*, 32–41; Lundeberg, "Underseas Warfare and Allied Strategy in World War I"; Lott, *Most Dangerous Sea*, 13, 23. R. Gardiner, *The Eclipse of the Big Gun*, 110 n. 33.

25. Chief of Naval Staff (Br) to CNO, Oct. 18, 1917, Roll 37, M1140; Sims to Dept., March 24, 1918, Reel 3, ME-11; memo for CNO, April 9, 1918, Reel 8, ibid.; Belknap testimony, Jan. 7, 1918, General Board Hearings; *New York Herald*, Nov. 12, 1919; Belknap to cousin Harry, Aug. 24, 1958; to Strauss, May 10, 1918, in Belknap Papers, NHF; Sims, *The Victory at Sea*, 297–98; Beals, "New England's Role in the Yankee Mining Squadron," 3–11; Belknap to Dept., Sept. 16, 1922,

Belknap Papers, NHF; Belknap, *The Yankee Mining Squadron*, 100–104; *Naval Ordnance Activities, World War, 1917–1918*, 122–24. See Navy Dept., *The Northern Barrage and Other Mining Activities*, 70–78; Mannix, *The Old Navy*, 21; Sims to Benson, June 14, 1918, copy in Pratt Papers, OA.

26. Browning to Jellicoe, July 20, 1917, in M. Simpson, *Anglo-American Naval Relations*, 90; Jellicoe to De Chair, June 7, 1917, ADM137/1436; ADM to C-in-C, and reply, June 7, 1917, ADM 137/1964; Dept. to Sims, July 5, 1917, file 25-9-2, Confidential Files, RG80; Summary of Messages received by Minister of Marine concerning augmentation of American naval forces in European waters, July 2, 1917 to January 14, 1918, French Naval Archives, Vincennes.

27. R. E. Johnson, *Guardians of the Sea*, 44–45; Scheina, "Coast Guard at War," *Commandant's Bulletin* 1987 (Feb.) 13: 27; Confidential Order No. 2, March 22, 1917, OK subj file, RG45.

28. Data on the cutters assigned to European waters from *DANFS* and *Jane's Fighting Ships of World War I*. See also Taylor to various shore facilities, April 21, 1917, Box 5, Entry 113, RG19; Niblack to Sims, July 29, 1918, P-Gibraltar subj file, RG45; Benson to Sims, Aug. 1, 1917, Reel 2, ME-11; Capt. Hertholf, USCG, to Chief, Bureau of Navigation, May 11, 1917, file 631, Records of the U.S. Coast Guard, RG26, NA.

29. Hellwig to Sims, June 2, 1918, OK subj file, RG45; Sims to CO USS *Marietta*, July 10, 1918, ibid.; Niblack to Sims, March 15, 1918, Box 76, Sims Papers, LC. See also comments on memo (n.d.) U.S. Ships to be Based at Gibraltar, ADM137/1437.

30. R. Gardiner, *The Eclipse of the Big Gun*, 124–25; Rousmaniere, "The Romance of the Subchasers," 42–43; Furer, "The 110-Foot Submarine Chasers and Eagle Boats," 753–54; Friedman, *U.S. Small Combatants*, 518.

31. Furer, "The 110-Foot Submarine Chasers and Eagle Boats," 755–59, 762–63; Freidel, *FDR: The Apprenticeship*, 310–13; Rousmaniere, "The Romance of the Subchasers," 43; R. Gardiner, *The Eclipse of the Big Gun*, 125; Friedman, *U.S. Small Combatants*, 518; Taylor, "The Design of War Ships as Affected by the World War," 179; Nutting, *The Cinderellas of the Fleet*, 57–59; Moffat, *Maverick Navy*, 149–50; Navy Dept., *The American Naval Planning Section in London*, June 12, 1918, 243–44. For a description of interior design and utilization of spaces, see Chambers, *Submarine Chasers in the Mediterranean*, 2–6; and *Annual Report Surgeon General, U.S. Navy 1918*, 264–65; *DANFS*, 6: 711–27.

32. For Sims's comments, see Sims to Belknap, July 11, 1917, in M. Simpson, *Anglo-American Naval Relations*, 244; to Bayly, Aug. 24, 1918, Box 24, Sims Papers, LC; to Niblack, May 23, 1918, Box 76, ibid.; to Dinger, Sept. 6, 1917, OH subj file, RG45. See also Halpern, *A Naval History of World War I*, 399; Babcock to Sims, n.d., but probably early 1918, Box 144, Sims Papers, LC; Taussig testimony, Dec. 4, 1917, General Board Hearings; Endorsement, May 29, 1917, file 420-14, Confidential Files, RG80; Cotten to wife, June 18, 1918, Cotten Papers, UNC-CH; Stone, "The Sub Chasers as Sea Boats," 57.

33. Fisher memos, Sept. 4, 8, 1917, in M. Simpson, *Anglo-American Naval Relations*, 253–54; De Chair to Greene, May 15, 1917, ibid., 46–47; Roskill, *Hankey, Man of Secrets*, 1: 453; *Pall Mall Gazette*, February 4, 1918; Benson to Sims, March 1918, U subj file, RG45.

34. Sims to Dept., March 28, 1918, Reel 4, ME-11; Sims to Admiralty, ibid., Sims to Secretary, Allied Naval Council, April 26, 1918, OR subj file, RG45; "Allocation of Submarine Chasers," May 20, 1918, ADM137/2709; memo no. 29, May 25, 1918, in Navy Dept., *The American Naval Planning Section in London*, 227–29; memo no. 34, June 7, 1918, ibid., 239–40; Sims to SecNav, June 1, 1918, Reel 4, ME-11; Minutes of Allied Naval Council, June 6, 1918, QC subj file, RG45; Sims to CNO, June 20, 1918, OD subj file, RG45; Twining to Sims, July 10, 1918, Reel 4, ME-11; Simsadus to Queenstown, Aug. 14, 1918, Reel 9, ibid.; Sims to Dept., Sept. 6, 1918, Reel 5, ibid.; Sims to Bayly, Sept. 14, 1918, Box 40, Sims Papers; Sims to Dept., Oct. 2, 1918, Reel 6, ME-11; Dept. to Sims, Oct. 3, 1918, ibid.; Thompson to Leigh, May 10, 1918, copy in Cotten Papers, UNC-CH. Concerning ASW craft and listening devices, see Naval Consulting Board to Dan-

iels, May 22, 1918, Box 47, Confidential Files, 1915–1922, RG80; Report of T. Robins, March 18, 1918, ibid.; Bulletin No. 2, May 18, 1918, LA subj file, RG45; Sims to Dept. April 15, 1918, ibid. For Captain Leigh and the listening devices, see chapter 18.

35. M. S. Brown, "The Experiences of a Yankee Sub-Chaser," 57; Moffat, *Maverick Navy*, 35; Blythe, "The Sea Terriers," 16; F. Green, *Our Naval Heritage*, 346; Hadley and Sarty, *Tin-Pots and Pirate Ships*, 224, 235; Rousmaniere, "The Romance of the Subchasers," 43; Chatterton, *Danger Zone*, 336; Stone, "The Sub Chasers as Sea Boats," 57–59; Sims to Admiralty, Oct. 30, 1918, Reel 6, ME-11; to Niblack, May 23, 1918, Box 76, Sims Papers, LC; Long memo to Chief of Staff, Simsadus, April 17, 1918, OD subj file, RG45; Wilbur questionnaire, WWI Research Collection, AMHI; *Annual Report Surgeon General, U.S. Navy 1919*, 263; Babcock to Sims, 1918, Box 144, Sims Papers, LC; Hepburn to Sims, Oct. 30, 1918, Reel 10, ME-11; Calthorpe to Geddes, June 5, 1918, in M. Simpson, *Anglo-American Naval Relations*, 277; Hayward testimony, Jan. 26, 1918, General Board Hearings; Chambers, *Submarine Chasers in the Mediterranean*, 2–6; extract of letter from British Admiral to Wemyss, copy in OD subj file, RG45; entries for July 29, Sept. 10, 1918, Kipp Diary, copy in author's possession; Babcock to Sims, n.d., Box 144, Sims Papers. LC; Medical officer, Plymouth Naval Base to Bureau of Medicine and Surgery, Feb., 1919, file 132564, RG52; Hepburn to Sims, Nov. 30, 1918, OD subj file, RG45.

36. Jackson to Wilson, Jan. 27, 1918, OD subj file, RG45; Chief of the 4th Section, Le Capitaine de Frigate, Report on the subchasers in French service, Dec. 15, 1917, copy in Box 10, Entry 113, RG19; Leyguis to Daniels, Dec. 7, 1918, Reel 36, Daniels Papers, LC; French naval attaché, London to Minister of Marine, n.d., but fall, 1918, French Naval Archives, Vincennes; Admiralty memo, Oct. 25, 1918, ADM137/947; "Report of an Italian Officer on Subchasers," Sept. 19, 1918, OD subj file, RG45; French naval attaché report, n.d., but fall, 1918, French Naval Archives, Vincennes.

37. *DANFS*, 6: 744–47; CNO to Sims, May 29, 1918, file 125138, Confidential Files, RG80; memo, March 28, 1918, OD subj file, RG45.

38. Donald Mitchell, *History of the Modern American Navy*, 142; Weir, *Building American Submarines*, 5–11. It was not until 1916 that the Navy contracted for "fleet submarines," that is, boats large enough and with speed and cruising radius capable of operating with a surface fleet. None were operational in time to participate in the war. For the problems with each submarine class, see Weir, *Building American Submarines*, 11, passim. See also H. E. Keisker, "U.S. Submarines in the War Zone," U.S. Naval Institute *Proceedings* 56 (Dec. 1930): 1132; Hart memo, n.d., copy in folder, "Allied Submarine Operations World War I," Box 1, OA; Dunn to Simsadus, May 20, 1918, Reel 20, ME-11; Sims to Dept., May 28, June 7, 1918, Reel 4, ibid.; Report, Nov. 23, 1917, Reel 14, ibid.; CO Submarine Flotilla Two to Commander, Submarine Force, Nov. 6, 1917, folder, "Allied Submarine Operations in World War I," Box 1, OA; Leigh, memo, Oct. 7, 1918, LA subj file, RG45. For fitting out British-type periscopes, see Sims to Dept., June 13, 1918, ME-11.

39. For Sims's quote, see *Naval Investigation*, 76–78. See also Sims to Daniels, June 28, 1917, in M. Simpson, *Anglo-American Naval Relations*, 233; Hart to Pratt, March 10, 1920, folder SM History, Box 2, OA; CNO order, July 2, 1917, folder "Allied Submarine Operations World War I," Box 1, OA; Daniels to Bureaus and Navy yards Boston, New York, Puget Sound, Aug. 15, 1917, in ibid.; Benson to Mayo, July 2, 1917, ibid.; Benson to Simsadus, Aug. 23, 1917, Reel 2, ME-11; Sims to Dept., Nov. 2, 1917, ibid.; Mayo to Dept., Aug. 27, 1917, Reel 3, ibid.; Benson to Mayo, Sept. 5, 1917, OH subj file, RG45; Sims to Bayly, Oct. 2, 1918, in M. Simpson, *Anglo-American Naval Operations*, 312; Benson to C.O. Submarine Force, Atlantic Fleet, et al., Sept. 5, 1918, OH subj file, RG45.

40. Dimensions, *DANFS*, 1: 232–35. See also Compton-Hall, *Submarines and the War at Sea*, 276–77.

41. For dimensions, see *Jane's Fighting Ships of World War I*, 133–36, and individual ship histories in *DANFS*. See also R. W. King, *Naval Engineering and American Seapower*, 69; *USS*

Nevada, *1916–1946*, 13; Power, *Battleship Texas*, 7; *USS* Nevada, *The Cheer Up Ship*, 4–5; Todd, USS *Oklahoma*, 19; Rickett Memoir, Smithsonian; Baker, "Historic Fleets," 60; Rossell, "Types of Naval Ships," 291–93; Perry, "Three Veterans of the United States Navy," 632–38; Lockwood, *Down to the Sea in Subs*, 18; J. W. Jones, "United States Battleship Operations in World War I," Ph.D. diss., 55–60.

42. Reilly and Scheina, *American Battleships 1886–1923*, 7–8, 154, 177–78, 241; Power, *USS* Texas, 9; C. King, *Atlantic Charter*, 200; Winterhalter testimony, Nov. 21, 1918, General Board Hearings; *ONI Monthly Bulletin* (Nov. 1, 1918): 2298; J. A. Goodwin to "Em," Nov. 21, 1918, in IWM. See also Stillwell, *Battleship* Arizona.

43. Friedman, *U.S. Battleships*, 177–78; Rowcliff to Vice Admiral Hoffman, May 11, 1918, USS *Arkansas* file, Ships History Branch, NHC; Attwood to Goodall, July 15, 1918, and Goodall to Attwood, June 28, 1918, in "Foreign Warship Covers," NMM; Attwood memo, 1918, in *New York* file, ibid.; Rodman to SecNav, Feb. 9, 1918, Reel 8, ME-11; Sims to CNO, Nov. 29, 1918, Box 9, entry 113, RG19; Capt. F. J. Egger to author, April 18, 1988, in author's possession; C. King, *Atlantic Charter*, 200.

44. Friedman, *U.S. Battleships*, 174–75; "Comparison of British and American Navigation Equipment," *ONI Monthly Bulletin* (Feb. 1918): 107; Schubert, *Come on Texas*, 173; Rowcliff, May 11, 1918, USS *Arkansas* File, Ships History Branch, NHC; Reilly and Scheina, *American Battleships*, 240–43; Attwood memo, 1918, in *New York* file, "Foreign Warship Covers," NMM Rodman to SecNav, Feb. 16, 1918, OB subj file, RG45; del Valle Oral History, Marine Corps Museum. For complaints about bridges in early classes, see Reilly and Scheina, *American Battleships*, 171.

45. Rodman to Benson, Jan. 19, 1918, in M. Simpson, *Anglo-American Naval Relations*, 342; Sims to Pringle, July 31, 1917, in ibid., 331; Sims to wife, July 30, 1917, Box 9, Sims Papers; Attwood memo on *New York*, "Foreign Warship Covers," NMM; Rodman to CNO, Feb. 9, 1918, Reel 8, ME-11; Power, *USS* Texas, 12; Friedman, *U.S. Battleships*, 175–77; Furlong, *Class of 1905*, 163; Thomas C. Kinkaid Oral History, USNI; Rodman to Benson, Dec. 30, 1917, Confidential Files, 1917–1919, RG80.

46. McCrea Oral History, USNI; DNC memo, 1918, "Foreign Warship Covers," NMM; E. L. Beach Memoir, in possession of the family of Captain Edward L. Beach.

47. See chapter 16.

48. "Comparison of British and American Gunnery Training, Fire Control, Control of Searchlights, and Control Stations," Jan. 1919, *ONI Monthly Bulletin* (Feb. 15, 1919): 67. This document gives a good explanation of gunnery training carried on by the battleships while with the Grand Fleet. Friedman, *U.S. Naval Weapons*, 30–34; Friedman, *U.S. Battleships*, 173. For development of fire control systems, see Mindell, "Datum for Its Own Annihilation," Ph.D. diss., 39–68. See also Hogg and Batchelor, *Naval Gun*, 108, 110, 116; R. W. King, *Naval Engineering and American Seapower*, 103–4; J. W. Jones, "U.S. Battleship Operations in World War I," Ph.D. diss., 162–68; Egerton to Bingham, July 21, 1918, Donald C. Bingham Papers, LC; Rodman to Bingham, March 16, 1918, ibid.; testimony of Kimmel, Feb. 28, March 25, 1918, Plunkett, Oct. 2, 1917; Castle, Sept. 29, 1917; Leahy, Oct. 2, 1918, all in General Board Hearings.

49. Mindell, "Datum for its Own Annihilation," Ph.D. diss., 65. See also J. W. Jones, "U.S. Battleship Operations in World War I," Ph.D. diss., 166; Castle testimony, Sept. 29, 1917, General Board Hearings.

50. Attwood memo on the *New York*, 1918, "Foreign Warship Covers," NMM; Sims to Benson, Dec. 20, 1917, in M. Simpson, *Anglo-American Naval Relations*, 340.

51. Report dated Dec. 10, 1918, in ibid., 358–59. See also *Naval Investigation*, 2796–97. "Comparison of Engineering Conditions in U.S. and Grand Fleet," Jan. 1919, *ONI Monthly Bulletin* (Feb. 15, 1919); Rodman Report, ibid., 15–26; Report on Rodman, March 1919, in "Foreign Warship Covers," NMM; edited copy of report in Friedman, *U.S. Battleships*, 178–79; Report on *New*

York in ibid.; *Daily Chronicle* (London), July 26, 1918; *Manchester Guardian*, Dec. 17, 1918. The Royal Navy did adopt the American refrigeration system for its ships serving in "hot climates." Memo, June 5, 1920, "Foreign Warship Covers," NMM. See also *Fleet Review* 9 (Oct. 1918), 13; *Naval and Military Record* (Aug. 7, 1918): 499.

52. Tobey to Rodman, Aug. 3, 1918, Box 63, Logistics file, RG45; Schoultz, *With the British Battle Fleet*, 301; R. W. King, *Naval Engineering and American Seapower*, 78. For the fire control systems (range finders, directors, etc.), see *Naval Ordnance Activities World War, 1917–18*, 151–57; Kimmel testimony, Feb. 22 1918, General Board Hearings; *ONI Monthly Bulletin* (Nov. 30, 1918): 89–91.

53. Minutes of Committee on Paravanes, n.d., ADM137/1967. *Arkansas* was the first U.S. battleship to have installed a gyroscope compass, which was developed by Elmer Sperry. The best account of the development of the Sperry gyroscope is Mindell, "Datum for Its Own Annihilation," Ph.D. diss., 50–74. See also Lockwood, *Down to the Sea in Subs*, 18.

54. Sims to Benson, Dec. 20, 1917, Box 49, Sims Papers, LC; Sims to Dept., Jan. 18, 1918, Reel 10, M1092; Benson to Sims, Jan. 5, 1918, LA subj file, RG45; memo by Admiralty Director of Plans, Jan. 13, 1918, in M. Simpson, *Anglo-American Naval Relations*, 343; Harry W. Hill Oral History, Columbia University; Wiley, *An Admiral from Texas*, 196; *ONI Monthly Bulletin* (Dec. 15, 1918): 2521–22; Simons, "Both by Land and by Sea"; Lieut. George L. Catlin, "Paravanes," April 22, 1919, copy in Navy Department Library; Stackhouse, "The Anglo-American Atlantic Convoy System in World War I," Ph.D. diss., 389; Moser Melia, *"Damn the Torpedoes,"* 33–34. Information on the use of paravanes on American warships operating in European waters is quite scarce. Because of the British demand for secrecy concerning this equipment, "it was a rule of the Navy Department that the word paravane should not be spoken on the telephone or written in dispatches." George Catlin, "Paravanes." For the development of the paravane, see Cornford, *The Paravane Adventure*, 31, 243–48; Hartcup, *The War of Invention*, 142–43; War Diary extract, June 15, 1918, LA subj file, RG45; Price to Daniels, June 30, 1917, ibid.; Pringle to Sims, July 21, 1917, ibid.; Sims to Dept., Jan. 28, 1918, ibid.; Pringle to Sims and endorsement, Jan. 23, 1918, ibid.; Sims to Bureau of Construction and Repairs, Sept. 11, 1918, ibid.; Sims to OpNav, Aug. 10, 1917, ibid.; Tobey to Dept., Aug. 27, 1917, Reel 2, ME-11.

55. Hill Oral History, Columbia University; Harrod, *Manning the New Navy*, 143; Edwards to Dorling, Oct. 26, 1918, ADM137/2710; John Hoover Oral History, Columbia University; Sims to Dept., Dec. 30, 1917, Reel 10, M1092; Report to OpNav, Aug. 24, 1918, ibid.; R. W. King, *Naval Engineering and American Seapower*, 1043; Weir, *Building American Submarines*, 70–71.

56. Marder, *From the Dreadnought to Scapa Flow*, 4: 71

57. Entries for May 24, 26, June 19, 1918, Latimer Diary, UVA; Moore Oral History, Columbia University; *Wadsworth* War Diary, May 5, 1917, copy in reel 8, ME-11; Pringle to Sims, July 15, 1917, Reel 3, ibid.; DeLany, *Bayly's Navy*, 2; "American Destroyers in the War," 88; Friedman, *U.S. Naval Weapons*, 123; *New York Herald*, April 11, 1919; *Harper's Pictorial Library of the World War*, 4: 330; Doughty, "The Effect of Depth Charges on Submarines," 353; W. H. Miller, *The Boys of 1917*, 60; Rose, *Brittany Patrol*, 81, 83–84; *Naval Ordnance War Activities, World War I, 1917–18*, 98–99; Niblack, "Putting Cargos Across," ZCP subj file, RG45; Wheeler Oral History, USNI; Carney Oral History, Columbia University; H. B. Wilson, *The American Navy in France*, 136; Sims to Benson, March 7, 1918, in M. Simpson, *Anglo-American Naval Relations*, 283; Pringle to Sims, July 15, 1917, C18-324 file, Confidential Files, RG80; Sims to Niblack, May 31, 1918, Reel 12, ME-11; *ONI Semi-Monthly Bulletin*, ser. 61 (Nov. 1918): 2295.

58. Doughty, "The Effect of Depth Charges on Submarines," 353; *Tucker* War Diary, July 5, 1917, OE subj file, RG45; *Naval Ordnance Activities, World War I, 1917–18*, 99, 101; Bureau of Ordnance memo, Oct. 24, 1917, Reel 10, M1092; Chief Gunner, *Prometheus*, to Wilson, June 18, 1918, Box 8, Logistics file, RG45; Sims to Bureau of Ordnance, July 8, 1918, Reel 4, ME-11; Price to CO

Submarine Detachment 3, Oct. 26, 1918, LA subj file, RG45; Dewey Watson letter to mother, n.d., War History Records, Indiana State Library; Friedman, *U.S. Naval Weapons*, 122; Fullinwider to Sims, Oct. 13, 1917, Fullinwider Papers, Smithsonian; Furlong testimony, Oct. 3, 1918, General Board Hearings.

59. *Naval Ordnance Activities, World War I, 1917–18*, 104–6; Fullam to Roger Welles, Jan., 1918, Box 5, William F. Fullam Papers, LC; Wheeler Oral History, USNI; W. H. Miller, *The Boys of 1917*, 60; "American Destroyers in the War," 86, 88–89; Sims to OpNav, May 14, 1918, Reel 4, ME-11; Sims to OpNav, March 24, 1918, Reel 3, ibid.

60. Sims to NavIntel, April 16, 1917, in M. Simpson, *Anglo-American Naval Relations*, 371; Dept. to Sims, Oct. 21, 1917, ibid., 380; Hartman, *Weapons That Wait*, 48; Ferrell, *Woodrow Wilson and World War I*, 44; Ohl, "Mines for the North Sea Barrage: A Study of the Navy and the Military-Industrial Complex," MS copy in possession of author. Earle to SecNav, Aug. 28, 1918, in Fullinwider Papers, Smithsonian; C.O. U.S. Naval Bases 17 & 18 to CO Mine Force, Sept. 21, 1918, ibid.; Fullinwider to Sims, Oct. 13, 1917, ibid.; Fullinwider memo, Oct. 16, 1917, ibid.; Cleary, "The Production of the Mines for the Northern Mine Barrage," 439; Grant, "The Use of Mines Against Submarines," 1275; F. H. Schofield, "Incidents and Present-Day Aspects of Naval Strategy," ibid., 49 (May, 1923): 794; *Naval Ordnance Activities, World War I, 1917–18*, 109–11; Friedman, *U.S. Naval Weapons*, 111; *The Northern Barrage and Other Mining Activities*, 42–49; Sims to CNO, July 18, 1917, Reel 1, ME-11. Commander Simon P. Fullinwider was in charge of the design and procurement of the Mark VI mines. Belknap to Sparkman, Dec. 5, 1956, Belknap Papers, NHF. This letter gives an interesting account of the development of mine operations during the early years of the twentieth century up to the U.S. entry into World War II. See also speech by Belknap, June 1, 1940, in ibid.

61. Ohl, "Mines for the North Sea Barrage"; R. A. Marr to Mrs. Shulte, n.d., in Norfolk folder, Virginia War History Commission Records, Virginia State Library; Ferrell, *Woodrow Wilson and World War I*, 44; Earle to SecNav, Aug. 7, 1918, in Fullinwider Papers, Smithsonian; Cleary, "The Production of the Mines for the Northern Mine Barrage," 441–45; Lott, *Most Dangerous Sea*, 15; *The Northern Barrage and Other Mining Activities*, 50–51.

62. Descriptions of the mines can be found in Duncan, *America's Use of Sea Mines*, 50–54; *Naval Ordnance Activities, World War I, 1917–18*, 111–12; The North Sea Mine Barrage, n.d., Roll 37, M1140; Belknap, *The Yankee Mining Squadron*, 25–28; *The Northern Barrage and Other Mining Activities*, 47–49. For the anchor decision, see Earle to Sims, Oct. 31, 1918, Reel 2, ME-11.

63. Quoted in T. Wilson, *The Myriad Faces of War*, 692. See also R. Gardiner, *The Eclipse of the Big Gun*, 116; Taffrail, *Swept Channels*, 325; Liddle, *The Sailor's War*, 186; memo by Admiralty Planning Division, Nov. 1, 1918, in M. Simpson, *Anglo-American Naval Relations*, 393; entries for Sept. 27, Oct. 4, 1918, Packer Diary, Packer MS, Churchill College, Cambridge.

64. Chack and Antier, *Histoire maritime de la première guerre mondiale*, 3: 456–58; Sims to OpNav, Nov. 5, 1918, Reel 8, ME-11; Michelsen, "The Submarine Warfare," 73–77; Grant, "The Use of Mines Against Submarines," 1275; *Naval Investigation*, 1512–13.

For discrepancies in American and British reports on premature explosions, see various reports in ADM137/1984. For American comments on premature explosions, see Strauss to Sims, June 20, 1918, Reel 8, ME-11; Strauss to CNO, March 7, 18, 1918, copy in Fullinwider Papers, Smithsonian; Sims to Bureau of Ordnance, June 17, 1918, Reel 4, ME-11; Sims to OpNav, Aug. 15, 1918, Reel 5, ibid.; Aug. 21, 1918, Reel 8, ibid.; Strauss to Earle, Aug. 22, 1918, AN subj file, RG45; Strauss to Sims, Sept. 6, 10, 26, 1918; Oct. 11, 19, 1918; Reel 8, ME-11. The fact that the British were having equal trouble with their mines was overlooked by Beatty. For this trouble, see correspondence in ADM137/1882; Sims to Benson, June 14, 1918, copy in Pratt Papers, OA; Fullinwider to Sims, Oct. 13, 1917, Fullinwider Papers, Smithsonian; Earle to CNO, Jan. 3, 1918, Reel 8, ME-11; Navy Dept., *The American Planning Section in London*, 168–69; Griff, *Surrendered*, 178; Halpern, *A Naval History of World War I*, 345. Not all British overlooked the Royal Navy's mine problems. See Marder, *From the Dreadnought to Scapa Flow*, 4: 87.

65. There is an impressive amount of literature on this. See, for example, Hartcup, *The War of Invention*, 129–40; Hackman, *Seek and Strike*, chap. 3; Lasky, "Review of World War I Acoustic Technology"; Lasky, "A Historical Review of Underwater Acoustic Technology." See also Marder, *From the Dreadnought to Scapa Flow*, 4: 75–77; memo on antisubmarine warfare, April 1918, ADM137/1548. Considerable information on hydrophone experiments in ADM137/2716; and in World War I records of the National Academy of Science, Washington, DC. See also Halpern, *A Naval History of the World War I*, 343–44; Friedman, *U.S. Naval Weapons*, 133–34; Terraine, *The U-Boat Wars*, 28–30. For experiments in "sound propagation underwater" by the Submarine Signal Company during the first decade of the twentieth century, see Navy Hydrographic Office, General Correspondence, 1907–1924, Box 193, Records of the Hydrographic Office, NA RG37. See also Lasky, "A Historical Review of Underwater Acoustic Technology," 597–608; Lasky, "Review of World War I Acoustic Technology," 363–85. See also Thomas Robbins to Daniels, March 8, 1918, Box 47, Naval Consulting Board, Confidential Files, 1915–1923, RG80.

66. The literature on this topic is also impressive. See Kevles, *The Physicists*, 118–22; Hackman, *Seek and Strike*, 40–43, 56–57; McBride, "The Navy's Academia Alliance"; *Washington Star*, March 29, 1919; Beach, "Hunting Submarines with a Sound Detector"; Beach, "The Wonderful Submarine Detector"; "Listening Devices in U-Boat War," in *Telephony* 76 (April 12, 1919): 23, 26–27; Merrill, "From the Heavens to the Depths," *Naval History* 14 (June 2000): 56–59; Report of Work of Anti-Submarine Division," n.d., LA subj file, RG45; Captain C. S. McDowell, "American Anti-Submarine Work during the [World] War, unpublished MS, 1977, copy in NDL. *History of the Bureau of Engineering during the War*, 47–56; Capt. J. T. Tompkins to Dept., "Development of Listening Devices," Dec. 10, 1919, Reel 114, M-1140; Weir, "The Submarine and the Ocean Environment," unpublished MS, copy in author's possession. See also Daniels to Naval Consulting Board, February 7, 1917, Box 47, Confidential Files, 1915–1923, RG80. For information on Daniels's failure to use academic scientists for work on detection equipment, see editorial in *Scientific American*, Aug. 11, 1917, 94.

67. None of the descriptions of the different American detectors are satisfactory. See, however, Hartcup, *The War of Invention*, 133–35; Kevles, *The Physicists*; notes on hydrophones, *ONI Monthly Bulletin* (Jan. 15, 1919): 71–77; Hayes, "Detection of Submarines," 21–39; Hackman, *Seek and Strike*, 56–58; Friedman, *U.S. Naval Weapons*, 133–34; memo no. 4, Feb. 4, 1918, in Navy Dept., *The American Naval Planning Section in London*; memo No. 23, Feb. 23, 1918, ibid., 117–20. For a discussion of the various types used, see Nutting, *The Cinderellas of the Fleet*, 71–79.

68. Correspondence concerning American destroyers in Queenstown using the gear in LA subj file, RG45. They received this equipment when they went into Cammell Laird shipyard for modifications. Sims to wife, July 6, 1917, Box 9, Sims Papers, LC; Benson to Sims, Nov. 19, 1917, Reel 2; ME-11; Sims to Dept., Jan. 8, 1918, Reel 3, ibid.; Sims to OpNav, Jan. 9, 1918, in M. Simpson, *Anglo-American Naval Relations*, 263; testimony of Dr. Whitney and Mr. Eveleth, Jan. 25, 1918, file 420-15, Box 108, General Board subj files, 1913–1919, RG80. For Leigh's report, see to Sims, Jan. 8, 1918, in LA subj file, RG45. Other correspondence and reports concerning the tests are in these files. Sims to Dept., Aug. 24, 1918, Reel 5, ME-11; Leigh to SecNav, with enclosure, Dec. 11, 1918, ZT subj file, ibid.; Beach, "The Wonderful Submarine Detector," 8–14.

69. Benson to Sims, Jan. 17, 1918, DD subj file, RG45; Sims to Benson, Jan. 14, 1918, Reel 3, ME-11; Benson to Sims, Jan. 12, 1918, and Sims to Leigh, Jan. 12, 1918, both in M. Simpson, *Anglo-American Naval Relations*, 264–65; Sims to OpNav, April 5, 1918, LA subj file, RG45; Pringle to Dunn, Aug. 20, 1918, ibid.; Sims to OpNav, July 22, 1918, Reel 4, ME-11.

70. For these tests, see the many reports dated Jan.-Nov. 1918 in LA subj file, RG45. See also Sims to OpNav, February 28, March 6, 23, 1918, Reel 3, ME-11; Report, April 23, 1918, Reel 4,

ibid.; Report, Aug. 4, 1918, Reel 5, ibid.; Report Nov. 14, 1918, Reel 6, ibid.; Stackhouse, "Anglo-American Atlantic Convoy system in World War I," Ph.D. diss., 354–59.

71. Memo, March 10, 1918, in M. Simpson, *Anglo-American Naval Relations*, 285. See also Sims to OpNav, Jan. 9, 1918, ibid., 263; ADM memo, May 3, 1918, ADM137/1538; memo, June 24, 1918, ADM116/1786; Report of work of Anti-Submarine Section, Dec. 11, 1918, ZT subj file, RG45; Sims to Dept., Jan. 8, 1918, Reel 3, ME-11; Leigh Report, n.d., LA subj file, RG45; Hackman, *Seek and Strike*, 59–60. For Asdic, see Sims to OpNav, Nov. 14, 1918, Reel 6, ME-11. Michelsen, "The Submarine Warfare," 66; see also testimony of Eveleth, Jan. 25, 1918, file 420-25, Box 108, General Board subj file, RG80; Terraine, *The U-Boat War*, 29; Kevles, *The Physicists*, 126; H. C. Hayes, "Detection of Submarines," 9; *History of the Bureau of Engineering during the War*, 58; memo of special board on anti-submarine detection to Operations, Aug. 21, 1917, file 127046, RG52; Sims to OpNav, Jan. 16, 1918, Reel 3, ME-11; Halligan to all destroyer commanders, Oct. 11, 1918, LA subj file, RG45; Sims to SecNav, Nov. 13, 1918, ibid. For other problems and limitations, see CO Subchaser Detachment 2 to Sims, Oct. 22, 1918, Reel 12, ME-11; Halpern, *A Naval History of World War I*, 342–43.

72. An excellent account of the early development of radio in the U.S. Navy is Douglas, "The Navy Adopts the Radio."

73. *History of the Bureau of Engineering during the War*, 125–26; Howeth, *History of Communication Electronics in the U.S. Navy*, 291 n. 99; entry June 24, 1918, Forbes diary in Box 58, Sims Papers, LC. Forbes was sent by the Bureau of Engineering to supervise the installation of electronics equipments. His diary is full of details about this work. Rodman to SecNav, March 30, Jan. 12, 1918, OB subj file, RG45; Todd testimony, April 20, 1918, General Board Hearings; F. T. Hunter, "Backing Beatty," 330; Blackford, *Torpedoboat Sailor*, 73. See also scattered documents in Reel 10, M-1092, particularly entries in C-29-C-30.

74. It was recommended that the British system be adopted by the U.S. Navy for the entire fleet after the war. McCormick to Hooper, March 28, 1918, Hooper Papers, LC. Beatty to Jellicoe, Jan. 12, 1918, 49008, Jellicoe Papers, British Museum. Beatty considered the wireless equipment on the American battleships to be "primitive." J. W. Jones, "American Battleship Operations in World War I," Ph.D. diss., 69.

75. In ADM137/1896 correspondence concerning the transfer of British signal books to American ships. See also Rodman to Dept., Jan. 25, 1918, OB subj file, RG45; Sims to Benson, Dec. 20, 1917, Box 49, Sims Papers, LC; Moore Oral History, Columbia University; McRae Oral History, USNI; Mayo to CNO, April 22, 1918, copy in Box 10, entry 113, RG19; C. King, *Atlantic Charter*, 201; cables from Beatty to Admiralty concerning signal books to U.S. Fleet, ADM 137/1964. For the British communication system, see *ONI Monthly Bulletin* (Jan. 1919): 49–55. For correspondence between naval officers concerning this change, see Bristol to Jackson, July 5, 13, 30, 1918, Mark Bristol Papers, LC.

76. Belknap, *The Yankee Mining Squadron*, 67; Belknap to Mayo, Jan. 1, 1919, Belknap Papers, NHF.

77. Stackhouse, "Anglo-American Atlantic Convoy System in World War I," Ph.D. diss., 232.

78. Memo, Oct. 10, 1918, ADM137/1510; Taylor, *Radio Reminiscence*, 64; Kenworthy, *The Real Navy*, 145; Niblack to Simsadus, July 28, 1918, Reel 9, ME-11; Howeth, *History of Communication Electronics in the U.S. Navy*, 291; "Report of an Italian Officer on Subchasers," Sept. 19, 1918, copy in OD subj file, RG45; *American Legion Monthly Magazine*, Aug. 1930, 40–41, 56; ibid., Jan., 1934, 36.

79. Entry for July 31, 1917, Merrill Diary, UNC-CH; Moore Oral History, Columbia University.

80. Quoted in Beston, *Full Speed Ahead*, 155–56.

Chapter 13. Return of the *Mayflower:* The Introduction of Convoying

1. Confidential order from Commander DD force to CO *Wadsworth*, April 13, 1917, Reel 1, Taussig papers, NDL, entry April 14, 1917, in Taussig, *The Queenstown Patrol*, 6–7.

2. For a biographical sketch of Taussig, see the introduction to Taussig's *The Queenstown Patrol*.

3. When the American destroyers arrived in Queenstown, Taussig had waiting for him a letter from Jellicoe. See Taussig, *The Queenstown Patrol*, 19.

4. Awarded for having done the most in his class for the promotion of athletics. Biographical sketch, Z file, OA.

5. Taussig, *The Queenstown Patrol*, 4.

6. *Pall Mall Gazette*, May 18, 1917; *Daily Chronicle* (London), May 18, 1917. *Cork Examiner*, May 17, 18, 1917; see also Perry, *Our Navy in the War*, 84.

7. Blackford, *Torpedoboat Sailor*, 75; entry for May 4, 1917, Fagan Diary, Mariners' Museum; Zogbaum, *From Sail to Saratoga*, 243. The arrival and presence of the American ships has not been forgotten in Queenstown, today Cobh, and nearby Cork. On the sixtieth anniversary of their arrival, the *Evening Echo* (Cork) carried articles and photographs of this event on May 4, 5, 1977.

8. Beecher, *The Story of Cork*, 94–95; *Cobh Annual*, 1978, 37; Chatterton, *Danger Zone*, 16; *Journal of Commerce* (Liverpool), Nov. 1, 1918; Ussler, *The Face of Ireland*, 302; Henderson, *A Question of Trust*, 110–16; Symington, "The Navy Way," LC.

9. FDR's naval aide, Commander Edward McCauley Jr., wrote in his diary, "on entering the harbor the most conspicuous thing in sight was the huge cathedral." Entry for July 1918, in Box 191, Assistant Sec of the Navy Files, FDR Library.

10. Ussler, *The Face of Ireland*, 303; Connolly, *The U-Boat Hunters*, 89; Henderson, *A Question of Trust*, 110–11.

11. Beecher, *The Story of Cork*, 94–95.

12. Blackford, *Torpedoboat Sailor*, 75–76; entry May 6, 1917, in Taussig, *The Queenstown Patrol*, 18–20; Thompson, *Take Her Down*, 221–22; Connolly, *The U-Boat Hunters*, 89; Churchill, *Traveller in War Time*, 41; Chapple, *We'll Stick to the Finish*, 214–16; Ussler, *The Face of Ireland*, 302; entry for July, 1918, McCauley Diary, Box 191, Assistant SecNav Files, FDR Library.

13. Sims requested that the traditional ceremonies expected by American diplomats—in this case, the consul in Queenstown—be abolished when additional American warships arrived so they could get into operation as quickly as possible. W. Page to Consul General, London, May 8, 1917, file 832, RG84.

14. See chapter 3 for an account of this meeting.

15. Fraser and Gibbons, *Soldier and Sailor Words*, 259; Whitaker, *Hunting the German Shark*, 15, 44.

16. Bayly, *Pull Together*, 221. U.S. destroyer skippers wrote their reports directly to Bayly (see ADM137/650). For a detailed breakdown of the command structure, see Cdr. Davy, Report on Personnel, June 27, 1918, NA subj file, RG45. The U.S. destroyers based at Queenstown became known in Great Britain as "The Queenstown Navy." See Fraser and Gibbons, *Soldier and Sailor Words*, 233. In the Sims Papers, two folders in Box 54, Special Correspondence, relate to Queenstown. See also Cooke, "Recollections," NDL.

17. Davy to Baldridge, May 17, 1918, copy in Box 47, Sims Papers, LC.

18. Report, collision between HMS *Zinnia* and USS *Benham*, file 26835-7361, Case 6972, Aug. 23, 1917, RG125; Sims to Admiral Wilson, Sept. 5, 1917, Box 23, Sims Papers, LC.

19. Blackford, *Torpedoboat Sailor*, 76. See also Sims to Dept., June 1, 1917, OE subj file, RG45; entry May 7, 1918, Merrill Diary, UNC-CH; Taussig, "Destroyer Experiences during the Great

War," 248; Schoeffel Oral History, USNI; Evans, *Keeping the Seas*, 146–47; DeLany, *Bayly's Navy*, 11.

20. Blackford, *Torpedoboat Sailor*, 77.

21. Evans, *Keeping the Seas*, 150.

22. Hashagen, *U-Boats Westward!*, 205, also entitled *The Log of a U-Boat Commander*.

23. After the initial patrols the American destroyer officers prepared a memo on ASW tactics that Sims later modified and adopted as a "Force Instruction." Memo dated July 6, 1917, copy in Davis Papers, ECU. A "Force Instruction," which included doctrine and general instructions for ASW operations and convoying, was promulgated by Simsadus in September 1917 and modified in August 1918. Copy of August 1918 Instruction in Rare Book Room, NDL. A separate one was put out by Admiral Wilson's headquarters in France, see Taussig. "Destroyer Experiences During the Great War," U.S. Naval Institute *Proceedings* 49 (March 1923): 406–8.

24. Taussig, "Destroyer Experiences during the Great War," 351–55; Zogbaum, *From Sail to Saratoga*, 249; Wheeler Oral History, USNI; Leighton, *Simsadus*, 4, 5–6. Taussig wrote that the patrol areas for individual ships were thirty to forty miles square. "Operations of American Destroyers Based on Queenstown," Taussig Collection, LC.

25. Lundeberg, "Underseas Warfare and Allied Strategy in World War I," pt. 2, "1916–1918," 60.

26. Strandmann, *Walter Rathenau*, 227; Marder, *From the Dreadnought to Scapa Flow*, 4: 277; Grant, *U-Boats Destroyed*, 41; Herwig and Trask, "The Failure of Imperial Germany's Underseas Offensive Against World Shipping," 619; Gretton, "The U-Boat Campaign in Two World Wars," 128–29. Marder, *From the Dreadnought to Scapa Flow*, 4: 146–48; Herwig, *"Luxury" Fleet*, 226.

27. "Defense of Trade in W.W. I & II," unpublished MS, May 3, 1968, copy in OA. The figures on German sinking are cited in most works on the naval side of the war. For the most recent studies of the U-boat campaign, see Tarrant, *The U-Boat Offensive*; and Terraine, *The U-Boat Wars*.

28. Wigfall, "Scientists and the Admiralty," Ph.D. diss., 20–40; Francis L. Keith, "Blindman's Bluff; Antisubmarine Warfare in the First World War," unpublished MS, University of Maryland, 1972, 9, copy in author's possession.

29. Quoted in Wigfall, "Scientists and the Admiralty," Ph.D. diss., 20.

30. Marder, *From the Dreadnought to Scapa Flow*, 4: 80. For the ineffectiveness of these small craft in antisubmarine warfare, see Corbett and Newbolt, *History of the Great War*, 4: 348.

31. Marder, *From the Dreadnought to Scapa Flow*, 4: 870.

32. "The Anti-Submarine War," ADM 137/1548.

33. Marder, *From the Dreadnought to Scapa Flow*, 4: 70–71.

34. Jellicoe quoted in ibid., 4: 70. See also ADM137/2664.

35. Terraine, *The U-Boat Wars*, 33.

36. Quoted in Marder, *From the Dreadnought to Scapa Flow*, 4: 97.

37. Ibid., 4: 79–80.

38. P. Kennedy, "Britain in the First World War," 60. See also Winton, *Convoy*, 49; Keith, "Blindman's Bluff," 17; ADM137/2664; R. C. Grady to CNO, June 6, 1917, LA subj file, RG45.

39. Gibson and Prendergast, *The German Submarine War*, 149. These authors, however, defended the patrol system as "the only possible and practical method of trade defense until such time as a sufficient number of fast vessels became available for convoy duty" (281). Fast vessels were available, but the majority of them were with the Grand Fleet.

40. Duff to Bethell, April 7, 1917, Duff MSS, NMM: Churchill quoted in Terraine, *The U-Boat Wars*, 47. See also Carr, *Good Hunting*, 14.

41. Sims to CNO, via Page, April 18, 1917, *Foreign Relations, 1917*, Supplement 2, 28–29. On November 20, 1917, he wrote, "The results obtained by this method [patrolling] were wholly unsatisfactory." To SecNav, Reel 2, ME-11.

42. Sims to SECNAV, Area file, RG45. See also report of Gunnery Department, US Destroyer Flotilla, Queenstown, Feb. 24, 1918, ZP subj file, RG45.

43. Niblack, "Putting Cargos Across," copy in ZCP subj file, RG45

44. Lecture by C. Davison, March 4, 1915, RG8 X-type files, NWC Files; Symington to Capt. Oliver, Dec. 10, 1914, ibid. See DeLany, *Bayly's Navy*, 2; Bowling, "The Negative Influence of Mahan on the Protection of Shipping in Wartime," Ph.D. diss., 196; *Naval Investigation*, 4, 1915, 1966.

45. Shafter, *Destroyers in Action*, 46.

46. Office of Naval Aeronautics to Commandant, US Naval Station, Pensacola, June 15, 1915, Box 4, Series I, Sub/Underseas Warfare Division, OA.

47. Quoted in McBride, "The Rise and Fall of a Strategic Technology," Ph.D. diss., 196.

48. See files including manuals in LA subj file, RG45.

49. Entry for June 19, 1917, Latimer Diary, UVA.

50. Falge, "Long and Arduous Duty," 35; Wheeler Oral History, USNI; Taussig, "Destroyer Experiences during the Great War," 349.

51. Bowling, "The Negative Influence of Mahan on the Protection of Shipping," Ph.D. diss., 250–53. There was considerable argument over whether convoying was offensive or defensive. Both Sims and the British Admiralty insisted that convoying was "an offensive measure." Sims to Daniels, June 29, 1917, in M. Simpson, *Anglo-American Naval Relations*, 72; memorandum to Allied Naval Council, January 22, 1918, in ibid., 267. See also Moore Oral History, Columbia University.

52. Bayly to Sims, July 6, 1917, in M. Simpson, *Anglo-American Naval Relations*, 240. See also Bayly to Admiralty, June 26, and July 13, 1917, ADM137/650; Bayly, *Pull Together*, 221.

53. Merrill Papers, UNC-CH.

54. Quoted in Frederick, *The Great Adventure*, 131.

55. Entry for May 12, Merrill Papers, UNC-CH. For wreckage, see Taussig, *The Queenstown Patrol*, 30, passim; and Zogbaum, *From Sail to Saratoga*, 251.

56. Blackford, *Torpedoboat Sailor*, 77.

57. Entry for May 8, 1917, in Taussig, *The Queenstown Patrol*, 30.

58. Halsey, *Admiral Halsey's Story*, 32; Moore Oral History, Columbia University; entry for July 4, 1918, Jenkins Diary, NWC.

59. Taussig, "Destroyer Experiences during the Great War," 56; entry for May 11, Merrill Diary, UNC-CH; Falge, "Long and Arduous Duty," 35.

60. Quoted in Coffman, *The War to End All Wars*, 109.

61. *Home Waters*, pt. 9, May 1, 1917, to July 31, 1917, *Naval Staff Monographs* 19: 90; Sims to Dept., May 21, 1917, Reel 8, ME-11. See also Paine, "Hide and Seek Afloat," 16.

62. Entry for May 15, 1917, R. Goodrich Diary, IWM; See also Duff to Bethel, May 17, 1917, Duff MS, NMM; and Captain F.S.W. deWinton recollections, Peter Liddle Archives.

63. M. Simpson, *Anglo-American Naval Relations*, 194–95.

64. Blackford, *Torpedoboat Sailor*, 77.

65. Marder, *From the Dreadnought to Scapa Flow*, 4: 97. See also Sprout and Sprout, *The Rise of American Naval Power*, 352–53.

66. QC subj file, RG45

67. Morison, *Sims*, 347. See also Sims, *The Victory at Sea*, 124; Sims to Dept., June 20, 1917, area file, RG45; Corbett and Newbolt, *History of the Great War*, 5: 56; "American Destroyers in the War," 14–15. Sims to SecNav, Nov. 20, 1917, Reel 2, ME-11.

68. To Gaunt, June 29, 1917, in M. Simpson, *Anglo-American Naval Relations*, 233; Sims to Navy Dept., June 24, 1917, Reel 1, ME-11; see also ibid., June 29, 1917; *Home Waters*, pt. 9, 161; *Naval Investigation*, 58–59; Taussig, "Destroyer Experiences during the Great War," 87–88; Testimony, Dec. 4, 1917, General Board Hearings.

69. Grant to Admiralty, August 7, 1917, copy in OF subj file, RG45; Winton, *Convoy*, 87.

70. Chack and Antier, *Histoire maritime de la premiere guerre mondiale*, 3: 166–67; George V to Beatty, April 27, 1917, in Ranft, *The Beatty Papers*, 1: 48. The literature on this topic is extensive. The most recent works are Winton, *Convoy*; Terraine, *The U-Boat War*; and Halpern, *A Naval History of World War I*, 355–60. See also Rutter, *Red Ensign*; Roskill, *Admiral of the Fleet Earl Beatty*, 219–20; Josephus Daniels, "The United States Navy in the War," 123; Roskill, *Hankey, Man of Secrets*, 380–83; Hankey, *The Supreme Command*, 2: 641–51; Josephus Daniels, *Cabinet Diaries*, entry for Feb. 23, 1919, 105; speech of FDR, Nov 11, 1920, in Jacoby, *Calendar of the Speeches of FDR*, 114; *Chicago Tribune*, Oct. 22, 1922.

71. Daniels to Sims, July 7, 1917, Sims to Daniels, July 11, 1917, in M. Simpson, *Anglo-American Naval Relations*, 240–41; Klachko, *Benson*, 70.

72. Roskill, "Capros Not Convoys, Counter Attack and Destroy," 1047.

73. Quoted in Semmel, *Liberalism and Naval Strategy*, 165.

74. Marder, *From the Dreadnought to Scapa Flow*, 4: 122–37, offers a good discussion of above arguments and others. See also Kenworthy, *The Real Navy*, 241–42.

75. Bone, *Merchantmen-at-Arms*, 244–47; notes of Admiralty conference, Feb. 22, 1917, ADM 137/2753.

76. Sims to SecNav, June 29, 1917, CP subj file, RG45; Roskill, "Capros Not Convoys," 1049; Gretton, *Convoy Escort Commander*, 194–201; McKillip, "Undermining Technology by Strategy," 18–37; Bowling, "The Negative Influence of Mahan on the Protection of Shipping in Wartime," Ph.D. diss., 16–18; Sims, *The Victory at Sea*, 103, 164–65. See also "Joint Memorandum by British and American Planning Division; Anti-submarine Attack by Coastal Escort," copy in Reel 4, ME-11, and Chief of Staff, Destroyer Flotillas, to Destroyer Flotillas, June 26, 1918, ibid.

77. For a discussion of these early convoys, see David Waters, "Notes on the Convoy System"; Stackhouse, "The Anglo-American Convoy System in World War I," Ph.D. diss., 30–31; and Kemp, *Convoy Protection*, 43–45.

78. Tarrant, *U-Boat Offensive*, 51; L. Gardiner, *The British Admiralty*, 335. For Jellicoe's explanation, see his *The Submarine War*, 130–31.

79. Marder, *From the Dreadnought to Scapa Flow*, 4: 158.

80. Knox Papers, LC; see also Morison, *Sims*, 347–48; L. Gardiner, *The British Admiralty*, 336. Commander David W. Waters, RN, an authority of the history of convoy, wrote the author on October 15, 1992, that Sims and Admiral Beatty were "the only two admirals in the 1914–18 war who understood the convoy system of warfare." See also Bowling, "Convoy in World War I," master's thesis, 214–23; Terraine, *The U-Boat Wars*, 92–93.

81. Josephus Daniels, "The United States Navy in the World War," 123. See also Josephus Daniels, *The Wilson Era: Years of War*, 68. Sims, *The Victory at Sea*, 111–13. For the April 19 report, see appendix 3, 376–84. See also *Naval Investigation*, 87; Morison, *Sims*, 348; A. H. Miles to Sims, March 16, 1920, Box 72, Sims Papers, LC.

82. Waters to the author, October 15, 1992; Lloyd George, *War Memoirs*, 3: 1161. See also Bowling, "Convoy in World War I," master's thesis, 76–77, 95–96, 202; Vice Admiral K.G.B. Dewar to Richmond, April 27, 1917, Dewar MS, NMM; Herbert Hoover, *Memoirs*, 1: 225. Even Vice Admiral Andreas Michelsen, the German naval officer and later historian on the submarine war, gives Sims considerable credit. "The Submarine Warfare," 79. Lord Salter, however, does not mention Sims in his recollections of the convoy controversy. See Salter, *Memoirs of a Public Servant*, 88.

83. To Babcock, March 28, 1924, Box 144, Sims Papers, LC.

84. Beloff, *Wars and Welfare*, 40.

85. Stackhouse, "The Anglo-American Convoy System in World War I," Ph.D. diss., 48–49. See also Josephus Daniels, *The Wilson Era: Years of War*, 67–68. See also Gaunt to Admiralty, ADM137/1322; Daniels to W. Wilson, July 14, 1917, in Link, *Wilson Papers*, 43, 178–79; Klachko,

Benson, 70; Churchill, *Thoughts and Adventures*, 138; Harries and Harries, *The Last Days of Innocence*, 81.

86. In M. Simpson, *Anglo-American Naval Relations*, 77. See also Miles to Sims, March 16, 1920, Box 72, Sims Papers, LC.

87. Daniels to Dill, March 6, 1921, Reel 54, Daniels Papers, LC; M. Simpson, *Anglo-American Naval Relations*, 119–20.

88. Box 49, Sims Papers, LC. See also Benson to Sims, June 24, 1917, ibid.; Parsons, *Wilsonian Diplomacy*, 57–58; Wilson to Wisenor, July 13, 1917, in Link, *Wilson Papers*, 43: 172–73.

89. Copy of Pratt's autobiography in OA; Wheeler, *Pratt*, 116–17; Eric Grove, "Reluctant Partner," unpublished paper, copy in author's hands. Admiral Gaunt, the British naval attaché in London, gives Pratt credit for persuading Benson to release warships for convoy work. See Gaunt to Jellicoe, July 5, 1917, in M. Simpson, *Anglo-American Naval Relations*, 235

90. "Historical Survey of Convoys," Dec 28, 1918, ADM137/2658; Marder, *From the Dreadnought to Scapa Flow*, 4: 187.

91. Sims to Navy Dept., July 11, 1917, OF subj file, RG45.

92. Corbett and Newbolt, *History of the Great War*, 5: 51; Bowling, "The Negative Influence of Mahan on the Protection of Shipping in Wartime," Ph.D. diss., 183. An analysis of submarine attacks for June-August 1917 convinced the Admiralty that nearly all the ships sunk during that period were unescorted. See *Home Waters*, pt. 9, *Naval Staff Monographs* 19, 160–61, 224–35.

93. The largest convoy, according to Stackhouse, was one of forty-seven ships plus escorts. "The Anglo-American Convoy System in World War I," Ph.D. diss., 81.

94. C-in-C Devonport to Admiralty, Jan. 16, 1918, ADM137/1505; H. Holt, "A Talk with Admiral Sims," 394; Taussig, "Destroyer Experiences during the Great War," 382.

95. Sims to Dept., Nov. 2, 1917, Reel 2, ME-11; Sims to Admiralty, June 22, 1917, Reel 8; ibid.; Sims to SecNav, Aug. 13, 1917, Reel 1, ibid.; Sims to SecNav, Oct. 3, 1917, Reel 18, ibid.; Sims to SecNav, Sept. 11, 1917, CP subj file, RG45; memo, Sept. 28, 1918, ADM137/2710; Report by C-in-C, Mitford Haven, Dec. 1918, ADM137/2659; Historical Report of Falmouth Convoys, Oct. 12, 1918, ADM137/1265; "Convoy System," ADM137/2659; Winton, *Convoy*, 79; Taussig, "Destroyer Experiences during the Great War," 376–78; Jellicoe, *The Submarine Peril*, 148–50; "We are Ready Now," 531.

96. "Escorting Formation," Box 1, Allied Submarine Operations, World War I, OA.

97. "Convoy System," March 1919, ADM137/2659; Corbett and Newbolt, *History of the Great War*, 5: 49; Winton, *Convoy*, 68–69.

98. Babcock to Sims, June 21, 1917, Box 3, Area file, RG45; ADM to C-in-C Queenstown, etc. June 22, 1917, ADM137/1327; to C-in-C Grand Fleet, June 30, 1917, ADM137/1899; Sims to Navy Dept., June 22, 1917, Reel 1, ME-11.

99. Babcock to Sims, June 21, 1917, Sims to Admiralty, June 21, 1921, Box 3, Area file RG45.

100. Winton, *Convoy*, 73, 94; Marder, *From the Dreadnought to Scapa Flow*, 4: 191–92.

101. "Historical Report of Convoys," Dec. 12, 1918, ADM137/2659.

102. Kemp, *Convoy Protection*, 55; Zogbaum, *From Sail to Saratoga*, 265; Cdr. Vernou testimony, Dec. 17, 1917, General Board Hearings.

103. Pratt to SecNav, Nov. 12, 1917, Reel 65, Daniels Papers, LC; Taussig, "Destroyer Experiences during the Great War," 367; Sims, *The Victory at Sea*, 356–57.

104. "Extension of North Atlantic Convoy System, July 8, 1918, Roll 40, M1140; Sims to Dept., July 14, 1918, Reel 9, ME-11; memo, Jan. 22–23, 1918, in M. Simpson, *Anglo-American Naval Relations*, 266–68. For the Allied Naval Council discussion, see report Jan. 17, 1918, in QC subj file, RG45. See also Fayle, *Seaborne Trade*, 3: 307.

105. Benson to Sims, Aug. 20, 2928, Reel 5, ME-11; Stackhouse, "The Anglo-American Atlantic Convoy System in World War I," Ph.D. diss., 274, 279.

106. Freidel, *Over There*, 65.

107. Sims to Dept., Oct. 19, 10, Nov. 8, 1917, Reel 2, ME-11; "Historical Report of O.F. Convoys, Falmouth," Dec. 12, 1918, ADM137/2659; Fayle, *Seaborne Trade*, 3:137; Corbett and Newbolt, *History of the Great War*, 5: 136.

108. Jellicoe, *The Crisis of the Naval War*, 135; ADM to C-in-C, Grand Fleet, July 4, 1917, ADM137/1899; ADM to C-in-C Devonport, Queenstown, and other commands, July 7, 1917, ibid.

109. Cochran MS, Cochran Papers, Coast Guard Library.

110. Niblack, "Putting Cargos Across," ZPA subj file, RG45.

111. Entries for June 1918, Bellitteri Diary, Bellitteri Papers, ECU. See also Stackhouse, "The Anglo-American Atlantic Convoy System in World War I," Ph.D. diss., 276.

112. W. J. Wheeler, "Reminiscences of World War Convoy Work," 385–87; see also Willoughby, Yankton—*Yacht and Man-of-War*, 200–203; and Evans, *Keeping the Seas*, 254.

113. Cochran MS, Cochran Papers, Coast Guard Library; Muhlhauser, *Small Craft*, 198

114. Testimony at *Naval Investigation*, 1008, OF subj file, RG45. See also Josephus Daniels, *Our Navy at War*, 116.

115. Notes on convoying, Dec. 27, 1917, OS subj file, RG45; Atterbury to Wilson, Feb. 14, 1918, CP subj file, ibid. See also Allen to Commander, Patrol Force, Jan.11, 1918, Reel 19, ME-11; and Oct. 10, 1917, Reel 2, ibid.

116. Stirling, "American Armed Yachts in the War Zone," 300. See also Berrien to Sims, May 28, 1919, Box 49, Sims Papers, LC; Stirling, "The Bridge across the Atlantic," 1681.

117. Twining to Admiralty, Feb. 11, 1918, ADM137/1534; Sims to Comfran, Brest, Oct. 28, 1918, Reel 10, ME-11; Sims to Dept., July 6, 1917, Reel 1, ibid.; to Comfran, Brest, Aug. 21, 1918, Reel 10; ibid.; memo, April 4, 1918, Reel 10, M1092; CO Hisco to Sims, April 4, 1918, Reel 19, ME-11; Courtney to Sims, Sept. 4, 1917, Reel 3, ibid.; War Diary of USS *Cushing*, entries for Aug. 30–31, 1917, Oct. 1, 1917, copy in OS subj file, RG45; CO *Christabel* to CO U.S. Patrol Squadron, Aug. 21, 1917, OS subj file, ibid.; War Diary of USS *Conyngham*, Sept. 8, 1917, ibid.; War Diary of USS *Rowan*, entry for Sept. 2, 1918, in Reel 10, ME-11. There is evidence that escorts were often guilty of using their radios as well as lights. See, for example, N. Collins, *Civilian Seamen in War*, 14.

118. *ONI Monthly Bulletin* (Feb. 1919): 43–49; Breckel, "The Suicide Flotilla," 663–64; Purdy to District Commander, Rochefort, France, March 20, 1918, OS subj file, RG45; Frederick, *The Great Adventure*, 60–61; Sims to Dept., Sept. 27, 1917, Reel 2, ME-11.

119. *American Legion Magazine*, April 1936, 51.

120. W. J. Wheeler, "Reminiscences of World War Convoy Work," 386.

121. Blackford, *Torpedoboat Sailor*, 129–31.

122. Entry for Nov. 10, 1918, Kurfess Diary, OA.

123. To Dept., July 30, 1918, Reel 4, ME-11; OpNav to Sims, July 15, 1918, ibid.; memo, Oct. 1918, ADM137/1510; memo, Dec. 28, 1918, ADM137/2658; Hosey to former crew members, April 6, 1950, copy in USS *Pocahontas* Collection, S-077-B., Photo Section, NHC; Munter to Simsadus, Dec. 11, 1917, OS subj file, RG45; entry for Sept. 27, 1918, Kurfess Diary, OA; Buettell, "Soldiers—Ships and the Sea," 23.

124. Leighton, *Simsadus*, 49–50. For a detailed discussion of zigzagging including various patterns, advantages, etc., see Stackhouse, "The Anglo-American Convoy System in World War I," Ph.D. diss., 137–52.

125. Sims to Dept., March 12, 1918, Reel 3, ME-11.

126. Taussig, "Destroyer Experience during the Great War," 387. See also Niblack, Putting Cargos Across," ZCP subj file, RG45.

127. *Home Waters*, pt. 9, *Naval Staff Monographs* 19: 161; Horton, *My Maiden Voyage*, 5.

128. F. H. Schofield, "Incidents and Present-Day Aspects of Naval Strategy," 797.

129. Wiggins to Rodgers, Feb. 6, 1918, Rodgers Family Papers, LC. For the British navy, see the documents in ADM137/2753. See also CO *Leviathan* to Dept, Sept. 20, 1918, reports of Cdr.

R.D. White, and other documents in LA subj file, RG45; Wiggins, *My Romance with the Navy*, 130–31; and Stackhouse, "The Anglo-American Atlantic Convoy System in World War I," Ph.D. diss., 137–52.

130. Leighton, *Simsadus*, 49–50.

131. Entry for Nov. 7, 1917, Morgan Diary, NHF.

132. Halsey Memoir, LC; Moore Oral History, Columbia University; Jarman Lynch Memoir, WWI Research Project, AMHI; Buchanan to Force Commander, Jan. 5, 1918, LA subj file, RG45; Hutchins to Force Commander, Nov. 19, 1917, LA subj file, ibid.; Benson to Commander Cruiser Force, Atlantic Fleet, April 13, 1918, Reel 4, ME-11.

133. Sims to Dept. (date not readable), Reel 4, ME-11; to patrol squadrons, Nov. 25, 1917, LA subj file, RG45.

134. Sims to Wilson, Feb. 24, 1918, Reel 19, ME-11. See also Benson to Simsadus, Feb. 13, 1918, Reel 19; OpNav to Simsadus, June 1, 1918, Reel 4; Wilson to Simsadus, April 2, 1918, Reel 19, all in ibid.

135. Sims to Adm., Queenstown, Nov. 28; Adm., Queenstown to Sims, Nov. 28, 1918, Reel 18, ME-11.

136. To Simsadus, Dec. 19, 1917, Reel 2, ME-11. See also Sims to OpNav, Nov. 26, 1917, Reel 18; Dec. 20, 1917, Reel 2; Dec. 13, 1917, Reel 2, ibid.; Marder, *From the Dreadnought to Scapa Flow*, 4: 272.

137. C-in-C Plymouth to Admiralty, Sept. 12, 1917, ADM137/1321; Bayly to Admiralty, July 20, 1917, ADM137/1327.

138. Sims to CO Patrol Sq. France, Sept. 26, 1917, Roll 40, M1140; Admiralty to Bayly, Nov. 9, 1917, ADM137/1328.

139. Pershing to Adjutant General, April 23, 1918, copy in CP subj file, RG45. See also Benson to Chief of Staff, Army, April 25, 1918, Pratt Papers, OA; Sims to OpNav, April 26, 1918, Reel 4, ME-11; to Benson, May 1, 1918, ibid.; Transport 4 to Amphibious Base, New York, May 4, 1918, ibid.; Sims to Commanding General, Base 3, May 21, 1918, CP subj file, RG45; Admiralty to C-in-Cs, Queenstown and Devonport, Aug. 11, 1917, ADM131/98. For Queenstown, see Reel 2, ME-11; Niblack to Simsadus, Dec. 1, 1917, 118, ibid.; Leonard to Navy Dept., Oct. 19, 1917, OS subj file, RG45; Marder, *From the Dreadnought to Scapa Flow*, 4: 273; Corbett and Newbolt, *History of the Great War*, 5: 98

140. ADM memo, April 8, 1918, ADM137/1535; Sims to Dept., Feb. 2, 1918, Reel 10, M1092; Corbett and Newbolt, *History of the Great War*, 5: 98

141. Admiralty Memorandum, July 17, 1918, in M. Simpson, *Anglo-American Naval Relations*, 300; Waters, "Notes on the Convoy System."

142. Soule, *Prosperity Decade*, 29.

143. D. M. Kennedy, *Over Here*, 326. See also L. D. Gibson with E. K. Gibson, *Over Seas*.

144. Parini, *Heir to Empire*, 44. See also Parsons, "Why the British Reduced the Flow of American Troops to Europe in August-October, 1918," 173–91.

145. Aug. 12, 1918, Reel 10, ME-11; see also Benson to Sims, Aug. 20, 1918, Reel 5, ibid.; Sims report, Sept. 5, 1918, Reel 5, ibid.; and Sims to Dept., Aug. 31, 1918, ibid.

146. For a detailed discussion of this topic, see Stackhouse, "The Anglo-American Atlantic Convoy System," Ph.D. diss., 233–42. This does not include French escorts.

147. See, for example, Jellicoe to Sims, July 11, 1917, in M. Simpson, *Anglo-American Naval Relations*, 243–44.

148. Michelsen, "The Submarine Warfare," 81. For details of this organization, see Fayle, *Seaborne Trade*, 3: 136–37; Jellicoe, *The Submarine Peril*, 181–202; Sims, *The Victory at Sea*, 122–30. For American insistence on troop convoys, see Bowling, "Convoy in World War I," master's thesis, 121–22, 142; Daniels to Sims, June 9, 1917, Reel 1, ME-11; Hurley, *The Bridge to France*, 235, and Stackhouse, "The Anglo-American Atlantic Convoy System in World War I," Ph.D.

diss., 61–62. Stackhouse refers to the system as an "umbrella." For British convoy officers in U.S. ports, see Report of Belknap, June 13, 1917, Reel 10, M1072.

149. Sims testimony, case 10622, RG125.

Chapter 14. Lafayette, We Are Here!: Convoys

1. Daniels to Sims, June 4, 1917, Reel 1, ME-11.

2. Sims order dated June 13, 1917, copy in Taussig papers, microfilm Reel 1, NDL.

3. *U.S.S.* Seattle *during the War*, 30–37; Stirling, "The Bridge across the Atlantic," 1064.

4. Entry for May 23, 1917, Gleaves Papers, LC. See also Gleaves, *The Admiral*, 140–41. For Gleaves orders, see June 5, 1917, Reel 13, ME-11.

5. Zogbaum, *From Sail to Saratoga*, 259.

6. June 25, 1917, Box 9, Sims Papers, LC.

7. Sayles to Sims, June 1, to Dept., June 9, 1917, TP subj file, RG45.

8. Russell Journal, USS *Walke* file, CZ file, OA.

9. *Fanning* War Diary, copy in Ships History Branch, NHC; Charles Moore Diary, OA, ibid. For the Gleaves quote, see Gleaves, *The Admiral*, 146; entry for June 18, 1917, in Taussig, *The Queenstown Patrol*, 66–67.

10. Quoted in F. D. Baldwin, "The American Enlisted Man in World War I," Ph.D. diss., 164; Marshall, *Memoirs of My Services in the World War*, 9. See also entry for June 23, 1917, Merrill Diary, UNC-CH; Freidel, *Over There*, 54; and Bone, *Merchantmen at Arms*, 290.

11. U.S. and British ships with the Queenstown command had escorted one or more ships when they passed through their patrol sector prior to June 23. See "Operation of American Destroyers Based on Queenstown," MS in Taussig Papers, LC.

12. Entry for June 30, 1917, Russell Journal in USS *Walke* file, CZ files, OA.

13. *U.S.S.* Seattle *during the War*, 39.

14. Creel, *Rebel at Large*, 190–93; Bayly to Admiralty, July 3, 1917, ADM137/650.

15. Quoted in Gleaves, *The Admiral*, 143. See also *ONI Monthly Bulletin* (June 15, 1919): 101–3.

16. Quoted in Albion and Pope, *Sea Lanes in Wartime*, 249.

17. Entry for July 2, 1917, Russell Journal, USS *Walke* file, CZ files, OA.

18. Zogbaum, *From Sail to Saratoga*, 259; Gleaves, *The Admiral,* 147; Stirling, "The Bridge across the Atlantic," 1671; entry for June 26, 1917, Merrill Diary, UNC-CH. Gleaves wanted the groups to sail independently with same number of destroyer escorts. See Gleaves Chief of Staff to CO *Charleston*, July 5, 1917, Reel 3, ME-11; Gleaves to Sims, via naval attaché in Paris, July 5, 17, 1917. See also French naval attaché to Paris (for Gleaves), June 29, 1917; Gleaves to SecNav, July 3, 1917; Sims to Admiralty, June 28, 1917, all in Reel 8, ME-11. See also Wiggins, *My Romance with the Navy*, 91–92; *Fanning* War Diary, Ships History Branch, NHC; entry July 3–4, 1917, Moore Diary, OA; Morison, *Sims*, 420–21; H. H. Staples Diary, LSU.

19. The *U.S.S.* Mount Vernon, 30–31.

20. "Summary of U.S. Naval Activities in European Waters," Z file, OA; *ONI Monthly Bulletin*, May 15, 1919, 34–35; H. B. Wilson, *The American Navy in France*, 67; Sims, *The Victory at Sea*, 129.

21. Entry for Aug. 1917, Merrill Diary, UNC-CH; see also entries for Aug. 3, 11, 1917, for his comments on convoying, Merrill Papers, UNC-CH, and Taussig, "Destroyer Experiences during the Great War," 376–77.

22. The *U.S.S.* Mount Vernon, 48.

23. Quoted in Josephus Daniels, *The Wilson Era: Years of War*, 95. See also "Summary of U.S. Naval Activities in European Waters," Z file, OA; Pratt, "Autobiography," copy in OA; Gleaves to Mayo, July 20, 1917, Reel 1 ME-11; Trask, "William Shepherd Benson," 15.

24. Bowling, "The Negative Influence of Mahan on the Protection of Shipping in Wartime," Ph.D. diss., 196.

25. Allard, "Anglo-American Naval Differences during World War I," 76.

26. Baker quote to SecNav, July 26, 1917, Box 14, Logistics file, RG45; entry for November 24, 1917, in Josephus Daniels, *Cabinet Diaries*, 241.

27. Minutes of the War Cabinet, CAB23/3.

28. Klachko, *Benson*, 108–9.

29. Pratt, "Autobiography," OA. See also Wheeler, *Pratt*, 99–100, 117; Klachko, *Benson*, 71, 108–9. See also M. Simpson, *Anglo-American Naval Relations*, 57–58; Beesley, *Room 40*, 259.

30. July 7, 1918, Box 82, Sims Papers, LC.

31. Trask, *Captains and Cabinets*, 160; see also Adm. M. Njegovan to C.O. U-boats Med., July 16, 1917, in Walton, *Over There*, 107.

32. Early Memoir, IWM.

33. Michelsen, "The Submarine Warfare," 83–84; Herwig, *Politics of Frustration*, 139–40; Sims, *The Victory at Sea*, 358–64.

34. Gibson and Prendergast, *The German Submarine War*, 298; Trask, *Captains and Cabinets*, 187; Halpern, *A Naval History of World War I*, 437. See also Scheer, *Germany's High Seas Fleet in the World War*.

35. June 5, 1917, OS subj file, RG45. See also Sims to Benson, April 2, 1918, in M. Simpson, *Anglo-American Naval Relations*, 159; and Marder, *From the Dreadnought to Scapa Flow*, 4: 285.

36. Hashagen, *U-Boats Westward!*, 224–25.

37. Bowling, "The Negative Influence of Mahan on the Protection of Shipping in Wartime," Ph.D. diss., 185–86; Keith, "Blindman's Bluff," 47–48.

38. On sailing vessels, see Sims to Jackson, Oct. 2, 1917, OH subj file, RG45; ADM137/1328; Herwig, *Politics of Frustration*, 132.

39. Doenitz, *Ten Years and Twenty Days*, 4. See also Spindler, *Der Handelskrieg mit U-Booten*, 4: 224.

40. Marder, *From the Dreadnought to Scapa Flow*, 4: 101. The Germans had 144 submarines in commission in January 1918.

41. Tarrant, *The U-Boat Offensive*, 49, 52. There are discrepancies in U-boat statistics. See Terraine, *The U-Boat Wars*, 65; Gibson and Prendergast, *The German Submarine War*, 355; Jameson, *The Most Formidable Thing*, 225; Herwig, *"Luxury" Fleet*, 220–21. See also Marder, *From the Dreadnought to Scapa Flow*, 4: 105–6.

42. Marder, *From the Dreadnought to Scapa Flow*, 5: 80–82.

43. Sims to Dept. for War Dept., Sept. 7, 1917, Reel 3, MS-11; ADM to Gaunt, October 10, 1917, Reel 2, ibid., Sims to Dept., October 24, 1917, CG subj file, RG45; Sims to Dept., Nov. 20, 1917, Roll 40, M1140; Rose, *Brittany Patrol*, 123.

44. Sims to Dept., Dec. 25, 1917, Reel 18, ME-11; Sims to SecNav, Aug. 5, 1917, Reel 1, ME-11; Memo on Atlantic Convoy System, August 4, 1918, in M. Simpson, *Anglo-American Naval Relations*, 173.

45. Pershing to Sims, March 11, 1918, Reel 19, ME-11; Sims to Wilson, Aug. 3, 1918, Reel 4, ibid.; Benson to Simsadus, April 1, 1918, Reel 19, ibid.; Pershing to Biddle, April 2, 1918, Reel 4, ibid.; Sims to Wilson, April 2, 1918, Reel 19, ibid.; Sims to Dept., April 3, 1918, Reel 4, ibid.; Gleaves to Benson, June 10, 1918, ibid.

46. "Summary of U.S. Naval Activities in European Waters," Z file, OA; Dept. to Sims, July 1, 1917, Reel 1; Sims to Navy Dept., July 12, 18, 1917, all in ME-11.

47. To Jackson, July 11, 1917, TL subj file, RG45.

48. Ibid.; Jackson to Sims, July 11, 1917, Reel 2, ME-11.

49. Hurley, *The Bridge to France*, 235; Trask, *Captains and Cabinets*, 171–72, 182; Walton, *Over There*, 102–3.

50. Wilson to ALMA, Aug. 24, 1918, TT subj file; RG45; Sims to Wilson, Aug. 16, 1918, ibid.; Wilson to Sims, Aug. 23, 1918, ibid., Sims to Dept., Aug. 16, 1918, Reel 5, ME-11; Sims to Wilson, Aug. 27, 1918, Reel 10, ibid.; Benson to Simsadus, Aug. 27, 1918, ibid., Memo, Dec. 28, 1918, ADM137/2658.

51. Sims to Bayly, February 20, 1918, CP subj file, RG45; Sims to Wilson, February 20, 1918, Reel 19, ME-11; Atterbury to Sims, March 18, 1918, CP subj file, RG45; Sims to Dept., Feb. 12, 1918, ibid.; Pershing to Bartlett, Jan. 3, 1918, Reel 3; Sims to Pershing, Jan. 4, 1918, Reel 19; Sims to Dept., Jan. 7, 1918, ibid.; Sims to CNO, Jan. 8, 1918, Reel 3; Benson to Simsadus, Jan. 8, 1918, ibid., all in ME-11. See also Sims to Dept., Jan. 11, 1918, CP subj file, RG45. See also Repington, *The First World War*, 2: 244.

52. Daniels to Sims, Sept. 26, 1917, Case 10622, RG125.

53. Sims to Jackson, Sept. 1917, subj file TV, RG45. See also Babcock memo, Sept. 9, 1917, Logistics file, RG45; Sims to Jackson, Aug. 15, 1917, subj OF, RG45; War Diary *Wakiva II*, Oct. 24, 1917, in OS file, RG435.

54. Schwerer to Wilson, Feb. 18, 1918, CP subj file, RG45; Sims to Dept., Nov. 30, 1917, Box 54, Confidential Correspondence, 1917–1919, RG80; Wilson to Sims, Nov. 20, 1917, CO, *Wakiva II* to Wilson, Nov. 17, 1917, OS subj file, RG45.

55. Sept. 24, 1917, Case 10622, RG125; Sims to Fletcher, Sept. 11, 1917, Reel 3, ME-11. See also Daniels to Sims, Sept. 26, 1917, Case 10622, RG125. Steele memo, Oct. 17, 1917, Reel 3, ME-11; War Diary of Naval Patrol, France, Oct. 20, 1917, OF subj file, RG45; Sims to CNO, Oct. 17, Nov. 14, 1917, Reel 18, ME-11; Sims to Pratt, Oct. 19, 1917, Box 79, Sims Papers, LC.

56. For the Court of Inquiry, see Case 10622, RG125.

57. Schwerer to Minister, Oct. 28, 1917, with enclosures, "Plan of Order" in French Naval Archives, Vincennes; Magruder to Sims, Oct. 27, 1917, copy in case 10622, RG125.

58. Sims to Fletcher, Aug. 30, 1917, P-Brest subj file, RG45.

59. Entry for Oct. 6, 1918, Lawrence journal, WisHistSoc; Gaunt to Jellicoe, July 20, 1917, in M. Simpson, *Anglo-American Naval Relations*, 244–45; Commander Gay testimony, April 24, 1918, General Board Hearings; entry for Aug. 9, 1918, Taussig Diary, NWC; Richard L. Conolly Oral History, Columbia University.

60. See, for example, Sims to Dept., Oct. 4, 12, 25, 1917, in TT subj file, RG45.

61. G. W. Steele to CO Cruiser, Force, Sept. 21, 1917, P-Brest subj file, RG45; Report Dec. 14, 1917, in ADM137/650.

62. Quoted in Paine, *The Corsair in the War Zone*, 146–47. See also Sims to SecNav, Sept. 15, 1917, copy in Case 10622, RG125; Lawrence to Kate, Oct. 6, 1918, Lawrence Papers, WisHistSoc; entry for June 24, 1917, Merrill Diary, UNC-CH. See also Zogbaum, *From Sail to Saratoga*, 284–89.

63. Jackson to Sims, June 5, 1918, Reel 20, ME-11; Sims to "Am. Navy," Paris, June 8, 1918, Reel 4, ibid.; Sims to "Am Navy," Paris, May 25, 1918, Reel 20, ibid.

64. Oct. 12, 1917, P-Brest subj file, RG45. See, for example, Gleaves to Mayo, July 20, 1917, Reel 1, ME-11; memo to CNO, Aug. 30, 1917 Reel 3, ibid.; Dept. to Simsadus, Sept. 7, 1917, Reel 3, ibid.; Benson to Simsadus, Sept. 18, 1917, ibid.; Mayo report, Oct. 11, 1917, Box 104, Confidential Files, 1917–1919, RG80; Benson to Simsadus, Sept. 28, 1917, Reel 2, ME-11; Sims to Fletcher, Oct. 1, 1917, Reel 3, ibid.; CO naval detachment, *Edward Luckenbach* to CNO, Oct. 2, 1917, ibid.; Sims to CO "Am forces Brest," Oct. 25, 1917, Reel 18, ibid.; CO naval detachment, *City of Savannah*, to Dept., Nov. 7, 1917, ibid.; memo, CO Armed Guard on *Medina*, Nov. 22, 1917, CP subj file, RG45; Benson report of Nov. 1917 trip, Box 42, Benson Papers; Sims to CNO, Dec. 1, 1917, Reel 10, M1092. See also entry for April 14, 1918, Bathrop Diary, Smithsonian; James, *A Great Seaman*, 155–56; Murdock, *They Also Served*, 12.

65. Dec. 3, 1917, P-Brest subj file, RG45. See also Wilson to Sims, Nov. 11, 1917, OF subj file,

RG45; and Sims to Magruder, Oct. 23, 1917, Reel 2, ME-11. See also Fletcher to Sims, Sept. 9, 1917, Reel 3, ME-11; Daniels to Sims, Sept. 26, 1917, copy in Case 10622, RG125. Knox to Frothington, Sept. 30, 1924, Knox Papers, LC; *Naval Investigation*, 54–55, 385; G. E. Wheeler, *Pratt*, 90; Donald W. Mitchell, *History of the Modern American Navy*, 206; Page to Daniels, June 29, 1917, Reel 58, Daniels Papers, LC; Sims to Daniels, July 8, 1917, in M. Simpson, *Anglo-American Naval Relations*, 241–42; Baker to Daniels, July 26, 1917, Reel 1, ME-11; Daniels to Wilson, July 3, 1917, in Link, *Wilson Papers*, 43: 87; Sims to Pratt, Aug. 18, 1917, Box 78, Sims Papers, LC; Benson to Sims, Oct. 20, 1917, OE subj file, RG45; Pratt to Daniels, Nov. 12, 1917, Reel 65, Daniels Papers, LC.

66. Sims to Wilson, Nov. 3, 1917, P-Brest subj file, RG45; Wilson to Sims, Nov. 5, 1917, CP subj file, RG45; Wilson to Schwerer, Nov. 13, 1917, French Naval Archives, Vincennes; Minister of Marine to Admiralty, Dec. 21, 1917, ADM137/1534.

67. See French liaison officer to Fletcher, Sept. 11, 1997, forward to Sims, in Box 104, Confidential Correspondence, 1917–1919, RG80; Sims to Secretary, Allied Naval Council, March 9, 1918, CP subj file, RG45.

68. To Magruder, 23 Oct. 1917, Reel 2, ME-11; see also Sims to Fletcher, Oct. 1, 1917, Reel 3, ibid.; Sims to Dept., Oct. 1, 1917, ibid.

69. Reel 2, ME-11.

70. H. B. Wilson, *The American Navy in France*, 47.

71. Taussig Diary, NWC. See also Taussig, "Destroyer Experiences during the Great War," 405, 410; Battey, *70,000 Miles on a Submarine Destroyer*, 66; Adm. H. K. Hewitt Oral History, Columbia University, 93; H. B. Wilson, *The American Navy in France*, 31; Cobb, "The Tail of the Snake," 13; Murdock, *They Also Served*, 68–69.

72. Schwerer to Wilson, Jan. 20, 1918; Wilson to Sims, Dec. 14, 1917, CP subj file, RG45; Schwerer to Wilson, Nov. 12, 1917, ibid.; Wilson to Schwerer, Nov. 10, 1917, French Naval Archives, Vincennes. See also Wilson to Sims, Nov. 13, 1917, Reel 2, WE-11, and Schwerer to Minister of Marine, Jan. 14, 20, 1918, French Naval Archives, Vincennes.

73. Wilson to Sims, Jan. 27, 1918, OF subj file, RG45; Wilson to Simsadus, Dec. 2, 1917, Reel 18; Feb. 10, 1918, Reel 19, ME-11.

74. Murdock, *They Also Served*, 48.

75. *Havenhill (Pa.) Sunday Record*, Jan. 29, 1923, copy in Cooke Papers, LC.

76. Entry for Aug. 8, 1918, Taussig Diary, NWC; Vaughan, *The Gates Diaries and Letters*, 42–43.

77. Sims to SecNav, Oct. 1, 1917, CP subj file, RG45; Report on Personnel, June 27, 1918, NA subj file, ibid.; Commander Patrol Force to Jackson, Dec. 31, 1917, CP subj file, RG45; Ansel Oral History, USNI; Rose; *Brittany Patrol*, 63, 159–62, 177–78, 180–83; H. B. Wilson, *The American Navy in France*, 64–67; Pownall Oral History, USNI; entries for Feb.-Mar. 1918, Bathrop Diary, Smithsonian; Tibbott, "'Broadway' Sailors," 61; Beers, *U.S. Naval Port Offices in the Bordeaux Region*, 1917–1919, 34–37; Sims to CNO, Jan. 9, 1918, Reel 3; ME-11; Murdock, *They Also Served*, see especially entries for Jan. 9, 15, Feb. 8, and March 28, 1918, 40–43, 51, 57; Murray to C-in-C, Devonport, Jan. 14, 1918, ADM131/65; Schwerer to Minister of Marine, Dec. 6, 1917, Reel 18, ME-11.

78. Murdock, *They Also Served*, 48; Aug. 30, 1917, P-Brest subj file, RG45.

79. Entry for Aug. 8, 1918, Taussig Diary, NWC; Vaughan, *The Gates Diaries and Letters*, 42–43.

80. See, for example, Paine, *The Corsair in the War Zone*, 61; Murdock, *They Also Served*, 25, 28; Gleaves to CNO, Oct. 1, 1917, Reel 3, ME-11; Moore Oral History, Columbia University.

81. For background to these vessels, see chapter 12.

82. Sims to CNO, Sept. 15, 1917, Reel 2, ME-11; War Diary, Patrol France, Sept. 29, 1917,

OF subj file, RG45; Fletcher to Admiral Schwerer, Oct. 1, 1917, TT subj file, RG45; Fletcher to Schwerer, Oct. 10, 1917, CD subj file, RG45; Sims to CNO, Oct. 11, 1917, Reel 2, ME-11; Jackson to Sims, Oct. 18, 1917, OF subj file, RG45; Sims to CNO, Nov. 15, 1917, CP subj file, ibid.; Magruder to Wilson, Jan. 2, 1918, Confidential Files, 1917–1919, Box 104, RG80; Magruder, "The Navy in the War," 21–22, 74; Husband, *On the Coast of France*, 122–23.

83. Wilson to Sims, Dec. 10, 1917, OF subj file, RG45; H. B. Wilson, *The American Navy in France*, 125–29; Sims to OpNav, July 22, 1918, Reel 9, ME-11. For the story of these mine-sweepers, see Hinkamp, "Bringing in the Sheaves"; Hinkamp, "Pipe Sweepers," ibid.; "History of Squadron Four Patrol Force," OF subj file, RG45. See also Twining testimony, Case 10622, RG125; Hinkamp testimony, July 29, 1918, General Board Hearings; "Work of the American Mine-Sweeping Squadron," *Rudder* (April 1919): 180–81. For the comments of an illiterate sailor (formerly fisherman) on one of the sweepers, see Loder to wife, Oct. 31, Nov. 25, and Dec. 5, 1917, Loder Papers, Mariners' Museum.

84. July 10, 1917, Box 4, Sims Papers, LC; ADM to CNO, Grand Fleet, and other commands, July 7, 1917, ADM137/1899.

85. Aug. 11, 1917, copy in Reel 2, ME-11.

86. *ONI Monthly Bulletin* (May 15, 1919): 19. See also *American Legion Weekly*, March 7, 1925, 14.

87. Michelsen, "The Submarine Warfare," 97; *American Legion Weekly*, July 3, 1925, 16; Stackpole, "The Anglo-American Atlantic Convoy System in World War I," Ph.D. diss., 348.

88. Rose, *Brittany Patrol*, 96–101; "Life on the U.S.S. *Corsair*," 179–80.

89. Quoted in Freidel, *Over There*, 60.

90. Rose, *Brittany Patrol*, 254–57; Frederick, *The Great Adventure*, 139–40; Benson to Simsadus, June 8, 1918, Reel 4, ME-11; Foote, "Narrative of the *President Lincoln*"; Messimer, *Escape*, 1–19; Freidel, *Over There*, 58–61. The Percy Foote Collection in the Manuscript Collection, UNC-CH, has a folder on the *President Lincoln*'s sinking. There is an excellent account of the sinking in the William Search file, Spanish-American War Papers, AMHI. See also the papers of Karl Henry Newert in the Indiana War History Records, Indiana State Library. Newert was a wireless operator on the *Lincoln* and was one of the twenty-six that died in the sinking. A letter from one of the survivors in this collection attributed his death to the explosion of a boiler after they had abandoned ship and Newert was on a raft. More than likely it was the third torpedo that caused his death.

91. Messimer's *Escape* is an excellent, well-documented account of Isaacs. Hoehling interviewed Isaacs for his book *The Great War at Sea* and included Isaac's account of the sinking and his later exploits in an appendix (see 279–82).

92. To Dept., Reel 6, ME-11.

93. Entry for July 2, 1918, Brown Journal, WisHistSoc.

94. Ibid. Six out of a complement of 785 were lost; three in the boiler room when the torpedo exploded. Entry for July 6, 1918, Brown Journal, WisHistSoc; entry for July 6, 1918, Taussig Journal, NWC; Rose, *Brittany Patrol*, 268–71.

95. McCarthy, "When Torpedoes Struck," 26–28; Chatterton, *Danger Zone*, 330.

96. *ONI Monthly Bulletin* (May 15, 1917), 19; Grant, *U-Boat Intelligence*, 56.

97. Staton to father, Sept. 12, 1918, Staton Papers, UNC-CH. See also Wilson to Sims, Sept. 8, 1918, Reel 10, ME-11; CO, *Mount Vernon* to Wilson, Sept. 8, 1918, ibid. For accounts of other ships in the convoy see entry for Sept. 5, 1918, Slayback Memoir, NDL; CO USS *Winslow* to Sims, Sept. 5, 1918, Reel 10, ME-11; The Staton Papers, UNC-CH, have a large quantity of papers including statements of engine room survivors, lookouts, etc. as well as newspaper clippings about the incident.

98. Fix Oral History, "World War I Bluejacket," NHF.

99. Rose, *Brittany Patrol*, 104–5.

100. Hanks, "Fighting the U-Boats"; Alden and Westcott, *The United States Navy*, 348; Sims, *The Victory at Sea*, 148–49; Connolly, *Navy Men*, 208–18; Connolly, *Sea-Borne*, 201–3. Merrill in his diary mentions that his ship picked up the radio conversation between the *Luckenbach* and Nicholson. See entry for Oct. 1917, UNC-CH. See also *Naval Investigation*, 1006; Grant, *U-Boats Destroyed*, 118.

101. For the *Olympic* ramming the U-boat, see B. Hayes, *Hull Down*, 230–37.

102. Corbett and Newbolt, *History of the Great War*, 5: 136; Terraine, *The U-Boat War*, 90; Bowling, "Convoy in World War I," master's thesis, 169–70.

103. Authorities disagree on statistics of losses. See, for example, Winton, *Convoy*, 114–15; Stackpole, "The Anglo-American Convoy System in World War I," Ph.D. diss., 293; Marder, *From the Dreadnought to Scapa Flow*, 4: 277; Fayle, *Seaborne Trade*, 3: 251.

104. Marder, *From the Dreadnought to Scapa Flow*, 4: 281; Terraine, *The U-Boat Wars*, 86–88; Corbett and Newbolt, *History of the Great War*, 5: 137.

105. C-in-C, Devonport to ADM, Nov. 5, 1917, ADM131/98; Terraine, *The U-Boat Wars*, 98–99.

106. Quoted in Josephus Daniels, *The Wilson Era: Years of War*, 116.

107. Hashagen, *U-Boats Westward!*, 218–20. See also entry for January 8, 1918, in Goerlitz, *The Kaiser and His Court*. See also Sims to Dept., January 6, 1918, Reel 3, ME-11; Sims to Dunn, May 6, 1918, Reel 4, ibid.; Sims to Dept., May 9, 1918, Reel 20, ibid.; Sims to Dept., May 14, 18, June 13, 1918, Reel 4, ibid.; Benson to Sims, May 18, 1918, CP subj file, RG45; Benson to Sims, May 5, 1918, Reel 4, ME-11; War Diary, CO Azores, Jan. 19, 1918, P-Ponta Delgada, RG45.

108. Dunn to Sims, July 14, Oct. 14, 1918, Box 55, Sims Papers, LC; Leighton, *Simsadus*, 86; entry for July 1917, Brown Journal, Brown Papers, WisHistSoc; Sims to Wilson, Aug. 4, 1918, Reel 5, ME-11; Sims to Dunn, Aug. 2, 1918, ibid.

109. Sims would write Bristol, "the sending of the ships over here was not a part of a plan made on this side." This is not entirely correct, but the final decision, as usual, was in Washington. Sept. 2, 1918, Bristol Papers, LC. See also Sims to Bristol, Aug. 26, 1918, ibid.; Department's plan in Reel 5, ME-11. See also revised plan dated Aug. 6, 1918, ibid.; Sims to Admiralty, Aug. 10, 1918, TT subj file, RG45; Sims to Admiralty, Aug. 19, 1918, Reel 10, ME-11. Sims testimony, *Naval Investigation*, 171; Admiralty Plans Division Memorandum, May 6, 1918, in M. Simpson, *Anglo-American Naval Relations*, 344–46; Admiralty Memo, Nov. 4, 1918, ADM137/1899; Marder, *Portrait of an Admiral*, 322; Benson to Sims, July 30, 1918, Reel 4, ME-11; Sims to Benson, July 31, ibid.; Sims to Malvus, Queenstown, July 31, 1918, Reel 9; Sims to Benson, Aug. 2, 1918, ibid.; Memorandum Number 26, May 17, 1918, in Navy Dept., *The American Naval Planning Section in London*, 213–20; "Summary of U.S. Naval Activities in European Waters," Z file, OA; Trask, *Captains and Cabinets*, 218–19; Marder, *From the Dreadnought to Scapa Flow*, 5: 156–57. J. W. Jones, "U.S. Battleship Operations in World War I," Ph.D. diss., is the most thorough examination of this topic (see 174–203).

110. Extensive files on the raider problem can be found in CP subj file, RG45. For considerable discussion over where to base the various battleship divisions in North America and Europe, see Navy Dept., *The American Naval Planning Section in London*, 510–11; extract of July 20, 1920, statement by FDR in Jacoby, *Calendar of the Speeches of FDR*, 125; "The Atlantic Fleet in the War," unpublished paper, Mayo Papers, LC; Pratt, "Autobiography," OA; plan dated Oct. 10, 1918, in TT subj file, RG45; Sims testimony in *Naval Investigation*, 173–75; Sims to Benson, Aug. 3, 1918, in M. Simpson, *Anglo-American Naval Relations*, 348–49.

111. Sims to Dept., Aug. 5, Benson to Sims, Aug. 7, 1918, in Reel 5, ME-11.

112. Aug. 25, 1918, Box 81, Sims Papers, LC.

113. Aug. 8, 1918, ADM137/1622.

114. Bayly to Rodgers, Sept. 2, 1918, ADM137/1622; ADM memo, Sept. 1, 1918, ibid.; Bayly to ADM, Sept. 4, 1918, ADM137/1899; ADM to Bayly, Aug. 21, 1918, ADM137/1934; Rodgers to CNO, Sept. 16, 1918, OB subj file, RG45; Rodgers to Sims, Sept. 5, 1918, ibid.; Instructions No 1, Aug. 19, 1918, Reel 10, ME-11; Wemyss to Sims, Aug. 20, 1918, Box 24, Sims Papers; Twining memo to Sims, Aug. 20, 1918, ibid.

115. Long Memoir, UNC-CH; Bayly to Sims, Sept. 30, 1918, Box 47, Sims Papers, LC; Rodgers to Sims, Sept. 20. 1918, Box 81, ibid. See also Mayo to Benson, Sept. 18, 1918, Mayo Papers, LC.

116. See Mayo to Benson, Aug. 10, 1918, Reel 5, ME-11.

117. The American battleships, even the most modern ones, were considered too slow. Pratt, "Autobiography," OA; Benson to Sims, Aug. 30, 1918, Reel 5, ME-11; Sims to Benson, Aug. 31, ibid.; Benson to Sims, Sept. 3, 1918, ibid.; Grant to convoy officers in North America, Sept. 13, 1918, Roll 40, M1140; Sims to Rodgers, Sept. 25, Box 81, Sims Papers, LC.

118. Long Memoir, Long Papers, UNC-CH.

119. Oct. 30, 1918, William F. Fullam Papers, LC.

120. Fremantle to Beatty, Oct. 10, 1918, Ranft, *The Beatty Papers*, 1: 558, passim, for Grand Fleet sortie. Rodgers to Sims, Nov. 26, 1918, OB subj file; RG45; Sims to Rodgers, Oct. 14, 1918, Reel 10, ME-11; Sims to Dept., Oct. 16, 1918, Reel 8, ibid.; Wilkinson, *The USS* Nevada *and Her Experience in the War*, 7–8; Chatterton, *Danger Zone*, 364; Hustvedt Oral History, USNI; Thompson, *Take Her Down*, 262; "The Part the U.S.S. *Utah* played in the World War," OS subj file, RG45.

121. Salter, *Allied Shipping Control*, 125–28; Rutter, *Red Ensign*, 149; Bowling, "The Negative Influence of Mahan on the Protection of Shipping in Wartime," Ph.D. diss., 254. One historian, however, has suggested that it was American and Allied economic countermeasures that really made the difference. Among the measures he mentions are shifting the bulk of shipping from distant ports to North American ports; food rationing and control, and changes in agricultural production (103). See Olson, *The Economics of the Wartime Shortage*, 86–116.

122. Michelsen, "The Submarine Warfare," 81, 128; Goerlitz, *The Kaiser and His Court*, 369–70, 382, 384.

123. Goerlitz, *The Kaiser and His Court*, 369–70, 382, 384.

124. Sims, *The Victory at Sea*, 165.

Chapter 15. Escorts

1. Wemyss to Beatty, March 26, 1918, Beatty MS; Bayly to Adm. Milford Haven, June 1, 1918, ADM137/1512; G. Campbell, *Number Thirteen*, 122–24; Grasty, *Flashes from the Front*, 260; Sims to CNO, April 19, 1918, Reel 3, ME-11.

2. Ferrell, *Woodrow Wilson*, 38–39.

3. Sims to SecNav, April 24, 1917, CP subj file, RG45; to President, ibid.; Bowling, "The Negative Influence of Mahan on the Protection of Shipping in Wartime," Ph.D. diss., 90–91.

4. General Board letter, GB 425, series No. 7621, to SecNav, General Board Records, file January 1–30–June 30, 1917, RG80; SecNav to Sims, June 23, 1917, CP subj file, RG45. This file is replete with reports, correspondence concerning the developing submarine crisis and the recommended U.S. Navy response to it. See also Bowling, "The Negative Influence of Mahan on the Protection of Shipping in Wartime," Ph.D. diss., 93–94, 107–15, for a succinct analysis of the Board's concerns and recommendations.

5. Marder, *From the Dreadnought to Scapa Flow*, 4: 122–23; Jellicoe, *The Submarine Peril*, 113–15; and Jellicoe, *The Crisis of the Naval War*, 114–15, for this distribution and the defense of it.

6. Winton, *Convoy*, 70. See also Marder, *From the Dreadnought to Scapa Flow*, 4: 123–27. Not all historians agree with this assessment. See, for example, Gibson and Prendergast, *The*

German Submarine War, 175; and Carr, *Good Hunting*, 15. There is obviously a discrepancy in Marder's and Winton's total destroyers.

7. Entry for November 28, 1917, Larimer Diary, UVA; Knox to Frothingham, July 8, 1925, Knox Papers, LC.

8. M. Simpson, *Anglo-American Naval Relations*, 25–27, 480–81. At least one British journalist, Arthur Pollen, criticized the decision to build more destroyers, saying in effect that emphasis should be placed on constructing vessels that could be quickly built. To House, Aug. 27, 1917, Pollen Papers, copy provided by Professor Jon Sumida. Although the construction of destroyers was given priority during the war, fewer than 50 out of an authorized 260 were completed. This, of course, was a great disappointment to Sims and the British Admiralty. See M. Simpson, *Anglo-American Naval Relations*, 131, 504–39. After the war, Daniels would insist that before the United States entered the conflict "large numbers of antisubmarine craft were authorized." *Naval Investigation*, 2093. However, it was Assistant CNO Pratt who persuaded the naval secretary to delay the capital ship construction program in favor of destroyers. Ibid., 481.

9. Klachko, *Benson*, 63. See also Browning to Gaunt, April 3, 1917, in M. Simpson, *Anglo-American Naval Relations*, 28; entry for April 16, 1917, in Josephus Daniels, *Cabinet Diaries*, 135; Trask, *Captains and Cabinets*, 62–63. A detailed account of the Hampton Roads Conference can be found in a memo dated Feb. 26, 1921, in the Mayo Papers, LC, and a communication from Browning to Admiralty, April 13, 1917, ADM137/1436, copies in M. Simpson, *Anglo-American Naval Relations*, 33–37. See also Josephus Daniels, *Our Navy at War*, 45–49. The British and French naval attachés were also present at these meetings. See also Jellicoe to Beatty, April 6, 1917, ADM137/1964; Stackhouse, "The Anglo-American Atlantic Convoy System in World War I," Ph.D. diss., 38–39; Blumenthal, *Illusion and Reality in Franco-American Diplomacy*, 39; De Chair to Jellicoe, May 2, 1917, in M. Simpson, *Anglo-American Naval Relations*, 216–17.

10. For accounts of the conference, see C. H. Hunter, "Anglo-American Relations during the Period of Belligerency," 55–70; Willert, *The Road to Safety*, 73–81; De Chair, *The Sea Is Strong*, 230–33; Burk, *Britain, America, and the Sinews of War*, 125–35; Stackhouse, "The Anglo-American Atlantic Convoy System in World War I," Ph.D. diss., 40–42.

11. Gleaves, *The Admiral*, 138–39; De Chair, *The Sea Is Strong*, 231–32; Freidel, *FDR: The Apprenticeship*, 305; Trask, *Captains and Cabinets*, 74–75; K. Young, *Arthur James Balfour*, 384; De Chair to Jellicoe, April 28, 1917, in M. Simpson, *Anglo-American Naval Relations*, 21.

12. Benson memo of meeting with Chocheprat, April 27, 1917, in Box 37, Daniels Papers, LC; copy of Chocheprat's notes of meeting April 27, 1917, in Box 31, Assistant SecNav Files, Roosevelt Papers, FDR Library. See also French naval attaché, Washington, to Daniels, Oct. 20, 1917, Reel 36, Daniels Papers, LC; De Chair to Admiralty, April 27, 1917, in M. Simpson, *Anglo-American Naval Relations*, 210–11; Trask, *Captains and Cabinets*, 76; Willert, *The Road to Safety*, 80, 99; entry for April 22, 1917, in Josephus Daniels, *Cabinet Diaries*, 142, 144; memo of French naval attaché, Washington to Minister of Marine, n.d., but the file includes a number of cables concerning the meeting, French Naval Archives, Vincennes; Josephus Daniels, *Our Navy at War*, 99; Jusserand to Minister of Foreign Affairs, May 5, 1917, copy in French Naval Archives, Vincennes. Not all French naval officials opposed the decision to send the destroyers to British waters. The French naval attaché in London said that they should be based where they would be most useful—in Ireland. M. D. Lostende to Minister of Marine, April 27, 1917, French Naval Archives, Vincennes.

13. Bayly, *Pull Together*, 242.

14. Quoted in Bowling, "The Negative Influence of Mahan on the Protection of Shipping in Wartime," Ph.D. diss., 99. See also *Naval Investigation*, 4; Benson to Daniels, May 1, 1917, Reel 58, Benson Papers, LC; entry for April 24, 1917, in Josephus Daniels, *Cabinet Diaries*, 140; M. Simpson, *Anglo-American Naval Relations*, 479. Page to SecState and President, April 27, 1917,

CP subj file, RG45; Sims, *The Victory at Sea*, 48–49; Hendrick, *The Life and Letters of Walter Hines Page*, 2: 278–79. See also Page to SecState, July 11, 1917, *Foreign Relations, 1917*, Supplement 2, 124–26. Jellicoe to Beatty, April 12, 1917, in Patterson, *The Jellicoe Papers*, 2: 156; Sims to SecNav, April 14, 1917, CP subj file, RG45; copies of this communication can be found in Sims, *The Victory at Sea*, 374–76; and *Foreign Relations, 1917*, Supplement 2, 23–25; Sims to SecNav, April 18, 1918, in ibid., 28–29; Uhlig, *How Navies Fight*, 98; Trask, *Captains and Cabinets*, 67; Morison, *Sims*, 353; entry for April 17, 1917, in Josephus Daniels, *Cabinet Diaries*, 136; Hendrick, *The Life and Letters of Walter Hines Page*, 2: 198–99, 278; A. H. Miles to Sims, March 16, 1920, Box 72, Sims Papers, LC; W. F. Bell, "American Embassies in Belligerent Europe," Ph.D. diss., 154–55; Cooper, *Walter Hines Page*, 378–81; *Naval Investigation*, 4, 71; G. E. Wheeler, *Pratt*, 128, Hoover, *An American Epic*, 16. Sims asked Hoover to carry a message to the president about the submarine crisis.

15. To SecNav, CP subj file, RG45; see also Sims to SecNav, June 21, 1917, in Box 3, Area file, RG45.

16. To Daniels, in M. Simpson, *Anglo-American Naval Relations*, 241–42.

17. CP subj file, RG45. See also *Naval Investigation*, 51; and Sims to Page, June 25, 1917, in Box 3, Area file, RG45.

18. *Naval Investigation*, 55; Sims to Dept., June 25, 26, 1917, Box 3, Area file, RG45; Page to SecState, June 27, 1917, *Foreign Relations, 1917*, Supplement 2, 111–12; FO to British Ambassador, Washington, June 30, 1917, copy in Box 3, Area file, RG45; and British Embassy to Dept. of State, July 1, 1917, *Foreign Relations, 1917*, Supplement 2, 115; Trask, *Captains and Cabinets*, 72.

19. Benson to Sims, June 18, 1917, CP subj file, RG45; Benson testimony, *Naval Investigation*, 1908.

20. July 3, 1917, TP subj file, RG45. See also Trask, *Captains and Cabinets*, 89–90.

21. OF subj file, RG45. See also Daniels to President, July 3, 1917, in Link, *Wilson Papers*, 43: 87.

22. Quoted in Trask, *Captains and Cabinets*, 94.

23. Reel 3, ME-11.

24. See G. E. Wheeler, *Pratt*, 118.

25. Benson to Mayo, May 12, 1917, Reel 1, MS-11; *Naval Investigation*, 46–49; Knox to Frothington, July 16, 1925, Box 9, Knox Papers, LC.

26. Diary, May 5, 1917, Gleaves Papers, LC; Mayo, "Atlantic Fleet in the War," copy in Reel 57, Daniels Papers, LC.

27. June 13, 1918, Reel 15, ME-11.

28. Daniels, "The United States Navy in the World War," 121–22; Sims, *The Victory at Sea*, 40; Marder, *From the Dreadnought to Scapa Flow*, 4: 122–23, 145; Carr, *Good Hunting*, 15.

29. *ONI Monthly Information Bulletin*, May 15, 1919, 14; *Naval Investigation*, 258.

30. March 18, 1918, ADM137/1535.

31. Sept. 22, 1918, ADM137/2710.

32. Herwig, *Politics of Frustration*, 130, 138–39, 150.

33. Gaunt, British Embassy Washington to Benson, July 23, 1917, Box 4, Benson Papers, LC; Adm. H.S. Grant, C-in-C, Gibraltar to Admiralty, Aug. 7, 1917, copy in OF subj file, RG45.

34. Benson to Sims, Aug. 15, 1917, OF subj file, RG45.

35. Elderton, *Shipping Problems*, 28–31. For details of the expansion, see Winton, *Convoy*, 76, passim; and "convoy system," in ADM137/2659, and ADM137/1548.

36. Sims to CO *Melville*, Nov. 26, 1917, Reel 2, ME-11; Twining to *Melville*, Dec. 7, 1917, P-Brest subj file, RG45; Pringle to Sims, Oct. 11, 1917, OH subj file, RG45; Sims to CO, US Patrol Sq., Brest, Oct. 15, 1917, P-Queenstown subj file; Gaunt to Admiralty, July 19, 1917, copy in Reel 1, ME-11. For Gibraltar, see chapter 19.

37. This also is how Crowell and Wilson, in *The Road to France*, 2: 465, describe the impact of convoying.

38. Trask, *Captains and Cabinets*, 151–52, 181–82; Knox to Frothington, Sept. 30, 1914, Knox Papers, LC; Benson to Sims, Jan. 31, 1918, Reel 3, ME-11; *Naval Investigation*, 68–71. See also Taussig, "Destroyer Experiences in the Great War," 399; Jellicoe, *The Crisis of the Naval War*, 161; Sims to Bayly, May 19, 1918, Box 47, Sims Papers; Sims to Pringle, Dec. 7, 1917, OE subj file, RG45; H. B. Wilson, *The American Navy in France*, 26–27; Davy, Report on Personnel, June 27, 1918, NA subj file, RG45; McKean testimony, *Naval Investigation*, 1755.

39. R. A to Third Sea Lord, Dec. 3, 1917, ADM137/1437; Beatty to First Sea Lord, Dec. 16, 1917, ADM137/1962; Admiralty to Beatty, Jan 4, 1918, ibid.; memo on protection of minelayers, February 13, 1918, ADM137/1459; Twining to Admiralty, Feb. 13, 1918, ibid.; P.T.O. to C-in-C, February 16, 1918, ADM137/1898; Rear Admiral (Mines) C-in-C, Feb. 28, 1918, ADM137/1962; Bayly to Sims, Feb. 23, 1918, Box 47, Sims Papers, LC.

40. Rodman to SecNav, Jan 9, 1918; Beatty to Rodman, Jan. 11, 1918; Sims to SecNav, Jan 15, 1918, OpNav to Sims, Feb. 1, 1918; all in file 28754-18: 346, Confidential Files, 1917–1919, RG80; memo No.7, Jan. 14, 1918, in Navy Dept., *The American Naval Planning Section in London*, 35–36; memo, Nov. 26, 1917, ADM116/1567; Rear Adm. (Mines) to C-in-C, Feb. 28, 1918; memo, March, 1918, ADM137/1646; Sims to CNO, Jan. 15, 1918, copy in ADM137/1898; note, Jan. 21, 1918, ibid.; Sims to Fremantle and reply, June 29, 1918, ADM137/1459; memo, Feb. 8, 1918, ibid.; Sims to Wilson, Feb. 21, 1918, Reel 3, ME-11; memo, July 27, 1918, ADM137/21709; Fuller to First Lord, Sept. 8, 1918, ibid.; Beatty to Admiralty, Oct. 30, 1918, ADM137/1459. See also Roosevelt to Daniels, July 27, 1918, Box 45, Assist SecNav Files, FDR Library.

41. Sims to Pringle, March 29, 1918, Reel 4, ME-11; Rodman to SecNav, July 19, 1918, copy in ADM137/1898; Beatty to Admiralty, Oct. 12, 1918, ADM137/1984; Bowling, "The Negative Influence of Mahan on the Protection of Shipping in Wartime," Ph.D. diss., 497; Schoeffel Oral History, USNI; T. Wilson, *The Myriad Faces of War*, 635.

42. Report of 1917 trip, Box 42, Benson Papers, LC. See also entry for Dec. 20, 1917, in Josephus Daniels, *Cabinet Diaries*, 253. For the French navy, see Hood, *Royal Republicans*; 13; R. Gardiner, *The Eclipse of the Big Gun*, 113; Jenkins, *A History of the French Navy*, 316; Laurens, *Precis d'histoire de la guerre navale*, passim; Socas, "France, Naval Armaments, and Naval Disarmament," Ph.D. diss., 29–34; Halpern, *A Naval History of World War I*, 12–13. For the sailing fishing craft, see entry for Dec. 1, 1917, Brown Journal, WisHistSoc.

43. May 30, 1917, Box 25, Assistant SecNav Files, FDR Library. See also De Chair to Admiralty, April 27, 28, May 2, 1917, in M. Simpson, *Anglo-American Naval Relations*, 210–16. Why the minister addressed the letter to Roosevelt is unclear.

44. Box 53, Sims Papers, LC.

45. Daniels to Sims, June 20, 1917, copy in *Naval Investigation*, 46; Daniels to Fletcher, June 1, 1917, Reel 13, ME-11; Memo, May 3, 1917, File 144, Reel 40, M1140. The French minister of marine asked Roosevelt not to send the subchasers by way of Queenstown; "they might be retained." May 30, 1917, Box 25, Assistant SecNav Files, FDR Library.

46. Husband, *On the Coast of France*, 9–10.

47. "Nelson Goss," in Furlong, *Class of 1905*, 198.

48. Murdock, *They Also Served*, 30; Cooke, "Recollections of a Life in the Navy," Cooke MSS, LC.

49. Paine, *The Corsair in the War Zone*, 146–74; Breckel, "The Suicide Flotilla," 668–69; Stirling, "American Armed Yachts in the War Zone," 275; Tibbott, "'Broadway' Sailors," 63.

50. Entry for July 15, Taussig Diary, NWC Brown Journal, WisHistSoc. See also the *American Legion Magazine*, April 1930, 11; Wheeler Oral Interview, USNI; Alden and Westcott, *The United States Navy*, 351

51. Paine, *The Corsair in the War Zone*, 60. For the *Wakiva*, see Rose, *Brittany Patrol*, 249–50, and "Earl Farwell," in Furlong, *Class of 1905*, 129–30.

52. Cooke, "Recollections of a Life in the Navy," Cooke MSS, LC; "Earle Farwell" in Furlong, *Class of 1905*, 46, 129.

53. *Norma* War Diary, OR subj file, RG45; Paine, *The Corsair in the War Zone*, 60; Sims to Pringle, Sept. 6, 1917, P file-Brest subj file, RG45; Rose, *Brittany Patrol*, 205. Benson's biographer states that Sims ordered the transfer of these vessels from the Azores to Brest only after *Antilles* was sunk. This is not correct as *Antilles* was sunk in late October, a month after the destroyers received their orders to Brest. Klachko, *Benson*, 108–9.

54. Sims to SecNav, Sept. 13, 1918, Reel 4, ME-11.

55. Entry for Nov. 3, 1917, Fagan Diary, Mariners' Museum.

56. Sims to Dept., Sept. 13, 1917, Reel 2, ME-11; entry for July 11, Taussig Diary, NWC.

57. Sims to Pringle, Jan. 24, 1918, Box 79, Sims Papers, LC.

58. January 3, 1918, Box 79, Confidential Files, 1917–1919, RG80. See also Husband, *On the Coast of France*, 14.

59. For the reorganization, see chapter 3.

60. Sims to Wilson, Feb. 13, 1918, Reel 19, ME-11; Sims to Dept., Jan. 8, 1918, Reel 3, ibid.; Benson to Sims, Jan. 8, 1918, CP subj file, RG45; Jackson to Benson, Jan. 5, 1918, Box 6, Benson Papers; Wilson to Sims, Feb. 10, 1918, P-Brest subj file, RG45.

61. Feb. 21, 1918, Reel 3, ME-11.

62. Wilson to Sims, May 24, 1918, Sims to Wilson, May 24, 26, 1918, all in Reel 20, ME-11. See also Wilson to Sims, April 22, 1918, Reel 4, ibid.

63. Sims to AMNAPAR, Paris, May 25, 1918, Reel 4, ME-11; Sims to Pringle, May 18, 1918, Box 79, Sims Papers, LC; Sims to Benson, June 4, 1918, Box 49, ibid.; Sims to Dept., June 5, 1918, Reel 20, ME-11; Sims weekly report to SecNav, June 13, 1918, Reel 4, ibid.

64. Aug. 16, 1918, ADM137/1513.

65. Sims to Bayly, May 24, 1918, Box 47, Sims Papers, LC; Bayly to Admiralty, June 5, 1918, Reel 20, ME-11.

66. Sims to Dept., Aug. 19, 1918, Reel 9, ME-11; Sims to Wilson, Reel 10, ibid.; Rose, *Brittany Patrol*, 262.

67. Sims to Pringle, Jan. 12, 1918, OE subj file, RG45; Sims to Dunn, May 7, 1918, in M. Simpson, *Anglo-American Naval Relations*, 295–96; Sims to Murray, May 6, 1918, ibid., 295; Sims to Pringle, May 11, 1918, U subj file, RG45; Sims to Niblack, May 23, 1918, Box 76, Sims Papers, LC; Sims to Bayly, May 19, June 8, 1918, Box 47, ibid.; Bayly to Admiralty, June 5, 1918, OE subj file, RG45; Sims to Dept., Aug. 24, 1918, Reel 5, ME-11; Sims to Rodgers, Sept. 25, 1918, Box 24, Sims Papers; Sims to Dept., Oct. 9, 1918, Roll 12, ME-11; Marder, *From the Dreadnought to Scapa Flow*, 5: 98–99; Daniels to Wilson, July 3, 1917, in Link, *Wilson Papers*, 43: 87; "Joint Appreciation by the British and American Plans Divisions," March 28, 1918, in M. Simpson, *Anglo-American Naval Relations*, 287–90.

68. R. E. Johnson, *Guardian of the Seas*, 50–51.

69. Muhlhauser, *Small Craft*, 197–98; Roberts, *The Years of Promise*, 159. See also Sims to Dept., Oct. 24, 1917, subj file CG, RG45. For other comments concerning the Gibraltar-based American vessels, see chapters 12 and 19.

70. F. W. Brown, *Overseas, 1917–1918*, n.d., privately printed. Copy in Coast Guard Library, 3; *Seneca*'s history, copy in office of Coast Guard Historian. See also W. J. Wheeler, "Reminiscences of World War Convoy Work," 386–92.

71. For some examples, see entry for April 4, 1918, Halsey Memoir, LC; entry for Jan. 23–24, 1918, Moore Diary, NHF; Slayton to CO, Patrol Force, Dec. 22, 1917, Reel 18, ME-11; Wilson to all ships and District Commanders, July 25, 1918, Reel 9, ibid.; Port Officer, St. Nazaire to C.O. Patrol Squadron, Nov. 10, 1917, Reel 18, ibid.

72. Zogbaum, *From Sail to Saratoga*, 265–66. For examples of escorts missing convoys, see ADM to Adm. de Lostende, Jan. 26, 1918, ADM131/98; Pringle to Sims, Jan. 29, 1918, Box 79, Sims Papers, LC; Sims to Dept., Aug. 21, 1918, Reel 9, ME-11.

73. Sims to Wilson, April 4, 1918, Reel 19, ME-11; Admiralty to C-in-C Queenstown, Jan. 14, 1918, ADM137/1347; to C-in-C Devonport, Jan. 27, 1918, ADM137/1534; CO Harvard to Wilson, Feb. 4, 1918, OS subj file, RG45. For French concerns, see Salaun to DMM, Admiralty, Jan. 3, 1918, ADM131/98; Wilson to C-in-C Queenstown, Jan. 14, 1918, ADM137/1347.

74. To S. W. Bryant, Jan. 3, 1934, Queenstown Assn Files, NHF; Bayly to Sims, Oct. 20, 1918, in M. Simpson, *Anglo-American Naval Relations*, 315. See also entry for Nov. 17, 1917, Merrill Diary, UNC-CH; *American Legion Weekly*, July 13, 1923, 15.

75. March 28, 1918, Box 9, Sims Papers, LC. Evidently Berry's wife and Mrs. Sims were friends. See also Weaver, "An Incident of W.W.I.," 7–10. Weaver was *Manley*'s chief quartermaster. CO Terry to Sims, March 23, 1918, OS subj file, RG45; T. B. Brown, "Seventy-eight Thousand Miles in Search of German Submarines," 19–20.

76. Schoeffel Oral History, USNI; entry for Oct. 9, 1917, Moore Diary, NHF; *DANFS*, 6: 471.

77. Historical Sketch of the USS *Wakiva*, June 8, 1916, OS subj file, RG45; entry for May 22, 1918, Brown Journal, WisHistSoc; Rose, *Brittany Patrol*, 249–50.

78. File under *Benham* in file 26835-736:1, Case 6972, RG125. For the *Burrows* incidents, see entries for May 20 and Sept. 13, 1918, Lauer Journal, USS *Burrows* file, OA. See also Battey, *70,000 Miles on a Submarine Destroyer*, 230.

79. Harry B. Albright account, WWI Research Collection, AMHI.

80. Entry for Nov. 1917, Merrill Diary, UNC-CH. His papers also include his report of the incident, dated November 6, 1917.

81. Entry for Feb. 2, 1918, Halsey Journal, LC. For the *Alcedo* incident mentioned, see Ruth Wright Kauffman, "Small but Valiant," 69; and Breckel, "The Suicide Flotilla," 665.

82. To wife, Dec. 12, 1917, Box 9, Sims Papers, LC. See also Willoughby, *Yankton*, 205–6; and *DANFS*, 2: 89–90.

83. Entries for Jan. 9, 10, 1918, Brown Journal, WisHistSoc.

84. "Nelson Henry Goss," in Furlong, *Class of 1905*, 198.

85. Breckel, "The Suicide Flotilla," 664. See also Sims to Dept., Aug. 30, 1917, Reel 2, ME-11.

86. Entry for Jan. 16, 1918, Moore Diary, NHF; Doughty, "Mistaken Attacks in the World War," 1730. See also Niblack, "Putting Cargos Across," in ZPA subj file, RG45.

87. Doughty, "Mistaken Attacks in the World War," 1729.

88. Wiggins, *My Romance with the Navy*, 94.

89. For an example of an attack on a U.S. submarine, see R. Werner to CNO, July 21, 1918, Reel 9, ME-11.

90. Report of Court of Inquiry, Oct. 14, 1917, OS subj file, RG45; Daniels to Italian Minister of Marine, Oct. 9, 1917, 763.72/7185, NA microfilm M367; Train to NavIntel, Washington, Dec. 7, 1917, Reel 4, ME-11. For a description of the damage to the two submarines, see unknown seaman's diary, entry for Oct. 10, 1917, JOD/198, NMM.

91. Sims to Dept., May 5, 1918, Reel 12, ME-11; Doughty, "Mistaken Attacks in the World War," 1731.

92. Memo, Feb. 26, 1918, ADM137/1527; T. M. Jones, *Watchdogs of the Deep*, 158–59.

93. Blackford, *Torpedoboat Sailor*, 33.

94. Baker, *The Terror of Tobermory*, 69. See also Sims to Admiralty, July 27, 1918, Reel 12, ME-11; Extracts from Report, June 18, 1918, OD subj file, RG45.

95. Niblack War Diary, Nov.10, 1918, Reel 10, ME-11; Nutting, *The Cinderellas of the Fleet*, 92.

96. To Bayly, June 6, 1917, Reel 8, ME-11.

97. Willoughby, *Yankton*, 190–91. For another incident involving fishing vessels, see Wiggins, *My Romance with the Navy*, 98. For other examples, see Auten, *"Q" Boat Adventures*, 235–36; Sterne, *Over the Seas for Uncle Sam*, 122–23; N. Collins, *Civilian Seamen in War*, 12.

98. Quoted in Leighton, *Simsadus*, 47. See also Muhlhauser, *Small Craft*, 195, 197–98.

99. Taussig, "Destroyer Experiences during the Great War," U.S. Naval Institute *Proceedings* 49 (March 1923): 398–404.

100. Moore Oral History, Columbia University; entry for March 12, 1918, Moore Diary, NHF; *USS Walke* file, OA.

101. B. Hayes. *Hull Down*, 237.

102. Entry for Sept. 1917, Jenkins Diary, NWC.

103. Entry for April 14, 1918, Brown Journal, WisHistSoc. For the turtle, see statement of Albert J. Pyle in WWI Research Project, AMHI.

104. In Todd, *USS* Oklahoma, 19.

105. Halsey, *Admiral Halsey's Story*, 29; Rose, *Brittany Patrol*, 86–87; Whitaker, "Sims' Circus," 414; "With the Destroyers," *Our Navy* 12 (Feb. 1919): 33. For other accounts of porpoise problems, see Taussig, "Destroyer Experiences during the Great War," 61; M. S. Brown, "Life Overseas on the Yankee Sub-Chasers," 7; Moore Oral History, Columbia University.

106. Freidel, *Roosevelt: The Apprenticeship*, 346.

107. Entry for March 22, 1918, Halsey Journal, LC; Cochran MS, Coast Guard Library; Connolly, *Navy Men*, 221.

108. Battey, *70,000 Miles on a Submarine Destroyer*, 323. For other accounts of mistaken attacks, see entry Oct. 30, 1917, Marek Diary, Virginia War History Commission Records, Virginia State Library; entry for June 29, 1917, Merrill Diary, UNC-CH; Wiggins, *My Romance with the Navy*, 95; Bellitteri, "The Cruise of the U.S.S. *Chester* in European Waters," Bellitteri Papers, ECU; journal entry for Jan. 25, 1918, ibid.; Rose, *Brittany Patrol*, 168, G. U. Stewart file, Coast Guard Library; Cooke, "Recollections of a Life in the Navy," NDL; Murdock, *They Also Served*, 9–11; entry for June 14, 1918, Taussig Diary, NWC. See also his articles in U.S. Naval Institute *Proceedings*, particularly March 1923, 411–13.

109. Entry for June 1, 1917, in "A Destroyer on Active Service," 544, 545; Zogbaum, *From Sail to Saratoga*, 278, 280; Sims, *The Victory at Sea*, 143.

110. Cochran MS, Coast Guard Library.

111. Halsey Memoir, LC.

112. Both were on the *Nokomis*. See Lawrence to Kate, Dec. 2, 1918, Lawrence Papers, WisHistSoc; Miller, "A Yachtsman's Tale," 29. See also Blackford, *Torpedoboat Sailor*, 96; and Wheeler Oral History, USNI.

113. Freeman, *Sea-Hounds*, 139.

114. N.d., Jenkins Diary, NWC.

115. W. J. Wheeler, "Reminiscences of World War I Convoy Work," 388.

116. Hanks, "The Sinking of the *Alcedo*," 1762–63; Rose, *Brittany Patrol*, 111–21.

117. Sims, *The Victory at Sea*, 128.

118. Diary entries for Dec. 1917, in Merrill Papers, UNC-CH. See also F. A. Collins, *Naval Heroes of To-Day*, 22–26; *Literary Digest*, June 2, 1923, 47; and Bagley, "Torpedoed in the Celtic Sea." Admiral Bagley, the son of the *Jacob Jones* captain, wrote erroneously that the destroyer was the first U.S. warship sunk in World War I. A German newspaper account dated December 12, 1917, gives an excellent and accurate description of the *Jacob Jones* and the *Tucker* class. See OS subj file, RG45.

119. Connolly, *Navy Men*, 199–207; entry for Oct. 1917, Merrill Diary, UNC-CH.

120. See *Tampa* file in Office of the Historian, Coast Guard Headquarters; *Tampa* file, OA; *Tampa* file, OS subj file, RG45; Hunt Papers, Coast Guard Library; Charles Satterlee file, ibid.; Niblack to Satterlee, Sept. 5, 1918, CF subj file, RG45; Sims to Dept., Oct. 10, 1918, Reel 10, ME-

11; ADM Memo, Oct. 10, 1918, ADM137/1622; R. E. Johnson, *Guardians of the Sea*, 55. There is conflicting information on which U-boat torpedoed the *Tampa*. Early accounts based on British intelligence records indicate that it was *U-53*, but the War Diary of *UB-91* suggests that she was responsible for the sinking. See extract from *UB-91*'s War Diary in the Hunt Papers, Coast Guard Library. See also historical accounts of *Tampa* and Captain Charles Satterlee in Office of the Historian, U.S. Coast Guard Headquarters.

121. For a fairly typical description by a bluejacket of a sinking and its aftermath, see entry for July 20, 1917, Lauer Journal, USS *Burrows* files, CZ files, OA. See also Sims, *The Victory at Sea*, 143–47, and "Lawrence North McNair," in Furlong, *Class of 1905*, 324–25.

122. *ONI Monthly Bulletin* (May 15, 1919): 17.

123. Entries for June 21, and Sept. 16, 1917, Merrill Journal, UNC-CH; entries for June 21, and Sept. 16, 1917, ibid.; Wiggins, *My Romance with the Navy*, entry for Oct. 7, 1917, 196.

124. Grant found no evidence of a U-boat destroyed in French waters in November 1917 (see 186). See also *ONI Monthly Bulletin* (May 15, 1919): 18; *Naval Investigation*, 244; Stirling, "American Armed Yachts in the War Zone," 277–78; H. B. Wilson, *The American Navy in France*, 151.

125. Rose, *Brittany Patrol*, 246–47; Grant, *U-Boats Destroyed*, 120.

126. H. B. Wilson, *The American Navy in France*, 152; Sims to Wilson, May 18, 1918, Reel 19, ME-11; Address by Admiral Henry B. Wilson, *Transactions of the Society of Naval Architects and Marine Engineers* 27 (1919): 311–12.

127. Halpern, *A Naval History of World War I*, 400.

128. For the *Paducah*, see Morse, "When ASW was Young," 74; and J. J. Wheeler memoir on USS *Paducah*, J. J. Wheeler Papers, Coast Guard Library; for a copy of *Paducah*'s CO's report, dated Sept. 14, 1918, see J. J. Wheeler Papers. See also *Naval Investigation*, 2464; Sims, *The Victory at Sea*, 162–63. For confirmation of the two submarines destroyed, see Grant, *U-Boat Intelligence*, 188.

129. Rose, *Brittany Patrol*, 94. See also *ONI Monthly Bulletin* (May 15, 1919): 17. See also *Home Waters*, pt. 9, *Naval Staff Monograph* 19: 90–102, 155–256, for the Admiralty's brief analysis of each successful attack.

130. *American Legion Magazine*, Aug. 1940, 33; Coffman, *The War to End All Wars*, 112.

131. Cooke, "Recollections of Life in the Navy," NDL; Grant, *U-Boat Intelligence*, 170–71; entry for Feb. 2, 1918, Staples Diary, LSU.

132. "Hiram Leech Irwin," in Furlong, *Class of 1905*, 253; Grant, *U-Boat Intelligence*, 171; *ONI Monthly Bulletin* (May 15, 1919): 18; entry for May 16, Staples Diary, LSU.

133. Memoir of Henry M. Kieffer in USS *Parker* file, CZ file, OA; entry for Aug. 6, 1917, in Taussig, *The Queenstown Patrol*, 92.

134. For the *Lydonia*, see chapter 19.

135. See Carney, "The Capture of the *U-58*," U.S. Naval Institute *Proceedings* 61 (Jan. 1935): 99.

136. Quoted in Coffman, *The War to End All Wars*, 113.

137. There are a number of diaries and personal accounts of the *Fanning*'s crew, as well as nearby destroyers. See, for example, Wiggins, *My Romance with the Navy*, 110–11; entry for Nov. 17, 1917, Merrill Diary, UNC-CH; entries for Nov. 17–18, 1917, Arthur Carpender Diary, NHF; entries for Nov. 17–18, 1917, James Dolan Diary, NWC; Carney, "The Capture of the *U-58*," U.S. Naval Institute *Proceedings* 60 (Oct. 1934): 1401–4. See also Fort, "The Capture of the *U-58*," U.S. Naval Institute *Proceedings* 61 (Jan. 1935): 99–100; and War Log of USS *Fanning*, copy in Fanning file, Ships History Branch, NHC. The George Fort Collection in the Manuscript Collection at East Carolina University contains documents and correspondence concerning the incident. Sims's account in *The Victory at Sea* is fairly accurate (see 154–60). See also D. D. Lewis, *The Fight for the Sea*, 43–50; and Gibson and Prendergast, *The German Submarine War*, 227.

138. See, for example, entry for May 9, 1918, Wiggins, *My Romance with the Navy*, 126.

139. W. J. Wheeler, "Reminiscences of World War Convoy Work," 389. See also F. W. Brown, *Overseas, 1917–1918*, 6, privately printed. Copy in Coast Guard Library.

140. Sims to Senafloat, Gibraltar, Oct. 20, 1917, Reel 1, ME-11. To Admiralty, July 11, 1918, copy in ZP subj file, RG45.

141. Stirling, "American Armed Yachts in the War Zone," 278–80; H. B. Wilson, *The American Navy in France*, 151–52; Wilson to Sims, April 24, 1918, Reel 19, ME-11.

142. R. E. Johnson, *Guardians of the Sea*, 50–53; Niblack to Sims, July 8, 1918, CG subj file RG45; CO *Seneca* report, Sept. 16, 1918, OS subj file, ibid., extract from letter of Lt. Cdr. Van Deever, CO *Warrington*, Oct. 1, 1918, ibid.; documents concerning the *Seneca*'s rescue actions in the Fletcher Brown Papers, Coast Guard Library; Hurd and Bashford, *Sons of Admiralty*, 258–60; Ingraham, *First Fleet*, 61–70; unpublished Coast Guard History, copy in Coast Guard Historian's Office; *Seneca*'s History in ibid.; *Operations of the Coast Guard in Times of War*, 508. See also *Chicago Tribune*, Sept. 22, 1918.

143. Entry for Oct. 20, 1917, Merrill Journal, UNC-CH; Sims to Chief of Staff, Destroyer Flotilla, Nov. 9, 1917, Reel 18, ME-11. See also Blackford, *Torpedoboat Sailor*, 99–100; Kieffer, "The Orama Affair," 20–21; Connolly, *Navy Men*, 192–95; Connolly, *Sea-Borne*, 202–3.

144. Taussig, "Destroyer Experiences during the Great War," 383; Davy, Report on Personnel, July 27, 1918, NA subj file, RG45.

145. See chapter 7.

146. See, for example, Wilson to CO Tucker, Aug. 20, 1918, and CO Tucker to Wilson, Sept. 12, 1918, in Reel 9, ME-11. See Wilson letter and proceedings of Court of Inquiry, March 31, 1918, OS subj file, RG45; entry for June 21, 1917, Merrill Diary, UNC-CH.

147. Munro, Donald J. *Convoys, Blockades and Mystery Towers*, 133.

148. Berrien to Sims, May 28, 1919, Box 49, Sims Papers, LC.

149. Quoted in Connolly, *Navy Men*, 220.

150. Copy of address in Taussig Papers, LC.

151. Pringle to Sims, Oct. 25, 1917, Box 79, Sims Papers, LC.

152. Sims to Dept., Oct. 5, 1917, Reel 2, ME-11; Gleaves, "Orders for Ships in Convoy," Oct. 10, 1917, ibid.

153. Entry for June 28, 1918, Diary, NWC.

154. Entry for April 14, 1918, Slayback Memoirs, NDL; Sims to Dept., Oct. 8, 1917, Reel 2, ME-11; Taussig, "Destroyer Experiences during the Great War," 409.

155. Copy in Reel 1, ME-11.

156. Memorandum No. 20, April 3, 1918, in Navy Dept., *The American Naval Planning Section in London*, 194–95.

157. Admiralty Memo, May 21, 1918, ADM137/2753; Twining to Niblack, June 21, 1918, OD subj file, RG45; Sims to DD flotillas, U.S. Naval Forces in France, U.S. Patrol Squadrons based on Gibraltar, U.S. bases, Plymouth, and Corfu, July 15, 1918, Reel 4, ME-11; Sims to All Forces, July 17, 1918, Reel 20, ibid.

158. Wiggins, *My Romance with the Navy*, 129.

159. Memorandum No. 41, July 13, 1918, in Navy Dept., *The American Naval Planning Section in London*, 275. See also Zogbaum, *From Sail to Saratoga*, 277; F. W. Brown, *Overseas, 1917–1918*, 3; entry for Sept. 5, 1918, Journal, Bellitteri Papers, ECU; Louis Poisson Davis Sr. Oral History, ECU. For the quote from a former destroyer officer, see Friend, "The Rise and Fall of the *U-103*," 5, 62.

160. Furer, "The 110-Foot Submarine Chasers and Eagle Boats," 757; Sims to Pringle, Dec. 30, 1917, Reel 2, ME-11; Niblack to Senior Officer, Gibraltar, March 7, 1918, ZP subj file, RG45; Dept. to Sims, May 6, 1918, OK subj file, ibid.; Sims to Pringle, February 27, 1918, Reel 19, ME-11; Furlong, *Class of 1905*, 166; *Naval Ordnance Activities, War World I*, 1917–1918, 100; memo, depth charge tactics, Jan., 1918, Reel 4, ME-11; Sims to SecNav, Jan. 1, 1918, Box 5, Entry 113,

RG19; R. Gardiner, *The Eclipse of the Big Gun*, 115; Sims, *The Victory at Sea*, 95; Wheeler Oral History, USNI; Doughty, "The Effect of Depth Charges on Submarines," 353; Sims to All Forces, Jan. 7, Feb. 21, 1918, Reel 3, ME-11; Sims to Pringle, Jan. 4, 1918, ibid.; Bureau of Ordnance to Sims, March 4, 1918, ibid.; Sims to All Forces, April 18, 1918, LA subj file, RG45; Twining to DD Flotilla, June 5, 1918, ibid.; Pringle to Sims, April 19, 1918, Reel 19, ibid.; Sims to Pringle, April 3, 1918, ibid.; Pringle to Simsadus, May 10, 1918, Reel 20, ME-11; Pringle to Simsadus, May 13, 1918, ibid.; Sims to OpNav, May 24, 1918, Reel 4, ibid.; Sims to DD Flotillas, June 19, 1918, ibid.; Chief of Staff, DD Flotillas, to DD Flotillas, June 5, 1918, ibid.; Sims to CO submarine chasers, June 18, 1918, ibid.; Sims to OpNav, June 21, Aug. 24, 1918, ibid.; Sims to Bureau of Ordnance, July 8, 1918, ibid.; CNO to All Fleet Commanders, Sept. 5, 1918, Reel 5, ibid.; Sims to OpNav, Sept. 27, 1918, Reel 6, ibid.; Circular letter from Sims, Oct. 7, 1918, LA subj file, RG45; Wilson (Brest) to Sims, Oct. 11, 1918, ibid.; Pringle to Simsadus, Oct. 9, 1918, ibid.; SO Gibraltar to Simsadus, Oct. 10, 1918, ibid.; Sims to Dept., Oct. 24, 1918, Reel 6, ME-11. Terraine, *The U-Boat Wars*, 27. Germans interviewed after war were not impressed with them. See *ONI Monthly Bulletin* (April 15, 1919): 87–89. See also Munro to Admiralty, March 14, 1918, ADM137/1534, for a different opinion. Sims even recommended fitting depth charges; to Dept. July 11, 1918, LA subj file. Unfortunately, the executive officer of *Orizaba* tried to fire a depth charge using the vessel's saluting gun, killing him and several men. CO *Orizaba* to Gleaves, Aug. 17, 1918, Reel 10, ME-11.

161. Taussig, "Destroyer Experiences during the Great War," 406–7. See also Howe to Wilson, Oct. 28, 1918, LA subj file, RG45.

162. McNair to Sims, Aug. 6, 1919, Box 72, Sims Papers, LC; Sims to DD Flotilla, Queenstown, LA subj file, RG45.

163. Summary of U.S. Naval Activities in European Waters, Aug. 5, 1918, TL subj file, RG45; *ONI Monthly Bulletin* (May 15, 1919): 15–16; *Naval Investigation*, 2591; "British and American Naval Efforts," Sept. 22, 1918, ADM137/2710; Summary of U.S. Naval Activities in European Waters, Z File, OA; Winton, *Convoy*, 70. These figures do not include American ocean escorts, that is, those originating from North America. If these figures were included, statistics would show significant change. For example, American warships escorted sixty-one out of ninety-one of the New York H.M. convoys. See ADM137/2658.

164. Bayly, *Pull Together*, 242. See also Bowling, "Convoy in World War I," master's thesis.

Chapter 16. Comrades of the Mist: The North Sea

1. *Comrades of the Mist* is a term coined by American sailors in the Grand Fleet. Marder, *From the Dreadnought to Scapa Flow*, 4: 167; Beatty to Admiralty, Jan. 9, 1918, ADM116/1349; Roskill, *Admiral of the Fleet Earl Beatty*, 226–27; P. M. Kennedy, *The Rise and Fall of British Naval Mastery*, 250; Trask, *Captains and Cabinets*, 190–91. See also General Board Hearings for Oct. 16, 1917, for a synopsis of British naval plans. For Jellicoe's advocacy of the amphibious operation, see Wiest, *Passchendaele and the Royal Navy*. See also Marder, *From the Dreadnought to Scapa Flow*, 4: 167, 224; M. Simpson, *Anglo-American Naval Relations*, 203; *Daily Telegraph*, Nov. 2, 1917; "Inactivity of the British Navy," *Literary Digest*, Dec. 8, 1917; Roskill, *Admiral of the Fleet Earl Beatty*, 227; Marder, *Portrait of an Admiral*, 124.

2. *Naval Investigation*, 186; Trask, *Captains and Cabinets*, 64–65; Browning to Jellicoe, in Patterson, *The Jellicoe Papers*, 2: 181; Allard, "Anglo-American Naval Differences during World War I," 78.

3. Copy of Woodrow Wilson's speech in Josephus Daniels, *The Wilson Era: Yeas of War*, 43–45. For Wilson's views, see also Trask, *Captains and Cabinets*, 73, 131–33. For Sims's letter to Wilson, July 7, 1917, see CP subj file, RG45. See also C. Seymour, *The Intimate Papers of Colonel House* 3: 176–77; Jonathan Daniels, *The End of Innocence*, 244; Parsons, *Wilsonian Diplomacy*, 73–75; Allard, "Anglo-American Naval Differences during World War I," 78; Klachko, *Benson*, 81–82; entry for Aug. 16, 1917, in Josephus Daniels, *Cabinet Diaries*, 191.

4. Parsons, *Wilsonian Diplomacy*, 72–73; Jonathan Daniels, *End of Innocence*, 244–45; Trask, *Captains and Cabinets*, 132–33.

5. Jellicoe to Browning, July 7, 1917, in Patterson, *Jellicoe Papers*, 2: 181; Jellicoe to Beatty, July 31, 1917, ibid., 191; entry for Aug. 16, 1917, in Josephus Daniels, *Cabinet Diaries*, 191.

6. ZZ Operational Plan dated Aug. 7, 1917, in ADD 49008, Jellicoe Papers, British Museum. See also Marder, *From the Dreadnought to Scapa Flow*, 4: 232–35; Schoultz, *With the British Battle Fleet*, 285.

7. For the conference, see Trask, *Captains and Cabinets*, 150–53; Marder, *From the Dreadnought to Scapa Flow*, 4: 235–36. For Mayo's report and correspondence concerning the conference, see OC subj file, RG45. See also *Naval Investigation*, 2794; Schoultz, *With the British Battle Fleet*, 284–85; Allard, "Anglo-American Naval Differences during World War I," 78; testimony of Commander Pye, Oct. 16, 1917, General Board Hearings; Mayo to CNO, Sept. 6, 1917, Reel 3, ME-11.

8. Trask, *Captains and Cabinets*, 153–54; Allard, "Anglo-American Naval Differences during World War I," 78; entries for Oct. 13, 14, 1917, in Josephus Daniels, *Cabinet Diaries*, 220–21.

9. Allard, "Anglo-American Naval Differences during World War I," 79; Benson Testimony, *Naval Investigation*, 1852–53; C. Seymour, *American Diplomacy during the World War*, 242; Benson, "Report of the Activities of Admiral Benson While Serving as a Member of the American Mission Headed by Colonel House," Box 42, Benson Papers, LC; Trask, *Captains and Cabinets*, 179; General Board Hearings, April 25, 1918; Kenworthy, *The Real Navy*, 240; Conolly Oral History, Columbia University; Klachko, *Benson*, 93–94; C. Seymour, *Intimate Papers of Colonel House*, 3: 269. See also newspaper clipping from the *Sun* (date not legible) in Box 118, Sims Papers, LC. Beatty opposed an attack by surface vessels on the German submarine bases. He recommended that such an attack be carried out by aircraft. Beatty to Admiralty, Jan. 9, 1918, ADM116/1349. See also Klachko, *Benson*, 94; Patterson, *Jellicoe Papers*, 2: 201; Marder, *From the Dreadnought to Scapa Flow*, 4: 237. As late as June 1918, President Wilson and Pershing along with the Navy Department were still pushing for more aggressive naval action. See Smythe, *Pershing: General of the Armies*, 40. Sims never favored offensive operations against the submarine bases. He was totally committed to concentrating on convoying and ASW operations and in fact considered the convoy system an offensive measure. See Trask, *Captains and Cabinets*, 132–33; Dawson, *The War Memoirs of William Graves Sharp*, 176–77; Corbett and Newbolt, *History of the Great War*, 5: 132.

10. J. W. Jones, *U.S. Battleship Operations in World War I* is an excellent study of this squadron. However, I consulted Jones's Ph.D. dissertation on the same topic ("U.S. Battleship Operations in World War I, 1917–1918," North Texas State University, 1995). Historians disagree over whether *Delaware* (1906), *South Carolina* (1908) or *Michigan* (1908) was the first American dreadnought. See, for example, Sprout and Sprout, *The Rise of American Naval Power*, 263; Potter and Nimitz, *Sea Power: A Naval History*, 389; Hagan, *This People's Navy*, 240; Simons, "Both by Land and by Sea," 24, MS, NDL. See also P. M. Kennedy, *The Rise and Fall of British Naval Mastery*, 250; Trask, *Captains and Cabinets*, 190–91; General Board Hearings, Oct. 16, 1917, for a synopsis of British naval plans.

11. See Trask, *Captains and Cabinets*, 92–93, 131–32.

12. Ibid. See also 47–48, 301. For the fear of Japan, see Braisted, *The United States Navy in the Pacific*, especially chapters 3 and 8. See also 303–5. Pratt testimony, General Board Hearings, Oct. 19, 1917; Hagan, *This People's Navy*, 255; M. Simpson, *Anglo-American Naval Relations*, 303–5.

13. See Trask's introduction to Sims, *The Victory at Sea*, xvii; Braisted, *The United States Navy in the Pacific*, 301–2; Morison, *Sims*, passim; Klachko, *Benson*, 65–66; Sims testimony, *Naval Investigation*, 72–73; Sims to SecNav, April 14, 19, 1917, in Sims, *The Victory at Sea*, 374–84. Leighton in *Simsadus* wrote that in July Sims requested four dreadnoughts to be stationed on

the western coast of England or Ireland as protection against German commerce raiders. The author mistook the time; he probably meant 1918.

14. Memo, Oct. 26, 1917, Box 2, Assistant Secretary of Navy file, FDR Library; Sims to Dept., June 15, 1917, Reel 1, ME-11; Sims testimony, *Naval Investigation*, 74–75. See also *Naval Investigation*, 58, 644–45, 1904; Sims to OpNav, July 21, 1917, in M. Simpson, *Anglo-American Naval Relations*, 330, copy in TT subj file, RG45. Sims to Pratt, Aug. 18, 1917, Reel 2, ME-11; Benson to Sims, Aug. 19, 1917, ibid.; entry for Aug. 18, 1917, in Josephus Daniels, *Cabinet Diaries*, 192; Trask, *Captains and Cabinets*, 136, 151–53; Braisted, *The United States Navy in the Pacific*, 302–3. For Sims's response, see Sims to Benson, Sept. 1, 1917, in M. Simpson, *Anglo-American Naval Relations*, 331–32; Sims to Pratt, Sept. 27, 1917, Box 78, Sims Papers, LC.

15. Testimony of Pye, Schofield, and Pratt, Oct. 19, 1917, General Board Hearings. See also Braisted, *The United States Navy in the Pacific*, 304–5.

16. Hagan, *This People's Navy*, 257; M. Simpson, *Anglo-American Naval Relations*, 326; Jellicoe to Beatty, Nov. 9, 1917, in Patterson, *The Jellicoe Papers*, 2: 225; C. Seymour, *Intimate Papers of Colonel House*, 299; entry for Nov. 10, 1917, in Josephus Daniels, *Cabinet Diaries*, 235; G. E. Wheeler, *Pratt*, 103. See also Trask, *Captains and Cabinets*, 114–15. Benson, in a memo justifying the decision, used language quite similar to that used by Pye, Schofield, and Pratt in their testimonies before the General Board. See memo, Nov. 1917, in M. Simpson, *Anglo-American Naval Relations*, 333–34. See also memo of cooperation between the British and American battle fleets, Nov. 28, 1917, ADM137/2706; memo for Director of Plans, Nov. 19, 1917, in M. Simpson, *Anglo-American Naval Relations*, 335; Jellicoe to Beatty, Nov. 30, 1917, Beatty Papers, NMM; Marder, *Portrait of an Admiral*, 256; *Naval Investigation*, 600; Rodman to Sims, Dec. 24, 1917, Confidential Files, 1917–1919, RG80; Sims to Dept., Box 10, Entry 113, RG19.

17. Memo of Director of Plans, Nov. 19, 1917, in M. Simpson, *Anglo-American Naval Relations*, 335–37; Richmond to Dewar, Nov. 22, 1917, Dewar MS, NMM; *Naval Investigation*, 645; Mayo to CNO, Sept. 6, 1917, Reel 3, ME-11.

18. Sims to OpNav, December 20, 1917, Reel 8, ME-11; Sims to Benson, Jan. 8, 1918, Reel 3, ibid.; Sims to Rodman, Dec. 20, 1917, Box 81, Sims Papers, LC; Benson to Sims, Jan. 5, 1918, LA subj file, RG45; Sims to Benson, December 20, 1917, in M. Simpson, *Anglo-American Naval Relations*, 339–40; Rodman to Sims, Dec. 20, 1917, Box 49, Sims Papers, LC.

19. Rodman to SecNav, Feb. 28, 1918, copy in ADM137/1898; Aylmer to Capt. of the Fleet, March 2, 1918, ibid.; Sims to Dept., March 10, 1918, Reel 8, ME-11; Sims to OpNav, March 30, 1918, Reel 4, ibid.; communication between C-in-C, Grand Fleet, and Admiralty, March 1918, ADM137/1964; Admiralty to C-in-C, and reply, July 7, 1918, ADM137/1973; entry for July 20, 1918, Diary of Joseph Pressprick, copy in author's possession.

20. Sims to Rodman, Aug. 2, 1918, Box 24, Sims Papers, LC; Fremantle comment, June 12, 1918, ADM137/2709; memo No. 30, May 24, 1918, in Navy Dept., *The American Naval Planning Section in London*, 501; memo No. 47, Sept. 3, 1918, ibid., 329; Benson to Sims, Oct. 2, 1918, Reel 6, ME-11; Sims to Dept., Jan 8, 1918, Reel 3, ibid.; Rodman to Sims, Dec. 20, 1917, Box 49, Sims Papers, LC. Rodman also opposed rotating entire division.

21. *Naval Investigation*, 171–73, 230–31; Mayo, "The Atlantic Fleet in the War," copy in Reel 5, Daniels Papers, LC. See also Sims to Dept., July 31, 1918, Reel 4, ME-11; Sims to Pringle, July 31, 1918, Reel 19, ibid.; Sims to Benson, Oct. 27, Nov. 3, 1918, Reel 6, ibid.; Sims to Rodgers, Nov. 4, 1918, Reel 10, ibid.; M. Simpson, *Anglo-American Naval Relations*, 348–49; memo, Admiralty, July 27, 1918, ADM137/1898; memo, Admiralty, Oct. 15, 1918, ADM137/1622; Sims to Benson, Nov. 14, 1918, OS, *Arizona*, subj file, RG45.

22. Josephus Daniels, *The Wilson Era: Years of War*, 117–18. See entries for Nov. 11, 14, 1917, in Josephus Daniels, *Cabinet Diaries*, 235–37; Pratt, "Autobiography," OA; G. E. Wheeler, *Pratt*, 204. Pratt attended the meeting. See McCrea Oral History, USNI. Several publications have hinted that FDR was instrumental in Rodman's appointment, but this is doubtful. See N. Miller,

FDR, 142; Morrison, *Josephus Daniels*, 85; Richardson, *On the Treadmill to Pearl Harbor*, 439; Stiles, *The Man Behind Roosevelt*, 50; G. C. Ward, *A First-Class Temperament*, 493.

23. Rodman's autobiography is entitled *Yarns of a Kentucky Admiral*. For his career, see C. G. Reynolds, *Famous American Admirals*, 287–88; Stone, *Kentucky Fighting Men*, 219–31. See also Richardson, *On the Treadmill to Pearl Harbor*, 465; F. T. Hunter, "American Admirals at War," 35–37; McCrea Oral History, USNI; John McCrea to author, Sept. 1, 1986, copy in author's possession; Pratt, "Autobiography," OA; entry for Dec. 31, 1917, in Josephus Daniels, *Cabinet Diaries*, 258.

24. McCrea Oral History, USNI; F. T. Hunter, *Beatty, Jellicoe, Sims, and Rodman*, 43–44; Symington, "The Navy Way," NDL; Bernard H. Bieri Oral History, USNI; *U.S.S. Wyoming: At War in the North Sea*; Wiley, *An Admiral from Texas*, 194, 198; Stone, *Kentucky Fighting Men*, 30; E. E. Wilson, "Grand Fleet Morale," 6–7; Eugene E. Wilson Oral History, Columbia University; Pratt, "Autobiography," OA.

25. *Literary Digest*, Jan. 18, 1919; Ross letter to author, n.d.; Vlahos, *The Blue Sword*, 109–10; Symington, "The Navy Way"; Pratt, "Autobiography," OA

26. Josephus Daniels, *The Wilson Era: Years of War*, 119–20; Josephus Daniels, *The Wilson Era: Years of Peace*, 310; entry for July 1, 1919, Leahy Diary, William D. Leahy Papers, LC; McCrea Oral History, USNI; Chalmers, *The Life and Letters of David Beatty*, 300, hereafter cited as *David Beatty*; Rodman, *Yarns of a Kentucky Admiral*, 278; Blythe, "Ready!," 15; *Times* (London), March 23, 1919; Harry W. Hill Oral History, Columbia University; Wilson, *Hush of the Hydrophone Service*, 148. See also entry for May 31, 1918, Stuart Smith Diary, LC.

27. McCrea to author, Sept. 1, 1986, copy in author's possession. Rodman, *Yarns of a Kentucky Admiral*, 275; F. T. Hunter, *Beatty, Jellicoe, Sims, and Rodman*, 44; *New York Sun*, Dec. 27, 1918; Jameson, *The Fleet That Jack Built*, 238; Tweedie, *The Story of a Naval Life*, 184; Chatfield, *The Navy and Defense*, 164.

28. Knox to Dept., May 24, 1918, in M. Simpson, *Anglo-American Naval Relations*, 346–47; Chalmers, *David Beatty*, 299–300, 326; Sims to Benson, May 2, 1918, Box 49, Sims Papers, LC; Rodman, *Yarns of a Kentucky Admiral*, 266–67.

29. *Times* (London), Jan. 27, 1917; *Christian Science Monitor*, Jan. 13, 1919; George to Beatty, July 25, 1918, Beatty Papers, NMM; Wiley, *An Admiral from Texas*, 212; McCrea Oral History, USNI; *New York Herald*, European edition, Nov. 24, 1918; Dent, *The Life Story of King George V*, 280–81; Rodman, *Yarns of a Kentucky Admiral*, 273–74; A. E. Smith, "The Sixth Battle Squadron," 51. Rodman's knighthood was not approved by the U.S. government.

30. For Hughes, see Braisted, "Charles Frederick Hughes," 49–51; Pratt, "Autobiography," OA; McCrea Oral History, USNI; Stirling, *Sea Duty*, 200–201; Joseph M. Koch questionnaire, WWI Research Collection, AMHI; Symington, "The Navy Way," LC.

31. Interview with Captain Edward L. Beach, Oct. 19, 1889, copy in author's possession. See also Beach, *From Annapolis to Scapa Flow: The Autobiography of Edward L. Beach, Sr.*

32. Rodman to Benson, Dec. 19, 1917, Confidential Files, 1917–1919, RG80; A. E. Smith, "The Sixth Battle Squadron," 51; *Naval Investigation*, 612.

33. McClellan, "American Marines in the British Grand Fleet," 147–48; Simons, "Both by Land and by Sea," unpublished MS, NDL; L. Dawson, *Flotillas*.

34. McClellan, "American Marines in the Grand Fleet," 148. See also entry for Dec. 8, 1918, Witherspoon Journal, Witherspoon Family Papers, AMHI. A seaman on one of the British battleships later wrote, "We in the British Fleet taught them the art of fast coaling." Memoir of Victor Hayward, IWM. See also Bartimeus, "Admiral Sims and His Fleet," 577; R. F. Nichols Memoirs, Peter Liddell Archives; and Brown and Meehan, *Scapa Flow*, 123; entry for Dec. 1917, J. E. Attrill Diary, IWM; Liddle, *The Sailor's War*, 202; Orders for the C-in-C, Dec. 6, 1917, copy in the Boswell Papers, Peter Liddle Archives; entries for Dec. 6, 7, 1917, F. Bowman Diary, Peter Liddle Archives; Taylor, *Radio Reminiscences*, 64.

35. R. Miller, *Orkney*, 137; Bridges, *Scapa Ferry*, 14–17; Hewison, *This Great Harbour Scapa Flow*, 4–7; Muir, *Years of Endurance*, 133; Munro, *Scapa Flow*, 140, passim; Bayly, *Pull Together*, 128; Schoultz, *With the British Battle Fleet*, 29–31; Murmane, *Ground Swells*, 145–46; King-Hall, *Naval Memories and Traditions*, 273–74; McCrea Oral History, USNI; Brown and Meehan, *Scapa Flow*, 19. Rodman, in a detailed description of Scapa Flow, compared it very favorably to other anchorages used by the U.S. Navy including Guantanamo, Cuba. To CNO, April 13, 1918, PF subj file, RG45. See also Rodman, *Yarns of a Kentucky Admiral*, 282–83.

36. Quoted in Shepherd, "Death of a Fleet," Ph.D. diss., 83. Beatty quote cited in R. Miller, *Orkney*, 136. See also Cousins, *The Story of Scapa Flow*, 85.

37. Nicholson to author, Aug. 26, 1987, copy in author's possession; McCrea Oral History, USNI; *U.S.S. Wyoming: At War in the North Sea*. See also Symington, "The Navy Way," MS, LC; Wiley, *An Admiral from Texas*, 189–90.

38. H. H. Smith, *A Yellow Admiral Remembers*, 306–7; Muir, *Years of Endurance*, 200–201; Dawson, *Flotillas*, 166; Jose, *The Royal Australian Navy*, 303; *American Legion Magazine*, June 13, 1924; Rose letter to author; Simons, "Both by Land and by Sea," NDL; Koch questionnaire, WWI Research Collection, AMHI; entry for Dec. 10, 1917, Witherspoon Diary, Witherspoon Family Papers, AMHI; *U.S.S. Wyoming: At War in the North Sea*; entries for Dec. 17, 1917, and Sept. 28, 1918, McCrea Diary, WWI Research Project, AMHI; *Arklight*, Oct. 25, 1919, microfilm copy in Eugene Wilson Papers, NDL; *Dallas Times Herald*, Nov. 11, 1989; Rodman, *Yarns of a Kentucky Admiral*, 273–74; Rodman report dated Jan. 24, 1918, Reel 10, M1092; Schoultz, *With the British Battle Fleet*, 332–33; A. E. Smith, "The Sixth Battle Squadron," 53; Rodman to Sims, Dec. 24, 1917, Confidential Files, 1917–1919, RG80.

39. Entry for April 17, 1918, in Simons, "Both by Land and By Sea," NDL; Rodman, *Yarns of a Kentucky Admiral*, 273.

40. P. M. Kennedy, *The Rise and Fall of British Naval Mastery*, 246–50; Marder, *From the Dreadnought to Scapa Flow*, 5: 134–37. See also Admiralty memo, Jan. 9, 1918, ADM37/1459.

41. For the destroyer situation, see chapter 12. For the Grand Fleet, see also Memorandum No. 7, Jan. 1918, in Navy Dept., *The American Naval Planning Section in London*, 35–36; misc. documents, ADM137/1898; Marder, *From the Dreadnought to Scapa Flow*, 5: 131, 134–36; Rodman to CNO, Jan 9, 1918, Reel 3, ME-11. Beatty frequently complained about the need for destroyers including American. He even asked a visiting U.S. naval officer about obtaining some of the subchasers. Knox report to CNO, May 24, 1918, TX subj file, RG45. Rodman requested eight U.S. destroyers as late as November 5, 1918. To Sims, Reel 8, ME-11. No U.S. destroyers served with the Grand Fleet during the war.

42. USS *New York* War Diary, OB subj file, RG45; "The Grand Fleet," paper delivered at the Royal Naval Staff College, 1932, copy in John Creswell Papers, Churchill College.

43. Jellicoe to Beatty, Nov. 30, 1917, Beatty Papers, NMM; memo, Nov. 28, 1917, ADM137/2706; M. Simpson, *Anglo-American Naval Relations*, 327. Even George V wrote to Beatty expressing the importance of the American presence with the Grand Fleet. February 10, June 20, 1918, Beatty Papers. See also Fremantle memo, June 6, 1918, ADM137/2709; Beatty to wife, June 3, 1918, Beatty Papers; Wemyss to Beatty, Feb. 7, March 30, 1918, in Ranft, *Beatty Papers*, 1: 523; memo of conference with Deputy Chief of Naval Staff, February 25, 1918, ADM137/1646; R. F. Nichols memoirs, Peter Liddle Archives. At least one American officer agreed with Beatty: "When the U.S. battleships joined the Grand Fleet they were not a real addition of strength, but possibly even the reverse." Unsigned memo, May 6, 1918, TT subj file, RG45. See also Rodman to Mayo, June 15, 1918, Mayo Papers, LC. *Delaware* was nicknamed the "lone wolf" as she often became separated from the rest of the squadron and fleet. *The Big "D" Log* 11 (April 4, 1920): 9–10.

44. P. Kennedy, "Britain in the First World War," 62–63; Schoultz, *With the British Battle Fleet*, 325; Sims to Benson, April 2, 1918, in M. Simpson, *Anglo-American Naval Relations*, 159; Marder, *From the Dreadnought to Scapa Flow*, 5: 129; Vincent, *A Stoker's Log*, 215–36; Memoir of V. Hayward, IWM; Freeman, *Stories of the Ships*, F. T. Hunter, *Beatty, Jellicoe, Sims, and Rodman*, 14; Gaunt to Benson, Jan. 2, 1918, Box 6, Benson Papers, LC; Beston, *Full Speed Ahead*, 154; Madden to Jellicoe, Dec. 10, 1917; in Patterson, *The Jellicoe Papers*, 2: 239; Sims to Dept., Jan. 2, 1918. Reel 3, ME-11; Eugene Wilson Oral History, Columbia University; E. E. Wilson, "Grand Fleet Morale," 6–9; Bartimeus, *The Navy Eternal*, 237–38, 255–56; Cdr. Rowcliff to Coffman, May 18, 1918, in USS *Arkansas* file, Ships History Branch, NHC.

45. Sims to Benson, Feb. 25, 1918, Box 49, Sims Papers, LC; Rodman, *Yarns of a Kentucky Admiral*, 266; McCrea Oral History, USNI.

46. Pridham Memoir, Churchill College, Cambridge. See also entry for Dec. 7, 1917, Attrill Diary, IWM; M. Simpson, *Anglo-American Naval Relations*, 327; Rodman to Sims, May 23, 1918, ibid., 345; Wiley, *An Admiral from Texas*, 209–10; Marder, *From the Dreadnought to Scapa Flow*, 5: 125; Laurens, *Le commandement naval en Mediterranee*, 312; *Scotsman*, Dec. 2, 1918; Rodman to CNO, Feb. 28, 1918, in ADM137/1848. Parsons, *Wilsonian Diplomacy*, 118.

47. CDR Davy to Dept., June 27, 1918, Report on Personnel, N subj file, RG45; Mayo to wife, Sept. 26, 1918, Mayo Papers, LC. See also Mayo to CNO, Sept. 28, 1918, ibid.

48. McCrea Oral History, USNI; Mayo to wife, Sept. 26, 1918, Mayo Papers, LC; *New York Herald*, Dec. 27, 1919; Donald W. Mitchell, *History of the Modern American Navy*, 241; Capt. A. W. Clarke Memoir, Churchill College, Cambridge.

49. Rodman to C-in-C, Dec. 19, 1917, Confidential File 1917–1919, RG80; Murmane, *Ground Swells*, 149; Rodman to SecNav, Feb. 9, 1918, Reel 8, ME-11; Knox to CNO, June 14, 1918, copy in Pratt Papers, OA; Hill Oral History, Columbia University. For repairs, see chapters 5 and 7.

50. Hunter, *Beatty, Jellicoe, Sims, and Rodman*, 96, 113–14. See also Wiley, *An Admiral from Texas*, 190–91; *U.S.S. Wyoming: At War in the North Sea 1917–1918*; entry for Jan. 31, 1918, F. Bowman Diary, Peter Liddle Archives.

51. Beatty to wife, Jan 23, Feb. 20, 1918, Beatty Papers, NMM.

52. Copy of article for the *Outlook* in USS *Texas* Archives. "Walter Baldwin Crosby," in Furlong, *Class of 1905*, 82; *The Story of the USS* Texas, 28–31; Lewis Ross to author, n.d.; entry for Feb. 15, 1918, in Daniel Schenk Journal, Smithsonian; *Torch* 38 (June 1990): 11; *American Legion Monthly*, Sept. 1936, 16–17; Beatty to wife, Feb. 20, 1918, Beatty Papers, NMM.

53. Wiley, *An Admiral from Texas*, 198–99; Corbett and Newbolt, *History of the Great War*, 5: 220; F. T. Hunter, *Beatty, Jellicoe, Sims, and Rodman*, 99–101; Marder, *From the Dreadnought to Scapa Flow*, 5: 145–46; McCrea Oral History, USNI; entries for Joubert McCrea Diary, WWI Research Collection, AMHI. McCrea was an enlisted man from Georgia. For Rodman's order, see ADM137/1990. See also Beatty's memo, Jan. 26, 1918, in CP subj file, RG45; McClellan, "American Marines in the Grand Fleet," 150–52; Beatty to wife, Feb. 5, 1918, in Ranft, *The Beatty Papers*, 1: 508.

54. Pratt, "Autobiography"; OA; Klachko, *Benson*, 159; Parsons, *Wilsonian Diplomacy*, 113; David K. Brown, "Warfare and Escort Vessels," in R. Gardiner, *The Eclipse of the Big Gun*, 114.

55. Entry for March 13, 1918, in Josephus Daniels, *Cabinet Diaries*, 290; Benson to Sims, March 13, and Sims to Benson, March 17, 1918, Reel 3, ME-11.

56. Marder, *From the Dreadnought to Scapa Flow*, 5: 67–69; T. A. Thomson to Strauss, Oct. 22, 1918, AN subj file, RG45. For the North Sea Mine Barrage, see chapter 17.

57. In a letter to the author, a former junior officer on *Texas* claimed that Beatty did not want to risk his more modern oil-burning battleships in the shallow waters off Norway and Rodman volunteered his squadron for this work. Rose to author. I have found no supporting evidence for this.

58. Entry for July 2, 1918, A. Thesiger Diary, NMM; Rodman to CNO, July 6, 1918, Reel 8, ME-11; *The Story of the U.S.S.* Texas, 57–59; Wiley, *An Admiral from Texas*, 206–8; McClellan, "American Marines in the Grand Fleet," 155–58.

59. Halpern, *A Naval History of World War I*, 104.

60. For Rosyth, see Munro, *Scapa Flow*, 12–16; Beston, *Full Speed Ahead*, 150–52; Marder, *From the Dreadnought to Scapa Flow*, 5: 144–45.

61. Rodman, *Yarns of a Kentucky Admiral*, 281. See also Beston, *Full Speed Ahead*, 163–65, 167; Chapple, *We'll Stick to the Finish*, 206; entry for Oct. 18, 1918, H. A. Hill Diary, IWM; Herwig, *Politics of Frustration*, 142; Roskill, *Admiral of the Fleet Earl Beatty*, 258–59; Corbett and Newbolt, *History of the Great War*, 5: 130–237; Marder, *From the Dreadnought to Scapa Flow*, 5: 130, 144, 152–57.

62. McCrea Oral History, USNI; Marder, *From the Dreadnought to Scapa Flow*, 5: 168. Von Hipper quote in Herwig, *Politics of Frustration*, 147.

63. Tweedie, *The Story of a Naval Life*, 189; Herwig, *Politics of Frustration*, 148; Bywater and Ferraby, *Strange Intelligence*, 279–86; *The U.S.S.* Wyoming: *At War in the North Sea 1917–1918*; entry for Nov. 7, 1918, Pressprick Diary, copy in author's possession; Sims to Benson, Oct. 14, 1918, Reel 6, ME-11.

64. Murmane, *Ground Swells*, 176.

65. For a list of German submarines sunk in the war, probable date lost, and location, see Grant, *U-Boat Intelligence*, 182–90. See also "In the North Sea," 18; Murmane, *Ground Swells*, 175–77; Rodman, *Yarns of a Kentucky Admiral*, 271; *The Story of the U.S.S.* Texas, 16–17; Washington to Daniels, Feb. 10, 1918, Reel 64, Daniels Papers; Maxwell, *The Naval Front*, 179–81; Maguire, *Rig for Church*, 63–64; Alfred Stalbot to editor, *Veterans of Foreign Wars Magazine*, Dec. 1, 1977, copy in WWI Research Project, AMHI; *New York Herald*, European edition, Dec. 19, 1918; "Summary of Naval Forces Operating in European Waters," Z file, OA; entry for July 28, 1918, Pressprick Diary; CO USS *Florida* to Rodman, Feb. 10, 1918, Reel 8, ME-11; Rodman to CNO, Feb. 17, 1918, OB subj file, RG45; Rodman to Beatty, July 21, 1918, Reel 8, ME-11; Rowley, CO 16th Destroyer Squadron, to Tweedie, July 6, 1918, ibid.; McClellan, "American Marines in the British Grand Fleet," 157–58; Admiral reports of submarine attack, ADM137/1935; Wiley, *An Admiral from Texas*, 202–3; Hewison, *The Great Harbour Scapa Flow*, 122.

66. Rodman to Sims, Oct. 19, 1918, Reel 8, Me-11; Records of Court of Inquiry, File 187, RG125; *ONI Semi-Monthly Compilations*, ser. 64 (Dec. 15, 1918): 2522–24; McCrea Oral History, USNI; Alden and Westcott, *The United States Navy*, 360; *New York Herald*, Dec. 27, 1918; Grant, *U-Boat Intelligence*, 161.

67. McCrea Oral History.

68. Entry for July 27, 1918, Witherspoon Diary, Witherspoon Family Papers, AMHI. See also entry for July 23, 1918, Joubert McCrea Diary, WWI Research Collection, AMHI; A. E. Smith, "The Sixth Battle Squadron," 58–59; *American Legion Magazine*, July 1934, 36; Deck Log, 8, 9, 1918, USS *New York*, RG24; Sims Report, June 21, 1918, Reel 4, ME-11; Navy Dept., *The American Naval Planning Section in London*, 230–31, 329–30; McClellan, "American Marines in the Grand Fleet," 156; F. T. Hunter, "Kings, Princes, and American Sailors," 188–89.

69. Entry for July 27, 1918, Royal Archives, Windsor Castle. See also Rodman, *Yarns of a Kentucky Admiral*, 276–77; Boswell Papers, excerpted in Peter Liddle Archives; F. T. Hunter, *Beatty, Jellicoe, Sims, and Rodman*, 68–69, 139; F. T. Hunter, "Kings, Princes, and American Sailors," 193–94; entry for July 22, 1918, Witherspoon Diary, Witherspoon Family Papers, WWI Research Collection, AMHI; McClellan, "American Marines in the Grand Fleet," 157; *American Legion Magazine*, June 1936, 26–27; *Glasgow Herald*, July 24, 25, 1918; *Daily Mail* (London), July

24, 1918; *Linlithgowshire Gazette*, July 26, 1918, copy in Sims Papers, LC; *Scotsman*, July 25, 1918; *Naval and Military Record* (July 31, 1918); *New York Herald*, Jan. 4, 1919.

70. April 16, 1919.

Chapter 17. "The Pills of Perdition": The North Sea Mine Barrage

1. Duff to De Chair, May 13, 1917, Reel 1, ME-11; Daniels to Sims, May 10 1917, Area File, RG45; Daniels to Sims, April 17, May 11, 1917, in M. Simpson, *Anglo-American Naval Relations*, 371; Sims to Dept., May 11, 1917, ibid., 372–74; De Chair to Admiralty, May 10, 1917, ibid., 374; *Naval Investigation*, 188–89; Josephus Daniels, *The Wilson Era: Years of War*, 83–85; Daniels would later state that Sims and the Admiralty would hold up the barrage's approval for six months. *New York Evening Post*, May 11, 1920. See also Knox to Frothington, Jan. 11, 1926, Box 9, Knox Papers, LC; Navy Dept., *The American Naval Planning Section in London*, 493; Fremantle, *My Naval Career*, 248; Jellicoe, *The Crisis of The Naval War*, 166–67. Literature is extensive. The barrage was heavily covered in newspapers and other publications immediately after the war. U.S. Navy veterans of the barrage established an association that continued to exist until the 1970s. The association published two newsletters: *TNT*, followed by *Mine Barrage*. Several key figures associated with the barrage left important collections of papers. They include Rear Admiral Strauss, Rear Admiral Reginald Belknap, and Samuel P. Fullinwider. Published memoirs include Corrigan, *Tin Ensign*, and Mannix, *The Old Navy*. Other publications include *The Northern Barrage and Other Mining Activities*; *The Northern Barrage: Mine Force U.S. Atlantic Fleet*. For other accounts, see Joseph Strauss, Review of the North Sea Barrage, Dec. 9, 1919, AN subj file, RG45; *New York Herald*, Nov. 12, 30, 1918, Jan. 20, 1919; *New York Herald Magazine*, Jan. 26, 1919; *New York Times Magazine*, Sept. 14, 1919; *New York Post*, Feb. 1, 1919; *New York Times*, Oct. 28, 1918; *Torch*, Jan. 1977; K. Schofield, "The North Sea Gate Swings Shut," 23–27; Blythe, "The Pills of Perdition"; *American Legion Magazine*, Aug. 1941, 35–37. See also various publications by Reginald Belknap listed in bibliography.

2. Sims to Dept., May 14, 1918; Reel, ME-11.

3. Trask, *Captains and Cabinets*, 154–56; Freidel, *F.D.R.: The Apprenticeship*, 312; Elliott Roosevelt, *FDR: Personal Letters*, 355–56; G. C. Ward, *A First-Class Temperament*, 353–54; Coady, "Franklin D. Roosevelt's Early Washington Years," Ph.D. diss., 170–71; N. Miller, *FDR*, 142–44; Mannix, "The Great North Sea Mine Barrage," 37; *Washington Post*, Nov. 13, 1939; Kilpatrick, *Roosevelt and Daniels*, 39–43, 51; Jonathan Daniels, *The End of Innocence*, 246–47, 263; Fullinwider to E. K. Lindsey, May 31, 1931, Fullinwider Papers, Smithsonian. Daniels insisted that it was William Redfield who first suggested the idea to President Wilson, but his idea of using nets was considered impracticable by the Bureau of Ordnance. See Jonathan Daniels, *The End of Innocence*, 241; and Fullinwider letter cited above. For Wilson, see Josephus Daniels, *The Wilson Era: Years of War*, 47. See also Sims to Dept., May 11, 1917, in M. Simpson, *Anglo-American Naval Relations*, 272–73; Pratt testimony, Oct. 19, 1917, General Board Hearings; Sims to Pratt, June 6, 1917, Area File, RG45; Earle to Sims, June 11, 1917, Box 55, Sims Papers, LC; Fullinwider to Daniels, Aug. 7, 1918, Fullinwider Papers, Smithsonian; memo to Earle, Nov. 16, 1917, AN subj file, RG45; FDR to Wilson, June 5, 1917, in M. Simpson, *Anglo-American Naval Relations,* 377–78. For an early proposal submitted by Roosevelt, see memo, May 24, 1917, in ibid., 375–77.

4. Quoted in Marder, *From the Dreadnought to Scapa Flow*, 4: 227.

5. A. H. Miles to Sims, March 16, 1920, Box 72, Sims Papers, LC; Fullinwider memo for Chief, Bureau of Ordnance, June 8, 1917, Fullinwider Papers, Smithsonian; Earle to CNO, June 12, 1917, Reel 1, ME-11; Grady to CNO, June 6, 1917, in Reports by US S/M officers, WWI, Box 1, Command Files, OA. Daniels after the war would claim that David Lloyd George as early as April 1917 favored the barrage. If so, he had no influence with the Admiralty concerning this. See Josephus Daniels, *Our Navy at War*, 44. Ironically, while the United States was pushing for

the barrage, the Admiralty requested the use of the American minelayers at that time in commission. Gaunt to Daniels, July 6, 1917, Roll 37, M1140.

6. For the mine development, see chapter 12. See also Earle to Benson, July 18, 1917, Reel 1, ME-11.

7. Confidential notes, Sept. 4–5, 1917 in ADM137/847. See also Trask, *Captains and Cabinets*, 149–52; Schuyler to Fullinwider, Sept. 8, 1917, Fullinwider Papers, Smithsonian; memo of Fullinwider, July 28, 1918, ibid.; Patterson, *The Jellicoe Papers*, 2: 119–20; Dewar to Richmond, Aug. 18, 1917, Sir Herbert Richmond Papers, NMM. Sims always had reservations about the barrage, preferring to place total emphasis on antisubmarine warfare and convoying. For Sims's views, see Morison, *Sims*, 413–16; Leighton, *Simsadus*, 16–17; Sims to Earle, July 11, Sept. 25, 1917, Box 55, Sims Papers, LC; Mayo to A. Dunn, Feb. 15, 1931, Mayo Papers, LC; Trask, *Captains and Cabinets*, 87–88; Roskill, *Sea Power*, 135; Freidel, *FDR: The Apprenticeship*, 316. Daniels, despite his postwar publications, which emphasized his reservations about the barrage, castigated Sims for his opposition to it. See entry for Feb. 5, 1920, in Josephus Daniels, *Cabinet Diaries*, 49.

8. M. Simpson, *Anglo-American Naval Relations*, 368; Dewar, *The Navy from Within*, 233–35; Marder, *From the Dreadnought to Scapa Flow*, 4: 226; Mayo, "The Atlantic Fleet," 359–60; Belknap, *The Yankee Mining Squadron*, 19.

9. Freidel, *FDR: The Apprenticeship*, 316. See also Sims to Admiralty, Oct. 23, 1917, ADM 137/685; Trask, *Captains and Cabinets*, 154–55; Duncan, *America's Use of Sea Mines*, 50; Earle to SecNav, Aug. 7, 1918, copy in Fullinwider Papers, Smithsonian; Fullinwider memo, Dec. 17, 1917, ibid.; *Navy Ordnance Activities, World War I*, 110–11; General Board Memo, Oct. 24, 1917, in M. Simpson, *Anglo-American Naval Relations*, 381–82; Marder, *From the Dreadnought to Scapa Flow*, 4: 226; General Board Hearings, Oct. 19, 1917; Gaunt to Benson, Oct. 24, 1917, Roll 37, M1140; Elliott Roosevelt, *F.D.R.: Personal Letters*, 362–67; entries for Oct. 29, 30, 1917, in Josephus Daniels, *Cabinet Diaries*, 228–29; Senior Member, General Board to SecNav, Oct. 22, 24, 1917, Roll 37, M1140. Various authorities disagree on different dates that British authorities approved the project, and when the United States officially accepted it. The decisions were made sometime between October 15 and November 2, 1917.

10. For the mine planters, see chapter 12; for bases and other logistical requirements, see chapters 5, 6, and 8. See also Schuyler to Earle, Oct. 17, 1917, copy in Fullinwider Papers, Smithsonian; CNO to Bureau of Ordnance, Oct. 29, 1917, Reel 8, ME-11; memo for Admiral Earle, Nov. 16, 1917, AN subj file, RG45.

11. Benson to Sims, Oct. 21, 1917, in M. Simpson, *Anglo-American Naval Relations*, 379–80; Jellicoe to Benson, Oct. 22, 1917, ibid.; "Mining plan," n.d., an Admiralty memo in Roll 37, M1140; "American Consideration and Adoption of Project," unpublished MS in Fullinwider Papers, Smithsonian; Pye testimony, Oct. 19, 1917, General Board Hearings; Knox to Frothington, Sept. 8, 1925, Box 9, Knox Papers, LC.

12. Murfin to Fullinwider, Dec. 4, 1917, Fullinwider Papers, Smithsonian; Nicholson to Sims, Dec. 6, 1917, copy in ibid.; Admiralty to Sims, Dec. 7, 1917, ADM137/847; notes on conference, Aug. 26, 1918, ADM137/848; Beatty to Admiralty, Sept. 4, 1918, ADM137/1962. Sims endorsed changes in the plans. See Twining to CNO, Dec. 7, 1917, copy in Fullinwider Papers, Smithsonian. See also Fullinwider to Earle, Dec. 17, 1917, ibid.; Sims to Admiralty, Dec. 18, 1917, ADM 137/847; memo, Planning Section, Dec. 31, 1917, Roll 37, M1140; Sims to CNO, Dec. 7, 1917, ibid.; Duncan, *America's Use of Sea Mines*, 57–60.

13. Marder, *From the Dreadnought to Scapa Flow*, 4: 252–54; 5: 69–72; Riste, *The Neutral Ally*, 212–24, 268–69; Director of Plans memo, Nov. 5, 1917, ADM137/2706; memo, March 1, 1918, ADM 137/1646. See also cables from British minister to Norway in ADM 137/1888; cable for Barclay in Washington, Aug. 23, 1918, ADM1378/848; memo, July 31, 1918, in M. Simpson, *Anglo-American Naval Relations*, 391; Grant, *U-Boat Intelligence*, 102; undated cables from U.S.

naval attaché Christiania (today Oslo), roll 37, M1140; note from Navy Dept. to SecState, "Mining the Neutral Waters of Norway," in ibid.; Sims to naval attaché Christiania, July 10, 1918, Reel 8, ME-11; ibid., July 11, 1918, Reel 4, ME-11; Benson to Sims, Aug. 13, 1918, Reel 5, ibid.; Balfour to Robert Cecil, Aug. 22, 1918, in Ranft, *The Beatty Papers*, 1: 540–41; Wilson to Daniels, Aug. 22, 1918, in Link, *Wilson Papers*, 49: 312; memo for CNO, Aug. 22, 1918, copy in Fullinwider Papers, Smithsonian. Approximately thirty American manufactured mines washed ashore near Bergen. The Norwegian government believed that the Americans were mining their waters. The U.S. government sent a mine expert to Norway to investigate. Strauss says that the U.S. mines that washed ashore or were found in Norwegian waters were used by Norway for their mine barrage. During the last excursions, strong gales dashed U.S. mines ashore on Norwegian coast at times with spectacular explosions. Entry for Oct. 30, 1918, in Corrigan, *Tin Ensign*, 98. See also Strauss, "Recollections," OA; Sims to U.S. naval attaché Christiania, July 16, 18, 1918, Reel 8, ME-11; British minister, Norway, to Foreign Office, Aug. 9, 1918, copy in ADM137/848. Page to SecState, June 23, 1917, *Foreign Relations, 1917*, Supplement 2, 108–9; Evans, U.S. Embassy, Norway, to SecState, June 26, 1917, 763.72/5967, M367; entry for June 27, 1917, in Josephus Daniels, *Cabinet Diaries*, 169; memo, July 5, 1917, C-27-5, Box 75, Confidential File, 1917–1919, RG80; memo by the Admiralty Director of Plans, February 11, 1918, in M. Simpson, *Anglo-American Naval Relations*, 272; Pye testimony, Oct. 16, 1917, General Board Hearings; Marder, *From the Dreadnought to Scapa Flow*, 4: 252–54; J. W. Jones, "U.S. Battleship Operations in World War I," Ph.D. diss., 35–36; Riste, *The Neutral Ally*, 180–90. There are a number of memos on the Norwegian base idea in Box 42, Benson Papers, LC.

14. Sims to Admiralty, Dec. 18, 1917, ADM137/847; "remarks," Jan. 4, 1918, ibid. The British also advocated using a zigzag pattern in laying the mines, but the Americans preferred and followed straight lines in their patterns. Schuyler to Earle, Nov. 26, 1917, copy in Fullinwider Papers, Smithsonian. See also Admiral Sir Reginald Tupper, *Reminiscences*, 271–76; Admiralty to Sims, May 10, 1918, roll 21, M1140; Admiralty memo, Feb. 1, 1918, ADM137/847; memo for Chief of Bureau of Ordnance, Dec. 26, 1917, and Earle to CNO, Jan. 8, 1918, both in Fullinwider Papers, Smithsonian.

15. Quoted from an unpublished MS by Fullinwider in his papers. See also ADM to Beatty, Dec. 28, 1917, ADM137/1962; ibid., Jan. 27, 1918, ADM137/847; *Naval Ordnance Activities, World War*, 111; Leighton, *Simsadus*, 72.

16. FDR to Daniels, Oct. 16, 1918, in M. Simpson, *Anglo-American Naval Relations*, 180; Strauss, "Recollections," OA. The quote about officials in favor of the barrage is mentioned in Strauss testimony, 1919, General Board Hearings. See also *The Northern Barrage and Other Mining Activities*, 88; Beatty to Admiralty, July 7, 1918, ADM137/1984.

17. Wemyss to Beatty, Aug. 15, 1918, in Ranft, *The Beatty Papers*, 2: 536–38. See also Wemyss to Beatty, Aug. 23, 1918, ibid., 544–45; Flint to Sims, Sept. 18, 1918, Reel 8, ME-11; FDR to Daniels, Oct. 16, 1918, in M. Simpson, *Anglo-American Naval Relations*, 180; Beatty to Wemyss, Aug. 23, 1918, Beatty Papers, NMM.

18. Balfour to Cecil, Aug. 22, 1918, copy in Beatty Papers, NMM; Beatty to Wemyss, Sept. 1, 1918, ibid., 546; Wemyss to Beatty, Sept. 3, 1918, Wemyss Papers, microfilm, University of California at Irvine; Beatty to "Rosy," Sept. 25, 1918, ibid.; Fremantle, *My Naval Career*, 244; Thomson to Strauss, Oct. 22, 1918, AN subj file, RG45; Strauss to Simsadus, Oct. 19, 1918, Reel 8, ME-11.

19. Belknap to CNO, Jan 7, 1918, Reel 8, ME-11; Strauss Recollections, OA. See also Earle to CNO, Jan. 3, 1918, Reel 8, ME-11; Benson to Sims, Dec. 2, 1917, Reel 8, ME-11; Duncan, *America's Use of Sea Mines*, 60; Planning Section, memo, Dec. 31, 1918, roll 37; M1140; Joint memo by British and American planning "staffers," Jan. 12, 1918, in M. Simpson, *Anglo-American Naval Relations*, 389–90; Freidel, *FDR: The Apprenticeship*, 352; Earle to CNO, Jan. 3, 1918, Reel 8, ME-

11; Belknap to CNO, Jan. 5, 1918, ibid. See also Belknap testimony, Jan. 7, 1918, General Board Hearings; Navy Dept., *The American Planning Section in London*, 1.

20. Strauss reports on mine expeditions are in ADM137/1963. See also Corrigan, *Tin Ensign*, 77–84; *The Northern Barrage and Other Mining Activities*, 111–12; Mannix, *The Old Navy*, 228–29.

21. Beatty to Wemyss, Aug. 10, 1918, Wemyss MS, copy in Beatty Papers, NMM; Wemyss to Beatty, Aug. 15, 1918, Wemyss MS, microfilm, University of California Library; See also Beatty to Admiralty, Aug. 16, 1918, copy in Reel 5, ME-11; Beatty to Admiralty, Sept. 10, 11, 1918, to U.S. Navy Department; Admiralty to Beatty, Sept. 11, 1918, all in ADM137/1962. Beatty to Strauss, Sept. 29, 1918, ADM137/1984; Halpern, *A Naval History of World War I*, 439; Marder, *From the Dreadnought to Scapa Flow*, 4: 67–69. For other British comments on the mines, see ADM 137/1984; Corbett and Newbolt, *History of the Great War*, 5: 234–36.

22. Beatty to Wemyss, Sept. 11, 1918, ADM137/1984; Wemyss to Beatty, Aug. 10, 1918, Beatty Papers; Beatty to Wemyss, Aug. 10, 1918, in Ranft, *The Beatty Papers*, 2: 535; Lady Wemyss, *The Life and Letters of Lord Wester Wemyss*, 381. See also Marder, *From the Dreadnought to Scapa Flow*, 5: 68–69.

23. Strauss to CNO, March 7, 1918, copy in Fullinwider Papers, Smithsonian; *The Northern Mine Barrage and Other Mining Activities*, 105; Corbett and Newbolt, *History of the Great War*, 5: 334.

24. Isherwood to Fullinwider, Sept. 8, 1918, Fullinwider Papers, Smithsonian; Sims to Dept., June 24, 1918, Reel 4, ME-11; Rear Admiral J. D. McDonald, Commandant, Navy Yard, New York, to Belknap, May 9, 1918, Belknap Papers, NHF; Strauss testimony, 1919, General Board Hearings. Duncan quotes Strauss in *America's Use of Sea Mines* (62). See also Belknap to CNO, April 9, 1918, Reel 8, ME-11; memo, Admiralty Plans Division, July 24, 1918, in M. Simpson, *Anglo-American Naval Relations*, 389; memo to CNO, Feb. 11, 1918, Roll 37, M1140 Stirling, *Sea Duty*, 160.

25. Grant, *U-Boat Intelligence*, 102; Strauss to Sims, July 11, 1918, Strauss Papers, OA; Sims to Dept., July 9, 1918, Reel 4, ME-11; Wemyss to Beatty, Aug. 5, 1918, Beatty Papers, NMM; Sims to Fremantle, July 27, 1918, ibid.; Beatty to Admiralty, July 7, 1918, and reply same date, ADM 137/1984; Admiralty memo, July 15, 1918, ADM137/1968; Beatty to Admiralty, July 15, 1918, ADM 137/848; Walker to Beatty, July 25, 1918, ADM137/1962; Sims to Strauss, July 24, 1918, Reel 4, ME-11.

26. Strauss testimony, 1919, General Board Hearings; Strauss to Sims and reply, June 22, 1918, Reel 4, ME-11; *The Northern Barrage and Other Mining Activities*, 120; Admiralty to Beatty, July 17, 1918, ADM137/1984. A number of communications concerning British concerns over delays are found in ADM137/685 and 686. See also Belknap, *The Yankee Mining Squadron*, 81; Trask, *Captains and Cabinets*, 217; Rear Admiral, Mining to Third Sea Lord, Dec. 3, 1917, ADM 137/1437; memo, Feb. 11, 1918, ibid., 1459; memo, Dec. 22, 1917, ADM116/1567. See ADM137/2180 for these needs. Sims to Dept., March 3, 1918, Reel 3, ME-11; Memo No. 8, Jan. 31, 1918, in Navy Dept., *The American Naval Planning Section in London*, 51–53.

27. Strauss, "Recollections," OA; Marder, *From the Dreadnought to Scapa Flow*, 5: 67; F. H. Schofield, "Incidents and Present-Day Aspects of Naval Strategy," 794–95; Roskill, *Admiral of the Fleet Earl Beatty*, 256; Wemyss unpublished MS, Wemyss Papers, microfilm, University of California at Irvine; Stackhouse, "The Anglo-American Atlantic Convoy System in World War I," Ph.D. diss., 387.

28. Coffman, *The War to End All Wars*, 119; Cowie, *Mines, Minelayers, and Minelaying*, 69, 72; Trask, *Captains and Cabinets*, 217–18.

29. Sims to Dept., Dec. 12, 1917, Box 10, Logistics file, RG45; comments on Northern Mine Barrage, Jan. 12, 1918, ADM137/847; Belknap, *The Yankee Mining Squadron*, 92, passim; Strauss, "Recollections," OA.

30. A. W. Marshall, "Being an Account of Operations of the USS *Baltimore*, Mine Planter," OS subj file, RG45; Sims to CO *Baltimore*, March 21, 1918, AN subj file, RG45; Admiral, Grangemouth, to Simsadus, April 7, 1918, Reel 19, ME-11. Grangemouth was the Royal Navy's mine depot. See also CO Mine Force to Sims, May 1, 1918, Reel 20, ME-11; Marshall to Force CO, May 12, 1918, OS subj file, RG45; Marshall to Rear Admiral, Grangemouth, May 20, 1918, Reel 20, ME-11; Sims to Naval Base, Inverness, May 21, 1918, Reel 8, ibid.; *The Northern Barrage and Other Mining Activities*, 102–4.

31. Belknap to Sparkman, Dec. 5, 1956, Belknap Papers, NHF; Belknap speech, June 1, 1940, copy in ibid.

32. Entry for Oct. 31, 1917, in Josephus Daniels, *Cabinet Diaries*, 229; Pratt, "Autobiography," OA.

33. Felix Johnson Oral History, USNI; Pratt, "Autobiography," OA; Pratt to Daniels, Nov. 12, 1917, Reel 65, Daniels Papers, LC; Sims to wife, Jan. 10, 1919, Box 10, Sims Papers, LC. See also Andrews to Sims, June 10, 1927, Box 41, ibid. In 1925, after he was passed over a second time, Belknap appealed to former CNO Benson, who wrote an impressive recommendation for him. Belknap would in time be promoted to rear admiral before retiring in 1935. Belknap to Benson, Aug. 28, 1925, Benson to Belknap, Sept. 4, 1925, and Benson to SecNav, Sept. 4, 1925, all in Belknap Papers, LC.

34. Copy in AN subj file, RG45. For Belknap on Clinton-Baker, see letter to Rear Admiral Neil Dietrig, March 21, 1956, Belknap Papers, LC, and to "Bruce," July 13, 1958, ibid. See also Benson to Belknap, Oct. 23, 1918, Reel 8, ME-11; Magruder, "The Navy in the War," 131; Karsten, *The Naval Aristocracy*, 298. Rear Admiral Clinton-Baker was in command of British mining forces.

35. Howell, "A Horse Kicked Me," unpublished MS on microfilm, NDL; Conager to Belknap, July 4, 1958; Belknap to Bruce, July 13, 1958 in Belknap Papers, NHF; Andrews to Sims, Aug. 28, 1924, Box 41, Sims Papers. For assessments of Strauss's career after the war, see V. Davis, *The Admiral's Lobby*, 80–81; Braisted, *The United States Navy in the Pacific*, passim; and Tolley, *Yangtze Patrol*, passim.

36. Strauss, "Recollections," OA; Thomson to Strauss, Oct. 22, 1918, with enclosed memo regarding mining operations, AN subj file, RG45; Admiral to Beatty, Sept. 10, 1918, ADM137/1784; Sims to Strauss, Sept. 6, 1918, Reel 8, ME-11; Sims to Strauss, Oct. 17, 1918, ibid.; Strauss to Twining, Oct. 16, 1918, ibid.

37. Mannix, in *The Old Navy*, discusses weather and other problems, as does Corrigan in *Tin Ensign*. See also E. V. Whited Diary, Smithsonian; Belknap, *The Yankee Mining Squadron*, 20; John Young to Editor, *Torch*, Jan. 15, 1977, copy in WWI Research Project, AMHI; Freidel, *Over There*, 42–43, for *Housatonic* sailor's quote.

38. Strauss, "Recollections," OA; Corrigan, *Tin Ensign*, 71, 175–76; Furlong, *Class of 1905*, 51–53; Coffman, *The War to End All Wars*, 119; Belknap, *The Yankee Mining Squadron*, 14–15, 43–44, 60, 65, 75–76.

39. *Our Navy* 12 (Feb. 1919): 54; Cottman, *Jefferson County in the World War*, 99; Fraser and Gibbons, *Soldier and Sailor Words*; 163; Corrigan, *Tin Ensign*, 26–27.

40. Strauss, "Recollections," OA. See also Belknap, *The Yankee Mining Squadron*, 60.

41. Strauss to Earle, Jan. 25, 1919, copy in Belknap Papers, NHF. See also "Summary of U.S. Naval Activities in European Waters," Z file, OA; Josephus Daniels, *Our Navy at War*, 242; Mayo to SecNav, Nov. 20, 1918, Box 10, Logistics file, RG45; Benson to Sims, Oct. 19, 23, 1918, Box 49, Sims Papers, LC; "The Northern Sea Barrage—Its Wonderful Effectiveness," unpublished MS in Belknap Papers, NHF; Strauss, "Recollections," OA; Belknap, *The Yankee Mining Squadron*, preface; Capt. Thomas C. Hart, "Submarines," unpublished MS, Oct. 28, 1919, NWC; Josephus Daniels, *The Wilson Era: Years of War*, 89–91.

42. Roskill, *Admiral of the Fleet Earl Beatty*, 256–57. See also Fremantle, *My Naval Career*,

249; memo, Admiral Plans Division, Nov. 1, 1918, in M. Simpson, *Anglo-American Naval Relations*, 393–94. For American displeasure with British media giving Royal Navy credit for barrage, see Belknap, *The Yankee Mining Squadron*, 84; and Strauss, "Recollections," OA. Admiral Dreyer, who was in the Admiralty at the time, did say that the barrage was a source of "grave anxiety to U-boat crews." *The Sea Heritage*, 233.

43. Scheer, *Germany's High Sea Fleet in the World War*, 291; Michelsen, "The Submarine Warfare," 734–77; Bywater and Ferreby, *Strange Intelligence*, 267–68. See also Hashagen, *U-Boats Westward!*, 115–19, 217.

44. Marder, *From the Dreadnought to Scapa Flow*, 4: 225; Lundeberg, "Underseas Warfare and Allied Strategy in World War I," 65; M. Simpson, *Anglo-American Naval Relations*, 367; Lloyd, *The Nation and the Navy*, 259; Josephus Daniels, *The Wilson Era: Years of War*, 88. See also Pratt to Daniels, Nov. 12, 1917, Reel 65, Daniels Papers, LC.

45. Grant, *U-Boat Intelligence*, 104–5; Grant, *U-Boats Destroyed*, 107–8; Gibson and Prendergast, *The German Submarine War*, 320–21. For various conclusions on the number destroyed, see Marder, *From the Dreadnought to Scapa Flow*, 5: 73; Halpern, *A Naval History of World War I*, 440–41.

46. Trask, *Captains and Cabinets*, 218. See also Coletta, *Sea Power*, 72.

47. Grant, *U-Boats Destroyed*, 107–8; Hartman, *Weapons That Wait*, 53. See also Ferrell, *Woodrow Wilson and World War I*, 44; Cowie, *Mines, Minelayers, and Minelaying*, 71; and Duncan, *America's Use of Sea Mines*, 63.

48. Halpern, *A Naval History of World War I*, 440–41; Marder, *From the Dreadnought to Scapa Flow*, 5: 72–73; M. Simpson, *Anglo-American Naval Relations*, 370; Roskill, *Admiral of the Fleet Earl Beatty*, 257. See also T. Wilson, *The Myriad Faces of War*, 633.

49. "U.S. Naval Administration in World War II, Guide No. 15, Mine Warfare in the Naval Establishment," 3–9, NDL. Rear Admiral Kenneth L. Veth Oral History, USNI. The Allies considered a similar barrage using 181,000 mines to close the North Sea in World War II, but it was never put into effect.

Chapter 18. "Hunting the Huns"

1. Marder, *From the Dreadnought to Scapa Flow*, 4: 67–71, 134–35.

2. Bayly to Jellicoe, Oct. 3, 1917, ADD 49009, Jellicoe MSS, British Museum. For developing weapons and devices, see chapter 12.

3. Memo to Allied Naval Council, Jan. 22–23, 1918, in M. Simpson, *Anglo-American Naval Relations*, 266–67; Simpson in ibid., 202–3; Wemyss Memoir in Wemyss Papers, Microfilm, University of California at Irvine. See also lecture on antisubmarine warfare in Admiral John H. Godfrey Papers, Churchill College, Cambridge; Corbett and Newbolt, *History of the Great War*, 5: 124–27; Marder, *From the Dreadnought to Scapa Flow*, 4: 79–80; Roskill, *Admiral of the Fleet Earl Beatty*, 267.

4. A substantial number of booklets, pamphlets, monographs, and notes on submarine hunting by different types of vessels and aircraft as well as equipment in LA subj file, RG45.

5. See Leigh's report in LA subj file, RG45; Sims to Chief of Staff, Destroyer Flotillas, Feb. 22, 1918, OS subj file, ibid.; ibid., Aug. 16, 1918, Reel 10, ME-11; DeBreton to Leigh, April 18, 1918, OS subj file, RG45; entry for Oct. 2, 1918, Moore Diary, NHF; Schoeffel Oral History, USNI. See also letter of Floyd Roussin, n.d., in Floyd Roussin Papers, WWI Research Project, AMHI.

6. Johnson to Pringle, Aug. 30, 1918, copy in ADM137/947; Sims to CO *Parker*, Sept. 2, 1918, Reel 10, ME-11; Sims to Pringle, Aug. 16, 1918, Reel 9, ibid.; Buchanan to Sims, Feb. 23, 1918, ibid.; Pringle to Sims, report of operations, Feb. 22–28, 1918, Reel 19, ibid.; Sims to Dept., Feb. 28, 1918, Reel 3, ibid.; Bayly to Admiralty, Aug. 14, 1918, ADM137/1513; Pringle to Simsadus, Aug. 1918, LA subj file, RG45; Rice to Sims, Dec. 6, 1918, ibid.; Sims to Benson, Feb. 25, 1918, in M. Simpson, *Anglo-American Naval Relations*, 275–76.

7. Sims to Pringle, Sept. 5, 1918, Reel 10, ME-11; ibid., Aug. 16, 1918, Reel 9, ibid.; CO *Parker* to Sims, Sept. 8, 1918, LA subj file, RG45; Sims to CO subchaser detachment, Oct. 16, 1918, OD subj file, ibid.; ONI, Report of Submarine Attack, Oct. 17, 1918, in M. Simpson, *Anglo-American Naval Relations*, 312–14; Report of Admiralty conference on offensive actions against enemy submarines, May 3, 1918, ibid., 303; "Louis C. Farley," in Furlong, *Class of 1905*, 124–25; Sims to Admiralty, Sept. 7, 1918, ADM137/1622.

8. Memo of British and American Planning Sections, Oct. 11, 1918, ADM137/2709; Sims to Brady, Oct. 27, 1918, Reel 6, ME-11. See also memo No. 57, Oct. 1918, in Navy Dept., *The American Naval Planning Section in London*, 409–11; Sims to Dept., Oct. 19, 1918, Reel 6, ME-11.

9. Navy Dept., *The American Naval Planning Section in London*, 183–85; memo for Planning Section, June 14, 1918, LA subj file, RG45; memo on hunting groups, Allied Naval Council, June, 1918, QC subj file, RG45. Even First Sea Lord Geddes favored hunting rather than convoying. See Roskill, *Admiral of the Fleet Earl Beatty*, 267.

10. For discussion of these vessels, see chapter 12.

11. ADM memos, Feb. 8, 9, 1918, ADM116/1807; Sims to Benson, March 7, 1918, TT subj file, RG45; Benson to Sims, March, 1918, ibid.; Sims to Dinger, Sept. 6, 1917, OH subj file, ibid., Memo from Director Anti-Submarine Department (DASD) to First Lord, Sept. 8, 1917, in M. Simpson, *Anglo-American Naval Relations*, 254; Halpern, *A Naval History of World War I*, 398–99; Trask, *Captains and Cabinets*, 274–75; Sims to CNO, March 28, 1918, Reel 4, ME-11; Minutes of Director of Plans, March 1, 1918, in M. Simpson, *Anglo-American Naval Relations*, 277; Nicholson to Sims, Dec. 4, 1917, March 10, 1918, OD subj file, RG45; ADM Minutes, March 11, 1918, ADM137/1459; Minutes of Allied Naval Council, March 11–13, 1918, QC subj file, RG45; memo to War Cabinet, February 17, 1918, ADM116/1807; Sims to CNO, March 8, 1918, OD subj file, RG45; Murray to Sims, March 25, 1918, in M. Simpson, *Anglo-American Naval Relations*, 278–79; Sims to Murray, March 28, 1918, ibid., 279; Sims to CNO, March 16, 1918, Reel 3, ME-11; De Bon to Minister of Marine, March 16, 1918, French Naval Archives, Vincennes; Sims to Admiralty, March 28, 1918, Reel 4, ME-11.

12. Memos, Sept. 4, 1917, ADM137/1437.

13. Benson to Sims, March 1918, OD subj file, RG45; N. Chodson to Sims, March 10, 1918, OD subj file, ibid.; Sims to Benson, March 28, 1918, ibid.; De Bon to Director General of Anti-Submarine War (France), March 16, 1918, French Naval Archives, Vincennes; Murray to Sims, March 25, 1918, in M. Simpson, *Anglo-American Naval Relations*, 278; Minutes of Director of Planning, March 1, 1918, ibid., 277–78.

14. Biographical sketch in Robert H. Leigh file, ZB file, NDL. See also his unpublished autobiography, Florida State University; Murphy, *Fighting Admiral*, 77; Daniels to Sims, Jan. 15, 1918, OB subj file, RG45. Sims orders to Leigh, Jan. 12, 1918, copy in ADM137/1621. G. E. Wheeler, *Pratt*, 11, passim.

15. Sims, *The Victory at Sea*, 211–13.

16. Sims to ALUSNA, Lisbon, Sept. 10, 1918, Reel 10, ME-11; Sims to Dept., Nov. 11, 1918, ibid.; Leigh to Wilson, Oct. 9, 1918, OD subj file, RG45; Sims to Wilson, Aug. 9, 1918, ibid.; Twining to Cotten, July 17, 1918, ibid.; Wilson to Sims, Aug. 7, 1918, ibid.; Sims to Bayly, Aug. 24, 1918, Box 47, Sims Papers, LC.

17. Navy Dept., *The American Naval Planning Section in London*, 513.

18. For the crossing, see Moffat, *Maverick Navy*, 50–51; M. S. Brown, "The Experiences of a Yankee Sub-Chaser," 5; Blythe, "The Sea Terriers," 26; Sailing Master to Dunn, Feb. 18, 1918, Cotten Papers, UNC-CH; *Literary Digest*, Feb. 8, 1919, 63–64; Furer, "The 110-Foot Submarine Chasers and Eagle Boats," 262.

19. The CO of *Cyther* recommended that hunting squadrons accompany convoys, not as escorts but to search out and destroy U-boats waiting to attack. To Dept., May 18, 1918, Reel 10, M1092.

20. McCully to Pringle, April 17, 1918, CP subj file, RG45; "Employment of Submarine Chasers," March 19, 1918, OD subj file, ibid.; Nicholson to Sims, March 10, 1918, ibid.; Long to Pringle, April 17, 1918, ibid.; Pringle to Sims, July 16, 1918, ibid.; Sims to CO Subchaser Detachment 3, Aug. 16, 1918, ibid.; Sims to CO Subchaser Detachment 1, Aug. 26, 1918, ibid.; Minutes of Director of Planning, March 1, 1918, in M. Simpson, *Anglo-American Naval Relations*, 277–78; Sims to McCully, Aug. 4, 1918, ibid., 300–301; Cotten to wife, March 22, 1918, Cotten Papers, UNC-CH; M. S. Brown, "Life Overseas on the Yankee Sub-Chasers," 18; Sims to Bayly, Aug. 24, 1918, Box 47, Sims Papers, LC; Circular, Aug. 29, 1918, ADM 137/1947; "American Destroyers in the War," 90. The Admiralty later changed its opinion toward the use of the chasers and requested that they be used to escort convoys in the English Channel. Walker to Sims, Oct. 17, 1918, Reel 10, ME-11.

21. This was accurate as hydrophones could determine direction but not distance.

22. Sims, *The Victory at Sea*, 220.

23. There are excellent accounts by junior officers on these chasers, M. S. Brown, "Life Overseas on the Yankee Sub-Chasers" and "The Experience of a Yankee Sub-Chaser," and Moffat's *Maverick Navy*. See also Milholland, *The Splinter Fleet of the Otranto Barrage*; Chambers, *Submarine Chasers in the Mediterranean*; Twining to CO Aylwin, June 4, 1918, Reel 20, ME-11; Adam to C-in-C, Portsmouth, May 14, 1918, ibid.; Sims to Murray, May 6, 1918, in M. Simpson, *Anglo-American Naval Relations*, 295.

24. Cochran, "Plymouth in Civvi's," 15.

25. Ellyson to wife, Aug. 17, 1918, Ellyson Papers, NDL; Leigh to Sims, Aug. 14, 1917, Box 52, Sims Papers, LC; Moffat, *Maverick Navy*, 104; van Deurs, *Anchors in the Sky*, 188. For Cotten's career and comments about him, see biographical sketch in Governor Melvin Broughton Papers, North Carolina Division of Archives and History, Raleigh. See also Ellyson Papers, NDL, for his opinion of Cotten, especially letter to his wife, June 21, 1918. In the Cotten Papers at UNC-CH are copies of Cotten's compositions.

26. Leigh autobiography, Leigh Papers, FSU; Sims to Thursby, Sept. 19, 1924, Box 52, Sims Papers, LC; Cotten to Leigh, Aug. 30, 1918, OD subj file, RG45; Cotten to Leigh, July 30, 1918, OR subj file, ibid.; Thursby to Admiralty, Sept. 2, 1918, ADM131/65; Bristol to Sims, Nov. 6, 1918, Box 50, Sims Papers, LC; Cotten to wife, July 14, Aug. 4, 12, 1918, Cotten Papers, UNC-CH; entries for June 23–24, 1918, Cotten Diary, ibid.; Cotten to Hepburn, July 9, 1918, P-Plymouth subj file, RG45; Cotten to Leigh, Sept. 9, 1918, ibid.; Ellyson to wife, Aug. 3, 4, 7, Oct. 28, 1918, Ellyson Papers, NDL; Sims to Benson, July 28, 1918, in M. Simpson, *Anglo-American Naval Relations*, 167.

27. Cotten to wife, Sept. 7, Oct. 24, 1918, to Burrage, May 4, 1918, Cotten Papers, UNC-CH; Bristol, General Order No 1, Oct. 24, 1918, OD subj file, RGH45.

28. C. G. Reynolds, *Famous American Admirals*, 42–43; Braisted, "Mark Lambert Bristol," 331–70.

29. Pringle to Simsadus, Aug. 24, 1918, Reel 9, ME-11; Sims Report to Dept., Aug. 16, 1918, Reel 5, ibid.

30. Devonport (Naval District) General Order, June 14, 1918, ADM131/65; Sims to Admiralty, June 12, 1918, ADM131/1622; Moffat, *Maverick Navy*, 104; Cotten to Hepburn, July 9, 1918, P-Plymouth subj file, RG45; Cotten to Simsadus, June 14, 1918, Reel 20, ME-11; M. S. Brown, "Life Overseas on the Yankee Sub-Chasers," 7; Order for US subchasers, June 27, 1918, ADM 131/65; Cotten to wife, July 8, 1918, Cotten Papers, UNC-CH; Cotten to Hepburn, July 8, 1918, ibid.; Cotten to Leigh, July 22,30, 1918, OD subj file, RG45; memo, Aug. 4, 1918, ibid.

31. M. S. Brown, "Life Overseas on the Yankee Sub-Chasers," 7; quotes from Kohler report, n.d., copy provided author by Dr. Pete Capelotti. See also Moffat, *Maverick Navy*, 105–9.

32. Sims Report to Dept., Aug. 16, 1918, Reel 11, ME-11; Sims to subchaser detachment CO, Aug. 23, 1918, Reel 9, ibid.

33. Sims to Cotten, July 13, 1918, Reel 19, ME-11; Moffat, *Maverick Navy*, 93–94; Ellyson to wife, Aug. 3, 26, 1918, Ellyson Papers, NDL; Report of submarine attack, Aug. 25, 1918, Cotten Papers, UNC-CH; Leigh to COs, subchaser detachments 1, 2, and 3, Aug. 26, 1918, Reel 5, ME-11.

34. Bayly, *Pull Together*, 238; Bayly to Sims, Sept. 12, 1918, Box 47, Sims Papers, LC.

35. Bayly memo, Sept. 18, OD subj file, RG45; Hepburn Report, Nov. 30, 1919, ibid., Campbell in his published memoirs, *Number Thirteen*, wrote that twenty subchasers came under his command in June 1918. See also Kohler MS provided to the author by Dr. Pete Capelotti. For the codes and identification, see Hoehling, *The Great War at Sea*, 243; and Harries and Harries, *The Last Days of Innocence*, 81. See also Report to Dept., Sept 21, 1918, Reel 6, ME-11.

36. Sims to CO Subchaser Detachment One, Sept. 16, 1918, Reel 10, ME-11; CO Subchaser Detachment One to Sims, Sept. 6, 1918. ibid. Note at bottom of report was evidently written after the war was over. It said that *U-53*'s log recorded that she continued operating and made no repairs at her base. Unit CO to Cotten, Sept. 2, 1918, ibid.; officer in charge of listening, Unit 4 to Cotten, Sept. 6, 1918, ibid.; CO *Parker*, to Cotten, Sept. 6, 1918, ibid.; Leigh to Cotten, Sept. 14, 1918, ibid.; Cotten to wife, Sept. 1, 15, 1918, Cotten Papers, UNC-CH; W. H. Miller, *The Boys of 1917*, 128–29; Sims, *The Victory at Sea*, 226–27; M. S. Brown, "Life Overseas on the Yankee Sub-Chasers," 18; action report, Hearing Report, Unit A, Nov. 10, 1918, OD subj file, RG45.

37. CO, Div. 17 to Hepburn, Oct. 12, 1918, OD subj file, RG45; Hepburn Report, Nov. 30, 1918, ibid.; Walker (Admiralty) to Sims, Oct. 27, 1918, ibid.; Kohler to Aunt, n.d., copy provided to author by Dr. Pete Capelotti. See also Robbins to Capelotti, ibid.; an interview with German officer, Feb. 9, 1919, in LA subj file, RG45; Sweetman, "Aboard Subchaser 206," 69–71.

38. Thursby to Admiralty, Oct. 7, 1918. AMD137/1507.

39. Sims to Admiralty, Oct. 30, 1918, ADM137/1507, copy in Reel 10, ME-11. See also Thursby to Admiralty, Oct. 7, 1918, ADM137/1507; Admiralty to Thursby, Oct. 25, 1918, ADM137/1486; memo, Oct. 25, 1918, OD subj file, RG45; Leigh to Twining, Oct. 26, 1918, ibid.; Cotten to Sims, Oct. 28, 1918, ibid.; Bristol to Sims, Oct. 28, 1918, Bristol Papers, LC.

40. Michelsen, "The Submarine Warfare," 71. See also Nutting, *Cinderellas of the Fleet*, 81–82; "Summary of U.S. Naval Activities in European Waters," Z file, OA; interview with German officer, Feb. 12–13, 1919, in U.S. S/M officers, WWI, Box 1, WWII command file, OA. Subchasers deployed with the Otranto Barrage in the Adriatic Sea are discussed in chapter 19.

41. Eric Grove, "The Reluctant Partner: The United States and the Introduction and Extension of Convoy in 1917–1918," copy in author's possession.

42. Hall, "Life on a U.S. Submarine during the World War," 17–18, copy in Submarine Force Library and Museum. See also Keister, "U.S. Submarines in the War Zone," 1132; Hart to CO Submarine Force, Nov. 5, 1917, folder, Allied Submarine Operations, WWI, Box 1, OA; Hart to Pratt, March 10, 1920, Box 2, ibid.; Causey campaign order No. 10, Jan. 20, 1918, Box 3, Underseas Warfare Div., OA; Sims to Dept., Oct. 15, 1917, file C 48, Box 105, Confidential Files, RG80; Sims to Dunn, Oct. 16, 1918, Reel 14, ME-11; C. S. Alden, "American Submarine Operations in the War," 830–48; Sims to Dunn, May 19, 1918, Reel 4, ME-11; Sims to Dunn, May 18, 28, 1918, Reel 20, ibid.; Dunn to Sims, May 20, 1918, ibid.; Sims to Dept., June 7, 1918, ibid.; Sims to Admiralty, Oct. 22, 1918, P-Ponta Delgada subj file, RG45.

43. For the decision to deploy submarines in European waters, see chapter 12. This section on submarine warfare is primarily based on Grady, "War History of Submarine Division Five," n.d., copy in Allied Submarine Operations, WWI, Box 1, OA, also in *Nautilus* Memorial Museum; C. S. Alden, "American Submarine Operations in the War," 811–50, 1013–48; Barnes, *United States Submarines*, 104–11; Thompson, *Take Her Down*, passim; and Sims, *The Victory at Sea*, 263–84.

44. Bayly to Admiralty, Nov. 16, 1917, in M. Simpson, *Anglo-American Naval Relations*, 259. See also Bayly to Jellicoe, Dec. 19, 1917, ADD 49009, Jellicoe MS, British Museum; and Admiralty to Gaunt, Nov. 7, 16, 1917, Reel 10, ME-11. Queenstown, which did not impress Hart, who

called it a "one horse port," was to be the division's repair base. Entry Jan. 30, 1918, Hart Diary, OA.

45. Sims to Benson, April 7, 1918, Reel 19, ME-11.

46. Bayly to Admiralty, Feb. 19, 1918, ADM137/1538; entry for Jan. 29, 1918, Hart Diary, OA; Leutze, *A Different Kind of Victory*, 59.

47. Paine, *Roads to Adventure*, 447; Grady, "War History of Submarine Division Five"; C. S. Alden, "American Submarine Operations in the War," 1044; Furlong, *Class of 1905*, 147; Hart to Knox, April 5, 1918, OD subj file, RG45.

48. "Admiral" to Bayly, Aug. 13, 1918, ADM137/1527; Sims to Dept., Sept. 12, 18, 1918, Reel 5, ME-11; Sims to Hart, June 27, 1918, USS *Bushnell* file, Ships History Branch, NHC; Thompson, *Take Her Down*, 161; General Board Hearings, Jan. 25, 1918.

49. "Summary of U.S. Naval Activities in European Waters," Z File OA; Schoeffel Oral History, USNI; Sims, *The Victory at Sea*, 166, 272–73.

50. Grady, "War History of Submarine Division Five"; Leutze, *A Different Kind of Victory*, 60; C. S. Alden, "American Submarine Operations in the War," 1026; Barnes, *United States Submarines*, 106.

51. C. S. Alden, "American Submarine Operations in the War," 1020–22, 1032–35; W. H. Miller, *The Boys of 1917*, 119–20; Thompson, *Take Her Down*, 219, 220, 260, 263–64; Leighton, *Simsadus*, 87; Hall, "Life on a U.S. Submarine during the World War," 13, 18; *Klaxon* (Autumn 1993): 2; Dawson, *Flotillas*, 212–13; Sims, *The Victory at Sea*, 275–76; Grady, "War History of Submarine Division Five"; *Atlantic Monthly* 122 (July 1918): 693–96; Gibson and Prendergast, *The German Submarine War*, 314.

52. Sims to Dept., April 10, 1918, Reel 4, ME-11; Jusserand to SecState, June 11, 1918, ibid.; Sims to Dept., Oct. 2, 3, 1918, Reel 6, ibid.; Leighton to Twining, Oct. 7, 1918, LA subj file, RG45; Hart to Pratt, March 10, 1920, Box 2, SM History, OA; Sims to Bayly, Oct. 2, 1918, in M. Simpson, *Anglo-American Naval Relations*, 312.

53. Michelson, "The Submarine Warfare," 72; Sims, *The Victory at Sea*, 263, 280, 283; Alden and Westcott, *The United States Navy*, 354; Weir, *Building American Submarines*, 11. Even British submarines had little success in four years of war. In 1917–1918, they made 564 contacts, but only 19 hits. They sunk only 17 during the entire war. Marder, *From the Dreadnought to Scapa Flow*, 4: 84. For a different view, see Jellicoe, *The Crisis of the Naval War*, 97–98; Hart, "Submarine Operations," Box 2, SM file, OA.

54. For naval aviation in World War I, see Roscoe, *On the Seas and in the Skies*, 25–37; Van Wyen, *Naval Aviation in World War I*, passim. Turnbull and Lord, *History of United States Naval Aviation*, passim. The material on World War I in this volume is based to a considerable extent on Lord's manuscript administrative history. A recent book on naval aviation in World War I entitled *Naval Aviation in the First World War* by R. D. Layman has very little on U.S. naval aviation.

55. Taylor, *The Magnificent Mitscher*, 17; Rossano, *The Price of Honor*, 40; biographical sketch of Whiting in OA; *United States Naval Air Station Killingholme*.

56. Turnbull and Lord, *History of United States Naval Aviation*, 145; see also ibid., 120–21; Sims testimony, *Naval Investigation*, 128; Lord, "History of Naval Aviation," NDL. For the development of air stations, see chapters 5 and 6. This includes Whiting's plan.

57. Van Wyen, *Naval Aviation in World War I*, 12. See also entry for Dec. 17–22, 1917, in Sheely, *Sailor of the Air*; Sheely to Laura and Alice, April 10, 1918, ibid., 117; Moseley, *Extracts from Letters*, 147–50; Cunningham, "Report of an Aviator's Observation Trip to France and England," Jan. 1918, 1–3, Marine Corps Historical Center; Lord, "History of Naval Aviation," NDL.

58. For Callan, see Shirley, "John Lansing Callan—Naval Aviation Pioneer," 80–85.

59. Meals, "The American Station at Dunkirk," 13–14; Cagle, "A Caravan of Thieves," 24;

MacLeish to "Dearest Ones," May 6, 1918, in Rossano, *The Price of Honor*, 155–56; Progress Report, U.S. Naval Aviation Service, March 15, 1918, microfilm; NDL; Ashton W. Hardison letter to author, March, 1920, quoted in Chase, *Benjamin Lee, 2d*, 327–29; interview with Joseph A. Eaton, ACC #887072, OA. For technical information and a list by serial number of each aircraft flown in European waters, see "Naval Aviation Overseas, 1917–1918," copy in OA. The list includes which ones were wrecked, and so forth.

60. "U.S. Naval Air Station Arcachon," in ZPA subj file, RG45; Paine, *The First Yale Unit*, 24; Lord, "History of Naval Aviation," NDL; H. B. Miller, *Navy Wings*, 298–99; Cagle, "A Caravan of Thieves," 24–25; "History of U.S. Naval Aviation," NDL; Turnbull and Lord, *History of United States Naval Aviation*, 188; "History of U.S. Naval Air Station, Lough Foyle, Ireland," ZPA subj file, RG545; Roscoe, *On the Seas and in the Skies*, 94.

61. J. Harrison letter, n.d., in NHC, copy in author's possession; McKelvey, "Construction of the U.S. Naval Air Station L'Aber Vrach, France, World War I," OA; Van Wyen, *Naval Aviation in World War I*, 30; "World War I Diary Recounts Air/Sea Saga," in ibid., 46–47; H. B. Miller, *Navy Wings*, 235; "History of U.S. Naval Aviation," NDL; K. Hayes, *A History of the Royal Air Force and the United States Naval Air Service in Ireland*, 31, passim; Whitaker, "Flying Sailors," *Land and Water* 71 (May 2, 1918): 6; ibid. 72 (Oct. 17, 1918): 8.

62. For the history of these stations, see chapters 5 and 6.

63. Whitaker, "Flying Sailors," 12; B. Hayes, *Hull Down*, 228; *Flying Officers of the U.S. Navy*, 53–55; *American Legion Magazine*, Dec. 1929, 46; Maxfield to Cone, Aug. 17, 1918, GP subj file, RG45; memo of conference between Simsadus and Admiralty, Sept. 17, 1918, ibid.

64. Cone to Irwin, Sept. 24, 1918, TW subj file, RG45; Cone to Sims, Jan. 21, 1918, PP subj file, ibid.; Lord, "History of Naval Aviation," NDL; Sims to Dept., March 7, 1918, Reel 19, ME-11. See also Progress Report, U.S. Naval Aviation Foreign Service, March 15, 1918, microfilm, NDL.

65. Grossnick, *Kite Balloons to Airships*, 12, 14–16; K. Hayes, *A History of the Royal Air Force and United States Naval Air Service in Ireland*, 23–24, 29; Lord, "History of Naval Aviation," NDL; Spencer, "U.S. Naval Air Bases from 1914–1939," 1246; CO, U.S. Naval Air Stations Ireland to FDR, Jan. 27, 1919, ZPA subj file, RG45; establishment of kite balloons at Queenstown memo, June 22; Sept. 20, 1918, ADM137/1512; Cotten to Leigh, July 30, 1918, Cotten Papers, UNC-CH; "History of U.S. Naval Air Stations," n.d., ZPA subj file, RG45; memo, Admiralty Planning Division, March 15, 1918, in M. Simpson, *Anglo-American Naval Relations*, 157; M. Simpson, ibid., 203; memo, April 1, 1918, ibid., 290–91; Sims to Dept., July 3, 1917, ibid., 77–78. *ONI Monthly Bulletin* (Feb. 1919): 108; Gerken, *ASW versus Submarine Technology Battle*, 77; Murdock, *They Also Served*, 80–81; entry for July 9, 1918, Packer Diary, Packer MS, Churchill College; Rodman to Sims, Sept. 30, 1918, ZOB subj file, RG45; Corbett and Newbolt, *History of the Great War*, 5: 121.

66. Van Wyen, *Naval Aviation in World War I*, 77; "U.S. Naval Aviation Operations on the Coast of France," *ONI Monthly Bulletin* (May 15, 1919): 57; *The American Legion Magazine*, Dec. 1929, 46–49; entry for July 23, 1918, Latimer Journal; Grossnick, *Kite Balloons to Airships*, 14, 16.

67. "U.S. Naval Operations on the Coast of France," 48, 50. See also Lord in his "History of Naval Aviation," NDL. For Great Britain, see K. Hayes, *A History of the Royal Air Force and the United States Naval Air Service in Ireland*, 30–35. Van Wyen, in *Naval Aviation in World War I*, 76, concludes that U.S. naval aircraft made thirty attacks against German submarines of which ten were at least partially successful. Roscoe, in *On the Seas and in the Skies*, said that twenty-five attacks were made, eleven submarines damaged and one sunk (126). Josephus Daniels, in *The Wilson Era: Years of War*, claimed that two were sunk (122). See also Sitz, "A History of U.S. Naval Aviation," 32, NDL; History of the United States Naval Air Station, Wexford, Ireland, n.p., n.d., copy in the Mayo Papers; Stackhouse, "The Anglo-American Atlantic Convoy System in

World War I," Ph.D. diss., 396–400; Rose, *Brittany Patrol*, 218–20; 230–32; Winton, *Convoy*, 105.

68. Whiting to Sims, GP subj file, RG45. See also Lord, "History of Naval Aviation," NDL.

69. Cone to Sims, Oct. 6, 1917, GP subj file, RG45; Lord, "History of Naval Aviation," NDL. M. Simpson, *Anglo-American Naval Relations*, 65; see also memo of U.S. Naval Planning Section, London, Feb. 13, 1918, ibid., 156–57.

70. Price, *Aircraft versus Submarine*, 15; Kennett, *The First Air War*, 198–99.

71. Edwards, "The U.S. Naval Air Force in Action," 1864.

72. CO Richards memoirs, in author's possession. See also "History of the United States Naval Air Station, Ile-Tudy," copy in ZPA subj file, RG45; Sims, *The Victory at Sea*, 322; Rose, *Brittany Patrol*, 220–21, 230–32; Robert Mormon typed memoirs, in author's possession; Cagle, "A Caravan of Thieves," 25. For data on German submarines lost according to German records, see Grant, *U-Boat Intelligence*, 182–90.

73. Sheely, *Sailor of the Air*, 165.

74. For the development of the "Spider Web," see Gamble, *The Story of a North Sea Air Station*, 366–67; Price, *Aircraft versus Submarines*, 20–21; Terraine, *The U-Boat Wars*, 74–75; Grant, "Aircraft Against U-Boats," 824–25.

75. Gamble, *The Story of a North Sea Air Station*, 383–84, 388–91, 394–99; MacLeish to "Beloved," Feb. 25, 1918, in Rossano, *The Price of Honor*, 105–7; Sims, *The Victory at Sea*, 324–26.

76. Chase, *Benjamin Lee, 2d*, 327–29; interview with Joseph A. Eaton, copy in OA; Gamble, *The Story of a North Sea Air Station*, 392–93; Rear Admiral J. J. Schieffelin, "The Second Yale Unit," in Van Wyen, *Naval Aviation in World War I*, 58.

77. Admiralty memos, December 14, 1917, Jan. 24, July 6, 1918, ADM137/2241; Admiralty memos, June 20, July 7, 1918, ADM137/2706; Turnbull and Lord, *History of United States Naval Aviation*, 125–26; "Summary of U.S. Naval Activities in European Waters," Z file, OA; Admiralty memo Nov. 7, 1918, copy in Box 19, General Correspondence, U.S. Naval Forces Operating in European Waters, RG313; Sims to Dept., Aug. 14, 1918, Reel 5, ME-11; General Board Hearings, April 5, 1918; memo by U.S. Naval Planning Section in London, Feb. 15, 1918, in M. Simpson, *Anglo-American Naval Relations*, 156–57. R. D. Layman, in his recent book *Naval Aviation in the First World War* (190), refers to the lighter project as "grandiose."

78. Paine, *The First Yale Unit*, 80, 89, 298; Benson, Report of Conference, Nov. 12, 1917, Box 42, Benson Papers, LC; Lord, "History of Naval Aviation," NDL.

79. Cone to Irwin, Jan. 12, 1918, Box 104, Confidential Files, 1911–1919, RG80; *Flying Officers of the U.S.N.*, 24; Cunningham, "Report of Aviation Observation Trip, Jan. 1, 1918," microfilm, NDL, copy in the Marine Corps Historical Center; C. G. Reynolds, *Admiral John Tower*, 119; General Board Hearings, Jan. 24, 1918; Lord, "History of Naval Aviation," NDL.

80. MacLeish to family, March 24, April 11, 1918, in Rossano, *The Price of Honor*, 124–25, 137–38; Sheely to Lewis, Jan. 4, 1918, in Sheely, *Sailor of the Air*, 86–87. See also Davy's report on personnel, June 27, 1918, N subj file, RG45.

81. For MacLeish's experiences, see his letters of April 5, 11, 1918, in Rossano, *The Price of Honor*, 133–34, 137–38.

82. Cunningham, "Report of Aviation Observation Trip, Jan. 1, 1918, microfilm, NDL, copy in the Marine Corps Historical Center; *Marine Aviation in World War I, 1917–1918*, 15; H. B. Miller, *Navy Wings*, 263; Development of Northern Bombing Group, n.d., ZB subj file, RG45; General Board to SecNav, Feb. 26, 1918, Reel 3, ME-11; Lord, "History of Naval Aviation," NDL. This study is the most complete on the Northern Bombing project. See also Benson to Simsa-

dus, April 19, June 1, 1918, Reel 4, ME-11; Sims to Cone, May 17, 1918, ibid.; and Sims to Cone, June 4, 1918, Reel 20, ibid.; Cone to Simsadus, June 3, 1918, ibid.; Sims to SecNav, June 12, 1918, Reel 4, ibid.; Air Ministry to Admiralty, Aug. 13, 1918, in Roskill, *Documents Relating to the Naval Air Service*, 1: 699–700.

83. Cone to Wilson, May 22, 1918, GA subj file, RG45; Sims to Cone, June 5, 1918, Reel 4, ME-11; Cone to Sims, June 6, 1918, Reel 8, ibid.; Sims to Murray, June 12, 1918, in M. Simpson, *Anglo-American Naval Relations*, 161–62; Sims to Pratt, June 14, 1918, Pratt Papers, OA; Lord, "History of Naval Aviation," NDL; Progress Report, U.S. Naval Aviation, Foreign Service, Jan. 15, 1918, GA subj file, RG45.

84. Lord, "History of Naval Aviation," NDL; "Summary of U.S. Naval Activities in European Waters," Z file, OA; Daniels to SecWar, April, 4, 1918, Reel 4, ME-11; Davy's report on Personnel, June 27, 1918, N subj file, RG45.

85. "Summary of the Northern Bombing Group," n.d., ZGN subj file, RG45.

86. Sims to AMNSVPER, Paris, Nov. 4, 1918, Reel 8, ME-11; Naval attaché Paris to Benson, Oct. 25, 1918, ibid.; Sims to Dept., Aug. 25, 1918, ibid.; Sims to Wilson, Oct. 22, 1918, Reel 6, ibid.; Benson to Sims, Oct. 20, 1918, Reel 10, ibid.; Wilson to Sims, Aug. 17, 1918, Reel 9, ibid.; Lord, "History of Naval Aviation," NDL; *ONI Monthly Bulletin* (May 15, 1919): 137–41. For daily condition of aircraft in Northern Bombing Group, see the Message Book, U.S. Naval Aviation in Northern France, NHF.

87. Quoted in "Development of Northern Bombing Group," n.d., ZB subj file, RG45.

88. Grant, *U-Boat Intelligence*, 160–61. See also Turnbull and Lord, *History of United States Naval Aviation*, 136–39; Terraine, *The U-Boat Wars*, 125–26; Kennett, *The First Air War*, 198–99; Cone to Irwin, Sept. 24, 1918, GA subj file, RG45; Sims to Dept., Sept. 25, 1918, Reel 6, ME-11; Sims to SecNav, Sept. 26, 1918, ibid.; "Anglo-American Naval Policy," Sept. 27, 1918, in Roskill, *Documents Relating to the Naval Air Service*, 1: 734–36; "Notes on Proposed Agenda," Sept. 11, 1918, in M. Simpson, *Anglo-American Naval Relations*, 307–8; Lord, "History of Naval Aviation," NDL; Michelsen, "The Submarine Warfare," 68–69. For aircraft-subchaser tactics, see Cotten to CO, Royal Air Force, commanding No. 9, Sept. 14, 1918, OD subj file, RG45; Benson to Sims, Oct. 3, 1918, ibid.; CO Subchaser Detachment 3 to Sims, Nov. 30, 1918, OD subj file, ibid.; Cotten to C-in-C Plymouth, Aug. 19, 1918, ibid.; Admiralty to C-in-C Plymouth, July 15, 1918, ADM131/107.

89. April 7, 1918, in Rossano, *The Price of Honor*, 133–35.

90. Lord, "A History of Naval Aviation," NDL; Summary of U.S. Naval Activities in European Waters, Z file, OA; Roscoe, *On the Seas and in the Skies*, 124–26. The nineteen casualties do not include nine pilots killed while ferrying the Capronis from Italy to American airfields in France.

91. Following the Royal Navy's lead, the U.S. Navy was just beginning to place aircraft on warships. USS *Texas* with the Grand Fleet was equipped with aircraft shortly before the Armistice. Sims to CNO, Oct. 17, 1918, Box 6, RG19.

92. A detailed discussion of the report can be found in Lord, "History of Naval Aviation," NDL. See also Elliott Roosevelt, *F.D.R.: Personal Letters*, 436–37; Freidel, *FDR: The Apprenticeship*, 364–66; Roosevelt to Daniels, Oct. 16, 1918, Assistant SecNav Files, Box 46, FDR Library; Sims report to CNO, Aug. 24, 1918, Reel 5, ME-11; Roosevelt to Daniels, Aug. 18, 1918, Reel 10 ibid.

93. Halpern, *A Naval History of World War I*, 343.

94. Sims to Pringle, Oct. 23, 1917, Reel 10, ME-11; Sims to Benson, Oct. 16, 1917, ibid.; Mayo to Daniels, Sept. 8, 1917, in M. Simpson, *Anglo-American Naval Relations*, 103; Sims to Benson, July 30, 1917, ibid., 249.

95. Entry for Oct. 23, 1917, in Taussig, *The Queenstown Patrol*, 160. See Moore Oral History, Columbia University, for other comments; entry for Oct. 25, 1917, Merrill Journal, UNC-CH.

96. Entry for Oct. 23, 1917, in Taussig, *The Queenstown Patrol*, 160. See also biographical sketch in ZB files, NDL.

97. MacLeish to Beloved, Sept. 15, 1918, in Rossano, *The Price of Honor*, 215; Moore Oral History, Columbia University.

98. G. Campbell, *My Mystery Ships*, 220–21. See also Chatterton, *Q-Ships and Their Story*, 232; Sims, *The Victory at Sea*, 196; Wheeler Oral History, USNI; Sims to Dept., Nov. 1, 1917, OQ subj file, RG45.

99. Hanrahan's report, December 29, 1917, Reel 18, ME-11; Sims to wife, December 29, 1917, Box 9, Sims Papers, LC; Sims, *The Victory at Sea*, 197; Chatterton, *Q-Ships and Their Story*, 233; Zogbaum, *From Sail to Saratoga*, 261; Moore Oral History, Columbia University; Pringle to Sims, March 11, 1918, Box 79, Sims Papers, LC.

100. Copy of circular letter, Sept. 2, 1918, LA subj file, RG45. For analysis of ASW, see "Future Anti-Submarine Policy with Special Reference to Hunting Tactics," Oct. 30, 1918, ADM 137/2709; "Anti-submarine Warfare—Analysis of Methods of Attack," *ONI Monthly Bulletin* (March 15, 1919): 15; Crowell and Wilson, *The Road to France*, 2: 514–16; T. L. Hart, "Submarines," paper delivered at Naval War College, Oct. 28, 1919, in NWC; Bowling, "The Negative Influence of Mahan on the Protection of Shipping in Wartime," Ph.D. diss., 250–53.

Chapter 19. The Mediterranean

1. The best study of the war in the Mediterranean is Halpern, *Naval War in the Mediterranean*. See also Coletta, *Sea Power in the Atlantic and Mediterranean in World War I*.

2. Wilson to Sims, Aug. 20, 1917, P-Gibraltar subj file, RG45; Sims to Wilson, Aug. 10, 1917, ibid.

3. Cochran MS, Coast Guard Library.

4. Niblack, "Putting Cargos Across," ZCP subj file, RG45.

5. Niblack considered the Gibraltar command to be the highlight of his naval career and often wrote or spoke about it. See, for example, "Putting Cargos Across," copy in ZCP subj file, RG45; Niblack to Duncan, Oct. 15, 1919, NA subj file, RG45; "Gibraltar during the War," in *The Big U* (newsletter of USS *Utah*), Nov. 12, 1921, 2–3; address by Niblack in *Transactions of the Society of Naval Architects and Marine Engineers* 27 (1919): 323; and speech to English Speaking Union, Nov. 12, 1929, copy in WS subj file, RG45. For biographical sketches of Niblack, see C. G. Reynolds, *Famous Admirals*, 236–37; *DAB*, 7: 480–81. See also the Niblack papers in the Indiana Historical Society.

6. *Army and Navy Journal* 57 (Dec. 27, 1919): 524; *Our Navy* 13 (Oct. 1919): 22, Morison, *Sims*, 17; Zogbaum, *From Sail to Saratoga*, 346–57. Sims Papers, LC.

7. Sims to Niblack, July 15, Aug. 14, 1918, and Niblack to Sims, July 30, 1918, all in Box 24, Sims Papers, LC.

8. Niblack to Sims, Jan. 19, 1918, Box 76, Sims Papers, LC.

9. Sept. 3, 1918, Box 76, Sims Papers, LC.

10. Confidential note to Sims, n.d., Box 22, Sims Papers, LC.

11. Sims to Bullard, Sept. 19, 1918, Box 50, Sims Papers, LC; Bullard to Calthorpe, Oct. 23, 1918, NA subj file, RG45; Sims to Benson, Aug. 17, 1918, ibid.; to Benson, July 28, in M. Simpson, *Anglo-American Naval Relations*, 166–67; Benson to Bullard, Sept. 30, 1918, NA subj file, RG45S; Sims to Niblack, Sept. 1918, Box 24, Sims Papers, LC. In June, the American consul at Malta sent a message to the State Department urging this. June 28, 1918, file C20-234, Confidential Files, RG80.

12. Sims to Benson, March 28, 1918, OD subj file, RG45; Italian Naval Attaché to Sir Oswyn Murray and attached memo, Oct. 15 and 21, 1917, in Halpern, *The Royal Navy in the Mediterranean*, 284–85; Halpern, *Naval War in the Mediterranean*, 385–86.

13. Niblack to Sims, May 28, July 2, 1918, Box 76, Sims Papers, LC; Niblack to Sims, July 2,

and 29 Oct. 1918, ibid.; Niblack testimony, *Naval Investigation*, 1026–29. For Niblack's supposed anti-British views, see Sims to Mrs. Astor, Aug. 18, 1920, and to Mr. MacAfee, Aug. 18, 1920, both in Box 143, Sims Papers, LC.

14. Marder, *From the Dreadnought to Scapa Flow*, 1: 336. For a brief biographical sketch of Gauchet, see the entry under his name in Herwig and Heyman, *Biographical Dictionary of World War I*, 161.

15. Marder, *From the Dreadnought to Scapa Flow*, 4: 95. See also Maurice, *Lessons of Allied Co-Operation*, 176–77; and Wallach, *Uneasy Coalition*, 39–40.

16. Halpern, *The Royal Navy in the Mediterranean*, 210–11; Marder, *From the Dreadnought to Scapa Flow*, 4: 183.

17. Sims to Pratt, June 14, 1918, Pratt Papers, OA; Sims to Benson, April 20, 1918, Box 49, Sims Papers, LC; Trask, *Captains and Cabinets*, 186, 235–36; see also Parsons, *Wilsonian Diplomacy*, 83.

18. Quoted in Marder, *From the Dreadnought to Scapa Flow*, 5: 26. For Train's observation, see W. F. Bell, "American Embassies in Belligerent Europe," Ph.D. diss., 274.

19. Roskill, *Hankey: Man of Secrets*, 558; quote of Bliss in Petrie, *The Life and Letters of Austen Chamberlain*, 2: 122–23. See also Hardinge, *Old Diplomacy*, 227.

20. July 2, 1918, Box 76, Sims Papers, LC. For the Mediterranean command story, see Halpern, *Naval War in the Mediterranean*, passim.

21. To SecState, June 24, 1918, in *Foreign Relations, 1918*, Supplement 1, 264–65. See also Train to Sims, 25 June 1918, Box 88, Sims Papers, LC; Train to Sims, July 1, 1918, Reel 4, ME-11; Daniels to Sims, July 5, 1918, QQ subj file, RG45; Benson to Sims, Aug. 5, 1918, Reel 12, ME-11; entry for June 18, 1918, in Josephus Daniels, *Cabinet Diaries*, 312; see also Benson to SecState, June 20, 1918, 763.72/10605, in M367, Roll 96.

22. July 22, 1918, Box 15, Daniels Papers, LC.

23. Aug. 2, 1918 in M. Simpson, *Anglo-American Naval Relations*, 176.

24. Daniels to SecState, July 25, 1918, QQ subj file, RG45; Polk to Page, Aug. 1, 1918, Baker, *Wilson: Life and Letters*, 2: 310; *Foreign Relations, 1918*, Supplement 1, 1: 244–46, 295–96; Roosevelt to Daniels, Aug. 13, 1918, Box 15, Daniels Papers, LC; Roosevelt to Daniels, Oct. 16, 1918, Assistant SecNav Files, Box 46, FDR Library; entry for Sept. 5, 1918, in Josephus Daniels, *Cabinet Diaries*, 334; Ward, *A First-Class Temperament*, 390–91, 402–3; Josephus Daniels, *The Wilson Era: Years of War*, 264; entry for Aug. 11, 1918, in Elliott Roosevelt, *F.D.R.: Personal Letters*, 434–35; Trask, *Captains and Cabinets*, 268–69; Halpern, *Naval War in the Mediterranean*, 527–31; Freidel, *FDR: The Apprenticeship*, 350–51, 362–64.

25. Wayne to parents, Nov. 1917, Duffett Papers, Emil Buehler Naval Aviation Library; Pye testimony, General Board Hearings, Oct. 19, 1917. See also entry for Nov. 20, 1917, in Josephus Daniels, *Cabinet Diaries*, 239.

26. Sims to Dept., July 31, 1918, TT subj file, RG45; Benson to Sims, Nov. 20, 1917, Reel 12, ME-11; Sims to Benson, Feb. 15, 1918, file 220, Box 120, CNO Planning Division files, RG80; Memo, naval conf. 1917, Box 42, Benson Papers, LC; Memorandum by Italian representative, Allied Naval Council, Aug. 27, 1918, OC subj file, RG45; Train to Sims, May 11, 1918, Reel 12, ME-11; Sims to Train, May 23, 1918, TT subj file, RG45; Parsons, *Wilsonian Diplomacy*, 87, 94–95; Schoultz, *With the British Battle Fleet*, 295; Zivojinovic, *America, Italy, and the Birth of Yugoslavia*, 9–14, 119–20, Sims to Dept., March 26, 1918, Reel 12, ME-11; Trask, *Captains and Cabinets*, 229–33, 250, 256; M. Simpson, *Anglo-American Naval Relations*, 397–98; Navy Dept., *The American Naval Planning Section in London* 77; Halpern, *Naval War in the Mediterranean*, 401, 406–8; Coletta, *Sea Power in the Atlantic and Mediterranean in World War I*, 116–17.

27. Shirley, "John Lansing Callan—Naval Aviation Pioneer," 180–83. For the Italian request, see U.S. Naval Forces in Europe, History of Headquarters, Rome, Italy, ZGU subj file, RG45.

28. Train to Dept., Feb. 10, 1918, Reel 12, ME-11.

29. Benson to Sims, Feb. 18, 1918, Reel 3, ME-11; to Sims, March 16, 1918, Reel 12, ME-11; Lord, "History of Naval Aviation," NDL.

30. Lord, "History of Naval Aviation," NDL. See also the John L. Callan Papers in the Library of Congress for extensive correspondence concerning U.S. naval aviation in Italy.

31. Naval Air Station, Bolsena, Monthly Reports, PA subj file, RG45; von Doenhoff, "U.S. Naval Aviation in Europe during World War I," 225–29; Wayne to Norman and Winona, March 27, 1918, Duffett Papers, Emil Buehler Naval Aviation Library; Sitz, "A History of U.S. Naval Aviation," NDL.

32. *Flying Officers of the U.S. Navy*, 34.

33. Coletta and Bauer, "World War I U.S. Naval Air Stations in Europe," in Coletta and Bauer, *Bases, Overseas*, 373.

34. von Doenhoff, "U.S. Naval Aviation in Europe during World War I," 227. For the official account of the dogfight, see Naval Air Station, Porto Corsini, Weekly Report of Operations, 30 July 1918, PA subj file, RG45. See also H. B. Miller, *Navy Wings*, 245–47.

35. Bradford, *Gibraltar: The History of a Fortress*, 177; Josephus Daniels, *Our Navy at War*, 116. See also Dennis, *Gibraltar, the British Rock*, 86–87.

36. Report, Feb. 4, 1919, ADM137/1574.

37. For British reluctance, see Braisted, *The United States Navy in the Pacific*, 411.

38. De Chair to Admiralty, June 7, 1917, in M. Simpson, *Anglo-American Naval Relations*, 48; American Consul, Genoa to State Dept., June 25, 1917, file 20: 39, Box 54, Confidential Files, RG80; Pratt to Sims, July 2, 1917, copy in *Naval Investigation*, 1514; Mayo's letter of instruction, July 17, 1917, Reel 13, ME-11; Murray to Sen. officer, Gib., Aug. 19, 1917, Reel 3, ibid.; Grant to Admiralty, Aug. 20, 1917, copy in Reel 12, ibid.; Grant to Admiralty, Aug. 7, 1917, Reel 2, ibid. Admiralty to Sims, Sept. 20, 1917, P-Gibraltar subj file, RG45; Wilson to Sims, Aug. 20, 1917, Reel 12, ibid.; Wilson to Sims, Aug. 20, 1917, P-Gibraltar subj file, RG45; Ensign G. Chardenot, French liaison officer at Gibraltar, to Director General of the Anti-Submarine War, Aug. 28, 1917, French Naval Archives, Vincennes; Sims to Wilson, Sept. 5, 1917, P-Bases, RG45.

39. For these vessels, see chapter 13 on convoying in the Atlantic.

40. Falls, *The Great War*, 295. See also Corbett and Newbolt, *History of the Great War*, 5: 161.

41. Winton, *Convoy*, 94; Marder, *From the Dreadnought to Scapa Flow*, 4: 119; Bowling, "Convoy in World War I," master's thesis, 174.

42. May, "Convoy Sloop," 132.

43. Testimony of Niblack, *Naval Investigation*, 1029; Roper to Niblack, May 1, 1918, Reel 40, M1140.

44. For Admiralty instructions and writings on the introduction of Mediterranean convoys, see ADM137/2664; Confidential Memo, Sept. 20, 1917, ADM131/98. See also Winton, *Convoy*, 92–99; Halpern, *Naval War in the Mediterranean*, 386–87, 397; Corbett and Newbolt, *History of the Great War*, 5: 298; Kerr, *The Navy in My Time*, 206; Elliott, *The Cross and the Ensign*, 74.

45. Unknown seaman diary, entry for Sept. 18, 1917, JOD/198, NMM.

46. Niblack to Sims, May 28, 1918, Box 76, Sims Papers, LC: "Attack on Enemy Submarine by USS *Venetia*," May 11, 1918, OS subj file, RG45; CO *Venetia* to Niblack, July 28, 1918, OS subj file, RG45.

47. To Force CO June 2, 1918, CM subj file, RG45. See also Niblack test. *Naval Investigation*, 2802; Sims to Dept., Feb. 27, 1918, Reel 19, ME-11; Sims to Dept., Jan. 27, 1918, Reel 3, ibid.; Niblack to Sims, Jan. 19, 1918, Box 76, Sims Papers, LC; Niblack to Sims, Jan. 3, 1918, CK subj file, RG45; Grant to Admiralty, Aug. 10, 1917, copy in Reel 12, ME-11; Wilson to Sims, Aug. 25, 1917, ibid.; Wilson to Sims, Aug. 23, 1917, OF subj file, RG45; Sims to Dept., Nov. 20, 1917, OR subj file, RG45; Jellicoe to Wemyss, Dec. 2, 1917, in Halpern, *The Royal Navy in the Mediterranean*, 296; Halpern, *Naval War in the Mediterranean*, 214. See also Corbett and Newbolt, *History of*

the Great War, 5: 76. For Sims's response, see to CO *Marietta*, July 10, 1918, OF subj file, RG45; to Niblack, July 11, 1918, Reel 9, ME-11.

48. Niblack to Sims, March 29, June 21, 1918, Box 76, Sims Papers, LC; July 29, 1918, P-Gibraltar subj file, RG45; Halpern, *Naval War in the Mediterranean*, 446.

49. Cochran MS, Coast Guard Library; Whitaker, "The Mediterranean: The Last Stand of the Submarine," 50–51.

50. Niblack to Sims, Jan. 19, 1918, Box 76, Sims Papers, LC; *Naval Investigation*, 1029; Yamew, "Mediterranean Convoys," 242. For Grant's report, see to Admiralty, December 25, 1917, ADM 137/759.

51. C-in-C Fleet Commander to the commanders of U-boats in the Mediterranean, July 16, 1917, in Walton, *Over There*, 107.

52. To Simsadus, Reel 12, ME-11.

53. Sims to Niblack, Jan. 14, 1918, Reel 12, ME-11; Niblack to Sims, Jan. 31, Feb. 8, 1918, ibid., Godfrey to Henderson, Jan. 9, 1918, in Halpern, *The Royal Navy in the Mediterranean*, 364–65.

54. Niblack, "Putting Cargos Across," in ZCP subj file, RG45.

55. Entry for March 24, 1918, Quinn Diary, Duke University; Royall MS, Coast Guard Library; Speicher, "Some Experiences with Mediterranean Convoys during the World War," AMHI; entry for Oct. 25, 1918, Marek Diary, Virginia War History Commission Archives, Virginia State Library; C. V. Whited, Journal while on *Sacramento*, in Marie M. Wilson Collection, Smithsonian; Bellitteri, "Cruise of the U.S.S. *Chester* in European Waters, 1917–1918," Bellitteri Papers, ECU; French route officer to Grant, March 28, 1918, and letter from CO *Surveyor*, same date in ADM137/2176; Niblack to Force Commander, March 7, 1918, Reel 3, ME-11. For Admiralty orders concerning the use of Spanish waters, see memo "convoy Mediterranean 1918," in ADM137/2176, and Sims to SecNav, Feb. 19, 1918, Reel 12, ME-11.

56. "Genoa convoys," n.d., in CM subj file, RG45. This file contains considerable correspondence and reports on the convoy system in the Mediterranean, ASW policies and problems.

57. Niblack to Sims, July 29, 1918, P-Gibraltar subj file, bases, RG45; Sims to Dept., June 4, 1918, Reel 4, ME-11; Niblack to Sims, Sept. 13, 1918, Reel 10, ibid.; Sims to Dept., June 12, 1918, Reel 20, ibid.; Niblack to Sims, May 28, 1918, Box 76, Sims Papers, LC; Grant to Admiralty, July 22, 1918, and attachments, ADM137/760.

58. Niblack to Sims, OR subj file, RG45.

59. Quoted in Whitaker, "The Mediterranean: The Last Stand of the Submarine," 50.

60. T. Wilson, *The Myriad Faces of War*, 632; Trask, *Captains and Cabinets*, 226, 235.

61. Sims to Dept., Aug. 14, 1918, Reel 6, ME-11. See also Benson to Simsadus, June 9, Sims to Dept., June 12, 1918, Reel 4, ibid.

62. To Geddes, Sept. 4, 1918, in Halpern, *The Royal Navy in the Mediterranean*, 541. See also Pershing to Biddle, May 5, 1918, copy in Reel 20, ME-11; Pershing to Sims, May 17, 1918, Reel 12, ibid.; Sims to Pershing, March 9, 1918, CP subj file, RG45; Pershing to Sims, May 6, 1918, CP subj file, RG45; Sims to Dept. May 29, 1918, CP subj file, RG45; Sims to Dept., May 23, 1918, TV subj file, RG45; Halpern, *Naval War in the Mediterranean*, 514–15.

63. Niblack to Sims, July 11, 1918, Reel 12, ME-11; Adm to British C-in-C Mediterranean, July 14, 1918, Reel 12, ibid.; Sims to Niblack, July 14, 1981, ibid., Sims to Niblack, July 11, 1918, Reel 9, ibid.; Sims to Dept., Aug. 14, 1918, Reel 9, ibid.; Niblack to Sims, Oct. 18, 1918, Box 24, Sims Papers, LC; Sims to Admiralty, Sept.14, 1918, with comments, ADM137/760; "Mediterranean Convoys," Sept. 1914, ADM137/2176. See also Wilson to Sims, Sept. 1, 1918, Reel 12, ME-11; Baldwin to Wilson, Sept. 4, 1918, ibid.; Sims to Wilson, July 2, 1918, Reel 4, ME-11.

64. Sims to Niblack, May 23, 1918, in M. Simpson, *Anglo-American Naval Relations*, 413.

65. Entries for Nov. 2–9, 1918, Marek Diary, Virginia War History Commission Archives, Virginia State Library; Sims to Pringle, May 11, 15, 1918, OD subj file, RG45; to Dept., May 15, 1918, Reel 12, ME-11; Sims to Pringle, May 18, 1918, Box 79, Sims Papers, LC; Sims to Niblack,

May 23, Box 76, ibid.; Sims to Bayly, May 17, 1918, TP subj file, RG45; Sims to AMNAVPAR, Paris, Oct. 31, 1918, Reel 6, ME-11; Sims to Niblack, Nov. 6, 1918, OD subj file, RG45; Phillips to Force CO, Nov. 9, 1918, OD subj file, RG45; C.O. Subchaser unit C, Nov. 12, 1918, Reel 19, ME-11; CO Subchaser No. 331 to CO Special Submarine Chaser Detachment, Nov. 13, 1918, Reel 10, ibid.; Niblack to Sims, Oct. 29, 1918, Box 24, Sims Papers, LC; Niblack to Sims, Nov. 13, 1918, ibid.; CO Special Submarine Chaser Detachment to Force CO, Nov. 18, 1918, ibid.; Parker Oral History, Columbia University; Grant to Calthorpe, Nov. 27, 1918, ADM137/760; Niblack, "Putting Cargos Across," copy in ZCP subj file, RG45; Raguet, "United States Submarine Chasers at Gibraltar"; Nutting, *The Cinderellas of the Fleet*, 91–92; Chambers, *Submarine Chasers in the Mediterranean*, 28–30; Corbett and Newbolt, *History of the Great War*, 5: 859. For the Brazilian squadron, see documents in ADM137/1790.

66. Sokol, *The Imperial and Royal Austro-Hungarian Navy*, 120

67. Kerr, *The Navy in My Time*, 193; Marder, *From the Dreadnought to Scapa Flow*, 4: 262; Halpern, *Naval War in the Mediterranean*, 391–92; Bowling, "The Negative Influence of Mahan on the Protection of Shipping in Wartime," Ph.D. diss., 228. After the war, Calthorpe admitted that too much reliance was placed on the Otranto Barrage. See Marder, *From the Dreadnought to Scapa Flow*, 5: 36

68. Gibson and Prendergast, *The German Submarine War*, 246–47, 279; Halpern, *A Naval History of World War I*, 399. For the construction and evolution of the barrage, see Chrisman, "Naval Operations in the Mediterranean during the Great War," Ph.D. diss., 431–54, and Gould, "Submarine Warfare in the Adriatic."

69. Memorandum No. 9, Adriatic Situation, 30 Jan. 1918, in Navy Dept., *The American Naval Planning Section in London*, 59–77. The best accounts of the American proposal and its subsequent history are Halpern, *Naval War in the Mediterranean*, 434–41, 463–76; Trask, *Captains and Cabinets*, 240–51. See also Zivojinovic, *America, Italy, and the Birth of Yugoslavia*, 118–22. For Italian reaction, see Po, *Il grande ammiraglio Paolo Thaon di Revel*, 275–77.

70. Although Sir Herbert Richmond did not enter the Admiralty until April 1918, he had long favored amphibious operations in the Adriatic and in fact as early as September 1917 had suggested, "The Americans might manage it." His opinions were well known by Admiralty officials, and many favored them. Entry for Sept. 22, 1917, in Marder, *Portrait of an Admiral*, 273–74; Richmond to Keyes, Feb. 18, 1918, Halpern, *The Keyes Papers*, 1: 454–55; Marder, *From the Dreadnought to Scapa Flow*, 5: 306–7.

71. Trask, *Captains and Cabinets*, 240.

72. Sims to Dept., Feb. 14, 1918, Reel 12, ME-11; Sims to Wemyss, March 10, 1918, Box 23, Sims Papers, LC.

73. Memo for CNO, n.d., file 219-220-10, Office of Secretary and CNO correspondence, RG80

74. Halpern, *Naval War in the Mediterranean*, 436–38; Corbett and Newbolt, *History of the Great War*, 5: 298.

75. Sims to Dept., April 19, 1918, Reel 12, ME-11. See the series of documents in M. Simpson, *Anglo-American Naval Relations*, 409–11; Halpern, *Naval War in the Mediterranean*, 441. See also Trask, *Captains and Cabinets*, 246–47; Po, *Il grande ammiraglio Paolo Thaon di Revel*, 207–8; Ginocchietti, *La guerra sul mare*, 148–53.

76. Reel 4, ME-11.

77. Yarnell to Pratt, Sept.13, 1918, with attachment, Reel 64, M1140; Scott to CNO (War Plans Section), Nov. 9, 1921, ibid.

78. May 24, 1918, Reel 12, ME-11.

79. ADM memo, Jan. 22, 1918, Halpern, *The Royal Navy in the Mediterranean*, 372; Navy Dept., *American Naval Planning Section in London*, 74, passim; Benson to Sims, May 24, 1918, Reel 12; Sims to Dept., June 10, 1918, Reel 4, ME-11; entry for May 25, 1918, in Josephus Daniels,

Cabinet Diaries, 1918, 306; Halpern, *Naval War in the Mediterranean*, 508–9, Trask, *Captains and Cabinets*, 278–79. Detailed information on Mediterranean mining barrage proposals is found in QM file, subj. file, RG45.

80. Benson to Sims, Sept. 4, 1918, Reel 12, ME-11; Sims to Dept., May 6, 1918, Reel 12, ibid.; Admiralty to C-in-C Med., July 25, 1918, copy in Reel 4; Sims to C-in-C, Inverness, April 23, 1918, QM subj file, RG45; Sims to Dept., Sept. 1, 1918, Reel 12, ibid.; Strauss to Earle, 22 Aug. 1918, ibid.; Benson to Sims, Sept. 10, 1918, Reel 12, ibid.; Sims to Strauss, July, 1918, in M. Simpson, *Anglo-American Naval Relations*, 420–21; Sims to Dept., July 26, 1918, in ibid., 421–23; Godfrey to Ruck-Keene, July 31, 1918, in Halpern, *The Royal Navy in the Mediterranean*, 322–23; Calthorpe to Admiralty, Aug. 15, 1918, ibid., 528–29; Sims to Strauss, Aug. 3, 1918, QM file subj file, RG45; Strauss to Sims, Aug. 9, 1918, ibid.; Adm. Earle, Chief of BuOrd, to CNO, Aug. 4, 1918, CNO correspondence, 219-1 to 220-10, RG80; Dept. to Sims, Aug. 22, 1918, Reel 105, M1140; Strauss to Sims, Sept. 10, 1918, ibid.; Strauss, "Recollections," OA; Sims to CNO, Aug. 22, 1918, QM subj file, RG45; Marder, *From the Dreadnought to Scapa Flow*, 5: 35; Report of Proceedings of Allied Naval Council, Sept. 13–14, 1918, QC subj files, RG45; Sims to Benson, Oct. 15, 1918, AM subj file, RG45; Halpern, *Naval War in the Mediterranean*, 518–21. See also Daniels to Sec-State, Oct. 25, 1918, file 763.11896, M367; Dewar, *The Navy from Within*, 246–47.

81. ADM to C-in-C and reply, Sept. 15, 1918, ADM137/1984; Strauss, "Recollections," OA; Halpern, *Naval War in the Mediterranean*, 520.

82. Minutes by Captain Pound, Feb. 19, 1918, in M. Simpson, *Anglo-American Naval Relations*, 408–9; Leigh memoirs, "Whereas," FSU; Trask, *Captains and Cabinets*, 274–75.

83. To Admiralty, July 14, 1918, in Halpern, *The Royal Navy in the Mediterranean*, 510–11.

84. Sims to CNO, March 28, 1918, OD subj file, RG45; Murray to Sims, March 25, 1918, in M. Simpson, *Anglo-American Naval Relations*, 278–79; Trask, *Captains and Cabinets*, 275.

85. Sims to Murray, March 28, 1918, in M. Simpson, *Anglo-American Naval Relations*, 279–80; Wemyss to Secretary of Admiralty, April 13, 1918, OR subj file, RG45; Leigh to Force CO, April 17, 1918, Logistics file, RG45; Leigh to Tompkins, April 16, 1918, ibid.; Sims to CNO, April 16, 1918, OD subj file, RG45; Leigh memoirs, "Whereas," FSU; Usborne, *Blast and Counterblast*, 236; Senior British naval officer, Corfu to C-in-C Adriatic, June 15, 1918, ADM116/1650.

86. Leigh to Sims, April 17, 1918, Logistics file, RG45; ADM to Sims, March 16, 1918, OD subj file, RG45; Leigh to Tompkins, April 16, 1918, ibid.; Sims to CNO, April 16, 1918, OD subj file, RG45; Leigh memoirs, "Whereas," FSU; Sims to Aluana, Rome, May 6, 1918, Reel 12, ME-12; Spafford to Simsadus, May 18, 1918, ibid.; Sims to Leigh, May 31, 1918, ibid. Base 25 Report from conception to June 30, in P-Corfu subj file, RG45.

87. Entry for May 17, 1918, Kipp Diary, extracts in possession of author; Niblack to Sims, May 21, 1918, Reel 12, ME-11. See also Niblack to Sims, May 18, 1918, ibid.; Sims to Niblack, May 19, 1918, ibid.; Niblack to Sims, May 20, 1918, ibid.; Sims to Benson, Box 25, file C-3-1017, Confidential Files, RG80. For building the base, see chapter 5.

88. Chambers, *Submarine Chasers in the Mediterranean*, 36–37.

89. Sims to Italian government, May 5, 1918, OD subj file, RG45; Halpern, *Naval War in the Mediterranean*, 443; Chambers, *Submarine Chasers in the Mediterranean*, 33–37; Leigh memoirs, "Whereas," FSU; Niblack to Sims, May 14, 1918, Reel 12, ME-11; Calthorpe to Geddes, June 5, 1918, in M. Simpson, *Anglo-American Naval Relations*, 298; Keblinger to SecState, June 5, 1918, OS subj file, RG45.

90. Sims, *The Victory at Sea*, 214–15. See also R. W. Campbell, *Honor*, 56–57; CO Submarine Chasers, Distant Service, to Sims, July 1, 1918, copy in RG143. Loftin, "Subchasing at Otranto," 228; Usborne, *Blast and Counterblast*, 212–14.

91. Roussin questionnaire, WWI Research Collection, AMHI; Shaw, "Sanitary Report on the Island of Corfu"; Leigh memoirs, "Whereas," FSU; *Daily Mail*, Nov. 8, 1918.

92. For a similar recollection, see Roussin questionnaire, WWI Research Collection, AMHI.

93. Nelson to Sims, Sept. 28, 1918, Logistics file, RG45; Loftin, "Subchasing at Otranto," 231; Chambers, *Submarine Chasers in the Mediterranean*, 60–61; Leigh memoirs, "Whereas," FSU.

94. Chambers, *Submarine Chasers in the Mediterranean*, 41–42, 44–45; *Fleet Review* 10 (Sept. 1919), 24; Operation order for the Otranto Barrage, June 19, 1918, Reel 12, ME-11; Loftin, "Subchasing at Otranto," 230–31. See also Navy Dept., *The American Naval Planning Section in London*, 252–53; and Nutting, *The Cinderellas of the Fleet*, 99–101. For additional information on subchaser tactics, see the section on subchasers in chapter 12. The detailed reports of operations by the subchasers on the Otranto Barrage can be found in the OR subj file, RG45.

95. For this incident, see Mannix, *The Old Navy*, 49; W. H. Miller, *The Boys of 1917*, 129; and Usborne, *Blast and Counterblast*, 237.

96. Bassler, "Nelson," 29–30; Lockwood, *Down to the Sea in Subs*, 79; Oman, *Doctors Aweigh*, 205–6; biographical sketch in ZB files, NDL.

97. Sims, *The Victory at Sea*, 228–29; Groszman, "Reminiscences of Durazzo," 5. See also Loftin, "Subchasing at Otranto," Simons, "Both by Land and by Sea," MS, NDL; Moffat, *Maverick Navy*, 58–59; Milholland, *The Splinter Fleet*; Coffman, *The War to End All Wars*, 116–17. Lord Methuen, governor of Malta, described Nelson as "a fine fellow, with a great sense of humor." Anderson to Page, June 24, 1918, London Embassy Record 810/40, RG84. Secretary Daniels, in his various accounts of World War I, does not mention Nelson in command of the subchasers at Corfu. In *The Wilson Era: Years of War*, he writes that Leigh was in command (114). Daniels's slight may be attributed to the fact that Nelson was not the kind of officer he approved of. Commodore Kelly, the British commander-in-chief in the Adriatic, was not initially favorably impressed with Nelson, although he was to admire him in time. According to Leigh, Kelly considered him tactless and too fond of alcoholic beverages. See Usborn, *Blasts and Counterblasts*, 238–39; Leigh memoirs, "Whereas," FSU; Moffat, *Maverick Navy*, 238.

98. July 24, 1918, Reel 4, ME-11; Leigh to Sims, June 17, 1918, P-Corfu subj file, RG45.

99. Leigh memoirs, "Whereas," FSU; See also Sims to Nelson, Oct. 3, 1918, Reel 12, Me-11; Leigh to Sims, June 17, 1918, ibid.; Leigh to Sims, June 18, ibid.; Leigh to Sims, June 26, ibid.; July 4, ibid.; Nelson to Sims, Oct. 21, 18, ibid.; Leigh to Sims, July 1, 1918, ibid.; Sims to Benson, Aug. 16, 1918, Reel 5, ibid.

100. Loftin, "Subchasing at Otranto," 232; Leigh, "Whereas," FSU; Nutting, *The Cinderellas of the Fleet*, 103–4; Leigh to Sims, June 19, 1918, OD subj file, RG45.

101. Niemoller, *From U-Boat to Pulpit*, 106–8; Usborne, "The Anti-Submarine Campaign in the Mediterranean Subsequent to 1916," 439.

102. Halpern, *A Naval History of World War I*, 399; Usborne, *Blast and Counterblast*, 238; Leighton, *Simsadus*, 80. See also Shaw, *Knocking Around*, 314, for a British naval officer's assessment of American success on the barrage.

103. Kipp Journal, entry for July 23, 1918; *Our Navy* 12 (Aug. 1919): 62; Nutting, *The Cinderellas of the Fleet*, 101; Chambers, *Submarine Chasers in the Mediterranean*, 5152; Groszman, "Reminiscences of Durazzo," 7–8.

104. Entry for Aug. 24, 1918, Kipp Journal, extracts in possession of author.

105. Lt. Cdr. P. H. Bastedo, "Draft of Remarks on [Battle of Durazzo]," in OR subj file, RG45; Chambers, *Submarine Chasers in the Mediterranean*, 68–70; Jacoby, "How It Feels to Sink a Submarine," 19; "Bombarding Durazzo"; Nutting, *The Cinderellas of the Fleet*, 105.

106. Bastedo MS, OR subj file, RG45.

107. Chambers, *Submarine Chasers in the Mediterranean*, 75–76.

108. See Groszman, "Grand Work by the 110's," 519. There is considerable documentary information on this operation in OR subj file, RG45. It includes not only the American reports

but many Allied reports as well. For the British official report, see Kelly to Admiralty, Oct. 4, 1918, ADM137/2185. See also Manfroni, *Storia della marine Italiana, 1914–18*, 348–52; and Vicoli, *L'Azione navale di Durazzo*. See the appendix in Vicoli's work for reports of the units involved.

109. Breck to Sims, March 5, and Sims to Breck, April 10, 1922 in Box 50, Sims Papers, LC; ONI to Baer, Oct. 17, 1929; Durrigli (CO *U-29*) to Baer, May 22, 1930, and Baer to Simpson, Aug. 7, 1930, all in OR subj file, RG45. These letters insist that only one submarine was in action with the chasers, but two submarines were in the area, and the chasers were firing at anything that looked like a periscope. See also Sokol, *The Imperial Austrian and Hungarian Navy*, 135–36; and Sondhaus, *The Naval Policy of Austria-Hungary*, 136. In 1926, a former officer in the Austrian navy wrote to Admiral Keyes: "I just read Adm. Sims book on *The Victory at Sea*. . . . The American successes he claims in the Adriatic are absolute lies. . . . We hardly knew the presence of the Americans." Heyssler to Keyes, Dec. 21, 1926, in Halpern, *The Keyes Papers*, 2: 198–99.

110. Heyssler to Keyes, Dec. 21, 1926, in Halpern, *The Keyes Papers*, 2: 198–99.

111. See for example, *New York Times*, Oct. 4, 5, 6, 7, 12, 1918.

112. Heyssler to Keyes, Dec. 21, 1926, in Halpern, *The Keyes Papers*, 2: 198.

113. Sims to Benson, May 13, 1918, Reel 12, ME-11; undated memo, Box 42, Benson Papers, LC; Memo, "The Adriatic," May 16, 1918, in Navy Dept., *The American Naval Planning Section in London*, 224; Calthorpe to Admiralty, April 3, 1918; Lambert to Geddes, March 4, 1918; Geddes to Lloyd George and enclosure, April 6, 1918; Lambert to Calthorpe, April 14, 1918; Geddes to Lambert, April 15, 1918, all in Halpern, *The Royal Navy in the Mediterranean*, 429–45; Trask, *Captains and Cabinets*, 258–59; Halpern, *Naval War in the Mediterranean*, 458–59, 476–77, 480.

114. Kelley to Sims, July 18, 1918, Box 24; Sims to Kelley, July 24, 1918, both in Box 24, Sims Papers, LC; Leigh to Sims, July 3, 1918, Reel 12, ME-11; Sims to Naval attaché, Rome, Sept. 4, 1918, OD subj file, RG45.

115. Nelson to Sims, Oct. 19, 1918, P-Corfu subj file, RG45; Sims to Nelson, Oct. 22, 1918, Reel 6, ME-11; to Bulloch (at Malta), Oct. 22, 1918, Reel 12, ibid.

116. Sims to Dept., Nov. 3, 1918, WJ subj file, RG45. See also Roskill, *Hankey, Man of Secrets*, 626.

117. See, for example, Terraine, *The U-Boat War*, 115–16; T. Wilson, *The Myriad Faces of War*, 632; Halpern, *A Naval History of World War I*, 399; and Marder, *From the Dreadnought to Scapa Flow*, 5: 35–36; Trask, *Captains and Cabinets*, 281.

118. Niblack, "Putting Cargos Across," ZCP subj file, RG45; Winton, *Convoy*, 114.

119. Halpern, *Naval War in the Mediterranean*, 580; T. Wilson, *The Myriad Faces of War*, 633.

120. Sept. 4, 1918, UP subj file, RG45. See also Sims to Chief of Staff, DD flotillas, Logistics file, Box 7, RG45. A copy of the analysis of American naval presence in the Mediterranean dated November 1918 is in M. Simpson, *Anglo-American Naval Relations*, 429–34. Daniels wrote that the U.S. Navy in the Mediterranean furnished an average of 50 percent of the escort. See *Our Navy at War*, 122.

Chapter 20. The Eleventh Hour of the Eleventh Day of the Eleventh Month: The Armistice

1. Quoted in Marder, *From the Dreadnought to Scapa Flow*, 5: 169.

2. See, for example, James, *A Great Seaman*, 164.

3. Seldes, *Tell the Truth and Run*, 55.

4. The best account of the False Armistice is Weintraub, *A Stillness Heard Round the World*, 13–40. However, he ignores Great Britain. See also Toland, *No Man's Land*, 416–17; Crozier, *American Reporters on the Western Front*, 262–65.

5. Weintraub, *A Stillness Heard Round the World*, 39.

6. Wilson to Daniels, Jan. 1, 1934, copy in a number of documents together entitled "The False Armistice," located in OA. These documents, collected by Wilson, include letters from several of his subordinates as well as correspondence to and from Daniels, copies of articles written on the incident, and comments by the admiral himself on the incident.

7. Wilson's comments in his letter to Daniels cited above. Moreau's communication dated Nov. 8, 1918, in the French Naval Archives, Vincennes. See also entries for Nov. 13, 14, 1918, Brown Journal, WisHistSoc. Rumors among the Brest sailors were that "Wilson is in bad" and had asked to be relieved.

8. See 338–43. See also Sims to wife, Dec. 19, 1918, Box 10, Sims Papers, LC.

9. *American Legion Magazine*, March 1939, 60. Entry for Nov. 14, 1918, Brown Journal, Brown Papers, WisHistSoc; P to Jessie, Nov. 13, 1918, Post MS, LSU; Wheat, "The 'Sacred Drunk' of Brest When the War Was Over"; entry for Nov. 12, 1918, in Battey, *70,000 Miles on a Submarine Destroyer*, 236; entry for Nov. 13, 1918, Kurfess Diary, OA; Weintraub, *A Stillness Heard Round the World*, 244–45; autobiography of W. D. MacCourt, copy in author's possession.

10. Wheeler Oral History, USNI; entry for Nov. 12, 1918, in Shillinglaw, *An American in the Army and YMCA*, 128–29; *Literary Digest*, Feb. 1, 1919; Becker, *The Great War and the French People*, 320–21; Adam, *Paris Sees It Through*, 258; Weintraub, *A Stillness Heard Round the World*, 230–39. See also Weintraub's bibliography, 439–42, for other sources on Armistice Day in Paris.

11. Lawrence to Kate, Nov. 17, 1918, Lawrence Papers, WisHistSoc; Howard Johnson to author, Nov. 6, 1989, in author's possession. Entry for Nov. 11, 1918, Quinn Diary, Duke University; entries for Nov. 11, 12, 1918, Marek Diary, Virginia War History Commission Archives, Virginia State Library; entry for Nov. 28, 1918, Diary of unknown seaman, JOD/1`98, NMM; *Literary Digest*, Jan. 18, 1919.

12. Chambers, *Submarine Chasers in the Mediterranean*, 79–81; entries for Nov. 11, 12, 1918, Kipp Diary, extracts in author's possession. See also Halpern, *Naval War in the Mediterranean*, 564–68.

13. Moffat, *Maverick Navy*, 127; H. Kent Hewitt Memoirs, H. Kent Hewitt Papers, OA; Hewitt Oral History, Columbia University; Lawrence to Kate, Nov. 12, Dec. 2, 1918, Lawrence Papers, WisHistSoc. See also entry for Nov. 11, 1918, Brown Journal, WisHistSoc; Bellitteri, "The Cruise of the U.S.S. *Chester* in European Waters 1917–1919," Bellitteri Papers, ECU; memo, Nov. 2, 1918, ADM137/1527; Sims to Wilson, Oct. 28, 1918, Reel 8, ME-11; Wilson to Benson, Oct. 26, 1918, ibid. An American naval officer on a ship that reached *Britannia* later remarked how impressed he was when he observed the British sailors coiling lines and "leaving everything shipshape" before they abandoned ship. Parker Oral History, Columbia University.

14. Memoirs of Quartermaster Lynch, WWI Research Collection, AMHI; Moffat, *Maverick Navy*, 127; Ellyson to Nim, Nov. 11, 1918, Reel 1, Ellyson Papers, NDL; Rose, *Brittany Patrol*, 322; Furlong, *Class of 1905*, 199; Knowles, *Southampton*, 87; Weintraub, *A Stillness Heard Round the World*, 264–65, 270–71; Bludworth, *The Battle of Eastleigh*, 108.

15. Edwards to Cone, Nov. 12, 1918, Box 99, Area file, RG45; Sims to wife, Nov. 12, 1918, Box 10, Sims Papers, LC; Colgate W. Darden Jr. Oral History, USNI; Peel, *How We Lived Then*, 174–80; MacDonough, *In London during the Great War,* 332–33.

16. Zogbaum, *From Sail to Saratoga*, 292–93; Schoeffel Oral History, USNI; entry for Nov. 11, 1918, Forbes Diary, copy in Box 58, Sims Papers. LC. An officer on the *Dixie* has published memoirs suggesting that there was a celebration. See Levell, *"War on the Ocean,"* 46–47.

17. *USS* Nevada, *The Cheer Up Ship,* 9; Rickett Memoirs, Smithsonian; Hustvedt Oral History, USNI; Todd, *Oklahoma*, 18, 24.

18. Corrigan, *Tin Ensign*, 31–32; Mannix, *The Old Navy*, 241; "Exploits of a Yankee Sailor and a Scotch Soldier," *Rudder* (Feb. 1919): 77.

19. Harry Hill Oral History, Columbia University; Byrnes, *All in One Lifetime*, 44; McClellan, "American Marines in the British Grand Fleet," 160; Allen, *Sails to Atoms*, 33; Schubert, *Come On* Texas, 176; Bush, *Bless Our Ship*, 83; entry for Nov. 11, 1918, J. H. Hill Diary, IWM; Baynham, *Men from the Dreadnought*, 246; Lyman, "Which It Will Forget at Its Peril," 33.

20. Hayward, *HMS* Tiger *at Bay*, 171. For a slightly different version, see his unpublished memoir in IWM. See also the Pedro del Valle Oral History, Marine Corps Historical Center; Wilson Memoir, Reel 12, Eugene Wilson Collection, microfilm, NDL.

21. Entries for Nov. 11, 12, 1918, Witherspoon Diary, Witherspoon Family Papers, AMHI; James, *A Great Seaman*, 164. See also Dunn, *World Alive*, 278; F. T. Hunter, *Beatty, Jellicoe, Sims, and Rodman*, 170. On two of the American ships, the sailors broke into the torpedo alcohol locker in order to "splice the main brace." Murmane, *Ground Swells*, 430; Schubert, *Here Comes the* Texas, 177. For other accounts of the celebration, see *Glasgow Herald*, Nov. 12, 1918; entry for Nov. 11, 1918, Packer Diary, Packer MS, Churchill College; McClellan, "American Marines in the British Grand Fleet," 160; McCrea to mother and father, Nov. 12, 1918, Joubert McCrea Correspondence, WWI Research Project, AMHI; entry for Nov. 11, 1918, USS *Texas* deck log, RG24; Eugene Wilson Memoir, Eugene Wilson Collection, Reel 12, microfilm, NDL; Bush, *Bless Our Ship*, 83; entry for Nov. 11–18, 1918, Daniel Schenk Memoir, Smithsonian; "The Sea Lion's Roar," Nov. 11, 1918, copy of news release, USS *Texas* Archives; *The Story of the U.S.S.* Texas, 84; Baynham, *Men from the Dreadnoughts*, 246–47; Brown and Meechan, *Scapa Flow*, 123–24; entry for Nov. 11, 1918, Hill Diary, IWM.; Del Valle Oral History, Marine Corps Historical Center.

22. Signal from C-in-C to Grand Fleet, Nov. 11, 1918, copy in USS *Texas* Archives; Murmane, *Ground Swells*, 431; entry for Nov. 11, 1918, Parker Diary, Churchill College; *Glasgow Herald*, Nov. 12, 1918; Ross letter to author. See also entry for Nov. 9, 1918, McCrea Diary; World War I Research Project, AMHI; Marder, *From the Dreadnought to Scapa Flow*, 5: 185–86.

23. Trask, *Captains and Cabinets*, 343–54.

24. Shepherd, "The Death of a Fleet," 61, 76–77; Beatty General Order, Nov. 20, 1918, copy in USS *Texas* Archives. See also Van der Vat, *The Grand Scuttle* 130, passim; and Perrot, "Watching the Great Surrender"; Marder, *From the Dreadnought to Scapa Flow*, 5: 190–94.

25. Nov. 23, 1918, Box 10, Sims Papers, LC. For various accounts by Americans of the day, see *Arklight* 1, no. 20, copy in Reel 1, Wilson Papers; *Literary Digest*, Jan. 11, 1919, 564–65; Lewis Ross to Jim Stanfill, May 4, 1987, copy in author's possession; Quote of Admiral Harold R. Stark provided author by Mitchell Simpson III; *Stars and Stripes*, Nov. 29, 1918; Rodman, *Yarns of a Kentucky Admiral*, 289–90; G. Warren Clark, "World War One, Surrender of German Ships," copy in author's possession; *Great Lakes Bulletin*, Dec. 14, 1918; McClellan, "American Marines in the British Grand Fleet," 16; Lyman, "Which It Will Forget at Its Peril," 33.

26. McClellan, "American Marines in the British Grand Fleet," 161.

27. Behrens, "Goodbye Grand Fleet," 18, 53. Inset in this article is Beatty's farewell speech.

28. Harrod, *Manning the New Navy*, 144. Interestingly, the Coast Guard percentage-wise suffered more casualties than the Navy, primarily because of the loss of the cutter *Tampa*. See also Greene, "Navy 'Firsts' in the World War." See, for example, *Annual Report of the Secretary of the Navy*, 1918, 9–20; "Summary of Activities of U.S. Naval Forces in European Waters," copy in Z file, OA; *ONI Monthly Bulletin* (May 15, 1919): 7–14; Sims's testimony, *Naval Investigation*, 312–14. Members of Sims's staff periodically upgraded these statistics. See various reports in CZ subj file, RG45; and report dated Aug 5, 1918, in TL subj file, ibid.

29. *American Ship Casualties of the World War*; Donald W. Mitchell, *History of the Modern American Navy*, 248.

30. To Belknap, Feb. 5, 1919, Belknap Papers, NHC.

31. Showalter, "Towards a 'New' Naval History," 132. See also Walton, *Over There*, xxiii; and D. A. Brown, "Who Won the War?" 18–19, 47.

32. Churchill, *The World Crisis*, 831. See also "Naval Effort—Great Britain & United States of

America," an undated Admiralty memo to the War Cabinet, copy in the Grease Papers, Ministry of Defense Library, Scotland Yard; *Illustrated London News*, August 24, 1918; *New York Herald*, Dec. 29, 1918; Marder, *From the Dreadnought to Scapa Flow*, 5: 127.

33. Michelson, "The Submarine Warfare," 55. See also Herwig, *Politics of Frustration*, 148. For France, see Chack and Antier, *Histoire maritime de la premiere guerre mondiale*, 3: 460.

34. Sims to wife, Oct. 8, 1919, Box 10, Sims Papers, LC; Josephus Daniels, *The Wilson Era: Years of War*, 173. See also Knox to Frothington, July 9, 1925, Box 9, Knox Papers, LC.

35. Trask, *Captains and Cabinets*, 360.

36. "A Brief Summary of the U.S. Naval Activities in European Waters," Aug. 6, 1918, TL subj file, RG45. British records, especially the auxiliary patrol records in ADM137, clearly illustrate how subordinate they were.

37. See Sims to wife, Nov. 22, 1917, Box 9, Sims Papers, LC.

38. For an interesting analysis of Sims by one of his subordinates and critics, see Knox to Frothingham, Nov. 9, 1925, Box 9, Knox Papers, LC.

39. Marder, *From the Dreadnought to Scapa Flow*, 5: 298–99, 306; Hagan, *This People's Navy*, 254; Weigley, *The American Way of War*, 192–93. Captain Bowling in his dissertation writes that Admiral Beatty in January 1918 refuted Mahan's basic principles in order to "concentrate on a war against the U-boats." This is partly correct; however, Beatty continued to believe that a battle between his fleet and the German High Seas Fleet could be decisive. For Bowling, see "The Negative Influence of Mahan on Convoy Protection in Wartime," Ph.D. diss., 500. See also Roskill, *Admiral of the Fleet Earl Beatty*, 267.

40. Ferrell, *Woodrow Wilson and World War I*, 34; Trask, *Captains and Cabinets*, 363; Wayne P. Hughes Jr., "Tactics and Principles of Strategy," 30–31; and George H. Quester, "Naval Thought since 1914," 186–88, both in Hattendorf, *The Influence of History on Mahan*; Bowling, "The Negative Influence of Mahan on Convoy Protection in Wartime," Ph.D. diss., 264–65, 490–502; *New York Evening Post*, Nov. 21, 1918; J. W. Jones, "U.S. Battleship Operations in World War I," Ph.D. diss., 6. See also Bowling, "The Negative Influence of Mahan on the Protection of Shipping in the Battle of the Atlantic," paper, copy in author's possession.

41. Marder, *From the Dreadnought to Scapa Flow*, 5: 105. See also Ferrell, *Woodrow Wilson and World War I*, 38–39.

42. M. Simpson, *Anglo-American Naval Relations*, 198.

43. Ferrell, *Woodrow Wilson and the World War*, 38–39; June 19, 1919, Bayly Papers, IWM. See also Bowling, "Convoy in World War I," master's thesis, 262; and Marder, *From the Dreadnought to Scapa Flow*, 5: 322; Reiners, *The Lamps Went Out in Europe*, 217–21.

44. See, for example, Stevenson, *The First World War and International Politics*, 170; Howard, *War in European History*, 126–27. See also Parsons, *Wilsonian Diplomacy*, viii; and Taylor, *A History of the First World War*, 110; Olson, *The Economics of the Wartime Shortage*, 86–89, 96–97, 112–13.

45. Schmitt and Vedeler, *The World in the Crucible*, 305. See also Robbins, *The First World War*, 96–97.

46. For example, see H. W. Baldwin, *World War I*, 159; Roskill, *The Strategy of Sea Power*, 133; Hart, *The Real War, 1914–1918*, 471–72, 476; Brian Bond, introduction to *The First World War and British Military History*, 11; Coletta, *Sea Power in the Atlantic and Mediterranean in World War I*, 127; J. W. Jones, "U.S. Battleship Operations in World War I," Ph.D. diss., 43.

47. Grant, *Naval Intelligence*, 21, 45, 49–50, 55–56.

48. Uhlig, *How Navies Fight*, 100; V. Davis, *The Admiral's Lobby*, 135; Ballantine, *U.S. Naval Logistics in the Second World War*, 23.

49. Still, "Anglo-American Naval Logistic Cooperation in World War I."

50. Mayo testimony, *Naval Investigation*, 613.

51. Coffman, *The War to End All Wars*, 364.

Abbreviations

ADM	Admiralty
AEF	American Expeditionary Force
AMHI	American Military History Institute
ASW	Anti-Submarine Warfare
BuPers	Bureau of Personnel
BuS&A	Bureau of Supplies and Accounts
BuY&D	Bureau of Yards and Docks
CG	Coast Guard
C-in-C	Commander in Chief
CNO	Chief of Naval Operations
DAB	*Dictionary of American Biography*
DANFS	*Dictionary of American Naval Fighting Ships*
ECU	East Carolina University
FDR	Franklin D. Roosevelt
FO	Foreign Office
FSU	Florida State University
IWM	Imperial War Museum
LC	Library of Congress
LSU	Louisiana State University
MM	Mariners' Museum
MP	Military Police
NA	National Archives and Records Administration
NAS	Naval Air Station
NDL	Navy Department Library
NHC	Naval Historical Center
NHF	Naval Historical Foundation
NOTS	Naval Overseas Transportation Service
NWC	Naval War College
OA	Operations Archives
PRO	Public Records Office
RG	Record Group
SecNav	Secretary of the Navy
SP	Shore Patrol
UK	United Kingdom
UNC-CH	University of North Carolina, Chapel Hill
USNI	United States Naval Institute
USSB	United States Shipping Board
UVA	University of Virginia

Bibliography

As I mentioned in the introduction to this volume, little has been published about the United States Navy in World War I in the past quarter century. This paucity of writing about the Navy in that conflict is certainly not due to a lack of published and unpublished material (see William N. Still Jr., "World War I: A Bibliography of the Great War," *Naval History* [Spring 1992]: 59–61). As Edward M. Coffman writes in *The War to End All Wars* (369), there are "tons of World War I records in the National Archives." Naval participation in the conflict in terms of numbers was far less than that of the Army, but it did generate a massive amount of documentation, the largest collection in Record Group 45, particularly the subject file. Fortunately, Richard von Doenhoff, former archivist in charge of naval records in the National Archives, prepared the "United States Naval History Guide to Subject File, 1911–1927" (1965), an invaluable research tool.

Other National Archives record groups relating to the U.S. Navy include an impressive number of documents. World War I provided an impetus for the Navy's historical record collection practices (see William S. Dudley, "World War I and Federal Military History," *Public Historian* 12 [Fall 1990]: 37–39; William J. Morgan and Joye L. Leonhart, *A History of the Naval Historical Center and the Dudley Knox Center for Naval History*, Washington, DC: Naval Historical Foundation, 1983; Elizabeth B. Drewry, "Historical Units of Agencies of the First World War," *Bulletins of the National Archives* [July 1942]: 13–18; Dudley W. Knox, "Our Vanishing History and Traditions," U.S. Naval Institute *Proceedings* 52 [January 1926]: 15–25; and Ronald H. Spector, "An Improbable Success Story: Official Military Histories in the Twentieth Century," *Public Historian* 12 [Winter 1990]: 27–28).

Under orders from Secretary of the Navy Daniels, Admiral Sims created a historical section within Simsadus to collect war diaries, correspondent and cable files, operational reports, and other materials of historical significance. A similar section was created within the Navy Department. These records became the nucleus of the World War I records in RG45. Captain Dudley Knox, who had served on Sims's staff in London, in 1921 became the head of an Office of Naval Records and Library to oversee the Navy's records. He was also the head of the Navy's Historical Section, which would eventually become the Naval Historical Center. Knox's interest in documentaries resulted in the publication of the official records of the Navy in the Quasi-War with France. Knox also planned to publish a documentary series on the Navy in World War I. Members of his staff waded through Record Group 45's subject file and microfilmed thousands of documents. The publication never took place, however; the microfilm, some twenty rolls, is housed in the Navy Department Library. These documents, like those in *The Official Records of the Union and Confederate Navies in the War of the Rebellion* (thirty volumes, frequently cited as *ORN*), are a selection. Their strength, as in *ORN*, is in operations, neglecting other topics such as logistics and social history. (The microfilm is entitled "ME-11." There is a manuscript draft of a preface included in the microfilm that indicates that the compilation actually began in the 1920s.)

An important collection within RG45 is known as the "Z" file. These are unpublished naval histories of units, naval districts, stations, etc. for the World War I period. See

Checklist. Naval Histories in the "Z" File, Record Group 45 U.S. National Archives 1911–1927 (Operational Archives, Naval History Division, 1975).

I was disappointed with the records of the AEF (RG120), expecting to find considerable material on relations with the Navy. Very little was found. I discovered in RG125, case 10622, the records of a court of inquiry for Rear Admiral W. B. Fletcher, held after the war. It is a large file and most significant as it not only includes the testimony of Admiral Sims, Captain Twining, and other officers as to why Fletcher was relieved of his command but also at times provides considerable information on the force commander's policies as well as the Navy's efforts to establish a base in Brest, and elsewhere in France. File 14258, General Correspondence, 1912–1925, Records of the Bureau of Ships (RG19), contains manuscript histories of different types of naval vessels operating in European waters in World War I. The file includes a number of photographs.

The Naval Historical Center, located in the Washington Navy Yard, D.C., includes three branches that house unpublished materials relevant to this study: the Navy Department Library, the Operational Archives, and the Ships History Branch. Unpublished official reports and a few collections of private papers, including several on microfilm, can be found in the library's rare book and microfilm collections. Copies of the published annual reports of the secretary of the navy are located in the library. The General Board Records, 1917–1919, are on microfilm in the library. The library also has bound copies of the naval administrative histories of World War II. These histories contain information on World War I as well. See *Guide to United States Naval Administrative Histories of World War II* (Naval History Division, 1976). For manuscript holdings in the library, see George W. Emery, ed., *Historical Manuscripts in the Navy Department Library: A Catalog* (Naval Historical Center, 1994). The Ships History Branch has extensive files on every ship that has been commissioned in the Navy, including all of the nearly four hundred deployed to European waters in World War I. Much of the material in these files was collected for the extremely valuable publication *Dictionary of American Naval Fighting Ships*. Most of it comes from records in the National Archives and official ship logs, but occasionally a file includes personal papers and journal entries. The Operational Archives maintain large holdings of classified and unclassified records as well as historical documents and personal papers. Biographies and biographical material of most officers who served in the Navy are filed there. The archives have ships' history files, which, although not as extensive as the ones in the Ships History Branch, nevertheless are important. Although I was unable to examine the file of every ship that served in the European force in World War I, those that were examined included at times personal diaries and papers. The archives also hold copies of unpublished World War II histories and historical reports. These include material on World War I also. See *Partial Checklist: World War II Histories and Historical Reports in the U.S. Naval History Division* (Operational Archives, Naval History Division, 1977).

The Public Records Office (PRO) is the repository for official British records, including naval. Located in Kew, outside London, it is one of the most user-friendly repositories that this writer has ever used. There are detailed inventories of the different record groups. Most of the World War I naval records are found in Admiralty (ADM) 1, 116, and 137. There are some records identified as American, but by far most of them are buried in with the records of British naval commands, particularly the Grand Fleet, Queenstown, Gibraltar, Portsmouth, Falmouth, the Nore, the Irish Sea, etc. One large series of records, "The Auxiliary Patrol," includes weekly reports of the destroyers, subchasers, and other small craft operating in British waters. These reports include American vessels when they were involved and frequently include the reports of the commanders of American vessels. These reports from the U.S. commanders are addressed to the British admiral in command of the area where the ships were operating. They are important because in the majority of cases these reports were not sent to the force commander (Sims). These records (various commands) also include comments by the admirals on activities and operations in their commands, including at times comments about the Americans. They also sometimes include comments by Admiralty officials in notes attached to the reports (William N. Still Jr. to Dr. Dean Allard, June 19, 1990, copy in author's possession).

The official archives of the French navy are located at Vincennes in the suburbs of Paris. In 1986, I wrote the archivist about records of the American Navy in France during World War I. I was informed that there were disappointingly few. In 1990, I decided to include the French archives in a research trip to Europe. On this occasion and as an official representative of the Department of the Navy (I was the SecNav Scholar in Naval History at the time), I discovered they did have records of the U.S. Navy in France during World War I! At the time I was there, they were still being inventoried, so bunches (literally) of records were brought out to the search room where Dr. Tom Adams (a friend of mine, and a historian residing in Paris) and I went through as many of the documents as we could (I had allotted only one day there, believing that it was probably a waste of time) and separated the ones that we wanted copied. The archivist who helped me admitted that there were likely far more records, particularly documents concerning the construction of American naval air stations in France, and others relating to the Brittany Patrol, but I did not have time to examine them.

The practice of military and naval officers, particularly those in positions of command, of keeping possession of "official" records as well as personal papers was fortunately followed in World War I. The Library of Congress Manuscript Division is by far the most important repository of these collections. For the World War I period, there are more than thirty collections, including those of Secretary of the Navy Daniels, Chief of Naval Operations Benson, and European Naval Force Commander Sims, all important to this study. The majority of them were deposited in the Library of Congress by the Naval Historical Foundation. There are printed guides to many of these collections.

Personal papers relating to the naval side of World War I reside in state archives and libraries, historical societies, museums, and academic institutions through the United States and abroad. After the war, every state collected World War I materials of some sort. Some of them were simply an accumulation of documents concerning the state's activities during the war; others included personal papers and newspaper articles. Efforts were made to locate materials concerning naval activities, particularly diaries, correspondence, and letters to newspaper editors from sailors who served in the war zone. Unfortunately, a number of these collections were by county, as in the case of Colorado, or by individual name, place of service, and place of residence, as in Illinois. While I could not visit each locale, I was able to obtain some materials by mail. I actually examined the World War I collections in the Virginia State Library in Richmond, and although they were filed by county, I was able to locate and examine a number relating to naval activities in European waters. Both the Smithsonian and the Naval War College (Newport, R.I.) hold important collections of personal papers covering 1917–18.

Perhaps the most unique collection of personal papers relating to World War I is located at the U.S. Army Military History Institute, Army War College (Carlisle Barracks,

Pa.). In the late 1970s, the institute mailed more than ninety thousand questionnaires to the surviving World War I veterans. Of the more than seven thousand filled out and returned, approximately five hundred were from individuals who had served in the Navy. In addition, about sixty of these veterans had donated correspondence, journals, photographs, and newspaper articles relating to the Navy. As the institute's archivist, Dr. Richard Sommers, says, "This is, by far and away, the largest collection anywhere of personal papers of American servicemen in the Great War." Dr. B. Franklin Cooling used a large number of these questions for his article "It's a Long Way. . . ." in the November 1977 *VFW Magazine.* These questionnaires and other materials at the institute would make a fascinating quantitative study of World War I veterans.

In examining personal papers in British repositories, I was particularly interested in what Royal Navy sailors thought of American naval personnel and their ships. I discovered information related to this at the National Maritime Museum, Greenwich; the Imperial War Museum, London; the manuscript collections at Churchill College, Cambridge University; and the Peter Liddle "1914–1918 Personal Experience Archives." Mr. Liddle, of the Sunderland Polytechnic, has collected an impressive number of personal papers of both naval and army personnel. He has published a number of them in book form. When I posed my interest to him, he agreed to go through the papers and extract any and all comments concerning the U.S. Navy (Liddle to author, May 5, 1988, copy in author's possession). The National Maritime Museum has the Admiral David Beatty Papers. They have been edited by B. M. Ranft and published in the Naval Records Society Publications. Before the volume was published, Mr. Ranft kindly provided me with a list of the papers that included comments about the American Navy and/or its personnel. I examined the original papers, and my citations are to those rather than the published papers.

Newspaper files located in the Library of Congress, the British Newspaper Library, and other repositories are often duplicated in clipping files in the Admiral Sims Papers and other personal collections of private papers.

While research was in progress, the tabloid the *Torch* was published. The editor kindly provided a printout of World War I naval survivors and their addresses. I wrote to them, and many replied. Some included information about their services during the war. Articles and other publications written by war correspondents and reporters that appeared during and immediately after the war are included in primary sources.

Primary Sources
Unpublished
UNITED STATES

Government Repositories

American Military History Institute, Army War College, Carlisle Barracks, Pa.
World War I Research Collection.
Albright, Henry B. Papers.
Arnold, Walter. Papers.
Beatty, John R. Memoir.
Beavers, Ethan A. Letters to parents.
Berkovich, Solomon. Papers.
Blakely, J. R. Papers.

Goddard, Lt. Col. C. H. "Relations between American Expeditionary Forces and British Expeditionary Forces, 1917–1920." Army War College Historical Section Study No. 5. June 1942.

Graves, W. R. Diary.

Lynch, Jarmon A. Memoir.

McCrea, Joubert. Diary.

Merrill, Leslie. Papers.

Roussin, Floyd. Papers.

Schueler, Frank E. "A Gob's Letters Home during the World War, 1917–1919."

Search, William. File. Spanish-American War Papers.

Speicher, Cdr. P. E. "Some Experiences with Mediterranean Convoys during the World War." Lecture delivered at the Army War College, June 9, 1933.

Steen, Earl. Papers.

Witherspoon Family Papers.

Young, W. R. Diary.

Bureau of Medicine and Surgery, U.S. Navy, Washington, D.C.

Base Hospital No. 5. Historical Files.

Morgan, Major R. W. "Dr. James E. Talley, Lieutenant Commander (MC), USNR, A Navy Department in France, 1917–1918."

Emil Buehler Naval Aviation Library, National Museum of Naval Aviation, Pensacola, Fla.

Duffet, Wayne. Papers.

Franklin D. Roosevelt Library, Hyde Park, N.Y.

Assistant Secretary of the Navy Files.

Library of Congress, Manuscript Division, Washington, D.C., Personal Papers.

Belknap, Reginald R.

Benson, William S.

Bingham, Donald C.

Bliss, Tasker H.

Bristol, Mark L.

Callan, John L.

Cooke, Harold

Daniels, Josephus

Fahey, Charles. Diary.

Fullam, William F.

Gleaves, Albert

Halsey, William F.

Hooper, Stanford C.

King, Ernest J.

Knox, Dudley W.

Land, Emory Scott

Leahy, William D.

Lischiner, Jacob B. "Provost Marshal General's Department, A.E.F., World War I: A Story."

Long, Breckinridge

Mayo, Henry T.

McCully, Newton A.

McGowan, Samuel

Rodgers Family

Sims, William S.

Smith, Stuart Farrar

Standley, William

Strauss, Joseph

Symington, Powers. "The Navy Way." Copy in Navy Department Library.

Taussig, Joseph K.

Tumulty, Joseph

Marine Corps Historical Center, Washington Navy Yard, D.C.

Comford, Ralph Helm. Papers. Personal Papers Collection.

Cunningham, Captain Alfred A. "Report of an Aviator's Observation Trip to France and England." January 1918, microfilm, copy in NDL

National Archives and Records Administration, Washington, D.C.

RG19: Records of the Bureau of Ships

RG24: Records of the Bureau of Naval Personnel

RG26: Records of the U.S. Coast Guard

RG32: Records of the United States Shipping Board

RG37: Records of the Navy's Hydrographic Office

RG38: Records of the Office of the Chief of Naval Operations

RG45: Naval Records Collection of the Office of Naval Records and Library

RG52: Records of the Bureau of Medicine and Surgery

RG59: General Records of the Department of State

RG63: Records of the Committee on Public Information

RG71: Records of the Bureau of Yards and Docks

RG80: General Records of the Department of the Navy, 1798–1947

RG84: Records of the Foreign Service Posts of the Department of State

RG120: Records of the American Expeditionary Force (World War I), 1917–23

RG125: Records of the Office of the Judge Advocate General (Navy)

RG143: Records of the Bureau of Supplies and Accounts

RG200: National Archives Gift Collection (Red Cross Records)

RG313: Records of the Navy Operating Forces

National Museum of History and Technology, Smithsonian Institution, Washington, D.C.

Bathrop, Michael. Diary.

Fullinwider, Simon P. Papers.

Rickett, Guy. Diary and Memoir.

Schenk, Daniel. Memoir.

Whited, E. V. Diary.

Wilson, M. Collection.

Nautilus *Memorial and Submarine Force Library and Museum, Groton, Conn.*

Grady, R. C. "War History of Submarine Division Five." N.p., n.d.

Naval Historical Center, Washington Navy Yard, D.C.

Navy Department Library

Catlin, Lt. George L. "Paravanes." April 22, 1919.

Cunningham, Alfred A., "Report of Aviation Observation Trip, Jan. 1, 1918," microfilm, NDL.

Documents on U.S. Naval Operations in World War I. ME-11 (microfilm).

Ellyson, Theodore Gordon (microfilm).

Howell, Captain Glenn. "A Horse Kicked Me."

Laning, Harris. "An Admiral's Log." Vol. 2.

Lord, Christopher. "History of Naval Aviation, 1898–1939."

McDowell, Captain C. S. "American Anti-Submarine Work during the [World] War."

McNair, Francis V. Sims's Orders to London, England.

"Progress Report, U.S. Naval Aviation Forces, Foreign Service, Headquarters, Paris, France" (microfilm).

Simons, Robert Bentham. "Both by Land and by Sea."

Sitz, Walter H. "A History of Naval Aviation."

Slayback, George P., Jr. Memoir.

Tighe, Francis N. "Plunkett's Pirates."

"U.S. Bureau of Supplies and Accounts."

"U.S. Naval Administration in World War II." Series.

"U.S. Naval Administration in World War II: CNO Aspects of Logistic Planning."

"U.S. Naval Administration in World War II: CNO Base Maintenance Division: Mine Warfare in the Naval Establishment."

"U.S. Naval Aviation in World War II: DNCO (Air) Aviation Shore Establishments, 1911–1945."

Operational Archives

Allied Submarine Operations in World War I.

"A Brief History of U.S. Naval Forces in France, November 11, 1918–October 1, 1919."

Diamond, D. H. Scrapbook.

Fenny, Elizabeth. "History of Navy Nurse Corps."

Gill, Charles C. Memoirs.

Hewitt, H. Kent. Papers.

"Interview with Joseph A. Eaton."

Killingholme England Naval Air Station. ZE files.

Kittredge, Captain Tracy B. "United States–British Co-Operation, 1939–1942." COMNAVEUR Monograph.

Kurfess, William F. Diary.

McKelvey, Carlton A. "Construction of the U.S. Naval Air Station L'Aber Vrach, France, World War I." 1963.

Orr, Glenn R. "Aboard the USS *Harding*."

Pratt, William V. Papers.

Roskill, Stephen. "Defense of Trade in World War I." Lecture, May 3, 1968.

Stark, Harold R. Papers.

Strauss, Joseph. Recollections.

"Summary of Activities of U.S. Naval Forces Operating in European Waters." Z files.

Talley, Dr. James E. Papers.

USS *Burrows* file (Lauer Journal). ZC files.

USS *Parker* file (Henry Keiffer Memoir). ZC files.

USS *Walke* file (Charles Russell Journal). ZC files.

Wilson, Henry B. "The False Armistice." Copied from original papers in the Naval Academy Library, Annapolis, Md.

Photo Section

USS *Pocahontas* Collection

Ships History Branch

Ship Histories Files.

"U.S. Navy Ship Levels, 1917–1989."

"History of United States Naval Aviation French Unit," microfilm, NDL.

Naval War College, Newport, R.I.

Doland, James H. Journal.

File XTYU, Intelligence and Technology. Record Group 8

Jenkins, David. Diary.

Record Group 15.

USS *Little* War Diary.

Office of Coast Guard Historian, Coast Guard Headquarters, Washington, D.C.

USS *Seneca*'s History.

USS *Tampa* File.

U.S. Coast Guard Academy Library, Groton, Conn.
Brown, Fletcher. Papers.
Cochran, Hamilton. Papers.
Hunt, Fred. Papers.
Sattelee, Charles. Papers.
Stewart, Gustavus. Papers.
Royall, Hilary. Memoir.
Wheeler, J. J. Papers.

State and Private Repositories

Hill Memorial Library, Special Collections, Louisiana State University, Baton Rouge.
Post, Lauren Chester. Papers.
Staples, H. H. Diary.
Hoover Institution Archives, Stanford University, Palo Alto, Calif.
Keith, Gerald. Papers.
Woodworth, S. E. Diary.
Illinois State Historical Library, Springfield, Ill.
Berger, Louis. Letters.
Cohen, Sol and Julius. Letters.
Indiana Historical Society, Indianapolis, Ind.
Niblack, Albert. Papers.
Indiana State Library, War History Records, Indianapolis.
Bearswilt, F. Papers.
Neuert, Karl Henry. Papers.
Newspaper clippings.
Watson, Dewey. Letters.
Irish American Historical Society, New York, N.Y.
O'Connell, Daniel T. Collection.
J. Y. Joyner Library, Manuscript Collection, East Carolina University, Greenville, N.C.
Bellitteri, Marino. Papers.
Davis, Louis P. Papers.
Fort, George. Papers.
Taylor, John Clayton. Papers.
Mariners' Museum, Newport News, Va.
Fagan, Joseph. Diary.
Loder, Robert. Papers.
Minnesota Historical Society, St. Paul
Cathcart, Alexander, and Family. Papers.
Naval Historical Foundation, Washington Navy Yard, D.C.
Carpender, Arthur. Diary.
Dichman, Grattan C. Papers.
Fix, Paul Peter. "World War I Bluejacket." Oral History.
Moore, Charles. Diary.
Morgan, Junius. Diary.
Queenstown Association Files.
New Jersey Historical Society, Newark.
Carpender, Arthur. Papers.
North Carolina Division of Archives and History, Raleigh, N.C.
Broughton, Governor Melvin. Papers (biographical sketch of Lyman Cotten).

Ohio Historical Society, Columbus.
Harding, Warren G. Papers.
Robert Manning Strozier Library, Florida State University, Tallahassee.
Leigh, Richard H. Papers (typed memoir entitled "Whereas").
Seeley G. Mudd Manuscript Library, Princeton University Library, Princeton, N.J.
Fosdick, Raymond. Papers.
State Historical Society of Wisconsin, Madison.
Brown, Timothy. Journal.
Lawrence, George E. Papers.
University of California at Irvine.
Wemyss, Rosslyn. Papers (microfilm).
University of North Carolina Library, Manuscript Collection, Chapel Hill.
Alderman, W. Papers.
Anderson, Edwin. Papers.
Cotten, Lyman A. Papers.
Blue, Victor. Papers.
Foote, Percy. Papers.
Long, Andrew T. Papers.
Merrill, Aaron Stanton. Papers.
Staton, H. Papers.
Tomb, William. Diary.
University of Virginia Library, Charlottesville.
Latimer, M. W. Diary
USS Texas *Archives, San Jacinto, Texas.*
Virginia State Library, Richmond (Virginia War History) Commission, World War I Archives.
Kennedy, Edward L. Papers.
Marek, George. Diary.
Newspaper clippings.
William Perkins Library, Duke University, Durham, N.C.
Quinn, Clifton. Diary.
Yale University Library, New Haven, Conn.
House, Edward M. Papers.

GREAT BRITAIN

British Museum, London.
Jellicoe MSS.
Churchill College Library, Cambridge University, Cambridge.
Clarke, Arthur W. Memoir.
Cresswell, Captain John. Papers.
Godfrey, Admiral John H. Papers.
Harper, Geoffrey C. Diary.
Leslie, Sir John Randolph (Shane). Papers. "The System of Convoys for Merchant Shipping in 1917–1918."
Pridham, Vice Admiral Sir (Arthur) Francis. Memoir.
Packer, Admiral Sir Herbert. MSS.
Imperial War Museum, London.
Attrill, J. E. Diary.
Bayly, Lewis. Papers.
De Chair, Admiral Sir Dudley. Papers.

Dewar MSS.
Eady, C. M. Memoir.
Early MSS.
Gardner, Midshipman Lycelt. Diary.
Godwin, J. H. Letter, November 21, 1918.
Goodrich, Cdr. R. Diary.
Hayward, Victor. Memoir.
Hill, J. H. Diary.
National Maritime Museum, Greenwich, U.K.
Beatty, David. Papers.
Dewar, K.G.B. Papers.
Duff, Sir Alexander. Papers.
Foreign Warship Covers.
Hill, H. A. Diary.
Richmond, Sir Herbert. Papers.
Thesiger, Sir Bertram Sackville. Papers.
Unknown Seaman's Diary (JOD/198).
Peter Liddle 1914–1918 Archives, Leeds University.
Binney, Sir Thomas. Papers.
Boswell, F. Notes.
Foxton, F. Diary.
Gerrard, W. G. Memoir.
LeWinton, Captain F.S.W. Recollections.
Nichols, R. F. Memoir.
Salter, Vice Admiral J.S.C. Recollections.
Public Records Office, London.
Admiralty ADM116, ADM131, ADM137 Files
Cabinet CAB Files
Foreign Office FO Files
MT Files
Royal Archives, Windsor Castle, Windsor.
King George V. Diary.
Whitehall Library, Ministry of Defense, Scotland Yard, London.
Grease Papers.

Manuscript Material in Author's Possession

Allard, Dean C. "The Battle of the Atlantic: A United States Overview." May 1993.
Appleyard, Rollo. "The Elements of Convoy Defense in Submarine Warfare, April, 1918." Naval Historical Branch, Ministry of Defense, London.
Ashley, Ray. "The Return of the *Mayflower*." Graduate paper, May 3, 1991, East Carolina University.
Beach, Captain E. L. Memoir, in part concerning his command of battleship at Scapa Flow, provided by his son Capt. Edward Beach.
Clemens, Lt. Leon. Memoir notes.
Clark, G. Warren. "World War One, Surrender of German Ships."
Dawson, William H. Journal (typescript).
Gilbert, Robert. Memoir (typescript).
Grove, Eric. "The Reluctant Partner: The United States and the Introduction and Extension of Convoy in 1917–1918."

Hatton, Thomas. Diary.

Jackson, C. V. Memoir.

Kipp, W. D. Journal. Extracts provided author by his son.

Kleinstland, J. S. Letter. March 17, 1987, and manuscript, "A Saga of World War I."

Koehler, Hugo. Miscellaneous papers provided by Peter J. Capelotti.

MacCourt, W. D. Autobiography.

Momon, Robert. Memoir.

Ohl, John Kennedy. "Mines for the North Sea Mine Barrage: A Study of the Navy and the Military-Industrial Complex." Paper provided by the author.

Pollen, Arthur. Miscellaneous papers provided by Jon Sumida.

Pressprick, Joseph. Diary.

Rathbone, M. "Berehaven and West Cork Naval Operations." MSS.

Richards, CO Memoirs.

Ross, Lewis G. Letter and remembrances. January 12, 1987.

Taylor, J. Letter to author. March 8, 1988. Contains information on photographs of American warships repaired at Cammell Laid shipyard, 1917–18.

Letters to the Author

Cantrell, Ann. April 14, 1989 (about her father).

Egger, F. J. November 19, 1989.

Johnson, Howard. November 6, 1989.

Kinskey, James. April 25, 1987.

Latimer, L. November 19, 1989.

Neal, V. L. January 30, 1990.

Nicholson, Miller. July 20, 1987.

Parker, Michael. November 5, 1989.

Sweetman, Jack. February 11, 1985.

Taylor, John. March 8, 1988.

Tolley, Adm. Kemp. February 18, 1985.

Watters, Cdr. David N. October 15, 1992.

Oral Histories

Chaplain's Resource Board Archives, U.S. Navy Chaplain's Office, Norfolk, Va.

Edel, William.

Columbia University, Oral History Project Office, New York. (Copies held in Operational Archives and East Carolina University, Greenville, N.C.)

Carney, Robert B.

Conolly, Richard L.

Fife, James.

Fechteler, William M.

Hewitt, H. Kent.

Hill, Harry W.

Hoover, John H.

Land, Emory Scott.

Moore, Charles W.

Parker, Ralph C.

Wilson, Eugene E.

East Carolina University, Greenville, N.C.

Davis, Glenn.
Davis, Louis Poisson, Sr.
Helmick, Charles G.
Marine Corps Historical Center, Washington, D.C.
del Valle, Pedro.
U.S. Naval Institute, Oral History Office, Annapolis, Md.
Ansel, Walter C. W.
Bieri, Bernard H.
Bogan, Gerald F.
Darden, Colgate W., Jr.
Dyer, Thomas H.
Griffin, Charles G.
Hustvedt, Olaf M.
Johnson, Felix L.
Kinkaid, Thomas.
McCrea, John.
Pownall, Charles A.
Pyne, Schuyler Neilson.
Royar, Murrey L.
Schoeffel, Malcolm F.
Van Deurs, George.
Veth, Kenneth L.
Wheeler, Charles J.
Withington, Frederick Stanton.

U.S. Government Documents, Printed

Bureau of Engineering, Navy Department. *History of the Bureau of Engineering, Navy Depart-ment During the World War*. Washington, D.C.: GPO, 1922.

Bureau of Ordnance. Navy Department. *Navy Ordnance Activities, World War, 1917–1918*. Washington, D.C.: GPO, 1922.

Bureau of Yards and Docks. Navy Department. *Activities of the Bureau of Yards and Docks, Navy Department, World War, 1917–1918*. Washington, D.C.: GPO, 1921.

Congress, U.S. *Hearings before the Subcommittee of the Committee of Commerce, U.S. Senate*. 64th Cong., 1st sess. Washington, D.C.: GPO, 1916.

———. Subcommittee of the Committee on Naval Affairs. *Hearings: Naval Investigation*. 66th Cong., 2nd sess. Washington, D.C.: GPO, 1921.

Department of State. *Papers Relating to the Foreign Relations of the United States, 1917, The World War*. Supplement. 3 vols. Washington, D.C.: GPO, 1932.

———. *Papers Relating to the Foreign Relations of the United States, 1918, The World War*. Supplement. 3 vols. Washington, D.C.: GPO, 1933.

———. *Papers Relating to the Foreign Relations of the United States, Russia*. 3 vols. Washington, D.C.: GPO, 1931–32.

Navy Department. *The American Naval Planning Section in London*. Washington, D.C.: GPO, 1923.

———. *American Ship Casualties of the World War*. Washington, D.C.: GPO, 1923.

———. *Annual Report of the Secretary of the Navy*. Washington, D.C.: GPO, 1917–19.

———. *Annual Report Surgeon General U.S. Navy, 1918*. Washington, D.C.: GPO, 1919.

———. *Compilation of Court-Martial Orders for the Years 1915–1937*. 2 vols. Washington, D.C.: GPO, 1940.

———. *History of the Bureau of the Bureau Engineering*. Washington, D.C.: GPO, 1922.

———. *Navy Register*. 1916–18. 3 vols. Washington, D.C.: GPO, 1917–19.

———. *The Northern Barrage and Other Mining Activities*. Washington, D.C.: GPO, 1920.

———. *The United States Naval Railway Batteries in France*. Washington, D.C.: GPO, 1922; reprinted 1988 by the Naval Historical Center.

Naval Ordnance Activities, World War, 1917. Washington, D.C.: GPO, 1919.

Register of the Commissioned and Warrant Officers of the United States Navy and Marine Corps, 1918. Washington, D.C.: GPO, 1919.

Ships' Data. U.S. Naval Vessels, November 1, 1916. Washington, D.C.: GPO, 1917.

U.S. Statutes at Large. Vol. 39, part I, 556–619.

Microfilm Publications

National Archives and Records Administration, Washington, D.C.

Records of the Department of State Relating to World War I and Its Termination, 1914-1929 (Microcopy No. 367, 1962.)
  M1092
  M1140
  M316

Government Documents: British, Admiralty Library, London

Admiralty, *Supplement to the Monthly Navy List, Showing the United States Naval Forces Operating in European Waters, Corrected to November 1, 1918* (London: Harrison and Sons, 1918).

Home Waters. Part 9. May 1, 1917, to July 31, 1917. Naval Staff Monographs, vol. 19.

Published Diaries, Memoirs, and Papers

Adam, H. Pearl. *Paris Sees It Through: A Diary. 1914–1919*. London: Hodder and Stoughton, 1919.

Addison, Christopher. *Four and a Half Years*. 2 vols. London: Hutchinson, 1934.

Allen, George Washington. *Sails to Atoms: From Seaman to Admiral*. Philadelphia: Dorrance, 1975.

Arpee, Edward. *From Frigates to Flat-Tops: The Story of the Life and Achievements of Rear Admiral William Moffett, U.S.N., the Father of Naval Aviation, October 31, 1869–April 4, 1933*. Lake Forest, Ill., 1953.

Astor. Brooke. *Footprints: An Autobiography*. Garden City, N.Y.: Doubleday, 1980.

Baker, Ray Stannard. *American Chronicle: The Autobiography of Ray Stannard Baker*. New York: Charles Scribner's Sons, 1945.

Baldwin, Marian. *Canteening Overseas, 1917–1919*. New York: Macmillan, 1920.

Banks, Elizabeth. *The Remaking of an American*. Garden City, N.Y.: Doubleday, Doran, 1928.

Barclay, Harold. *A Doctor in France 1917–1919*. New York: privately printed, 1923.

Bartimeus [Lewis A. da Costa Ritchie]. *The Navy Eternal*. London: Hodder and Stoughton, 1918.

Bartlett, Squadron Leader CPO. *In The Teeth of the Wind: Memoir of the Royal Naval Air Service in the First World War*. Annapolis: Naval Institute Press, 1995.

Battey, George M., Jr. *70,000 Miles on a Submarine Destroyer*. Atlanta: Webb and Vary, 1919.

Bayly, Admiral Sir Lewis. *Pull Together: The Memoirs of Admiral Sir Lewis Bayly*. London: Harrap, 1939.

Beach, Edward L., Sr. *From Annapolis to Scapa Flow: The Autobiography of Edward L. Beach, Sr.* Annapolis: Naval Institute Press, 2003

Beaverbrook, Lord. *Men and Power 1917–1918*. London: Hutchinson, 1936.

Belknap, Captain Reginald R. *The Yankee Mining Squadron or Laying the North Sea Mine Barrage*. Annapolis: Naval Institute Press, 1920.

Beston, Henry B. *Full Speed Ahead*. Garden City, N.Y.: Doubleday, Page, 1919.

Blackford, Charles Minor. *Torpedoboat Sailor*. Annapolis: Naval Institute Press, 1968.

Bludworth, T. Francis. *The Battle of Eastleigh, England, U.S.N.A.F.* New York: Thomson, 1919.

Blumenfeld, Ralph D. *All in a Lifetime*. London: Ernest Benn, 1931.

Bone, David. *Landfall at Sunset: The Life of a Contented Sailor*. London: Gerald Duckworth, 1955.

Borden, Henry, ed. *Robert Laird Borden: His Memoirs*. Toronto: Macmillan of Canada, 1938.

Borden, Raymond D. Maggie *of the Suicide Fleet*. Garden City, N.Y.: Doubleday, Doran, 1930. See also Buranelli.

Bridges, Sir Tom. *Alarms and Excursions: Reminiscences of a Soldier*. London: Longmans Green, 1938.

A Brief History of the U.S.S. Texas *and Life Generally in the North Sea during the War*. N.p., n.d.

Brittain, Sir Harry. *Pilgrims and Pioneers*. London: Hutchinson, n.d.

Broome, John Egerton. *Make A Signal!* London: Putnam, 1955.

Brown, Fletcher W.. *Overseas, 1917–1918*. Privately printed. Copy in Coast Guard Library.

Brownrigg, Rear Admiral Sir Douglas. *Indiscretions of the Naval Censor*. London: Cassell, 1920.

Buena Vista's Part in the World War. Storm Lake, Iowa: Tom D. Eilers, 1920.

Buenzle, Fred J. *Bluejacket: An Autobiography of a Chief Yeoman, USN, Ret'd*. New York: W. W. Norton, 1939.

Bullard, Robert Lee. *Personalities and Reminiscences of the War*. Garden City, N.Y.: Doubleday, Page, 1925.

Buranelli, Prosper. Maggie *of the Suicide Fleet*. Garden City, N.Y.: Doubleday, Page, 1930.

Bush, Captain Eric. *Bless Our Ship*. London: Allen and Unwin, 1958.

Byrne, William. *The Deck Log of the Naval Auxiliary Reserve*. N.p., 1978.

Byrnes, James F. *All in One Lifetime*. New York: Harper and Brothers, 1958.

Bywater, Hector C., and H. C. Ferraby. *Strange Intelligence: Memoirs of Naval Secret Service*. London: Constable, 1934.

Campbell, Rear-Admiral Gordon. *My Mystery Ships*. Garden City, N.Y.: Doubleday, Doran, 1929.

———. *Number Thirteen*. London: Hodder and Stoughton, 1932.

Cannon, James, Jr. *Bishop Cannon's Own Story: Life As I Have Seen It*. Edited by Richard L. Watson Jr. Durham, N.C.: Duke University Press, 1955.

Capper, Henry D. *Aft-From the Hawsehole: Sixty-two Years of Sailors' Evolution*. London: Faber and Gwyer, 1927.

Carr, William Guy. *Good Hunting*. London: Hutchinson, 1940.

Chambers, Hilary R., Jr. *United States Submarine Chasers in the Mediterranean, Adriatic, and the Attack on Durazzo*. New York: Knickerbocker Press, 1920.

Chapple, Joe Mitchell. *We'll Stick to the Finish*. Boston: Chapple, 1918.

Chatfield, Lord Alfred E. *The Navy and Defense*. London: William Heinemann, 1942.

Chase, Mary Justice, ed. *Benjamin Lee, 2d. Letters and Sketches*. Boston: Cornhill, 1920.

Christie, Guy. *Harbours of the Forth*. London: Christopher Johnson, n.d.

Churchill, Hon. Winston S. *Thoughts and Adventures*. London: Thornton Butterworth, 1932.

Churchill, Winston. *A Traveller in War Time*. New York: Macmillan, 1918.

Clark, Alan, ed. *"A Good Inning": The Private Papers of Viscount Lee of Farcham*. London: John Murray, 1974.

Clark, Andrew. *Echoes of the Great War*. New York: Oxford University Press, 1985.

Complete Presidential Press Conferences of Franklin D. Roosevelt. Vols. 9 and 10. New York: DaCapo Press, 1972.

Connolly, James B. *Sea-Borne: Thirty Years Avoyaging*. Garden City, N.Y.: Doubleday, Doran, 1944.

Coontz, Robert E. *From the Mississippi to the Sea*. Philadelphia: Dorrance, 1930.

Corday, Michel. *The Paris Front, An Unpublished Diary: 1914–1918*. New York: E. P. Dutton, 1934.

Cornford, L. Cope. *The Paravane Adventure*. London: Hodder and Stoughton, 1919.

Corrigan, John P. *Tin Ensign: Mine Planting in the North Sea*. New York: Exposition Press, 1971.

Creel, George. *Rebel at Large: Recollections of Fifty Crowded Years*. New York: G. P Putnam's Sons, 1947.

Cronon, E. David, ed. *The Cabinet Diaries of Josephus Daniels 1913–1921*. Lincoln: University of Nebraska Press, 1973.

Cunningham, Captain Alfred A. *Marine Flyer in France*. Washington, D.C.: History of Museums Division, U.S. Marine Corps, 1974.

Cutchins, John A. *An Amateur Diplomat in the World War*. Richmond, Va.: American Legion, 1938.

Daniels, Josephus. *The Cabinet Diaries of Josephus Daniels 1913–1921*. Edited by E. David Cronon. Lincoln: University of Nebraska Press, 1973.

———. *The Wilson Era: Years of Peace, 1910–1917*. Chapel Hill: University of North Carolina Press, 1944.

———. *The Wilson Era: Years of War and After, 1917–1923*. Chapel Hill: University of North Carolina Press, 1946.

Daniels, Mrs. Josephus. *Recollections of a Cabinet Minister's Wife, 1913–1921*. Raleigh, N.C., 1945.

Davies, Vice-Admiral Richard Bell. *Sailor in the Air*. London: Peter Davies, 1967.

Dawes, Charles G. *A Journal of the Great War*. 2 vols. Boston: Houghton Mifflin, 1921.

Dawson, Captain Lionel. *Flotillas: A Hard-Lying Story*. London: Rich and Cowan, 1933.

Dawson, Warrington. *The War Memoirs of William Graves Sharp*. London: Constable, 1931.

De Chair, Admiral Sir Dudley. *The Sea is Strong*. London: George G. Harrap, 1961.

Dewar, Vice Admiral K.G.B. *The Navy from Within*. London: Victor Gollancz, 1939.

Doenitz, Karl. *Ten Years and Twenty Days*. London: Weidenfeld and Nicolson, 1959.

Dunn, Robert. *World Alive*. New York: Crown, 1956.

Esher, Viscount Oliver. *Journals and Letters of Reginald Viscount Esher*. Vol. 4. London: Ivor Nicholson and Watson, 1938.

Evans, Captain E.R.G.R. *Keeping the Seas*. London: Sampson Low, Marston, n.d.

Extracts from the Letters of George Clark Moseley during the Period of the Great War. Privately printed, 1930.

Fiske, Bradley. *From Midshipman to Rear Admiral*. New York: Century, 1919.

Fitch, Henry. *My Mis-Spent Youth: A Naval Journal*. London: Macmillan, 1937.

Flower, Newman, ed. *The Journals of Arnold Bennett, 1911–1921*. London: Cassell, 1932.

Fosdick, Raymond B. *Chronicle of a Generation*. New York: Harper and Brothers, 1958.

Freeman, Lewis R. *Sea-Hounds*. New York: Dodd, Mead, 1919.

Fremantle, Admiral Sir Sydney Robert. *My Naval Career, 1880–1928*. London: Hutchinson, 1949.

Gamble, C. F. Snowden. *The Story of a North Sea Air Station*. London: Neville Spearman, 1967.

Gibbons, Floyd. *And They Thought We Wouldn't Fight*. New York: George H. Doran, 1918.

Gibbons, Helen D. *A Little Gray Home in France*. New York: Century, 1919.

Gleaves, Albert. *The Admiral: The Memoirs of Albert Gleaves, USN*. Pasadena, Calif.: Hope, 1985.

Goerlitz, Walter, ed. *The Kaiser and His Court. The Diaries, Note Books and Letters of Admiral Georg Alexander Von Muller, Chief of the Naval Cabinet, 1914–1918*. New York: Harcourt, Brace and World, 1964.

Goodenough, Admiral Sir William. *A Rough Record*. London: Hutchinson, 1943.

Grasty, Charles. *Flashes from the Front*. New York: Century, 1918.

Gretton, Vice-Admiral Sir Peter. *Convoy Escort Commander*. London: Cassell, 1964.

Griff [pseud.]. *Surrendered*. Published by author, n.d.

Gulick, Luther. *Morals and Morale*. New York: Association Press, 1919.

Gwatkin-Williams, Captain R. S. *Under the Black Ensign*. London: Hutchinson, 1918.

Hagood, General Johnson. *The Services of Supply: A Memoir of the Great War*. Boston: Houghton Mifflin, 1927.

Hallam, Squadron Leader T. D. *The Spider Web*. Annapolis: Nautical and Aviation Publishing, 1979.

Halpern, Paul G., ed. *The Keyes Papers, 1914–18*. Vol. 1. London: Naval Records Society, 1972.

———, ed. *The Royal Navy in the Mediterranean, 1915–1918*. London: Navy Records Society, 1987.

Halsey, Fleet Admiral William F., and Lieutenant Commander J. Bryan III. *Admiral Halsey's Own Story*. New York: McGraw-Hill, 1947.

Hankey, Lord. *The Supreme Command*. Vol. 2. London: Allen and Unwin, 1961.

Harbord, Major General James G. *Leaves from a War Diary*. New York: Dodd, Mead, 1925.

Hardinge, Lord of Penshurst. *Old Diplomacy*. London: John Murray, 1947.

Harrison, Carter H. *With the American Red Cross in France, 1918–1919*. Chicago: Ralph Fletcher Seymour, 1947.

Hartford, Commander G. B. *Commander, R.N.* London: Arrowsmith, 1957.

Hashagen, Ernest. *U-Boats Westward!* New York: G. P. Putnam's Sons, 1931. Also entitled *The Log of a U-Boat Commander*.

Hayes, Sir Bertram. *Hull Down*. New York: Macmillan, 1925.

Haygood, General Johnson. *The Service of Supply: A Memoir of the Great War*. Boston: Houghton Mifflin, 1927.

Hayward, Victor. *HMS* Tiger *at Bay: A Sailor's Memoir, 1914–18*. London: William Kimber, 1977.

Henderson, Loy W. *A Question of Trust. The Origins of U.S.–Soviet Diplomatic Relations. The Memoirs of Loy W. Henderson*. Palo Alto: Hoover Institution Press, 1986.

A History of the U.S.S. Mount Vernon. N.p., n.d.

Holleran, Owen C. *Holly, His Book*. Privately printed, 1924.

Holt, R. B. *History of the U.S.S.* Harrisburg. N.p., n.d.

Hoover, Herbert. *An American Epic*. Vol. 2. Chicago: Henry Regency, 1960.

———. *The Memoirs of Herbert Hoover: Years of Adventure, 1874–1920*. 3 vols. New York: Macmillan, 1951–53.

Huddleston, Sisley. *In My Time*. London: Jonathan Cape, 1938.

Hunt, Frazier. *One American*. New York: Simon and Schuster, 1938.

Hurley, Edward N. *The Bridge to France*. Philadelphia: J B. Lippincott, 1927.

Husband, Joseph. *On the Coast of France*. Chicago: A. C. McClurg, 1919.

———. *A Year in the Navy*. Boston: Houghton Mifflin, 1919.

Jacoby, Robert L., comp. *Calendar of the Speeches and Other Published Statements of Franklin D. Roosevelt, 1910–1920*. Hyde Park, N.Y.: Franklin D. Roosevelt Library, 1952.

Janis, Elsie. *The Big Show: My Six Months with the American Expeditionary Forces*. New York: Cosmopolitan, 1919.

———. *So Far, So Good: An Autobiography*. New York: E. P. Dutton, 1932.

Jeffery, Keith, ed. *The Military Correspondence of Field Marshal Sir Henry Wilson 1918–1922*. London: Army Records Society, 1985.

Jellicoe, Admiral of the Fleet Earl. *The Crisis of the Naval War*. London: Cassell, 1920.

———. *The Submarine Peril*. London: Cassell, 1931.

Jones, T. M. *Watchdogs of the Deep*. Sydney, Australia: Angus, Robertson, 1935.

Kauffman, Reginald Wright. *Our Navy at War*. Indianapolis: Bobbs-Merrill, 1918.

Kenworthy, Hon. J. M. *The Real Navy*. London: Hutchinson, 1932.

Kerr, Admiral Mark. *The Navy in My Time*. London: Hutchinson, 1933.

King, Ernest J., and Walter M. Whitehill. *Fleet Admiral King: A Naval Record*. New York: Norton, 1952.

King-Hall, Admiral Sir Herbert. *Naval Memories and Traditions*. London: Hutchinson, 1926.

Land, Emory Scott. *Winning the War with Ships*. New York: Robert M. McBride, 1958.

Link, Arthur S., ed. *The Papers of Woodrow Wilson*. Vols. 42–58. Princeton, N.J.: Princeton University Press, 1983–85.

Lloyd George, David. *War Memoirs of David Lloyd George*. 6 vols. Boston: Little, Brown, 1936.

Lockwood, Charles A. *Down to the Sea in Subs*. New York: W. W. Norton, 1967.

The Log of the USS Northern Pacific *during the Great War*. N.p., n.d.

Long, John D. *The New American Navy*. New York: Outlook, 1903.

Long, Walter. *Memories*. London: Hutchinson, 1923.

Longworth, Alice Roosevelt. *Crowded Hours*. New York: Charles Scribner's Sons, 1933.

Lovell, Robert O. *"War on the Ocean": A Sailor's Souvenir*. Newcastle, Ind.: privately printed, 1937.

MacDonough, Michael. *In London during the Great War*. London: Eyre and Spottiswoode, 1935.

Maguire, Doris D., ed. *French Ensor Chadwick, Selected Letters and Papers*. Washington, D.C.: University Press of America, 1981.

Maguire, William A. *Rig for Church*. New York: Macmillan, 1942.

Mannix, Rear Admiral Daniel P., III. *The Old Navy*. New York: Macmillan, 1983.

Marder, Arthur J., ed., *Fear God and Fear Nought: The Correspondence of Admiral of the Fleet Lord Fisher*. 3 vols. London: Cape, 1952–57.

Marshall, George C. *Memoirs of My Services in the World War 1917–1918*. Boston: Houghton Mifflin, 1976.

Martin, Dr. Franklin H. *The Joy of Living: An Autobiography*. Garden City, N.Y.: Doubleday, Doran, 1933.

Maxwell, Gordon S. *The Naval Front*. London: A. and C. Black, 1920.

Michelsen, Andreas. *The Submarine Warfare, 1914–1918*. Translated copy in ZCP subj file, RG45.

Mitchell, William. *Memoirs of World War I*. New York: Random House, 1960.

Moffat, Alexander W. *Maverick Navy*. Middletown, Conn.: Wesleyan University Press, 1976.

Moffatt, James S. *King George Was My Shipmate*. London: Stanley, Paul, 1940.

Moseley, George Clark. *Extracts from the Letters of George Clark Moseley during the Period of the Great War*. Printed for private distribution, 1923.

Mountevans, Admiral Lord. *Adventurous Life*. London: Hutchinson, 1946.

Muir, John R. *Years of Endurance*. London: Philip Allan, 1936.

Munro, Donald John. *Convoys, Blockades and Mystery Towers*. London: Sampson Low, Marston, 1932.

———. *Scapa Flow, A Naval Retrospect*. London: Sampson Low, Marston, 1932.

Munson, James, ed. *Echoes of The Great War: The Diary of the Reverend Andres Clark, 1914–1919*. New York: Oxford University Press, 1985.

Murdock, Lawrence B. *They Also Served*. New York: Carlton Press, 1967.

Murmane, Mark R. *Ground Swells*. New York: Exposition Press, 1949.

Murray, Lady (Oswyn). *The Making of a Civil Servant: Sir Oswyn Murray, G.C.B., Secretary of the Admiralty, 1917–1936*. London: Methuen, 1940.

Murray, Lt.-Col. Hn. Arthur C. *At Close Quarters*. London: John Murray, 1946.

New Brunswick, New Jersey in the World War. S. M. Christie Press, 1921.

Newton, Joseph F. *Preaching in London: A Diary of Anglo-American Friendship*. New York: George H. Doran, 1922.

Niemoller, Martin. *From U-Boat to Pulpit*. Chicago: Willett, Clark, 1937.

O'Hara, Edward. *World War at Its Climax: Being Personal Imprints of the Great Conflict and Close Up Glimpses of the World Tragedy*, East Aurora, N.Y.: Roycrofters, 1922.

Paine, Ralph D. *Roads to Adventure*. Boston: Houghton Mifflin, 1922.

Palmer, Frederick. *With My Own Eyes*. Indianapolis: Bobbs-Merrill, 1933.

Patterson, A. Temple, ed. *The Jellicoe Papers*. 2 vols. London: Navy Records Society, 1966–68.

Peel, Mrs. C. S. *How We Lived Then, 1914–1918*. New York: Dodd, Mead, 1929.

Pepper, George Wharton. *Philadelphia Lawyer*. Philadelphia: J. B. Lippincott, 1944.

Petrie, Sir Charles, ed. *The Life and Letters of Austen Chamberlain*. 2 vols. London: Hutchinson, 1939–40.

Playne, Caroline E. *Britain Holds On, 1917, 1918*. London: Allen and Unwin, 1933.

Ranft, B. McL. *The Beatty Papers*. Vol. 1, *1902–1918*. London: Naval Records Society, 1989.

Rathenau, Walter. *Walter Rathenau: Industrialist, Banker, Intellectual, and Politician*. Edited by Hartmut Pogge von Strandmann. Oxford: Clarendon Press, 1985.

Repington, Lieut. Col. C. A. Court. *The First World War 1914–1918*. 2 vols. Boston: Houghton Mifflin, 1921.

Richardson, James O. *On the Treadmill to Pearl Harbor*. Washington, D.C.: Naval History Division, Department of the Navy, 1973.

Riddell, Lord. *Lord Riddell's War Diary, 1914–1918*. London: Ivor Nicholson and Watson, 1933.

Roberts, Cecil. *The Years of Promise, 1908–1919: Being the Second Book of an Autobiography*. London: Hodder and Stoughton, 1968.

Robertson, Sir William. *From Private to Field Marshal*. Boston: Houghton Mifflin, 1921.

Robien, Lewis. *The Diary of a Diplomat in Russia, 1917–1918*. Translated from French by Camilla Sykes. New York: Praeger, 1969.

Rodman, Hugh. *Yarns of a Kentucky Admiral*. Indianapolis: Bobbs-Merrill, 1928.

Romis, D. K. *The United States Ship* Great Northern. N.p., 1919.

Roosevelt, Eleanor. *The Autobiography of Eleanor Roosevelt*. New York: Harper and Brothers, 1958.

Roosevelt, Elliott, ed. *F.D.R.: His Personal Letters, 1905–1928*. New York: Duell, Sloan, and Pearce, 1970.

Roosevelt, Mrs. Theodore, Jr. *Day Before Yesterday*. Garden City, N.Y.: Doubleday, 1959.

Rose, H. Wickliffe. *Brittany Patrol*. New York: W. W. Norton.

Roskill, Captain S. W., ed. *Documents Relating to the Naval Air Service*. Vol. 1, *1908–1918*. London: Navy Records Society, 1989.

Rossano, Geoffrey L. *The Price of Honor: The World War One Letters of Naval Aviator Kenneth MacLeish*. Annapolis: Naval Institute Press, 1991.

Ruggles, Logan E. *The Part the U.S.S.* Von Steuben *Played in the Great War*. N.p., n.d.

Salter, Lord. *Memoirs of a Public Servant*. London: Faber and Faber, 1961.

The Saranac, U.S. Mine Squadron One: Northern Barrage, 9 April '18[–]3 January '19. Saratoga Springs, N.Y.: E. H. Holland, printer, 19??.

Scheer, Admiral Reinhard. *Germany's High Seas Fleet in the World War*. London: Cassell, 1920.

Schoultz, Commodore G. von. *With the British Battle Fleet; War Recollections of a Russian Naval Officer*. London: Hutchinson, 1925.

Schubert, Paul. *Come On* Texas. New York: Jonathan Cape and Harrison Smith, 1930.

Scott, Admiral Sir Percy. *Fifty Years in the Royal Navy*. London: John Murray, 1919.

Scott, Hugh L. *Some Memories of a Soldier*. New York: Century, 1928.

Seldes, George. *Tell the Truth and Run*. New York: Greenberg, 1953.

Service Record of Men of the Hanover National Bank of the City of New York. N.p., 1920.

Seymour, Charles, ed. *The Intimate Papers of Colonel House*. Vol. 3. Boston: Houghton Mifflin, 1928.

Shaw, Frank H. *Knocking Around*. New York: Dodd, Mead, 1927.

Sheely, Lawrence D. *Sailor of the Air: The 1917–1919 Letters and Diary of USN CMM/A Irving Edward Sheely*. Tuscaloosa: University of Alabama Press, 1993.

Shillinglaw, David Lee. *An American in the Army and YMCA, 1917–1920*. Edited by Glen E. Holt. Chicago: University of Chicago Press, 1971.

Simpson, Michael, ed. *Anglo-American Naval Relations 1917–1919*. London: Navy Records Society, 1991.

Sims, William S. *The Victory at Sea*. Annapolis: Naval Institute Press, 1984.

Smith, Holland M. *Coral and Brass*. Washington, D.C.: Zinger, 1979.

Smith, Humphrey Hugh. *A Yellow Admiral Remembers*. London: Edward Arnold, 1932.

Sowden, W. J. *The Roving Editors*. Adelaide, Australia: W. K. Thomas, 1919.

Sterne, Elaine. *Over the Seas for Uncle Sam*. New York: Britton, 1918.

Still, William N., Jr., ed. *The Queenstown Patrol, 1917: The Diary of Commander Joseph Knefler Taussig, U.S. Navy*. Newport, R.I.: Naval War College Press, 1996.

Stirling, Yates. *Sea Duty: The Memoirs of a Fighting Admiral*. New York: G. P. Putnam's Sons, 1939.

Strandmann, Hartmut Pogge von. *Walter Rathenau*. Oxford: Clarendon Press, 1985.

Sullivan, Vincent F. *With the Yanks in France*. Privately printed, 1921.

Summerbell, Carlyle. *A Preacher Goes to War*. Norwood, Mass.: Ambrose Press, 1936.

Taffrail [Henry Taprell Dorling]. *Endless Story*. London: Hodder and Stoughton, 1931.

———. *Swept Channels*. London: Hodder and Stoughton, 1935.

Tallens, Sir Stephen. *Man and Boy*. London: Faber and Faber, n.d.

Taylor, A. Hoyt. *Radio Reminiscences: A Half Century*. Washington, D.C.: U.S. Naval Research Laboratory, 1960.

Taussig, Joseph Knefler. *The Queenstown Patrol, 1917: The Diary of Commander Joseph Knefler Taussig, U.S. Navy*. Edited by William N. Still Jr. Newport, R.I.: Naval War College Press, 1996.

Thompson, Commander T. B. *Take Her Down: A Submarine Portrait*. New York: Sheridan House, 1942.

Townsend, Allan R. *One Man's Navy*. New York: Carlton Press, 1970.

Tupper, Admiral Sir Reginald. *Reminiscences*. London: Jarrolds, 1929.

Tweedie, Admiral Sir Hugh. *The Story of a Naval Life*. London: Rich and Cowan, 1939.

United States Naval Air Station, Killingholme. Killingholme: The Station, 1918.

Usborne, Vice Admiral C. V. *Blast and Counterblast*. London: John Murray, 1935.

———. *Smoke on the Horizon: Mediterranean Fighting 1914–1918*. London: Hodder and Stoughton, 1933.

USS Nevada, 1916–1946. San Francisco: James H. Barry, 1946.

U.S.S. Seattle during the War. Brooklyn: Brooklyn Daily Eagle, 1919.

U.S.S. Wyoming: At War in the North Sea, 1917–1918. N.p., 1919.

Vaughan, David K., ed. *An American Pilot in the Skies of France: The Diaries and Letters of Lt. Percival T. Gates, 1917–1918*. Dayton, Ohio: Wright State University Press, 1992.

Venzon, Anne Cipriano, ed. *General Smedley Darlington Butler: The Letters of a Leatherneck, 1898–1931*. New York: Praeger, 1992.

Vincent, Henry. *A Stoker's Log.* London: Jarrolds, 1929.

Virginia War History Commission. *Virginia War Letters, Diaries and Editorials.* Vol. 3, edited by Arthur K. Davis. Richmond: Virginia State Library, 1925.

Wallace, Lew B. *A Sailor's Log.* Privately published, 1919.

Walton, Robert C. *Over There: European Reaction to Americans in World War I.* Itasca, Ill.: F. E. Peacock, 1971.

War Log of the U.S.S. St. Louis, *February 4, 1917–July 2, 1919.* New York: Wynkoop Hallenbeck Crawford, 1919.

White, L.G.W. *Ships, Coolies, and Rice.* London: Sampson Low, Marston, 1936.

Wiggins, Angus W. *My Romance with the Navy.* Daytona Beach, Fla.: Hall, 1975.

Wile, Frederic William. *News Is Where You Find It.* Indianapolis: Bobbs-Merrill, 1939.

Wiley, Henry A. *An Admiral from Texas.* Garden City, N.Y.: Doubleday, 1934.

Wilkinson, Syd E. *The U.S.S.* Nevada *and Her Experiences in the War.* N.p., 1918.

Willert, Sir Arthur. *Washington and Other Memories.* Boston: Houghton Mifflin, 1972.

Wilson, H. W. *Hush of The Hydrophone Service.* London: Mills and Boon, 1920.

Wilson, Lieut. Comdr. Eugene E. *Comrades of the Mist and Other Rhymes of the Grand Fleet.* New York: George Sully, 1919.

———. *Wings of the Dawn.* Palm Beach, Fla.: Literary Investment Guild, 1950.

Winn, H. W. *Fighting the Hun on the U.S.S.* Huntington. Privately printed, 1919.

World War at Its Climax. East Aurora, N.Y.: Roycrofters, 1922.

Wright, Rear Admiral Noel. *Sun of Memory.* London: Ernest Benn, 1947.

Young, Hugh. *A Surgeon's Autobiography.* New York: Harcourt, Brace, 1940.

Zogbaum, Rufus Fairchild. *From Sail to Saratoga: A Naval Autobiography.* N.p., Rome, 1961.

Articles

"Admiral Sims as Much an Enemy of Red Tape as of the German U-Boats." *Current Opinion* 63 (August 1917): 88–89.

"Admiral Sims in the Team-work for Victory." *Scientific American* 120 (April 12, 1919): 374.

"The American and British Navies in the War." *Literary Digest,* November 23, 1918, 17–18.

"The American Destroyers." *Scientific American* (Dec. 28, 1918): 515.

"American Destroyers in the War." *Sea Power* 6 (February 1919): 88–92.

"An American Naval Air Base." *Sphere* (October 26, 1918): 66–67

Beach, Brewster. "Hunting Submarines with a Sound Detector." *Scientific American* 73 (April 5, 1919): 335, 353–54.

———. "The Wonderful Submarine Detector." *American Marine Engineer* 14 (April 1919): 8–9.

Behrens, O. W. "Goodbye Grand Fleet." *Navy Life,* June 1919: 18, 63.

Belknap, Capt. Reginald R. "The Auxiliary Squadron." U.S. Naval Institute *Proceedings* 43 (April 1917): 639–54.

———. "The North Sea Mine Barrage." *National Geographic* 35 (February 1919): 85–110.

———. "The North Sea Mine Barrage." *Scientific American* 120 (March 15–22, 1919): 250–51, 288–89.

———. "The Yankee Mining Squadron." U.S. Naval Institute *Proceedings* 45 (1919): 1973–2012; 46 (1920): 5–32, 197–230.

Beston, Henry. "My Friends, The Gobs." *Red Cross Magazine* 13 (December 1918): 62–63.

———. "On Night Patrol: A Tale of the American Destroyers." *Outlook* 120 (October 2, 1918): 172–74.

———. "With the American Submarines." *Atlantic Monthly* 122 (November 1918): 688–97.

Boland, M. "The U.S.S. *Pocahontas* during the War." *United States Naval Medical Bulletin* 14 (July 1920): 462–94.

"Bombarding Durazzo: A Letter." *Broadside* (December 6, 1918): 10, 45.

Braisted, William C. "Medical Department Activities during the War." *Military Surgeon* (June 1920).

Breckel, H. F., "The Suicide Flotilla." Naval Institute *Proceedings* 53 (June 1927): 661–70.

"Brest and Le Havre." *Nautical Magazine* 104 (1920): 474–76.

Brown, E. W. "Submarine Division Five." *United States Naval Medical Bulletin* (October 1919): 849–90.

Brown, M. S. "The Experiences of a Yankee Sub-Chaser." *Pacific Motor Boat* 11 (April 1919): 5–8.

———. "Life Overseas on the Yankee Sub-Chasers." *Pacific Motor Boat* 12 (April 1920): 3–10, 17–20.

Brown, T. B. "Seventy-eight Thousand Miles in Search of German Submarines." *Lamp* 1 (August 1919): 19–20.

———. "Building a Pipe Line across Scotland." *Lamp* 1 (August 1919): 16–18.

Burns, J. E. "The Flotilla Disbursing Office." *Marksman* 1 (April 20, 1919): 1–2.

Blythe, Samuel G. "At a Naval Base." *Saturday Evening Post,* September 18, 1918: 21, 106–7.

———. "The Breton Patrol." *Saturday Evening Post*, December 7, 1918: 7, 68, 70, 72.

———. "Contact!" *Saturday Evening Post*, October 12, 1918: 89–92.

———. "Deep Sea Scouting." *Saturday Evening Post*, October 20, 1917: 29–30, 33–34.

———. "The Pills of Perdition." *Saturday Evening Post,* November 9, 1918: 14, 34, 37, 40.

———. "Ready!" *Saturday Evening Post*, November 2, 1918: 15–16.

———. "Removing the Mufflers." *Saturday Evening Post*, February 1, 1919: 72–77.

———. "The Sea Terriers." *Saturday Evening Post*, October 19, 1918: 16–17, 83.

"The *Calhoun* during the War." *Fleet Review* 2 (May 1920): 18–19.

Carney, Bill. "The Gob's Log." *Newport Recruit* (October 1918): 27, 89–90.

Carney, Robert B. "The Capture of the *U-58*." U.S. Naval Institute *Proceedings* 60 (1934): 1401–10.

———. "The Capture of the *U-58*." *Shipmate* 49 (August 1986): 7–10.

Catlin, George L. "Paravanes." U.S. Naval Institute *Proceedings* 45 (July 1919): 1135–57.

Claudy, C. H. "In a Certain Well-known Ocean." *St. Nicholas Magazine* 45 (July 1918): 770–74.

Cleary, F. J. "The Production of the Mines for the Northern Mine Barrage." *Journal of the American Society of Naval Engineers* 24 (August 1922): 438–51.

Cluverius, Capt. Watt T. "Planting a War Garden." U.S. Naval Institute *Proceedings* 45 (1919): 333–38.

Cochran, Hamilton. "Plymouth in Civvis." *American Legion Magazine*, January 27, 1924: 15–16.

Connolly, James B. "Our Dauntless Destroyer Boys." *Colliers Weekly*, June 15, 1918: 9–11.

Cooling, H. L. "Making Morale on a Man O' War." *Navy Life*, August 1918: 30–32.

Copeland. D. Graham. "Steel Tower Construction at the World's Greatest Radio Station." U.S. Naval Institute *Proceedings* 46 (December 1920): 1903–20.

Cornfold, L. C. "The United States Navy." *Living Age* 299 (November 2, 1918): 264–69.

Cross, Marty. "Fists across the Sea." *American Legion Magazine*, May 1935, 28–29, 31.

Cunningham, Bill. "K.O. by Sailor Guns," *American Legion Magazine*, Aug., 1939, 44–45.

Davis, G. T. "Paris Leave." Supplement to the *United States Naval Medical Bulletin* 14 (July 1920): 56.

"A Destroyer on Active Service." *Atlantic Monthly* 121 (April 1918): 542–46.

Dinger, H. C. "Fueling at Sea." U.S. Naval Institute *Proceedings* 45 (September 1919): 1607–12.

Dunbar, A. W. "The Hospital Ship *Comfort*." *United States Navy Medical Bulletin* (1919): 591–602.

Duncan, Raymond H. "Before and After." *Marksman* 1 (April 20, 1919): 1–2.

Dyer, George. "The Supply Department in War Time." U.S. Naval Institute *Proceedings* 46 (March 1920): 372–92.

"Edinburgh's Poor Bairns." *Fleet Review* 9 (September 1918): 39–40.

Ellicott, J. M. "Recollections of Admiral Sims." Naval Institute *Proceedings* 78 (March 1952): 319–24.

Foote, Percy W. "Narrative of the *President Lincoln*." U.S. Naval Institute *Proceedings* 48 (July 1922): 1073–86.

Fort, George. "The Capture of the *U-58*." U.S. Naval Institute *Proceedings* 61 (January 1935): 99–100.

Freeman, Lewis R. "Getting Together: How the Officers and Men of the British and American Ships in European Waters Are Making Acquaintance." *Outlook* 119 (July 17–August 7, 1918): 451–53, 564–65.

———. "Out with the Yanks." *National Review* (1918): 76–90.

———. "The United States Navy." *Land and Water* 71 (May 2, 1918): 19–20.

Friend, John. "The Rise and Fall of the *U-103*." *American Legion Magazine*, July 1936: 5, 62.

Furer, J. H. "The 110-Foot Submarine Chasers and Eagle Boats." U.S. Naval Institute *Proceedings* 45 (May 1919): 743–57.

Garrison, H. A. "The United States Naval Air Station, Pauillac, Gironde, France." *United States Naval Medical Bulletin* (July 1918): 611–17.

Glassford, William A. "A Leader of Men." *Avodo Record*. Copy in Lewis Bayly Papers, IWM.

"Grand Fleet Canteen Ship SS *Borodino*." *Navy* 24 (April 1919): 17–23.

Groszman, "Grand Work by the 110's." *Rudder* (November 1918): 519–21.

———. "Reminiscences of Durazzo." *Motorboat* 13 (January–March 1919): 5–9.

———. "A Yachtsman at Durazzo." *Yachting* (February 1919): 61, 81.

Hall, R. E. "Life on a Submarine during the World War." *General Electric News. Erie Works* 14 (July 17, 1931): 13, 18. Copy in the *Nautilus* Memorial and Submarine Museum Archives.

Hanks, Carlos. "Fighting the U-Boats." U.S. Naval Institute *Proceedings* 62 (December 1936): 1685–88.

———. "The Sinking of the *Alcedo*." U.S. Naval Institute *Proceedings* 63 (December 1937): 1762–63.

Hawks, Wells. "The Battle of Trompeloup." *Fleet Review* 10 (July 1919): 1–2.

Herman, Dr. Leon. "Naval Base Hospital No. 5." In *Philadelphia in the World War*, 322–29. New York: Philadelphia War History Committee, 1922.

Hinkamp, C. N. "Bringing in the Sheaves." U.S. Naval Institute *Proceedings* 45 (1919): 1117–33.

———. "Pipe Sweepers." U.S. Naval Institute *Proceedings* 46 (September 1920): 1477–84.

Holloway, Admiral J. L. "Recollections, 1915–20." *Shipmate* 47 (April 1984): 17–19.

Holt, Hamilton. "Behind the British Fleet." *Independent* 96 (December 28, 1918): 425–26.

———. "A Talk with Admiral Sims." *Independent* 96 (December 21, 1918): 394.

Hooper, Stanford. "The Lafayette Radio Station and its Relation to the United States Naval Communication Service and the World War." *Journal of the American Society of Naval Engineers* 33 (August 1920): 97–219, 387–415.

Horton, Roy. "My Maiden Voyage." *American Legion Weekly*, May 8, 1925, 4–5, 19–20.

Hunter. Francis. "Backing Beatty." *World's Work* (July 1919): 329–36.

Hutchinson, Palmer H. "The Sixth Battle Squadron." *Sea Power* 6 (December 1919): 265–67; and 7 (January 1920): 266–68.

"In the North Sea." *Marine Magazine*, February 1919, 17–18.

Jackson, Chester. "Mission to Murmansk." U.S. Naval Institute *Proceedings* 95 (February 1969): 82–89.

Jacoby, McClear. "How It Feels to Sink a Submarine." *Motorboat* 13 (October 10, 1919): 19–21.

Jenkins, Albert. "Why Hard-Boiled Crews Liked Plunkett." *Journal of the Switchman's Union of North America* (June 1935): 178–79, 185.

Johnson, John W. "In the Navy during the World War." *Granite Monthly* 52 (February 1920): 58–61.

Johnson, Lucius W. "A Junior Doctor with Admiral Sims." U.S. Naval Institute *Proceedings* 77 (1951): 1089; and 78 (1952): 319, 1140–43.

Johnson, Lucius W., and Raymond Miller. "A Navy Base Hospital Overseas." *Modern Hospital* 12 (April 1919).

Kauffman, Ruth Wright. "Small but Valiant." *Red Cross Magazine* 14 (March 1919): 68–72.

Lake, Governor. "Giving the Boys His Best." *Associated Men* 43 (March 1918): 593–94.

"Life on the U.S.S. *Corsair*." *Rudder* (April 1918).

"Listening Devices in U-Boat War." *Telephony* 76 (April 12, 1919): 23, 26–27.

Loftin, Frank. "Subchasing at Otranto." *Sea Power* (May 1921): 228–31.

Mason, Gregory. "Out with the Fog Hounds." *Outlook* 120 (November 13, 1918): 412, 417–18.

May, W. E. "Convoy Sloop, 1917–1918." *Mariner's Mirror* 70 (May-August 1984): 169, 226, 320–22, 431–33.

Mayo, Henry T. "The Atlantic Fleet in The Great War." In *What Really Happened at Paris*, edited by Edward House and Charles Seymour, 348–69. New York: Scribner's Sons, 1921.

McCarthy, Dan. "When Torpedoes Struck." *VFW Magazine*, November 1985, 26–28.

McClellan, Major Edward N. "American Marines in the British Grand Fleet." *Marine Corps Gazette* 7 (June 1922): 147–64.

Meals, Robert W. "The American Station at Dunkirk." *Hospital Corps of the Navy*. Supplement to *United States Navy Medical Bulletin* (January 1920): 9–22.

Meriwether, Walter Scott. "An American Sailor's Story." *Munsey* 63 (March 1918): 233–52.

———. "Four American Admirals." *Munsey* 63 (May 1918): 809–11.

Miles, Frank. "Ain't It the Truth?" *American Legion Weekly,* September 14, 1923: 12–14.

Moore, Joseph E. "Venereal Campaign in Paris District of the American Expeditionary Force." *Journal of the American Medical Association* (April 24, 1920): 1158–62.

Nelson, Harvey. "Uncle Sam—He Also Ran." *Our Navy* 13 (July 1919): 1–4.

"*New York*'s Christmas Party." *Fleet Review* 9 (Dec. 1918): 21–22.

Niblack, Albert. "Address." *Transactions of the Society of Naval Architects and Marine Engineers* 27 (1919): 323–24.

Nichols, Robert H. "Comrades of the Mist." *American Legion Magazine*, October 1940, 35–36, 46.

Nimitz, Chester. "The Navy's Secret Weapon." *Petroleum Today* (Spring 1961) Unpaginated reprint in author's possession.

Nutting, William W. "Squelched by the Censor." *Motor* 14 (July 10, 1917): 3–5.

Odell, Joseph H. "Spiritual Realities and High Explosives." *Atlantic Monthly* 122 (Nov. 1918): 697–704.

Paine, Ralph, D. "Hide and Seek Afloat." *Saturday Evening Post,* January 26, 1918: 16, 17, 45, 49.

———. "Our Navy on the French Coast." *Saturday Evening Post*, April 20, 1918, 14–15, 88, 90–93.

Perrot, F. "Watching the Great Surrender." *Living Age* 300 (January–March 1919): 5–10.

Perry, Lawrence. "They're in the Navy Now." *New Country Life*, August 1918: 33–38.

Philbrick, Clarence. "Navy Undress Blues." *American Legion Magazine*, August 1934, 20–21.

———. "Pharmacist's Mate 3d Class." *American Legion Magazine*, December 1935: 55–57.

Pugh, W. S. "Education and Sanitation Aboard Ship." *United States Naval Medical Bulletin* 13 (July 1919): 254–66.

Raguet, Commander Edward C. "United States Submarine Chasers at Gibraltar, November 1918." U.S. Naval Institute *Proceedings* 62 (December 1936): 1703–11.

Reuterdahl, Henry. "Admiral Sims." *Land and Water* (July 19, 1917): 9–11.

Richardson, Anna Steese. "My Visit to Our Sailor Boys." *Woman's Home Companion* 45 (June 1918): 26.

Rodman, Hugh. "The Christmas Ship." U.S. Naval Institute *Proceedings* 57 (July 1931): 888.

———. "Deeds of the American Battle Squadron." *Current History* 9 (February 1919): 254–57.

Rodriques, Gustave. "Americans as They Seem to a Frenchman." *Scribner's Magazine* 64 (July–December 1918): 554–56.

Scofield, Kendrick. "The North Sea Gate Swings Shut." *Sea Power* 6 (January 1919): 23–27.

Shaw, H. "Sanitary Report on the Island of Corfu." *United States Naval Medical Bulletin* (January 1919): 163–64.

"A Sick Bay in Scotland." *American Legion Magazine*, November 1921, 36–41.

Smith, Vice Admiral Allan E. "The Sixth Battle Squadron: A Reminiscence." *American Neptune* 40 (January 1980): 50–62.

Stanley, Frank. "War Time Repairs in the Navy." *American Machinists* 48 (May 1918): 731–32.

Stephenson, C. S. "With a Naval Railway Battery in France." *United States Naval Medical Bulletin* 13 (October 1919): 840–43.

Stirling, Archibald. "American Armed Yachts in the War Zone." *Yachting* 29 (May 1921): 275–78.

———. "The Bridge across the Atlantic." U.S. Naval Institute *Proceedings* 51 (September 1925): 1669–73.

Stone, Herbert L. "The Sub Chasers as Sea Boats." *Yachting* 28 (February 1920): 55–58.

Stuart, Robert. "All for 'Our Boys' in London." *Associated Men* 43 (May 1918): 686–87.

Taylor, David Watson. "The Design of War Vessels as Affected by the World War." *Journal of the Franklin Institute* 190 (August 1920): 157–85.

Taussig, Joseph. K. "Destroyer Experiences during the Great War." U.S. Naval Institute *Proceedings* 48 (December 1922): 2015–40; 49 (January 1923): 39–69; 49 (February 1923): 221–48; 49 (March 1923): 383–408.

Tinker, C. A. "Naval Flyers Abroad." *Navy Review* 10 (November 1919): 30–31.

Tunis, John. "Three Armistice Days." *American Legion Magazine*, November 1936, 14–15.

Vandercook, D. C. "The Greatest Battle of the War." *Associated Men* 43 (April 1918): 590–91, 690.

———. "The Man from Home." *Associated Men* 43 (May 1918): 410.

"Veteran Tars of 1917–18: A Yarn of the Good Old Days. Paris, Landlubbers, and Submarines." *Literary Digest*, August 24, 1918, 44.

"We Are Ready Now—American Destroyers on Duty." *Review of Reviews* 57 (May 1918): 531–32.

Weaver, Frank W. "An Incident of World War I." *Shipmate* 29 (January 1966): 7–10.

Wheat, George S. "The 'Sacred Drunk' of Brest When the War Was Over." *New York Herald Magazine*, January 12, 1918: 11, 13.

Wheeler, William J. "Reminiscences of World War Convoy Work." U.S. Naval Institute *Proceedings* 55 (May 1929): 385–92.

Whitaker, Herman. "Flying Sailors." *Land and Water* 71 (May 2, June 27, 1918): 6; and 72 (October 17, 1918): 8.

———. "How We Beat the U-Boats." *Independent* 96 (October 19, 1918): 84–85.

———. "The Mediterranean: The Last Stand of the Submarine." *Century Magazine* 97 (November 1918): 50–58.

———. "Our Tin Fleet in the First Battle Line." *New York Sun*, October 20, 1918: 18–19.

———. "Our Toy Dreadnoughts." *Century Magazine* 96 (June 1918): 791–804.

———. "Shore Leave." *Land and Water* 71 (July 11, 1918): 5–7.

———. "Sims' Circus When It Gets Shore Leave." *New York Sun Magazine*, April 28, 1918: 358–59, 404–5.

———. "Smashing Hun Submarines with Sims." *New York Sun Magazine*, April 14, 1918: 21–24.

———. "Toy Dreadnoughts." *Century* 96 (Oct., 1918): 997–804.

———. "With the American Fleet." *Land and Water* 71 (August 8, 1918): 13–14.

Williams, I. W. "With Destroyers in the War Zone." *United States Naval Medical Bulletin* (July 1918): 403–5.

Wilson, Admiral Henry B. "Address." *Transactions of the Society of Naval Architects and Marine Engineers* 27 (1919): 311–12.

"With the yankee 'suicide fleet' in French waters." *Literary Digest* (March 22, 1919): 19–20.

"Work of the American Mine Sweeping Squadron." *Rudder* (April, 1919): 180–81.

Wygant, Benyaurd. "Admiral Sims as I Knew Him." U.S. Naval Institute *Proceedings* 77 (1951): 1088–92.

Yamew [pseudo.]. "Mediterranean Convoys." *Naval Review* 53 (July 1965): 141–45.

Secondary Sources

Books, Monographs, and Studies

Abrahamson, James L. *America Arms for a New Century*. New York: Free Press, 1981.

Abrams, Ray H. *Preachers Present Arms*. New York: Round Table Press, 1933.

Adams, Henry H. *Witness to Power: The Life of Fleet Admiral William D. Leahy*. Annapolis: Naval Institute Press, 1985.

Albion, Robert G. *Makers of Naval Policy, 1798–1947*. Edited by Rowena Reed. Annapolis: Naval Institute Press, 1980.

Albion, Robert G., and Jennie B. Pope. *Sea Lanes in Wartime: The American Experience, 1775–1945*. 2nd ed. Hamden, Conn.: Archon, 1968.

Alden, Carroll Storrs, and Allan Westcott. *The United States Navy: A History*. Chicago: J. B. Lippincott, 1943.

Alden, Carroll Storrs, and Ralph Earle. *Makers of Naval Tradition*. Boston: Ginn, 1942.

Alden, John D. *Flush Decks and Four Pipers*. Annapolis: Naval Institute Press, 1965.

Allston, RADM Frank J., SC, USNR (Ret.). *Ready for Sea: The Bicentennial History of the U.S. Navy Supply Corps*. Annapolis: Naval Institute Press, 1995.

Anderson, Oscar E. *Refrigeration in America: A History of a New Technology and Its Impact*. Princeton: Princeton University Press, 1953.

Arnold, Craig. *Medea: The Classic Steam Yacht*. San Diego: Maritime Museum Association of San Diego, 1994.

Arthur, Reginald W. *Contact! Naval Aviators Assigned Numbers 1 to 2000*. Washington, D.C.: Naval Aviation Register, 1967.

Auten, Lt. Commander Harold. *"Q" Boat Adventures*. London: Herbert Jenkins, 1919.

Baker, Ray Stannard, ed. *Woodrow Wilson: Life and Letters*. 8 vols. Garden City, N.Y.: Doubleday, Page, 1927–39.

Baker, Richard. *The Terror of Tobermory: An Informal Biography of Vice-Admiral Sir Gilbert Stephenson*. London: W. H. Allen, 1972.

Baldwin, Hanson W. *World War I*. New York: Harper and Row, 1962.

Ballantine, Duncan S. *U.S. Naval Logistics in the Second World War*. Princeton: Princeton University Press, 1947.

Balliano, Adolfo, and Soavi, Giuseppe. *L'Italia sul mare nella grande Guerra*. Torino: Successore Loescher Ermanno, 1934.

Barnes, Robert H. *United States Submarines*. New Haven, Conn.: H. F. Morse, 1944.

Baynham, Henry. *Men from the Dreadnoughts*. London: Hutchinson, 1976.

Beatty, Charles. *Our Admiral: A Biography of Admiral of the Fleet Earl Beatty*. London: W. H. Allen, 1980.

Becker, Jean-Jacques. *The Great War and the French People*. New York: St. Martin's Press, 1986.

Beecher. Sean. *The Story of Cork*. Cork: Mercier Press, 1971.

Beers, Henry P. *U.S. Naval Forces in Northern Russia: Archangel and Murmansk, 1918–1919*. Administration Reference Service Report No. 5. Washington, D.C.: Office of Records Administration, U.S. Navy, 1943.

———. *U.S. Naval Port Offices in the Bordeaux Region, 1917–1919*. Administrative Reference Service Report No. 3. Washington, D.C.: Office of Records Administration, Navy Department, September 1943.

Beesly, Patrick. *Room 40*. New York: Harcourt Brace Jovanovich, 1982.

———. *Very Special Admiral: The Life of Admiral J. H. Godfrey*. London: Hamish Hamilton, 1980.

Beloff, Max. *Wars and Welfare, Britain 1914–1945*. London: Edward Arnold, 1984.

Bennett, Geoffrey. *'Charlie B.': The Life of Admiral Lord Beresford*. London: Peter Dawnay, 1968.

Besch, Michael D. *A Navy Second to None: The History of U.S. Naval Training in World War I*. Westport, Conn.: Greenwood Press, 2002.

Betts, John R. *America's Sporting Heritage, 1850–1950*. Menlo Park, Calif.: Addison-Wesley, 1974.

Bird, James. *The Major Seaports of the United Kingdom*. London: Hutchinson, 1963.

Blumenthal, Henry. *Illusion and Reality in Franco-American Diplomacy, 1914–1945*. Baton Rouge: Louisiana State University Press, 1986.

Bond, Brian, ed. *The First World War and British Military History*. Oxford: Clarendon Press, 1991.

Bone, David W. *Merchantmen-At-Arms: The British Merchants' Service in the War*. New York: E. P. Dutton, 1919.

Borden, Penn. *Civilian Indoctrination of the Military: World War I and Future Implications for the Military-Industrial Complex*. Westport, Conn.: Greenwood Press, 1989.

Bradford, Ernle. *Gibraltar: The History of a Fortress*. New York: Harcourt Brace Jovanovich, 1971.

Bradford, James C., ed. *Admirals of the New Steel Navy: Makers of American Naval Tradition, 1880–1930*. Annapolis: Naval Institute Press, 1990.

Braganca-Cunha, V. De. *Revolutionary Portugal*. London: James Clarke, 1937.

Braisted, William R. *The United States Navy in the Pacific, 1909–1922*. Austin: University of Texas Press, 1971.

Brandt, Allan M. *No Magic Bullet: A Social History of Venereal Disease in the United States since 1880*. New York: Oxford University Press, 1985.

Brassey, Earl, and John Leyland. *The Navy Annual, 1919*. London: William Clowes and Sons, 1919.

Braynard, Frank O. *The Story of the* Leviathan. Vol. 1. New York: South Street Seaport Museum, 1972.

Bridges, Antony. *Scapa Ferry*. London: Peter Davies, 1957.

Brown, D. K. *A Century of Naval Construction*. London: Conway Maritime Press, 1983.

Brown, Lt. (jg) F. W., USCG. *Overseas, 1917–1918*. Privately printed. Copy in CG Library.

Brown, Malcolm. *The Imperial War Museum Book of the First World War*. Norman: University of Oklahoma Press, 1993.

————. *Scapa Flow*. London: Penguin, 1968.

Buell, Thomas B. *Master of Sea Power: A Biography of Ernest J. King*. Boston: Little, Brown, 1980.

Burger, Katherine Johnson. *Called to Serve: American Nurses Go to War, 1914–1918*. Ann Arbor, Mich.: U.M.I., 1993.

Burke, Kathleen. *Britain, America, and the Sinews of War, 1914–1918*. Boston: Allen and Unwin, 1985.

Burrows, C. W. *Scapa Flow and a Camera*. New York: Charles Scribner's Sons, 1921.

Byrne, William J. *The Deck School Log of the Naval Auxiliary Reserve*. New York: Wynkoop Halleneck Crawford, 1920.

Calhoun, Frederick S. *Power and Principle: Armed Intervention in Wilsonian Foreign Policy*. Kent, Ohio: Kent State University Press, 1986.

Campbell, R. Wright. *Honor*. New York: Tom Doherty, 1987.

Capoletti, Peter, ed. *Our Man in the Crimea: Commander Hugo Koebler and the Russian Civil War*. Columbia, S.C.: University of South Carolina Press, 1991.

Carew, Anthony. *The Lower Deck of the Royal Navy, 1900–39*. Manchester: Manchester University Press, 1981.

Carroll, F. M. *American Opinion and the Irish Question 1910–23*. London: Gill and Macmillan, 1978.

Carter, Rear Admiral Worrall Reed. *Beans, Bullets, and Black Oil*. Washington, D.C.: GPO, 1953.

Carver, Thomas Nixon. *Government Control of the Liquor Business in Great Britain and the United Sates*. Carnegie Endowment for International Peace Preliminary Economic Studies of the War. New York: Oxford University Press, 1919.

Chack, Paul, and Jean-Jacques Antier. *Histoire maritime de la premiere guerre mondiale*. Vol. 2, *1916–1918*. Paris: Editions France-Empire, 1971.

Chalmers, Rear Admiral W. S. *The Life and Letters of David Earl Beatty*. London: Hodder and Stoughton, 1951.

Chapin, W.A.R. *The Lost Legion: The Story of the Fifteen Hundred Doctors Who Served with the B.E.F. in the Great War*. Springfield, Mass., 1926.

Chatterton, E. Keble. *Amazing Adventure*. London: Hurst and Blackett, 1936.

————. *Danger Zone: the Story of the Queenstown Command*. Boston: Little, Brown, 1934.

————. *Gallant Gentlemen*. London: Hurst and Blackett, 1931.

————. *Q-Ships and Their Story*. London: Sidgwick and Jackson, 1922.

————. *Seas of Adventure: The Story of the Naval Operations in the Mediterranean, Adriatic, and Aegean*. London: Hurst and Blackett, 1942.

Chevrillon, André. *Les Americains a Brest*. Paris: Librairie Chapelot, 1920.

Christian Science War Time Activities. Boston: Christian Science Publishing Society, 1922.

Churchill, Hon. Winston. *The World Crisis*. New York: Charles Scribner's Sons, 1923.

Clark, Elmer T. *Social Studies of the War*. New York: George H. Doran, 1919.

Clephane, Lewis P. *History of the Naval Overseas Transportation Service in World War I*. Washington, D.C.: Naval Historical Center, 1969.

Coffman, Edward M. *The War to End All Wars*. New York: Oxford University Press, 1968.

Cogar, William B. *Dictionary of Admirals of the U.S. Navy*. Vol. 2, *1901–1918*. Annapolis: Naval Institute Press, 1989.

Coleman, James. *History of the Great Island, Ancient Cove, and Modern Queenstown*. Cork: Guy, 1923.

Coletta, Paolo E. *Allied and American Naval Operations in the European Theatre in World War I*. Lewiston, Md.: Edwin Meller Press, 1996.

———. *The American Naval Heritage in Brief.* Lanham, Md.: University Press of America, 1987.

———, ed. *American Secretaries of the Navy.* Vol. 2, *1913–1972.* Annapolis: Naval Institute Press, 1980.

———. *Sea Power in the Atlantic and Mediterranean in World War I.* Lanham, Md.: University Press of America, 1989.

Coletta, Paolo E., and K. Jack Bauer. *United States Navy and Marine Corps Bases, Overseas.* Westport, Conn.: Greenwood Press, 1985.

Collier, Richard. *The Plague of the Spanish Lady: The Influenza Pandemic of 1918–1919.* New York: Atheneum, 1974.

Collins, Francis A. *Naval Heroes of To-Day.* New York: Century, 1918.

Collins, L. J. *Theatre at War, 1914–18.* New York: St Martin's Press, 1998.

Collins, Nelson. *Civilian Seamen in War.* [Alpena, Mich.]: League of Civilian Seamen: United States Section: Pamphlet II: 1924.

Collis, Maurice. *Nancy Astor.* New York: E. P. Dutton, 1960.

Compton-Hall, Richard. *Submarines and the War at Sea 1914–18.* London: Macmillan, 1991.

Connolly, James B. *Navy Men.* New York: John Day, 1939.

———. *The U-Boat Hunters.* New York: Charles Scribner's Sons, 1918.

Cooper, John Milton. *Walter Hines Page.* Chapel Hill: University of North Carolina Press, 1977.

Corbett, Julian, and Henry Newbolt. *History of the Great War: Naval Operations.* 5 vols. London: Longmans, Green, 1920–31.

Cornebise, Alfred E. *The Stars and Stripes: Doughboy Journalism in World War I.* Westport, Conn.: Greenwood Press, 1984.

———. *War As Advertised: The Four Minute Men and America's Crusade, 1917–1918.* Philadelphia: American Philosophical Society, 1984.

Costello, John. *Virtue under Fire.* Boston: Little, Brown, 1985.

Cottman, George S. *Jefferson County in the World War.* Madison, Ind.: Jefferson County Historical Society, 1920.

Courteault, Paul. *La vie economique Bordeaux pendant la guerre.* Paris: Les Presses Universitaires De France, 1977.

Cousins, Geoffrey. *The Story of Scapa Flow.* London: Frederick Muller, 1965.

Cowie, Captain J. S. *Mines, Minelayers, and Minelaying.* London: Oxford University Press, 1949.

Cozens, Frederick W., and Florence Scovil Stumpf. *Sports in American Life.* New York: Arno Press, 1976.

Crosby, Alfred W. *America's Forgotten Pandemic: The Influenza of 1918.* New York: Cambridge University Press, 1989.

———. *Epidemic and Peace, 1918.* Westport, Conn.: Greenwood Press, 1976.

Crowell, Benedict, and Robert Forrest Wilson. *The Road to France.* Vol. 2, *The Transportation of Troops and Military Supplies 1917–1918.* New Haven, Conn.: Yale University Press, 1921.

Crozier, Emmet. *American Reporters on the Western Front 1914–1918.* New York: Oxford University Press, 1959.

Cuff, Robert D. *The War Industries Board.* Baltimore: Johns Hopkins University Press, 1973.

Dabney, Virginius. *Dry Messiah: The Life of Bishop Cannon.* Westport, Conn.: Greenwood Press, 1949.

Daniels, Jonathan. *The End of Innocence.* Philadelphia: J. B. Lippincott, 1954.

———. *Washington Quadrille.* Garden City, N.Y.: Doubleday, 1968.

Daniels, Josephus. *Our Navy at War.* New York: George H. Doran, 1922.

Davenport, E. H., and Sidney R. Cooke. *The Oil Trusts and Anglo-American Relations.* Westport, Conn.: Hyperion Press, 1976.

Davies, Pete. *The Devil's Flu: The World's Deadliest Influenza and the Scientific Hunt for the Virus That Caused It.* New York: Henry Holt, 2000.

Davis, George T. *A Navy Second to None.* New York: Harcourt, Brace, 1940.

Davis, Vincent. *The Admiral's Lobby.* Chapel Hill: University of North Carolina Press, 1967.

Davison, Henry P. *The American Red Cross in the Great War.* New York: Macmillan, 1920.

Deacon, Richard. *The Silent War: A History of Western Intelligence.* London: David and Charles, 1978.

DeLany, Vice Admiral Walter S. (Ret.). *Bayly's Navy.* Washington, D.C.: Naval Historical Foundation, 1980.

Dennis, Philip. *Gibraltar, the British Rock.* London: David and Charles, 1977.

Denny, Ludwell. *America Conquers Britain: A Record of Economic War.* New York: A. A. Knopf, 1930.

Dent, Richard C. *The Life Story of King George V.* New York: E. P. Dutton, n.d.

Dictionary of American Fighting Ships. 9 vols. Washington, D.C.: Naval Historical Center, 1959–93.

Dock, Lavinia L., Sarah Elizabeth Pickett, Clara D. Noyes, Fannie F. Clement, Elizabeth G. Fox, and Anna R. Van Meter. *History of American Red Cross Nursing.* New York: Macmillan, 1922.

Dodson, Christopher, and John Miller, *The Day They Almost Bombed Moscow.* New York: Atheneum, 1986.

Donnachie, Ian. *A History of the Brewing Industry in Scotland.* Edinburgh: John Donald, 1979.

Don Passos, John. *Mr. Wilson's War.* Garden City, N.Y.: Doubleday, 1962.

Dorwart, Jeffery M. *Conflict of Duty: The U.S. Navy's Intelligence Dilemma, 1919–1945.* Annapolis: Naval Institute Press, 1983.

———. *The Office of Naval Intelligence.* Annapolis: Naval Institute Press, 1979.

Dougan, David. *A History of North East Shipbuilding.* London: Allen and Unwin, 1968.

Dreyer, Admiral Sir Frederic C. *The Sea Heritage.* London: Museum Press, 1955.

Drury, Clifford Merrill. *The History of the Chaplain Corps, United States Navy.* Vol. 1, *1778–1939.* Washington, D.C.: GPO, 1983.

Dulles, Foster Rhea. *A History of Recreation.* New York: Appleton-Century Crofts, 1965.

Duncan, Robert C. *America's Use of Sea Mines.* Silver Springs, Md.: United States Naval Ordnance Laboratory, 1962.

Duroselle, Jean Baptista. *France and the United States.* Chicago: University of Chicago Press, 1978.

Dyer, Vice Admiral George C. *Naval Logistics.* Annapolis: Naval Institute Press, 1962.

Ebbert, Jean, and Marie-Beth Hall, *The First, the Few, the Forgotten: Navy and Marine Corps Women in World War I.* Annapolis: Naval Institute Press, 2002.

Eccles, Henry E. *Logistics in the National Defense.* Harrisburg, Pa.: Stackpole Co., 1959.

———. *Operational Naval Logistics.* Washington, D.C.: Bureau of Naval Personnel, GPO, 1950.

Egan, Maurice F., and John B. Kennedy. *Knights of Columbus in Peace and War.* Vol. 1. New Haven, Conn.: Knights of Columbus, 1920.

Eilers, Tom D. *Buena Vista's Part in the World War.* Storm Lake, Iowa: privately published, 1920.

Elderton, W. Palin. *Shipping Problems, 1916–1921.* London: A. and C. Black, 1928.

Elliott, Peter. *The Cross and the Ensign: A Naval History of Malta, 1798–1979.* Annapolis: Naval Institute Press, 1980.

Ellis, Hamilton. *British Railway History.* London: Allen and Unwin, 1959.

Evans, James E., and Captain Gardner L. Harding. *Entertaining the American Army*. New York: Association Press, 1921.

Falls, Cyril. *The Great War*. New York: Capricorn, 1959.

Fayle, C. Ernest. *Seaborne Trade*. Vol. 3. London: John Murray, 1924.

Ferraby, Hubert C. *The Grand Fleet*. London: Herbert Jenkins, 1916.

Ferrell, Robert H. *Woodrow Wilson and World War I 1917–1921*. New York: Harper and Row, 1985.

Fife, George Buchanan. *The Passing Legions*. New York: Macmillan, 1920.

Filene, Peter. *Him/Her/Self: Gender Identities in Modern America*. Baltimore: Johns Hopkins University Press, 1998.

Finnegan, John Patrick. *Against the Specter of a Dragon: The Campaign for American Military Preparedness, 1914–1917*. Westport, Conn.: Greenwood Press, 1974.

Firkins, Peter. *Of Nautilus and Eagles: History of the Royal Australian Navy*. Sydney: Hutchinson of Australia, 1983.

Flying Officers of the U.S. Navy. Washington, D.C.: Naval Aviation War Book Committee, 1919.

Forbes, John D. *J. P. Morgan, Jr., 1867–1943*. Charlottesville: University Press of Virginia, 1981.

Forrest, Wilbur. *Behind the Front Page*. New York: D. Appleton-Century, 1934.

Fraser, Edward, and John Gibbons. *Soldier and Sailor Words and Phrases*. London: George Routledge and Sons, 1925.

Frederick, Pierce G. *The Great Adventure*. New York: Ace, 1960.

Freeman, Lewis R. *Stories of the Ships*. London: John Murray, 1919.

Freidel, Frank. *Franklin D. Roosevelt: The Apprenticeship*. Boston: Little, Brown, 1952.

———. *Over There: The Story of America's First Great Overseas Crusade*. Boston: Little, Brown, 1964.

Friedman, Norman. *U.S. Battleships*. Annapolis: Naval Institute Press, 1985.

———. *U.S. Destroyers*. Annapolis: Naval Institute Press, 1982.

———. *U.S. Naval Weapons*. Annapolis: Naval Institute Press, 1987.

———. *U.S. Small Combatants*. Annapolis: Naval Institute Press, 1987.

Frothington, Thomas G. *The Naval History of the World War: The United States in the War 1917–1918*. Cambridge: Harvard University Press, 1927.

Furer, Julius. *Administration of the Navy Department in World War II*. Washington, D.C.: GPO, 1959.

Furlong, William Rae. *Class of 1905, United States Naval Academy*. Annapolis: Naval Institute Press, 1930.

Gabriel, Richard A., and Karen S. Metz. *A History of Military Medicine*. Vol. 2, *From the Renaissance through Modern Times*. Westport, Conn.: Greenwood Press, 1992.

Gardiner, Leslie. *The British Admiralty*. London: William Blackwood and Sons, 1968.

Gardiner, Robert, ed. *The Eclipse of the Big Gun: The Warship 1906–45*. London: Conway Maritime Press, 1992.

Garnett, Laurie. *The Coming Plague*. New York: Penguin Books: 1994.

Garratt, G. T. *Gibraltar and the Mediterranean*. New York: Coward-McCann, 1939.

Garrison, Lieut. Col. Fielding H. *Notes on the History of Military Medicine*. Washington, D.C.: Association of Military Surgeons, 1922.

Gerken, Louis. *ASW versus Submarine Technology Battle*. Chula Vista, Calif.: American Scientific Corp., 1986.

Gibbons, Herbert Adams. *Ports of France*. New York: Century, 1926.

Gibson, Charles Dana, with E. Kay Gibson. *Over Seas: U.S. Army Maritime Operations 1898 through the Fall of the Philippines*. Camden, Maine: Ensign Press, 2001.

Gibson, R. H., and Maurice Prendergast. *The German Submarine War 1914–1918*. London: Constable, 1931.

Gilbert, Martin Winslow. *Winston S. Churchill: The Challenge of War, 1914–1916*. Boston: Houghton Mifflin, 1971.

Gill, Crispin. *Plymouth: A New History*. London: David and Charles, 1979.

Ginocchietti, Angelo. *La guerra sul mare*. Rome: Libreria Del Victtorie, 1930.

Gleichauf, Justin F. *Unsung Sailors: The Naval Armed Guard in World War II*. Annapolis: Naval Institute Press, 1990.

Godson, Susan H. *Serving Proudly: A History of Women in the U.S. Navy*. Annapolis: Naval Institute Press, 2001.

Goldhurst, Richard. *The Midnight War: The American Intervention in Russia, 1918–1920*. New York: McGraw-Hill, 1978.

Goldrick, James. *The King's Ships Were at Sea*. Annapolis: Naval Institute Press, 1984.

Gordon, Dennis, ed. *Quartered in Hell: The Story of the American North Russian Expeditionary Force, 1918–1919*. Missoula, Mont.: Doughboy Historical Society, 1982.

Gramling, Oliver. *AP: The Story of News*. New York: Farrar and Rinehart, 1940.

Grant, Robert M. *U-Boat Intelligence 1914–1918*. Hamden, Conn.: Archon Books, 1969.

———. *U-Boats Destroyed: The Effect of Anti-Submarine Warfare 1914–1918*. London: Putnam, 1964.

Graves, Robert, and Alan Hodge. *The Long Weekend: A Social History of Great Britain, 1918–1939*. New York: Macmillan, 1941.

Gray, Edwyn. *The Killing Time*. New York: Charles Scribner's Sons, 1972.

Green, Fitzhugh. *Our Naval Heritage*. New York: Century, 1925.

Greenville, John A. S., and George B. Young. *Politics, Strategy, and American Diplomacy: Studies in Foreign Policy, 1873–1917*. New Haven: Yale University Press, 1966.

Gretton, Vice Admiral Sir Peter. *Winston Churchill and the Royal Navy*. New York: Coward McCann, 1969.

Grossnick, Roy A., ed. *Kite Balloons to Air Ships . . . The Navy's Lighter-than-Air Experience*. Washington, D.C.: Deputy Chief of Naval Operations (Air Warfare) and the Commander, Naval Air Systems Command, n.d.

Guinn, Paul. *British Strategy and Politics, 1914–1918*. London: Oxford University Press, 1965.

Hackmann, Willem. *Seek and Strike: Sonar, Anti-submarine Warfare, and the Royal Navy 1914–54*. London: Her Majesty's Stationery Office, 1984.

Hadley, Michael L., and Roger Sarty. *Tin-Pots and Pirate Ships: Canadian Naval Forces and German Sea Raiders 1880–1918*. Montreal: McGill-Queens University Press, 1991.

Hagan, Kenneth J. *The People's Navy: The Making of American Sea Power*. New York: Free Press, 1991.

Halpern, Paul G. *A Naval History of World War I*. Annapolis: Naval Institute Press, 1994.

———. *The Naval War in the Mediterranean, 1914–1918*. Annapolis: Naval Institute Press, 1987.

Harbord, James G. *The American Army in France 1917–1919*. Boston: Little, Brown, 1936.

Hardach, Gerd. *The First World War 1914–1918*. Berkeley and Los Angeles: University of California Press, 1977.

Harper's Pictorial Library of the World War. Vol. 4, *The War on the Sea*. New York: Harper and Brothers, 1920.

Harries, Meirion, and Susie Harries. *The Last Days of Innocence: America at War, 1917–1918*. New York: Random House, 1997.

Harrod, Frederick S. *Manning the New Navy: The Development of a Modern Naval Enlisted Force, 1899–1940*. Westport, Conn.: Greenwood Press, 1978.

Hart, B. H. Liddell. *The Real War, 1914–18*. Boston: Little, Brown, 1930.

Hartcup, Guy. *The War of Invention: Scientific Developments, 1914–18*. London: Brassey's Defence Publishers, 1988.

Hartley, Stephen. *The Irish Question as a Problem in British Foreign Policy, 1914–18*. New York: St. Martin's Press, 1987.

Hartmann, Gregory K. *Weapons That Wait: Mine Warfare in the U.S. Navy*. Annapolis: Naval Institute Press, 1979.

Hassler, Warren W., Jr. *With Shield and Sword: American Military Affairs, Colonial Times to the Present*. Ames: Iowa State University Press, 1982.

Hattendorf, John B. *The Influence of History on Mahan*. Newport, R.I.: Naval War College Press, 1993.

———. *Sailors and Scholars: The Centennial History of the Naval War College*. Newport, R.I.: Naval War College Press, 1984.

Hayes, Karl. *A History of the Royal Air Force and United States Naval Air Service in Ireland 1913–1923*. Dublin: Irish Air Letter, 1988.

Hayes, Ralph A. *Secretary Baker at the Front*. New York: Century, 1918.

Hendrick, Burton J. *The Life and Letters of Walter Hines Page*. 2 vols. New York: Doubleday, Page, 1922.

Herwig, Holger H. *"Luxury" Fleet: The Imperial German Navy, 1888–1918*. London: Ashfield Press, 1987.

———. *Politics of Frustration: The United States in German Naval Planning, 1889–1941*. Boston: Little, Brown, 1976.

Herwig, Holger H., and Neil M. Heyman. *Biographical Dictionary of World War I*. Westport, Conn.: Greenwood Press, 1982.

Hewison, W. S. *This Great Harbour, Scapa Flow*. Stromness, Orkney: Orkney Press, 1985.

Hibbert, Christopher. *The English: A Social History*. New York: W. W. Norton, 1987.

Hicken, Victor. *The American Fighting Man*. New York: Macmillan, 1969.

Hoehling, A. A. *The Great Epidemic*. Boston: Little, Brown, 1961.

———. *The Great War at Sea*. London: Corgi, 1967.

Hofman, Erik. *The Steam Yachts*. Tuckahoe, N.Y.: John De Graff, 1970.

Hogg, Ian, and John Batchelor. *Naval Guns*. Poole Dorset, U.K.: Blandford Press, 1979.

Hood, Ronald C. *Royal Republicans: The French Naval Dynasties between the World Wars*. Baton Rouge: Louisiana State University Press, 1985.

Hopkins, C. Howard. *History of the Y.M.C.A. Movement in North America*. New York: Association Press, 1951.

Horsfield, John. *The Art of Leadership in War: The Royal Navy from the Age of Nelson to the End of World War II*. Westport, Conn.: Greenwood Press, 1981.

Hough, Richard. *The Great War at Sea 1914–1918*. New York: Oxford University Press, 1983.

Howard, Michael. *War in European History*. London: Oxford University Press, 1976.

Howell, Glenn. *Medals of Honor*. New York: Dial Press, 1931.

Howeth, Lindwood S. *History of Communication Electronics in the United States Navy*. Washington, D.C.: GPO, 1963.

Hoy, Hugh Cleland. *40 O.B.* London: Hutchinson, 1932.

Hunter, Lieut. Francis T. *Beatty, Jellicoe, Sims, and Rodman*. Garden City, N.Y.: Doubleday, Page, 1919.

Hurd, Archibald. *The Merchant Navy*. Vol. 3. London: John Murray, 1929.

Hurd, Archibald, and H. H. Bashford. *Sons of Admiralty: A Short History of the Naval War 1914–1918*. London: Constable, 1919.

Huston, James A. *The Sinews of War: Army Logistics 1775–1953*. Washington, D.C.: Office of the Chief of Military History, United States Army, 1966.

Hutchinson, John F. *Champions of Charity: War and the Rise of the Red Cross*. Boulder, Colo.: Westview Press, 1996.

Hutton, Patrick H., ed. *Historical Dictionary of the Third French Republic, 1870–1940*. Westport, Conn.: Greenwood Press, 1986.

Ingraham, Reg. *First Fleet: The Story of the U.S. Coast Guard at War*. Indianapolis, Ind.: Bobbs-Merrill, 1944.

Ireland, John deCourcy. *Ireland and the Irish in Maritime History*. Dublin: Glendale Press, 1986.

The Irish Mess and an Attack on the U.S. Navy. Boston: Advisory Committee, Irish Victory Fund, 1919.

The Irish World and American Ireland Liberation. N.p., February 12, 1920.

Jackson, Captain Orton P., and Colonel Frank E. Evans. *The New Book of American Ships*. New York: Frederick A. Stokes, 1926.

Jackson, Robert. *The Prisoners 1914–18*. London: Routledge, 1989.

James, Admiral Sir William. *The Code Breakers of Room 40*. New York: St. Martin's Press, 1956.

———. *The Eyes of the Navy: A Biographical Study of Admiral Sir Reginald Hall*. London: Methuen, 1956.

———. *A Great Seaman: The Life of Admiral of the Fleet Sir Henry F. Oliver*. London: H. F. and G. Witherby, 1956.

Jameson, William. *The Fleet That Jack Built*. London: Rupert Hart-Davis, 1962.

———. *The Most Formidable Thing*. London: Rupert Hart-Davis, 1965.

Jenkins, E. H. *A History of the French Navy*. Annapolis: Naval Institute Press, 1973.

Jestin, Alain. *Histoire vecue du camp Americians de Pontanezer pendant la guerre de 1914–1918*. Brest, 1968.

Johnson, Lieut. Col. Edward C. *Marine Corps Aviation: The Early Years, 1912–1940*. Washington, D.C.: History and Museums Division, Headquarters, U.S. Marine Corps, 1977.

Johnson, Robert E. *Guardians of the Sea: History of the United States Coast Guard, 1915 to the Present*. Annapolis: Naval Institute Press, 1987.

Jones, Jerry W. *U.S. Battleship Operations in World War I*. Annapolis: Naval Institute Press, 1998.

Jones, T. M. *Watchdogs of the Deep*. Sydney: Angus and Robertson, 1932.

Jose, Arthur W. *The Royal Australian Navy, 1914–1918*. Sydney: Angus and Robertson, 1928.

Karsten, Peter. *The Naval Aristocracy: The Golden Age of Annapolis and the Emergence of Modern American Navalism*. New York: Free Press, 1972.

Kaspi, André. *Le temps des Americains: Le concours Americain a la France en 1917–1918*. Paris: Sorbonne, 1976.

Kaufman, Barton. *Efficiency and Expansion: Foreign Trade Organization in the Wilson Administration, 1913–1921*. Westport, Conn.: Greenwood, 1974.

Kemp, Paul. *Convoy Protection: The Defense of Seaborne Trade*. London: Arms and Armour, 1993.

Kemp, Tom. *The French Economy, 1913–39*. New York: St. Martin's Press, 1972.

Kennan, George F. *The Decision to Intervene*. New York: Atheneum, 1967.

Kennedy, David M. *Over Here: The First World War and American Society*. New York: Oxford University Press, 1980.

Kennedy, Paul M. *The Rise and Fall of British Naval Mastery*. New York: Charles Scribner's Sons, 1976.

Kennett, Lee. *The First Air War, 1914–1918*. New York: Free Press, 1991.

Kenworthy, John. *The Real Navy*. London: Hutchinson, 1932.

Kernodle, Portia B. *The Red Cross Nurse in Action, 1882–1948*. New York: Harper and Brothers, 1949.

Kevles, Daniel J. *The Physicists*. Cambridge: Harvard University Press, 1987.

Kilpatrick, Carroll. *Roosevelt and Daniels: A Friendship in Politics.* Chapel Hill: University of North Carolina Press, 1952.

King, Cecil. *Atlantic Charter.* London: Studio, 1943.

King, Rear Admiral Randolph W., ed. *Naval Engineering and American Seapower.* Baltimore: Nautical and Aviation Publication Co. of America, 1989.

Kittredge, Tracy Barrett. *Naval Lessons of the Great War.* Garden City, N.Y.: Doubleday, Page, 1921.

Klachko, Mary, with David Trask. *Admiral William Shepherd Benson, First Chief of Naval Operations.* Annapolis: Naval Institute Press, 1987.

Knock, Sidney. *"Clear Lower Deck."* London: Philip Allan, 1932.

Knowles, Bernard. *Southampton: The English Gateway.* London: Hutchinson, 1951.

Kobler, John. *Ardent Spirits: The Rise and Fall of Prohibition.* New York: G. P. Putnam's Sons, 1973.

Lajugie, Joseph. *Bordeaux au XX siecle.* Bordeaux, 1932.

Langhorne, Elizabeth. *Nancy Astor and Her Friends.* New York: Praeger, 1974.

Langley, Harold. *Social Reform in the Navy, 1798–1862.* Urbana: University of Illinois Press, 1967.

Larzelere, Alex R. *The Coast Guard in World War I: An Untold Story.* Annapolis: Naval Institute Press, 2003.

Laurens, Adolphe. *Le commandement naval en Mediterranee, 1914–1918.* Paris: Payot, 1931.

———. *Precis d'histoire de la Guerre navale, 1914–1918.* Paris: Payot, 1927.

Layman, R. D. *Naval Aviation in the First World War.* Annapolis: Naval Institute Press, 1995.

Lee, J. J. *Ireland, 1912–1985.* Cambridge: Cambridge University Press, 1989.

Leighton, John Langdon. *Simsadus: London.* New York: Henry Holt, 1920.

Lepotier, Comtre-Amiral. *Brest, porte oceane.* Paris: Editions France-Empire, 1968.

LeRoy, Thierry. *La Guerre Sous-marine en Bretagne, 1914–1918: Victoire de L'Aeronavale.* N.p., 1990.

Leutze, James. *A Different Kind of Victory: A Biography of Admiral Thomas C. Hart.* Annapolis: Naval Institute Press, 1981.

Lewis, Brian. *Our War: Australia during World War I.* Melbourne: Melbourne University Press, 1980.

Lewis, Commander David D. *The Fight for the Sea.* New York: Collier, 1961.

Liddle, Peter H. *The Sailor's War, 1914–18.* Dorset: Blandford Press, 1985.

Link, Arthur S. *Wilson: Campaigns for Progressivism and Peace, 1915–1917.* Princeton, N.J.: Princeton University Press, 1965.

———. *Wilson, Confusion and Crisis 1915–1916.* Princeton, N.J.: Princeton University Press, 1964.

———. *Woodrow Wilson and the Progressive Era, 1910–1917.* New York: Harper Torchbooks, 1954.

Lloyd, Christopher. *The Nation and the Navy.* London: Cresset Press, 1961.

Lohbeck, Don. *Patrick J. Hurley.* Chicago: Henry Regnery, 1956.

Lott, Arnold S. *Most Dangerous Sea.* Annapolis: Naval Institute Press, 1959.

Love, Robert W., Jr. *History of the U.S. Navy, 1775–1941.* Vol. 1. Harrisburg, Pa.: Stackpole, 1992.

Low, A. M. *Mine and Countermine.* New York: Sheridan House, 1940.

Lyons, F.S.L. *Ireland since the Famine.* London: Fonana/Collins, 1971.

MacDougall, Philip. *Royal Dockyards.* London: David and Charles, 1982.

Macksey. Kenneth. *For Want of a Nail: The Impact on War of Logistics and Communications.* London: Brassey's, 1989.

Manfroni, Camilla. *Storia della marine italiana, durante la guerra mondiale, 1914–1918*. 2nd ed. Bologna: Nicola Zanichell, 1925.

Marcosson, Isaac F. *S.O.S. America's Miracle in France*. New York: John Lane, 1919.

Marder, Arthur J. *From the Dreadnought to Scapa Flow. The Royal Navy in the Fisher Era, 1904–1919*. 5 vols. London: Oxford University Press, 1961–70.

———. *Portrait of an Admiral: The Life and Papers of Sir Herbert Richmond*. London: Jonathan Cape, 1952.

Marshall, S.L.A. *World War I*. New York: Houghton Mifflin, 1985.

Marwick, Arthur. *The Deluge: British Society and the First World War*. New York: W. W. Norton, 1965.

Maurice, Sir Frederick. *Lessons of Allied Co-Operation: Naval Military and Air, 1914–1918*. London: Oxford University Press, 1942.

Maxwell, Gordon S. *The Naval Front*. London: A. and C. Black, 1920.

Mayo, Katherine. *"That Damn Y."* Boston: Houghton Mifflin, 1920.

McClellan, Major Edwin N. *The United States Marine Corps in the World War*. Washington, D.C.: Historical Branch, G-3 Division, Headquarters, U.S. Marine Corps, 1968.

McDowell, Robert. *The Irish Convention 1917–1918*. London: Routledge and Kegan Paul, 1970.

McNeill, William. *Plagues and People*. Garden City: Anchor, 1976.

Meigs, Montgomery C. *Slide Rules and Submarines: American Scientists and Subsurface Warfare in World War II*. Washington, D.C.: National Defense University Press, 1990.

Messimer, Dwight R. *Escape*. Annapolis: Naval Institute Press, 1994.

Michelsen, Vice Admiral Andreas. *Der U-Bootskrieg, 1917–1918*. Leipzig: Koehler, 1925. An English translation, "The Submarine Warfare," is in *ONI Monthly Information Bulletin*, January 1926.

Milholland, Ray. *The Splinter Fleet*. Indianapolis, Ind.: Bobbs-Merrill, 1936.

Miller, Harold Blaine. *Navy Wings*. New York: Dodd, Mead, 1937.

Miller, Nathan. *FDR: An Intimate History*. Garden City, N.Y.: Doubleday, 1983.

Miller, Ronald. *Orkney*. London: B. T. Batsfod, 1976.

Miller, Warren Hastings. *The Boys of 1917*. Boston: L. C. Page, 1939.

Millett, Allan R. *Semper Fidelis: The History of the United States Marine Corps*. New York: Macmillan, 1980.

———, and Murray Williamson, eds., *Military Effectiveness*. Vol. 1, *The First World War*. Boston: Allen and Unwin, 1988.

Mitchell, David. *Women on the Warpath: The Story of the Women of the First World War*. London: Jonathan Cape, 1966.

Mitchell, Donald W. *History of the Modern American Navy*. New York: Knopf, 1946.

Mitchell, W. H., and L. A. Sawyer. *Sailing Ship to Supertanker*. Suffolk: Terence Dalton, 1987.

Mock, James R. *Censorship 1917*. Princeton, N.J.: Princeton University Press, 1941.

Mock, James R., and Cedric Larson. *Words That Won the War: The Story of the Committee on Public Information 1917–1919*. Princeton: Princeton University Press, 1939.

Moore, Joel R., et al. *The History of the American Expedition Fighting the Bolsheviks: Campaigning in North Russia, 1918–1919*. Detroit: Polar Bear, 1920.

Moore, John E. *Jane's Fighting Ships of World War I*. Reprint. New York: Military Press, 1990.

Morison, Elting E. *Admiral Sims and the Modern American Navy*. Boston: Houghton Mifflin, 1942.

Morrison, Joseph L. *Josephus Daniels, The Small-d Democrat*. Chapel Hill: University of North Carolina Press, 1966.

Moser Melia, Tamara. *"Damn the Torpedoes": A Short History of U.S. Naval Mine Countermeasures, 1777–1991*. Washington, D.C.: Naval Historical Center, 1991.

Muhlhauser, G.H.P. *Small Craft*. London: J. Lane, Bodley Head, 1924.

Muir, John R. *Years of Endurance*. London: Philip Allan, 1936.

Murphy, Francis X. *Fighting Admiral: The Story of Dan Callaghan*. New York: Vantage Press, 1952.

Murray, Arthur C. *Master and Brother. Murrays of Eubank*. London: John Murray, 1945.

Nalty, Bernard C., ed. *Blacks in the U.S. Military: Essential Documents*. Wilmington: Scholarly Press, 1991.

The Naval Staff of the Admiralty: Its Work and Development. Naval Staff Monographs. London: Training and Staff Duties Division, Admiralty, September 1929.

Neeser, Robert Wilden. *Our Many-Sided Navy*. New Haven, Conn.: Yale University Press, 1914.

Norton, Grace. *The Odyssey of a Torpedoed Transport*. Boston: Houghton Mifflin, 1918.

Nouailhat, Yves-Henri. *Les Americains a Nantes et Saint-Nazaire 1917–1919*. Paris: Les Belles Lettres, 1972.

Nutting, William S. *The Cinderellas of the Fleet*. Jersey City, N.J.: Standard Motor Construction Co., 1920.

Olson, Mancur, Jr. *The Economics of the Wartime Shortage*. Durham, N.C.: Duke University Press, 1963.

Oman, Rear Admiral Charles M. *Doctors Aweigh*. Garden City, N.J.: Doubleday, Doran, 1943.

Operations of the Coast Guard in Times of War. Washington, D.C.: U.S. Coast Guard, 1940.

Owen, Charles. *No More Heroes, The Royal Navy in the Twentieth Century: Anatomy of a Legend*. London: Allen and Unwin, 1975.

Pack, S.W.C. *Sea Power in the Mediterranean*. London: Arthur Baker, 1971.

Packard, Captain Wyman H. *A Century of U.S. Naval Intelligence*. Washington, D.C.: Naval Historical Center and Office of Naval Intelligence, 1996.

Padfield, Peter. *Aim Straight: A Biography of Admiral Sir Percy Scott*. London: Hodder and Stoughton, 1966.

Paine, Ralph D. *The Corsair in the War Zone*. Houghton Mifflin, 1920.

———. *The First Yale Unit: A Story of Naval Aviation 1916–1919*. 2 vols. Cambridge, Mass.: Riverside Press, 1925.

Palmer, Frederick. *Bliss, Peacemaker. The Life and Letters of General Tasker Howard Bliss*. New York: Dodd, Mead, 1934.

———. *Newton D. Baker: America at War*. 2 vols. New York: Dodd, Mead, 1931.

Parkinson, John, Jr. *The History of the New York Yacht Club*. New York: New York Yacht Club: 1975.

Parkinson, J. R. *The Economics of Shipbuilding in the United Kingdom*. Cambridge: Cambridge University Press, 1960.

Parini, Carl P. *Heir to Empire: United States Economic Diplomacy, 1916–1923*. Pittsburgh: University of Pittsburgh Press, 1969.

Parsons, Edward B. *Wilsonian Diplomacy: Allied-American Rivalries in War and Peace*. New York: Forum Press, 1978.

Parsons, William B. *The American Engineers in France*. New York: D. Appleton, 1920.

Patterson, A. Temple. *Jellicoe: A Biography*. London: Macmillan, 1969.

———. *Portsmouth: A History*. London: Moonraker Press. 1976.

———. *Tyrwhitt of the Harwich Force*. London: MacDonald, 1973.

Paxson, Frederick L. *America at War 1917–1918*. Boston: Houghton Mifflin, 1939.

Peebles, Hugh B. *Warshipbuilding on the Clyde*. Edinburgh: John Donald, 1987.

Perry, Lawrence. *Our Navy in the War*. New York: Charles Scribner's Sons, 1918.

Philadelphia in the World War, 1914–1919. Philadelphia: Philadelphia War History Committee, 1922.

Pilat, Oliver. *Pegler: Angry Man of the Press*. Westport, Conn.: Greenwood Press, 1963.

Po, Commandante Guido. *Il grande ammiraglio Paolo Thaon di Revel*. Turin: S. Lattes and C. Editori, 1936.

Pollen, Anthony. *The Great Gunnery Scandal: The Mystery of Jutland*. London: Collins, 1980.

Pollen, Arthur H. *The Navy in Battle*. London: Chatto and Windus, 1919.

Polmar, Norman, and Thomas B. Allen. *Rickover*. New York: Simon and Schuster, 1982.

Potter, E. B., and Chester W. Nimitz, eds. *Sea Power: A Naval History*. Englewood Cliffs, N.J.: Prentice Hall, 1960.

Power, Irvin. *Battleship* Texas. College Station: Texas A&M University Press, 1993.

Preventive Medicine in World War II. Washington, D.C.: Office of Surgeon General, U.S. Army, 1958.

Price, Alfred. *Aircraft versus Submarine*. Annapolis: Naval Institute Press, 1973.

Puleston, Captain W. D. *Annapolis: Gangway to the Quarterdeck*. New York: D. Appleton-Century, 1942.

Ratcliffe, Mike. *Liquid Gold Ships: A History of the Tanker, 1859–1984*. London: Lloyd's of London Press, 1985.

Reeves, Nicholas. *Official British Film Propaganda during the First World War*. London: Croom Helm, 1986.

Reilly, John D., Jr., and Robert Scheina. *American Battleships, 1886–1923*. Annapolis: Naval Institute Press, 1980.

Reiners, Ludwig. *The Lamps Went Out in Europe*. Cleveland, Ohio: World, 1966.

Requin, Lieut. Col. E. *America's Race to Victory*. New York: Frederick A. Stokes, 1919.

Reynolds, Clark G. *Admiral John Towers*. Annapolis: Naval Institute Press, 1991.

———. *Famous American Admirals*. New York: Van Nostrand Reinhold, 1978.

Reynolds, David. *Rich Relations: The American Occupation of Britain, 1942–1945*. New York: Random House, 1995.

Rhodes, Benjamin. *The Anglo-American Winter War with Russia, 1918–1919*. Westport, Conn.: Greenwood Press, 1988.

Riske, Milt. *United States Hospital Ships*. Washington, D.C.: Naval Historical Foundation, 1973.

Riste, Olav. *The Neutral Ally: Norway's Relations with Belligerent Powers in the First World War*. London: Allen and Unwin, 1965.

Robbins, Keith. *The First World War*. New York: Oxford University Press, 1984.

Roddis, Louis H. *A Short History of Nautical Medicine*. New York: Paul B. Hoeber, 1942.

Roger, Paul. *Les Americains a le Brest pendant la premiere guerre mondiale*. Brest, n.d.

Roscoe, Theodore. *On the Seas and in the Skies: A History of the U.S. Navy's Air Power*. New York: Hawthorn, 1970.

Roskill, Stephen. *Admiral of the Fleet Earl Beatty: The Last Naval Hero: An Intimate Biography*. New York: Atheneum, 1981.

———. *Hankey: Man of Secrets*. Vol. 1. New York: St. Martin's Press, 1970.

———. *The Strategy of Sea Power*. London: Collins, 1962.

Russell, Sir Herbert. *Sea Shepherds*. London: John Murray, 1941.

Rutter, Owen. *Red Ensign: A History of Convoy*. London: Robert Hale, 1943.

Safford, Jeffrey J. *Wilsonian Maritime Diplomacy, 1913–1921*. New Brunswick, N.J.: Rutgers University Press, 1978.

Salaun, Le Vice-Amiral. *La marine Francaise*. Paris: Les Editions De France, 1934.

Salter, J. A. *Allied Shipping Control*. Oxford: Clarendon Press, 1921.

Sammons, Jeffrey T. *Beyond the Ring: The Role of Boxing in American Society*. Urbana: University of Illinois Press, 1988.

Schaffer, Ronald. *America in the Great War: The Rise of the War Welfare State*. New York: Oxford University Press, 1991.

Scheer, Admiral. *Germany's High Seas Fleet in the World War*. London: Cassell, 1920.

Schmidt, Hans. *Maverick Marine: General Smedley D. Butler and the Contradictions of American Military History*. Lexington: University Press of Kentucky, 1987.

Schmitt, Bernadotte E., and Harold C. Vedeler. *The World in the Crucible, 1914–1919*. New York: Harper and Row, 1984.

Schneider, Dorothy, and Carl J. Schneider. *Into the Breach: American Women Overseas in World War I*. New York: Viking, 1991.

Scott, W. R., and J. Cunninson. *The Industries of the Clyde Valley during the War*. Oxford: Clarendon Press, 1924.

Semmel, Bernard. *Liberalism and Naval Strategy*. Boston: Allen and Unwin, 1986.

Seymour, Charles. *American Diplomacy during the World War*. Baltimore: Johns Hopkins University Press, 1934.

Seymour, Harold. *Baseball: The People's Game*. Vol. 1. New York: Oxford University Press, 1990.

Shafter, Richard. *Destroyers in Action*. New York: Cornell Maritime Press, 1945.

Shaw, G. C. *Supplying Modern War*. London: Faber and Faber, 1938.

Silverston, Paul H. *U.S. Warships of World War I*. Garden City, N.Y.: Doubleday, 1970.

Simpson, B. Mitchell, III. *Admiral Harold R. Stark: Architect of Victory, 1939–1945*. Columbia: University of South Carolina Press, 1989.

Sinclair, Andrew. *Era of Excess: A Social History of the Prohibition Movement*. New York: Harper Colophon, 1962.

Sinclair, David. *Dynasty: The Astors and Their Times*. New York: Beaufort, 1981.

Slosson, Preston W. *The Great Crusade and After, 1914–1928*. New York: Macmillan, 1931.

Smellie, John. *Shipbuilding and Repairing in Dublin: A Record of Work Carried Out by the Dublin Dockyard Co. 1901–1923*. Glasgow: McCorquodale, 1935.

Smout, T. C. *A Century of the Scottish People 1830–1950*. New Haven, Conn.: Yale University Press, 1986.

Smythe, Donald. *Pershing: General of the Armies*. Bloomington: Indiana University Press, 1986.

Sokol, Anthony E. *The Imperial and Royal Austro-Hungarian Navy*. Annapolis: Naval Institute Press, 1968.

Sondhaus. Lawrence. *The Naval Policy of Austria-Hungary, 1867–1918*. West Lafayette, Ind.: Purdue University Press, 1994.

Soule, George. *Prosperity Decade: From War to Depression, 1917–1929*. New York: Harper and Row, 1951.

Spector, Ronald. *Professors of War: The Naval War College and the Development of the Naval Profession*. Newport, R.I.: Naval War College Press, 1977.

Sprout, Harold, and Margaret Sprout. *The Rise of American Naval Power, 1776–1918*. Princeton: Princeton University Press, 1946.

Stafford, Captain Lawrence F. *A History of Communications Intelligence in the United States with Emphasis on the United States Navy*. Denver, Colo.: Naval Cryptologic Veterans Association, 1982.

Stallings, Laurence. *The Doughboys*. New York: Popular Library, 1964.

Stenson, Patrick. *The Odyssey of C. H. Lightoller*. New York: W. W. Norton, 1984.

Stevenson, David. *The First World War and International Politics*. New York: Oxford University Press, 1988.

Stiles, Lela. *The Man Behind Roosevelt: The Story of Louis McHenry Howe*. Cleveland, Ohio: World, 1954.

Still, William N., Jr. *American Sea Power in the Old World: The United States Navy in European and Near Eastern Waters, 1865–1917*. Westport, Conn.: Greenwood Press, 1980.

Stillwell, Paul. *Battleship* Arizona: *An Illustrated History*. Annapolis: Naval Institute Press, 1991.

Stone, Richard G., Jr. *Kentucky Fighting Men 1861–1945*. Lexington: University Press of Kentucky, 1982.

The Story of the USS Texas. Houston, Tex.: Battleship Texas Commission, 1964.

Strauss, David. *Menace in the West: The Rise of French Anti-Americanism in Modern Times*. Westport, Conn.: Greenwood Press, 1976.

Sweetman, Jack. *The U.S. Naval Academy: An Illustrated History*. Annapolis: Naval Academy Press, 1979.

Sumida, Jon Teteuro. *In Defense of Naval Supremacy: Finance, Technology, and British Naval Policy, 1889–1914*. Boston: Unwin Hyman, 1989.

Summary of World War Work of the American YMCA. N.p.: International Committee of Young Men's Christian Association, 1920.

Sykes, Christopher. *Nancy: The Life of Lady Astor*. Chicago: Academy, 1972.

Taft, William Howard. *Service with Fighting Men*. 2 vols. New York: Association Press, 1922.

Taillemite, Etienne. *Dictionnaire des Marins Francais*. N.p.: Editions Maritimes et Outre-Mer, 1982.

Tarrant, V. E. *The U-Boat Offensive, 1914–1945*. Annapolis: Naval Institute Press, 1989.

Taussig, Betty Carney. *A Warrior for Freedom*. Manhattan, Kans.: Sunflower Press, 1995.

Taylor, A.J.P. *The First World War*. New York: Capricorn Press, 1972.

Taylor, Theodore. *The Magnificent Mitscher*. New York: W. W. Norton, 1954.

Terraine, John. *The U-Boat War, 1916–1945*. New York: G. P. Putnam's Sons, 1989.

Thevenot, Roger. *A History of Refrigeration throughout the World*. Paris: International Institute of Refrigeration, 1979.

Thomas, Lowell. *Old Gimlet Eye: The Adventures of Smedley D. Butler*. New York: Farrar and Rinehart, 1933.

Thorpe, George C. *Pure Logistics: The Science of War Preparation*. Washington, D.C.: National Defense University Press, 1986.

Thoumin, General Richard. *The First World War*. New York: G. P. Putnam's Sons, 1964.

Till, Geoffrey. *Air Power and the Royal Navy 1914–1945*. London: Janes, 1979.

Timberlake, James H. *Prohibition and the Progressive Movement, 1900–1920*. Cambridge: Harvard University Press, 1966.

Titus, Warren I. *Winston Churchill*. New York: Twayne, 1963.

Todd, Joe L., comp. USS Oklahoma: *Remembrance of a Great Lady*. Oklahoma City: USS *Oklahoma* Association, 1990.

Toland, John. *No Man's Land: 1918, The Last Year of the Great War*. New York: Ballantine, 1980.

Tomazi, Auguste. *La guerre naval dans l'Adriatique*. Paris: Payot, 1925.

Trask, David F. *The AEF and Coalition Warmaking, 1917–1918*. Lawrence: University of Kansas Press, 1993.

———. *Captains and Cabinets: Anglo-American Naval Relations, 1917–1918*. Columbia: University of Missouri Press, 1972.

The Truth about Ireland in the Great War. Washington, D.C.: Irish National Bureau, 1919.

Turnbull, Archibald D., and Clifford L. Lord. *History of United States Naval Aviation*. New Haven, Conn.: Yale University Press, 1949.

Uhlig, Frank, Jr. *How Navies Fight: The U.S. Navy and Its Allies*. Annapolis: Naval Institute Press, 1993.

United States Naval Aviation, 1910–1980. 3rd ed. Washington, D.C.: Naval Historical Center, 1981.

Ussler, Arland. *The Face and Mind of Ireland.* London: Victor Gollanz, 1950.

USS Nevada, *The Cheer Up Ship.* N.p., n.d.

Van der Vat, Dan. *The Grand Scuttle: The Sinking of the German Fleet at Scapa Flow in 1919.* London: Hodder and Stoughton, 1982.

Vandiver, Frank E. *Black Jack: The Life and Times of John J. Pershing.* Vol. 2. College Station: Texas A&M University Press, 1977.

Van Deurs, George. *Anchors in the Sky: Spuds Ellyson, the First Naval Aviator.* San Rafael, Calif.: Presidio Press, 1978.

Van Wyen, Adrian O. *Naval Aviation in World War I.* Washington, D.C.: Office of the Chief of Naval Operations, Navy Department, 1969.

Venn, Fiona. *Oil Diplomacy in the Twentieth Century.* New York: St. Martin's Press, 1985.

Vicoli, Fulvio. *L'Azione navale di Durazzo.* Milan: Arti Grapiche O. Maranconi, 1933.

Vlahos, Michael. *The Blue Sword: The Naval War College and the American Mission, 1919–1941.* Newport, R.I.: Naval War College Press, 1980.

von Doenhoff, Richard A., and Janet McIntire von Doenhoff. *Patriots and Guardians: The New York Yacht Club and the United States Navy since 1846.* New York: New York Yacht Club, 1994.

Walker, George. *Venereal Disease in the American Expeditionary Forces.* Baltimore: Medical Standard, 1922.

Wall, Richard, and Jay Winter, eds. *The Upheaval of War: Family, Work and Welfare in Europe, 1914–1918.* Cambridge: Cambridge University Press, 1988.

Wallach, Jehuda L. *Uneasy Coalition: The Entente Experience in World War I.* Westport, Conn.: Greenwood Press, 1993.

Waller, P. J. *Democracy and Sectarianism. A Political and Social History of Liverpool 1868–1939.* Liverpool: Liverpool University Press, 1981.

Walling, R.A.J. *The Story of Plymouth.* New York: William Morrow, 1950.

Walworth, Arthur. *America's Moment: 1918.* New York: W. W. Norton, 1977.

———. *Woodrow Wilson.* 2 vols. Baltimore: Penguin, 1969.

Ward, Alan J. *Ireland and Anglo-American Relations 1899–1921.* Toronto: University of Toronto Press, 1969.

Ward, Geoffrey C. *A First-Class Temperament. The Emergence of Franklin Roosevelt.* New York: Harper and Row, 1989.

Waters, Cdr. David W. *Notes on the Convoy System of Naval War, Thirteenth to Twentieth Centuries.* Part 2, *First World War, 1914–18.* Copy provided author by Cdr. Waters.

Watt, D. Cameron. *Personalities and Policies.* South Bend, Ind.: University of Notre Dame Press, 1965.

———. *Succeeding John Bull: America in Britain's Place, 1900–1975.* Cambridge: Cambridge University Press, 1984.

Weeks, Charles J. *An American Naval Diplomat in Revolutionary Russia: The Life and Times of Vice Admiral Newton A. McCully.* Annapolis: Naval Institute Press, 1994.

Weigley, Russell F. *The American Way of War: A History of United States Military Strategy and Policy.* New York: Macmillan, 1967.

Weintraub, Stanley. *A Stillness Heard Round the World: The End of the Great War: November 1918.* New York: Oxford University Press, 1985.

Weir, Gary E. *Building American Submarines, 1914–1940.* Washington, D.C.: Naval Historical Center, 1991.

Wemyss, Lady. *The Life and Letters of Lord Wester Wemyss.* London: Eyre and Spottiswoode, 1935.

Wheeler, Gerald. E. *Admiral William Veazie Pratt, U.S.N.: A Sailor's Life*. Washington, D.C.: Naval History Division, 1974.

Whitaker, Herman. *Hunting the German Shark*. New York: Century, 1918.

White, Lillian C. *Pioneer and Patriot: George Cook Sweet, Commander, U.S.N., 1877–1953*. Delray Beach, Fla.: Southern, 1953.

Wiest, Andrea. *Passchendaele and the Royal Navy*. Westport, Conn.: Greenwood Press, 1985.

Wildenberg, Thomas. *Gray Steel and Black Oil: Fast Tankers and Replenishment at Sea in the U.S. Navy, 1912–1992*. Annapolis: Naval Institute Press, 1996.

Wile, Frederic William. *Explaining the Britishers*. New York: George H. Doran, 1919.

Willert, Arthur. *The Road To Safety: A Study in Anglo-American Relations*. London: Derek Verschoyle, 1952.

Williams, John. *The Home Fronts: Britain, France, and Germany, 1914–1918*. London: Constable, 1972.

Williamson, Harold and Arnold R. Daum. *The American Petroleum Industry*. Evanston, Ill.: Northwestern University Press, 1963.

Willoughby, Malcolm F. Yankton—*Yacht and Man-of-War*. Cambridge, Mass.: Crimson Printing, 1935.

Wilson, Admiral Henry B. *An Account of the Operations of the American Navy in France during the War with Germany*. N.p., 1919.

Wilson, Derek. *The Astors: 1763–1992*. New York: St. Martin's Press, 1993.

Wilson, George B. *Alcohol and the Nation*. London: Nicholson and Watson, 1940.

Wilson, Trevor. *The Myriad Faces of War: Britain and the Great War, 1914–1918*. London: Policy Press, 1986.

Winslow, Richard E., III. *"Do Your Job!" An Illustrated Bicentennial History of the Portsmouth Naval Shipyard, 1800–2000*. Portsmouth, N.H.: Portsmouth Marine Society, 2000.

Winter, J. M. *The Experience of World War I*. New York: Columbia University Press, 1989.

Winton, John. *Convoy: The Defense of the Sea Trade*. London: Michael Joseph, 1983.

Wycoff, Minnie Elizabeth. *Ripley County's Part in the World War 1917–1918*. Batesville, Ind.: Ripley County Historical Society, 1920.

Yardley, Herbert O. *The American Black Chamber*. Indianapolis, Ind.: Bobbs-Merrill, 1931.

Young, Kenneth. *Arthur James Balfour*. London: Bell, 1963.

Young, S. *Pen and Pictures of the Great War*. N.p., n.d.

Zahniser, Marvin R. *Uncertain Friendship: American-French Relations through the Cold War*. New York: John Wiley and Sons, 1975.

Zimmerman, Phyllis A. *The Neck of the Bottle: George W. Goethals and the Reorganization of the U.S. Army Supply System, 1917–1918*. College Station: Texas A&M University Press, 1992.

Zivojinovic, Dragan R. *America, Italy, and the Birth of Yugoslavia (1917–1919)*. New York: Columbia University Press, 1972.

Articles and Essays

Albion, Robert G. "Logistics in World War II: A Bibliography." U.S. Naval Institute *Proceedings* 84 (January 1957): 97–102

Alden, C. S. "American Submarine Operations in the War." U.S. Naval Institute *Proceedings* 46 (1920): 811–50, 1013–48.

Alden, John D. "The Yacht That Was a Destroyer." U.S. Naval Institute *Proceedings* 93 (December 1967): 156–59.

Allard, Dean C. "Admiral William S. Sims and United States Naval Policy in World War I." *American Neptune* 35 (April 1975): 97–110.

———. "Anglo-American Naval Differences during World War I." *Military Affairs* 44 (April 1980): 75–81.

Allston, Rear Admiral Frank J. USNR (Ret.). "Live Wire of the Navy." *Navy Supply Corps Newsletter*, March/April 1994, 35–38.

Ambrose, Stephen. "Seapower in World Wars I and II." In *War, Strategy, and Maritime Power*, edited by B. Mitchell Simpson III, 175–98. New Brunswick, N.J.: Rutgers University Press, 1977.

Anderson, Bern. "The Protection of Commerce in War." U.S. Naval Institute *Proceedings* 88 (1952): 881–87.

——. "The U.S. Navy's Attitude on Convoys." U.S. Naval Institute *Proceedings* 83 (July 1957): 782–83.

Anonymous. "The Very Human Admiral." *Independent* (April 19, 1919): 93–96.

"Auxiliary Ship Navy—Mobile Logistic Support Force." *All Hands* (January 1976): 3–13.

Bagley, Admiral Worth. "Torpedoed in the Celtic Sea." *Naval History* 14 (May/June 1997): 36–40.

Baker, A. D., III. "Historic Fleets." *Naval History* 10 (August 1995): 60.

Baldridge, Harry A. "Sims—The Iconoclast." U.S. Naval Institute *Proceedings* 63 (February 1937): 183–90.

Bartimeus [Rice, Lewis]. "Admiral Sims and His Fleet." *Living Age* 297 (June 8, 1918): 577–83.

——. "Admiral Sir Lewis Bayly and the American Navy." *Landmark*. Copy in the Lewis Bayly Papers, IWM.

Bartlett, Merrill. "Secretary of the Navy Josephus Daniels and the Marine Corps, 1913–21." In *New Interpretations in Naval History*, edited by William B. Cogar, 190–208. Annapolis: Naval Institute Press, 1989.

Bassler, Robert E. "Charles Preston (Juggy) Nelson: A Real Character of the Old Navy." *Shipmate* 45 (October 1982): 29–30.

Beals, Victor. "New England's Role in the Yankee Mining Squadron." *New England Galaxy* 10 (1968): 3–11.

Beardsley, Edward H. "Allied Against Sin: American and British Responses to Venereal Disease in World War I." *Medical History* 20 (April 1976): 189–202.

Bemend, Alan. "Principles Underlying Ship Camouflage." *International Marine Engineering* (Feb. 1919): 90–93.

Bieg, V. N. "War and Naval Engineering." U.S. Naval Institute *Proceedings* 46 (April 1920): 539–44.

"Bound for Bantry Bay." *Oklahoma General Recall* (September 1977): 7–8.

Bradford, James C. "Henry T. Mayo: Last of the Independent Naval Diplomats." In *Admirals of the New Steel Navy*, edited by James C. Bradford, 253–81. Annapolis: Naval Institute Press, 1990.

Braisted, William. "Charles Frederick Hughes," In *The Chiefs of Naval Operations*, edited by Robert W. Love Jr., 49–68. Annapolis: Naval Institute Press, 1980.

——. "Mark Lambert Bristol: Naval Diplomat Extraordinary of the Battleship Age." In *Admirals of the New Steel Navy*, edited by James Bradford, 331–73. Annapolis: Naval Institute Press, 1990.

Breemer, J. S. "Defeating the Submarine—Choosing ASW Strategy." Part 1, "The First World War." *Naval Forces* 9 (1988): 34–41.

Breckel, H. L. "The Suicide Flotilla." U.S. Naval Institute *Proceedings* 53 (June 1927): 661–70.

Brown, David A. "Who Won the War?" *Foreign Service* (October 1938): 18–19, 47.

Buckley, Suzann. "The Failure to Resolve the Problem of Venereal Disease among the Troops in Britain during World War I." In *War and Society: A Yearbook of Military History*, 2: 65–85. New York: Holmes and Meier, 1977,

Buettell, Roger B. "Soldiers—Ships and the Sea." *VFW Magazine*, February 1971, 22–23, 33.

Bunkley, Commander J. W. "The Woozlefinch: The Navy's 14-Inch Railway Guns." U.S. Naval Institute *Proceedings* 57 (May 1931): 584–98.

Burch, Marybelle. "'I Don't Know Only What We Hear!': The Soldier's View of the 1918 Influenza Epidemic." *Indiana Medical History Quarterly* 4: 23–27.

"The Bureau in World War I." *Navy Supply Corps Newsletter*, February 1970: 100–103.

Bywater, Hector C. "Notes on the American Navy." *Navy* (1921).

Cagle, Maury. "A Caravan of Thieves." *Naval Aviation News* (March/April 1985): 23–25.

"Captain Henry T. Settle, Eighty Years at Sea and Ashore." *Shipmate* 51 (May 1988): 17–18.

Chandler, T. E. "American and British Destroyers." U.S. Naval Institute *Proceedings* 48 (April 1922): 585–91.

Churchill, Winston. "Naval Organization, American and British." *Atlantic Monthly* 120 (1916): 277–84.

Cobb, Irvin S. "The Tail of the Snake." *Saturday Evening Post*, August 31, 1918, 12–13, 37.

Coletta, Paolo E. "Daniels." In *American Secretaries of the Navy*, edited by Paolo Coletta, 2: 525–81. Annapolis: Naval Institute Press, 1980.

———. "The Destroyer Tender." U.S. Naval Institute *Proceedings* 84 (May 1958): 51.

———. "Naval Lessons of the Great War: The William Sims–Josephus Daniels Controversy." *American Neptune* 51 (Fall 1991): 241–51.

———. "The American Naval Leaders' Preparation for War." In *The Great War, 1917–1918: Essays on the Military, Political, and Social History of the First World War*, edited by R.J.Q. Adams, 161–82. College Station: Texas A&M University Press, 1990.

———. "The United States Navy in the Adriatic in World War I." In *Ships, Seafaring, and Society: Essays in Maritime History*, edited by Timothy J. Runyon, 339–54. Detroit: Wayne State University Press, 1987.

Cope, H. F. "U.S. Submarines in the War Zone." U.S. Naval Institute *Proceedings* 56 (1930): 711–16, 1132.

Cornford, L. C. "The United States Navy." *Living Age* 291 (October-December 1918): 264–67.

Cunningham, A. C. "The Moveable Base." U.S. Naval Institute *Proceedings* 30 (March 1904): 181–95.

Daniels, Josephus. "The United States Navy in the World War." *North Carolina Historical Review* 4 (January 1927): 115–26.

Davis, Kenneth S. "No Talent for Subordination: FDR and Josephus Daniels." In *FDR and the U.S. Navy*, edited by Edward J. Marolda, 1–11. New York: St. Martin's Press, 1998.

DeLany, Vice Admiral Walter S. "Pull Together." *Shipmate* 40 (October 1977): 19–22.

DeNovo, John. "Petroleum and the United States Navy." *Mississippi Valley Historical Review* 41 (March 1935): 641–56.

Dewey, Peter. "Nutrition and Living Standards in Wartime Britain." In *The Upheaval of War: Family, Work and Welfare in Europe, 1914–1918*, edited by Richard Wall and Jay Winter, 192–222. Cambridge: Cambridge University Press, 1988.

Doughty, L. "The Effect of Depth Charges on Submarines." U.S. Naval Institute *Proceedings* 61 (1935): 353–57.

———. "Mistaken Attacks in the World War." U.S. Naval Institute *Proceedings* 60 (December 1934): 1729–34.

Douglas, Susan. "The Navy Adopts the Radio, 1899–1919." In *Military Enterprise and Technological Change*, edited by Merrit Roe Smith, 117–73. Cambridge: MIT Press, 1985.

Draper, Robert. "Ghosts of Centuries." *American Way*, December 15, 1990, 42–49, 78.

Durlacher, A. J. "The Phantom Whistle." U.S. Naval Institute *Proceedings* 74 (June 1948):721.

Edwards, LCDR Walter. "The U.S. Naval Air Force in Action, 1917–18." U.S. Naval Institute *Proceedings* 48 (1922): 1863–82

"Exploits of a yankee sailor and a Scotch soldier." *The Rudder* (Feb. 1919): 76–77.

Falge, CDR John H. "Long and Arduous Duty: Queenstown Destroyers in World War I." *Shipmate* 40 (April 1977): 35–36.

Field, James. "Sims." *Dictionary of American Biography.* Supplement 2, 614–15.

Foley, Paul. "The Cruiser *Dixie*: Tender to the Atlantic Fleet." *Journal of the American Society of Naval Engineers* 22 (November 1910): 1244–59.

———. "Petroleum Problems of the World War." U.S. Naval Institute *Proceedings* 50 (1924): 1802–31.

Freeman, Lewis R. "Coaling the Fleet." *Land and Water* 71 (July 18, 1918).

Fridenson, Patrick. "The Impact of the War on the French Worker." In *The Upheaval of War: Family, Work, and Welfare in Europe, 1914–1918*, edited by Richard Fall and Jay Winter, 235–48. Cambridge: Cambridge University Press, 1988.

"Front Line Sailors of the A.E.F." *Foreign Service* (October 1937): 20–27.

Gault, P. F. "A Tragic War Time Convoy." *Cavalry Journal* 18 (1932): 194–297.

Gosnell, H. A. "War Losses of the United States Navy." U.S. Naval Institute *Proceedings* 63 (1937): 1169–70.

Gould, S. W. "Submarine Warfare in the Adriatic: The Otranto Barrage, 1915–1918." U.S. Naval Institute *Proceedings* 70 (June 1944): 683–89.

Grant, Robert M. "Aircraft against U-Boats." U.S. Naval Institute *Proceedings* 64 (June 1937): 824–28.

———. "The Use of Mines against Submarines." U.S. Naval Institute *Proceedings* 65 (September 1938): 1275–79.

Gray, George W. "The Red Cross and the Navy." *Red Cross Magazine* 12 (October 1917): 424–27.

"The Great War: The Great Boom." *Cobh Annual* (1978): 32–39.

Greene, F. V. "Navy 'Firsts' in the World War." *Foreign Service* (1938): 14–15, 25.

Gretton, Peter. "The U-Boat Campaign in Two World Wars." In *Naval Warfare in the Twentieth Century 1900–1945*, edited by Gerald Jordan, 128–40. London: Croom Helm, 1977.

Gurney, Fred, "The U.S. Dispatch Agency in London." U.S. Naval Institute *Proceedings* 62 (February 1936): 189–92.

Hagan, Kenneth. "The Critic Within." *Naval History* 12 (November-December 1998): 20–25.

Halpern, Paul. G. "Comparative Naval History." In *Doing Naval History: Essays Toward Improvement*, edited by John B. Hattendorf, 75–92. Newport, R.I.: Naval War College Press, 1995.

Hamilton, James E. "A Short History of the Naval Use of Fuel Oil." *Journal of the American Society of Naval Engineers* 47 (1935): 36–56.

Hanks, Carlos C. "Fighting the U-Boats." U.S. Naval Institute *Proceedings* 62 (December 1936): 1685–88.

———. "Two Tugs and a Freighter." U.S. Naval Institute *Proceedings* 65 (June 1937): 810–12.

Hattendorf, John. "Technology and Strategy." In *Strategy and Power*, edited by B. Michael Simpson III, 111–38. New Brunswick, N.J.: Rutgers University Press, 1977.

Haves, T. A. "Coal Wagons of the Sea." *Navy Life* (November 1918): 18–21.

Hayes, Harvey C. "Detection of Submarines." *Proceedings American Philosophical Society* 59 (1920): 1–47.

Hayes, John D. "Logistics—The Word." *Naval Research Logistics Quarterly* 1 (September 1954): 182–90.

Henrizi, John T. "U.S. Navy Colliers." U.S. Naval Institute *Proceedings* 93 (May 1967): 163–64.

Herwig, Holger H., and David Trask. "The Failure of Imperial Germany's Underseas Offensive against World Shipping, February 17 to November 1918." *Historian* 38 (August 1971): 611–36.

Hunter, Francis T. "American Admirals at War." *World's Work* 37 (May 1918): 35–39.

———. "Backing Beatty." *World's Work* 38 (July 1919): 329–35.

———. "Kings, Princes, and American Sailors." *World's Work* 38 (June 1919): 184–94.

Jackson, Chester V. "Mission to Murmansk." U.S. Naval Institute *Proceedings* 95 (February 1969): 82–89.

Jones, Geoffrey. "Admirals and Oil Men: The Relationship between the Royal Navy and the Oil Companies, 1900–1924." In *Charted and Uncharted Waters: Proceedings of a Conference on the Study of British Maritime History*, edited by Sarah Palmer and Glyndwr Williams, 107–121. Queen Mary College, London, September 8–11, 1981.

———. "The British Government and the Oil Companies, 1912–1924: The Search for an Oil Policy." *Historical Journal* 20 (1977): 651–59.

Keister, H. E. "U.S. Submarines in the War Zone." U.S. Naval Institute *Proceedings* 56 (December 1930): 1132.

Kennedy, Paul. "Britain in the First World War." In *Military Effectiveness*, edited by Allan Millett and Murray Williamson, vol. 1, *The First World War*, 31–79. Boston: Allen and Unwin, 1988.

Kieffer, Henry M. "The *Orama* Affair." *Shipmate* 41 (October 1978): 20–22.

Lang, R. G. "The Supply Ship." U.S. Naval Institute *Proceedings* 51 (February 1925): 269–73.

Lasky, Marion. "A Historical Review of Underwater Acoustic Technology, 1916–1939, with Emphasis on Underseas Warfare." *Journal of Underwater Acoustics* 25 (October 1974): 597–624.

———. "Review of World War I Acoustic Technology." *Journal of Underwater Acoustics* 24 (July 1973): 363–85.

"Listening Devices in U-Boat War." *Telephony* 76 (April 12, 1919): 23, 26–27.

Livermore, Seward W. "The Azores in American Strategy Diplomacy, 1917–1919." *Journal of Modern History* 20 (September 1948): 197–211.

Long, John W. "American Intervention in Russia: The North Russian Expedition, 1918–19." *Diplomatic History* 6 (Winter 1982): 45–68.

Lundeberg, Philip K. "Underseas Warfare and Allied Strategy in World War I." Part 2, "1916–1918." *Smithsonian Journal of History* 1–30 (1966): 49–72.

Lyman, Charles H. "Which It Will Forget at Its Peril." *Sea Power* 15 (September 1972): 33.

Maurer, John H. "American Naval Concentration and the German Battle Fleet, 1900–1918." *Journal of Strategic Studies* 6 (1983): 147–81.

———. "Fuel and the Battle Fleet: Coal, Oil, and American Naval Strategy." *Naval War College Review* 34 (November-December 1981): 60–77.

Magruder, T. P. "The Navy in the War." *Saturday Evening Post*, January 26–April 27, 1929, 3–4, 20–21, 29, 33, 42–45.

Mannix, Rear Admiral Daniel P., 3rd. "The Great North Sea Mine Barrage." *American Heritage* 34 (April/May 1983): 36–48.

McBride, William M. "The Navy's Academia Alliance, 1896–1923." *Journal of Military History* 56 (Jan. 1992): 28–34.

McCarthy, Dan B. "When Torpedoes Struck." *VFW Magazine*, November 1985, 26–28.

McKay, Colin, "America's Part in the Naval War." *Nautical Magazine* 104 (1920): 319–22.

McKenna, Richard. "The Wreck of Uncle Josephus." In *The Left-Handed Monkey Wrench*, edited by Robert Shenk, 155–84. Annapolis: Naval Institute Press, 1984.

McKillip, LCDR Robert W. H. "Undermining Technology by Strategy: Resolving the Trade Protection Dilemma of 1917." *Naval War College Review* 44 (Summer 1991): 18–37.

Meriwether, Walter Scott. "Four American Admirals." *Munsey* 63 (May 1918): 798–812.

Merrill, John. "From the Heavens to the Depths." *Naval History* 14 (June 2000): 56–59.

Mims, Lt. Col. Floyd C. "Take Me Out to the Ball Game." U.S. Naval Institute *Proceedings* 108 (February 1982): 110–12.

Mitchell, John B. "Admiral McGowan." *Forum* 62 (June 1919): 93–97.

Moore, E. "The Navy's Mobile Shipyards." *BuShips Journal* 4 (October 1955): 2–8.

Moore, R. R. "*Corsair*, Most Famous of Steam Yachts." *Nautical Research Journal* 15 (1968): 18–28.

Morrisey, Carla R. "The Influenza Epidemic of 1918." *U.S. Navy Medicine* (May-June 1986): 11–19.

Morse, Anthony, Sr. "When ASW Was Young." *Naval History* 4 (Spring 1990): 72–74.

Morse, Stephan S., and Robert D. Brown. "The Enemy Within: As Civilization Spreads, So Do Viruses." *Modern Maturity* 26 (June-July 1993): 52–53.

Murphy, Robert C. "Marine Camouflage." *Sea Power* 6 (January 1919): 28–32.

Neeser, Robert W. "Les patrouilleurs Americains sur les cotes de France (1917–1918)." *La Revue Maritime Nouvelle* Serie, Tome 2, 1st Semester (January-June, 1921): 234–42.

Nenninger, Timothy K. "American Military Effectiveness in the First World War." In *Military Effectiveness*, edited by Allan Millett and Murray Williamson, vol. 1, *The First World War*, 116–56. Boston: Allen and Unwin, 1988.

Neuhaus, Henry. "Fifty Years of Naval Engineering in Retrospect." *Journal of the American Society of Naval Engineers* 50 (August 1938): 22–26.

"Old Salts Hark Back to World War I." *American Legion Magazine*, November 1977, 8–10, 24.

Owen, C.V. "The United States Navy and the Allied Blockade in the Last War." *Royal United Service Institute Journal* 85 (1940): 206–12.

Parsons, Edward B. "Why the British Reduced the Flow of American Troops to Europe in August-October 1918." *Canadian Journal of History* 12 (December 1977): 173–91.

Perry, Lyman S. "Three Veterans of the United States Navy." U.S. Naval Institute *Proceedings* 57 (1931): 632–38.

Petrie, C. "The Mediterranean in Two Wars." *Quarterly Review* 271 (October 1943): 164–75.

Pollen, Arthur. "America and the Naval Revolution." *Metropolitan* (September 1918): 59–60.

Porch, Douglas. "The French Army in the First World War." In *Military Effectiveness*, edited by Allan Millett and Williamson Murray, vol. 1, *The First World War*, 190–228. Boston: Allen and Unwin, 1988.

Reed, Alastair. "The Impact of the War on the British Workers." In *The Upheaval of War: Family, Work and Welfare in Europe, 1914–1918*, edited by Richard Wall and Jay Winter, 221–34. Cambridge: Cambridge University Press, 1988,

Reed, Percy. "The *Bridgeport*." *Shipmate* 47 (June 1984): 17–18.

Robinson, S. M. "The Evolution of the Destroyer." *Journal of the American Society of Naval Engineers* 31 (November 1919): 900–910.

Roskill, Stephen W. "Capros Not Convoy: Counter Attack and Destroy." U.S. Naval Institute *Proceedings* 83 (October 1956): 1047–53.

Rossell, H. E. "Types of Naval Ships." In *The Society of Naval Architects and Marine Engineers Historical Transactions, 1893–1943*, 248–329. New York: Society of Naval Architects and Marine Engineers, 1945.

Rousmaniere, John. "The Romance of the Subchasers." *Naval History* 6 (Summer 1992): 42–45.

Sanderson, Debra. "The Worst Disaster in Recorded History." *Old Farmer's Almanac* (1993): 114–17.

Scheina, Robert L. "Coast Guard at War." *Commandant's Bulletin* 4 (Feb. 1987): 133–40.

Schilling, Warner. "Civil-Naval Politics in World War I." *World Politics* 7 (July 1955): 572–91.

Schofield, Frank H. "Incidents and Present-Day Aspects of Naval Strategy." U.S. Naval Institute *Proceedings* 49 (1923): 777–800.

Schofield, Kendrick. "The North Sea Gate Swings Shut." *Sea Power* 6 (January 1919): 23–27, 68, 71.

Shillman, J. H. "The Evolution of the Navy Ration." U.S. Naval Institute *Proceedings* 60 (1934): 1678–81.

Shirley, Noel. "John Lansing Callan—Naval Aviation Pioneer. *Over the Front* 21 (Summer 1987): 180–85.

Showalter, Dennis E. "Towards a 'New' Naval History." In *Doing Naval History: Essays Toward Improvement*, edited by John Hattendorf, 129–37. Newport, R.I.: Naval War College Press, 1995.

Shrader, Charles R. "'Maconochie's Stew.'" In *The Great War, 1914–18, Essays on the Military, Political, and Social History of the First World War*, edited by R.J.O. Adams, 103–22. College Station: Texas A&M University Press, 1990.

Simpson, Michael. "William S. Sims, U.S. Navy, and Admiral Sir Lewis Bayly, Royal Navy: An Unlikely Friendship, and Anglo-American Cooperation." *Naval War College Review* 41 (Spring 1988): 60–80.

"Sinking of *Jacob Jones*." *Literary Digest*, June 2, 1923, 47.

Smith, Captain Roy C. "A Grand Old Man: Admiral Richard Harrison Jackson, Centenarian Plus." *Shipmate* 51 (January–February 1988): 18–19.

Smythe, Donald. "Venereal Disease: The AEF's Experience." *Prologue* 9 (Summer 1977): 65–74.

Sokol, A. E. "Naval Strategy in the Adriatic Sea during the World War." U.S. Naval Institute *Proceedings* 63 (August 1937): 1077–92.

Spector, Ronald. "Josephus Daniels, Franklin Roosevelt and the Reinvention of the Naval Enlisted Man." In *FDR and the U.S. Navy*, edited by Edward Marolda, 19–33. New York: St. Martin's Press, 1998.

Spencer, Ivor D. "U.S. Naval Air Bases from 1914–1939." U.S. Naval Institute *Proceedings* 75 (1949): 1242–55.

Sprague, George E. "Flying Gobs." *Liberty Magazine*, January 7–21, 1939, 14–16, 24–27, 51–53.

Still William N., Jr. "Albert Gleaves." In *American National Biography*, 9: 114–15. New York: Oxford University Press, 1999.

———. "Anglo-American Naval Logistic Cooperation in World War I." *American Neptune* 55 (1995): 213–21.

———. "Logistical Support for U.S. Naval Forces Operating in European Waters in World War I." In *XVIII Congresso Internazionale Di Storia Militare*, 283–87. Rome: International Committee for Military History, 1993.

Sumida, Jon. "British Naval Administration and Policy in the Age of Fisher." *Journal of Military History* 54 (January 1990): 1–26.

———. "British Naval Operational Logistics, 1914–1918." *Journal of Modern History* 57 (July 1993): 447–80.

———. "Forging the Trident: British Naval Industrial Logistics, 1914–1918." In *Feeding Mars: Logistics in Western Warfare from the Middle Ages to the Present*, edited by John Lynn, 217–50. Boulder, Colo.: Westview Press, 1993.

Sumrall, R. E. "Ship Camouflage, Deceptive Art." U.S. Naval Institute *Proceedings* 74 (July, 1971): 68–71.

Sweetman, Jack. "Aboard Subchaser 206." U.S. Naval Institute *Proceedings* 102 (September 1976): 69–72.

Taylor, David W. "The Design of Warships as Affected by the World War." *Journal of the Franklin Institute* 190 (August 1920): 157–85.

Thelander, Theodore A. "Josephus Daniels and the Publicity Campaign for Naval and Industrial Preparedness before World War I." *North Carolina Historical Review* 43 (Summer 1966): 316–32.

Thomas, Deborah. "Women and Work in Wartime Britain." In *The Upheaval of War, Work, and*

Welfare in Europe, 1914–1918, edited by Richard Wall and Jay Winter, 297–326. Cambridge: Cambridge University Press, 1988.

Tibbott, David W. "'Broadway' Sailors." U.S. Naval Institute *Proceedings* 107 (June 1981): 58–65.

Trask, David. "FDR at War." In *FDR and the U.S. Navy,* edited by Edward J. Marolda, 13–18. New York: St. Martin's Press, 1998.

———. Introduction to *The Victory at Sea,* by William S. Sims. Garden City, N.Y.: Doubleday, Page, 1920. Reprint, Annapolis: Naval Institute Press, 1964, with new introduction by Trask.

———. "William Shepherd Benson." In *The Chiefs of Naval Operations,* edited by Robert W. Love Jr. Annapolis: Naval Institute Press, 1980.

———. "William Sowden Sims: The Victory Ashore." In *Quarterdeck and Bridge,* edited by James C. Bradford, 275–90. Annapolis: Naval Institute Press, 1997.

Urofsky, J. Melvin. "Josephus Daniels and the Armor Trust." *North Carolina Historical Review* 45 (July 1968): 240–52.

Usborne, Capt. C. V. "The Anti-Submarine Campaign in the Mediterranean Subsequent to 1916." *Journal of the Royal United Service Institution* 69 (February to November 1921): 444–64.

Van Deurs, Rear Admiral George. "What Happened to *Cyclops, Nereus,* and *Proteus—Langley's* Missing Sisters?" *Naval Engineers Journal* (October 1974): 60–64.

"The Very Human Admiral." *Independent* 98 (1919): 93.

"Vice Admiral Joel Roberts Poinsett Pringle, U.S. Navy." *Naval War College Review* 22 (January 1970): 1–21.

von Doenhoff, Richard. "U.S. Naval Aviation in Europe during World War I." *XVIII Congresso Internazional Di Storia Militare.* Rome: International Commission for Military History, 1993.

Warner, Allen H. "The American Military Achievement: A British View. *Living Age* (July 5, 1919): 28–36.

Weeks, Charles J. "A Samaritan in Russia: Vice Admiral Newton A. McCully's Humanitarian Efforts, 1914–1920." *Military Affairs* 52 (January 1988): 12–17.

Weigley, Russell F. "The Principle of Civilian Control." *Journal of Military History* 57 (October 1993): 27–58.

"What the American Soldiers Think of the French." *Literary Digest* (June 28, 1919): 48.

Wheeler, Gerald. "William Veazie Pratt, U.S. Navy: A Silhouette of an Admiral. *Naval War College Review* 22 (May 1969): 37–61.

Whitaker, Herman. "The Mediterranean: The Last Stand of the Submarine." *Century* 97 (November 1918): 50–56.

Wildenberg, Thomas. "Chester Nimitz and the Development of Fueling at Sea." *Naval War College Review* 46 (Autumn 1993): 52–62.

Williams, William J. "Josephus Daniels and the U.S. Navy's Shipbuilding Program during World War I." *Journal of Military History* 60 (January 1996): 7–38.

Wilson, Eugene E. "Grand Fleet Morale." *Shipmate* 27 (January 1964).

Wilson, Robert F. "Sims, of the Successful Indiscretions." *World's Work* 34 (July 1917): 333–40.

Woodward, David R. "The Military Role of the U.S. in World War I." In *The American Military Tradition From Colonial Times to the Present,* edited by John M. Carroll and Colin F. Baxter, 117–34. Wilmington, Del.: Scholarly Resources, 1993.

Yerxa, Donald A. "The United States Navy in Caribbean Waters during World War I." *Military Affairs* (October 1987): 182–87.

Dissertations and Theses

Adams, W. E. "André Tardieu and French Foreign Policy, 1902–1919." Ph.D. diss., Stanford University, 1959.

Bacon, Eugene Hayward. "Russian-American Relations." Ph.D. diss., Georgetown University, 1951.

Baldwin, Fred Davis. "The American Enlisted Man in World War I." Ph.D. diss., Princeton University, 1964.

Barboo, Samuel H. "A Historical Review of the Hygiene of Shipboard Food Services in the United States Navy, 1775–1965." Doctor of Public Health, UCLA, 1966.

Bell, Lewis Baker. "Samuel H. McGowan." Master's thesis, Princeton University, 1947.

Bell, Walter Fulghum. "American Embassies in Belligerent Europe, 1914–1918." Ph.D. diss., University of Iowa, 1983.

Bowling, Roland Alfred. "Convoying in World War I: The Influence of Admiral William S. Sims, U.S. Navy." Master's thesis, San Diego State University, 1975.

———. "The Negative Influence of Mahan on the Protection of Shipping in Wartime: The Convoy Controversy in the Twentieth Century." Ph.D. diss., University of Maine at Orono, 1980.

Brooke, Edward Howard. "The National Defense Policy of the Wilson Administration." Ph.D. diss., Stanford University, 1950.

Chrisman, Herman Henry. "Naval Operations in the Mediterranean during the Great War, 1914–1918." Ph.D. diss., Stanford University, 1931.

Coady, Joseph W. "Franklin D. Roosevelt's Early Washington Years 1913–1920." Ph.D. diss., St. John's University (New York), 1968.

Costello, Daniel J. "Planning for War: A History of the General Board of the Navy, 1900–1914." Ph.D. diss., Fletcher School of Law and Diplomacy, 1968.

Easerling, Verlin R. "Great Britain's Peril and the Convoy Controversy: A Study of the Intended Results of Unrestricted U-Boat Warfare and the Convoy System as a Counter-Measure, World War I." Ph.D. diss., University of Colorado, 1951.

Green, James R. "The First Sixty Years of the Office of Naval Intelligence." Master's thesis, American University, 1963.

Hickey, Demott V. "The First Ladies in the Navy." Master's thesis, Columbia College, 1965.

Hunter, Charles H. "Anglo-American Relations during the Period of American Belligerency, 1917–1918." Ph.D. diss., Stanford University, 1935.

Jones, Jerry W. "U.S. Battleship Operations in World War I, 1917–1918." Ph.D. diss., University of North Texas, 1995.

Killen, Landa. "The Search for a Democratic Russia: The Wilson Administration's Russian Policy, 1917–1920." Ph.D. diss., University of North Carolina at Chapel Hill, 1975.

Long, John W. "Civil War and Intervention in North Russia, 1918–1920." Ph.D. diss., Columbia University, 1972.

McBride, William M. "The Rise and Fall of a Strategic Technology: The American Battleship from Santiago Bay to Pearl Harbor, 1898–1941." Ph.D. diss., Johns Hopkins University, 1989.

Mindell, David A. "'Datum for its Own Annihilation': Feedback, Control, and Computing, 1916–1945." Ph.D. diss., Massachusetts Institute of Technology, 1996.

Olszewski, George J. "Allied Intervention in North Russia, 1918–1919." Ph.D. diss., Georgetown University, 1958.

Ramsey, Robert D., III. "Delivering the Goods: The Development of an American Logistical System in France, May 1917–March 1918." Ph.D. diss., Rice University, 1977.

Schilling, Warner R. "Admirals and Foreign Policy, 1913–1919." Ph.D. diss., Yale University, 1953.

Shepherd, David N. "Death of a Fleet: Responsibility for the Scuttling of the German High Seas Fleet at Scapa Flow, June 21, 1919." Ph.D. diss., Texas Christian University, 1973.

Socas, Roberto F. "France, Naval Armaments, and Naval Disarmament 1918–1922." Ph.D. diss., Columbia University, 1955.

Stackhouse, Glenn. "The Anglo-American Atlantic Convoy System in World War I, 1917–1918." Ph.D. diss., University of South Carolina, 1993.

Watson, Griff. "A Profile of the Tennessee Servicemen in World War I." Ph.D. diss., Middle Tennessee State University, 1985.

Weeks, Charles J. "An American Naval Diplomat in Revolutionary Russia: The Life and Times of Newton A. McCully." Ph.D. diss., University of Georgia, 1975.

Wigfall, Michael B. "Scientists and the Admiralty: Conflict and Collaboration in Anti-Submarine Warfare." Ph.D. diss., University of London, 1987.

Zimmerman, Phyllis A. "George W. Goethals and the Reorganization of the United States Army Supply System, 1917–1918." Ph.D. diss., Indiana University, 1987.

Periodicals and Magazines

All Hands

American Legion Magazine

Army & Navy Journal, 1917–21

Army & Navy Register

Arklight (USS *Arkansas*)

Atlantic Monthly

Big "D" Log

Broadside

Fixen (copy in Reginald Belknap Papers, LC)

Great Lakes Bulletin

Land and Water

Landmark

L'Illustration

Literary Digest

National Geographic Magazine

Naval and Military Record

Naval Reserve

New Country Life

Oklahoma General

Our Navy

Pauillac Pilot

Recall

Rudder

Scientific American

Shipmate

Sphere

Syren and Shipping

Torch (Veterans of World War I of the U.S.A., Inc.)

U.S. Naval Institute *Proceedings*

VFW Magazine

Newspapers

Baltimore Sun
Boston Globe
Chicago News
Chicago Tribune (Paris edition)
Christian Advocate
Christian Science Monitor
Cork Examiner
Daily Chronicle (London)
Daily Graphic (London)
Daily Herald (London)
Daily Mail (London)
Daily News (London)
Daily Telegraph (London)
Edinburgh *Evening News*
Evening Echo (Cobh)
Glasgow Herald
Inverness Courier
Irish Independent
Journal of Commerce (Liverpool)
Le Figaro
Le Matin
Manchester Guardian
New York Evening Mail
New York Herald
New York Telegram
New York Times
Norfolk Virginia Pilot
Observer (London)
Orcadian
Pall Mall Gazette
Philadelphia Public Ledger
Portsmouth Herald
Sporting News (London)
Stars and Stripes
Scotsman
Times (London)
Washington Post
Westminster Gazette

Fiction

Wouk, Herman, *The Glory*. Boston: Little, Brown, 1994.

Index

Page numbers in italics indicate illustrations.

William N. Still Jr. is professor emeritus of maritime history from East Carolina University. He served as codirector of the Program in Maritime History and Underwater Research at ECU. He is a past president of the North American Society for Oceanic History, former member of the Secretary of the Navy's subcommittee on naval history, and was the secretary of the Navy's research scholar in naval history in 1989–1990. Dr. Still is the author and editor of a number of publications including *Confederate Shipbuilding: American Sea Power in the World; Why the South Lost the Civil War*, and *The Queenstown Patrol, 1917* (editor).